The Routledge Research Companion to Johann Sebastian Bach

The Routledge Research Companion to Johann Sebastian Bach provides an indispensable introduction to the Bach research of the past thirty to fifty years. It is not a lexicon providing information on all the major aspects of Bach's life and work, such as the *Oxford Composer Companion: J. S. Bach*. Nor is it an entry-level research tool aimed at those making a beginning of such studies. The valuable essays presented here are designed for the next level of Bach research and are aimed at masters and doctoral students, as well as others interested in coming to terms with the current state of Bach research. Each author covers three aspects within their specific subject area; firstly, to describe the results of research over the past thirty to fifty years, concentrating on the most significant and controversial, such as: the debate over Smend's NBA edition of the B minor Mass; Blume's conclusions with regard to Bach's religion in the wake of the "new" chronology; Rifkin's one-to-a-vocal-part interpretation; the rediscovery of the Berlin Singakademie manuscripts in Kiev; the discovery of hitherto unknown manuscripts and documents; and the reevaluation of previously known sources. Secondly, each author provides a critical analysis of current research being undertaken that is exploring new aspects, reinterpreting earlier assumptions, and/or opening-up new methodologies. For example, Martin W. B. Jarvis has suggested that Anna Magdalena Bach composed the cello suites and contributed to other works of her husband—another controversial hypothesis, whose newly proposed forensic methodology requires investigation. On the other hand, research into Bach's knowledge of the Lutheran chorale tradition is currently underway, which is likely to shed more light on the composer's choices and usage of this tradition. Thirdly, each author identifies areas that are still in need of investigation and research.

Robin A. Leaver is Professor Emeritus of sacred music, Westminster Choir College, Princeton; currently visiting professor at the Institute of Sacred Music, Yale University, and Honorary Professor at Queen's University, Belfast, Northern Ireland. He has written the program notes for the Bach Choir of Bethlehem since 1984 and contributes from time to time to the program books of the Bach Collegium Japan. Past president of the American Bach Society, Dr. Leaver is the editor of monographs in the series *Contextual Bach Studies* (Scarecrow/Rowman & Littlefield 2006–), and the General Editor of *The Yale Journal of Music and Religion*. Recent Bach studies include contributions to *Exploring Bach's B-Minor Mass* (Cambridge University Press, 2013), which he coedited with Yo Tomita and Jan Smaczny; the *Bach-Jahrbuch* (2013); *Bach: The Journal of the Riemenschneider Bach Institute* (2014), and *Bach Perspectives 10* (2016). He is currently researching the liturgical contexts of Bach's music.

The Routledge Research Companion to Johann Sebastian Bach

Edited by Robin A. Leaver

LONDON AND NEW YORK

First published 2017
by Routledge
2 Park Square, Milton Park, Abingdon, Oxon OX14 4RN

and by Routledge
711 Third Avenue, New York, NY 10017

Routledge is an imprint of the Taylor & Francis Group, an informa business

© 2017 Robin A. Leaver

The right of Robin A. Leaver to be identified as author of this work
has been asserted by him in accordance with sections 77 and 78 of the
Copyright, Designs and Patents Act 1988.

All rights reserved. No part of this book may be reprinted or reproduced
or utilised in any form or by any electronic, mechanical, or other means,
now known or hereafter invented, including photocopying and recording,
or in any information storage or retrieval system, without permission in
writing from the publishers.

Trademark notice: Product or corporate names may be trademarks
or registered trademarks, and are used only for identification and
explanation without intent to infringe.

British Library Cataloguing-in-Publication Data
A catalogue record for this book is available from the British Library

Library of Congress Cataloging-in-Publication Data
Names: Leaver, Robin A., author.
Title: The Routledge research companion to Johann Sebastian Bach /
Robin A. Leaver.
Description: New York, NY: Routledge, 2017. | Includes index.
Identifiers: LCCN 2016019404 | ISBN 9781409417903 (hardback) |
ISBN 9781315452814 (ebook)
Subjects: LCSH: Bach, Johann Sebastian, 1685–1750—Criticism and
interpretation. | Bach, Johann Sebastian, 1685–1750—Bibliography. |
Music—Germany—18th century—History and criticism.
Classification: LCC ML410.B13 L382 2017 | DDC 780.92—dc23
LC record available at https://lccn.loc.gov/2016019404

ISBN: 978-1-409-41790-3 (hbk)
ISBN: 978-1-315-45281-4 (ebk)

Bach musicological font developed by © Yo Tomita

Typeset in Times New Roman
by codeMantra

Printed and bound by CPI Group (UK) Ltd, Croydon, CR0 4YY

Contents

List of Illustrations	viii
Foreword CHRISTOPH WOLFF	ix
Preface ROBIN A. LEAVER	xi
Abbreviations	xiii
Contributors	xix
1 Introduction ROBIN A. LEAVER	1
PART I **Sources**	23
2 Documents HANS-JOACHIM SCHULZE	25
3 Manuscripts YO TOMITA	47
4 Printed Editions GREGORY BUTLER	89
PART II **Contexts**	97
5 Households TANYA KEVORKIAN	99

vi   *Contents*

6 Schools   116
MARKUS RATHEY

7 Churches   142
ROBIN A. LEAVER

8 Courts   191
ANDREW TALLE

PART III
Musical Influences   211

9 The Alt-Bachisches Archiv   213
STEPHEN ROSE

10 Other Composers   237
KIRSTEN BEIßWENGER

PART IV
Genres and Forms   265

11 Vocal Music   267
MARK A. PETERS

12 Keyboard Music   295
DAVID YEARSLEY

13 Instrumental Chamber and Ensemble Music   317
DAVID LEDBETTER

14 Chorales   358
ROBIN A. LEAVER

15 Counterpoint, Canons and the Late Works   377
PAUL WALKER

16 Compositional Technique   398
ULRICH SIEGELE

Contents vii

PART V
Dissemination

435

17 Sons, Family and Pupils

437

STEPHEN ROE

18 Early Posthumous Printed Editions

464

MATTHEW DIRST

19 Recent Research Developments

475

MANUEL BÄRWALD

PART VI
Chronology

485

20 Life and Works 1685–1750

487

ROBIN A. LEAVER

Index

541

List of Illustrations

Music Examples

9.1 Johann Christoph Bach, "Ach, daß ich Wassers gnug hätte," bars 1–11. — 225

9.2 Johann Christoph Bach, "An Wasserflüssen Babylon," bars 1–5. — 226

9.3 Johann Christoph Bach, "Ach, daß ich Wassers gnug hätte," bars 16–19. — 227

9.4 Johann Sebastian Bach, "Ich hab mein Sach Gott heimgestellt" (BWV 1113), bars 37–41. — 229

Tables

9.1 Contents of the Alt-Bachisches Archiv — 214

16.1 Categories of formal construction in the Fugues of the Well-Tempered Clavier — 416

16.2 Fugue in A major, *WTC* II (BWV 888/2): Basic Proportional Pattern and its Individualization — 421

16.3 Fugue in A major, *WTC* II (BWV 888/2): Inner Structure of the Halves — 421

16.4 Six-part Ricercar of the Musical Offering (BWV 1079/2): Basic Proportional Patterns — 422

16.5 The System of Time Structure in Bach's Music — 432

Foreword

Within the academic discipline of musicology, Bach scholarship has always played a major role, owing primarily to the historical preeminence of the composer Johann Sebastian Bach. More often than not, advances in Bach research acted as stimulus for methods and approaches throughout the field as demonstrated, for example, in Philipp Spitta's magisterial *Johann Sebastian Bach* (1872/79) that served as a model for historical-critical biography in music, or the groundbreaking studies in the chronology of Bach's works by Alfred Dürr (1957) and Georg von Dadelsen (1958), who laid the foundation for modern music philology. The same is generally true of the game-changing editorial achievements made by the two editions of the complete works, the *Bach-Gesellschaft* edition of 1851–99 and the *Neue Bach-Ausgabe* of 1954–2007, both of which were of seminal importance for the design of scholarly editions in music.

Off and on, Bach scholarship set the pace for and defined the depth and breadth of musicological inquiry up to the present day and including gender or cultural studies as well as other branches of what has become known as "New Musicology." Published and online Bach bibliographies document an immense and sheer limitless field indeed. Nevertheless, Bach scholarship shows its great strength and genuine vitality primarily along the more traditional paths and methods of historical and interdisciplinary studies, which increasingly integrate the innovative features of the digital humanities. The present book reflects this in an exemplary way as the editor's general introduction, with its comprehensive retrospective of Bach studies from their earliest beginnings through the twentieth century, sets the tone for the book's twenty chapters, all written by distinguished and internationally recognized experts.

The editor's introduction will make it abundantly clear how vast and complex a field Bach scholarship has become, how challenging it is for even the better prepared, and how nearly impenetrable it has become for the uninitiated. A well-designed and comprehensive research guide, therefore, is more or less a *sine qua non* for all those in need for basic information, direction, and assistance on the basis of the present state of scholarship. Hence, the organization of the volume focuses on the "classic" areas of Bach studies and follows a pragmatic system of topical subjects.

x *Foreword*

Part I of the book points at the fundamental importance of, and pilots through the study of documentary and musical sources—always the core of serious Bach research—and Part II introduces the institutional context for Bach's lifelong and variegated activities as a musician. Part III illuminates the various spheres of stylistic influences on his music and Part IV advises on the principal genres, types, and techniques of composition Bach engaged in. Part V finally addresses Bach's legacy and early reception history and then turns to current affairs: first the ambitious research projects underway at the Leipzig Bach Archive and second the ongoing concern regarding the difficult issues of Bach chronology.

This modern research guide lends itself to serving as a reliable, encompassing, and up-to-date companion for all who are interested in Johann Sebastian Bach and one of the most fascinating and rewarding areas of musical scholarship.

Christoph Wolff
Harvard University and
Bach-Archiv Leipzig

Preface

According to Carl Philipp Emanuel Bach—as reported by Johann Nikolaus Forkel—his father, Johann Sebastian Bach, when asked how he achieved such mastery of compositional excellence modestly replied, "I was obliged to be industrious; whoever is equally industrious will succeed equally well."[1] Of course Bach was referring to the complexities of composition but his understatement of industriousness applies equally well to those who would undertake research in order to understand, analyze, explain, promulgate, interpret, expose, discover, identify, etc., the remarkable music of Bach that continues to intrigue and astonish performers, audiences, musicologists and music theorists alike.

The Research Companion provides an overview of Bach research of the past generation. The authors cover three aspects of research in their assigned chapters. First, they describe the results and impact of various types of research over the past thirty to fifty years, concentrating on the most significant and controversial. Second, where possible, they outline current research being undertaken that is exploring new aspects, reinterpreting earlier assumptions, and/or opening-up new methodologies. Third, they pinpoint areas that are still in need of investigation and research.

Given the heavily bibliographic content of the chapters, it was thought to be more practical to include full annotations in the footnotes, where the information is presented topically, instead of including abbreviated citations in the notes with an extensive, cumulative, and alphabetical bibliography at the end of the volume. A significant number of the seminal articles discussed in this Research Companion are reprinted in Bach, ed. Yo Tomita, volume 4 of *The Baroque Composers*, ed. David Ledbetter (Farnham: Ashgate, 2011). For a cumulative and continuous database of Bach research, see the online *Bach Bibliography* created by Yo Tomita (www.qub.ac.uk/~tomita/bachbib/) administered by the Bach-Archiv, Leipzig.

I acknowledge with gratitude the advice and assistance of many people, more than can all be named here. First and foremost is Heidi Bishop, who invited me to edit the Research Companion to Johann Sebastian Bach in the first place,

---

1 NBR 459; Dok 7: 57.

xii *Preface*

and then waited patiently for me to decide whether I really wanted to do this, which, eventually, I discovered I did! I am similarly most grateful to all the authors who have written for this volume: your expertise, insight, and patience are much appreciated. But there are several I must single out, notably: my Queen's Belfast colleague, Yo Tomita, whose clear thinking and unstinting assistance have been a constant stimulus; and my Yale colleague, Markus Rathey, whose expertise, encouragement, and translation skills have proved invaluable. I am also grateful to Christoph Wolff not only for writing the Foreword but also for his advice concerning the structure of the volume. I am particularly indebted to Reiko Füting and Emerson Morgan for the clarity of their translations from German.

When I was still teaching musicology, I would begin a new class by telling the students that if they were to succeed in musicology they needed to make friends with a music librarian—better still, marry one! I have never regretted such action and thus this volume, like others, has been brought to fruition with the patience, support, and expertise of Sherry L. Vellucci.

Robin A. Leaver

Abbreviations

AcM	*Acta Musicologica* (1931–).
AfMw	*Archiv für Musikwissenschaft* (1931–).
A-Wn	Osterreichische Nationalbibliothek, Musiksammlung, Vienna.
BACH	*The Journal of the Riemenschneider Bach Institute* (1970–).
B-Bc	Brussels, Conservatoire Royal de Musique, Bibliothèque.
BC	*Bach Compendium. Analytisch-bibliographisch Repertorium der Werke Johann Sebastian Bach*, 4 vols., ed. Hans-Joachim Schulze and Christoph Wolff (Leipzig: Peters, 1985–1989).
Beißwenger BNB	Kirsten Beißwenger, *Johann Sebastian Bachs Notenbibliothek* (Kassel: Bärenreiter, 1992).
BG	[Bach Gesamtausgabe.] *Johann Sebastian Bachs Werke. Gesamtausgabe der Bachgesellschaft* (Leipzig: Bachgesellschaft, 1851–1899).
BJ	*Bach-Jahrbuch*, ed. Arnold Schering, 1904–1939; ed. Max Schneider, 1940–1952; ed. Alfred Dürr and Werner Neumann, 1953–1974; ed. Hans-Joachim Schulze and Christoph Wolff, 1975–2004; ed. Peter Wollny, 2005–.
BJHM	*Basler Jahrbuch für historische Musikpraxis* (1977–).
BP	*Bach Perspectives*, American Bach Society (Lincoln: University of Nebraska, 1995–1999; Urbana: University of Urbana Press, 2003–).

1: *Bach Perspectives*, ed. Russell Stinson (1995).

2: *J. S. Bach, the Breitkopfs, and Eighteenth-Century Music Trade*, ed. George B. Stauffer (1996).

3: *Creative Responses to Bach from Mozart to Hindemith*, ed. Michael Marissen (1998).

4: *The Music of J. S. Bach: Analysis and Interpretation*, ed. David Schulenberg (1999).

5: *Bach in America*, ed. Stephen A. Crist (2003).

6: *J. S. Bach's Concerted Ensemble Music: the Overture*, ed. Gregory G. Butler (2007).

7: *J. S. Bach's Concerted Ensemble Music: the Concerto*, ed. Gregory G. Butler (2008).

xiv *Abbreviations*

 8: *J. S. Bach and the Oratorio Tradition*, ed. Daniel R. Melamed (2011).

 9: *J. S. Bach and His German Contemporaries*, ed. Andrew Talle (2013).

 10: *Bach and the Organ*, ed. Matthew Dirst (2016).

BR-JCFB *Bach-Repertorium 4. Johann Christian Friedrich Bach: Thematisch-systematisches Verzeichnis der musikalischen Werke*, ed. Ulrich Leisinger (Stuttgart: Carus, 2013).

BR-WFB *Bach-Repertorium 2. Wilhelm Friedemann Bach: Thematisch-systematisches Verzeichnis der musikalischen Werke*, ed. Peter Wollny (Stuttgart: Carus, 2012).

BWV^2 [Bach-Werke-Verzeichnis.] Wolfgang Schmieder, ed., *Thematisch-systematisch Verzeichnis der musikalischen Werke von Johann Sebastian Bach*. (Leipzig: Breitkopf & Härtel, 1950; rev. ed. Wiesbaden: Breitkopf & Härtel, 1990). *Das neue Bach-Werke-Verzeichnis* is forthcoming.

BWV^{2a} *Bach-Werke-Verzeichnis. Kleine Ausgabe (BWV 2a)*, ed. Alfred Dürr, Yoshitake Kobayashi, and Kirsten Beißwenger (Wiesbaden: Breitkopf & Härtel, 1998).

CBH *Cöthener Bach-Hefte* (1981–).

CPEB NV *Verzeichniß des musikalischen Nachlasses des verstorbenen Capellmeisters Carl Philipp Emanuel Bach* (Hamburg: Scheibes, 1790). Facsimiles: *The Catalog of Carl Philipp Emanuel Bach's Estate: A Facsimile of the Edition by Scheibes, Hamburg, 1790*, annotated, with a Preface by Rachel W. Wade (New York: Garland, 1981); Carl Philipp Emanuel Bach, *Autobiography [&] Verzeichniß des musikalischen Nachlasses*, annotations in English and German by William S. Newman (Buren: Knuf, 1991); Carl Philipp Emanuel Bach, *The Complete Works*, Series VIII, *Supplement: C. P. E. Bach's Nachlaß Verzeichnis* (1790), ed. Peter Wollny (Los Altos: Packard Humanities Institute, 2014).

D-B Staatsbibliothek zu Berlin – Preußischer Kulturbesitz, Musikabteilung mit Medelssohn-Archiv.

D-Bsa Library of the Berlin Singakademie (deposited in D-B).

DBF [Deutsches Bachfest, Neue Bachgesellschaft]. *Fest- und Programmbuch*, cited by city and year.

D-Dl Dresden Sächsische Landesbibliothek – Staats- und Universitätsbibliothek, Musikabteilung.

Dok *Bach-Dokumente, Supplement zu NBA*, ed. Bach-Archiv Leipzig.

 1: *Schriftstücke von der Hand Johann Sebastian Bachs*, ed. Werner Neumann and Hans-Joachim Schulze (Kassel: Bärenreiter, 1963).

2: *Fremdschriftliche und gedruckte Dokumente zur Lebensgeschichte Johann Sebastian Bachs 1685–1750*, ed. Werner Neumann and Hans-Joachim Schulze (Kassel: Bärenreiter, 1969).

3: *Dokumente zum Nachwirken Johann Sebastian Bachs 1750–1800*, ed. Hans-Joachim Schulze (Kassel: Bärenreiter, 1969).

4: *Bilddokumente zur Lebensgeschichte Johann Sebastian Bachs*, ed. Werner Neumann (Kassel: Bärenreiter, 1979).

5: *Dokumente zu Leben, Werk und Nachwirken Johann Sebastian Bachs 1685–1800. Neue Dokumente. Nachträge und Berichtigungen zu Band I-III*, ed. Hans-Joachim Schulze and Andreas Glöckner (Kassel: Bärenreiter, 2007).

6: *Ausgewählte Dokumente zum Nachwirken Johann Sebastian Bachs 1801–1850*, ed. Andreas Glöckner, Anselm Hartinger and Karen Lehmann (Kassel: Bärenreiter, 2007).

7: Johann Nikolaus Forkel, *Ueber Johann Sebastian Bachs Leben, Kunst und Kunstwerke (Leipzig 1802). Edition. Quellen. Materialien*, ed. Christoph Wolff and Michael Maul (Kassel: Bärenreiter, 2008).

8: *Ausgewählte Dokumente zum Nachwirken Johann Sebastian Bachs 1801–1850*, ed. Peter Wollny (Kassel: Bärenreiter, forthcoming).

Dürr Chr	Alfred Dürr, "Zur Chronologie der Leipziger Vokalwerke J. S. Bachs," BJ 44 (1957): 5–162.
Dürr Chr 2	Alfred Dürr, *Zur Chronologie der Leipziger Vokalwerke J. S. Bachs. Zweite Auflage: Mit Anmerkungen und Nachträgen versehener Nachdruck aus Bach-Jahrbuch* (Kassel: Bärenreiter, 1976).
Dürr K	Alfred Dürr, *Die Kantaten von Johann Sebastian Bach* (Kassel: Bärenreiter, 1971; 10th ed., 2010).
Dürr K, ET	Alfred Dürr, *The Cantatas of J. S. Bach with their Librettos in German-English Parallel Text*, rev & trans. Richard D. P. Jones (Oxford: Oxford University Press, 2005).
Dürr St	Alfred Dürr, *Studien über die frühen Kantaten J. S. Bachs* (Leipzig: Breitkopf & Härtel, 1951).
Dürr St 2	Alfred Dürr, *Studien über die frühen Kantaten J. S. Bachs. Verbesserte und erweiterte Fassung der Jahr 1951 erschienenen Dissertation* (Wiesbaden: Breitkopf & Härtel, 1977).
ECM	*Eighteenth-Century Music* (2004–).
EM	*Early Music* (1973–).
ET	English translation.
FK	Martin Falck, "Katalog," in *Wilhelm Friedemann Bach: Sein Leben und seine Werke* (Leipzig: Kahnt, 1913; 2nd ed. 1919).
GB-Lbl	British Library, London.

xvi *Abbreviations*

GB-Ob	Bodleian Library, Oxford.
H	E. Eugene Helm, *Thematic Catalogue of the Works of Carl Philipp Emanuel Bach* (New Haven: Yale University Press, 1989).
I-Bc	Museo internazionale e biblioteca della musica di Bologna.
JAMS	*Journal of the American Musicological Society* (1948–).
JM	*Journal of Musicology* (1982–).
KB	*Kritischer Bericht* of NBA.
Kobayashi	Yoshitake Kobayashi, "Zur Chronologie der Spätwerke Johann Sebastian Bachs. Kompositions- und Aufführungstätigkeit von 1736 bis 1750," BJ 74 (1988): 7–72.
Kobayashi/Herz	Gerhard Herz, "Yoshitake Kobayashi's Article 'On the Chronology of the Last Phase of Bach's Work. Compositions and Performances: 1736 to 1750.' An Analysis with Translated Portions of the Original Text," BACH 21/1 (1990): 3–25.
LBB	*Leipziger Beiträge zur Bach-Forschung*, Bach-Archiv Leipzig (Hildesheim: Olms, 1995–).

> 1: *Passionmusiken im Umfeld Johann Sebastian Bachs/ Bach unter den Diktaturen 1933–1945 und 1945–1989*, ed. Hans-Joachim Schulze, Ulrich Leisinger and Peter Wollny (1995).
>
> 2: *Die Bach-Quellen der Bibliotheken in Brüssel: Katalog*, ed. Hans-Joachim Schulze, Ulrich Leisinger and Peter Wollny (1997).
>
> 3: *Die Briefentwürfe des Johann Elias Bach (1705–1755)*, ed. Evelin Odrich and Peter Wollny, 2nd expanded ed. (2005).
>
> 4: *Carl Philipp Emanuel Bach: Dokumente zu Leben und Wirken aus der zeitgenössischen hamburgischen Presse*, ed. Barbara Wiermann (2000).
>
> 5: *Bach in Leipzig – Bach und Leipzig: Konferzbericht Leipzig 2000*, ed. Ulrich Leisinger (2002).
>
> 6: *Die Anfänge einer Bach-Gesamtausgabe*, ed. Karen Lehmann (2004).
>
> 7: *Musik, Kunst und Wissenschaft im Zeitalter J. S. Bachs*, ed. Ulrich Leisinger and Christoph Wolff (2005).
>
> 8: *Die Bach-Quellen der Sing-Akademie zu Berlin: Katalog*, 2 vols., ed. Wolfram Enßlin (2005–2006).
>
> 9: *Johann Christoph Friedrich Bach: Briefe und Dokumente*, ed. Ulrich Leisinger (2011).
>
> 10: *Die Bach-Quellen in Wien und Alt-Österreich: Katalog*, 2 vols., ed. Christine Blanken (2011).
>
> 11: *Die ältere Notenbibliothek der Thomasschule zu Leipzig: Verzeichnis eines weitgehend verschollenen Bestands*, ed. Andreas Glöckner (2011).

LQ	*Lutheran Quarterly* (1987–).
Mf	*Die Musikforschung* (1948–).

Abbreviations xvii

MGG	*Die Musik in Geschichte und Gegenwart. Allgemeine Enzyklopädie der Musik,* ed. Friedrich Blume (Kassel: Bärenreiter, 1949–1986).
MGG[2]	*Die Musik in Geschichte und Gegenwart. Allgemeine Enzyklopädie der Musik. Begrundet von Friedrich Blume,* ed. Ludwig Fincher (Kassel: Bärenreiter, 1994–2007).
ML	*Music & Letters* (1920–).
MQ	*Musical Quarterly* (1915–).
MT	*The Musical Times* (1844–).
MuK	*Musik und Kirche* (1929–).
NBA	[Neue Bach-Ausgabe.] *Johann Sebastian Bach: Neue Ausgabe sämtliche Werke,* ed. Johann-Sebastian-Bach-Insitut, Göttingen and the Bach-Archiv, Leipzig (Kassel: Bärenreiter, 1954–2007).
NBA[rev]	*Johann Sebastian Bach: Neue Ausgabe sämtliche Werke – Revidierte Edition,* ed. Bach-Archiv, Leipzig (Kassel: Bärenreiter, 2010–).
NBR	Hans T. David and Arthur Mendel, *The New Bach Reader: A Life of Johann Sebastian Bach in Letters and Documents,* revised and enlarged by Christoph Wolff (New York: Norton, 1998; first published in 1945, 2nd ed. 1966).
NG[1]	*The New Grove Dictionary of Music and Musicians,* ed. Stanley Sadie (London: Macmillan, 1980).
NG[2]	*The New Grove Dictionary of Music and Musicians: Second Edition,* ed. Stanley Sadie (London: Macmillan, 2001).
NG[Online]	*Grove Music Online,* ed. Dean Root. Part of *Oxford Music Online* http://www.oxfordmusiconline.com
RISM	*Répertoire International des Sources Musicales* (1971–).
Schulze	Hans-Joachim Schulze, *Studien zur Bach-Überlieferung im 18. Jahrhundert* (Leipzig: Peters, 1984).
Spitta	Philipp Spitta, *Johann Sebastian Bach* (Leipzig: Breitkopf & Härtel, 1873–1880; reprint, Wiesbaden: Breitkopf & Härtel, 1864).
Spitta ET	Philipp Spitta, *Johann Sebastian Bach, His Work and Influence on the Music of Germany, 1685–1750,* trans. Clara Bell and J.A. Fuller-Maitland, John Alexander (London: Novello, 1884; reprint, New York: Dover, 1951).
TBSt 1, 2/3, 4/5	*Tübinger Bach-Studien,* ed. Walter Gerstenberg. 1: Georg von Dadelsen, *Bemerkungen zur Handschrift Johann Sebastian Bachs, seiner Familie und seines Kreises* (Trossingen: Hohner, 1957). 2/3: Paul Kast, *Die Bach-Handschriften der Berliner Staatsbibliothek* (Trossingen: Hohner, 1958). 4/5: Georg von Dadelsen, *Beiträge zur Chronologie der Werke Johann Sebastian Bachs* (Trossingen: Hohner, 1958).

xviii   *Abbreviations*

UB
Understanding Bach, open access journal of Bach Network UK (2006–) http://www.bachnetwork.co.uk/understanding-bach/

WA
[Weimarer Ausgabe] *Luthers Werke: Kritische Gesamtausgabe* (Weimar: Böhlau, 1883–1993).

WA BR
Luthers Werke: Kritische Gesamtausgabe. Briefwechsel (Weimar: Böhlau, 1930–1985).

WA TR
Luthers Werke: Kritische Gesamtausgabe. Tischreden (Weimar: Böhlau, 1912–1921).

Weiß
Katalog der Wasserzeichen in Bachs Originalhandschriften, ed. Wisso Weiß and Yoshitaki Kobayashi, NBA IX/1 (1985).

Wolff BLM
Christoph Wolff, *Johann Sebastion Bach: The Learned Musician,* "updated" ed. (New York: Norton, 2013).

Wolff Essays
Christoph Wolff, *Bach: Essays on His Life and Music* (Cambridge: Harvard University Press, 1991).

Wolff St. ant.
Christoph Wolff, *Der Stile antico in der Musik Johann Sebastian Bachs. Studien zu Bachs Spätwerk* (Wiesbaden: Steiner, 1968).

Wq
Alfred Wotquenne, *Thematische Verzeichnis der Werke von Carl Philipp Emanuel Bach* (Leipzig: Breitkopf & Härtel, 1905; reprint, Wiesbaden: Breitkopf & Härtel, 1968).

WTC
Well Tempered Clavier.

Zahn
Johannes Zahn, *Die Melodien der deutschen evangelischen Kirchenlieder, aus den Quellen* (Gütersloh: Bertelsmann, 1889–1893; reprint, Hildesheim: Olms, 1997).

Zedler
Johann Heinrich Zedler, *Grosses vollständiges Universal-Lexicon aller Wissenschafften und Künste ...* (Halle: Zedler, 1732–1754; reprint, Graz: Akademische Druck- und Verlagsanstalt, 1999) = http://www.zedler-lexikon.de/

Contributors

Manuel Bärwald studied musicology and philosophy in Leipzig. He has been a research fellow at the Bach-Archiv Leipzig since 2009. Within the research projects "Expedition Bach" and "Bachs Thomaner," he has been responsible for investigating archival documents relating to the Bach family and the history of baroque music in Central Germany. Recent articles have appeared in *Understanding Bach* (2011) and *Bach Jahrbuch* (2012 and 2013). In 2013, he completed his doctoral dissertation: "Italienische Oper in Leipzig: 1744–1756" (Leipzig University).

Kirsten Beißwenger completed her doctoral studies at Johann-Sebastian-Bach-Institut, Göttingen University, with the ground-breaking dissertation, *Johann Sebastian Bachs Notenbibliothek* (1991, published by Bärenreiter in 1992), that identified and catalogued Bach's knowledge and use of the works of other composers. Between 1991 and 1993, she was a research assistant at the Johann-Sebastian-Bach-Institut and the editor of a number of volumes of the NBA, notably NBA IX/3, a catalogue and documentation of Bach's copyists that she edited with her husband, the late Yoshitake Kobayashi. In addition to creating editions of musical scores for Carus, she was a contributing editor of the *Bach-Werke-Verzeichnis. Kleine Ausgabe* (BWV 2^{2a}). From 1993, Dr. Beißwenger was a professor at Dokkyo University, Soka/Tokyo, Japan. At the time of her untimely death in 2013, she was working on a multidisciplinary project of music, literature, and culture in seventeenth- and eighteenth-century Germany.

Gregory Butler is professor emeritus of music at the School of Music, University of British Columbia, Vancouver, Canada, and past president of the American Bach Society. He is the author of *J. S. Bach's Clavier-Übung III: The Making of a Print* (Duke University Press, 1990) and numerous articles on the first editions of Bach's works. He has also written extensively on Bach's concertos and a book-length study on the concerted works is presently nearing completion. He is collaborating with his wife, Lynn Edwards Butler, on a study of the Leipzig organs and organ works of Bach. His interest in the instrumental music of Mozart's Salzburg years has led most recently to research on the Mannheim-Paris trip of 1777–1778.

xx   *Contributors*

Matthew Dirst is professor of music at the Moores School of Music, University of Houston, and also serves as artistic director of the period-instrument group Ars Lyrica Houston. His research interests include Bach and Bach reception, while his performing activities encompass diverse activities as an organist, harpsichordist, and conductor. A recent Grammy nominee for his work with Ars Lyrica, his recordings on the Sono Luminus, Centaur, and Naxos labels feature music by J. S. Bach, Johann Adolf Hasse, Joseph Bodin de Boismortier, Johann Jakob Walther, and the Scarlatti and Couperin families; and his publications include *Engaging Bach: The Keyboard Legacy from Marpurg to Mendelssohn* (Cambridge University Press, 2012).

Tanya Kevorkian is an associate professor of history at Millersville University. She received her doctorate from Johns Hopkins University in 1997. Her areas of interest include Baroque music history, the social history of religion, and colonial Pennsylvania. Her first book, *Baroque Piety: Religion, Society, and Music in Leipzig, 1650–1750* (Ashgate, 2007), was awarded the American Bach Society's 2008 William Scheide prize. Other awards include a National Endowment for the Humanities Fellowship for 2012–2013 and a Summer Faculty Fellowship at the McNeil Center for Early American Studies at the University of Pennsylvania in 2010. Recent publications include "Pietists and Music," in Douglas Shantz, ed., *A Companion to German Pietism, 1660–1800* (Brill, 2015), "Town Musicians in German Baroque Society and Culture," in *German History* (2012), and "The Church, the Street, the Tower, and the Home as Sites of Religious Music-Making in Urban Baroque Germany," in Stefanie Beghein and Bruno Blondé, eds, *Music and the City: Perspectives on Musical Cultures and Urban Societies in the Southern Netherlands and Beyond, c. 1650–1800* (Leuven University Press, 2013). In addition to delivering papers at a range of history and music conferences, she has given preconcert lectures for Tempesta di Mare (Philadelphia), Ars Lyrica Houston, and other ensembles. Dr. Kevorkian is currently at work on her second book, *Music and Urban Life in Baroque Germany, a Comparative Study of Musical Life in Augsburg, Erfurt, Gotha, Leipzig, and Munich.*

Robin A. Leaver is professor emeritus of sacred music, Westminster Choir College, Princeton; and currently visiting professor at the Institute of Sacred Music, Yale University, and Honorary Professor at Queen's University, Belfast, Northern Ireland. He has written the program notes for the Bach Choir of Bethlehem since 1984 and contributes from time to time to the program books of the Bach Collegium Japan. Past president of the American Bach Society, Dr. Leaver is the editor of monographs in the series *Contextual Bach Studies* (Scarecrow/ Rowman & Littlefield 2006–), and the General Editor of *The Yale Journal of Music and Religion*. Recent Bach studies include contributions to *Exploring Bach's B-Minor Mass* (Cambridge University Press, 2013), which he co-edited with Yo Tomita and Jan Smaczny; the *Bach-Jahrbuch* (2013); *Bach: The Journal of the Riemenschneider Bach Institute* (2014), and *Bach Perspectives 10* (2016). He is currently researching the liturgical contexts of Bach's music.

David Ledbetter is an independent researcher in seventeenth- and eighteenth-century keyboard music and performance practice, with a particular interest in how an understanding of context and structure may deepen and enrich performance. Recent publications include: *Unaccompanied Bach: Performing the Solo Works* (Yale University Press, 2009); "Fugal Improvisation in the Time of J. S. Bach and Handel," *The Organ Yearbook* 42 (2013): 53–75; and the final volumes of a performing edition of the String Quartets of Joseph Haydn (with Simon Rowland-Jones, Peters Edition, 2009, 2014). He was series editor of *The Baroque Composers* (5 vols., Ashgate, 2010–2011).

Mark Peters is professor of music at Trinity Christian College, Palos Heights, Illinois. His primary area of research is sacred music of the Baroque period, and he is the author of the monograph *A Woman's Voice in Baroque Music: Mariane von Ziegler and J. S. Bach* (Ashgate, 2008). His other publications include articles in *Bach: Journal of the Riemenschneider Bach Institute* and the monograph *Claude Debussy As I Knew Him and Other Writings of Arthur Hartmann* (University of Rochester Press, 2003), with Samuel Hsu and Sidney Grolnic. In 2006, Peters received the William H. Scheide prize from the American Bach Society for his article, "A Reconsideration of Bach's Role as Text Redactor in the Ziegler Cantatas" (*Bach: The Journal of the Reimenschneider Bach Institute*, 2005). He has presented his research at meetings of the American Musicological Society, American Bach Society, Bach Colloquium, and the Society for Christian Scholarship in Music. Peters has served as secretary-treasurer of the American Bach Society and on the executive committee of the Society for Christian Scholarship in Music. His current research project explores theological, liturgical, poetic, and musical perspectives on the Magnificat in eighteenth-century Germany.

Markus Rathey is professor of music history at Yale University. His research focuses on music in the second half of the seventeenth century, Johann Sebastian Bach, and the Bach family. He taught at the Universities of Mainz and Leipzig and was a research affiliate at the Bach Archive in Leipzig. Professor Rathey's publications include books about Johann Rudolph Ahle, Carl Philipp Emanuel Bach, and an edition of the music theoretical writings by Johann Georg Ahle. His most recent publications are a study of Bach's Christmas Oratorio (published by Oxford University Press) and an introduction to *Bach's Major Vocal Works* (Yale Universty Press). His articles have appeared in journals such as *18th Century Music, Early Music History, Bach-Jahrbuch*, and *Schütz-Jahrbuch*. He is the current president of the American Bach Society and serves on the editorial boards of the *Bach: The Journal of the Riemenschneider Bach Institute* and the *Yale Journal for Music and Religion*.

Stephen Roe worked for more than 35 years at Sotheby's where he founded regular sales of printed and manuscript music and was worldwide Head of Books and Manuscripts from 2009 to 2015. During his time there, he discovered new works and manuscripts by Beethoven, Mozart, César Franck, xxii *Contributors*

J. C. Bach, C. F. Abel, Mahler, Richard Strauss, and many others. He is now a consultant at Sotheby's and a freelance writer on music, concentrating on the Bach family, and in particular on Johann Christian Bach. He has written extensively about J. C. Bach and is currently engaged on a descriptive catalogue of all his autograph manuscripts and preparing a biography. He has also written about Carl Friedrich Abel and is planning to write a monograph on the great viol da gamba player and composer. He is also particularly interested in music printing in London in the second half of the eighteenth century and on the Welcker family in particular. He is a member of the Kuratorium of the Bach Archiv, Leipzig, and was a Senior Research Fellow there in 2013.

Stephen Rose is a reader in music at Royal Holloway, University of London. His research focuses on German music between 1550 and 1750, including its social and cultural contexts, creativity and authorship, and aspects of printing and publishing. Publications include *The Musician in Literature in the Age of Bach* (Cambridge University Press, 2011) and *Leipzig Church Music from the Sherard Collection: Eight Works by Sebastian Knüpfer, Johann Schelle, and Johann Kuhnau* (A-R Editions, 2014). His articles appear in such journals as *Early Music, Journal of the Royal Musical Association, Music & Letters,* and the *Schütz-Jahrbuch.* Currently, he is completing a monograph on music and authorship in the era between Heinrich Schütz and Johann Sebastian Bach. He directs two collaborative projects with the *British Library: Early Music Online* (which has digitized more than 320 books of sixteenth-century music) and *A Big Data History of Music* (which analyses bibliographical records as big data). He is reviews editor of the journal *Early Music,* and is active as a harpsichordist and organist.

Hans-Joachim Schulze studied at the Musikhochschule and the University of Leipzig (1952–57), specializing in musicology and German language and literature. Among his teachers were Heinrich Besseler, Rudolf Eller, Paul Rubardt, Walter Serauky, and Hellmuth Christian Wolff. In 1979, he received his doctorate at the university of Rostock with "Studien zur Bach-Überlieferung im 18. Jahrhundert." In 1990, he was made honorary lecturer at the Martin Luther University of Halle-Wittenberg, and in 1993, honorary professor at the Hochschule für Musik und Theater in Leipzig. He became assistant at the Bach-Archiv in Leipzig in 1957, Acting Director from 1974 to 1979, and in 1992 he became director and project leader of the Neue Bach-Ausgabe, a position from which he retired in 2000. Schulze's publications include *Bach-Dokumente* 1–3, and 5 (1963–72, 2007, vols. 1–2 with Werner Neumann); *Bach Compendium* 1–4 (1986–89, with Christoph Wolff), as well as numerous papers and commentaries to facsimile editions. During 1975–2004, he also served with Christoph Wolff as editor of the *Bach-Jahrbuch,* and in 2007 he translated Kerala J. Snyder's *Dieterich Buxtehude* into German. He is an honorary member of the American Bach Society and the Neue Bachgesellschaft, Leipzig.

Contributors xxiii

Ulrich Siegele was born in 1930 at Stuttgart (Germany). He studied musicology, classics and history mainly at Tübingen University, where he received his doctorate in 1957 and the *venia legendi* (Habilitation) in 1965; subsequently, he taught musicology there, since 1971 as professor, until his retirement in 1995. His main interests in research are the history of compositional techniques, especially the construction of form with regard to duration and functional differentiation (in J. S. Bach, Monteverdi, Schütz, Beethoven, Wagner, and the serial music of the past century), and biography in its historical, political, and economic context (J. S. Bach, Telemann). He has edited and commented on the two seminal publications of the Stuttgart organist Johann Ulrich Steigleder (1593–1635). For more than fifty years, he has worked on tempo and duration in J. S. Bach's music on the premises that the tempo of a piece of music, just as the other parameters, is laid down in its notation. He has recently published a book dealing with the foundations of the Goldberg-Variations, which Bach disposed, with all repetitions, to the duration of exactly 90 Minutes, divided into two halves of 45 Minutes: *Johann Sebastian Bach komponiert Zeit: Tempo und Dauer in seiner Musik*, vol. 1: *Grundlegung und Goldberg-Variationen* (Hamburg: Tredition, 2014). Vol. 2: *Joannes- und Matthäus Passion* (Hamburg: Tredition, 2016).

Andrew Talle has been a full-time member of the musicology faculty at the Peabody Conservatory since 2004, a senior fellow at the Bach-Archiv Leipzig since 2010, and a Gilman Scholar at The Johns Hopkins University since 2011. He studied linguistics and cello performance at Northwestern University and historical musicology at Harvard University, completing his doctorate with Professor Christoph Wolff in 2003. Dr. Talle has published articles in the *Bach-Jahrbuch*, the *Cöthener Bach-Hefte*, and *Stadtgeschichte: Mitteilungen des Leipziger Geschichtsvereins*, among others. He is the editor of *Bach and His German Contemporaries* (University of Illinois Press, 2013). The same press will publish his monograph on keyboard culture in the time of J. S. Bach in 2016. His research on travel diaries from the first half of the eighteenth century is supported by a grant from the Alexander von Humboldt Foundation.

Yo Tomita is professor of Musicology at School of Creative Arts, Queen's University Belfast, Northern Ireland, and senior fellow of the Bach-Archiv, Leipzig. Tomita received his doctorate from the University of Leeds in 1991 with a dissertation on the sources of Bach's *The Well-Tempered Clavier*, part II. Since its release on the internet in May 1997, his Bach Bibliography (www.music.qub.ac.uk/tomita/bachbib/) has been widely recognized as an essential resource among fellow scholars, the development of which, from 2012, comes under the oversight of the Bach-Archiv. Tomita organized the international symposium "Understanding Bach's B-minor Mass" at Queen's University Belfast in 2007, and in 2010 he chaired the Fourteenth Biennial International Conference in Baroque Music in Belfast. In 2012, he was named the third Gerhard Herz Visiting Professor in Bach Studies at the University

xxiv   *Contributors*

of Louisville. With Ruth Tatlow, he currently holds the joint editorship of *Understanding Bach*, the online journal of Bach Network UK. His recent publication includes essays in *The English Bach Awakening. Knowledge of J. S. Bach and his Music in England 1750–1830*, ed. Michael Kassler (Ashgate, 2004), *The Piano in Nineteenth-Century British Culture. Instruments, Performers and Repertoire*, eds. Therese Ellsworth and Susan Wollenberg (Ashgate, 2007), a critical edition of *The Well-Tempered Clavier*, part II (Henle, 2007); and edited books *Bach: The Baroque Composers* (Ashgate, 2011) and *Exploring Bach's B-minor Mass* (Cambridge University Press, 2013). Tomita is currently working on a two-volume monograph *The Genesis and Early History of Bach's Well-tempered Clavier, Book II: a Composer and his Editions, c.1738–1850* (Ashgate), and *The Cambridge Bach Encyclopedia* (Cambridge University Press).

Paul Walker is associate professor of Music at the University of Notre Dame, Indiana, where he teaches studio organ, organ literature, and other courses in the graduate program of Sacred Music. His scholarly work focuses on the early history of fugue and more generally on the music of the sixteenth and seventeenth centuries. He authored the articles on fugue and related topics for *New Grove II*, and his book *Theories of Fugue from the Age of Josquin to the Age of Bach* (University of Rochester Press, 2000) won the American Bach Society's biennial William H. Scheide Prize in 2002. He has also published editions of music by Samuel Capricornus and Marc-Antoine Charpentier, and is a member of the editorial board for the *Collected Works of Dieterich Buxtehude* published by Broude Brothers. For twenty years before coming to Notre Dame, Walker directed the Charlottesville, Virginia-based vocal ensemble Zephyrus, which specializes in early music and which he founded in 1991. Current projects include a complete edition of a Venetian printed chansonnier of 1535 (to be published by A-R Editions), the final two vocal volumes of the Buxtehude Complete Works, and a book-length history of the fugue before Bach.

Christoph Wolff Adams University professor emeritus at Harvard University, the eminent musicologist, is the recipient of various international prizes and several honorary degrees. He also holds an honorary professorship at the University of Freiburg and memberships in the American Academy of Arts and Sciences, the American Philosophical Society, and the Sächsische Akademie der Wissenschaften, and has served as director of the Bach-Archiv in Leipzig and president of the Répertoire International des Sources Musicales. He has written many books and articles on the history of music from the fifteenth to the twentiethth centuries, with notable contributions to Bach and Mozart studies, such as *Bach: Essays on His Life and Music* (Harvard University Press, 1991), *Mozart's Requiem* (University of California Press, 1994), *The New Bach Reader* (Norton, 1998), and *Johann Sebastian Bach: The Learned Musician* (Norton, 2000, and translated into eight languages).

David Yearsley was educated at Harvard College and Stanford University, where he received his doctorate in music history. He is author of the widely praised *Bach and the Meanings of Counterpoint* (Cambridge University Press, 2002) and *Bach's Feet: The Organ Pedals in European Culture* (Cambridge University Press, 2012), which received the Ogasapian Book Award from the Organ Historical Society. Among his honors as an organist are all major prizes at the Bruges Early Music Festival. He has been an Alexander von Humboldt Foundation Fellow at the Humboldt University in Berlin, a Wenner-Gren Foundation Fellow at the University of Gothenburg, and recipient of an American Council of Learned Societies Fellowship. An active journalist, he has been music critic for the Anderson Valley Advertiser for more than two decades. A long-time member of the pioneering synthesizer trio, Mother Mallard's Portable Masterpiece Company, he teaches at Cornell University.

1 Introduction

Robin A. Leaver

Bach studies have their origin in the activities of his sons and pupils, such as Wilhelm Friedemann and Carl Philip Emanuel in Dresden, Halle, Berlin and Hamburg, and Heinrich Nicolaus Gerber, Lorenz Christoph Mizler, Johann Philipp Kirnberger, Johann Christian Kittel, among others, in Leipzig, Berlin, Erfurt, etc. These in turn influenced others, such as: Baron van Swieten in Vienna who drew around him an influential circle of musicians—including Mozart, Haydn and Beethoven—to perform and discuss the music of Bach; A. F. C. Kollmann in London who promoted and published Bach's keyboard music and encouraged others, such as Samuel Wesley, Karl Friedrich Horn, and Benjamin Jacob, to study, perform and publish Bach's music; and Johann Nikolaus Forkel, the pioneering music historian and bibliographer of Göttingen University, who brought a systematic aesthetic and analytic approach to the music of Bach, which he saw as the climax of European music.

A primary concern of the emerging Bach movement was the search for as much of the music of the master that could be recovered; thus, at an early stage there was much sharing and copying of manuscripts. At the same time, some of the early Bach enthusiasts, such as Marpurg and Adlung, discussed and analyzed his music in their treatises of music theory and performance practice, and from the early decades of the nineteenth century there was a steady stream of publications of Bach's music, with a particular emphasis on the keyboard and organ music, though an increasing number of the vocal works were also being issued. The second half of the nineteenth century saw an intensification of Bach studies, fueled by the steady stream of the volumes of the collected edition of the Bachgesellschaft, and the comprehensive biographical and analytical volumes of Carl Heinrich Bitter and Philipp Spitta. By this time, of course, a significant amount of Bach's music was known, performed and venerated, garnering epithets and superlatives from leading composers, performers and theorists, as well as from the general concert-going public, though much of this music was actually heard in churches and chapels.

At the beginning of the nineteenth century Bach's music had been promoted and studied in semi-private groups of professional and accomplished amateur musicians, but now, as the century began to draw to its close, much of Bach's

2   Robin A. Leaver

music had become public and popular, especially in Germany where political, artistic and cultural concerns were becoming fused together with nationalistic aspirations. Bach studies that had originated from internal imperatives that sought to understand the music of Bach on its own terms became increasingly subject to external pressures.

Germany in the later nineteenth century had only recently become a unified country, under Kaiser Wilhelm I, and the ethos of the newly integrated nation was decidedly Protestant. The Prussian court preacher, Adolf Stoecker, immediately following unification in 1871, declared: "Das heilige evangelische Reich deutscher Nation vollendet sich" (The holy Protestant empire of the German nation is now complete).[1] The use of the term "evangelische"—meaning Protestant and not simply Lutheran—recalled and contrasted the earlier term "Römisches" in the title that was forcibly abandoned in 1806: "Heiliges Römisches Reich Deutscher Nation" (Holy Roman Empire of the German Nation).[2] The distinction between "evangelische" and "Römische" had clear anti-Catholic overtones as Prussian Protestantism was energetically promoted. A larger-than-life image of the reformer Martin Luther was created as the symbol of this "Nationalreligiosität," an amalgam of nationalism and politicized Christianity that was widely disseminated in popular culture.[3] This was particularly intensified in 1883, the year in which the 400th anniversary of Luther's birth was celebrated with all kinds of events, including specially composed oratorios,[4] and the publishing of the first volume of what was to become the monumental Weimarer Ausgabe of Luther's works, which was issued with a kind of Prussian imprimatur.[5] A Luther cult was developed and promoted in which the reformer

---

1   Cited Heinrich August Winkler, *Der lange Weg nach Westen: Deutsche Geschichte vom Ende des Alten Reiches bis zum Untergang der Weimarer Republik*, 4th ed. (Munich: Beck, 2002), 214. Bach had long been extolled as a hero of Prussian Protestantism; see the comment of Ferdinand Adolph Gelbcke (1841), Dok 6: 211 (No. B14).

2   For the background, see Heinz Schilling, ed., *Heiliges Römisches Reich Deutscher Nation 962 bis 1806: Altes Reich und neue Staaten 1495 bis 1806* (Dresden: Sandstein, 2006).

3   See the relevant contemporary literature assembled by Dieter Langewiesche, "Nation, Nationalism, Nationalstaat: Forschungsstand und Forschungsperspektiven," *Neue Politische Literatur* 40 (1995): 190–236.

4   See Linda Maria Koldau, "Träger nationaler Gesinnung: Luther-Oratorien im 19. Jahrhundert," *Musik zwischen ästhetischer Interpretation und sozilogischen Verständnis*, eds. Tatjana Böhme-Mehner and Motje Wolf (Essen: Blau Eule, 2006), 55–84; an abbreviated and revised ET: "Singing Luther's Praises in 1883 with L. Meinardus," LQ 25 (2011): 279–297. See also the lecture that political historian Heinrich von Treitschke gave in Darmstadt in 1883, "Luther and the German Nation" (*Germany, France, Russia, and Islam* (London: Jarrold, Allen & Unwin, 1915), 223–255), that included such phrases as: "our Protestant nation" (p. 224); "the Reformer of our Church [Luther] was the pioneer of the whole German nation" (p. 225); "lady Music, the most German of all the arts" (p. 249).

5   At the head of the list of subscribers, in a separate section, two Prussian princes appear—crown prince Friedrich Wilhelm, who received three copies and prince Albrecht who received one—and the Prussian ministry responsible for religious affairs—Das Königlich Preußische Ministerium der geistlichen, Unterrichts- und Medical-Angelegenheiten (Prussian Ministry of Religious, Educational and Medical Affairs)—received 25 copies; see WA 1: iii.

Introduction 3

was seen as the prophet and hero of the German nation, supremely in his nailed protest of the ninety-five theses of 1517, which was interpreted as a defiant anti-Catholic action.[6] However, it was a carefully constructed image of Luther that exaggerated some aspects and eliminated others, for example, while the ninety-five theses were published in the first volume of the Weimarer Ausgabe in 1883,[7] Luther's own critical evaluation of them was effectively suppressed and not included in the collected edition until 1967.[8]

The Bach movement in many respects became a subset of the nationalist Luther cult. Bach the supreme Protestant cantor was venerated alongside Luther, the supreme Protestant reformer. The concept was fueled by Philipp Spitta, who in the preface to his monumental study hailed Bach as "Germany's greatest church composer."[9] Of course German nationalism was not new or new to the Bach movement, as Forkel's pioneering study of 1802 clearly demonstrates, especially his final sentences,[10] but the intensity and scope of the popular movement under the influence of Prussian Protestantism was something more broadly based and more widely disseminated:[11] Bach's music was understood and heard as the "audible Fatherland."[12]

The Bachgesellschaft came into existence in 1850 with the aim to publish the complete works of the composer. When the final volume appeared in 1900 the old society was disbanded and replaced by the Neue Bachgesellschaft. In May that year, Julius Smend reported:

> Under the chairmanship of Professor Kretzschmar in Leipzig a new Bachgesellschaft has been formed. Its purpose is "to create a reviving power for the works of the great German composer among the German people and

---

6 The concepts of Luther as hero and prophet of the German nation were not new; see Robert Kolb, *Martin Luther as Prophet, Teacher and Hero: Images of the Reformer 1520–1620* (Grand Rapids: Baker Academic, 1999); but the political and popular way in which Luther was presented in the aura of late-nineteenth-century Romanticism was new.

7 WA 1: 233–238.

8 WA BR 12: 2–10.

9 "Deutschlands größten Kirchencomponisten." Spitta, 1: xxvii; the preface was not translated for the English edition. See also Wolfgang Sandberger, *Das Bach-Bild Philipp Spittas: Ein Beitrag zur Geschichte der Bach-Rezeption in 19. Jahrhundert* (Stuttgart: Steiner, 1997), 19–20.

10 "Und dieser Mann – der größte musikalische Dichter und der größte musikalischer Declamator, den es je gegeben hat, und den es wahrscheinlich je geben wird – war ein Deutscher. Sey stolz auf ihn, Vaterland; sey auf ihn stolz, aber, sey auch seiner werth!" Dok 7: 89; "And this man, the greatest musical poet and the greatest musical orator that ever existed, was a German. Let his country be proud of him; let it be proud, but, at the same time, worthy of him!" NBR 479.

11 For the background, see Markus Rathey, "Bach-Renaissance, Protestantismus und nationale Identität im deutschen Bürgertum des 19. Jahrhunderts," *Protestantische Identität und erinnerung: Von der Reformation bis zur Bürgerrechtsbewegung in der DDR*, eds. Joachim Eibach and Marcus Sandl (Göttingen: Vandenhoeck & Ruprecht, 2003), 177–190.

12 Rathey, "Bach-Renaissance," 189: "auditives Vaterland," a pun on Heinrich Heine's name for the Jewish Torah, "portatives Vaterland" (portable Fatherland).

4   Robin A. Leaver

in those countries that are receptive to serious German music." Now that the Bachgesellschaft has finished its task of publishing the complete critical edition of the works of Bach, a new [society] steps forth, which has the goal, through regular migrating Bachfests, by publishing popular cheap editions [of music], and by the founding of this affiliated society, to make fully accessible Bach's music to our people and the Protestant churches.[13]

In the revised regulations (Satzungen) of 1907 the desire to make Bach's music accessible to the churches was advanced from the last item to the second, that a primary aim of the Neue Bachgesellschaft was "in particular to make it possible for those works he wrote for the church to be used in worship."[14] Thus a notable feature of the Bachfest of the Neue Bachgesellschaft was (and remains) that Bach's vocal and organ works should be heard within liturgical worship, together with other music and preaching. At the second Bachfest in Leipzig in 1904, the influence of the Luther cult was plain. Since it took place at the beginning of October, when the annual Reformation festival was usually held at the end of that month, the worship service at the Bachfest was a reconstruction of a Leipzig Lutherfest service. Bach's Reformation cantata, *Gott der Herr ist Sonn und Schild* (BWV 79) was performed, together with concerted music by Johann Christoph Altnickol, a motet by Hassler—*Deus noster refugium*, Psalm 46, the Psalm from which Luther created his *Ein feste Burg*—and organ music by Pachelbel as well as by Bach.[15] At the same Bachfest, Karl Greulich, a pastor in Thuringia, gave a keynote address, "Bach and Lutheran Worship," which was published a few months later in the first issue of the *Bach-Jahrbuch*. It was clearly an exposition of the aim of the leading members of the Neue Bachgesellschaft to promote Bach's

---

13 *Monatschrift für Gottesdienst und kirchliche Kunst* 5 (1900): 145: "Unter dem Vorsitz von Professor Kretzschmar in Leipzig hat sich eine neue Bachgesellschaft gebildet. Ihr Zweck ist, 'den Werken des großen deutschen Tonmeisters eine belebende Macht im deutschen Volke und in den ernster deutscher Musik zugänglich Ländern zu schaffen.' Nachdem die Bachgesellschaft mit der Veröffentlichung der kritischen Gesamtausgabe der Werke Bachs ihre Aufgabe erfüllt hat, tritt die neue auf den Plan, um durch regelmäßige wandernde Bach-Feste, durch Veranstaltung volkstümlicher billiger Ausgaben und durch Begründig von Zweigvereinen die Bachsche Musik unser Volke und den evangelischen Kirchen vollends zugänglich zu machen."

14 "2. Zweck. Der Zweck der Neuen Bachgesellschaft ist, den Werken des große deutschen Tonmeisters Johann Sebastian Bach eine belebende Macht im deutschen Volke und in dem ernster deutscher Musik zugängigen Länden zu schaffen, insbesondere auch seine für die Kirche geschaffenen Werke dem Gottesdienste nutzbar zu machen." DBF Eisenach (1907), 8. Earlier statements regarding the aims and objectives of the Neue Bachgesellschaft make no reference to the liturgical use of Bach's vocal works; see, for example, DBF Leipzig (1904), 123.

15 DBF Leipzig (1904), 103–110. The liturgy, its chants, chorales and scores of the other music were published the following year by Neue Bachgesellschaft: *Fest-Gottesdienst zum* [Zweites] *deutschen Bachfeste in der Thomaskirche zu Leipzig* [1904], ed. Georg Rietschel (Leipzig: Breitkopf & Härtel, 1905). The Deutsche Bachfest *Festschrift* included a detailed explanation of the liturgy by Georg Rietschel, "Der Gottesdienst des zweiten Bachfestes am Sonntag, den 2. Oktober" (DFB Leipzig (1904), 73–83), which was reprinted as the introduction to the *Fest-Gottesdienst zum deutschen Bachfeste in der Thomaskirche zu Leipzig*, ii–vi.

Introduction 5

music within liturgical worship. Greulich concluded that the new society had a message for the nation: "'Bach for the German people!' is even more important than the enthusiasts' cry 'Dürer for the German people!' And further, 'Bach in Lutheran worship' is yet more important than the narrow-minded intolerant cry 'Parsifal for Bayreuth!'"[16] Here Greulich was giving rhetorical resonance to a primary principle that the Direktorium of the Neue Bachgesellschaft defined in the Satzungen of the new society.

The Direktorium in the early years included such musicians as Joseph Joachim, Siegfried Ochs, Hermann Kretzschmar and Karl Straube, but they were balanced by theologians and churchmen such as Friedrich Spitta, Julius Smend and Georg Rietschel.[17] These three were involved in liturgical studies as well as Lutheran church music. Friedrich Spitta, younger brother of Philipp Spitta, was professor of theology and university preacher in Straßburg, who wrote on Bach, Handel, and Schütz, as well as Luther.[18] Julius Smend, father of Friedrich Smend, was a colleague of Friedrich Spitta in Straßburg and was also particularly involved in liturgical studies.[19] In 1896, Friedrich Spitta and Julius Smend co-founded and co-edited the *Monatschrift für Gottesdienst und kirchliche Kunst* that from time to time included articles and reports on Bach and Bach festivals.[20] Georg Rietschel, then pastor of the St. Matthäuskirche (the Neukirche of Bach's day) and professor of practical theology in Leipzig, was close to the Luther cult.[21] His *magnum opus* was *Lehrbuch der liturgik*, a comprehensive and detailed study of Lutheran liturgy in which he declared that Bach "through the cantatas he composed for the worship of Sundays and Festivals [of the church year] ... reached

---

16 Karl Greulich, "Bach und der evangelische Gottesdienst," BJ 1 (1904): 34: "'Bach dem deutschen Volke!' das ist ebensowenig Schwärmerei wie der Ruf 'Dürer dem deutschen Volke!' Und weiter 'Bach im evangelischen Gottesdienst!' das ist noch viel weniger engherzige Intoleranz als der Ruf 'Den Parsifal für Bayreuth!'"

17 For the general background of the founding and early years, see Rudolf Eller, ed., *100 Jahre Neue Bachgesellschaft: Beiträge zu ihrerGeschichte* (Leipzig: Evangelische Verlag, 2001).

18 Representative works by Friedrich Spitta include: *Händel und Bach. Zwei Festreden* (Bonn: Hochgürtel, 1885); *Die Passionen nach den vier Evangelisten von Heinrich Schütz: ein Beitrag zur Feier d. 300-jährigen Schütz-Jubiläums* (Leipzig: Breitkopf & Härtel,1886); and *"Ein feste Burg ist unser Gott": Die Lieder Luthers in ihrer Bedeutung für das evangelische Kirchenlied* (Göttingen: Vandenhoeck & Ruprecht, 1905).

19 Representative works by Julius Smend include: *Die evangelischen deutschen Messen bis zu Luthers Deutscher Messe* (Göttingen: Vandenhoeck & Ruprecht, 1896; reprint, Nieuwkoop: de Graaf, 1967); and *Der evangelische Gottesdienst: eine Liturgik nach evangelischen Grundsätzen* (Göttingen: Vandenhoeck & Ruprecht, 1904).

20 For example, Julius Smend, "Die Matthäus-Passion von Bach und ihre mancherlei Aufführungen," *Monatschrift für Gottesdienst und kirchliche Kunst* 4 (1899): 139–148; Friedrich Spitta, "Bach und Luther," ibid., 5 (1900): 216–219.

21 See, for example, the following books by Rietschel: *Luther und die Ordination* (Wittenberg: Herrosé, 1883); *Luther und sein Haus* (Halle: Verein für Reformationsgeschichte, 1888); and *Luthers seliger Heimgang* (Halle: Verein für Reformationsgeschichte 1890). Rietschel also wrote a study of the role of the organ in Lutheran worship: *Die Aufgabe der Orgel im Gottesdienste bis in das 18. Jahrhundert* (Leipzig: Dürr, 1893).

6   *Robin A. Leaver*

the highest perfection."[22] For the reconstructed Reformation day service of the 1904 Bachfest, Georg Rietschel was responsible for the details of the liturgy[23] and Julius Smend preached the sermon.[24]

The first president of the Neue Bachgesellschaft was Hermann Kretzschmar,[25] an influential figure in German musical life as a writer, teacher and performer, in Leipzig until 1904 and then as the first professor of music in Berlin and later also the director of the Berlin Church Music Institute, among other responsibilities.[26] In two influential articles published in the *Jahrbuch der Musikbibliothek Peters* in 1902 and 1905,[27] Kretzschmar developed his theories of musical hermeneutics. The goal was to reveal the meaning of music, its essential inner essence—not just its outward manifestation of form and structure. The aim was "to penetrate the sense and ideational content that the forms enclose, to search out everywhere the soul under the body, to reveal in every part of a work of art the pure kernel of thought, to explain and interpret the whole."[28] The content of such hermeneutics was characterized by an adjectival vocabulary that expressed categories of feeling.[29] Critics, notably Heinrich Schenker,[30] thought such hermeneutics too subjective and indeterminate to be of much use; nevertheless, Kretzschmar's

---

22   "Durch J. S. Bach, der für die Sonn- und Festtagsgottesdienste diese Kantaten komponierte, erreichten sie die höchste Blüte." Georg Rietschel, *Lehrbuch der liturgik. Erster Band: Die Lehrer vom Gemeindegottesdienst* (Berlin, Reuther & Reichard, 1900), 587. For an evaluation of Rietschel's contribution to liturgical theory and practice in Germany, see Wolfgang Ratzmann, "Die Liturgiewissenschaftler Georg Rietschel in Leipzig: Gottesdiensttheologie zwischen Luther und Schleiermacher," *Die Theologische Fakultät der Universität Leipzig: PersonenProfile und Perspektiven aus sechs Jahrhunderten Fakultätsgeschichte*, ed. Andreas Gösner (Leipzig: Evangelische Verlagsanstalt, 2005), 277–287.

23   See note 15.

24   BJ 1 (1904): 11–18.

25   Kretzschmar alternated with Georg Rietschel as president and was followed by Julius Smend: Kretzschmar, 1900–1902, 1912–1924; Rietschel, 1902–1912; and Smend, 1924–1930; see Eller, *100 Jahre Neue Bachgesellschaft*, 139.

26   See Martin Pfeffer, *Hermann Kretzschmar und die Musikpädagogik zwischen 1890 und 1915* (Mainz: Schott, 1992).

27   "Anregungen zur Förderung musikalischer Hermeneutik," and "Neue Anregungen zur Förderung musikalischer Hermeneutik," reprinted in Hermann Kretzschmar, *Gesammelte Aufsätze über Musik und Anderes* (Leipzig: Breitkopf & Härtel, 1910–1911), 2: 168–192 and 280–293, respectively; translated in Edward A. Lippman, *Musical Aesthetics: A Historical Reader* (New York: Pendragon Press, 1986–1990), 3: 5–30 and 31–45, respectively.

28   Lippman's trans. in *Musical Aesthetics*, 3: 6.

29   See the following analyses: Edward A. Lippman, *A History of Western Musical Aesthetics* (Lincoln: University of Nebraska Press, 1992), 354–355; Lee A. Rothfarb, "Hermeneutics and Energetics: Analytical Alternatives in the Early 1900s," *Journal of Music Theory* 36 (1992): 43–68, esp. 54–55; Lee A. Rothfarb, "Music and Mirrors: Misconceptions and Misrepresentations," *Music in the Mirror: Reflections on the History of Music Theory and Literature for the Twenty-First Century*, eds. Andreas Giger and Thomas J. Matthiesen (Lincoln: University of Nebraska Press, 2002): 233–246, esp. 234–235;

30   See, for example, Nicholas Cook, "Playing God: Creativity, Analysis, and Aesthetic Inclusion," *Musical Creativity: Multidisciplinary Research in Theory and Practice*, eds. Irène Deliège and Geraint Wiggens (Hove: Psychology Press, 2006), 9–24, esp. 13.

Introduction   7

theories proved to be widely popular,[31] not least in Bach circles within which Kretzschmar was prominent.

The Neue Bachgesellschaft exercised considerable influence on Bach research during the first half of the twentieth century. With the combination of having been strongly affected by the Luther cult of the previous quarter of a century or so, being so closely connected with Kretzschmar's subjective musical hermeneutic that was susceptible to theological interpretation, and also being conditioned by the liturgical and theological agendas of Julius Smend, Friedrich Spitta and Georg Rietschel, meant that an exaggerated, one-sided image of Bach was universally projected: Bach, the supreme Lutheran Cantor who was fundamentally and almost exclusively seen as a composer for the church. Ulrich Siegele has characterized this development as the theologization of the Neue Bachgesellschaft.[32] On the one hand, much Bach literature was predicated on the Luther cult, as is witnessed to, for example, in the sequence of books on Luther and Bach by Hans Preuß.[33] On the other hand, there were extravagant statements about Bach, the most notable being his elevation to the "Fifth Evangelist," an epithet that seems to have been created either by Nathan Söderblom, Swedish bishop of Uppsala, or Julius Smend, sometime around 1920.[34] Such sentiments gave rise to a flood of more popular literature in the first half of the twentieth century in which facts were confused by fictions, and subjective interpretations

31 Such ideas were popular in England, as, for example, in Donald Tovey's *Essays in Musical Analysis* (Oxford: 1935–1939, 6 vols., frequently reprinted); see Joseph Kerman, *Contemplating Music: Challenges to Musicology* (Cambridge: Harvard University Press, 1985), 74–75.

32 Ulrich Siegele, "Johann Sebastian Bach – 'Deutschlands größter Kirchenkomponist': Zur Entstehung und kritik Identifikationsfigur," *Gattungen der Musik und ihr Klassiker*, ed. Hermann Danuser (Laaber: Laaber, 1988), 59–86, esp. 68–69.

33 Books by Hans Preuß: *Unser Luther* (Leipzig: Deichert 1917); *Johann Sebastian Bachs Bibliothek* (Leipzig: Scholl, 1928); *Martin Luther, der Künstler* (Gütersloh: Bertelsmann, 1931); *Martin Luther, der Prophet* (Gütersloh: Bertelsmann, 1933); *Martin Luther, der Deutsche* (Gütersloh: Bertelsmann, 1934); *Johann Sebastian Bach, der Lutheraner* (Erlangen: Verlag der Martin-Luther-Bundes, 1935). See also: Julius Smend, *Luther und Bach: Ein Vortrag* (Leipzig: Breitkopf & Härtel, 1917); Philip Wolfrum, *Luther und die Musik: Luther und Bach* (Heidelberg: Pfeiffer, 1917); and Friedrich Smend, *Luther und Bach* (Berlin: Haus & Schule, 1947).

34 See Anders Jarlert, "Bach – ein 'fünftes Evangelium' mit oder ohne einen 'fünften Evangeliste'? Zum Bach-Verständnis Nathan Söderbloms," *Hof- und Kirchenmusik in der Barockzeit: Hymnologische, theologische und musikgeschichtliche Aspekte*, eds. Friedhelm Brusniak und Renate Steiger (Sinzig: Studio, 1999), 51–70. Smend used the epithet in a sermon at the ninth Bachfest in Hamburg in 1921, BJ 18 (1921): 6; see Ruth Tatlow, *Bach and the Riddle of the Number Alphabet* (Cambridge: Cambridge University Press, 1991), 18. Ironically, the concept can be possibly traced back to a letter Friedrich Nietzsche wrote to Erwin Rohde, 20 April 1870: "In dieser Woche habe ich dreimal die Mattäuspassion des göttlichen Bach gehört, jedesmal mit demselben Gefühl der unermeßlichen Verwunderung. Wer des Christenthum völlig verlernt hat, der hört es hier wirklich wie ein Evangelium," *Friedrich Nietzsches Briefwechsel mit Erwin Rohde*, eds. Elisabeth Förster-Nietzsche and Fritz Schöll, 2nd ed. (Berlin: Schuster & Loeffler, 1902), 197. [This week I have heard the Matthew Passion three times by the divine Bach, every time with the same feeling of infinite wonder. Whoever has totally unlearned Christianity truly hears it here as a gospel.]

8   Robin A. Leaver

were preferred to objective investigations.[35] As a result, according to Friedrich Blume writing in 1947, "the journalistic portrait of Bach... became more and more vague and lifeless [and] the portrait drawn by the theologians became increasingly pale and colourless."[36]

These essentially romanticized and theologized images of the Thomascantor had significant ramifications for Bach research. Frequently, it was what was regarded as self-evident that determined what were thought to be the substance and details of Bach's life and works, rather than the substance of researched evidence creating the image of the man and his music. The following are some of the more important misconceptions that were fostered by a distorted image of the composer.

It was regarded that any church musician worth his salt would carefully and methodically compose for the church throughout his life. Thus it was assumed that during Bach's twenty-seven years in Leipzig his output remained at the same rate, which, given the number of extant cantatas, must mean that he composed around one cantata each month. This was drawn from Spitta, whose carefully researched conclusions were simplified and popularized, such as the view that because the Lutheran chorales, and especially the chorales of Luther, were considered to be the glory of the German Reformation, most of Bach's chorale cantatas must have been composed during his mature years, towards the end of his life (between 1735 and 1744 according to Spitta[37]), and were thus to be seen as the culmination of his work as the supreme Lutheran church composer.

The Luther cult fostered by Prussian Protestantism stressed the Germanness of worship, with the consequence that Latin was effectively banished as being the language of Catholicism. Thus Bach's Latin Masses (BWV 233–236) were, for quite some time, undervalued because of their Latin text. Because they were parodied works, it was reasoned that the original German "Protestant" cantatas must be superior to their "Catholic" re-workings as settings of parts of the Latin Ordinary of the Mass. The B minor Mass (BWV 232) could not be so easily dismissed, but at least it was possible to stress its Lutheran character. Thus, Friedrich Smend, among others, insisted that the B minor Mass could not be considered a single unified work but that it had to be regarded as

---

35 A representative example is the romantic fictive autobiography by Esther Meynell, *The Little Chronicle of Anna Magdalena Bach* (London: Chatto & Windus, 1925, with many reprints in England and America). It was translated into German as *Die kleine Chronik der Anna Magdalena Bach* (Leipzig: Koehler & Amelang, 1930; 200,000 copies had been issued by 1936).

36 Friedrich Blume, *Two Centuries of Bach: An Account of Changing Taste*, trans. Stanley Godman (London: Oxford University Press, 1950), 70; originally published as *J. S. Bach im Wandel der Geschichte* (Kassel: Bärenreiter, 1947); reprinted in Friedrich Blume, *Syntagma musicologicum* [1]: *gesammelte Reden und Schriften*, ed. Martin Ruhnke (Kassel: Bärenreiter, 1963), 412–447; 897–898. The essay must have been written during the time Blume was working on the entry "Johann Sebastian Bach," published a few years later: MGG 1 [issued in the first installment published in 1949], cols. 962–1047.

37 Spitta 2: 569; Spitta ET 3: 91.

Introduction 9

four distinct works designed for use at various junctures within the Lutheran liturgy of Bach's day.[38]

It was thought that although Bach could take music originally composed for a secular occasion and re-work it for a sacred purpose, he would never parody a sacred work for secular use; indeed, it was considered an immutable principle. The fact that movements of the St. Matthew Passion (BWV 244) also occur in the Trauer-Music Bach composed for the funeral service for Prince Leopold of Anhalt-Cöthen, performed on 24 March 1729 (BWV 244a), was taken as irrefutable evidence that the first performance of the Passion could not have taken place earlier than Good Friday, 15 April 1729.[39]

All of these "facts," with others that were also thought to be self-evident, have subsequently been proved to be unfounded assumptions.

Two world wars interrupted the exchange of Bach scholarship, though, to judge by the break in the sequence of Bachfests, it would seem that recovery after the First World War took less time, a mere six years (between 1914 and 1920, with a "Kleines Bachfest" in 1917), compared with almost twice the length of time of the interruption created by the Second World War (between 1939 and 1950). The map of Europe was being re-drawn after the Second World War, especially that of Germany, which was divided into two states in 1948: the Bundesrepublik Deutschland in the West and the Deutsche Demokratik Republik (DDR) in the East. Most of the Bach towns and cities, especially in the areas of the former Saxony and Thuringia, were then in the DDR, which was founded as an atheist, communist state.

The international Bach community was ahead of post-war politicians and diplomats, since already in 1946 they had created the Internationale Bach-Gesellschaft, based in Schaffhausen in Switzerland, the country that had maintained its neutrality during the Second World War. Under the presidency of Albert Schweitzer, leading international musicians, such as Ernest Ansermet, Wilhelm Backhaus, Benjamin Britten, Pablo Casals, among others, set up an organization that holds a Bachfest every few years, similar to that of the Neue Bachgesellschaft. Each Bachfest in Schaffhausen included a symposium at which leading scholars presented papers on Bach and his music. Over the years, these symposia have been addressed by such scholars as Rudolf Steglich, Walter Blankenburg, Kurt von

---

38 See NBA KB II/1. Unlike others, Smend was well aware that Luther had not abrogated the use of Latin for Lutheran worship; see Friedrich Smend, "Bachs h-moll-Messe: Entstehung, Überlieferung, Bedeutung," BJ 34 (1937): 58. Although much of Friedrich Smend's work on the B minor Mass has been, rightly, severely criticized, Bach scholarship is nevertheless deeply indebted to him for his careful scholarship that revealed the detail and significance of Bach's use of symmetry and parody in his extended works; see Friedrich Smend, *Bach-Studien: Gesammelte Reden und Aufsätze*, ed. Christoph Wolff (Kassel: Bärenreiter, 1969); Rudolf Elvers, "Bibliographie Friedrich Smend," *Festschrift für Friedrich Smend zum 70. Geburtstag dargebracht von Freunden und Schülern* (Berlin: Merseburger, 1963), 98–100; see also Christoph Wolff, "Die Rastrierungen in den Originalhandschriften Joh. Seb. Bach und ihre Bedeutung für die diplomatische Quellenkritik," ibid., 80, note 1.

39 See, for example, Spitta 2: 568; Spitta ET 2: 398. The year 1729 was also apparently confirmed by the fact that this was the year the libretto was published.

10   *Robin A. Leaver*

Fischer, Alfred Dürr, Hans-Joachim Schulze, among many others,[40] including Friedrich Blume who gave the most far-reaching paper on Bach in the second half of the twentieth century, and did so on the only occasion that the Internationale Bach-Gesellschaft did not meet in Schaffhausen (see further later in this chapter).

The commemoration of the bicentenary of Bach's death in 1950 had enormous repercussions.[41] In the DDR, the Bach-Archiv came into being in Leipzig; in the Bundesrepublik Deutschland, the Johann-Sebastian-Bach-Institut was founded at Göttingen University. The two institutions soon joined forces to exercise editorial oversight of a completely new edition of Bach's works: the Neue Bach Ausgabe.[42] The volumes of the old Bachgesellschaft edition, some nearly a hundred years old, were out of date. Editorial procedures had changed with the passage of time, important manuscripts had either been unknown or inaccessible to the editors of the old edition and some editorial decisions were clearly wrong. Even though the two institutions were committed to the collaborative venture, there was more than a hint of rivalry and competition between them. For example, the respective Bach festivals in Leipzig and Göttingen in 1950 were held on exactly the same dates: 23–30 July.[43] As with earlier Bachfests, these bicentenary festivals were a mixture of concerts, recitals, and cantatas presented within worship services and lectures.[44] There were some indications of where Bach research might be headed at the 1950 Bachfests, such as the volume of documents prepared to accompany the exhibition at the Göttingen Bachfest, a kind of foretaste of the *Bach Dokumente* volumes that would eventually supplement NBA.[45] The primary image of Bach, however, at least in the West, was little altered:[46] in the East, a significant shift in emphasis had begun. The central

---

40   Diethard Hellmann, "Neue Bachgesellschaft und Internationale Bach-Gesellschaft," Eller, *100 Jahre Neue Bachgesellschaft*, 131–133.

41   For a review of the literature generated by the bicentenary, see Friedrich Smend, "Vom literarischen Ertrage des Bach-Gedenkjahres," *Theologischen Literaturzeitung* 76 (1951), cols. 593–600; and Walter Blakenburg, "Theologische und geistesgeschichtliche Problem der gegenwärtigen Bachforschung," *Theologische Literaturzeitung* 78 (1953), cols. 391–410.

42   *Die Neue Bach-Ausgabe 1954–2007: Eine Dokumentation vorgelegt zum Abschluß von Johann Sebastian Bach Neue Ausgabe Sämtlicher Werke herausgegeben von Johann-Sebastian Bach-Institut Göttingen und vom Bach-Archiv Leipzig*, ed. Uwe Wolf (Kassel: Bärenreiter, 2007).

43   DBF Leipzig (1950); *Zum 200. Todestag von Johann Sebastian Bach: Bachfest 1950. Göttingen 23–30 July* (Kassel: Bärenreiter, 1950). On the background, see Elizabeth Janik, *Recomposing German Music: Politics and Musical Tradition in Cold War Berlin* (Leiden: Brill, 2005), 221–228.

44   For example, at the Göttingen Bachfest Christhard Mahrenholz gave a lecture on "Johann Sebastian Bach und der Gottesdienst seiner Zeit"; it was later published in *Musik und Kirche* 20 (1950): 145–158, and reprinted in *Musicologica et liturgica: gesammelte Aufsätze von Christhard Mahrenholz*, ed. Karl Ferdinand Müller (Kassel: Bärenreiter, 1960), 205–220.

45   *Johann Sebastian Bach Documenta, herausgegeben durch die Niedersächsische Staats- und Universitätsbibliothek von Wilhelm Martin Luther zum Bachfest 1950 in Göttingen* (Kassel: Bärenreiter, 1950).

46   See, for example, the essays published under the auspices of the Internationale Bach-Gesellschaft, *Bach-Gedenkschrift*, ed. Karl Mattaei (Zurich: Atlantis, 1950). The book-jacket carried the additional information: "Siebsehn hervorragende Mitarbeiter aus der ganzen Welt vereinigen sich in deisem Band zu einer einzigartigen Huligung and den Genius des Thomas-Kantors."

Introduction   11

committee of the Sozialistische Einheitspartei Deutschlands, the East German communist party, in preparing for the Bach celebrations in 1950, declared that Bach had "burst the church's musical restraints and replaced dead formulas with human feeling and experience, thereby expressing the bourgeois humanist opposition to the declining feudal society."[47]

Around the same time as the bicentenary commemoration, Walther Vetter, professor of music history at Humboldt University, East Berlin (DDR), published *Der Kapellmeister Bach,* in which he called into question Bach's religiosity and presented the composer as being primarily concerned with musical opportunities and being indifferent to specific religious concerns.[48] As evidence, Vetter, for example, cited Bach's willingness to serve the Calvinist court in Cöthen. It was no accident that the title page of Vetter's book twice used the term "Kapellmeister," in contrast to the usual "Kantor" that had until then been the title almost universally applied to Bach. Something of a firestorm ensued. Among the first to register objection was Friedrich Smend in his book on Bach in Cöthen published the following year. In a footnote extending over five pages of small print, Smend challenged much in Vetter's book, especially his reinterpretation of the traditional view of Bach as the Lutheran Cantor *par excellence*:[49] "I must... contradict more forcefully and fundamentally what Vetter has to say on the subject of Bach's religious beliefs and his attitude towards the churches and various denominations."[50] Controversy ensued. In the years that followed, writings on Bach published in the DDR tended to diminish the significance of religion for Bach and promoted the "Kapellmeister" rather than the "Kantor,"[51] whereas in the West the traditional view of the Lutheran "Thomaskantor" generally prevailed.

A few years before the outbreak of the Second World War, Arnold Schering defined the aims and objectives of Bach research:

> Bach research proceeds in three ways in the lively appreciation of the great master. It makes available the original compositions in the form of critical editions; it studies the historical principles upon which stylistically appropriate performance is based; and finally, by revealing the

---

[Seventeen foremost contributors from the whole world join together in this volume to present a singular homage to the Thomas-Kantor.]

47   Cited Janik, *Recomposing German Music,* 225; see also the series of articles under the title "Bach unter den Diktaturen 1933–1945 und 1945–1989," LBB 1 (1995): 105–241.

48   Walther Vetter, *Der Kapellmeister Bach: Versuch einer Deutung Bachs auf Grund seines Wirkens als Kapellmeister in Köthen* (Potsdam: Athenaion, 1950).

49   Friedrich Smend, *Bach in Köthen* (Berlin: Christlicher Zeitschriftenverlag, 1951), 144–149; ET, Friedrich Smend, *Bach in Köthen,* trans. John Page (St. Louis: Concordia, 1985), 183–187.

50   Smend, *Bach in Köthen,* 147: "Noch tiefer aber und grundsätzlicher ist dem zu widersprechen, was Vetter über Bach's Glauben und über sein Verhältnis zu den Kirchen und Konfessionen sagt." ET, 185.

51   See, for example, Meinrad Walter, "J. S. Bach und die Aufklarung? Kritische Bemerkungen zum Bachverstandnis der DDR-Musikwissenschaft," AfMw 42 (1985): 229–240.

12   Robin A. Leaver

characteristic mind-set of Bach's time it establishes the intrinsic value of his creativity.[52]

Of these three research areas, the third, contextual studies, was underdeveloped when Schering wrote and would not become a primary concern until much later; the second, studies of historical performance practices, was in many respects pioneered by Schering and became a significant, if controversial, research area in the second half of the twentieth century; the first, philological research in connection with the production of accurate editions, continued to absorb most of the attention in the post-war decades, linked as it was to the editing of the NBA volumes.

The first volume of the NBA to be published was devoted to Bach's Advent cantatas (NBA I/1) and appeared in 1954. Later the same year, Friedrich Smend's edition of the B minor Mass was published (NBA II/1), well-received to begin with, but as time passed it increasingly became the subject of intense criticism and debate.[53] Bach research was thus again subjected to controversy, which resulted in a significant review of the editorial procedures to be followed by the editors in the subsequent volumes of the NBA.

More controversy was created in 1957–58 by the publication of the groundbreaking research into the chronology of Bach's vocal works by two scholars of the Johann-Sebastian-Bach-Institut, Göttingen: Alfred Dürr's "Zur Chronologie der Leipziger Vokalwerke J. S. Bachs,"[54] and Georg von Dadelsen's *Beiträge zur Chronologie der Werke Johann Sebastian Bachs.*[55] Based on painstaking philological investigations into the handwriting of Bach and his copyists, paper watermarks, and other diplomatic methodologies, research overturned the pioneering chronological conclusions that Spitta had been able to draw from the information that was available to him. The "new chronology"—as it is still called today even though it is half-a-century old—demonstrated that rather than regularly composing one cantata each month Bach was composing at a much more intensive rate and that most were composed during his early years in Leipzig. In the first three years or so of his tenure as the Thomaskantor, Bach's output was more like one cantata each week, though some weeks he must have been working on two or more simultaneously. Further, rather than being the culmination of his mature years, the

---

52 Arnold Schering, *Johann Sebastian Bachs Leipziger Kirchenmusik: Studien und Wege zu ihrer Erkenntnis* (Leipzig: Breitkopf & Härtel, 1936), 1: "In drei Punkten tritt die Bach-Forschung in den Dienst der lebendigen Pflege des großen Meisters. Sie hat die Urschrift seiner Werke in der Form kritischer Ausgaben vorzulegen; sie hat die geschichtlichen Grundlagen zu erforschen, auf denen eine stilgemäße Wiedergabe beruht, und endlich soll sie durch Bloßlegen der eigentümlichen Denkformen des Bachschen Zeitalters ein besonderes Verständnis für die Eigenwerte seines Schaffens vorbereiten."

53 For the points at issue with Smend's edition, see Georg von Dadelsen, "Friedrich Smends Ausgabe der h-moll-Messe von J. S. Bach," Mf 12 (1959): 315–334; ET: "Friedrich Smend's Edition of the B-minor Mass by J. S. Bach," [trans. by James A. Brokaw II], *BACH* 20/2 (Summer 1989): 49–74.

54 Dürr Chr.

55 TBSt 4/5.

Introduction   13

majority of the chorale cantatas were found to have been composed mostly during Bach's second year in Leipzig, 1724–25. The combined evidence showed that most of the church cantatas had been composed between 1723 and 1727.[56] The ramifications of these discoveries took time to be assimilated because they called in question many assumptions that had become widely accepted. For example, Donald Mintz, in a review of von Dadelsen's *Beiträge zur Chronologie,* wrote: "At the present stage, the results of these investigations, massive and well-informed as they are, cannot be accepted without some slight reservations."[57]

In September 1961, the Eighth Congress of the International Musicological Society was held in and around New York. On the fifth day (September 9), the congress met in Princeton and one of the symposia was devoted to "Bach Problems," a session chaired by Arthur Mendel, professor of music at Princeton University. One of the two papers discussed was by Georg von Dadelsen, who gave a summary of recent research into the chronology of Bach's works.[58] Four other briefer presentations, similarly mostly concerned with the implications of the new chronology, were also featured.[59] In one of these, Friedrich Blume juxtaposed the chronological findings of Dürr and von Dadelsen with Smend's discoveries with regard to Bach's parody process to suggest the possibility that, given the intensity of cantata composition in his early years in Leipzig, more of them may have been parodies of earlier composed music.[60] It is clear that Blume was coming to terms with the implications of the new chronology and was working towards the conclusions he would make public in the following year, at the seventh Bachfest of the Internationale Bach-Gesellschaft, held that year in Mainz rather than in Schaffhausen.

The paper that Friedrich Blume gave in Mainz, June 1962, was cataclysmic in its impact because he presented what he regarded as the consequences of the new chronology: "Umrisse eines neuen Bachbildes" (Outline of a New Picture of Bach). He stunned his hearers by his demolition of the popular image of Bach. As soon as the paper appeared in print, it spread like wildfire: published later in 1962 in a German journal;[61] issued the same year as a separate pamphlet;[62] in

---

56 English summaries of the findings Dürr and von Dadelsen were provided, for example, by Arthur Mendel, "Recent Developments in Bach Chronology," MQ 46 (1960): 303–336, and Gerhard Herz, "The New Chronology of Bach's Vocal Music," *Bach Cantata No 140 Wachet auf, ruft uns die Stimme: the Score of the New Bach Edition, Backgrounds, Analysis, View and Comments,* ed. Gerhard Herz (New York: Norton, 1972), 3–50.

57 *MLA Notes* 17 (1960): 572.

58 *International Musicological Society. Report of the Eighth Congress: New York 1961,* ed. Jan Larue (Kassel: Bärenreiter, 1961), 1: 236–249.

59 *Report of the Eighth Congress: New York 1961,* 2: 127–131.

60 *Report of the Eighth Congress: New York 1961,* 2: 128–129.

61 Friedrich Blume, "Umrisse eines neuen Bach-Bildes," *Musica* 16/4 (1962): 169–176; reprinted in Blume, *Syntagma musicologicum* [1]: 466–479; 898–899.

62 Friedrich Blume, *Umrisse eines neuen Bach-Bildes* (Kassel: Bärenreiter, 1962); membership gift of the Internationalen Bach-Gesellschaft.

14 *Robin A. Leaver*

English translation in 1963;[63] and subsequently in other translations and reprints. The "New Picture of Bach" that Blume presented was very different from the old image:

> How disappointed he [Bach] was with Leipzig is attested clearly and beyond dispute by the letter to Erdmann of 1730. Did Bach have a special liking for church work? Was it a spiritual necessity for him? Hardly. There is at any rate no evidence that it was. Bach the supreme cantor, the creative servant of the Word of God, the staunch Lutheran, is a legend. It will have to be buried along with all the other traditional and beloved romantic illusions.... A landslide has taken place in the wake of the new chronology of the Leipzig vocal works established by Georg von Dadelsen and Alfred Dürr.[64]... Spitta's picture of the supreme cantor toiling away for years on end at the task of supplying his Leipzig congregations with cantatas has been destroyed.... On the basis of this one-sided inheritance ... there arose ... [an] over-simplified conception that has dominated the Bach image to the present time. This conception is now being shaken, but the Bach we are beginning to see is certainly no less great than the previous one. At the same time he is more down-to-earth, more human, more tied to his own period.... Those who see Bach as the mere guardian of tradition misinterpret him just as much as those who try to see him exclusively as a pioneer; and those who see in him only the churchman just as much as those who characterize him one-sidedly as the court *Kapellmeister*; and those who see him only as the learned musician in his study just as much as those who lower him to the level of the mere virtuoso, conductor and hack. He was all these things, and his greatness lies not least in the fact that he was able to combine them all in himself and to integrate them, from the power of his own spirit, in a work of absolutely unique quality.[65]

Blume's deconstructionism polarized Bach studies to a considerable degree, and a flood of reviews and articles appeared in popular newspapers and magazines as well as in scholarly journals. On the one hand, there were those who were scandalized by Blume's apparent capitulation to the DDR-Marxist image of Bach as a non-religious, secular composer. Notable among such responses to

---

63 Friedrich Blume, "Outlines of a New Picture of Bach," trans. by Stanley Godman, ML 44 (1963): 214–227.

64 Later he adopts a different metaphor: "What has happened here is the equivalent of an earthquake. Its centre is a new conception of history, and its epicentre the new chronology of the Leipzig choral works by Georg von Dadelsen and Alfred Dürr. This must now be regarded as fully established: a conference of specialists which met at Princeton University in the autumn of 1961 was unable to suggest any objections." Blume, "Outlines of a New Picture of Bach," 222; Blume, *Syntagma musicologicum* [1]: 475.

65 Blume, *Syntagma musicologicum* [1], 470–471, 479; Blume, "Outlines of a New Picture of Bach," 218–219, 227.

Introduction 15

Blume's minimalism was Friedrich Smend who asked "What's Left?"[66] On the other hand, there were others, perhaps mainly music theorists and performers, who welcomed Blume's re-interpretation, because it appeared to give greater attention to Bach's music rather than to what Bach's personal beliefs might have been. One unfortunate byproduct of the debate was the tendency by many of those who adhered to a traditional view of Bach to reject the new chronology simply on the grounds that Blume's new image of Bach was based upon it. Thus books and articles, certainly in the English-speaking world, continued to promote both the image and chronology found in Spitta's study of Bach. For example, the manuscript of W. G. Whittaker's study of Bach's cantatas, issued posthumously in 1959 and reprinted several times over the next thirty years,[67] was completed too early to have incorporated the new chronology.[68] It would be another twelve years before Alfred Dürr would publish his book on the cantatas of Bach, in which the new chronology was consistently presented,[69] and a further thirty-four years would elapse before Dürr's book would appear in English translation.[70]

The divide within Bach scholarship, which Christoph Wolff has characterized as "the completely artificial juxtaposition of Bach the church musician vs. Bach the secular artist,"[71] continued to dominate much of the literature. However, there were moderate voices that pointed out that although Blume was basically right in his condemnation of a mythological Bach image, he nevertheless overstated his case and did not take into account all the available evidence. Alfred Dürr, for example, referred to Bach's letter of resignation from his position in Mühlhausen in 1708[72] in which he expressed his goal of "a well-regulated church music, to the Glory of God."[73] Walter Blankenburg, who some ten years earlier had warned against a distorted image of Bach,[74] reviewed

---

66 Friedrich Smend, "Was bleibt? Zu Friedrich Blumes Bach-Bild," *Der Kirchenmusiker* 13 (1962): 178–190; also issued as *Was bleibt? Zu Friedrich Blumes Bach-Bild* (Berlin: Merseburger, 1962).

67 William Gillies Whittaker, *The Cantatas of Johann Sebastian Bach: Sacred and Secular* (London: Oxford University Press, 1959).

68 When first published, it contained the following note: "In the years since the book was completed, much research has been carried out into the dating of Bach's cantatas, and a number of revised dates have been suggested. At present, however, no final agreement seems to have been reached on this matter, and it has therefore been decided to leave Dr. Whittaker's text unaltered." Whittaker, *The Cantatas of Johann Sebastian Bach*, 1: ix.

69 Dürr K.

70 Dürr K, ET.

71 Christoph Wolff, "Images of Bach in the Perspective of Basic Research and Interpretive Scholarship," JM 22 (2005): 507.

72 Alfred Dürr, "Zum Wandel des Bach-Bildes. Zu Friedrich Blumes Mainzer Vortrag," *MuK* 32 (1962): 145–152.

73 NBR 57 (No. 32); BD 1: 19 (no. 1): "den Endzweck, nemlich eine regulirte kirchen music zu Gottes Ehren."

74 Walter Blankenburg, "Handreichung zum Bach-Jahr 1950 für Pfarrer, Organisten und Chorleiter ...," MuK 19 (1949): 175: "... Gleichzeitig muß jedoch vor einem falschen

16   Robin A. Leaver

and integrated the views of Dürr and Smend, and in particular stressed that Bach's use of parody in his sacred vocal music cannot be construed as evidence that he was disinterested in creating such works.[75] Gerhard Herz, who wrote almost a decade later, was able to point to the Bible commentary edited by Abraham Calov once owned by Bach that only came to light sometime after Blume's Mainz lecture, volumes which contain the composer's underlinings and annotations.[76]

In 1976, Walter Blankenburg, with others, founded the Internationale Arbeitsgemeinschaft für theologische Bachforschung with the aim of exploring the theological and liturgical contexts for which much of Bach's music was created. It was to some degree a response to the challenge of Blume's 1962 Mainz lecture, but in terms of its agenda, it was closer to Blume's call for research that he made a decade-and-a-half earlier. Towards the end of *J. S. Bach im Wandel der Geschichte* (1947), Blume wrote:

> With great courage Schering attempted a completely new interpretation of Bach's music and in his discovery of Bach's use of symbolism he opened up a new approach to Bach's innermost conception of religion and dogma.[77] Schering was able to show that Bach in his vocal works was not merely aiming, as Schweitzer had thought, at translating the words into the language of musical sound, but, in addition to that, as Dilthey had surmised intuitively,[78] he was symbolizing in his music the hidden relationships, the ultimate ideas, in fact the *coincidentia oppositorum* itself, which elude the untutored reader and listener, since to understand them a whole training in the subtleties and sophistications of the old-Lutheran scholasticism is required. This

---

Persönlichkeitskult und einer nach rückwärts gewandten Heldenverehrung gewarnt werden. Die Bezeichnung Bachs als fünfter Evangelist zeugt von einem gefährlichen Mißverständnis seiner Musik: diese dient dem Evangelium, es ist aber nicht selbst. Nicht die Person Bachs, sondern sein Werk ist das Entscheidende." The passage was repeated in *Evangelische Welt* 4 (1950): 26–27, and translated in *Concordia Theological Monthly* 21 (1950): 366: "We must warn against a false personality cult and a backward-looking hero worship. To designate Bach as the fifth evangelist witnesses to a dangerous misunderstanding of his music, which serves, but is not in itself, the gospel. It is not the person of Bach but his work that is decisive."

75 For a review of the initial scholarly debate, see Walter Blankenburg, "Zwölf Jahre Bachforschung," *AcM* 37 (1965): 120–125.

76 Gerhard Herz, "Toward a New Image of Bach," BACH 1/4 (1970): 9–27, and 2/1 (1971): 7–28; reprinted in Gerhard Herz, *Essays on J. S. Bach* (Ann Arbor: UMI Research Press, 1985), 149–184. See Herz's earlier essay, "Bach's Religion," *Journal of Renaissance and Baroque Music* 1 (1946): 124–138, which is an expansion of a section of his doctoral dissertation; Gerhard Herz, *Johann Sebastian Bach im Zeitalter des Rationalismus und der Frühromantik: Zur Geschichte der Bachbewegung von ihren Anfängen bis zur wiederaufführung der Matthäuspassion im Jahre 1829* (Kassel: Bärenreiter, 1935; reprint, Leipzig: Zentralantiquariat, 1985), 2–4; Herz, *Essays on J. S. Bach*, 2–4.

77 For example, Arnold Schering, "Bach und das Symbol," BJ 22 (1925): 40–63; BJ 25 (1928): 119–137; BJ 34 (1937): 83–95.

78 See Wilhelm Dilthey, *Von deutscher Dichtung und Musik; aus den Studien zur Geschichte des deutschen Geistes*, 2nd ed. (Stuttgart: Teubner, 1957), 205–248.

Introduction   17

interpretation seems to open a door on the whole world of Bach's innermost conceptions and ideas. To open it still farther must now be one of the most urgent concerns of future Bach research.[79]

The Internationale Arbeitsgemeinschaft für theologische Bachforschung held regular conferences, published the papers presented at these gatherings and sponsored a number of other publications,[80] including my own bibliography of Bach's personal library,[81] and Elke Axmacher's dissertation on the Passions.[82] The conferences in the early years were generally effective and productive, attended from time to time by such Bach luminaries as Alfred Dürr, Klaus Hofmann, Yoshitake Kobayashi, Hans-Joachim Schulze, among others, in addition to the regular membership—though the continued participation of such Bach scholars declined largely as the result of the non-scientific speculations of some of the members who insisted on such things, for example, as the view that every blot and scribal error in Bach's manuscripts were intentional and held hidden meanings.

Blankenburg's concerns and leadership were of a different order. He had sought to mediate over the Blume controversy and his extensive review articles of Bach literature had already become increasingly comprehensive in scope, going beyond the narrowly theological and embracing more broadly based musicological concerns, articles that first appeared in the *Theologische Rundschau* that were later transferred, expanded and extended in *Acta Musicologica*.[83]

---

79 Blume, *Two Centuries of Bach*, 84; Blume, *Syntagma musicologicum* [1]: 447. See also his earlier comment, after criticizing "snobbish aesthetes" of the earlier decades of the twentieth century, Blume wrote: "No attempt was made even to undertake a thorough scientific study of Bach from the theological point of view, and the Evangelical [Lutheran] church has still to pay a debt of honour in this respect." Blume, *Two Centuries of Bach*, 70; Blume, *Syntagma musicologicum* [1]: 441.

80 See Walter Blankenburg,"Theologische Bachforsching heute," *Bach und die Nachwelt. Band 4: 1950–2000*, ed. Joachim Lüdtke (Laaber: Laaber, 2005), 375–389 (originally given as a guest lecture at Augsburg University in 1985); Renate Steiger, ed., *Theologische Bachforshung heute: Dokumentation und Bibliographie der Internationalen Arbeitsgemeinschaft für theologische Bachforschung 1976–1996* (Berlin: Galda & Wilch, 1998).

81 Robin A. Leaver, *Bachs theologische Bibliothek: eine kritische Bibliographie* [Beiträge zur theologischen Bachforschung; 1] (Stuttgart: Hänssler, 1983).

82 Elke Axmacher, *"Aus Liebe will mein Heyland sterben": Untersuchungen zum Wandel des Passionsverständnisses im frühen 18. Jahrhundert* [Beiträge zur theologischen Bachforschung; 2] (Stuttgart: Hänssler, 1984; reprint, Stuttgart: Carus, 2005); see also Elke Axmacher, "Ein Quellenfund zum Text der Matthäus-Passion," BJ 64 (1978): 181–191.

83 Walter Blankenburg, "Zehn Jahre Bachforschung," *Theologische Rundschau* 29 (1963): 335–358; and 30 (1964: 237–268; Walter Blankenburg, "Zwölf Jahre Bachforschung," AcM 37 (1965): 95–158; Walter Blankenburg, "Die Bachforschung zeit etwa 1965: Ergebnisse–Probleme–Aufgaben," AcM 50 (1978): 93–154; 54 (1982): 162–207; 55 (1983): 1–58. See also Walter Blankkenburg, "Tendenzen der Bachforschung seit den 1960er Jahren, insonderheit im Bereich der geistlichen Vokalmusik," *Bachforschung und Bachinterpretation heute: Wissenschaftler und Praktiker im Dialog. Bericht über das Bachfest-Symposium 1978 der Philipps-Universität Marburg* (Leipzig: Neue Bach Gesellschaft, 1981), 86–93.

18   Robin A. Leaver

After Blankenburg's death, the emphasis changed in the Arbeitsgemeinschaft and the perspective became more narrowly focused. To many in the wider Bach world, it appeared that the old image of Bach the supreme Lutheran Cantor was being repristinated.[84] Ultimately when it became clear that the wider cultural religious issues such as those pursued by Tanya Kevorkian,[85] or the Anti-Judaism explored by Michael Marissen,[86] were not being encouraged, a few of the established members of the Arbeitsgemeinschaft took action that eventually led to the demise of the working group.[87] A possible replacement society has been subsequently discussed, but the prevailing view is that Bach's religious environment, although clearly extremely important, is but one of a variety of different contexts that shaped his approach to composition, contexts that together form a complex matrix of influences that need to be considered in relation to each other rather than in isolation.[88]

Such an integrated approach to Bach studies was Blume's ideal. For him, there was no single key that could unlock the secrets of Bach's life and music, be it theology, philology, rhetoric, or some other discipline or methodology. For him, what was needed was a systematic and multi-disciplinary approach, something that he thought had been neglected in previous Bach research. In October 1968, Blume gave a paper at four North American universities in which he addressed "The Present State of Bach Research." The paper has been largely ignored, partly because its publication was delayed,[89] partly because it remained in

84 Rebecca Joanne Lloyd, "Bach Among the Conservatives: The Quest for Theological Truth," PhD thesis (King's College, London University, 2006) is highly critical of the writings of members of the Arbeitsgemeinschaft. Hans-Joachim Hinrichsen, "Universalität uns Zersplitterung: Wege der Bachforschung 1945–2005," *Johann Sebastian Bach und die Gegenwart: Beiträge zur Bach-Rezeption 1945–2005*, eds. Michael Heinemann and Hans-Joachim Hinrichsen (Cologne: Dohr, 2007), 143–154, offers a more balanced evaluation. However, a primary criticism of Lloyd, that the Arbeitsgemeinschaft was heavily weighted towards theological concerns almost to the exclusion of musical matters, was right on target. Indeed, the weakness was recognized by some of the members and was a major factor in the dissolution of the working group.

85 Tanya Kekorkian, *Baroque Piety: Religion, Society, and Music in Leipzig, 1650–1750* (Aldershot: Ashgate, 2007).

86 Michael Marissen, "Blood, People, and Crowds in Matthew, Luther, and Bach," LQ 19 (2005): 1–22.

87 Something of the internal problems and the over-emphasis on theological concerns can be seen in the highly critical review by Renate and Lothar Steiger of Martin Petzoldt's *Bach-Kommentar* – all three members of the Arbeitsgemeinschaft: Renate and Lothar Steiger, *"... den Bach runter." Protokoll einer Enttäuschung in Briefen an einen befreundeten Autor. Eine gegen die ursprüngliche Absicht doch notwendig gewordene Veröffentlichung, zu Martin Petzoldts Bach Kommentar* (Heidelberg: Paulus, 2004), http://www.palatina-verlag.de

88 Substantial investigations into the theological issues relating to Bach's music continue to appear, such as three major studies of the St. John Passion: Michael Marissen, *Lutheranism, Anti-Judaism, and Bach's "St. John Passion"* (New York: Oxford University Press, 1998); Eric Chafe, *J. S. Bach's Johannine Theology: The St. John Passion and the Cantatas for Spring 1725* (New York: Oxford University Press, 2014); and Andreas Loewe, *Johann Sebastian Bach's St. John Passion (BWV 245): A Theological Commentary* (Leiden: Brill, 2014).

89 Friedrich Blume, *Syntagma Musicologicum II: Gesammelte Reden und Schriften 1962–1972*, eds. Anna Amalie Abert and Martin Ruhnke (Kassel: Bärenreiter, 1973), 281–292; the North American universities were Columbia, Harvard, Binghamton and Toronto, ibid., 404.

Introduction 19

English, partly because it questioned the dominance of philology in Bach studies, and partly because, unlike his 1962 Mainz paper, it contained no burning controversial issue. Yet, his assessment of where Bach studies were around fifty years ago is perceptive and revealing. His conclusion was that "While Bach research has been remarkably revived and enlivened within these 17 or 18 years [1950–1968], it has more and more lost its wide horizon."[90] By this, he meant that philology, the primary tool of the NBA editors, had tended to crowd out biographical, analytical, stylistic, interpretive, archival, cultural, historical and other methodologies.

> This is what happened after 1950. All reverence to Spitta notwithstanding a growing gang of younger labourers went to work with pick-axe and spade and dug the ground on which Spitta had built, wondering whether his fundaments were or were not still sound and whether they would or would not stand for another century. The result was surprising: under the weight of new methods the old masonry crumbled away. Neither was Spitta's knowledge of the sources exhausting nor was his method of criticism satisfying. Bach's handwriting and its development over roughly forty years had to be re-checked. The sorts of paper he used could now be ascertained much more accurately than 60 or 70 years earlier, since research on papers and watermarks had meanwhile grown into an independent field of scholarship.... For the first time in Bach research an organized search was undertaken to trace the copyists of Bach's works and to distinguish the various persons concerned with extracting the parts from his scores... etc.... On the other hand, however, these same methods of research, have, by their accumulation of data and by the one-sidedness of their use, also led into formal philogism. This philogism is the dominant school in present Bach research. Its use is indefinite and it actually serves as a panacea for all scruples and doubts.[91]

Blume is fully appreciative of the radically new information revealed by philological research but is nevertheless aware of its short-comings. On the one hand, he can write: "This new chronology of Bach's vocal works is, in my view, the first important and incisive result of all Bach research within the past 15 or 20 years. It has caused a landslide in the sum of our knowledge on Bach."[92] On the other hand, he can also write: "It is however one of the inherent attributes of philogism that it tends to exaggeration, to perfectionism and to intolerance."[93] On the negative consequences of philogism, Blume registers his concern at what he saw as the decline of investigations into "Figurenlehre" and rhetorical interpretations in general, the lack of appropriate studies of Bach's recurrent use of basic numbers

90 Blume, *Syntagma Musicologicum II*, 290.
91 Blume, *Syntagma Musicologicum II*, 283–284.
92 Blume, *Syntagma Musicologicum II*, 284.
93 Blume, *Syntagma Musicologicum II*, 286.

20   *Robin A. Leaver*

and proportions in his musical structures, the verging on non-existent research into connections between meaning and compositional technique in Bach's works, and the almost abandonment of archival studies.[94]

On the positives that philology brings to Bach research, Blume points to three important areas: biography, *stile antico* and contexts.[95] Blume recognized the biographical consequences of the new chronology. Much of Bach's music was composed earlier than previous research had concluded; therefore, the basic understanding of Bach's development as a composer, especially in his younger years, needed re-evaluation. Similarly, the last decade of Bach's life also needed re-interpretation now that a different picture of his compositional activity had been revealed, especially in light of the researches of Christoph Wolff into Bach's use of the *stile antico* in his own music and of his study of the music of composers such as Palestrina, Bassani, Lotti, Caldara, among others.[96] Blume's final sentences of his 1968 paper focused on what had not yet been accomplished especially with regard to contextual issues.

> There is one fact that often irritates me, but it is not bound up with Bach research in particular: it is the fact that all attempts fail to touch the larger contexts of history. Where is the modern history of Bach as a cantata composer? Or the book on Bach in the history of the mass? Where is the book on so interesting a subject as Bach and French music? Let alone a book on Bach's position in the history of music or his impact on the music of the past two centuries? We are drowned in details of conventional investigation, some useful, some not, we are throttled in the noose of breathtaking subtleties and sophistries but cannot breathe freely the air of wide surveys and comprehensive outlooks. We are captives in the nets and traps of our own anxieties. And this is what we do hope the next generation will achieve: to free us from the tyranny of self-chosen restriction.[97]

The past half century since Blume wrote these words has seen a complete sea-change for musicology in general and Bach research in particular. Waves of iconoclasm have washed away old parameters and methodologies. The new broom of modernism has itself been swept away by postmodernism, which has been pushed aside by a kind of post-postmodernism, as our modern preoccupations, like the "self-chosen restrictions" of Blume's day, still condition how we

---

94   Blume, *Syntagma Musicologicum II*, 286–287, 291. On the latter point concerning archival studies, at the time Blume wrote only Dok 1 had been published.

95   Blume, *Syntagma Musicologicum II*, 290–292.

96   Wolff St. ant; Blume, *Syntagma Musicologicum II*, 291. That a major study of Bach's understanding and use of the *stile antico* had not appeared earlier is in large measure due to the pervasive Protestantism of many Bach scholars who were reluctant to concede that Bach could have been influenced by Catholic composers.

97   Blume, *Syntagma Musicologicum II*, 292.

Introduction 21

investigate the past.[98] Questions that would almost certainly never occur to Bach scholars of Blume's generation have been persistently asked during these years, be they the political inquiries of Susan McClary,[99] the social and cultural perspectives of Lawrence Kramer,[100] the gender queries of Suzanne Cusick,[101] the religious enquiries into perceived non-religious music by Michael Marissen,[102] or the Newtonian explorations of Christoph Wolff.[103]

On the other hand, many of the items on Blume's agenda for future Bach research have been fulfilled. As already noted, one of his concerns was the need to revise the biography of the composer, especially his earlier years, now that the chronology of his compositional output is more accurately known.[104] Important recent biographical studies include the significant volumes on Bach's early life by Konrad Küster and Reinmar Emans,[105] the two short studies of the composer by both Martin Geck and Peter Williams that were followed by full-scale biographies from the same authors,[106] and Christoph Wolff's comprehensive biography that has become the most widely used.[107]

Blume would presumably have been pleased to see the many studies of rhetoric that have appeared in recent decades,[108] though he would not have endorsed

---

98 See, for example, John Butt, "The Post Modern Mindset, Musicology and the Future of Bach Scholarship," UB 1 (2006): 9–18.

99 Susan McClary, "The Blasphemy of Talking Politics during the Bach Year," *Music and Society: the Politics of Composition, Performance and Reception*, eds. Richard Leppert and Susan McClary (Cambridge: Cambridge University Press, 1987), 13–62.

100 Lawrence Kramer, *Classical Music and Postmodern Knowledge* (Berkeley: University of California Press, 1995), 233–242.

101 Suzanne G. Cusick, "On Lesbian Relation with Music: A Serious Effort not to Think Straight," *Queering the Pitch: the New Gay and Lesbian Musicology*, eds. Philip Brett, Elizabeth Wood and Gary C. Thomas (London: Routledge, 1994), 67–83.

102 See note 85.

103 For example, Christoph Wolff, "Bach's Music and Newtonian Science: A Composer in Search of the Foundations of His Art," *UB* 2 (2007):

104 Friedrich Blume, *Der junge Bach* (Wolfenbüttel: Möseler, 1967); Blume, *Syntagma Musicologicum II*, 167–189; ET " J. S. Bach's Youth," *MQ* 54 (1968): 1–30. On writing of contemporary biographical studies, see Robert L. Marshall, "Toward a Twenty-First-Century Bach Biography," *MQ* 84 (2000): 497–525.

105 Konrad Küster, *Der junge Bach* (Stuttgart: Deutsches Verlags-Anstalt, 1996); Reinmar Emans, ed., *Der junge Bach: weil er nicht aufzuhalten .... Begleitbuch* (Erfurt: Thüringer Landesausstellung, 2000).

106 Martin Geck, *Johann Sebastian Bach* (Reinbek: Rowohlt, 1993), ET *Bach*, trans. Anthea Bell (London: Haus, 2000); Martin Geck, *Bach: Leben und Werk* (Reinbek: Rowohlt, 2000), ET *Johann Sebastian Bach: Life and Work*, trans. John Hargreaves (Orlando: Harcourt, 2006). Peter F. Williams, *The Life of Bach* (Cambridge: Cambridge University Press, 2003), Peter F. Williams, *J.S. Bach: A Life in Music* (Cambridge: Cambridge University Press, 2007).

107 Wolff BLM.

108 Representative literature includes: Alan Street, "The Rhetorico-Musical Structure of the 'Goldberg' Variations: Bach's Clavierübung IV and the *Institutio Oratoria* of Quintilian," *Music Analysis* 6 (1987): 89–131; Paul Walker, "Rhetoric, the Ricercar, and J. S. Bach's Musical Offering," *Bach Studies 2*, ed. Daniel R. Melamed (Cambridge: Cambridge University Press, 1995): 175–191; Paul Walker, "Fugue in the Music-Rhetorical Analogy and Rhetoric in the

22   Robin A. Leaver

the opinion of some who insist that rhetoric is the only key to understand Bach's music.[109] Similarly, Blume would no doubt have applauded the significant studies of numerical structures and proportion in Bach's music that have been a feature of recent research,[110] though not the esoteric expositions of number symbolism that purport to reveal cabalistic secrets.

What was at the heart of Blume's agenda for the future of Bach research was above all that it should "breathe freely the air of wide surveys and comprehensive outlooks."[111] By this, I take it that he hoped that Bach would be examined, interpreted, and evaluated not in isolation of disciplines, methodologies and procedures, but rather in an integrated approach to the multiple contexts within which Bach can only be truly approached—historical and contemporary, secular and religious—making full use of archival and documentary sources, the analyses of music theory, the insights of performance practices, as well as the complexities of our virtual world by which new technologies proliferate.[112]

The starting point of this Research Companion is the post-Blume half-century of Bach research. Whether the authors here have proved as far-sighted as Blume was in his day will not be known for some time, but the hope is that what is written here will encourage and inform the continuing quest of Bach research to understand more effectively the man and the music of this remarkable composer.

Development of Fugue," *Bach Perspectives* 4 (1999), 159–179; Warren Kirkendale, "On the Rhetorical Interpretation of the Ricercar and J. S. Bach's Musical Offering," *Studi Musicali* 26 (1997): 331–376; Bettina Varwig, "One More Time: J. S. Bach and Seventeenth-Century Traditions of Rhetoric," ECM 5 (2008): 179–208; Reinhold Kubik and Margit Legler, "Rhetoric, Gesture and Scenic Imagination in Bach's Music," UB 4 (2009): 55–76.

109 See also Peter F. Williams, "The Snares and Delusions of Musical Rhetoric: Some Examples from Recent Writings on J. S. Bach, BJHM. *Sonderband* (1983): 230–240.

110 Representative literature includes: Ruth Tatlow, *Bach and the Riddle of the Number Alphabet* (Cambridge: Cambridge University Press, 1991); Ruth Tatlow, "The Use and Abuse of Fibonacci Numbers and the Golden Section in Musicology Today," UB 1 (2006): 69–85; Ruth Tatlow, "Collections, Bars and Numbers: Analytical Coincidence or Bach's Design?," UB 2 (2007): 37–58; Ruth Tatlow, *Bach's Numbers: Compositional Proportion and Significance* (Cambridge: Cambridge University Press, 2016). Ulrich Siegele, "Proportionierung als kompositorisches Arbeitsinstrument in Konzerten J. S. Bachs," *Dortmunder Bachforschung* 1 (1997): 159–171; Ulrich Siegele, "Taktzahlen als Schlüssel zur Ordnung der 'Klavierübung III' von J. S. Bach. Ein Vorschlag für die Aufführung," MuK 76 (2006): 344–351; Ulrich Siegele, "Taktzahlen als Ordnungsfaktor in Suiten- und Sonatensammlungen von J. S. Bach. Mit einem Anhang zu den Kanonischen Veränderungen über 'Vom Himmel hoch,'" AfMw 63 (2006): 215–240; Ulrich Siegele, "Taktzahlen der Präludien und Fugen in Sammlungen mit Tastenmusik von J. S. Bach," *Dortmunder Bachforschung* 9 (2009): 77–108. Don O. Franklin, "Aspekte von Proportion und Dimension in Johann Sebastian Bachs Missa von 1733," LBB 5 (2002): 235–272; Don O. Franklin, "Composing in Time: Bach's Temporal Design for the Goldberg Variations," *Bach Studies from Dublin* [Irish Musical Studies 8], eds. Anne Leahy and Yo Tomita (Dublin: Four Courts Press, 2004), 103–128; Don O. Franklin, "Das Verhältnis zwischen Taktart und Kompositionstechnik im Wohltemperierten Klavier I," *Musikwissenschaftliche Schriften* 38 (2002): 147–160.

111 See note 97.

112 See, for example, Ruth Tatlow, "Challenging Virtuality: A Personal Reflection," *UB* 7 (2012): 57–60.

Part I
Sources

2 Documents

Hans-Joachim Schulze
Anne Leahy (1961–2007) in memoriam

Any study of the life, work and historical significance of a personality—especially in the arts—has to broadly (though not exclusively) depend on sources that are subject to the contingencies of tradition and the availability of documentation, whether it be fragmentary and inadequate as with Homer or Shakespeare, overflowing and barely manageable as with Mendelssohn and Goethe, or extensive but not overwhelming as with Mozart and Johann Sebastian Bach. The extent of the documentation depends on whether the aim is to organize an exhaustive collection of sources or to limit the selection to what is thought to be important.

Collection and Publication

With regard to the collation of handwritten and printed sources relating to the life, work and reception history of individual composers or performers, musicology has had particular success. Following the pioneering work initiated by Otto Erich Deutsch, documentary anthologies of Franz Schubert, Handel and Mozart need to be mentioned. With regard to Johann Sebastian Bach until the mid-twentieth century, however, only inadequate experiments appeared in German literature. The first authoritative representative collection of Bach documents came instead from the English-speaking world, *The Bach Reader: A Life of Johann Sebastian Bach in Letters and Documents* (New York: Norton, 1945), edited and translated by Hans Theodor David and Arthur Mendel, with later reprints and expansions.

In response a comparable anthology from J. S. Bach's homeland did not begin until 1960. The original plan of a new edition of J. S. Bach's letters, proposed by the Bach-Archiv, Leipzig, was expanded to become an annotated edition of all hand-written documents by Bach (including printed documents that originated with Bach). It appeared as *Schriftstücke von der Hand Johann Sebastian Bachs* in 1963, the first volume of Supplements to the Neue Bach Ausgabe (Dok 1). Volume 2 appeared in 1969: *Fremdschriftliche und gedruckte Dokumente zur Lebensgeschichte Johann Sebastian Bachs 1685–1750* (Dok 2). Volume 3 was issued in 1972, continuing the coverage to the end of the eighteenth century: *Dokumente zum Nachwirken Johann Sebastian Bachs 1750–1800* (Dok 3). Volume 5, published in 2007, incorporated documents newly identified after 1972, and also included a comprehensive index of persons covering all the *Dokumente*

26   *Hans-Joachim Schulze*

volumes together with a chronological overview: *Dokumente zu Leben, Werk und Nachwirken Johann Sebastian Bachs 1685–1800* (Dok 5).

From continuing research undertaken since 2007, there is the possibility of a further supplementary volume ("Dok 5a"), but it remains an open question whether it will be published in the foreseeable future. Another sequel was published in 2007, *Ausgewählte Dokumente zum Nachwirken Johann Sebastian Bachs 1801–1850* (Dok 6), which—in contrast to the chronological organization of the previous two volumes (Dok 2 and 3)—a topical arrangement as used in the first volume (Dok 1) is followed for the period between the beginning of the nineteenth century and the appearance of Bach-Gesellschaft Ausgabe, now referred to as the "Old Bach Edition," that began publication in 1850. In 2008, Volume 7 appeared with an annotated edition of Johann Nikolaus Forkel's manifesto *Ueber Johann Sebastian Bachs Leben, Kunst und Kunstwerke* of 1802 (Dok 7). Yet to appear is Volume 8, a summary of documents (especially catalogs) that establish the early transmission of the works of J. S. Bach (Dok 8), and a revised edition of Volume 4, published in 1979, a collection of photographic illustrations, which both in terms of its content and technical quality needs to be upgraded.

Although together these volumes present the evidence of handwritten and printed documents, nevertheless individual volumes have different emphases that cannot be overlooked. Although Volume 1 (Dok 1) deals with Bach's own writings and documents, Volume 2 (Dok 2) offers a bewildering diversity of material— from individual receipts to broad musical-aesthetic expositions—and attempts to make them available in an accessible way. Volume 3 (Dok 3) is similar but here the desire for completeness of documentation reveals a certain apologetic stance. It attempts to refute the persistent yet faulty assumption that after Bach's death he was entirely forgotten until Felix Mendelssohn's revival of the St. Matthew Passion (1829) moved him into the consciousness of posterity. Thus documents are presented year by year that together refute the common view that the knowledge of Bach and his music existed for decades only in a gray area. Located in the border region between the foothills of continuing tradition and the altitude of the historian is Forkel's manifesto (and its commentary) (Doc 7), whereas the selection of material in Volume 6 (Dok 6) is almost exclusively devoted to historical review.

Use and Interpretation

In his *Tonkünstler-Lexikon* (Leipzig, 1790) the Sondershausen court organist Ernst Ludwig Gerber (son of Bach's pupil Heinrich Nicolaus Gerber) made the apt comparison: "this great artist [Bach]" has bequeathed to us "the following works to test our talent, just like the bow of Ulysses."[1] That Bach has left us *Works* has to be understood in the most literal sense: in spite of diligent searches, the documentary traces are disappointingly small. We know almost nothing about him as a human being. We know a little more about the context of his work. But even here most

---

1   Dok 3: 469 (No. 948).

of the information concerns official matters, next to nothing is known about the performance and the reception of his works. However, the sharpening of scholarly tools in the recent decades was not deterred by the permanent "nescimus" (unknowing). Scholars approach the limited corpus of documents with sophistic arguments and everything is being interrogated, turned around, evaluated, questioned, and, if necessary, also turned into its complete opposite. Popular are especially falsification, in the footsteps of Karl Popper, and deconstruction, in the tradition of Martin Heidegger. However, it is never being asked whether the authors of the historical texts and Bach in particular might have made provisions for such an interpretative approach. What the authors of the historical texts, and especially Bach himself, may have made of such treatments is, of course, not asked.[2]

One unfortunate side effect of the attempt to document everything that can be found about Bach is that some exegetes use the (apparent) silence of the sources for very creative interpretations to fill these voids. Almost everything that cannot be outright refuted has been proposed. As a consequence, we have plenty of interpretations: Bach the theologian, the mathematician, the philosopher, the physicist, the rhetorician, poet, art historian, politician. These images are being highlighted as essential, but instead often obscure the image of Bach as the musician. The result of such hypothetical interpretations is that the Thomascantor mutates into a super-human, artificial character.

The relatively small corpus of documents regarding Bach's life, and here particularly the few autograph or authorized letters by Bach, show that its language, with the typical mixture of German and Latin and the few French and Italian words, is mostly clear and understandable. Grammatically, however, the texts are not without faults, and Bach's language is a far cry from the attempts of reforming the German language we find in the writings of Leipzig literary pundit Johann Christoph Gottsched. This is rather surprising, considering that Johann Sebastian Bach showed a keen sense for high linguistic quality when he chose the texts for his compositions.

Relatively few oral statements by the Thomascantor are known and they are exclusively transmitted by hearsay, several degrees removed from Bach.

Polemic writings from the 1730s and 40s, both in manuscript and in print, reveal, if we approach them from a neutral distance, that the supposed universal genius was easily overwhelmed in his struggles with academically trained adversaries, since he himself lacked academic training. As a consequence, he easily found himself in a position where he had to defend himself. A case in point is the so-called "Präfektenstreit" in 1736–38. It was a drawn-out conflict between the rector of the Thomas School and his cantor about authority within the school. It essentially revolved around whether academic or musical matters should have priority.[3] The

---

2 See Hans-Joachim Schulze, "Zur Kritik des Bach-Bildes im 20. Jahrhundert," LBB 5 (2000): 13–25; ET: "Bach at the Turn of the Twenty-first Century," *Bach Studies from Dublin*, ed. Anne Leahy and Yo Tomita (Dublin: Four Courts, 2004), 247–260; and *The Worlds of Johann Sebastian Bach*, ed. Raymond Erickson (Amadeus: New York, 2009), 291–305.

3 Dok 1: Nos. 32–35, 39–41; Dok 2: Nos. 382, 383, 394, 398, 403, 406, 412; NBR, 172–185, 189–196 (Nos. 181–186, 192–196).

28   Hans-Joachim Schulze

same applies to the Scheibe-Birnbaum dispute (1737–1745), in which Bach's interests were (more or less successfully) represented by Bach's friend, the Leipzig magister Birnbaum.[4] Finally, in a school pamphlet from 1749, the Freiberg Rector Johann Gottlieb Biedermann had criticized music and has interpreted the term "musike vivere" as living in a disorderly and hedonistic manner. During the last months of his life, Bach was involved in this controversy in a quite embarrassing way. The Nordhausen organist Christoph Gottlieb Schröter had reacted to Biedermann's invectives against music with a pamphlet that defended music by referring to classical authors, biblical sources as well as contemporary scholarly works. Bach effected several changes to Schröter's text, including the following argument:

> And finally (by saying a lot with only a few words) the above program [pamphlet] contradicts the high Duke's [Electoral] Church-Order, pleasure, and interests. Since if nobody (according to the author's critical remarks) would study music, what would happen to church music? Where would one find opera singers and orchestra musicians? and how would the alcohol tax be affected by this?[5]

These questions have their merit, without doubt, but they are out of place in an academic pamphlet. It is impossible to reconstruct whether Bach made these changes himself or whether someone incorporated his oral remarks into the printed version of Schröter's text. In the eyes of those involved, Bach was in part held accountable for these inappropriate changes and only his death saved him from further, unappealing controversies.[6]

For our own time, preoccupied with the revelations of investigative journalism, Bach's quite unremarkable biography (as far as we have any information at all) only rarely provides details that could be viewed as being sensational.

Completeness/Asymmetrical Transmission

An observer will notice the uneven density of known events in the *Kalendarium zur Lebensgeschichte Johann Sebastian Bachs*.[7] Continuity, as we know it from Goethe[8] or in a similar way from Mendelssohn,[9] is unthinkable in the case of J. S. Bach.

---

4   Dok 2: Nos. 400, 409, 410, 413, 417, 420, 432, 436, 441, 442, 446, 476, 530, 533, 552; NBR 337–353.

5   "Und endlich (mit wenigen viel gesagt) so laufft oben besagtes Programma wider hohe Landes-Fürstliche Kirchen-Ordnung, Plaisirs und Interesse; Denn wann niemand mehr (nach des Autoris Abmahnung) Musicam studiren soll, wo bliebe die Kirchen-Musick? wo würde man Operisten und Cappelisten hernehmen? und was würde die Tranck-Steuer darzu sagen?"

6   Dok 1: 121–122, 124–126 (Nos. 52, 53, 55); Dok 2: 461–464 (No. 592); NBR 241–243 (No. 268); Ulrich Leisinger, "Biedermann und Bach: Vordergründe und Hintergründe eines gelehrten Streites im 18. Jahrhundert," LBB 7 (2005): 141–167.

7   *Kalendarium zur Lebensgeschichte Johann Sebastian Bachs: Erweiterte Neuausgabe*, ed. Andreas Glöckner (Leipzig: Evangelische Verlagsanstalt, 2008); first published in 1970; 2nd ed. 1979.

8   Johann Wolfgang Goethe. *Tagebücher. Historisch-kritische Ausgabe* (Stuttgart: Metzler, 1998–).

9   See especially Felix Mendelssohn Bartholdy, *Sämtliche Briefe*, eds. Helmut Loos and Wilhelm Seidel (Kassel: Bärenreiter, 2008–).

Documents 29

With regard to the printed sources published in *Bach Dokumente* volumes 1–3 and 5 (covering the years 1685–1800), we can assume that in some areas the desired completeness has almost been accomplished. This is true in particular for the music theoretical publications as with all the "official" newspapers. Almost completely lost, however, are advertisements (such as for concerts) in local newspapers (Leipzig, Dresden), because only fragments of these have been preserved. Great losses (albeit partly of known extent) appear in the area of printed texts of Bach's musical performances from the time between 1707 and 1750 (i.e., prints of the texts set to music for birthdays, weddings, honorific tributes, and funerals from Mühlhausen, Weimar, Cöthen, and Leipzig). Also lost are numerous textbooks for performances of cantatas, oratorios, passions, and compositions for the annual inauguration of the town council from Bach's time in Weimar (1714–17) and Leipzig (1723–50).

It is difficult to decide whether popular or scholarly journals from the second half of the eighteenth century contain any material that would be comparable to the reviews in Friedrich Nicolai's *Allgemeine Deutsche Bibliothek*. Rare prints of poems with either humorous or homage character sometimes mention the name Bach briefly and contribute details to our knowledge; however these details do not affect the general picture of Bach.

It is much more difficult to determine the extent of the loss of handwritten documents. Almost completely lost is Bach's private correspondence. Carl Philipp Emanuel Bach's remark, that his father had barely the time for the necessary correspondence and thus did not have more extensive written exchanges,[10] has sometimes been misunderstood by later interpreters as if Bach had only rarely written letters at all. This is not the case. The remark by Bach's son only refers to more extensive exchanges of letters as we know them between Telemann and Carl Heinrich Graun,[11] or the extensive reports Johann Gottfried Walther sent between 1729 and 1744 from Weimar to Heinrich Bokemeyer in Wolfenbüttel.[12]

None of the original copies of the private and official letters Bach must have received have been preserved and only a few of the private letters he wrote himself are extant. In this latter group are two letters Bach wrote in 1726 and 1730 to his former classmate Georg Erdmann, who would later become Russian Emissary Agent in Danzig.[13] Those letters survived because the Russian government safeguarded his letters as part of the estate of a government official. Four letters from the years between 1736 and 1738 directed to the family Klemm in Sangerhausen, dealing with Bach's recommendation of his third-oldest son, Johann Gottfried Bernhard, for the position as organist, and his subsequent unexplained

---

10 Dok 3: 290 (No. 803); NBR 400 (No. 395).
11 Georg Philipp Telemann, *Briefwechsel. Sämtliche erreichbare Briefe von und an Telemann*, eds. Hans Große and Hans Rudolf Jung (Leipzig: Deutscher Verlag für Musik, 1972), 264–306.
12 Johann Gottfried Walther, *Briefe*, eds. Klaus Beckmann and Hans-Joachim Schulze (Leipzig: Deutscher Verlag für Musik, 1987).
13 Dok 5: 85–86 (No. A 13); Dok 1: 67–70 (No. 23); NBR 125–126 (No. 121), 151–152 (No. 152). The context shows that Bach did not write any other letters to Erdmann during his time in Leipzig.

30 *Hans-Joachim Schulze*

disappearance without covering his debts, were only discovered in 1900 in the city archive of Sangerhausen.[14] The letters were probably preserved because of the financial obligations of Bach's son, which the father refused to cover. Two letters from 1748, sent to the former Leipzig student of theology and Bach's personal secretary, Bach's cousin, Johann Elias Bach (who from 1743 served as cantor in his hometown Schweinfurt),[15] were preserved by J. E. Bach's heirs for more than a century and only then sold to a collector. With less than ten private letters, the bounty is less than meager—especially compared with almost 4700 letters that were addressed to Johann Christoph Gottsched, and that the poet kept in meticulous order.[16] The number of Bach's letters also pales in comparison to the huge number of letters by Felix Mendelssohn Bartholdy or Richard Wagner.

Some remarks in the "Briefentwürfe des Johann Elias Bach" (letter drafts by J. E. Bach) suggest the previous existence of some private correspondence within J. S. Bach's family, especially in regard to the journey to Berlin Bach made in 1741 and his wife Anna Magdalena's health problems during his absence.[17] We do not know whether and for how long the Bach family kept letters like this after 1750. Contrary to Goethe, who had made plans years before his death, Bach did not make any arrangements to keep important letters and documents in case of his passing. More likely, it was something similar to Carl Philipp Emanuel Bach's request to his publisher Breitkopf in 1786 for a general discharge to be able to get rid of letters and other documents that had accumulated over several decades.[18]

Part of such correspondence within the family would be, hypothetically, a group of letters regarding baptisms ("Gevatterbriefe"). The request to serve as godfather was probably, as usual at that time, made in writing and in the case of Bach's family there would have been letters for 20 children, born during his two marriages. Another group of documents, belonging to his private correspondence, even though they also affected a significant part of his income, were written agreements with private students and other collaborators.[19] The occasional mention of contracts

---

14 Dok 1: 91–95 (Nos. 37–38), 107–110 (Nos. 42–43); NBR 186–188 (Nos. 188–189), 200–202 (Nos. 203–204.

15 Dok 1: 117–121 (Nos. 49–50); NBR 234–235 (Nos. 257–258).

16 *Johann Christoph Gottsched Briefwechsel: Historisch-kritische Ausgabe*, eds. Detlef Döring and Manfred Rudersdorf (Berlin: de Gruyter, 2007–). For a comparable collection in the area of music, see Anne Schnoebelen, *Padre Martini's Collection of Letters in the Civico Museo Bibliografico Musicale in Bologna: An annotated Index* (New York: Pendragon, 1979).

17 Dok 2: 391–393 (Nos. 489–490); NBR 212–213 (Nos. 222–223).

18 Carl Philipp Emanuel Bach, *Briefe und Dokumente: Kritische Gesamtausgabe*, ed. Ernst Suchalla, (Göttingen: Vandenhoeck & Ruprecht, 1994), 1116; *The Letters of C. P. E. Bach*, trans. & ed. Stephen L. Clark (Oxford: Clarendon, 1997), 237.

19 For the "Contract" with Philipp David Kräuter, see Dok 5: 118–119 (No. B 53c). What proportion of the "Informiren," the teaching private students, made to J. S. Bach's entire workload—and therefore also to his income—cannot now be judged. For examples of the excessive teaching by his contemporaries, see Johann Gottfried Walther, *Musicalisches Lexicon* (Leipzig: Deer, 1732; facsimile, Kassel: Bärenreiter, 1953), 656–657 (Johann Gotthilf Ziegler); also Jacob Adlung's autobiography: *Musica Mechanica Organoedi* (Berlin: Birnstiel, 1768), 2: ii–xiv, esp. xi.

Documents 31

("Contracte") suggests that agreements for musical lessons (length and cost of the lessons), and also the lending of musical instruments, were made in writing and not just orally. Johann Sebastian Bach's own contracts of this kind have not been preserved; however, some receipts from 1747 related to Bach's keyboard lessons for Graf von Würben (Wrbna) (who would later be one of Mozart's supporters in Vienna) suggest that written agreements of this kind must have existed.[20]

As mentioned previously, the transmission of documents pertaining to Johann Sebastian Bach often has the character of isolated islands. The examples mentioned here could easily be expanded: the different struggles with the consistory in Arnstadt (1705–06),[21] the documents pertaining to the education of Philipp David Kräuter in Weimar (1712/13),[22] in Leipzig the documents pertaining to the music performances in the "new service" ("neuer Gottesdienst") at the university church and the income connected with it (1725/26),[23] the funerary arrangements for the Saxon Electress Christiane Eberhardine (1727) and the question of whether the Thomascantor was allowed to produce the music and to perform it.[24]

Such "islands" contrast often with considerable gaps, so that completeness is mostly an exception. One exception from the transmission of documents that is normally one-sided is the correspondence between Bach and the town council of the city of Plauen in connection with Bach's recommendation of Georg Gottfried Wagner for the position of cantor in Plauen.[25] Visible gaps, besides the complete loss of documents mentioned earlier, are also lacunae within material that is otherwise mostly complete. An example is the documentation of the deliberations regarding the search for a new Cantor at St. Thomas school in 1722/23.[26] During the meeting of the city council on 9 April 1723, the recorder was called away.[27] The minutes on loose, individual sheets have not yet been found and therefore the exact terms the members of the council agreed to concerning Bach's duties at the school are unknown. More serious is that it is unknown how far the position in Leipzig had been described to Bach as "beneficial" ("favorable"). We have to rely on remarks by Georg Philipp Telemann and Christoph Graupner in this regard. In both cases, annual sums of 1000 Taler had been mentioned.[28]

---

20 Dok 1: 204–206 (Nos. 130–132, 135), Dok 5: 107–108 (Nos. A 134, A 135a).
21 Dok 2: 15–18 (No. 14), 19–22 (Nos. 16–17); NBR 43–48 (Nos. 19–21).
22 Dok 5: 116–122 (Nos. B 53a-c, B 54a, B 56a, B 57a, B 58a); NBR 318–320 (No. 312).
23 Dok 1: 30–45 (Nos. 9–12); Dok 2: 149–153, 155–157 (Nos. 192, 194–198, 202, 203, 205); NBR 118–125 (Nos. 119–120).
24 Dok 2: 169–177 (Nos. 225–235); NBR 135–137 (135–137). Bach's contract with Hans Karl von Kirchbach, who had commissioned the music, is nowhere to be found.
25 Dok 1: 46–53 (Nos. 14–17); Dok 3: 627–628 (No. 56a); NBR 126–129 (Nos. 123–126); see also Hans-Joachim Schulze, "Johann Sebastian Bach und Georg Gottfried Wagner: Neue Dokumente," *Bach-Studien 5: Eine Sammlung von Aufsätzen* (Leipzig: Breitkopf & Härtel, 1975), 147–154.
26 Dok 1: 175–178 (Nos. 91–92); Dok 2: 88–112, 114–115, 138–139 (Nos. 119, 121–125, 127–148, 152, 177–178); NBR 99–110 (Nos. 93–107).
27 Dok 2: 92–93 (No. 127).
28 Letter of Telemann, dated 15 October 1722, to the Collegium Scholarchale in Hamburg, Joachim Kremer, *Das norddeutsche Kantorat im 18. Jahrhundert: Untersuchungen am Beispiel*

32   Hans-Joachim Schulze

This sum is probably based on the assumption that it would be possible to recruit affluent students in a university city like Leipzig in order to earn money by teaching music.

The most deplorable gaps are found in the documents listing J. S. Bach's estate and its distribution among the heirs, the widow Anna Magdalena, and the nine surviving children, a document that is a copy of the no-longer-extant original.[29] Musical scores, collections of cantata libretti, hymnals and probably other books (with the exception of theological works) were apparently distributed and are not mentioned in the estate catalog. Therefore, the list of works in the later obituary[30] has only a summary character, leaves many questions open and had to be amended later by C. P. E. Bach.[31]

Among the gaps in the transmission of documents, the most deplorable are those that have happened later and partly for unknown reasons. One document that disappeared after 1872 is a volume, begun in Ohrdruf in 1685, in which pastors, cantors, organists and others wrote their own biographies.[32] Before 1900, the secondary literature on collections of autographs and the practice of autograph collection sometimes mentions a journal of C. P. E. Bach, which had been destroyed because its significance had not been understood. In 1905, Rudolf Bunge mentioned a Lautenclavicimbel (lute-harpsichord) Bach had commissioned in Cöthen from a master carpenter for 60 Taler.[33] In the correspondence of Bohemian Graf Johann Adam von Questenberg, there were (allegedly) two letters by Bach that had already been lost before 1930.[34]

Several documents were lost during and after 1945 because of World War II and its aftermath. Bach's letter from 27 July 1733, which had accompanied the vocal and instrumental parts for the Missa the composer sent to the Saxon Elector (BWV 233^1)[35], was laying on the desk of the director of the music department of the Sächsische Landesbibliothek and thus presumably burnt during the bombing of Dresden on 13–14 February 1945. A letter of reference for his student and later son-in-law Johann Christoph Altnickol, dated 1 January 1748 (contemporary copy), was destroyed during a fire in the church of Lower-Silesian Niederwiesa.[36] On the other hand, three documents pertaining to Christoph Gottlob Wecker (two letters and one letter of reference) survived World War II

Hamburgs (Kassel: Bärenreiter, 1995), 422–423; letter of landgrave Ernst Ludwig and his son, Darmstadt, 3 May 1723, *Christoph Graupner, Hofkapellmeister in Darmstadt 1709–1760*, ed. Oswald Bill (Mainz: Schott, 1987), 145.

29 Dok 2: 490–512 (Nos. 627–628); NBR 250–255 (No. 279).

30 Dok 3: 85–86 (No. 666); NBR 303–304. (No. 306).

31 Dok 3: 243–248 (No. 776), 284–287 (No. 801); NBR 396 (No. 394). Surprisingly, the B Minor Mass is not mentioned.

32 Dok 2: 202–203 (No. 277).

33 Rudolf Bunge, "Johann Sebastian Bachs Kapelle zu Cöthen und deren nachgelassene Intrumente," BJ 2 (1905): 29.

34 Dok 5: 265 (Appendix No. 7).

35 Dok 1: 74–75 (No. 27); NBR 158 (No. 162).

36 Dok 1: 150–151 (No. 82); NBR 231 (No. 252).

Documents 33

unharmed.[37] Sometime after the war, an unknown person who pretended to be on an official mission asked for the autographs to transfer them to a safe place; since then, these documents have disappeared. Published libretti of cantatas performed in Weimar in 1715, which Philipp Spitta was able to examine,[38] were thought to be lost in 1950 but were subsequently rediscovered in the 1990s in the Herzogin Anna Amalia Bibliothek in Weimar, only to be destroyed in the devastating fire of 2004.

Not everything that has been thought to be lost has disappeared for good. Unexpected rediscoveries are not rare. Letters by Bach student Johann Philipp Kirnberger addressed to the Berlin publisher Georg Jacob Decker—in connection with the publishing of *Wahre Grundsätze zum Gebrauch der Harmonie*— had still been in possession of the publishing house in the nineteenth century.[39] However, they were nowhere to be found when Ernst Fritz Schmid asked to see them.[40] What he did not know was that they had already been sold to the Preussische Staatsbibliothek in 1927. Around 1950, two letters of reference by J. S. Bach, owned by the city archive of Torgau,[41] were considered to have been burned; however, in 1960, they were exactly where they were supposed to be. The director of the archive in 1960 explained:[42] After the end of the war, some over-eager people had aimed for a complete new beginning and had therefore declared the holdings of the city archive (including treasures on the history of Saxony and especially the Reformation) as products of a bureaucracy that had been defeated. Therefore, they had piled up these documents in the court yard of the city hall and set them on fire. Only the intervention of the archivist had averted their complete destruction. Bach's letter of reference for his student Bernhard Dieterich Ludewig, dated 10 October 1737,[43] had been lost since 1950 and it was assumed that it had been destroyed. However, in 2009, it was rediscovered in Zörbig, where it had been all the time. It had accidentally been tucked into a book after it had been part of an exhibition.

Lost in a similar way was the only copy of the printed libretto of Bach's cantata for the organ inauguration in Störmthal, *Höchsterwünschtes Freudenfest* (BWV 194). It had originally been part of the performance material but then the Staatsbibliothek zu Berlin had integrated it into a collection of text prints without leaving a note at the original place. This print has been accessible to scholarship again only since 1997.[44] The matriculation register of the Leipzig

---

37 Dok 1: 53–54, 57–58, 129 (Nos. 18, 20, 60); NBR 131–132 (Nos. 129–131). The documents were in the "Alten Archiv" of Friedenskirche von Schweidnitz (Lower Silesia, today belonging to Poland).
38 Dok 3: 651 (No. 74a).
39 Dok 3; 257–258 (No. 780).
40 Ernst Fritz Schmid, *Carl Philipp Emanuel Bach und seine Kammermusik* (Kassel: Bärenreiter, 1931), 34.
41 Dok 1: 138–139, 146–147 (Nos. 69 and 79; NBR 153–154, 219 (Nos. 154 and 231).
42 In a conversation with the author around 1960.
43 Dok 1: 142–143 (No. 74); NBR 196–197 (No. 198).
44 Peter Wollny, "Neue Bach-Funde," BJ 83 (1997), 21–26.

34   Hans-Joachim Schulze

Thomas School, which reached back to 1640, in which the students of the school had to sign in their own handwriting, had not been accessible to Philipp Spitta. The two volumes had been lent to someone but nobody knew to whom.[45] Only after return of the manuscripts was Bernhard Friedrich Richter able to compile his register of Thomas alumni.[46] Around 1950/60, the older matriculation register (1640–1729) was still available but the newer volume, begun by Johann Matthias Gesner in 1730, was nowhere to be found. The latter had been given to the Leipzig city archive in 1960 but without leaving a paper trail indicating the transfer of the document. Staff members of the history department of Leipzig University discovered the manuscript, which was made difficult by the cryptic and difficult-to-understand entry in the catalogue of the archive.[47] Since 2012, the second volume has been accessible to Bach scholars again.

We should also mention the significant new discoveries that have been made. A receipt, published in 1967, provides evidence that Bach served as middle-man for the sale of a *Piano et Forte* to northeast Poland.[48] In 1979, Leipzig Superintendent Herbert Stiehl was able to find the "Taufzettel" (registration for an upcoming baptism) for those of Bach's children who were born in Leipzig during his marriage with Anna Magdalena; the documents are partly in Bach's own hand.[49] A thorough search in the archives pertaining to the employment of the cantors in the city of Salzwedel has uncovered several documents, some of them autograph letters by J. S. Bach, which document Bach's support for his student Johann Friedrich Doles.[50] Research in the Leipzig University archives was able to locate documentation for the "Stipendium Hammerianum," which had been given to students for several decades; some of these documents are Bach's own testimonials for prefects of the Thomas school.[51] During his research into the history of the Thomas choir, Michael Maul was able to find an undated memorandum

---

45 Bernhard Friedrich Richter, "Die Alumnen der Thomasschule zu Bachs Zeit," BJ 4 (1907): 43.

46 Richter, "Alumnen der Thomasschule," 66–76, here 21, 26.

47 Personal communication with Thomas Töpfer, Leipzig, 20 March 2012.

48 Dok 3: 633 (No. 142a); NBR 239 (No. 262).

49 Herbert Stiehl, "Taufzettel für Bachs Kinder," BJ 65 (1979): 7–18; see also Martin Petzoldt, *Bachs Leipziger Kinder: Dokumente von Johann Sebastian Bachs eigener Hand/ Bach's Children in Leipzig: Documents in Johann Sebastian Bach's Own Hand* (Leipzig: Evangelische Verlagsanstalt, 2008). The existence of such documents was already known earlier, as is documented in the study by Walter Lange, *Richard Wagner und seine Vaterstadt* (Leipzig: Siegel, 1921), in which are published such "Taufanmeldung" (registration for upcoming Wagner's baptism of 1813 including an official confirmation from 1889).

50 Dok 5: 269–272, 275–276 (Nos. A 45c, A 45d, B 517a); see. Steffen Langusch, "'...auf des Herrn Capellmeisters Bach recommendation...' Bachs Mitwirken an der Besetzung des Kantorats der Altstadt Salzwedel 1743/44," BJ 93 (2007): 9–43. A request to the Stadtarchiv Salzwedel had been unsuccessful; see Dok 1: 272 (Incerta 7).

51 Andreas Glöckner, "Johann Sebastian Bach und die Universität Leipzig. Neue Quellen [I]," BJ 94 (2008): 159–201, here 187–201; *Johann Sebastian Bach. Vier Zeugnisse für Präfekten des Thomanerchores 1743–1749. Faksimile und Transkription*, ed. Andreas Glöckner (Kassel: Bärenreiter, 2009).

by the teachers of the Thomas school.[52] The text, probably written in the 1720s, seems to anticipate some passages from Bach's "Entwurff einer wohlbestallten Kirchenmusic" and sheds new light on the negative effect a new school order had on the musical practice at the school.

Credibility

The essential aspects of a famous event in Bach's biography, the encounter with the Prussian King Friedrich II in May 1747 in Potsdam, are sufficiently documented by contemporary sources: the improvisation of a fugue based on a given theme, the examination of the forte pianos in the palace. However, the descriptions of the surrounding circumstances are somewhat contradictory. A newspaper article appeared on 11 May 1747 in the Berlin newspapers, which was subsequently reprinted without changes in Hamburg, Magdeburg and Frankfurt/M and which found its way (in slightly revised form) also into the newspapers of Leipzig and Munich.[53] According to these articles, Bach had traveled to Potsdam to hear the excellent music at the court. However, the king had immediately demanded that he improvise a fugue "without any preparation" on a given subject. Afterwards, Bach announced that he would elaborate a regular fugue based on this subject and publish this composition. The sources continue that, on the following day, Bach had played a fugue on a subject given allegedly "without preparation." In 1774, King Friedrich II told Gottfried van Swieten that the old Bach had improvised fugues for four, five, and even eight voices based on the given subject.[54]

These reports differ significantly from the one given by Johann Nikolas Forkel in 1802. According to Forkel, Bach's visit to Potsdam had happened at the behest of the Prussian monarch and Carl Phillipp Emanuel had had to urge his father in letters until he had agreed to the journey. After his arrival, J. S. Bach had not even had the time to change into a proper dress, so that the encounter between the cantor and the king had started with extensive apologies by Bach. The first performance of a fugue had only taken place after Bach had tested and fantasized on the forte pianos from Gottfried Silbermann's workshop that were in the palace. Furthermore, the six-part fugue, which the king had urged Bach to improvise, had been based on a subject chosen by the composer himself. In the following days, Bach had to play in the presence of the king "on all organs in Potsdam."[55]

One could say that Forkel's report and the historical event in 1747 are separated by more than five decades and that therefore the newspaper article from 1747 had

---

52 Michael Maul, *"Dero berühmbter Chor": Die Leipziger Thomasschule und ihre Kantoren (1212–1804)* (Leipzig: Lehmstedt, 2012), 186–191. ET forthcoming.

53 Dok 2: 434–435 (No. 554), Dok 5: 297–298 (No. 554); NBR 224 (No. 239); and Markus Rathey, "Bachs Besuch in Potsdam und dessen Rezeption in der Münchner Presse," BJ 97 (2011): 269–271.

54 Dok 3: 276 (No. 790); NBR 366–367 (No. 360).

55 Dok 7: 21–23; NBR 429–430.

36   Hans-Joachim Schulze

more credibility,[56] especially if we also include a passage from the obituary,[57] which seems to confirm the article. However, one should not forget that the newspaper article from 1747 is a typical example of court reporting, in which it would have been inappropriate to depict the king as someone asking Bach for a favor. The same applies to the obituary: Johann Friedrich Agricola and C. P. E. Bach were subjects of the Prussian King and they had to make sure not to depict their superior in an unfavorable light. But in 1802, it was unnecessary for Forkel to continue such deference. Additionally, he had two eyewitnesses on his side, who had observed the events before and behind the scenes: Wilhelm Friedemann, who had accompanied his father on his journey, and C. P. E. Bach, who was chamber musician of the Prussian King. Therefore, the later report is—with certain limitations—more credible than the earlier one.

Consideration of living persons comes into play in many texts of this kind. The same applies to notes by former student at the Thomas school, Johann Friedrich Köhler, begun in 1776 and which contain information about conflicts between the rector of the school and the cantor;[58] and an anecdote, published in 1810, about a physical altercation between C. P. E. Bach and Johann Christian Kittel (who had died the previous year, 1809) on the day of Johann Sebastian Bach's funeral.[59]

To what degree these anecdotes reflect historical events, and to what degree they are just a form of literary fiction, has to be decided for each case individually. A classic example is the encounter between the Weimar court organist J. S. Bach and the French organist and harpsichordist Louis Marchand. All known descriptions of this encounter[60] originate, as has been shown by Werner Breig,[61] with one single witness, Johann Sebastian Bach himself, who must have told different versions at different times of his life. Therefore, other Bach anecdotes have to be approached in a similarly critical way, even though it is not necessary to turn what they try to report into their complete opposite.[62]

"According a certain tradition" (meaning, a tradition that is indeed certain), Bach wrote his Well-tempered Clavier at a place of "ennui, boredom, and the

---

56 Konrad Küster, "Zum Umgang mit Musikeranekdoten des 18. Jahrhunderts: Das Beispiel Bach," *Biographie und Kunst als historiographisches Problem. Bericht über die Intern. Wiss. Konferenz anläßlich der 16. Magdeburger Telemann-Festtage Magdeburg, 13. bis 15. März 2002* (Hildesheim: Olms, 2004), 142–160.

57 Dok 3: 85 (No. 666); NBR 302–303 (No. 306).

58 Dok 3: 312–315 (No. 820); NBR 172 (No. 180).

59 Dok 6: 164–166 (No. A 34).

60 To list a few: Dok 2: 348 (No. 441); Dok 3: 83–84 (No. 666); Dok 3: 443 (No. 927); Dok 3: 424–425 (No. 914); NBR 79–80, 301–302, 408 (Nos. 67, 306, 396).

61 Werner Breig, "Bach und Marchand in Dresden. Eine überlieferungskritische Studie," BJ 84 (1998): 19–33.

62 See, for instance, Konrad Küster, *Der junge Bach* (Stuttgart: Deutsche Verlags-Anstalt, 1996), who suggests that Bach had been admitted at the school in Lüneburg as a bass singer; see also my review in BJ 83 (1997): 203–205.

Documents 37

absence of any kind of musical instrument."[63] Earlier Bach scholarship did not understand the reference; only the publication of notes by the Weimar court secretary about a "dishonorable" dismissal of Bach after four weeks of arrest at the end of 1717[64] made the remark clearer. We do not know whether Bach in his later years told more about his treatment in Weimar. However, if the roots of the Well-tempered Clavier reach back to November 1717, C. P. E. Bach's remark, made to Charles Burney, must be wrong. He had told the English music historian that his father had composed the twenty-four preludes and fugues, with their difficulties and their (allegedly) five voices, as an exercise for him (C. P. E. Bach).[65] We know from other documents that C. P. E. Bach sometimes treated the truth quite liberally.[66]

Some written remarks by Bach also raise critical questions. This is true even for his *Entwurff einer wohlbestallten Kirchen Music* from 23 April 1730.[67] It is very clear that Bach's goal was to write a text that is, in spite of its brevity, a concise and unambiguous guideline for the organization of church music in Leipzig. However, writing letters or appeals to the authorities was not exactly Bach's strong suit. Some of the information in the document is still quite imprecise or even questionable, even though the neat handwriting suggests that it must have been preceded by a draft (in which Bach had an opportunity for corrections and revisions). It might be in part due to his character that Bach did not make his text "bullet proof" and that his text has the appearance of being written spontaneously and that he used arguments to make points that were sometimes quite risky;[68] but the vague character of his text is also partially due to Bach's inability to craft a sophisticated argument. Primarily, however, this might be due to his self-image as someone with infallible competence in all musical things and in all questions of how to organize music.[69] In a similar way, one could criticize details in Bach's autograph letter to Georg Erdmann;[70] for instance, the recorded details regarding his income in Leipzig, or the chronological order of the events during the search for a new Thomascantor in 1722/23.

---

63 Dok 3: 468 (No. 948); NBR 372 (No. 370).
64 Dok 2: 65–66 (No. 84); NBR 80 (No. 68).
65 Dok 3: 252 (No. 778); see the different phrase in the German Version: Dok 3: 253 (No. 778).
66 See, for instance, his letters to the publisher Artaria in Vienna (10 or 16 November 1779) and Breitkopf in Leipzig (25 December 1779): C. P. E. Bach, *Briefe und Dokumente*, 795–796, and 810; *Letters of C. P. E. Bach*, 148–149 and 153.
67 Dok 1: 60–66 (No. 22); NBR 145–151 (No. 151).
68 Regarding financial issues, see Hans-Joachim Schulze, "Studenten als Bachs Helfer bei der Leipziger Kirchenmusik," BJ 70 (1984): 45–52, and Hans-Joachim Schulze, "Besitzstand und Vermögensverhältnisse von Leipziger Ratsmusikern zur Zeit Johann Sebastian Bachs," *Beiträge zur Bach-Forschung* 4 (1985): 33–46.
69 See Hans-Joachim Schulze, "Bachs Aufführungsapparat: Zusammensetzung und Organisation," *Die Welt der Bach-Kantaten*, ed. Christoph Wolff (Stuttgart: Metzler, 1996–1999), 3: 143–155, here 147.
70 Dok 1: 67–70 (No. 23); NBR 151–152 (No. 152).

38   *Hans-Joachim Schulze*

Even documents that seem to be unproblematic often have to be evaluated critically. Johann Salomon Riemer's notes from 8 June 1749,[71] regarding Gottlob Harrer's "trial performance for the future appointment as Cantor of St. Thomas's, in case the Capellmeister and Cantor Herr Sebastian Bach should die," appear less tasteless if we take into account that Riemer apparently collected individual notes and only later transferred the information into large tomes. We have reason to assume that he transferred the information only after Bach had already died. More difficult is the case of the basso continuo treatise (Generalbasslehre), to which the former student at the Thomas school and later deputy rector, Karl August Thieme, added a title page that referred to J. S. Bach and the year 1738.[72] We have reason to assume that the title page was written later than the manuscript contents and that the connection with Bach is dubious.[73]

Equally problematic is the "last warning" regarding a harpsichord, written by an unknown hand, and addressed to Herrn Martius in spring 1748.[74] Earlier scholarship had assumed that the addressee had been a concert organizer who had borrowed a keyboard instrument but had failed to return it. More recent studies, however, suggest that the tardy borrower was a student.[75] Possible candidates are a Johann Christoph Gottfried Martius (Mertz) from Gräfenheinichen (born 1726), who began his studies in Wittenberg and then transferred to Leipzig in 1747. Later he became teacher at the Gymnasium zum Grauen Kloster in Berlin (sources document his presence until 1774). Bach, who was always busy, might have asked his youngest son, Johann Christian, to write the "last reminder" (which is only transmitted in a later copy). Johann Christian's authorship would explain the grammatical and orthographical errors in the text. There is no reason at this point to assume that the text is a forgery.[76]

Some publicity surrounded Michael Maul's discovery of a letter he found in the church archive of St. Nikolai, Döbeln. The former member of the Thomas choir, Gottfried Benjamin Fleckeisen (1719–86), had applied for the position of town cantor in Döbeln in 1751 and he mentioned that he had for "4 years been prefect of the *chorus musicus*" and for "two whole years [he had] performed and directed the music in the main churches St. Thomas and St. Nicholas in place of the Capellmeister."[77] If this is correct, Fleckeisen might have been Bach's substitute in the middle of the 1740s. This, however, would contradict a remark by Johann Christoph Altnickol, who states in 1747 that he had sung bass under

---

71 Dok 2: 457 (No. 584); NBR 240 (No. 266).
72 Dok 2: 333–334 (No. 433), and the illustration before p. 400; also Dok 5: 295 (No. 433); Spitta 2: 913; Spitta ET 3: 315; *The Bach Reader... Revised*, ed. Hans T. David and Arthur Mendel (London: Dent, 1966), 392; *J. S. Bach's Precepts and Principles For Playing the Thorough-Bass or Accompanying in Four Parts. Leipzig, 1738*, ed. Pamela L. Poulin (Oxford: Clarendon, 1994).
73 See Schulze, 126–127.
74 Dok 3: 627 (No. 45c); NBR 233–234 (No. 256).
75 Michael Maul, "Ein neues Dokument zu Bachs Instrumentenverleih," BJ 95 (2009): 226, 228.
76 For a more skeptical assessment, see Tatjana Schabalina, "Zur Echtheit von zwei Briefen aus dem Glinka-Museum in Moskau," BJ 93 (2007): 179–196.
77 See the reduced reproduction in *Bach Magazin*, Heft 23 (Frühjahr/Sommer 2014), 25.

Documents 39

Bach's direction for three years during the performance of vocal and instrumental music in the two main churches of Leipzig.[78] We have two contradictory witnesses; and we have to be careful if we want to draw conclusions about Bach's lack of interest in his position or about Bach's health in these years. Conclusive evidence is still lacking.

Correctness

We normally expect historical documents to be reliable with regard to names, dates and circumstances. However, upon closer examination and if compared critically with other documents, it regularly becomes clear that historical documents are not completely reliable. This also holds true for documents regarding Bach and his circle, as the following examples will show.

One source of errors is the insufficient knowledge of names; a problem that Bach had as well. When Georg Gottfried Wagner, a former student in Leipzig who had participated for years in performances of church music, asked Bach in November 1723 for a reference for an application (it is not known for what position), Bach wrote the letter for a "Johann Gottlieb" Wagner and Wagner himself subsequently corrected his error.[79] In October 1726, Bach was more careful: in a letter, in which he recommended Wagner for a position as cantor in Plauen, he only wrote the last name of the applicant and left space so that the first name could be entered later.[80] One month later, Bach still was not able to remember the first name of his student and in another letter to Plauen he simply called him "Mons.Wagner."[81]

Bach was not the only one who struggled with these kinds of lapses of memory. When his student Lorenz Christoph Mizler intended to dedicate his dissertation in 1734 to four well-known musicians, he mentioned an Ansbach Capellmeister with the name "Johann Benedict" Bümler.[82] Only in the new edition of 1736 was the mistake corrected and Georg Heinrich Bümler appeared with his correct name. Johann Gottfried Walther had been quite confused by the wrong name and Mizler apologized by saying that he had not known the correct name of the Capellmeister.[83] This is at least a bit surprising. Mizler could have easily avoided the mistake if he had consulted his copy of Walter's *Musicalisches Lexicon* (1732) to check the correct name.

Errors and mistakes with regard to first names occur quite frequently in historical sources. Especially prone to mistakes are records of baptisms, weddings and funerals in church registers. In order to avoid those mistakes altogether,

---

78 Dok 2: 434 (No. 553); see also Dok 1: 148–149 (No. 81).
79 Dok 3: 627–628 (No. 56a); NBR 112–113 (No. 112); see Hans-Joachim Schulze, "Studenten als Bachs Helfer bei der Leipziger Kirchenmusik," BJ 70 (1984), 45–52.
80 Dok 1: 49–51 (No. 16); NBR 128 (No. 125).
81 Dok 1: 51–53 (No. 17); NBR 128–129 (No. 126).
82 Dok 2: 247–248 (No. 349); NBR 163 (no. 168).
83 Walther, *Briefe*, 201.

40 *Hans-Joachim Schulze*

contemporaries frequently abbreviated the first same simply with the letter *N.* (= *Nomen nescio*; name unknown). Therefore, the records of Mühlhausen mention in May 1707, June 1708, and July 1708 a certain "*N.* Pach," which refers to Johann Sebastian Bach as well as his cousin and successor as organist Johann Ernst Bach.[84] Anna Magdalena Bach in September 1747 appears as "*N.* Bachin" in the records for the baptism of her granddaughter Anna Carolina Philippina Bach.[85] The index of names in Johann Mattheson's *Grundlage einer Ehren-Pforte* (Hamburg, 1740) presents quite frequently the "*N.*" Obviously, the wish of having a complete index collided with the incomplete information provided by the authors of the biographies in the book.[86]

A second group of mistakes is incorrect or missing dates. In the short overview of his career, which Bach probably gave his cousin Johann Gottfried Walter for his *Musicalisches Lexicon* (1732), the beginning of Bach's tenure in Arnstadt is listed correctly as 1703.[87] When Bach wrote the *Ursprung der musicalisch-Bachischen Familie* (probably in fall 1735), he gave the date as 1704.[88] At the beginning of Bach's work in Arnstadt, there is the examination of the recently completed organ in the Neue Kirche (New Church). The record in the files of the city from 13 July 1703 calls the 18-year-old Bach "Fürstlich Sächsischer HoffOrganiste von Weimar" (Ducal Saxon court organist from Weimar).[89] Originally, Weimar court organist Johann Effler had been expected to examine the organ, but had cancelled. The sloppy record-keeping in Arnstadt gave Bach a title he had not earned yet!

A mysterious detail missing from the history of the Bach family is the date of Carl Philipp Emanuel Bach's birth. In the *Ursprung der musicalisch-Bachischen Familie* (1735), Johann Sebastian Bach gives the date as 14 March 1714; however, this is the birthday of Georg Philipp Telemann, who stood godfather for Bach's second son. A later autobiography, written by Carl Philipp Emanuel, integrated into the German Version of Charles Burney's *Tagebuch seiner musikalischen Reisen*, only contains the vague remark "in March 1714."[90] Only Philipp Spitta in 1873[91] was able to find the correct date in the Weimar records: the birth took place on 8 March 1714, and the baptism was two days later.[92]

A special case in terms of unreliable dates concerns the matriculation records of the Thomas school, in which the students had to enter their own information. Here, every record has to be verified by information from other sources. One

---

84 Dok 2: 22–23, 33–34 (Nos. 19, 36, 37); NBR 49, 58 (Nos. 22a, 34).
85 Dok 2: 437 (No. 558).
86 Newer publications sometimes hastily replace the letter "*N.*" in a source with "Nikolaus."
87 Dok 2: 231–232 (No. 323); NBR 294–295 (No. 304).
88 Dok 1: 259 (No. 184); NBR 290 (No. 303).
89 Dok 2: 10–11 (No. 7); NBR 40 (No. 15).
90 Dok 3: 255–257 (No. 779).
91 Spitta 1: 620; Spitta ET 2: 8.
92 Dok 2: 54 (No. 67); NBR 72 (No. 55).

characteristic example is Maximilian Nagel, whose resignation from his post as prefect (most likely for health reasons) had led to the so called "Präfektenstreit" in the summer of 1736. Nagel, descendent of a Thuringian family of musicians, entered in the matriculation records in 1730 that he had been born in Nuremberg on 23 November 1714.[93] The correct date, however, is 22 November 1712. It is not known whether the large discrepancy is based on lack of knowledge on the side of Nagel or whether he intentionally cheated on his age. However, when Nagel died in Ansbach in 1748, the local church recorded his correct age.

A third source for errors has acoustical reasons. Information can be wrong because of misunderstandings in oral communication. When Johann Andreas Silbermann, organ builder in Straßburg, nephew of Gottfried Silbermann, visited Leipzig in spring 1741 during a journey to Berlin that also brought him through Saxony, he was shown the organs of the churches of St. Paul (the University church) and St. Nicholas. On the first instrument, he complained of the heavy mechanics, remarked on further technical defects and also made critical comments about Johann Sebastian Bach's examination report from 1717.[94] The name of the organist who assisted him is listed in Silbermann's travel diary[95] and in a later, calligraphic copy, as "Emilius" and "Aemilius," who was supposed to be the organist at St. Nicholas. This "Emilius" must have been the Bach student Gottfried August Homilius, who at this time still lived in Leipzig.[96]

Critical remarks on Bach as an examiner of organs were also made by Johann Christian Kluge. In 1746, Kluge got into a dispute with Gottfried Silbermann over the newly erected organ at St. Wenzeslas in Naumburg built by Zacharias Hildebrand. Kluge, the organist of the church, had previously worked in Weißenfels and Wiehe/Unstrut; later, he would move to Altenburg and finally to Dresden.[97] In 1748, Zittau was looking for a successor for former Bach student Carl Hartwig, who had to resign from his position for psychological reasons. Possible applicants that were being discussed were Johann Sebastian Bach's two oldest sons, but the minutes from 13 February 1748 also mention a "Herr Johann Christian Kluge, Organist zu St. Nikolai in Hamburg."[98] The reason for this mistake: the recorder understood "Hamburg" instead of "Naumburg" and instead of "St. Wenzeslas" he heard the more common "St. Nikolai."

A special case is the mistaken consonants and vowels because of dialectal differences or because the writer (unsuccessfully) tried to write a name in High German. An extreme case is a nuptial record from 1642 in Arnstadt, which lists

---

93 Richter, "Alumnen der Thomasschule," 70; see also the illustrations in Hans-Joachim Schulze, *Bach in Ansbach* (Leipzig: Evangelische Verlagsanstalt, 2013), 125.

94 Dok 2: 389–390 (No. 486); Dok 5: 162–163 (No. B 485a).

95 The diary had been owned by a private collector but towards the end of 2014 was acquired by the Sächsische Landesbibliothek Universitätsbibliothek, Dresden, from a Sotheby auction.

96 Dok 5: 386 and 402.

97 Dok 5: 407.

98 C. P. E. Bach, *Briefe und Dokumente*, 19.

42   Hans-Joachim Schulze

the husband of a Christiana Bach as "Ritze Fokke."[99] The proper version of the name would be "Moritz Vogt" (or Voigt). A student who is listed in the records of Leipzig University as "Herr Etzmann" in 1749/50 borrowed a keyboard instrument from Bach. The identification of the student was only possible after transforming the name into its High German equivalent: "Oetzmann."[100] The opposite of such mistakes are attempts of eighteenth-century scribes to "correct" names that seem to need correction. A Johann Friedrich Drobisch, a student of Bach, is listed in the *Tabula Musicorum* of the Leipzig "Großes Conzert" from 1746 through 1748 as "Trobisch;"[101] and a town administrator (Amtmann) in Langensalza around 1740 with the name Johann Carl Wilhelm Dumpf is listed as "Tumpf."[102]

For a long time, theologians were unable to identify two titles in Bach's estate catalogue from 1750, "Heinischii Offenbahrung Joh," and "Jauckleri Richtschnur der Christlichen Lehre." The identification becomes easy if we assume that two people were involved in compiling the list of books: one (Anna Magdalena Bach?) probably read a short version of the title, tinted by today's typical dialect of Sachsen-Anhalt, while a second person wrote down what he or she had heard. This turned the name of (Caspar) "Heunisch" into "Heinisch" and (Georg) Gaugler into "Jauckler."[103]

A fourth category of errors is the forgetfulness of the people involved in the historical events. A well-known example is the *Trauer-Ode* (BWV 198), which, according to almost all contemporary sources, was performed in the Leipzig University Church on 17 October 1727.[104] However, the title page of Bach's autograph score gives the date as 18 October.[105] Bach probably added the title some time later when he did not have access to the original printed libretto or the report in the relevant Leipzig newspaper. Almost equally well-known is Bach's assertion made in the famous letter to Georg Erdmann from 28 October 1730 that he had delayed ("trainieret"[106]) his decision to apply for the cantorate at St. Thomas for three months. After all we know about the search for the new Thomascantor in 1723, such a delay is rather unlikely. Similarly astonishing and hard to explain

---

99 Karl Müller and Fritz Wiegand, *Arnstädter Bachbuch. Johann Sebastian Bach und seine Verwandten in Arnstadt*, 2nd ed. (Arnstadt: [s.n.], 1957), 140.

100 Michael Maul, "'Die große catholische Messe': Bach, Graf Questenberg und die Musicalische Congregation in Wien," BJ 95 (2009): here 229; ET, "'The Great Catholic Mass': Bach, Count Questenberg and the Musicalische Congregation in Vienna," *Exploring Bach's B-minor Mass*, eds. Yo Tomita, Robin A. Leaver and Jan Smaczny (Cambridge: Cambridge University Press, 2013), 84–104.

101 Dok 5: 184–185 (No. C 650aa).

102 Hans-Joachim Schulze, "Johann Sebastian Bachs Himmelfahrts-Oratoriums und Picanders Geburtstags-Kantate für 'Herrn J. W. C. D.,'" BJ 95 (2009): 191–199.

103 Thomas Wilhelmi, "Bachs Bibliothek. Eine Weiterführung der Arbeit von Hans Preuß," BJ 65 (1979): 119; see a facsimile of the entries, Robin A. Leaver, *Bachs theologische Bibliothek* (Stuttgart: Hänssler, 1983), 33.

104 Dok 2: 173–177 (Nos. 229–235).

105 Dok 1: 228–229 (No. 161); NBR 136–137 (No. 136).

106 Dok 1: 67 (No. 23); NBR pp. 151–152 (No. 152).

is a mistake on the wrapper for the parts of the B Minor Mass (BWV 232[1]) Bach sent to the Elector of Saxony. The title, written by an authorized Dresden scribe, lists the vocalists and instrumentalists but does not notice that violin I and II as well as viola are missing. Instead of eighteen voices, as listed on the title page, the number should have been 21.[107]

During the so-called "Präfektenstreit" (1736/38), Bach meant to remember that Johann Gottlob Krause had been promoted to his position only towards the end of 1735 and that he, as third prefect, had only been entrusted with minor musical duties at the New Church in Leipzig.[108] However, the rector at the Thomas School, Johann August Ernesti, either kept more detailed records, or simply had a better memory: he remarked that Krause had only been fourth prefect. This awarded him a dual victory: he could accuse the Thomascantor of a lie[109] and he was able to show that his protégé had a rapid career, ascending within only three-quarters of a year from fourth prefect to first prefect. However, the exact circumstances are not mentioned. The three other prefects were all unavailable: Maximilian Nagel was ill, Gotthelf Engelbert Nitsche graduated from the school on Easter 1736 and the third, Gottfried Theodor Krauß, had fled from the school after the rector had threatened him with corporal punishment (a beating).

A fifth source for errors is inadequate copies of documents. Detrimental to biographical research is the common practice of the university in Bach's time to copy into the official matriculation records the information provided by the students at the end of the semester. It is impossible to judge whether the numerous mistakes were made by the eighteenth-century copyists or whether editions of the matriculation records in the early twentieth century have added further errors; this is a question that will need to be explored in detail in the future. A student who Bach explicitly calls a *J. U. Studiosus* is Johann Georg Heinrich, who was impossible to find in the matriculation records until it finally turned out that he had been listed there as "Hemrich."[110] Johann Friedrich Helbig, who was a member of Telemann's *Collegium musicum*, the author of the libretto of Cantata BWV 47, is listed in the records as "Hemsig." Carl Ephraim Haupt, a student at the Thomas school in the 1740s, who was often sent by Bach to get the wine the Cantor had earned when providing the music for weddings,[111] is listed in the university records as being from "Hohenficla," which can be translated as "Hohenfichte," probably a place in southern Saxony. However, Haupt came from "Hohenthecla"; Thekla is now part of the city of Leipzig.

Bach's student Christoph Nichelmann came to Leipzig from the Brandenburg town of Treuenbrietzen on the recommendation of his relative Johann Christian

---

107 Dok 1: 233–234 (No. 166); NBR 156–158 (No. 161).
108 Dok 1: 87 (No. 34); NBR 175 (No.183).
109 Dok 2: 275 (No. 383); NBR 185 (No. 186).
110 Dok 1: 146–147 (No. 79); Dok 5: 281 (No. 79).
111 Dok 3: 342 (No. 851).

44   Hans-Joachim Schulze

Krüger, who had some knowledge of music and mentioned that he had studied in Leipzig.[112] Misleading in this case is the printed edition of the matriculation record that adds a third first name as well as a strange place in Brandenburg. Instead of "Fr[ie]dr[ich] Obricen," the correct version should be "Fidobricen," that is "Treuenbrietzen." Unresolved is still the question of the hometown of Bach's flutist and harpsichordist Friedrich Gottlieb Wild[113] from "Grünhan. Lus." A town of this name is not known in the region of Lausitz.

Additional difficulties occur if documents are changed intentionally. I have already mentioned the possibility of faulty information in the matriculation records of the Thomas school. Bach's letter of reference for Johann Georg Heinrich (which I have also mentioned) was originally written in May 1742 for an unknown job application;[114] later changes, probably made by Heinrich himself, now state the date as 13 May 1744. The manipulation was without consequence as Heinrich did not get the position he had applied for.

At the end of this section, I would like to return to mistakes that are due to a lack of knowledge of seventeenth- and eighteenth-century German. Carl Philipp Emanuel Bach occasionally made comments in the *Ursprung der musicalisch-Bachischen Familie*:[115] "Den ersten Aufsatz machte mein seeliger Vater vor vielen Jahren." ("The first draft was written by my late father many years ago").[116] This remark has occasionally been understood as if J. S. Bach had only written the first paragraph about Veit Bach. What C. P. E. Bach means, however, is that his father wrote the first version of the genealogy. The second Bach son also bemoaned that his father "nie selbst von seinem Leben etwas aufgesetzet" ("Since he never wrote down anything about his life")[117] and therefore gaps in his biography could not be closed. Giovanni Battista Martini's comment about J. S. Bach, "che stimo difficile trovare un Professore che lo superi"[118] cannot be translated with the common dictionaries. A solution was provided by Jacob von Stählin, who used the phrase "Virtuosen, oder nach Italienischer Art zu reden, Professoren" ("Virtuosi, or according to Italian speech, professors"),[119] which made clear that Martini was talking about virtuosos when he used the term "professore."

The derogatory term "Zippel fagotist," which has frequently been discussed[120] and which earned the twenty-year-old Bach a fistfight with an older student in

---

112   Dok 3: 106–107 (No. 674).
113   Dok 1: 127–128 (No. 57); NBR 134–135 (No. 134), 321 (No. 315).
114   Kobayashi 11.
115   Dok 1: 255–267 (No. 184); NBR 283–294 (No. 303).
116   Dok 3: 287–288 (No. 802); NBR 282 (introduction to Nos. 302–303).
117   Dok 3: 290 (No. 803); NBR 400 (No. 395).
118   Dok 2: 469 (No. 600); NBR 386 (No. 385).
119   Jacob von Stählin, "Nachricht von der Tanzkunst und Balleten in Rußland," Johann Joseph Haigold, *Beylagen zum Neuveränderten Rußland. Zweiter Theil* (Riga: Hartknoch, 1770; reprint, Leipzig: Peters, 1982), 83.
120   For example, Sara Botwinick, "Fear not the Zippel Fagottist!" *Bach Notes. The Newsletter of the American Bach Society* 4 (Fall 2005): 8–9.

Documents   45

Arnstadt,[121] could have easily been understood in its scatological meaning if interpreters had consulted the article "Zippel" (onion) in Zedler's *Universal Lexicon*.[122]

Bach wrote on the title page of his *Orgel-Büchlein* "Autore Joanne Sebast: Bach p.t. Capellæ Magistro S. P. R. Anhaltini-Cothenisis."[123] Charles Sanford Terry suggested that p[ro] t[empore] meant that Bach would be music director in Cöthen in the future, so that—contrary to earlier assumptions—Bach had worked on the *Orgel-Büchlein* during his arrest in 1717, and not on the *Wohltemperiertes Clavier*. If Bach had wanted to refer to his current employment in Cöthen, he would have had to write "eo tempore."[124] Although this argument sounded compelling, it is based on a lack of knowledge of eighteenth-century conventions.[125]

Similar to this misunderstanding is the transcription of a frequently used sign that indicates the continuation of a thought, resembling the letter "p" in German script (it sometimes resembles the letter "f" in cyrillic). Numerous publications therefore transcribe the sign as "p" and resolve the abbreviation as "perge" (continue).[126] However, the sign in question would have to resemble a Latin "p" if it were to be resolved as a Latin word. Therefore it is more likely that the letter in question is a quickly written "C" or a "c" and that it means "cetera"—as in *et cetera*.[127]

An astonishing and quite embarrassing example should be mentioned at the end of this chapter, although it is only loosely related to the matter of Bach documents. It regards the text for the *Trauer-Ode* (BWV 198), performed in October 1727 in commemoration of the death of Saxon Electress Christiane Eberhardine. According to all extant reports, this event was exceptional and not considered an official ceremony of the state because the Elector had converted to Catholicism, and therefore a Protestant funeral was problematic. The seventh stanza in Johann Christoph Gottsched's ode (movement 8 in Bach's cantata) reads thus:

---

121 Dok 2: 17 (No. 14); NBR 45 (No. 19c).
122 The small Anhalt town of Zörbig had the nickname "Zippel-Zerbst" in the seventeenth century; allegedly because if the numerous onion fields in the nearer vicinity; see Zedler, 63 (1750): col. 83. Robert L. Marshall has drawn attention to an obviously nasty meaning of the term, as documented in Grimm's *Deutsches Wörterbuch*; Robert L. Marshall, "Toward a Twenty-First Century Bach Biography," MQ 84 (2000): 497–525, esp. 501.
123 Dok 1: 214–215 (No. 148); NBR 80–81 (No. 69).
124 Charles Sanford Terry, "The 'Orgelüchlein': Another Bach Problem," *The Musical Times* 58 (1917): 9–11, 60–62, 107–109.
125 Regarding the date for the composition of the *Orgel-Büchlein* and the genesis of the title page in Cöthen, see Georg von Dadelsen, "Zur Entstehung des Bachschen Orgelbüchleins," *Festschrift Friedrich Blume zum 70. Geburtstag*, eds. Anna Amalie Abert and Wilhelm Pfannkuch (Kassel: Bärenreiter, 1963), 74–79.
126 See NBA IV/1 KB, 23.
127 Transcribed thus in Dok 1–5. See also Klaus Beckmann's interpretation, Walther, *Briefe*, 16.

46   *Hans-Joachim Schulze*

Der Ewigkeit Saphirnes Haus   Eternity's sapphire house
Zieht Deiner heitern Augen-Blicke Attracts your serene view
Von der verschmähten Welt zurücke Away from the azure world
Und tilgt der Erden Denckbild aus.[128] And effaces the image of the earth.

Bach's barely legible text has been transcribed "Dreckbild" (image of dirt) instead of "Denkbild" ("image/ monument/ memorial").[129] Even a brief consultation of the contemporary sources would have helped avoid this awkward mistake.[130]

Translated by Markus Rathey

---

128 Johann Christoph Gottsched, *Oden Der Deutschen Gesellschaft in Leipzig In vier Bücher abgetheilet* (Leipzig: Gleditsch, 1728), 80; Michael Ranft, *Necrologium Domus Saxonicæ Coævum. Oder Vollständige Lebens-Geschichte Aller In diesem ietztlauffenden XVIII. Seculo Verstorbenen Herzoge von Sachsen...* (Leipzig: Martini, 1728), 408.

129 NBA I/38: 234 (Werner Neumann); Werner Neumann, *Johann Sebastian Bach sämtliche Kantatentexte* (Leipzig: Breitkopf & Härtel, 1967), 400; Melvin P. Unger, *Handbook to Bach's Sacred Cantata Texts* (Lanham: Scarecrow, 1996), 696.

130 After having mentioned my discovery in a conversation, a *Plagiarius* published my finding in 1975 under his own name; a reference to the relevant essay is therefore obsolete.

3 Manuscripts

Yo Tomita[1]

Any consideration of Bach manuscripts must begin with the work of two scholars: Georg von Dadelsen (1918–2007), who broke new ground in Bach scholarship by dating Bach's manuscripts through analysis of the handwriting of Bach and his copyists;[2] and Alfred Dürr (1918–2011), who was able to establish a new chronology of Bach's vocal works composed in Leipzig by studying watermarks and identifying the individual copyists.[3] For those who accepted the validity of the old chronology proposed by Philipp Spitta (1841–94) in the late nineteenth century, which until then had been considered unassailable, it was an earth-shattering realization that the foundation of their scholarship had been removed. A half-century has passed, and although a number of refinements have been made to the findings of Dadelsen and Dürr (and others), their theories and methodologies have remained broadly unchallenged. There is, however, every reason to believe that future generations will develop new techniques and methodologies that will re-evaluate existing evidence and discover new perspectives in Bach research.

The aim of this chapter is three-fold: first, to explain systematically the multiple disciplines that have to be used in the study of manuscripts; second, to review the evolution and development of methodologies used by the scholars who have shaped the present form of scholarship, and to chart outstanding problems that have yet to be resolved; and third, to offer some ideas of what future research might entail and in what way scholarship might develop. Because numerous and disparate methodologies are used in the study of Bach manuscripts, the discussions that follow will take nothing for granted, but will describe and define each

---

1 I am most grateful to Nobuaki Ebata, David Ledbetter and Richard Rastall, whose comments on an early version of this chapter were invaluable. I am also indebted to Tanja Kovačević and Robin A. Leaver for their editorial work on this chapter.

2 TBSt 1 and TBSt 4/5.

3 Dürr Chr 2. The work of Dadelsen and Dürr was further refined by Yoshitake Kobayashi; see Kobayashi, and Yoshitake Kobayashi, "Quellenkundliche Überlegungen zur Chronologie der Weimarer Vokalwerke Bachs," Karl Heller and Hans-Joachim Schulze, eds., *Das Frühwerk Johann Sebastian Bachs* (Cologne: Studio, 1995), 290–310; and NBA IX/1 (1985), IX/2 (1989), and IX/3 (2007).

48   Yo Tomita

one as it relates to understanding and reproducing, with as much accuracy as possible, Bach's intentions in the manuscripts that contain his music.

Manuscript Study

Bach research has traditionally placed a great emphasis on studying manuscripts. The fact that most of Bach's works have been transmitted in manuscript form is the obvious justification for such studies. But, crucially, there are broader musicological research goals than simply deciphering the music of a manuscript. Not only is there the music but also evidence of both writer(s) and user(s) that witness to the origin and dissemination of the composition(s). A manuscript may contain additional important details, such as interventions by later owners, individual and institutional, auctioneers and antiquarian music dealers. Whether or not such information can be retrieved and decoded successfully depends on the methodology and research techniques used. Even if the significance is not immediately apparent the information should nevertheless be recorded, opening the possibility for future discovery. Scholarly advancement moves forward in this perpetual cycle, building on the discoveries of one's predecessors.

Every music manuscript contains a wide range of information manifested not only in its written contents, such as the various inscriptions including the title, movement headers, or the composer's name and, of course, the actual musical contents in notational form, but also in its existence as a whole, which reveals the circumstances of its production. This includes the physical makeup of the score and/or a set of parts, the identity of the writer, when and why it was produced, and evidence of its subsequent ownership and use. If the manuscript was written by the composer himself, considerable insights into his creative process might be gained through a careful exploration for traces of composition and revision that it might contain. Manuscripts are indeed a treasure-house of information, and from them one may learn many fascinating historical details. A manuscript may offer clues that disclose the date of composition and performance(s), or information about its background, the person(s) who inherited it, and how it has been used or appreciated by subsequent musicians and collectors. This kind of information may not be accessible from the study of the surviving letters and documents alone. In this way, manuscripts may provide fresh perspectives on Bach's biography as well as the reception history. Manuscript studies will therefore continue to attract scholars eager to unveil quiescent pieces of evidence waiting to be brought to light.

Approaches and Terminologies

The study of a manuscript usually begins with an assessment of the manuscript itself as a physical artifact. This involves examining diplomatic evidence, that is, all its material features such as paper; the implements used in its production such as quill, pencil, rastrum, ruler and knife; the types of ink used; foliation of paper and binding; as well as any significant features in the handwriting specific to time and region, each of which supplies an independent set of chronological and locational information with which to profile the circumstances of the source's production. Although this phase of examination, when conducted on a single source, may not immediately produce definitive evidence about its origins, it is vital that one takes this step properly from the outset because the evidence garnered through this process becomes the basis for interpreting evidence acquired through subsequent phases of examination. Quite separately, this step needs to be undertaken as part of a large schematic research examining all related sources. The greater the volume of diplomatic evidence gathered, the greater the possibility of ascertaining the origins and contexts in which the sources were made.

The next phase of inquiry is text criticism, the evaluation of the written contents using philological methodologies. The procedure normally begins with an assessment of the broader issues, such as obvious notational features, and gradually narrows down to a detailed discussion of the specifics of musical content, such as corrections and revisions, incrementally building on observations made in the previous phases of study. When examining a work that is transmitted in multiple sources, one of the primary aims is to establish which source gives the closest readings to the original even if the original is no longer extant and has to be reconstructed hypothetically. Ultimately, the study should establish a firmer ground to assess the content of a manuscript and establish what the composer intended when the document was being written.

It is not always straightforward to retrieve the information one expects to find. To successfully locate the information and make sense of it, it is usually necessary to examine widely and systematically not only the source in question, but also all the other sources that are considered related for specific enquiries. Furthermore, the sources should be evaluated both externally (the physical makeup such as paper, ink, foliations of the manuscript, etc.) and internally (the manner in which they were written as well as the written contents of the manuscripts). Imagine that each manuscript represents a collection of various tiny fragments of knowledge: it resembles a multi-dimensional jigsaw puzzle—each fragment may provide crucial information for reconstructing the image, but the same piece of information may also support the reconstruction of another picture. For example, a variant reading in one source can provide evidence for tracing the transmission route of related manuscripts, but the same information can also be seen as evidence for reconstructing the profile of the scribes (how reliably they reproduced their model, which aspects of the musical text they altered and why). Information retrieval from the music manuscript needs to be conducted in such a way that allows for subsequent analyses and verification.

Locating Sources

The usual starting point for Bach scholars has been to consult the relevant volume of the NBA *Kritische Berichte* that attempts to trace, describe and assess

50   *Yo Tomita*

all the known manuscript sources for specific works of Bach.[4] These volumes provide the background to the decisions behind the edition of music in the specific volume of the NBA. However, one must be aware that, because the NBA project ran for over half a century and involved many scholars, the quality and the state of scholarship in each volume are not uniform, which has resulted in many of the earlier volumes requiring major updates. More recently, scholars have increasingly been using online databases of sources, such as the Source Catalogues of Bach-Digital (2008–),[5] which succeeds the Göttinger Bach-Katalog (1999–2008).[6] In addition to the basic search facility, such databases allow filtering the information by scribe, approximate date of copying, Bach's compositions contained in the source, and other basic source information. The databases also offer high-resolution color scans of Bach's original manuscripts held in public libraries in Germany. Although the amount of detail available in online databases is limited—and for this reason the NBA *Kritische Berichte* retain their usefulness—the value of the databases is unquestionable, as their data can be frequently updated, errors corrected and new records added. They have become the preferred initial source reference tool for most Bach scholars. In the past, one had to write to the holding library to request microfilms or photocopies to obtain reproductions of sources that were not commercially available in facsimile[7] or microfilm/microfiche.[8] The Bach-Archiv Leipzig library possesses a comprehensive collection of photographic reproductions of manuscripts. Today, color scans of manuscripts can be obtained on CD-ROM or downloaded from the internet, and, once scanned in this manner, they are often made available to other readers—sometimes free of charge—from the library's website.[9] Because of the

---

4   Concise summaries of the main sources of vocal works that were known by the late 1980s are found in BC. A brief list of all the sources of Bach's entire oeuvre is found in BWV[2] (1990); one must, however, exercise caution when using it, as it merely lists the sources, without applying rigorous source-critical considerations.

5   www.bachdigital.de.

6   www.bach.gwdg.de.

7   Particularly important is the series of facsimiles issued by Insel Verlag in the 1920s. Made before ink corrosion had damaged them even further, they preserve the clearest images of Bach's autographs. Another representative collection of Bach's autographs was published in a series called "Faksimile-Reihe Bachscher Werke und Schriftstücke" (1954–88), and its successor "Faksimile-Reihe Bachscher Werke und Schriftstücke. Neue Folge" (2001–). Anyone using a facsimile edition should be alert to any errors or imperfections that might have crept in during its preparation and production. See, for example, Albi Rosenthal, "Facsimiles as Sources of Error," Paul Brainard and Ray Robinson, eds., *A Bach Tribute: Essays in Honor of William H. Scheide* (Kassel: Bärenreiter, 1993), 205–207.

8   The most important is Die Bach-Sammlung: Musikhandschriften der Staatsbibliothek zu Berlin – Preußischer Kulturbesitz, Teil 1 (Munich: Saur, 1997–2003; Supplement [I] (2000), and Supplement II, 2003).

9   Some of the most prominent at present are: Staatsbibliothek zu Berlin (digital.staatsbibliothek-berlin.de), Bayerische Staatsbibliothek (www.digitale-sammlungen.de) and Sächsische Landesbibliothek – Staats- und Universitätsbibliothek Dresden (digital.slub-dresden.de). See also note 5.

speed at which digital images are becoming available on various websites, it is increasingly difficult to keep track of the newly digitized sources.[10]

To locate sources that have not yet been reported in Bach literature, other channels such as RISM and individual library catalogues that may have escaped the notice of Bach scholars need to be investigated. It is, of course, possible to stumble upon new sources in archives or auction houses purely by accident. Vague descriptions are common in nineteenth-century catalogues of sources and auctions, and it requires considerable knowledge about the many aspects of music manuscripts to develop an instinct for evaluating what the cataloguer was attempting to describe, and piece together numerous minute fragments to reveal the hitherto invisible historical information.

Classifying Sources

Sources can be classified in a number of ways, determined by the nature and purpose of the enquiries. Classification of sources can be confusing; any study of a particular composer tends to generate its own distinct source types and tailor its jargon accordingly, which has resulted in an extensive accumulation of terminology.[11] Many of the source type descriptions—sketch, draft, composing score, fair copy, etc.—were devised for the purposes of scholarly discourse, and were not necessarily used by the composers themselves. It is therefore of utmost importance that in source scholarship a distinction be made between our later categories and those of Bach's day.

Primary and Secondary Sources

The common practice in manuscript studies is to divide sources into two categories: primary and secondary. *Primary* sources are those shortlisted as priority subjects because they are believed to contain the original information, so that the remaining sources that do not contain any original information from the time period of enquiry, that is, the *secondary* sources, can be set aside from the main target of research.

The majority of studies of music manuscripts are conducted with a view to producing reliable editions of music. One of the most important tasks of the editor is to establish the composer's intended text through the examination of the surviving sources.[12] The primary sources consulted for this purpose include everything that directly reflects the composer's intentions. This includes scores

---

10 For a discussion of this issue, see Yo Tomita "Challenging Virtuality: A Response to Ruth Tatlow," *Bach Notes: The Newsletter of the American Bach Society* 18 (Spring 2013): 3–6.

11 For example, the term "discarded autograph" represents one of the five categories of sources used in Chopin studies. It refers to a manuscript that Chopin initially intended as a clean copy for the engraver, but as he subsequently revised the score, the copy, no longer suitable for its original purpose, was discarded.

12 See further "Critical Editions" in this chapter.

52   *Yo Tomita*

written in his own hand as well as performance parts supervised by the composer. These are more commonly referred to as "original manuscripts" (see the following section). Also included in this category are prints published during Bach's lifetime, especially by Bach himself (i.e., "original prints"), that may contain information not found in the surviving manuscripts.[13] In reception studies, the category of primary sources is accordingly broadened to include sources of the period on which the study is focused. For example, a manuscript copy of Bach's Schübler chorales (BWV 645–650), once owned by Mendelssohn (GB-Ob, MS. Deneke Mendelssohn c.71), would be regarded as a primary source by someone studying Mendelssohn's involvement with the publication of the work, whereas someone preparing an edition of the Schübler chorales would consider it a secondary source.[14]

The classification of sources is an important part of a scholar's work, and false assessment at this stage could jeopardize the outcome of the discussion in a catastrophic way. A well-known case is Friedrich Smend's evaluation of two specific manuscript copies of the B-minor Mass, Source C (D-B, Am. B. 3) and Source D (a three-volume manuscript consisting of D-B, Mus. ms. Bach P 572, P 23 and P 14). Smend considered both these manuscripts to be primary sources dating from Bach's lifetime (i.e., written before the autograph was modified), whereas later scholars found that they were copied after Bach's death (the alteration of the autograph having already begun). The damage, however, had been done and, consequently, the NBA edition of the Mass incorporated numerous posthumous additions as if they were Bach's own.[15]

Autographs, Copies and Original Manuscripts.

When the writer is the author of the work, the manuscript is termed *autograph* (or less often *holograph*).[16] All the other manuscripts are thus called *copies*. Copies (*Abschriften*) usually contain a greater number of errors of various kinds. Actually, it is a somewhat shocking revelation to find that a number of the original parts of Bach's cantatas contain uncorrected errors, some of which

---

13 Distinction is also made between a corrected "personal copy" (*Handexemplar*) and a copy in which corrections were transferred from an authentic source by another hand. In many cases, *Handexemplars* survive while the original manuscripts themselves do not. See Butler in Chapter 2.

14 See Nobuaki Ebata, Yo Tomita and Ian Mills, "Mendelssohn and The Schübler Chorales (BWV 645–650): A New Source found in the Riemenschneider Bach Institute Collection," BACH 44/1 (2013): 1–45.

15 See the critical review of NBA II/1 (1954) and NBA II/1 KB (1956), by Georg von Dadelsen: Mf 12 (1959): 315–34; ET "Friedrich Smend's Edition of the B-minor Mass by J. S. Bach," BACH 20/2 (Summer 1989): 49–74.

16 Although both terms basically mean the same thing, "autograph" is generally the preferred term in manuscript studies. For a debate on the terms, see mssworkinggroup.pbworks.com/w/page/26216258/Holograph%20vs%20Autograph (accessed 26 February 2014).

Manuscripts 53

so serious, that they surely must have caused problems when they were used for performance.[17]

In Bach literature, there are a few other terms that are commonly used to distinguish the finer nuances between sources. Partial autograph (*Teilautograph*) is a hybrid type of which there are two possible materializations. The first is a manuscript that was written by more than one writer, one of which is Bach himself. A typical example is the score of Cantata 61 (D-B, Mus. ms. Bach P 45, Faszikel 6), which was started as a fair copy by Bach's copyist, with Bach himself taking over from the second movement.[18] There are also cases where Bach embarked on making the fair copy, which he then passed on to his assistant for completion. The score of the St. John Passion (D-B, Mus. ms. Bach P 28) is an interesting example. Having copied the work neatly up to page 20, in mid-March 1739 Bach suddenly stopped copying, possibly because he learnt that the Passion performance had been canceled for that year.[19] The manuscript was completed in 1749, by one of Bach's principal copyists, Johann Nathanael Bammler (1722–84), who seems to have used the draft score of 1724 that contained revisions made before 1739.[20] The second manifestation of a partial autograph is a copy that contains Bach's later additions or corrections. Examples are both numerous and wide-ranging, and include the original score—a revision copy—of BWV 875/1 and a sales copy of BWV 1021 (see discussion later in this chapter).

Some confusion exists over Bach's copies of other composers' works, either the copies he made himself or those he owned, but did not copy: they should never be referred to as Bach's autographs, even if they are entirely in Bach's handwriting. When discussing Bach's transcriptions of other composers' works, the distinction becomes even more confusing, as a transcription may denote anything from a straightforward re-setting for a different instrument or instruments to more involved re-compositions of a piece. In principle, a straightforward re-setting for a different instrument should be called "copy" or "transcription manuscript." This applies when discussing the non-extant manuscript in Bach's hand of the Aria (BWV 587), a transcription of Couperin's Trio movement from the Suite *L'impériale* for two violins and continuo. On the contrary, when discussing the score of the D-minor

---

17 See Alfred Dürr's humorous article "De vita cum imperfectis," Robert L. Marshall, ed. *Studies in Renaissance and Baroque Music in Honor of Arthur Mendel* (Kassel: Bärenreiter, 1974), 243–53.

18 Wollny identifies the scribe as Johann Lorenz Bach (1695–1773), grandson of an elder brother of J. S. Bach's father. Peter Wollny, "Einführung" / "Introduction," *Johann Sebastian Bach: 'Nun komm, der Heiden Heiland' BWV 61. Faksimile der Originalpartitur* (Laaber: Laaber, 2000), vii and xii–xiii.

19 See NBR 204 (No. 208) and Dok 2: 338–9 (No. 439) for the account recorded by a clerk of the Leipzig town council dated 17 March 1739. See also Kobayashi, 44.

20 Peter Wollny, "Neue Bach-Funde," BJ 83 (1997): 7–50, esp. 42–3; Peter Wollny, "Vorwort," Peter Wollny, ed., Johannespassion: Passio secundum Joannem, Fassung IV (1749), BWV 245/ BC D 2d, mit der unvollendeten Revision BC D 23 (1739) im Anhang, für Soli (SATBB), Chor (SATB), 2 Traversflöten, 2 Oboen/Oboe d'amore, Oboen da caccia, Viola da gamba, 2 Violinen, Viola und Basso continuo / Johann Sebastian Bach (Stuttgart: Carus, 2002), vii and ix.

54 Yo Tomita

Concerto for organ (BWV 596; D-B Mus. ms. Bach P 330), which is a more involved re-composition of Antonio Vivaldi's D-minor Concerto for two violins and cello from *L'Estro Armonico*, Op. 3, No. 11, RV 565, it should be referred to as "autograph" (of Bach's arrangement), and not "copy" (of Vivaldi's composition).[21]

The *original manuscript* (also *original score* and *original parts*) is another conceptual term used in Bach scholarship. It refers to a manuscript prepared for Bach's own use, his personal copy for that matter, which could have been made either by Bach himself or another copyist (the question of penmanship is immaterial here). However, as Bach himself did not make any remarks that would indicate that the manuscript was his personal copy, this can only be found out through studying the surviving sources systematically and carefully. One of the best-known examples of this kind is the so-called "London autograph" of WTC II (GB-Lbl, Add. MS 35021), which is a partial autograph, mostly in Bach's hand, but some movements are in the hand of his second wife, Anna Magdalena Bach, who assisted her husband in the production of fair copies.[22] A question such as that concerning the division of their labor becomes an important issue when evaluating the source: Anna copied from Bach's revision copy that needed to be produced in fair copy, while Bach took on the portion he felt he still needed to revisit from the compositional aspect. The concept of *original manuscript* is crucial when discussing the sources of Bach's ensemble music, particularly those for a vocal ensemble with an orchestra, such as the sacred cantatas. Bach composed his music as scores, from which sets of parts were then produced, often by his copyists. When he subsequently inspected the parts, he supplied performance-related indications, such as slurs and ornaments, but also further developed some of the musical ideas. And, normally, these were not transferred to his own scores. For this reason, in Bach scholarship it is more productive to discuss the sources from Bach's perspective rather than from our own arbitrary distinction between autographs and copies.

Compositional Stages and Neatness of Handwriting

Manuscripts are customarily described in pre-classified categories of notional compositional stages from general appearance, namely, sketch (*Skizze*), draft (*Entwurf*), composing score (*Konzeptschrift*) and fair copy (*Reinschrift*).[23] In Bach's case, the first two of these types do physically exist, but only within composing scores, as can be observed in the composing scores of some cantatas, for which Bach did not produce fair copies. It appears that his standard practice was

---

21 See James B. Welch, "J. S. Bach's Concerto in D minor, BWV 596, after Vivaldi: its Origin, Questioned Authorship, and Transcription," *Diapason* 74 (May 1983): 6–7. For further discussion of Bach's transcriptions of works by his fellow composers, see Chapter 10.

22 "London original manuscript" (*Londoner Originalhandschrift*, as used in NBA V/6.2) would be a more precise designation than this English nickname introduced by Richardson and Emery in their respective articles published in *Music & Letters* and used widely since at least 1953.

23 See Robert L. Marshall, *The Compositional Process of J. S. Bach. A Study of the Autograph Scores of the Vocal Works*, 2 vols. (Princeton: Princeton University Press, 1972), 1: 3–6 and 31–32, for definitions.

Manuscripts   55

to write out a score directly, without relying on sketches or drafts,[24] by seeking to develop the pieces from ideas already present in the composing score. By and large, this worked well, although the existence of sections laden with revisions indicates that Bach occasionally struggled to arrive at a satisfactory text. Yet in the case of instrumental compositions, especially the keyboard works from the late Leipzig period, for which Bach wrote out fresh fair copies, it may be assumed that he destroyed the composing scores containing sketches and drafts when he no longer needed them.[25] Due to Bach's process of revision, which led to the creation of new fair copies and rendered early sketches and drafts redundant, keyboard works tend to be preserved in multiple copies. Therefore, Bach studies normally deal with just two types of manuscript: although *composing scores* contain a considerable number of corrections of a formative nature, the *fair copies* contain very few or none, and where corrections are found, they are usually limited to rectifying copying errors or slips of the pen.[26] A broader survey of Bach's autographs indicates that Bach saw in the production of fair copies another opportunity for engagement with the compositional possibilities of the pieces, and continued to revise them as he wrote them out.[27]

Sometimes further distinctions are made within these categories. One of these is a *revision copy*, which lies halfway between a composing score and a fair copy.[28] The score of "Gloria in excelsis Deo" (BWV 191; D-B, Mus. ms. Bach P 1145) is one such example. Evidently working from the score of the *Missa* (BWV 232[1]; D-B, Mus. ms. Bach P 180) sometime ca. 1743–6,[29] Bach made multiple minor

---

24 Marshall, *Compositional Process*, 2 transcribes all the known sketches and drafts. NBA Supplement (Wollny and Maul, 2012) reproduces them in facsimile. The nature of the discarded readings is wide-ranging. One of the most fascinating examples includes the draft of BWV 149, the paper of which was used for the score of BWV 201 (D-B, Mus. ms. Bach P 175) several weeks later.

25 See, for example, Yo Tomita, "Bach and His Early Drafts: Some Observations on Little Known Early Versions of Well-Tempered Clavier II and the Goldberg Variations from the Manfred Gorke Collection," BACH 30/2 (1999): 49–72.

26 Dadelsen TBSt 4/5: 58–72; Marshall, *Compositional Process*, 1: 4.

27 This observation is particularly relevant to the manuscripts of solo keyboard works. There are only a few fair-copy scores of his ensemble music, as Bach presumably considered the production of parts to be the equivalent of making a fair copy.

28 Marshall, *Compositional Process*, 1: 5, 18–20.

29 This dating is by Kobayashi, 52. For a long time, the year 1745, as proposed by Butler, has been known as the possible date of performance, but recent studies by Rathey and Leaver propose that the revision copy of the "Gloria" originated a few years earlier, namely in 1742. Gregory Butler, "Johann Sebastian Bachs Gloria in excelsis Deo BWV 191: Musik für ein Leipziger Dankfest," BJ 78 (1992): 65–71; Markus Rathey, "Zur Entstehungsgeschichte von Bachs Universitätsmusik 'Gloria in Excelsis Deo' BWV 191," BJ 99 (2013): 319–28; and Robin A. Leaver, "Bachs lateinische Kantate 'Gloria in Excelsis Deo' BWV 191 und eine lateinische Rede über Lukas 2:14," BJ 99 (2013): 329–34. However, Rathey and Leaver's new dating is not without problems. A careful consideration of the evidence presented by Kobayashi and his dating "von etwa 1743 bis etwa 1746," especially in conjunction with watermark evidence (Weiß 21) and Bach's G-clef, renders 1742 to be too early. Future research must include a reassessment of watermarks to see whether or not the paper is a variant of Weiß 21.

56 *Yo Tomita*

corrections of a revisionary nature in the score of the "Gloria." If the appearance of an autograph suggests that it is a revision copy, then it is possible to infer that the music is either a parody or a transcription, even if no such version of the piece is known among the surviving sources. It thus follows that a *transcription score* is effectively a revision copy. In the score of the harpsichord concertos (D-B, Mus. ms. Bach P 234) traces of Bach's compositional adjustments can be identified, which are especially numerous within BWV 1052; having carefully studied these, Siegele proposed that it was transcribed from a lost violin concerto.[30] Among the revision copies are also scores in which revisions were worked out at chronologically differing stages. For example, the original manuscript of the D-minor Prelude of WTC II (BWV 875/1: GB-Lbl, Add. MS 35021, f. 4r) was initially produced by Anna Magdalena as a fair copy, which Bach later decided to substantially revise, extending the movement from 53 to 61 bars in length.

Rough and *neat* are often crucial distinctions when discussing Bach's handwriting, not only because of the radical differences between the script forms, which may affect the identification of the writer as well as the dating of the handwriting,[31] but also because it reflects how much time and care Bach was able to devote to writing the manuscript. This distinction often goes hand in hand with the compositional stages—the handwriting is rough in composing scores and neat in fair copies.[32] This, however, is not always the case. The calligraphic appearance of the original manuscript of the Prelude in F-sharp minor (BWV 883/1, GB-Lbl, Add. MS. 35021, f. 10r) is quite deceptive; in fact, it contains a number of notational adjustments that Bach had made while producing this score, which strongly suggests that he was not copying from a fully written-out draft, but was more likely writing straight from his head.

Bach's Own Classification

It is not very clear how Bach classified his scores and parts. The earliest reference to Bach's musical library is a list of works included in the obituary written by Carl Philipp Emanuel Bach and Johann Friedrich Agricola. The list is, unfortunately, too general to allow any firm conclusions as to the library's organization.[33] Still, the mention of "five full annual cycles (*Jahrgänge*) of church pieces, for all the Sundays and holidays," the first on the list totalling sixteen items, has several important implications. First, it suggests that Bach reused

---

30 Ulrich Siegele, *Kompositionsweise und Bearbeitungstechnik in der Instrumentalmusik Johann Sebastian Bachs* (Stuttgart: Hänssler, 1975), esp. 101–16; see also NBA KB VII/7 (1971): 36–40. The lost but reconstructed concertos were published as NBA VII/7 (Supplement), and BWV² (1990) indicated them by R-numbers, such as BWV 1052R. R-numbers were abandoned in BWV²ᵃ (1998).

31 Dadelsen uses the terms working script (*Gebrauchsschrift*) and calligraphic script; see TBSt 4/5: 71–2; see also Marshall, *Compositional Process*, 1: 4.

32 See, for example, Bach's autograph score of the Christmas Oratorio (D-B, Mus. ms. Bach P 32), which includes many parody movements from secular cantatas.

33 NBR 304 (No, 306); Dok 3: 86 (No. 666).

his scores and parts more than a few times during the twenty-seven years of his office in Leipzig; if so, it is reasonable to assume that he had an efficient filing system of all the pieces in the library. Second, the list implies that the original sources of nearly two full annual cycles of cantatas were lost after Bach's death, as only three annual cycles survive. However, the letter of Johann Elias Bach to Johann Wilhelm Koch, dated 28 January 1741,[34] hints that a large number of cantatas from the two missing annual cycles may have already been removed from Bach's library in 1740. Such a significant loss of original material has serious implications for Bach scholarship and must be taken into account when interpreting Bach's creative activities. Whether or not Bach indeed composed all five annual cycles of cantatas will undoubtedly remain a pressing question for future Bach studies.

It is also necessary to consider the origin of manuscripts from Bach's point of view. Were they the result of the initial composition or were they later fair-copy versions made for the purpose of preservation? Were they intended for Bach's own library or made for someone else? Regarding the manuscripts that Bach kept in his library, it is likely that he distinguished between two types: (1) original manuscripts, whether complete and incomplete, such as the *Orgelbüchein*, comprising his personal reference copies; and (2) multiple copies for use by students, or manuscripts that might have been original sources, but were subsequently downgraded to be given away to students or admirers when new versions were created. Awareness of such distinctions is often crucial when evaluating the musical contents of copies made by Bach's students. For some of his major keyboard works such as WTC, Bach seems to have had multiple copies often containing different versions of the pieces, and his tendency to let his students make copies of earlier versions suggests that he kept his personal copy, containing the most up-to-date shape of the compositions, separate from the multiple copies. The possibility of lost sources cannot be discounted when considering such issues.

As is evident from some of the surviving sources, Bach did not retain all of his manuscripts for his library; some were given away or sold, while others, such as his drafts, have been lost or disposed of. The most important among these will probably have been dedication copies, made with a view of securing a better social status or new employment. The fair-copy score of the Brandenburg Concertos (BWV 1046–1051; D-B, Am. B. 78) and the performance parts of the *Missa* of 1733 (BWV 232[I]; D-Dl, Mus. 2405-D-21) are the best-known surviving examples of this kind. Bach would probably also have had fair copies made for private sale. Although no certain sample of this kind exists in Bach's own hand, a number of copies made by Anna Magdalena, some of which are partial autographs (for example, BWV 1021: D-LEb, Go. S. 3, Faszikel 1), are presumed to have been made for this purpose.[35] Bach is also known to have loaned manuscripts, some of which, such as the original parts of the *Sanctus* (BWV 232[III]) sent to Count Franz

---

34 NBR 210 (No. 219); Dok 2: 388 (No. 484).
35 See Yo Tomita, "Anna Magdalena as Bach's Copyist," UB 2 (2007): 59–76, esp. 71.

58   *Yo Tomita*

Anton von Sporck in 1725 or 1726,[36] were never returned, or simply given them away as occasional gifts. Such gifts may in fact be crucial when interpreting how collections such as Bach's WTC II were compiled and kept together. The source transmission of the F-minor pair (BWV 881) is unique within the collection: its early version was transmitted exclusively in sources connected with Kirnberger, and there are sufficient grounds to speculate that he acquired their autograph while studying with Bach.

Bach must also have distinguished his copies in terms of neatness and general appearance. Those that he considered worthy of sale or presentation to potential patrons or friends, such as the partial autograph score of the Brandenburg Concertos which he dedicated to the Margrave Christian Ludwig of Brandenburg in 1721, could be studied to determine how many errors Bach could tolerate in a presentation copy.

Diplomatic Evidence

The study of manuscripts usually begins with the examination of the document itself using the methodology developed in codicology and diplomatics, scholarly disciplines that critically analyze historical documents by focusing on the conventions, protocols and formulae used by document creators in order to gain an understanding of the process of their creation. In this case, the focus is on the paper, the implements used for writing and erasure and the manner in which the document was crafted and finished. The study of written contents is therefore set aside until the next stage of study.

Paper and Watermarks

It was Spitta who introduced "paper study" to Bach scholarship as an integral part of evaluating the sources.[37] It was an attractive proposition as it offered a new kind of information based on the identification of the approximate time and place of paper manufacture independent of the contents of the document, a study that could be managed entirely objectively. However, as is evident from some of Spitta's mistakes, the study requires tremendous effort and patience to bear fruit.[38]

Until the beginning of the nineteenth century, paper was made by hand in small batches. In Europe, paper makers customarily added watermarks to their

---

36 Or more precisely, after Christmas 1724 and before Easter 1727; see Dürr Chr 2, 77 and 93.

37 Spitta is enthusiastic in relating his theory of using watermarks in Bach source studies; Spitta 2: 775–776; Spitta ET 2: 680.

38 Even though Spitta believed his method was vigorous and thorough, conclusions he drew from incomplete and imperfect data led him astray; for instance, he failed to recognize some of the crucial features of watermarks, such as the three variants of the watermark "MA" (small, middle and large). Awareness of such features allowed Wisso Weiß to classify and date Bach's paper more precisely than Spitta. See Dürr Chr 2, 35, 126, 138–141.

Manuscripts 59

paper as trademarks. The designs of watermarks vary widely, some simply comprising the letters indicating the names of the maker (often in initial or in a monogram form), or the region and ruler, while others include elaborate shapes such as coats of arms, plants, animals, tools, etc. The possibilities are endless, but currently no single standard exists to describe each watermark. A common practice in Bach studies is to refer to the catalogue number of Wisso Weiß's *Katalog der Wasserzeichen in Bachs Originalhandschriften* (NBA IX/1);[39] other watermark catalogues that can be consulted include the series *Papyraceae Historiam Illustrantia* published by the Paper Publications Society.[40]

Watermarks are created by wireworks mounted in the paper mold. The wireworks (or the paper mold itself, for that matter) did not last very long. The shape of the watermark would have become distorted through repeated use, and when the mold became defective, it was either repaired or replaced. As is often the case with handicrafts, wireworks were never exactly the same, and even minute variations can be detected and evaluated. Because paper makers normally used a pair of molds to increase productivity, another watermark, which may only be slightly different in shape, may reappear in a source in regular sequence.

The chronology of paper production can be pursued only when an adequate sample of watermarks has been gathered. Finding an exact match for a watermark is vital: when the same watermark is found in more than one source, the likelihood that the leaves (folios) containing identical watermarks were manufactured in close proximity, in both time and place, increases significantly. The same inference may then also be extended to the written contents. However, this only allows determining a *terminus post quem*, that is, the earliest point in time the entries may have been made; the latest possible point, or *terminus ante quem*, will remain open-ended unless additional evidence becomes available. Bach seldom inscribed dates in his music manuscripts, but because he tended to use the same batch of paper for writing letters and other documents that included dates, it is often possible to narrow down the dating of his music manuscripts to a year or two.

Watermark evidence is not always straightforward to interpret. Research can be impeded if a watermark is partially cut off when the manuscript was trimmed or if it has been concealed within the binding. Watermarks are normally placed in the middle of an uncut, unfolded sheet of paper, and in many instances a sheet was folded and cut before it was used, which would have eliminated or truncated

---

39 Weiß.

40 Volumes that are most commonly referred to in Bach scholarship are: Edward Heawood, ed., *Watermarks: mainly of the 17th and 18th centuries.* Monumenta chartae papyraceae historiam illustrantia, I (Hilversum: Paper Publication Society, 1957); Émile Joseph Labarre, ed., *The Nostitz papers: Notes on Watermarks found in the German Imperial Archives of the 17th & 18th centuries, and Essays Showing the Evolution of a Number of Watermarks.* Monumenta chartae papyraceae historiam illustrantia, V (Hilversum: Paper Publication Society, 1956); see also the database *Musik der Dresdner Hofkapelle. Schrank II. Die Instrumentalmusik zur Zeit der sächsisch-polnischen Union. Wasserzeichenkataloge.* www.schrank-zwei.de/recherche/schreiber-wasserzeichenkataloge

60 *Yo Tomita*

the watermark.[41] Even when watermarks are not physically severed or concealed, they can be difficult to discern if a large amount of ink has been deposited on the paper. Radiographic photography can be used to reveal the images clearly, though very few libraries in the world are equipped to provide this service. Double paper poses an even greater challenge in watermark research. This is an extra-thick sheet of paper that was made by overlaying two sheets before their drying out and designed to prevent ink from bleeding through to the other side while at the same time allowing the writer to scratch out small mistakes with a knife. It may contain two overlaid watermarks, which can be extremely difficult to distinguish due to the paper's thickness. It is to be hoped that an automatic identification system of digitized watermarks modelled on the Integrated Automated Fingerprint Identification System (IAFIS), or something similar, would become available to researchers in the future. A catalogue of the leaves of Bach's original sources could then be produced, which would reveal the minute variations in watermarks and help to date the papers of his manuscripts more precisely.

Due to the various sizes and formats in which paper occurs, form, as in studies of other composers, is an essential part of paper studies. Although in Bach studies Weiß's comprehensive catalogue of watermarks has made this process somewhat redundant,[42] research on non-original manuscript copies on paper not covered by Weiß is yet to be undertaken. Ideally, source studies of secondary copies, including those of works by other composers, should gradually be extended into the same rank as the original manuscripts in order to build up a more comprehensive pool of information concerning the origins of a wide range of papers.

Collation and Binding

The way in which sheets of paper are collated into manuscripts is an essential point for examination. Just like stave ruling (see the "Rastrum and Ruler" in this chapter), it can offer additional clues for a clearer understanding of the writer's intentions. In the majority of cases, the sheets (*Bögen*) that form a manuscript are bifolios (double leaves, *Doppelblätter*), with each sheet folded down the middle to create four sides.[43] Staves are usually ruled after the sheet has been folded. When only two sides are needed—for instance, to insert a newly composed section that would occupy less than two sides, such as the "Et incarnatus" of Bach's B-minor Mass—a single half-sheet (folio, single leaf) would be used.

---

41 See note 45.

42 Weiß 1: 14, for a general discussion of this issue.

43 Here the term "sides" has been used instead of "pages," as manuscripts are normally counted by leaves (= folios). Each folio has two sides: recto (facing side) and verso (reverse side). These are customarily foliated by the librarian in pencil in the top right-hand corner when the manuscript is acquired, even where it contains original pagination. Note that "sheet" is a unit for counting paper as a physical object, whereas "folio" refers to the same physical object when forming part of a manuscript. (NB. "folio" may also be used to describe a particular paper size.)

Manuscripts 61

Bach's standard practice, as regards the organization of his music paper (or, more technically, "fascicle structure"), was a binio,[44] or two bifolios stacked up to provide eight usable sides.[45] Departures from this standard practice were probably occasioned by Bach's circumstances at the time. On the one hand, a typical composing score is a successive gathering of unios, because the composer would not know in advance the exact number of leaves that would be needed. This is the case with Bach's earliest surviving composing scores (F-Pn MS-2; BWV 134a, performed on 1 January 1719), and became custom practice within a few months upon his appointment as Thomascantor in Leipzig, when he undertook the enormous task of producing a large number of new works. The autograph score of Cantata 105, "Herr, gehe nicht ins Gericht," for example, is written on five successive bifolios (abbreviated as 'I × 5' or '5 I').[46] On the other hand, fair-copy scores of instrumental works from any period often consist of a gathering of quarternios,[47] which is stronger when bound as well as more convenient for handling.

Sometimes the fascicle structure can reveal important facts. The original performance parts of the 1733 *Missa*, which Bach dedicated to the Saxon elector Friedrich August II on 27 July 1733, were prepared under Bach's supervision. His family travelled with him to Dresden and assisted him in creating the parts from his score. Carl Philipp Emanuel helped his father with the soprano parts; however, he could not copy all the notes in the planned space of a binio fascicle (eight sides) for the part of Soprano 1, so Bach intervened; he copied from bar 60b to the end using a new bifolio. He ruled twelve systems on its first page, and finished the rest using eleven systems, leaving one unused system below; the three remaining pages were left blank.[48] In practice, this meant that, as a result, the singer would have been holding two physical objects together—a binio fascicle plus a unio—which would have been very awkward in performance, especially at page turns.

---

44 Fascicles are described in Latin by the number of bifolios: unio (1), binio (2), ternio (3), quarternio (4), quinio (5), senio (6) and so on. They are also expressed in abbreviated form in Roman numerals, e.g., 6 IV + 2 + 3 II (6 quarternios, 2 single leaves, 3 binios). Note that the German term *Faszikel* does not have the same meaning: it refers to the entire gathering of fascicles created by the writer, the actual German equivalent of fascicle being *Lage*.

45 When Bach made a bifolio, he would have usually folded an uncut sheet once, a binio thus requiring two separate sheets. (Exceptions are limited to smaller bound oblong volumes, such as the *Orgelbüchlein* and the family anthologies discussed below.) Other composers, research has found, would have often cut one sheet and folded it to make two bifolios or a binio fascicle. This is particularly important for scholars studying the watermarks in Mozart's scores; see Alan Tyson, *Mozart: studies of the autograph scores* (Cambridge: Harvard University Press, 1987), 5.

46 Marshall, *Compositional Process*, 1: 61–63. For a detailed observation of Bach's compositional process, see Robert Marshall's commentary accompanying the facsimile published jointly by Zentral-Antiquariat der DDR in Leipzig and Hänssler in Neuhausen-Stuttgart in 1983, reprinted in Robert Marshall, *The Music of Johann Sebastian Bach. The Sources, The Style, The Significance* (New York: Schirmer, 1989), 131–42.

47 See note 44.

48 NBA KB II/1a (2005): 16.

62   Yo Tomita

They would also have had to take great care not to drop the loose leaves! This hypothetical reading of the performance situation is suggested by the present structure of the source (II+I). However, Bach would have probably expected the singer to fold the unio fascicle the other way round and wrap the binio fascicle around it to make a ternio fascicle. This example illustrates the importance of planning the score layout and the collation of sheets together. The fascicle structure thus often reveals the predicted number of leaves required for a manuscript as well as any subsequent adjustments to accommodate new circumstances.

The binding of a manuscript can also expose some fascinating details of the history of its making. An act of affirming a collation of leaves as the final arrangement, it reflects the owner's expectation for the manuscript to last. A relatively small number of manuscripts were bound by Bach. Known specimens are limited to the keyboard collections and family anthologies such as the *Clavierbüchlein* for W. F. Bach (US-NH, Music Deposit 31), the same for Anna Magdalena Bach (of both 1722 and 1725, D-B, Mus. ms. Bach P 224 and P 225, respectively), and possibly also *Orgelbüchlein* (D-B, Mus. ms. Bach P 283), Inventions and Sinfonias (D-B, Mus. ms. Bach P 610), WTC I (D-B, Mus. ms. Bach P 415)[49] and WTC II (the 1744 copy by Altnickol, D-B, Mus. ms. Bach P 430). The last-mentioned volume has a new title page pasted over the original, with an indication that it was to be furnished with a different wording.[50] The change of wording alluded to suggestions that it was Bach who commissioned this copy and requested the change.[51] Indeed, a title page could have been accommodated in the initial plan of collation as fol. 1r of the quarternio fascicle of the fair copy of WTC I as well as of the binio fascicle of WTC II. However, in many instances, title pages were added to the already bound manuscripts at a later stage. The title pages of the four sections of the B-minor Mass (D-B, Mus. ms. Bach P 180), for instance, were once presumably the front parts of the original wrappers[52] for each section; the wrappers would have been cut in half and their (blank?) back parts discarded when the sections were bound in the nineteenth century, possibly during Nägeli's ownership.

Bindings by later owners, including libraries, can cause difficulties for research. Sometimes the paper has been over-trimmed, with marginal instructions such as movement headers, and even parts of the musical text itself, cut off. Tight binding also makes it extremely difficult to ascertain how a manuscript has been

---

49 The present brown leather binding dates, according to Dürr, from the mid-nineteenth century; it probably replaced Bach's more modest original binding, which may have consisted of paper boards, as is the case with Altnickol's copy of WTC II. NBA KB V/6.1 (1989): 20.

50 NBA KB V/6.2 (1996): 81.

51 This manuscript was reported bound ("eingebunden") when it was listed in CPEB NV, 66; see Peter Wollny, "Zur Überlieferung der Instrumentalwerke Johann Sebastian Bachs: Der Quellenbesitz Carl Philipp Emanuel Bachs," BJ 82 (1996): 7–21, esp. 13–14.

52 Many of Bach's original manuscripts were furnished with a wrapper (*Umschlag*), which kept together the score and a set of parts. The first page of the wrapper would have been made into a title page for the music. Later entries by subsequent owners, such as signatures, stamps, and auction lot numbers, which are very useful in researching reception history, may also have been added on the wrapper.

Manuscripts 63

collated. There are also instances where the original collation has been violated, for instance where *Auflagebögen*[53] (for example, D-B, Mus. ms. Bach P 416, Faszikel 4) have been bound into a volume for the sake of safe keeping, thereby countermanding their practical use.

Rastrum and Ruler

In Bach's time, music sheets were usually ruled by the writer using a rastrum. Bach, too, would have bought a stock of plain, unruled paper,[54] and prepared his music manuscript paper using an implement with five nibs, drawing one staff at a time.[55] In some instances, he used two implements of different sizes on the same page, accentuating the layout of his score. Two of the best-known examples are the 1736 score of the St. Matthew Passion (BWV 244; D-B, Mus. ms. Bach P 25) and that of the Fifth Brandenburg Concerto (BWV 1050) dedicated to Margrave Christian Ludwig in March 1721 (D-B, Am. B. 78): these show that Bach often had a good plan of the score layout, but had not always executed it perfectly.[56] Occasionally, Bach used a narrower implement to rule additional staves in the bottom margin when he needed to write more notes than he had initially envisaged; sometimes, he also drew a staff line by line with a ruler, or, less frequently, freehand.

---

53 *Auflagebogen* is a bifolio manuscript made for performance purposes that is supposed to be used in an opened state (*Pultanlage*). It requires only one turn of the entire leaf (i.e., 2v+1r; 1v+2r), rather than two page turns necessary with a normal bifolio manuscript (1r, 1v+2r, 2v). *Auflagebögen* cannot be read in the correct musical sequence if they are bound at the spine. The so-called "London autograph" of WTC II is a typical example of unbound *Auflagebögen*, and P 416/4 is its copy.

54 The only known exception is the score of BWV 195 (D-B, Mus. ms. Bach P 65), which uses printed manuscript sheets. Kobayashi speculates that they were provided by the printer who prepared the publication of *The Art of Fugue*; see Yoshitake Kobayashi, *Bach to no Taiwa: Bach Kenkyu no Saizensen* / バッハとの対話: バッハ研究の最前線 [Conversation with Bach: the Frontline of Bach Research] (Tokyo: Shogakukan, 2002), 147.

55 For a detailed discussion of Bach's stave-ruling practices, see Marshall, *Compositional Process*, 44–7.

56 Taking the case of the Fifth Brandenburg Concerto, it would seem that Bach's initial plan was to copy the first movement (219 bars) from the model (D-B, Mus. ms. Bach St 130) into the space of 24 pages (ff. 58r–69v) that were ruled with eight staves—six narrower staves for melody instruments and two wider staves for solo harpsichord below them. He needed to write roughly 9 bars of music per page (24 × = 216), but having copied the first five pages, he found it impossible to maintain this due to the extensive use of demisemiquaver (thirty-second note) runs in the harpsichord part. He was forced to revise his original one-system layout for the harpsichord cadenza. Instead of leaving blank staves for the *tacet* instruments, he reconfigured the staves on three pages (ff. 67r–68r) to a four-system layout, three narrow staves and a wide one. The remaining three pages (ff. 68v–69v) were occupied by the second movement, where the staves were configured in two systems (four plus four) of uneven appearance. This theory of Bach's copying process emerged from a private discussion with Nobuaki Ebata, to whom I am very grateful.

64 *Yo Tomita*

In his younger years, Bach tended to draw staves neatly, perhaps using a ruler, a habit that he gradually grew out of. A careful study of Bach's choice of implement and layout may reveal both his changing attitude to writing scores and the compositional stage at which he arrived having embarked on writing out a manuscript.[57] Instances also exist where Bach had ruled the staves carelessly and unsuccessfully, which prevented him from using the defective area. Perhaps the most famous example is the so-called "unfinished fugue" of *The Art of Fugue* (BWV 1080/20; D-B, Mus. ms. Bach P 200, Appendix 3, 5). Christoph Wolff argues that Bach stopped writing out this quadruple fugue at bar 239 not because of the reasons C. P. E. Bach cited on the page ("N.B. While working on this fugue, in which the name BACH appears in the countersubject, the author died."[58]), but because he was aware of the poor stave ruling in the lower part of the page. Hence from the outset he never intended to write more than he had done, as he had already drafted the so-called "fragment x," now lost, for the concluding section of the fugue on another sheet.[59]

Bach's rastrum does not seem to have lasted for more than a year, which necessitated him to regularly make or acquire replacements.[60] It would therefore be theoretically possible to reconstruct the chronology of his rastrum usage, very much in the same way as it would be in the study of watermarks: although watermark evidence points to the time of purchase of the paper, rastrum evidence indicates the time the manuscript was prepared. Studying the two sets of chronological evidence together could provide finer details of the activities that took place in the composer's workshop. For this reason and in consequence of the 1963 publication of an influential article on this subject by Christoph Wolff, the potential value of rastrology is now widely recognized.[61]

---

57 See Marshall, *Compositional Process*, 47–61.

58 Dok 3: 3 (No. 631).

59 Christoph Wolff, "The Last Fugue: Unfinished?" *Current Musicology* 19 (1975): 71–77; also in Christoph Wolff, *Bach. Essays on His Life and Music* (Cambridge: Harvard University Press, 1991), 259–264 and 423.

60 This conclusion can be drawn from a study of the "London autograph" of WTC II. See Chapter 2 of Yo Tomita, "J. S. Bach's Well-Tempered Clavier, Book II: A Study of its Aim, Historical Significance and Compiling Process," (PhD diss., University of Leeds, 1990), and Yo Tomita and Richard Rastall, *The Genesis and Early History of Bach's Well-tempered Clavier, Book II: A Composer and his Editions, c.1738–1850* (Aldershot: Ashgate, forthcoming). It is quite possible that Bach replaced rastra every one or two months during the period from 1723 to 1725, when he was preparing weekly cantata performances, which generally featured newly composed works.

61 Christoph Wolff, "Die Rastrierungen in den Originalhandschriften Joh. Seb. Bachs und ihre Bedeutung für die diplomatische Quellenkritik," *Festschrift für Friedrich Smend zum 70. Geburtstag dargebracht von Freunden und Schülern* (Berlin: Merseburger, 1963), 80–92. Although Emery criticized Wolff's theory for the uncertainties surrounding the stave measuring (see ML 45 (1964): 167–170), the value and validity of rastorology undoubtedly remain. It was unfortunate that at the time of Wolff's proposal, the only comprehensive attempt by Hans Otto Hiekel on Bach's original manuscripts, *Katalog der Rastrierungen in den Originalhandschriften Johann Sebastian Bachs* (Göttingen, unpublished typescript, 1965) did not produce significant results, mainly due to the imprecise method of measurement. It should, however, be possible to produce a new and more reliable catalogue of Bach's rastra using the latest information technology equipment, as discussed later in this chapter.

As no specimen of a rastrum used by Bach survives, research on rastra has to be carried out by measuring the thickness of each line, spaces between them and the overall height of the staves drawn. This actually represents the main impediment for such research: owing to inevitable variations conceivably affected by such factors as the thickness of ink, differences in the skills and habits of the users of the implements, especially the pressure applied to the rastra and angle at which they were held, the surface on which the drawing was done, and so on. It is far from straightforward to work with such a dataset even if the information has been collected thoroughly and comprehensively. Yet by combining this information with other identifiable features, such as the unique defects of each implement (for example, the tendency to fail while drawing specific lines or uneven spacing between the lines) and the unique habits of the user of the rastrum (perhaps the tendency to leave ink blots or bending the implement at the start or end of ruling), future research may be able to arrive at an adequate algorithm to compute distortions in the measurements by taking all these factors into consideration.

Quills, Ink, Pencil and Knife

Quills

Although Bach's quills, like his rastra, have not survived, it is possible to deduce how they were made and used from studying what was written with them. A quill needs to be cut when the tip becomes too soft to write firmly and replaced when further cutting becomes impractical. It is possible to detect the places where Bach sharpened or replaced his quill mid-way through a page, which could offer additional evidence to trace the sequence of his writing.[62] According to Kobayashi, it should be possible to find out both the angle at which the quill was held and the pressure that was applied to it by examining the handwriting using infrared reflectography; the ultimate goal would be to identify the writer.[63] More recently, a statistical approach for writer identification using image processing and machine learning has been proposed by Masahiro Niitsuma.[64]

Ink

Unlike Bach's rastra and quills that no longer survive, ink is deposited on paper and can therefore be studied directly. The study of ink is particularly important

---

62 For example, D-B, Mus. ms. Bach P 25, f. 37v, lower system (BWV 244/29, at b. 69). NBA KB II/5 (1974): 24.

63 Kobayashi, *Bach to no Taiwa*, 149.

64 Masahiro Niitsuma, Lambert Schomaker, Jean-Paul van Oosten and Yo Tomita, "Writer Identification in Old Music Manuscripts Using Contour-Hinge Feature and Dimensionality Reduction with an Autoencoder," Richard Wilson, et al., eds., *Computer Analysis of Images and Patterns: 15th International Conference, CAIP 2013, York, UK, August 27–29, 2013, Proceedings* (Berlin and Heidelberg: Springer, 2013), 2: 555–62.

66   Yo Tomita

when distinguishing the layers of revisions as well as identifying subsequent entries made by someone other than the composer.

Ink study has commonly been carried out with the naked eye, but it requires caution. Exposure to oxygen and moisture in the atmosphere over the years affects the chemical composites of iron-gall ink, causing it to fade or change color. In more severe cases, acid contained in the ink can corrode the paper (*Tintenfraß*). Wide-ranging shades of ink found in eighteenth-century manuscripts can be deceptive and potentially misleading. In fact, a wide range of browns—from very dark, almost black, to light brown—can now be observed on a page on which the writing was originally uniformly black. Thus the evidence gathered by visual impression should be treated with care and, wherever possible, corroborated using scientific, analytical techniques such as spectroscopy and infrared reflectography.

Among the several notable attempts in the recent past to analyze ink using scientific equipment, the first and most rigorously documented was reported by Howard Cox in the mid-1980s. A scientific team in California analyzed the chemical constituents of the ink used in the marginal annotations and the underlinings found in the annotations in the Calov Bible once owned by Bach. Using a method known as PIXE (particle induced X-ray emission), the team concluded that "with high probability, Bach was also responsible for the underlinings and marginal marks."[65] More recently, Uwe Wolf used a micro X-ray fluorescence analysis technique on the autograph score of the B-minor Mass (D-B, Mus. ms. Bach P 180) to identify and distinguish the inks used by Bach in Leipzig and C. P. E. Bach in Hamburg. Wolf found that the differing amounts of lead contained in the ink they used respectively were a determining factor.[66] Attempts to use spectral analysis of inks on Bach manuscripts, commonly used by forensic document examiners, have produced no significant results.[67]

Pencil

Pencil entries are rarely found in original Bach manuscripts and are not easy to identify with the naked eye because they have faded and are barely visible. A few

---

65 Bruce Kusko, "Proton Milloprobe Analysis of the Hand-Penned Annotations in Bach's Calov Bible," Howard H. Cox, ed., *The Calov Bible of J. S. Bach* (Ann Arbor: UMI Research Press, 1985), 31–106, esp. 42.

66 Uwe Wolf, Oliver Hahn and Timo Wolff, "Wer schrieb was? Röntgenfluoreszenzanalyse am Autograph von J. S. Bachs Messe in h-Moll BWV 232," BJ 95 (2009): 117–34; Uwe Wolf, "Many Problems, Various Solutions: Editing Bach's B-minor Mass," Yo Tomita, Robin A. Leaver and Jan Smaczny, eds., *Exploring Bach's B-minor Mass* (Cambridge: Cambridge University Press, 2013), 165–85, esp. 178–184.

67 For example, the review of Rainer Kaiser's doctoral thesis "Tintenanalytische Untersuchungen an Bachschen Originalhandschriften mit Hilfe reflexionsspektroskopischer Methoden. Ein Beitrag zur archäometrischen Bach-Forschung" (Berlin: Technische Universität, 1987) in Yoshitake Kobayashi's monograph *Bach: Densho no Nazo o ou* / バッハ: 伝承の謎を追う [Bach: Pursuing the Mystery of Transmission] (Tokyo: Shunju sha, 1995), 21, and my own experiments on Bach's autograph of BWV 872/2 as reported in "Analysing Bach's ink Through a Glass Darkly," MT 139 (Winter 1998): 37–42, esp. 41–2.

reported instances of accidentals written in pencil in the original parts suggest that they were added during rehearsal. The best-known example must be Bach's annotation in the score of *The Art of Fugue*, an instruction, presumably to his assistant, on how to notate Contrapunctus 8, which Christoph Wolff deciphered using infrared photography.[68] Kobayashi speculates that Bach was compelled to use a pencil as he was bed-ridden at that time.[69] More instances of Bach's use of pencil may be found in future research using infrared reflectography.

Knife

A knife was used both for sharpening the quill and scratching out symbols in need of deletion, which was possible as the paper was usually sufficiently thick and strong. Bach's knives do not survive, and the matter has, to my knowledge, never been raised as a subject for research in Bach studies.

Notational Evidence

Once the physical and material features of a manuscript have been studied, the investigation turns to the writer of the manuscript and its written contents, especially the notational evidence contained in the source itself. The aim is to broadly assess the circumstances of its production in order to establish who wrote it and when it was written, and to begin to consider for what purpose it was written. All the information gained thus far comes into play for interpreting the musical evidence in this next phase of research.

Bach's Handwriting—Its Identification and Chronology

Is the manuscript in the hand of Bach or someone else? If it is not Bach, can the scribe be identified? Identification of writers through handwriting analysis is a delicate matter, as graphology is by and large a pseudoscience. Yet with sufficient caution and rigor, it is possible to identify Bach's handwriting from that of other scribes and establish its detailed chronology.

Nineteenth-century scholars were aware of the potential value of this type of study, but in the process they mistakenly declared more manuscripts to be Bach's autographs than have subsequently been authenticated. Spitta was aware of the differences between the handwritings of Bach and his second wife, Anna Magdalena,[70] whereas many of his fellow scholars could not tell the difference.

---

68 Wolff, "The last fugue unfinished?" 71–7.

69 Kobayashi, *Bach to no Taiwa*, 154. A sketch of a fugue in pencil exists; see Marshall, *Compositional Process*, 1: 32; 2: No. 150.

70 Spitta's description of Anna's handwriting is given in Spitta 1: 754–755; Spitta ET 2: 147–148. It should be noted, however, that some of his attributions to her appear to be incorrect: for example, the portion of Brockes Passion (D-B, ms. 9002/10) was, according to Dürr Chr 2, 119 and Kobayashi, 33 and 62, copied by principal copyist (*Hauptkopist*) H (= Johann Nathanael

68   *Yo Tomita*

Today, it is widely acknowledged that, in addition to Anna Magdalena, several of Bach's students likewise developed handwriting very similar to that of their master. One of them is Christian Gottlob Meißner (1707–60),[71] a student of Bach's whose copies were regarded as Bach's autographs throughout the nineteenth century and beyond. Examining his handwriting, Dürr observed:

> Certainly his writings initially show no particular affinity to those of Bach. Only in the course of the years, one symbol after another starts to transform after the model of Bach's handwriting, and we would have hardly been inclined to recognise the same writer in the earliest and latest shapes, had the ongoing transition of individual forms not been established. The changes, as opposed to the those in the handwriting of the principal copyist A [J. A. Kuhnau], are mostly continuous, less disjointed, and are indeed so numerous that one can recognise, especially in relation to the time he first emerged, a series of characteristic stages of development.[72]

Similarly, Anna Magdalena's music handwriting appears to have gradually transformed in the first couple of years of her marriage to Bach, whose own handwriting went through significant changes during the hectic period of his new career in Leipzig.[73]

The present methodology used for identifying Bach's handwriting and establishing its chronology developed gradually in the first half of the twentieth century,[74] and crystallized in the 1950s in the research of Walter Emery[75] and

---

Bammler, identified by Wollny, "Neue Bach-Funde," BJ 83 (1997), 36ff; see also NBA IX/3, 173ff.), while the score of BWV 165 (D-B, Am. B. 105) was, according to Dürr Chr 2, 71 and 150, copied by Anon. Id (= Johann Christian Köpping, identified by Schulze, "Beiträge zur Bach-Quellenforschung," Carl Dahlhaus, Reiner Kluge, Ernst Hermann Meyer and Walter Wiora, eds. *Gesellschaft für Musikforschung. Bericht über den Internationalen Musikwissenschaftlichen Kongress Leipzig 1966* (Kassel: Bärenreiter, 1970), 269–275; see also Dürr Chr 2, 173 n.51 and NBA IX/3, 55f.).

71 Identified by Hans-Joachim Schulze, "Johann Sebastian Bach und Christian Gottlob Meißner," BJ 54 (1968): 80–88; also see Schulze, 101–110 and Dürr Chr 2, 163, n.4. In the 1950s Meißner was known as "Anon. 1" (Dadelsen, TBSt 1) and Hauptkopist B (Dürr Chr).

72 "Freilich zeigen seine Schriftzüge zunächst noch keine sonderliche Verwandtschaft mit denen Bachs. Erst im Laufe der Jahre beginnt sich ein Zeichen nach dem andern nach dem Leitbild der Bachschen Handschrift umzuformen; und wir wären schwerlich bereit, in den Ausgangs- und Endformen denselben Schreiber wiederzuerkennen, ließe sich nicht der Übergang der einzelnen Formen laufend belegen. Dabei vollziehen sich die Veränderungen im Gegensatz zu denen in der Schrift des Hauptkopisten A meist kontinuierlich, weniger sprunghaft; doch sind sie so zahlreich, daß sich besonders für die erste Zeit seines Auftretens eine Reihe charakteristischer Entwicklungsstadien aufzeigen läßt." Dürr Chr 2, 26.

73 Dadelsen TBSt 1, esp. 32–33; Yo Tomita, "Anna Magdalena as Bach's Copyist," 59–76, esp. 67; NBA IX/3, 20–21.

74 For the summary of this development, see Dadelsen TBSt 1: 10–11, and NBA IX/3 (2007): xix–xxi.

75 Walter Emery, "The London Autograph of 'The Forty-Eight,'" ML 34 (1953): 106–123.

Georg von Dadelsen.[76] Dadelsen's monograph of 1958 is a compendium of methodologies for chronological research into Bach's works. In it, he demonstrates the approaches to the study of Bach's handwriting, especially its chronology, which in turn plays a central role in establishing the chronology of Bach's works.

Starting with a detailed study of Bach's handwriting and using the methodology he had developed, which is still in use today, Dadelsen focused not only on Bach himself, but extended his inquiry to the handwritings of his wife, the two eldest sons and several other copyists from Bach's circle.[77] The work involved the extraction of a range of specific symbols representative of the writer's habits and style of writing, such as clefs, minims (half-notes), flagged notes and crotchet (quarter-note) rests, from all the original manuscripts samples known at the time. He then systematically sifted through the samples in order to identify the writer and, at the same time, observe changes in the handwritings. In doing so, he managed to distinguish Bach's handwriting from those of his copyists, whose handwriting resembled that of their master's, a task that had previously not been possible.

Having pinpointed the chronological shifts in Bach's handwriting in the manuscripts that included a date in his own hand, Dadelsen cautiously extended his study to autographs that could be dated according to the circumstances of their production. Having accumulated a sufficient body of reliable evidence, he was able to identify the main features of Bach's handwritings at various periods of his life. Using this evidence, he further extended the search to autographs that clearly demonstrate the recognizable calligraphic features of each period,[78] although he found a relatively few distinct calligraphic features with which to further distinguish Bach's handwriting in the manuscripts written between 1724 and ca. 1740. Dadelsen's work was subsequently improved by Kobayashi, who charted the finer details of Bach's handwriting from the Arnstadt period to his final years in Leipzig.[79] Sporadic additions of symbols such as accidentals and ornaments continue to be investigated as they have proven to be difficult to identify and analyze.[80]

Studying Bach's handwriting, as well as that of his copyists, involves a careful examination of both Bach's original manuscripts and those of his copyists (see "Bach's copyists" later in this chapter). The ultimate aim of such a study is the establishment of the chronology of Bach's works. Spitta, who could not develop an effective methodology for the study of handwriting,

---

76 Dadelsen, TBSt 1 and TBSt 4/5.

77 Dadelsen, TBSt 1. This methodology was subsequently significantly refined by Kobayashi; see NBA IX/3 (2007): xxi–xxiii.

78 Young age until ca. 1713, the second half of Weimar years 1714–16, Cöthen 1717–23, Leipzig (1723 to January 1724; 1724–34; 1735–ca. 1744/46; the final years).

79 See note 3; see the summary in NBA IX/2 (1989).

80 See, for example, the added sharp in b. 78 of "Et in unum Dominum" in Bach's autograph of the B-minor Mass (D-B, Mus. ms. Bach P 180) as discussed by Joshua Rifkin in "Blinding Us with Science? Man, Machine and the Mass in B Minor," ECM 8 (2011): 77–91, esp. 78.

70   *Yo Tomita*

based his inquiries on watermark evidence. Dadelsen, aware that no one had done a thorough and systematic study in this area since Spitta's time, undertook his chronological study with Bach's handwriting as the starting point. Around the same time, Alfred Dürr, who had already completed his doctoral research into Bach's early cantatas,[81] was making significant progress in his study of Bach's vocal works of the entire Leipzig period, transmitted mostly in the original manuscripts, by focusing on both watermarks (citing the findings by Weiß) and scribes (i.e. Bach's copyists).[82] The bulk of sources from this period is made up of vocal works, especially sacred cantatas, for which Bach engaged a number of assistants to produce the necessary performance parts. Having examined the numerous copies made by the two principal copyists,[83] Dürr noticed that their handwriting underwent significant changes over the years. Following Dadelsen's approach, Dürr arrived at the chronology of three annual cycles of cantatas and dated the sources produced in the early Leipzig period;[84] he then mapped out the chronology of the entire Leipzig period (mainly until 1735). Later, Kobayashi applied this methodology to all the original manuscripts, and came up with a new chronology of Bach's works written between 1736 and 1750.[85] An area in which there is still scope for this type of investigation concerns Bach's works from his Cöthen period, which could not be dated using diplomatic methods due to insufficient information.

Research into music handwriting has made a significant impact on Bach scholarship in various areas. The identification of a scribe often influences the judgment of the authenticity of a version of a work, a problem faced by the editors of the NBA, as Klaus Hofmann and Yoshitake Kobayashi have outlined.[86] A good example of this is BWV 1050a (D-B, Mus. ms. Bach St 132, Faszikel 1), the evaluation of which has changed after Dürr identified the scribe of the part to be

---

81 Dürr St; see also Dürr St 2.

82 Dürr Chr 2.

83 Hauptkopist A (Anon. 3) and Hauptkopist B (Anon. 1) were later identified as Johann Andreas Kuhnau and Christian Gottlob Meißner respectively by Schulze. See Dürr Chr 2, 163; see also NBA IX/3 (2007): xx n.9.

84 The result was essentially the same as that of Dadelsen. See Georg von Dadelsen, "Bachforschung in Tübingen," Arnold Feil and Thomas Kohlhase, eds., *Über Bach und anderes: Aufsätze und Vorträge 1957–1982* (Laaber: Laaber, 1983), 159–167, esp. 163.

85 Kobayashi. See also his two catalogues, NBA IX/2 and IX/3 (with Kirsten Beißwenger) that, together with NBA IX/1, manifest the result of research on Bach's original manuscripts carried out in the second half of the twentieth century. See "Bach's copyists" in this chapter.

86 Klaus Hofmann, "Bach oder nicht Bach? Die Neue Bach-Ausgabe und das Echtheitsproblem. Mit einem Beitrag von Yoshitake Kobayashi über 'Diplomatische Mittel der Echtheitskritik,'" Hanspeter Bennwitz, ed., *Opera incerta: Echtheitsfragen als Problem musikwissenschaftlicher Gesamtausgaben. Kolloquium Mainz 1988, Bericht. Akademie der Wissenschaften und der Literatur, Mainz. Im Auftr. des Ausschusses für Musikwissenschaftliche Editionen der Konferenz der Akademien der Wissenschaften in der Bundesrepublik Deutschland* (Stuttgart: Steiner, 1991), 9–48.

Manuscripts 71

Bach's son-in-law Johann Christoph Altnickol,[87] and not Gottlob Harrer, Bach's successor as Thomascantor, as claimed earlier by Heinrich Besseler.[88] Although the identity of the writer has been questioned by Peter Wollny, who identifies him as Johann Christoph Farlau (ca. 1735–after 1770), one of Altnickol's students in Naumburg,[89] the authenticity of the version, which has to date remained intact, has not yet been challenged. Among the remaining tasks is the investigation of a collection commonly known as the "Great Eighteen" Chorales (BWV 651–668), known to us through a partial autograph (D-B, Mus. ms. Bach P 271, Faszikel 2). The identity of the anonymous copyist and his relationship with the other scribes is crucial for the authentication of the collection as a whole. The first fifteen of the "Great Eighteen" (BWV 651–665) are in Bach's hand.[90] Of the remaining preludes, two (BWV 666–667) are in the hand of Johann Christoph Altnickol, whose handwriting Wollny has dated to 1751 as *terminus ante quem*.[91] The final prelude ("Vor deinen Thron tret ich," BWV 668, survived only fragmentarily), appended at the end of the manuscript,[92] was written by an unknown copyist, known as Anon. Vr or Anon. 12. The first task that Bach entrusted to this scribe was to make a copy of the original manuscript of WTC II around 1742.[93] The copyist carried it out with little respect towards his model, leaving ink marks at page breaks throughout the manuscript.[94] This series of observations supports Kobayashi's suggestion that the scribe could be identified as Frau Altnickol, Bach's daughter Elisabeth ("Lieschen") Juliana Friederica (1726–81).[95] However, the handwriting of Anon. Vr also appears among Bach's original parts from his

87 Alfred Dürr, "Zur Entstehungsgeschichte des 5. Brandenburgischen Konzerts," BJ 61 (1975): 63–69, esp. 64–65.

88 NBA KB VII/2 (1956): 103.

89 On the evidence of the similarities between their handwritings, Wollny suggests that Farlau studied with Altnickol in Naumburg before the former had commenced his university studies at Jena University in 1756. Peter Wollny, "Tennstädt, Leipzig, Naumburg, Halle: Neuerkenntnisse zur Bach-Überlieferung in Mitteldeutschland," BJ 88 (2002): 29–60, esp. 43–44.

90 Through handwriting analysis, Kobayashi dated the first thirteen ca. 1739–42, and the remaining two ca. 1746–7. Kobayashi, 45 and 56.

91 Peter Wollny, "Einführung" and "Introduction," Peter Wollny, ed., Die Achtzehn Grossen Orgelchoräle BWV 651–668 und Canonische Veränderungen über 'Vom Himmel Hoch' BWV 769. Faksimile der Originalhandschrift (Laaber: Laaber, 1999), ix (German) and xvii (English).

92 That is, after the Canonic Variations (BWV 769a).

93 This copy was split into four portions after Bach's death, presumably while in the possession of W. F. Bach: (1) D-B, Mus. ms. Bach P 416, Faszikel 4; (2) Newberry Library, Chicago, Case MS 6A 72; (3) GB-Lbl Add MS 38068; and (4) the portion once housed in D-Dl lost during WWII; see also Kobayashi, 29–30, and NBA IX/3 (2007): 171.

94 These can be identified by studying the ink. Some of them were later scratched out; for details, see Yo Tomita, *J. S. Bach's 'Das Wohltemperierte Clavier II': A Critical Commentary, vol. I: Autograph Manuscripts* (Leeds: Household World, 1993).

95 Kobayashi, Bach to no Taiwa, 260, 344–345; Yoshitake Kobayashi, "Exkurs über den Schreiber Anonymus Vr bzw. Anonymus 12," Siegbert Rampe, ed., *Bach: Das Wohltemperierte Klavier I: Tradition, Entstehung, Funktion, Analyse. Ulrich Siegele zum 70. Geburtstag* (Munich: Katzbichler, 2002), 14–16.

72   Yo Tomita

final years,[96] and after that, in the copies prepared for C. P. E. Bach in Berlin from the summer of 1749 onwards,[97] which contradicts Kobayashi's hypothesis, because Lieschen presumably lived in Naumburg with her husband Altnickol, who had been organist there since 30 July 1748. They were married in St. Thomas's in Leipzig on 20 January 1749.[98] Their son, whom they named Johann Sebastian, was born on 4 October of the same year in Naumburg, but sadly passed away in less than three weeks.[99] No record exists of another child born to the couple until 30 May 1751.[100] Did she really copy manuscripts for both her father in Leipzig and her step-brother in Berlin during her pregnancy? Could the family's closer ties around the time of her father's ill health and subsequent death, and the fact that her little brother, Johann Christian, was to be looked after by C. P. E. Bach until 1755, imply that Lieschen offered to help her half-brother as copyist? In addition, because Bach's collection of music manuscripts appears to have been distributed outside of the legal procedure, the possibility that she, rather than Wilhelm Friedemann,[101] inherited the manuscript cannot be ruled out.[102] If so, C. P. E. Bach obtained the manuscript from her later (i.e., after Altnickol's death in 1759).

In any case, further evidence is required to argue for or against Kobayashi's suggestion. A fresh study of Bach's life in connection with the anecdotal episode involving the "death-bed" chorale, which Bach supposedly dictated,[103] or a study of the reasons for its inclusion at the end of the first edition of *The Art of Fugue* published in 1751,[104] might uncover such evidence.

Accurate identification of scribes plays an important role in evaluating the contents of a manuscript, especially within the revised passages. Future Bach studies need some form of grapho-analysis capable of examining the subject

---

96 The latest version of BWV 195 (D-B, Mus. ms. Bach St 12) is dated by Kobayashi, 61–3, "between August 1748 and October 1749"; the fourth version of BWV 245 (D-B, Mus. ms. Bach St 111) was prepared for the performance on 4 April 1749.

97 The score of Wq. 215 (D-B, Am. B. 170), copied on Berlin paper (NB. Wq 215 was composed in August 1749); Wq 65/25, 65/27 (on Berlin paper), 65/30 (with C. P. E. Bach's corrections; the work was composed in 1758). These were found in D-B, Mus. ms. Bach P 789 and P 776. See Christine Blanken, "Zur Werk- und Überlieferungsgeschichte des Magnificat Wq 215 von Carl Philipp Emanuel Bach," BJ 92 (2006): 229–71, esp. 236f.; also Kobayashi, 30.

98 Dok 1 (No. 50).

99 Dok 2 (No. 587).

100 Dok 3 (No. 640). Their second child, named Augusta Magdalena, was born and baptized in Naumburg with Anna Magdalena and Johann Gottfried Müthel among the godparents.

101 Christoph Wolff, "The Deathbed Chorale: Exposing a Myth," *Bach: Essays on His Life and Music*, 282–294.

102 Yoshitake Kobayashi, "Zur Teilung des Bachschen Erbes," *Acht kleine Präludien und Studien über BACH. [Festschrift für] Georg von Dadelsen zum 70. Geburtstag am 17. November 1988* (Wiesbaden: Breitkopf & Härtel, 1992), 67–75. See also Peter Wollny, "Überlegungen zur Bach-Überlieferung in Naumburg," BJ 86 (2000): 87–100.

103 Forkel names Altnickol as the person to whom Bach dictated this chorale. NBR, p. 466; Dok 7, p. 66 n.143.

104 Kobayashi, *Bach to no Taiwa*, 260.

Manuscripts 73

objectively and scientifically. A recent demonstration by Martin Jarvis, relying on forensic document examination techniques, was an interesting attempt to distinguish between the handwritings of Bach and Anna Magdalena.[105] Although it fell short in its argument that the portion copied by Anna had in fact been "composed" by her, it nevertheless raised renewed hopes of further developments in the improvement of the methodology of grapho-analysis. As Masahiro Niitsuma has recently demonstrated, handwriting analysis in Bach studies will before long be carried out by a computer-driven application that can measure and objectively verify the corpus of handwriting samples.[106]

Notational Convention and Chronology

The study of the chronology of handwriting can also inform the chronology of notational practice and vice versa. This is most clearly reflected in the way accidentals were used. Until the beginning of the eighteenth century, the symbol to cancel a pitch raised by a sharp was not a natural, as is customary today, but a flat. According to Dürr, this is a common occurrence in Bach's autographs written up to 1713, which started to wane in 1714, becoming almost totally extinct after 1715.[107]

Another accidental, the older form of which in Bach's manuscripts over time gave way to modern usage, is the double sharp, an x-shaped symbol raising by a semitone a pitch that has already been raised by a sharp in the key signature. Bach began to change his ordinary sharps ($\sharp$) to the modern symbol of the double sharp from around 1736. In the autograph fair copy of the St. Matthew Passion (D-B, Mus. ms. Bach P 25) the double sharp is indicated by a large $\sharp$ tilted to the right.[108] It settles into its modern form around 1739, as can be seen in the autograph fair copies of the "London autograph" WTC II (GB-Lbl, Add. MS. 35021). The E-major prelude and fugue of the same set, copied by Anna Magdalena, still used an ordinary sharp to indicate f-double sharp, hinting that

---

105 Martin W. B. Jarvis, "Did Johann Sebastian Bach Write the Six Cello Suites?" (PhD diss., Faculty of Law Business & Arts, Charles Darwin University, 2007); see also Jarvis, "The Application of Forensic Document Examination Techniques to the Writings of J. S. Bach and A. M. Bach," UB 3 (2008): 87–92. Here the point is to draw attention to the possibilities presented by a new methodology, not the erroneous conclusion drawn from it; see Ruth Tatlow, "A Missed Opportunity: Reflections on *Written by Mrs. Bach*," UB 10 (2015): 141–157.

106 Masahiro Niitsuma and Yo Tomita, "Classifying Bach's Handwritten C-clefs," Anssi Klapuri and Colby Leider, eds., *Proceedings of the 12th International Society for Music Information Retrieval Conference, ISMIR 2011, Miami, Florida, USA, October 24–28, 2011* (Miami: University of Miami, 2011), 417–21.

107 NBA KB I/35 (1964, Alfred Dürr, ed.): 40–41, and NBA KB I/14 (1963, Alfred Dürr and Arthur Mendel, eds.): 106. One of the few exceptions is the harpsichord part of BWV 1050 in Bach's handwriting of ca.1721 (D-B, Mus. ms. Bach St 130), where the pitch of $f\sharp^1$ indicated by the key signature is cancelled by a flat in bb. 198–9.

108 See, for example, BWV 244/29, bb. 51–3: f. 36v in the autograph.

74   *Yo Tomita*

Anna's model—Bach's autograph score, which may have been Bach's composing score—predated 1736.

In a similar way, Bach changed his notation of the double flat from an ordinary flat to a larger, plumper symbol, around 1736, as seen in his fair copy of the St. Matthew Passion.[109]

Extending the study beyond Bach's original manuscripts and examining a piece through distant copies, notational practice can sometimes be indicative of a composition's time of origin, which in turn supports the argument for the work's authenticity. For example, Bach's best known organ work, the Toccata in D minor (BWV 565), is only known through copies, the earliest of which—and also the common source for all the other surviving copies—was written by Johannes Ringk (1717–78), a student of Johann Peter Kellner (1705–72), a well-known admirer and collector of Bach's works (mainly organ music), who claimed to have met Bach.[110] Ringk's copy (D-B, Mus. ms. Bach P 595, Faszikel 8) uses a modal key signature and 3-shaped flags on semiquavers (sixteenth-notes), notational conventions that had petered out by the middle of the eighteenth century.[111]

Bach's Copyists

The identification of Bach's copyists (i.e., those who participated in the production of the original manuscripts) and an understanding of the extent of their involvement and quality of work is an important part of research, as it paints a vivid picture of the actual practical situations in which the manuscripts were made and used. It also provides crucial evidence for chronology research, as already discussed within the section "Bach's Handwriting—Its Identification and Chronology," while an insight into a copyist's habitual errors would offer valuable clues for textual analysis.

The copyists involved in the production of Bach's Leipzig cantatas have been particularly well researched. The scores—often composing scores, especially in the case of the early Leipzig cantatas—are usually in Bach's hand, whereas the performance parts were entrusted to his copyists, although Bach may subsequently have made small corrections and added performance-related marks. Bach's copyists were normally drawn from the ranks of the pupils at the St. Thomas School, family members and private students. Dürr's main contribution to this aspect of research was the identification of their roles and distribution

---

109   See BWV 244/59, b. 2 in the alto: f. 67v in the autograph. NBA KB II/5 (1974): 209.

110   Dok 3: 77 (No. 663). For a comprehensive study on Ringk's copying of Bach's works, see Dietrich Killian, NBA KB IV/5+6 (1978): 198–205; see also Russell Stinson, *The Bach Manuscripts of Johann Peter Kellner and His Circle. A Case Study in Reception History* (Durham: Duke University Press, 1989.

111   See the table listing the instances of flats used in place of natural signs as well as uses of the old semiquaver form and in 37 manuscripts copied by Ringk in Killian, NBA KB IV/5+6 (1978): 204: it shows that Ringk's copy of BWV 565 was written before ca. 1740. See also Rolf Dietrich Claus, *Zur Echtheit von Toccata und Fuge d-moll BWV 565*, 2nd ed. (Cologne: Dohr, 1998), in which Claus argues against this view from the standpoint of style criticism.

of work, classified into two types: principal copyists (*Hauptkopisten*), to whom Bach entrusted the preparation of entire sets of parts (without duplicates) from scores,[112] and other copyists, who made duplicate parts. The most important of Bach's principal copyists were: Johann Andreas Kuhnau (= Hauptkopist A), C. G. Meißner (= Hauptkopist B), and Johann Heinrich Bach (= Hauptkopist C) from the early Leipzig period; Johann Ludwig Krebs and Johann Ludwig Dietel (= Hauptkopist F) from the middle Leipzig period; and Johann Nathanael Bammler (= Hauptkopist H) from the late Leipzig period.[113] Some of his family members— Anna Magdalena, Wilhelm Friedemann, Carl Philipp Emanuel, Johann Christoph Friedrich and Johann Christian—also served Bach faithfully as his copyists. Although a number of anonymous copyists have been named since the publication of the second revised edition of Dürr's seminal work in 1976,[114] a comprehensive list of scribes is yet to be assembled. Their names and work were updated and summarized in a catalogue of Bach's copyists by Kobayashi and Beißwenger, published in 2007 (NBA IX/3).[115] Statistical data, for example, on the copyists' habitual errors—essential for evaluating the quality of text in the copies—are some of the issues that remain to be investigated in future studies.

Other Scribes of Bach's Works

The previously mentioned catalogue of Bach's copyists does not include information about the non-original manuscript copies of Bach's works that were not made for the composer's own use, such as the copies of keyboard music his students created as part of their studies with him. While a comprehensive catalogue of all the scribes and their copies is yet to be compiled,[116] there are some notable studies on key scribes. The most important scribe from Bach's youth is his eldest brother, Johann Christoph (1671–1721) of Ohrdruf, whose hand appears together

---

112 Strictly speaking, the copyist who made the entire set of parts (without duplicates) from a score is called the Hauptschreiber. Hauptkopist is a specific term proposed by Dürr to refer to the scribe whom Bach employed to act as Hauptschreiber. Bach scholars have hence taken a stance to recognise those main scribes as Hauptkopisten when there is evidence of their making of multiple sets of parts.

113 Dürr Chr 2, esp. 145f.

114 Dürr Chr 2. Nearly all the Hauptkopisten have been identified, the most recent being Hauptkopist H = Johann Nathanael Bammler. Wollny, "Neue Bach-Funde," 36–50. On the contrary, the identification of assistant copyists (*Nebenkopisten*) proved to be more difficult, because of a relatively fewer number of known specimens of their handwriting.

115 Yoshitake Kobayashi and Kirsten Beißwenger, *Die Kopisten Johann Sebastian Bachs. Katalog und Dokumentation*, 2 vols. (Kassel: Bärenreiter, 2007). Concordances of copyists with various anonymous codes given by earlier scholars, including Paul Kast and Eva Renate Blechschmidt, are given on pp. 216–218. In addition, Maul suggests that more names might be identified by a careful study of a recently uncovered notebook that belonged to a pupil of St Thomas.' Michael Maul, "'welche ieder Zeit aus den 8 besten Subjectis bestehen muß' – Die erste 'Cantorey' der Thomasschule - Organisation, Aufgaben, Fragen," BJ 99 (2013): 11–77, esp. 15–19.

116 The Bach Digital's online source catalogue (www.bachdigital.de/content/bachsourcejs.xml) does contain a certain amount of such information and can be used for this purpose.

76   Yo Tomita

with Bach's in two well-known anthologies—the so-called "Möller manuscript" (D-B, Mus. ms. 40644) and the "Andreas Bach Book" (D-LEm, III.8.4), which are believed to have been copied between 1705 and 1713.[117] These are important sources for understanding Bach's creative development, which is explored in Section IV of this volume. Among the best known scribes of Bach's works from his immediate circle are: Johann Gottfried Walther (1684–1748),[118] Johann Tobias Krebs (1690–1762)[119] and Johann Caspar Vogler (1696–1763)[120] from the Weimar period; Heinrich Nikolaus Gerber (1702–75)[121] and Bernhard Christian Kayser (1705–58)[122] from the early Leipzig period; and Johann Friedrich Agricola (1720–74)[123] and Johann Christoph Altnickol (1719–59) from the later Leipzig period. Johann Christian Kittel (1732–1809)[124] and Christian Friedrich Penzel (1737–1801),[125] pupils of Bach in the final years of his life, continued to copy his works after his death, and promoted their master's works in Erfurt and Merseburg, respectively.

Whereas much of the research on copies made after Bach's lifetime belongs to the study of the reception of Bach's works, a number of them attest to the early shapes of the compositions, thus providing an additional insight into Bach's creative process. Notable examples include the manuscript score of the early version of the St. Matthew Passion (BWV 244b; D-B, Am. B. 6 and Am. B. 7), published in facsimile in NBA II/5a as a copy in the hand of Johann Christoph Altnickol,[126] but which, according to Peter Wollny, was copied by Altnickol's

---

117 For example, Schulze, 46f.; Hans-Joachim Schulze, "Johann Christoph Bach (1671–1721), 'Organist und Schul Collega in Ohrdruf', Johann Sebastian Bachs erster Lehrer", BJ 71: 55–81; Robert Hill, "The Möller Manuscript and the Andreas Bach Book: Two Keyboard Anthologies from the Circle of the Young Johann Sebastian Bach,'" (PhD diss., Harvard University, 1987), 2 vols.

118 For example, Hermann Zietz, *Quellenkritische Untersuchungen an den Bach-Handschriften P 801, P 802 und P 803 aus dem 'Krebs'schen Nachlass' unter Berücksichtigung den Choralbearbeitung des jungen J. S. Bach* (Hamburg: Wagner, 1969).

119 For example, Hans Löffler, "Johann Tobias Krebs und Matthias Sojka, zwei Schüler Johann Sebastian Bachs," BJ 37 (1940–48): 136–148.

120 For example, Hans-Joachim Schulze, "'Das Stück in Goldpapier': Ermittlungen zu einigen Bach-Abschriften des frühen 18. Jahrhunderts," BJ 64 (1978): 19–42, and Schulze, 59ff.

121 For example, Alfred Dürr, "Heinrich Nicolaus Gerber als Schüler Bachs," BJ 64 (1978): 7–18.

122 Kayser has long been known as Anonymous 5 (= Anon. Ih), whose handwriting was very similar to Bach's. He was identified by Talle. Andrew Talle, "Nürnberg, Darmstadt, Köthen: Neuerkenntnisse zur Bach-Überlieferung in der ersten Hälfte des 18. Jahrhunderts," BJ 89 (2003): 143–172 esp. 155f.

123 Dürr Chr 2, 44–65.

124 For example, Ulrich Leisinger, "Johann Christian Kittel und die Anfänge der sogenannten späteren thüringischen Bach-Überlieferung," Rainer Kaiser, ed., *Bach und seine mitteldeutschen Zeitgenossen. Bericht über das internationale musikwissenschaftliche Kolloquium, Erfurt und Arnstadt 13. bis 16. Januar 2000* (Eisenach: Wagner, 2001), 235–251.

125 See, for example, Kobayashi Yoshitake, "Franz Hauser und seine Bach-Handschriftensammlung," (PhD diss. University of Göttingen, 1973), 109–112.

126 Dürr, "Zur Chronologie der Handschrift Johann Christoph Altnickols und Johann Friedrich Agricolas," and NBA KB II/5 (1974): 62f.

Manuscripts 77

student Farlau.[127] Other examples include Johann Christoph Oley's (1738–89) copy of the Italian Concerto (BWV 971),[128] and Christoph Ernst Abraham Albrecht Freiherr von Boineburg-Lengsfeld's (1752–1840) copies of the WTC II and Goldberg Variations.[129]

Musical Evidence

Having established the diplomatic and notational evidence, evaluation of the writer's activity can proceed through an examination of musical evidence manifested in the form of written contents. This needs to be approached from the actual context of the manuscript production by piecing together the evidence already gathered, and to take into consideration a range of issues. These range from the manner in which the manuscript was prepared and its purpose, to the actual act of committing the notes to paper, or the way in which they were written and revised, with the ultimate aim of reconstructing the sequence of events to reveal the intentions of the writer. The study of the composition and revision processes is absolutely central in manuscript studies, as it harbors a compelling story about the composer and his work, including the context of its creation and revision,[130] its history built on factual evidence. However, one should be aware of potential pitfalls when attempting to interpret information flowing from the composer's brain to his hand, and on to paper, as the written contents cannot convey everything the composer imagined. For instance, some ideas will inevitably be lost when they are committed to paper (although, of course, there is no way to prove it), while others may not be fully formulated;[131] some may have been written inaccurately,[132] or incompletely,[133] and in some the errors may have been rectified when the composer had subsequent opportunities to check or write the

---

127 Wollny, "Tennstädt, Leipzig, Naumburg, Halle," 36–47.

128 Boston Public Library M.200.12 (2); NBA KB V/2 (1981): 39–47.

129 Bach-Archiv, Leipzig, Go. S. 19; Yo Tomita, "Bach and His Early Drafts: Some Observations on Little Known Early Versions of Well-Tempered Clavier II and the Goldberg Variations from the Manfred Gorke Collection," BACH 30/2 (1999): 49–72.

130 This includes the internal logic of the composition itself, which the composer felt was still lacking, and any external circumstances, such as the setting of a piece for a new context, which may necessitate transcribing or transposing it for a different instrument or expanding it to fit into a new work, as is the case with many movements of WTC II.

131 The best-known examples are the early versions of Inventions in C minor (BWV 773) and G minor (BWV 797) found in the *Clavierbüchlein* for Wilhelm Friedemann, in which we find evidence of Bach adjusting the melodic shape of the theme to ensure dramatic cohesiveness.

132 See the variants of the A-minor prelude in WTC II (BWV 889/1), b. 30. The initial reading found in his autograph (GB-Lbl, Add. MS 35021) gives a passage of weaker contrapuntal logic, which Bach adjusted in his later (lost) copy, as can be observed in Altnickol's 1744 copy (D-B, Mus. ms. Bach P 430), among others.

133 See the textural clarification Bach makes in the Prelude in F minor in WTC II (BWV 881/1), bb. 38–9; compare the Prelude in F-sharp minor in WTC II (BWV 883/1), b. 20.

78   *Yo Tomita*

piece out afresh.[134] A good example is the way in which Bach treated articulation and phrasing marks in his scores: he seldom fully wrote them out. Occasionally, however, Bach does the opposite and supplies "unexpected extra" instructions that cannot be explained with logic or consistency.[135] All this may be appreciated from a broader historical context according to which in Bach's time notated music was not expected to represent a work in every detail, but was merely a kind of template into which performers were expected to inject "life" by providing articulations, embellishments, phrasing, and even improvisation.

In addition to the study of the processes of composition and revision, manuscript studies offer further avenues to gain new knowledge from the sources with regard to performance implications, Bach's teaching, critical editions, and, finally, transmission and reception history.

Performance Implications

Bach's original manuscripts reveal information from which conclusions can be drawn with regard to the way in which he expected his works to be performed in terms of his performing forces, articulation, phrasing and possibly other aspects. Arguably the most intensely debated, as well as the most consequential for the performance of Bach's vocal works in the past three decades, is Joshua Rifkin's revolutionary idea that Bach's vocal works were routinely sung by one singer per part,[136] which contradicts the standard and traditional interpretations (e.g., three singers per part). Rifkin claims that this is manifested in the surviving original parts, although from the viewpoint of source study, his assertion lacks conviction, and has consequently attracted numerous objections from other scholars.[137] The argument is complex, as source evidence is sometimes incomplete and ambiguous. For example, the absence from the surviving vocal parts of indications that would specify which movements are to be sung by the concertists alone and which are to be joined by ripienists may be interpreted as a specific instruction for not using ripienists in the piece, or perhaps as Bach's desire to maintain flexibility, which would allow him to reuse the parts, possibly in different settings, in the future. Possible deformations of source evidence, for instance, the disposal

---

134 See, for example, how BWV 831 was gradually clarified notationally. Walter Emery, "An Introduction to the Textual History of Bach's Clavierübung, Part II," MT 92 (May 1951): 205–209; and 92 (June 1951): 260–262.

135 See, for example, the slur provided for the demisemiquaver (thirty-second note) flourish in the bass in b. 21 of BWV 870/1 in Altnickol's 1744 copy: there is no slur in the corresponding passage in the earlier part of the prelude in b. 6. Logically, the placement should be reversed. A possible explanation of such an anomaly is that additions were made during a lesson.

136 Joshua Rifkin, "Bach's Chorus: A preliminary Report," MT 123 (November 1982): 747–754; see also Andrew Parrott, *The Essential Bach Choir* (Woodbridge: Boydell, 2000).

137 See, for example, Uwe Wolf, "Von der Hofkapelle zur Stadtkantorei: Beobachtungen an den Aufführungsmaterialien zu Bachs ersten Leipziger Kantatenaufführungen," BJ 88 (2002): 181–191, esp. 187–191; for a fair summary of the ensuing debate, see Robin A. Leaver, "Performing Bach: One or Many?" *Choral Scholar* 1/1 (Spring 2009): 6–15.

by subsequent owners of duplicate parts that were once kept together, must also be considered.[138] Each piece of evidence must therefore be interpreted within its own broader historical context, which in itself is in need of clarification and further research.[139]

The performance markings Bach himself added to the original manuscripts, such as ornaments, slurs and dots, have been reasonably well-researched[140] and understood, and it has become standard procedure among the circles of early music performers today to examine the original sources in order to understand Bach's approach to performance issues. Particularly notable is the shift in recent decades from scores that are often available in facsimile editions to the reproductions of original performance parts that have not been easily obtainable. This is necessary because Bach added to the individual parts performance-related marks that are not indicated in his original scores, and is therefore another area requiring further research.[141]

The high visibility of such issues does not mean that everything is clearly understood and that no room is left for further study. Many questions remain unresolved. One such question concerns the placement of slurs—how many notes are covered by a single stroke: even in some of the most exquisite autograph fair copies, such as that of the Violin Solos (BWV 1001–1006; D-B, Mus. ms. Bach P 967), this is not always clear.[142] When it comes to works for which Bach's autograph scores do not survive, such as the Cello Suites (BWV 1007–1012), we have to rely on copies in which the accuracy of a slur's placement is often highly questionable.[143] In a set of parts made by Bach and his copyists, one may find that the placement of a slur varies from one part to the next, thus posing a problem

---

138 One such example that came to light with recent source recoveries are the ripieno parts of Cantata 23 that once completed the original set. The parts were separated after the Berlin Singakademie obtained the manuscript. See Christoph Wolff, "Zurück in Berlin: Das Notenarchiv der Sing-Akademie. Bericht über eine erste Bestandsaufnahme," BJ 88 (2002): 165–169.

139 This includes research on Bach's changing attitudes to performances in response to varying and evolving circumstances, iconographical evidence found in the engravings in the contemporary sources, and documentary evidence referring to the size of choir and how the choir held the parts sharing or not sharing with fellow singers. One must be aware that the weight of support gained from this type of evidence is still very small and requires further systematic study.

140 For example, John Butt, *Bach Interpretation. Articulation Marks in Primary Sources of J. S. Bach* (Cambridge: Cambridge University Press, 1990).

141 For example, Masaaki Suzuki has written "Seisaku Noto /制作ノート" (Production Notes) in the concert program booklets of Bach Collegium Japan since 1995, in which he often discusses the original parts in the context of his own interpretation.

142 Frederick Neumann, "Some Performance Problems of Bach's Unaccompanied Violin and Cello Works," Mary Ann Parker, ed., *Eighteenth-Century Music in Theory and Practice: Essays in Honor of Alfred Mann* (Stuyvesant: Pendragon Press, 1994), 19–46, esp. 37. For a discussion from a source-critical perspective on wider editorial issues, see Georg von Dadelsen, 'Die Crux der Nebensache – Editorische und praktische Bemerkungen zu Bachs Artikulation' BJ 64 (1978): 95–112.

143 See "Commentary" in Bettina Schwemer and Douglas Woodfull-Harris, eds., *6 Suites a Violoncello Solo senza Basso. BWV 1007–1012. / J. S. Bach* (Kassel: Bärenreiter, 2000), 6–7.

80   Yo Tomita

for the editor of a critical edition.[144] It seems that Bach was aware of the inherent problem of the notational system in this regard. From around 1746, he began to use dots as articulation marks to indicate the notes that did not belong with the slurred notes, probably to overcome this problem; this can be seen in the performance parts of BWV 8 (later version in D; Bach-Archiv Leipzig, Thomana 8), in which the principle is followed through with particular meticulousness in the traverso part.[145] The dots found in Altnickol's 1744 copy of WTC II, as later additions to the subjects of the A-minor and B-flat-minor fugues, probably date from the same period. Given the new role the dots assumed around that time, caution is required when interpreting their meaning.[146]

The subtleties in Bach's beaming of quavers (eighth-notes) suggest that his phrasing and articulation indications went beyond the use of symbols.[147] Following the convention of his time, Bach normally wrote beams for a succession of quavers longer than the unit of a beat: for example, one beam was applied for six quavers in 3/4 ($\sqrt{}$) and two for eight quavers in 4/4 ($\sqrt{}$). It is rare to find Bach consistently writing quaver beams over a one-beat unit (e.g., in 3/4: $\sqrt{}$). When he does so, his choice of notation seems to imply that he wanted to stress a specific mood or the character of the movement. Study of these exceptional cases has revealed that these were used to indicate two types of situations: (1) a lively execution of leaping quavers; as in WTC I, Fugue in C-sharp major (BWV 848/2); Prelude in F-sharp minor (BWV 859/1); Prelude in G major (BWV 860/1); Prelude in B-flat major (BWV 866/1); Variations 28 and 29 of the Goldberg Variations (BWV 988): and (2) a plodding mood in quavers of the same pitch or in step-wise motion, as in WTC I, Prelude in F minor (BWV 857/1), Prelude in G minor (BWV 861/1); WTC II, Prelude in F minor (BWV 881/1), Prelude in A minor (BWV 889/1); Orgelbüchlein, "Da Jesus an dem Kreuze stund"(BWV 621), "Es ist das Heil uns kommen her" (BWV 638), "Ich ruf zu dir, Herr Jesu Christ" (BWV 639); and Invention in B minor (BWV 786). In the majority of movements, however, Bach uses both types of quavers discreetly to convey extra nuances, be it to distinguish two contrasting motifs, to articulate structurally at cadential passages with default beams, or to indicate the increase of attention to the local passage with extended beams. Bach's quaver beams may be a new resource for finding out how Bach responded to his pieces in performance. Although the process of *writing* music cannot be translated directly into how the writer actually *performed* the piece, we may have come one step closer to learning how Bach

---

144   See NBA II/5 KB, 129–130 (Dürr); see also Dürr "De vita cum imperfectis."

145   Kobayashi, *Bach to no Taiwa*, 224–227.

146   Schulenberg's explanation appears to be the most likely. He interprets the dots added in the B-flat minor fugues "to mean accentuation and separation, rather than staccato in the modern sense," and to "reinforce the subject's declamatory quality." David Schulenberg, *The Keyboard Music of J. S. Bach*, 2nd ed. (New York: Routledge, 2006), 271.

147   For further discussion, see Yo Tomita, "Reading Soul from Manuscripts: Some Observations on Performance Issues in J. S. Bach's Habits of Writing His Music," Thomas Donahue, ed., *Essays in Honor of Christopher Hogwood. The Maestro's Direction* (Lanham: Scarecrow, 2011), 13–40.

Manuscripts 81

engaged with his music, or at least acquired an additional means to read Bach's intentions as to how he perceived his music at multiple layers of compositional thought process from motivic to structural levels.[148]

Bach's Teaching

Some of Bach's manuscripts, particularly those for keyboard works, document how and what he taught his students, among whom were his own sons and wife. As has been demonstrated by numerous scholars since the time of Spitta, considerable insights into Bach's pedagogical methods and educational philosophy can be gained by careful study.[149] Perhaps the most important source that epitomizes Bach's systematic teaching program is the *Clavierbüchlein* for Wilhelm Friedemann Bach (Yale University Library, New Haven, Music Deposit 31), a notebook he gave in January 1720 to his then nine-year-old son. The manner in which the pieces were entered into the notebook reveals how Bach taught this gifted child in the course of several years. Comparison with later collections that evolved from this notebook, namely WTC I and the Inventions and Sinfonias, shows that Bach adapted and improved his earlier teaching materials as tools for teaching advanced students. In addition to these two well-known collections, there are other collections of keyboard works—the Six Small Preludes (BWV 933–938), English Suites and French Suites, as well as those that appear in C. P. E. Bach's *Nachlass*,[150] namely "5 Präludien und 5 Fugen,"[151] "Suite pour

---

148 Modern critical editions, including NBA, tend to normalize inconsistencies in beaming, treating it as something that requires editorial arbitration, even though their editorial guidelines advise editors to retain Bach's own grouping of notes under beams as it may convey articulation. See the section "Balkensetzung" in "Editionsrichtlinien. Johann Sebastian Bach. Neue Ausgabe sämtlicher Werke," Georg von Dadelsen, ed., *Editionsrichtlinien musikalischer Denkmäler und Gesamtausgaben* (Kassel: Bärenreiter, 1967), 61–80, here 66; revised and updated version in Frauke Heinze and Uwe Wolf, *Gesamtregister*, NBA IX/4 (2010): 319–335 at 325: "Da die Bachsche Notengruppierung unter Umständen für die Artikulation von Bedeutung ist, ist sie nach Möglichkeit beizubehalten." Indeed, Bach's notation of quaver beaming is often inconsistent, and the problem is felt even more acutely when dealing with copies. Although a reliable way of extracting such information is yet to be devised, the possibility of rediscovering Bach's intentions should not be ignored. Future critical editions must address this issue seriously. For further discussion on this issue, see Tomita, "Reading Soul from Manuscripts" and "Deciphering J. S. Bach's Performance Hints Hidden in J. S. Bach's Quaver Beams," EM 44 (2016): 89–104.

149 See Chapter 6, "Bach as Teacher" in David Ledbetter, *Bach's Well-tempered Clavier: The 48 Preludes and Fugues* (New Haven: Yale University Press, 2002), 126–140.

150 CPEB NV 66–69. Note that the third item was listed at the very end of Bach's vocal works ("Singstücke") on p. 81. See also Dok 3: 491–501 (No. 957).

151 Most likely D-B, N. Mus. ms. 10490, containing BWV 870a, 899, 900, 901 and 902, a collection first publicly discussed by Klaus Hofmann "'Fünf Präludien und fünf Fugen': Über ein unbeachtetes Sammelwerk Johann Sebastian Bachs," Winfried Hoffmann and Armin Schneiderheinze, eds., *Bach-Händel-Schütz-Ehrung 1985 der Deutschen Demokratischen Republik. Bericht über die Wissenschaftliche Konferenz zum V. Internationalen Bachfest der DDR in Verbindung mit dem 60. Bachfest der Neuen Bachgesellschaft. Leipzig, 25. bis 27. März 1985*

82   *Yo Tomita*

le Clavecin"[152] and "Einige Clavierstücke und Fugen von Joh. Seb. und Wilhelm Friedem. Bach."[153]—that require further study so that a broader view of Bach's pedagogy can be attained, or even just to establish whether some of them are indeed genuine products of Bach.

Occasionally, copies made by Bach's students contain sporadic additions of performance-related marks such as slurs, ornaments and fingerings, as manifested, for example, in Johann Caspar Vogler's copy of the early version of the opening prelude of WTC II (BWV 870a/1, D-B, Mus. ms. Bach P 1089, f. 4v).[154] Because these symbols do not contain sufficient calligraphic information to connect them to Bach, it is necessary for these additions and their musical context to be studied.[155]

Critical Editions

Most of Bach's works are known to us through manuscripts, some of which are autograph or original manuscripts (e.g., performance parts with autograph revisions), while others survive only in copies. The quality and reliability of text transmitted in manuscript copies vary. As a result of this varied nature of manuscripts arose the idea of a critical edition, an attempt to produce a definitive engraved version of the music, accompanied by a critical commentary that explains the reasons behind the choice of a particular version or versions and lists alternative readings. Such editions are one of the primary means by which the work of musicologists reaches performers.

One of the first tasks for an editor is to identify the most reliable source among the surviving sources by carefully assessing them (*recensio*) to establish their common readings and variants, together with the origins and chronology of these readings. This is described in a tree diagram (*stemma*),[156] which elucidates the relationship of sources (*filiation*). The primary sources, containing the composer's original version(s) of text,[157] are distinguished from the rest, the secondary sources. This can be a very lengthy process because evidence is often both

---

(Leipzig: VEB Deutscher Verlag für Musik, 1988), 227–235; see also James Brokaw, "Recent Research on the Sources and Genesis of Bach's Well-tempered Clavier, Book II," BACH 16/3 (July 1985): 17–35. The pieces in question were published together with WTC II in NBA V/6.2 (1995).

152 Most likely D-B, Mus. ms. Bach P 563, containing BWV 844a, 933, 872a/2 (in C), 901/1, Wq 111.

153 Most likely D-B, Mus. ms. Bach P 226, containing BWV 872a/1 (in C), 875 and Fk 26–28.

154 See, for example, Mark Lindley "Early fingering: Some Editing Problems and Some New Readings for J.S. Bach and John Bull," EM 17 (1989): 60–69, esp. 65; Peter Le Huray, "Bach's C major Prelude BWV 870 and 870a," in Peter Le Huray, ed., *Authenticity in Performance: Eighteenth-Century Case Studies* (Cambridge: Cambridge University Press, 1990), 5–23, esp. 10f.

155 See Alfred Dürr, "Ein Dokument aus dem Unterricht Bachs?" *Musiktheorie* 1/2 (1986): 163–170.

156 For further discussion, see "Transmission and Reception History" in this chapter.

157 Original musical text does not necessarily imply a single version. Various issues may arise, ranging from differences in versions to discrepancies in readings between the score and performance parts.

Manuscripts 83

extensive and complex. Separating Bach's revisions from alterations by others (and identifying the hand where someone else entered the revisions/alterations), distinguishing the layers of revisions Bach entered in a single manuscript or identifying the number of copies in which Bach entered his revisions, including those that are no longer extant, are among the most challenging tasks. Ideally, answers should be drawn using philological methodologies, which include studying the patterns of errors and variants reflected in subsequent generations of copies, and combined with the study of ink[158] and calligraphy.[159] However, due to a lack of evidence, our findings are often conditioned by our received understanding of Bach's compositional process. (On the other hand, the same understanding may also color our perceptions and make us biased.)

The notion of versions and variant readings (or variants) as well as their differences is important. Both concern situations where the musical text of the same piece is handed down to us through the surviving sources in non-unanimous form. A *version* is a difference observed at a large scale, such as the length, form or textural shape of the composition, whereas a *variant* is a smaller-scale discrepancy manifested among the surviving sources that belong to the same version of the composition, in features such as pitch and rhythm.[160] A *new version* may have been produced when Bach had fresh motivation. Such an occurrence, however, may never be ratified, and can therefore not be considered in the production of an edition. One of the most fundamental tasks of an editor is to assess all the differences found in the sources and determine whether they make up multiple versions or are merely variants. Ideally, critical editions should produce different versions in full, while variants should be dealt with in a critical report in list or table form, with the more important variants considered as alternative readings and supplied to the respective musical pages as footnotes.

Under the banner of a critical edition, mixing variants from different versions, called conflation of texts (*contaminatio*), is considered a violation of editorial rules, as it creates a new "hybrid" version of the text, which the composer probably never considered.[161] Producing a single version of the text from a pool of multiple

---

158 For example, Wolf, Hahn and Wolff, "Wer schrieb was?" 117–134.

159 A revised reading can be difficult to decipher accurately. For example, the natural Bach wrote on beat 2 of bar 10 of the Sarabande in Partita 2 in D minor (BWV 1004/3) has frequently been misinterpreted by scholars as a flat. See Neumann, 'Some Performance Problems of Bach's Unaccompanied Violin and Cello Works," 22–23, and Martin Jarvis, "Is Anna Magdalena's Manuscript of the Violin Sonatas & Partitas a Copy of the '1720 Autograph' of the Unaccompanied Violin Sonatas & Partitas of J. S. Bach?" *Stringendo* 29/2 (2007): 41–42.

160 See Dadelsen, "Editionsrichtlinien," 63, and Heinze and Wolf, *Gesamtregister*, 333.

161 However, in situations where multiple sources exist for the same version of a piece, it is essential to assess every variant in order to determine which readings originated from the composer and which did not, or which reading the composer decided to replace with a new one. Choosing a single source in such a situation and producing its text faithfully to avoid conflation of text represents a mere transcription (with no editing involved), and therefore cannot be regarded as a critical edition. For this reason, I would remonstrate against the editorial principles adopted in Peters' *The Complete Chopin: A New Critical Edition.*

84   Yo Tomita

versions therefore requires great caution and sufficient justification for the choice of one version over another. Once these necessary steps have been completed, the next phase, aimed at establishing whether the musical texts of the selected primary sources were really intended by the composer (*examinatio*), can then proceed. Contrary to common belief, Bach did make occasional mistakes, ranging from simple grammatical errors, such as parallel fifths and octaves or inaccurately notated rhythm of a complex constellation of beamed notes (lacking a beam, for instance) to notational oversights such as missing or inaccurate accidentals caused, for instance, by a confusion between modal and modern key signatures[162] or in places in which a piece would temporarily modulate.[163] Occasionally, the received understanding of Bach's compositional logic and procedure influences text-critical judgment, and results in the correction of a grammatically valid pitch. This tendency was particularly strong in the editorial decisions of the NBA.

Bach scholarship has greatly benefited from the NBA project, which, in addition to producing definitive versions of Bach's music for further study, has provided scholars with an array of valuable insights acquired during the process of its making, as has already been touched upon. However, the process has not finished with its completion in 2008.[164] Volumes of the revised edition of NBA (NBA[rev]) have been published since 2010 to replace those that needed to be re-edited as a result of advancements made since the time of their original publication both in terms of the concept of a critical edition and the state of scholarship. In addition, a number of hitherto unknown sources and those once considered lost have resurfaced. The mounting successes of scholars and their promotion of scholarship have resulted in a growing desire among the general public to hear unusual versions of well-known pieces, for example, an early version of the St. Matthew Passion (BWV 244b). The need for further research seems to continue without end as research reveals new insights. As our understanding of Bach's music continues to develop, our notion of what a critical edition should be will also change. Scholars in the future will undoubtedly discover new ways of presenting the complex yet fascinating continuum in the transformation and maturing of a work in the hands of its composer, which the sources harbor, but which tends to get buried in the dense, utilitarian and often not easily digestible make-up of critical reports.[165]

---

162   Perhaps the best-known example is the 1720 autograph of Violin Solos. In b. 3 (the beginning of the second system) of the opening G-minor Adagio (BWV 1001/1), Bach omits the flat for $e_\flat^1$. Numerous examples can also be found in the original manuscript of WTC II, hinting that earlier versions of some movements were written in modal key signatures.

163   Two specific instances are found in WTC II: Fugue in D major (BVW 874/2; autograph missing), b. 45 tenor ($g\sharp$ – Bach, for a while, forgot to write the sharp as the passage modulated to A major); Fugue in G minor (BWV 885/2), b. 64 alto ($a_\flat^1$ – Bach forgot to add the flat as the passage modulated to C minor).

164   Strictly speaking, the eighth volume of its supplement series *Bach-Dokumente*, "Materialien zur Quellen-Überlieferung bis 1850," is yet to appear.

165   For further discussion on this issue, see Yo Tomita, "'Rotancho Misakyoku" to Bach Kenkyu: Sakuhin no Densho to Gakufu Henshushi kara miru Kenkyujo no Shomondai' /《ロ短調ミサ

Transmission and Reception History

Transmission (*Überlieferung*) is a term used in manuscript studies to describe the way in which works were disseminated through the act of copying, as this was the only practical means available at the time. Just as the biological features of living creatures are passed on to their offspring, each of which, however, is born into this world different from the other, so too do music manuscripts, which, although fundamentally retaining nearly all the genetic information from their parental source, undergo modification in the process of copying. The reasons behind the newly introduced changes are numerous, and unmasking them is one of the primary objectives for establishing a *stemma*.[166] A lack of competence on the writer's part to accurately reproduce (or properly update the notational convention of) the model or a change of score layout necessitated by the size of notation or paper, are among those reasons. Variants could also have been introduced deliberately, where the writer wished to correct or modernize some of the notational or musical properties of the written contents. The modifications are then evaluated as either *errors* or *variants*, depending on the musical context. For example, pitch variants will always be examined within the context of both the generic harmonic grammar and specific stylistic traits, such as the motives and figures used within the piece.

A careful evaluation of the musical text is sometimes extended to cover the people involved, copyists, users and owners. When the subject touches upon the biographical sphere, the study, exploring the musical lives of individuals and their engagement with the works in question within the contexts of a particular time and region, becomes one of *reception history*. A notable example from recent scholarship that successfully illuminates how tracing the sources' transmission can contribute to our better understanding of the reception history is a study of a group of recently resurfaced manuscript sources of Bach's Sonatas and Partitas for Solo Violin (BWV 1001–1006): it examines their provenance, some of which are linked to eminent figures such as Carl Friedrich Zelter (1758–1832) and Louis Spohr (1784–1859), establishes a textual link between them, traces the origin of this branch of transmission to Bach's autograph and manages to paint a lively picture of how this celebrated work of Bach's had been valued by many.[167] The nature of reception study often requires scholars to branch out into spheres

---

曲》とバッハ研究：作品の伝承と楽譜編集史からみる研究上の諸問題 [The B-minor Mass and Bach Research: Various research questions posed by the work's transmission and the history of editing], *Ongaku Kenkyujo Nenpo / Kunitachi College of Music Research Institute Bulletin* 24 (March 2012): 145–182, esp. 164.

166 By carefully examining the stemma of secondary sources it is sometimes possible to discover the variants once contained in a lost original manuscript, which would otherwise be inaccessible. Charting the process of transmission can thus become a twoway street, at the same time moving ahead towards subsequent related sources and back towards the composer's original text.

167 Tanja Kovačević and Yo Tomita, "Neue Quellen zu Johann Sebastian Bachs Violinsoli (BWV 1001–1006). Zur Rekonstruktion eines wichtigen Überlieferungszweigs," BJ 95 (2009): 49–74.

86   Yo Tomita

of research that lie outside their main subject area (i.e., spheres that focus on the individuals and situations to which a particular source is linked), so its future lies in the collaboration between scholars with different specialist backgrounds. The knowledge gained through the exploration of specific people, periods and regions should then be reassessed in context of the placement of its subject within broader current of musical scenes and trends.

Future Work

The breadth and depth of detail at which each scholar engages with Bach manuscripts as discussed in this chapter gives the impression that it is impossible for any one scholar to be fully cognizant of every new development in research as well as the past achievements. Yet it is imperative that we are aware of the complexity of the subject. Even when engaging with a specific field of manuscript study, crucial evidence often comes from a holistic and systematic investigation, as was repeatedly demonstrated by scholars in the past. As research grows ever more specialized and segmented, the future calls for a research environment in which scholars will share work and knowledge for their mutual benefit, while focusing on their particular research interests. Only in this way shall we avoid losing touch with one another's achievements. As I suggested in 2002, Bach scholars need to consider creating a flexible, stable and dynamic global research infrastructure for sharing data, computing, and other resources via the internet. Using the recently established e-Science model is, in my view, the most attractive option.[168]

The course of study is affected, often fundamentally, by new source finds. The discovery of Bach's personal copy of the Goldberg-Variations in 1974, which included a hitherto-unknown set of Fourteen Canons (BWV 1087)[169] in his hand at the back of the volume, provided rich biographical material to repaint the picture of Bach in the last few years of his life.[170] The rediscovery by Christoph Wolff and his colleagues at the Ukrainian Research Institute, Harvard University, of the Berlin Sing-Akademie collection in Kiev in 1999 likewise shook the foundation of C. P. E. Bach studies, which subsequently became the main fuel for *Carl*

---

168 Yo Tomita, "Breaking the Limits: Some Preliminary Considerations on Introducing an e-Science Model to Source Studies," *Ongakugaku to Globalization: Nihon Ongaku Gakkai Soritsu 50 Shunen Kinen Kokusai Taikai: Shizuoka 2002. Hokokusho = Musicology and globalization: proceedings of the International Congress in Shizuoka 2002 in celebration of the 50th anniversary of the Musicological Society of Japan* (Tokyo: Nihon Ongaku Gakkai, 2004), 233–237; see also Tomita, "Challenging Virtuality," 4–6.

169 Two of these canons (nos. 11 and 13) were known in slightly different versions, BWV 1077 and 1076 respectively.

170 For an account of the circumstances of its discovery, see Olivier Alain, "Un supplément inédit aux Variations Goldberg de J. S. Bach," *Revue de Musicologie* 61 (1975): 244–245; see also Christoph Wolff, "Bach's Handexemplar of the Goldberg Variations," JAMS 29 (1976): 224–241. This copy is presently held by the Bibliothèque Nationale de France in Paris under the shelfmark: MS 17 669.

Philipp Emanuel Bach: The Complete Works, the volumes of which started to appear from 2005 at an astonishing pace.[171] Wolff's next project was *Expedition Bach* at the Bach-Archiv Leipzig. Since its inception in 2002, his team has been systematically searching for historical documents in federal, communal and church archives in the historical territories of Saxony, Thuringia and Anhalt, and has already reported a number of significant finds including a hitherto-unknown autograph of the Weimar aria "Alles mit Gott und nichts ohn' ihn" (BWV 1127) in 2005,[172] and, in the following year, the so-called "Weimar Organ Tabulature" bearing Bach's own signature. Having been widely accepted as the earliest manuscript copy in Bach's hand, and containing the organ music of Reincken and Buxtehude, the Tabulature provides us with concrete material to reassess the ability of the teenage Bach, the young organ scholar.[173] Naturally, the net ought to be cast wider in the future. The source hunt in the archives in Central and Eastern Europe, as outlined by Szymon Paczkowski in his keynote paper entitled "Bach and Poland in the 18th century," read at the Bach Network UK dialogue meeting in Warsaw in July 2013,[174] will soon be launched with the hope of uncovering more evidence relating to the early reception of Bach's works by Kirnberger in Częstochowa, Podhorce, Równe and Lwów, and Mizler in Końskie and Warsaw. Further discoveries of Bach's original manuscripts are anticipated in the future from pursuing these teacher-pupil connections.[175] Meanwhile, revisiting already known collections and archives has proven to be useful. Among the collections housed in the Staatsarchiv Leipzig, a branch of the Sachsische Staatsarchiv, are the sources that have been transferred from the company archives of music publishers such as Breitkopf & Härtel and C. F. Peters, which were for some unknown reason overlooked by the editors of NBA, despite having been long available to scholars.[176] It was only in 2013 that the vast corpus of Bach sources housed there came to be known, and the process of reevaluation began. Among the first fruits of this fresh investigation was the recovery by Christine Blanken of Breitkopf's house copies, which include a very early fair copy of the keyboard Toccatas in the hand of a Bach pupil and containing Bach's autograph revisions, many early copies of the compositions of the Bach family, J. S. Bach's organ chorales copied

---

171 *Carl Philipp Emanuel Bach: The Complete Works* published by the Packard Humanities Institute in Los Altos, CA.

172 Michael Maul, "'Alles mit Gott und nichts ohn' ihn' – Eine neu aufgefundene Aria von Johann Sebastian Bach," BJ 91 (2005): 7–34.

173 Michael Maul and Peter Wollny, eds. *Weimarer Orgeltabulatur. Die frühesten Notenhandschriften Johann Sebastian Bachs sowie Abschriften seines Schülers Johann Martin Schubart. Mit Werken von Dietrich Buxtehude, Johann Adam Reinken und Johann Pachelbel*, Faksimile-Reihe Bachscher Werke und Schriftstücke. Neue Folge, III; Documenta Musicologica. Zweite Reihe: Handschriften-Faksimiles, 39 (Kassel: Bärenreiter, 2007).

174 A revised version is published in UB 10 (2015): 123–137.

175 This research should also include the eastern areas of formerly German lands (Prussia) that are parts of Poland and Russia today where Bach's students worked after studying with Bach.

176 Thekla Kluttig, "Nur Briefe berühmter Komponisten? Archivgut von Leipziger Musikverlagen als Quelle für die Musikwissenschaften," Mf 66/4 (2013): 391–407.

88 Yo Tomita

by C. G. Gerlach and J. L. Krebs and copies of Bach's organ works published by A. B. Marx in the 1830s.[177] Without doubt, further progress will be made in the near future, and the report is keenly awaited by many scholars. Alongside the recovery of physical sources, we will learn more about the lost sources by piecing together various fragments of information arrived at through a systematic investigation of known sources. For example, the systematic research of Nobuaki Ebata on manuscript sources of the Four-Part Chorales may well lead to the identification of some that originated from the chorale movements of the lost Picander-Jahrgang cantatas (the fourth annual cycle, of which presently only approximately ten cantatas are known to have survived), and possibly offer further possibilities of identifying the chorale movements from the cantatas of the fifth Jahrgang and two passions, all of which have completely disappeared.[178]

Equally important is the establishment of the e-Science environment with new methodologies and research techniques using Artificial Intelligence techniques to extract more data from the existing sources and to carry out more powerful analyses. The new analyses may yield connections impossible to make through our cognitive power alone. For example, they will hopefully show the relationships between all the variants found in sources of a single work and how to measure the strength of these relationships, with all that this implies for their provenance. In this light, nearly every area of source study needs to be revisited to ensure that every new research resource, knowledge or analytical technique will be integrated dynamically into the system, so that it will be available to everyone in real time.

---

177 Christine Blanken, "Ein wieder zugänglich gemachter Bestand alter Musikalien der Bach-Familie im Verlagsarchiv Breitkopf & Härtel," BJ 99 (2013): 79–128..

178 See the forthcoming article by Nobuaki Ebata in UB.

4 Printed Editions

Gregory Butler

As is so often the case in the domain of Bach studies, Philipp Spitta was the pioneer in research on the early printed editions. Before the publication of his ground-breaking biography, Bach scholars knew of the existence of the printed editions that had served as primary sources for the publication of certain collections of the composer's keyboard music but no one had undertaken an in depth study of any of them. Spitta's research on the *Musical Offering*[1] marked an important turning point. He noted the existence of the oversize dedicatory copy and raised the issue of the survival of the print in incomplete exemplars leading him to the "installment" theory. After Spitta in the years before the First World War, the major contribution to the field was that of Gustav Wustmann.[2] The bulk of his study of Leipzig engravers through the eighteenth century was devoted to those artisans active during the time of Bach and his work was of immense value. Because he dealt with engravers as a whole instead of specifically with music engravers he alerted scholars who followed him to important sources for concordances of unidentified engravers responsible for those of Bach's original prints engraved before 1740.

In the years leading up to and following the war, a number of general studies on music engraving, printing, and the book trade laid the foundation for the first monograph on the printed editions by Georg Kinsky.[3] In his book, Kinsky offered a salient biographical description including the date of publication for each of the original editions of Bach's works as well as detailed information on all the particulars of his subject: the engraving and format, the various engravers, printers and publishers involved, sales, distribution and marketing, and reports and commentaries from the time. In addition, he raised important issues not dealt with before: the existence of *Handexempläre* and of two previously undiscovered original editions. He also drew on important peripheral prints from the 1730s

---

1 See Spitta 2: 843–845; Spitta ET 3: 292–294.
2 See Gustav Wustmann, *Der Leipziger Kupferstich im 16., 17. und 18. Jahrhundert* (Leipzig: Hirschfeld, 1907).
3 Georg Kinsky, *Die Originalausgaben der Werke Johann Sebastian Bachs: ein Beitrag zur Musikbibliographie* (Vienna: Reichner, 1937; reprint, Hilversum: Knuf, 1968).

90   *Gregory Butler*

to which Bach contributed, the Schemelli *Gesangbuch* and Sperontes' *Singende Muse an der Pleisse*.

At the same time as Kinsky was at work on his monograph, other researchers were making important contributions. Notable among these was Friedrich Smend, who published his research on the original print of the *Canonic Variations on "Vom Himmel hoch"* (BWV 769) in connection with his edition of the work for the *Neue Bachgesellschaft*.[4] Smend's bias in favor of the autograph led to his unfair dismissal of the print as "clumsy" and a "distortion" and to his unfounded conclusion that Bach had been excluded by the engraver Schmid from the editorial process. Nevertheless, his integration of a study of the engraving in critical source studies was important and ahead of his time.

In the years immediately following the Second World War, there was little research on the printed editions. It was not until the mid-1950s when Hans Klotz was preparing his edition of the organ chorales from Bach's original Leipzig manuscript for the NBA that the subject was addressed anew. Klotz offered a convincing argument against Smend's relegation of the original print of the *Variations on "Vom Himmel hoch"* to the status of a source of peripheral importance. As part of the scholarly apparatus in the critical notes to his edition published in 1957, he made the decision to include a list of all the known exemplars of the original print.[5] In so doing, he made his intent clear: the importance of the original print as a source was equal to that of the autograph version in D-B Mus. Ms. Bach P 271 (BWV 769a). This is clear from his source critical study of the work in which, for the first time, he gives a detailed comparison of readings from both the original print and Bach's autograph.[6] The reading arrived at was challenged by the British musicologist, Walter Emery,[7] in a paper read before the Eighth Congress of the International Society in New York[8] in which he took issue with Klotz's interpretation of the source critical evidence. Klotz had argued that the order in which the five variations appeared in the original print was that intended by Bach as the definitive scheme while Emery, as Smend before him, insisted on the ordering in the autograph.

The debate with Klotz led Emery to focus on the engraver of the *Variations on "Vom himmel hoch,"* Balthasar Schmid.[9] He was one of the first researchers to hunt for and discover engraving concordances in other prints. While Emery's

---

4 Friedrich Smend, "Bach's Kanonwerk über 'Vom Hommel hoch da komm ich her,'" BJ 30 (1933): 1–29.
5 NBA IV/1, KB, 52.
6 NBA IV/1, KB, 86–101.
7 A decade earlier, Emery had become involved in a study of an exemplar of the original print of Bach's *Klavierübung II* in the British Library; see Walter Emery, "An Introduction to the Textual History of Bach's Clavierübung Part II," MT 92 (1951): 205–209, 260–262. This ultimately led to his edition of the work for the NBA.
8 Walter Emery, "On Evidence of Derivation," *International Musicological Society. Report of the Eighth Congress: New York 1961*, ed. Jan Larue (Kassel: Bärenreiter, 1961), 1: 249–252.
9 See Walter Emery, "The Goldberg Engraver," MT 104 (1963): 875; and Walter Emery, "Schmid and the Goldberg," MT 105 (1964): 350.

Printed Editions 91

researches were preliminary, another researcher, Horst Heussner, had embarked on a detailed biographical study of Schmid that included extensive lists both for Schmid's publications of other composers' works as well as for those of his own works.[10] In his study, Heussner called on publisher's plate numbers as well as catalogues in an attempt to arrive at a chronology for Schmid's publications. Heussner went on to widen his studies to take in music engraving, publishing, and distribution as a whole in early eighteenth-century Nuremburg.[11] Work on Schmid culminated in the early 1970s with Willi Wörthmüller's important facsimile edition of the *Variations on "Vom himmel hoch."*[12] Flanking the facsimile reproduction are two articles, one by Lothar Hoffmann-Erbrecht on the relation of Schmid to the Bach family[13] and a second by Hans Klotz on the source history of the variations.[14] As bookends, there are two lists, the first by the editor, of all the publications by Schmid of music composed by the Bach family and the second, by Christoph Wolff, of all of the original editions of the works of J. S. Bach including title, printer, date, format, and a list of known exemplars.

At this point, Wolff's groundbreaking edition of the *Musical Offering* for the NBA had been published for five years and two years before he had published his findings in English.[15] Going beyond Klotz, Wolff's study took into account watermarks, paper formats and qualities, and engraving corrections. It also dealt with such aspects as Bach's marketing strategy, print runs, distribution, and so forth. Most important, Wolff challenged Spitta's installment concept in favor of an ingenious "wrapper" theory in which printing units in upright portrait format were enclosed in those in oblong landscape format. Based on his research, Wolff conducted a graduate seminar at Columbia University during the fall semester of 1972 with a source critical study of the *Art of Fugue* as its subject. Of the students' papers, subsequently published in the 1975 issue of *Current Musicology*, that of Richard Kaprowski[16] was of particular interest. In it, Kaprowski applied graphological analysis in his minute scrutiny of the various engraving styles in an attempt to establish a relative chronology. In so doing, he suggested that more than one engraver was involved in the project.

---

10 See Horst Heussner, "Der Musikdrucker Balthasar Schmid in Nürnberg," Mf 16 (1963): 348–62.

11 Horst Heussner, "Nürnberger Musikverlag und Musikalienhandel im 18. Jahrhundert," *Musik und Verlag. Karl Vötterle zum 65. Geburtstag am 12. April 1968*, ed. Richard Baum and Wolfgang Rehm (Kassel: Bärenreiter, 1968), 319–341.

12 See Willi Wörthmüller, *Die Nürnberger Musikverleger und die Familie Bach: Materialien zu einer Ausstellung des 48. Bach-Fests der Neuen Bach-Gesellschaft; Mit der Faksimile-Ausgabe des Erstdrucks der Kanonischen Veränderungen über "Vom Himmel hoch" von Johann Sebastian Bach BWV 769* ([Leipzig?]: Zirndorf Bollmann, 1973).

13 Lothar Hoffmann-Erbrecht, "Johann Sebastian und Carl Phlipp Emanuel Bachs Nürnberger Verleger," Wörthmüller, *Die Nürnberger Musikverleger*, 5–10.

14 Hans Klotz, "Die 'Kanonische Veränderungen' in Entwurf, Reinschrift und Druck," Wörthmüller, *Die Nürnberger Musikverleger*, 11–14.

15 See Christoph Wolff, "New Research on Bach's Musical Offering," MQ 57 (1971): 379–408.

16 See Richard Kaprowski, "Bach 'Fingerprints' in the Engraving of the Original Edition," *Current Musicology* 19 (1975): 61–67.

92   *Gregory Butler*

The findings of Wolff and his students kindled interest in the engraving of the *Art of Fugue* (BWV 1080), leading Wolfgang Wiemer to extend the kind of evidence called on by Kaprowski and apply it to the perennial question of the ordering scheme intended by Bach.[17] Gregory Butler, another student attending Wolff's seminar, proposed, on the basis of the erasure of pagination apparent in the original print, an ordering scheme in which the augmentation canon came last instead of first in the series of four, a finding now generally accepted by Bach scholars.[18]

After publishing a general survey of the engraving of the earlier original prints concentrating on the Leipzig engraving shop of Johann Gottfried Krügner[19] and a more detailed study of the engraving in the Schemelli *Gesangbuch*,[20] Butler set out to examine every extant exemplar of the original prints of Bach's music. His initial goal was to identify engravers not yet identified; to do so, he widened the search for engraving concordances to include besides music, engraved illustrations, and portraits in printed books. He succeeded in identifying the engravers of the *Six Partitas*—a Weimar student of Bach, Johann Gotthilf Ziegler, and the young Balthasar Schmid—and the engraver of the titles for *Klavierübung I*—Johann Gottfried Krügner[21]—as well as those of *Klavierübung II*, two Nuremberg engravers with links to Leipzig—Johann Georg Puschner (Italian Concerto) and Jean Christoph Dehné (French Ouverture).[22]

In the course of his research, Butler became involved in an extended study of the original print of *Klavierübung III*, which he eventually published as a monograph.[23] Largely through paper studies, he was able to determine that the two sections engraved by the Krügner shop in Leipzig and by Schmid in Nuremberg were printed separately and also identified two proof copies of the Krügner section and a partial engraver's copy of the Schmid section. Through erasures in page numbers and by analyzing the engraving of the titles, he was able to point to changes in the concept and scale of the collection as it evolved.

In the mid-1980s, attention had begun to shift back to the prints from Bach's last decade. In part, this interest was spurred by the publication of complete facsimile editions of high quality. Wolff's facsimile edition of the *Musical*

---

17 Wolfgang Wiemer, *Die wiederhergestellte Ordnung in Johann Sebastian Bachs Kunst der Fuge: Untersuchungen am Originaldruck* (Wiesbaden: Breitkopf & Hartel, 1977).

18 See Gregory Butler, "Ordering Problems in Bach's *Art of Fugue* Resolved," MQ 69 (1983): 44–61.

19 Gregory Butler, "Leipziger Stecher in Bachs Frühdrucken," BJ 66 (1980): 9–26.

20 Gregory Butler, "J. S. Bach and the Schemelli *Gesangbuch* Revisited," *Studi Musicali* 13 (1984): 241–257.

21 Gregory Butler, "The Engraving of J. S. Bach's *Six Partitas*," *Journal of Musicological Research* 7 (1986): 3–27.

22 Gregory Butler, "The Engravers of Bach's *Clavier-Übung II*," *A Bach Tribute: Essays in Honor of William H. Scheide*, ed. Paul Brainard and Ray Robinson (Kassel: Bärenreiter, 1993), 57–69.

23 Gregory Butler, *Bach's Clavier-Übung III: The Making of a Print* (Durham: Duke University Press, 1990).

Offering as part of the Peters reprint series[24] was followed two years later by that of both the autograph manuscript and the original print of the *Art of Fugue* edited by Hans Gunter Hoke.[25] Finally, with Wolff's facsimile edition of *Klavierübung I-IV*,[26] virtually all of the original prints were available in high definition facsimiles. Studies focusing on the Schübler shop also acted as a stimulus. Notable among these was Wiemer's detailed biographical study of the family of engravers in which, through engraving concordances, he was able not only to identify Johann Georg as the engraver of the *Art of Fugue* but his younger brother, Johann Heinrich, as a second engraver involved in the engraving of the *Musical Offering*.[27]

During the 1990s, Butler revisited three of the late prints as an extension of his earlier work. In a study on the *Variations on "Vom Himmel hoch,"*[28] he presented evidence suggesting that the versions of the variations in both the autograph and the original print represented different stages in the source history and by so doing called into question the whole *Fassung letzter Hand* concept. In a second on the *Musical Offering*,[29] he pointed to the involvement of a third engraver from the Schübler family, Johann Jacob Friedrich, in the project. He suggested that the collection underwent a longer gestation period than previously projected and that in Bach's original concept it included only the three printing units in oblong format preserved in the dedicatory copy—the title page and the three- and six-part ricercars with their appended canons—and that only later did he decide to add the two printing units in upright portrait format—the other canons and the trio sonata.[30] This ordering of the printing units supported that put forward by Michael Marissen. He revived Spitta's "installment" theory holding that the reason for the collection's piecemeal survival was because the consumer had the choice of buying any of one, two, three, or all four printing units along with the title page. Finally, in a study on the *Art of Fugue*,[31] extending Kaprowski's

---

24 Johann Sebastian Bach, *Musicalisches Opfer* BWV 1079, ed. Christoph Wolff (Leipzig: Peters, 1977).

25 Johann Sebastian Bach *Kunst der Fuge* BWV 1080, ed. Hans Gunter Hoke (Leipzig: Peters, 1979).

26 Johann Sebastian Bach *Clavier Übung* Teil I-IV, ed. Christoph Wolff (Leipzig: Peters, 1984).

27 See Wolfgang Wiemer, "Johann Henrich Schübler, der Stecher der Kunst der Fuge," BJ 65 (1979): 75–95.

28 See Gregory Butler, "J. S. Bach's Kanonische Veränderungen über "Vom Himmel hoch" (BWV 769). Ein Schlußstrich unter die Debatte um die Frage der "Fassung letzter Hand," BJ 86 (2000): 9–34.

29 Gregory Butler, "The Printing of J. S. Bach's *Musical Offering*: New Interpretations," JM 19 (2002): 306–331.

30 See Michael Marissen, "More Source Critical Research on Bach's *Musical Offering*," BACH 25 (1994): 11–27. Marissen's claim that certain plates were engraved freehand instead of by the *Abklatschvorlage* method, although intriguing, is not supported by the appearance of the engraving.

31 Gregory Butler, "Scribes, Engravers, and Notational Styles: The Final Disposition of Bach's Art of Fugue" in *About Bach*, ed. Gregory Butler, George B. Stauffer, and Mary Dalton Greer (Urbana: University of Illinois Press, 2008), 111–123.

94   *Gregory Butler*

work on the engraving, Butler suggested that the collection was engraved in two installments and demonstrated the point in the project where Bach was no longer supplying engraver's copy beginning with Contrapunctus 13.2. He argued that the *Fuga à tre* (unfinished fugue) was never intended to be part of the collection and that the unfinished work was, in fact, a third mirror fugue.

A critical and sometimes contentious issue surrounding the original prints is the identification of Bach's personal copies or *Handexempläre*. It is important because such exemplars may, as in the case of the two *Handexempläre* of the *Schübler Chorales* (BWV 645–650), one of which came to light in 1975 and the other more recently, present revised readings and corrections in Bach's hand.[32] Even more spectacularly, in the case of the *Handexemplar* of the *Goldberg Variations*, which resurfaced in 1975, a previously unknown set of fourteen canons was appended to the print.[33] But it is perplexing that, in some cases, in exemplars known to have been in Bach's possession, such as the *Handexemplar* of *Klavierübung III*, the musical text is perfectly clean. It is for this reason that Butler has suggested that a distinction be made between those exemplars that may have been kept by Bach as remainders from an edition and those in which he entered corrected or revised readings and that only the latter be referred to as *Handexemplar*.[34] Provenance of certain exemplars though is an issue of the greatest importance for in some cases, revised readings not in Bach's hand may well stem from the composer. A good example is an exemplar of the *Goldberg Variations* once belonging to Bach's student, Johann Friedrich Agricola.[35] Not only does this copy contain important annotations by Agricola, it also confirms the identity of its owner and the date of publication of the printed edition to the year 1741.

A case that has aroused considerable controversy is *Klavierübung I*. Even though Bach's hand appears in none of the extant exemplars of the original print, the editor of the work for the NBA, Richard Jones, held that one of the exemplars in the British Library was the *Handexemplar* on the basis of the revised readings it contained and promoted these readings in his edition.[36] Christoph Wolff took issue with Jones' identification of this exemplar as the *Handexemplar*, arguing that it was hypothetical and that Jones had ignored important revised readings in

---

32 See Christoph Wolff, "Bach's Personal Copy of the Schübler Chorales," *Bach the Organist: His Instruments, Music, and Performance Practices*, ed. George B. Stauffer and Ernest May (Urbana-Champaign: Indiana University Press, 1985), 121–132. A further *Handexemplar* of the *Schübler Chorales* has recently been discovered; see George B. Stauffer, "Noch ein 'Handexemplar': der Fall der Schübler Choräle," BJ 101 (2015): 177–192.

33 See Christoph Wolff, "Bach's *Handexemplar* of the Goldberg Variations: A New Source," JAMS 29: (1976): 224–241.

34 See Gregory Butler, "*Handexemplar*," *Oxford Composer Companions: J. S. Bach*, ed. Malcolm Boyd (Oxford: Oxford University Press, 1999), 206.

35 See Gregory Butler, "Neues zur Datierung des Originaldrucks Bachs *Goldberg Variationen*," BJ 74 (1988): 19–24.

36 NBA V/1, KB (1978), 18–23.

Printed Editions   95

four other heavily corrected exemplars.[37] Jones responded by including a section comparing readings in his doctoral dissertation and in a supplement in the critical notes to his edition. Recently, Andrew Talle has come up with an intriguing interpretation that none of the heavily corrected exemplars is the *Handexemplar*, but rather that the readings, although they originate with Bach, were entered as exercises by students into copies in Bach's possession as solutions to readings which the composer found problematic.[38] Of course, this is of the greatest importance in establishing definitive readings for the works these prints contain. At the same time, it indicates that for Bach, who was an inveterate tinkerer, the reading of a work at the time of its engraving represented a stage in its evolution which in turn would be superseded by a later reading.

Recently, there has been a turn towards placing the original prints in their social context. Talle has become interested in tracing the provenance of certain exemplars in an attempt to discover who the buyers were and what motivated them as consumers. He has also looked at Sperontes' *Singende Muse an der Pleisse* and the economics around the publication of its many editions in the 1730s and 1740s.[39] This work is important because it seeks to understand the wider social and cultural milieu in which the original editions were produced. This approach could be broadened to focus on Bach and his publishers and how these publications impacted on the composer economically and artistically in much the same way as Steven Zohn's recent study on Telemann in the marketplace.[40] At the same time, the recent discovery of autograph entries in an exemplar of *Klavierübung III* by George Stauffer[41] has once again raised great interest in the original prints as primary sources of the utmost importance, particularly in such a case where no other source material in Bach's hand has survived.

At first glance, the editions of Bach's works from his lifetime would seem to be as immutable as fair apographic copies of other works of the composer. However, they have revealed much to Bach scholars over the years, and it is a fair bet that they will continue to do so in the future.

---

37 Christoph Wolff, "Textkritische Bemerkungen zum Originaldruck der Bachschen Partiten," BJ 63 (1979): 65–74.

38 Andrew Talle, "A Print of *Clavierübung* I from J. S. Bach's Personal Library," *About Bach*, ed. Butler, et al, 157–168.

39 Talle's findings were presented in a paper entitled "A New Look at Sperontes' *Singende Muse an der Pleisse* delivered at the biennial meeting of the American Bach Society at Madison, Wisconsin on May 8, 2010.

40 See Steven Zohn, *Music for a Mixed Taste: Style, Genre, and Meaning in Telemann's Instrumnetal Works* (New York: Oxford University Press, 2008), 335–390.

41 See George Stauffer, "Ein neuer Blick auf Bachs 'Handexemplar': Das Beispiel Clavier-Übung III," BJ 96 (2010): 29–52.

Part II
Contexts

5 Households

Tanya Kevorkian

Johann Sebastian Bach lived in a number of households in the course of his life. Most of them, ranging from his birthplace in a town musician's household in Eisenach, to the cantor's service apartment in Leipzig, were typical of early modern urban households in two important respects. First, they included not only members of the immediate family, but also various other people. Second, these households were not just places of residence, but also sites of work and production: of musical learning, composition, and the copying of manuscripts. As historians have found, people's roles in the family, in the household, and in the economy overlapped. Bach's households during his shorter stints at the courts of Weimar and Cöthen also shared these characteristics.

Several historiographical traditions can help us reconstruct how household organization structured Bach's life and work. Musicologists have written extensively about town musicians, about cantors and organists, and about Bach's family itself. These studies provide insight into the sizes of the households, the duties of various members, and the hardships and advantages of the musician's life. Editions of primary sources relating to Bach are also important. Next, many strands of scholarship by historians provide context for musicians' households. The literatures on guild and merchant households, women, marriage, family, childhood, "house fathers" and "house mothers," demography, and on urban history more generally are all valuable. Work by historians can help us understand how musicians' households, and their members' life trajectories, fit into the society around them. How typical were Bach's placement with his brother in Ohrdruf after the death of his parents, his two marriages, and his lifespan? To what extent did town musicians' households resemble those of more formally organized guildspeople? What differences were there among cantors', organists', and town musicians' households, and how did they compare to non-musicians' households?

It will be useful to first examine Bach and his wives as they moved through the stages of their lives; then, we can consider how Bach's various households shaped his working life. The biographical literature on J. S. Bach and his family gives us plentiful detail on the specifics of his life. Christoph Wolff's *Johann Sebastian Bach: The Learned Musician* (Wolff BLM) is a meticulous guide with copious references to earlier literature. *The New Grove Bach Family* is also a reliable

100 *Tanya Kevorkian*

primer.[1] The *New Bach Reader* (NBR) includes a number of contemporary documents in translation relating to the household. Most of these are taken from the *Bach-Dokumente* (Dok).

In the older literature, and in the popular imagination, Bach often is seen not only as frustrated and underappreciated in his professional life, but also as someone who had an exceedingly difficult personal life. Bach did experience a huge amount of personal pain. His parents, Maria Elisabeth and Johann Ambrosius, had eight children and outlived four before dying within a year of each other at the ages of forty-nine and fifty.[2] Just short of his tenth birthday when he was orphaned in 1695, J. S. was the youngest of the children; he also had a new step-sister the same age, and another who was two years older, because his father had remarried just twelve weeks before his death. Bach also lost his first wife, and he outlived eleven of the twenty children to whom his two wives gave birth.[3] The physical and probably emotional toll on his wives was even greater. His first wife, Maria Barbara, who herself was orphaned by the age of twenty, bore seven children in just under ten years, all by the age of thirty-four, losing three by the age of one; she died at age thirty-five. Likewise, his second wife, Anna Magdalena, became a step-mother to four children who were younger than age twelve when she married at twenty, and bore thirteen children of her own in just under nineteen years. She lost five at the age of one or younger, two others before the age of five, and a step-son at the age of twenty-four, thus outliving six of her biological children and three step-children. She was widowed at the age of forty-nine, never to remarry, living in part on alms for the last ten years of her life.

Music historians point out that high child mortality rates, being widowed, and remarrying were all common to the era, and they are right. An extensive literature by historians, linked with the specifics of the Bach family, can greatly expand our insights into the survival and family formation strategies of the Bachs. It shows that the Bachs were typical of families of their time in some regards, and actually quite fortunate, when considered in context, in other ways. The leading historical demographer of Germany, Arthur Imhof, notes that "life was insecure for everyone,"[4] regardless of sex, social status, or age, but especially for infants. Rather than the modern Western expectation of a long life, people in the early modern period lived with the expectation that they could pass away at any time. The survival rates of Johann Sebastian's siblings and children, at about 50%, were typical of the times. Infant mortality, especially up to the age of five, was very high, and half of all children never reached the age of fifteen.[5]

---

1 Christoph Wolff, Walter Emery, et al., *The New Grove Bach Family* (New York: Norton, 1983).

2 For a table with information on J. S. Bach's siblings, see Wolff BLM, 19.

3 For a table with biographical information on the children, see Wolff BLM, 396–398.

4 Arthur Imhof, *Lebenserwartungen in Deutschland vom 17. bis zum 19. Jahrhundert* (Weinheim: VCH Verlagsgesellschaft, 1990), 38. The preface and introduction of this book, along with explanations of charts and graphs, are translated into English.

5 Joel Harrington, *The Unwanted Child. The Fate of Foundlings, Orphans, and Juvenile Criminals in Early Modern Germany* (Chicago: University of Chicago Press, 2009), 214.

What of the fates of children who were orphaned? Joel Harrington has productively applied the concept of the "circulation of children," first developed by anthropologists, to early modern German families.[6] Along with providing a case study of Nuremberg, he synthesizes much literature on childhood and the family for Germany and Europe. Although the title of his book, *The Unwanted Child*, is a misnomer in cases like J. S. Bach's, where an inability to provide economic support or the death of parents, rather than a lack of desire to keep a child, was the issue, the Bach family definitely circulated its children in the ways that Harrington depicts. He emphasizes that family members, godparents, and even neighbors frequently took in children, often informally, when parents either could not afford to keep them or passed away. It speaks not only to the cohesiveness of the Bach family, then, but also to that of early modern families more generally that Bach's oldest brother, Johann Christoph—aged twenty-four, newly married, about to become a father, and installed as organist in the small nearby town of Ohrdruf since 1690—took in Johann Sebastian and his next-older brother, Johann Jacob, then aged thirteen. Older siblings, along with godparents or other relatives, most commonly took in orphans. Indeed, J. S.'s first wife, Maria Barbara, along with her two older sisters, was herself taken in by her maternal aunt and the aunt's husband, who was also her godfather, after she was orphaned. And after J. S. died, his second-oldest son, Carl Philipp Emanuel, took in his half-brother Johann Christian, who was then fifteen years old and twenty-one years his junior. As C. P. E. himself noted in the family genealogy, in the second and third person but with a hint of pride, Johann Christian "[w]ent, after our late father's death, to his brother C. P. E. in Berlin, who gave him his upbringing and his education. Journeyed in 1754 to Italy. Is now in England in the service of the Queen..."[7]

Often, foster parents were not able to financially support their charges. Johann Christoph obtained support from the Ohrdruf gymnasium (Latin school), where Johann Sebastian, known for his fine soprano, became a choral scholar, earning free board at the school and an income from singing. Johann Jacob, who also probably received free board, was sent back to Eisenach after about a year, at the age of fourteen, as an apprentice to the town musician who had succeeded Ambrosius Bach.[8] Apprenticing arrangements for boys, and placement in domestic service for girls, often for children as young as twelve, were a very common method of child circulation. Parents or guardians no longer had to pay for the child's upkeep, and the child could learn skills and perhaps an income that would set him or her on the road to independence. There actually was a shortage of apprenticing arrangements from the sixteenth century onward, and many children without family connections, good personal reputations, or with physical handicaps ended up begging on the streets instead.[9]

---

6 For a definition, see Harrington, *Unwanted Child*, 7 ff.
7 NBR 293 (No. 303); Dok 1: 267 (No. 184).; addendum to J. S. Bach's "Origin of the Musical Bach Family."
8 Wolff BLM, 37–38.
9 Harrington, *Unwanted Child*, esp. Ch. 4.

102   Tanya Kevorkian

The next step in J. S. Bach's education shows how community members as well as family could help to circulate children. In March 1700, just before his fifteenth birthday, he left with his fellow Ohrdruf choral scholar Georg Erdmann for Lüneburg to finish his studies at the prestigious St. Michael's school. His boarding opportunities in Ohrdruf had run out, but the Ohrdruf cantor, the young Elias Herda, was an alumnus of St. Michael's and likely the person who helped get Bach and Erdmann choral scholarships in Lüneburg.[10] Johann Sebastian's move to Lüneburg also supports Harrington's argument that along with broader social norms and structures, "individual agency, contingency, and personal dispositions" were important in determining outcomes for individual youths.[11] Bach's older brother, Johann Jacob, sent back to Eisenach as an apprentice, followed well-trodden family footsteps in becoming a town musician in small-town central Germany. In contrast, Johann Sebastian moved unusually quickly through his schooling in both Eisenach and Ohrdruf, and then made the leap of finishing gymnasium in northern Germany. As Wolff notes, his family could have easily found him an apprenticeship in the area. However, his intelligence, voice, and willingness to travel more than 200 miles to Lüneburg helped set him on the path towards much greater prominence.

What of Bach's life once he entered the workforce? His marriage to his second cousin Maria Barbara Bach in 1707, four years after he began as organist in Arnstadt, was typical in that many men, including musicians, married around the time they started their first regular positions. Second-cousin marriages also were not uncommon. Guild masters were actually required to marry at the time they became masters, partly because the guild household required a female head of household and partly, as Lyndal Roper has shown, because the guild master's position as head of a married household was central to guild ideology.[12] Clerics also generally married close to the time when they attained regular positions.[13] Only a handful did not marry.[14] We do not know enough about how close other musicians' weddings were to their taking a first position to know how typical Bach was of his peers.

---

10 Wolff BLM, 39 ff.

11 Harrington, *Unwanted Child*, 285.

12 Lyndal Roper, *The Holy Household: Women and Morals in Reformation Augsburg* (Oxford: Oxford University Press, 1989); Heide Wunder, *He is the Sun, She is the Moon: Women in Early Modern Germany*, trans. Thomas Dunlap (Cambridge: Harvard University Press, 1998), 72 ff., and passim. On musicians, see Stephen Rose, *The Musician in Literature in the Age of Bach* (Cambridge: Cambridge University Press, 2011), Ch. 3.

13 Luise Schorn-Schütte, "Pfarrfrauen in der hansestädtischen Gesellschaft der Frühen Neuzeit," Barbara Vogel and Ulrike Weckel, eds., *Frauen in der Ständegesellschaft. Leben und Arbeiten in der Stadt vom späten Mittelalter bis zur Neuzeit* (Hamburg: Krämer, 1991), 201–225. For an overview of research on the clergy, see Luise Schorn-Schütte, "Priest, Preacher, Pastor: Research on Clerical Office in Early Modern Europe," *Central European History* 33 (2000): 1–37; Luise Schorn-Schütte and C. Scott Dixon, eds., *The Protestant Clergy of Early Modern Europe* (Houndmills: Palgrave Macmillan, 2003).

14 For example, the Leipzig cleric Adam Bernd; see Adam Bernd, *Eigene Lebens-Beschreibung* (Leipzig: Heinsius, 1738; reprint, Munich: Winkler, 1973).

Households 103

Bach remarried about a year and a half after losing his first wife. This was a bit under the average time that elapsed for urban professional and elite men between the time they were widowed and when they remarried. It was also typical that Anna Magdalena Wilcke was significantly younger than her husband. Arthur Imhof has found that more than 80% of men who were widowed before the age of fifty-five remarried; in their second marriages, they tended to marry young women who had not previously been married.[15] In contrast, only about 15–30% of women who were widowed before age fifty-five, and 7–15% of all widows, remarried. It is not clear whether this was because men favored younger women without their own children, or because widows preferred not to remarry; likely both issues were a factor.[16] Widows who did remarry also waited longer than men: about three to four years in contrast to about two for men. Anna Magdalena's not remarrying was thus typical of the times. Johann Sebastian's step-mother Margaretha, in contrast, had bucked the trend by remarrying twice by the age of thirty-six, although it was typical that her second husband was almost thirty years older than she was, and that her third (Ambrosius) was also older by fourteen years.[17]

Finally, what about Bach's lifespan of sixty-five years? J. S. lived far longer than any of his siblings, although four of his children lived longer than he. In the early modern period, fewer than one in 100 people lived past the age of sixty-five,[18] although survival rates were beginning to rise in the eighteenth century. This helps explain the very hearty language of Georg Philipp Telemann's long-time friend and colleague Johann Georg Pisendel as he congratulated Telemann on his sixty-eighth and seventieth birthdays in 1749 and 1751.[19] Neither Pisendel nor Telemann could know that Telemann would live another seventeen years, to the almost unbelievable age of eighty-seven.

Historians have debated the emotional lives of early modern families heatedly and in depth since the publication of Philippe Aries' *Centuries of Childhood* in French in 1960 and English in 1962.[20] Parents' bonds to their children have been the especial focus of interest. Aries argued that until the seventeenth century, parents had little emotional attachment to their children, and indeed perceived them as little adults. This began to change, initially among the nobility and wealthy, as infant and child mortality gradually dropped, the home and workplace separated, and people gained more privacy in their homes. Numerous scholars modified but

---

15 Arthur Imhof, "Wiederverheiratung in Deutschland zwischen dem 16. und dem Beginn des 20. Jahrhunderts," Rudolf Lenz, ed., *Studien zur deutschsprachigen Leichenpredigt der frühen Neuzeit* (Marburg: Schwarz, 1981), 185–222.

16 Also see Wunder, *He is the Sun, She is the Moon*, 30–31 and 134 ff.

17 Wolff BLM, 34.

18 Harrington, *Unwanted Child*, 97.

19 Pisendel to Telemann, letters of 16 April 1749 and 26 March 1751, Georg Philipp Telemann, *Briefwechsel*, eds. Hans Grosse & Hans Rudolf Jung (Leipzig: VEB Deutscher Verlag für Musik, 1972), 347–352 and 356–369.

20 Philippe Aries, *Enfant et la vie familiale sous l'Ancien Regime* (Paris: Plon, 1960); ET, *Centuries of Childhood: A Social History of Family Life* (New York: Vintage, 1962).

104   *Tanya Kevorkian*

essentially supported, and even sharpened, Aries' thesis in the 1970s, including Michael Mitterauer and Reinhard Sieder. More recently, some historians have argued that there is much evidence to the contrary, for example of parental grieving at the death of a child. Currently, a more nuanced picture which acknowledges elements of both arguments prevails. Also, there is now a consensus that the modern family started to emerge in the course of the eighteenth rather than seventeenth century.[21]

Johann Sebastian Bach famously left very little personal testimony or, indeed, detailed writing on any subject. Even musicians of the time who did write more extensively, such as Telemann or Johann Mattheson, recorded very little of their emotional lives, and in this, they were typical of their contemporaries. Thus, for the most part, one must guess regarding this subject. There are some clues, though. The very intense, graphic nature of many Baroque cantata and hymn texts, which often stress individuals' difficulties (usually described in generic terms), and how one can overcome those difficulties by relying on God and Christ, tells us that people did experience a full range of emotions, and that they often processed them in a religious framework.

We also have some more specific references. Several of these show that the Bach family identified itself by, and bonded around, music. They suggest that the Bachs' collective music-making created bonds that were stronger than those among many other families. Even accounting for the post-1750 mystique around J. S. Bach, they are noteworthy. In 1730, Bach wrote to his former schoolmate Georg Erdmann requesting help in finding a new job. In the last paragraph of the letter, Bach updates his friend about his family, mentioning his marriages and surviving children. He then writes in more descriptive language, "they are all born musicians, and I can assure you that I can already form an ensemble both *vocaliter* and *instrumentaliter* within my family, particularly since my present wife sings a good, clear soprano, and my eldest daughter, too, joins in not badly."[22] In his 1735 genealogical notes on the "Origin of the Musical Bach Family," Bach traced the family's musical impulse back four generations to the baker Veit Bach, who "found his greatest pleasure in a little cittern, which he took with him even into the mill and played upon while the grinding was going on.... And this was, as it were, the beginning of a musical inclination in his descendants."[23] In his 1802 biography of Bach, which relied on a variety of evidence that he gathered from Bach's sons, Johann Nikolaus Forkel wrote,

> the different members of this family had a very great attachment to each other ... they resolved at least to see each other once a year and fixed a certain day upon which they had all to appear at an appointed place. ... Their

---

21   For a review of the literature, see Harrington, *Unwanted Child*, introduction, or Hugh Cunningham, *Children and Childhood in Western Society Since 1500*, 2nd edition (New York: Pearson, 2005), introduction.

22   Letter to Erdmann, 28 October 1730, NBR 152 (No. 152); Dok 1: 68 (No. 23).

23   NBR 283 (No. 303).

Households 105

amusements, during the time of their meeting, were entirely musical. As the company wholly consisted of cantors, organists, and town musicians … and as it was besides a general custom at the time to begin everything with Religion, the first thing they did, when they were assembled, was to sing a chorale. From this pious commencement they proceeded to drolleries which often made a very great contrast with it. For now they sang popular songs, the contents of which were partly comic and partly naughty, all together and extempore … and not only laughed heartily at it themselves, but excited an equally hearty and irresistible laughter in everybody that heard them.[24]

Get-togethers might also be smaller in scale, and held at the Bach home, which functioned as a musical open house. In 1739, for example, Johann Sebastian's cousin's son Johann Elias, who lived with the family while he studied in Leipzig, serving as a correspondent and tutor, wrote, "just at that time something extra fine in the way of music was going on, my honored cousin from Dresden [Wilhelm Friedemann Bach], who was here for over four weeks, having made himself heard several times at our house along with the two famous lutenists Mr. Weise [Silvius Leopold Weiss] and Mr. [Johann] Kropffgans."[25]

The family's self-identification by music extended to collecting the compositions of forbears, a collection now called the Alt-Bachisches Archiv. J. S. passed this to C. P. E. Bach. Forkel wrote that C. P. E. "had a particular esteem for" Johann Christoph Bach, a town and court organist in Eisenach who was his first cousin twice removed and had died in 1703. Forkel wrote, "it is still quite fresh in my remembrance how good-naturedly the old man smiled at me at the most remarkable and hazardous passages when he once gave me the pleasure, in Hamburg, of letting me hear some of those old pieces."[26] In an addendum to his father's entry on Johann Christoph in the "Origin" (which included J. S.'s assessment, "He was a profound composer"), C. P. E. himself had noted, "This is the great and expressive composer."[27]

Although entries in the "Origin" are generally recorded without embellishment, two do note unusually intense emotions or bonds. Of a great-uncle, Johann, who had been a town musician and then organist in Erfurt and had died in 1673, J. S. wrote that he "[w]as twice married: first to Mistress Barbara Hoffmann, daughter of his beloved master, by whom he had one stillborn son, whom the mother followed in death half an hour later …"[28] Johann's attachment to his master, who J. S. notes "persuaded his father to let [Johann's] son be apprenticed to him," and the short interval between the death of Johann's stillborn son and wife, stood out sufficiently in family lore to be recorded a century later. The story was likely passed on through Ambrosius, who had worked with Johann (his uncle)

---

24 *On Johann Sebastian Bach's Life, Genius, and Works*; NBR 424; Dok 7: 16.
25 Letter of August 11, 1739; NBR, 204 (No. 209); Dok 2: 366 (No. 448).
26 NBR 423; Dok 7: 15. This Johann Christoph is no. 13 in the genealogical chart in NBR 285.
27 NBR 288 (No. 303); Dok 1: 265 (No. 184).
28 NBR 286; Dok 1: 256. Johann was no. 4 in the genealogical chart.

106   Tanya Kevorkian

as a young man in Erfurt.[29] And in another addendum to his father's genealogy, C. P. E. wrote of Ambrosius and his twin brother Johann Christoph,

> [t]hese twins are perhaps the only ones of their kind ever known. They loved each other extremely. They looked so much alike that even their wives could not tell them apart. ... Their speech, their way of thinking – everything was the same. In music, too, they were not to be told apart: they played alike and thought out their performances in the same way. If one fell ill the other did, too. In short, the one died soon after the other.[30]

The earliest generations of German musicologists already showed an interest in the social organization of musicians, especially of town musicians. Examining household sizes, duties of the town musicians and their assistants, and sources of income helped them to determine the numbers and competence of musicians, as well as the forces available to perform specific works. Also from the beginning, a direct or indirect interest in J. S. Bach's life and work drove some important research. In his 1921 article on Leipzig town musicians, Arnold Schering delineated working conditions, organization, relationships with the city council, household structures, and competition among wind and string players.[31] Several early articles in the *Bach-Jahrbuch*, for example those by Bernhard Friedrich Richter on town musicians and externally housed students at the school of St. Thomas in Leipzig, Schering's on the cornettist and trumpeter Gottfried Reiche, and Fritz Rollberg's on J. S. Bach's father Ambrosius, also provide valuable material.[32] Like these articles, Schering's volumes of the history of music in Leipzig and other early book-length works are based on extensive archival research, and show a real interest in musicians' household organization, work schedules, and relations with the authorities.[33]

These early musicologists built a detailed picture of the musician's household. It included apprentices, sometimes journeymen, and often extended family members. The male members of the household shared performance duties. In smaller towns, the head of household was also the head of the ensemble, which consisted of the master and his apprentices and journeymen; in larger towns with more than one town musician, the other ensemble members, who were more often regularly appointed town musicians themselves, did not live together. Apprentice and journeymen members of the household in smaller towns were sent to

---

29 Wolff BLM, 16.

30 NBR, 288; Dok 1: 258. This Johann Christoph was no. 12 in the genealogical chart.

31 Arnold Schering, "Die Leipziger Ratsmusik von 1650 bis 1775," AfMw 3 (1921): 17–53.

32 Bernhard Friedrich Richter, "Stadtpfeifer und Alumnen der Thomasschule in Leipzig zu Bachs Zeit," BJ 4 (1907): 32–78; Arnold Schering, "Zu Gottfried Reiches Leben und Kunst," BJ 15 (1918): 133–140; Fritz Rollberg, "Johann Ambrosius Bach: Stadtpfeifer zu Eisenach von 1671–1695," BJ 24 (1927): 133–152.

33 Arnold Schering, *Musikgeschichte Leipzigs*, Vol. 2: *Von 1650 bis 1723* and Vol. 3, *Johann Sebastian Bach und das Musikleben Leipzigs im 18. Jahrhundert* (Leipzig: Kistner & Siegel, 1926 and 1941).

perform watch duty and to play daily from church and council hall towers. In larger towns, watch duty was performed by non-musicians, although town musicians still had to play regularly from towers. The majority of the household's income was not the salary paid by the town, but rather "accidental" fees from weddings in particular, and also for playing at banquets, at New Year's, and other occasions. Incomes were usually barely enough to feed all mouths around the table. During mourning periods for nobles, when musicians were not allowed to play at weddings or other festive occasions for six months or even a full year, the household often fell into debt.

Post-World War II Germany saw the emergence of new leaders such as Walter Salmen, whose work explores musicians' incomes, working conditions, and relations with the authorities.[34] Although more work was done in the former West Germany, Leipzig in particular continued to be an East German center of research on the social history of musicians.[35] In the past twenty years, there has been a new wave of interest in town musicians. Studies have emphasized many of the same themes as older ones, but they offer detailed information about places for which there was no previous in-depth knowledge, such as Minden, Braunschweig, Rain am Lech in Bavaria, and the Bavarian Imperial cities.[36] In addition, some works offer imaginative approaches to the subject. Walter Salmen's *Zu Tisch mit Johann Sebastian Bach* provides a detailed examination of the households of J. S. Bach from the perspective of living space, diet, and leisure time.[37] And Stephen Rose examines the status and reputation of town musicians, organists, and cantors from the vantage point of Baroque novels, linking issues musicians faced in their

---

34 Walter Salmen, ed., *The Social Status of the Professional Musician from the Middle Ages to the 19th Century*, trans. Herbert Kaufmann and Barbara Reisner (New York: Pendragon, 1983); German original, *Der Sozialstatus des Berufsmusikers vom 17. bis zum 19. Jahrhundert* (Kassel: Bärenreiter, 1971). See especially the articles by Heinrich Schwab, "Zur sozialen Stellung des Stadtmusikanten," Salmen, ed., *Social Status*, 9–25, and Dieter Krickeberg, "Zur sozialen Stellung des deutschen Spielmanns im 17. und 18. Jahrhundert, besonders im Nordwesten," ibid., 26–42.

35 See the collected articles by Reinhard Szeskus: *Bach in Leipzig. Beiträge zu Leben und Werk von Johann Sebastian Bach* (Wilhelmshaven: Noetzel, 2003); see also Steffen Lieberwirth, *Die Entwicklung des Stadtpfeiferamtes der Stadt Leipzig unter Berücksichtigung des sozialen Status der Musiker* (Leipzig: Karl-Marx-University, 1979).

36 See Jürgen Brandhorst, *Musikgeschichte der Stadt Minden: Studien zur städtischen Musikkultur bis zum Ende des 19. Jahrhunderts* (Hamburg: Wagner, 1991); Werner Greve, *Braunschweiger Stadtmusikanten: Geschichte eines Berufstandes 1227–1828* (Braunschweig: Stadtarchiv und Stadtbibliothek, 1991); Christoph Lang, "Kirchen-, Turm- und Tanzmusik. Profil des Türmerberufes am Beispiel der Stadt Rain am Lech," *Musik in Bayern* 67 (2004): 39–77; Helen Green, "Musiker zwischen Stadt und Hof. Die Stadtpfeifer der bayerischen Reichsstädte und ihre Arbeitsstätten zur Zeit Maximilians I," *Musik in Bayern* 69 (2005): 5–28; Tanya Kevorkian, "Town Musicians in German Baroque Society and Culture," *German History* 30 (2012): 350–371.

37 Walter Salmen, *Zu Tisch mit Johann Sebastian Bach: Einnahmen und "Consumtionen" einer Musikerfamilie* (Hildesheim: Olms, 2009).

108   *Tanya Kevorkian*

professional lives, and those discussed by musicologists, to broader questions of early modern historiography.[38]

There is also a literature on organists and cantors. Much of it focuses on individuals rather than on the occupations as a social group. This is partly because, in a given town, there was usually only one cantor, and only one or a few organists. Histories of music in a given town generally feature detailed discussions of local cantors and organists. Separate studies of prominent individuals, ranging from Buxtehude to Telemann to J. S. and C. P. E. Bach, are also useful.

There is also a tradition of more general work on these groups. Arnfried Edler's 1982 work on north German organists remains a classic; some of its findings are summarized in English in the translation of Salmen's *Social Status of the Professional Musician*.[39] For cantors, Dieter Krickeberg's 1965 study and the multi-author *Struktur, Funktion und Bedeutung* of 1997 stand out.[40] Arno Werner's much older *Vier Jahrhunderte im Dienste der Kirchenmusik*, which addresses all of the urban musical occupations, comes from the same generation as the works of Schering.[41] Primary sources, notably Johann Mathheson's *Vollkommener Capellmeister*, are also instructive. Much like research on town musicians, these studies detail the musicians' education, duties, relationships with urban and court authorities, and social status and income. By the end of the seventeenth century, both cantors and organists had high status in mid-sized and larger towns, as well as at courts; they often had a university education. The studies examine cantors' and organists' music to a greater degree than research on town musicians, simply because far more of their manuscripts and printed scores survive. However, there is much less emphasis on their households. In part, this is because the apprentices and journeymen who lived with town musicians performed with them. They thus appear as urban employees in some records, and were also more clearly part of the town musicians' working lives.

The differences in emphasis in research on town musicians as opposed to organists and cantors are also a reflection of archival material available. Town musicians' activities were minutely regulated, and the monitoring generated many city council files. Town musicians also regularly did battle (sometimes physical) with competitors for wedding and other engagements. The competitors included country, court, and regimental musicians, as well as "beer fiddlers" living in

---

38 Rose, *The Musician in Literature in the Age of Bach*, especially Ch. 3, 4, and 6.

39 Arnfried Edler, *Der nordelbische Organist. Studien zu Sozialstatus, Funktion und kompositorischer Produktion eines Musikerberufes von der Reformation bis zum 20. Jahrhundert* (Kassel: Bärenreiter, 1982); idem, "The Social Status of Organists in Lutheran Germany from the 16th through the 19th Century," in Salmen, ed., *Social Status*, 61–93.

40 Dieter Krickeberg, *Das Protestantische Kantorat im 17. Jahrhundert: Studien zum Amt des deutschen Kantors* (Berlin: Merseburger, 1965); Wolf Hobohm, et. al., eds., *Struktur, Funktion und Bedeutung des deutschen protestantischen Kantorats im 16. bis 18. Jahrhundert* (Oschersleben: Ziethen, 1997).

41 Arno Werner, *Vier Jahrhunderte im Dienste der Kirchenmusik: Geschichte des Amtes und Standes der evangelischen Kantoren, Organisten und Stadtpfeifer seit der Reformation* (Leipzig: Merseburger, 1932).

Households 109

towns. Officially appointed wind and string players also competed with one another. Because the town musicians were defending privileges issued by town councils, their cases were handled by councilors, often in great detail. In contrast, while organists and cantors in Lutheran areas were appointed and paid by city councils, their legal jurisdiction lay primarily with the consistories. Organists and cantors did not have natural competitors of the types that plagued town musicians. Further, because of their higher social status and the settings in which they performed (church or at the homes or banquets of the wealthy), when and where they performed was not as tightly regulated. Fights with colleagues, consistories, and councilors over *what* they played—issues such as the choice of hymns or the style of organ accompaniment—were more frequent. In contrast, the types of pieces that town musicians played do not seem to have been challenged.

Research on town musicians, organists, and cantors has some drawbacks. There is still much less work on Catholic and Calvinist areas than on Lutheran areas. Musicians' relations with townspeople generally, apart from the urban authorities, have been neglected. Individual studies, which are numerous, could be synthesized to provide a more general picture. And there is very little emphasis on women or gender. There has been very little research even on Anna Magdalena Bach, who played distinct roles in the musical production of J. S. Bach's households, until very recently. Hans-Joachim Schultze wrote a thoughtful essay in 1990; the first scholarly book-length collection of documents relating to her, along with essays including recent research by Maria Hübner, and an article by Yo Tomita on Anna Magdalena as a copyist have appeared in recent years.[42] Women did not usually hold regular positions or perform, but their work in the household, as we will see, was indispensable. Studying gender involves examining relations between men and women, and expectations of male as well as female behavior. If one reconstructs a broader social history of music, including examining lyrics, audience makeup, and patronage, not only do women appear, but gender relations emerge as an important dynamic in the production and reception of music.[43]

A long historiographical tradition has examined the economic, social, and familial functions of early modern households. There have been several points of consensus across time. One is that the household rather than the family was the unit that was most important to contemporaries. This was especially true for

---

42 Maria Hübner, ed., *Anna Magdalena Bach: Ein Leben in Dokumenten und Bildern* (Leipzig: Evangelische Verlagsanstalt, 2004). The essay by Hans-Joachim Schultze, "Zumahln da meine itzige Frau gar einen sauberen Soprano singet," is included in this collection, 11–24. Yo Tomita, "Anna Magdalena as Bach's Copyist," UB 2 (2007): 59–76. Anna Magdalena was "copyist" not "composer," as sensationally claimed by Martin Jarvis, whose claims are academically discredited; see Ruth Tatlow, "A Missed Opportunity: Reflections on 'Written by Mrs. Bach,'" UB 10 (2015): 141–157.

43 The symposium "Poets, Mothers, and Performers: Considering Women's Impact on the Music of J. S. Bach," held at the Yale University Institute of Sacred Music in October 2009, was a significant event; see review by Tanya Kevorkian in *Bach Notes: Newsletter of the American Bach Society*, No. 12 (Winter 2010): 2–3.

110　*Tanya Kevorkian*

references to everyday life; when they thought in terms of long stretches of time, people tended to think more along the lines of direct descent, as we see with stories from the Bach family. When heads of households referred to "me and mine," they meant all residents: they often did not clearly distinguish among the "subject" members of the house: children, servants, tutors, and apprentices. In part, this was because the members' everyday lives were similar: except in wealthy households, they worked, ate, and often slept together. Also, servants and apprentices were often related to the heads of households.

Another point of consensus is that there was a reliance on every member of the household, apart from the very young and old, to work. Yet another is that the head of household, or *Hausvater*, ruled over all other residents; his wife, the *Hausmutter*, was a secondary authority figure with rights of her own, especially over children and apprentices. Finally, in early modern political thought, the household was the smallest political unit, and the house father a representative of the urban or rural authorities. Conversely, city councillors and nobles were conceived in paternalistic terms themselves.

Along with these broad areas of consensus, there have been shifts over time. Otto Brunner, whose term *das ganze Haus* is still invoked, wrote an early, influential article on the subject.[44] He worked primarily with the printed literature on the subject; his approach was through *Begriffsgeschichte*, or conceptual history, and he traced the history of the household from ancient times through the Middle Ages into the early modern period. Since the 1960s, historians have emphasized the distinctions between the prescriptive ideal found in the printed literature of the day, for example *Hausvaterliteratur*, and everyday realities. Through demographic and other archival studies, they have built a much more specific picture of rural, urban artisanal, urban elite, and noble households. They have examined how labor in and outside the household was conducted along lines of gender and status. Studies of architecture, diet, and leisure time have provided a better idea of the everyday life within a household. Several still-important studies emerged around 1990, following years of intensive research in the field. These include the first volume of Richard van Dülmen's *Kultur und Alltag*, which also provides a good overview; Lyndal Roper's *The Holy Household*, on gender, guild households, and the Reformation; and Heide Wunder's *He is the Sun, She is the Moon*, who also provides a general overview, along with an emphasis on interactions and distinctions among men and women.[45]

How can historians' insights into the household help us to understand musicians' households, lives, and work? Studies of urban households are most relevant here. Town musicians' households can best be compared to those of guildspeople, and cantors' and organists' to those of urban professionals. Musicians' households at

---

44　Otto Brunner, "Das 'ganze Haus' und die alteuropäische 'Ökonomik,'" Otto Brunner, *Neue Wege der Verfassungs- und Sozialgeschichte* (Göttingen: Vandenhoek & Ruprecht, 1956), 33–61; 2nd edition, 1968.

45　Van Dülmen, *Kultur und Alltag in der Frühen Neuzeit*. Vol. I, *Das Haus und seine Menschen, 16.–18. Jahrhundert* (Munich: Beck, 1990).

courts differed in several ways from them. However, some dynamics were common to most types of household. Similarities in J. S. Bach's own throughout his life exemplify these dynamics. After examining the commonalities, we will look at differences among occupations.

All households included a rotating cast of servants and/or relatives. Except for brief periods after house fathers Ambrosius and J. S. died, after which their households were dissolved (in some other cases, widows remarried within their previous husband's occupation, which allowed them to retain their households), a man was the head of household. A woman's presence was so important that after Ambrosius and J. S. were widowed, both men remarried relatively quickly. The male head of household had a specific work position and duties, and a direct relationship to the authorities. His wife bore children, supervised them and other household members with her husband, and was a source of flexible labor in her husband's field.

Education and training were important functions of the household. This was even more true for musicians than for guildspeople, merchants, clerics, and bureaucrats. Early training in music is key to attaining proficiency, and the early modern musical household provided an ideal training ground for budding musicians. Children not only received lessons, but were constantly exposed to performance in and outside the household. Boys in particular were likely dragooned into early service as instrument carriers, performers, and copyists. By their teens, boys might receive further, more formal training as apprentices in other households or Latin schools. If they were choristers, their training could begin earlier. Girls did not have these opportunities, but they were educated at home, and there are numerous examples, apart from Anna Magdalena Bach, of musicians' families at courts whose daughters became professional singers, often marrying other musicians.[46] Another major difference between boys and girls was that while musically gifted boys from families of non-musicians—Telemann and the Haydn brothers are examples—could become musicians because of the formal schooling available to them, girls from non-musical families were extremely unlikely to. Virtually all female professional musicians came from musicians' families. The same applied to female professional painters, engravers, and actresses,[47] again attesting to the power of training received in one's birth household.

The background of the household helps to explain why so many members of the Bach family became musicians. Although the Bachs were an extreme example, there were many other families who produced musicians across several generations. Members of many of these families intermarried. For example, Anna Magdalena Wilcke came from a family of court trumpeters and organists; Maria Barbara Bach's father was a musician; and the Strunck and Döbricht sisters, who dominated among the female singers at the Leipzig opera and were active at

---

46 On the Strunck and Döbricht sisters, who also worked as producers and librettists, see Michael Maul, *Barockoper in Leipzig (1693–1720)* (Freiburg: Rombach, 2009), 2 volumes, passim.

47 Wunder, *He is the Sun, She is the Moon*, 104–112.

112   *Tanya Kevorkian*

other operas, came from and married into musical families. Similarly, sons of jurist, clerics, and merchants often followed directly in their fathers' footsteps. Alternatively, they might become members of other professions in which relatives were active. For example, the son of a merchant might become a jurist, joining uncles or grandfathers in that profession, because the elites intermarried. Although some guildspeople followed directly in their fathers' footsteps, it was just as likely that they would enter other trades. For example, the son of a baker might become a wig maker. Intermarriage among children of guildspeople of different trades was the rule. In Leipzig, only a few trades, including tanners and printers, produced dynasties within one trade.

What of the role of women in the household? Historians have differed, sometimes sharply, on this point. Some, including Lyndal Roper, have emphasized the subjugation of women in the patriarchal structure, ideology, and everyday life of the household, pointing to the Reformation as a time when the household generally received an upward valuation in politics and religion (a point on which all historians agree), as well as an increase in emphasis on the subordination of women in the household. Others, including Heide Wunder and Luise Schorn-Schütte, emphasize the roles and rights that women did have, and the respect that they received for these.

We have little evidence for how J. S. Bach's mother, Maria Elisabeth, stepmother Margaretha, or two wives valued themselves or were valued by those around them. We do have indications of their roles, though. In Eisenach, Maria Elisabeth and (briefly) Margaretha would have helped supervise a larger and more directly work-related town musician's household than did Maria Barbara or Anna Magdalena in Cöthen. This meant acting as a surrogate mother to the apprentices, and seeing to the upbringing of children and step-children. In Eisenach and elsewhere, it also meant supervising cooking, cleaning, and laundry: all labor-intensive, time-consuming processes. Until her death in 1729, Maria Barbara's older sister Friedelena, who stayed with the family after Johann Sebastian's remarriage and moved to Leipzig, would have helped with all of this.

The Cöthen court's regular employment of Anna Magdalena as a singer made a huge difference in her role compared to that in Leipzig. This well-paying job had almost as high a salary as her husband's: 300 Thaler compared to 400 for Johann Sebastian[48] (although she would not have had most of the additional sources of accidental income that he did). With no comparable positions available in Leipzig, which is typical in this regard of other towns, Anna Magdalena lost not only income but also a public performance platform. She is documented as singing three times as a guest performer in Cöthen and Weissenfels to 1729,[49] well into her childbearing years, and thus must have continued to keep her voice in shape until then. We have no evidence of further public performances by her, but Johann Sebastian's reference in his 1730 letter to Erdmann, the status of

---

48 Wolff BLM, 204–05.
49 Hübner, *Anna Magdalena Bach*, 49–56.

Households   113

the Bach home as a musical open house, and Anna Magdalena's own history of training and performance since childhood make it likely that she continued to sing at home and in other homes. Hans-Joachim Schultze points out, though, that mundane household burdens on Anna Magdalena in Leipzig must have been considerable, and may have drained her of energy for musical activities.[50]

All of the women would have served as a source of flexible labor, a role identified by Roper and other historians. Although they did not have a formal title or certificate, women were generally familiar with the work processes of a household, and participated especially when there were shortages of labor. We see this in particular for Anna Magdalena's activities as a copyist. She made fair copies and doublets of many of J. S. Bach's most important works, especially in the winter, a time when musicologists speculate that the St. Thomas school students were most likely to be ill.[51] The timing does not clearly line up with her pregnancies; as Tomita notes, she was six and eight months pregnant, respectively, when she copied two scores,[52] and at other times had given birth just a few months earlier. Thus it was a need or desire for her copying skills that led to her activity.

What were the roles of the male head of household? Many of these roles had little to do with their occupations. They disciplined other household members when necessary, especially children, apprentices, and servants, brought up children, especially boys, and led domestic religious life. The house father was also responsible for the whereabouts of residents, especially for ensuring that they were not out and about at night and in tumultuous times. Thus, during times of unrest, city councils routinely reminded heads of household not to let their children, servants, or other residents of the house go out.

Even institutional living arrangements such as the St. Thomas school, and some public spaces, provided for paternalistic oversight. Tavern owners were responsible for keeping the peace in their taverns.[53] Orphanages and houses of correction in Leipzig and elsewhere had house fathers and mothers.[54] The St. Thomas school did not, but the office of inspector mimicked that of the house father. When Bach was cantor, he alternated with the school's rector and two teachers who did not live in the school building, in serving as inspector. Part of that once-monthly stint of a week involved making sure that the boys did not stay or sneak out on the streets at night. The inspector was also to supervise a student called the *calefactor* who woke the other students, and to supervise the students at their prayers, mealtimes, and singing hours.[55] Bach apparently refused to carry

---

50   Schultze, "Zumahln da meine itzige Frau," Hübner, *Anna Magdalena Bach*, 14.

51   See Tomita, "Anna Magdalena as Bach's Copyist," 63.

52   Tomita, "Anna Magdalena as Bach's Copyist," 64.

53   Ann Tlusty, *Bacchus and Civic Order: The Culture of Drink in Early Modern Germany* (Charlottesville: University of Virginia Press, 2001), 160–61.

54   See Tanya Kevorkian, "The Rise of the Poor, Weak, and Wicked: Poor Care, Punishment, Religion, and Patriarchy in Leipzig, 1700–1730," *Journal of Social History* 34 (2000): 163–181; Harrington, *Unwanted Child*, esp. Ch. 3 and 5.

55   *E.E. Hochweisen Raths der Stadt Leipzig Ordnung der Schule zu St. Thomae* (Leipzig: Tietze, 1723; facsimile, ed. Hans-Joachim Schultze, Leipzig: Zentralantiquariat, 1985), 27–32.

114   *Tanya Kevorkian*

out his inspection duties after 1730, and was joined by the rector in this by 1734,[56] but he likely performed them until then. City councilors took his refusal seriously as they accused him of not doing his job.

Other duties of the house father were more directly connected to his occupation. The male head of household supervised and taught apprentices and journeymen the skills of their trade; Ambrosius Bach and other family members who were town musicians would have spent considerable time with this, in addition to performing with the young men outside the home. J. S. Bach did not have apprentices, but he supervised copyists for the steady stream of cantata parts and scores, as well as for his other works, assigning work and then checking it. Copyists included schoolboys, his sons, and Anna Magdalena. He also gave his sons, perhaps his daughters, and university students music lessons in the cantor's service apartment, which was actually an entire wing of the school building and included fifteen rooms on five floors.[57] Not least, Bach composed, spending many hours in the composition study that was on the main (second) floor of the apartment.[58]

Comparisons of musicians' households to those of other occupations have hovered around the edges of this study. In conclusion, let us compare more specifically. In the urban context, town musicians' households, and their identities more generally, were most like those of guildspeople. As Stephen Rose emphasizes, musicians' novels and musicians' own testimony stressed guild morals and ideals: the regulated, thorough acquisition of skills; legitimate birth; honorable behavior in the urban context; and contrast to dishonorable interlopers such as "beer fiddlers."[59] As we have seen, the membership of the household, especially of apprentices and journeymen, was also similar. However, there were also major differences. Although town musicians showed some guild-like features, they rarely formed an actual guild.[60] In part, this may have been because there were not enough musicians. Small towns often only had one; even in the large town of Leipzig, there were only about eight altogether, and only one apprentice at a time. Unlike most guildspeople, the town musicians were city council employees, receiving part of their income and sometimes payment in kind from the council.

Perhaps most important, what town musicians offered was not a finished product but a public performance. They did produce, reproduce, and own scores, but they were not primarily composers; many did not compose at all. Their most prominent roles were as markers and keepers of public time: playing from towers and in the street, celebrating festive occasions and helping make church services memorable. Their other most frequent performances, at weddings, New Year's, and at celebrations such as church fairs, also marked special occasions or festivities. Although the authorities regulated the prices musicians could charge for weddings and other gigs, just as they regulated the prices of bread, saddles, and

---

56 NBR, 172 (No. 180; Dok 3: 314 (No. 820); Wolff BLM, 346, 350.
57 Salmen, *Zu Tisch*, 13–14.
58 Salmen, *Zu Tisch*, 13.
59 Rose, *The Musician in Literature in the Age of Bach*, esp. Ch. 3.
60 For this issue in Leipzig, see Schering, "Die Leipziger Ratsmusik."

wigs, a performance was a more transient, less substantial, and at the same time a more public and prominent product. What the town musician's household thus most importantly produced was musical skill. The distinction between typical guilds and musicians was not absolute: recent literature on guilds has emphasized artisans' roles in passing on skills;[61] but the difference in the households' products remains.

If town musicians can be compared most directly to artisans, cantors' and organists' households can best be compared to those of clerics and school teachers. Like clerics and teachers, they were church employees, appointed and regulated by the secular authorities, often lived in service apartments, generally did not have burgher or citizen status (unless they owned a home of their own), and thus were not, like other male heads of household, part of the burgher militia, subject to being mustered and called up for ceremonial and chaotic occasions. Payment in kind, especially of firewood, beer, and sometimes grain, was essential to the running of their households.[62] They often had a university education. Their households included wives, children, often servants, and also often university students who served as copyists and tutors. One thing their households produced was literate artifacts, especially scores, since composition was an important part of their occupation, at least in larger towns; most organists and cantors also had music libraries, just as a cleric generally had his theological library.

Another thing that cantors and organists produced was public performance. In this regard, they resembled town musicians; differences in status were balanced by similarities in product. In addition, members of all these groups worked closely together, especially in church. This brings us to a final research desideratum. The literature on the different musical occupations has for the most part been separate. This reflects real differences in activities, household composition, status, and musical relevance, as well as distinct source bases. However, we should remember more often that members of these groups not only frequently played together, but also had training that overlapped in many ways. Socially, too, they were connected: there was intermarriage among the groups, and one individual might shift from one occupation to another. It is useful to ask, then, how much commonality members of these occupations perceived among one another; what parallels there were between their overlapping occupations and, for example, printers, book binders, and publishers, who also often worked together, and whose occupations were linked; and what new insights such an examination might provide into the social history of music.

---

61 S.R. Epstein and Maarten Prak, eds., *Guilds, Innovation, and the European Economy* (Cambridge: Cambridge University Press, 2008).
62 For Bach and payment in kind, see Salmen, *Zu Tisch, passim.*

6 Schools

Markus Rathey

Johann Sebastian Bach spent almost half of his life at schools, first as a schoolboy in a number of central and north German cities and then, from 1723 until the end of his life, as a teacher at the Thomas School in Leipzig. Even between these two framing periods, he collaborated with boys' choirs and music teachers at local schools in Arnstadt and Mühlhausen. Only during the fifteen years at the courts in Weimar and Cöthen (1708–1723), Bach was without a position that was directly linked to an institution of learning. But even in Weimar, cantor Georg Theodor Reineccius supplied boys from the school to sing with the court chapel musicians.[1]

The early modern school was not only a house of learning but also an important source for religious formation and the place where lifelong contacts and friendships were forged. Bach met his friend Georg Erdmann (1692–1736) at the Lyceum in Ohrdruf; the friendship continued when both moved to Lüneburg and lasted until Erdmann's untimely death.[2] Schools taught the basics of knowledge and laid the epistemological groundwork for the understanding of the world. The schools were also the main carriers of musical life in Protestant German cities from the Reformation until the second half of the eighteenth century. A familiarity with traditions and conventions of music education and musical practice is therefore essential for an understanding of the institutional and performative contexts for Bach's works.

Music lessons were an integral part of the curriculum, and school choirs represented the main body of singers for Protestant church services in Bach's time. Schools also provided basic introductions in music theory and performance practice. Treatises published for use in schools were a valuable source for the performance and understanding of music in the seventeenth and early eighteenth centuries. Furthermore, theater plays and even singspiels were performed at schools. Christian Weise (1642–1708) was one of the most influential authors of school plays and had an important impact on authors of dramas and opera

---

1 See Chapter 7.
2 See the two [extant] letters Bach sent to Erdmann in NBR 125–126 (No. 120) and 151–152 (No. 152); Dok 5: 85 (No. A13); Dok 1: 67–68 (No. 23).

librettos in the latter part of the seventeenth century. Although Bach never composed nor produced an opera, he would have performed plays during his time at school, some of them surely with incidental music. Information about Bach's involvement in these activities is lost but these activities were such an integral part of the education that it is feasible to assume his involvement either way.

Bach's time at school and the curriculum under which he spent his years of education has been covered in several important studies. The most important recent publications on this topic are Peter Lundgren's article "Schulhumanismus, pädagogischer Realismus und Neuhumanismus. Die Gelehrtenschule zur Zeit J. S. Bachs"[3] and Martin Petzoldt's "'Ut probus & doctus reddar'. Zum Anteil der Theologie bei der Schulausbildung Johann Sebastian Bachs in Eisenach, Ohrdruf und Lüneburg."[4] Both provide a wealth of information about the content and context of Bach's education and on shifts in pedagogy during his lifetime.[5]

Bach spent most of his working life at the Thomas School in Leipzig. The school orders for this institution have been edited by Hans-Joachim Schulze (who also provides an excellent commentary).[6] A recent collection of essays on the relationship among music, arts, and sciences in the time of Johann Sebastian Bach (*Musik, Kunst und Wissenschaft im Zeitalter Johann Sebastian Bachs*), published in 2005, is an invaluable resource for the study of Bach as a student and as a teacher.[7]

Finally, more general studies of the German school system in the early modern period are available.[8] Despite their early publication years, Friedrich Paulsen's *Geschichte des gelehrten Unterrichts* from 1919 through 1921[9] as well Otto Kaemmel's *Geschichte des Leipziger Schulwesens* from 1909[10] remain important sources. The views of education promoted in the two books are outdated and

---

3 Peter Lundgren, "Schulhumanismus, pädagogischer Realismus und Neuhumanismus. Die Gelehrtenschule zur Zeit J. S. Bachs," LBB 7 (2005): 25–38.

4 Martin Petzoldt, "'Ut probus & doctus reddar'. Zum Anteil der Theologie bei der Schulausbildung Johann Sebastian Bachs in Eisenach, Ohrdruf und Lüneburg," BJ 71 (1985): 7–42.

5 A recent study exploring Bach's life and work from a music-pedagogical perspective does not provide new information but consists, at least for the biographical part, mainly of paraphrases and quotations from the Bach biographies by Christoph Wolff and others; Suzanne van Kempen, *Bach–musikpädagogisch betrachtet* (Frankfurt: Lang, 2009).

6 For a recent overview of the life at the schools of St. Thomas and St. Nicholas in Leipzig that does not focus on Bach and his legacy, see Annemarie Mieth, "Die Leipziger Schulen Thomana und Nicolaitana im Spiegel humanistischer, aufklärerisch-pietistischer und neuhumanistischer Entwicklungen," *Pensée pédagogique: enjeux, continuités et ruptures en Europe du XVIe au XXe siècle*, eds. Monique Samuel-Scheyder and Philippe Alexandre (Bern: Lang, 1999), 23–37.

7 LBB 7 (2005).

8 For a bibliographical overview of the development of the schools between the end of the Thirty Years' War and the end of the eighteenth century, see Anton Schinding, *Bildung und Wissenschaft in der Frühen Neuzeit 1650–1800* (Oldenbourg: München, 1994).

9 See Friedrich Paulsen, *Geschichte des gelehrten Unterrichts auf den deutschen Schulen und Universitäten vom ausgange des Mittelalters bis zur Gegenwart*, 3rd ed. (Leipzig: Veit, 1919–1921; reprint Berlin: de Gruyter, 1965).

10 Otto Kaemmel, *Geschichte des Leipziger Schulwesens vom Anfange des 13. bis gegen die Mitte des 19. Jahrhunderts (1214–1846)* (Leipzig: Teubner, 1909).

118   *Markus Rathey*

the interpretations are not always correct; however, both provide valuable selections of sources that are otherwise not easily available. The most recent survey of the history of German schools is the multivolume *Handbuch der deutschen Bildungsgeschichte*, edited by Notger Hammerstein and others. Relevant for Bach's time in particular are the first two volumes, which cover the fifteenth through eighteenth centuries.[11] The collection is the most up-to-date study of education and schooling in Germany between the Reformation and the end of the eighteenth century. The most current and comprehensive study on the history and practice of music education in Bach's time is John Butt's *Music Education and the Art of Performance in the German Baroque* (1994), which covers a wide array of topics including the role of practical music in education, the content of instruction books, and the implications for performance practice.[12]

As Wolfgang Neugebauer warned in his article in the *Handbuch der deutschen Bildungsgeschichte*, it would be a critical mistake to approach the school system of the seventeenth and eighteenth centuries with a modern mindset and the expectation to find the degree of organization and structure that was only accomplished over the course of the nineteenth century.[13] Attempts for organization via school orders and reforms by princes and dukes were one thing, but much depended on the willingness of local authorities and even more on the abilities of the individual teachers, who mostly lacked a pedagogical education and were freshly minted young theologians eager to move on to a parish. School orders, curricula, and textbooks can only provide a framework for what Bach (and his classmates) might have learned but they are not always a reliable reflection of the actual lessons.

Scholars rarely bridge the gap between general topics of academic education and music education. Most studies on music education in the baroque mention the important pedagogical reformers Reyher and Comenius only in passing, whereas music education is rarely brought up in studies on education in the seventeenth and eighteenth centuries (this is even the case for the otherwise excellent *Handbuch der deutschen Bildungsgeschichte*). It would be desirable to see these two aspects as a unit and to explore the influence of pedagogical concepts and reforms on music education in the time of Bach.

The following overview will first outline the pedagogical concepts of the Lutheran Reformation, which guided the way for the next 250 years of German

---

11 Notker Hammerstein, et al, *Handbuch der deutschen Bildungsgeschichte* (Munich: Beck, 1987–): *Band I: Das 15. bis 17. Jahrhundert: Von der Renaissance und der Reformation bis zum Ende der Glaubenskämpfe* (1996); *Band II: 18. Jahrhundert: Vom späten 17. Jahrhundert bis zur Neuordnung Deutschlands um 1800* (2005). A short and comprehensive overview of the schools in central Germany is the following article: Andreas Lindner, "Stationen der Geschichte des evangelischen Schulwesens der Frühen Neuzeit in Mitteldeutschland," *Das evangelische Schulwesen in Mitteldeutschland. Stationen und Streifzüge*, eds. Andreas Lindner and Andrea Schulte (Münster: Waxmann, 2007), 11–67.

12 John Butt, *Music Education and the Art of Performance in the German Baroque* (Cambridge: Cambridge University Press, 1994).

13 Wolfgang Neugebauer, "Niedere Schulen und Realschulen," *Handbuch der deutschen Bildungsgeschichte*, 2: 213.

Schools   119

school history; then I will turn to the seventeenth century school reforms, which led to the forms and ideals of teaching Bach would have experienced in the 1690s. Bach's own time as a student will be the focus of the third part of this essay before we finally turn to Bach as a teacher in Leipzig. This last section will combine an analysis of the pedagogical reforms in Leipzig and Bach's own duties as a teacher at the Thomas School.

Schools During the Lutheran Reformation

The Protestant Reformation in the first half of the sixteenth century had not only shattered the religious and social foundations of Germany, but had also made necessary a reform of the educational system, as most of the schools in the Middle Ages had been controlled by the church.[14] The Reformation, for a short time, caused a crisis in the schools and universities in Germany; however, this situation was soon resolved.[15] Spearheaded by Luther's friend and collaborator, the humanist Philipp Melanchton, the schools in the Lutheran territories of Germany underwent a thorough reform that began in the middle of the 1520s.[16] Luther's treatise "An die Ratsherren aller Städte deutschen Landes, daß sie christliche Schulen aufrichten und erhalten sollen" from 1524 marks the beginning of the reforms, but the practical realization lay in the hands of Melanchthon. The latter was often called "Praeceptor Germaniae" (teacher of Germany), a name that reflects his importance for the reform.[17] One of Luther's and Melanchthon's primary goals was to raise the general level of education and to enable the students to read the essential documents of Christian faith (Bible and catechism). On a larger scale (as part of Lutheran work ethics), the goal was to educate the pupils to be able to make significant contributions to society within their divinely ordained occupations. In Melanchthon's view of a reformed school, he emphasized the "*artes dicendi*," the proficiency in subjects like Latin and rhetoric, while deemphasizing the role of math and history.[18]

---

14 For a short systematic overview of the medieval school system from a musicological perspective, see Leeman L. Perkins, *Music in the Age of the Renaissance* (New York: Norton, 1999), 55–87.

15 See Notker Hammerstein, "Die historische und bildungsgeschichtliche Physiognomie des konfessionellen Zeitalters," *Handbuch der deutschen Bildungsgeschichte*, 1: 68–70.

16 Some of the ideas for the reforms were, of course, already prepared by pre-reformatory humanist thinkers; see Arno Seifert, "Das höhere Schulwesen. Universitäten und Gymnasien," *Handbuch der deutschen Bildungsgeschichte*, 1: 226–253.

17 See the excellent chapter on Melanchthon's reforms in Heinz Scheible, *Melanchthon. Eine Biographie* (Munich: Beck, 1997), 28–56; for the theological context of the reforms, see Markus Wriedt, "Die theologische Begründung der Schul- und Universitätsreform bei Luther und Melanchthon," *Humanismus und Wittenberger Reformation. Festgabe anläßlich des 500. Geburtstages des Praeceptor Germaniae Philipp Melanchthon am 16. Februar 1997*, eds. Michael Beyer and Günther Wartenberg (Leipzig: Evangelische Verlagsanstalt, 1996), 155–183.

18 Arno Seifert, "Das höhere Schulwesen. Universitäten und Gymnasien," *Handbuch der deutschen Bildungsgeschichte*, 1: 281.

120 *Markus Rathey*

The Reformation knew two different types of schools: the Latin and the German. While the Latin schools had their roots in the Middle Ages and were only reformed by Melanchthon, the German schools emerged during the sixteenth century as an attempt to elevate the level of literacy among the population and to enable them to read the Bible and the catechism.[19] While compulsory schooling existed as an ideal, it was not widely realized in Germany before the nineteenth century.[20] The German school had, since the sixteenth century, normally consisted of one room where boys[21] of different ages and knowledge were educated together by a schoolmaster. Larger cities also had a number of so-called "Winkelschulen" (hedge-schools, literally "corner-schools"), small schools privately run by schoolmasters but not supervised by the authorities. These schools were frequently criticized and sometimes closed by the authorities; however, they constituted an important part of the education of wide parts of the population.[22]

The main focus of the educational reforms, however, was on the reorganization of the Latin schools. Melanchthon laid the groundwork for his reforms during his participation in the Saxon Church and School Visitation in 1527–28. In his *Unterricht der Visitatoren*,[23] Melanchthon develops a model according to which the children should be divided into three groups: the elementary level, where the pupils learned to read, write, and sing; acquired a basic understanding of faith; and learned the foundations of Latin.[24] On the second level, the students were taught Latin grammar (based on some canonical antique texts) and received further teaching in Christian faith by reading biblical texts from the Old and New Testaments. The majority of students left school after this level because they had learned everything they would need for a future profession in trade or crafts. On the third level (which was only intended for the most accomplished), the pupils received further training in Latin grammar and were taught rhetoric and

---

19 Lundgren, "Schulhumanismus," 26.

20 James Van Horn Melton, *Absolutism and the Eighteenth-Century Origins of Compulsory Schooling in Prussia and Austria* (Cambridge: Cambridge University Press, 1988). The book begins with a short but useful introduction into educational reforms under Luther and Melanchthon and explains the later reforms of the German schools in the seventeenth century.

21 Most of the school reforms during the early modern period focused on the schooling of boys; however, girls' schools also existed and were of increasing importance; see Christine Mayer, "Erziehung und Schulbildung für Mädchen," *Handbuch der deutschen Bildungsgeschichte*, 2: 188–211.

22 For the German "Winkelschulen," see Christopher R. Friedrichs, "Whose House of Learning? Some Thoughts on German Schools in Post-Reformation Germany," *History of Education Quarterly 22/3*, (1982): 371–377, *Special Issue: Educational Policy and Reform in Modern Germany.* See also Wolfgang Neugebauer, "Niedere Schulen und Realschulen," *Handbuch der deutschen Bildungsgeschichte*, 2: 215.

23 Published in Emil Sehling, *Die Kirchenordnungen des XVI. Jahrhunderts, Erste Abtheilung, Erste Hälfte* (Leipzig: Reisland 1902), 149–174; for a modern edition see *Melanchthons Werke in Auswahl*, ed. Robert Stupperich, 7 vols. (Gütersloh: Bertelsmann/ Mohn, 1951), 1: 216–271.

24 For an overview on basic schooling and literacy among German children in the early modern period, see Richard Gawthrop and Gerald Strauss, "Protestantism and Literacy in Early Modern Germany," *Past & Present* 104 (1984): 31–55.

dialectic. The goal was to enable them to write and speak Latin, which was the language of the international intellectual discourse and an indispensable basis for studies in theology, law, and medicine.[25] It is important to note that the three levels do not necessarily reflect the pupils' age; students ascended to a higher grade based on their accomplishments and not based on the years they had spent in school. Music was part of the education on all three levels[26] and the students were expected to sing in the school choir (*Cantorei*) on Sundays, feast days, and special occasions during the week. Already during the early Reformation, music teachers published treatises for use at the Latin schools, which taught the basics of music notation, singing, and (especially later in the seventeenth century) also elementary rules of performance practice.[27]

The curriculum of the Latin schools was based on the model of the medieval system of the seven liberal arts (*septem artes liberales*). The emphasis of the teaching was on the arts of the *trivium*, the language-related arts, and on grammar and rhetoric in particular. The third element of the *trivium*, dialectics, was not taught at every school, but was sometimes included in the curriculum.[28] The teaching was based on two basic texts—the catechism and the Latin grammar—representing the two ideals of early modern education, *pietas* (piety) and *eloquencia* (eloquence).[29] The latter was further accomplished by studying canonical classical authors. The reading of these authors focused mainly on the study of grammatical rules and constructions as well as the identification and application of phrases and rhetorical figures that could be used for the pupils' own speeches. In other words, the texts were not studied as esthetical objects or for their historical value but as models for the acquisition of a good Latin style.

The subjects of the *quadrivium* (arithmetic, geometry, astronomy, and the theory of music) were not taught extensively; often, the schools limited the teaching of this sector of knowledge to basic math and music, theoretical knowledge that was necessary to sing in the choir.[30] The emphasis of the school education during and after the Reformation was on language and language-related subjects.

---

25 For the importance of Latin in the early modern university and the scholarly discourse see the excellent overview by Manfred Fuhrmann, *Latein und Europa. Geschichte des gelehrten Unterrichts in Deutschland. Von Karl dem Großen bis Wilhelm II* (Cologne: DuMont, 2001).

26 For music education in German Latin schools, see the older but still reliable study by Klaus Wolfgang Niemöller, *Untersuchungen zu Musikpflege und Musikunterricht an den deutschen Lateinschulen vom ausgehenden Mittelalter bis um 1600* (Regensburg: Bosse, 1969).

27 The most influential book in the time of the Reformation was the treatise by Heinrich Faber, *Compendiolum musicae pro incipientibus* from 1548, which was repeatedly reprinted, plagiarized, and paraphrased in the next 150 years. A reprint of a later edition of the book appeared in 1980: *Henrici Fabri Compendiolum musicae pro incipientibus, Bibliotheca musica bononiensis*, II/20 (Nuremberg: Paul Kauffmann, 1594; reprint, Bologna: Forni, 1980). For an overview of the music-theoretical context of the school books, see Werner Braun, *Geschichte der Musiktheorie 8: Deusche Musiktheorie des 15. bis 17. Jahrhunderts, 2 vols.* (Darmstadt: Wissenschaftliche Buchgesellschaft, 1994).

28 Lundgren, "Schulhumanismus," 26.

29 Paulsen, *Geschichte des gelehrten Unterrichts* 2: 48.

30 Lundgren, "Schulhumanismus," 26.

122   Markus Rathey

This would become one of the targets of major criticism during the reform of the school system in Germany from the middle of the seventeenth century.

School Reforms in the Seventeenth Century

The school system in the seventeenth and eighteenth centuries underwent a dramatic change, which in turn had an impact on Bach's own education. A target of criticism was in particular the strong focus on grammar instead of more practical subjects. The goals of these reforms can be summarized in the short phrase *realia, non verba* (concrete things, not words). Reformers demanded, as Paulsen has summarized, that the schools not only teach Latin, but also include practical subjects such as math, sciences, history, and geography.[31] The shift is a fundamental one. Instead of teaching language as a tool to understand the world, the school reformers demanded direct access to methods and paradigms that led to an understanding of the world.

The demand for reforms reflected several developments that took place in the decennia after the reformation. One of these was the increasing importance of the natural sciences in the late sixteenth and early seventeenth centuries, fueled by new discoveries and the proliferation of the experimental sciences. But the push for educational reform also had economic reasons, as trade became increasingly international and German merchants were challenged by their Dutch competitors. Educators felt the need to teach a practical knowledge that could secure success in an international market, which included practical abilities like math, geography, and modern languages.[32] Finally, the paradigm shift towards a more practical approach also had a religious component, as theologians after the turn of the century placed a stronger emphasis on a *praxis pietatis*, the living of faith in everyday life. Although Lutheran orthodoxy had stressed the "true faith" (while often neglecting the "practical faith"), reform theologians like Johann Valentin Andreae (1586–1654) and Johann Arndt (1555–1621) highlighted the practical side of Christianity. The two theologians were not necessarily leading figures in the school reforms of the seventeenth century, notwithstanding Andreaes's criticism that Latin was the goal of teaching instead of being just the language of teaching;[33] however, both of them strongly influenced later thinkers. Andreae had a strong impact on the ideas and reforms of Jan Amos Comenius,[34] and both Andreae and especially Johann Arndt with his books on

---

31 Paulsen, *Geschichte des gelehrten Unterrichts*, 1: 483.

32 Wilhelm Kühlmann, "Pädagogische Konzeptionen," *Handbuch der deutschen Bildungsgeschichte*, 1: 177–178.

33 Kühlmann, "Pädagogische Konzeptionen," 168–169.

34 Martin Brecht, "'Er hat uns die Fackel übergeben...' Die Bedeutung Johann Valentin Andreaes für Johann Amos Comenius," *Das Erbe des Christian Rosenkreuz* (Amsterdam: de Pelikaan, 1988), 28–47; and a short summary of Brecht's observations in his history of Pietism: Martin Brecht, ed., *Der Pietismus vom siebzehnten bis zum frühen achtzehnten Jahrhundert (Geschichte des Pietismus 1)* (Göttingen: Vandenhoeck & Ruprecht, 1993), 165–166.

Schools 123

"true Christianity" helped shape the religious and pedagogical reforms of August Hermann Francke's Halle Pietism towards the turn of the next century.[35]

The leading figures in the reform programs during the early and mid-seventeenth century were the northern German educator Wolfgang Ratke (or Ratchius; 1571–1635) and the Moravian theologian and teacher Jan Amos Comenius (1592–1670), followed by Andreas Reyher (1601–1673) and Johann Buno (1617–1697) in the next generation. The new views of education found their way into school ordinances that were issued during the seventeenth century and also into new school books such as Comenius's *Janua linguarum reserata* and *Vestibulum*, two books for the teaching of Latin that Bach would have used as a student in his Latin lessons.[36] Most successful was Comenius's influential *Orbis sensualium pictus*, a schoolbook for the lower grades, in which all facets of the material and spiritual world were depicted and clearly labeled in Latin and the vernacular.[37] The book, first published in Nuremberg in 1657, saw numerous editions in the following decades, and was translated into several languages.[38] The book is paradigmatic for the shift in education from the focus on grammar to the "things of the world." The topics covered in the book include the description of God and the world, images depicting the human body and its parts, husbandry, baking and fishing, religion (including Christianity and Islam), and finally the Last Judgment. The book is an encyclopedia of early modern knowledge and is important not only for our understanding of education in the seventeenth century but also for our understanding of the early modern period worldview.[39]

A historiographic counterpart to Comenius's *Orbis sensualium pictus* is the *Idea historiae universalis* (Lüneburg 1672), by Johann Buno, a comprehensive and highly influential history book (with a natural emphasis on Germany) that covers the span of human history from creation to the most recent times. Buno employs an effective mnemonic device by using images that refer to certain letters of the alphabet, which in turn identify the century. It is significant that Buno places a similar emphasis on pictorial representation as Comenius does, albeit

35 Erhard Peschke, *Bekehrung und Reform. Ansatz und Wurzeln der Theologie August Hermann Franckes (Arbeiten zur Geschichte des Pietismus 15)* (Bielefeld: Luther-Verlag, 1977), 115–135.

36 Raymond Erickson, "Introduction: The Legacies of J. S. Bach," *The World of Johann Sebastian Bach*, ed. Raymond Erickson (New York: Amadeus, 2009), 22–23.

37 For a general overview of the form, style, and use of textbooks in schools during the early modern period, see the collection of essays *Scholarly Knowledge: Textbooks in Early Modern Europe*, eds. Emidio Campi, Simone de Angelis, Anja-Silvia Goeing and Anthony Grafton (Geneva: Droz, 2008). Wilhelm Kühlmann gives a short account of the different types of pedagogical texts, ranging from treatises of pedagogy to textbooks for school children in his chapter "Pädagogische Konzeptionen," *Handbuch der deutschen Bildungsgeschichte*, 1: 156–159.

38 Kühlmann points out that the book was successful until the time of Goethe in the second half of the eighteenth century; Kühlmann, "Pädagogische Konzeptionen," 171.

39 For Comenius see Daniel Murphy, *Comenius: A Critical Reassessment of His Life and Work* (Dublin: Irish Academic Press, 1995); and M. W. Keatinge, *The Historical Life of John Amos Comenius* (Whitefish: Pessinger, 2005). A reprint of Comenius' *Orbis Pictus* was published by Keatinge, *Comenius, Orbis Pictus* (Whitefish: Kessinger Publishers, 2007).

124   Markus Rathey

now functionalized for mnemonic purposes. Bach, (already) during his studies at Ohrdruf, would have used this school book.[40] And John Butt has recently pointed out that the presentation of knowledge (and of history in particular) in books like this shaped Bach's own perception of human history and of historical development.[41]

The most influential reformer for the central German territory was Andreas Reyher, who was one of the disciples of Comenius. Reyher was serving as rector at the St. Michael's School in Lüneburg when Duke Ernst the Pious of Saxony-Gotha employed him as rector at the Latin school (Gymnasium) in Gotha and, even more importantly, as adviser to the Duke for a groundbreaking reform of the schools in the territory.[42] The school reforms in Saxe-Gotha were a part of a larger scale reform of society including religion, social control of the subjects, and a redesign of the administrative structure towards an early-absolutist model spearheaded by Veit Ludwig of Seckendorf (1626–1692).[43]

Reyher published a treatise on education, the *Methodus oder Bericht wie [die] Schuljugend [...] unterrichtet werden soll* (Gotha 1642, with numerous later editions), which served as a model for the reforms in Gotha and other territories in Germany.[44] Like Comenius, Reyher emphasized the teaching of *"realia"* in the schools of the Gotha territory, without neglecting the classical Latin and the teaching of religion. In a teaching plan developed for the schools in Gotha, he demanded that one of the main parts of the Small Catechism be taught to the children each day.[45] He furthermore reworked Comenius's already revolutionary Latin

---

40 Wolff BLM, 40.

41 John Butt, *Bach's Dialogue with Modernity. Perspectives on the Passions* (Cambridge: Cambridge University Press, 2010), 118–119; see also the earlier study, Jan Chiapusso, "Bach's Attitude towards History," MQ 39 (1953): 396–414.

42 For the reforms of Ernst the Pious, see the recent study Veronika Albrecht-Birkner, *Reformation des Lebens. Die Reformen Herzog Ernst des Frommen von Sachsen-Gotha und ihre Auswirkungen auf Frömmigkeit, Schule und Alltag im ländlichen Raum* (Leipzig: Evangelische Verlags, 2002).

43 For a recent assessment of von Seckendorf's impact on the reforms see Andreas Klinger, "Veit Ludwig von Seckendorff's 'Fürsten Stat' and the Duchy of Saxe-Gotha," *European Journal of Law and Economics*, 19 (2005): 249–266.

44 On Reyher and his reforms, see Gerd Hohendorf, "Über den Einfluß ratichianischer und comenianischer pädagogischer Theorien auf den Gothaer Schulmethodus des Andreas Reyher (1642)," in *Diesterweg verpflichtet. Beiträge zur deutschen Bildungsgeschichte*, ed. Gerd and Ruth Hohendorf (Köln: Böhlau, 1994), 36–43 and *Andreas M. Reyher: Magister, Pädagoge, Schulreformer 1601–1673. Festschrift zum 400. Geburtstag am 4. Mai 2001* (Suhl: Suhl-Information, 2001); an interesting overview on Reyher's impact on the teaching of math is provided by Manfred Weidauer, "Andreas Reyher (1601–1673): Rechenbuchautor und Reformpädagoge," in *Rechenbücher und mathematische Texte der frühen Neuzeit*, ed. Rainer Gebhardt (Annaberg-Buchholz 1999), 323–330. For source studies on Reyher see the excellent publication: Annette Gerlach, Cornelia Hopf, Susanne Werner, *Magister Andreas Reyher (1601–1673). Handschriften und Drucke. Bestandsverzeichnis* (Gotha: Forschungs- und Landesbibliothek, 1992).

45 Robin A. Leaver, *Luther's Liturgical Music. Principles and Implications* (Grand Rapids, MI: Eerdmans, 2007), 112–113.

textbook *Janua Linguarum* (1631). Comenius's book contained 1000 sentences in Latin, topically arranged in chapters on topics of religion (the creation of the world), the human body (for instance on the external senses), or on aspects of everyday life (like cattle or sports). The book bridges the gulf between *"verbae"* of classical, humanist education, and *"realia"* of seventeenth-century reform pedagogy. The arrangement of knowledge resembles that of Comenius's *Orbis sensualium pictus*, albeit without the use of images. Although Comenius's *Janua* still has an encyclopedic perspective, spanning the gamut of all human knowledge, Reyher drastically cut the number of chapters and topics, instead focusing on those things he thought were suitable and necessary for the education of young school children.[46] Instead of beginning with a cosmological view of God the creator and the world, Reyher's revision begins with the immediate environment of the young student: the school and the things of his world.[47]

The reforms by Comenius, Reyher, and others were important but did not entirely change the face of education. The changes were not as rapid as most of them would have wished, and the schools still emphasized the learning of Latin grammar[48] more than the sciences of life. Even in the territory of Saxe-Gotha, the reforms by Reyher and Ernst the Pious were not as successful as some of the sources might suggest. As Neugebauer points out, the introduction of *"realia"* was met by citizens' resistance.[49]

Martin Petzoldt has suggested, in his article "'Ut probus & doctus reddar.' Zum Anteil der Theologie bei der Schulausbildung Johann Sebastian Bachs,"[50] that Reyher's "Kleine Dialoge" (1653) had to be seen as a backbone for Bach's early education in *quarta* and *quinta*, combining the study of language with religious education.[51] However, Lundgren challenges Petzoldt's assessment that Reyher was the "Schulvater der Bildung" (school father of education) for Bach who left his mark on the composer for the rest of his life. Lundgren points out that the "Kleine Dialoge" was only used in the lower classes of the Latin school. But since Bach did not leave school after *quinta*, the assessment of Reyher's book as a key text for his schooling seems exaggerated to Lundgren, who suggests that other books also have to be taken into account.[52] The dissent between Lundgren and Petzoldt makes clear that the study of the influence of the worldview and perception of reality presented in these school books is still at its infancy. John Butt has, as mentioned previously, related Buno's history textbook to Bach's view of

---

46 Erickson, "Introduction: The Legacies of J. S. Bach," 23–24.

47 Walter Sparn, "Religiöse und theologische Aspekte der Bildungsgeschichte im Zeitalter der Aufklärung," *Handbuch der deutschen Bildungsgeschichte*, 2: 136.

48 See the overview on grammar textbooks in the seventeenth century by Nicola McLelland, "Authority and Audience in Seventeenth-Century German Grammatical Texts," *The Modern Language Review* 100 (2005): 1025–1042.

49 Wolfgang Neugebauer, "Niedere Schulen und Realschulen," *Handbuch der deutschen Bildungsgeschichte*, 2: 223.

50 Petzoldt, "Ut probus," 7–42.

51 Petzoldt, "Ut probus," 37f.

52 Lundgren, "Schulhumanismus," 35.

126   *Markus Rathey*

history; it would further be necessary to scrutinize the textbooks that were most likely read by Bach and explore possible influences on his thinking.

An important influence on the school reforms in the early modern period were the Pietist movements in the late seventeenth and early eighteenth centuries. The leader of Halle Pietism, August Hermann Francke, had been a pupil of Reyher in the 1670s, and, like Comenius and Reyher before him, emphasized the importance of practical education.[53] He also founded an institution for the training of teachers, the Halle Paedagogium in 1696, called the *Seminarium selectum praeceptorum*.[54] Traditionally, teachers had been trained at universities and were able to teach in the lower classes of a Latin school if they had acquired a bachelor's degree (for grades *sexta* to *quarta*)[55] or, for the higher classes *tertia* to *prima*, a master's degree.[56] Often the position of a teacher was only a transitory stage on the way to becoming a pastor at a church.[57] The quality of teaching was therefore not always guaranteed. As Jens Bruning has pointed out, it sometimes came to a negative selection as theologians who had not been able to land a position at a church remained as teachers at a school.[58] Francke's Halle Paedagogium, however, paid attention to the preparation of the teachers and their specific needs as educators. It was the first pedagogical institute in central Europe and served as a model for the training of teachers throughout the eighteenth century.

Besides the schoolbooks mentioned previously, the schools in the late seventeenth century still used Luther's Small Catechism for basic religious education as well as a theological compendium published by the Lutheran orthodox theologian Leonhard Hutter (or Hutterus, or Hütter) (1563–1616).[59] The influential

---

53   For Francke's educational concept see the short summary in Ulrich Hermann's article in *Handbuch der deutschen Bildungsgeschichte* 2: 101–102, and the article by Anthony J. La Vopa, "Vocations, Careers, and Talent: Lutheran Pietism and Sponsored Mobility in Eighteenth-Century Germany," *Comparative Studies in Society and History* 28 (1986): 255–286.

54   Lundgren, "Schulhumaniusmus," 29–30; see also Walter Sparn, "Religiöse und theologische Aspekte der Bildungsgeschichte im Zeitalter der Aufklärung," *Handbuch der deutschen Bildungsgeschichte*, 2: 140–141.

55   The classes in the Latin schools were counted in descending order; the lowest class was *sexta*, the followed *quinta, quarta, tertia, secunda*, and finally *prima*.

56   Lundgren, "Schulhumaniusmus," 26–27.

57   Notker Hammerstein, "Die historische und bildungsgeschichtliche Physiognomie des konfessionellen Zeitalters," *Handbuch der deutschen Bildungsgeschichte*, 1: 69. This was even the case for cantors, who were often (at least ideally) the most musically skilled graduates from the theological faculties; for some middle German examples, see my article on the Erfurt theologian and musician Nicolaus Stenger: "'Die Heiligkeit der edlen Musik'. Frömmigkeit und musikalische Praxis im Werk Nicolaus Stengers," *Nicolaus Stenger (1609–1680). Beiträge zu Leben, Werk und Wirken*, ed. Michael Ludscheid (Erfurt: Ulenspiegel, 2011), 79–99.

58   Jens Bruning, "Das protestantische Gelehrtenschulwesen im 18. Jahrhundert: Pietismus – Aufklärung – Neuhumanismus," in *Handbuch der deutschen Bildungsgeschichte*, 2: 306. Two of Bach's teachers in Ohrdruf, Kiesewetter and Herda, respectively rector and cantor, originally sought ordination; see the discussion in Chapter 7.

59   For a modern edition with German and English translations, see Leonhard Hutter, *Compendium locorum theologicorum ex scripturis sacris et libro concordiae*, ed. by Johann Anselm Steiger (Stuttgart: Frommann-Holzboog, 2006).

schoolbook was frequently reprinted and shaped the fundamental theological training of numerous generations of Lutheran schoolboys. The book follows the Trinitarian structure of the Christian Creed (God the Father – Christ the Son – Holy Spirit), but interjects other dogmatically essential topics, such as the doctrine of the two natures of Christ, the problem of free will, good works, Christian marriage, etc. The *Compendium* is divided into thirty-four chapters, each with questions and answers of varying difficulty and complexity, so that students on different levels of knowledge could work with the book. Every student was expected to have worked through the compendium several times during his time at school.[60] It is important for the theological concept of the *Compendium* that the book does not begin with the chapter on the triune God but on the Holy Scripture as divinely inspired and as the only form of divine revelation. It manifests and confirms the scripture-centeredness of seventeenth century Lutheranism.[61] Students (and so Bach) had to learn Hutter's *Compendium* by heart and would thus have acquired a solid knowledge of Lutheran orthodox theology. Although it is difficult, and probably impossible, to name the influence of texts like this on individual faith and personal piety, it would also be inaccurate to rule out an influence.

The knowledge of theology Bach would have received through the study of Hutter explains how he could excel in his theological examination when he applied for the position as Cantor at St. Thomas. Even though he did not have university training as applicants for similar positions usually had, he had acquired a solid grounding in Lutheran doctrine during his years at school. As Martin Petzoldt has pointed out, Bach had to answer questions on the Bible and dogmatics, and the exam was held in Latin.[62] Ulrich Siegele has attempted to relate theological paradigms from Hutter's compendium to Bach's theological understanding of form in his Duet in F-Major (BWV 803).[63] Even if some of his interpretations might be disputable, Siegele surely refers to one of the essential theological sources for Bach, a text that was probably more influential for Bach's early religious formation than most writings by Luther.

---

60 For an overview see the partly outdated article by Paul Nebel, "Leonard Hutters *Compendium Locorum Theologicorum,*" *Neue Jahrbücher für Pädagogik* 5 (1902): 327–361. A more recent study of Hutter and Bach is provided by Reinhard Kirste, "Theologische und spirituelle Ermöglichungsansätze für Bachs Werk unter besonderer Berücksichtigung des Verständnisses von Wort und Geist bei Leonhart Hutter und Johann Arnd," *Bach als Ausleger der Bibel,* ed. Martin Petzoldt (Berlin: Evangelische Verlagsanstalt, 1985), 77–95.

61 See Markus Rathey, "Heinrich Schütz, 'Selig sind die Toten' (1648). Musikalische Syntax als Bedeutungsträger," *Jahrbuch 1999 der Ständigen Konferenz Mitteldeutsche Barockmusik* (Eisenach: Wagner, 2000), 39–50, which gives an overview of this doctrine and also an example how texts like Hutter's book might have influenced a musician.

62 Martin Petzold, "Bachs Prüfung vor dem Kurfürstlichen Konsistorium zu Leipzig," BJ 84 (1998): 19–30.

63 Ulrich Siegele, *Bachs theologischer Formbegriff und das Duett F-dur. Ein Vortrag (Tübinger Beiträge zur Musikwissenschaft 6)* (Stuttgart: Hänssler, 1978).

Bach as Student

The pedagogical concepts that were formed during the seventeenth century were still in place when Johann Sebastian Bach went to school in the last decade of the century. Further reforms would take place when Bach was a teacher in Leipzig. We will therefore focus on Bach the student for a while and explore the specific contexts in which Bach went to school and how the developments explained previously affected him. After that, we will return to the pedagogical reforms that took place during Bach's time at the St. Thomas School.

The earliest source for Bach's attendance of a school is from 1693, when he entered the Latin school in Eisenach, beginning in the *quinta*. It is possible that he attended another school before in Eisenach.[64] Rainer Kaiser has suggested that the composer did attend a "German school" in Eisenach and outlines what he might have learned;[65] however, sources for this do not exist. Kaiser's assumption was recently rejected by Lundgren in his article *Schulhumanismus*;[66] as Latin schools did not necessarily require that students attend an elementary school to learn reading and writing before enrollment, it is possible that Bach in fact did not go to a German school.[67]

School attendance was mandatory in Eisenach, which, since 1680, had belonged to the duchy of Gotha and was therefore to follow the rules instituted by Reyher. Students had to attend school between the ages of 5 and 12, but because the Latin school only accepted boys between the ages of 7 and 24,[68] the boys were (at least in theory) expected to attend a German school beforehand to acquire basic knowledge, especially in reading, writing, religion, and some math. We can assume that Bach, if he attended a German school, was taught based on the three main books of religious education: Bible, hymnal, and catechism, which were used as textbooks for reading as well. In Bach's time, Eisenach had at least eight German schools, which were very small and often were only run by a single teacher.[69] Christoph Wolff, based on the research by Kaiser, suggests that Bach might have attended the school in the Fleischgasse, where he lived between the ages of five and seven before he moved on to the Latin school.

Bach's Latin school had six classes; students normally stayed for two years in a grade before they moved on to the next one. But only a small number actually went through all of the six grades: some entered later, as Bach did, and even more left school before finishing the final grade.[70] In spite of the reforms by Comenius and Reyher, the education at Bach's school still centered on the learning of Latin.

---

64 Martin Geck, *Bach. Leben und Werk* (Reinbek: Rowohlt, 2000), 49.

65 Rainer Kaiser, "Johann Sebastian Bach als Schüler einer 'deutschen Schule' in Eisenach?" BJ 80 (1994): 177–84.

66 Lundgren, "Schulhumanismus," 35.

67 Arno Seifert, "Das höhere Schulwesen. Universitäten und Gymnasien," *Handbuch der deutschen Bildungsgeschichte* I, 281.

68 Wolff BLM, 26.

69 See Wolff BLM, 26.

70 Wolff BLM, 26.

The lessons were based on the *Vestibulum* by Comenius,[71] which Bach must have studied diligently and, since he finished his classes with success, also quite commendably. Besides the academic training, the students of the Latin School formed the basis for the *chorus musicus* or *Cantorey* at the St. Georg Church in Eisenach.[72] From the outset, Bach would have received a solid basis in both the academic language (actively and passively) and in music.

We are informed about some of the topics that were taught by Bach's teacher, Johann Christian Juncker; the plan of lessons prescribed Luther's catechism, the psalms, exercises in writing and reading, and grammar, all, of course, in Latin.[73] The lessons started very early in the morning. During the summer months, school was in session from 6 to 9 am and from 1 to 3 pm; during winter, the classes met later, from 7 to 10 am and from 1 to 3 pm. The rehearsals of the *chorus musicus* were on Tuesdays, Thursdays, and Fridays from noon to one, the time during which music had been traditionally taught in German Latin schools since their inception during the Reformation. On Wednesdays and Saturdays, there were no afternoon sessions.[74]

In 1694, Bach finished the *quinta* as fourth-best student, attesting to his intellectual curiosity and diligence beyond the sphere of music. In the next year, however, 1695, his grades dropped dramatically and he found himself in twenty-third place. The reason for this is easy to divine, as it was the year in which both of his parents died.[75] The death of his parents caused Bach, as is well-known, to move to Ohrdruf to live with his older brother Johann Christoph.[76] In Ohrdruf, Bach continued his education at the Lyceum, a well-regarded Latin school. The curriculum was basically the same as in Eisenach. He would probably even have used the same set of schoolbooks: language manuals by Comenius and Reyher, and Hutter's *Compendium*.

When Bach entered the *tertia* in 1695, he had exercises in Latin based on *Dialogi seu Colloquia puerilia*, a book by the school reformer Reyher, first published in Gotha in 1653. In addition to Latin, Bach also had reading exercises in Greek. In the *secunda*, Bach had to study Hutter's *Compendium*, Cornelius Nepos's *Biographien führender Gestalten*, and the letters by Cicero. In the *prima*, the curriculum prescribed the historical writings by Curtius Rufus, Johannes Buno's *Idea historiae universalis* and the comedies by the Latin poet Terence.[77] Furthermore, he would have had lessons in arithmetic.

---

71 Geck, *Bach. Leben und Werk*, 48.
72 Wolff BLM, 25–26.
73 Wolff BLM, 27.
74 See the overview in Wolff BLM, 28.
75 Wolff BLM, 27.
76 Johann Christoph's influence on his younger brother is analyzed by Hans-Joachim Schulze, "Johann Christoph Bach (1671–1721), 'Organist und Schul Collega in Ohrdruf,' Johann Sebastian Bachs erster Lehrer," BJ 71 (1985): 55–81.
77 Wolff BLM, 40.

130   *Markus Rathey*

Bach was aided economically, as he received a "Freistelle" (free board) and was a member of the *Currende*, a chorus that sang for alms on the streets and in front of the houses of citizens.[78] When he lost his "Freistelle" in 1700, Bach left Ohrdruf (he may even have made this decision for lack of an economic basis), and went to Lüneburg. The school records for Ohrdruf state in March 1700: "Luneburgum ob defectum hospitiorum se contulit d. 15. Martii 1700" (Left for Lüneburg, in the absence of free board"[79]).

But let us stay with Bach in Ohrdruf for another moment. The move to the new city and the care of his brother enabled Bach to improve his grades immediately and he was soon again one of the best students in his class. The detailed lists of Bach's standing in his class have survived and are easily accessible in *The New Bach Reader*.[80] In the larger picture, the individual grades do not matter much. We would appreciate the composer Bach even if he had been a poor student. However, his excellent grades in school reveal him as a fine and diligent learner. Even after the school reforms in the seventeenth century, education favored rote learning and the imitation of classical models. School education was not geared towards the development of the individual. Bach's grades show that he must have been skillful at learning; one might even see a connection to his later compositions, in which Bach easily adopts musical styles and forms and uses them creatively. He was also well-versed in arts like rhetoric[81] and theology, two subjects that were emphasized at all the schools he attended. Although his school education did not necessarily make Bach an accomplished composer, his success at school reveals some of the intellectual traits that also formed the basis for his prowess as a composer.

While we are well-informed about the subjects that were taught at Bach's schools, and can partially reconstruct their impact on his development, not much is known about the influence individual teachers had on the young student. Our knowledge is still fragmentary in this respect and further research might reveal more information. The Lyceum in Ohrdruf was led by rector Johann Christoph Kiesewetter (since 1696). He taught the students of the *prima*, whereas the deputy rector Johann Jeremias Böttiger taught the students in the *secunda*. During his tenure, Kiesewetter fought vehemently against problems of discipline. The main target of his criticism was the music teacher, cantor Johann Heinrich Arnold, who was called by Kiesewetter "pestis scholae" and "scandalum ecclesiae et carcinoma civitatis."[82] Kiesewetter's anger, calling

---

78 Markus Rathey, "Kurrende," *Lexikon der Musik der Renaissance*, 2 vols., ed. Elisabeth Schmierer (Laaber: Laaber, 2012), 1: 700–701.

79 NBR, 34 (No. 8e); Dok 2: 7 (No. 4).

80 Ibid., NBR, 34 (No. 8a-f).

81 For two recent accounts of Bach and rhetoric, see Markus Rathey, "Textsyntax und Prosodie in der Aufklärung und bei Johann Sebastian Bach," *Musik und Ästhetik* 8 (2004): 24–39, and Bettina Varwig, "One More Time: J. S. Bach and Seventeenth-Century Traditions of Rhetoric," ECM 5 (2008): 179–208.

82 Quoted after Wolff BLM, 40.

Schools 131

Arnold a disease and a disgrace, betrays some of the tensions between individual teachers at the Lyceum. We do not know how successful Arnold was in his teaching—he taught Bach during the two years in the *tertia*—and we are also unaware of how important he was for Bach's musical education;[83] we can, however, assume that the tensions between rector and teacher had a negative effect of some sort on the education of the young students. Consequently, Arnold was replaced in 1698 with Elias Herda, who came from Gotha, the center of the school reform in the seventeenth century. Herda had musical training and had also studied theology at the University of Jena. A letter of recommendation for Herda, written by Johann Andreas Danz, professor at Jena, describes Herda as an excellent musician but even more as a teacher with profound theological training. Konrad Küster's study on the young Bach provides the entire text of the letter as well as evaluations of Herda by Ohrdruf superintendent Kromayer and a report about his audition.[84] All in all, Herda seems to have been a solid, though not superior musician, whose strength was more theological and pedagogical. The arrival of Herda was also a lucky coincidence for Bach, because the cantor had been a student at St. Michael's in Lüneburg from 1689 to 1695 and probably made Bach and his friend Erdmann aware of the availability of free board at the school in Lüneburg when the financial situation in Ohrdruf had changed in 1700.

It is remarkable that Bach stayed in school that long and that in 1700 he did everything to overcome the obstacle of a lack of financial support in Ohrdruf. As pointed out earlier, it was not unusual for a student to leave school before finishing the upper grades, especially if the students did not intend to pursue an academic career but, as in the case of Bach, stayed in the "family business."[85] Christoph Wolff reflects on this issue when he suggests that Johann Sebastian's older brother, Johann Christoph, might have entertained the possibility that young Sebastian might leave school to begin an apprenticeship with a musician (as he himself had done with the organist Johann Pachelbel), but that he must have noticed the exceptional academic abilities of his younger sibling.[86] Whatever the case, Bach left for Lüneburg to continue his schooling.

Seen in retrospect, losing the free board in Ohrdruf turned out as luck for Bach, because it forced him to go to a school that was more rigorous than the Lyceum in Ohrdruf.[87] The school in Lüneburg was housed in the old St. Michael's monastery.[88] It consisted of three separate entities, the "Ritteracademie," a boarding school for

---

83 Christoph Wolff points out that Arnold was indeed a good scholar; Wolff BLM, 40.
84 Konrad Küster, *Der junge Bach* (Stuttgart: Deutsche Verlags-Anstalt, 1996), 72–75.
85 For the education and training of Bach's brother, Johann Christoph, see his short biographical sketch from 1700; NBR 35–36 (No. 9); Schulze, "Johann Christoph Bach," 60.
86 Wolff BLM, 41.
87 See Wolff's assessment, Wolff BLM, 55–56.
88 For Bach's time in Lüneburg, see Gustav Fock, *Der junge Bach in Lüneburg* (Hamburg: Merseburger, 1950). The book is only in part outdated and still provides the most comprehensive collection of material on the intellectual and musical life in Lüneburg during Bach's time.

132   *Markus Rathey*

the sons of the nobility; the Latin school, which Bach attended; and the *Collegium academicum*, an institution that resembled a university. Even though the three entities were kept separate, the proximity ensured contact between the pupils and might have led to an intellectual and social exchange. Bach, who had already finished about half of the first year of the *prima* in Ohrdruf (where the school year began in the fall), had to begin from scratch again in Lüneburg (where the school year started at Easter);[89] however, what he lost in time by changing schools, he gained in quality of education.

The Latin school offered a dozen scholarships for poorer students (like Bach), who had to sing in the so-called "Mettenchor," the members of which sang in the morning and evening services (matins and vespers) and also constituted a part of the *chorus symphoniacus*, the main chorus, which sang figural music in the Mass services on Sundays and feast days; this chorus had 20 members.[90] Lüneburg had a long musical tradition, which is documented by a catalog of the musical sources in the town library, published by Friedrich Welter in 1950.[91] An extensive overview of the musical culture at St. Michael's Lüneburg and Bach's involvement in the "Mettenchor" and the *chorus symphoniacus* has been published by Konrad Küster in his study on the young Bach.[92]

The emphasis of the education in Lüneburg was, as can be expected for the late seventeenth century, on old languages, theology, and classical literature, but also included the "*realia*" like history, geography, and physics.[93] We are well-informed about the subjects taught in Lüneburg. The most comprehensive exploration of this topic (and of the subjects that Bach had to take during his school days) can be found in the article by Martin Petzold, "'Ut probus & doctus reddar' Zum Anteil der Theologie bei der Schulausbildung J. S. Bachs" from 1985.[94] A short summary of the information relevant for Bach's time in Lüneburg is given by Christoph Wolff in his Bach biography.[95]

Bach's main teacher at Lüneburg was the rector, Magister Johannes Büsche, who taught religion, logic, and Latin. Bach's second teacher in Lüneburg was Magister Eberhard Joachim Elfeld, who taught Latin and Greek; arithmetic was taught by the cantor of the school, August Braun. Further lessons, held by the two primary teachers, would have focused on history, geography, genealogy, heraldry, German poetry, math, and physics. Martin Petzoldt further suggests that

---

89 Wolff BLM, 54.

90 Geck, *Bach. Leben und Werk*, 53.

91 Friedrich Welter, *Katalog der Musikalien der Ratsbücherei Lüneburg* (Lippstadt: Kistner & Siegel, 1950); for a more recent study and reconstruction of the repertoire at the St. Michael's School in Lüneburg, see Friedrich Jekutsch, *Rekonstruktion der Chorbibliothek von St. Michaelis zu Lüneburg: Ein Beitrag zum Bachjahr 2000* (Lüneburg: Ratsbücherei, 2000).

92 Küster, *Der junge Bach*, 85–97; Küster's list of the members of the Mettenchor is reprinted in NBR 37 (No. 11).

93 See Wolff BLM, 55–56.

94 Petzoldt, "Ut probus," 7–42.

95 Wolff BLM, 57–58.

Schools   133

Bach might have taken private lessons in theology with the pastor at St. Michael's and the "inspector" of the school, Martin Georg Hülsemann.[96]

The curriculum of the St. Michael's school for the year 1695 listed the following school books for the primary subjects:

> Leonard Hutter, *Compendium locorum theologicum*
> Andreas Reyher, *Systema logicum* (Gotha 1691)
> Heinrich Tolles, *Rhetorica Gottingensis* (Göttingen 1680) (a short summary of Aristotelian rhetoric)
> Virgil, *Bucolica*
> Virgil, *Aeneis*, book IV
> Cicero, *De Catalina*
> Quintus Curtius Rufus's book about Alexander the Great
> Cicero, *De officiis*
> Cicero, *Epistolae* (extracts)
> Horace, *Carmina*

The books reflect a solid theological education but also show that Bach was trained to have basic knowledge of the principles of classical rhetoric and logic. In the books by Virgil, Bach would also have found plots and characters of classical literature and mythology—some of which would later appear in the librettos he used for his secular cantatas.[97] Further textbooks included philosophical texts by Kebes of Theben (Cebetis Tabula), Phokylides, Isokrates, and Theognis. Bach's reading list was not different from that of most other pupils at Latin schools; it reflects the shared knowledge of the educated class in Germany around 1700. It is hard to determine how influential most of the texts were on Bach's own thinking and worldview. However, a systematic study of the books could reveal some interesting insights that might even shed some light on compositional procedures, though this is only speculation. What is certain is that Bach's thorough academic education went far beyond what most of his family members would have received before him; and it was more than most town musicians and organists would have learned. The excellent academic training would enable him later to become cantor at St. Thomas in Leipzig, a position that was traditionally held by musicians with a university degree. Even without the degree, Bach was able to master the exam before he took his position in Leipzig.[98]

When Bach left the school in Lüneburg in 1702, he did not hold an official position related to a school until he moved to Leipzig in 1723. However, his duties as organist in Arnstadt and Mühlhausen required him to collaborate

---

96 Petzoldt, "Ut probus," 28f.

97 See for the texts of these cantatas and their literary background: Z. Philip Ambrose, "Klassische und neue Mythen in Bachs weltlichen Kantaten," *Die Welt der Bach Kantaten II: Johann Sebastian Bachs weltliche Kantaten*, ed. Christoph Wolff (Stuttgart/Kassel: Metzler/ Bärenreiter, 1997), 139–155.

98 For Bach's exam in Leipzig, see Petzold, "Bachs Prüfung," 19–30.

134   *Markus Rathey*

with the cantors of the local schools and with their students, who formed the school choir.[99] After being a court musician in Weimar and Köthen, it must have been quite a step for Bach to become a schoolteacher in Leipzig.[100] And that he paid someone to teach the Latin lessons that were required of him shows that he was more invested in the musical aspects of the office than the academic side.

Bach as Teacher in Leipzig

When Bach became cantor at the Thomas School in Leipzig, he assumed a position at an institution that could trace its history back to the thirteenth century. Founded as a school associated with an Augustinian monastery, it became Protestant in the course of the Reformation.[101] The school was the most demanding and selective Latin school of the area, and put a strong emphasis on the quality of music, which was performed by students in the local churches in Leipzig. The names of some of the cantors during the sixteenth and seventeenth centuries resemble a "who's who" of the leading German Protestant composers of their time: Sethus Calvisius (1594–1615), Johann Hermann Schein (1615–1630), Sebastian Knüpfer (1657–1676), Johann Schelle (1677–1701), and Johann Kuhnau (1701–1722). The school was supported by the city council, but it also had a sizable endowment through bequests and charitable gifts by Leipzig citizens who supported those boys in need of financial support.[102] During the time of Bach and his predecessor Johann Kuhnau, the school had 55 resident students (*alumni*) in the classes *quarta* through *prima* (the four upper classes); additionally, the school admitted up to twice the number of external students (*externi*) who lived with their families in Leipzig. In return for room and board, the *alumni* had to sing in the Thomas choirs that provided the liturgical music for four of the churches in the city: St. Thomas, St. Nicholas, the New Church, and St. Peter's.[103] Additionally, the singers earned money by performing at weddings and funerals, and in the *Currende*, where they sang on special occasions on the streets and in front

---

99   Peter Wollny, "Über die Hintergründe von Johann Sebastian Bachs Bewerbung in Arnstadt," BJ 91 (2005): 83–94.

100   A fact that is reflected by the composer himself in the second letter to his friend Georg Erdmann from 1730.

101   Manfred Mezger and Bernhard Knick, eds., *St. Thomas zu Leipzig. Schule und Chor. Stätte des Wirkens von Johann Sebastian Bach. Bilder und Dokumente zur Geschichte der Thomasschule und des Thomanerchores mit ihren zeitgeschichtlichen Beziehungen* (Wiesbaden: Breitkopf & Härtel, 1963); Stefan Altner and Martin Petzoldt, eds., *800 Jahre Thomana... Festschrift zum Jubiläum von Thomaskirche, Thomanerchor und Thomasschule* (Wettin-Löbejün: Stekovics, 2012); Michael Maul, *"Dero berümbter Chor': Die Leipziger Thomasschule und ihre Kantoren 1212–1804* (Leipzig: Lehmstedt, 2012), ET forthcoming.

102   See Stefan Altner, "Wiedergewonnene Dokumente über 'gangbare' Legate für die Thomasschule zur Bach-Zeit," LBB 5 (2002): 455–463; and Hans-Joachim Schulze, *Das Quittungsbuch des Nathanischen Legats* (Berlin: Kulturstiftung der Länder, 1995).

103   For the duties of the choirs see Wolff BLM, 250–251.

of the houses of wealthy citizens; one of the regular tasks was the annual New Year's singing.

As cantor, Bach ranked third among the four main teachers.[104] Ahead of him were the rector and the conrector, and on fourth rank was the tertius; also, the school employed additional teachers, the *"collegae ordinarii."* Bach's tasks at the Thomas School included, besides his musical obligations, participation in admissions where he had to examine the musical proficiency of the applicants, and one week each month he served as inspector of the school dormitories. Bach's (and his pupils') day looked as follows according to the school order from 1723:[105]

5:00 am	Wake-up call (in winter: 6:00)
7:00 am	Academic lectures
10:00 am	Study period
11:00 am	Lunch
12:00 pm	Singing lessons
1:00 pm	Academic lectures
3:00 pm	Study period (3:00–4:00 often singing at funerals)
6:00 pm	Dinner
8:00 pm	Study period
9:00 pm	Bedtime

Bach held his "musical exercises with all classes" on Mondays, Tuesdays, and Wednesdays at 9:00 am and 12:00 pm; on Fridays, he met his pupils only at 12:00 noon. No music classes were scheduled for Thursdays and Saturdays.[106] As Wolff points out, "the classes were compulsory for all resident and nonresident students, altogether some 150 youngsters, so Bach was assisted by the four choral prefects appointed by him from among the senior and musically expert students."[107]

As musicologists, our view of the Thomas school as a place of learning is slightly distorted because the focus scholars have put on Bach and his time in Leipzig sometimes overshadows the strong academic profile of the school outside of the music lessons. The study by Otto Kaemmel, *Geschichte des Leipziger Schulwesens* from 1909, still provides some good sources for life outside of the

---

104 For the history of the Thomas school and its organization in Bach's time see the overview in Wolff BLM, 237–253.

105 Schulze, *Die Thomasschule in Leipzig*, 27–32; here reproduced after Wolff's translation in: "Bach in Leipzig," in *The Worlds of Johann Sebastian Bach*, ed. Raymond Erickson (New York: Amadeus Press, 2009), 273.

106 Wolff BLM, 248.

107 Wolff BLM, 248.

136　*Markus Rathey*

music lessons.[108] A recent article by Stefan Altner about the teachers at the school during Bach's time is also helpful.[109]

Although Bach's time as a pupil was influenced by the reforms spearheaded by Comenius and Reyher in the middle of the seventeenth century (the sheer number of textbooks Bach would have read reflects their influence, not to mention their impact on the curriculum), he would have experienced another school reform that was connected with the two rectors of the Thomas School, Johann Matthias Gesner (1691–1761) and Johann August Ernesti (1707–1781). The latter questioned current pedagogical concepts that (even after the reforms in the middle of the seventeenth century) still focused too much on imitating the classical authors instead of understanding them from an esthetical and literary perspective. In a fundamental speech from 1736, Ernesti criticized the *stupor paedagogicus*, the stupidity of schooling. He emphasized that the primary goal of learning should be to understand the Latin (= classical) authors and not just the mastery of Latin.[110] One demand of the reforms Ernesti was about to initiate was to read not only snippets of classical texts in order to imitate their style, but also to read complete texts (or at least larger coherent sections) with the goal of learning from their content.[111]

At Bach's arrival in Leipzig in 1723, the Thomas School was still following the old humanist ideals of pedagogy; this can be seen from a teaching plan from 1676 that was based on the reform plans of then rector Jakob Thomasius (1622–1684). The textbooks were, as Otto Kaemmel outlines in his *Geschichte des Leipziger Schulwesens*, memorized, repeated, examined, and analyzed according to the rules of grammar, style, rhetoric, and logic and the results were collected in exercise books to be used for imitation in the pupil's own writing and oratory.[112] Attempts to modernize the curriculum had been made around 1714,[113] and another attempt was made in 1723 when a new school order ("Schulordnung") was published;[114] yet, it would take until the 1730s for the rectors of the school to

---

108　The Thomas School was, of course, an exception among the schools in Saxony; for the "normal" situation of school education, see Katrin Keller, "'... daß wir ieder zeith eine feine lateinische schul gehabt haben.' Beobachtungen zu Schule und Bildung in sächsischen Kleinstädten des 17. und 18. Jahrhunderts," *Kleine Städte im neuzeitlichen Europa*, ed. H. Th. Gräf (Berlin: Spitz, 1997), 137–168.

109　Stefan Altner, "Die Lehrer der Thomasschule zur Zeit des Kantorats von Johann Sebastian Bach. Quellenauszüge aus dem Archiv des Thomaschores," *Im Klang der Wirklichkeit. Musik und Theologie. Martin Petzoldt zum 65. Geburtstag*, eds. Norbert Bolin and Markus Franz (Leipzig: Evangelische Verlagsanstalt, 2011), 28–38.

110　See the short summary in Lundgren, "Schulhumanismus," 31–32 and the more extensive treatment in Paulsen, *Geschichte des gelehrten Unterrichts* 2: 30f.

111　Lundgren, "Schulhumanismus," 32.

112　See Otto Kaemmel, *Geschichte des Leipziger Schulwesens vom Anfange des 13. bis gegen die Mitte des 19. Jahrhunderts (1214–1846)* (Leipzig/Berlin: Teubner, 1909), 263; see also the summary in Lundgren, "Schulhumanismus," 33.

113　See Lundgren, "Schulhumanismus," 33.

114　See Hans-Joachim Schulze, *Die Thomasschule Leipzig zur Zeit Johann Sebastian Bachs. Ordnungen und Gesetze 1634. 1723. 1733* (Leipzig: Zentralantiquariat, 1985).

Schools 137

embark on some groundbreaking changes. The attempted reforms in 1723 were initiated by the town council but the teachers, led by the rector Johann Heinrich Ernesti (1652–1729) and supported by the cantor Johann Sebastian Bach, resisted; as Schindel points out, they objected not for fundamental pedagogical reasons, but because they feared that the new rules could impede their additional income by reducing the extracurricular activities of the students.[115] Thus the reforms were not implemented until after the arrival of Gesner in 1730 when the new "Schulordnung" was published in 1733.

Both Gesner and Johann August Ernesti emphasized the importance of the "*realia*." Reading Latin and Greek was still considered essential, of course, but the practical disciplines become more important. Representative of Gesner's view is the *Braunschweigisch-Lüneburgische Schulordnung* from 1737, a document written after he had left Leipzig but that nonetheless well reflects his view of education during his short tenure at the Thomas School: "Who reads their writings and understands them, enjoys the company of the greatest and most noble souls who have ever been; and he acquires, as happens in all conversations, beautiful thoughts and impressive words."[116]

Gesner's pedagogical concept and his importance for the school reforms in the eighteenth century in general (and for the Thomas School in particular) has been analyzed in an article by Ulrich Schindel, *Johann Matthias Gesners aufgeklärte Pädagogik*.[117] Gesner had come to Leipzig in 1730 as successor to the older Johann Heinrich Ernesti who had died at the age of seventy-seven after forty-five years in office. Gesner stayed only for four years before he left for the newly founded Georgia Augusta in Göttingen, but he still had a lasting impact on the pedagogical culture of the Thomas School. Johann Sebastian Bach and Gesner had a very good relationship, which is reflected in a remark in Gesner's Quintilian-commentary from 1738 in which he called Bach a "vielfältigen Orpheus und zwanzigfachen Arion" ("a versatile Orpheus and twentyfold Arion"); in other words, a god-like musical genius.[118] He also describes Bach's playing and conducting providing a valuable source for Bach as a performer in the 1730s.

When Gesner came to Leipzig, he was already known as a school reformer— in fact, this was probably one of the reasons he was hired in the first place. In 1715, he had published a treatise with suggestions regarding the reform of Latin schools, "*Institutiones Rei Scholasticae*" (Jena 1715). In six chapters, Gesner outlines his ideal of a teacher—his character, talents, knowledge, and abilities. He also devotes space to the explanation of good and successful teaching methods

---

115 Ulrich Schindel, "Johann Matthias Gesners aufgeklärte Pädagogik," LBB 7 (2005): 44.
116 "Wer also ihre Schriften lieset und verstehet, der genießet des Umgangs der größten und edelsten Seelen, die jemals gewesen, und nimmt dadurch auch selbst, wie es bei aller Konversation geschiehet, schöne Gedanken und nachdrückliche Worte an." Quoted after Lundgren, "Schulhumanismus," 32; see also Paulsen, *Geschichte des gelehrten Unterrichts* 2: 21.
117 Schindel, "Johann Matthias Gesners aufgeklärte Pädagogik," 39–49.
118 NBR 328–329 (No. 328); Dok 2: 331–332 (No. 432).

138   *Markus Rathey*

and the demeanor a teacher should show in the classroom. However, Gesner is also realistic as to concede that there is no "perfect teacher."[119]

Gesner's interest in pedagogy and the proper methods of teaching was influenced by contemporary Pietism. Gesner had studied with the Pietist theologian Johann Franz Buddeus and was acquainted with the Paedagogium in Halle, which had been founded by Pietist August Hermann Francke. Even though Gesner does not appear to follow the Pietist movement theologically, he was most definitely influenced by their modern pedagogical concepts. In his suggestions for a reform, Gesner provides a long list of abilities and knowledge a teacher should have: proficiency in old and modern languages (Latin, Greek, French, English, Dutch, Italian, Spanish, German), eloquence, poetry, history (including German history), math, astronomy, chronology, geography, architecture, music, and philosophy.[120]

An important source for Gesner's reform ideas for Leipzig is some written comments he made about the Leipzig "Schulordnung" (school order) from 1723.[121] One remark pertains to the students during the colder part of the year; Gesner suggests that they should be allowed to leave the church during Sunday sermons if it is very cold and instead go to a warmer classroom where a sermon would be read to them. Students should also be able to check out books from the school library; previously, they were only allowed to read them on the premises. Reading is also involved in a third suggestion: it was customary that the students listened to readings during their meals. However, instead of the New Testament, which was traditionally read and already well known to the students, Gesner suggests readings from classical authors instead.[122]

Gesner's ambitious reforms, however, are not directly reflected in the school order from 1733. It focuses mainly on disciplinary aspects but leaves out the contents of teaching as well as the qualifications and demeanor of the teacher, which had been of major importance to him in his treatise from 1715. Ulrich Schindel suspects, probably correctly, that Gesner left these contentious points out and only focused on those aspects that were of importance to the city government while he intended to deal with the other issues on an internal basis.[123] And that he did: new textbooks were introduced (some of them edited by Gesner himself), and even some contemporary German poets found their way onto the reading list, like Gellert and Gottsched.[124]

One of the most striking innovations by Gesner was the introduction of a so-called "Fragekolleg"; twice a week, the rector was available for his students to answer questions about texts they had read or, more generally, about rhetoric or poetry. Gesner explained this idea in his treatise *Programma de interrogandi in*

---

119   See Schindel, "Johann Matthias Gesners aufgeklärte Pädagogik," 41.

120   Listed in Schindel, "Johann Matthias Gesners aufgeklärte Pädagogik," 42.

121   The *adnotationes* are published in Schulze, *Die Thomasschule Leipzig*, Appendix A; for a short summary, see Schindel, "Johann Matthias Gesners aufgeklärte Pädagogik," 44.

122   Schindel, "Johann Matthias Gesners aufgeklärte Pädagogik," 44–45.

123   Schindel, "Johann Matthias Gesners aufgeklärte Pädagogik," 45.

124   Comprehensive listed in Schindel, "Johann Matthias Gesners aufgeklärte Pädagogik," 45.

studiis litterarum ratione atque utilitate" from 1734.[125] This system is a clear departure from the tradition of purely rote learning students would have experienced for the most part of the seventeenth century.

The pedagogical reforms were continued under Gesner's successor Johann August Ernesti, who emphasized the importance of the *"realia"* even more. Ernesti published in 1736 a comprehensive text book of essential knowledge for the students, the *Initia doctrinae solidioris*, a book that saw several editions until the end of the eighteenth century. The mere fact that it begins with arithmetic and geometry before it moves on to the metaphysics shows the practical focus of the book. In the final chapters, the textbook treats the art of rhetoric extensively, but with a much more practical focus than the traditional textbooks. Music, on the other hand, traditionally part of the seven liberal arts and treated in conjunction with mathematics and astronomy, no longer retains a central place in Ernesti's system of education.

Bach got along very well with Gesner, which can be seen not only from the teacher's favorable mention of Bach in his Quintilian-commentary but also from the lack of evidence for any conflict between the cantor and his superior. This does not mean that Bach wholeheartedly subscribed to Gesner's reforms, but that Bach did not think that the reforms impeded on his authority and his additional income. Did Bach share Gesner's pedagogical views? There is no evidence to prove or disprove a stance either way. More problematic, however, was Bach's relationship with Gesner's successor Ernesti. The subject of the dissent was not the curriculum or the pedagogical mission of the Thomas School but an infringement upon Bach's responsibilities and his authority.

I refer to the so-called "Präfektenstreit," the quarrel about the selection of the prefects, which dragged on for about two years from 1736 to 1738. The quarrel is well-accounted for in numerous documents, which are printed in *The New Bach Reader*[126] and in Hans-Joachim Schulze's collection of documents about Bach's time at St. Thomas.[127] The struggle was also analyzed from a sociological perspective by Frank Mund in his study *Lebenskrisen als Raum der Freiheit*.[128] Although the study provides a fresh and interesting view of the conflict, it sometimes lacks historical precision and historical perspective and attempts a psychological interpretation that is based on an insufficient basis of sources.[129]

The root for the quarrel was that Bach was responsible for the music in four of Leipzig's churches and therefore depended on his "prefects" (students who

---

125 Reprinted in Gesner, *Opuscula Minora Varii Argumenti*, Breslau 1734, 37–44; see the short overview in Schindel, "Johann Matthias Gesners aufgeklärte Pädagogik," 47.

126 NBR 172–185 (Nos. 180–187); Dok 1: 82–90 (Nos. 32–35) and Dok 2: 268–276 (Nos. 382–383). NBR 189–196 (Nos. 192–196); Dok 1: 97–106 (Nos 40–41).

127 Schulze, *Die Thomasschule in Leipzig*; for a short summary, see also Wolff BLM, 349–350.

128 Frank Mund, *Lebenskrisen als Raum der Freiheit. Johann Sebastian Bach in seinen Briefen* (Kassel: Bärenreiter 1997).

129 See also reviews by Bernd Heyder, *Concerto* 14/127 (1997): 18–20, and Martin Geck Mf 53 (2000): 97–98.

140   *Markus Rathey*

served as substitute conductors) to lead the ensembles in the churches where he could not be present. He also relied on them for singing and instrumental lessons as well as rehearsals. Ernesti had in 1736 appointed the first, or general, prefect against Bach's objections and this unfurled into a struggle over Bach's prerogative to appoint the prefects. The surviving documents contain four letters of complaint by Bach to the city council, the rector's rebuttal, a decree issued by the council, two appeals by Bach to the consistory, and a decree by the Elector of Saxony and King of Poland. The outcome of the conflict is somewhat ambiguous. The king asked the consistory in Leipzig to resolve the issue according to what they saw fit but at the same time the monarch also expressed that he was leaning towards Bach's position.[130] Even though we are not informed how the issue of the selection of the prefects was handled in the future, it is clear that the dispute strained the relationship between Bach and Ernesti. Christoph Wolff states, "The conflict destroyed what must initially have been a good relationship between rector and cantor: Ernesti had served in 1733 and 1735 as godfather to Bach's children."[131]

Perspectives

Johann Sebastian Bach lived during a time of fundamental shifts in pedagogy in the seventeenth and eighteenth centuries. His own time at school fell in the wake of the reforms of the second half of the seventeenth century, which attempted to shift the emphasis from an understanding of the structures of language to an understanding of the structures of the world. That this shift was only partly successful necessitated further reforms, which, in Leipzig, occurred in Bach's time as cantor and teacher at the Thomas School. It is beyond our knowledge how Bach personally assessed these reforms. His ambitions as a schoolteacher (outside of his music lessons) were rather limited. Already in Arnstadt, he was reluctant to work with the students of the local school, and in Leipzig he made sure that he did not have to teach Latin. The reason for this was not that he objected to learning of Latin as the core of school education (which would make him a proponent of the newer pedagogical strands), but because he had no interest in teaching it and rather focused on the one thing he could do best: compose and direct music. Bach did not support the attempts to reform the Thomas School in 1723; however, he got along well with the reformer Gesner, who initiated some changes at the school. When Gesner's successor Ernesti continued the reforms and infringed upon Bach's authority, the cantor stood up and fought for his interests. There is no indication that Bach shared Ernesti's view for reforms of the curriculum; the reason for the conflict was a question of authority and not of the content of education. As a music teacher, Bach was successful, as a large number of students can attest, but their teaching took place mostly outside of the core curriculum.

---

130 NBR 195–196 (No. 196); Dok 2: 293 (No. 406).
131 Wolff BLM, 349.

Bach's seeming reluctance to reforms aside, the Thomas School was the environment in which he lived and worked (even his apartment was in the school building). Also, his own education at the Latin schools in Eisenach, Ohrdruf, and Lüneburg not only provided him with a solid religious education (as the exam from 1723 shows), but also shaped his thinking and his understanding of the world. Bach's education put a strong emphasis on grammar on the one hand (that is, on structures that could and should be replicated) and on the other hand, on a form of creativity that focused on the collection and imitation of models. Students read classical texts, collected rhetorical tropes, and used them for their own rhetorical exercises.

The "grammatical world" was not the only one to follow clear rules and patterns; even the proponents of the "*realia*," such as Comenius and Reyher, presented a world that was clearly structured and could be learned and approached in neatly defined categories, as Comenius *Orbis sensualium pictus* shows. It is the understanding of the world, which Foucault has labeled as "representation" and characterized as typical for the seventeenth and eighteenth centuries.[132] The view of the world was slowly changing in Bach's lifetime but the composer was still very much part of this episteme.

Further research on Bach and schools will, first of all, have to shed light on more details of his education at the schools he attended. The question of whether he did go to a German school is still undecided and the content of his education (based on curricula and his school books) needs further scrutiny. But even more important would be to explore how the way in which knowledge was transmitted, taught, and structured affected the way he approached his own material, music. This is not a task for musicologists alone. We rather have to rely on research done by historians, and historians of pedagogy in particular. Jens Bruning reminds us in his article from 2005 that the seventeenth century is still the least researched century in the history of schools in Germany during the early modern period (sixteenth through eighteenth centuries)[133] and the way modern scholars approach the school systems during this period is still very much influenced by standards that were established in the nineteenth and twentieth centuries. Things were much less organized and institutionalized in Bach's times and research into his schooling would do well to treat the sources very cautiously not to impose anachronistic expectations.

---

132 Michel Foucault, *The Order of Things. An Archaeology of the Human Sciences* (New York: Vintage, 1994).

133 Jens Bruning, "Das protestantische Gelehrtenschulwesen," *Handbuch der deutschen Bildungsgeschichte*, 2: 280–281.

7 Churches

Robin A. Leaver
Martin Petzoldt (1946–2015) in memoriam

Johann Sebastian Bach was born and brought up within the Lutheran Church and he remained a member for the whole of his life. Apart from just five and a half years, his professional life was engaged in service to the church. However, the Lutheran church of the eighteenth century was neither the church of the Reformation *per se*—though many have thought that it remained substantially unchanged from Luther's day—nor was it the same as the German Protestantism of the later nineteenth century—though this was a common impression conveyed in early Bach studies. More recent research has sought to reveal and understand, from printed and archival sources, the cross-currents of thought and practice within the Lutheran Church of Bach's time. This chapter explores aspects of the Bach family's connection with the church, Bach's relationships with the clergy of the churches he either attended or served, especially in his formative years, and presents an evaluation of Bach as a Lutheran churchman.

The Bach Family and the Church

The Bach family was Lutheran. Professionally and personally, its Lutheran faith and commitment were of fundamental significance. At a funeral of a member of the Bach family in Eisenach in 1679, the preacher said of Bach's father and his brothers that they were "gifted with a good understanding, with art and skill which makes them respected and listened to in the churches, schools, and in all the townships, so that through them the Master's work is praised."[1]

Forkel, on the basis of what he had learned from Bach's sons, Carl Philipp Emanuel and Wilhelm Friedemann, described the annual family gatherings of the wider Bach family that usually took place in either Erfurt, Eisenach, or Arnstadt, the three towns where the family was most numerous:

---

1 Valentin Schrön, *Der Göttliche wohlgegründete Schluß wegen viel oder wenig gegebener Güter und Gaben/ Nach Anleitung der Wort des Herrn Christi.... Zum täglichen Memorial und güldenen Regel vorgestellet/ bey der Leichbestattung Dorotheen Marien Bachin... Welche den 6. Febr. Anno 1679. alhier in Eisenach im Herrn seelig entschlaffen...* ([Eisenach]: Kolb, 1679); cited Spitta 1: 172; Spitta ET 1: 174. Dorothee Marie Bach (1652–1679) was the physically and mentally handicapped sister of Ambrosius Bach who cared for her within his family circle.

Churches 143

Their amusements, during the time of their meeting, were entirely musical. As the company wholly consisted of cantors, organists, and town musicians, *who had all to do with the Church*, and as it was besides a general custom at the time to begin everything with Religion, the first thing they did, when they were assembled, was to sing a chorale.[2]

The professional and private lives of the Bachs were thus closely associated with the church that bore the name of Martin Luther, even though at this time the church was more commonly referred to as "Evangelisch" rather than "Lutherisch." Nevertheless, Luther's influence was ubiquitous. The three primary Lutheran documents for church, school, and home were the Bible, the Small Catechism, and the hymnal, often with all three being bound together in one volume. These three documents were reprinted continuously, each area or local town or city producing its own editions, which had title pages such as these: *Die gantze Heil. Schrifft... Verdeutscht durch D. Martin Luthern*; *Der kleine Catechismus D. Martini Lutheri*; *Geistliche Kirchenlieder und Psalmen, D. Martini Luthers.*

Lutheran clergy, teachers, and musicians worked closely together in church, school and township. Many clergy had been organists in churches and/or cantors (foremost teachers) in Latin schools before ordination. Many teachers had studied theology at university and had considered ordination before pursuing their vocation in education. Cantors were not only responsible for teaching music in schools, but also the basic theology of Luther's Small Catechism, in addition to providing appropriate music for worship in the churches. The connection between theology and music, between music and ministry, can be traced back to Luther, especially the statement in his *Tischreden* (Table Talk) where he expressed his view that a teacher must be able to sing and a pastor must have prior practical musical experience in schools:

Music I have always loved. Whoever knows this art is a good sort, fit for anything. It is imperative that music be kept in schools. A schoolmaster must be able to sing, or I will not consider him, and a young man should not be ordained into the preaching ministry without first experiencing and practicing it [music] in school.[3]

Luther's reforming colleagues, notably Philipp Melanchthon, were also of the same mind, and the Lutheran church in general developed a particularly positive approach to music in church and school, creating a distinctive musical tradition that contrasts with the more circumscribed approach of other branches of Protestantism.[4] This tradition in general, as well as its more specific features,

2 NBR 424 (emphasis added); Dok 7: 16.
3 WA TR No. 6248.
4 See the collected essays, *Singen, Beten, Musizieren: Theologische Grundlagen der Kirchenmusik in Nord- und Mitteldeutschland zwischen Reformation und Pietismus (1530–1750)*, eds., Jochen M. Arnold, Konrad Küster, and Hans Otte (Göttingen: V & R unipress, 2014).

144   *Robin A. Leaver*

together with Bach's place within it, has been explored from various points of view in recent literature.[5]

The Swiss cultural historian, Kaspar von Greyerz, draws a distinction between macrohistory and microhistory, the former relating to the larger political and economic developments, the "official" understanding of cultural interaction, and the latter to the "actual" cultural experiences of everyday life.[6] In religious terms, Greyerz points, on the one hand, to the macrohistory of the great festivals of the church year at Christmas, Easter, Ascension and Pentecost, which need to be balanced, on the other hand, by the microhistory of the actuality of personal and family devotional life.[7] Much of the earlier literature on the religious and liturgical life of Bach's time has been essentially exercises in macrohistory, studies of mostly printed sources of such official documents as *Kirchen-Ordnungen* and *Kirchen-Agenden*,[8] but Tanya Kevorkian has created new perspectives on the contemporary Lutheranism of Bach's time, by examining archival sources to discover how everyday life was impacted by the church and its music, and how the people received or modified (or ignored) what the church promoted.[9] At the same

---

5 A representative listing includes: Carol K. Baron, ed., *Bach's Changing World: Voices in the Community* (Rochester: University of Rochester Press, 2006); John Butt, *Music Education and the Art of Performance in the German Baroque* (Cambridge: Cambridge University Press, 1994); John Butt, "Emotion in the German Lutheran Baroque and the Development of Subjective Time Consciousness," *Music Analysis* 29/1–3 (2010): 19–36; Eric T. Chafe, "Luther's 'Analogy of Faith' in Bach's Church Music," *Dialog* 24 (1985): 96–101; Eric T. Chafe, *Tonal Allegory in the Vocal Music of J. S. Bach* (Berkeley: University of California Press, 1991); Eric T. Chafe, *Analyzing Bach Cantatas* (Oxford : Oxford University Press, 1999); Joyce L. Irwin, *Neither Voice nor Heart Alone: German Lutheran Theology of Music in the Age of the Baroque* (New York: Lang, 1993); Joyce L. Irwin, "Bach in the Midst of Religious Transition," *Bach's Changing World*, ed. Baron, 108–126; Robin A. Leaver, "Music and Lutheranism," *The Cambridge Companion to Bach*, ed. John Butt (Cambridge: Cambridge University Press, 1997), 35–45, 253–256; Robin A. Leaver, "Music and the Reformation," *European Music, 1520–1640*, ed. James Haar (Rochester: Boydell Press, 2006), 371–400; Robin A. Leaver, *Luther's Liturgical Music: Principles and Implications* (Grand Rapids: Eerdmans, 2007); Robin A. Leaver, "Religion and Religious Currents," *The Worlds of Johann Sebastian Bach*, ed. Raymond Erikson (New York: Amadeus Press, 2009), 105–139; Michael Marissen, *Lutheranism, Anti-Judaism, and Bach's St. John Passion* (New York: Oxford University Press, 1998); Michael Marissen, "On the Musically Theological in J. S. Bach's Cantatas," *LQ* 16 (2002): 48–64; Michael Marissen, "Blood, People, and Crowds in Matthew, Luther, and Bach," *LQ* 19 (2005): 1–22.

6 Kaspar von Greyerz, *Religion and Culture in Early Modern Europe, 1500–1800*, trans. Thomas Dunlap (New York: Oxford University Press, 2008), 8–11.

7 Greyerz, *Religion and Culture*, 5.

8 For example: Charles Sanford Terry, *Cantata Texts, Sacred and Secular, With a Reconstruction of the Leipzig Liturgy of his Period* (London: Constable, 1926; reprint, London: Holland, 1964); Günther Stiller, *Johann Sebastian Bach und das Leipziger gottesdienstliche Leben seiner Zeit* (Kassel: Bärenreiter, 1970), ET, *Johann Sebastian Bach and Liturgical Life in Leipzig*, ed. Robin A. Leaver (St. Louis: Concordia, 1984); Martin Petzoldt, "Liturgie und Musik in den Leipziger Hauptkirchen," Christoph Wolff, ed., *Die Welt der Bach Kantaten*, Bd. 3: *Johann Sebastian Bachs Leipziger Kirchenkantaten* (Stuttgart: Metzler, 1999), 69–94.

9 Tanya Kevorkian, "The Reception of the Cantata during Leipzig Church Services, 1700–1750," *Bach's Changing World*, ed. Baron, 174–189; Tanya Kevorkian, *Baroque Piety: Religion, Society, and Music in Leipzig, 1650–1750* (Aldershot: Ashgate, 2007).

Churches 145

time, she has heightened the awareness of the importance of social and cultural history for Bach research.

In light of this, one might, for example, look again at Forkel's account of the annual gatherings of the wider Bach family. The implication one draws from this is that these meetings were specially created events. But were they? It would seem most likely that these gatherings coincided with the observance of ecclesiastical rites of passage in the lives of individual family members—baptisms, weddings, and funerals—and therefore more research into the social mores of such church-connected occasions might help to illuminate these musical gatherings of the Bachs. Weddings would seem to be the most likely of the three possibilities, because they were generally planned some time in advance.[10] There was much music-making associated with weddings, including the bride's and groom's processions to the church, the service in the church,[11] and the following celebratory banquet and dance that might extend over two days.[12] The fragmentary *Quodlibet* (BWV 524), in Bach's hand dating from 1707, was almost certainly intended for a wedding banquet. Baptisms and funerals could have shorter preparation times given the uncertainties of their happenings, although births were known some time in advance and deaths were sometimes preceded by protracted illnesses, which would allow time for planning activities surrounding a baptism or a funeral. Details of the rite of baptism, such as the provision of godparents, the giving of names, and the recording of the details in the official registers of the church,[13] are all well-known. But customs surrounding baptism—such as the fact that it was usual for the new mother not to attend the rite, because she was confined to the house until "churched;"[14] or the custom of placing a Bible and hymnal in the cradle of the newborn in the days before baptism[15]—are less well-known, as is the role of the town musicians and the nature of musical celebrations around the time of baptism.[16] Burials had to be speedily arranged and could be simple affairs. But sometimes the funeral, or a later memorial service,

---

10 At least three weeks' notice had to be given because banns were required to be announced from the pulpit on three consecutive Sundays before the wedding; see *Leipziger Kirchen-Andachten* (Leipzig: Würdig, 1684), 18; Terry, *Cantata Texts, Sacred and Secular*, 38.

11 Some of the cantatas Bach composed for wedding ceremonies have survived: BWV 34a, 120a, 195, 196, 197. Wedding services of widows or widowers were generally held in a house rather than in church.

12 See the ground-breaking article on the role of town musicians in German society, especially at weddings, Tanya Kevorkian, "Town Musicians in German Baroque Society and Culture," *German History* 30 (2012): 350–371, esp. 362–365. Bach's extant cantatas composed for wedding banquets, the Hochzeit cantatas, are: BWV 202, 210a, 216.

13 Baptism records of the Bach family, as well as the occasions when Bach was a godparent, are reproduced in Dok 2, No. 1 being the record of Bach's baptism in the Georgenkirche, Eisenach.

14 On the custom, see Paul Graff, *Geschichte der Auflösung der Alten Gottesdienstlichen Formen in der evangelischen Kirche Deutschlands* (Göttingen: Vandenhoeck & Ruprecht, 1937–39), 1: 311–313.

15 See Robert William Scribner, *Religion and Culture in Germany (1400–1800)*, ed. Lyndal Roper (Leiden: Brill, 2001), 292.

16 See Kevorkian, "Town Musicians," 361.

146   *Robin A. Leaver*

to judge from published funeral sermons, could be quite elaborate affairs, with the deceased being honored with specially written poetry and specially composed music. So what were some of the customs surrounding baptisms, weddings and funerals that might shed more light on these gatherings of the wider Bach family?[17]

There may still be more to discover from Forkel's reference to the Bach family meetings. For instance, he draws attention to the improvised *quodlibets* sung by the Bachs:

> they sang popular songs, the contents of which were partly comic and naughty, all together and extempore, but in such a manner that the several parts thus extemporized made a kind of harmony together, the words, however, in every part being different. They called this kind of extemporary harmony a *quodlibet*, and not only laughed heartily at it themselves, but excited an equally hearty and irresistible laughter in everybody that heard them.... such *quodlibets* were usual in Germany at a much earlier period – I possess, myself, a printed collection of them which was published in Vienna in 1542.[18]

The *quodlibet* fragment (BWV 524) was obviously connected with a wedding, and seems to confirm that the annual Bach gatherings, at least on some occasions, did take place when such ecclesiastical rites of passage were being observed. This wedding *quodlibet*, as well as the more refined *quodlibet* in the Goldberg Variations (BWV 988/var. 30), is clearly light-hearted and humorous, as most of them were, but not exclusively so. Michael Praetorius defined *quodlibet* thus:

> It consists of a great variety of half and complete lines of text extracted from motets [sacred music], madrigals [secular music], and other secular, also humorous, German songs together with their melodies...[19]

17 See the forthcoming book, Tanya Kevorkian, *The Musical Experience in German Baroque Towns*. There is also the related question concerning the relationship between the gatherings of the Bach family and the existence of guild-like organizations of town musicians, given that Bach's father, Johann Ambrosius Bach, was a leading town musician, and that in Erfurt— where Ambrosius had been a town musician—one group of town musicians was known as "Bache" because of the high proportion of members of the Bach family within its ranks; see Kevorkian, "Town Musicians," 354; see also Stephen Rose, *The Musician in Literature in the Age of Bach* (Cambridge: Cambridge University Press, 2011), 75–112, esp. 95, where a contemporary source contrasts the primary role of town musicians – serving God by playing in church—with the more mundane role of "beer fiddlers."

18 NBR 424; Dok 7: 16. The reference is apparently to the part-books of Wolfgang Schmeltzl, who coined the term *quodlibet*: *Guter seltzamer und kunstreicher teutscher Gesang, sonderlich etliche künstlicher Quodlibet...* (Nuremberg: Petreius, 1544). See Hans-Joachim Schulze, "Notizen zu Bachs Quodlibets," BJ 80 (1994): 171–175.

19 Michael Praetorius, *Syntagma Musicum III*, trans. and ed. Jeffery Kite-Powell (Oxford: Oxford University Press, 2004), 33; Michael Praetorius, *Syntagmum Musicum: Tomus tertius* (Wolfenbüttel, 1619; reprint, Kassel: Bärenreiter, 1954), 17.

Churches 147

Even though Praetorius suggests that the associated texts were mostly humorous, the examples he gives in detail are not:

> I particularly like the one I found in which the first voice sings *Erhalt uns Herr* [Luther], the second *Ach Gott vom Himmel* [Luther], the third *Vater unser im Himmelreich* [Luther], the fourth *Wir glauben* [Luther], the fifth *Durch Adams Fall* [Lazarus Spengler]; by an unknown composer.
>
> Another one and containing the five principal sections of the Catechism, has five different voices as follows:
> 1 [Commandments] *Mensch wiltu leben seliglich* [Luther] in the bass
> 2 [Creed] *Wir glauben all an einen Gott* [Luther] in the second *cantus*
> 3 [Lord's Prayer] *Vater unser im Himmelreich* [Luther] in the first *cantus*
> 4 [Baptism] *Christ unser Herr zum Jordan kam* [Luther] in the tenor
> 5 [Lord's Supper] *Jesus Christus unser Heiland* [Luther] in the alto
> Composed by Johannes Göldel.[20]

Because it was essentially an improvised tradition, it is not surprising that there are so few written-out examples of chorale *quodlibets*.[21] The sole example of a collection of such settings appears to be Johannes Christenius, *Kirchen Quotlibet, in welchen die gewöhnlichsten Psalmen... des... lutherischen Gesangbuchs... begriffen* (Gera: Mamitzsch, 1624). However, there are some hints that the tradition of improvising combinations of different chorales continued. For example, Andreas Hammerschmidt juxtaposes two chorales in his *Kirchen- und Tafel-Music* (Zittau: Dehnen, 1662), No. 22: *Gott hat das Evangelium* and *Ach Gott vom Himmel sieh darein*.[22] There are also two notable examples in Bach's music. In the first movement of Cantata 127, three chorale melodies are combined: *Herr Jesu Christ, wahr' Mensch und Gott, Christe, du Lamm Gottes*, and the first line of *Herzlich tut mich verlangen* (in the *basso continuo*).[23] The *Canonic Variations* include a chorale *quodlibet* in which all four lines of the chorale melody *Vom Himmel hoch* are combined together (BWV 769/5 = BWV 769a/3). Thus when the Bachs came together for their family gatherings, they very possibly sang more than just one chorale at the beginning of their proceedings, and that

---

20 Praetorius, *Syntagma Musicum III*, trans. Kite-Powell 33–34; *Syntagmum Musicum: Tomus tertius*, 18, 258; see Carl von Winterfeld, *Der evangelische Kirchengesang und sein Verhältnis zur Kunst des Tonsatzes* (Leipzig: Breitkopf & Härtel, 1843–1847; reprint, Hildesheim: Olms, 1966), 2:14.

21 Carl Ludwig Hilgenfeldt, *Johann Sebastian Bach's Leben, Wirken und Werke: Ein Beitrag zur Kunstgeschichte des achtzehnten Jahrhunderts* (Leipzig: Hofmeister, 1850; reprint, Hilversum: Knuf, 1965), 8, and Tab. 1, was only able to cite A. A. H. Redeker's reconstruction of Praetorius's description of Göldel's catechism chorale quodlibet.

22 See Friedhelm Krummacher, *Die Choralbearbeitung in der protestantischen Figuralmusik zwischen Praetorius und Bach* (Kassel: Bärenreiter, 1978), 62, 71.

23 The setting of *Christe, du Lamm Gottes* (BWV 233a)—later used for the *Kyrie* of the Missa in F (BWV 233/1)—incorporates the *Kyrie* from the Litany in the bass line.

148   *Robin A. Leaver*

their *quodlibets* were not exclusively jocular and secular but may well have been based on different chorales, similar to the examples given by Praetorius.

Bach's Connections with Individual Clergy

Bach's association with the clergy of the churches he either attended or served has usually been given only passing attention by Bach scholars. An exception is Martin Petzoldt, who has researched and published important brief studies of the life and works of many of these pastors and theologians.[24] Nevertheless, it would seem that there is more to be revealed for Bach studies from continued research in this area.

Eisenach

Johann Sebastian Bach was baptized by the Eisenach archdeacon (later superintendent), Johann Christoph Zerbst (1643–1719), on 23 March 1685, two days after his birth.[25] As a boy, Zerbst had been a pupil at the Latin school in Eisenach where he exhibited significant musical ability. He was first a member, then prefect, of the *chorus musicus* and was sufficiently accomplished to be able to substitute for the organist, Andreas Oswald [Ußwalt] (1634–1665),[26] when he was incapacitated by gout.[27] After studying theology at Jena University, he was ordained and become the deacon in Eisenach in 1671, then archdeacon and inspector of the Latin school in 1675, becoming superintendent in 1691.[28] Zerbst was the editor of the *Neues vollständiges Eisenachisches Gesangbuch Worinnnen...*

24   See, for example: Martin Petzoldt, "'Ut probus & doctus reddar.' Zum Anteil der Theologie bei der Schulausbildung Johann Sebastian Bachs in Eisenach, Ohrdruf und Lüneburg," BJ 71 (1985): 7–42; Martin Petzoldt and Joachim Petri, *Johann Sebastian Bach: Ehre sei dir Gott gesungen. Bilder und Texte zu Bachs Leben als Christ und seinem Wirken für die Kirche* (Göttingen: Vandenhoeck & Ruprecht, 1988); Martin Petzoldt, "Bach in theologischer Interaktion. Persönlichkeiten in seinem beruflichen Umfeld," *Über Leben, Kunst und Kunstwerke: Aspekte musikalischer Biographie Johann Sebastian Bach im Zentrum* [Festschrift für Hans-Joachim Schulze zum 65. Geburtstag], ed. Christoph Wolff (Leipzig: Evangelische Verlagsanstalt, 1999), 133–159.

25   Dok 2: 3 (No. 1). On the background, see Angelika Marsch, "Johann Sebastian Bach und die St. Georgenkirche zu Eisenach," *Nordost-Archiv: Zeitschrift für Kulturgeschichte und Landeskunde* 18 (1985): 169–185.

26   Wolff BLM, 26, suggests that Zerbst substituted for Johann Christoph Bach, who became organist after Oswald's death in 1665, by which time Zerbst had left Eisenach and was studying theology in Jena.

27   Johanne Sigismund Moench, *Johannes Theologus, Das ist, Der... Herr Johann Christoph Zerbst, Hochfürsl. Sachsen-Eisenachischer Hochverordneter General-Superintendens... (Welcher den 31. Maji 1719. im 76sten Jahr seines... Lebens... entschlaffen,) Wurde Bey seinem den 31. Junii darauf, als am S. Trinitatis-Fest angestellten solennen Leichen-Begängniß Aus dem Spruche I. Joh. IV. v. 9–11. als ein Denckmahl seiner hier gehaltenen geistreichen Predigten Zum steten Nachruhm vorgestellet In der Kirchen zu St. Georgen...* (Eisenach: Boetius, 1719), 47.

28   *Thüringer Pfarrerbuch*, ed. Bernhard Möller, et al (Neustadt an der Aisch: Degener, 1997–2000; Leipzig: Evangelische Verlagsanstalt, 2004–), 1: 473–474; Petzoldt, "Bach in theologischer Interaktion," 159.

so wol die alte/ als neue/ doch mehrenteils bekante Geistliche Kirchenlieder und Psalmen/ D. Martin Luthers/ und anderer Gottseeligen Männer befindlich (Eisenach: Rörer, 1673).[29] This hymnal, created by Zerbst, was the first collection of hymns that Bach would have used in public worship in church and school, and probably also in private at home in Eisenach.[30] Zerbst's sermons were similarly the first that Bach heard regularly Sunday by Sunday, and therefore the preacher must have had a formative influence on the young Bach. A few years after Bach had left Eisenach, Zerbst was responsible for the publication of a new quarto edition of the Bible: *Biblia, Das ist: Die gantze Heil. Schrifft Alten und Neuen Testaments, Verdeutscht durch D. Martin Luthern....* (Eisenach, 1704). Zerbst's preface is a summary of what Bach would have learned about Scripture from the superintendent in his preaching in church and in his involvement in the Latin school that Bach attended. The preface begins and ends with 1 Maccabees 12: 9: "Wir haben Trost an Gottes Wort das wir täglich lesen" (We have comfort in God's word which we daily read). The final paragraph begins with a desire that this Bible should promote the indwelling richness of the word of Christ, and refers to Colossians 3:16, a passage that continues with one of the primary verses in the New Testament that has musical significance: "singing psalms and hymns and spiritual songs."[31] It is not without significance that the Eisenach superintendent had experience as an organist in his earlier years and therefore must have been sympathetic and supportive of the ministry of music in the church.

Other clergy that Bach must have encountered in Eisenach were the archdeacon Valentin Schrön (1627–1706)—who preached the sermon at the funeral of Dorothee Marie Bach in 1676[32]—and deacons Sebastian Schramm (1652–1719)[33] and Johann Sigismund Coberger (1658–1719),[34] who all began their respective ministries in 1691.[35]

Ohrdruf

After his parents' deaths, Bach went to live with his oldest brother, Johann Christoph Bach (1671–1721), in Ohrdruf, where he attended the Latin school and sang in the *chorus musicus* in the Michaeliskirche between 1695 and 1700.[36]

---

29 See Conrad Freyse, "Sebastians Gesangbuch," BJ 45 (1958): 123–26; Conrad Freyse, "Johann Sebastian Bachs erstes Gesangbuch," *Jahrbuch für Liturgik und Hymnologie* 6 (1961): 138–42; Hans Dieter Ueltzen, "Johann Sebastian Bachs Kinder-Bilder-Gesangbuch," *Gottesdienst und Kirchenmusik* 5 (1986): 143–44; Petzoldt and Petri, *Ehre sei dir Gott gesungen*, 24–28.

30 See Chapter 14.

31 *Biblia, Das ist: Die gantze Heil. Schrifft Alten und Neuen Testaments* (Eisenach: Urban, 1704), fol.) (2^r–)(4^v.

32 *Thüringer Pfarrerbuch* 3: 392–393; see also note 1.

33 *Thüringer Pfarrerbuch* 3: 390–391.

34 *Thüringer Pfarrerbuch* 3: 116.

35 The archdeacon studied at Wittenberg University; the two deacons at Jena University.

36 Hartmut Ellrich, "Johann Sebastian Bach in Ohrdruf (1695– 1700)," *Johann Sebastian Bach und seine Zeit in Arnstadt*, eds. Matthias Klein and Janny Dittrich (Rudolstadt: Hain, 2000), 31–38.

150   *Robin A. Leaver*

The superintendent was Johann Abraham Kromayer (1665–1733) who, like other clergy Bach encountered early in life, studied theology at Jena University. He was ordained in 1692 to serve as deacon under his father Melchior Kromayer, the superintendent, whom he succeeded on his father's death in 1696.[37] Other clergy that Bach is likely to have encountered at the Michaeliskirche, Ohrdruf, are Johann Christoph Wolf (1638–1707), archdeacon since 1676,[38] and Georg Michael Lehmus (1666–1721), deacon since 1696.[39]

In the Ohrdruf church library, there exists a manuscript collection of sermons by J. A. Kromayer covering two complete annual cycles that were preached in Ohrdruf during 1696 and 1697, entitled: "Nachfolge Christi und die ersten Christen."[40] It appears that they were prepared for publication but were never issued in print.[41] These sermons are important because Bach must have heard Kromayer preach them from the Ohrdruf pulpit and therefore they are in need of serious study.

Also in the Ohrdruf church library is a copy of Caspar Heunisch's *Haupt-Schlüssel über die hohe Offenbahrung S. Johannis* (Schleusingen: Göbel, 1684) with a manuscript dedication from the author to Melchior Kromayer on the title page.[42] Because Bach is known to have owned a copy of this book later in life,[43] several questions are raised. When did Bach begin to collect such books? How influential in his choice of books were the clergy that Bach knew? Did any of these clergy present books to Bach? There is evidence that Bach received at least one book from a pastor, probably early in his career. Spitta records a detached flyleaf from an octavo book that has the inscription: "ex libera donatione Dn. [Deacon] Oehmii me possidet Joh. Seb. Bach."[44] Unfortunately, the current

---

37   Zedler 15: cols. 1962–1963; *Thüringer Pfarrerbuch* 1: 416–417; Petzoldt, "Bach in theologischer Interaktion," 146. For a discussion of a hymn sermon by Melchior Kromayer, see Markus Rathey, "Two Unlikely Sisters: The 'Cross' and the 'Crosses' in BWV 12 and 69a," BACH 38/1 (2007): 8–13.

38   *Thüringer Pfarrerbuch* 1: 726–727.

39   *Thüringer Pfarrerbuch* 1: 434.

40   Michaelisbibliothek Ohrdruf, Ms. Sig. Q321; see Petzoldt and Petri, *Ehre sei dir Gott gesungen*, 37.

41   There were discussions some years ago about the possibility of publication, given their importance as sermons heard by the young Bach, but nothing appeared. Perhaps the costs of transcribing the lengthy manuscript for a publication that would have had limited circulation proved prohibitive; hopefully, a digital copy of the manuscript can be made available in due course.

42   Michaelisbibliothek Ohrdruf, Sig. Q131; see Petzoldt and Petri, *Ehre sei dir Gott gesungen*, 36. Melchior Kromayer published his own study of the book of Revelation: *Kirchen-Chronica des Neuen Testaments. Oder Die Offenbahrung S. Johannis auf eine neue Lehr-Art... erklähret. Bey jetzigen denckwürdigen Zeiten... ans Licht gegeben* (Leipzig: Groß & Braun, 1708).

43   See Robin A. Leaver, *Bachs theologische Bibliothek: Eine kritische Bibliographie* (Stuttgart: Hänssler, 1983), No. 33.

44   Spitta 1: 354; Dok 1: 268.

Churches 151

whereabouts of the fragment is unknown, as is the identity of the donor[45] and the book from which it was taken.

The rector of the Ohrdruf Lyceum (Latin school) during Bach's time in the school was Johann Christoph Kiesewetter (1666–1744), the grandson of an archdeacon in Arnstadt.[46] He studied theology at Jena University and on the completion of his studies returned to Arnstadt in 1696 with the view of becoming the pastor of the Neue Kirche—where Bach a few years later would serve as organist—but instead accepted the position of rector in Ohrdruf later the same year, a position he held until he moved to Weimar in 1712.[47]

Elias Herda (1674–1728), cantor for most of Bach's time in Ohrdruf, had a similar experience. After being a choral scholar at St. Michael's Lüneberg between 1689 and 1695, Herda attended Jena University (1695–1697), where he studied theology with the intention of being ordained. In the same way that Kiesewetter was briefly in the running for a pastorate in Arnstadt, Herda was being considered for a similar position in Gotha in 1697, but instead accepted the position of cantor in Ohrdruf.[48] It must have been through Herda's influence that Bach was able to make the next move in his education in Lüneburg, and, given that he had seriously considered ordination, Herda probably had as much theological as musical influence on the young Bach. Indeed, the combined theological influence of superintendent, rector and cantor in Ohrdruf must have made a distinctive impression on the young musician.

Lüneberg

With the loss of financial support in Ohrdruf, the so-called *hospitia liberalia*, Bach could no longer continue his education at the Lyceum. Hence the move to Lüneberg where he could finish his schooling in return for singing in the *Mettenchor*,[49] following in the footsteps of Herda. The pastor of the Michaeliskirche was Martin Georg Hülsemann (1654–1738), whose biographical details are hard to come by.[50] He probably studied at Wittenberg University, after which he was a deacon in Hamburg before moving to a similar position at the Michaeliskirche, Lüneburg,

---

45 Spitta noted that a succession of burgermasters in Mühlhausen came from the Oehme family and therefore suggests that the book was given to Bach during his time in Mühlhausen. However, there were other branches of the Oehme family in Thuringia.

46 Johann Christoph Olearius, *Historia Arnstadiensis, Historie der alt-berühmten Schwartzburgischen Residentz Arnstadt* (Arnstadt: Bielcke, 1701; facsimile, Arnstadt: Donhof, 1998), 108, see also 111.

47 Petzoldt, "Bach in theologischer Interaktion," 145–146; Olearius, *Historia Arnstadiensis*, 114.

48 Petzoldt, "Bach in theologischer Interaktion," 144; Gustav Fock, *Der junge Bach in Lüneberg: 1700 bis 1702* (Hamburg: Merseburger, 1950), 38; Konrad Küster, *Der junge Bach* (Stuttgart: Deutsche Verlags-Anstalt, 1996), 72–75; Wolff BLM, 39–41.

49 Bach sang under the leadership of the cantor Johann Conrad Dreyer rather than his predecessor, August Braun; see Küster, *Der junge Bach*, 86.

50 Petzoldt, "Ut probus & doctus reddar," 28, note 94; Petzoldt, "Bach in theologischer Interaktion," 145.

152   Robin A. Leaver

in 1695; two years later, he became the *pastor primarius* (1697). Petzoldt suggests that Bach may have had private lessons in theology from Hülsemann, but gives no sources.[51] The deacon of the Michaeliskirche during Bach's time was Johann Jacob Boje (1671–1729), who, like Hülsemann, is biographically elusive, except that he apparently studied theology with Elias Herda and J. A. Kromayer in Jena,[52] which may prove to be significant if more can be discovered about him. No doubt in their regular catechetical preaching, these clergy made significant use of Joachim Lütkemann's *Corpus Doctrinae Catecheticae Augustum*, first issued in 1656 for use in church and school throughout the principalities of Braunschweig, Lüneburg, and Wolfenbüttel, being continuously reprinted well into the eighteenth century.[53] Lütkemann's concern was to restore effective catechetical teaching disrupted and neglected during the Thirty Years' War.

Arnstadt

With Bach's move to Arnstadt in 1703,[54] as the organist of the Neuen Kirche, his relationship with clergy was significantly changed: instead of being a pupil and parishioner, he was now a professional colleague. The Neuen Kirche in Arnstadt was a kind of proving ground for newly ordained clergy, who usually held the position of pastor for no more than a year, although in some cases it extended to three or even four years.[55] When Bach began his appointment in August 1703, the pastor was Johannes Andreas Emmerling (1672 –1743),[56] but he left the following year and on New Year's Day 1705 he was replaced by Justus Christian Uthe (1680–1716), who remained in the position until 1709.[57] Uthe apparently exercised pastoral oversight with regard to Bach to judge from the consistory minute concerning the "frembde

---

51 Petzoldt, "Ut probus & doctus reddar," 28.

52 Fock, *Der junge Bach in Lüneburg*, 42; Küster, *Der junge Bach*, 72–73.

53 Joachim Lütkemann, *Corpus Doctrinae Catecheticae Augustum. Das ist: Anleitung zur Catechismus-Lehr/ Wie dieselbe in des Fürstenthumbs Braunschweig-Lüneburg-Wolfenbüttelschen Theils Schulen und Kirchen einfältig und erbawlich zu treiben...* (Lüneburg: Stern, 1656); see Christian Deuper, *Theologe, Erbauungsschriftsteller, Hofprediger: Joachim Lütkemann in Rostock und Wolfenbüttel* (Wiesbaden: Harrassowitz, 2013), 285–314. For the background of Lutheran catechetical instruction, see Gerhard Bode, "Instruction in the Christian Faith by Lutherans and Luther," *Lutheran Ecclesiastical Culture 1550–1675*, ed. Robert Kolb (Leiden: Brill, 2008), 159–204.

54 Hannelore Wallendorf, "Die Bache in Arnstadt," *Bach und seine Zeit in Arnstadt*, eds. Klein and Dittrich, 63–70.

55 See *Thüringer Pfarrerbuch* 2: 20.

56 *Thüringer Pfarrerbuch* 2: 133–134. Emmerling studied at Jena University 1661–1664. Sophia Dorothea Emmerling, a cousin of Bach's first wife, Maria Barbara, was godmother to Johann Gottfried Bernhard Bach, baptized in the Stadtkirche Weimar in May 1715; see Dok 2: 58 (No. 74).

57 *Thüringer Pfarrerbuch* 2: 397–398. Uthe was later deacon of Langensalza (1709–1716), and appointed superintendent in Freiburg/Unstrut in 1716, but died soon after. A member of the Uthe family, Mathes Uthe, was Stadtpfeiffer in Mühlhausen in the seventeenth century; see Markus Rathey, *Johann Rudolph Ahle 1625–1673: Lebensweg und Schaffen* (Eisenach: Wagner, 1999), 41, 45.

Churches 153

Jungfer" in the organ loft in November 1706.[58] Not a great deal is known about him, although he had a reputation of opposing those whose views went beyond the theological parameters of the Lutheran confessions.[59]

The Neuen Kirche pastor did not have exclusive use of the church's pulpit, since the town's clergy would preach each of their sermons in all of the town churches on different days throughout the week.[60] In Arnstadt in addition to the successive pastors of the Neuen Kirche, Emmerling, and Uthe, Bach found himself working with the other Arnstadt clergy, notably two members of the numerous Olearius family of pastors, theologians, professors, and lawyers, with branches in Halle and Leipzig.[61] They were father and son: the superintendent and pastor of the Barfüsserkirche, Johann Gottfried Olearius (1635–1711), and the deacon, Johann Christoph Olearius (1668–1747), who had been pastor of the Neuen Kirche in 1694. The superintendent had previously worked with two organists from the Bach family in Arnstadt. Sebastian's great uncle, Heinrich Bach (1615–92), had been the organist of the Barfüsserkirche for almost fifty years when Olearius became superintendent in 1688. But a year later (1689), it was clear that his blindness was preventing him from continuing his duties and Sebastian's oldest brother, Johann Christoph, who would later take responsibility for his younger brother in Ohrdruf, was brought in as an able substitute.[62] When Heinrich Bach died in 1692, the superintendent preached the funeral sermon.[63]

Johann Gottfried Olearius was born and brought up in Halle, where his father, Gottfried Olearius (1604–1685), was pastor and superintendent of the Liebfrauenkirche, commonly known as the Marktkirche. After studies at various universities across Germany, including Leipzig and Jena, he was ordained and assisted his father as deacon in Halle, then, when his father died in early 1685, succeeded him as the pastor of the Marktkirche. Later, in 1688, he was called to become superintendent in Arnstadt, where he served for the rest of his life.[64] He published a steady stream of devotional prose and poetry, which

---

58 Dok 2: 21–22 (No. 17), NBR 47–48 (No. 21).

59 Carl Friedrich Göschel, *Chronik der Stadt Langensalza in Thüringen. Dritter Band* (Langensalza: Knoll, 1842), 460.

60 The preaching responsibilities are set out in Olearius, *Historia Arnstadiensis*, 47–50.

61 Wolfgang Tittelbach-Helmrich, "Die Olearius Pastoren als Geistliche der Bachkantoren in Arnstadt," Klein and Dittrich, *Bach und seine Zeit in Arnstadt*, 63–70, and 196.

62 Karl Geiringer, *The Bach Family: Seven Generations of Creative Genius* (New York: Oxford University Press, 1954), 20–23.

63 Johann Gottfried Olearius, *I.N.J. Der Hier zeitlich- und dort ewiglich Reichbeseligte Lebens-Bach/ Nach seinem Herfliessen/ Ergiessen/ und Geniessen/ Aus des 91sten Psalms letzten Vers : Bey ... Leichbestattung Des ... Herrn Heinrich Bachs/ An die 51. Jahr Wohlverdient-gewesenen Organisten un[d] Wohlbeliebten Stadt-Musici allhier zu Arnstadt/ Welcher am 10. Iulii ... im 77. Jahre seines mit Ehren hochgebrachten Alters ...* (Arnstadt: Meurer, 1692). See also Heinrich Beyer, "Leichensermone auf Musiker des 17. Jahrhunderts," *Monatshefte für Musikgeschichte* 7 (1875): 171–175, 177–188, esp. 178–179; Ulrich Konrad, "Instrumentalkompositionen von Heinrich Bach (1615–1692). Zwei bislang unbeachtete Sonaten in einem Gothaer Partiturbuch," BJ 81 (1995): 93–113, esp. 100–102, 104–105.

64 Zedler 25: cols. 1187–1189; *Thüringer Pfarrerbuch* 2: 298; Petzoldt, "Bach in theologischer Interaktion," 148; see also Tittelbach-Helmrich, "Die Olearius Pastoren," 144–149.

154   Robin A. Leaver

included some seventy hymn texts.[65] But he was also an accomplished musician. For more than ten years, between 1660 and 1672, he combined the functions of deacon and director of music at the Marktkirche, Halle.[66] This was a church that had a prestigious tradition of church music, with one of his predecessors being Samuel Scheidt (1687–1654), and one of his successors, Handel's teacher Friedrich Wilhelm Zachow (1663–1712). This "Directorium Musices" involved the direction of concerted music by such contemporary composers as Andreas Hammerschmidt (1612–1675), Wolfgang Carl Briegel (1626–1712), and Samuel Capricornus (1628–1665), among others.[67] Therefore, when towards the end of 1705, Bach made his request to the Arnstadt superintendent to visit "Lübeck in order to comprehend one thing and another about his art,"[68] he was addressing someone who knew exactly the importance and significance of such a visit. Johann Gottfried Olearius was not someone who simply knew about music but rather someone who had the experience of performing and directing music in a church that had a significant musical tradition.

Johann Christoph Olearius[69] attended the university at Jena (1687–1693) where he studied a wide variety of subjects. In later years, he issued a significant sequence of substantial publications on local history, numismatics,[70] antiquities, homiletics, bibliography, etc.,[71] and especially on the history and use of hymnody,[72] which established him as one of the pioneer Lutheran hym-

---

65   Emil Eduard Koch, *Geschichte des Kirchenlieds und Kirchengesangs der christlichen, insbesondere der deutschen evangelischen Kirche*, 3rd ed. (Stuttgart: Belser, 1866–1877), 3: 350–352. Twenty-eight hymn texts are found in Albert Fischer and Wilhelm Tümpel, *Das deutsche evangelische Kirchenlied des 17. Jahrhunderts* (Gütersloh: Bertelsmann, 1904–1916; reprint, Hildesheim: Olms, 1964), 4: 381–393 (Nos. 469–486). Bach composed a melody and setting for one of these hymn texts, "Dich bet ich an, mein höchster Gott," included in the Schemelli *Gesangbuch* (BWV 449).

66   Walter Serauky, *Musikgeschichte der Stadt Halle: Von Samuel Scheidt bis an die Zeit Georg Friedrich Händels und Johann Sebastian Bachs* (Halle: Buchhandlung des Waisenhauses, 1935–1943; reprint, Hildesheim: Olms, 1971) 2/1: 293–295.

67   Serauky, *Musikgeschichte der Stadt Halle*, 2/1: 292: "1663 10 Musicalische sachen, welche H. M. Olearius zu Leipzig gekaufft" [1663 10 musical pieces which Herr Magister Olearius bought in Leipzig].

68   NBR 46 (No. 20); Dok. 2, 19 (No. 16).

69   The following paragraphs are substantially based on Robin A. Leaver, "The Organist Encounters the Hymnologist: J. S. Bach and J. C. Olearius in Arnstadt," *Understanding Bach* 7 (2012): 21–28; see also Zedler 25: cols. 1176–1184; *Thüringer Pfarrerbuch* 2: 297; Petzoldt, "Bach in theologischer Interaktion," 147–148; Tittelbach-Heinrich, "Die Olearius Pastoren," 150–156.

70   In 1693, on completing his studies at Jena, he became curator of the numismatic collection of Graf Anton Günther II of Schwarzburg-Sonderhausen in Arnstadt; see Peter Berghaus, "Numismatiker im Porträt: 38. Johann Christoph Olearius, 17.9.1668 Halle - 31.3.1747 Arnstadt," *Geldgeschichtliche Nachrichten*, 31 (1996): 276–285.

71   See *Catalogus Scriptorum, welchem, auf Begehren redlich gesinnter Freunde und besonderer Liebhaber der Hist. Literariae, zum Andencken seiner wenigen und geringen Schrifften, wie sie von A. C. 1690. bis A. C. 1727. in Druck gegangen, wohlmeynend communiciren wollen, Io. Christoph. Olearius* ([Arnstadt]: [s.n.], [1727]).

72   The pastors and theologians of the Olearius family made significant contributions to Lutheran hymnody; see Johann Bernhard Liebler, *Hymnopoeographia Oleariana, oder Olearische*

nologists of the early eighteenth century.[73] He was also the editor of the hymnal that Bach must have used during his time as the organist of the Neuen Kirche: *Neu-verbessertes Arnstädtisches Gesangbuch/ Darinnen Eine vergnügliche Anzahl von Geistlichen und erbaulichen Liedern zufinden/ welche nicht allein von reinen Evangelischen Lehrern und andern rechtgläubigen verfertiget* (Arnstadt: Bachmann, 1701; further editions in 1703 and 1705, with a slightly different title). The hymnal included quite a number of his father's hymn texts, as well as his own parody of Luther's *O Gott vom Himmel sieh darein*, written against Pietism.[74]

J. C. Olearius appears to have had a musical background. He was born in Halle when his father was directing the music of the Marktkirche, so it seems most likely that his first lessons in music came from his father.[75] He also collected music, especially part books of Italian motets,[76] as well as numerous hymnals, many of which included music. Although his many writings on the Lutheran chorale concentrate on texts, from time to time he does include references to music. For example, his discussion of the music associated with the Passion hymn *Jesu, meines Lebens-Leben*, includes the notation of two preferred melodies that are given with their respective figured basses.[77] Similarly, at the beginning of his preface to the *Arnstadtisches Gesangbuch*, dated 8 December 1700, Olearius wrote:

> Hymns have their great usefulness as much for their beautiful melodies as for their pleasing poetry and edifying content. The melody, or art of song, is the power of music which has such an undeniable effect that even the devil himself must acknowledge it.[78]

Many of the hymnals that Olearius collected are to be found in the Forschungs-bibliothek Gotha. Among them is a copy of the Schemelli *Musicalisches Gesangbuch* (Leipzig: Breitkopf, 1736), attested by the signature on the title

---

Lieder-Historie, darinnen unterschiedene Olearii, als berühmte Lieder-Dichter und Lieder-Freunde ...(Naumburg: Boßögel, [1727]), 11–12 (Johann Gottfried Olearius) and 14–20 (Johann Christoph Olearius).

73 See Martin Rößler, "Die Frühzeit hymnologischer Forschung," *Jahrbuch für Liturgik und Hymnologie* 19 (1975): 123–186, esp. 134–137.

74 Liebler, *Hymnopoeographia Oleariana,* 15–16; Koch, *Geschichte des Kirchenlieds und Kirchengesangs,* 5: 357–358.

75 Petzoldt, "Bach in theologischer Interaktion," 147.

76 See Leaver, "The Organist Encounters the Hymnologist," 22.

77 Johann Christoph Olearius, *Betrachtung des bekannten Passion-Liedes/ Jesu meines Lebens-Leben* ... (Jena: Bielcke, 1704), 17–22.

78 *Arnstadtisches Verbessertes Gesangbuch* (Arnstadt: Bachmann, 1705), sig. a 2r: "Lieder haben ihren grossen Nutzen sowohl wegen der schönen Melodien als auch angenehmen Poësie und erbaulichen Innhalts. Die Melodie oder Gesang-Art hat Krafft der Music eine solche unwiedersprechliche Würckung daß der Teufel selbst solche bezeugen muß..."

156   *Robin A. Leaver*

page,[79] for which Bach was the musical editor, and thus a copy that could quite possibly have been a gift from Bach.

While Bach was in Arnstadt, J. C. Olearius was at work on a significant hymnological project, a commentary on the primary chorales sung throughout the church year: his *Evangelischer Lieder-Schatz,* published in Jena, issued in four parts between 1705 and 1707.[80] But these hymn commentaries also included sermon outlines, some of which were based on sermons that Olearius had preached in Arnstadt and which Bach is likely to have heard. For the young Bach, working alongside J. C. Olearius gave him an extraordinary opportunity to learn from one of the leading authorities of the day, piling up an enormous amount of information on the Lutheran chorale, its history in general as well as the background of individual hymns. The fruits of Bach's Arnstadt experience are not hard to find. A few years after leaving Arnstadt, he planned to create what in many ways amounts to a musical counterpart of Olearius's *Evangelischer Lieder-Schatz*: his projected *Orgelbüchlein,*[81] especially the first section of church year chorales. Similarly, the chorale cantatas that Bach composed in Leipzig mostly between 1724 and 1725 (Jahrgang II) may well have been influenced by his experience in Arnstadt. It is no coincidence that this sequence of chorale cantatas was begun in 1724, exactly two hundred years after the first hymns of Luther and others were published. Most of the chorales of this Jahrgang are the classic, first-generation Lutheran hymns that Olearius wrote about so often. For example, for the bicentenary of the Lutheran Reformation in 1717—a celebration that had been years in preparation—Olearius reissued the contents of the earliest Lutheran hymnals published between 1524 and 1525. In the preface to that volume, Olearius observed that these hymns had been sung continuously in Lutheran churches and homes for "almost two hundred years" (fast auf 200. Jahr).[82]

Then there is Bach's visit to Lübeck. Was this his own idea or was it suggested to him by J. C. Olearius? To judge from the consistory interrogation after his return, it does not seem likely that superintendent Olearius initiated the possibility, though he must have been supportive of the journey and its purpose.[83] But J. C. Olearius may well have planted the seed of the idea in the mind of the young Bach, since ten years or so earlier (1694–1695), at the beginning of his career, he had made a similar excursion from Arnstadt to Hamburg, Lübeck, and Travemünde in order to visit pastors and theologians, and especially those with extensive libraries.[84] The possibility that J. C. Olearius influenced Bach's decision

---

79 Forschungsbibliothek Gotha, shelfmark: Cant. spir. 8° 00265.

80 See Rößler, *Die Bibliographie der deutschen Liedpredigt,* 132–134; Leaver, "The Organist Encounters the Hymnologist," 25–27.

81 See my earlier discussion: Robin A. Leaver, "Bach and Hymmnody: The Evidence of the *Orgelbüchlein,*" EM 13 (1985): 227–236.

82 Johann Christoph Olearius, *Jubilirende Lieder-Freude/ Bestehend in erster Aufflage derer allerersten A.C. 1524. und 1525. in Druck gegangenen Lutherischen Gesängen zur Vermehrung schuldigster Devotion und Danckbarkeit, bey dem Andern von Gott verliehenen Lutherischen Reformations-Jubilaeo, nebst einer Vorrede* (Arnstadt: Meurer, 1717), sig.)2(^{v} –)3(^{r}.

83 Dok 2: 19–21 (No.16); NBR 46–47 (No. 20).

84 See further, Leaver, "The Organist Encounters the Hymnologist," 23.

Churches 157

to make the trip to Lübeck becomes more likely when the connection between Olearius and the Lübeck superintendent, Georg Heinrich Götze (1667–1728),[85] is considered. Götze had been appointed to the Lübeck position a few years earlier in 1702 and like Olearius had already begun to publish significant books on hymnology. Also, like Olearius, he edited a hymnal, the first official hymnal for Lübeck: *Lübeckisches Gesang-Buch ...* (Lübeck: Wiedemeyer, 1703).[86] The Gesangbuch was introduced on the third Sunday in Advent (16 December 1703), when Buxtehude would have played the Marienkirche organ and Götze preached the sermon. The sermon was published the following year, and it included an open letter addressed to Johann Christoph Olearius: *Christliche Lieder-Predigt, Nach Anleiting der Worte Davids Ps. XLV.v.2. ...Am dritten Advent-Sonntage, Den XVIden Decembr. A. MDCC.III. Als das Lübeckische Gesang-Buch Der Christl. Gemeinde zu St. Marien bekandt gemacht wurde, In der Furcht des Herrn gehalten, und nebst einem besondern Send-schreiben, an den Verfasser der Lieder-Bibliothec (Tit.) Herrn M. Joh. Christoph Olearium, Wohlverordneten Prediger und Bibliothec. in Arnstadt...* (Lübeck: Wiedermeyer, 1704).[87] In return, Olearius dedicated the first volume of his *Evangelischer Lieder-Schatz* (1705) to the Lübeck superintendent. Given this connection between Götze and Olearius, it does not seem unreasonable to suppose that the Arnstadt deacon had some involvement in Bach's decision to go to Lübeck in the first place, nor perhaps too speculative to suggest that Bach may well have taken with him a letter of introduction from Johann Christoph Olearius addressed to superintendent Götze.

Although it was during his Mühlhausen years that Bach felt secure enough to embark on marriage, the ceremony was conducted in a church close to Arnstadt rather than in the church he was serving as organist in Mühlhausen. He married his distant relative, Maria Barbara, the daughter of Johann Michael Bach (1648–1694), his father's cousin. The wedding took place in the small village church of nearby Dornheim:

> On October 1707 the worthy Johann Sebastian Bach, bachelor, organist of the church of Divii Blasii, Mühlhausen, lawfully begotten son of the deceased honourable and distinguished Ambrosius Bach, town's organist and musician in Eisenach, to the virtuous Maria Barbara, spinster, youngest surviving daughter of the late right worthy and distinguished Bach, organist at Gehren, here in the house of God [Bartholomäuskirche, Dornheim], by permission of his lordship the Count [of Schwartzburg], and after banns duly called in Arnstadt.[88]

---

85 Zedler 11: cols. 87–89; Rößler, "Die Frühzeit hymnologischer Forschung," 138–139.

86 The earliest known extant imprint dates from 1716.

87 See Martin Rößler, *Die Bibliographie der deutschen Liedpredigt* (Nieuwkoop: de Graaf, 1976), 205; and Rößler, "Die Frühzeit hymnologischer Forschung," 138–139; see also J. C. Olearius, *Betrachtung des bekannten Passion-Liedes/ Jesu meines Lebens-Leben ...* sig. a1ᵛ.

88 Charles Sanford Terry, *Bach: A Biography*, 2nd ed. (London: Oxford University Press, 1933), 77. Similar entries occur in both Arnstadt and Dornheim church registers: Dornheim, Dok 2: 28 (No. 29); Arnstadt, Dok 2: 28 (No. 28), NBR 51–52 (No. 26). The entry in the Arnstadt

158   *Robin A. Leaver*

The couple was married by the Dornheim pastor, Johann Lorenz Stauber (1660–1723), who was appointed in 1705 after having been a pastor in Rudisleben.[89] Stauber seems to have had a special relationship with the Bach family, which would explain why the wedding did not take place in one of the more commodious Arnstadt churches, and why it was necessary to obtain special permission from the Count of Schwartzburg. Although not a great deal is known about Stauber, he was born in Arnstadt, studied in Wittenberg,[90] and had a continuing connection with the Bachs. After the death of his first wife, Stauber married Regina Wedemann, Maria Barbara Bach's aunt, and after Regina Stauber's death in 1730—ten years after Maria Barbara's death—Sebastian Bach was named in connection with the dispersal of her estate.[91] According to Bitter, Bach got to know Stauber in Arnstadt when the former was the organist of the Neuen Kirche and the latter was a candidate for the ministry.[92] Bach may well have befriended Stauber during his time in Arnstadt, but Stauber was then no longer a theological student preparing for ordination, having been a pastor since 1687.

Wilhelm Rust concluded that Bach's cantata *Der Herr denket an uns* (BWV 196), a setting of Psalm 115: 12–15, was composed for a wedding, a reasonable conclusion because the text speaks of the blessing of two houses or families.[93] Spitta thought that the reference to children made the cantata more likely to have been intended for the second wedding of a widower, and the reference to the priestly "house of Aaron" suggested to him that it was intended for the wedding of a pastor. Because it is clearly an early cantata, Spitta thought it likely that Bach composed it for Stauber's second marriage, to Regina Wedemann on 5 June 1708.[94] Spitta's arguments are not conclusive, because references to the prospect of children were common at first weddings,[95] and when the "house of Aaron" is juxtaposed with "house of Israel," as it is in the psalm, there is no overwhelming reason to suppose that the cantata was composed for a pastor. Thus Mary Greer, in drawing a parallel between the house of Aaron and the

---

register is headed "Dom: XV. p. Trin," that is, fifteenth Sunday after Trinity = 2 October 1707, presumably recording that the banns had been read for the third consecutive Sunday and no impediment was raised. On the Dornheim church, see Siegfried Neumann, "Die Kirche St. Bartholomäus zu Dornhein – Traukirche von Johann Sebastian Bach," *Bach und seine Zeit in Arnstadt*, eds. Klein and Dittrich, 165–171.

89 Neumann, "Die Kirche St. Bartholomäus zu Dornhein," 170–171.

90 *Schediasma Historico-Criticum De Apophthegmate Ignatii: O Emos Eros Estaurotai, publicae ventilationi subiiciendum a Praeside M. Wilhelmo Ernesto Tentzelio, Thur. Respondente Johanne Laurentio Staubern/ Arnstadiensi. Ad d. XIV. Mart. A. MDCXXCIII* (Wittenberg: Brüning, 1683). I am grateful to Joshua Rifkin for locating this dissertation.

91 Dok 2: 212–213 (No. 293).

92 Carl Hermann Bitter, *Johann Sebastian Bach*, 2nd ed. (Dresden, Bänsch, 1880), 1:84; no source cited.

93 Rust included the cantata with other "Trauungs-Cantaten" in BG 13/1.

94 Spitta 1: 369–370; Spitta ET 1: 370–371.

95 For example, Psalm 128, with its reference to wife, children, and children's children, was commonly used at weddings.

Churches   159

"house of Bach" (and following a hint by Christoph Wolff[96]), suggests that the cantata was perhaps more likely to have been composed by Bach for his own wedding to Maria Barbara in October 1707. It is suitably lightly scored for the small Bartholomäuskirche, Dornheim, where Stauber was pastor. Greer writes:

> As far as we know, the wedding... is the only instance in which two members of the Bach clan married one another. It would be hard to imagine a more appropriate text for the nuptial celebration of two members of the Bach family, nearly all of whom were employed as church musicians.[97]

Mühlhausen

The position of organist at the Blasiuskirche, Mühlhausen, a large church of cathedral-like dimensions, must have seemed very attractive to Bach, especially as he had the opportunity of playing on the recently renewed instrument that was larger than any of the organs in Arnstadt.[98] But the churches of the town were disturbed by a controversy that may well have been a significant factor in his decision to leave the position barely a year later. The controversy in Mühlhausen concerned the influence of Halle Pietism[99] that Spitta characterized in largely black and white terms, with superintendent Johann Adolph Frohne (1652–1713),[100] pastor of the Blasiuskirche, on the Pietist side, and archdeacon Georg Christian Eilmar (1665–1715),[101] pastor of the Marienkirche, on the Orthodox side.[102] Stemming from Spitta's characterization of this controversy, Bach literature has been flooded with misinformed and misleading interpretations regarding the significance of the Pietist/Orthodox confrontation with regard to Bach. Briefly stated, the common viewpoint is: that only Pietists promoted warm devotional piety, whereas the Orthodox were committed to an intellectual formalism; that the Orthodox were doctrinally pedantic to the exclusion of all else, whereas only the Pietists sought to work out their faith practically and ethically; that the Pietists opposed all elaborate church music, whereas the Orthodox

---

96 Wolff BLM, 91–92.
97 Mary Dalton Greer, "From the House of Aaron to the House of Johann Sebastian: Old Testament Roots for the Bach Family Tree," *About Bach*, ed. Gregory Butler, George B. Stauffer, and Mary Dalton Greer (Urbana: University of Illinois Press, 2008), 24–25.
98 See Christoph Wolff and Markus Zepf, *The Organs of J. S. Bach: A Handbook*, trans. Lynn Edwards Butler (Urbana: University of Illinois Press, 2012), 8–13 (Arnstadt), 71–74 (Mühlhausen, Blasiuskirche). The organ of the Marienkirche, Mühlhausen, was similarly larger than the Arnstadt instruments; ibid., 69.
99 In this chapter, the terms Pietism/Pietist are capitalized in order to convey that the subject concerns a specific movement within Lutheranism and not just simply a general movement for "piety." Similarly, Orthodox/Orthodoxy is also capitalized in order to convey the *status quo* of Lutheran polity that the Pietists reacted against.
100 Petzoldt, "Bach in theologischer Interaktion," 140–141.
101 Petzoldt, "Bach in theologischer Interaktion," 138.
102 Spitta 1: 354–365; Spitta ET 1: 358–366.

160   *Robin A. Leaver*

vigorously promoted such music. But the Pietists did not have a monopoly on piety; for example, Erdmann Neumeister is sometimes called a Pietist because of his emotionally charged cantata libretti and because some of his hymn texts appear in Freylinghausen's Pietist hymnal, but Neumeister was staunchly Orthodox theologically and he campaigned most vigorously against the Pietists. Similarly, while it is true that some Pietists did oppose elaborate church music, others did not, and while some Orthodox did enthusiastically endorse the new type of concerted cantatas, as epitomized by the libretti of Neumeister, there were those who were against their use.[103] The Orthodox/Pietist controversy is much more nuanced than is often presented in Bach studies.

Lutheran Pietism, as a specific movement, was many faceted.[104] Its inspiration was found in the writings of Philipp Jacob Spener (1635–1705), which led to the formation of Bible study groups (referred to as *collegium pietatis*, or *ecclesiolae in ecclesia*, little churches within the church), with later leadership being assumed by August Hermann Francke (1663–1727), centered in Glaucha near Halle, in the Waisenhaus with its effective printing and publishing, and also to some degree in Halle University. At the beginning, it appeared to be a movement for the intensification of spiritual life and as such it was welcomed. But when it took on a decidedly anticlerical stance, and many Pietists began calling for the dismantling of distinctive Lutheran patterns of worship, and other aspects of Christian life and practice, there was a significant reaction from the Lutheran Orthodox establishment.

For Bach, Mühlhausen could not have been his introduction to the Pietist/ Orthodox controversy, because Pietists, mostly laity, had been active in Thüringia for some time.[105] It is possible that later Pietist elements in Ohrdruf had their origin during Bach's time there,[106] and similarly Pietists had also been active in and around Arnstadt,[107] but the clergy and schoolteachers in both places opposed

---

103 See Robin A. Leaver, "Oper in der Kirche: Bach und der Kantatenstreit im frühen 18. Jahrhundert," BJ 99 (2013): 171–203.

104 Pietism in general is extraordinarily diverse, involving different countries, different languages, and different confessional contexts; see *Geschichte des Pietismus*, ed. Martin Brecht, et al, 4 vols. (Göttingen: Vandenhoeck & Ruprecht, 1993–2004). German Pietism that relates to Bach is specific to time, place and confession. The background is covered in the first volume of *Geschichte des Pietismus – Der Pietismus vom siebzehnten bis zum frühen achtzehnten Jahrhundert*, and an invaluable introduction is Johannes Wallmann, *Der Pietismus* (Göttingen: Vandenhoeck & Ruprecht, 2005). For a general overview of the issues, see Robin A. Leaver, Bach and Pietism," *Concordia Theological Quarterly* 55 (1991): 5–22.

105 See Theodor Wotschke, "Der Pietismus in Thüringen," *Thüringisch-Sächsische Zeitschrift für Geschichte und Kunst* 18 (1929): 1–55. Much in Leo Schrade's "Bach, the Conflict Between the Sacred and the Secular," *Journal of the History of Ideas* 7 (1946): 151–194, is based on Wotschke's article. The most comprehensive discussion of Bach's experience in Mühlhausen is Johannes Wallmann, "Neues Licht auf die Zeit Johann Sebastian Bachs in Mühlhausen. Zu den Anfängen des Pietismus in Thüringen," *Pietismus und Neuzeit ein Jahrbuch zur Geschichte des Neueren Protestantismus* 35 (2009):46–114.

106 Wotschke, "Der Pietismus in Thüringen," 42.

107 Valentin Ernst Loescher, *The Complete Timotheus Verinus* [1718–1721], trans. James L. Langebartels and Robert J. Koester (Milwaukee: Northwestern, 1998), 1: 21. Loescher, superintendent

Churches 161

them. Eilmar had experienced Pietists in Langensalza, where he was deacon between 1691 and 1696, but apparently did not start writing against them until after he had moved to Mühlhausen;[108] however, once started he did not stop. At first his opposition to Pietists was of a general nature, such as his *Gülden Kleinod Evangelischer Kirchen* (Leipzig: Neuenhahn, 1701),[109] which was severely criticized by Johann Anastasius Freylinghausen (1670–1739),[110] Pietist theologian in Halle, the compiler of the influential Pietist hymnal, *Geist-reiches Gesang-Buch*, first published by the Halle Waisenhaus in 1704 and reprinted numerous times. Among other things, Eilmar was affronted by the way in which some Pietists were employing Article XXVIII of the Augsburg Confession—the article that condemned the power of Catholic bishops in the sixteenth century—using it to criticize contemporary Lutheran clergy and the liturgies of baptism, confession and the sacrament of the altar. Later, Johann Matheson made significant use of Eilmar's *Gülden Kleinod*, in his *Musicalische Patriot* (1728) to argue that this Pietist agenda undermined the music ministry of the church.[111] Issues became more personal when in 1703 Frohne published a small book on the spiritual priesthood of all true believers, a primary Pietist tenet.[112] Eilmar responded, in a book published in Wittenberg rather than Mühlhausen, with a refutation in which he charged Frohne with misunderstanding Scripture.[113] Over the following few years, Frohne and Eilmar exchanged their differences in print, Frohne insisting that he remained Orthodox in his theology[114] and Eilmar persistently attacking

---

in Dresden, was the primary Orthodox spokesman against Pietism through his writings in the theological journal, *Unschuldige Nachrichten von alten und neuen theologischen Sachen*, he edited in the first decades of the eighteenth century and later. The *Vollständiger Timotheus Verinus*, published in Wittenberg, was an expanded compilation of the articles and book reviews on Pietism that had appeared in *Unschuldige Nachrichten* since 1701.

108 For example, Georg Christian Eilmar, *Des Pietisten L. Kletwichs zu Langensalza ganz Unsinnige Raserey...* ([Mühlhausen]: [s.n.], 1704); see Wallmann, "Neues Licht auf die Zeit Johann Sebastian Bachs in Mühlhausen," 71–84.

109 Eilmar's later publications include *Anatomie der pietistischen Fledermaus* (Mühlhausen: Käyser, 1704), and *Die Pietisterey als das größte Hinderniß wahrer Gottseeligkeit aus der Lehre von der Buße erwiesen* (Wittenberg: Hake, 1705).

110 Johann Anastasius Freylinghausen, *Entdeckung Der Falschen Theologie, Womit Einige so genannte Evangelisch- Lutherische Lehrer, insonderheit Herr Doct. Georg Christian Eilmar... In seinem also titulirten Güldenen Kleinod der Evangelischen Kirchen...* (Halle: Waisenhaus, 1704).

111 Johann Matheson, *Der Musicalischen Patriot, Welcher seine gründliche Betrachtungen, über Geist- und Weltl. Harmonien* (Hamburg: [Matheson], 1728; facsimile, Leipzig: Zentralantiquariat, 1978), 149–152.

112 Johann Adolpn Frohne, *Gründlicher Beweiß des Geistlichen Priesterthums* (Mühlhausen: Brückner, 1703).

113 Georg Christian Eilmar, *Gründliche Erörterung der Lehre vom geistlichen Priesterthum nach dessen in der Heiligen Schrift abgemessenem Gebrauch ...* (Wittenberg: Hake, 1704).

114 See Martin Pezoldt, *Bachstätten aufsuchen* (Leipzig: Verlag Kunst und Touristik, 1992), 133–137; see also Küster, *Der junge Bach*, 161–165. Wallmann, "Neues Licht auf die Zeit Johann Sebastian Bachs in Mühlhausen," 53–56, and *passim*, takes issue with some of Petzoldt's conclusions.

162   *Robin A. Leaver*

him for what he saw as the errors of Pietism.[115] Thus by the time Bach arrived in Mühlhausen, there was a clear division among the people, but it was more complex than Spitta suggested. Instead of being a two-way split there was also a third party that attempted to remain impartial. One faction comprised those who supported the superintendent and called themselves "Frohnlisch"; another more numerous faction stood with archdeacon Eilmar; and a third group followed Benjamin Eisenhardt, pastor in Felchta on the outskirts of Mühlhausen, who in 1711 became deacon of the Marienkirche in Mühlhausen, the assistant to pastor Eilmar.[116]

The evidence does seem to point to Bach being closer to Eilmar than to Frohne, even though the latter was the pastor of the church where he was organist. Perhaps Frohne was somewhat indifferent to music. When he republished the Mühlhausen hymnal (originally issued in 1686) edited by his father—whom he succeeded as superintendent—Frohne wrote a new preface that is silent concerning the role of music in hymnody, a topic commonly explored in many other hymnal prefaces.[117] Eilmar, on the other hand, took a close interest in music. Over the years, Bach's predecessor in Mühlhausen, Johann Georg Ahle (1651–1706), had issued a sequence of four publications on various aspects of music theory. The last, *Winter Gespräche* (1701), primarily concerned with intervals and modes, was prefaced by a celebratory poem by Eilmar that began: "Golden poetry and sweet music, these are truly gifts from God...."[118] It was presumably this interest in music that led Eilmar to commission Bach to compose the cantata *Aus der Tiefen rufe ich* (BWV 131). At the end of the autograph score, there is the following note: "At the request of Dr Georg Christian Eilmar set to music by Johann Sebastian Bach (Organist at Mühlhausen)."[119] Martin Petzoldt has suggested that the libretto of the fragmentary cantata *Meine Seele soll Gott loben* (BWV 223),

---

115   The flow of publications by Frohne, Eilmar, and others, is charted in Johann Georg Walch, *Bibliotheca theologica selecta litterariis adnotationibus instructa* (Jena: Croecker, 1757–1765), 2: 765–766. See also Ernst Koch, "Ostergedanken: Kontroversen um den 'neuen Menschen' in der frühen pietistischen Bewegung in Mühlhausen/Thüringen," *Alter Adam und Neue Kreatur: Pietismus und Anthropologie. Beiträge zum II. Internationalen Kongress für Pietismusforschung 2005*, ed. Udo Sträter (Halle: Niemeyer, 2009), 173–177.

116   Reinhard Jordan, *Chronik der Stadt Mühlhausen in Thüringen 3: 1600–1770* (Mühlhausen: Danner, 1906), 139–140. On Eisenhardt, see the funeral sermon by Johann Jakob Lungershausen, *Die Beschaffenheit des Hertzens Jacobs, bey der Wiederkehre in sein Vaterland, als der weyland... Hr. Beniamin Eisenhardt, Hochverdienter Prediger... zu Mühlhausen* (Mühlhausen: Brückner, 1723). Eisenhardt preached Eilmar's funeral sermon: Benjamin Eisenhardt. *Der Theure Gottes-Mann und Prophete Samuel... Des Hochwürdigen, Magnifici und Hochgelahrten Herrn, Herrn Georg Christian Eilmars...* (Mühlhausen: Brückner, 1715).

117   *Vermehrtes Gesang-Buch/... Geistreiche Lieder* (Mühlhausen: Petri, 1697), no pagination.

118   Johann Georg Ahle, *Winter Gespräche/ darinnen ferner vom grund- und kunstmäßige Componiren gehandelt wird* (Mühlhausen: Bruckner, 1701; facsimile in Johann Georg Ahle, *Schriften zur Musik*, ed. Markus Rathey, 2nd ed., Hildesheim: Olms, 2008), [v–vi]: "Die güldne Poësi, und suße Musica, | Dieselben sind wohl recht des Gottes Gaben..."

119   NBA I/34, KB, 49; Dok 3: 638: "Auff Begehren Tit: Herrn D: Georg Christ: Eilmars in die Music gebracht von Joh. Seb. Bach. Org. Molhusino." Eilmar was godfather to Bach's firstborn child, Catharina Dorothea, baptized in the Stadtkirche, Weimar, 29 December 1708.

Churches 163

known only from a later copy,[120] may have been written by Eilmar,[121] which may be the case, but the work has since been removed from the Bach canon.[122]

There is an intriguing connection between Eilmar and the Arnstadt superintendent Johann Gottfried Olearius. As the general superintendent of Schwarzburg-Sondershausen, Olearius had quasi-episcopal oversight for the churches of the principality. In August 1690, it was necessary for him to visit the parish of Keula, north of Mühlhausen. Eilmar, who was then the pastor of the small parishes of Groß- and Kleingrabe, near Mühlhausen, wrote and published a celebratory poem of eleven stanzas welcoming the general superintendent.[123] The poem, a mixture of classical and biblical allusion, reveals that the author had some detailed knowledge of Olearius's career that suggests that the two were known to each other. If so, then it is also possible that Bach had some awareness of Eilmar even before moving to Mühlhausen.

How Frohne and Eilmar were able to work together in Mühlhausen over these years is something of a mystery, but it may be that although they were in conflict over Pietism, there was some kind of mutual respect in other areas of theology and pastoral practice. It is significant that when Frohne died in 1713 Eilmar preached the funeral sermon in which he likened Frohne to the prophet Haggai, "the angel of the Lord who spoke the Lord's message to the people: 'I am with you,' says the Lord" (Haggai 1: 13).[124] Whatever working relationship the two opposing clergy were able to develop, it would seem that the atmosphere in Mühlhausen was not conducive for Bach to accomplish his "goal of a well-regulated church music," the phrase that occurs twice in his letter of resignation from the position in Mühlhausen.[125] He therefore moved on to the Weimar court, though retained positive connections with the town, composing two companion cantatas to *Gott ist mein König* (BWV 71) in honor of the Mühlhausen town council in 1709 and 1710 but which are no longer extant.

Weimar

As court organist (and chamber musician[126]) in Weimar, Bach was involved not only with the court chapel (Himmelsburg) but also with the churches in the town,

---

120 Spitta 1: 339–340; Spitta ET 1:343–344.
121 Martin Petzoldt, "Liturgical and Theological Aspects," *The World of Bach Cantatas: Johann Sebastian Bach's Early Sacred Cantatas*, ed. Christoph Wolff (New York: Norton, 1997), 115.
122 See Hans-Joachim Marx, "Finderglück: eine neue Kantate von J. S. Bach? von G.F. Händel? – Meine Seele soll Gott loben (BWV 223)," *Göttinger Händel-Beiträge* 10 (2004): 179–204.
123 Georg Christian Eilmar, *Der Den Kirchen Himmel stützende Oelbaum Bey erfreulicher Ankunft Des Hoch Ehrwürdigen... Herrn Johann Gottfried Olearii... den 6ten Aug. dieses 1690. Jahres in dem Hoch-Gräftlichen Amt Keula...* (Mühlhausen: Paul, [1690]). "Oelbaum" (olive-tree) is a pun on the superintendent's family name "Olearius," a Latinization of "Oehlschlaeger" ([olive-]oil-presser).
124 Georg Christian Eilmar, *Evangelisches Mühlhausen/... Leichen-Begängnis/ Des weyland HochEhrwürdigen/ in Gott Andächtigen/ und Hochgelahrten Herrn/ Herrn D. Joh. Adolph Frohnens... Gedächtnis Predigt/...* (Mühlhausen: Brückner, [1713]).
125 Dok 1: 19–21 (No. 1); NBR 36–37 (No. 32).
126 Dok 5: 113 (No. B 35a); NBR 59 (No. 35).

164   *Robin A. Leaver*

the Jakobskirche and especially the Stadtkirche of SS. Peter and Paul, where many ducal events, church synods and ordinations took place, where his cousin Johann Gottfried Walther (1684–1748) was organist (from 1707), and where Bach's children were baptized.[127] There was similarly an overlap between court and town clergy. The pastor of the Stadtkirche was also general superintendent and primary court preacher (Oberhofprediger) and thus regularly occupied both pulpits. During most of Bach's years at the court, these church and court positions were held by Johann Georg Lairitz (1647–1716), who had studied at Jena University and had held a number of pastoral positions before taking up responsibilities in Weimar in 1697.[128] Lairitz oversaw the creation of the new edition of the Weimar hymnal: *Schuldiges Lob Gottes, Oder: Geistreiches Gesang-Buch... So in Kirchen und Schulen des Fürstenthums Weimar... zu gebrauchen* (Weimar: Mumbach, 1713). In the preface, Lairitz wrote the following: "The church... has written spiritual songs by which her spirit is edified... powerfully rich words... which she ornaments with gracious and pleasing melodies."[129] When Bach evaluated the organ and gave the dedicatory recital in the newly built parish church of Taubach near Weimar, on Sunday 26 October 1710 (Trinity 19), Lairitz was present and, because he received a fee greater than Bach's, presumably preached the dedication sermon.[130] But Bach would have regularly heard his sermons in both the court chapel and Stadtkirche in Weimar. On Lairitz's death in 1716, he was succeeded by Johann Philipp Treuner (1666–1722),[131] formerly professor of metaphysics and logic at Jena University, but because he did not take up his appointments in Weimar until early in 1717, a few months before Bach was actively looking for another position, it is not likely that the new superintendent made much impression on the court musician. Similarly, it is not clear how the lives and ministries of the archdeacon and deacon of the Stadtkirche, respectively Anton Günther Faselius (1649–1727) and Georg Wilhelm von der Lage

---

127   Wilhelm Friedemann, 24 November 1710, Dok 2: 43 (No. 51); NBR 63 (No. 41); Maria Sophia and Johann Christoph, 23 February 1713, Dok 2: 45–46 (No. 56), twins that lived for no more than a few days; Carl Philipp Emanuel, 10 March 1714, Dok 2: 54 (No. 67); Johann Bernard Bach, 12 May 1715, Dok 2: 58 (No. 74). Bach was also godparent for two or three children baptized in the Stadtkirche, including the son of Johann Gottfried Walther, 27 Sept 1712, Dok 2: 44 (No. 54). For church life in Weimar, see Ernst Koch, "'Jakobs Kirche' – Erkundungen im gottesdienstlichen Arbeitsfeld Johann Sebastian Bachs in Weimar," BJ 92 (2006): 37–64.

128   Zedler 16: cols. 1238–1240; Gottfried Albin Wettin, *Historische Nachrichten Von der berühmten Residentz-Stadt Weimar...* (Weimar: Hoffmann, 1737), 384; Petzoldt, "Bach in theologischer Interaktion," 146; Koch, "Jakobs Kirche," 49–51.

129   *Schuldiges Lob Gottes, Oder: Geistreiches Gesang-Buch: Ausgebreitet, durch Hrn. D. M. Luthern, und andere vornehme Evangelische Lehrer, So in Kirchen und Schulen des Fürstenthums Weimar... zu gebrauchen* (Weimar: Mumbach, 1713), sig. A4[r].

130   Dok 2: 42–43 (Nos. 50 and 50a); see also Wolff and Zepf, *The Organs of J. S. Bach*, 90–91. Because superintendent Layritz had oversight of the rebuilding of old organs and the installation of new ones, it is likely that there were other occasions where Layritz and Bach collaborated at the dedication of such instruments.

131   Zedler 45: cols. 551–554; Wettin, *Historische Nachrichten Von... Weimar*, 384–385; Koch, "Jakobs Kirche," 54–55.

Churches 165

(uncertain dates),[132] intersected with Bach, though the latter administered emergency baptism to one of Bach's twins, daughter Maria Sophia, on 23 February 1713, but she died soon afterwards.[133]

A regular preacher in the court chapel during Bach's time was Johann Klessen (1669–1720),[134] who had studied at Jena and Wittenberg Universities before being ordained in Weimar where he was successively Stifts-prediger, deacon of the Stadtkirche, before becoming the under-court-preacher in 1707. The main task of the Stifts-prediger was the preaching and teaching of Luther's Small Catechism.[135] In 1702, under the ducal authority of Wilhelm Ernst and Johann Ernst, Klessen published the substance of his Stifts-prediger catechism preaching as: *Die Weimarische Kleine Bibel: Darinn Der Unterricht Christlicher Lehre, nach Anleitung D. Martin Luthers Kleinen Catechismi, deutlich und erbaulich gezeiget wird* (Weimar: Müller, 1702).[136] The title linked this detailed exposition of the Catechism with the so-called *Weimarische Grosse Bibel*, the complete Scripture commentary by significant seventeenth-century theologians, prepared under the leadership of Johann Gerhard (1582–1637) and published for lay use.[137] The assistant court preacher, Johann Wilhelm Hecker (1668–1743), had attended Jena University and served various churches in Erfurt as deacon before, like Klessen, he became in turn Stifts-prediger then court-preacher.[138]

Towards the end of the year 1713, a sequence of celebrations took place in Weimar within days of each other. They included the older duke's fifty-second birthday on 30 October—for which Bach composed the strophic aria, *Alles mit Gott und nicht ohn' ihn* (BWV 1127), discovered in recent years[139]— Reformation Day on 31 October, the opening of the new orphanage sometime that week, and especially the dedication of the new Jacobskirche on 6 November, an occasion that served to emphasize belief and practice associated with every

---

132   Wettin, *Historische Nachrichten Von... Weimar*, 398, 403.

133   Dok 2: 45 (No. 56).

134   Johann Friedrich von Werther, *Ein rechter Evangelischer Hof-Prediger in redlicher Ausrichtung seines Amts, wurde, als... Herr Joh. Klessen... selig verstorben.... In der Stadt-Kirche, zu St. Petri und Pauli [Weimar]...* (Erfurt: Limprecht, 1720); Wettin, *Historische Nachrichten Von... Weimar*, 406; Koch, "Jakobs Kirche," 51–53, 58–63.

135   See Wettin, *Historische Nachrichten Von... Weimar*, 50, 404–406. The successive Stift-prediger during Bach's time were Johann Andreas Lossius, about whom little is known, and Johann David Baier (1681–1752); see Wettin, *Historische Nachrichten Von... Weimar*, 407. Baier was the son of the influential Jena theologian, Johann Wilhelm Baier (1647–1695), author of the widely used *Compendium Theologiae Positivae* (first published in 1686, with eleven further editions by 1750), who was appointed general superintendent and Oberhofprediger in 1695 but died soon after arriving in Weimar; Wettin, *Historische Nachrichten Von... Weimar*, 382–383.

136   Zedler 55: col. 1407.

137   Zedler 55: cols. 1337–1407; Herbert von Hintzenstern, "Die 'Weymarische Bibel': ein riesiges Kommentarwerk Thüringer Theologen aus den Jahren 1636 bis 1640," *Herbergen der Christenheit: Jahrbuch für deutsche Kirchengeschichte* (1971): 175–[183].

138   Wettin, *Historische Nachrichten Von... Weimar*, 407; Koch, "Jakobs Kirche," 53–54.

139   See Michael Maul, "'Alles mit Gott und nichts ohn' ihn' – Eine neu aufgefundene Aria von Johann Sebastian Bach," BJ 91 (2005): 7–34.

166   *Robin A. Leaver*

Lutheran place of worship. On the dedication day, a procession of various dignitaries and clergy made its way from the ducal palace to the Jacobskirche, led by boys of the gymnasium singing chorales, who would have been directed by the cantor Georg Theodor Reineccius (1687–1726).[140] The Weimar clergy formed a significant group and processed in the following order:

> General superintendent and Oberhofprediger Lairitz, carrying a silver crucifix;
> Hofprediger Klessen with a complete Bible of both Old and New Testaments;
> Unter-Hofprediger Hecker with the "Große Weimar Biebel," that is, the lay Bible commentary;
> Archdeacon of the Stadtkirche, Faselius, with the "Weimarische kleine Biebel," that is, Klessen's extensive exposition of the Catechism;
> Deacon von der Lage with the *Formula of Concord*, the specific Lutheran confession;
> Stifts-prediger Baier with the 1664 Weimar *Kirchen-Ordnung*;
> Pastor of the Jacobskirche, newly appointed, Ludwig Friedrich Rothmaler (1679–1739),[141] with the *Kirchen-Agenda*;
> Substitute deacon of the Stadtkirche, Johann Friedrich Hebenstreit (1691–1731),[142] with the new "Weimarische Gesang-Buch";
> these were followed by three church assistants carrying paraments for altar and pulpit.[143]

One of the sources gives a fuller account of the procession and names more of the participants. In this source, the eleven "Musici von der Capelle" are named in two groups, numbered 34–37 and 40–46; Bach was number 44.[144] Five were singers:

> ALTO: Gottfried Blühnitz, Johann Jakob Graf
> TENOR: Andreas Ablinger, Johann Döbernitz[145]
> BASS: Gottfried Ephraim Theile

---

140 Johann Gottfried Walther, *Musikalisches Lexicon oder Musikalische Bibliothec* (Leipzig: Deer, 1732; facsimile, Kassel: Bärenreiter, 1967), 517–518. Reineccius was godfather to Bach's daughter Maria Sophia, 23 February 1713; Dok 2: 45–46 (No. 56).

141 Rothmahler studied at Jena University; Wettin, *Historische Nachrichten Von... Weimar*, 452–453.

142 Hebenstreit studied at Jena University where his father, Johann Paul Hebenstreit, was then professor of theology; he was later pastor of the Jacobikirche, Weimar; Wettin, *Historische Nachrichten Von... Weimar*, 453.

143 Wettin, *Historische Nachrichten Von... Weimar*, 432–434; Zedler, *Universal-Lexicon*, 55: cols. 1304–1305; Johann Christian Lünig, *Theatrum Ceremoniale Historico-Politicum, Oder Historisch- und Politischer Schau-Platz Aller Ceremonien... Anderer Theil* (Leipzig: Weidmann, 1720; facsimile, Vienna: [s.n.], 1953), 353–354.

144 Lünig, *Theatrum Ceremoniale Historico-Politicum*, 358; Dok 2: 48 (No. 60).

145 He was also a bassoonist as well as a singer.

Churches 167

Five were string players:

> VIOLINS: Johann Georg Hoffmann, August Gottfried Denstedt
> Andreas Christoph Ecke, Johann Sebastian Bach.[146]
> VIOLONE: Johann Andreas Ehrbach

The Vice-Capellmeister, Johann Wilhelm Drese, presumably played harpsichord continuo, seeing that at this stage there was no organ in the church. The omission of the Capellmeister's name, Johann Samuel Drese, may well have been due to ill health, a persistent problem with him.

The service that followed was a clear demonstration of "a well-regulated church music." Chorales were sung unaccompanied, the collect and other liturgical texts were intoned by respective clergy, and the court Capelle performed a concerted setting of a Missa (Kyrie and Gloria), as well as a three-movement cantata composed for the occasion, presumably by either the Capellmeister or Vice-Capellmeister:

> 1 Chor. Hilf, laß alles wohl gelingen...
> 2 Aria. Herr ich habe lieb die Städte deines Hauses... (Psalm 26: 8)
> 3 Aria. Hier ist das Hauß, da Gottes Ehre wohnet...[147]

Because cantor Reineccius regularly arranged for boys to sing in the concerted music of the court chapel he must have supplied such singers to join with the "Musici von der Capelle" on this occasion in the concerted Missa (perhaps the E major Missa by Reineccius mentioned in Walther's *Musicalisches Lexicon*) and first movement of the cantata, the arias being sung by one or two of the court singers. After the singing of two hymns—*Wir glauben all an einen Gott*, and *Ach [Herr] Jesu Christ dich zu uns wend*—the dedication sermon was preached by superintendent Lairitz, on Psalm 122: "I was glad when they said unto me, 'Let us go into the house of the Lord.'"[148] In the sermon, he drew attention to the significance of each of the items the clergy had carried in procession to the church, stressing the importance of the Bible, its text and commentary, the Catechism and its exposition, the church order and liturgy, the purity of doctrine as expressed in confessional writings, and the new Weimar *Gesang-Buch*, which, he said, "reminds us that we should here laud the name of the Lord with praise and thanks, with singing and playing (Singen und Spielen) to exalt his goodness."[149] After the sermon, there was a special dedicatory prayer followed by the singing of the *Te Deum*, that is, Luther's German version, *Herr Gott dich loben wir*, with trumpets and drums. The service ended with a collect, benediction, and

---

146 It possible that two played viola, following late seventeenth-century scoring of violin 1 and 2 and viola 1 and 2.

147 Wettin, *Historische Nachrichten Von... Weimar*, 437–439; Zedler 55: cols. 1305–1306.

148 An outline of the content is given in Wettin, *Historische Nachrichten Von... Weimar*, 439.

149 Wettin, *Historische Nachrichten Von... Weimar*, 434–435.

168   *Robin A. Leaver*

hymn—Luther's *Erhalt uns, Herr, bei deinem Wort*—and the people departed to the accompaniment of trumpets and drums and the ringing of all the bells in Weimar.[150]

The rich experience that the Weimar court offered Bach was intensified three months later when the terms of his employment were modified. His title was changed to Concertmaster and in addition to his role as court organist he was now not only responsible for composing a cantata each month but also for directing rehearsals of the court musicians.[151] Although in terms of rank, he was below both Capellmeister and Vice-Capellmeister, in practical terms he was on an equal footing. No doubt the fact that the Markt-Kirche in Halle had wanted to appoint him as Zachau's successor as organist and director of music the previous December[152] was a major factor in the duke's decision to promote him and keep him in Weimar. Bach was now able to regularly compose and perform in the conducive religious atmosphere of the court that was theologically Orthodox but expressed in the warm and intimate spirituality that is often mistakenly thought to be exclusive to the Pietists. Like most of the clergy that Bach had dealt with in his life thus far, the clergy in Weimar were mostly graduates of Jena University, noted for its mild and moderate Orthodoxy,[153] which was different from the more hard-edged Orthodoxy that frequently emanated from Wittenberg. Another former student of Jena University who held several positions at court, including consistorial secretary, ducal librarian, and custodian of the duke's collection of medals and coins, was Salomon Franck (1659–1725), who had studied law and theology.[154] He was also a poet who had recently begun writing cantata libretti in the new style, incorporating recitatives and da capo arias, following the example of Erdmann Neumeister. Most of Bach's cantata libretti during this creative period between 1714 and 1717 came from Franck's pen. Franck provided a poetic meditation on the biblical pericope assigned for the day or celebration, usually the gospel, which Bach then expressed in musical form. Thus in the service on the day in question, the biblical pericope was read then expounded by preacher, poet and composer in rhetoric, poetry and music in the sermon from the pulpit and the cantata from the musicians' gallery. In many respects, it was an ideal church environment in which Bach could work and thrive, especially with supportive colleagues. These not only included Franck and the Weimar clergy, but also the gymnasium faculty, where Kiesewetter, whom Bach had known in

---

150 Lünig, *Theatrum Ceremoniale Historico-Politicum*, 359.

151 See Dok 2: 53–54 (No. 66); NBR 70–71 (Nos. 51–52).

152 Dok 2: 49–52 (Nos. 62–63); NBR 66–68 (No. 48). Since father and son Johann Gottfried Olearius and Johann Christoph in Arnstadt had strong connections with Halle they may have had some influence on Bach's visit to Halle.

153 See Karl Heussi, *Geschichte der theologischen Fakultät zu Jena* (Weimar: Böhlaus, 1954), especially chapters 4 and 5, which discuss the professors who taught the clergy known to Bach.

154 Petzoldt, "Bach in theologischer Interaktion," 140. Franck was also connected with Arnstadt, having been consistorial secretary there between 1689 and 1697, when he moved to the similar position in Weimar.

Churches 169

Ohrdruf, was rector, Johann Matthias Gesner (1691–1761),[155] with whom Bach would work closely in Leipzig, was conrector, and Reineccius was cantor.

Given the persistent illness of the Capellmeister and the limitations of the Vice-Capellmeister, Bach must have thought that he would be in line to become the successor of the elder Drese. But when Johann Samuel Drese died, 1 December 1716, the duke acted according to precedent and would declare that Johann Wilhelm Drese would succeed his father as Capellmeister. Before the decision about the succession was made known, Bach composed cantatas on a weekly basis: *Wachet! betet! betet! wachet!* (BWV 70a) and *Ärgre dich, O Seele, nicht* (BWV 186a) were performed on the Second and Third Sundays of Advent (6 and 13 December 1716, respectively), and *Herz und Mund und Tat und Leben* (BWV 147a), was intended for the Fourth Sunday in Advent (20 December) but was not performed because it was only partially composed. Thereafter there is no direct evidence that Bach ever composed another cantata for the Weimar court chapel.[156] Because the new Capellmeister was then 40 and Bach was 32, it was clear that if he was to become a Capellmeister then he would have to seek that future somewhere other than at the Weimar court.[157]

One possibility was the court of Saxe-Gotha where the Capellmeister, Christian Friedrich Witt (1660–1717),[158] was seriously ill. Bach, already known at the court for at least one organ recital in 1711,[159] was invited to direct and possibly compose passion music in the Friedenstein court chapel in Gotha on Good Friday, 26 March 1717, just eight days before Witt's death. The ducal accounts record the honorarium Bach received together with the expenses of printing copies of the passion libretto.[160] In the following eighteen months, nine more musicians performed music at the court, suggesting that they were being con-

---

155 Petzoldt, "Bach in theologischer Interaktion," 142–143; Reinhold Friedrich, *Johann Matthias Gesner: Sein Leben und sein Werk* (Roth: Genniges, 1991). Poet and philologist, Gesner studied theology at Jena university, where he lived with Johann Franz Buddeus (1667–1729), professor of theology; in Weimar from 1715 he was also ducal librarian.

156 There is indirect evidence that he may have composed a cantata for the celebration of the bicentenary of the Reformation, 31 October 1717; see Robin A. Leaver, "Bach and the Bicentenary of the Reformation, 1717," *Im Klang der Wirklichkeit: Musik und Theologie*, ed. Norbert Bolin and Markus Franz (Leipzig: Evangelisches Verlaganstalt, 2011), 49–62.

157 See Andreas Glöckner, "Gründe für Johann Sebastian Bachs Weggang von Weimar," *Bericht über die Wissenschaftliche Konferenz zum V. Internationalen Bachfest der DDR in Verbindung mit dem 60. Bachfest der Neuen Bachgesellschaft, Leipzig, 25. bis 27. März, 1985*, eds. Winfried Hoffman and Armin Schneiderheinze (Leipzig: Deutscher Verlag für Musik, 1988), 137–143.

158 In older literature, the date of Witt's death is given as 13 April 1716, but the register of deaths in Gotha records the date as 3 April 1717; see Andreas Glöckner, "Neue Spuren zu Bachs 'Weimarer' Passion," LBB 1 (1995): 33.

159 Dok 5: 273 (No. B52b); and Christian Ahrens, "Neue Quellen zu J. S. Bachs Beziehungen nach Gotha," BJ 83 (2007): 45–54.

160 Dok 5: 126 (No. B81a); Glöckner, "Neue Spuren zu Bachs 'Weimarer' Passion," 35; NBR 78–79 (Nos. 63–65); BC 3: 983–984 (No. [D 1]). None of the copies of the printed libretto is apparently extant.

170   *Robin A. Leaver*

sidered as candidates for the vacant position. They included Augustin Reinhard Stricker, Capellmeister in Cöthen (who died ca. 1718); Georg Philipp Telemann (1681–1767), Capellmeister in Frankfurt; Johann Friedrich Fasch (1688–1758), Concertmaster in Gera (later Capellmeister in Zerbst); and Gottfried Heinrich Stölzel (1690–1749), Capellmeister in Gera, who was eventually appointed Witt's successor late in 1720.[161]

The prospect of possibly becoming the Gotha Capellmeister in succession to Witt may have seemed an attractive one for Bach, given the situation in which he found himself in Weimar. The Gotha court chapel had an enviable tradition of supporting high standards in church music. The Oberhofprediger in Gotha was Albrecht Christian Ludwig (1667–1733),[162] who had worked closely with Witt. Together they had produced the impressive hymnal, *Psalmodia Sacra* (Gotha 1715), which included many new chorale melodies by Witt.[163] But Ludwig was also a poet and librettist, and among his published works is a birthday cantata for Friedrich II of Saxe-Gotha in 1721,[164] and a complete annual cycle of cantata texts for Stölzel in 1725.[165] So if Bach had become the Gotha Capellmeister, he could have developed a partnership with Ludwig similar to the one he had with Franck in creating cantatas in Weimar. However, in 1717, this possibility was not an obvious one and perhaps it was already clear that the appointment of Witt's successor was going to be a protracted affair—there were three years between Witt's death and Stölzel's appointment—and Bach's concern to secure a position was much more immediate.

Cöthen

Details concerning Bach's transition from Weimar to Cöthen are either nonexistent, contradictory, or enigmatic. Prince Leopold of Anhalt-Cöthen (1694–1728) had taken the opportunity of bringing to his court the core of the excellent musicians of the Berlin court capelle when it was disbanded in 1713. They included Augustin Reinhard Stricker, who became the Cöthen Capellmeister;

---

161 Ahrens, "Neue Quellen zu J. S. Bachs Beziehungen nach Gotha," 49–51.

162 Ludwig studied theology at the universities of Wittenberg, Jena, and Leipzig, and was successively a pastor in Auligk, Frauenpreißnitz, and Zeitz, before becoming Oberhofprediger in Gotha in 1713; *Thüringer Pfarrerbuch* 1: 448–449.

163 *Psalmodia Sacra, Oder: Andächtige und schöne Gesänge, So wohl des... Lutheri als anderer Geistreichen Männer... In dem Fürstenthum Gotha und Altenburg, auf nachfolgende Art zu singen und zu spielen* (Gotha: Reyher, 1715); See Zahn 6: 298–300 (No. 877). After Witt's death Ludwig edited a supplement: *Anhang, An das Gothaisches Cantional... Die in dem Andern Theile Des Gothaischen Gesang-Buchs* (Gotha: Reyher, 1726); see Zahn 6: 306 (No. 895).

164 Albrecht Christian Ludwig, *Die unter einem friedliebenden Salomo beglückte Unterthanen: als zu des durchlauchtigsten Fürsten und Herrns, Herrn Friedrich, Herzog zu Sachsen... hohen Geburts-Feste* (Gotha: Reyher, [1721].

165 Albrecht Christian Ludwig, *Musicalischen Kirchen-Andachten: welche in Hochfürstl. Schloß-Kirche zum Friedenstein, vom Advent 1725. bis 1726.... Aufgeführet werden* (Gotha: Reyher, [1725]).

Churches 171

now, just three-and-a-half years later he was giving up the position. Did Stricker think he could do better elsewhere? But after moving away from Cöthen, apart from a few references to him in 1718, nothing more is known about Stricker. Another possibility is that Leopold dismissed him once he knew that Bach was available.[166] It seems that Bach visited Prince Leopold in August 1717 when he entered into some kind of agreement to become Stricker's successor, but there was no announcement at that time.[167] Bach's obituary suggests that the formal invitation to become Capellmeister was not made until after Bach had returned to Weimar following his visit to Dresden.[168] So the possible scenario seems to be that Bach's appointment as Cöthen Capellmeister was not announced until Stricker's dismissal had been effected, which also would explain why Bach's detention in Weimar came late in the year, when the duke discovered Bach's intentions.

Up until this point in his life, Bach was both professionally and personally connected with the Lutheran church. During the six years of his time in Cöthen, these two aspects would be separated: professionally, he served the Calvinist court; personally, he and his family attended the local Lutheran church. Professionally, he had the highest status a musician could aspire to at that time, a body of musicians that were second to none, and a prince who was actively involved in the music of his court. However, apart from the annual New Year celebrations and Leopold's birthdays, sacred cantatas were not a common feature of the worship of the Calvinist court chapel. Thus Bach's goal of "a well-regulated church music" had to be put to one side while he explored the enormous possibilities of composing chamber music for the talented musicians of the Cöthen capelle. But he remained a committed Lutheran.

Confessionally, there were significant differences, both theological and practical, between Calvinists and Lutherans, especially with regard to liturgy and music. Among other things, Calvinists charged Lutherans of retaining many unreformed Roman Catholic practices, and Lutherans accused Calvinists of legalistic interpretations of Scripture that resulted in restrictive and minimalist worship. The Cöthen court, Calvinist since the late sixteenth century, was perhaps not as strict in its practice of Calvinism as elsewhere in that, for example, instruments were employed in the chapel from time to time, but this was a long way from Lutheran traditions of church music.

Leopold's father, Emanuel Lebrecht (1671–1704), had married Gisela Agnes von Rath (1669–1740), who was from an aristocratic Lutheran family, in 1692, but on her marriage she did not convert to Calvinism but remained staunchly Lutheran. With her husband's consent, Gisela Agnes arranged for a church to be built

---

166 See the discussion in Wolff BLM 195. That Bach's salary was twice what Stricker received (Wolff BLM, 188–189) supports the conjecture that Stricker was dismissed so that Bach could become the Capellmeister. It seems likely that Bach had made the acquaintance of Prince Leopold in January 1716 when Ernst Augustus I, duke of Saxe-Weimar, married Leopold's sister, Eleonore Wilhelmine, at his mother's estate in Nienburg.

167 Dok 2: 67 (No. 86); NBR 82 (No. 70).

168 Dok 3: 84 (No. 666); NBR 302 (No.306).

172   *Robin A. Leaver*

for the Lutheran minority in Cöthen, with the unsubtle dedication to St. Agnus in 1669,[169] to which was added a school that Bach's children later attended, and a Lutheran cemetery (dedicated in June 1703),[170] where Bach's first wife was laid to rest on 7 July 1720, when Bach was away in Carlsbad with Prince Leopold and other members of the capelle.[171] What remains unknown is the extent to which Bach and his family were involved in the music of the Agnuskirche.[172]

When Gisela Agnes's husband died in 1704, Leopold was only ten years old and thus she ruled the principality as regent—from a modest house opposite the Agnuskirche—while Leopold finished his schooling, mostly in Berlin, and completed a grand tour. When he came of age in 1715, he returned to Cöthen and assumed his birthright, and Gisela Agnes withdrew to her residence in Nienburg. The Calvinism of his forbears, with which he was in total sympathy, was often at variance with his mother's Lutheranism and her advocacy of the concerns of the worshipers at the Agnuskirche, which led to bitter arguments between mother and son.

The pastor of the Agnuskirche during Bach's time in Cöthen was Paulus Berger (ca. 1670–1732),[173] who had studied at Halle and Wittenberg Universities. He was previously pastor in Groß Rosenburg before becoming the Lutheran court preacher and pastor of the Agnuskirche, and also the father-confessor (Beichtvater) to Gisela Agnes, in 1712. Berger and Bach seem to have been closely associated because there is the possibility that at some point they lived at the same address in Cöthen.[174] There was also a close affinity with the deacon, Georg Friedrich Zeidler (1684–1745),[175] appointed in 1719, who officiated at Bach's marriage to Anna Magdalena Wilcke, on 3 December 1721, which, according to the custom of a second marriage, took place in a house rather than in the church.[176] The

---

169 The dedication sermon was later published, with other sermons preached in Cöthen; see *Unschuldige Nachrichten* (1745): 372–379.

170 *Unschuldige Nachrichten* (1745): 377.

171 Dok 2: 76 (No. 100); NBR 88 (No. 80).

172 Cantata 21 was apparently performed in the Reformed "Cathedral Church" in Cöthen; see Michael Maul and Peter Wollny, "Quellenkundliches Bach-Aufführungen in Köthen, Ronneburg und Leipzig zwischen 1720 und 1760," BJ 89 (2003): 97–99. Similarly, there is evidence that Cantata 199 was performed in the Cöthen sometime around 1720; see Tatjana Schabalina, "Ein weiteres Autograph Johann Sebastian bachs in Rußland: Neues zur Entstehungsgeschichte der verschiedenen Fassungen von BWV 199," BJ 90 (2004): 11–40.

173 Zedler, Supplement 3: cols. 790–791; Petzoldt, "Bach in theologischer Interaktion," 135. On the clergy who served the Agnus-Kirche in the first half of the eighteenth century, see *Unschuldige Nachrichten* (1745): 378.

174 See Herbert Zimpel and Günther Hoppe, "Stiftstraß 11 – eines der Köthener Bachhäuser?" *Cöthener Bach-Heft* 6 (1994): 83–88. However, the question of Bach's residence(s) in Cöthen is fraught with complexity and uncertainty; see Georg Heeg, "Wohnung J. S. Bachs in Köthen," http://www.heeg.de/images/Bachhaus-klein.pdf. I am grateful to Robert L. Marshall for this information.

175 Petzoldt, "Bach in theologischer Interaktion," 158. It is possible that George Friedrich Zeidler was a relative of Christian Zeidler (ca. 1650–1707), rector of the Latin school in Eisenach when Bach was a boy; see Petzold, *loc. cit.*

176 Dok 2: 83 (No. 110); NBR 93 (No. 86).

Churches 173

prickly nature of the relationship between the two confessions in Cöthen can be seen in the dispute that arose when the Calvinist church charged that customary fees had not been paid for Bach's marriage.[177] Bach clearly understood these tensions between the two confessions, since he noted on the title page of the 1722 manuscript *Clavier-Büchlein für Anna Magdalena Bachin* (P 224) three short titles of books by August Pfeiffer, which were possibly already in his library, that deal with the theological differences between Lutheranism and Calvinism, especially with regard to the doctrine of predestination: *Anti-Calvinismus* a comprehensive study; *Christen Schule* a series of sermons that address Calvinism from time to time; and *Antimelancholicus* that includes a series of extended dialogs between a Lutheran believer and a Calvinist preacher.[178] The listing of these books—by the most numerous author after Luther in Bach's personal library—is usually explained as Bach wanting to commend these books to his young wife. But Eric Chafe has suggested an alternative interpretation. He notes that there are several details—such as *Ante Calvinismus* instead of *Anti Calvinismus*, and that *Christen Schule* is an incomplete title—that seem to suggest that the information was communicated to him aurally, implying that he did not yet own these books, and was jotting down the titles for future reference.[179] Further, because Bach the Capellmeister of the court of Calvinist Cöthen was about to apply for the position of cantor and director of music in Lutheran Leipzig, his knowledge of the anti-Calvinist stance of the famously Orthodox Lutheran theologian, August Pfeiffer, who had been archdeacon of the Thomaskirche in Leipzig, would help to relieve any doubts about his religious affiliation.

Leopold's marriage to his cousin, Frederica Henrietta, princess of Anhalt-Bernburg, on 11 December 1721, had negative repercussions for Bach and his fellow court musicians. As he explained in his letter to his school friend Georg Erdmann, dated 28 October 1730, "It must happen, however, that the said *Serenissimus* [prince Leopold] should marry a princess of Berenburg, and... the musical interests of the said prince had become somewhat lukewarm, especially as the new princess seemed to be unmusical..."[180] What had begun with great promise now looked more and more doubtful, and thus Bach turned his attentions to Leipzig. He stressed that a secondary reason for the move to Leipzig was the education of his sons. However, it has been suggested that there may have been yet another reason for him wanting to move: the possible presence of Pietism in Cöthen. In 1721, Gisela Agnes came under the influence of Halle Pietism, and the following year August Hermann Francke spent three days with her and other women of her court, which ultimately led to the appointment in 1726 of

---

177 Dok 2: 120 (No. 158); see Wolf BLM, 219.

178 Leaver, *Bachs theologische Bibliothek*, No. 37 (*Anti-Calvinismus*), Nos. 14 or 36 (*Christen Schule*), and No. 39 (*Antimelancholicus*).

179 Eric Chafe, *J. S. Bach's Johannine Theology: The St. John Passion and the Cantatas for Spring 1725*, (Oxford: Oxford University Press, 2014), 40.

180 NBR 151 (No. 152); Dok 1: 67 (No. 23). Another pressure on music at court was Leopold's increased expenditure on his troops.

174   *Robin A. Leaver*

Francke's protégé, Johann Konrad Ludwig Allendorf (1693–1773) as Lutheran court preacher in Cöthen. Allendorf was the author of the so-called *Cöthenisch Lieder* of 1736, a controversial collection of hymns that was accused of blurring the theological differences between Lutherans and Calvinists.[181] But it is clear that there was no Pietist influence in Cöthen during Bach's tenure at the court. Gisela Agnes met with Francke at her residence in Nienburg, not in Cöthen, and Allendorf's influence postdates Bach's time at the court.[182]

Leipzig

When Bach arrived in Leipzig, he assumed a significant leadership role in a complex ecclesiastical environment that included two primary churches, several other parish churches, and a university church, to which were each assigned various levels of clergy. There were also the theological professors of the university, *ordinarius* and *extra-ordinarius*, some of whom were also active clergy in the city churches. Some of the teachers in the church-schools had theological backgrounds and at least two, at different periods, were simultaneously the Sunday Vespers preacher in the Nikolaikirche as well as teaching in the Nikolaischule.[183] Thus during Bach's twenty-seven years in Leipzig, he must have encountered something in excess of forty different clergy, together with many others who had an interest and expertise in theology and ecclesiastical affairs. There are basic studies of some of these clergy and theologians,[184] but more research needs to

---

181   The collection was originally published under the title, *Einige gantz neue Lieder zum Lobe des Dreyeinigen Gottes...* (Cöthen: Jordan, 1736); see Koch, *Geschichte des Kirchenlieds und Kirchengesangs*, 4: 433–445. That these hymns were compromised from a Lutheran point of view appeared to be confirmed when they were published as an appendix to the Moravian hymnal: *Das Gesang-Buch der Herrnhut: und anderer Brüder-Gemeinen. Mit denen Cöthenischen Liedern vermehret* ([Löbau]: [s.n.], 1741).

182   See Gertraud Zaepernick and Johannes Wallmann, "Fromme Höfe im 18. Jahrhundert," *Pietismus und Neuzeit* 32 (2006): 213–219, esp. 218–219.

183   Georg Christoph Wintzern, *Reverendum Ministerium Lipsiense, Oder Eigentliches Verzeichniß Derer Prediger, Welche Seit der Reformation des seeligen Lutheri bis hieher, Nemlich von Anno 1539. bis Anno 1722...* ([Leipzig]: [s.n.], 1722); *Vollständiges Verzeichniß der Prediger in Leipzig... von dem 1539 bis zu dem ietzigen 1777 Jahre zum Predigt-Amte beruffen worden...* 3rd ed. (Leipzig: Dürr, [1777]); Stefan Altner, "Die Lehrer der Thomasschule zur Zeit des Kantorats von Johann Sebastian Bach: Quellenauszüge aus dem Archiv des Thomanerchores," Bolin and Franz, *Klang der Wirklichkeit: Musik und Theologie*, 28–38. A few years before Bach's appointment in Leipzig, it was reported that the Leipzig Consistory comprised 775 clergy, of which 91 served in and around the city of Leipzig; see Iconder [= Johann Christian Crell], *Das gesambte jetzt- Lebende Geistliche Ministerium Im Gantzen Churfürstenthum Sachsen... In Jar 1720* (Leipzig: Martini, [1720]), 53, 156.

184   Brief biographies of many of these clergy can be found in the appendixes of *800 Jahre Thomana, Glauben – Singen – Lernen: Festschrift zum Jubiläum von Thomaskirche, Thomanerchor und Thomasschule*, ed. Stefan Altner and Martin Petzoldt (Wettin-Löbejün: Stekovics, 2012), 428–463. See also Friedrich Osterhild, *St. Nikolai zu Leipzig: Geschichte des Gotteshauses und der Gemeinde 1160–1960* (Berlin: Evangelische Verlagsanstalt, 1964), 93–103, and Petzoldt, "Bach in theologischer Interaktion," *passim*. See also Martin Petzoldt,

Churches 175

be done in order to create a clearer picture of the ecclesiastical and theological environment in Leipzig during Bach's time. Of course, some of these clergy had only a peripheral connection with Bach, but others were closer to their cantor and his family; of these, the following should be noted.

First, there were the two professors of theology who examined Bach in May 1723 for his understanding of biblical theology and his commitment to confessional Lutheranism.[185] One was Johann Schmid (1649–1731), who studied at Leipzig University, becoming professor of eloquence in 1684, then professor of theology in 1700, nine times dean of the theological faculty, and eight times rector of the University. He was a typical erudite academic and advocate of Lutheran Orthodoxy.[186] The examination of Bach was similar to that required of clergy entering into a new pastoral office and was no *pro forma* exercise. The previous year, 1722, a candidate for the position of cantor in Zwickau was examined by professor Schmid, who failed the would-be cantor on account of his inadequate understanding of biblical theology, and thus, even though he was musically qualified, was never appointed to the position.[187] The other professor was Salomon Deyling (1677–1755), who was also the pastor of the Nikolaikirche and the superintendent during the whole of Bach's time in Leipzig. Deyling studied theology at Wittenberg University, where he became adjunct professor of philosophy, and after other pastoral positions was appointed professor and superintendent in Leipzig in 1721. Over the years, he was dean of the theological faculty eight times.[188] Like Schmid, Deyling was an advocate of Lutheran Orthodoxy, but unlike Schmid he was not exclusively an academic but combined his scholarship with the pastoral oversight of the Leipzig churches as superintendent. Bach had to have worked closely with Deyling in connection with providing suitable music for the two principal churches. For example, libretti for the proposed cantatas for upcoming Sundays and celebrations had to be submitted in advance to Deyling for his imprimatur that they were theologically sound and liturgically appropriate. Deyling, as superintendent not only of the city churches but also of the surrounding parishes, had oversight over practical matters, such as the installation of new organs. There is at least one recorded example, the proposed new organ for the church in Stötteritz in 1748, in which both Deyling and Bach were involved.[189] There may well have been other years when both men were together concerned with such proposals for new organs. Another type of collaboration

---

Bach-Kommentar: theologisch-musikwissenschaftliche Kommentierung der geistlichen Vokalwerke Johann Sebastian Bachs (Kassel: Bärenreiter, 2004–), who, where possible, identifies the Leipzig clergy who preached at the services in which Bach's cantatas were heard.

185 Dok 2: 99–100 (No. 134); NBR 103 (No. 101).

186 Zedler 35: col. 384–390; Petzoldt, "Bach in theologischer Interaktion," 151.

187 See Martin Petzoldt, "Bachs Prüfung vor dem Kurfürstlichen Konsistorium zu Leipzig," BJ 84 (1998): 19–30.

188 Petzoldt, "Bach in theologischer Interaktion," 137–138.

189 See Lynn Edwards Butler, "Four Sources Relating to Bach, Organ Builder Johann Scheibe, and the Organs in Zschortau and Stötteritz," BACH 44/2 (2013): 3–5. The death of the organ builder, Scheibe, prevented the proposed organ from being built.

176   Robin A. Leaver

between Bach and Deyling occurred in connection with the university church of St. Paul, which also doubled as the university's aula, where theological debates, doctoral defenses, and orations of various kinds were held. It now appears that Bach's Latin cantata, *Gloria in excelsis Deo* (BWV 191), was performed in the Paulinerkirche on Christmas Day 1742, in connection with a Latin oration by Deyling on Luke 2: 14.[190] Although the author of numerous theological treatises and tracts, Deyling does not appear to have written about church music *per se*. However, in his book on pastoral theology, first published in 1734, in the section devoted to liturgical practice, he writes about the theological importance of the classic hymns of the sixteenth century, especially the hymns of Luther.[191] Thus it would seem that Bach's second Jahrgang of 1724–1725, cantatas mostly based on the chorales of Luther and his contemporaries, was something that Deyling fully appreciated and supported.

Leipzig clergy that were obviously close to Bach and his family were those who were successively the family's Beichtvater, that is, the pastor who heard their confessions before they attended communion and penitential observances. The choice of these clergy was Bach's own. The first was Christian Weiss, Sr. (1671–1736), an alumnus of Leipzig University who had been pastor of the Thomaskirche since 1714.[192] Weiss presided over Bach's installation as cantor, in the absence of superintendent Deyling, who was protesting at the Leipzig council's failure to involve him in Bach's appointment.[193] Weiss's Orthodoxy was often expressed polemically against Pietism on the one hand and Roman Catholicism on the other. The latter was especially marked after the Saxon Elector, August the Strong, converted to Roman Catholicism in order to secure the Polish crown in 1697. When Weiss was deacon in Torgau, he frequently preached before August the Strong's estranged wife, Christiane Eberhardine, who had remained a committed Lutheran. Thus it would seem likely that Weiss was involved in some way in the memorial service in the Paulinerkirche after the Electress's death in 1727, for which Bach composed the Trauer-Ode (BWV 198).[194] After Weiss's death, Romanus Teller

---

190   See Markus Rathey, "Zur Entstehungsgeschichte von Bachs Universitätsmusik Gloria in excelsis Deo BWV 191," BJ 99 (2013): 319–328; Robin A. Leaver, "Bachs lateinische Kantata 'Gloria in excelsis Deo' BWV 191 und eine lateinische Rede über Lukas 2:14," BJ 99 (2013): 329–334.

191   Salomon Deyling, *Institutiones Prudentiae Pastoralis... editio secunda* (Leipzig: Lanckisch, 1739), 598–607.

192   Petzoldt, "Bach in theologischer Interaktion," 156–157; see also Martin Petzold, "Christian Weise d.Ä. und Christoph Wolle – zwei Leipziger Beicht-Väter Bachs, Vertreter zweier auslegungsgeschichtlicher Abschnitte der ausgehenden lutherischen Orthodoxie," *Bach als Ausleger der Bibel: Theologische und musikwissenschaftliche Studien zum Werk Johann Sebastian Bachs* (Göttingen: Vandenhoeck und Ruprcht, 1985), 109–129, esp. 119–123.

193   See Dok 2: 107–109 (No. 145); NBR 106–108 (No. 104).

194   There are other connections between the Weiss and the Bach families. Examples include: in 1728 Bach composed a cantata (see NBA I/33, KB, 14) for the wedding of Johanna Elizabeth Weiss to Friedrich Schulze, deacon in Naumburg, who later collaborated with Bach in the creation of the 1736 Schemelli Gesangbuch; in 1732 another daughter, Dorothea Sophia Weiss, was godmother to Johann Christoph Friedrich Bach; and in 1737, Christian Weiss, Jr., deacon of the Nikolaikirche, was godfather to Johanna Carolina Bach.

Churches 177

(1703–1750) became the Bachs' Beichtvater between 1738 and 1740.[195] Teller, an alumnus of Leipzig University, was successively subdeacon, deacon, and, from 1745, pastor of the Thomaskirche. Teller was also professor of theology and the editor of a new edition of the basic theological textbook used in the university, David Hollaz's *Examen theologicum acromaticum* (1750),[196] the last classic statement of Orthodox Lutheran dogmatics. Johann Paul Ram (1701–1741), an alumnus of Wittenberg University, subdeacon of the Thomaskirche, was briefly the Bachs' Beichtvater from 1740 until his death in 1741.[197] Bach's fourth and final Beichtvater in Leipzig was Christoph Wolle (1700–1761), a former Thomaner who sang under Johann Kuhnau, an alumnus of Leipzig University, successively deacon and archdeacon of the Thomaskirche, and professor of theology, who officiated at the wedding of Elisabeth Juliana Friederica Bach to Johann Christoph Altnikol, organist in Naumburg, on 20 January 1749,[198] and who brought the sacrament of the altar to Bach in his home for the last time on 22 July 1750.[199]

A third group of Leipzig clergy who were close to the Bach family were the five pastors who baptized the twelve children born between 1724 and 1742.[200]

Urban Gottfried Seiber (1669–1741), alumnus of Wittenberg University, successively subdeacon, deacon, archdeacon and pastor of the Thomaskirche, baptized Gottfried Heinrich (27 February 1724), Johann August Abraham (5 November 1733) and Johann Christian (7 September 1735).[201]

Justus Gotthard Rabener (1688–1731), Leipzig University alumnus, successively subdeacon and deacon of the Thomaskirche, baptized Christian Gottlieb (14 April 1725), Elisabeth Juliana Friederica (5 May 1726), Regina Johanna (10 October 1728),[202] and Christiana Dorothea (18 March 1731).[203]

---

195 Petzoldt, "Bach in theologischer Interaktion," 154–155; Petzoldt and Petri, *Ehre sei dir Gott gesungen*, 133. It is possible that Bach already knew members of Teller's family since his mother was the sister of Johann Abraham Kroymayer, superintendent in Ohrdruf when Bach was living with his brother; see Zedler 42: col. 679.

196 David Hollaz, *Examen theologicum acroamaticum universam theologiam thetico-polemicam complectens*, ed. Romanus Teller (Leipzig: Kiesewetter, 1750), originally published in 1707.

197 Petzoldt, "Bach in theologischer Interaktion," 149.

198 Dok 2: 454 (No. 579a).

199 Petzoldt, "Bach in theologischer Interaktion," 157–158; Petzold, "Christian Weise d.Ä. und Christoph Wolle – zwei Leipziger Beicht-Väter Bachs," 123–124.

200 Dok 5: 89–98 (Nos. A92a-Ap2m); see Martin Petzoldt, *Bachs Leipziger Kinder: Dokumente von Johann Sebastian Bachs eigener Hand* (Leipzig: Evangelische Verlagsanstalt, 2008), text in both German and English. Thirteen Bach children were born in Leipzig but no baptismal record survives for Christiana Sophia Henrietta, who died on 29 June 1726 aged 3¼; Petzoldt, *Bachs Leipziger Kinder*, 22–23.

201 Petzoldt, "Bach in theologischer Interaktion," 153–154.

202 Because this was an emergency baptism, done in the home rather than church by either the midwife or perhaps even Bach himself, pastor Rabener's role would have been to confirm that the baptism was valid when the child was presented in church as soon as possible after the baptism; see Petzoldt, *Bachs Leipziger Kinder*, 57–63.

203 Petzoldt, "Bach in theologischer Interaktion," 148–149.

178 *Robin A. Leaver*

Johann Gottlob Carpzov (1679–1767), alumnus of Leipzig and Altdorf Universities, archdeacon of the Thomaskirche and professor of Hebrew, baptized Ernestus Andreas (30 October 1727), and Christiana Benedicta (1 January 1730), for whom Carpzov's daughter, Sophia Benedicta, was godparent.[204]

Gottlieb Gaudlitz (1694–1745), alumnus of Leipzig and Wittenberg Universities, successively subdeacon, deacon, archdeacon and ultimately pastor of the Thomaskirche,[205] baptized Johann Christoph Friedrich (23 June 1732), and Johanna Carolina (30 October 1737).

Christian Gottlob Eichler (1711–1785), alumnus of Leipzig University, deacon of a number of Leipzig churches, ultimately becoming the pastor of the Nikolaikirche after Deyling's death,[206] baptized Regina Susanna (22 February 1742).

Of these clergy, one is known to have expressed positive views on church music from the pulpit of the Thomaskirche. In 1714, archdeacon Carpzov preached a series of eighty-four weekday sermons in the Thomaskirche under the general title "Gewissens-Unterricht" (Conscience instruction). Although they were not published until after Carpzov became the superintendent of Lübeck in 1730,[207] they nevertheless clearly reveal the style, form and content of Carpzov's preaching that Bach would have frequently heard until Carpzov left for Lübeck. After six introductory sermons defining the parameters of "Gewissen," the following thirty are headed "Conscience instruction on God, religion, and worship." Sermon 22 is titled: "Of public church-songs and church music," and is based on the Pauline text "Be filled with the Spirit; speaking to yourselves in psalms and hymns and spiritual songs, singing and playing to the Lord in your hearts" (Ephesians 5:18–19).[208] The King James Version translates ψαλλοντες (psallontes) as "making melody" but Luther translated it as "spielet," creating the comprehensive statement "singet und spielet" (singing and playing), which Lutheran commentators and preachers expounded as vocal and instrumental music in worship—and Carpzov was no exception. Much of his sermon is taken up with promoting classic Lutheran chorales, but he goes on to ask whether figural music has a legitimate place in the Lutheran church, or is it to be feared as papal yeast ("Päpstlicher Sauerteig") that infects the whole?[209] Carpzov argues against

---

204 Petzoldt, "Bach in theologischer Interaktion," 136–137.

205 Petzoldt, "Bach in theologischer Interaktion," 141–142. In 1728, there was a dispute between Bach and Gaudlitz in which Bach charged the deacon of usurping his responsibility of choosing Vesper hymns; see Dok 1: 54–57 (No. 19).

206 Petzoldt, *Bachs Leipziger Kinder*, 111.

207 Succeeding Georg Heinrich Götze, the hymnological colleague of Johann Christoph Olearius, whom Bach may have encountered in 1705; see page 157 above.

208 Johann Gottlob Carpzov, *Unterricht vom Unverletzten Gewissen beyde gegen Gott und Menschen, in vier und achtzig Predigten, Vormahls der Gemeine Gottes zu St. Thomas in Leipzig vorgetragen, und nun auf vielfältiges Verlangen in Druck gegeben* (Leipzig: Martini, 1733), 409–434.

209 Carpzov, *Unterricht vom Unverletzten Gewissen*, 413.

Churches   179

Andreas Carlstadt and Ulrich Zwingli who in Luther's day either limited or eliminated worship music, and explores the biblical—and therefore prepapal—record that establishes the legitimacy of a wide range of vocal and instrumental music for worship. However, he warns against superficial "theatralische Music" that tickles the ears but does not awaken devotion, because the sounds obscure the text.[210] It needs to be born in mind that when Carpzov preached this sermon in 1714, opera in Leipzig was particularly prominent, and many of its musicians were also involved in the operatic style of church music then current in the Neukirche, much to the consternation of Bach's predecessor Kuhnau.[211] Carpzov was therefore supporting Kuhnau in this sermon and it would seem likely that he would have similarly supported Bach in his provision of music for the Leipzig churches. One wonders whether Bach was aware that the archdeacon considered each of the three biblical leaders of Old Testament music, Asaph, Heman, and Jeduthun, as a Capellmeister and *Director chori musici*—the same titles that Bach held in Leipzig.[212]

Bach as a Lutheran

When Bach died in 1750, because he had made no will, an inventory of his estate was drawn up. It was hardly complete, because, for example, Bach's clothes must have consisted of more than the eleven shirts, three coats, and one pair of silver shoe buckles that it records.[213] Chapter XII is a short-title listing of the theological books in Bach's library, comprising 52 titles in 81 bound volumes,[214] but because the custom of the time was to include several books within a single binding, Bach's collection was probably somewhat greater than the inventory suggests. All except two of the titles listed in the inventory are theologically Lutheran. The exceptions are the works of the Jewish historian Josephus and the sermons of the Dominican Johannes Tauler,[215] both of which were widely read in Lutheran circles. As has been noted earlier in this chapter, Bach seems to have developed an interest in such literature early in life and over the years amassed his modest but by no means insignificant library. Librarians with whom he had worked could have advised him on his choices, such as Johann Christoph

---

210 Carpzov, *Unterricht vom Unverletzten Gewissen*, 425.
211 See Leaver, "Oper in der Kirche," 171–203.
212 Carpzov, *Unterricht vom Unverletzten Gewissen*, 411; see 1 Chronicles 25; see also Greer, "From the House of Aaron to the House of Johann Sebastian," *passim*.
213 Dok 2: 494 (No. 627); NBR 252–253 (No. 279).
214 Dok 2: 494–496 (No. 627); NBR 253–254 (No. 279). For identification of the short titles see: Thomas Wilhelmi, "Bachs Bibliothek: Eine Weiterführung der Arbeit von Hans Preuß," BJ 65 (1979): 107–129; Leaver, *Bachs theologische Bibliothek*, passim; Johannes Wallmann, "Johann Sebastian Bach und die 'Geistlichen Bücher' seiner Bibliothek," *Pietismus und Neuzeit* 12 (1986): 162–181. It is necessary to consult all three works as, while many of the titles and editions are easily identifiable, some are ambiguous and could refer to different books because of the title abbreviations.
215 Leaver, *Bachs theologische Bibliothek*, 74–75 (No. 9) and 85–91 (No. 13).

180 *Robin A. Leaver*

Olearius in Arnstadt and Salomo Franck in Weimar, or clergy he worked with who had significant theological libraries of thousands of volumes could have similarly shared their bibliographical expertise, such as Bach's first Beichtvater in Leipzig, Christian Weiss, Sr., pastor of the Thomaskirche,[216] or the Leipzig superintendent, Salomon Deyling, pastor of the Nikolaikirche.[217] Bach's own library was, of course, much smaller than the massive collections of these professional theologians but compares quite favorably with the books used most often by clergy in small towns and villages, as evidenced in eighteenth-century visitation returns in the dukedom of Saxe-Gotha; indeed, Bach owned a significant number of the frequently cited titles, including the following:[218]

Martin Luther	Sermons (*Postillen*)	2, 3, 28
Heinrich Müller	*Evangelische Schluß-Kette*	8, 20
Martin Geier	*Zeit und Ewigkeit*	25
August Pfeiffer	*Anti-Melancolicus*	39
Johann Gerhard	*Schola Pietatis*	45
Johann Arndt	*Wahres Christenthum*	51[219]

Such devotional books were quarried by preachers for their sermons and read aloud in homes as part of daily devotions. At the end of his Small Catechism, Luther directs that there should be morning and evening prayers and thanksgivings before and after meals in the home, what came to be considered the Hauskirche. These devotions were to be led by the Hausvater or Hausmutter, and in practice also included Bible reading, the singing of hymns, a portion of the catechism, and reading of a passage from a devotional book.[220] It is clear that Bach and his wife, Anna Magdalena, continued to acquire such literature for their own devotional use and personal study, for family devotions as well as gifting such volumes to family and friends.

The writings of Luther made up a substantial part of Bach's library. He presumably already owned the eight volumes of the Jena German edition of the collected works (No. 3), when in September 1742 he purchased the Altenburg edition of Luther's writings (No. 2) at the auction of the library of the Leipzig theologian, Andreas Winckler (1684–1742).[221] In many respects, the Altenburg edition is

216 *Catalogvs Bibliothecæ B. Christiani Weisii... cum selecto omnis generis dissertationum... in collegii rubri vaporario auctionis lege vendendae* ([Leipzig]: Cruciger, 1744).

217 *Catalogus Bibliothecae Deylingiae auctionis lege in collegii rubri vaporario die seqq vendendae* (Leipzig: Cruciger, 1756).

218 Numbers on the right in the list, and in parenthesis in the following paragraphs, refer to those in Leaver, *Bachs theologische Bibliothek*.

219 See Ernst Koch, "Dorfpfarrer als Leser: Beobachtungen an Visitationsakten des 18. Jahrhunderts im Herzogtum Sachsen-Gotha," *Pietismus und Neuzeit* 21 (1995): 274–298. Bach also owned four more titles by Heinrich Müller (Nos. 19, 41–43), and eight by Pfeiffer (Nos. 14–18, 36–38).

220 See Kolb, *Lutheran Ecclesiastical Culture 1550–1675*, 193, 277.

221 Dok 1: 199 (No. 123); *Catalogus bibliothecae selectae beati Andreae Winckleri Catalogus bibliothecae selectae b. Andreae Winckleri: qui Lipsiae die III. & sqq. Sept. hujus 1742. anni ... auctionis lege vendentur* (Leipzig: [Cruciger], 1742).

Churches 181

a reprint of the Jena edition, but the Altenburg edition includes such things as Luther's lengthy commentary on the book of Genesis that was not included in the Jena edition. This suggests that Bach was concerned to own as many of the works of the reformer as he could, even if it meant duplicating what he already had. He also owned Luther's *Tischreden* (No. 4), the third volume of the Wittenberg German edition of Luther's works, mostly commentaries on the Psalms (No. 6), and two different editions of Luther's *Hauspostille* (Nos. 7 and 28). The only substantial work of Luther he did not own was the *Kirchenpostille*, which was not included in any of Luther's collected works until a later period.[222]

The inventory does not list copies of the Bible, catechism, hymnals,[223] and other books that Bach must have owned,[224] implying that they were divided among the family before the inventory was drawn up. It is likely that there were several Bibles in the Bach home in Leipzig. Among them was the folio *Biblia, Das ist/ Die gantze Heilige Schrifft... Verteutscht durch D. Martin Luther... Zumalen mit Mattäi Merians sel. schönen lebhafften Original-Kupffer-Stucken gezieret* (Frankfurt: Merian, 1704), which Bach acquired in 1744 and that only came to light in recent years.[225] It was already at that time a collector's item, notable for the inclusion of more than 200 superb engravings by Matthäus Merian (1593–1650) originally published in Strassburg between 1625 and 1630.[226] Another Bible that had come into the Bach home in 1738 was an edition published in Eisleben in 1736 that was later inscribed and given to Johann Christoph Friedrich by his mother, Anna Magdalena—at Christmas 1749 when Bach was seriously ill—a few weeks before he left home to become chamber musician to the court at Bückeburg.[227] But other copies of the Bible must have been in the cantor's apartment in the Thomasschule.

Bach was clearly a student of the Bible and it is highly likely that, like his contemporary Johann Mattheson, he set aside time for regular reading of Scripture.[228] He owned two commentaries on the complete biblical text: Johann Olearius, *Biblische Erklarung Darinnen nechst dem allgemeinen Haupt-Schlüssel Der*

---

222 See note 233.

223 An exception is the final item listed in the inventory (No. 52), the eight-volume anthology, *Andächtiger Seelen geistliches Brand- und Gantz-Opfer/ Das ist vollständiges Gesangbuch* (Leipzig: Zedler, 1697).

224 See Martin Petzoldt, "Über Johan Sebastian Bachs nichtfestgestellte kirchlich-theologische Bibliothek," *Johann Sebastian Bachs Kantaten zum Thema Tod und Sterben und ihr literarisches Umfeld*, ed. Renate Steiger (Wiesbaden: Harrassowitz, 2000), 283–318.

225 See Peter Wollny, "Fundstücke zur Lebensgeschichte Johann Sebastian Bachs 1744–1750," BJ 97 (2011), 37–39, 47–48.

226 Matthäus Merian, *Icones biblicæ præcipuas Sacræ Scripturæ historias eleganter & graphicè repræsentante* (Strassburg: Zetzner, 1625–1630); Matthäus Merian, *Great Scenes from the Bible: 230 Magnificent 17th-Century Engravings* (Mineola: Dover, 2002).

227 *Biblia, Das ist: Die gantze Heilige Schrifft... verdeutscht durch D. Martin Luthern...* (Eisleben: Schul-Lotterie, 1736); Dok 1: 124 (No. 54); Petzoldt and Petri, *Ehre sei dir Gott gesungen*, 148, 212. The front of the binding is impressed with the initials "A.M.B" and the back with "1738."

228 See Beekman C. Cannon, *Johann Mattheson: Spectator in Music* (New Haven: Yale University Press, 1947), 100–102, 219–220, 224.

182   Robin A. Leaver

gantzen heiligen Schrifft (Leipzig: Tanoven, 1678–1681) (No. 12), and Abraham Calov, *Die Deutsche Biebel/ D. Martini Lutheri... Mit Beyfügung der Aulegung/ die in Lutheri Schrifften zu finden* (Wittenberg: Schröter, 1681–1682) (No. 1). The latter three volumes, the only books listed in the inventory known to have survived, are particularly significant. On each of the title pages Bach inscribed his monogram and the year of acquisition, as he would do in the Merian Bible in 1744 (see previous): "J. S. Bach [with intertwined initials] 1733." The volumes are extremely important because they contain Bach's marginal notes and underlinings, markings he made for his own reference that most likely date from the middle to late 1730s.[229] Here is revealed a Lutheran musician who is concerned with understanding the biblical and theological meaning of his art, most notably with his comment alongside 2 Chronicles 5: 13: "NB Where there is devotional music, God with his grace is always present."[230] There is evidence that Bach continued to hold the Calov volumes in high regard. When he bought the Altenburg edition of Luther's works towards the end of 1742, he noted in his receipt that these volumes were once owned by Abraham Calov, and that Calov had used them as his primary source to create the *Deutche Bibel*, a set of which volumes Bach had obtained some nine years earlier:

> These *Teütsche und herrliche Schrifften des seeligen Dr. M. Lutheri* (which stem from the library of the eminent Wittenberg general superintendent and theologian Dr. Abraham Calov, which he supposedly used to compile his great *Teütsche Bibel*; also after his death, they passed into the hands of Dr. J. F. Mayer[231]), I have acquired at an auction for 10 thlr., anno 1742, in the month of September.
>
> Joh. Sebast. Bach[232]

Towards the end of the final volume of the Altenburg Luther edition, there is an index to Luther's writings in the sequence of the books of the Bible. Thus using this index, Calov compiled much of the *Deutsche Bibel,* extracting passages from Luther's writings and rearranging them in biblical order, only writing his own

---

229   See Howard H. Cox, ed., *The Calov Bible of J. S. Bach* (Ann Arbor: UMI Research Press, 1985); Robin A. Leaver, *J. S. Bach and Scripture: Glosses from the Calov Bible Commentary* (St. Louis: Concordia, 1985).

230   "NB Bey einer andächtigen Musique ist allezeit Gott mit seiner Gnadengegenwart." Dok 3: 636 (No.183a); Leaver, *J. S. Bach and Scripture*, 97–98; Cox, *The Calov Bible of J. S. Bach*, 112.

231   Johann Friedrich Mayer (1666–1712), born in Leipzig, studied at the university, was professor of theology in Wittenberg where he was a colleague of Calov, and ultimately became pastor primarius in Hamburg. He assembled what was probably the largest personally owned library at that time; see Volker Gummelt, "Der Maßlose: Johann Friedrich Mayer – Wächter der Orthodoxie, virtuoser Prediger, Bibliomane," Irmfried Garbe, Tilman Beyrich and Thomas Willi, eds., *Greifswalder theologische Profile: Bausteine zur Geschichte der Theologie an der Universität Greifswald* (Frankfurt: Lang, 2006), 45–56.

232   NBR 218 (No. 228); Dok 1: 199 (no. 123).

Churches 183

commentary where none by Luther could be found.[233] It is a measure of the value that Bach put on both the Altenburg Luther edition and Calov's use of it as his starting point for compiling the *Deutsche Bibel* that he felt it necessary to record the information in the lengthy parenthesis of the 1742 auction receipt.

Bach also owned other biblical handbooks, including August Pfeiffer's commentary on the Old Testament (No. 18), Johann Christian Adami's commentary on the Song of Solomon (No. 31), Caspar Heunisch's commentary on Revelation (No. 33), and Heinrich Bünting's travelog of the journeys of biblical personalities, together with geographical, monetary and mensural statistics (No. 11).

Collected sermons on the biblical lections of epistle or gospel (or both) throughout the church year form a significant part of Bach's library, ten volumes—some running into thousands of pages—in addition to the two editions of Luther's *Hauspostille*: four by August Pfeiffer (Nos. 14, 15, 17, 36), three by Heinrich Müller (Nos. 8, 19, 20), and one each by Nicolaus Stenger (No. 23), Martin Geier (No. 25), and possibly August Hermann Francke (No. 35). The one-year cycle of biblical readings—especially the gospels—for the Sundays, festivals, and other celebrations of the church year was not simply a liturgical necessity but was culturally imbedded into the social fabric of everyday life. Bibles and New Testaments generally included an index to the specific passages appointed for the epistles and gospels throughout the year. The Leipzig yearbook, a directory begun in 1750, contained useful information regarding the structure and personnel of the Saxon and local governments, the University, the churches, local businesses, and other vital data, especially the postal service.[234] The yearbook began with a calender of the year in question in which each week is named by the church year Sunday, followed by a brief summary of the gospel for that day, together with its biblical reference. For example, in January: "3. Woche. 2. n[ach]. Epiph. Hochzeit zu Cana, Joh. 2." These passages of Scripture were therefore extremely well-known, not only for the published homilies but also for the expositions heard in the Sunday sermons, customarily on the gospel at the morning Hauptgottesdienst and on the epistle at the afternoon Vespers. Thus these books in Bach's home not only supplied biblical devotions for himself and his family but also provided the biblical and theological context within which his cantatas were heard week by week in the churches.

Among other devotional books in the Bach household, the collected sermons on the Passion by Johann Jacob Rambach (1693–1735) stand out (No. 26). In my 1983 study of Bach's library, I simply recorded that because the inventory listed the volume as "Rambachii Betrachtung," and that Rambach authored a number of books with "Betrachtung" prominent in the title, it was not possible to

---

233 In a sense the Calov volumes formed another edition of Luther's writings. One major source that Calov used extensively in the *Deutsche Bibel* was Luther's *Kirchenpostille*, which was otherwise absent from Bach's library.

234 *Leipziger Adreß- Post- und Reise-Kalender, auf das Jahr Christi...* (Leipzig: Neubert, 1750–).

184   *Robin A. Leaver*

identify which one Bach owned. But I now think that the volume in question was Rambach's most popular book: *Betrachtungen über das gantze Leiden Christi... Nach der Harmonischen Beschreibung der vier Evangelisten abgehandelt. Vormals eintzeln* [1722–1729], *itzt zusammen herausgegeben, Auch mit einigen Kupfern gezieret* (Jena: Hartung, 1730). It seems to have been a book that was prized in the Bach household because, in 1742, Anna Magdalena Bach presented a copy of the second edition (Jena 1732) to Christiana Sybilla Bose.[235] Whether Bach knew of parts I and II (originally published in 1722 and 1723, respectively) of Rambach's exposition of the Passion when composing his John and Matthew Passions is an open question.[236]

Another popular devotional book, especially in Leipzig, was Friedrich Werner's *Der richtige und untrügliche Himmels-Weg eines Christen*, first published in 1704, reprinted numerous times, reaching a twenty-second edition in 1771, and described as a "highly edifying and beloved book."[237] Friedrich Werner (1659–1741) was another Leipzig pastor whom Bach must have known, because he was deacon of the Nikolaikirche when Bach arrived in Leipzig in 1723 and later (from 1737 until his death) the archdeacon, who was noted for his effective preaching.[238] Werner's book is not listed in the inventory, but because Wilhelm Friedemann Bach owned a copy of the 1710 edition, it seems most likely that it was known to the Bach family.[239] Wilhelm Friedemann's copy is inscribed with the year 1733, which is the year he left Leipzig to begin his first professional appointment as organist of the Sophienkirche, Dresden. Thus Werner's book was possibly a gift from his parents, in the same way that his brother Johann Christoph Friedrich received the gift of a Bible in 1749 before he left home for his appointment in Bückeburg.[240]

Other books in Bach's library also strongly reflect his Lutheran identity. Already noted are the books by Pfeiffer that express the differences between Lutherans and Calvinists.[241] There are other books that similarly take issue with Roman Catholicism as against Lutheranism: notably Martin Chemnitz's *Examen Concilii Tridentini* (No. 5), the classic Lutheran argument, point by point, against the decrees of the Council of Trent; Nicholas Hunnius's briefer *Apostasia Ecclesiae Romanae* (No. 49); and Philipp Jacob Spener's *Gerechter Eifer wider das Antichristische Pabstthum* (No. 48), which is mostly Reformation Day sermons, and not the kind of devotional writing one might have expected from this pioneer of Pietism. Among other Lutheran books are: the sermons of

---

235 Hans-Joachim Schulze, "Anna Magdalena Bachs 'Herzens Freündin." Neues über die Beziehungen zwischen den Familien Bach und Bose," BJ 83 (1997): 151–153.

236 Rambach's *Betrachtungen über das gantze Leiden Christi*, is one of the primary sources Chafe uses in discussion of the St. John Passion in *Bach's Johannine Theology*.

237 Zedler 55: 454. In a section warning against hypocrisy, Werner stresses the need for one's praying and singing to come from the heart; see Friedrich Werner, *Der richtige und untrügliche Himmels-Weg eines Christen... Zwanzigste Auflage* (Leipzig: Weidmann, 1755), 225–240.

238 Zedler 55: cols. 451–455.

239 See Wollny, "Fundstücke zur Lebensgeschichte Johann Sebastian Bachs 1744–1750," 36.

240 See note 239.

241 See note 179.

Christoph Scheibler, *Aurifodina Theologica* (No. 10), a Lutheran dogmatic theology in homiletic form; the sermons on the Augsburg Confession by August Pfeiffer, *Evangelische Aug-Apfel* (No. 17), and Nicolaus Stenger, *Grund-Feste der Augspurgischer Confession* (No. 24); and catechism sermons by Erdmann Neumeister, *Tisch des Herrn* [sacrament of the altar] (No. 46) and *Wasserbad im Worte* [baptism] (No. 47), volumes that also included sermons on hymns.

A Conflict About Theology or Music?

Towards the end of 2013, the Bach-Archiv Leipzig announced the discovery of a letter written by a former pupil of Bach at the Thomasschule that sheds new light on the last decade of Bach's life.[242] It was written by Gottfried Benjamin Fleckeisen (1719–1789) on 27 February 1751 and addressed to the municipal authorities of Döbeln, where his recently deceased father, Gottfried Fleckeisen, had been cantor since 1704.[243] The letter was written by Fleckeisen to commend himself as his father's successor. In the event, the application was unsuccessful and instead Fleckeisen became the cantor of Roßwein, a position he held for the rest of his professional life.[244]

According to the records, Fleckeisen was a Thomaner between 1732 and 1746,[245] that is a period of fourteen years, longer than any of his contemporaries who mostly spent between two and five years at the school, though a few stayed eight or nine years.[246] But Fleckeisen's letter clarifies his time at the school: nine years as a Thomaner and a further four years as a *chorus musicus* prefect, after which he spent five years at Leipzig University. But without mentioning Bach's name, he also adds that for "two whole years," presumably 1744 to 1746, as prefect, "in the place of the Capellmeister, and without glory" he had to "lead and conduct" the music of the two principal churches in Leipzig, the Thomaskirche and Nikolaikirche, and that he had done so "honourably."[247]

Fleckeisen's self-promoting letter implies that Bach had withdrawn from an important part of his responsibilities in Leipzig for at least two years. Although Fleckeisen gives no reason why it was necessary for him to replace Bach, there are some significant details in the letter that strongly suggest that the so-called "Praefektenstreit" of 1736–1738[248] was never fully resolved. The dispute was over the appointment of the prefects whose function was to direct the

---

242 See Michael Maul, "zwey ganzer Jahr die Music an Statt des Capellmeisters aufführen, und dirigiren müssen'—Überlegungen zu Bachs Amtsverstandnis in den 1740er Jahren," BJ 101 (2015): 75–97. I am grateful to Michael Maul for supplying me with a transcription of the letter before its publication.

243 Reinard Vollhardt, *Geschichte der Cantoren un Organisten von den Städten im Königriech Sachsen*, ed. Eberhard Stimmel (Leipzig: Peters, 1978), 59.

244 Vollhardt, *Cantoren und Organisten... im... Sachsen*, 288, 474.

245 Bernhard Friedrich Richter, "Stadtpfeifer und Alumnen der Thomasschule in Leipzig zu Bachs Zeit," BJ 4 (1907): 71.

246 Richter, "Stadtpfeifer und Alumnen," 68–76. Fleckeisen's time at the school was so long that Richter had to add an exclamation point after the terminal year of 1746.

247 John Eliot Gardiner, *Bach: Music in the Castle of Heaven* (New York: Knopf, 2013), 541.

248 NBR 172–185 (Nos. 180–187); Dok 1: 82–90 (Nos. 32–35) and Dok 2: 268–276 (Nos. 382–383). NBR 189–196 (Nos. 192–196); Dok 1:97–106 (Nos. 40–41).

186   Robin A. Leaver

secondary choirs in three of the churches at the same time as Bach was directing the primary choir in either the St. Thomas or the St. Nicholas church. Traditionally, the cantor had always chosen these prefects because of the musical leadership they were expected to fulfill. However, the rector, Johann August Ernesti, took the matter into his own hands and appointed these prefects himself without consulting Bach. Bach protested several times to the Leipzig town council, a body he had described in 1730 as "odd and little interested in music, so that I must live amid almost continual vexation, envy, and persecution."[249] Charges and countercharges were issued by the two protagonists and, until now, it has been assumed that the matter simply petered out and a working relationship was restored between the two men. But the discovery of Fleckeisen's letter suggests that the matter may never have been settled. Two documents support the concept of continued antipathy between rector and cantor. One is the summary of the prefect dispute, published in 1776, that reported on the aftermath:

> From that time on, though there have been several incumbents of both posts, little harmony has been observed between the Rector and the Cantor.[250]

The other source is Quantz's treatise, *Versuch einer Anweisung die Flöte traversiere zu spielen*, written about ten years or so after the dispute began. Although it purports to be a general statement, the details reflect with some accuracy the situation in Leipzig:

> If a cantor is found here and there who understands his duties, and wants to administer his musical office honestly, at many places the authorities of the school... seek to hinder the practice of music. And even in those schools which, as their laws attest, have been established principally with the aim that music should be taught and learned, and *musici eruditi* should be trained, the rector supported by the director [Vorsteher] is often the most open enemy of music.[251]

In Leipzig, the Vorsteher—school superintendent—was Christian Ludwig Stieglitz (1677–1758), a powerful man in Leipzig politics: town councilor from 1715, judge from 1725, lawyer to the royal Polish and Saxon electoral courts in Dresden, and six times Leipzig Burgermeister between 1741 and 1757.[252] Johann

---

249 NBR 152 (No. 152); Dok 1: 67 (No. 23); see Robin A. Leaver, "Leipzig's Rejection of J.S. Bach," BACH 3/ 3 (July 1972): 27–39; 3/4 (October 1972): 3–7.

250 NBR 172 (No. 180); Dok 3: 314 (No. 820).

251 Johann Joachim Quantz, *Versuch einer Anweisung die Flöte traversiere zu spielen* (Berlin: Boß, 1752; facsimile, Wiesbaden: Breitkopf & Härtel, 1988), 326 (Hauptstück XVIII, § 80); ET *Johann Joachim Quantz On Playing the Flute*, trans. and ed. Edward R. Reilly, 2nd ed. (Boston: Northwestern University Press, 2001), 337.

252 Karin Kühling and Doris Mundus, eds., *Leipzigs Regierende Bürgermister vom 13. Jahrhundert bis zur Gegenwart: Eine Übersichtsdarstellung mit biographischen Skizzen* (Beucha: Sax, 2000), 44.

Churches 187

August Ernesti (1707–1781),[253] philologist and educator, was Stieglitz's protégé. While a student at Leipzig University, Ernesti was private tutor in the Stieglitz household. On obtaining his master's degree in 1731, through Stieglitz's influence, Ernesti was appointed conrector of the Thomasschule, to work alongside the rector, Johann Matthias Gesner, another philologist and colleague of Bach at the Weimar court who extolled the Leipzig cantor's musical gifts.[254] One suspects that Stieglitz was behind the decision not to grant Gesner permission to become a professor at the university while continuing as the rector of the school—as previous rectors had done. This meant that Gesner left Leipzig in 1734 to become a professor at the newly founded University of Göttingen, and Ernesti, who was still only 27, became the rector of the Thomasschule.

It is clear that Steiglitz and Ernesti were in league with each other. For example, Ernesti was given preferential treatment, such as being released from otherwise obligatory menial oversight tasks in the school, a privilege also claimed by Bach but not accorded to him.[255] Stieglitz and Ernesti were intent on working together to change the educational philosophy of the school, moving it away from its previous primary focus on music in favor of a rigorous curriculum that stressed mathematics, philosophy, dialectics, ethics, natural sciences, and natural theology. These are the subjects covered by the basic textbook that Ernesti published as *Initia doctrinae solidioris* (1736, with six more editions by 1783). Music is mentioned only once in this curriculum of Ernesti, and then only in passing, within the context of mathematics and acoustics.[256] Stieglitz was at best lukewarm towards music, who after Bach's death declared "the school needs a cantor [i.e., teacher] and not a Capellmeister, though he must understand music."[257] Ernesti was openly hostile towards music. If he came across a Thomaner practicing an instrument, he would castigate the student with, "What? You want to be a beer fiddler, too?"[258]

The root cause of the conflict between Ernesti and Bach has frequently been explained as the collision of two theologies, Bach representing Lutheran Orthodoxy and Ernesti manifesting the emerging theology of the Enlightenment.[259] The argument is based on Ernesti's *Institutio interpretis novi testamenti* published in 1765, some years after Bach's death, in which he argued that the documents of the New Testament should be studied in exactly the same way as the Greek and Latin

---

253 *Allgemeine Deutsche Bibliographie* (ADB) 6 (1877: 235–241); http://www.deutsche-biographie. de/sfz13604.html
254 See NBR 328–329 (No. 328); Dok 2: 331–333 (No. 432).
255 See NBR 172 (No. 180); Dok 3: 314 (No. 820).
256 Johann August Ernesti, *Initia doctrinae solidioris... editio altera* (Leipzig: Wendler, 1745), 7.
257 NBR 246 (No.274a); Dok 2: 479 (No. 614).
258 NBR 172 (No. 180); Dok 3: 314 (No. 820).
259 See, for example, "Bach's Quarrel with the Rector of St. Thomas School," Robert M. Stevenson, *Patterns of Protestant Church Music* (Durham: Duke University Press, 1953), 67–77; "The Musician Versus the Grammarian: an Early Storm Warning," Paul S. Minear, *The Bible and the Historian: Breaking the Silence about God in Biblical Studies* (Nashville: Abingdon, 2002), 25–36, 264–265.

188   *Robin A. Leaver*

classics. Ernesti's monograph became the foundation stone of the so-called "historical-grammatical method" of biblical interpretation in the nineteenth century. However, the edition that was widely used was the fourth edited by Christoph F. Ammon in 1792, which was twice the length of Ernesti's original monograph, and it is Ammon's additions rather than Ernesti's original text in which overt rationalism is found. Ernesti was thus viewed through the lens of the expansions of the later editions of his monograph, whereas he himself, in his stress on the literal interpretation of the biblical text, had more in common with Salomon Glassius's *Philologia sacra* (1623 and many later reprints),[260] the classic Lutheran textbook on biblical linguistics, than with the later editors of his *Institutio*.[261] Further, his view that the New Testament should be treated like any classic document was also misunderstood when it was thought that he meant that the Scriptures should be considered no different from any other writings of human composure. But this was not his meaning. In an oration he gave at the Thomasschule in April 1736, Ernesti fulminated against the current practice, what he termed the *stupor paedagogicus*, the stupidity of reading Latin authors piecemeal simply to master a superior Latin style. Instead, he called for the reading of complete texts, or at least substantial portions of them, so that one could learn the substance rather than simply the style of these documents.[262] Seen in this light his later call for reading the New Testament like non-sacred literature was almost certainly meant as an encouragement for people to read substantial and consecutive passages of Scripture rather than simply relying on the fragmented epistle and gospel passages assigned to the Sundays and celebrations of the church year. And more fundamentally, Ernesti was criticized by those who followed him for his adherence to the Orthodox Lutheran position on biblical inspiration and the primacy of Scripture.[263] Therefore the conflict between the two men was not over differences in theology: they both held substantially the same basic beliefs. It was, rather, a fundamental disagreement over the role of music in education that had significant ramifications for the Leipzig churches as well as the Thomasschule, and in personal terms it undermined Bach's sense of vocation.

Festivals and Special Occasions More than Sundays?

Although one would need more than one document to construct a firm hypothesis regarding the final years of Bach's life, Fleckeisen's letter does seems to suggest

---

260 Editions in print during Bach's day included an additional treatise by Glassius on sacred logic, edited by Johann Gottfried Olearius, superintendent in Arnstadt during Bach's time there; for example: Salmon Glassius, *Philologia sacra* (Amsterdam: Wolters, 1711), 975–990.

261 For the background, see William Baird, *History of New Testament Research. Volume One: from Deism to Tübingen* (Minneapolis: Fortress, 1992), 108–115.

262 "De intereuntium humaniorum literarum caussis," Johann August Ernesti, *Opuscula varii argumenti* (Leipzig: Fritsch, 1794), 36–50; see also Peter Lundgreen, "Schulhumanismus, pädagogischer Realismus. Die Gelehrtenschule zur Zeit J. S. Bachs," LBB 7 (2005): 31–32; the year is wrongly recorded as 1738 instead of 1736.

263 See John H. Sailhamer, "Johann August Ernesti: the Role of History in Biblical Interpretation," *Journal of the Evangelical Theological Society* 44/2 (2001): 206.

Churches 189

that in the prefect dispute, neither Ernesti nor Bach would back down. The result appears to be, at least from time to time, both rector and cantor appointed their own prefects, with Bach refusing to work with Ernesti's choices, choosing instead to work with his own "prefects." Ernesti's prefects, of which Fleckeisen was one, would then be responsible for the weekly church music in the two principal churches when Bach refused to work with these prefects, such as between 1744 and 1746. Bach's "prefects," such as Johann Nathanael Bammler (1722–1784),[264] worked with Bach mostly on the special church music for major festivals and observances.[265] Bach thus apparently distanced himself from the weekly performance of cantatas in the church services, either by his nonattendance or by re-performing earlier-composed cantatas,[266] but continued to compose other music with intensified contrapuntal complexity. These were the years in which he produced the Canonic Variations on *Vom Himmel hoch* (BWV 769), Clavierübung IV (BWV 988; Goldberg Variations), the Art of Fugue (BWV 1080), and the Musical Offering (BWV 1079). Given the situation with regard to the prefect dispute, there was little encouragement to compose new cantatas.

His Lutheran identity appears to have weathered the storm during these years. His manuscript marginalia in the Calov *Deutsche Bibel* volumes, which came into his possession in 1733, are likely to have been penned sometime around the beginning of the prefect dispute. Then there was the Altenburg edition of Luther's writings he purchased in 1742, and the illustrated Bible he bought in 1744. However, there was a significant shift in his thinking and practice that is clearly observable in these years.

There are two aspects of this change in emphasis. On the one hand, Bach significantly intensified the repertory of Latin music by other composers for use in the Leipzig churches from the 1730s onwards, the extent of which has only become apparent in recent research.[267] On the other hand, during the same period, he recomposed his own cantata movements in which the original German texts were replaced by Latin, mostly texts of the Ordinary of the Mass (see later). Latin liturgical texts were not regularly used in the Sunday worship in Leipzig, but were a significant feature of the celebrations on the major festivals of the church year. There is therefore the suggestion that, although Bach was *persona non grata* with the rector, Vorsteher, and some of the town councilors, the Leipzig clergy, especially superintendent Deyling, had a different opinion. Traditional liturgy, together with its Latin language and music, were constantly attacked by the Pietists, so this increased usage of Latin liturgical-musical settings might have been part of a reaction to these aspects of Pietism by the largely Orthodox

---

264 Richter, "Stadtpfeifer und Alumnen," 73.

265 During the 1740s Bammler was involved in creating scores and/or parts for performances of the St. John Passion (BWV 245^{IV}), Easter Oratorio (BWV 249), and the anonymous Sanctus (BWV 239).

266 For an overview of the years 1738–1750 see the Chronology, Chapter 20.

267 See Peer Wollny, "Zwei Bach-Fund in Mügeln. C.P.E. Bach, Picander und die Leipziger Kirchenmusik in den 1730er Jahren," BJ 96 (2010): 111–151, esp. 114–116; Christoph Wolff, *Johann Sebastian Bach: Messe in h-Moll* (Kassel: Bärenreiter, 2009): 21–30.

190 *Robin A. Leaver*

Leipzig clergy.[268] What is clear is that this was not an innovation but rather an intensification of a long-standing tradition. In Leipzig, as elsewhere in Lutheran Germany, concerted settings of the Missa (Kyrie and Gloria) had long been performed, especially on major festivals, together with such settings of other parts of the *Ordinarium*, Credo, Sanctus and Agnus Dei.[269]

For Bach, the shift in emphasis from German to Latin was momentous. As he reviewed his substantial corpus of vocal works from the vantage point of his later years, his perspective changed from the homiletical to the liturgical. Cantatas that were originally conceived as sermons in sound directed to the gathered congregation were reworked to become liturgical prayers and praises directed to God. These are the parodies Bach created in his later years in which movements from the cantatas were recomposed into new works, notably the four short Masses (BWV 233–236) created between 1738 and 1739, the Latin cantata, *Gloria in excelsis Deo* (BWV 191), dating from 1742, and supremely the B minor Mass (BWV 232), finally assembled together between 1748 and 1749. There was of course a practical reason for the parodies. The cantatas on which they were based were composed as *Proprium* music, that is, closely associated with the biblical lections—especially the gospel—of a particular Sunday, celebration or observance in the church year. As such, they were restricted to the occasion for which they were composed and could only usually be used once each year. But by recomposing the movements and adapting them to *Ordinarium* texts—that is, the fixed liturgical texts that were used on the principal feasts and saints' days— then the music could be heard several times in any year. Bach therefore made his music more accessible by transforming some of his finest compositions from *Proprium* to *Ordinarium*, changing their function from proclamation to prayer.

---

268 Deyling certainly had a comprehensive view of liturgy; see Deyling, *Institutiones Prudentiae Pastoralis*, 593.

269 On Lutheran use of the Latin *Ordinarium*, see Robin A. Leaver, "Bach's Mass: 'Catholic' or 'Lutheran'?" *Exploring Bach's B-minor Mass*, eds. Yo Tomita, Robin A. Leaver and Jan Smaczny (Cambridge: Cambridge University Press, 2013), 28–36. Jeffrey S. Sposato has independently come to similar conclusions regarding the Latin works of Bach's later years; see Jeffrey S. Sposato, *Leipzig After Bach: Church and Concert Life in a German City, 1743–1847*, forthcoming. See also the relevant sections in Chapter 10.

8 Courts

Andrew Talle

Johann Sebastian Bach spent his entire life within the Holy Roman Empire of the German Nation (*Heiliges Römisches Reich teutscher Nation*), a patchwork of around 1800 territories varying in size and shape that encompassed most of central Europe, including all of modern Germany and Austria, and portions of modern Italy, France, Belgium, Luxemburg, Lichtenstein, Switzerland, the Netherlands, Poland, the Czech Republic, and Slovenia. Officially, the Emperor in Vienna was at the very top of the hierarchy, followed by the Prince Electors (*Kurfürsten*)— the Archbishops of Mainz, Cologne, and Trier, the King of Bohemia, the Count Palatine of the Rhein, the Duke of Saxony, and the Margrave of Brandenburg, and later the Duke of Bavaria and the Duke of Brunswick-Lüneburg. In practice, however, the Emperor was quite weak, leaving the electors and other local rulers—princes, feudal lords, clerics, ecclesiastical institutions, city and village governments—a large measure of autonomy.[1]

The destruction of the Thirty Years' War (1618–1648) brought with it a consolidation of power. Only the most powerful rulers—those with access to extensive natural resources or foreign precious metals—were able to maintain their independence. Members of the lower, landed nobility, reduced to a state of destitution by the war, found themselves in an awkward position; survival demanded that they generate some income and yet social status did not permit them to engage in productive work. Some solved this problem by joining a religious body and donating their lands to the church, but most opted to go into the service of the more powerful noble families, who offered them economic security and titled sinecures in courtly bureaucracies in exchange for undying loyalty. The resulting circumstance is what we now refer to as *Absolutism*, in which the power of the ruling families that came out on top of this historical process went largely unchecked by the lower nobility.[2]

---

1 For a useful survey of the Holy Roman Empire, its history, and institutions, see Peter H. Wilson, *The Holy Roman Empire 1495–1806* (New York: St. Martin, 1999). Thomas Höckmann has prepared excellent maps of the Empire as it existed in the eighteenth century; see http://www.hoeckmann.de/deutschland/index.htm

2 Modern research on absolutist representation was effectively founded in the 1960s by Norbert Elias, whose *Die höfische Gesellschaft. Untersuchungen zur Soziologie des Königtums und der*

192   Andrew Talle

This consolidation of power established a rough equilibrium; independent potentates had little hope of improving their circumstances by declaring war on one another.[3] Cultural representation, rather than violence, became the primary means of establishing authority. The courtly residence of each potentate was not only the seat of politics and diplomacy in his territory, it was also the center for elite cultural competition. Elaborate hunts, dances, operas, palaces, gardens, and art collections enabled potentates to make their power palpable for the citizens and farmers in their own realms, as well as for visiting dignitaries. The number of court employees who helped the potentate actually govern remained relatively constant between 1650 and 1750, whereas the number of employees charged with representation—chambermaids, seneschals, hunt masters, gardeners, poets, and singers—increased tremendously.[4]

Music was among the most important forms of courtly representation.[5] Trumpeters and timpanists in particular were absolutely indispensable at virtually all courts, and their services were required more often than those of any other court musicians.[6] Members of the court chapel (*Hofkapelle*) were regularly called upon to entertain guests in concerts or at meals or to provide music for

---

    höfischen Aristokratie, (Darmstadt: Luchthand, 1969) and his earlier *Über den Prozeß der Zivilisation* (Basel: Falken, 1939), ET *The Civilizing Process*, trans. Edmund Jephcott (New York: Pantheon, 1982), remain seminal works. For an overview of the noble court system in the Holy Roman Empire, see Jürgen Freiherr von Kruedener, *Die Rolle des Hofes im Absolutismus* (Stuttgart: Fischer, 1973). Some have argued that Elias's focus on the court of the King of France, Louis XIV, is not directly transferable to the courts of the Holy Roman Empire; see in particular Volker Bauer, *Die höfische Gesellschaft in Deutschland von der Mitte des 17. bis zum Ausgang des 18. Jahrhunderts. Versuch einer Typologie.* (Tübingen: Niemeyer, 1993), and Aloys Winterling, *Der Hof der Kurfürsten von Köln, 1688–1794. Eine Fallstudie zur Bedeutung 'absolutistischer' Hofhaltung* (Bonn: Röhrscheid, 1986). For an excellent survey of the literature, see Barbara Stollberg-Rilinger, "Hofzeremoniell als Zeichensystem. Zum Stand der Forschung," Jiliane Riepe, ed., *Musik der Macht - Macht der Musik: Die Musik an den sächsisch-albertinischen Herzogshöfen Weißenfels, Zeitz und Merseburg.* (Schneverdingen: Wagner, 2003), 11–22. A still-useful account in English of German social hierarchies in this period is provided by Walter H. Bruford, *Germany in the Eighteenth Century – The Social Background of the Literary Revival* (Cambridge: Cambridge University Press, 1935, and later reprints).

3 Mack Walker, *German Home Towns: Community, State, and the General Estate, 1648–1871* (Ithaca: Cornell University Press, 1971), 12–20.

4 Kruedener, *Die Rolle des Hofes*, 8.

5 Music historians have increasingly devoted their attentions to the details of musical life at the courts in central Germany. Some recent examples of note include Karla Neschke & Helmut Köhler, *Residenzstadt Sondershausen – Beiträge zur Musikgeschichte* (Sondershausen: Starke, 2004); Karla Neschke, *Johann Balthasar Christian Freislich (1687–1764) – Leben, Schaffen, und Werküberlieferung* (Oschersleben: Ziethen, 2000); Hans Rudolf Jung, *Musik und Musiker im Reußenland* (Weimar: Hain, 2007); Christian Ahrens, *"Zu Gotha ist eine gute Kapelle..." – aus dem Innenleben einer thüringischen Hofkappe des 18. Jahrhunderts* (Stuttgart: Steiner, 2009); and Samantha Owens, Barbara Reul, and Janice B. Stockigt, eds., *Music at German Courts, 1715–1760: Changing Artistic Priorities* (Woodbridge: Boydell, 2011).

6 Sabine Henze-Döhring, "Der Stellenwert der Musik im höfischen Zeremoniell," Jiliane Riepe, ed., *Musik der Macht - Macht der Musik: Die Musik an den sächsisch-albertinischen Herzogshöfen Weißenfels, Zeitz und Merseburg.* (Schneverdingen: Wagner, 2003): 23–32.

religious services. Those rulers who invested heavily in music could sometimes reap political rewards. Ernst August of Brunswick-Calenberg had aspirations in 1689 to become a Prince Elector, so he built an opera house like those otherwise found only at electoral courts. Having raised himself culturally to the status of a Prince Elector, the Emperor offered him the political title the following year.[7]

Young musicians—like young lawyers, preachers, and administrators—dreamed of joining prestigious courtly establishments. Georg Philipp Telemann wrote in 1718 that gaining "the grace of great lords, the courtesy of nobles, and the love and deep respect of other servants" in a court *Kapelle* was the best motivation for improving one's musical skills, "especially when one is still young enough to have the necessary fire for such undertakings."[8] Courtly life also presented its hazards, however. Telemann acknowledged that "at court one is worked too hard, the masters are not all music lovers, and one can all too easily fall into disfavor."[9] Musicians were not always or even usually held in high regard. Even the leader of the court musical establishment, the Capellmeister, was ordinarily consigned to the lower third of the ceremonial ranking system of court employees, behind the master of ceremonies (*Ceremonienmeister*), the master of hunts (*Hof-Jägermeister*), and court medical doctors (*Hofärtzten*), the court architect (*Bau-Director*), but ahead of the master chef (*Küchenmeister*), the court fencing master (*Hof-Fechtmeister*), and the court chamber musicians (*Cammer-Musicanten*).[10] Musicians with extensive training and expertise were often supplemented by local boys or sons of other court employees, whose skills and pay were generally quite meager.[11] A court musician with a knack for negotiating tricky political situations could sometimes gain favor that could lead to additional, non-musical appointments. Johann Christian Edelmann wrote that because his father "had an excellent alto voice and could play the lute well," he was appointed chamber musician (*Cammer-Musicus*) to Duke Christian of Weißenfels, but when the duke moved to Sangerhausen in 1711 he was promoted "to serve as Court Secretary (*Hof-Secretarius*)."[12] Both Telemann and Gottfried Heinrich Stölzel enjoyed the rank of courtly secretary while serving at the courts in Eisenach and Gotha, respectively.[13]

---

7 Juliane Riepe, "Hofmusik in der Zeremonialwissenschaft des 18. Jahrhunderts," *Händel Jahrbuch*, 49 (2003): 36.

8 See Steven Zohn, "'Die vornehmste Hof-Tugend': German Musicians' Reflections on Eighteenth-Century Court Life," Owens, Reul, Stockigt, *Music at German Courts*, 416.

9 Owens, Reul, Stockigt, *Music at German Courts*, 418.

10 Riepe, "Hofmusik in der Zeremonialwissenschaft," 44–47.

11 Christoph-Hellmut Mahling, "Herkunft und Sozialstatus des höfischen Orchester-musikers im 18. und frühen 19. Jahrhundert in Deutschland," Walter Salmen, ed., *Der Sozialstatus des Berufsmusikers vom 17. bis 19. Jahrhundert.* (Kassel: Bärenreiter, 1971), 103–136.

12 Carl Rudolph Wilhelm Klose, ed., *Joh. Chr. Edelmann's Selbstbiographie. Geschrieben 1752* (Berlin: Wiegandt, 1849), 6–7.

13 Zohn, "Die vornehmste Hof-Tugend," 417. Johann Mattheson, *Grundlage einer Ehren-Pforte woran der Tüchtigsten Capellmeister, Componisten, Musikgelehrten, Tonkünstler & c. Leben, Wercke, Verdienste & c. erscheinen sollen* (Hamburg: Mattheson, 1740), 346.

194   *Andrew Talle*

Courts were of central importance to J. S. Bach, particularly during the middle part of his career (1708–1723) while he resided at the courts of Dukes Ernst Ludwig and Wilhelm Ernst of Saxe-Weimar and Prince Leopold of Anhalt-Cöthen. Before and after this period too, Bach enjoyed regular and profitable contact with members of the nobility, who commissioned him to compose new works (for example, Johann Adam, Count of Questenberg[14]), hired him to teach keyboard lessons (such as Eugen Wentzel, Imperial Count of Wrbna[15]), and attended his performances (such as the Princes of Hessen-Kassel[16]). Bach also maintained connections with numerous court musicians who worked in places he is not known to have visited (for example, Christoph Graupner in Darmstadt,[17] Heinrich Gerber in Sondershausen,[18] and Johann Ludwig Bach in Meiningen[19]). He undoubtedly enjoyed much more contact with the noble courts and court musicians of his time than we presently know to be documented.[20] In the discussion that follows, I will devote a section to each court with which Bach is known to have had direct contact, beginning with those at which he resided.

Courts at Which Bach Resided

Weimar (1703, 1708–1717)

Weimar during Bach's time there had a population of just under 5000.[21] Before 1707, the territory of which it was the capital city was ruled by two brothers, Wilhelm Ernst, Duke of Saxony-Weimar, and Johann Ernst III, Duke of Saxe-Weimar. Upon the death of the latter in 1707, his position was inherited by his son, Ernst August I, Duke of Saxe-Weimar (1688–1748), who thereafter co-ruled with his uncle. The personalities of Wilhelm Ernst and Ernst August were radically different, and led repeatedly to conflicts, which often made it difficult for their musicians and other employees.[22]

---

14 Dok 5: 171–172 (No. B 581a); see also Michael Maul, "'The Great Catholic Mass': Bach, Count Questenberg and the Musicalische Congregation in Vienna," Yo Tomita, Robin A. Leaver, and Jan Smaczny, *Exploring Bach's B-minor Mass* (Cambridge: Cambridge University Press, 2013), 84–104.

15 Dok 1: 204–207 (Nos. 130–132, 134–135) and Dok 5: 107–108 (Nos. A 134, A 135a).

16 Dok 2: 410–411 (No. 522).

17 Dok 2: 98 (No. 132).

18 Dok 3: 476–477 (No. 950).

19 Dok 1: 264 (No. 184).

20 It has been argued that Bach visited the court in Arnstadt while serving as organist of the St. Blasius Church. This is indeed likely, but so far only circumstantial evidence has come to light; see Markus Schiffner, "Johann Sebastian Bach in Arnstadt," *Beiträge zur Heimatgeschichte Stadt und Kreis Arnstadt* 4 (1985): 24–26; and Wolff BLM, 83–89.

21 Alex Stelzner, "Die staatliche Ordnung im Weimarer Herzogtum zu Zeiten Johann Sebastian Bachs," Helen Geyer, ed., *Johann Sebastian Bach in Weimar (1708–1717)* (Göttingen: Hainholz, 2008), 135.

22 For profiles of the two dukes, see Rudolf Herrmann, "Die Bedeutung des Herzogs Wilhelm Ernst von Sachsen-Weimar (1683–1728) für die Weimarische evangelische Kirche," *Zeitschrift des Vereins für thüringische Geschichte und Altertumskunde* 30/2 (1915): 225–278; and

Bach's first stay in Weimar began in January 1703, shortly after he left the Michaelisschule in Lüneburg, and lasted for roughly six months. Court payment records refer to him as a *Laquey*,[23] but the record of his organ test in Arnstadt in the same year describes him as the "Fürstlich Sächsischer HoffOrganiste zu Weimar,"[24] and the obituary of 1754 refers to him as *Hoff Musicus*.[25] Whatever Bach's official title, his duties are entirely obscure, he was paid quite poorly (6 Florins and 18 Groschen per quarter[26]), and he left after six months to serve as organist at the Neuen Kirche in Arnstadt.

Bach returned to the court in Weimar in the summer of 1708, this time with the unambiguous title of *Hoforganist*. His base salary was now considerably higher (37 Florins, 10 Groschen, and 6 Pfennige per quarter[27] plus allowances for wood and coal[28]), and he received small bonus payments from a courtly foundation,[29] and for maintaining the keyboard instruments.[30] In March 1714, Bach's salary in Weimar was raised and he was given the additional title of *Concert-meister*, with a rank just below that of the Capellmeister, Johann Samuel Drese. He received an additional compensation for strings and music paper,[31] and funeral clothing,[32] and his bonus payments (*Naturalien* and the traditional supplement at the New Year) were raised to match those of the Capellmeister.[33] Bach's new appointment required him to perform new works on a monthly basis, and the musicians of the capelle were required to rehearse these works upon his request.[34] He was also required to perform at court functions and ceremonies; for example, the presentation of *Hofmarschälle*[35] and official birthday celebrations for members of the ducal family.[36]

Hagen Jäger, "Alchemie, Theosophie und Frömmigkeit bei Herzog Ernst August von Sachsen-Weimar-Eisenach," Geyer, *Johann Sebastian Bach in Weimar (1708–1717)*, 143–167. For the conflicts between them that made life difficult for musicians, see Andreas Glöckner, "Gründe für Johann Sebastian Bachs Weggang von Weimar," Winfried Hoffmann and Armin Schneiderheinze, eds., *Bericht über die Wissenschaftliche Konferenz zum V. Internationalen Bachfest der DDR in Verbindung mit dem 60. Bachfest der Neuen Bachgesellschaft. Leipzig, 25. bis 27. März 1985.* (Leipzig: Deutscher Verlag für Musik, 1988): 137–144.

23 Dok 2: 10 (No. 6).
24 Dok 2: 10 (No. 7). It has been recently suggested that authorities in Arnstadt may have confused Bach with Johann Effler, who likely recommended him for the position there. This would explain why they accorded him the title of court organist in Weimar. See Peter Wollny, "Über die Hintergründe von Johann Sebastian Bachs Bewerbung in *Arnstadt*" BJ 91 (2005): 90.
25 Dok 3: 82 (No. 666).
26 Dok 2: 10 (No. 6).
27 Dok 2: 35–36 (No. 39).
28 Dok 2: 36–37 (Nos. 40, 41).
29 Dok 2: 41 (No. 48).
30 Dok 2: 41 (No. 49).
31 Dok 2: 56–57 (No. 71).
32 Dok 2: 58–59 (No. 75).
33 Dok 2: 57–58, 64 (Nos. 73, 81).
34 Dok 2: 53–54 (No. 66).
35 Dok 2: 55–56 (No. 69).
36 Dok 5: 123 (No. B 59a).

196   *Andrew Talle*

Which works Bach composed in Weimar and when he composed them is far from clear. The authors of Bach's obituary asserted that most of his organ works were produced during this period,[37] but not a single instrumental composition can be securely dated to a particular year. Analysis of Bach's handwriting suggests that he set down much of the *Orgelbüchlein* (BWV 599–644) during this period, and analyses of the handwriting of his associates, Johann Tobias Krebs Sr. and Johann Gottfried Walther, place a number of additional keyboard works in the Weimar era.[38] Some, if not all, of the Brandenburg Concertos (BWV 1046–1051) were probably composed here, although we cannot know exactly when.[39] The vocal works can be dated with a little more confidence because the paper and handwriting of about twenty cantatas can be securely connected with Weimar.[40] On the basis of Bach's 1714 contract, which specified that he was to "perform new pieces monthly," scholars have attempted to attach cantatas to particular Sundays in the church calendar. The cantatas do in many cases seem to fit into four-week intervals, but not always.[41] The "Hunt Cantata" (BWV 208) was composed in Weimar, though it was first performed in Weissenfels.[42] The biggest Bach-related sensation of the century thus far has been the discovery of a previously unknown aria, *Alles mit Gott und nichts ohn' ihn* (BWV 1127), in the *Herzogin Anna Amalia Bibliothek* in Weimar, which was composed for Duke Wilhelm Ernst's fifty-third birthday celebrations in 1713.[43] The difficulties with chronology have made the study of Bach's stylistic development a particular challenge, but some brave authors have made attempts.[44]

37   "Hier hat er auch die meisten seiner Orgelstücke gesetzet." Dok 3: 83 (No. 666).
38   BWV 538, 540, 569, 572a, 574a, 574b, 653a, 653b, 665a, 666a, 667b, 721, 770, 806a, 951, 965, 966, 981, 996. See Hermann Zietz, *Quellenkritische Untersuchungen an den Bach-Handschriften P801, P802, und P803 aus dem "Krebs'schen Nachlass" unter Berücksichtigung den Choralbearbeitung des jungen J. S. Bach* (Hamburg: Wagner, 1969); Stephen Daw, "Copies of J. S. Bach by Walther & Krebs: a Study of the Manuscripts P801, P802, P803," *Organ Yearbook* 7 (1976): 31–58; and Kirsten Beißwenger, "Zur Chronologie der Notenhandschriften Johann Gottfried Walthers," *Acht kleine Präludien und Studien über BACH. Georg von Dadelsen zum 70. Geburtstag am 17. November 1988*, ed. Göttingen Kollegium des Johann-Sebastian-Bach-Instituts (Wiesbaden: Breitkopf & Härtel, 1992), 11–39.
39   Wolff BLM, 169.
40   See Dürr St, 64–65; and Klaus Hoffmann, "Neue Überlegungen zu Bachs Weimarer Kantaten-Kalender," BJ (1993): 28–29.
41   Dürr St; Andreas Glöckner, "Zur Chronologie der Weimarer Kantaten Johann Sebastian Bachs," BJ 71 (1985): 159–164; Alfred Dürr, "Merkwürdiges in den Quellen zu Weimarer Kantaten Bachs," BJ 73 (1987): 151–158; Yoshitake Kobayashi, "Quellenkundliche Überlegungen zur Chronologie der Weimarer Vokalwerke Bachs," Karl Heller and Hans-Joachim Schulze, eds., *Das Frühwerk Johann Sebastian Bachs: Bach-Kollegium Rostock 1990* (Cologne: Schewe, 1995): 290–308; Daniel R. Melamed, "Mehr zur Chronologie von Bachs Weimarer Kantaten," BJ 79 (1993): 213–216; Andreas Glöckner, "Neue Spuren zu Bachs 'Weimarer' Passion," LBB 1 (1995): 33–46.
42   See the following sections for information on Weissenfels.
43   See Michael Maul, "'Alles mit Gott und nichts ohn' ihn' – Eine neu aufgefundene Aria von Johann Sebastian Bach," BJ 91 (2005): 7–34.
44   See Peter Williams, *The Organ Music of Johann Sebastian Bach,* 2nd ed. (Cambridge: Cambridge University Press, 2004); Richard Douglas Jones, *The Creative Development of Johann Sebastian*

Courts 197

Little is known of Bach's life beyond the court during this period. He lived for a time in the home of the countertenor and master of courtly pages, Adam Immanuel Weldig.[45] A rare bit of documentary evidence relating to Bach's first wife, Maria Barbara, was recently discovered: a 1708 reference to her seat in Weimar's *Schloßkirche*.[46] Throughout his time in Weimar, Bach earned income beyond his salary by offering private lessons, both to aristocrats[47] and to pre-professional musicians.[48] We have a student from Augsburg, Philipp David Kräuter, to thank for some of the most detailed documentation of J. S. Bach's teaching practices. In 1712, Kräuter traveled to Weimar with a stipend from the *Augsburger Scholarchat* and regularly reported back to his patrons about his lessons with Bach.[49]

Little concrete information is known of Bach's working conditions in Weimar,[50] but at some point he seems to have become disappointed with them. The dukes were not always kind to those in their employ.[51] Bach's frustration may have been exacerbated by his having been passed over as the replacement for Capellmeister Johann Samuel Drese, who died in December 1716. An opportunity to move to another court presented itself in the person of Prince Leopold of Anhalt-Cöthen, who likely heard Bach perform at the wedding celebrating his sister Eleonore Wilhelmine of Anhalt-Cöthen's marriage to Duke Ernst August of Saxony-Weimar on 24 January 1716. When Leopold's Capellmeister, August Reinhard Stricker, left in 1717, the Prince offered the open position to Bach. Perhaps emboldened by his famous triumph in a 1717 keyboard competition with Louis Marchand, Bach accepted Leopold's offer and sought his release from service in Weimar. What exactly transpired during these discussions remains shrouded in mystery, but allegedly as a result of his "obstinate testimony and too-stubborn demands for release," Bach was imprisoned in the *LandRichter-Stube*

Bach (Oxford: Oxford University Press, 2007–2013); and Jean-Claude Zehnder, "Zu Bachs Stilentwicklung in der Mühlhäuser und Weimarer Zeit," Schulze and Heller, *Das Frühwerk J. S. Bachs*, 311–338; Siegbert Rampe, "'Monatlich neüe Stücke' – Zu den musikalischen Voraussetzungen von Bachs Weimarer Konzertmeisteramt," BJ 88 (2002): 61–104.

45   Dok 2: 39 (No. 45). Bach is documented to have lived in Weldig's home in 1709, though he was likely there already in 1708. Weldig left Weimar in 1713, at which point Bach probably moved, if he had not done so earlier; see Karl Bechstein, "Johann Sebastian Bachs Wohnung in Weimar," *Landeszeitung Deutschland* 81 (1929): 216.

46   The discovery was made by Michael Maul; see Dok 5: 114 (No. B 38a).

47   See Dok 2: 44 (No. 53) for Bach's payments for instructing the courtly page, Adam Friedrich Wilhelm von Jagemann.

48   Johann Lorenz Bach studied for several years with J. S. Bach in Weimar beginning in or after 1713 and continuing until 1717, at the latest; see Dok 2: 64–65 (No. 82). Johann Tobias Krebs Sr. also studied with Bach between 1710 and 1717; see Dok 3: 123 (No. 694).

49   Dok 2: 46–47 (No. 58); Dok 3: 649–650 (Nos. 53a, 53b, 58); Dok 5: 116–122 (Nos. B 53a, B 53b, B 53c, B 54d, B 56a, B 57a, B 58a).

50   For a few hints, see Herbert Heyde, "Über die Streichinstrumente der Weimarer Hofkapelle im 18. Jahrhundert," *Studien zur Aufführungspraxis und Interpretation der Musik des 18. Jahrhunderts* 29 (1986): 32–43; and Jörg Arnold, "Raumakustische Rekonstruktion der 'Himmelsburg' – Ein Diskussionsbeitrag zu den musikalischen Aufführungsbedingungen Bachs," Geyer, *Johann Sebastian Bach in Weimar (1708–1717)*, 105–125.

51   See Glöckner, "Gründe für Johann Sebastian Bachs Weggang von Weimar, 137–144.

198   *Andrew Talle*

from 6 November to 12 December 1717.[52] Upon being released, Bach and his family moved immediately to Cöthen.

Cöthen (1717–1723)

Cöthen then counted around 3000 citizens and served as the central residence of the territory of Prince of Anhalt-Cöthen.[53] Prince Leopold of Anhalt-Cöthen assumed power in 1715. Music played a central role in his early life; at the age of eight, he was already studying with the *Hofmusikus*, Christoph Krull, and continued his musical training while studying at the *Ritterakademie* in Berlin (1707–1710). While on the Grand Tour (1710–1713), he attended numerous operas in Italy and the Netherlands and gave performances of his own at the courts of high potentates.[54] A court capella was established in Cöthen since 1702, but it was much improved in 1713 when Leopold heard the news that Friedrich Wilhelm I of Prussia had fired his musicians and immediately had his mother hire as many as he could for his own court, bringing Capellmeister Augustin Reinhard Stricker, gambist Christian Ferdinand Abel, and cellist Christian Bernhard Linicke, among others.[55]

Bach's time in Cöthen is in most respects even more poorly documented than his time in Weimar. The *Cammer-Rechnungen* of the court reveals that he was given a signing bonus of 50 Thaler and thereafter paid 33 Thaler per month.[56] He was compensated an extra 12 Thaler for costs related to rehearsing with the court musicians in his own home,[57] an activity that gained him admirers in other

---

52 Dok 2: 65–66 (No. 84).
53 Günther Hoppe, "Die Bachgedenkstätte im Historischen Museum Köthen," *Cöthener Bach-Hefte* 2 (1983): 5–6.
54 Günther Hoppe, "Köthener politische, ökonomische und höfische Verhältnisse als Schaffensbedingungen Bachs (Teil 1)," *Cöthener Bach-Hefte*, 4 (1986): 26–31.
55 The best sources of information on the *Hofkapelle* within the context of court and city culture in Cöthen remain the path-breaking articles by Günther Hoppe and Hans-Joachim Schulze, most of which appeared in the *Cöthener Bach-Hefte* series. See Günther Hoppe's "Köthener politische, ökonomische und höfische Verhältnisse als Schaffensbedingungen Bachs (Teil 1)," *Cöthener Bach-Hefte* 4 (1986): 12–62; "Köthener Kammerrechnungen – Köthener Hofparteien. Zum Hintergrund der Hofkapellmeisterzeit Johann Sebastian Bachs," Hoffmann and Schneiderheinze, *Bericht über die Wissenschaftliche Konferenz ... 1985*, 145–154; "Zu musikalisch-kulturellen Befindlichkeiten des anhalt-köthnischen Hofes zwischen 1710 und 1730," *Cöthener Bach-Hefte* 8 (1998): 9–52; and "Die konfessionellen Gegensätze zur Bach-Zeit in Köthen, Paulus Berger und Johann Conrad Lobethan," *Cöthener Bach-Hefte* 11 (2003): 136–208. Hans-Joachim Schulze's major contributions include "'... aus einem Capellmeister ein Cantor zu werden...' – Fragen an Bachs Köthener Schaffensjahre," *Cöthener Bach-Hefte* 1 (1983): 4–16; "Von Weimar nach Köthen – Risiken und Chancen eines Amtswechsels," *Cöthener Bach-Hefte* 11 (2003): 9–27; and "Johann Sebastian Bach und Köthen – Wege und Irrwege der Forschung," *Cöthener Bach-Hefte* 12 (2004): 9–28. See also Maik Richter, *Die Hofmusik in Köthen von den Anfängen (um 1690) bis zum Tod Fürst Leopolds von Anhalt-Köthen (1728)* (Saarbrücken: Müller, 2008).
56 Dok 2: 67–67 (No. 86) and Dok 1: 190 (No. 110).
57 Dok 2: 70 (No. 91).

Courts 199

arenas of Cöthen's musical life.[58] Bach's duties included maintaining the court harpsichords,[59] and in early 1719 he was compensated for a trip to Berlin during which he purchased a two-manual harpsichord built by Michael Mietke.[60] It was also part of the Capellmeister's job to arrange for guest musicians to perform at court, and Bach brought guest musicians from Rudolstadt and Merseburg.[61] He was also obliged more than once to travel with Leopold and six other members of the *Hofkapelle* to Carlsbad, where the Prince liked to relax in the summer.[62]

Bach's personal life in Cöthen is equally opaque to historians. The exact location of his home, in which all of those rehearsals took place, remains a matter of speculation, though we do know that he had at least one servant.[63] Bach rented seats and attended services at the Lutheran Agnuskirche.[64] Baptismal records reveal that he developed close relationships not only with his patrons,[65] but also with members of the court capelle.[66] The most famous emotional moment in Bach's documented life occurred in the summer of 1720; when he returned from a trip to Carlsbad, he entered his home to learn that his wife of 13 years, Maria Barbara Bach, whom he had left "healthy and fresh," had died and already been buried.[67] After a decent interval, he married Anna Magdalena Wilke, a court soprano in Cöthen and daughter of a trumpeter at the court in Weissenfels.[68]

Teaching seems to have played an important role in Bach's life during his years in Cöthen, as it had in Weimar. He instructed both local boys[69] and others who traveled to study with him and lived in his home, following the traditional apprenticeship model.[70] For his eldest son, the nine-year-old Wilhelm Friedemann Bach, he began a series of lessons documented by a *Clavier-Büchlein* dated

---

58 Dok 5: 129 (No. B 115a). Bach was praised in 1722 by Johann Jeremias Göbel, the cantor of the *Jacobskirche* in Cöthen, for rehearsing diligently with his musicians, unlike some of those for whom Göbel was responsible.

59 Dok 2: 86 (No. 115).

60 Dok 2: 73–74 (No. 95).

61 Dok 2: 72 (No. 93).

62 Dok 2: 67–68 (No. 86); see Maria Hübner, "Neues zu Johann Sebastian Bachs Reisen nach Karlsbad," BJ 92 (2006): 93–107.

63 Bach's servant girl, Anna Elisabeth, was godmother to a soldier's son; Dok 2: 81 (No. 106).

64 Dok 2: 71 (No. 92) and 79–80 (No. 103).

65 Dok 2: 73 (No. 94). Bach's relationship with Princes Leopold and August Ludwig was such that he invited them to serve as godparents to his son, whom he named Leopold August Bach in their honor.

66 Dok 2: 76 (No. 99). Bach served as godfather to Christian Ferdinand Abel's daughter.

67 Dok 2: 76 (No. 100) and Dok 3: 87 (No. 666). Maria Barbara Bach was buried on 7 July 1720. Her date of death is unknown. The fact that J. S. Bach was not informed of her death in Carlsbad suggests that he returned not long after her burial, and there had been no time to send him a notice by post.

68 Dok 2: 83 (No. 110) and Dok 2: 83–84 (No. 111).

69 Andrew Talle, "Nürnberg, Darmstadt, Köthen – Neuerkenntnisse zu Bach-Überlieferung in der ersten Hälfte des 18. Jahrhunderts," BJ 89 (2003): 143–172.

70 Dok 5: 126–127 (No. B 90a); see Michael Maul, "Rolle contra Räder. Einblicke in den Himmelfahrtsgottesdienst der Agnuskirche im Jahr 1718," *Cöthener Bach-Hefte* 13 (2006): 147–162.

200 *Andrew Talle*

22 January 1720.[71] The book is dominated by the *Inventionen und Sinfonien* (BWV 772–801), which on the title page of another autograph manuscript Bach suggests were intended to help "keyboard enthusiasts, particularly those inclined to learning" how to play in two and three voices, and to come up with good ideas and develop them. Most importantly they were to develop a "singing" style of performance and a "foretaste of composition."[72] The primary autograph manuscript of these pieces is dated 1723, and they belong to a group of works which Bach systematically finalized in Cöthen, though all were likely begun in Weimar. Others in this group include the chorale preludes of the *Orgelbüchlein* (BWV 599–644; signed "Capellæ Magistri S. P. R. Anhaltini-Cotheniensis"), *Sei Solo a Violino senza Basso accompagnato* (BWV 1001–1006; signed "Cöthen 1720"), and the first twenty-four Preludes and Fugues of the Well-Tempered Clavier (BWV 846–869; signed "Cöthen 1723").[73] A particularly tantalizing clue as to the Weimar roots of this last-mentioned work was provided by the music historian Ernst Ludwig Gerber, whose father studied with Bach, and whose *Historisch-Biographisches Lexicon der Tonkünstler* (Leipzig, 1790) asserts that Bach wrote the Well-Tempered Clavier "in a place, where depression, boredom, and the lack of any type of musical instrument made this pastime necessary."[74] Where might Bach have been subjected to such a torment except during the month he was confined in the *LandRichter-Stube* in Weimar? All of these works—as well as the French Suites (BWV 812–817), five of which appear for the first time in Anna Magdalena's *Clavier-Büchlein* of 1722[75]—were put to pedagogical use, and were likely conceived with teaching in mind. Their title pages suggest that they are to be employed in training young musicians and the first works they present are always simpler than those that follow.

Bach was responsible in Cöthen for composing cantatas celebrating the New Year as well as the Prince's birthday (10 December). Only two survive with both text and music intact (BWV 134a and 173a).[76] The texts of four more survive (BWV 66a; Anh. 5, 6, and 7), but only the music of BWV 66a is reconstructible on the basis of parody (BWV 66). Two additional cantatas (BWV 184a and 194a) lack texts entirely but can be musically reconstructed on the basis of later parodies (BWV 184 and 194). The title page of a cantata Bach composed to celebrate Leopold and his wife at the New Year in 1723 (BWV Anh. 8) also survives, though both music and text have been lost.[77] Bach no doubt produced numerous other instrumental and vocal works for the court in Cöthen, some of which have

---

71 Dok 1: 215 (No. 149). The book is now at Yale University's Beinicke Library (no call number).

72 Dok 1: 220–221 (No. 153).

73 For the *Orgelbüchlein* see Dok 1: 214 (No. 148); for the Well-Tempered Clavier see Dok 1: 219–220 (No. 152). The manuscript of the violin soli—D-B: Mus.ms.Bach.P967—is dated 1720.

74 Dok 3: 468 (No. 948).

75 D-B, Mus.ms.Bach.P224.

76 Dok 1: 218–219 (No. 151).

77 Dok 2: 88–89 (No. 120). Both BWV 66a and Anh. 5 were performed on December 10, 1718, for Prince Leopold's birthday; see Dok 2: 72 (No. 93).

Courts 201

been lost without a trace, but others of which no doubt survive in earlier or later versions.[78]

In one of his only surviving personal letters, written to Georg Erdmann on 28 October 1730, Bach suggests that he was unusually content at the beginning of his time in Cöthen, and that he could have imagined serving this Prince, who "both loved and knew music" for the remainder of his career. He goes further to suggest, however, that eventually Prince Leopold's enthusiasm for music became somewhat more tepid as a result of his 1721 marriage to Frederika Henrietta of Anhalt-Bernburg—whom Bach described as an *amusa* (that is, she was amusical)—prompting him to leave the court.[79] This explanation for Bach's having left the court of his "dearly beloved"[80] Prince Leopold has never been very persuasive, not least because Bach was already applying for positions elsewhere well before the marriage,[81] and because the Princess died before Bach actually left Cöthen.[82] Günther Hoppe has demonstrated that the prince did indeed begin devoting less money to music after his marriage in 1721, not so much because of his wife's expensive tastes or amusical character, but because of the long-term loss of income from ancillary territories, and the introduction of a palace guard around the same time.[83]

Whatever the reasons, Bach applied for and was officially granted dismissal from his duties in Cöthen on 4 April 1723.[84] After moving to Leipzig, Bach maintained a good relationship with Prince Leopold and his court musicians, regularly returning to perform celebratory cantatas (such as BWV 36a), often together with his wife.[85] He also presented a gift of the first Keyboard Partita (BWV 825) to Leopold's newborn son and would-be heir, Emanuel Ludwig, upon its release in 1726,[86] and composed and performed the music for Leopold's funeral in 1728.[87]

---

78 For the challenges of settling chronological questions regarding the concertos, see Hans-Joachim Schulze, "Johann Sebastian Bachs Konzerte - Fragen der Überlieferung und Chronologie," *Bach Studien* 6 (1981): 9–26; Karl Heller, "Zur Chronologie des Bachschen Konzertschaffens. Versuch einer Bestandsaufnahme," *Abhandlungen der Akademie der Wissenschaften zu Göttingen, Philologisch-Historische Klasse* 3/240 (2001): 185–208; and Christoph Wolff, "Bach in Köthen – ein erledigtes Thema?" Peter Wollny, ed., *Musikgeschichte im Zeichen der Reformation. Magdeburg – ein kulturelles Zentrum in der mitteldeutschen Musiklandschaft. Ständige Konferenz Mitteldeutsche Barockmusik. Jahrbuch 2005* (Beeskow: Ortus, 2006), 307–318.
79 Dok 1: 67 (No. 23).
80 Dok 3: 84 (No. 666).
81 Dok 2: 77–79 (No. 102). In 1720, Bach applied and auditioned for the position of organist at Hamburg's Jakobikirche.
82 Friederica Henrietta of Anhalt-Cöthen died on 4 April 1723. Bach himself did not move to Leipzig until 22 May 1723, though he had applied for the Thomaskantorat already in December 1722; see Dok 2: 88 (No. 119).
83 Hoppe, Günther. "Köthener politische, ökonomische und höfische Verhältnisse... (Teil 1)," 35–41.
84 Dok 2: 93 (No. 128).
85 Dok 2: 144, 153, and 181 (Nos. 184, 199, and 244).
86 Dok 1: 223–224 (No. 155) and Dok 5: 145 (No. B 262a).
87 Dok 2: 189–190 (No. 258) and Dok 3: 84 (No. 666). Only the text survives, though some of the music was used in the St. Matthew Passion (BWV 244) and the *Trauerode* (BWV 198).

202   *Andrew Talle*

Sometime before 1729, there was a performance at the Jacobskirche in Cöthen of BWV 21,[88] and Bach's colleagues and former students continued to work at the court until the 1750s.[89]

Additional Courts with Which Bach Had Contact

Lüneburg (1700–1702)

Bach's obituary, written largely by his son Carl Philipp Emanuel, includes the following remarks about his time as a pupil of the *Michaelisschule* in Lüneburg (1700–1702):

> From here he had regular opportunities to hear a then-famous *Capelle* maintained by the Duke of Celle, which consisted for the most part of Frenchmen, allowing him to develop a solid familiarity with the French style, which in those lands at that time was something quite new.[90]

For decades, it was assumed that Bach had actually traveled to Celle to hear this ensemble, but the city is too far from Lüneburg to have made this practicable on a regular basis. Christoph Wolff has argued persuasively that Bach must instead have heard the ensemble of Georg Wilhelm, Duke of Brunswick-Lüneburg (1624–1705), at his newly built castle in Lüneburg.[91]

Gotha (1711, 1717)

The court in Gotha is unusually well-documented and thus proven particularly inviting for historians and musicologists.[92] Bach visited the court at least twice,

---

88   See Michael Maul and Peter Wollny, "Quellenkundliches zu Bach-Aufführungen in Köthen, Ronneburg und Leipzig zwischen 1720 und 1760," BJ 89 (2003): 97–142.

89   See Talle, "Nürnberg, Darmstadt, Köthen," BJ 89 (2003): 155–172; and Maik Richter, "Die Köthener Hofmusik zur Zeit des Fürsten August Ludwig," *Musik an der Zerbster Residenz. Bericht über die Internationale wissenschaftliche Konferenz vom 10. bis 12. April 2008 im Rahmen der 10. Internationalen Fasch-Festtage in Zerbst*, ed. Internationalen Fasch-Gesellschaft (Beeskow: Ortus, 2008), 167–182.

90   Dok 3: 82 (No. 666): "Auch hatte er von hier aus Gelegenheit, sich durch öftere Anhörug einer damals berühmten Capelle, welche der Hertzog von Zelle unterhielt, und die mehrentheils aus Frantzosen bestand, im Frantzösischen Geschmacke, welcher, in dasigen Landen, zu der Zeit was ganz Neues war, fest zu setzen."

91   Wolff BLM, 65–66. Although the possibility remains, there is no evidence that the duke ever visited Lüneburg with his ensemble during the time Bach was a student there. It is at least as possible that Bach heard the ducal Celle ensemble in the town of Ebstorf, just 26 km south of Lüneburg, where the duke regularly spent several months during hunting season. This possibility is discussed in Robert L. Marshall and Traute M. Marshall, *Exploring the World of J. S. Bach: A Traveler's Guide* (Urbana: University of Illinois Press, 2016), 110–114.

92   For background on Gotha and its musicians, see Christian Ahrens, *"Zu Gotha ist eine gute Kapelle..." – aus dem Innenleben einer thüringischen Hofkappe des 18. Jahrhunderts* (Stuttgart: Steiner, 2009); Helga Raschke, *Bevölkerung und Handwerk einer Thüringischen Residenzstadt. Gotha zwischen 1640 und 1740* (Bucha: Quartus, 2001); Rolf Dietrich Claus, "Die

Courts 203

both times while employed in Weimar. In 1711, he was paid 12 Thaler, presumably for performances at the keyboard, since he is described in the records as an organist.[93] In 1717, Bach received an additional 12 Thaler from the court in Gotha, probably to give a performance of a *Passionsmusik* on Good Friday of that year (26 March).[94] Though this "Weimar Passion" is lost, some of its music may appear in the St. John Passion (BWV 245) and *Ich armer Mensch, ich Sündenknecht* (BWV 55).[95]

Weissenfels (1713, 1729)

Bach performed *Was mir behagt, ist nur die muntre Jagd!* (BWV 208) at the court in Weißenfels in celebration of Duke Christian of Saxony-Weißenfels's thirty-first birthday (23 February 1713).[96] The text of this cantata was written by the Weimar court poet, Salomo Franck, suggesting that the presentation was a gift from the Weimar court more broadly. Musical arrangements were likely aided by Bach's former landlord in Weimar, Adam Immanuel Weldig, who had by this point moved to Weissenfels.[97]

In 1721, Bach married Anna Magdalena Wilke, whose father was a trumpeter at the court in Weissenfels. He may have visited the city again on the way to or from nearby Schleiz in August 1721, refreshing the acquaintance with her family or perhaps formally asking for her hand in marriage.

In 1729, Bach performed again at the court in Weissenfels.[98] It was probably on this occasion that he was granted the title of nonresident court composer by Duke Christian of Saxon-Weißenfels.[99] Further relationships with the city

---

Bachs, die Musik und das Militär in Sachsen-Gotha. Jacob Bach als Mitinitiator der Militärdienstbefreiung für junge Musiker," BJ 83 (1997): 193–197; and Bert Siegmund, "The Court of Saxony-Gotha-Altenburg," Owens, Reul, and Stockigt, *Music at German Courts, 1715–1760*, 197–222.

93 Christian Ahrens, "Neue Quellen zu J. S. Bachs Beziehungen nach Gotha," BJ 93 (2007): 45–60.

94 Armin Fett noted in his 1951 dissertation that a *ConcertMeister* named Bach was paid 12 Thaler for a visit to the court of Friedrich II, Duke of Saxony-Gotha-Altenburg, in 1717; see Armin Fett, "Musikgeschichte der Stadt Gotha. Von den Anfängen bis zum Tode Gottfried Heinrich Stölzels (1749). Ein Beitrag zur Musikgeschichte Sachsen-Thüringens," (Dissertation: Universität Freiburg, 1951), 141; Dok 5: 126 (No. B 81a). It remained for Eva-Maria Ranft to argue in 1985 that this most likely referred to J. S. Bach: Eva-Maria Ranft, "Ein unbekannter Aufenthalt Johann Sebastian Bachs in Gotha?" BJ 71 (1985): 165–166.

95 Andreas Glöckner, "Neue Spuren zu Bachs 'Weimarer' Passion," 33–46.

96 Dok 2: 45 (No. 55); see Hans-Joachim Schulze, "Wann entstand Johann Sebastian Bachs 'Jagdkantate'?" BJ 86 (2000): 301–305.

97 Wolff BLM, 134–135; see also Dok 2: 54 (No. 68).

98 Dok 2: 189 (No. 258).

99 Dok 1: 129, 136–138 (No. 60, 68–69), and Dok 2: 235 (No. 327). For general information on the court musical establishment in Weissenfels, see Wolfgang Ruf, "The Courts of Saxony-Weißenfels, Saxony-Merseburg, and Saxony-Zeitz," Owens, Reul, and Stockigt, *Music at German Courts, 1715–1760*, 223–255; Arno Werner, *Städtische und fürstliche Musikpflege in Weissenfals bis zum Ende des 18. Jahrhunderts* (Leipzig: Breitkopf & Härtel, 1911); Torsten Fuchs, *Studien zur Musikpflege in der Stadt Weissenfels und am Hofe der Herzoge*

204   *Andrew Talle*

are suggested by text concordances with works performed in the Weissenfels *Stadtkirche.*[100]

Dresden (1717, 1733, 1736)

The Dresden court of Augustus the Strong, Elector of Saxony, was among the leading musical centers of Bach's time,[101] and was also the site of one of Bach's most famous musical triumphs. Sometime towards the end of 1717, he visited Dresden and was expected to engage in a musical competition with the French organist, Louis Marchand. The account of this encounter, which appears in Bach's obituary, is the one most commonly cited, but it is not necessarily the most reliable. A more logical account appeared in Friedrich Wilhelm Marpurg's *Legende einiger Musikheiligen* (Berlin, 1786).[102] Because Marpurg's text does not usually appear in English, I take the liberty of including it here:

> The year 1717 gave our already so famous Bach a new opportunity to achieve still further honor. Marchand, the clavier player and organist famous in France, had come to Dresden, had let himself be heard by the King with exceptional success, and was so fortunate as to be offered a highly paid post in the Royal service. The Concertmaster in Dresden at the time, Volumier,

---

von Sachsen-Weissenfels (Lucca: Libreria musicale italiana, 1997); Eva-Maria Ranft, "Zum Personalbestand der Weissenfelser Hofkapelle," *Beiträge zur Bach-Forschung* 6 (1987): 5–36.

100 Hans-Joachim Schulze, "Musikaufführungen in der Weißenfelser Stadtkirche von 1732 bis 1736," Roswitha Jacobsen, ed., *Weißenfels als Ort literarischer und künstlerischer Kultur im Barockzeitalter* (Amsterdam: Rodopi, 1994), 121–131.

101 The electoral court in Dresden and its musical establishment are among the most well-researched topics in eighteenth-century German music history. For general information, see Karl Czok, "Sächsischer Landesstaat zur Bachzeit," *Beiträge zur Bachforschung* 1 (1982): 25–31; Karl Czok, "Zum Problem des aufgeklärten Absolutismus in Sachsen in der ersten Hälfte des 18. Jahrhunderts," Hoffmann and Schneiderheinze, *Bericht über die Wissenschaftliche Konferenz ... 1985*, 35–40; Kai Köpp, *Johann Georg Pisendel (1687–1755) und die Anfänge der neuzeitlichen Orchesterleitung* (Tützing: Schneider, 2005); Ulrike Kolmar, *Gottlob Harrer (1703–1755), Kapellmeister des Grafen von Brühl am sächsisch-polnischen Hof und Thomaskantor in Leipzig. Mit einem Werkverzeichnis und einem Katalog der Notenbibliothek Harrers* (Beeskow: Ortus, 2006); Janice B. Stockigt, *Jan Dismas Zelenka: A Bohemian Musician at the Court of Dresden* (Oxford: Oxford University Press, 2000); Janice B. Stockigt, "The Court of Saxony-Dresden," Owens, Reul, and Stockigt, *Music at German Courts, 1715–1760*, 17–49; Mary Oleskiewicz, "'For the Church as Well as For the Orchestra': J. S. Bach, the Missa, and the Dresden Court, 1700–50," BACH 38/2 (2007): 1–38, esp. 4–5; Ortrun Landmann, "Die Dresdner Hofkapelle zur Zeit J. S. Bachs," *Concerto*, 51 (1990): 7–16; Ortrun Landmann, ed., *Johann Georg Pisendel – Studien zu Leben und Werk ; Bericht über das internationale Symposium vom 23. bis 25. Mai 2005 in Dresden* (Hildesheim: Olms, 2010); Ortrun Landmann, "The Dresden Hofkapelle During the Lifetime of Johann Sebastian Bach," EM 17 (1989): 17–30; Panja Mücke, *Johann Adolf Hasses Dresdner Opern im Kontext der Hofkultur* (Laaber: Laaber, 2003).

102 For a study of the transmission of this anecdote, see Werner Braun, "Bach und Marchand in Dresden. Eine überlieferungskritische Studie," BJ 84 (1998): 7–18.

wrote to Bach, whose merits were not unknown to him, at Weimar, and invited him to come forthwith to Dresden, in order to engage in a musical contest for superiority with the haughty Marchand. Bach willingly accepted the invitation and journeyed to Dresden. Volumier received him with joy and arranged an opportunity for him to hear his opponent first from a place of concealment. Bach thereupon invited Marchand to a contest, in a courteous letter in which he declared himself ready to execute *ex tempore* whatever musical tasks Marchand should set him and, in turn, expressed his expectation that Marchand would show the same willingness – certainly a proof of great daring. Marchand showed himself quite ready to accept the invitation. The time and place were set, not without the foreknowledge of the King. Bach appeared at the appointed time at the scene of the contest, in the home of a leading minister of state, where a large company of persons of high rank and of both sexes was assembled. There was a long wait for Marchand. Finally, the host sent to Marchand's quarters to remind him, in case he should have forgotten, that it was now time for him to show himself a man. But it was learned, to the great astonishment of everyone, that Monsieur Marchand had, very early in the morning of that same day, left Dresden by special coach. Bach, who thus remained sole master at the scene of the contest, accordingly had plentiful opportunities to exhibit the talents with which he was armed against his opponent. And this he did, to the astonishment of all present. The King had intended to present him on this occasion with 500 thaler; but through the dishonesty of a certain servant, who believed that he could use this gift to better advantage, he was deprived of it, and had to take back with him, as the sole reward of his efforts, the honor he had won. Strange Fate! A Frenchman voluntarily abandons a permanent salary offered to him, amounting to more than a thousand thaler, and the German, to whom the former by his flight certainly seemed to have conceded the preference, cannot even obtain possession of the one special gift intended for him by the favor of the King. For the rest, our Bach willingly credited Marchand with the reputation of fine and very proper playing. Whether, however, Marchand's Musettes for Christmas Eve, the composition and performance of which is said to have contributed most to his fame in Paris, would have been able to hold the field before connoisseurs against Bach's multiple fugues: that may be decided by those who heard both men in their prime.[103]

Bach arrived in Dresden and was allowed, with permission of the King but without Marchand's knowledge, to witness the French virtuoso's next performance at court. After Marchand played, among other things, a number of variations on a little French song – which were well

---

103 Dok 3: 83–84 (No. 666). The translation here is adapted from that which appears in NBR 300–301 (No. 306).

206   *Andrew Talle*

applauded owing to their artfulness and also his neat and fiery performance style – Bach, who was standing next to him, was asked to take his turn at the harpsichord. He accepted the challenge, preluded briefly with masterful chords, and before anyone could grasp what was going on played the same little French song and varied it a dozen times with an artfulness no one had ever heard before. Marchand, who had to this point always triumphed over all organists with which he had been confronted, had to acknowledge in this case the superiority of his competitor. Bach then took the liberty of inviting Marchand to a friendly competition at the organ, and to this end submitted to him a piece of paper with a theme sketched out in pencil to be improvised upon freely. He also offered to accept any theme Marchand wished to put forward. But it seemed to Monsieur Marchand that rather than compete with Bach it would be in his interest to leave Dresden by express post coach. This anecdote is told in various ways, but the version above comes straight from the composer, who told it to me himself. By the way, Bach always praised the skills of this French virtuoso and expressed regret that he himself had never heard Marchand perform at the organ.[104]

On 14 September 1731, Bach performed at the *Sophienkirche* in Dresden, though no court visit is documented.[105] With the ascendance of Elector Friedrich August II (1696–1763), in February 1733 Bach began an intensive campaign to acquire the official title of composer to the Dresden court, most explicitly by his presentation of the Kyrie and Gloria of the B minor Mass (BWV 232) on 27 July 1733, with an accompanying letter humbly requesting the title.[106] Between December 1733 and October 1734, Bach's Leipzig *Collegium Musicum* performed no fewer than five times in honor of the Elector and his wife,[107] including an original cantata in honor of Maria Josepha's thirty-fourth birthday in December 1733[108] and a celebratory cantata for the couple performed during the *Michaelis* fair in October 1734.[109] In September 1736, Bach formally renewed his petition for the title of court composer, which was finally granted on 19 November 1736. He performed on the afternoon of 1 December 1736 (from 2 to 4 pm) in Dresden's *Frauenkirche* before a distinguished assembly that included many courtiers.[110]

---

104 Dok 3: 424–425 (No. 914).
105 Dok 3: 653–654 (No. 294b).
106 Dok 1: 74 (No. 27).
107 Dok 2: 244–252 (Nos. 344–348; 350–353).
108 Dok 2: 244 (No. 344). The "Dramma per Musica" which Bach dedicated to Maria Josepha on her birthday (8 December 1733) was "Tönet, ihr Pauken! Erschallet, Trompeten!" (BWV 214).
109 Dok 249–252 (No. 351–353). The cantata was "Preise dein Glücke, gesegnetes Sachsen" (BWV 215). Ludwig Siegfried Vitzthum von Eckstädt was incidentally involved in this performance.
110 Dok 1: 91 (No. 36) and Dok 2: 278–280 (Nos. 388, 389).

Berlin (1719, 1747)

As noted previously, Bach was compensated in early 1719 by the court in Cöthen for a trip to Berlin during which he purchased a harpsichord from Michael Mietke.[111] It has long been assumed that on this visit Bach also performed for Margrave Christian Ludwig of Brandenburg, an event to which he alludes in the dedication of the *Six Concerts* he sent the Margrave in March 1721 (BWV 1046–1051).[112]

Bach traveled to Berlin again in August 1741, though no court visit is documented.[113] He was back in May 1747, this time as a guest of honor of Friedrich II ("The Great") of Prussia, who then employed his son, Carl Philipp Emanuel.[114] This event was widely reported and discussed at the time, but the fullest account was narrated to Johann Nikolaus Forkel by Wilhelm Friedemann Bach, who accompanied his father to Friedrich's court.[115] Bach arrived at his son's apartment in Berlin on Sunday, May 7, but did not have time to exchange his traveling clothes for cantor's black frock before he was called to appear at court. Forkel enjoyed Friedemann's recreation of the comical dialog between the King and Bach, as the latter tried profusely to apologize for his appearance. After a tour of the palace, in several rooms of which Bach was asked to improvise on a different keyboard instrument, including a number of Silbermann fortepianos, Friedrich played Bach a chromatic theme of his own invention, which Bach then developed in his contrapuntal manner. The King requested a fugue in six voices, but in order to satisfy him, Bach was obliged to invent a theme that lent itself to such treatment. The following day, Bach was similarly obliged to perform on several organs in Potsdam. After returning to Leipzig, he worked out Friedrich's theme in a variety of ways—including as a chamber music work featuring the King's favorite instrument, the flute—and had it published, primarily in order to give it away to friends as a memento. Bach's dedication highlights his subservience and desire merely to promote Friedrich's genius by making public his royal theme.[116]

---

111 Dok 2: 73–74 (No. 95).

112 Dok 1: 216–218 (No. 150). For background on the Margrave's court and its musical establishment see Heinrich Besseler, "Markgraf Christian Ludwig von Brandenburg," BJ 43 (1956): 18–35.

113 Dok 2: 391–393 (Nos. 489, 490, 491). It has been argued that the scoring of the Brandenburg Concertos was intended as a critique of courtly culture; see Michael Marissen, *The Social and Religious Designs of J. S. Bach's Brandenburg Concertos*. (Princeton: Princeton University Press, 1995).

114 For background on the court and its musical establishment, see Ellen Elizabeth Exner, "The Forging of a Golden Age: King Frederick the Great and Music for Berlin (1732 to 1756)," (Dissertation: Harvard University, 2010); and Mary Oleskiewicz, "The Court of Brandenburg-Prussia," Owens, Reul, and Stockig, *Music at German Courts, 1715–1760*, 79–130.

115 The account is recorded in Forkel's *Ueber Johann Sebastian Bachs Leben, Kunst und Kunstwerke* (Leipzig, 1802); Dok 7: 22–23.

116 See Dok 1: 117–118, 241–243 (Nos. 49, 173); Dok 2: 434–435, 437, 454 (Nos. 554, 557, 580); Dok 3: 623, 657 (Nos. Anh I 3, 594a); Dok 5: 169–170 (No. B 568a). For information on the

208   Andrew Talle

Schleiz (1721)

Bach was paid for a guest performance in Schleiz at the court of Heinrich XI, Count of Reuß, between 7 August and 13, 1721.[117] He visited nearby Gera between May 30 and 6 June 1725, to test the organ of the Johanniskirche.[118] That he was not compensated for food on June 1 or 2 makes it plausible that he used this occasion once again to perform at the court in Schleiz.[119]

Zerbst (1722)

In 1722, Bach composed a cantata—*O vergnügte Stunden, Da mein Hertzog funden seinen Lebenstag*—celebrating the forty-fifth birthday of Johann August of Anhalt-Zerbst.[120] That Bach was actually present in Zerbst on the Prince's birthday (August 9) is unlikely; indeed, even the Prince himself was elsewhere.[121] The librettist of Bach's cantata is unknown, but the work was most likely commissioned and handed over to Prince Johann August by Georg Rudolph von Kayn.[122] A number of text concordances with Leipzig cantatas— including Bach's *Ich hatte viel Bekümmernis* (BWV 21)—have been discovered in the court library, suggesting that Bach's collaborations with Zerbst may have been more extensive than previously imagined.[123]

---

creation and publication of the Musical Offering, see Gregory Butler, "The Printing History of J. S. Bach's Musical Offering: New Interpretations," JM 19 (2002): 306–331; Michael Marissen, "More Source-Critical Research on J. S. Bach's Musical Offering, BACH 25/1 (Spring-Summer 1994): 11–27; Hans-Joachim Schulze, "Johann Sebastian Bachs 'Musikalisches Opfer': Bemerkungen zu seiner Geschichte und Aufführungspraxis," *Studien zur Aufführungspraxis und Interpretation der Musik des 18. Jahrhunderts* 25 (1985): 11–15; Wolff Essays, 239–258.

117 Dok 2: 81–82 (No. 107). For general information on the court in Schleiz, see Hans Rudolf Jung, Musik und *Musiker im Reußenland* (Weimar: Hain, 2007).

118 Dok 2: 143, 144 (Nos. 183, 183a).

119 See Michael Maul, "Johann Sebastian Bachs Besuche in der Residenzstadt Gera," BJ 90 (2004): 101–120.

120 Dok 2: 85–86 (No. 114); see Barbara Reul, "'O vergnügte Stunden / Da mein Hertzog funden seinen Lebenstag': Ein unbekannter Textdruck zu einer Geburtstagskantate J.S. Bachs für den Fürsten Johann August von Anhalt-Zerbst," BJ 85 (1999): 7–18. For general information about the court at Zerbst, see Dirk Herrmann, "Die Barockresidenz Zerbst als Wirkungsstätte von Johann Friedrich Fasch," in Internationalen Fasch-Gesellschaft (ed.), *Musik an der Zerbster Residenz. Bericht über die Internationale wissenschaftliche Konferenz vom 10. bis 12. April 2008 im Rahmen der 10. Internationalen Fasch-Festtage in Zerbst* (Beeskow: Ortus, 2008): 21–36; Barbara Reul, "Musical Life at the Court of Anhalt-Zerbst. An Examination of Unknown Primary Sources at the Landeshauptarchiv Sachsen-Anhalt, Abteilung Dessau," *Musik an der Zerbster Residenz*, 197–222; Barbara Reul, "The Court of Anhalt-Zerbst," Owens, Reul, and Stockigt, *Music at German Courts, 1715–1760*, 259–286.

121 Hans-Joachim Schulze, "Johann Sebastian Bach und Zerbst 1722: Randnotizen zu einer verlorenen Gastmusik," BJ 90 (2004): 209–214.

122 Michael Maul, "Neues zu Georg Balthasar Schott, seinem Collegium musicum und Bachs Zerbster Geburtstagskantate," BJ 93 (2007): 61–104.

123 Peter Wollny, "Neue Ermittlungen zu Aufführungen Bachscher Kirchenkantaten am Zerbster Hof," Rainer Kaiser, ed., *Bach und seine mitteldeutschen Zeitgenossen. Bericht über das*

Directions for Future Research

Music historians interested in early eighteenth-century Germany have focused increasingly on illuminating the social and political environments in which musicians worked. The courts have proven a rewarding object of inquiry. Recent collections of essays, such as those edited by Helen Geyer[124] and Samantha Owens, Barbara Reul, and Janice Stockigt,[125] exemplify the new approach in offering historical depth and incorporating the work of historians and scholars in fields other than music. Because of a lack of documentation, Bach's connections with the courts of his time, and particularly his daily activities in Weimar and Cöthen, remain poorly understood. A collection of essays to be produced by Michael Maul and Peter Wollny has been promised in the *Schriftenreihe des Bach-Archivs Leipzig* and will represent a major contribution to the literature on Bach and the musical environment in Weimar.[126] Scholars, performers, and music lovers at large would welcome virtually any further archival discoveries that shed new light on Bach's relationships with the courts of his time.

---

  internationale musikwissenschaftliche Kolloquium Erfurt und Arnstadt (Eisenach: Wagner, 2002), 199–217.

124 Helen Geyer, *Johann Sebastian Bach in Weimar (1708–1717)*.

125 Owens, Reul, and Stockigt, *Music at German Courts, 1715–1760*.

126 See Michael Maul, "Zwei Clavierbücher aus der Herzogen Anna Amalia Bibliothek Weimar als Quellen zur Zerbster Musikpflege um 1680," *Musik an der Zerbster Residenz: Bericht über die internationale wissenschaftliche Konferenz... 2008 im Rahmen 10. Inernationale Fasch-Festtage*, eds. Konstanze Musketa and Barbara M. Reul (Beeskow: Ortus, 2008), 41–67, esp. 42, n. 7.

Part III
Musical Influences

9 The Alt-Bachisches Archiv

Stephen Rose

"Johann Sebastian Bach belongs to a family that seems to have received a love and aptitude for music as a gift of Nature to all its members in common."[1] Thus begins the Obituary of J. S. Bach, which then traces the family's history back to Veit Bach, a sixteenth-century Lutheran exiled from Hungary to Thuringia. A similar concern for the family's origins and lineage was felt by J. S. Bach during the last decades of his life. In 1735, he made a family tree, with accompanying genealogical commentary describing "The Origin of the Bach Family of Musicians."[2] At about the same time, he began acquiring manuscripts of sacred vocal music by his forebears, a collection that later became known as the Alt-Bachisches Archiv. In charting his ancestors and their musical accomplishments, Bach addressed the potent question of his musical origins. What and where were his roots as a man and a musician? Had he inherited a hereditary gift for music? What was the historical and musical significance of his family and his own place in it? What biographical and compositional continuities did he feel with previous musicians in his family?

Bach's interest in the music of his ancestors focused on the twenty vocal pieces (listed in Table 9.1) that comprise the Alt-Bachisches Archiv. The Archiv is dominated by two members of the family, both sons of the Arnstadt organist Heinrich Bach (1615–1692): Johann Christoph Bach (1642–1703), who was organist in Eisenach from 1665 until his death; and Johann Michael Bach (1648–1694), who was organist and town clerk in Gehren from 1673 until his death. Both men were cousins of J. S. Bach's father, Johann Ambrosius; and Johann Michael was also Johann Sebastian's father-in-law via his first wife Maria Barbara, an act of interbreeding that drew two lines of the family together. Also represented in the Alt-Bachisches Archiv are Johann Bach (1604–1673), organist in Erfurt from 1636 until his death, and Georg Christoph Bach (1642–1697), cantor in Schweinfurt from 1684 until his death.

During the eighteenth century, the Alt-Bachisches Archiv manuscripts were not regarded as museum pieces, but gained many accretions as the pieces were

---

1 NBR 297 (No. 306); Dok 3: 80 (No. 666).
2 Dok 1: 255–267 (No. 184); NBR 283–94 (303).

Table 9.1 Contents of the Alt-Bachisches Archiv

This table lists the 20 pieces of the Alt-Bachisches Archiv as itemized in C. P. E. Bach's 1790 estate inventory, arranged alphabetically according to the composer attributions established by current scholarship. Manuscripts copied after 1750 are excluded. All sources listed are currently held in the Staatsbibliothek zu Berlin. Information about sources and copyists from LBB 8.

Composer	Title	Scoring	Genre	Manuscript	Principal scribe(s)
Georg Christoph Bach	Siehe, wie fein und lieblich	T, T, B, vn, 3 va da gamba, bc	Family composition	SA5163	Georg Christoph Bach
Johann Bach	Sei nun wieder zufrieden	8vv, bc	Motet	SA5151	Jonas de Fletin
Johann Bach	Unser Leben ist ein Schatten	9vv, bc	Motet	SA5140	Heindorff
Johann Bach	Weint nicht um meinen Tod	4vv	Chorlied	SA5150	Heindorff
Johann Christoph Bach	Ach, daß ich Wassers gnug hätte	A, vn, 3 va da gamba, bc	Concerto	SA5160	Unknown
Johann Christoph Bach	Der Gerechte, ob er gleich zu zeitlich stirbt	5vv, bc	Motet	SA702 SA5154	Johann Sebastian Bach Heinrich Bach
Johann Christoph Bach	Es erhub sich ein Streit	10vv, 4 tpt, timp, 2 vn, 4 va, bc	Concerto	SA5166	Unknown; underlay by Heindorff
Johann Christoph Bach	Es ist nun aus mit meinem Leben	4vv, bc	Chorlied	SA5157	Heindorff
Johann Christoph Bach	Lieber Herr Gott, wecke uns auf	8vv, bc	Motet	SA5142 SA5143, SA5144 P4/2	Heinrich Bach Johann Sebastian Bach; Johann Nathanael Bammler Johann Christoph Bach
Johann Christoph Bach	Meine Freundin, du bist schön	4vv, vn, 3 va da gamba, bc	Family composition	SA5161	Johann Ambrosius Bach
Johann Christoph Bach	Mit Weinen hebt sichs an	4vv, bc	Chorlied	SA5159	Heindorff
Johann Michael Bach	Ach, wie sehnlich wart ich der Zeit	S, vn, 3 va da gamba, bc	Concerto	SA5148	Unknown

Composer	Title	Scoring	Genre	Manuscript	Principal scribe(s)
Johann Michael Bach	Auf, laßt uns den Herren loben	A, vn, 3 va da gamba, bc	Concerto	SA5138	Unknown
Johann Michael Bach	Das Blut Jesu Christi	5vv, bc	Motet	SA5147	Heindorff; Johann Michael Bach
Johann Michael Bach	Die Furcht des Herrn	9vv, 2 vn, 2 va, bc	Concerto	SA5149	Johann Christoph Bach
Johann Michael Bach	Herr, wenn ich nur dich habe	5vv, bc	Motet	SA5146	Heindorff
Johann Michael Bach	Ich weiß, daß mein Erlöser lebt	5vv, bc	Motet	SA5146	Heindorff
Johann Michael Bach	Nun hab ich überwunden	8vv, bc	Motet	Missing	
Johann Sebastian Bach	Ich lasse dich nicht, BWV Anh.159	8vv	Motet	P4/1	Johann Sebastian Bach; Philipp David Kräuter
Adam Drese	Nun ist alles überwunden	4vv	Chorlied	SA5137	Drese; Heindorff

216   *Stephen Rose*

repeatedly studied and performed. From Johann Sebastian, the Archiv manuscripts passed to Carl Philipp Emanuel Bach, who made the first known reference to them as the Alt-Bachisches Archiv.[3] The twenty pieces in the Archiv were itemized in the 1790 auction catalog of Emanuel's estate,[4] and the Archiv was offered again for sale in 1805 on the death of his daughter.[5] The manuscripts were acquired by the collector Georg Poelchau, who eventually passed most of them to the choral society in Berlin, the Sing-Akademie, apart from a few manuscripts sold to the Berlin Royal Library (now the Staatsbibliothek zu Berlin).[6]

Subsequently, the Alt-Bachisches manuscripts underwent a checkered history. At the Sing-Akademie, they remained inaccessible and unknown even to that indefatigable researcher of Bach sources, Philipp Spitta, who listed them as lost in his Bach biography of 1873–1880.[7] Shortly after the outbreak of World War I, Max Schneider succeeded in "rediscovering and piecing together the manuscripts, piece by piece and often page by page."[8] But in 1944, the Sing-Akademie library became inaccessible again, after it was evacuated from Berlin to avoid war damage. For decades, the manuscripts were presumed lost, until in 1999 they were rediscovered in Kiev by Christoph Wolff and Patricia Grimsted of Harvard University. In 2002, the manuscripts were repatriated to Berlin, where they are now housed in the Staatsbibliothek.[9] This tale of loss and rediscovery has added to the mystery and allure of the Alt-Bachisches Archiv.

This chapter starts by summarizing recent source-critical scholarship on the manuscripts of the Alt-Bachisches Archiv. It then considers topics that have been less prominent in recent research, such as: the musical genres included in and excluded from the Archiv; whether there was a compositional style shared by seventeenth-century members of the Bach family; how the young Johann Sebastian might have been influenced by the compositions of his forebears; and the reception of the Archiv from the eighteenth to early twentieth centuries. It should be noted that the term "Alt-Bachisches Archiv" has been used elastically in some editions and recordings to refer to any vocal pieces by seventeenth-century members of the Bach family.[10] This chapter uses the term

---

3   Letter from C. P. E. Bach to J. N. Forkel, 20 September 1775; Dok 3: 292 (No. 807).

4   CPEB NV, 83–85.

5   Elias N. Kulukundis, "Die Versteigerung von C. P. E. Bachs musikalischem Nachlaß im Jahre 1805," BJ 81 (1995): 145–176, esp. 157.

6   Daniel Melamed, *J. S. Bach and the German Motet* (Cambridge: Cambridge University Press, 1995), 169–170.

7   Spitta 1: 58–59, 73; Spitta ET, 1: 59–60, 75.

8   "[E]s mir… glückte, Stück für Stück der Handschriften, oft blattweise, nach und nach wiederzufinden." *Altbachisches Archiv* (*Das Erbe deutscher Musik* 1–2), ed. Max Schneider (Leipzig: Breitkopf & Härtel, 1935), 1: 112.

9   Patricia Grimsted, "Bach is Back in Berlin: The Return of the Sing-Akademie Archive from Ukraine in the Context of Displaced Cultural Treasures and Restitution Politics"; Christoph Wolff, "Recovered in Kiev: Bach et al. A Preliminary Report on the Music Archive of the Berlin Sing-Akademie," *Notes* 58 (2001): 259–271.

10 As in Schneider's edition, see later; or recordings such as *Altbachisches Archiv*, Cantus Cölln and Concerto Palatino, directed by Konrad Junghänel (Harmonia Mundi 901783.84, recorded in 2002).

"Alt-Bachisches Archiv" to refer specifically to the twenty vocal pieces as listed in Carl Philipp Emanuel Bach's estate catalog (see Table 9.1), although it considers the wider compositional output of the Bach family when probing their musical style and their possible influence.

Sources

Recent research on the Alt-Bachisches Archiv has focused on the manuscripts, including their provenance and the authorship of pieces in them. This focus reflects the preoccupation with source-critical work in Bach studies, as well as the scholarly desire to reveal the origins of manuscripts that had been inaccessible for most of the twentieth century.

The critical edition of the music of the Alt-Bachisches Archiv remains that by Max Schneider, published as the two inaugural volumes of the series *Das Erbe deutscher Musik* in 1935. Although this series was a product of the nationalist movement in German musicology (as discussed at the end of this chapter), with a mission to provide critical editions suitable for performers, much of Schneider's scholarship remains valuable today. Unlike other editions that sought to be of practical use (such as early volumes of the *Neue Schütz Ausgabe*), Schneider retained the original note-values and key-signatures. His musical text is reasonably reliable, although his account of the sources is brief, with inadequate detail about the scribal hands and the many chronological layers within each bundle of manuscripts. Schneider's critical commentary has been superseded by Wolfram Enßlin's 2006 catalog of the recovered Bach sources of the Berlin Sing-Akademie, which contains accurate and detailed descriptions reflecting the latest codicological research.[11] Up-to-date descriptions of the manuscripts are also available via the open-access online database of RISM.[12]

The scope and contents of Schneider's edition need to be clarified, because it does not correspond to the twenty pieces listed as the Alt-Bachisches Archiv in C. P. E. Bach's estate inventory. Schneider included thirteen Bach family pieces from other sources, such as the library of the Michaeliskirche in Erfurt (now held in the Staatsbibliothek zu Berlin). But he omitted four pieces in the Archiv that had already been published in editions of the early twentieth century: Johann Christoph Bach's *Lieber Herr Gott, wecke uns auf, Es erhub sich ein Streit im Himmel* and *Ach, daß ich Wassers gnug hätte*, as well as *Ich lasse dich nicht* (nowadays reascribed to J. S. Bach, see later). More recent editions of these pieces can be found in the *Stuttgarter Bach Ausgabe* (published originally by Hänssler, now by Carus), along with many other Bach family compositions. A new comprehensive edition of the Alt-Bachisches Archiv is under preparation by Peter Wollny and Christoph Wolff.

Another area of recent research concerns the provenance of the manuscripts in the Alt-Bachisches Archiv. In 1935, Schneider suggested that most of the

---

11 LBB 8 (2006).

12 http://opac.rism.info

218   *Stephen Rose*

manuscripts originated "as a collection begun by Johann Ambrosius Bach of choice works by his closest relatives."[13] He surmised that the collection passed somehow from Johann Ambrosius to his son Johann Sebastian and then on to Carl Philipp Emanuel. In 1995, Daniel Melamed cast doubt on Schneider's hypothesis, noting that because Johann Ambrosius died in 1695, he cannot have been responsible for those manuscripts dated in the late 1690s. Furthermore, most evidence of Bach's use of the Alt-Bachisches Archiv dates from the 1740s, whereas if Bach had acquired it from his father, one might expect indications that he used it earlier in his career.[14]

Dramatic discoveries about the collection's provenance were made by Peter Wollny in the late 1990s, initially working from photographs of the then-lost manuscripts. By comparing these photographs with the scribal hands found in documents in various Thuringian archives, Wollny showed that most of the manuscripts were copied by Arnstadt musicians. Eight motets are in the hand of Ernst Dietrich Heindorff (1651–1724), town cantor in Arnstadt from 1681 until his death. Johann Bach's motet *Sei nun wieder zufrieden* is in the hand of Jonas de Fletin (1610–55), town and court cantor in Arnstadt from 1644 until his death. And manuscripts of two motets—Johann Christoph Bach's *Lieber Herr Gott, wecke uns auf* and *Der Gerechte, ob er gleich zu zeitlich stirbt*—are in the hand of his father Heinrich Bach.[15] After the rediscovery of the Sing-Akademie manuscripts in Kiev, Wollny was able to confirm these findings; he also identified the score of Johann Michael Bach's motet *Das Blut Jesu Christi* as the composer's autograph.[16] Table 9.1 lists the principal scribes of the manuscripts in the Alt-Bachisches Archiv.

Wollny's discoveries have two important implications. First, much of the Alt-Bachisches Archiv originated not as a family archive but as a working repertory used by the Arnstadt cantor Heindorff. Arnstadt was where Heinrich Bach lived and where his sons Johann Christoph and Johann Michael grew up, so it is unsurprising that their music continued to be used there. Johann Michael Bach maintained close links with Heindorff, writing the motet *Herr, wenn ich nur dich habe* for the funeral in 1690 of his son Friedrich Ernst.[17] Dates on some manuscripts of pieces in the collection (such as "1699," found on Johann Michael Bach's *Das Blut Jesu Christi*, and also Johann Bach's *Weint nicht um meinen Tod*) show that Heindorff continued to use these motets for several years after the deaths of their respective composers.

---

13 "[N]ach von Johann Ambrosius Bach begonnenen Sammlung erlesener Werke seiner nächsten Anverwandten." Schneider, *Altbachisches Archiv*, 1: 111.
14 Melamed, *J. S. Bach and the German Motet*, 178–179.
15 Peter Wollny, "Alte Bach-Funde," BJ 84 (1998): 137–148.
16 Peter Wollny, "Geistliche Musik der Vorfahren Johann Sebastian Bachs. Das Altbachische Archiv," *Jahrbuch des Staatlichen Instituts für Musikforschung Preußischer Kulturbesitz* (2002): 41–59, esp. 48–50.
17 Wollny, "Alte Bach-Funde," 146.

The Alt-Bachisches Archiv 219

Second, Wollny's work on the provenance of the manuscripts supports Melamed's hypothesis that Johann Sebastian Bach obtained the Archiv relatively late in his career. Wollny suggests that Johann Sebastian gained the manuscripts from Heindorff only after the latter's death in 1724, possibly via Johann Ernst Bach (1683–1739), who was organist at Arnstadt's Neuen Kirche from 1707, and the only Bach in Arnstadt at this time.[18] By contrast, Konrad Küster has pointed to the marital links between the Heindorff and Bach families to suggest that Johann Sebastian obtained the Alt-Bachisches Archiv early in his career, perhaps as part of the "good store of choicest church compositions" he acquired in Mühlhausen.[19] However, Küster's hypothesis has not drawn any support from other scholars.

A final area of recent research on the Alt-Bachisches sources concerns the composer attributions. This is a perennial problem in research on manuscripts of Bach family music, given the presence of so many Bachs with similar forenames, and the often casual attitude to attribution. In many sources of keyboard works, the ascriptions may simply say "Bach" (which could indicate many members of the Bach family, or possibly also "Bachelbel") or merely give the initials of the composer.[20] In the case of the manuscripts in the Alt-Bachisches Archiv, *Die Furcht des Herrn* is transmitted without attribution, whereas other pieces (such as *Nun ist alles überwunden*) merely bear the initials of their composer. Confusion can also arise because pieces often survive in the hand of another family member, as with Johann Christoph Bach's *Der Gerechte* transmitted in a score written by his father Heinrich, or Johann Michael Bach's *Die Furcht des Herrn*" preserved in parts written by his brother Johann Christoph (see Table 9.1).

In 1999, Daniel Melamed probed the uncertainties over the authorship of much of the music customarily attributed to the Eisenach organist Johann Christoph Bach (1642–1703). Many of these confusions might result from the fact that there were several Bach family members with this name; Melamed also argued that previous generations of scholars were unduly keen to attribute pieces to a composer hailed as "expressive" and "profound" in the eighteenth century.[21] In relation to the Alt-Bachisches Archiv, Melamed noted the conflicting ascriptions for several pieces usually assigned to Johann Christoph: thus, *Ach, daß ich Wassers gnug hätte* is attributed to Heinrich Bach in a copy in the Düben Collection, Uppsala;[22] and *Es erhub ein Streit* is ascribed to Johann Michael in a 1686 inventory from

---

18 Wollny, "Alte Bach-Funde," 148.

19 Konrad Küster, "Bachs Umgang mit Vokalmusik Thüringer Komponisten," Rainer Kaiser, ed., *Bach und seine mitteldeutschen Zeitgenossen: Bericht über das internationale Musikwissenschaftliche Kolloquium, Erfurt und Arnstadt, 13. bis 16. Januar 2000* (Eisenach: Wagner, 2001), 112–126, esp. 118, 122). The quotation is from NBR 57 (No. 32); Dok 1: 19 (No. 1).

20 Wolff Essays, 117.

21 Daniel Melamed, "Constructing Johann Christoph Bach (1642–1703)," ML 80 (1999): 345–365. For a more recent view on the authorship of Johann Christoph's keyboard works, see Pieter Dirksen, "Zur Echtheit der Johann Christoph Bach (1642–1703) zugeschriebenen Klavierwerke," BJ 96 (2010): 217–248.

22 Uppsala Universitetsbiblioteket vok.mus.i.hs. 003:001. The *Stuttgarter Bach Ausgabe* ascribes "Ach, daß ich Wassers gnug hätte" to Heinrich Bach (Stuttgart: Hännsler, 1976).

220   Stephen Rose

the Ansbach court.[23] In his earlier study of Bach's motets, Melamed attributed the motet *Ich lasse dich nicht* BWV Anh.159 to Johann Sebastian Bach. The piece had been ascribed to Sebastian in Johann Gottfried Schicht's edition of 1802, but since Johann Friedrich Naue's edition of 1821–1823 it had generally been ascribed to Johann Christoph Bach. Melamed rehabilitated Schicht's attribution on the basis of source-critical evidence (the survival of the score in the hands of Johann Sebastian and his Weimar pupil Philipp David Kräuter), stylistic criteria (the sophisticated counterpoint), and an apparent quotation of a gavotte from Jean-Baptiste Lully's 1686 opera *Armide* (Melamed suggests that Johann Sebastian might have obtained a copy of this gavotte in 1713 via Prince Johann Ernst of Weimar).[24]

Further insights into the authorship of items in the Alt-Bachisches Archiv have been gained by Peter Wollny. He has shown that an anonymous piece in the collection, the choral lied *Nun ist alles überwunden* (which Schneider tentatively ascribed to Heinrich Bach) is by Adam Drese (ca. 1620–1701), Capellmeister to the Duke of Schwarzburg in Arnstadt from 1678.[25] The discovery of another composer's work in the Alt-Bachisches Archiv raises questions about the extent and scope of the collection. When Bach acquired these manuscripts from Arnstadt, did they include many works by composers outside the Bach family? Melamed showed that a score of Sebastian Knüpfer's motet *Erforsche mich, Gott*, used by Bach for performance in 1740s Leipzig, has a title-page in the scribal hand that Wollny subsequently identified as Heindorff's.[26] Might this manuscript have once belonged to the Archiv? And did Johann Sebastian intend the Archiv to contain examples of his own works apart from *Ich lasse dich nicht*? Peter Williams speculates that Bach perhaps contributed some of his early autographs to it, such as the score of Cantata 71.[27] Possibly many of the Archiv's manuscripts were lost or dispersed before C. P. E. Bach obtained them and gave them the designation of "Alt-Bachisches Archiv." More research is thus required to establish the original extent of the collection by searching for manuscripts in other libraries whose provenance lies with the Bach family or with Arnstadt musicians such as Heindorff.

The Music of the Alt-Bachisches Archiv

The Alt-Bachisches Archiv offers an invaluable but one-sided view of the music of Bach's ancestors. Most of Bach's forebears worked as organists or instrumentalists; writing or performing vocal music was not part of their regular duties. Yet

---

23 Richard Schaal, *Die Musikhandschriften des Ansbacher Inventars von 1686* (Wilhelmshaven: Heinrichshofen, 1966), 57.

24 Melamed, *J. S. Bach and the German Motet*, 45–59.

25 Wollny, "Alte Bach-Funde," 139, 146.

26 Staatsbibliothek zu Berlin, Mus. ms. autogr. Knüpfer; see Melamed, *J. S. Bach and the German Motet*, 196.

27 Peter Williams, *J. S. Bach: A Life in Music* (Cambridge: Cambridge University Press, 2007), 3.

The Alt-Bachisches Archiv 221

the Archiv contains only vocal works, with none of the keyboard music that was the Bach family's usual fare. Many of these vocal pieces were written for special occasions such as funerals; perhaps as a result, they show an unusually high level of craftsmanship and expressive richness. The following paragraphs comment on the genres of music included in and omitted from the Archiv, and then probe the compositional style of members of the Bach family as demonstrated by the Archiv.

The Alt-Bachisches Archiv contains three categories of compositions: this heterogeneity reflects the varied provenance of the manuscripts, some copied by Heindorff and others with as yet unknown origins. The largest category of items are motets and strophic choral lieder—settings of Biblical or chorale texts with no independent instrumental parts apart from continuo (although the voices might be doubled by instruments, as in Johann Michael Bach's *Das Blut Jesu Christi*). Such pieces belonged to a Thuringian tradition of simple motets that could be sung by amateur choirs. Many of these motets and *Chorlieder* were written for funerals, as indicated by their text or details of the occasion preserved on the manuscripts (as with Johann Michael Bach's *Herr, wenn ich nur dich habe*, mentioned previously). Almost all of these pieces were transmitted by Heindorff, who as a cantor would have required a working repertory of funeral music.

Second, there are vocal concertos—pieces for solo voices and obbligato instruments. Most are small-scale works transmitted in copies made by scribes other than Heindorff.[28] This was a repertory more closely associated with organists; indeed, pieces in the concerted style have been dubbed "organist music" by Martin Geck, who contends they were directed by the organist rather than the cantor in church.[29] Among these concertos are two pieces that may have been the most widely disseminated Bach family compositions in the seventeenth century: the Michaelmas concerto *Es erhub sich ein Streit*, which also survives in a copy in the Berlin Amalienbibliothek (Staatsbibliothek zu Berlin Ms.AmB.91) and is listed in inventories at Ansbach (1686) and Schweinfurt (1688);[30] and *Ach, daß ich Wassers gnug hätte*, which also survives in Uppsala and is listed in inventories from Schweinfurt (two copies, 1688) and Lüneburg (1696).[31]

A final category of the Alt-Bachisches Archiv consists of two pieces written for events in the Bach family. First, there is Georg Christoph Bach's *Siehe wie fein und lieblich*, written for the get-together of the composer with his brothers Johann Ambrosius Bach and the Arnstadt town musician Johann Christoph Bach (1645–1693), as the title page records. Second, there is Johann Christoph

---

28 The one exception is that Heindorff added text-underlay to Johann Christoph Bach's twenty-two-part vocal concerto *Es erhub sich ein Streit*. LBB 8 (2006): 497.

29 Martin Geck, *Die Vokalmusik Dietrich Buxtehudes und der frühe Pietismus* (Kassel: Bärenreiter, 1965), 60–67.

30 Peter Wollny, "Materialien zur Schweinfurter Musikpflege im 17. Jahrhundert," *Schütz-Jahrbuch*, 19 (1997): 113–163, esp. 143; Schaal, *Die Musikhandschriften*, 57.

31 Uppsala Universitetsbiblioteket vok.mus.i.hs. 003:001; Wollny, "Materialien zur Schweinfurter Musikpflege," 139, 160; Max Seiffert, "Die Chorbibliothek der St. Michaelisschule in Lüneburg zu Seb. Bach's Zeit," *Sammelbände der Internationalen Musikgesellschaft* 9 (1907–8): 593–621, esp. 594).

222   *Stephen Rose*

Bach's *Meine Freundin, du bist schön*, presumably written for a family wedding such as that of the Arnstadt town musician Johann Christoph Bach and Martha Elisabeth Eisentraut on 5 April 1679. The manuscript has programmatic annotations describing an amorous encounter between a young man and woman.[32] The sources of both pieces are copied by members of the Bach family and were probably transmitted to J. S. Bach via his relations.

Equally revealing is what the Alt-Bachisches Archiv excludes. The Archiv has none of the large-scale vocal concertos known to have been written by Bach family members, apart from Johann Christoph's twenty-two part *Es erhub sich ein Streit* and Johann Michael's fourteen-part *Die Furcht des Herrn*. Yet, large-scale concertos were a major aspect of Johann Michael's output. Twelve such pieces are ascribed to him in the 1686 inventory from the Ansbach court, and a copy of one of these (*Der Herr ist König*, for SSATB soloists, ripieno choir, four trumpets, two violins, two violas, timpani, and continuo) survives in the Großfahner/Eschenbergen collection.[33] Perhaps these large-scale concertos are less well-represented in the Archiv because they may have held limited interest to Heindorff or J. S. Bach; by the mid-eighteenth century, such vocal concertos were more likely to sound obsolete than the simple textures of the Thuringian motet.

The Archiv also omits instrumental ensemble music. Johann Michael Bach wrote "starcke *Sonaten*" (large-ensemble sonatas) as well as "Clavier Sachen" (keyboard pieces) according to Johann Gottfried Walther,[34] and his sonata *Revange* is mentioned by Johann Heinrich Buttstett.[35] A "lovely sonata on various instruments" by Johann Michael was performed during a 1671 dedication service at the Kaufmannskirche, Erfurt.[36] None of this chamber music survives; as with the vocal concertos, it may have been excluded from the Archiv because J. S. Bach had little interest in it in the 1740s or was unable to obtain copies.

The biggest omission from the Alt-Bachisches Archiv, however, is keyboard music. Many organ chorales survive by members of the Bach family, including twenty-six such pieces attributed to Johann Michael Bach. A manuscript of *44 Choräle zum Praembulieren* is ascribed to "Johann Christoph Bachen / Organ: in

---

32   For an analytical account, see Peter Wollny, "Johann Christoph Bachs Hochzeitsdialog *Meine Freundin, du bist schön*," Michael Märker and Lothar Schmidt, eds., *Musikästhetik und Analyse. Festschrift für Wilhelm Seidel zum 65. Geburtstag* (Laaber: Laaber, 2002), 83–98.

33   Schaal, *Die Musikhandschriften des Ansbacher Inventars*, 57. The Großfahner/Eschenbergen copy survives in the Weimar Hochschule für Musik, Ms.GF107/BaJM; see Rainer Kaiser, "Unbekannte Kompositionen der Bach-Familie des 17. Jahrhunderts in Thüringer Archiven," *Ständige Konferenz Mitteldeutsche Barockmusik Jahrbuch* (2000): 56–73; and Hans Rudolf Jung, *Thematischer Katalog der Musikaliensammlung Großfahner / Eschenbergen in Thüringen* (Kassel: Bärenreiter, 2001), 126–127.

34   Johann Gottfried Walther, *Musicalisches Lexicon* (Leipzig, 1732), 64.

35   Johann Heinrich Buttstett, *Ut, mi, sol, re, fa, la, tota musica et harmonia æterma* (Erfurt: Werther, ca. 1716), 88.

36   "[S]chöne Sonate... auf unterschiedlichen Instrumenten," quoted in Helga Brück, "Eine 'Verordnung der Music' der Kaufmannskirche zu Erfurt von 1671 als Nachweis unbekannter Kompositionen von Johann Michael Bach (1648–1694)," BJ 84 (1998): 183–185.

Eisenach,"[37] although several scholars argue that the simplicity of these fughettas suggests that they were composed by another Johann Christoph in the family, such as Johann Sebastian's Ohrdruf brother (1671–1721).[38] Other keyboard works known to have been composed by Bach family members are now lost. For instance, the funeral sermon for Heinrich Bach mentions his chorales, preludes, and fugues,[39] but no keyboard works can be securely attributed to him.

It is likely that the young J. S. Bach had access to his family's organ music via the Eisenach organist Johann Christoph Bach, with whom he presumably spent time during his childhood in Eisenach.[40] Albums of his ancestors' keyboard works also circulated within the extended Bach family. Ernst Ludwig Gerber (1746–1819) owned a manuscript from a Bach family member that contained settings of more than 200 chorale melodies, including seventy-two chorales by Johann Michael Bach and eight by Johann Christoph Bach, plus settings by J. S. Bach, Johann Ludwig Bach, and Thuringians such as Buttstett.[41] The "Neumeister" collection (Yale University Library Ms. LM 4708), containing chorales by Johann Michael, Johann Christoph, and Johann Sebastian Bach, among others, was probably copied from a manuscript originally within the Bach family circle.[42]

Despite the presence of these Bach family manuscripts of keyboard chorales, there is no evidence that J. S. Bach wished to include his ancestors' organ music in the Alt-Bachisches Archiv. By the time he was compiling the Archiv in the late 1730s or 1740s, he was a cantor, so his performing interests were mainly in vocal music. He may have considered that his ancestors' organ music lacked the artistic ambition and expressive intensity of their vocal works; many of the organ chorales attributed to Johann Michael and Johann Christoph are modest settings, probably written for everyday use rather than special occasions. Indeed, the simple Thuringian organ chorale of the late seventeenth century did not appeal to mid-eighteenth century ears. In 1758, Jakob Adlung wrote that Johann Michael Bach's "chorales mean little nowadays."[43] There is no sign that the mature Bach

---

37 Berlin, Universität der Künste, Ms. 1491; the only modern edition is a performer's edition of limited scholarly value: Johann Christoph Bach, *44 Choräle zum Präambulieren*, ed. Martin Fischer (Kassel: Bärenreiter, 1930).

38 Jean-Claude Zehnder, *Die frühen Werke Johann Sebastians Bach. Stil – Chronologie – Satztechnik*, 2 vols. (Basel: Schwabe, 2009), 378; Rainer Kaiser, "Johann Christoph Bachs *Choräle zum Präambulieren* – Anmerkungen zu Echtheit und Überlieferung," BJ 87 (2001): 185–189; Dirksen, "Zur Echtheit," 239.

39 Quoted in Ulrich Konrad, "Instrumentalkompositionen von Heinrich Bach (1615–1692). Zwei bislang unbeachtete Sonaten in einem Gothaer Partiturbuch," BJ 81 (1995): 93–115, esp. 105.

40 Wolff BLM, 28–30.

41 Ernst Ludwig Gerber, *Neues historisch-biographisches Lexikon der Tonkünstler*, 4 vols (Leipzig: Kühnel, 1812–14), 1: cols. 209–210, 213; see also the 1791 list of Bach works owned by Gerber, Dok 5: 252 (No. C967a).

42 Wolff Essays, 112.

43 "[S]eine Chorale bedeuten heutiges Tages nicht viel." Jakob Adlung, *Anleitung zu der musikalischen Gelahrtheit* (Erfurt: Jungnicol, 1758), 690.

224   *Stephen Rose*

made his "Neumeister" chorales—his youthful foray into this Thuringian style (discussed later)—available to his pupils or colleagues for copying.[44]

Despite omitting all instrumental works, the Alt-Bachisches Archiv still allows an investigation of whether the Bach family had a distinctive compositional style. Jean-Claude Zehnder has recently argued that these Bach family compositions are characterized by a "melodically oriented form" and a delight in "the chordal-harmonic colour of sonorities."[45] Such a combination of features is suggested by the Obituary's description of Johann Christoph Bach as writing "in a galant and cantabile style, yet uncommonly full-textured."[46] The melodiousness of the Bach family compositions is evident in strophic choral lieder such as Johann Christoph's "Es ist nun aus," where the lower three voices support an arching melody in the soprano part. Even in the more contrapuntal of motets, the top voice usually carries the melodic interest, as in Johann Michael's *Herr, wenn ich nur dich habe*, with its predominantly conjunct lines in lilting triple-time. Often the ends of phrases are reinforced by an echo, as in Johann Bach's *Unser Leben ist ein Schatten* or Johann Christoph's *Es ist nun aus*.[47] Such melodiousness was a common characteristic of late seventeenth-century music; it reflects the importance of strophic song in the period and also the influence of the music of Giacomo Carissimi, Vincenzo Albrici, and Giuseppe Peranda.[48]

This melodic emphasis also occurs in the instrumental introductions to vocal concertos, which often feature a declamatory or fantasia-like line for solo violin against a viol accompaniment. In Johann Christoph's Lamento *Ach, daß ich Wassers gnug hätte*, the violin anticipates the "tear" motif of a diminished fourth that is later sung to "Wassers gnug" (Example 9.1). In Johann Michael's *Ach, wie sehnlich wart ich der Zeit,* and *Auf, laßt uns den Herrn loben*, the solo violin creates an anguished mood through its jagged ornamentation in the initial sinfonia, in contrast to the syllabic text-setting, regular phrase-lengths, and even rhythms of the vocal strophes. Violin solos also occur in Georg Christoph's *Siehe wie fein und lieblich ist* and Johann Christoph's *Meine Freundin*. Such violin solos with viol accompaniment are relatively rare in the works of other late seventeenth-century German composers;[49] perhaps the Bach family's skills as instrumentalists and instrument-builders encouraged them to explore these rich scorings.

Coupled with this melodic impulse, the compositions of the Bach family also show a love of vertical sonorities. Their organ chorales often use a simple four-part

---

44   Wolff Essays, 118.

45   "'[M]elodie-orientierte' Gestaltung" and "akkordisch-harmonischen Farbe der Klänge." Zehnder, *Die frühen Werke*, 376–377.

46   Dok 3: 80 (No. 666); translation modified from NBR 298 (No. 306).

47   Zehnder, *Die frühen Werke*, 402–405.

48   On these Italian influences, see Peter Wollny, "Italian and German Influences in the Thuringian Motet Repertoire of the Late Seventeenth Century," Alberto Colzani, et al., eds., *Relazioni musicali tra Italia e Germania nell'età barocca* (Como: Antiquae Musicae Italicae Studiosi, 1997), 201–215.

49   A similar texture can be found in the sinfonia to the anonymous cantata "Gott sei mir gnädig"; Sächsische Landesbibliothek-Staats- und Universitätsbibliothek Dresden, Mus Ms.2-E-558.

The Alt-Bachisches Archiv 225

Example 9.1 Johann Christoph Bach, "Ach, daß ich Wassers gnug hätte," bars 1–11. Uppsala Universitetsbiblioteket, Vok.mus.i.hs. 003:001.

texture enriched by suspensions and passing-notes, as with the piquant dissonances in Johann Christoph Bach's *An Wasserflüssen Babylon* (Example 9.2).[50] Johann Christoph also used dissonance in his vocal works for expressive effect: in *Ach, daß ich Wassers gnug hätte*, the sense of lamentation is intensified by the high level of dissonance, with seventh chords repeatedly sounded in the viols in

---

50 Modern edition in Johann Michael Bach, *Sämtliche Orgelchoräle mit einem Anhang (Orgelchoräle des Bach-Kreises, hauptsächlich aus der Neumeister-Sammlung)*, ed. Christoph Wolff (Stuttgart: Hänssler, 1988), 72.

Example 9.2 Johann Christoph Bach, "An Wasserflüssen Babylon," bars 1–5. Yale University Library, Ms. LM 4708, 100.

bars 3–4 and unprepared seventh chords in bars 7–8 (Example 9.1). Similarly bold harmonies and progressions are found in his motet *Der Gerechte*.

Such a love of rich sonorities would seem to be the germ of two anecdotes in the Obituary, both making dubious claims about Johann Christoph Bach. The Obituary asserts that "on the organ and on the keyboard he never played in fewer than five real parts."[51] In fact, most of Johann Christoph's surviving organ chorales are in four parts. And to support its claim that Johann Christoph was "strong... in the expression of the meaning of the words," the Obituary states that in "a motet written seventy-odd years ago... he had the courage to use the augmented sixth."[52] As Mark Ellis notes, no augmented sixths can be found in the surviving output of Johann Christoph Bach.[53] But the anecdote may allude to the bold harmonic progressions found in some of his music, for instance the circle-of-fifths in bars 16–19 of *Ach, daß ich Wassers gnug hätte* (Example 9.3). Here the voice sings in canon with the solo violin, pushing the progression onwards by adding sevenths to each chord; but whereas the versions of the circle-of-fifths recommended in thorough-bass treatises of the early eighteenth century stay within a single key, Johann Christoph's version moves from an E major chord to F major chord. Creating a musical outpouring akin to the tears described in the penitential text, this passage exemplifies the expressivity and harmonic inventiveness for which Johann Christoph was posthumously celebrated. Further analysis of Bach family compositions in the context of other seventeenth-century music would help refine our understanding of their output and compositional style.

Influence

Scholars of the nineteenth and early twentieth centuries were primarily interested in the Alt-Bachisches Archiv as a possible influence on J. S. Bach's musical style. Philipp Spitta probed the works of Johann Christoph and Johann Michael Bach for "germ[s] of the spirit of Sebastian Bach."[54] Albert Schweitzer and Karl

---

51 NBR 298 (No. 306); Dok. 3: 80–81 (No. 666).
52 *Loc. cit.*
53 Mark Ellis, *A Chord in Time: The Augmented Sixth from Monteverdi to Wagner* (Farnham: Ashgate, 2010), 88–89; see also Melamed, *J. S. Bach and the German Motet*, 166.
54 Spitta 1: 65; Spitta ET, 1: 66.

Example 9.3 Johann Christoph Bach, "Ach, daß ich Wassers gnug hätte," bars 16–19.

Geiringer saw *Es erhub sich ein Streit* as presaging Bach's own setting of these words (BWV 19).[55] More recently, Daniel Melamed argued that there are few continuities between Bach's own vocal style and the works of his forebears.[56] The Alt-Bachisches Archiv exemplifies late seventeenth-century styles of vocal composition in central Germany. In the 1700s, many of these styles were swept away by the Italianate innovations that formed the basis of Bach's mature style, namely the ritornello techniques of Antonio Vivaldi and the structure of cantata librettos pioneered by Erdmann Neumeister (where recitatives alternate with arias). Consequently, any traces of a Bach family influence are likely to be found in Bach's earliest works, where they mingle with inspiration from other figures such as Georg Böhm, Dieterich Buxtehude, and Johann Pachelbel.

Bach's compositions that show the strongest influence of his ancestors are his organ chorales in the "Neumeister" collection (Yale University Library Ms. LM 4708). These are among Bach's earliest extant works, with some of them probably dating back to his time in Ohrdruf.[57] Although the "Neumeister" chorales are the work of a fledgling composer, they still show an intriguing variety of stylistic and formal strategies, as recently investigated by Richard Jones and Jean-Claude Zehnder.[58]

---

55 Albert Schweitzer, *J. S. Bach*, ET, 2 vols (Leipzig: Breitkopf & Härtel, 1911), 1: 74; Karl Geiringer, *The Bach Family: Seven Generations of Creative Genius* (London: Allen & Unwin, 1954), 58.
56 Melamed, *J. S. Bach and the German Motet*, 186.
57 Wolff Essays, 118. Scholars continue to dispute J. S. Bach's authorship of some of the "Neumeister" chorales: see Michael Heinemann, "Neumeisters Choräle: Zu einer Sammelhandschrift 'früher' Bach-Werke," *Organ Yearbook*, 29 (2000): 7–18; Zehnder, *Die frühen Werke*, 358.
58 Richard D. P. Jones, *The Creative Development of Johann Sebastian Bach* (Oxford: Oxford University Press, 2007), 1: 72–86; Zehnder, *Die frühen Werke*, passim.

228   *Stephen Rose*

Seven of Bach's "Neumeister" chorales are four-part settings of the chorale melody, sometimes with an imitative treatment prefacing the initial line. This was a style favored by Johann Michael Bach, combining a prominent upper-voice melody with the harmonic richness favored by the Bach family. In *Christus, der ist mein Leben* (BWV 1112), Zehnder detects the influence of Johann Michael in "the flowing form of the interludes" and the plain yet sonorous handling of the cantus firmus.[59] In other pieces, the young Bach used a four-part texture to explore dissonances, either via suspensions and figuration in the inner parts, such as in *O Jesu, wie ist dein Gestalt* (BWV 1094), or via homophonic use of the diminished seventh, as in bar 37 of *Ich hab mein Sach Gott heimgestellt* (BWV 1113, Example 9.4). Such harmonic richness points back to Bach's ancestors, but also creates a feature that Peter Williams identifies as characteristic of the collection—the diminished seventh chord held against a tonic pedal (see the penultimate chord of Example 9.4).[60]

Another fingerprint of Bach's "Neumeister" chorales, but rare in his later keyboard chorales, is the echo effect. As mentioned previously, echoes are common in the melodious style of late seventeenth-century vocal music, including pieces in the Alt-Bachisches Archiv. In *Ich hab mein Sach Gott heimgestellt*" (BWV 1113) the ends of chorale lines are echoed (Example 9.4), similar to Bach family motets, such as Johann Bach's *Unser Leben ist ein Schatten*. In *Christ, der du bist der helle Tag* (BWV 1120) the opening homophonic introduction incorporates echoes. And in *Herr Gott, nun schleuß den Himmel auf* (BWV 1092), fragments of the chorale melody are echoed at a lower octave. Each of these settings has a four-part homophonic texture reminiscent of Bach family motets, although Richard Jones notes that the use of echoes in keyboard chorales might also follow the model of Bach's Lüneburg teacher Georg Böhm.[61]

In many of Bach's early works, it can be hard to identify influences as specifically from the Bach family, as opposed to central German music more generally in the period. In the *Capriccio sopra il lontananza del suo fratello dilettissimo* (BWV 992), a keyboard sonata representing the departure of "the most beloved brother," the use of programmatic rubrics to represent a family event recalls Johann Christoph's wedding concerto *Meine Freundin*. Yet a closer model for the *Capriccio* can be found in Johann Kuhnau's Biblical Sonatas (1700), in which programmatic keyboard music represents well-known Old Testament stories rather than events comprehensible only to family members.

Similarly, Bach's early vocal works (those written in Arnstadt and Mühlhausen) show some likenesses with pieces in the Alt-Bachisches Archiv, but rather than being cases of verifiable influence, these likenesses are common traits of German vocal concertos at the end of the seventeenth century. The anguished mood of several of Bach's early cantatas may seem to echo pieces in the Alt-Bachisches

---

59 Zehnder, *Die frühen Werke*, 26.

60 Peter Williams, *The Organ Music of J. S. Bach*, 2nd ed. (Cambridge: Cambridge University Press, 2003), 543.

61 Jones, *Creative Development*, 1: 84.

Example 9.4 Johann Sebastian Bach, "Ich hab mein Sach Gott heimgestellt" (BWV 1113), bars 37–41. Yale University Library, Ms. LM 4708, 123.

Archiv. The melancholic impatience with the world in Cantata 106, *Gottes Zeit ist die allerbeste Zeit*, recalls the mood of Johann Michael Bach's *Ach, wie sehnlich wart ich der Zeit*. Cantata 106 also has similarities with Johann Bach's motet *Unser Leben ist ein Schatten*: both quote the chorale melody *Ich hab mein Sach Gott heimgestellet*, and Johann Bach's motet incorporates stanza 8 of this hymn ("Ach Herr, lehr uns bedenken wohl"), a paraphrase of Psalm 90: 12, one of the texts used in Cantata 106. There are similarities of compositional technique too between Bach's early vocal works and those of his ancestors. Bach's Cantata 150 uses a modulating ostinato bass in its final movement, similar to the central section of Johann Christoph Bach's *Meine Freundin*; and in the first aria of the cantata, the soprano soloist is echoed by the violins in a way also found in Johann Michael Bach's *Auf, laßt uns den Herrn loben*.[62] But these features are part of the common language of late seventeenth-century music, and also occur in the output of composers such as Buxtehude. Indeed, the relationship of the Alt-Bachisches Archiv with the wider repertory of late seventeenth-century music remains to be fully explored, and such an investigation would help give a more nuanced notion of how far Bach's ancestors influenced his own compositions.

Reception

Even when pieces in the Alt-Bachisches Archiv had ceased to be a compositional inspiration to J. S. Bach, they continued to be performed by members of the Bach family throughout the eighteenth century, and then in wider musical circles in the nineteenth century. Studies of the reception of the Alt-Bachisches Archiv have focused on J. S. Bach's interest in the collection, with less attention being given to subsequent uses of it. Research in this area raises many questions about performance practice, changing conceptions of the musical past, and shifting notions of church music and German music.

The stereotyped attitude in early eighteenth-century Germany was that old music (particularly vocal concertos) had little value and should not be performed. In 1753, Caspar Ruetz, the Lübeck cantor, described how he had disposed of

---

62 Zehnder, *Die frühen Werke*, 190.

230 *Stephen Rose*

manuscripts of church music by his father-in-law and grandfather-in-law: "But who will give anything for it, other than someone who needs scrap paper, for nothing is more useless than old music."[63] Sometimes he used it as kindling in his stove, although he also felt an antiquarian interest: "I have tried to keep most of the scores of the old pieces on account of their antiquity and in order to see from them the style and disposition of the music of those times."[64] J. S. Bach superficially adhered to such attitudes. He showed no interest in acquiring the musical estate of his Leipzig predecessor Johann Kuhnau (whereas Kuhnau had obtained for the Thomasschule the musical estate of his own predecessor Johann Schelle).[65] In the 1730 *Entwurff,* he wrote that "the former style of music no longer seems to please our ears."[66] Yet, within a few years, Bach's attitude to "old music" (particularly that of his family) had changed.

Bach's interest in the Alt-Bachisches Archiv has been investigated by Melamed and Wollny; it is documented primarily by his additions (mostly dating from the 1740s) to the manuscripts.[67] Some of Bach's changes suggest an antiquarian interest, such as making a new title-page for *Meine Freundin, du bist schön*. Other additions imply that Bach performed these pieces, including his insertion of text underlay in Johann Christoph Bach's *Es ist nun aus* and *Es erhub sich ein Streit*; C. P. E. Bach records that his father performed the latter piece "in Leipzig in the church; everyone was astonished by the effect."[68] Bach also made or supervised the copying of performing parts of Johann Christoph's *Der Gerechte* and *Lieber Herr Gott*.

Scholars have speculated about Bach's reasons for his interest in the Alt-Bachisches Archiv. His assembly of these manuscripts coincided with him making the Genealogy and family tree, which themselves may have been spurred by him reaching the age of fifty. Peter Williams conjectures that "fifty was an important age in Thuringian/Saxon tradition."[69] Mary Greer suggests that by making the Genealogy, Bach was following the instruction in Leviticus 25.10 that: "You shall hallow the fiftieth year... It should be a jubilee for you: you shall return, every one of you, to your property and every one of you to your family."[70]

---

63 Caspar Ruetz, *Widerlegte Vorurtheile von der Wirkung der Kirchenmusic und von den darzu erforderten Unkosten* (Rostock: Berger, 1753), 113: "Wer will aber, wo er nicht Maculatur von nöthen hat, das geringste darfür geben; weil nichts unbrauchbarer als alte Noten."

64 Ruetz, *Widerlegte Vorurtheile*, 112: "Nur die meisten Partituren der alten Stücke habe beyzubehalten gesucht, um des Alterthums willen, und den Geschmack und die Beschaffenheit der damahligen Music daraus zu sehen."

65 Wolff BLM, 269, 332, 498.

66 NBR 149 (No.151); Dok 1: 62–63 (No. 22).

67 Melamed, *J. S. Bach and the German motet*, 180–188; Wollny, "Geistliche Musik," 50–55. Bach's additions to the manuscripts are listed in LBB 8.

68 Dok 3: 292 (No. 807).

69 Williams, *J. S. Bach: A Life in Music*, 2.

70 Mary Dalton Greer, "From the House of Aaron to the House of Johann Sebastian. Old Testament Roots for the Bach Family Tree," Gregory G. Butler, George B. Stauffer and Mary Dalton Greer, eds., *About Bach* (Urbana: University of Illinois Press, 2008), 15–34.

The Alt-Bachisches Archiv 231

Another possible reason was the trend among musicians to write autobiographies for publication in Mattheson's *Grundlage einer Ehrenpforte* (1740); these life-stories usually described the musician's origins and the emergence of his talent.[71] Bach did not contribute to Mattheson's project, but the Genealogy was an analogous (if private) way for him to explore his lineage and assert his self-identity as a musician.

In the 1740s, Bach's work on the Alt-Bachisches manuscripts paralleled his assembling and revising of his own compositions such as the Eighteen Chorales and the B Minor Mass. Putting his own works in order for posterity must have made him think of his own historical position within his dynasty. As Bach approached death, he seems to have looked back to his ancestors with particular intensity. Wolff has argued that the parts of *Lieber Herr Gott*—"among the latest samples of Bach's handwriting... reveal[ing] that the ailing old man clearly had trouble writing"—were prepared for possible use at Bach's own funeral.[72]

Bach was not the only member of his family to show interest in the dynasty's genealogy and musical accomplishments. Hans-Joachim Schulze has shown that Johann Nicolaus Bach (1669–1753, organist in Jena) mentioned in a 1728 letter that he was descended from the Hungarian Veit Bach.[73] Peter Williams suggests that Bach's genealogical list must have drawn on "an older document begun by a previous member of this large family."[74] The Alt-Bachisches Archiv also shows that previous generations of the family valued the compositions of their kin: the earliest surviving manuscripts of Johann Christoph's *Lieber Herr Gott* and *Der Gerechte* were copied by the composer's father Heinrich,[75] perhaps as a proud reflection of his son's achievements.

Less research has been done on C. P. E. Bach's use of the Alt-Bachisches Archiv, although he too was profoundly aware of his musical ancestry. His 1773 autobiography starts by drawing attention to his place in the musical dynasty, tracing his lineage back to his maternal grandfather Johann Michael Bach.[76] Concerned to secure his family's place in the emerging discipline of music history, he supplied Johann Nicolaus Forkel with biographical material about Johann Sebastian's forebears, including an annotated copy of the Genealogy and copies of motets from the Alt-Bachisches Archiv.[77] Forkel recorded how on a visit to Hamburg, C. P. E. Bach let him hear performances of "the most remarkable and hazardous passages" of Johann Christoph Bach's pieces.[78] The Archiv manuscripts suggest that Emanuel performed Johann Christoph's *Lieber*

---

71 Stephen Rose, *The Musician in Literature in the Age of Bach* (Cambridge: Cambridge University Press, 2011), 179–213.

72 Wolff BLM, 451–452.

73 Hans-Joachim Schulze, "'Die Bachen stammen aus Ungarn her': ein unbekannter Brief Johann Nikolaus Bachs aus dem Jahre 1728," BJ 75 (1989): 213–220.

74 Williams, *J. S. Bach: A Life in Music*, 1.

75 Staatsbibliothek zu Berlin, Mss. SA 5142 and 5154; LBB 8 (2006): 481, 489.

76 Dok 3: 225 (No. 779).

77 Dok 1: 261 (No. 184); Dok 3: 288–290 (No. 801), 3: 292 (No. 807).

78 NBR 423; Dok 7: 15.

232   Stephen Rose

Herr Gott (for which he made additions to the parts prepared by J. S. Bach, and had extra parts prepared by his copyist Johann Heinrich Michel).[79] Michel also made scores of Johann Michael's *Auf, laßt uns den Herrn loben* and Johann Christoph's *Ach, daß ich Wassers gnug hätte*,[80] possibly implying that Emanuel wished to study these vocal concertos that otherwise existed only in parts. Most intriguingly, C. P. E. Bach used Johann Christoph's motet *Der Gerechte* as the opening and concluding movements in a 1774 cantata of the same name (H 818). An extreme example of Emanuel's habit of borrowing other composers' music, this cantata warrants further investigation, in particular to probe the stylistic disjunction between Emanuel's arias and a motet written almost a century earlier.

Beyond these demonstrations of family loyalty, there were wider factors that gave continuing relevance to the Alt-Bachisches Archiv through the nineteenth and twentieth centuries. Two of these factors merit further research: the longevity of motets amid changing notions of church music and the growth of German nationalism.

Throughout the eighteenth century, old-fashioned motets were regularly performed in Lutheran churches. Until the 1790s, sixteenth-century motets from the printed anthology *Florilegium portense* (1618–1621) were performed in Leipzig church services as introits. Polyphonic motets were the favored repertory at funerals and burials: the archaic sound of the genre suited the solemnity of these occasions and the scoring complied with the prohibitions on obbligato instruments at funerals.[81] (As already noted, many of the Alt-Bachisches Archiv motets transmitted via Heindorff were intended for funerals.) The motet was thus an exception to the mid-eighteenth-century indifference to "old music." In this context, Bach's performances of Johann Christoph Bach's motets (and also Sebastian Knüpfer's *Erforsche mich, Gott*) were not particularly remarkable. The preference for the motet may also explain why Bach seems not to have performed any vocal concertos by his ancestors, apart from *Es erhub sich ein Streit*.

By the late eighteenth century, German musicians increasingly regarded the unaccompanied motet as the ideal of church music. Whereas cantatas were regarded as showcasing the individual singers and instrumentalists, the motet presented timeless texts from the Bible or chorales, with no distracting displays of solo virtuosity. Motets occupy a prominent place in the output of such composers as Gottfried August Homilius (1714–1785) and Johann Friedrich Doles (1715–1797).[82] Such a climate favored the motets of Johann Christoph Bach and Johann Michael Bach: the melodic appeal of their works coincided so closely with contemporary taste that the Obituary described Johann Christoph Bach as "galant" (see previous); and the straightforward vocal lines of these motets suited

---

79 Staatsbibliothek zu Berlin, Mss. SA 5143–45; LBB 8 (2006): 482–483.

80 Staatsbibliothek zu Berlin, Mss. SA 5139, 5160; LBB 8 (2006): 480, 493.

81 Stephen Rose, "Lutheran Church Music," Simon P. Keefe, ed., *The Cambridge History of Eighteenth-Century Music* (Cambridge: Cambridge University Press, 2009), 137–167, esp. 155–159.

82 Ibid.

The Alt-Bachisches Archiv   233

amateur choirs more than the florid writing of J. S. Bach's motets. The preference for the simplicity of the motet, however, could arouse suspicion of the harmonic intensity of Johann Christoph's vocal concertos. In his copy of Forkel's 1802 biography of J. S. Bach, Carl Friedrich Zelter annotated disapprovingly the anecdote about Johann Christoph using the augmented sixth. "The merit of such a daring piece should not be over-exaggerated. In this and similarly adventurous pieces lies the decline of a pure church style."[83]

A selection of nine motets attributed to Johann Christoph and Johann Michael Bach was published by Johann Friedrich Naue in 1821–1823. Thereafter these motets were performed regularly in concerts of sacred polyphony, often alongside contrapuntal classics such as Antonio Lotti's *Crucifixus*. In April 1828, a Passiontide concert in Breslau featured Johann Michael Bach's *Das Blut Jesu Christi* and, in March 1838, a similar concert included Johann Michael Bach's *Nun hab ich überwunden* and Johann Christoph Bach's *Lieber Herr Gott* alongside vocal works by Johann Eccard, Giovanni Rovetta, and Leonardo Leo.[84] *Ich lasse dich nicht*, ascribed sometimes to Johann Christoph and sometimes to Johann Sebastian Bach, was sung in concerts in Königsberg in September 1826 and in Halle's Marktkirche in November 1836, on both occasions with Lotti's *Crucifixus*; it also featured in Mendelssohn's "historic concert" of works by Bach and Handel in Leipzig on 21 January 1841.[85] These references are taken from the accounts of early nineteenth-century performances of Sebastian's works collected in *Bach-Dokumente* vol. 6; it would be an interesting research project to undertake a comprehensive study of nineteenth-century performances of pieces by Bach's ancestors.

A second factor in the continuing longevity of the Alt-Bachisches Archiv was German nationalism. Myths of origin, descent, and kinship are central to discourses of nationalism,[86] and in this respect the Bach lineage provided a compelling symbol for Teutonic cultural pride. Whereas at the start of the eighteenth century, earlier generations of Bachs were scorned as unduly provincial (thus Mattheson mocked Johann Michael Bach for his bad French[87]), by the end of the century attitudes had changed. Most scholars highlight Forkel's 1802 biography of Bach—with its description of Bach's works as "an invaluable national patrimony"—as the moment when Bach reception became fully aligned with German nationalism.[88] Yet in his description of Bach's forebears, Forkel's account recapitulates an incipient nationalism already found in the 1754 Obituary of J. S. Bach. (This similarity is not surprising, given that C. P. E. Bach wrote the Obituary and also supplied Forkel with material for his account.) The Obituary

---

83   Dok 7: 148 (No. D4): "Das Verdienst eines solchen Wagstücks ist übrigens nicht hoch zu taxiren. In diesem und ähnlichen Wagstücken liegt der Untergang eines reinen Kirchenstyls."
84   Dok 6: 55 (No. D39), and 705 (No. D199).
85   Dok 6: 593–594 (No. D46), 707 (No. D201), and 721 (No. E2).
86   Anthony D. Smith, *The Antiquity of Nations* (Cambridge: Polity, 2004), 47.
87   Johann Mattheson, *Das beschützte Orchestre* (Hamburg: Schiller, 1717), 221–223.
88   NBR 419; Dok 7: 9–10.

234   *Stephen Rose*

praises "these honest Thuringians [who] were so well satisfied with their native land and with their station in life" that "they gladly preferred… the approval of a throng of their faithful countrymen," rather than travelling abroad to seek praises "from a few (perhaps even envious) foreigners."[89] Other early biographical documents such as the Genealogy show that members of the Bach family were already being praised for attributes that later became central to notions of German music. J. S. Bach described Johann Christoph as "a profound composer" and C. P. E. Bach praised his grandfather Johann Michael Bach as "a thorough [*gründlich*] composer."[90] As Bernd Sponheuer notes, by the nineteenth century an "ideal type of 'the German' in music" had emerged that included many of the same qualities, including *Tiefsinn* (profundity), *Arbeit* (hard work) and *Gründlichkeit* (thoroughness).[91] It remains an open question as to how far Johann Sebastian's and Emanuel's descriptions of their forebears shaped the emergence of this "ideal type" of Teutonic music.

By the time of Philipp Spitta's Bach biography of 1873–1880, the nationalist significance of the seventeenth-century Bachs had increased further. Evidently unaware of the music of such composers as Sebastian Knüpfer or Johann Schelle, Spitta saw the period 1650–1675 as one of "profound exhaustion," with "no new or fresh growth" in German music. In these difficult times, the Bach family showed a racial superiority in rising above the norm: "such a complete insensibility to the… universal degeneracy… necessarily leads us to infer their descent from a race of the greatest health and vigour." Whereas early eighteenth-century German composers would adopt musical innovations from the "blossoming field of art" of Italy, Johann Christoph and Johann Michael Bach preserved "the precious essence of German national feeling in a pure vessel."[92] Spitta's account of the brothers' music emphasizes their settings of the Lutheran Bible and of chorales, those musical symbols of German Protestantism. He makes little reference to the strong Italian influences that scholars such as Peter Wollny have detected in Bach family compositions.[93]

In the 1930s, the Alt-Bachisches Archiv aroused a powerful brand of nationalist zeal. It was no coincidence that Schneider's edition of the Alt-Bachisches Archiv formed the first two volumes of the flagship of the Third Reich's musicological enterprises, the collected edition *Der Erbe deutscher Musik* (The Heritage of German Music). The series replaced the *Denkmäler deutscher Tonkunst*

---

89 NBR 298 (No. 306); Dok 3: 81 (No. 666).

90 Dok 1: 258 (No. 184); Dok 3: 225 (No. 779).

91 Bernd Sponheuer, "Reconstructing Ideal Types of the 'German' in Music," Celia Applegate and Pamela Potter, eds., *Music and German National Identity* (Chicago: University of Chicago Press, 2002), 36–58, esp. 40.

92 Spitta ET, 1: 41–42; Spitta 1: 40–41.

93 Wollny, "Italian and German Influences in the Thuringian Motet"; on the Monteverdian flavor of Heinrich Bach's *Ich danke dir, Gott*, see Peter Wollny, "The Distribution and Reception of Claudio Monteverdi's Music in Seventeenth-Century Germany," Silke Leopold and Joachim Steinhauer, eds., *Monteverdi und die Folgen* (Kassel: Bärenreiter, 1998), 51–75.

(Monuments of German Composition); its new name reflected a desire to connect the nation's musical heritage to its living present.[94] Heinrich Besseler, director of the Musikdenkmäler committee at the Staatliches Institut für Deutsche Musikforschung, explained that: "Heritage (*Erbe*) in its full sense means the entirety of music that has grown from our soil and that through the centuries has fulfilled and clarified the life of the nation."[95] As a repertory of old music performed repeatedly across two centuries, the Alt-Bachisches Archiv exemplified this living heritage. Moreover, as Besseler commented, "it shows the foundations that support the immortal works of [Johann Sebastian] Bach: the cantors' and organists' art of the Bach clan, already—as with Johann Michael and Johann Christoph Bach—lit up with flashes of genius."[96] Schneider's introduction to his edition implied that the creative gifts of the Bach family were not exclusive to musicians but could be found more widely among Thuringians of other occupations: "In Johann Sebastian Bach culminated the creative gifts of an old family, spread across Thuringia, of peasants, artisans and musicians."[97]

More sinister views were found in a 1932 book on music and race by the musical dilettante and Nazi party member Richard Eichenauer. Seeking to show how a composer's style could be shaped by the "racial soul," he viewed the Bach family as a "particularly good example of how intellectual qualities can be inherited."[98] Citing Spitta's study of the similarities between the music of Bach and that of his ancestors, Eichenauer viewed such likenesses as proof "that not only a general aptitude such as 'musicality' is inherited, but also the style of this aptitude."[99] A few years later, the musicologist and Nazi sympathizer Hans Joachim Moser described J. S. Bach's relationship with his ancestors via a comparison with the German landscape. For Moser, Bach was "no fantastic crag" but the dominating figure in a veritable mountain-range of talent, just "as in his Thuringian Forest the Inselberg curves powerfully upwards as the highest peak in the lovely chain of mountains, then falls away to a second, always substantial series of peaks on

---

94 Pamela Potter, *Most German of the Arts: Musicology and Society from the Weimar Republic to the End of Hitler's Reich* (New Haven: Yale University Press, 1998), 72–74.

95 Heinrich Besseler, "Das Erbe deutscher Musik," *Deutsche Musikkultur* 1 (1936/37): 16: "... nur die Gesamtheit der Musik, die auf unserem Boden gewachsen ist und Jahrhunderte hindurch das Leben der Nation erfüllt und verklärt hat, bildet das 'Erbe' im vollen Sinne."

96 Besseler, "Das Erbe deutscher Musik," 16: "Sie zeigt den Untergrund, der das unvergängliche Werk Bachs trägt: die Kantoren- und Organistenkunst der Bachischen Sippe, in der schon hier und dort, wie bei Johann Michael und Johann Christoph Bach, Genieblitze wetterleuchten."

97 Schneider, *Altbachisches Archiv*, 1: v: "In Johann Sebastian Bach gipfelt die schöpferische Begnadung eines alten, über Thüringen weitverzweigten Geschlechts von Bauern, Handwerkern und Musikern."

98 Richard Eichenauer, *Musik und Rasse* (Munich: Lehmann, 1932), 158: "... besonders gutes Beispiel für die Vererbbarkeit geistiger Eigenschaften."

99 Ibid.: "... daß nicht nur ganz allgemeine Anlagen wie 'Musikalität' vererbt werden, sondern auch der Stil dieser Anlagen."

236 *Stephen Rose*

the other side."[100] Further research is required to shed more light on how the Alt-Bachisches Archiv was appropriated as a symbol of German nationalism.

Thus the Alt-Bachisches Archiv raises many questions about the changing place of music within German culture from the seventeenth century to the present day. Although many details of the manuscripts' provenance and attributions have been disclosed, much research remains to be done on how the Bach family's music relates to other late seventeenth-century composers, and on the cultural significance of this unique collection.

---

100 Hans Joachim Moser, *Joh. Seb. Bach* (Berlin: Hesse, 1935), 34: "...keine phantastische Felszack, sondern, wie in seinem Thüringer Waldland aus all den lieblich-wohligen Bergketten sich der Inselsberg als weithin beherrschender Gipfel gewaltig emporwölbt, um dann nach einer zweiten, noch immer stattlichen Bergreihe ins jenseitige rasch abzufallen."

10 Other Composers

Kirsten Beißwenger[†]

This chapter addresses the question of Bach's knowledge of the works of other composers, their influence on his own compositions, and the works he collected in his own personal music library.

When dealing with the question of the influence exerted by composers on another, several layers of inquiry need to be explored. First and foremost are the specific works studied at some point during the life of the composer. Sources for this information will be found in letters, journal entries, autobiography, or other similar documents written by the composer. Where such direct statements cannot be found there is the possibility of discovering indirect information from contemporaries or family members. Then there are the composers with whom the composer in question studied at an early stage of his career, as a kind of apprenticeship, as well as the specific music these teachers commended to their pupil. A composer progressing through his career will encounter others who will influence his musical development, either personally or through their compositions. All of these avenues need to be explored. But perhaps the surest way to discover the influence of other composers upon another, in the absence of direct statements from the composer himself, is to investigate his library, the collection of musical scores, assembled either for performance or study, or, which is often the case, a mixture of both. However, few musical collections survive intact and only in a few rare cases are the performing and study scores of the former owner known and readily accessible.

When the specific question about the influence other composers exerted upon Johann Sebastian Bach is addressed, an impressive image of his engagement with other composers emerges, despite the paucity of actual source documents. There are no statements by Bach himself about his teachers or about exchanges with other composers that would reveal his study interests in the music of others. His son, Carl Philipp Emanuel Bach, supplied the first references to this issue in the Obituary, drafted jointly with Johann Friedrich Agricola,[1] which was later expanded in his correspondence with Johann Nikolaus Forkel who was at work

---

1 Dok 3: 81–82 (No. 666).

---

† Deceased.

238   *Kirsten Beißwenger*

on his study of Bach's life and works.[2] These statements refer to the composers whom Bach "loved and studied" during his years of apprenticeship, but also to those of his contemporaries whom he held in the highest esteem. These statements are complemented by various source documents of his life, especially his early years. But Bach's own music reveals in no small measure which composers he studied and who thus exerted an influence upon him. This is particularly the case when specific works of these other composers were either the foundation of his own compositions or when he arranged their works.

Ultimately, the evidence of the influence of other composers will be primarily found in the surviving remnants of Bach's music library. But there is the secondary evidence of musical materials that he encountered, either at the direction of his teachers or through his own curiosity. Thus transcriptions he made as a pupil should be accorded a high priority, because they may well be traced back to models in his library.

The possible ways of answering the question of the influence of other composers on Johann Sebastian Bach are presented in this chapter. The starting point is Bach's music library, because it contained the compositions that Bach assembled and possessed. In the reconstruction of this music library works that are indirectly attributed to his collection are to be included because they were clearly known to Bach since he used them as models for his own compositions.

Johann Sebastian Bach's Music Library

To speak of Johann Sebastian Bach's music library today, one must be aware of the fact that this collection of music has not been transmitted intact. Its holdings were—like Bach's own works—divided among family members outside official inheritance regulations.[3] Because there is no estate inventory or similar catalog, the reconstruction of the library is dependent on various established pieces of information that establish specific works to the collection. Evidence is only accepted as authentic if a work in question is preserved in a source in Bach's hand and has passed through a chain of provenance that can be traced back to the Bach household. Similarly, attribution to his library is likewise confirmed when the source was copied by a family member at a point in which the copyist lived in the Bach household. In these cases, the line of provenance of the source gives definitive information that the source actually descended from the collection of the cantor of St. Thomas. Finally, several works are counted among this collection when their inclusion is confirmed by reliable evidence, even though today the actual copies are no longer extant.

Following Wilhelm Rust's first listing of works from Bach's music library, in connection with questions concerning authenticity,[4] and Christoph Wolff's

---

2 Dok 3: 288–289 (No. 803); also Dok 3: 292 (No. 807).

3 Dok 2: 490–498 (No. 627); NBR 250–256 (No. 279): *Die Specificatio der Verlaßenschafft des am 28. July. 1750 seelig verstorbenen Herrn Johann Sebastian Bachs.* The inventory lists only household objects, instruments and the religious books in Bach's library.

4 BG XI/1, foreword, xivf.

Other Composers 239

catalog of the Latin church music in Bach's library,[5] my 1992 dissertation recorded all the works of Bach's library known at that time.[6] There were 113 works or collections of works that, based on source studies, were able to be assigned as secure attributions. An extensive discussion preceded construction of the catalog, in which all theses and hypotheses posited in the 150-year history of Bach research were scrutinized with the aim of deciding whether a work should be attributed to the library or excluded.[7] The works confirmed by source studies are registered in the first part of my catalog of the music library.

Besides these holdings in the Bach music library that are confirmed by source studies, many additional works can be attributed to the library in other ways. Several compositions located in this chapter are rich in information for our inquiry. These are the compositions by others that Bach took as the basis for his adaptations. First and foremost are his works that adapt concertos by Alessandro and Benedetto Marcello, Guiseppe Torelli, Georg Philipp Telemann, and Antonio Vivaldi in the concertos for organ or harpsichord (BWV 592–596 and BWV 972–987), as well as the *Hortus musicus* by Johann Adam Reinken (model for the fugues BWV 954, 965/2, 966/2), the trio in b minor from Opus 3 by Arcangelo Corelli (model for the fugue BWV 579), or the trios in A major, b minor and B major from Opus 1 of Tomaso Albinoni (model for the fugues BWV 946, 950, 951).

An indirect attribution of a work to Bach's music collection can be given when a composition exists in a transcription by a pupil, under the assumption that the copy was prepared while the teacher-pupil relationship was active. Because Bach's pupils seem to have had free access to the music cabinet of his teacher,[8] the copy would most likely have been produced from a manuscript in Bach's possession. Another way works can be indirectly attributed to Bach's music library is by consulting the compositions that Bach sold on commission; exemplars of such works were therefore accessible in his private collection. Finally, also included in the reconstruction of the library are those works that were mistakenly transmitted under his name when they came into other hands via his estate or that of his heirs. Such a case exists, for example, in some of the compositions in the possession of the Breitkopf printing house: many works, especially cantatas and Latin church music, were associated with the name Bach, and it is clear that many of the attributions to Bach were made under the assumption that the works must have been his, since the sources were previously owned by the Bach family.[9]

Even though it is not possible to illustrate here every single example by which a work can be indirectly attributed to the Bach music collection, nevertheless it is necessary to recognize the complexities of such reconstruction.

---

5 Wolff St. ant, 159–162.
6 Beißwenger BNB.
7 See Beißwenger BNB, esp. 19–43.
8 See Kirsten Beißwenger, "Erwerbsmethoden von Musikalien im frühen 18. Jahrhundert am Beispiel Johann Sebastian Bachs und Johann Gottfried Walthers," *Fontes* 45 (1998): 240–242.
9 Beißwenger BNB, 71–78.

240   *Kirsten Beißwenger*

Inventory of Works in the Bach Music Library

The fragment of Bach's music library that survives today is the product of chance because the transmission of these sources was neither systematic nor deliberate on the part of successive owners, even owners from within the family circle. Nevertheless, the surviving remnant supplies representative examples of music with which Bach was engaged over the course of his life. With the exception of opera and oratorio, the essential genres of vocal and instrumental music by predecessors, contemporaries, and younger colleagues of the three most important musical nations—Germany, France and Italy—have survived. In the past two decades, it has become increasingly evident that only a provisional assessment of the inventory of works could have been assembled in the catalog of Bach's library in my 1992 dissertation, because several discoveries of works that can be assigned to his library have since appeared. These not only expand the existing picture with regard to repertory, but also present new insight into Bach's engagement with particular genres in detail, and as a consequence lead in part to some surprising discoveries. In order to be able to integrate these discoveries into the complete overview of Bach's study of works by other composers, these works along with information about their sources are briefly presented here. In the compilation that follows, some compositions already known are also included since new information has been forthcoming.

Newly Discovered Works and New Insights into Known Works from Bach's Music Library

Antonio Biffi, cantata *Amante moribondo* (Fragment)
  Transmission: from Bach's library: D-B Mus. ms. 1812, contains only recitative with cavatina, movement 1, and aria, movement 2, mm. 1–9, in a copy by JSB before 1712.
  Notes: Copy by JSB with shortening of figures in contrapuntal excerpts of the composition. In the surviving parts, the work is composed for soprano and basso continuo.
  Literature: Peter Wollny, "Neue Bach-Funde," BJ 83 (1997): 7–20.

Dietrich Buxtehude, chorale prelude *Nun freut euch, lieben Christen g'mein* (BuxWV 210).
  Transmission: from Bach's library?: D-WRa fol. 49/11, tablature transcription in unknown hand (JSB?)
  Notes: Copy passed down together with the chorale prelude *An Wasserflüssen Babylon* by J. A. Reinken, which has a colophon in JSB's hand. It is thus confirmed that the Reinken copy was in the possession of JSB, at least temporarily, and along with it the copy of Buxtehude's chorale prelude. According to the study of the script by Maul and Wollny, the copy is supposed to have been prepared by JSB, namely in Ohrdruf in 1698/99, thus in a period from which no written documents by Bach heretofore are known.

Other Composers 241

Whether, however, Bach is the copyist of the source is not certain from the research conducted to date. Additional pages in the tablature contain works by Pachelbel (copyist: Anonymous M 1 = Johann Martin Schubart?).
Literature: Martin Staehelin, "Beweis oder Vermutung? Zur Publikation der Bach zugeschriebenen Weimarer Orgeltabulaturblätter," Mf 61 (2008): 319–329; Michael Maul and Wollny, "Replik," Mf 62 (2009): 37; Martin Staehelin, "Duplik," Mf 62 (2009): 150–151; Michael Maul and Peter Wollny, "The Weimarer Organ Tablature," UB 3 (2008): 67–74.

François Couperin, Allemande for two keyboards from the *Second Livre des Pièces de Clavecin*, Paris: author [1717].
Transmission: from a print in Bach's library? D-B Mus. ms. 4222, copy in the hand of C. P. E. Bach, ca. 1729/30; additional sources: D-B Mus. ms. 4222/3, D-B SA 3916 (copy by Johann Friedrich Hering).
Notes: Copy of the young C. P. E. Bach, probably from a print in his father's library. This source is therefore a second piece that now exists from the *Second Livre des Pièces de Clavecin* by Couperin that was copied by a member of Bach's household. Before this discovery only the copy of a rondeau made by Anna Magdalena Bach, dated between 1725 and 1734, was known, which is found in her notebook (D-B Mus. ms. Bach P 225, 46–48). As a consequence, it is strongly assumed that Bach possessed an exemplar of the print.
Literature: Peter Wollny, "Zur Rezeption französischer Cembalo-Musik im Hause Bach in den 1730er Jahren: Zwei neu aufgefundene Quellen," *In organo pleno: Festschrift für Jean-Claude Zehnder zum 65. Geburtstag*, ed., Luigi Collarille and Alexandra Nigito (Frankfurt: Lang, 2007), 265–270.

François Couperin, *L'Impériale*, Sonata no. 3 from *Les Nations Sonades; et Suites de Simphonies en Trio... Paris, auteur, Boivin, 1726*
Transmission: from Bach's library: no recorded sources; additional sources: D-Dl Mus. 2162-Q-2, copy of an early version of the sonata entitled *La Convalescente. Sonnade. Del S. Couprin* in the hand of Johann Georg Pisendel.
Notes: The fourth movement of the sonata is the model for Bach's aria in F major for organ (BWV 587). Bach evidentially did not use the 1726 imprint as a model for the setting, but rather he seems to have had access to the manuscript source of the work mentioned previously, which Pisendel possibly had brought back on his journey from Paris to Saxony (May to October 1714). The fourth movement—designated *Légèrement* in the print version of 1726—appears here as the fifth movement entitled *Air gracieusement* and Bach's setting corresponds in the musical structure, a regular arch-form, to this version. Owing to the discovery of this source it is conceivable that Bach undertook the setting as early as his time in Weimar, contemporaneous with the decline during this period in concerto settings (BWV 592–596 and 972–987).

242 *Kirsten Beißwenger*

Literature: Kersten Delang, "Couperin - Pisendel - Bach. Überlegungen zur Echtheit und Datierung des Trios BWV 587 anhand eines Quellenfundes in der Sächsischen Landesbibliothek - Staats- und Universitätsbibliothek Dresden," BJ 93 (2007): 197–204.

Johann Pachelbel, chorale prelude *An Wasserflüssen Babylon*, *Kyrie Gott Vater in Ewigkeit*, *Fuga*
Transmission: From Bach's library or after a model from Bach's library?: D-WRa fol. 49/11, tablature transcription in the hand of Anonymous M 1 (Johann Martin Schubart?)
Notes: The tablature transcription is included with the chorale setting *An Wasserflüssen Babylon* by J. A. Reinken, the copy that bears a colophon in JSB's hand, which indicates that it was a former possession of Bach. Pachelbel's works were transcribed by Bach's copyist Anonymous M 1. That the copyist might be identified with Bach's pupil Schubart is plausible, since as a pupil he had access to the manuscripts in Bach's music cabinet.
Literature: See under Couperin, Allemande.

Giovanni Pierluigi da Palestrina, Missa *Ecce sacerdos manos* for SATB
Transmission: from Bach's library: D-B collection of the Sing-Akademie SA 424ZC 629, set of parts in the hands of JSB and Johann Christoph Altnickol, prepared around 1745.
Notes: The vocal parts written out by Altnickol encompass the entire Mass with the exception of the Agnus Dei III; a "Fondament" voice likewise prepared by Altnickol contains only the sections Kyrie – Christe – Kyrie. In JSB's hand are a fragmentary part for oboe I (which breaks off in the Gloria, m. 31) and the title page. The set of parts leaves behind the impression that it was never fully completed, for various reasons: the thoroughbass part does not include the short Protestant Mass requisite for worship at Leipzig, consisting of the Kyrie and Gloria. The fragmentary oboe voice suggests that an additional Mass was planned, in which instrumental scoring doubled the vocal lines.
Literature: Barbara Wiermann, "Bach und Palestrina. Neue Quellen aus Johann Sebastian Bachs Notenbibliothek," BJ 88 (2002): 9–14.

Giovanni Pierluigi da Palestrina, first book of masses, 4th edition: *Missarum liber primus cum quatuor, quinque, ac sex vocibus, liber primus* (Rome: Gardano, 1591) (Missa *Ecce sacerdos magnus*, Missa [*sine nomine*] à 6, Missa *O Regem coeli*, Missa *Virtute magna*, Missa *Gabriel Archangelus*, Missa *Ad coenam agni providi*, Missa *Pro defunctis*).
Transmission: from Bach's library: D-B Mus. ms. 16695, score copy of the mass book in largely incomplete transcription by an unknown hand with autographed addendum by JSB to the title of the Missa [*sine nomine*], around 1745.
Notes: The score was the copying model for Bach's transcription of the Missa *Ecce sacerdos magnus* as well as for the Missa *Sine nomine*. They originally belonged to Johann Gottfried Walther's collection of music, from which Bach may have obtained them during his Weimar years.
Literature: Wiermann, "Bach und Palestrina," 14–28.

Other Composers   243

Marco Gioseppe Peranda, Missa in a (Kyrie and Gloria) for SSATTB, V, I, II, Va I-III, bassoon, and basso continuo.

Transmission: sources from Bach's library: D-B Mus. ms. 17079/11, set of parts only for the Kyrie from the hand of JSB during the Weimar period, between 1714 and 1717; additional sources: D-B Mus. ms. 30098/6, score by unknown hand from the first half of the eighteenth century? (model for Bach's copied parts?), D-B Mus. ms. 17079/12, set of parts from the nineteenth century of the Kyrie and Gloria by a copyist for the Voss collection with variant instrumental setting.

Notes: As with the Kyrie in C by Peranda, which survives in copyist's transcription from Bach's music library, Bach apparently was interested only in the Kyrie of the Mass; dated between 1714 and 1717 in Weimar. The title page of the parts in the hand of the later owner, Breitkopf, however, alludes in its wording, "Missa Kyrie cum Gloria...," to the former existence of parts for the Gloria. It eludes our knowledge whether Bach also wrote out parts for the Gloria in Weimar at the same time as the Kyrie, which parts later went missing. Wollny considers the score by unknown hand D-B Mus. ms. 30098/6, which indeed contains no entries by Bach, to be the model for Bach's copied parts, but this without citing text-critical evidence that would prove this dependency. According to Wollny, Bach should have altered the textual underlay extensively while copying, changed major thirds to minor thirds at cadences of the provided model, and written out trill signs.[10]

Literature: Peter Wollny, *Marco Gioseppe Peranda, Missa in a* (Stuttgart: Carus 2000).

Jean Philippe Rameau, *Nouvelles Suites de Pieces de Clavecin*, Paris: Roussel 1729/30.

Transmission: after a model from Bach's library? D-B Mus. Ms. 18106, copy by Johann Friedrich Agricola, ca. 1738.

Notes: complete copy of the book of suites possibly after a model from Bach's library.

Literature: Wollny, "Zur Rezeption französischer Cembalo-Musik," 271–272.

Johann Adam Reinken, chorale prelude *An Wasserflüssen Babylon*.

Transmission: from Bach's library: D-WRa fol. 49/11, copy in an unknown hand (JSB?) with a colophon in the hand of JSB.

---

10   This is not the place to explore a discussion about the dependency of the two sources, in which such considerations would receive a secure text-critical basis. It should be briefly observed, however, that in addition to a few corrections in Bach's copy of the parts (which indicates that the parts were copied from the score), there are many deviations in the notation of both sources that seem to render such a dependency as at least debatable. It is at any rate very risky to attribute all correction-free differences in voice leading or beaming of eighth notes (instead of a flagged eighth-note notation as is common in the score) to Bach's role as copyist. The text-setting as adduction of an outstanding act of editing is problematic in this respect, because the score is not always completely texted. Thus anyone preparing a copy of parts from this model would need to proceed independently. A detailed analysis of the sources would be necessary in order to gain clarity for this set of questions.

244 *Kirsten Beißwenger*

Notes: The copy exhibits a colophon at the end in the hand of JSB, with the inscription, "Il Fine / â Dom: Georg Böhme / descriptum ao. 1700 Lunaburgi." By this it is confirmed that the Reinken copy was in the possession, at least temporarily, of JSB. According to Maul/Wollny's examination of the script the copy is taken to have been prepared by JSB, namely in Lüneburg in 1700, thus in a period from which no written documents by Bach heretofore are known. Whether, however, Bach is the copyist of the source is not determined with certainty from the research conducted to date. Additional pages in the tablature contain works by Pachelbel (copyist: Anonymous M 1 = Johann Martin Schubart?) and the chorale prelude *Nun freut euch lieben Christen g'mein* by Buxtehude.
Literature: See under Couperin, Allemande, above.

Gottfried Heinrich Stölzel, cantatas for the thirteenth to nineteenth Sundays after Trinity and for the Feast of St. Michael, from the Jahrgang of cantata libretti, *Das Saiten-Spiel des Hertzens, am Tage des Herrn, oder Sonn- und Fest-tägliche Cantaten*, by Benjamin Schmolck (Breslau: Rohrlach, 1727).

Transmission: from Bach's library: no sources recorded; additional sources: D-HAu 76 L 1034, printed libretti from Leipzig from the collection of Balthasar Hoffman, later rector of the Merseburger Gymnasium, containing the cantata texts for the thirteenth to sixteenth Sundays after Trinity, bound in Hoffmann's collection of printed cantata texts from Merseburg for the liturgical year 1734/35; D-LEm I B 2e, undated libretti from the archive of St. Nicholas Church in Leipzig, containing the texts of four cantatas for the Feast of St. Michael and the seventeenth to nineteenth Sundays after Trinity.
Notes: Both printed libretti books, without title pages, contain the texts of the respective cantatas. Pagination, contents and graphic design prove that both booklets are to be considered chronologically as consecutive libretti. Based on the classification in the liturgical year of 1734/35 at Merseburg by Hoffmann, the performances can be dated to 1735. The libretti from Benjamin Schmolck's *Saiten-Spiel* are expanded and divided in Stölzel's cantatas for Gotha by the use of chorale stanzas. It is conceivable that Bach may have performed the complete Jahrgang in Leipzig.
Literature: Marc-Roderich Pfau, "Ein unbekanntes Leipziger Kantatenheft aus dem Jahr 1735," BJ 94 (2008): 99–122; Peter Wollny, "'Bekennen will ich seinen Namen': Authentizität, Bestimmung und Kontext der Arie BWV 200. Anmerkungen zu Johann Sebastian Bachs Rezeption von Werken Gottfried Heinrich Stölzels," BJ 94 (2008): 137–146.

Gottfried Heinrich Stölzel, cantata Jahrgang *Das Namen-Buch Christi und der Christen, zu Heiliger Erbauung hiebevor in einem Jahr-Gange eröffnet* by Benjamin Schmolck (Breslau: Rohrlach, 1731).

Other Composers   245

Transmission: no sources recorded from Bach's library; additional sources: D-SHs.

Notes: Although no sources in Bach's possession have survived, two title pages, without author inscription, written by JSB (D-B P 1230 und P 1130), for cantatas *à 4 Voci e 4 Stromenti*, possibly indicate previously existing performance materials from this Jahrgang in Bach's music collection. The scoring for the two cantatas for the fifth and sixth Sundays after Trinity corresponds to the setting of the entire Jahrgang (excluded are the festive settings of the cantatas for the first day of Christmas and for the first day of Easter). Stölzel's Jahrgang originated in Gotha in 1731/32, and the Bach title pages are dateable 1732–1735.

Literature: Andreas Glöckner, "Ein weiterer Kantatenjahrgang Gottfried Heinrich Stölzels in Bachs Aufführungsrepertoire?" BJ 95 (2009): 95–115.

Gottfried Heinrich Stölzel, Passion oratorio, *Ein Lämmlein geht und trägt die Schuld.*

Transmission: no sources recorded from Bach's library; additional sources: RUS-SPsc 6.46.9.47, libretto entitled *Der Gläubigen Seele Geistliche Betrachtungen Ihres leidenden Jesu So am Charfreytage, vor und nach der Vesper-Predigt in der Kirche zu St. Thomae musiciret worden. Leipzig 1734.*

Notes: Bach performed the Passion oratorio by Stölzel in St. Thomas Church on Good Friday in 1734. This is the first Passion that Stölzel composed as Capellmeister at Gotha, performed in 1720. A copy of this Passion oratorio, which potentially originated from Bach's time as cantor of St. Thomas, was in the holdings of the library of St. Thomas School until 1945. Bach's aria *Bekennen will ich seinen Namen* (BWV 200; D-B N. Mus. ms. 307), is an arrangement from a movement in Stölzel's Passion oratorio, the aria of the Faithful Soul, "Dein Kreuz, o Bräutigam meiner Seelen," for tenor, oboe, violin, bassoon, and basso continuo. The adaptation was completed in 1742.

Literature: Tatjana Schabalina, "'Texte zur Music' in Sankt Petersburg Neue Quellen zur Leipziger Musikgeschichte sowie zur Kompositions- und Aufführungstätigkeit Johann Sebastian Bachs," BJ 94 (2008): 77–84; Wollny, "'Bekennen will ich seinen Namen,'" 125–136.

Gottfried Heinrich Stölzel, aria for soprano and basso continuo *Bist du bei mir* from the opera *Diomedes oder die triumphierende Unschuld.*

Transmission: sources from Bach's library: D-B P 225, 75 and 78, Klavierbüchlein for Anna Magdalena Bach, inscribed by AMB herself; additional sources: D-B, collection of the Sing-Akademie SA 8087. Libretto: D-Bhu, Musiksammlung, 47/LR 53 500 B 361.

Notes: The aria—at least its text—comes from Stölzel's opera, *Diomedes oder die triumphierende Unschuld*, which is known from the opera libretto originating in Bayreuth. The occasion was a performance given on the fortieth birthday of the Margrave Georg Wilhelm, celebrated on November 16, 1718, "Auf dem großen Theater zu Bayreuth." The music of the opera

246 *Kirsten Beißwenger*

is lost. Individual arias, including *Bist du bei mir*, are found in the aria collection of the holdings of the Sing-Akademie in Berlin.

Literature: Andreas Glöckner, "Neues zum Thema Bach und die Oper seiner Zeit," BJ 88 (2002): 172–174; LBB 8 (2006): 157.

Silvius Leopold Weiss, lute suite in A major.

Transmission: sources from Bach's library: none recorded; additional sources: D-Dl Mus 2841-V-1, "*Suonata del Sigre. S. L. Weiß*" with movements Entree, Courante, Rondeau, Sarabande, Menuet, Allegro. Lute tablature, written by unknown copyist.

Notes: The lute suite is the model for the harpsichord part in movements 2–6 of the Trio in A for violin and harpsichord (BWV 1025; D-B P 226). The harpsichord part represents an overall faithful transcription of the lute solos. The closing section of the fantasia, movement 1, shows a relationship to the prelude for lute, held in Wrocław, Diözesanarchiv Mf 2002. Whether this represents a piece by Weiss and is the basis of the Bach adaptation remains uncertain at present. The dating of the setting is unknown; the harpsichord part partially written by JSB in P 226 perhaps indicates 1746/47.

Literature: Christoph Wolff, "Das Trio A-Dur BWV 1025: Eine Lautensuite von Silvius Leopold Weiss bearbeitet und erweitert von Johann Sebastian Bach," BJ 79 (1993): 47–67; Karl-Ernst Schröder, "Zum Trio A-Dur BWV 1025," BJ 81 (1995): 47–60.

Anon., Mass (Kyrie and Gloria) in e (Fragment).

Transmission: Source from Bach's library: D-MÜG Mus. ant. 374, copy in the hand of J. S. Bach ca. 1738/39.

Notes: Kyrie-Gloria Mass of an unknown composer copied in fragments.

Literature: Perter Wollny, "Zwei Bach-Funde in Mügeln. C. P. E. Bach, Picander und die Leipziger Kirchenmusik in 1730er Jahren," BJ 96 (2010): 114–116.

St. Mark Passion, Passion pastiche in various versions (formerly attributed to Reinhard Keiser).

Transmission: sources from Bach's library: D-B Mus. ms. 11471/1 (copy of parts, partially prepared in Weimar before 1712, partially in Leipzig in 1726), D-B N. Mus. ms. 468 (harpsichord part for the pastiche setting with insertions of arias from the Brockes Passion by Georg Friedrich Handel, prepared in Leipzig between 1743 and 1748), Thiele private collection (bassoon part of an aria from Handel's Brockes Passion, copied by JSB between 1743 and 1748); additional sources: D-B N. Mus. Ms. 10624, D-Gs Cod. Ms. Philos. 84^e: Keiser 1, D-B Mus. ms. 11471, printed text of a performance from 1707 in Hamburg cathedral: D-Hs A/70002.

Notes: Only in the copy of parts from Bach's library for the performance of 1726 is the St. Mark Passion ascribed to Reinhard Keiser; all other sources are without author inscriptions. Whether the work is actually by Keiser has been the subject of heavily debated research centered on stylistic issues. Due to the

Other Composers   247

printed text for a performance in the Hamburg cathedral it is assumed that the Passion originated in Hamburg. The work was performed by cathedral music director Friedrich Nicolaus Braun in 1707, which is made explicit from the title of the printed text: "...abgesungen von Friedr. Nicol. Brauns..." Because Reinhard Keiser is excluded as the composer, perhaps—if the attribution of Bach's set of parts bears influence in any way—another Keiser could have been the composer of the work. In that case the father of Reinhard—according to one hypothesis of Christine Blancken and Daniel R. Melamed—is the most likely possibility: Gottfried Keiser (ca. 1650–before 1732) sojourned in different places, and he was purportedly a fine composer. Alternatively, the composer could have been Reinhard's successor, "the erstwhile cantor at the cathedral, Friedrich Nicolaus Brauns... [who] composed many pieces of church music" (Johann Mattheson, *Grundlage einer Ehrenpforte* (Hamburg: Mattheson, 1740), 126). It is possible that the Passion was known in the Bach household as a work of Keiser's only by hearsay and that it was consequently erroneously ascribed to the most famous member of the family.

Literature: Daniel R. Melamed, *Hearing Bach's Passions* (Oxford: Oxford University Press, 2005), 81; Christine Blancken, CD booklet for the recording *Markus-Passion: Passions-Pasticcio mit Arien von Georg Friedrich Handel. Beararbeiter Johann Sebastian Bach*. St. Mauritius Kantorei Hardegsen, directed by Gerhard Ropeter (CD 080308).

Bach's Engagement with Works of Other Composers

In the letter to Forkel previously referred to, Carl Philipp Emanuel Bach mentions the names of composers that his father had studied: "besides Froberger, Kerl and Pachelbel, he heard and studied the works of Frescobaldi, the Baden Capell-meister Fischer, Strunck, some old and good Frenchmen, Buxtehude, Reincken, Bruhns, the Lüneburg organist Böhm."[11] With these words the son established the parameters surrounding the influence of practical composers whom he additionally designated as strong writers of fugues ("starcke Fugisten").

It is assumed that Bach copied works of all the composers whom he had studied in his years of apprenticeship. Until a few years ago, it was in large part an exercise in speculation in order to establish the repertory with which Bach was familiar during these formative years. The earliest composite manuscripts with organ works permit inferences to be drawn from the broad circle of music that surrounded the young Bach. The first independently arranged collection of works by Johann Pachelbel, Johann Caspar Kerl and Johann Jacob Froberger, which Bach copied at night by moonlight in the home of his brother, Johann Christoph, is lost,[12] as is original manuscript that he copied from. It is most likely, however, that the repertory of this collection is revealed in the surviving tablature

---

11   NBR 398 (No. 395); Dok 3: 288 (No. 803). C. P. E. Bach crossed out "his Lüneburg teacher Böhm" and replaced it with "the Lüneburg organist Böhm"; see also *The Letters of C. P. E. Bach*, trans. and ed. Stephen L Clark (Oxford: Clarendon, 1997), 73.

12   Dok 3: 81f (No. 666): NBR 299 (No. 306).

248   *Kirsten Beißwenger*

book (1692) of Valentin Eckelt, who, like Johann Christoph Bach, was a pupil of Pachelbel.[13] Much more extensive, however, are the two anthologies with music for keyboard arranged by Johann Christoph Bach well after 1700, the Möller Manuscript (Mö) and the Andreas Bach Book (ABB),[14] with works by northern, central, and southern German composers as well as by representatives from Italy and France: Georg Böhm, Dietrich Buxtehude, Johann Caspar Ferdinand Fischer, Peter Heidorn, Johann Kuhnau, Johann Adam Reinken, Tomaso Albinoni, Agostino Steffani, Nicolas Antoine Le Bègue, Jean-Baptiste Lully, und Marin Marais.[15] The copy of Buxtehude's Prelude and Fugue in g minor (BuxWV 148), passed down as a single leaf in the hand of Johann Christoph Bach (also includes an unknown secondary copyist), is one of the few but very important sources known to have circulated in the environment of the young Bach. A precise dating of the source is not possible, but must have originated—according to Schulze— before both great anthologies.[16]

Only in the most recent times has a source been identified that enables a direct glimpse into this repertory in Bach's music library. Michael Maul and Peter Wollny discovered in the Anna Amalia Library, Weimar, the "Weimarer Orgeltabulatur," four pages of organ tablature with works by Reinken, Buxtehude and Pachelbel. According to the research of Maul and Wollny, the copies of Reinken's *An Wasserflüssen Babylon* and Buxtehude's *Nun freut euch lieben Christen gmein* are the earliest musical manuscripts of Bach,[17] but the status of the copyist in the ensuing discussion has not met with entire agreement.[18] For our connection the question of copyist is, however, secondary. Crucial is the colophon beneath the transcription of the Reinken piece, the inscription, "Il Fine / â Dom. Georg: Böhme / descriptum ao. 1700 Lunaburgi." This confirms that

---

13 On the repertory of this manuscript, Pl-Kj Mus. ms. 40035, see Christoph Wolff, "Johann Valentin Eckelts Tabulaturbuch von 1692," *Festschrift Martin Ruhnke zum 65. Geburtstag*, ed. Mitarbeitern des Instituts für Musikwssenschaft der Universität Erlangen-Nürnberg (Stuttgart: Hänssler 1986), 374–386.

14 Möller manuscript, D-B Mus. ms. 40644; Andreas Bach Book D-LEm, Sammlung Becker III.8.4.

15 See Schulze, 41–45; Robert Stephen Hill, "The Möller Manuscript and the Andreas Bach Book: Two Keybord Anthologies from the Circle of the Young Johann Sebastian Bach," PhD diss. (Harvard University, 1987).

16 Hans-Joachim Schulze, "Bach und Buxtehude: Eine wenig beachtete Quelle in der Carnegie Library zu Pittsburgh/PA," BJ 77 (1991): 177–181. Dating is difficult, since the first entries in both anthologies (Mö and ABB) are not clear. Schulze surmises "hardly before 1705" (Schulze, ibid., 178), and Wolff gives the beginning as "around 1700" (Wolff BLM, 50).

17 Peter Wollny and Michael Maul, eds., *Weimarer Orgeltabulatur. Die frühesten Notenhandschriften Johann Sebastian Bachs sowie Abschriften seines Schülers Johann Martin Schubart. Mit Werken von Dietrich Buxtehude, Johann Adam Reinken und Johann Pachelbel* (Kassel: Bärenreiter 2007), xxi.

18 Martin Staehelin, "Beweis oder Vermutung? Zur Publikation der Bach zugeschriebenen Weimarer Tabulaturblätter," Mf 61 (2008): 319–329; see also the reply by Maul/Wollny in Mf 62 (2009), 37, and Staehelin's rejoinder, Mf 62 (2009): 150–151.

Other Composers 249

the manuscript—comprising both Reinken and Buxtehude pieces—was at least temporarily located in the possession of Bach.[19]

The works by Pachelbel—the chorale prelude *An Wasserflüssen Babylon*, and *Kyrie Gott Vater in Ewigkeit*, and a *Fuga*—are transmitted in transcriptions of the Bach copyist Anonymous M 1. This copyist may be either Bach's spouse Maria Barbara or his pupil Johann Martin Schubart.[20] A definitive clarification of this question of copyist, contrary to the opinion of Maul/Wollny, is not yet possible, despite the discovery of the "Weimarer Tabuatur," because there are no written documents clearly signed by either Maria Barbara or by Schubart. This source also provides no new insights. Its line of provenance cannot be traced back into the eighteenth century, so that nothing can be clarified about the way in which it passed into the possession of the library at Weimar.[21] That this manuscript is an example of organ tablature, copied more likely by a prospective organist than by a spouse, indicates that there is rather, in connection with identifying the copyist, more to think about Schubart than about Maria Barbara. According to the study of the handwriting by Maul and Wollny, the two pages ought to have originated around 1707/08 or 1708/09 respectively, thus to a period in which Schubart was Bach's pupil.[22] Assuming that Anonymous M 1 is indeed identical with Schubart, it could be that he prepared the copy based on originals in the musical resources of his teacher. In Mühlhausen we know, through his petition for release in 1708, that he had been collecting music: "[I] have acquired from far and wide, not without cost, a good store of the choicest church compositions..."[23] Other than these examples, there is no specific information of the extent or scope of Bach's knowledge of the works of other composers during his years in Arnstadt and Mühlhausen, materials that might well have been more a matter of performance material than of study scores. Evidence for the wide-ranging transmission of works of other composers dates from Bach's Weimar years. Here the variety that is altogether symptomatic of Bach's music library in later years is already apparent. Alongside works for organ and harpsichord and settings for instrumental ensembles, both German and Latin sacred musical works are found in his inventory, as well as Latin and Italian chamber cantatas. As for Bach's copies of collections of organ works only the *Premier Livre d'Orgue* by Nicolas de Grigny is represented, consisting of an organ mass and five hymns, but there are other works for organ identifiable among the indirectly classifiable works of the library. A copy of the *Fiori musicali* of Frescobaldi with, according to Spitta, the signature "J. S. Bach 1714" in Bach's own hand is no longer extant.[24] Similarly, according to Johann Abraham Birnbaum, Bach possibly also owned at least one

---

19 Many questions remain unresolved or partially resolved concerning the identities of owners and scribes of the "Weimarer Tabulatur."

20 NBA IX/3.1, 1. In research the scribe was known heretofore as Anon. Weimar 1.

21 The earliest indication found in the catalog is traceable back to the 1840s.

22 Wollny/Maul, *Weimarer Orgeltabulatur*, xxiii.

23 NBR 57 (No. 32); Dok 1: 19.

24 Spitta 1: 418; Spitta ET 1: 420–421.

250   *Kirsten Beißwenger*

volume of the *Livre d'Orgue* of Pierre Du Mage (ca. 1676–1751).[25] A toccata and a passacaglia by Bernardo Pasquini were apparently copied by Bach, according to a remark made by Franz Hauser, as an addendum to the entry for BWV 536 in his thematic catalog: "Angehaengt von Bachs Hand: Toccata u. Passacaglia von Bernardo Pasquini."[26] As for copies made by pupils, probably from models in Bach's library, alongside the aforementioned Pachelbel transcription from Weimar in organ tablature also by Anonymous M 1, the toccata in G major by Dietrich Buxtehude (BuxWV 164), as well as the *Premier Livre d'Orgue* and the *Second Livre d'Orgue* by Jacques Boyvin (copyist Johann Caspar Vogler between 1710 and 1715) survive.

Music for harpsichord is only represented by works of French clavecinists. Bach demonstrably transcribed the *Six Suittes de Clavessin* by François Dieupart[27] (after 1667–1740) for himself between 1709 and 1712, and dating from the same period is his copy of the table of ornaments from the *Pièces de Clavecin* by Jean Henri d'Anglebert (1628–1691), that had appeared in 1689 and are among the classics of French suites of dance movements for harpsichord. That French music was a major point of study in Bach's Weimar period is reinforced also by the aria in F major for organ (BWV 587)—though indeed controversial regarding its authenticity—an adaptation of the fourth movement of the third sonata *L'Impériale* from the publication *Les Nations. Sonades et Suites de Simphonies en Trio* (Paris, 1726) by François Couperin. Bach used an early version for his adaptation of this trio sonata, which he almost certainly received via the concertmaster of Dresden, Johann Georg Pisendel, on his return from Paris in 1714, when he stayed at Buttelstedt, near Weimar, on 15 October. It is possible that Bach availed himself of the opportunity to renew his acquaintance with Pisendel, which had ended in 1709, and thereby review the musical treasure that had been brought along from Paris.[28]

Bach did not confine himself to French instrumental music, however, but also explored Italian works. Alongside the transcription of a concerto for two solo violins, strings and basso continuo by Georg Philipp Telemann, dated ca. 1709, around the same time Bach copied the *Concerto a cinque* from Tomaso Albinoni's Op. 2 (BWV Anh. I 23).[29] Most traces of Bach's engagement with the Italian solo concerto lead to his concerto transcriptions for harpsichord or organ (BWV 592–596 and BWV 972–987) with works by Vivaldi (including several concertos from his pathbreaking *L'Estro armonico*, Op. 3), Torelli, as well as Alessandro and Benedetto Marcello. These concerto settings were less a matter of material

---

25   Dok 2: 304 (No. 409); NBR 346 (No. 344).
26   Yoshitake Kobayashi, "Franz Hauser und seine Bach-Handschriftensammlung," PhD diss. (Göttingen 1973), 233.
27   Beißwenger BNB, 280–282.
28   Kerstin Delang, "Couperin – Pisendel – Bach. Überlegungen zur Echtheit und Datierung des Trios BWV 587 anhand eines Quellenfundes in der Sächsischen Landesbibliothek – Staats- und Universitätsbibliothek Dresden," BJ 93 (2007): 197–204.
29   Op. 2, No. 2; only the continuo part is extant; see Schulze, 28.

Other Composers 251

for study than for performance, which is particularly apparent in Bach's choice of concertos by his pupil, Prince Johann Ernst of Saxony-Weimar, as models for such adaptations.

The concertos of Telemann are also counted among the models; the setting of the concerto in g minor for violin concertato, strings and basso continuo (BWV 985) is widely known, and yet another concerto by Telemann may be found among the settings. In the 20 March 1810 catalog of the auction house of Strigelius, Erfurt, is the following entry: "Telemann, Concerto appropriato all'organo di J. S. Bach, f-dur, geschr."[30]

It is difficult to assign a conclusive chronological sequence for Bach's fugues on the themes of others, because none of the works is found in autograph sources, although there are early copies in general that date from 1707–1713 and also extend into the late Weimar period. The same is true for the concerto settings which reveal the works that were encountered. The models consist of sonatas by Albinoni, namely the trio sonatas from his Op. 1 (BWV 946, 950, 951), from Corelli's Op. 3 (BWV 579), as well as the *Hortus musicus* of Reinken (BWV 954, 965, 966).[31] The fugue BWV 532 traces back not to a sonata but to a canzonetta, a short, simple and song-like piece. This fugue, dated by George B. Stauffer to 1708–1712,[32] could have been based on a fugue in D by Pachelbel, but the relationship between the theme of Buxtehude's canzonetta and BWV 532 is closer.[33]

Concerning the surviving vocal compositions from Bach's music library, there is no clear picture of the genres with which Bach was predominantly engaged during his Weimar years. However, the repertory does point to Bach's occupation with several sacred and secular works. Through the discoveries of the last two decades, the picture becomes even more complex and former propositions have become questionable. What is striking are the relatively numerous individual Kyrie compositions among the works of the Weimar period. Bach transcribed in score format the Kyrie of the Mass in A major by Johann Baal, a Franconian composer who was active between 1677 and 1685 as organist and composer at the court of the prince-bishop of Bamberg, and afterward joined the Benedictine order as a monk in Münsterschwarzach. All further movements in the score, from Gloria

---

30 *Verzeichnis von Musikalien und musikalischen Schriften nebst andern gebundenen Büchern aus allen Wissenschaften, welche den 20. März 1810 u. folg. Tage... in dem Strigelius'schen Hause... versteigert werden sollen. / Erfurt 1810*, 7 (No. 82); see Beißwenger BNB, 378–379.

31 While only "Weimar?" is stated for the dating of BWV 579, and BWV 946 and BWV 954 are examples of early works of uncertain date of origin, three fugues survive in the transcript of Johann Gottfried Walther, dated 1714–1717, namely the fugues BWV 951, 965, 966; see Kirsten Beißwenger, "Zur Chronologie der Notenhandschriften Johann Gottfried Walthers," *Acht kleine Präludien und Studien über BACH. Georg von Dadelsen zum 70. Geburtstag am 17. November 1988*, ed. Kollegium des Johann-Sebastian-Bach Instituts Göttingen (Wiesbaden: Breitkopf & Härtel 1992), 27. On Bach's engagement with Reinken, see Christoph Wolff, "Bach and Johann Adam Reinken: A Context for the Early Works," Wolff Essays, 56–71.

32 George B. Stauffer, "The Free Organ Preludes of Johann Sebastian Bach," PhD diss. (Columbia University, New York 1978), 147.

33 Beißwenger BNB, 51.

252 *Kirsten Beißwenger*

to Agnus Dei, in Bach's music library (D-B Mus. ms. 30091, No. 1) are in the hand of Johann Gottfried Walther.[34] While in Weimar Bach also copied the Kyrie of the *Missa San Lamberti*, published in *Jubilum missale sextuplex* (Augsburg 1706), by Johann Christoph Pez, the pupil of Kerll active in southern Germany, and Bach later completed the transcription, from the Gloria to Agnus Dei, in Leipzig in 1724.[35] Another transcription of a Kyrie in Bach's music library is that in C major by Marco Gioseffo Peranda, the Capellmeister of Dresden, which is in the hand of an unknown copyist (Anonymous W 1, D-B Mus. ms. 17079/10).[36] A further Kyrie composition of Peranda in Bach's hand was identified in 2000 by Peter Wollny (D-B Mus. ms. 17079/11).[37] It derives from the Mass in a, from which the Gloria was copied in other sources (see previous). If one were to ignore the Kyrie in C by Peranda, the copy of which is dated sometime around 1709 on the basis of its watermarks,[38] the chronological origin of copies of other Kyrie compositions lies between 1714 and 1717. Also to be included among these works is the anonymous Kyrie-Gloria Mass in c minor (BWV Anh. II 29, Pl-Kj St 547), which survives only in the violoncello part. It is therefore assumed that these works are to be connected with Bach's appointment as Concertmaster in Weimar in 1714 with the responsibility of performing new pieces monthly ("monatlich neüe Stücke uf[zu]führen").[39] It is conceivable that in addition to this assignment he was also required to perform Kyrie compositions in the worship of the court chapel. German composers, or Italians active in German-speaking regions, were particularly esteemed by Bach, another discovery of recent years that shows that Bach's interest in Latin church music was not limited to such works as he potentially needed for a performance repertory, but rather that he was already engaged during the Weimar period with compositions that were modeled on the irrefutable authority of the classical vocal polyphony of Giovanni Pierluigi da Palestrina. Among the Palestrina works in Bach's library, Barbara Wiermann discovered a transcribed score of the first book of masses (4th ed., Rom 1591, D-B Mus. ms. 16695), mostly of incomplete transcriptions. Bach received this score by an unknown copyist from the collection of Johann Gottfried Walther, which is an indication that Bach probably took possession of it during his time at Weimar.[40] This means that by this time he was already aware of the music of Palestrina, perhaps not yet for performance reasons, as it was in the 1740s, when he produced the set of parts for the *Missa sine nomine*, and the recently discovered incomplete set of parts for the *Missa Ecce Sacerdos Magnus*.[41] Rather, it was his interest in the

---

34 Beißwenger BNB, 228–229.
35 Beißwenger BNB, 308–309.
36 Beißwenger BNB, 306.
37 Marco Gioseppe Peranda, *Missa in a*, ed. Peter Wollny (Stuttgart: Carus 2000).
38 Beißwenger BNB, 63.
39 Dok 2: 53 (No. 66); NBR 70 (No. 51).
40 Barbara Wiermann, "Bach und Palestrina. Neue Quellen aus Johann Sebastian Bachs Notenbibliothek," BJ 88 (2002): 14ff.
41 Wiermann, "Bach und Palestrina," 9–14.

Other Composers 253

older style—like that of Walther—that arose out of music-theoretical curiosity and led him to secure scores of seven masses.

In contrast to masses, only scattered examples survive from other vocal genres. These include the St. Mark Passion, formerly ascribed to Reinhard Keiser and copied in 1711/12 or as early as 1710; the cantata *Auf Gott hoffe ich* by the Dresden Capellmeister, Johann Christoph Schmidt (1714–16);[42] as well as the Latin cantata *Languet anima mea* by Viennese court theorbist and later court composer Francesco Conti (Partiturabschrift, D-B Mus. ms. 30098, Nr. 7, original date of the source: 1716).[43] The repertory was enlarged with the recently discovered chamber cantata *Amante moribondo*, copied before 1712 and surviving in fragments, by Antonio Biffi, the pupil of Legrenzi active in Venice as *maestro de capella* at San Marco and *maestro di coro* at the Conservatorio dei Mendicanti.[44]

From the Cöthen period nothing survives except one set of parts of the Conti cantata (D-B Mus. ms. 4081). With regard to the number of vocal works, the picture changes with Bach's Leipzig period starting in 1723, compared to those of the Weimar years. Bach, from that time on cantor of the St. Thomas Church and *Director musices* of the city of Leipzig, managed his obligation of weekly performances of cantatas not only with the composition of separate cycles of church cantatas, but he also gathered works by other composers into the performance calendar. Thus in the first months of 1726 he turned to cantatas by his relative in Meiningen, Johann Ludwig Bach, together with at least one by Telemann, namely the cantata *Der Herr ist König* from 1724/25, a score transcribed by Bach's copyists.[45] The Advent cantata *Machet die Tore weit*, heard on 28 November 1734, is another Telemann cantata Bach performed.[46] It is open to speculation regarding the possibility of additional cantatas by Telemann used by Bach. Thus Wolf Hobohm argues that at least some of the texts he discovered in *Texten Zur Leipziger Kirchen Music* (1725) are to be identified with cantatas by Telemann.[47] The collection of cantatas by other composers in Bach's music library suggests that it was essentially compiled for performance rather than study. This conclusion is reinforced by the published cantata texts by Benjamin Schmolck, *Das Saiten-Spiel des Hertzens* (Breslau and Leipzig, 1720; with later reprints), which were set to

---

42 Beißwenger BNB, 311–312.
43 Beißwenger BNB, 278–279.
44 Peter Wollny, "Zwei Bach-Funde in Mügeln," 7–20.
45 Beißwenger BNB, 315–316 (*Thematisches Verzeichnis der Vokalwerke von George Philipp Telemann*, 2nd ed, ed. Werner Menke (Frankfurt: Klostermann, 1988 and 1995): 8:6.
46 Beißwenger BNB, 316–317 (TVWV 1:1074).
47 Among the texts, three are from the third Jahrgang by Erdmann Neumeister, *Geistliches Singen und Spielen. Das ist: Ein Jahrgang von Texten, welche ... in Eisenach musikalisch aufgeführt werden von Georg Philipp Telemann* (Gotha, 1711), which were demonstrably not set by Bach. Since the text Jahrgang had been written for Telemann, it is natural to assume—according to Hobohm—that the texts imply cantatas by Telemann. See Wolf Hobohm, "Neue 'Texte zur Leipziger Kirchen-Music,'" BJ 59 (1973): 5–32. For further consideration of Bach's ownership of Telemann's music, see Beißwenger BNB, 68–71.

254   *Kirsten Beißwenger*

music by the Gotha court Kapellmeister, Gottfried Heinrich Stölzel. Two Leipzig libretto booklets containing cantata texts for the thirteenth to nineteenth Sundays after Trinity, and for the Feast of St. Michael, attest to performances in Leipzig in 1735.[48] It is quite possible that the complete Jahrgang of the Schmolck/Stölzel cantatas was performed by Bach that year.[49] And perhaps the *Saiten-Spiel* Jahrgang was not the first group of Stölzel cantatas that Bach brought to Leipzig for the worship of the two principal churches. There is evidence to suggest that Bach also performed the *Nahmen-Buch* Jahrgang (1731/32) in Leipzig.[50] As discovered by Andreas Glöckner, Stölzel's *Nahmen-Buch* Jahrgang was at one time in the possession of the St. Thomas School in Leipzig (there until 1943), so that it is conceivable that, either complete or in part, these cantatas were sung during the time of Johann Sebastian Bach. Evidence for this supposition is found in two surviving individual title pages in Bach's hand that have neither composer nor work identification, but which conform in detail with cantatas in this cycle.

By 1726 Bach had already gathered a large number of compositions—larger than any other master—for the fulfillment of his official duty of the weekly Sunday cantata performances, that is, the cantatas of Johann Ludwig Bach. This therefore undergirds the hypotheses of Pfau, Wollny, and Glöckner with regard to Bach's performances of complete annual cycles by other composers in the 1730s, to augment the repertory of his own cantatas. But this is in apparent contrast to the claim he made to the Leipzig city council, 15 August 1736, that "the concerted pieces... performed by the First Choir... are my own compositions...."[51] With composers such as Johann Ludwig Bach, Stölzel and Telemann, Bach remained within the context of contemporaries of his immediate geographical and familial environment. A similar picture emerges when attention is turned to passions. The St. Mark Passion (BWV 247), copied during the Weimar period, underwent its first re-performance in Leipzig in 1726. The anonymous St. Luke Passion (BWV 246), long attributed to Bach, followed in 1730 as the next passion composition by another composer.[52] Both works were heard again in the middle 1740s, the St. Luke Passion with only one slight change—Bach inserted the chorus *Aus der Tiefen* (BWV 246/40a) as the

---

48   Concerning this see Marc-Roderich Pfau, "Ein unbekanntes Leipziger Kantatentextheft aus dem Jahr 1735," BJ 94 (2008): 99–122; and Peter Wollny, "'Bekennen will ich seinen Namen.' Authentizität, Bestimmung und Kontext der Arie BWV 200. Anmerkungen zu Johann Sebastian Bachs Rezeption von Werken Gottfried Heinrich Stölzels," BJ 94 (2008): 137–146.

49   Pfau, "Ein unbekanntes Leipziger Kantatentextheft," 113f.

50   *Benjamin Schmolckens Nahmen-Buch Christi und der Christen, zu heiliger Erbauung in einem Jahr-Gange eröffnet, und in Hochfürstl. Schloß-Capelle zum Friedenstein von Advent. 1731 bis dahin 1732. musicalisch aufgeführet. GOTHA, Druckts Johann Andreas Reyher, F. S. Hof-Buchdr.* Copy of the printed text in D-GOl, sig. Cant. Spir. 8° 176. See Andreas Glöckner, "Ein weiterer Kantatenjahrgang Gottfried Heinrich Stölzels in Bachs Aufführungsrepertore?" BJ 95 (2009): 95–115.

51   Dok I, 88 (No. 34); NBR, 176 (No. 183). The performance of the entire cycle by the second choir would not have been possible as this choir sang cantatas "only on Feast Days," ibid.

52   For discussions of research and authenticity, see NBA II/9, KB, 69–74 (Beißwenger).

Other Composers 255

closing movement of the first part[53]—and the St. Mark Passion with extensive revisions, since some of the arias were replaced with arias from the Brockes Passion by Handel, and other arias appended from works by Handel, with the result that the work experienced a considerable expansion.[54] In addition to both these oratorio passions with biblical texts, a copy of the Brockes Passion by Handel was known as well (D-B Mus. ms. 9002/10), a manuscript that Bach began himself in 1746/47, but completed, after August 1748, by Johann Nathanel Bammler (Hauptkopist H). Whether the copy of the score was prepared for performance evades our knowledge. However, two factors would seem to militate against the possibility. First, it is striking that it lacks the necessary reference to the division of the work into two parts, Part I being heard before the Vespers sermon, and Part II after it, on Good Friday in one of the two main churches. Second, a performance in Leipzig was highly improbable because the Brockes Passion replaced the biblical text with a poetic version of the passion narrative, something that was inadmissible for the conservative authorities in Leipzig. Whether Bach offered extra-liturgical presentations of passion music, in addition to the liturgical passion performances, there is no indication, but perhaps is something that should not be entirely ruled out.[55] Stölzel's passion oratorio, *Ein Lämmlein geht und trägt die Schuld*, first performed in 1720—Stölzel's first year as court Capellmeister in Gotha—was performed on 23 April 1734 in St. Thomas Church, as is evidenced by the recently discovered printed libretto.[56] Bach appears to have returned to Stölzel's passion in the 1740s, since around 1742 Bach adapted the aria of the faithful soul ("Gläubigen Seelen") for tenor, oboe, violin, bassoon, and basso continuo, "Dein Kreuz, o Bräutigam meiner Seelen," for alto, viola, violins I and II, and basso continuo, with a new text beginning: "Bekennen will ich seinen Namen" (D-B N. Mus. ms. 307).[57]

---

53 Yoshitake Kobayashi, "Zu einem neu entdeckten Autograph Bachs – Choral: Aus der Tiefen," BJ 57 (1971): 5–12.

54 NBA II/9, KB, 106–109 (Beißwenger).

55 Alfred Dürr, *Die Johannes-Passion von Johann Sebastian Bach* (Kassel: Bärenreiter, 1988), 144.

56 Tatjana Schabalina, "'Texte zur Music' in Sankt Petersburg. Neue Quellen zur Leipziger Musikgeschichte sowie zur Kompositions- und Aufführungstätigkeit Johann Sebastian Bachs," BJ 94 (2008): 77–84.

57 Wollny, "Bekennen will ich seinen Namen," 123–136. Beyond the passions firmly ascribed to Bach's performance and study repertory, two additional works are repeatedly considered in connection with the corpus of Bach's passion music: the passion cantata *Ein Lämmlein geht und trägt die Schuld* by Carl Heinrich Graun, in an expanded pastiche version, and *Das Selige Erwägen* by Georg Philipp Telemann (TVWV 2:5). Graun's passion cantata is in a score format transcribed by Altnickol and an unknown copyist (D-B *Mus. ms. 8155*). Here various enlargements are found, such as, among others: the introductory movement of the psalm cantata *Wer ist der, so von Edom kömmt* by Telemann (TVWV 1:1586) as the opening movement; the adapted first movement of Bach's cantata *Herr Jesu Christ, wahr' Mensch und Gott* (BWV 127) and the arioso definitely attributed to Bach *So heb ich denn mein Auge sehnlich auf* (BWV 1088) as the introduction to the second part. The interpolation of movements by Bach, as well as the provenance of the score from the direct milieu of Bach—additionally, a libretto (D-Gs *8° Cod. Ms. Philos. 84ᵉ Graun 3*)—survives in Thuringian Frankenhausen: a single performance of a largely identical pastiche version under the direction of Johann Wilhelm Cunis, confirmed

256 *Kirsten Beißwenger*

In contrast to cantatas and passions, many works of Latin figural music from Bach's music library remain extant. These possess—aside from the possibility that they were also performed[58]—much more the character of study than does the surviving repertory of cantatas. This connects with the fact that most of the copies date from the years 1732 to 1742 and thus stand in immediate proximity to Bach's own mass compositions: the Kyrie and Gloria, dedicated in 1733 to the Elector of Saxony, later incorporated into the B-minor mass (BWV 232), and the four so-called Lutheran masses (BWV 233–236), which date from the late 1730s. However, from the 1720s is the Gloria of the Mass by Pez from which Bach copied the Kyrie in Weimar.[59] In 1727, this was followed by the Mass *Allein Gott in der Höh sei Ehr* by Johann Ludwig Bach,[60] and between 1725 and 1729 the Mass in g minor by Johann Hugo von Wilderer (1671–1724),[61] Capellmeister at the court of the Electoral Palatinate in Düsseldorf. These composers were German, but the picture diametrically changes with copies of works made from the 1730s. Insofar as the composers can be identified, they are all Italian: Giovanni Battista Bassani (1647–1716), *maestro di cappella* at the cathedral in Ferrara, and after 1712 at Santa Maria Maggiore in Bergamo; Antonio Caldara (1670–1736), after various occupations in different Italian states, including Rome, deputy Capellmeister at the Viennese court; Francesco Durante (1684–1755), various responsibilities as teacher and Capellmeister in Naples; Antonio Lotti (1666–1740), organist and after 1736 *maestro di cappella* at San Marco in Venice, and from 1717 to 1719 on leave as visitor at the court in Dresden; and finally Giovanni Pierluigi da Palestrina, the past master of classical vocal polyphony. From Bassani Bach had

---

alumnus from 1741 to 1747, later cantor and music director of St. Thomas School. This points to the origin of the pastiche in the environment of Bach, but there is no longer evidence that would prove Bach's ownership and performance of Graun's work (NBA I/41, KB, 56–66). Until 1943, the collection of the St. Thomas School in Leipzig contained an additional score copy of Graun's passion cantata, in which entries by Bach were to have been found, according to Carl Hermann Bitter (see NBA I/41, KB, 58f.). More recently Peter Wollny has brought *Das Selige Erwägen* by Telemann – in a copy by Johann Andreas Kuhnau, Christian Gottlob Meißner, Bernhard Dietrich Ludewig, and Anonymous Vs (D-Gs *2° Cod. Ms. philos. 84ᵃ*)— into the arena of Bach's passion performances. These parts by copyists, that had both copied for Bach and for the Neukirche in Leipzig, were previously assigned chiefly to the repertory of the Neukirche, since only oratorio passions based on the biblical passion narratives were understood to be performed in the two main churches in Leipzig (Wollny, "Bekennen willl ich seinen Namen," 136). But it has now been demonstrated from Stölzel's passion that Bach also incorporated such passion oratorios at Vespers on Good Friday in the 1730s. Therefore, according to Wollny, the possibility should be reconsidered that the sources for Telemann's *Das Seligen Erwägen* could have been prepared for Bach's repertory. The connection in this respect is debatable, since the copy dates to around 1730, according to Glöckner (Glöckner, "Neukirche," 131); Kuhnau, however, worked for Bach only from 1723 to 1725 and occasionally in 1727 (NBA IX/3.1, 27).

58 This is assumed, because some of the works only survive as scores, whereas others exist as scores and parts, or only as parts.
59 Beißwenger BNB, 308–309.
60 Beißwenger BNB, 243–244.
61 Beißwenger BNB, 322–323.

Other Composers 257

the *Acroama missale* (Augsburg, 1709), encompassing six masses, as transcribed in 1735 by a copyist (D-B Mus. ms. 1160).[62] Alongside the title page of the fifth mass Bach composed a Credo intonation (BWV 1081). Durante's Kyrie-Gloria Mass in c minor (D-LEbh *Mus. ms. 10*), to be dated between 1727 and 1732 from the watermarks,[63] contains a newly composed Christe by Bach (BWV 242).[64] The *Missa à 4, 5, et 6 voci* by Lotti (D-B Mus. ms. 13161) copied in 1732/35—apart from one inserted measure in *Domine fili unigenite*—remained unchanged. It reflects the performance style of the Dresden court: Bach transcribed it from Zelenka's copy of the mass (D-Dl Mus. 2159-D-4), under the title *Missa Sapientiae*;[65] he undertook numerous changes to the instrumentation, mostly woodwinds, in order to be able to utilize the rich array of timbre of the famous court orchestra at Dresden.

Although these works represent examples of the "stile misto" of the Bolognese, Venetian, and Neapolitan mass tradition, from around 1742 Bach turned towards the mass tradition of Palestrina, and did so for the purpose of performance. From the mass book of 1591, of which he probably possessed the copy of the score from his time in Weimar, he arranged the Kyrie and Gloria from the *Missa sine nomine* for performance.[66] The set of parts (D-B Mus. ms. 16714) includes *colle parte* for cornetto and trombone, with a figured-bass continuo part that is patterned as a *basso seguente*. Around 1745, a vocal part of a mass from the mass book that followed was made from the Missa *Ecce Sacerdos Magnus*, although it is unclear why this copy remained an incomplete fragment.[67]

Alongside the masses by well-known composers, between 1739 and 1742, Bach also copied a Magnificat in C major by Caldara, in which an adaptation of the *Suscepit Israel* is attested.[68] This repertory of identified works of church music was supplemented by a series of anonymously transmitted compositions: the four-voice Mass in C major (BWV Anh. II 25, 1740/42); and the two works for double chorus, the Mass in G major (BWV Anh. II 167, 1732/35 and 1738/39), and the Magnificat in C major (BWV Anh. II 30, ca. 1742). Additionally two individual Sanctus compositions survive, in d minor (BWV 239, 1738/41) and in G major (BWV 240, ca. 1742).[69]

Finally, Bach's setting around 1747 of the Sanctus from the *Missa superba* by Johann Caspar Kerll (BWV 241) stands alone, for which he may have used the copy that was in the music library of the St. Thomas School. With this composition by Kerll (1627–1693), who was principally active in Munich, we find

---

62 Beißwenger BNB, 272–275.
63 A) MA (oder AM?) double-line letters of medium size, each lying in the gutter; b) empty; Weiß, 122.
64 Beißwenger BNB, 282–283.
65 Beißwenger BNB, 303–304.
66 Beißwenger BNB, 305–306.
67 Wiermann, "Bach und Palestrina," 10ff.
68 Beißwenger BNB, 277–278.
69 Beißwenger BNB, 323–336.

258   Kirsten Beißwenger

ourselves again with the work of a seventeenth-century German composer, who however did not remain in isolation in Bach's collection of later years, if one considers other genres. Around 1746/47, Bach copied the motet *Erfosche mich, Gott* by a predecessor in the cantorate at St. Thomas, namely Sebastian Knüpfer (1633–1676).[70] In addition, most copies—in Bach's hand—of works in the *Alt-Bachisches Archiv*, dating from Bach's later years in Leipzig, form a group of sacred compositions by Bach's ancestors.[71] That Bach in his later years was not solely pre-occupied with music of his forebears, however, is made clear by the psalm-cantata *Tilge, Höchster, meine Sünden*, the adaptation, around 1746/47, of the *Stabat Mater* of Giovanni Battista Pergolesi (1710–1736). If this is the sole surviving example of Bach's involvement with modern Italian vocal compositions, it nevertheless represents one of the most significant works of its time; according to Francesco Degrada, it is the work upon which—besides the *Salve regina*—Pergolesi's fame is founded.[72]

Instrumental music dating from the Leipzig period also survives from Bach's collection of music. Pieces by various composers are found in the keyboard books of Anna Magdalena Bach and Wilhelm Friedemann Bach that date from the 1720s.[73] There are copies, prepared by Bach and Bernhard Christian Kayser in 1723, of Inventions 2, 5, 6, and 7 for violin and continuo from *La Pace*, Op. 10 (Bologna 1712) by Francesco Bonporti (1672–1749).[74] Instrumental music does not generally appear until the 1730s in Bach's collection of music, which evidently is to be attributed to Bach's acceptance of the *Collegium musicum* in 1729. Bach was director of the student ensemble from 1729 to 1737 and once more from 1739 to at least 1741, and perhaps also until 1744, when the direction was assumed by Carl Gotthelf Gerlach, the music director of the Neukirche in Leipzig, who under Bach's leadership had also been entrusted with various tasks, such as violist, violinist, and harpsichordist.[75] Immediately in Bach's first year as director of

---

70 Beißwenger BNB, 301–302.

71 On the Alt-Bachisches Archiv, see Chapter 9.

72 Francesco Degrada, "Pergolesi, Giovanni Battista," MGG[2] Personenteil, 13: col. 315. Considerations by Yoshitake Kobayashi point towards a rhythmic and melodic correspondence between "O clemens" from Pergolesi's *Salve Regina* and *Et incarnatus est* from Bach's B-minor Mass, which raises the question whether Bach also possessed this work at one time. Philological knowledge could support this thesis; see Yoshitake Kobayashi, "Bach und der Pergolesi-Stil – ein weiteres Beispiel der Entlehnung?" *Bach und die Stile: Bericht über das 2. Dortmunder Bach-Symposion 1998*, ed. Martin Geck, (Dortmund: Klangfarben, 1999), 147–160.

73 The second *Clavierbüchlein* of Bach's spouse contains minuets by "Monsieur" Böhm and Christian Petzold; in the *Clavierbüchlein* of Bach's oldest son contains the *Pièce pour le Clavecin* by J. Chr. Richter, the partita in g minor by Gottfried Heinrich Stölzel, and the suite in A major by Telemann (TWV 32:14).

74 It is possible that a copy of Bach's Invention No. 1 in A major with thoroughbass had also existed at one time, according to Forkel (fragment, D-B *Mus. ms. autogr. Forkel*); Beißwenger BNB, 343.

75 Glöckner, "Neukirche," 89f.

Other Composers   259

the student ensemble (1729/30) are found the copies of overtures by the Eisenach organist, Johann Bernhard Bach (1676–1749).[76] Of the five total sets of parts of these overtures, mentioned in the catalog of Carl Philipp Emanuel Bach's estate,[77] three survive: in D major, G major, and g minor.[78] Similarly, a set of parts survives of the overture in G major (D-B St 319)—the overture *La Tempête* to the opera *Il zelo di Leonato* (1691)—by Agostino Steffani (1654–1728).[79] Around 1734/35 Bach (with copyists) made a set of parts of the Concerto grosso in f minor Op. 1, No. 8, by Pietro Antonio Locatelli (1695–1764).[80] Also to be associated with Bach's activity with the *Collegium musicum* is his adaptation of Vivaldi's concerto in b minor for four violins concertati, strings, and basso continuo, Op. 3, Nr. 10 (RV 580) to become the concerto for four harpsichords (BWV 1065).[81] And last to be mentioned is Bach's transcription in 1731 of Handel's chamber cantata *Armida abbandonata* (D-DS Mus. ms. 986), which was almost certainly for performance with the *Collegium musicum*.[82]

Apart from the concerto in a minor for harpsichord and orchestra (Wq 1 / H 403) by Carl Philipp Emanuel Bach, which survives in a set of parts dating from 1746/47 (Pl-Kj St 495), after 1738 only instrumental works for small ensembles

---

76 Beißwenger BNB, 232–235.

77 CPEB NV, 83.

78 The original parts for the overture in e minor and a second in g minor are lost, but in both cases it is assumed that their provenance matches those of the others. Although there is no longer any evidence of the g minor overture, beyond the entry in the catalog of Carl Philipp Emanuel Bach's estate, a copy of the score of the e minor overture in the hand of S. Hering still exists (D-B P 291, 160–172, together with the overtures in G major and g minor); see Beißwenger BNB, 233 and 235. Joshua Rifkin suggests that the g minor overture has similarities with the first movement of Bach's overture in b minor (BWV 1067); see Joshua Rifkin, "The 'B-Minor Flute Suite' Deconstructed. New Light on Bach's Ouverture BWV 1067," BP 6 (2007): 1–98.

79 Beißwenger BNB, 313–314.

80 Beißwenger BNB, 302–303.

81 Schulze, 171.

82 Six chamber cantatas by Nicola Antonio Porpora and one cantata by Alessandro Scarlatti are attributed by Glöckner (Glöckner, "Neukirche," 89f.) and Wolff (Wolff BLM, 355) to have been performed by the *Collegium musicum* under Bach's directorship, a work recorded in the library of the music director of the Neukirche in Leipzig, Carl Gotthelf Gerlach (D-LEm, Sammlung Becker *III.5.24* and *III.5.25* (Porpora); D-LEm, Sammlung Becker *III.5.27* (Scarlatti)). Glöckner supports this attribution with Gerlach's various functions in the *Collegium musicum*. Wolff also considers Gerlach to be an assistant director (Wolff BLM 354). George B. Stauffer shares this view and sets out to incorporate additional works in the performance circle of the *Collegium musicum* in Bach's time that could have been in the possession of Gerlach, namely two arias from Handel's opera *Alcina* (HWV 34), as well as a cantata by Handel, and three additional arias, one of which is not found among Handel's known works. As tempting as these considerations are, the attributions must remain—and Stauffer indicates as much— hypothetical, until Gerlach's role as assistant director in the *Collegium musicum* in Bach's time is clarified by documentation. See George B. Stauffer, "Music for 'Cavaliers et Dames.' Bach and the Repertoire of His Collegium Musicum," Gregory G. Butler, George B. Stauffer, Mary Dalton Greer, eds., *About Bach* (Urbana: University of Illinois Press, 2008), 135–156.

260   *Kirsten Beißwenger*

are known: the *Harmonische Denck- und Danckmahl* (Augsburg 1738) by Johann Gottfried Walther, an exemplar of which Bach had received as a gift, according to a letter from Walther to his correspondent Heinrich Bokemeyer, 30 July 1738;[83] a print of the quartet for flute, violin, violoncello, and continuo (Paris Quartets, Paris 1738) by Telemann, to which Bach subscribed;[84] the concerto for two harpsichords in F major (Fk 10), and three pieces for keyboard by Wilhelm Friedemann;[85] and the adaptation of a suite for lute in A major by Silvius Leopold Weiß (1787–1750)[86] of uncertain date, although there is possible evidence that it is to be dated 1746/47.[87] If this is correct then it would offer significant evidence that Bach was engaged his entire life as a musician and composer with works of his colleagues, in order to clothe them in new sonority, yet also in a more sophisticated compositional body of sound. As with the other adaptations of works mentioned in the present overview, it also establishes that Bach strove for compositional intensification by the addition of contrapuntal voices, and through rhythmic differentiation or harmonic-melodic profiling with respect to the original.[88]

The Influence of Other Composers on J. S. Bach: Some Marginal Notes

Even though we know only a small part of Bach's library of music by other composers, the collection he compiled for both study and performance, there is still a sufficient corpus from which to draw conclusions concerning his particular interests. In contrast, the question of the influence these composers exerted on Bach's compositions and stylistic development is much more difficult to answer.

Philipp Spitta demonstrated, by his extensive and sophisticated survey of the organ music of the late seventeenth century, the importance of the organ masters from southern, central, and northern Germany, as well as those from France, for

---

83   Johann Gottfried Walther, *Briefe*, eds. Klaus Beckmann and Hans-Joachim Schulze (Leipzig: VEB Deutscher Verlag für Musik 1987), 214.

84   Dok 2: 328 (No. 425).

85   One *Bourleska* (*L'imitation de la chasse*) (Fk 26), *La Reveille* in C major (Fk 27), and one Gigue in G major (Fk 28). The works of Friedemann and Carl Philipp Emanuel Bach as well as Telemann's Paris Quartets are attributed by Stauffer ("Music for 'Cavaliers and Dames,'" 142–43; Wolff also attributes the Telemann quartets, see Wolff BLM, xxix) to the performance circle of the *Collegium musicum*, or the concert by Emanuel Bach to that of the *Große Konzerte* founded in 1744. Whether Bach was actually interested for this reason in the Paris Quartets requires further explanation, since they were produced in 1738 and were acquired by Bach when he was presiding over the *Collegium musicum*.

86   Christoph Wolff, "Das Trio A-Dur BWV 1025: Eine Lautensuite von Silvius Leopold Weiss bearbeitet und erweitert von Johann Sebastian Bach," BJ 79 (1993): 47–67; see also Karl-Ernst Schröder, "Zum Trio A-Dur BWV 1025," BJ 81 (1995): 47–59.

87   On the dating, see NBA IX/3.1, 181 and especially 205. In the source (D-B P 226, 33–40) small treble clefs are written in Bach's hand, but these are too uncertain as material for establishing an unequivocal dating.

88   Wolff, "Das Trio A-Dur BWV 1025," 54–58.

Other Composers 261

the young Bach. If the general circle of central German organists—the organist/ composers of his own family, together with Johann Pachelbel,[89] whose combined influence was significant and formative—is taken for granted, then for Spitta the one composer who stands at the epicenter, to whom he concedes an irrevocable influence on Bach, is Georg Böhm, and supremely his chorale arrangements.[90] Spitta judges Buxtehude somewhat differently, whose importance for Bach he saw in a different light: "There can be no doubt that [Bach] far surpassed Buxtehude, but his advance was, at the same time, a step in another direction, although he used and appropriated the acquisitions of the earlier master."[91] Johann Adam Reinken—to mention the third northern German organ master that was important for Bach—plays no role in Spitta's monograph. Christoph Wolff proposes that the reason for this is that Spitta was not yet familiar with Bach's adaptation of the *Hortus musicus* of Reinken at the time he was working on the first volume of his monograph.[92] Subsequent research concerning the influence of these three masters on Bach has significantly nuanced the inter-relationships: Jean-Claude Zehnder has dealt with the musical influence of Georg Böhm,[93] and Christoph Wolff has illustrated the importance of Reinken for the development of the tonal language of the young Bach by reference to the adaptation of the sonata from *Hortus musicus*; indeed he considers Reinken to be the most significant teacher of Bach and the most important facilitator of northern German organ playing.[94] Concerning the influence of Buxtehude on Bach, Wolff draws into the discussion salient analogies between works by both masters.[95]

In the case of Böhm, Buxtehude and Reinken, it is useful to establish them as role models, because Bach is known not only to have studied their works, but also to have been personally acquainted with all three, and—as various studies have revealed—their personal style is attested in Bach's works. If the primary concern, however, is to scrutinize which composers, or which compositions, exerted influence on Bach, works that are not traceable to the library will be frequently mentioned. Such considerations, of course, lack philological grounding.

---

89 See Jean-Claude Zehnder, "'Des seeligen Unterricht in Ohrdruf mag wohl einen Organisten zum Vorwurf gehabt haben…' Zum musikalischen Umfeld Bachs in Ohrdruf, insbesondere auf dem Gebiet des Orgelchorals," Geck, *Bach und die Stile*, 169–191. Zehnder concludes that the influence of the Bach family was more important than that of Pachelbel. See also Christoph Wolff, "Pachelbel, Buxtehude und die weitere Einfluß-Sphäre des jungen Bach," Karl Heller and Hans-Joachim Schulze, eds., *Das Frühwerk Johann Sebastian Bachs* (Cologne: Studio 1995), 21–32.

90 Spitta 1: 207ff; Spitta ET 1: 210ff.

91 Spitta 1: 282; Spitta ET 1: 283.

92 Christoph Wolff, "Johann Adam Reinken und Johann Sebastian Bach: Zum Kontext des Bachschen Frühwerks," BJ 71 (1985): 100; Wolff Essays, 57.

93 Jean-Claude Zehnder, "Georg Böhm und Johann Sebastian Bach. Zur Chronologie der Bachschen Stilentwicklung," BJ 74 (1988): 72--110.

94 Wolff, "Johann Adam Reinken," 109–114; Wolff Essays, 63–71. On the significance of Reinken, see also Wolff BLM, 62–65.

95 Christoph Wolff, "Buxtehude, Bach, and Seventeenth-Century Music in Retrospect," Wolff Essays, 41–55.

262   Kirsten Beißwenger

However, to preclude such works from the discussion at the outset—especially if the modeling function is well established—would be tantamount to a positivistic restriction in perception, as it were, to deal only with what is verifiable by specific sources. Bach's music library can be further reconstructed by including works that are stylistically connected with Bach's music. But if such works are to be considered a clear distinction should be made between what is speculative and what is documented.

One genre in which various new paths have been taken in past years in order to determine the influence upon Bach's creative work is the instrumental concerto or the concerto-like movements in Bach's cantatas, keyboard and organ works. That Vivaldi's concerto form has a crucial influence in this respect on Bach's compositions has been continuously discussed in scholarship since Forkel.[96] Special attention was given to the Bach–Vivaldi connection in Bach research in the post-war studies of Rudolf Eller[97] and Hans-Günter Klein, whereby the later Vivaldi concerto form assumes the character of a "Leitform" in the work of Bach.[98] The origin for the occupation with this form is found in Bach's adaptations of Vivaldi's violin concertos for organ or harpsichord, even if today they must be considered less as study compositions than as commissions.[99] In the laying out of concerto movements or concerto-like movements Bach drew on other composers as well as Vivaldi,[100] as explored in the extensive studies by Jean-Claude Zehnder and Dominik Sackmann, even if both researchers include works in their discussions for which there is no evidence that Bach ever possessed them. The same holds true for Gregory Butler's conclusion with regard to the similarities between concertos from Albinoni's Op. 7 and Op. 9 and concertos by Bach.[101] Zehnder sees in the form of Bach's Weimar concertos with short

---

96 Dok 7: 36; NBR, 441.

97 Rudolf Eller, "Die Konzertform Johann Sebastian Bachs," Ph. D. diss. Leipzig University (1947); Rudolf Eller, "Zur Frage Bach–Vivaldi," Walter Gerstenberg, Heinrich Husmann, Harald Heckmann, eds., *Bericht über den Internationalen Musikwissenschaftlichen Kongresss Hamburg 1956* (Kassel: Bärenreiter, 1957), 80–85; Rudolf Eller, "Geschichtliche Stellung und Wandlung der vivaldischen Konzertform," Erich Schenk, ed., *Bericht über den internationalen musikwissenschaftlichen Kongress Wien. Mozartjahr 1956 3. bis 9. Juni* (Graz: Böhlaus, 1958), 150– 155; Rudolf Eller, "Vivaldi–Dresden–Bach," *Beiträge zur Musikwissenschaft* 3 (1961): 31–48.

98 Hans-Günter Klein, *Der Einfluss der vivaldischen Konzertform im Instrumentalwerk Johann Sebastian Bachs* (Strasbourg: Heitz, 1970), 11.

99 Schulze, 156–163, esp. 156–158; see Hans-Joachim Schulze, "J. S. Bach's Concerto-arrangements for Organ – Studies or Commissioned Works," *Organ Yearbook* 3 (1972): 4–13.

100 Also included among concerto adaptations are concertos by Torelli as well as by Alessandro and Benedetto Marcello, who until recently were not included in stylistic comparisons.

101 Gregory G. Butler, "J. S. Bach's Reception of Tomaso Albinoni's Mature Concertos," *Bach Studies 2*, ed. Daniel R. Melamed (Cambridge: Cambridge University Press, 1995), 20–46. In the concertos Op. 7, No. 8/1 and Op. 7, No. 9/1 Butler sees comparable ritornello schemes in the Brandenburg concerto No. 6/3 (BWV 1051) and the Brandenburg concerto No. 1/3 (BWV 1046). Motivic relationships connect Albinoni's concerto Op. 9, No. 3/1 with the third movement of the concerto for harpsichord and strings in E major (BWV 1053).

Other Composers 263

ritornellos[102] an influence of Torelli's *Concerti grossi* Op. 8 (Bologna 1709), of which the first concerto has a similar ritornello structure as found in works by Bach.[103] Dominik Sackmann sees in Bach's slow concerto movements an influence of the slow movements of Corelli's violin sonatas Op. 5, to which Corelli subsequently created ornamented versions of the violin part as late as 1710.[104] In the newly developed expressivity of Corelli's melodic line, Sackmann sees the model for Bach's own expressive style, which he fostered in various genres, such as the slow concerto or sonata movement, cantata sinfonia, aria, or organ chorale.[105]

Even if the work of Corelli mentioned here is a collection of sonatas, Bach was particularly occupied around 1714 with the modern Italian concerto. The engagement with this concerto literature led—according to Christoph Wolff—to Bach's distinctive personal style, blending the Italian elements with a complex and elegant counterpoint that was pervaded with thoughtfulness and subtlety: "Italian models... trained the young Bach in consistent and logical part writing, the design of closed and rounded movements, the differentiation between thematic expositions and related yet nonthematic episodes, and the integrated use and expansion of sequential patterns."[106] The transformation of other styles into a personal style spares no tradition. Thus he incorporated the motet movement of the seventeenth century, equally the style of Palestrina and denoted *stile antico*, into his own musical language.[107] The *stile antico* is seen by Christoph Wolff as independent contact with the traditional musical language of classical vocal polyphony, to be clearly separated from motet form, of which the "Allabreve movements" are the most strict.[108] The Credo and Confiteor movements, designated as *stile antico* by Wolff from the B-minor Mass (BWV 232),[109] exhibit—according to Siegfriend Oechsle—elements that were not inherited from the "historical style of Palestrina," but rather reveal a radical confrontation of phrase-structural

---

102 Belonging to this are, according to Zehnder, the Toccata in G major (BWV 916); the Toccata in C major (BWV 564); Trio on *Herr Jesu Christ, dich zu uns wend* (BWV 655 and 655a); the sonata of the cantata *Himmelskönig sei willkommen* (BWV 182), as well as Aria No. 4 of the same cantata; the instrumental movement in F major (BWV 1040); and the Aria No. 13 from the Hunt cantata (BWV 208).

103 *Concerti grossi con una Pastorale per il Santissimo Natale ... opera ottava* (Bologna: Silvani, 1709); see Jean-Claude Zehnder, "Giuseppe Torelli und Johann Sebastian Bach. Zu Bachs Weimarer Konzertform," BJ 77 (1991): 33–95.

104 Dominik Sackmann, "Bachs langsame Konzertsätze unter dem Einfluß von Arcangelo Corelli: Vom Ostinatoprinzip zum Primat der expressiven Solostimme, Geck, *Bach und die Stile*, 303–326; see also Dominik Sackmann, *Bach und Corelli. Studien zu Bachs Rezeption von Corellis Violinsonaten op. 5 unter besonderer Berücksichtigung der 'Passaggio-Orgelchoräle' und der langsamen Konzertsätze* (München: Katzbichler, 2000).

105 Sackmann, "Bachs langsame Konzertsätze," 324.

106 Wolff BLM, 64–65.

107 See Wolff St. ant.; and Wolff Essays, 84–104.

108 Wolff St. ant., 119–122.

109 Wolff St. ant., 15.

264   Kirsten Beißwenger

contrasts.[110] Oechsle draws attention to several features of compositional structure in the Credo movement of the B-minor Mass that do not hark back to the Palastrina style itself, but rather are formations of a later reception of various stylistic traditions of the seventeenth century.[111] Yet, Bach in his later years engaged with the musical techniques of composition of the late sixteenth and seventeenth centuries, his orientation towards contrapuntal directions of style is intensified at that time—whether in reaction to modernity remains undecided—and manifests here as elsewhere his reflective reworking of traditions of style and genre.

Translated by Emerson Morgan

110 Siegfried Oechsle, "Johann Sebastian Bachs Rezeption des stile antico. Zwischen Traditionalismus und Geschichtsbewußtsein," Geck, *Bach und die Stile*, 103–122.
111 Oechsle, "Johann Sebastian Bachs Rezeption des stile antico," 113–119.

Part IV
Genres and Forms

11 Vocal Music

Mark A. Peters

In his 1835 introduction to the "Crucifixus" of Johann Sebastian Bach's B-minor Mass, the English music editor William Ayrton stated: "[Bach's] vocal works are much more likely to convey his name to distant ages than those of the instrumental kind.... [They] show he possessed genius as well as science."[1] Indeed, the vocal music of J. S. Bach has long fascinated performers and scholars alike. To cite further just two of the most famous examples, it is through his vocal compositions that we mark moments among the most significant in Bach reception in the past 200 years. Consider first Felix Mendelssohn's famous 1829 performance of the St. Matthew Passion, often cited as the beginning of a "rediscovery" of Bach by performers and concert audiences and as the initiation of Bach's widespread acclaim as one of the greatest composers in the Western art music tradition. Likewise, it is Alfred Dürr and Georg von Dadelsen's revised chronology of Bach's vocal music in the 1950s which has inspired—we might even say required—entirely new considerations of Bach's compositional output.[2] In both cases, new perspectives on Bach's vocal music have contributed to an outpouring of new interest in, and discoveries about, the composer and his works.

It is the latter of these two defining moments which concerns us most in this chapter, as we consider the immense amount of scholarship undertaken on Bach's vocal music since the 1950s. For the new chronology by Dürr and Dadelsen, with important additions and clarifications by Yoshitake Kobayashi,[3] was just a beginning. Significant contributions to the literature on Bach's vocal music have been made over recent decades by scholars such as Elke Axmacher, John Butt, Eric Chafe, Stephen Crist, Don Franklin, Andreas Glöckner, Robin A. Leaver, Michael Marissen, Robert Marshall, Daniel Melamed, Martin Petzoldt, Markus

---

1 William Ayrton, *Sacred Minstrelsy: A Collection of Sacred Music by the Great Masters of All Ages and Nations*, vol. 2 (London: Parker, 1835), ix., cited in Robin A. Leaver, "An Early English Imprint of the 'Crucifixus' of the *B minor Mass* (BWV 232^{II}/5)," *Understanding Bach* 3 (2008): 46.

2 Dürr Chr 2, and TBSt 4/5.

3 See especially Kobayashi, and Yoshitake Kobayashi, "Quellenkundliche Überlegungen zur Chronologie der Weimarer Vokalwerke Bachs," *Das Frühwerk Johann Sebastian Bachs*, ed. Karl Heller and Hans-Joachim Schulze (Cologne: Studio, 1995), 290–308.

268   Mark A. Peters

Rathey, Joshua Rifkin, William H. Scheide, Hans-Joachim Schulze, George B. Stauffer, Renate Steiger, Christoph Wolff, and Peter Wollny, among others. In addition to monographs, articles, and presentations on Bach's vocal music by these and other scholars, significant attention has been devoted to this repertory both in Bach journals (including BJ and BACH) and serials (including BP, *Beiträge zur Bach-Forschung*, and LBB). Focus on Bach research was particularly intense around the years 1985 (celebrating 300 years since Bach's birth) and 2000 (celebrating 250 years since Bach's death).

With so much written about Bach's vocal music and by such eminent scholars, it seems fair to at least pose the question of what more can possibly be studied in relation to these works. Yet questions, even fundamental ones, still abound in Bach scholarship. For example:

How many cantatas did Bach compose? J. S. Bach's obituary notice (Nekrolog), prepared by Carl Philipp Emanuel Bach and Johann Friedrich Agricola, refers to five cantata Jahrgänge, which seems to imply a total of about 300 cantatas.[4] Yet only about 200 are extant. Have 100 Bach cantatas been lost? Is the "five" of the Nekrolog a misprint? Or is our method of tallying incorrect and Bach's cantata oeuvre practically complete?

How may passion settings did Bach compose? The Nekrolog likewise refers to five passion settings by Bach, whereas we can identify only two (the St. John and St. Matthew Passions) and the existence of a third (the St. Mark Passion); have the other settings been lost? Is this "five" a misprint? Or were C. P. E. Bach, Agricola, and Mizler perhaps including different versions of the St. John and St. Matthew passions in their total?

How many singers per voice part performed Bach's compositions under his direction? Since Joshua Rifkin's now-legendary paper at the annual meeting of the American Musicological Society in 1981, this question has been the one most hotly contested in Bach scholarship. For Rifkin's proposal, that one singer performed each vocal part, holds far-reaching implications for both performance and scholarship. Is Rifkin correct, or should we hold to the alternate view of three singers per part?

What is the definitive score for the B-minor Mass? One of Bach's most celebrated works, but one apparently never performed in its entirety during his lifetime, presents a long and complex publication history in which every edition has been questioned or challenged on significant points of interpretation. The debate over the critical score of the B-minor Mass continues even today, as Joshua Rifkin edited a critical edition of the Mass in 2006 and the Bach-Archiv in Leipzig has prepared a new version for the revised *Neue Bach-Ausgabe*.[5]

---

4 Originally published in Lorenz Christoph Mizler, *Neu eröffnete musikalische Bibliothek* IV/1 (Leipzig, 1754): 158–76; transcription in Dok 3: 80–93 (No. 666); NBR 295–307 (No. 306).

5 NBA^{rev} 1, ed. Uwe Wolf (2010). The publication history of the B minor Mass is reviewed in George B. Stauffer, *Bach, The Mass in B Minor: The Great Catholic Mass* (New Haven: Yale University Press, 2003 [1997]), 267–69. See also, Joshua Rifkin, ed., *Johann Sebastian Bach: Messe h-moll* (Wiesbaden: Breitkopf & Härtel, 2006); Uwe Wolf, Oliver Hahn, and Timo Wolff, "Wer schrieb was? Röntgenfluoreszenzanalyse am Autograph von J. S. Bachs

Vocal Music 269

In addition, new discoveries, such as the recovery of the collection of the Sing-Akademie zu Berlin in Kiev in 1999, continue to inform our understanding of Bach and his vocal compositions.[6] New understandings of the contexts in which Bach lived and composed further illuminate our understanding of Bach's vocal music.[7] Various analytical approaches continue to reveal new meanings and processes in these compositions. And new research into the works of Bach's contemporaries not only illuminates the works of these composers and their relation to Bach's compositions, but also provides us with a broader and richer perspective on music-making in eighteenth-century Germany.[8] In short, this is an exciting time for the study of Bach's vocal music. Although much significant research has been done that continues to engage us, we recognize as well seemingly endless possibilities for engaging this repertory.

Given the vast amount of research that has been done on Bach's vocal music, my goal in the present chapter is not to attempt a comprehensive overview of this scholarship or to provide a research guide for the various genres within Bach's output (i.e., cantata, passion, oratorio, mass, motet). The chapter is rather presented in two parts: the first provides a chronological overview of Bach's vocal works while noting some of the most important sources for further research into particular issues, genres, and pieces; the second provides an overview of various approaches scholars are taking to Bach's vocal music and discusses representative examples of each approach.

A Chronological Overview of J. S. Bach's Vocal Works

The current section provides a brief overview of the chronology of Bach's vocal works as presented by Dürr, Dadelsen, and Kobayashi and continually refined by later scholars.[9] One important consideration is that the new chronology was indeed focused on Bach's vocal music and particularly the sacred cantatas. Although Philipp Spitta had placed Bach's composition of cantatas primarily in the 1730s and 1740s, Dürr and Dadelsen demonstrated that the majority of Bach's cantatas were composed during his first two years in Leipzig (1723–1725) and that Bach likely did not regularly compose sacred cantatas again after 1727. Rather than occupying the composer throughout his Leipzig tenure then, the composition of cantatas largely took place during a fairly circumscribed period early in his Leipzig years.[10]

Messe in h-Moll BWV 232," BJ 95 (2009): 117–33; Joshua Rifkin, "Blinding Us with Science? Man, Machine and the Mass in B Minor," ECM 8 (2011): 77–91; and *Exploring Bach's B-minor Mass*, ed. Yo Tomita, Robin A. Leaver and Jan Smaczny (Cambridge; Cambridge University Press, 2013).

6 In the present volume, see Chapter 9, "The Alt-Bachisches Archiv" and Chapter 19, "Recent Research Developments."

7 See Chapters 5–8 of the present volume.

8 See Chapters 9, 10, and 17 in the present volume.

9 See Chapter 20: "Chronology."

10 Good general sources on Bach's cantatas include: Dürr K; Dürr K, ET; Martin Petzoldt, *Bach-Kommentar: Theologisch-Musikwissenschaftliche Kommentierung der Geistlichen*

270   *Mark A. Peters*

Bach's earliest vocal works, of course, date from a much earlier time, as he composed cantatas in both Arnstadt (1703–1707) and Mühlhausen (1707–1708). Appointed to the post of organist in both cities, Bach did not hold any official responsibility for composing or performing vocal music. Bach's few surviving cantatas from this period are either for special occasions or to texts that could be used on a variety of occasions in the church year. Bach's next appointment, in Weimar (1708–1717), was also as organist and likewise allowed at first little opportunity for the composition of vocal music. In March 1714, however, Bach was promoted to the position of Concertmaster, with an increased salary and with the added duty of composing one cantata each month for performance in the Weimar court chapel.[11]

Bach began his new responsibilities as Concertmaster of the Weimar court with the performance of *Himmelskönig, sei willkommen* (BWV 182) on Palm Sunday 1714. With some exceptions, such as the period of mourning for Prince Johann Ernst of Saxe-Weimar in 1715, Bach continued with the monthly composition of sacred cantatas until December 1716. With the death of Weimar court Capellmeister Johann Samuel Drese on 1 December 1716, Bach appears to have temporarily assumed duties of the Capellmeister for a few weeks. Bach apparently would not have expected to be appointed to the post permanently, since Drese's son, Johann Wilhelm Drese, served as vice-Capellmeister (and was, in fact, subsequently appointed Capellmeister). But Bach did apparently compose cantatas for the three Sundays following the elder Drese's death, for the first three Sundays of Advent, 1716.[12] But following this period and for reasons today unknown, Bach did not compose any more sacred cantatas for the Weimar court, and he left for a new appointment in Cöthen a year later, in December 1717.

As court Capellmeister to Prince Leopold of Anhalt-Cöthen, Bach was primarily responsible for the performance of instrumental music. Because the court chapel was Calvinist, Bach did not hold any responsibilities for providing regular

---

Vokalwerke Johann Sebastian Bachs, 3 vols. (Kassel: Bärenreiter, 2004–); Hans-Joachim Schulze, *Die Bach-Kantaten: Einführungen zu sämtlichen Kantaten Johann Sebastian Bachs* (Leipzig: Evangelische Verlagsanstalt, 2006); and Christoph Wolff, ed., *Die Welt der Bach-Kantaten*, 3 vols. (Stuttgart: J. B. Metzler, 1996–1999).

11 On Bach's pre-Leipzig cantatas, see (in addition to the general sources on Bach's cantatas cited previously): Dürr St; Karl Heller and Hans-Joachim Schulze, eds., *Das Frühwerk Johann Sebastian Bachs* (Cologne: Studio, 1995); Friedhelm Krummacher, "Bachs frühe Kantaten im Kontext der Tradition," Mf 44 (1991): 9–32; and Jean-Claude Zehnder, *Die frühen Werke Johann Sebastian Bachs: Stil—Chronologie—Satztechnik*, 2 vols. (Basel: Schwabe, 2009). On the chronology of Bach's Weimar cantatas, see also Andreas Glöckner, "Zur Chronologie der Weimarer Kantaten Johann Sebastian Bachs," BJ 71 (1985): 159–64; Klaus Hofmann, "Neue Überlegungen zu Bachs Weimarer Kantaten-Kalender," BJ 79 (1993): 9–30; Daniel R. Melamed, "Mehr zur Chronologie von Bachs Weimarer Kantaten," BJ 79 (1993): 213–16; and Yoshitake Kobayashi, "Quellenkundliche Überlegungen zur Chronologie der Weimarer Vokalwerke Bachs," in Heller and Schulze, eds., *Das Frühwerk Johann Sebastian Bachs*, 290–308.

12 BWV 70a, 186a, and 147a. The manuscript of BWV 147a, however, was left incomplete, and the cantata appears not to have been performed in Weimar.

Vocal Music 271

church music in Cöthen. But while we do not often think of Cöthen in conjunction with vocal music, Bach did compose a number of occasional cantatas during his tenure there, most of them for Leopold's birthday (December 10) and for New Year's Day.[13]

Bach's relative focus on instrumental music in Cöthen (1717–1723) was immediately followed by his most intensive interactions with vocal music during his first two years as Leipzig town cantor, a position he officially began on 30 May 1723 with the performance of the cantata *Die Elenden sollen essen* (BWV 75). In fact, our view of Bach's first years in Leipzig was monumentally altered through Dürr and Dadelsen's revised chronology. Two elements of this new chronology are particularly revealing in relation to Bach's composition of vocal music. The first is the sheer number of cantatas Bach composed during his first two years in Leipzig. In addition to reworking earlier cantatas for performance in Leipzig (sometimes with significant changes), Bach composed about eighty-eight new cantatas in this two-year period. The second, and complementary, element is Bach's lack of focus on sacred cantata composition for the remainder of his Leipzig tenure. By 1729, Bach never again dedicated himself with any regularity to the composition of new sacred cantatas. While he continued to perform a sacred cantata in Leipzig's principal churches for every Sunday and feast day (about sixty liturgical occasions each year, a requirement of his position as Thomascantor), Bach either reperformed his own earlier compositions or performed works by other composers. His compositional efforts were focused elsewhere.[14]

As noted previously, Bach's obituary by C. P. E. Bach and Agricola indicates that the elder Bach composed five complete annual cantata cycles (Jahrgänge). A cantata Jahrgang included all the Sundays and feast days of the church year, in Bach's Leipzig about sixty cantatas annually (in Leipzig, no concerted music was performed during the Second, Third, and Fourth Sundays of Advent or during Lent). The first two of these cycles encompass Bach's first two years in Leipzig. Jahrgang I began with BWV 75 on the First Sunday after Trinity 1723 and continued until Trinity Sunday 1724. During this year, Bach presented a varied approach to cantata performance. He reused his earlier cantatas to the greatest extent possible, through reperformance, revision, and parody. For those occasions for which he did not have a suitable cantata extant, he composed new cantatas. The result is a somewhat heterogeneous cycle incorporating a variety of text types and musical styles.[15]

---

13 On Bach's Cöthen cantatas, see (in addition to the general sources on Bach's cantatas cited previously): Andreas Glöckner, "Anmerkungen zu Johann Sebastian Bachs Köthener Kantatenschaffen," CBH 4, 89–95; and Friedrich Smend, *Bach in Köthen* [1951], trans. John Page, ed. and rev. Stephen Daw (St. Louis: Concordia, 1985).

14 A good, though now somewhat dated, overview of large-scale trends in Bach's Leipzig years is Rudolf Eller's "Gedanken über Bachs Leipziger Schaffensjahre," *Bach-Studien* 5 (1975): 7–27; ET "Thoughts on Bach's Leipzig Creative Years," trans. and annotated by Stephen A. Crist, BACH 21/2 (1990): 31–54.

15 On Bach's first Leipzig Jahrgang, see Martin Geck, ed., *Bachs 1. Leipziger Kantatenjahrgang: Bericht über das 3. Dortmunder Bach-Symposion 2000*, Dortmunder Bach-Forschungen

272   *Mark A. Peters*

By contrast, Bach began his Jahrgang II (1724–1725) with an ambitious and systematic approach to cantata composition, in which he wrote a new cantata based on a Lutheran hymn (chorale) for each liturgical occasion from 11 June 1724 to 25 March 1725. These chorale cantatas represent the most intensive and unified approach to the sacred cantata in Bach's compositional output. For reasons scholars today can only speculate, Bach abandoned his chorale cantata project after Lent 1725. After reperforming some earlier cantatas and composing three new works in the style of his Jahrgang I cantatas, Bach concluded his second Jahrgang with nine cantatas to texts by Leipzig poet Christiane Mariane von Ziegler.[16]

Upon completion of Jahrgang II on Trinity Sunday 1725, Bach halted his regular composition of sacred cantatas, either reperforming his own earlier works or performing cantatas by other composers. Bach began his third Jahrgang with *Unser Mund ist voll lachens* (BWV 110) on Christmas Day 1725, but continued only until 27 January 1726, after which he instead performed cantatas by his cousin Johann Ludwig Bach.[17] Bach resumed cantata composition with the Ascension cantata *Gott fährt auf mit Jauchzen* (BWV 43) and continued with new cantatas throughout most of the Trinity season. Bach essentially completed his Jahrgang III in 1727, during which he composed new cantatas for many of the liturgical occasions for which he had not written a new cantata the previous year.

Bach's first three cantata Jahrgänge are thus relatively straightforward and clearly defined. But with the fourth and fifth Jahrgänge we enter the realm of much greater speculation and scholarly debate. It is unclear whether Bach did indeed compose five complete cantata cycles as the obituary states (in which case about 100 cantatas must be lost) or whether most of Bach's cantatas are extant and the obituary's account inaccurate. Speculation about Jahrgang IV is centered around Picander (Christian Friedrich Henrici), the librettist who provided the text for the St. Matthew Passion and other of Bach's works.[18] In 1728, Picander

---

3 (Dortmund: Klangfarben, 2002). Despite all that has been written on Bach's first year in Leipzig and on his sacred cantatas, no other single volume devoted to the Jahrgang exists. A detailed study of Bach's first Leipzig Jahrgang addressing textual, musical, and contextual features of the works would be a significant contribution to Bach research.

16 On the chorale cantatas, see Renate Steiger, ed., *Johann Sebastian Bachs Choralkantaten als Choral-Bearbeitungen*, Internationale Arbeitsgemeinschaft für Theologische Bachforschung Bulletin 3 (Heidelberg: Manutius, 1991); Friedhelm Krummacher, *Bachs Zyklus der Choralkantaten: Aufgaben und Lösungen* (Göttingen: Vandenhoek & Ruprecht, 1995); Sachiko Kimura, *Die Choralkantaten Johann Sebastian Bachs: Kompositorische Struktur und Stellum im Kantatenwerk* (Kassel: Bärenreiter, 2011). On the cantatas to texts by Mariane von Ziegler, see Mark A. Peters, *A Woman's Voice in Baroque Music: Mariane von Ziegler and J. S. Bach* (Aldershot: Ashgate, 2008).

17 See William H. Scheide, "Johann Sebastian Bach's Sammlung von Kantaten seines Vetters Johann Ludwig Bach," BJ 46 (1959): 52–94; 48 (1961): 5–24; and 49 (1962): 5–32.

18 On the Picander Jahrgang (Jahrgang IV), see Klaus Häfner, "Der Picander-Jahrgang," BJ 61 (1975): 70–113; William H. Scheide, "Bach und der Picander-Jahrgang—Eine Erwiderung," BJ 66 (1980): 47–51; Klaus Häfner, "Picander, der Textdichter von Bachs viertem Kantatenjahrgang: Ein neuer Hinweis," Mf 35 (1982): 156–62; William H. Scheide, "Eindeutigkeit und

published his *Cantaten Auf die Sonn- und Fest-Tage durch das gantze Jahr*, a complete cycle of cantata texts. In the volume's preface, Picander writes about the cycle: "I undertook the design the more readily, because I flatter myself that the lack of poetic charm may be compensated for by the loveliness of the music of our incomparable Capellmeister Bach, and that these songs may be sung in the main churches of our pious Leipzig."[19] It is not known whether Bach did indeed compose cantatas for this complete cycle as Picander hoped: Bach's settings of only nine of the texts are extant, and only one of these settings can be securely dated to the 1728–1729 liturgical year. Although earlier scholars have pondered whether a great number of Bach's cantatas to Picander's texts have been lost, Peter Wollny has recently posited that Bach undertook the Picander cycle as a joint venture with his two oldest sons and possibly other students, as well.[20]

A fifth cantata Jahrgang composed by Bach is even more speculative than the Picander cycle, for there is hardly any source evidence for such a Jahrgang beyond the statement by C. P. E. Bach and Altnikol in J. S. Bach's obituary and no evidence of significant cantata production by Bach after 1729. Christoph Wolff has suggested the possibility that because Bach began Jahrgang I as a double cycle (with either cantatas in two parts or two separate cantatas for each liturgical occasion), the fifth Jahrgang could be the second half of that cycle.[21] Other possibilities include the consideration of the Weimar cantatas as a cycle, a significant loss of cantata sources from after 1729, or a misprint in the obituary.[22]

Scholars have observed a number of reasons for Bach's turn from sacred cantata composition after 1729. One element of this change was Bach's focus on instrumental music when he took over the directorship of Leipzig's *Collegium Musicum* in 1729. But vocal music likewise continued to occupy Bach's compositional efforts. In addition to continuing to compose and perform cantatas for special occasions (annual installation ceremonies for the Leipzig town council, birthdays, weddings, name days, funerals) and to perform a sacred cantata for each Sunday and feast day and a passion for each Good Friday, Bach focused his compositional activities on the creation of unique, large-scale masterworks.

Mehrdeutigkeit in Picanders Kantatenjahrgangs—Vorbemerkung und im Werkverzeichnis des Nekrologs auf Johann Sebastian Bach," BJ 69 (1983): 109–13; Klaus Häfner, *Aspekte des Parodieverfahrens bei Johann Sebastian Bach: Beiträge zur Wiederentdeckung verschollener Vokalwerke* (Laaber: Laaber, 1987); and Klaus Hofmann, "Anmerkungen zum Problem 'Picander-Jahrgang'," LBB 5 (2002): 69–87.

19 Cited in Wolff BLM, 285.
20 Peter Wollny, "Zwei Bach-Funde in Mügeln: C. P. E. Bach, Picander und die Leipziger Kirchenmusik in den 1730er Jahren," BJ 96 (2010): 111–51.
21 Wolff BLM, 286.
22 On the possible existence and nature of Jahrgang V, see William H. Scheide, "Ist Mizlers Bericht über Bachs Kantaten korrekt?" Mf 14 (1961): 60–63; Alfred Dürr, "Wieviel Kantatenjahrgänge hat Bach komponiert? Eine Entgegnung." Mf 14 (1961): 192–95; William H. Scheide, "Nochmals Mizlers Kantatenbericht—Eine Erwiderung." Mf 14 (1961): 423–27; Christoph Wolff, "Wo blieb Bachs fünfter Kantatenjahrgang?" BJ 68 (1982): 151–52; and Alfred Dürr, "Noch einmal: wo blieb Bachs fünfter Kantatenjahrgang?" BJ 72 (1986): 121–22.

274   *Mark A. Peters*

Such a focus was, of course, not a new one for Bach, for his responsibilities as Leipzig town cantor included the performance of a passion setting every year for the Good Friday Vespers service. In contrast to composers such as Georg Philipp Telemann who generally composed a new passion setting each year, Bach focused his efforts on the composition, revision, and perfection of his two masterpieces, the St. John Passion (BWV 245) and St. Matthew Passion (BWV 244). Bach composed the first version of the St. John Passion for his first Leipzig Good Friday Vespers (1724) and performed subsequent versions of it in 1725 (version II), 1732 (version III), and ca. 1749 (version IV). Bach's St. Matthew Passion is documented in two versions, the earlier version performed in 1727 and 1729 and the later version in 1736 and again in the 1740s.[23] The same process was followed with regard to Bach's St. Mark's Passion (music lost), the early version of which was performed in 1731 and a revised version in 1744. Bach also performed passions by other composers, including the anonymous St. Mark Passion (formerly attributed to Reinhard Keiser but now considered anonymous; performed by Bach in 1726 and again in the 1740s), possibly an anonymous St. Luke Passion, and Gottfried Heinrich Stölzel's *Der Gläubigen Seele Geistliche Betrachtungen Ihres leidenden Jesu* (performed by Bach in 1734).[24]

---

23 Scholarship on Bach's passions is vast and spans a wide array of approaches, and it is therefore not possible to mention more than a few sources here. For a good introduction to Bach's passions, see Daniel R. Melamed, *Hearing Bach's Passions* (Oxford: Oxford University Press, 2005). For annotated texts with English translations, see Michael Marissen, *Bach's Oratorios: The Parallel German-English Texts with Annotations* (Oxford: Oxford University Press, 2008). An excellent study of the St. John Passion is Alfred Dürr, *Die Johannes-Passion von Johann Sebastian Bach: Entstehung, Überlieferung, Werkeinführung* (Kassel: Bärenreiter, 1988); ET *Johann Sebastian Bach's "St. John Passion": Genesis, Transmission and Meaning*, trans. Alfred Clayton (Oxford: Oxford University Press, 2000). For theological perspectives on the passions, see Elke Axmacher, *"Aus Liebe will mein Heyland sterben": Untersuchung zum Wandel des Passionsverständnisses im frühen 18. Jahrhundert* (Stuttgart: Hänssler, 1984); Michael Marissen, *Lutheranism, Anti-Judaism, and Bach's St. John Passion* (Oxford: Oxford University Press, 1998); and Eric Chafe, *J. S. Bach's Johannine Theology: The St. John Passion and the Cantatas for Spring 1725* (Oxford: Oxford University Press, 2014). Just a few of the most significant articles on the passions are: Joshua Rifkin, "The Chronology of Bach's Saint Matthew Passion," MQ 61 (1975): 360–87; Eric Chafe, "J. S. Bach's *St. Matthew Passion*: Aspects of Planning, Structure, and Chronology," JAMS 35 (1982): 49–114; and Christoph Wolff, "Musical Forms and Dramatic Structure in Bach's Saint Matthew Passion," BACH 19/1 (1988): 6–20. Important collections of essays on Bach's passions include Ulrich Prinz, ed., *Johann Sebastian Bach, Matthäus-Passion, BWV 244: Vorträge der Sommerakademie J. S. Bach 1985* (Kassel: Bärenreiter, 1990); Ulrich Prinz, ed., *Johann Sebastian Bach, Johannes-Passion, BWV 245: Vorträge des Meisterkurses 1986 und der Sommerakademie J. S. Bach 1990* (Kassel: Bärenreiter, 1993); and Hans-Joachim Schulze, Ulrich Leisinger, and Peter Wollny, eds., *Passionsmusiken im Umfeld Johann Sebastian Bachs / Bach unter den Diktaturen, 1933–1945 und 1945–1989*, LBB 1 (1995). Two significant studies discussing Bach's passions in broad historical perspective are Karol Berger, *Bach's Cycle, Mozart's Arrow: An Essay on the Origins of Musical Modernity* (Berkeley: University of California Press, 2007); and John Butt, *Bach's Dialogue with Modernity: Perspectives on the Passions* (Cambridge: Cambridge University Press, 2010).

24 On the anonymous Mark and Luke passions, see Daniel R. Melamed, *Hearing Bach's Passions*. On Stölzel's *Der Gläubigen Seele*, see Tatiana Schabalina, "'Texte zur Music' in Sankt

Vocal Music   275

In addition to the revised versions of the St. John Passion and St. Matthew Passion, three large-scale vocal works from Bach's final two decades warrant special attention, and are indeed among the best known of Bach's compositions: the Magnificat in D Major (BWV 243), the Christmas Oratorio (BWV 248), and the B-minor Mass (BWV 232). Bach seems especially to have turned to the composition of vocal music in the years 1733 and 1734, when he not only revised the Magnificat and composed the *Missa* (the Kyrie and Gloria of what would become the B-minor Mass) and Christmas Oratorio, but also composed several secular cantatas for performance by his *Collegium Musicum*.

Bach's festive Magnificat in D Major is a revised version of his Magnificat in E-flat Major (BWV 243a). Bach composed the earlier version for the Feast of Mary's Visitation in 1723, less than two months after his arrival in Leipzig, and performed it again with four interpolated Christmas movements on Christmas Day 1723.[25] Bach revised the Magnificat in its D Major version possibly for performance on the Feast of Visitation on 2 July 1733, which would place it during a period of his intensive interest in sacred Latin settings which culminated with his composition of the *Missa* (BWV 232[1]), whose dedication to Friedrich August II is dated 27 July 1733.

The years 1733 and 1734 likewise saw Bach's composition of several secular cantatas to be performed by his *Collegium Musicum*. Although we most often think of the *Collegium Musicum* in association with instrumental music, the ensemble also performed vocal music, particularly for special occasions or in honor of distinguished guests. Bach's occasional cantatas performed by the *Collegium Musicum* in 1733 and 1734 include such notable works as *Laßt uns sorgen, laßt uns wachen* (BWV 213) for the birthday of the electoral prince, Friedrich Christian; *Tönet, ihr Pauken! Erschallet, Trompeten* (BWV 214) for the birthday of the Electress, Maria Josepha; *Blast Lärmen, ihr Feinde! verstärket die Macht* (BWV 205a) in celebration of the coronation of Friedrich Augustus II as King of Poland; the "Coffee Cantata," *Schweigt stille, plaudert nicht* (BWV 211); and *Preise dein Glücke, gesegnetes Sachsen* (BWV 215), marking the first anniversary of the election of Friedrich Augustus II as King of Poland.[26]

Petersburg: Neue Quellen zur Leipziger Musikgeschichte sowie zur Kompositions- und Aufführungstätigkeit Johann Sebastian Bachs," BJ 94 (2008): 33–98.

25 Andreas Glöckner, "Bachs Es-Dur-Magnificat BWV 243a—eine genuine Weihnachtsmusik?" BJ 89 (2003): 37–45. On Bach's Magnificat, see also Robert M. Cammarota, "The Repertoire of Magnificats in Leipzig at the Time of J. S. Bach: A Study of the Manuscript Sources" (Ph.D. diss., New York University, 1986); and Robert L. Marshall, "The Origin of the *Magnificat*: A Lutheran Composer's Challenge," in *The Music of Johann Sebastian Bach: The Sources, the Style, the Significance* (New York: Schirmer, 1989), 161–73; originally published in *Bach Studies*, ed. Don O. Franklin (Cambridge: Cambridge University Press, 1989), 36–53.

26 Relatively little research has been focused on Bach's occasional cantatas. A good general source is Hans-Joachim Schulze's "Bach's Secular Cantatas: A New Look at the Sources," BACH 21/1 (1990): 26–41. More focused studies include Stephen A. Crist, "The Question of Parody in Bach's Cantata *Preise dein Glücke, gesegnetes Sachsen*, BWV 215," BP 1 (1995): 135–62; and Szymon Paczkowski, "A Polonaise Duet for a Professor, a King and a Merchant:

276   Mark A. Peters

Because of the specific occasional texts of these cantatas, at times addressing the occasion or the honoree by name, they were most often not appropriate for repeat performance. For many of the works, Bach chose to parody certain movements in order to preserve them in a more lasting form. For Bach, this most often consisted of transferring movements from the secular cantatas into sacred works which could be performed for recurring liturgical occasions. This process is most thoroughly demonstrated in the years 1733 and 1734 with Bach's choice to parody almost all the choruses and arias from the cantatas BWV 213 and 214 for his Christmas Oratorio. Bach composed the six cantatas of the Christmas Oratorio for the Christmas season 1734–1735, with one cantata performed on each of the three days of Christmas, on New Year's Day, on the Sunday after New Year, and on Epiphany. In the Christmas Oratorio, Bach displays masterful use of parody, as he drew most of the choruses and arias from earlier sources, while reworking and reordering them for their new texts and liturgical occasions and interweaving them with newly composed recitatives and chorale settings. The result is not only six exemplary individual cantatas, but also a masterful large-scale structure spanning the six liturgical occasions of the Christmas season.[27]

Bach's final large-scale vocal work, and indeed his final composition, was the B-minor Mass, among the best loved and most researched of all his works. As noted previously, Bach composed the *Missa* (Kyrie and Gloria) in 1733. The composer traveled to Dresden in July 1733 and sent the performing parts of the *Missa* to Friedrich Augustus II accompanied by a letter (dated 27 July) requesting a court title. Bach returned to the project in the final years of his life, apparently completing the manuscript score of the Mass Ordinary between August 1748 and October 1749. Like the Christmas Oratorio, much of the Mass employs parodies of earlier compositions, with Bach adapting many movements from occasional works for this more lasting context (indeed, several scholars have noted that Bach may have considered the Latin Mass Ordinary a text that would endure in later generations even more so than the German sacred texts of parodied works such as the Christmas Oratorio).

---

on Cantatas BWV 205, 205a, 216 and 216a by Johann Sebastian Bach," *Understanding Bach* 2 (2007): 19–36. More scholarly attention has been paid to those occasional cantatas that Bach used as models for sacred compositions. See especially the literature on the Christmas Oratorio and the B-minor Mass.

27   For an annotated text of the Christmas Oratorio with English translation, see Marissen, *Bach's Oratorios*. For a good broad introduction to Bach's three oratorios (Christmas, Easter, and Ascension), see Christoph Wolff, "Under the Spell of Opera? Bach's Oratorio Trilogy," BP 8 (2011), 1–12. For an overview of Bach's parody process drawing examples primarily from the *Christmas Oratorio*, see Hans-Joachim Schulze, "The Parody Process in Bach's Music: An Old Problem Reconsidered," BACH 20/1 (1989): 7–21. Recent handbooks on the *Christmas Oratorio* include Ignace Bossuyt, *Johann Sebastian Bach: Christmas Oratorio. BWV 248*, trans. Stratton Bull (Leuven: Leuven University Press, 2004); and Meinrad Walter, *Johann Sebastian Bach: Weihnachtsoratorium* (Kassel: Bärenreiter, 2006).

Vocal Music 277

Despite the popularity of the Mass with modern performers and concert audiences and the wealth of scholarly writing dedicated to the work, Hans-Joachim Schulze's 1985 statement still holds true today:

> The composition that the Zurich publisher Hans Georg Nägeli called in 1818 'the greatest musical artwork of all time and of all nations' ('das grösste musikalische Kunstwerk aller Zeiten und Völker') is not only the latest but still the most puzzling and controversial amongst the oratorio-like works of the Leipzig *Thomaskantor*.[28]

Many questions about the Mass remain without definitive answer: Was the *Missa* performed in Dresden in 1733? If so, where and by whom? What motivated Bach to return to the work and compose a complete Mass Ordinary? Did Bach envision a performance of the complete Mass? If so, in what context? Furthermore, as noted previously, the publication history of the B minor Mass has been long and complex, with debate over the definitive score continuing today. Given the ongoing popularity of the B-minor Mass, the wealth of research that has been completed on it, and the many questions surrounding the work, the Mass will no doubt continue, in Schulze's words, as "perpetual touchstone for Bach research."[29]

---

28 Hans-Joachim Schulze, "The B minor Mass—Perpetual Touchstone for Bach Research," *Bach, Handel, Scarlatti: Tercentenary Essays*, ed. Peter Williams (Cambridge: Cambridge University Press, 1985), 311.

29 Given the vast amount of research into the B minor Mass from a wide variety of perspectives, it is not possible to mention more than a few sources here. Important introductory essays include Schulze, "The B minor Mass—Perpetual Touchstone for Bach Research;" Yoshitake Kobayashi, "Die Universalität in Bachs h-moll-Messe: ein Beitrag zum Bach-Bild der letzten Lebensjahre," MuK 57 (1987): 9–24, ET "Universality in Bach's B Minor Mass: A Portrait of Bach in His Final Years," BACH 24/2 (1993): 3–25; and Christoph Wolff, "Bach the Cantor, the Capellmeister, and the Musical Scholar: Aspects of the B-Minor Mass," BACH 20/1 (1989): 55–64. Monographs dedicated to the B-minor Mass and addressing many issues of chronology, context, performance, meaning, and composition include John Butt, *Bach: Mass in B Minor* (Cambridge: Cambridge University Press, 1991); Stauffer, *Bach, The Mass in B Minor*; Christoph Wolff, *Johann Sebastian Bach: Messe in h-Moll* (Kassel: Bärenreiter, 2009); and Tomita, Leaver, Smaczny, *Exploring Bach's B-minor Mass*. A significant collection of essays on the Mass is Ulrich Prinz, ed., *Johann Sebastian Bach, Messe h-Moll "Opus ultimum," BWV 232: Vorträge der Meisterkurse und Sommerakademien J. S. Bach 1980, 1983 und 1989* (Kassel: Bärenreiter, 1990). Some of the most notable among recent articles include: Peter Wollny, "Ein Quellenfund zur Entstehungsgeschichte der h-Moll-Messe." BJ 80 (1994): 163–69; Joshua Rifkin, "Eine schwierige Stelle in der h-Moll-Messe," LBB 5 (2002): 321–31; Szymon Paczkowski, "On the Problems of Parody and Style in the 'Et resurrexit' from the Mass in B minor by Johann Sebastian Bach," BACH 37/2 (2006): 1–44; Reinhard Strohm, "Transgression, Transcendence and Metaphor—the 'Other Meanings' of the B-Minor Mass," *Understanding Bach* 1 (2006): 49–68; Mary Oleskiewicz, "'For the Church as Well as for the Orchestra': J. S. Bach, the *Missa*, and the Dresden Court, 1700 to 1750," BACH 38/2 (2007): 1–38; Peter Wollny, "Beobachtungen am Autograph der h-Moll-Messe," BJ 95 (2009): 135–51; and Michael Maul, "'Die große catholische Messe': Bach, Graf Questenberg und die Musicalische Congregation in Wien," BJ 95 (2009): 153–75, ET "'The Great Catholic Mass': Count Questenberg and the

278   *Mark A. Peters*

Approaches to the Study of Bach's Vocal Music

As the previous section has made clear, scholars have approached Bach's vocal music from a wide variety of perspectives, exploring issues such as chronology, musical style, meaning, compositional history, performance history, and reception. The following section aims to introduce some of the principal approaches to Bach's vocal music and to discuss one or two recent examples of each.

Source Study

Long a cornerstone in Bach research, source study continues to serve the field in important ways. The celebrated place of the interpretation of primary sources for Bach studies is evidenced not only by the monumental studies of chronology by Dürr, Dadelsen, and Kobayashi cited above, but also by such works as Robert L. Marshall's *The Compositional Process of J. S. Bach: A Study of the Autograph Scores of the Vocal Works* (1972) and Laurence Dreyfus's *Bach's Continuo Group: Players and Practices in His Vocal Works* (1987). And one need only peruse the most recent issue of *Bach-Jahrbuch* for examples of multiple ways in which the discovery and interpretation of primary sources continues to prove valuable for the study of Bach's vocal music.

A recent example not only of an exciting new discovery related to Bach's vocal music but also of the ways in which such a discovery can inform our understanding of the composer and his works is provided by Tatiana Schabalina's research at the National Library of Russia in St. Petersburg. Schabalina's work has focused on printed texts for the vocal music of Bach and his contemporaries. In Leipzig, as in many other German cities, booklets containing the texts of concerted music were available for purchase by the congregation. Leipzig chronicler Christoph Ernst Sicul describes this practice in his 1717 statement:

> So that this polyphonic music, especially on high festivals, may be heard with greater devotion, it has become custom for some time for the honorable cantor to have the texts of the music printed beforehand... under the title *Kirchen-Music*, so that everyone can provide himself with these and read along.[30]

Schabalina observes that such text booklets are important sources not only for the texts they contain, but also because they usually indicate both date and location

---

Musicalische Congregation in Vienna," Tomita, Leaver, Smaczny, *Exploring Bach's B-minor Mass*, 84–104.

30   Christoph Ernst Sicul, *New annali Lipsiensium Continuation II: Oder des mit 1715ten Jahre Neuangegangenen Leipziger Jahrbuchs Dritte Probe* (Leipzig, 1717), 570; cited in Günther Stiller, *Johann Sebastian Bach and Liturgical Life in Leipzig*, trans. Herbert J. A. Bouman, Daniel F. Poellot, and Hilton C. Oswald, ed. Robin A. Leaver (St. Louis: Concordia, 1984), 121–22. See also Martin Petzoldt, *Texthefte zur Kirchenmusik aus Bachs Leipziger Zeit* (Stuttgart, 2000) for an introduction to the text booklets and for facsimiles of the books known in 2000 to be extant from Bach's tenure in Leipzig.

of the original performance, details not usually included in manuscript sources such as scores and performing parts.[31] Unfortunately, such booklets were clearly considered ephemeral by Bach and his contemporaries, for by the year 2000 researchers had only discovered six such booklets from Bach's Leipzig tenure.[32] Schabalina, however, recently discovered more than 300 printed sources related to J. S. Bach and his German contemporaries in the National Library of Russia. More than fifty of these are connected to Bach's Leipzig.[33]

In a series of recent articles, Schabalina has detailed some of the most significant of her discoveries and has begun to explore the ways in which these printed text sources inform our understanding of Bach, particularly in relation to the chronology of his vocal works.[34] The most significant of Schabalina's findings include previously unknown text booklets for church music by Bach from the years 1724, 1725, 1727, and 1728; the printed text to a passion oratorio by Gottfried Heinrich Stölzel performed at the Thomaskirche on Good Friday 1734; and an original edition of Picander's 1728/29 cantata Jahrgang, now the only known extant copy of this important source.

One important initial task of these articles was simply to report on and provide basic descriptions of these newly discovered sources, and Schabalina naturally focused on such details in her earlier articles. Her "'Texte zur Music' in Sankt Petersburg," for example, provides an overview of her findings related to Leipzig, first providing basic bibliographic information for fifty Leipzig sources from the years 1693 to 1765 in the following categories: texts to church music; texts to secular cantatas; and libretti for opera and musical theatre.[35] Schabalina goes on to describe the church music sources in greater detail, including those containing texts of music by Bach and those with texts of compositions by his predecessors, contemporaries, and successors.

In her later articles, Schabalina both describes additional sources she has found since her 2008 article was published and explores in more detail what her findings contribute to our understanding of Bach and his vocal works. In "Recent Discoveries in St Petersburg" and "'Texte zur Music' in Sankt Petersburg: Weitere Funde," for example, Schabalina examines the meanings and significance of the Picander cycle, calling for a reconsideration of details of Bach's interactions with Picander and his texts on the basis of this discovery.[36] And in "Neue Erkenntnisse zur Entstehungsgeschichte der Kantaten BWV 34 und 34a," she argues for a

---

31 Schabalina, "Recent Discoveries in St Petersburg," 77.
32 Wolff BLM, 259–60.
33 Schabalina, "Recent Discoveries in St Petersburg," 77.
34 Tatiana Schabalina, "'Texte zur Music' in Sankt Petersburg: Neue Quellen zur Leipziger Musikgeschichte sowie zur Kompositions- und Aufführungstätigkeit Johann Sebastian Bachs" BJ 94 (2008): 33–98; Schabalina, "Recent Discoveries in St Petersburg"; Schabalina, "'Texte zur Music' in Sankt Petersburg: Weitere Funde," BJ 95 (2009): 11–48; and Schabalina, "Neue Erkenntnisse zur Entstehungsgeschichte der Kantaten BWV 34 und 34a," BJ 96 (2010): 95–109.
35 Schabalina, "'Texte zur Music' in Sankt Petersburg," 35–43.
36 Schabalina, "Recent Discoveries in St Petersburg," 87–92; and Schabalina, "'Texte zur Music' in Sankt Petersburg: Weitere Funde," 20–30.

280   *Mark A. Peters*

revised chronology of these cantatas. Based both on study of a newly discovered text booklet and on detailed analysis of the surviving manuscript sources for the compositions, Schabalina argues that BWV 34a is in fact a parody of BWV 34, not vice versa as has traditionally been thought to be the case.[37]

Schabalina's findings in St. Petersburg are among several notable recent discoveries related to Bach's vocal music.[38] Other of the most significant findings include Michael Maul's discovery of a previously unknown aria by Bach[39] and Patricia Kennedy Grimstead and Christoph Wolff's rediscovery in Kiev of the Sing-Akademie zu Berlin archive, whose location had been generally unknown since the end of World War II.[40] The highly publicized finding of the Sing-Akademie archive in particular has opened up a wealth of research possibilities into the works of Bach's predecessors, contemporaries (especially Telemann), and successors (especially C. P. E. Bach).[41]

Schabalina sums up well the current excitement generated by discovery of new sources and their significance for Bach research:

> Judging by all the recent events, Bach research worldwide is now entering a new phase of development, when unknown Bach autographs, unknown works and texts are constantly appearing. No doubt, each of them widens and enriches our knowledge and understanding of Bach's life work. Let us hope that this process continues further and brings us new fresh and important advances.[42]

Musical Analysis

As with source studies, musical analysis has long served an important role in Bach research. Scholars have pursued a wide variety of analytical approaches, while emphasizing the importance of a close reading of Bach's compositions.

---

37 Schabalina, "Neue Erkenntnisse," 95–109.
38 See Chapter 19 of the present volume, "Recent Research Developments."
39 Michael Maul, "'Alles mit Gott und nichts ohn' ihn'—Eine neue aufgefundene Aria von Johann Sebastian Bach," BJ 91 (2005): 7–34.
40 See Patricia Kennedy Grimstead, "Bach Is Back in Berlin: The Return of the Sing-Akademie Archive from Ukraine in the Context of Displaced Cultural Treasures and Restitution Politics," http://www.ucis.pitt.edu/nceeer/2003_816_03_Gromsted.pdf.
41 See Christoph Wolff, "Recovered in Kiev: Bach et al.: A Preliminary Report on the Music Archive of the Berlin Sing-Akademie," *Notes* 58 (2001): 259–71; Christoph Wolff, et al, "Zurück in Berlin: Das Notenarchiv der Sing-Akademie. Bericht über eine erste Bestandsaufnahme," BJ 88 (2002): 165–80; the report of a roundtable discussion on the Sing-Akademie archive and its possibilities for further research moderated by Ulrich Leisinger, "Die Handschriftensammlung der Sing-Akademie zu Berlin im 'Archiv-Museum für Literatur und Kunst der Ukraine' in Kiew und ihre Bedeutung für künftige Forschungsvorhaben," LBB 5 (2002): 333–84; LBB 8 (2006); and Axel Fisher and Matthias Kornemann, eds., *The Archive of the Sing-Akademie zu Berlin: Catalogue / Das Archiv der Sing-Akademie zu Berlin: Katalog* (Berlin: De Gruyter, 2010).
42 Schabalina, "Recent Discoveries in St Petersburg," 92.

Vocal Music 281

As in other fields of musicology, musical analysis is often combined with other approaches, such as source studies, textual studies, or studies of compositional process.

An important trend in analytical studies of Bach's vocal music is the relationship of Bach's compositions to those of his predecessors, including not only internationally acclaimed composers such as Palestrina but also members of his own family as represented in the Alt-Bachisches Archiv. Christoph Wolff has published extensively on Bach's interactions with earlier musics.[43] Two other significant analytical studies have focused on dance rhythms in Bach's compositions, one by Doris Finke-Hecklinger and the other by Meredith Little and Natalie Jenne.[44] Other exemplary analytical studies of Bach's vocal music include those by Stephen A. Crist, Rebekka Bertling, and Richard Jones.

One scholar who has most consistently and extensively applied analytical methods to the study of Bach's vocal works is Eric Chafe. Over the past three decades, Chafe has pursued a distinctive approach to analyzing Bach's vocal works, which interweaves the study of text, music, historical music theory, historical theology, and meaning, to reveal significant new insights into these compositions.[45] The focus of Chafe's analytical system is on tonal language and structure, as well as on the ways in which interpretations of tonal structure articulate theological content. Chafe summarizes the importance of such an approach particularly in relation to Bach's cantatas in the statement: "Understanding the way that our modern concepts of relative major and minor keys, of key relationships, and of dominant/subdominant polarity within the key arose from the older theory is, in my view, essential to understanding how the relationship of music and theology conditioned Bach's cantata designs."[46] Chafe interprets such musical structures and the meanings they convey through the framework of what he calls "tonal allegory," a concept he has explored not only in Bach's vocal works but also in the music of Claudio Monteverdi and in Richard Wagner's *Tristan und Isolde*. Chafe has explained the concept most thoroughly in relation to Bach in his monograph

---

43 See, for example, Wolff St. Ant.; Christoph Wolff, "J. S. Bach and the Legacy of the Seventeenth Century," *Bach Studies 2*, ed. Daniel R. Melamed (Cambridge: Cambridge University Press, 1995), 192–201; and Wolff Essays, 84–104.

44 Doris Finke-Hecklinger, *Tanzcharaktere in Johann Sebastian Bachs Vokalmusik* (Trossingen: Hohner, 1970); Meredith Little and Natalie Jenne, *Dance and the Music of J. S. Bach*, expanded edition (Bloomington: Indiana University Press, 2001 [1991]).

45 Although Chafe's early research was focused on Bach's passions, his more recent studies have been dedicated primarily to the sacred cantatas. Chafe's most extensive treatments of Bach's music have been four monographs: *Tonal Allegory in the Vocal Music of J. S. Bach* (Berkeley: University of California Press, 1991); *Analyzing Bach Cantatas* (Oxford: Oxford University Press, 2000); *J. S. Bach's Johannine Theology* (2014); and *Tears into Wine: J. S. Bach's Cantata 21 in its Musical and Theological Contexts* (Oxford: Oxford University Press, 2015). Chafe's articles on Bach's sacred vocal music include "J. S. Bach's *St. Matthew Passion*: Aspects of Planning, Structure, and Chronology," JAMS 35 (1982): 49–114; "The St. John Passion: Theology and Musical Structure," Franklin, *Bach Studies*, 75–112; and "Bach's *Ascension Oratorio*: God's Kingdoms and Their Representation," BP 8 (2011), 122–45.

46 Chafe, *Analyzing Bach Cantatas*, xi.

282 Mark A. Peters

Tonal Allegory in the Vocal Music of J. S. Bach. Chafe presents the concept in the book's preface, where he explains: "Allegory expresses the spiritual life, a way of thought in music, and in the other arts, as well as in religion, and it is fundamental to my argument that tonality acts as a central, if not the central, means by which music becomes allegorical."[47] Chafe goes on in the volume's first chapter to investigate the concept of musical allegory both in historical context of Bach's time and in later scholarly inquiry into Bach's music. He proceeds, through careful study of both historical music theory and historical theology, to present allegory as a hermeneutical tool by which the meanings in a piece of music can be explicated. Following chapters dedicated to study of the B-A-C-H motive and to tonal theory in the early eighteenth century, the bulk of the book presents careful analyses of Bach cantatas, of the Christmas Oratorio, and of the St. John Passion and St. Matthew Passion.

An article that provides a straightforward introduction to some aspects of Chafe's approach to analyzing Bach's vocal music is his "Bach's *Ascension Oratorio*: God's Kingdoms and Their Representation." Although Chafe does not use the term "tonal allegory" in the article, his approach here clearly draws upon his earlier studies and his analytical system combining elements of historical theology, historical music theory, and tonal features of a composition. Chafe summarizes his approach to analyzing the Ascension Oratorio in the article's introduction:

> The musical and textual design of the oratorio relates closely to the liturgical and scriptural background for Ascension Day, and to contemporary theological perspectives that can be gleaned from writings by Lutheran authors of the seventeenth and eighteenth centuries. The tonal plan of the oratorio reflects its theological meaning.... The theological meaning of the oratorio revolves around the relationship of the two arias [movements 4 and 8] and their placement in the design of the whole. In their different ways the two halves of the oratorio mirror the theological presentation of God's kingdoms as worlds "above" and "below," united for the faithful through Jesus's ascension.[48]

Chafe goes on to provide a detailed analysis of the Ascension Oratorio, which addresses the liturgical and scriptural background of Ascension Day within contemporary Lutheran theology, the musical and textual design of the Ascension Oratorio, and the tonal design of the work. Both this article and Chafe's other writings on Bach's vocal works demonstrate the ways in which historical theology, historical music theory, and tonal structures can provide insights into the meanings of Bach's compositions.

---

47 Chafe, *Tonal Allegory*, vii.
48 Eric Chafe, "Bach's *Ascension Oratorio*: God's Kingdoms and Their Representation," BP 8 (2011): 122.

Vocal Music 283

Performance Practice

Musicological studies related to performance practice have been not only among the most fruitful, but also among the most controversial, in recent decades, and studies of Bach's vocal music have been no exception. Both scholarship and performances of Bach's music related to the "early music" movement and to "authentic" or "historically informed" performance have gained recognition and sometimes notoriety. Issues of performance practice and historically informed renderings were brought to the fore in Bach circles through the recording of Bach's complete cantatas by Gustav Leonhardt and Nikoloaus Harnoncourt (begun in 1971, completed in 1990) and have continued to provide inspiration for scholars and performers alike.

Despite the many facets of historically informed performance related to Bach's vocal music, the one that has most engaged researchers is the size of Bach's vocal ensemble. In 1920, Arnold Schering proposed that Bach's standard vocal ensemble consisted of twelve singers, three for each of the four vocal parts, and this view came to be the one generally accepted by Bach scholars.[49] But in 1981, Joshua Rifkin proposed that Bach's standard vocal ensemble consisted rather of four singers, one for each vocal part.[50] The issue has been hotly debated since, with many scholars and performers accepting Rifkin's evidence and others rejecting it in favor of Schering's hypothesis.[51] The vitriolic nature of the debate

---

49 Arnold Schering, "Die Besetzung Bachscher Chöre," BJ 17 (1920): 77–89.

50 Joshua Rifkin, "Bach's Chorus," paper presented at the Annual Meeting of the American Musicological Society, Boston, 1981. Reprinted in Andrew Parrot, *The Essential Bach Choir* (Woodbridge: Boydell, 2000), 189–208.

51 Joshua Rifkin, "Bach's Chorus: A Preliminary Report," MT 123 (1982): 747–54; Robert L. Marshall, "Bach's Chorus: A Preliminary Reply to Joshua Rifkin," MT 124 (1983): 19–22. The principal sources in support of Rifkin's view include: Joshua Rifkin, "From Weimar to Leipzig: Concertists and Ripienists in Bach's 'Ich hatte viel Bekümmernis'," EM 24 (1996): 583–603; John Butt, "Bach's Vocal Scoring: What Can It Mean?" EM 26 (1998): 99–107; Parrott, *The Essential Bach Choir*, German translation, *Bachs Chor: Zum neuen Verständnis*, trans. Claudia Brusdeylins (Kassel: Bärenreiter, 2003); Joshua Rifkin, *Bach's Choral Ideal* (Dortmund: Klangfarben, 2002); Joshua Rifkin, "Bach's Chorus: Some New Parts, Some New Questions," EM 31 (2003): 573–80; Daniel R. Melamed, *Hearing Bach's Passions* (Oxford: Oxford University Press, 2005); and Andrew Parrott, "Vocal Ripienists and J. S. Bach's Mass in B Minor," ECM 7 (2010): 9–34.

The principal sources in opposition to Rifkin's view include: Hans-Joachim Schulze, "Studenten als Helfer bei der Leipziger Kirchenmusik," BJ 70 (1984): 45–52; Ton Koopman, "Recording Bach's Early Cantatas," EM 24 (1996): 605–21; Ton Koopman, "Bach's Choir, an Ongoing Story," EM 26 (1998): 109–21; Uwe Wolf, "Von der Hofkapelle zur Stadtkantorei: Beobachtungen an den Aufführungsmaterialien zu Bachs ersten Leipziger Kantatenaufführung," BJ 88 (2002): 181–91; Andreas Glöckner, "Alumnen und Externe in den Kantoreien der Thomasschule zur Zeit Bachs," BJ 92 (2006): 9–36, ET "Alumni and Externals in the Choirs of the Thomas School during Bach's Time," BACH 40/1 (2009): 1–34; and Andreas Glöckner, "'Derer Ripienisten müssen wenigstens auch achte seyn, nehmlich zu ieder Stimme zwey': Bemerkungen Zur Besetzung der Leipziger Kirchenmusiken Johann Sebastian Bachs," *Im Klang der Wirklichkeit: Musik und Theologie. Martin Petzoldt zum 65. Geburtstage*, eds. Norbert Bolin and Markus Franz (Leipzig: Evangelische Verlagsanstalt, 2011).

284 *Mark A. Peters*

has at times reached surprising levels. Although it began in print calmly enough with Rifkin's 1982 article "Bach's Chorus: A Preliminary Report" and Robert L. Marshall's gracious disagreement in his "Bach's Chorus: A Preliminary Reply to Joshua Rifkin," the fight over the nature of Bach's chorus has unfortunately at times been characterized by fierce jibes, mocking replies, and ad hominem attacks by scholars and performers on both sides of the issue.

It is interesting that most of the publishing on the topic of Bach's vocal forces has been done by Rifkin and others arguing that Bach's concerted music was originally performed with one singer per part. Indeed, the first full-length article opposing this view was Ton Koopman's "Bach's Choir: An Ongoing Story" of 1998, seventeen years after Rifkin had first proposed it.[52] Rifkin and Parrott have argued convincingly and at great length for one-on-a-part performance, and I believe that John Butt's 1991 statement on Rifkin is still true today: "Although this view continues to be opposed by some of the most important figures in Bach research, there have been no convincing arguments, based on meticulous source-study, actually to prove him wrong."[53]

The very intensity of the debate, in addition to its long life, demonstrates that the issue is a central one for our understanding of Bach's vocal music. Andrew Parrott describes it as "not a minor historical point, a detail of purely academic interest, but a fundamental principle of performance—and of composition— running right through Bach's (and others') creative output, and consequently something which [contributes] to a significantly fuller understanding of his music."[54] Also at stake are the ways in which musicological research can, or should, inform modern performance. Although both Rifkin and Parrott have taken pains to express that Bach's original performing forces need not be repli-cated by all modern conductors and ensembles, it is clear that a recognition that Bach employed one singer per vocal part should at least inform modern perfor-mances, even those employing larger vocal ensembles.

Perhaps most at stake is the nature of source studies and their interpretation, for scholars espousing opposing viewpoints in the debate not only focus on dif-ferent primary sources but also draw very different conclusions from the same sources. The principal sources and topics debated include the following.[55]

1   *The various repertories sung by choirs under Bach's purview.* As town can-tor, Bach was responsible for the music at five of Leipzig's churches and oversaw four choirs composed of students of the Thomasschule. Only the

---

For a discussion of the debate, see *The Essential Bach Choir*, 209–11; for a chronological bibliography, see Robin A. Leaver, "Performing Bach: One or Many?" *The Choral Scholar: the Online Journal of the National Collegiate Choral Organization* 1 (2009): 6–15.

52 Koopman had introduced the topic and stated his disagreement with Rifkin earlier, in his 1996 article "Recording Bach's Early Cantatas," 612–13.

53 John Butt, *Bach: Mass in B Minor*, 40.

54 Parrott, *The Essential Bach Choir*, 2.

55 For the sake of brevity, in the current summary I will refer only to practices in Bach's Leipzig, not in the earlier stages of his career. For this summary, I have principally drawn upon Parrott, *The Essential Bach Choir*; Rifkin, *Bach's Choral Ideal*; and the Appendix to Parrott, "Vocal Ripienists and J. S. Bach's Mass in B Minor," 25–34.

first choir sang Bach's own complex music, while the remaining choirs sang the progressively simpler genres of motet, chorale, and chant. A significant distinction in Rifkin's argument is that the one-to-a-part practice applies only to Bach's own concerted music, not to the other, simpler repertories.

2 *The differing roles of concertists and ripienists.* It is widely recognized that in concerted music of the Baroque period, concertists sang throughout, including not only what are today seen as solo numbers (such as recitatives and arias) but also in choruses. The concertists were thus essential to all movements. Ripienists, on the other hand, were usually optional. They were either silent or doubled music already being sung by the concertists. Furthermore, ripienists stood in a different location than the concertists.[56]

3 *Copies and copy sharing.* The physical distance of ripienists from concertists required that each group be provided with its own performing parts. However, ripieno parts are not extant for the majority of Bach's cantatas. Rifkin's opponents have posited the large-scale loss of ripieno parts, and have also argued that ripienists could, indeed, have shared parts with concertists. Rifkin and Parrott, on the other hand, believe that ripieno parts have survived at the same rate of success as other parts and that primary sources argue against any practice of sharing copies.

4 *Bach's memorandum of 1730, "Entwurff einer wohlbestallten Kirchen Music."* In August 1730, Bach composed a memorandum to the Leipzig town council detailing the state and structure of Leipzig's church music. For proponents of Schering's view, this is a key piece of evidence, for they interpret Bach here as arguing for an ideal of three or four singers per part for choirs with twelve or sixteen members. However, Rifkin and Parrott have argued both that the "Entwurff" addresses motet singing and not concerted music and that Bach was arguing not for performance by choirs with twelve or sixteen members but for a larger pool of singers upon which he could draw for performance.

5 *Rosters of Leipzig choirs and additional singers who may have been available to perform.* Most of the serious published literature opposing Rifkin has focused especially on this point, arguing that far greater numbers of singers were available to Bach and so he must naturally have used them. Rifkin and Parrott have argued against the assumption that Bach considered one-to-a-part performance of his concerted vocal music as inadequate and rather that such performance was the norm for concerted music. They further argue that groups of singers enumerated by other scholars were not available or musically adequate for the performance of Bach's concerted vocal works.

6 *Known instrument/singer ratios in comparable Baroque ensembles.* A final issue raised is that of balance: how could four singers compete with a known instrumental ensemble of up to approximately twenty-one performers? Parrott convincingly shows that such a ratio was a common one in the Baroque period and that the use of twelve or sixteen singers would create instrument/singer ratios otherwise unknown in the period.

---

56 Parrott, *The Essential Bach Choir*, 54–57.

286   Mark A. Peters

The debate over Bach's vocal forces has been a fruitful one for Bach research, one that has contributed significantly to our understanding of Bach's vocal works, their sources, and their performance contexts, while also informing and inspiring countless modern performances. Scholars on both sides of the debate, but especially Rifkin and Parrott, have employed source study to reveal new findings that have not only challenged traditional understandings of Bach's vocal music but have also helped us to hear these works in new ways. And recent supporters of Rifkin's view, most notably John Butt and Daniel R. Melamed, have begun to explore more fully the implications of the size of Bach's choir for understandings and interpretations of particular Bach compositions.[57] In disagreeing with Rifkin, scholars such as Andreas Glöckner, Hans-Joachim Schulze, and Uwe Wolf have significantly enlarged our understanding of the performers available to Bach and of the challenges Bach faced in presenting his vocal music.[58] Their studies have helped to put human faces not only on Bach himself, but also on his original performers. Although we can little expect agreement over the size of Bach's choir, we continue to benefit from ongoing scholarly investigations into the topic.

Theology

Johann Sebastian Bach's sacred vocal music has long been a source for theological scrutiny and reflection. Indeed, one can argue that such theological—or perhaps devotional—consideration fits closely with the original contexts and intentions of these works. With the notable exception of his B-minor Mass, for which no clear intended performance context is evident and which was apparently never performed completely during the composer's lifetime, Bach's sacred vocal music was composed for the Lutheran liturgy. The cantatas, for example, were performed for the principal services of each Sunday and feast day, in close connection with the assigned Gospel reading and the sermon. Bach's oratorios were designed to take the place of the cantata in the feast day liturgies for the Christmas season, Easter, and Ascension; the passions formed the core of the annual Good Friday Vespers liturgy; the Magnificat was a central element in Vespers liturgy for each Sunday and feast day. And Bach himself clearly recognized and embraced the liturgical nature and theological import of these compositional efforts.

With the growing recognition of the importance of contextual studies in musicology in recent decades, many scholars have explored Lutheran theology as one of the primary contexts by which we should understand the sacred music

---

57 See, for example, John Butt, *Bach's Dialogue with Modernity: Perspectives on the Passions* (Cambridge: Cambridge University Press, 2010), 197–209; and Daniel R. Melamed, *Hearing Bach's Passions* (Oxford: Oxford University Press, 2005), 19–46.

58 See, for example, Schulze, "Studenten als Helfer bei der Leipziger Kirchenmusik," 45–52; Wolf, "Von der Hofkapelle zur Stadtkantorei," 181–91; and Glöckner, "Alumnen und Externe," 9–36. More recent literature on the continuing research and debate includes: Robert L. Marshall, "Belated Thoughts on Bach's Chorus," *Early Music America* 15 (2009): 24–28; and Michael Maul, "'Welche ieder Zeit aus dem besten Subjectis bestehen muß': Die erste 'Cantorey' der Thomasschule – Organisation, Aufgaben, Fragen," BJ 99 (2014): 11–77.

Vocal Music   287

of J. S. Bach. Naturally, many of the studies done on theological contexts for understanding Bach's compositions are focused on his vocal music. Important fundamental studies of Bach's theological contexts include Günther Stiller on liturgical life in Leipzig,[59] Robin A. Leaver on Bach's theological library,[60] and Leaver and Howard H. Cox on Bach's personal copy of the Bible commentary edited by Abraham Calov, now in the library of Concordia Seminary, St. Louis.[61] A new work of monumental significance for understanding Bach's vocal works in theological perspective is Martin Petzoldt's *Bach-Kommentar*, the first handbook of Bach's vocal music to systematically incorporate theological sources and perspectives.[62] Other scholars who have employed historical theology in the study of Bach's vocal music include Elke Axmacher, Eric Chafe, Stephen A. Crist, Don O. Franklin, Michael Marissen, Markus Rathey, Renate Steiger, Isabella Van Elferen, and Meinrad Walter. Given the scope and number of such studies, this section will briefly discuss three exemplary recent studies.[63]

Stephen A. Crist's "Historical Theology and Hymnology as Tools for Interpreting Bach's Church Cantatas: The Case of *Ich elender Mensch, wer wird mich erlösen*, BWV 48" provides a good introduction to theological Bach research, as Crist's stated goal in the article is to offer a case study on how information from the perspectives of historical theology and hymnology can inform our interpretation of a Bach cantata.[64] Crist not only provides significant insights into Cantata 48, but even more importantly both demonstrates and argues for the importance of such an approach. He concludes his article with the statement: "Only by pursuing an integrated approach, which draws upon these sources as well as musical analysis and manuscript study, will it be possible to achieve a full-orbed understanding of these incomparably rich compositions."[65]

---

59   See note 30. The study was originally Stiller's doctoral dissertation, published as *Johann Sebastian Bach und das Leipziger gottesdienstliche Leben seiner Zeit* (Berlin: Evangelische Verlagsanstalt, 1970).

60   Robin A Leaver, *Theologische Bibliothek: Eine kritische Bibliographie / Bach's Theological Library: A Critical Bibliography* (Stuttgart: Hänssler, 1983).

61   Robin A. Leaver, *J. S. Bach and Scripture: Glosses from the Calov Bible Commentary* (St. Louis: Concordia, 1985); Howard H. Cox, ed., *The Calov Bible of J. S. Bach* (Ann Arbor: UMI Research Press, 1985).

62   See note 10.

63   Although Eric Chafe is one of the principal scholars writing on Bach in theological perspective, this section does not address his writings because they are the focus of the "Musical Analysis" section earlier in this chapter.

64   Stephen A. Crist, "Historical Theology and Hymnology as Tools for Interpreting Bach's Church Cantatas: The Case of *Ich elender Mensch, wer wird mich erlösen*, BWV 48," *Historical Musicology: Sources, Methods, Interpretations*, ed. Stephen A. Crist and Robert Montemorra Marvin (Rochester: University of Rochester Press, 2004), 57–84. The article was first published in German as Stephen A. Crist, "Historische Theologie und Hymnologie als Interpretationshilfen für Bachs Kantate *Ich elender Mensch, wer wird mich erlösen* (BWV 48)," *Bachs 1. Leipziger Kantatenjahrgang: Bericht über das 3. Dortmunder Bach-Symposion 2000*, ed. Martin Geck, (Dortmund: Klangfarben, 2002), 303–27. Stephen A. Crist is currently completing a monograph with the provisional title: *Originality and Convention in the Arias of J. S. Bach*.

65   Crist, "Historical Theology," 79.

288   *Mark A. Peters*

The primary sources Crist engages are ones with close connections to Bach, primarily titles listed in the inventory of Bach's theological library. These include biblical commentaries by Abraham Calov, Johann Olearius, and August Pfeiffer; sermons for the Nineteenth Sunday after Trinity by Martin Luther, Heinrich Müller, August Hermann Francke, and Martin Geier; and hymnological sources by Johann Christoph Olearius, Johann Avenarius, and Caspar Binder. After a brief introduction to his methodology and sources, the bulk of the article is a movement-by-movement exposition of Cantata 48 in which the cantata's text and music are probed on the basis of these theological sources. Crist not only discusses contemporary theological understandings of the Gospel reading for the Nineteenth Sunday after Trinity and the text of Cantata 48, but also demonstrates the ways in which Bach provides an exposition of the cantata's text through his compositional choices in setting it.

Don O. Franklin's "The Role of the 'Actus Structure' in the Libretto of J. S. Bach's Matthew Passion" provides a second example of how historical theology can broaden our understanding of Bach's vocal works, in particular the way in which the analysis of a single source of historical theology can provide a rubric for interpreting a particular composition.[66] Franklin highlights the importance of Johann Olearius's *Biblische Erklärung*, a five-volume biblical commentary published between 1678 and 1681 and owned by Bach, for our understanding of the text and structure of the St. Matthew Passion.[67] In discussing the six successive "acts" that correspond to the primary events of the passion as defined by Lutheran tradition (the "Actus structure"), Franklin demonstrates that Picander's libretto for the St. Matthew Passion as set by Bach is modeled not on Martin Luther's understanding of the "Actus structure" but on that of Johann Olearius. A close reading of Olearius's commentary on the passion story in Matthew's Gospel in light of the "Actus structure" reveals significant insights into the way in which Bach and Picander understood and structured the story in their St. Matthew Passion.

A final example of a theological perspective on Bach's vocal music is Markus Rathey's "Drama and Discourse: The Form and Function of Chorale Tropes in Bach's Oratorios," an excellent example of the interweaving of contextual studies, musical and textual analysis, and theological understanding to reveal new

---

66   Don O. Franklin, "The Role of the 'Actus Structure' in the Libretto of J. S. Bach's Matthew Passion," *Music and Theology: Essays in Honor of Robin A. Leaver*, ed. Daniel Zager (Lanham: Scarecrow, 2007), 121–39.

67   Both Franklin and Petzoldt have argued convincingly for the significance of Olearius's *Biblische Erklärung* for theological understandings of Bach's vocal works. See, for example, Don O. Franklin, "The Libretto of Bach's John Passion and the Doctrine of Reconciliation: An Historical Perspective," *Das Blut Jesu und die Lehre von der Versöhnung im Werk Johann Sebastian Bachs*, ed. Albert A. Clement (Amsterdam: North-Holland, 1995), 179–203; Don O. Franklin, "'Recht glauben, Christlich leben, seelig sterben': Johann Olearius and Johann Sebastian Bach," *Die Quellen Johann Sebastian Bachs: Bachs Musik im Gottesdienst*, ed. Renate Steiger (Heidelberg: Manutius, 1998), 229–48; and Petzoldt, *Bach-Kommentar*, see note 10.

Vocal Music 289

insights into Bach's vocal works.[68] Rathey's study focuses on Bach's treatment of chorale tropes (movements which combine a newly written text with a traditional hymn) in the St. John Passion, St. Matthew Passion, and Christmas Oratorio. Through musical and textual analysis, Rathey demonstrates his thesis that in Bach's oratorios, "Chorale tropes appear at crucial moments, mostly at points where the doubt of the individual, ignited by the biblical narrative, must be overcome by the faith of the congregation."[69] Although the newly written text interpolations (recitatives and arias) represent the individual response of the Christian believer to the biblical story, chorales represent instead the collective response of the Christian congregation. Rathey explains further the theological significance of chorale tropes, in which there is a dialogue between the individual (recitative or aria) and the congregation (chorale): "In most cases they transform the individual by contrasting his or her doubts about the paradox of the incarnation or Christ's suffering with the position and knowledge of the congregation as it is spelled out (and codified) in the congregational hymns."[70]

To cite just one of Rathey's examples, Bach combines aria and chorale in "Mein teurer Heiland" of the St. John Passion. The movement, immediately following Jesus's death, juxtaposes an aria for bass modeled after an aria by Barthold Heinrich Brockes with the thirty-fourth stanza of the passion hymn *Jesu Leiden, Pein und* Tod in a four-part setting. Rathey shows that while the aria text expresses until the very end a lack of understanding of Jesus's passion, the individual (represented by the bass) is transformed by the Christian congregation (represented in the chorale), which "is already aware of Christ's resurrection and of the salvific and soteriological meaning of his death."[71]

As demonstrated by these examples, theological perspectives have much to contribute to our understanding of Bach's vocal music. Despite all the research on Bach in theological context, much remains to be done in this field as scholars continue to probe theological sources and the ways in which they can reveal new meanings for Bach's music. To date, relatively few book-length studies of Bach's music in theological perspective have been published. Most books on Bach and theology are either general reference works or collections of essays by different authors, although notable exceptions include Elke Axmacher's *"Aus Liebe will mein Heyland sterben": Untersuchung zum Wandel des Passionsverständnisses im frühen 18. Jahrhundert* (1984), Meinrad Walter's *Musik-Sprach des Glaubens: Zum geistlichen Vokalwerk Johann Sebastian Bachs* (1994), Michael Marissen's *Lutheranism, Anti-Judaism, and Bach's St. John Passion* (1998), and Eric Chafe's *Analyzing Bach's Cantatas* (2000).[72] In addition, several scholars

---

68 Markus Rathey, "Drama and Discourse: The Form and Function of Chorale Tropes in Bach's Oratorios," BP 8 (2011), 42–68.

69 Rathey, "Drama and Discourse," 44.

70 Rathey, "Drama and Discourse," 68.

71 Rathey, "Drama and Discourse," 45–47.

72 For Axmacher, Marissen, and Chafe, see notes 23 and 45; Meinrad Walter, *Musik-Sprach des Glaubens: Zum geistlichen Vokalwerk Johann Sebastian Bachs* (Frankfurt: Knecht, 1994).

290   *Mark A. Peters*

are currently researching particular repertories of Bach's vocal music informed by theological perspectives with the goal of publishing monographs on these topics. These include Robin A. Leaver on the passions, Markus Rathey on the Christmas Oratorio, and myself on Bach's settings of the Magnificat in German (BWV 10) and Latin (BWV 243 and 243a). It is to be hoped that these are only a few of many new studies that will reveal new understandings of Bach's vocal music and of the theological perspectives of Bach and his contemporaries.

Text

Closely related to theological perspectives on Bach's vocal music are studies of text, and indeed there is much overlap between the two. In addition to the various theological approaches discussed in the previous section, studies of text can be categorized as addressing three particular issues: meaning, poetry, and librettists. And although much has been done on Bach's vocal music in theological perspective, relatively few studies focus on these textual issues.

The study of text meaning is the area with the closest connection to theological research, as many theological studies are closely concerned with the meanings of texts and how they are realized in Bach's compositions. The many studies of theological sources important for our understanding of the texts Bach set and his musical realizations of them have drawn attention to the need for understanding such texts, and even their individual works, in eighteenth-century perspectives. Although modern meanings and later perspectives are certainly important in ongoing understanding of Bach's works, it is crucial also that we recognize the meanings these texts would have held for Bach and his contemporaries. Given the introduction to such studies in the previous section, I will not address further such detailed studies of sacred music. A few important sources for meanings of Bach's sacred vocal works do, however, warrant further mention.

Two recent studies have begun to address the need for greater attention to the understanding of the texts Bach set within the context of eighteenth-century theology and poetry. The first is Michael Marissen's *Bach's Oratorios: The Parallel German-English Texts with Annotations* (2008),[73] which provides German texts with English translations for the Christmas Oratorio, St. Matthew Passion, St. Mark Passion (by an anonymous composer, but performed at least twice by Bach), St. John Passion, Easter Oratorio, and Ascension Oratorio. In addition to providing lucid English translations that seek to convey as accurately as possible the sense of the original German, Marissen provides detailed footnotes on biblical contexts for understanding the texts as well as on how particular words and theological concepts were understood by Luther, Calov, and Olearius and as they have been understood also by modern biblical commentators.[74]

---

73   See note 23.

74   Marissen further describes his methodology and its importance within the contexts of the sacred cantatas in Michael Marissen, "Historically Informed Rendering of the Librettos from Bach's Church Cantatas," *Music and Theology*, ed. Daniel Zager, 103–20.

Lucia Haselböck's *Bach-Textlexikon: Ein Wörterbuch der religiösen Sprach-bilder im Vokalwerk von Johann Sebastian Bach* (2004),[75] likewise proves a valuable resource for understanding the theology and poetry of Bach's vocal works in contemporary context. Haselböck begins with a helpful introduction to German Baroque poetry in relation to the texts Bach set. The majority of the book is then a lexicon of key theological terms that appear in Bach's vocal music. Haselböck not only provides contemporary understandings for these terms, but also discusses the ways in which the term is used in Bach's vocal works.

Given the close attention to text meaning in Bach's sacred vocal music, it is somewhat surprising that little parallel study has been done of the secular can-tatas (as mentioned previously, studies of the secular cantatas tend to focus on their sacred parodies, in which the text is replaced in the process of a move-ment's reworking). That such studies can provide significant new understandings of Bach's works and compositional contexts is revealed in Szymon Paczkowski's 2007 article,[76] one of few studies to take seriously the texts of Bach's secular can-tatas. Paczkowski argues convincingly that a proper understanding of *Zerreißet, zersprenget, zertrümmert die Gruft* (BWV 205) not only informs our interpre-tation of the cantata itself but also of its later manifestation as BWV 205a and of Bach's reuse of its music in the cantatas BWV 216 and 216a. Paczkowski provides a fascinating contextual study of the text and its contemporary meanings within the framework of the occasions for which the cantatas were first performed.

Although trends towards understanding contemporary meanings of the texts Bach set are encouraging, there has been an almost complete lack of attention to the poetic nature of such texts. Little scholarly attention has been paid to the poetic qualities of Bach's texts outside of Harald Streck's classic study.[77] More recently, however, Isabella van Elferen has researched the background of seventeenth-century devotional poetics and their influence on the music of Bach and his predecessors.[78] The field of Bach research would benefit greatly from scholars of eighteenth-century German poetry turning their attention to the po-etic texts Bach set, as well as from Bach scholars examining more closely Bach's texts as poetry and not merely as conveyors of meaning.

A final issue related to the texts Bach set is that of librettists, and here, too, there is much opportunity for further research. It is true that the librettists are not known for many of Bach's vocal works. But little still has been done on

---

75 Lucia Haselböck, *Bach-Textlexikon: Ein Wörterbuch der religiösen Sprachbilder im Vokalwerk von Johann Sebastian Bach* (Kassel: Bärenreiter, 2004).

76 Szymon Paczkowski, "A Polonaise Duet for a Professor, a King and a Merchant: on Cantatas BWV 205, 205a, 216, and 216a by Johann Sebastian Bach," *Understanding Bach* 2 (2007): 19–36. See also Szymon Paczkowski, *Styl polski w muzyce Johanna Sebastiana Bacha* (Lublin: Polihymnia, 2011); ET: Szymon Paczkowski, *Polish Style in the Music of Johann Sebastian Bach*, trans. Piotr Szymczak (Lanham: Roman & Littlefield, 2017).

77 Harald Streck, *Die Verskunst in den poetischen Texten zu den Kantaten J. S. Bachs* (Hamburg: Verlag der Musikalienhandlung, 1971).

78 Isabella van Elferen, *Mystical Love in the German Baroque: Theology, Poetry, Music* (Lanham: Scarecrow, 2009).

292   Mark A. Peters

those librettists who are identified, including Salomo Franck, Johann Christoph Gottsched, Christian Friedrich Henrici (Picander), Johann Oswald Knauer, Georg Christian Lehms, Erdmann Neumeister, and Christiane Mariane von Ziegler. Although a number of articles introduce these poets and their connections with Bach and his vocal music,[79] the only book-length account of a single librettist connected with Bach is my study of Mariane von Ziegler.[80] It is hoped that more studies of Bach's librettists will be undertaken, providing further biographical, poetic, and contextual insights into the lives and works of these important individuals.

Contextual Studies

The preceding two sections, on theology and text, have demonstrated multiple ways in which our understanding of Bach's music has been broadened through contextual study. As scholars in the field of musicology have in recent decades emphasized such broad contextual understandings of music and musicians, many Bach scholars have likewise begun to incorporate such methodology. Recent collected essays that expand our understanding of contexts in which Bach lived, worked, and composed include those edited by Carol Baron and Raymond Erickson,[81] and three volumes edited by Christoph Wolff particularly introduce such contextual study in relation to Bach's sacred and secular cantatas.[82] The present volume is itself a testimony to the ways in which Bach research is being informed by contextual study. Although studies of sources and genres are well represented, likewise are contextual studies (Chapters 5–8), studies of Bach's music within broader compositional contexts (Chapters 9–10), and studies of how Bach's music and compositional style have been received and disseminated (Chapters 17–19). Given the nature of this volume as highlighting such contextual study and the

---

79 The standard overview of Bach's librettists, now quite dated, is Ferdinand Zander, "Die Dichter der Kantatentexte Johann Sebastian Bachs: Untersuchungen zu ihrer Bestimmung," BJ 54 (1968): 9–64. Articles on particular librettists include Elisabeth Noack, "Georg Christian Lehms, ein Textdichter Johann Sebastian Bachs," BJ 56 (1970): 7–18; Helmut K. Krausse, "Eine neue Quelle zu drei Kantatentexten Johann Sebastian Bachs [on Knauer]," BJ 67 (1981): 7–22; Helmut K. Krausse, "Erdmann Neumeister und die Kantatentexte Johann Sebastian Bachs," BJ 72 (1986): 7–31; Elke Axmacher, "Erdmann Neumeister: Ein Kantatendichter J. S. Bachs," MuK 60 (1990): 249–302; and Robin A. Leaver, "Oper in der Kirche: Bach und der Kantatenstreit im frühen 18. Jahrhundert, BJ 99 (2013): 171–203. Picander is the librettist most discussed in the Bach literature, most often in discussions of chronology (speculations of Bach's fourth cantata Jahrgang as the "Picander Jahrgang") or of the St. Matthew Passion.

80 Mark A. Peters, *A Woman's Voice in Baroque Music: Mariane von Ziegler and J. S. Bach* (Aldershot: Ashgate, 2008).

81 Carol K. Baron, ed., *Bach's Changing World: Voices in the Community* (Rochester: University of Rochester Press, 2006); Raymond Erickson, ed., *The Worlds of Johann Sebastian Bach* (New York: Amadeus, 2009).

82 Christoph Wolff, ed., *Die Welt der Bach-Kantaten*, 3 vols. (Stuttgart: Metzler, 1996–1999); also issued in Dutch and Italian; ET of the first volume: *The World of the Bach Cantatas: Johann Sebastian Bach's Early Sacred Cantatas* (New York: Norton, 1995).

Vocal Music   293

extent to which such studies are addressed in other chapters, I will only briefly mention here a few recent exemplary studies that relate to Bach's vocal music.

One excellent example of how our understanding of Bach's vocal music is expanded through studies of historical context and reception is Tanya Kevorkian's *Baroque Piety*.[83] By exploring Leipzig's religious and musical culture through social history, Kevorkian broadens our view of the city and its religious and musical life in the period leading up to and including Bach's time as cantor. The book presents three main theses that are intertwined throughout: that the church was the main public arena for the regular negotiation of fundamental issues; that Baroque music was both embedded in religious culture and likewise helped to structure that culture; and that the conflict between the Pietists and non-Pietists shook the entire religious system.[84] Kevorkian likewise brings into conversation with each other three fields of scholarly inquiry: the social history of religion, musicology, and Pietist history.

Kevorkian presents a complex and intriguing picture of the ways in which negotiations took place in the arena of Leipzig's public religious life. She considers a variety of groups involved in such negotiations (property-owning inhabitants [burghers], non-property owners, city councilors, clerics, musicians, the Saxon Electors, and consistory officials), as well as of concrete practices through which negotiations were carried out (pew-holding, education, and clerical and musical appointments). As Kevorkian explains, "Ordinary people and authorities alike, with the partial exception of Pietists, made little effort to avoid secular categories of status, gender, property, and other forms of hierarchy, which were openly carried over into the religious arena."[85] By considering new sources and varied modes of inquiry, Kevorkian opens up a wealth of new insights into Leipzig during the years 1650–1750.

One fascinating example that certainly places Bach's vocal music in a new light is Kevorkian's picture of how congregants experienced the church service, including congregants' practices of arrival, departure, seating, and other behaviors, their reception of and participation in music, and their reception of the sermon. Kevorkian explains:

> If the service is regarded as an arena in which interactions among inhabitants, visitors, and urban authorities were negotiated and reproduced, a complex picture emerges. Congregants did their best to display a variety of social, occupational, and gender differences. Far from passively receiving the messages that the producers of the service meant to convey, congregants timed their arrival and departure and paid attention selectively, according to their varying social, musical, religious, and political interests.[86]

---

83 Tanya Kevorkian, *Baroque Piety: Religion, Society, and Music in Leipzig, 1650–1750* (Aldershot: Ashgate, 2007).
84 Kevorkian, *Baroque Piety*, 1–2.
85 Kevorkian, *Baroque Piety*, 5–6.
86 Kevorkian, *Baroque Piety*, 51.

294   *Mark A. Peters*

Although we think of Bach's sacred vocal music in light of modern standards of concert listening (remaining seated, listening in silence, devoting full attention to the music) such standards were simply not in place in Bach's Leipzig. By revealing significant new details about musical production and reception, Kevorkian's book gives us a much more complex—and much richer—understanding of Bach's role in Leipzig's musical and religious culture.

Another important category of contextual studies related to Bach's vocal music is that of the later reception of Bach's vocal works. Much of this research has focused on the 1829 performance of Bach's St. Matthew Passion at the Sing-Akademie zu Berlin, a performance led by Carl Friedrich Zelter and Felix Mendelssohn.[87] Such studies are representative of one important trend in the study of reception history: contextual studies of performances of Bach's vocal music, which often focus on motivation for and details of the performance and on popular and critical response. Another important field of inquiry in Bach reception is that of Bach's influence on later composers. In addition to the recent wealth of new studies of Bach's sons and students, Bach's vocal music has, for example, been studied extensively in light of Johannes Brahms's interactions with it as a performer, scholar, editor, and composer.[88]

Another exciting aspect of research in Bach studies is the relationship of Bach's works to those of his contemporaries. Scholars are just beginning to study the vast repertories of vocal music by such composers as Georg Philipp Telemann, Christoph Graupner, Gottfried Heinrich Stölzel, Johann Friedrich Fasch, and Carl Philipp Emanuel Bach. Although it lies beyond the scope of the present chapter to even begin to address the works of such composers, the recent attention by scholars to their works offers vast possibilities for research into the vocal music of the early eighteenth century. And continued studies of the vocal music of Bach's contemporaries will not only inform our understanding of Bach's own vocal works, but will introduce to scholars and concert audiences alike a wealth of compositions little known before.

---

87 Studies include Barbara David Wright, "Johann Sebastian Bach's *Matthäus-Passion*: A Performance History 1829–1854" (Ph.D. diss.: University of Michigan, 1983); Michael Marissen, "Religious Aims in Mendelssohn's 1829 Berlin-Sing-Akademie Performances of Bach's *St. Matthew Passion*," MQ 77 (1993): 718–26; Andreas Glöckner, "Zelter und Mendelssohn—Zur 'Wiederentdeckung' der Matthäus-Passion im Jahre 1829," BJ 90 (2004): 133–55; and Celia Applegate, *Bach in Berlin: Nation and Culture in Mendelssohn's Revival of the* St. Matthew Passion (Ithaca: Cornell University Press, 2005).

88 See, for example, Virginia Hancock, *Brahms's Choral Compositions and His Library of Early Music* (Ann Arbor: UMI Research Press, 1983); Virginia Hancock, "Brahms's Performances of Early Choral Music," *Nineteenth-Century Music* 8 (1984): 125–41; Daniel Beller-McKenna, "The Great *Warum?* Job, Christ, and Bach in a Brahms Motet," *Nineteenth-Century Music* 19 (1996): 231–51; Michael Musgrave, *Brahms: A German Requiem*, Cambridge Music Handbooks (Cambridge: Cambridge University Press, 1996); and Robin A. Leaver, "Brahms's Opus 45 and German Protestant Funeral Music," JM 19 (2002): 616–640.

12 Keyboard Music

David Yearsley

Bach composed a large and diverse body of music playable on keyboard instruments. His fame during his lifetime and his posthumous reputation were built on this corpus, coupled with his abilities as an organist and his dedication as a teacher—pedagogical purposes having motivated the composition (and copying) of much of his oeuvre.[1] The number of "keyboard" entries in the flawed, but still-preferred catalog of his works, Wolfgang Schmieder's *Bach-Werke-Verzeichnis* (BWV), first published in 1950, approaches half of the entire list, which, at this point, ends with BWV 1128. The keyboard music runs from the first of the set of six organ Trio Sonatas (BWV 525), through the free organ works, to the chorale-based preludes in the 600s and 700s; many of these pieces are without pedal (*manualiter*) but have retained, often by force of convention, their identity as "organ" works. The treatment of chorale melodies in these preludes associates them with the church service, though playing such pieces on harpsichord or clavichord was a common feature of Lutheran domestic piety and of musical training. What are most often now called the "harpsichord" or "keyboard" works commence with BWV 772, the first of the two-part *Inventions*. The 800s are taken up mostly by the great collections of suites and the two books of the Well-Tempered Clavier, with the 900s consumed by miscellaneous works and more than a few spurious intruders into the Bach canon. The BWV returns to the keyboard with 1079 and 1080, the Canonic Variations on *Vom Himmel hoch* and the *Art of Fugue*, accorded a single entry. Almost all of the rediscoveries of Bach's music over the past half-century have been of keyboard music: the "Neumeister" Chorales (BWV 1090–1120) were brought to light in 1985; the Fantasia in C Minor (BWV 1121), an early autograph in German organ tablature discovered in 1982; and, more recently, the 2008 reappearance of an impressive chorale fantasia, also an early work, on *Wo Gott der Herr nicht bei uns hält* (BWV 1128), currently the terminus of the meandering BWV itinerary. The placement of the keyboard duets (BWV 802–805) reflects the Procrustean nature of this (or perhaps any) catalog: they were published by Bach in the *Clavierübung III*,

---

1 George Stauffer, "J. S. Bach as Organ Pedagogue," *The Organist as Scholar: Essays in Memory of Russell Saunders* (Stuyvesant: Pendragon Press, 1994): 25–44.

296   *David Yearsley*

which names on its title-page the organ; yet they were nested by the architect of the 1950 BWV catalog, Wolfgang Schmieder, among the "harpsichord" works because they are without pedals and do not treat a chorale. Whether these criteria were shared by, or particularly relevant to, Bach's view of the appropriateness of one keyboard instrument over another for a given piece seems doubtful.

In light of the sheer quantity of this body of music, a complete perusal of the shelves of scholarship it has inspired would be impossible here. Yet this survey of the catalog has already engaged, if obliquely, some of the important issues confronted by Bach scholarship over the past few decades. The first of these is more than simply terminological: what is meant by "keyboard music"? I will begin by examining some of the crucial implications of this question and its relation to Bach's oeuvre and scholarship. I will then turn to related organo- logical issues and their ramifications for performance. Scholarly inquiry into these matters has generally relied on source studies, a perennial strength of Bach scholarship, and I will turn to this area before moving to more recent work that adopts a more overtly hermeneutic approach. In conclusion, I present a short case study of the debate over the authenticity of Bach's most famous "organ" work, the *Toccata and Fugue in D Minor* (BWV 565): this controversy was joined over aspects of style and source studies, and, indeed, the question as to what consti- tutes "keyboard" music. In revisiting these scholarly tests and triumphs, I hope also to point towards some potentially rewarding directions for further research into Bach's keyboard works. My central claim—hardly objectionable—is that the cooperation not only among these fields, but also between performance and scholarship, has led to some of the most important work in recent decades, and will continue to map out the productive territory ahead.

Hierarchies

The two most important modern surveys of Bach's works for keyboard instru- ments are Peter Williams, *The Organ Music of J. S. Bach,* and David Schulen- berg's *The Keyboard Music of J. S.* Bach; both are available in recently revised editions that reflect many new findings in the field.[2] Tellingly, both of these books are organized according to the distinction embedded in the BWV between "or- gan" and "keyboard," the latter implying that no pedals are used and bringing to mind the harpsichord, and the former suggesting pedals and/or treatment of cho- rale melodies. Although both are indispensable as reference tools, each is much more than simply that, and is filled with unique insights, and usefully unsettling questions (especially in the case of Peter Williams' book). Another still more re- cent and extremely valuable compendium and sourcebook is *Bachs Klavier- und Orgelwerke* edited by Siegbert Rampe; its two volumes also accept the category of "keyboard" and "organ," even if the contents of the essays are not necessarily

---

2 Peter Williams, *The Organ Music of J. S. Bach* (Cambridge: Cambridge University Press, 2004); David Schulenberg, *The Keyboard Music of J. S. Bach*, 2nd ed. (New York: Routledge, 2006).

divided according to the *pedaliter / manualiter* dichotomy, but more along the lines of genre and compositional construction; indeed, these stylistic and historical connections work against the division implicit in the book's title.[3] Although the titles and concerns of all of these books are adopted partly as a matter of marketing and utility, the authors themselves register the many problems with the general taxonomy, and recognize the fluidity of the repertoire across these often-arbitrary boundaries. Still, the distinction between "keyboard" and "organ" retains currency, and it would indeed be hard from our twenty-first-century position to imagine an alternative approach. This vantage point is fundamentally different from that of the eighteenth century.

Most modern listeners, players, and scholars come to Bach's keyboard music first through the modern piano, often learning pieces from the Inventions and Sinfonias, before moving on to the Well-Tempered Clavier, the Suites and Partitas, and, if continuing onward to the heights of Bachian achievement, to the Goldberg Variations—although there has been a rapid increase in the number of historically informed performances and recordings of this *Clavierübung* IV on old eighteenth-century harpsichords or modern copies of historic instruments; the recordings on modern piano of Glenn Gould from 1955 and 1981[4] remain a kind of reference point, definitive in spite, or perhaps largely because, of their bracing eccentricity. General knowledge of the organ works among Bach devotees is much more limited, with celebrity in that area of his corpus largely monopolized by the *Toccata and Fugue in D Minor* (BWV 565). The piano is the basic keyboard resource for Bach's music, as in Joseph Kerman's endearing portrait of his readership of Bach enthusiasts at their instruments—

> home pianists who have often found themselves drawn to Bach over the years, often to pieces they have known for as long as they can remember, and whose deep pleasure in them is not blunted too much by cautious tempos, uneven articulation, or even a certain amount of stumbling. This community is said to be dead or dying, but I reckon the reports are exaggerated.[5]

In the eighteenth century, the keyboard landscape was far more varied, but the basic instruments available to students, amateurs, and professionals were the one- or two-manual harpsichord, and the more utilitarian, and indeed more expressive clavichord, claimed by Bach's first biographer, Johann Nikolaus Forkel, to have been the instrument Bach favored for "private musical entertainments."[6]

---

3 Siegbert Rampert, ed., *Bachs Klavier- und Orgelwerke: Das Handbuch*, 2 vols. (Laaber-Verlag: Laaber, 2008); see also the earlier study, Paul Badura-Skoda, *Interpreting Bach at the Keyboard* (Oxford: Oxford University Press, 1993).

4 A photo of Gould graces the cover of Rampe's second volume.

5 Joseph Kerman, *The Art of Fugue: Bach Fugues for Keyboard, 1715–1750* (Berkeley: University of California Press, 2005), xvii.

6 Johann Nikolaus Forkel, *Ueber Johann Sebastian Bachs Leben, Kunst und Kunstwerke* (Leipzig: Hoffmeister & Kühnel, 1802; reprinted., Kassel: Bärenreiter, 1999), 17; Dok 7: 29; NBR, 436.

298   *David Yearsley*

The eighteenth century was itself a rich period for innovation and invention of new keyboard instruments: Bach owned a *Lautenwerk*, an instrument with gut strings, and endowed with a lush, mellower sound than the harpsichord. Bach's colleague, the organ-maker Gottfried Silbermann, invented a *Cembalo d'amore*, a clavichord with strings that were not fixed to the bridge, and would be raised by the tangents when struck, allowing them to ring more freely. Other experiments included the *Tangentenflügel*, a kind of keyboard variant of the hammer dulcimer, and credited to another Bach contemporary and acquaintance, Pantaleon Hebenstreit;[7] Silbermann also made these instruments. Bach himself played some of the first early pianos in Germany, those made by the immensely capable Silbermann. The German word "Clavier" tends to refer to the clavichord, especially towards the end of the eighteenth century; but the term can be ambiguous, sometimes purposefully so. When we refer to "keyboard" music, and therefore to "keyboard" instruments, we should remember that the situation in Bach's day was wonderfully chaotic, and therefore all the richer. Long misunderstood by modernists, this diverse instrumentarium and the range of sonorities it produced endured attacks on the very use of "inexpressive" historic instruments, most infamously in Theodor Adorno's essay, "Bach Defended Against His Devotees," which decried the "acoustically static character of the harpsichord and organ."[8] Ten years later, Friedrich Blume was similarly dismissive with his strident answer to his own rhetorical question, aimed primarily at severing any affinity between Bach and the church: "Was Bach particularly attached to the organ? Hardly."[9]

The keyboard operated with hands alone is the prime conduit through which to hear Bach's "keyboard" music, whereas the organ has to some degree been displaced to the sidelines in twentieth- and twenty-first-century culture and this must have an effect, even if indirect, on scholarly attitudes. The modern primacy of domestic keyboard instruments over the church organ inverts the aesthetic hierarchy that prevailed in Bach's time. His contemporary, the Hamburg music theorist Johann Mattheson, began his first book, *Das neu-eröffnete Orchestre* of 1713, by proceeding through the accepted retinue of instruments and crowning it with the organ—"the most perfect" member of the European instrumentarium.[10] Mattheson carried this view through his life asserting in his masterpiece, *Der vollkommene Capellmeister* of 1740, that "no single instrument can compare with the organ."[11] There are any number of sources that espouse this same view. Closer to J. S. Bach's time and circle, Jakob Adlung's *Anleitung zu der*

---

7 Christian Ahrens, "Pantaleon Hebenstreit und die Frühgeschichte des Hammerklaviers," *Beiträge zur Musikwissenschaft* 29 (1987): 37–48.

8 Theodor Adorno, "Bach Defended Against His Devotees," *Prisms*, trans. Samuel and Sherry Weber (Cambridge: MIT Press, 1981), 141.

9 Friedrich Blume, "Outlines of a New Picture of Bach," ML 44 (1963): 217.

10 Joann Mattheson, *Das neu-eröffnete Orchestre* (Hamburg: [the author], 1713; reprint Hildesheim: Olms, 1991), 256.

11 Johann Mattheson, *Der vollkommene Capellmeister* (Hamburg: Herold, 1739; reprint Kassel: Bärenreiter, 1954), 479; ET Ernest C. Harriss, *Johann Mattheson's Der vollkommene Capellmeister* (Ann Arbor: UMI, 1981), 861.

Keyboard Music 299

musikalischen Gelahrtheit of 1758 begins the treatment of practical music with the organ, devoting to it 200 of the volume's 800 pages.[12] Adlung's discussion of the previously mentioned *Lautenwerk* reflects this hierarchy, when he described it as "the most beautiful of all keyboard instruments *after* the organ"[13] (emphasis added). It was assumed by these writers – and one must infer, Bach himself—that the organ marked the summit of keyboard culture.

Bach's early livelihood and burgeoning reputation derived from his mastery both as a player of the organ and an expert in its construction. The importance of these skills, ones that sent him climbing so quickly up the ladder of professional advancement in his native central Germany, had to do not least with the expense of the organ. Faced with the capital costs of organ projects, church committees needed reliable experts such as Bach, who could inspect these instruments and then bring them to musical life in the divine service. Thus the title of the Obituary, written by C. P. E. Bach, J. F. Agricola, and L. C. Mizler and published in 1754 in the latter's periodical, *Die Musicalische Bibliothek*, described the deceased as "The World Famous Organist."[14] Nowadays the keyboard for the feet—the pedalboard—so essential to the specifically German way of playing the organ is not so much forgotten, as it is considered an almost secondary phenomenon.[15] Although it is true that in the eighteenth century far less organ music was published than *manualiter* works, this was due to the fact that while there was a burgeoning market for domestic keyboard collections, there was little demand for printed organ music, as organists largely improvised or circulated their music in manuscript copies. The four parts of Bach's *Clavierübung* series show this: the first (the Partitas), second (the French Overture and Italian Concerto), and the fourth (the "Goldberg" Variations) list harpsichord on their title-pages; only the third part is expressly intended for organ and its difficulty is emphasized in the title-page, which claims that the works contained are especially suited to "Connoisseurs" (Kenner). The organ was harder, more complicated, and more costly than all of the other keyboard instruments—but its rewards were deemed greater.

Forkel's account of Bach's organ music begins with a forceful assertion of the centrality of the pedal to the German organ:

> The pedals are an essential part of the organ: by them alone is it exalted above all other instruments, for its magnificence, grandeur, majesty depend upon them. Without the pedals, this great instrument is no longer great: it approaches the little positives, which are of no value in the eyes of competent judges. But the great organ, provided with pedals, must be so managed that

---

12 Jakob Adlung, *Anleitung zu der musicalischen Gelahrtheit* (Erfurt: Jungnicol, 1758; reprint, Kassel, Bärenreiter, 1953), 337–550.

13 Jakob Adlung, *Musica mechanica organoedi* (Berlin: Birnstiel, 1768; reprint Kassel: Bärenreiter, 1931), 2: 133.

14 Dok 3: 80 (No. 666); NBR 297 (No. 306).

15 See David Yearsley, *Bach's Feet: the Organ Pedals in European Culture* (Cambridge: Cambridge University Press, 2012).

300 *David Yearsley*

> its whole compass is brought into action: in other words, the composer and
> the player must require from it all that it can perform. Nobody has ever done
> this more than J. S. Bach.[16]

To claim yourself as a complete keyboard player in eighteenth-century Germany was to be able to play the organ with obbligato pedal.

Though I am being more than a little polemical in adjusting the historiographical frame around the landscape of Bach keyboard studies, I do believe that an organ-centered revision of scholarly approaches to the field is long overdue. It is not that we are lacking important studies of many aspects of Bach's organs and his music, but rather that the kinds of questions one asks as a professional musician, scholar or amateur player are necessarily shaded by one's mode of access to the music and the relative prestige of the recognized instruments now in use.

This state of affairs helps to explain the impact of Robert Marshall's 1986 article, "Organ or 'Klavier'? Instrumental Prescriptions in the Sources of Bach's Keyboard Works," but also some of its seemingly anachronistic attitudes.[17] The essay constituted a major challenge to then current notions of the instruments Bach might have had in mind when conceiving of a range of works to be played at the keyboard, either with the hands alone or with both hands and feet. Marshall's essay came partly in response to Heinz Lohmann's somewhat controversial complete edition of the "organ works" published between 1968 and 1979;[18] this edition included many *manualiter* works, including the "keyboard" Toccatas (BWV 910–916). Although praising some of Lohmann's inclusions because they upended the division between organ and keyboard, Marshall rightly criticized his edition for its often arbitrary assignment of some fifty new works to the organ. According to Marshall, Lohmann relied too heavily on his own tastes and inclinations rather than the indications of the source materials and eighteenth-century notions regarding the relationships of the instruments. While acknowledging that most scholars of Bach's music have long operated under the premise that all keyboard instruments "shared a common repertoire,"[19] Marshall argued that even though Bach often wrote pieces for a "universally available medium" (that is, clavichord, harpsichord, or organ), he did conceive of them for particular instruments, even if, as Marshall also noted, the composer would have readily sanctioned performance on any of them. For example, while early sources of the "keyboard" Toccatas do not survive in autograph copies, the sources are close enough to Bach to render the instrument indications of considerable value; the use of the term *manualiter* in these sources is an anomaly rarely found in

---

16 Forkel, *Bachs Leben, Kunst und Kunstwerke*, 59; Dok 7: 76–77; NBR, 470.

17 Robert L. Marshall, "Organ or 'Klavier'? Instrumental Prescriptions in the Sources of Bach's Keyboard Works," *J. S. Bach as Organist: His Instruments, Music, and Performance Practices*, ed. George Stauffer and Ernest May (London: Batsford, 1986), 212–240.

18 J. S. Bach, *Sämtliche Orgelwerke*, 10 vols., ed. Heinz Lohmann (Wiesbaden: Breitkopf & Härtel, 1968–1979).

19 Marshall cites Willi Apel's *The History of Keyboard Music to 1700* (Bloomington: Indiana University Press, 1972), 3.

non-pedal pieces, such as the suites, works that seem clearly to be intended for the harpsichord or clavichord. Marshall therefore draws the inference that Bach had the organ in mind for the Toccatas.

Marshall's most radical suggestion, however, was that both books of the Well-Tempered Clavier, spanning some two decades of Bach's life from the early 1730s into the 1740s could have been conceived as organ pieces, for hands alone—a path that even Lohmann was apparently unwilling to tread.[20] While Marshall's boundaries between the various instruments and their repertoire is fluid, and although he cites the free-ranging modes of transcription typical of Bach and his contemporaries, he does not reject all distinctions between them. Further, Marshall argues that the harpsichord was hardly a solo "recital" instrument. It was at the organ that Bach and his contemporaries were heard as virtuosos in public; this had to do not just with the higher decibel power of which the organ was capable, but because of the prestige of its technological complexity, sonic variety, and extended contrapuntal capabilities.

Marshall's essay marks a crucial contribution to the field because it both embraces the dynamic nature, and ecumenical approach to writing for keyboard characteristic of the age, but it also argues that in spite of its more limited manual compass in comparison to most harpsichords (and harpsichord music by Bach), the organ was the dominant public instrument and one on which much *manualiter* music long associated with the harpsichord (and later the piano) was appropriate, even to be preferred. Taken for granted in Marshall's argument is that *manualiter* meant that the feet were not deployed; as I touch on later in this essay, there is a rich performance tradition of adding pedal to pieces that have no explicit indications in the original sources for use of the feet. We have Marshall largely to thank for orienting us towards this more eighteenth-century attitude. Another aspect of eighteenth-century keyboard culture, also touched on by Marshall, has to do with the fact that the organ was the transcription instrument par excellence; nothing prevented the organist from colonizing other repertories, indeed, he was encouraged to do so. Distinctions between keyboard instruments were ones of convenience or marketability rather than hard-and-fast barriers of any kind. Marshall's essay was so useful—and so provocative—partly because it challenged the marginalization of the organ. Ironically, it was a provocation that would have been utterly lost on eighteenth-century professional keyboardists. The way to be freed from the obsession with the question as to which instrument is "intended" or most "appropriate" is to adopt an all-embracing attitude across the spectrum of keyboard instruments, with the organ as an encompassing ideal. This is not to claim that Bach undervalued the clavichord (another long-neglected instrument) and its unmatched intimacy, or the harpsichord, but merely that the heavenly organ was most prized. This broader, yet also more hierarchized, view of eighteenth-century keyboard culture will, I believe, lead to some new questions for scholarship to pursue.

---

20 Marshall says nothing of the possible involvement of the pedal in these pieces, a common enough practice in "manualiter" repertoire of Bach's time.

302   *David Yearsley*

Organological Matters

Marshall uses Alfred Dürr's study of the compasses of keyboards played by Bach in exploring the issue of the composer's "intended" keyboard instruments.[21] The underlying assumption is that when Bach composed a piece, he had the local instruments in mind. In the case of organs, this method assigns, even if tentatively, a piece to a particular period in Bach's career by ascertaining the range of the works and relating this to organological facts: the Neue Kirche in Arnstadt, where Bach worked from 1703 to 1707, had a manual compass from C to c3 and the pedal from C to d1; the organ at his next post at St. Blasius, in Mühlhausen, where he lived from 1707 to 1708, had a range of C to d3 in the manual and from C to d1 in the pedal; the instrument in the Schlosskirche in Weimar, where Bach took up his post as Court Organist in 1708 and where, according to his Obituary, he composed most of his organ works, went only to c3 in the manuals; the pedal compass at Weimar ran from C to e1. This organological evidence helps establish links between Bach's compositional output and particular instruments, and therefore contributes to attempts at establishing a chronology for the repertoire.

Bach's *Toccata in F Major* (BWV 540) is the most obvious and oft-used example. Uniquely, this piece reached way up to f3 in the manuals and f1 in the pedal, most famously and arduously in one of the two solos for feet alone. The only instrument with this manual and pedal range was that in the court chapel in Weißenfels, to which Bach had close ties; the obvious conclusion is that Bach composed the flamboyant piece with this organ in mind. What this plainly shows is that, at least in some cases, there is a connection between instrument and the origins of, and impulse behind, a piece. Yet one should remember that this does not define or circumscribe the work, but rather is only a part of its larger reception and performance history.[22] Adaptability and transformation were not only the right of Bach as composer, but of all who took an interest in his music and played it. Bach was the greatest master of just this kind of adaptability; indeed, recent work on his instrumental music shows him to be one of the greatest and most opportunistic practitioners of this aspect of the musical craft of the eighteenth century.[23]

According to his Obituary, Bach took a keen interest in music technology; his work as an organ consultant, and his responsibilities for organ and harpsichord

---

21 Alfred Dürr, "Tastenumfang und Chronologie in Bachs Klavierwerken," *Festschrift George von Dadelsen zum 60. Geburtstag*, ed. Thomas Kohlhase and Volker Scherliess (Stuttgart: Hänssler, 1978), 73–88.

22 Bach's student, Johann Ludwig Krebs, owned a version of the famous Toccata probably copied in the second decade of the eighteenth century by his father Johann Tobias, who had also been a pupil of Bach; this reading of the piece (D-B Mus. Ms. Bach P 803) kept the pedal part within a compass of C to c1 and the manuals between C and c3, thus rendering the piece playable on all central German organs, including the famous instrument by Tobias Heinrich Gottfried Trost made between 1735 and 1739 for the Altenburg castle chapel where Johann Ludwig Krebs was long organist. See Dietrich Kilian, NBA IV: 5–6, KB, 405–408.

23 See, for example, BP 7.

Keyboard Music 303

maintenance, bear this out. According to Adlung, he also played an important role in the early development of the fortepiano in Germany.[24] Bach is known to have acted as agent for the sale of one of Silbermann's pianos in May 1749.[25] He was apparently keen to embrace and encourage new developments, especially when they fulfilled his high standards for musical expression. The crucial studies of instrument-makers closely associated with Bach are Ulrich Dähnert's monographs on the work of organ builders Gottfried Silbermann and Zacharias Hildebrandt; Bach acted as consultant for the latter's magnum opus in Naumburg (40 km from Leipzig), which was dedicated in 1746.[26] That this great organ, as well as other important instruments known to, and admired by Bach, are still extant and indeed playable in restored condition encourages further research, particularly in relation to performance. Quentin Faulkner's work, which combines a reading of relevant theoretical sources with organological expertise and first-hand experience with the instruments, has yielded important insights, not only for performance practice, but also with regard to organ design and its relation to compositional style; one of the objects of study becomes the nature of eighteenth-century sonority, something that only direct experience can provide.[27] Faulkner's work draws extensively on Jakob Adlung's *Musica mechanica organoedi* of 1768, which Faulkner has translated, and that contains, as mentioned previously, exceptionally valuable information on the keyboard instruments of Bach's time.[28] Peter Williams has also confronted the notion of the "Bach" organ in his study of the organ works. Also important is Lynn Edwards Butler's ongoing work on central German organs.[29] As Adlung and modern scholars such as those just mentioned have noted, Bach ardently admired the instruments of Hamburg, much different than those of central Germany.[30] What these important studies investigate is the changing aesthetic of the organ during Bach's time, and both the specificity and wide-ranging nature of his tastes.

An outstanding example of the interplay between organology, source studies, and the critical reading of the musical texts can be found in George Stauffer's important work on the organ preludes. Combining a thorough investigation into

---

24 NBR, 365–6 (No. 358b); Dok 3: 194–195 (No. 743).

25 NBR, 239 (No. 262), 365–366 (No. 358d); Dok 3: 194 (No. 743), 633 (No. 142a)

26 Ulrich Dähnert, *Der Orgel- und Instrumentenbauer Zacharias Hildebrandt: Sein Verhältnis zu Gottfried Silbermann und Johann Sebastian Bach* (Leipzig: Breitkopf & Härtel,1962); Ulrich Dähnert, *Die Orgeln Gottfried Silbermanns in Mitteldeutschland* (Leipzig: Koehler & Amelang, 1953). See also Christoph Wolff and Markus Zepf, *The Organs of J. S. Bach: A Handbook*, trans. Lynn Edwards Butler (Urbana: University of Illinois Press, 2012), 70–73.

27 Quentin Faulkner, "Jakob Adlung's *Musica Mechanica Organoedi* and the 'Bach Organ'" BACH 21/1 (1990): 42–59; see also Quentin Faulkner, *The Registration of J. S. Bach's Organ Works* (Colfax: Leupold, 2008).

28 See Jacob Adlung, *Musica mechanica organoedi: Musical Mechanics for the Orgnist*, trans. Quentin Faulkner (Lincoln: Zea E-Books, 2011).

29 Lynn Edwards, "The Thuringian Organ, 1702–1720: "...Ein wohlgerathenes gravitätisches Werk," *Organ Yearbook* 22 (1991): 119–150.

30 NBR, 364 (Nos 358a-b); Dok 3: 191–192 (Nos. 739–740).

304 *David Yearsley*

contemporary theoretical sources with careful analysis of the notation of the sources of the preludes, Stauffer concluded that these free works were played on a single manual without changes, on large registrations (indicated by the phrase *pro organo pleno*—"for full organ"—itself not a prescriptive label, but one with many subtle variations). Stauffer's convincing thesis transformed contemporary practice, which had typically involved multiple changes of manuals and stops in an approach that amounted to orchestrating the works.[31] Stauffer shows that the creative scholarly perspective involving treatises, sources, and the old instruments themselves has produced vital new ways of understanding and performing Bach's organ works. As Dähnert and others showed, the inclusion of thirds in the mixtures of many central German organs made polyphony for *Organo pleno* rich and clear; this aesthetic judgment in turn made great practical sense of the historical and analytical research in Stauffer's book. Such studies should not be thought of as specialized work directed at organists and organ builders, but rather as crucial research into Bach's sound-world and into the impact, and indeed meanings, of his largest-scale keyboard music.

Another essential contribution to our increasing awareness of the rich diversity of Bach's keyboard culture has come with Joel Speerstra's important work on the pedal clavichord.[32] In "Klavier or Organ" Marshall had rightly conjectured that the "three claviers" (3. Clavire) listed in the specification of Bach's estate referred to a pedal clavichord (one pedalboard, with two manuals stacked above it).[33] Such instruments were apparently common; Johann Gottfried Walther also owned one; these pedal clavichords were crucial to their own practice, and were eventually passed on to a son pursuing a career as an organist. Although pedal harpsichords had been built, and performed and recorded on in the twentieth century, few if any pedal clavichords constructed according to eighteenth-century models had been heard or played. Only the fewest historical exemplars of the pedal clavichord have survived. The pedal clavichord was a ghost of history, one that spurred Schmieder's assignment, questioned by Marshall, of several pieces to the "Pedalcembalo." A builder, performer, and scholar, Speerstra demonstrates in a single person the fruitful interaction between historical scholarship, organology, and performance. Speerstra's multifaceted work also shows that, although Marshall's insights were crucial and necessary, we have now largely moved beyond an approach that finds interest in ascribing repertoire to one or another of the keyboard instruments available to Bach. By contrast, Speerstra has shown that the pedal clavichord was a crucial training apparatus for organists; anything could be played on it, as was certainly the case in the Bach household. That the instrument served as a necessary tool for the organist did not diminish the value accorded it for its own expressivity.

---

31 George Stauffer, *The Free Organ Preludes of Johann Sebastian Bach* (Ann Arbor: UMI, 1978).

32 Joel Speerstra, *Bach and the Pedal Clavichord* (Rochester: Rochester University Press, 2004).

33 Marshall, "Organ or 'Klavier'?," 220–221.

Keyboard Music 305

New avenues for the organ's involvement in Bach's oeuvre continue to be opened up. In a recent article, Christoph Wolff has argued that Bach played solo organ concertos with string orchestra.[34] What is so thrilling about Wolff's article is not the details of this interesting, if recondite, debate over the original versions of the harpsichord concertos BWV 1052 and BWV 1053, but the way Wolff links, admittedly in a speculative fashion, the hypothetical original form of these works with the recitals Bach gave on the new Silbermann organ in Dresden's Sophienkirche in the Fall of 1724.[35] According to a contemporary newspaper report these programs included "preludes and various concertos, with intervening soft instrumental music."[36] Wolff argues that this phrase must refer to solo organ concertos with string accompaniment. How strange that this possibility has never been explored before, especially given the encouragement it offers to present-day organists to play Bach's "harpsichord" concertos on the organ, as for example, Johann Wilhelm Hässler, a student of Bach's student Johann Christian Kittel, did in the 1780s. Wolff musters a convincing array of supporting evidence for his conjectures, examining key relationships, musical style, temperament, pitch standards, and keyboard compasses, among other factors. Regardless of whether the hypothesis is ever "proved"—and it seems unlikely that it will be by any juridical standard—we can for the first time imagine fully-fledged organ concertos by the instrument's greatest master. I see the historical report on the Dresden recitals not so much as evidence in a scholarly back-and-forth but as an invitation to reinvigorate this aspect of keyboard culture through the cooperation of scholarship and performance.

Similarly, the research of Greg Crowell provides a welcome challenge to modern conventions of continuo playing, another of the essential skills of the eighteenth-century keyboardist.[37] Crowell has convincingly argued that small positive organs (what he calls "trunk" organs) were rarely used in performances of Bach's vocal music in the eighteenth century, even though these instruments are nearly ubiquitous on modern recordings, even those that are "historically informed." Instead, it was the large church organ, often with many stops pulled and with the feet playing demanding running passages at sixteen-foot pitch, which provided the backdrop and fundament for Bach's concerted vocal music. This kind of research not only rebuts Adorno's dismissal of "mechanically squeaking *continuo*-instruments,"[38] but also constitutes a fundamental transformation of the role of the organ in the cantatas. This research shows that continuo playing at the organ was physically more demanding for the organist and sonically enriched

---

34 Christoph Wolff, "Sicilianos and Organ Concerts," BP 7 (2008): 97–114.

35 For Butler's view of the prehistory of BWV 1053 see "Bach the Cobbler: the Origins of J. S. Bach's E-Major Concerto (BWV 1053)," BP 7 (2008): 1–20.

36 Wolff, "Sicilianos and Organ Concerts," 107; see also NBR, 117 (No. 118); Dok 2: 150 (No. 193).

37 Gregory Crowell, "Registration and Sonority in J. S. Bach's Continuo Practice," *Diapason*, 93 (2002): 19–21.

38 Adorno, "Bach Defended Against His Devotees," 145.

306   *David Yearsley*

the entire texture in ways that prevailing practice does not come close to. Further research into continuo realization techniques of this kind of complexity also drastically alters our understanding of the sound of Bach's vocal works.[39]

Source Studies

Source studies continue to be a vital area of the scholarship devoted to Bach's keyboard music. One of the most important figures in this field over the past decades has been Russell Stinson, who, among other work, has produced monographs on Bach's two most important collections of chorale preludes—the *Orgelbüchlein* (599–644) and the so-called "Great Eighteen" (BWV 651–668).[40] Both of Stinson's studies illuminate Bach's working methods, his creative goals, and his sense of the artistic potential of the genre. The precision of Stinson's analysis, particularly regarding the autograph sources, impresses most: he has painstakingly examined every page of both precious manuscripts in search of corrections, erasures, emendations, and other signs of hesitation, changes of mind, or improvement. Stinson excels in sifting through the residue left by the working composer; indeed, he is fascinated by the meanderings of Bach's pen, searching out every overcrowded measure, oversized note head, poorly aligned inner part, and the like. Stinson refused to accept prior assertions about the uniformity of Bach's handwriting during his Weimar years (1708–1717), and modestly informs the reader that by comparing the *Orgelbüchlein* "with Bach's script in *all* manuscripts written before 1718" (emphasis added) he has been able to forge an admittedly provisional, but still convincing, chronology. This chronology lays out an early phase of fifteen chorales written between 1708 and 1712; an initial "middle" phase dating from the years 1712–13 that produced another nineteen chorales; a concluding middle phase of four chorales composed in 1715–16; a late Weimar phase of 1716–17 yielding six chorales; and finally, as is already well-known, three chorales completed in Leipzig sometime after 1726. Organological information especially having to do with the Weimar organ allowed Stinson further insight into performance and dating with respect to the *Orgelbüchlein*. These are not merely arcane details, but build a larger picture, useful to chronology but also, ultimately, to a broader context for, and performance of, this music.

Another landmark of source studies, reflecting an unmatched commitment to detail and a comprehensive knowledge of the dissemination of Bach's music, is Yo Tomita's monumental study of the Well-Tempered Clavier II.[41] This study painstakingly details all emendations in the autograph score, noting later accretions by Bach, and even other hands. Tomita is comprehensive and exacting in

---

39 See also Laurence Dreyfus, *Bach's Continuo Group* (Cambridge: Harvard University Press, 1987).

40 Russell Stinson, *Bach: the Orgelbüchlein* (New York: Schirmer, 1996); Russell Stinson, *J. S. Bach's Great Eighteen Organ Chorales* (Oxford: Oxford University Press, 2001).

41 Yo Tomita, *J. S. Bach's "Das Wohltemperierte Clavier II": A Critical Commentary* (Leeds: Household World, 1992–1995).

Keyboard Music 307

his treatment of all the extant manuscripts, and is able to provide a broad account of reception—of the origins and longevity of alternate readings. What Tomita's study also shows is the composer at work—the many decisions taken and turned away from, the flashing insight and careful consideration that yield compositional choices of great depth and ingenuity. Though the source materials for the Well-Tempered Clavier II are particularly rich, Tomita's methods could be applied across the keyboard works.

Groundbreaking research not into manuscripts, but original prints comes from Gregory Butler, whose study of the *Clavierübung III* and the *Canonic Variations on "Vom Himmel hoch"* is a model of source analysis in which the scholar teases out analytical and historical insights.[42] Before Butler's investigations, prints such as these were taken to be essentially static entities. To the contrary, Butler demonstrated that the printed pages were rich in details that reveal much about their compilation, and Bach's ever-changing conception of his works. Butler shows that both collections went through evolving conceptual phases, and that the composer added pieces to them while the publication process was still underway. Butler is able to demonstrate, for example, that the four *Duettos* (BWV 802–805) were a late addition to the *Clavierübung III*. This in turn sheds light on the curious inclusion of this quartet of non–chorale-based *manualiter* pieces in a collection of chorale preludes framed by a monumental *pedaliter* prelude and fugue (BWV 552). In demonstrating the fluidity of Bach's conception of his own works, Butler was able to make substantive arguments about the notion of textual finality. Butler's work embodies a dynamic approach with respect to instrumentation: Bach may have added the quartet of *Duettos* into the sublime mix of the *Clavierübung* partly for domestic players not up to the demands of the massive *Prelude and Fugue in E-flat* and the large-scale chorale preludes; still, the *Duettos* are not easy and are as difficult as many of the small-scale *manualiter* chorale settings in the collection. The fluid conception of the collection parallels a fluid conception of appropriate instruments: the organ was the ideal option (as the title-page suggests), but other instruments were more than simply secondary alternatives.

Having illuminated Bach's elastic approach to his printed collections, Butler argues in a follow-up essay to his *Canonic Variations* book that we should discard the notion that either one of the two versions of this set should hold primacy over the other. This amounts to a critique of the notion of a "definitive" text, a concept to which generations of scholars had been strongly attached.[43] Butler's work strengthens the image of Bach as obsessive tinkerer and reviser, a

---

42 Gregory Butler, *Bach's Clavier-Übung III: the Making of a Print, with a Companion Study of the Canonic Variations on "Vom Himmel hoch," BWV 769* (Durham: Duke University Press, 1990); see also Chapter 4.

43 Gregory Butler, "J. S. Bachs Kanonische Veränderungen über 'Vom Himmel hoch' (BWV 769). Ein Schlußstrich unter die Debatte um die Frage der 'Fassung letzter Hand,'" BJ 86 (2000): 9–34.

308   David Yearsley

musician continually trying to implement new ideas into his prints until at last they appeared.

Yet scholarship has shown that the process of revision continued even after publication. The work of Christoph Wolff and others on Bach's personal copies of his prints shows him to have continued the revising at home.[44] Bach's own copy of the *Schübler Chorales* (BWV 645–650) shows substantial and unexpected revisions to the note text and detailed information regarding performance and registrations, contributing yet again to the dynamic nature of performance and text. The rediscovery of Bach's copy of the *Goldberg Variations* (BWV 988) brought with it fourteen new canons, and showed that publication also did not mean the end of the composer's imaginative engagement with his material.[45] All of these findings produce a dynamic picture of Bach's creative process and its relationship to instruments and to the imperatives of production. Doubtless the manuscript and print sources of Bach's keyboard music will continue to yield new findings about Bach's musical laboratory, his aesthetic inclinations, and his approach to performance, among many other topics.

Influences and Contemporaries

Continued archival work into, and edition-making of, the keyboard music of the seventeenth and eighteenth centuries yields an ever-expanding view of the contexts for Bach's achievements and for the possible influences which might have shaped them. The music of well-known, and lesser-known, predecessors and contemporaries continues to reveal much about the ways Bach learned and created.[46] For example, Bach's keyboard transcriptions of orchestral music, especially of works of Antonio Vivaldi and Giuseppe Torelli, are a crucial part of this story.[47] Studies of musical influence rely on both a command of sources and dissemination, but even more importantly on a critical ear. Investigations into the music of Bach's contemporaries have revealed a great deal, and have much more still to tell us. In his tour-de-force of textual analysis, Butler also showed how the music of Bach's contemporary C. F. Hurlebusch, the butt of an unflattering vignette in which Bach laughs smugly at Hurlebusch's keyboard works,[48]

---

44 Christoph Wolff "Bach's Personal Copy of the Schübler Chorales," Wolff Essays, 178–187; see also Wolff's "The Handexemplar of the Goldberg Variations," Wolff Essays, 162–177. A second Handexemplar has been discovered; see George B. Stauffer, "Noch ein 'Handexemplar': Der Fall der Schübler-Choräle," BJ 101 (2015): 177–192.

45 On the rediscovery of the Goldberg Handexemplar, see Olivier Alain, "Un supplement inédit aux 'Variations Goldberg' de Jean-Sebastien Bach," *Revue de musicologie* 61 (1975): 244–294.

46 See, for example, Peter Williams, "Some Observations on Three Keyboard-Composers: Frescobaldi, J. S. Bach and Domenico Scarlatti," *Litterae organi: Essays in Honor of Barbara Owen*, ed. John Ogasapian, et al (Richmond: OHS Press, 2005), 53–71.

47 Luigi Ferdinando Tagliviani, "Bach's Organ Transcription of Vivaldi's 'Grosso Mogul,'" Stauffer and May, *J. S. Bach as Organist*, 212–239. See also Jean-Claude Zehnder, "Giuseppe Torelli und Johann Sebastian Bach: Zu Bachs Weimarer Konzertform," BJ 77 (1991): 33–95.

48 NBR, 408 (No. 396); Dok 3: 443 (No. 927); Forkel, *Bachs Leben, Kunst und Kunstwerke*, 46; Dok 7: 58–59; NBR, 460.

exerted an important influence on one of Bach's great organ pieces, the *Prelude and Fugue in E-Flat Major* (BWV 552).[49] Butler was able not only to discover an important impetus for Bach, but also to confirm one way in which, not unlike his great contemporary Handel, the music of others served as an inspiration for, if not an outright challenge to, Bach's own compositional aims.

John Butt's study of Bach's late style examines the influence of another "lesser" contemporary, G. F. Kauffmann, another example of how filling out the context of a well-known masterpiece can illuminate it anew.[50] Looking west out of the window of the second floor composing room in his apartment in the St. Thomas School building in Leipzig, Bach could, on clear days, see the distant spire of Merseburg Cathedral where Kauffmann was organist and, later, director of church music to the Duke of Saxe-Merseburg. Kauffmann is now chiefly remembered as one of Bach's competitors for the cantor's position in Leipzig. In spite of his obscurity, it is still somewhat surprising that neither of Stinson's books mentions Kauffmann's *Harmonische Seelenlust*, one of the most important collections of chorale preludes from the period.[51] Published in twelve installments between 1733 and 1740 and engraved in Leipzig by J. G. Krügner (also the engraver of Bach's *Clavierübung I* and *II*, as well as, as Butler showed, some pages of the *Clavierübung III*), the *Harmonische Seelenlust* probably helped encourage Bach to publish his own collection of chorale preludes in the *Clavierübung III*, which appeared in 1739 as Kauffmann's project was being completed by his widow. Butt shows how Kauffmann's gallant, but often challenging, music inspired Bach to new heights of elegance and refinement in his own late works, especially the *Canonic Variations* (BWV 769). George Stauffer's important article on Bach's assimilation of French Classical organ music, another influence mentioned by his son C. P. E. Bach in an important letter with biographical information sent to J. N. Forkel in 1775,[52] proceeds from an examination of the sources to imaginative and useful interpretation of the ways in which Bach used them and expanded on their lessons.[53]

Questions of influence are raised by Robert Hill's important work on two diverse collections of keyboard music from the Bach circle stemming from the early years of the eighteenth century. Hill's study examines in great detail the Möller Manuscript (Staatsbibliothek zu Berlin, Mus. ms. 40644) and the Andreas Bach Buch (MB Lpz III.8.4) largely copied by Bach's older brother Johann Christoph,

---

49 Butler, *Bach's Clavier-Übung III*, 4–18.

50 John Butt, "J. S. Bach and G. F. Kauffmann: Reflections on Bach's Later Style," *Bach Studies 2*, ed. Daniel Melamed (Cambridge; Cambridge University Press, 1995): 47–61.

51 Georg Freidrich Kauffmann, *Harmonische Seelen Lust Musikalischer Gönner und Freunde* (Leipzig; Krügner, [1733–1740]; facsimile, Courlay: Fuzeau, 2002).

52 NBR, 398–400 (No. 395); Dok 3: 288–290 (No. 803).

53 George Stauffer, "Boyvin, Grigny, D'Angelbert, and Bach's Assimilation of French Classical Organ Music," EM 21 (1993); 83–96. See also Victoria Horn, "French Influence in Bach's Organ Works," Stauffer and May, *J. S. Bach as Organist*, 256–273.

310   *David Yearsley*

with whom Johann Sebastian went to live on the death of his parents in 1695.[54] In another impressive demonstration of source-critical analysis, Hill showed that the two collections were compiled between about 1703 and about 1713; many of the pieces must have been supplied to Johann Christoph by his younger brother, Johann Sebastian. The sprawling repertoire contained in these manuscripts ranged from Johann Caspar Ferdinand Fischer in South Germany to Dieterich Buxtehude in the North, and to many other important keyboard players of the seventeenth century; these collections provide perhaps the best view into Bach's keyboard background, one fostered by his older brother, but also nourished by J. S. Bach's own indefatigable copying and his travels to the north to Lüneburg in 1700 to study and, five years later, to Lübeck to learn from Buxtehude himself. Much is still to be learned about patterns of dissemination, and the intricate web of stylistic relationships from which Bach's music emerged. That both manuscripts contain *pedaliter* and *manualiter* pieces again speaks to the fluidity of the notion of "keyboard"; this repertoire spans both home and church and allows for the widest possible instrumental realizations.

The recent discoveries of Bach's earliest autographs have contributed further to this picture of Bach's early influences. In 2006, Michael Maul and Peter Wollny exhumed Bach's personal copies of two monumental keyboard pieces: a complete copy of Johann Adam Reincken's *An Wasserflüssen Babylon* and a single page of Dieterich Buxtehude's *Nun freut auch lieben Christen g'mein*, both written in German organ tablature.[55] The autographs of these giant chorale fantasias are so moving not only because of the graceful, if sometimes unsure, ductus of the young Bach's calligraphy, but also because of the unmatched industry—Bach's own explanation for his success—they represent. Bach's closing inscription to the Reincken chorale fantasia indicates that the manuscript dates from 1700, and was made in Lüneburg in the home of Georg Böhm, confirming a suspicion of Bach scholarship that Böhm was Bach's teacher.[56] Confirmed by impressive archival research on the part of Maul and Wollny, the close personal connection between Bach and Böhm parallels musical influences reflected in these early manuscripts and in other sources of Bach's own music.

What did Bach do with the knowledge born of all this copying? Still another recent discovery gives us a lasting impression of how study and creativity were two sides of the Bachian coin. In August 2008, Bach's chorale fantasia on *Wo Gott der Herr nicht bei uns hält* (given the next available catalog entry of BWV 1128) for two manuals and pedal turned up at a Leipzig auction. Not as ambitious

---

54 Robert Hill, ed., *Keyboard Music from the Andreas Bach Book and the Möller Manuscript* (Cambridge: Harvard University Press, 1991). See also Hill's "The Möller Manuscript and the Andreas Bach Book: Two Keyboard Anthologies from the Circle of the Young Johann Sebastian Bach," Ph.D. diss. (Harvard University, 1987).

55 *Weimarer Orgeltabulatur*, facsimile and modern edition, ed. Michael Maul and Peter Wollny (Kassel: Bärenreiter, 2007).

56 Jean-Claude Zehnder, "Georg Böhm und Johann Sebastian Bach: Zur Chronologie der Bachschen Stilentwicklung," BJ 74 (1988): 73–110.

Keyboard Music 311

as the chorale fantasias of Buxtehude and Reincken that Bach copied, BWV 1128 is clearly inspired by its northern antecedents.[57] The relationship between these kinds of early attempts at lavish expression, and the rich milieu of contemporaries, competitors, and teachers, will continue to be a productive object of scholarship. As an increasing number of scholars and players become more intimately acquainted with previously distant corners of the contemporary repertoire, new perspectives on Bach's music will open up before us. Influences do not lurk everywhere, but there are clearly many more to be found. Archival work accompanied by modes of scholarship that relate instruments, sources, and performance will add to our ever-expanding appreciation of Bach's achievement.

Hermeneutics

Discussions of influence and style depend not only on familiarity with sources and repertories, but also on interpretation: what particular musical strands might be seen to connect, whether tenuously or firmly, one composer's music to that of another? Biographical and musical findings play an important part in such assessments, but ultimately there is a premium on the subjective critical faculties of the scholar. A brilliant example of hermeneutic criticism is Laurence Dreyfus's 1996 *Bach and the Patterns of Invention*, a book that adopts new critical methodologies based in part on eighteenth-century ways of thinking. Dreyfus's approach is, as he puts it, a "process of 'pulling pieces apart' by identifying and examining the leading inventions"; this "mirrors to some meaningful extent what the composer would recognize as the reverse of the way he has put the pieces together. Analysis, in this rather literal sense, is the inverse of synthesis or composition."[58] Dreyfus shows that Bach's process of invention was one that entailed more than simply discovering a good musical idea—i.e., motive—and meant exploring the combinatorial and elaborative patterns that such an idea necessarily brought with it. Although "Bach maintains a distinction between a basic idea and its development, the surface appearances tend to suggest that both contain a similar degree of artifice."[59] Though not exclusively devoted to keyboard music, Dreyfus's work compellingly describes the modes of thought that created two of Bach's best-loved and most well-known keyboard works—the C-major Invention (BWV 772) and the Fugue in C major (BWV 845/1). Dreyfus shows how Bach rationally exploits the rich possibilities of his inventions, and how these primary inventive schemes are stitched together and elaborated. In laying bare, often with startling results, the relationship between invention and elaboration, Dreyfus demonstrates the potential of a very eighteenth-century way of hearing

---

57 J. S. Bach, *Choralfantasie für Orgel, BWV 1128: Wo Gott der Herr nicht bei uns halt*," eds. Stephen Blaut and Michael Pacholke with a preface by Hans-Joachim Schulze (Beeskow: Ortus-Verlag, 2008).

58 Laurence Dreyfus, *Bach and the Patterns of Inventions* (Cambridge: Harvard University Press, 1996), 10.

59 Ibid.

312 *David Yearsley*

and understanding Bach's music, one that is never fustily antiquarian, but instead strikes one as highly modern; the utility of his analytical methods, he argues, surpasses later organicist approaches, particularly those descending from Heinrich Schenker. The implications of Dreyfus's work—arguably the most important contribution to Bach studies in the past two decades—have yet to be completely digested by the scholarly community. Because Dreyfus considers relatively few pieces in his pursuit of Bach's modes of invention, similar analytical studies would doubtless pay dividends across the keyboard repertory. These methodologies also have profound implications for Bach's aesthetics, as they illuminate the composer's often cantankerous attitudes towards contemporary aesthetics.

Although Dreyfus's work draws abundantly on eighteenth-century perspectives, it is also marked by an enviable ability to exploit methodologies from scholars working in other fields of the humanities. Dreyfus turns for help to literary scholars, particularly Alistair Fowler, in order to investigate the ways genres coalesce and are articulated, and can be transformed by the contributors to them.[60] Fowler theorizes a "generic repertoire," which in the case of Bach's music, can be constructed by many factors, from "gross size" to "harmonic vocabulary," to "contrapuntal devices"—just to list a few of the aspects touched on by Dreyfus. Fugue is not a "style, a texture... or only a technique," but a genre, an "intuitive notion" fleshed out without a set of "eternally valid criteria." With his keen historical knowledge of contemporary repertories and music theory, Dreyfus unpacks the constituent features of various genres, from fugues to concertos, and demonstrates that generic considerations are crucial to the way Bach elaborates his musical inventions. For this reason, Dreyfus cautions against collapsing technique and style, a tendency that mars so much modern analysis of Bach's music. He also attacks formalist approaches to the analysis of fugue, which is not, he argues, a form—not "an empty vessel into which genre is poured."[61] It is also wrong, he says, to assume that a given mode of elaboration or technique is specific to a single genre or even set of genres; this dynamic, eighteenth-century attitude, allows Dreyfus to highlight the ways in which Bach expressed his critical attitude towards rationalist taxonomies prevalent in the music theory of the period. In Dreyfus's thought-provoking treatment of the *Echo* from the *French Overture* (BWV 831), an apparently slight dance movement is revealed as camouflaging beneath its coy surface a complex concerto movement. Dreyfus's Bach is a critic of Enlightenment categorization; the composer's most artificial creations can appear in gallant guises, that is, in many genres traditionally resistant to the level of complexity Bach subjects them to. Dreyfus's work provides a model not only for a mode of analysis informed by eighteenth-century approaches, but also for the potential expansion of the sometimes narrow disciplinary boundaries of Bach scholarship.

---

60 Alastair Fowler, *Kinds of Literature: an Introduction to the Theory of Genres and Modes* (Cambridge: Harvard University Press, 1982).

61 Dreyfus, *Bach and the Patterns of Invention*, 139.

Dreyfus's critical approach to genre and style shares its attention to musical detail with Joseph Kerman's previously mentioned readings of Bach's keyboard music. Both Dreyfus and Kerman share a commitment to interpreting the musical texts not as static objects but vibrant entities. Kerman's call for what he calls music criticism, practiced in his book on Bach's keyboard fugues, has not received much support in Bach scholarship, but could, I believe, be of great use. I would see the wider introduction of something like Kermanian criticism into Bach studies, not so much as a turn away from archival and source studies, but as a valuable aspect of any persuasive account of individual pieces or larger repertories and genres.

The historically grounded hermeneutic impulse behind Dreyfus's work motivates other important contributions to our understanding of Bach's music. Theological perspectives have provided valuable contexts for understanding his chorale-based keyboard music, illuminating many possible layers of complementary meaning. Robin A. Leaver's comprehensive knowledge of doctrinal contexts of, and specific theological influences on, Bach's music has been crucial to these explorations.[62] Musical rhetoric and theological meaning can be seen and heard to inform one another in Bach's oeuvre, and although meaning can be slippery, it is nonetheless rich in potential concerning the complex relationship between invention, religious belief, and the projection of "extra-musical" ideas. Chorale texts and the theological literature provide powerful traction for making sense of Bach's compositional decisions—and for uncovering the composer's hermeneutic contributions to the meanings of chorale, and to larger theological questions.[63] Alternate modes of interpretation, such as numerological attempts at uncovering hidden, mystical meaning, have in my opinion been less rewarding than those involving theological, literary, and cultural approaches. Other methodologies from other disciplines will continue to present themselves for the enterprising and creative Bach scholars. Further reading in theology and liturgical practice along the lines Leaver and others have laid out will doubtless be productive in as yet unforeseen ways.[64]

Hermeneutic approaches such as these become much more difficult in the case of "textless" free works, and in "secular" repertories such as the suites. In these areas social contexts seem the more promising way forward, not just in matters of moral uplift and musical education, but in the reception and understanding of these works, as Andrew Talle's study of the *Social Background for Bach's*

---

62 Robin A. Leaver, "Bach's 'Clavierübung III': Some Historical and Theological Considerations," *Organ Yearbook* 6 (1975): 17–32.

63 Bach's historical position with respect to such important liturgical developments as the *Deutsche Messe* and the use of the organ in the divine service have also been the object of some of Leaver's scholarship; see his *Luther's Liturgical Music: Principles and Implications* (Grand Rapids: Eerdmans, 2007).

64 Exploration of other methodologies include Stephen Rose, *The Musician in Literature in the Age of Bach* (Cambridge: Cambridge University Press, 2011); and Ruth Tatlow, *Bach's Numbers: Compositional Proportion and Significance* (Cambridge: Cambridge University Press, 2016).

314   *David Yearsley*

Partitas powerfully demonstrates.[65] I like to think that my own work drawing on theological and cultural literature of the period has outlined some of the domestic, moral, and pedagogical dimensions of the Anna Magdalena Bach Book of 1725—and by extension other collections from the inner Bach circle. This and future research will articulate previously neglected meanings and uses of Bach's keyboard music.[66] Scholarship can productively draw not only on musical theoretical sources, but also on related literatures: moral writings, travel books, and cultural polemics, among others. A vast amount of literature was produced by the bibliophilic Enlightened culture of the book-fair city of Leipzig and its environs, and as more of this material is researched we will continue to learn ever more about the situations and sentiments which allowed Bach's music to flourish—and to come in for criticism. Although source studies will continue to be relevant, the fleshing out of social, literary, and theological contexts will contribute substantially to hermeneutic endeavors that try to find larger and deeper meanings.

The Toccata and Fugue in D Minor

Long cherished for its fiery intensity, the Toccata in Fugue in D Minor (BWV 565) provides a useful lens through which to view the current state of Bach keyboard scholarship. Though other works have been dislodged from the Bach catalog for less secure bona fides,[67] the famous Toccata remains a warhorse of the repertoire. But however dramatic and original, it is an odd, even eccentric, piece, in many ways unique in Bach's output. No autograph survives, and the best source is from the mid-eighteenth century. Accordingly, Peter Williams questioned its authenticity along with the idea that the piece, whoever the composer, was originally for the organ. The impetuous figures in parallel octaves in the Toccata; the minimal use of the pedal; the endless echoes; and the sparseness of the counterpoint in the fugue: all these features make it seem more like a transcription and, indeed one done more in the style of the later eighteenth century.[68] These observations and questions amounted to a kind of heresy, so embedded is the work in scholarship and in the wider cultural image of Bach's music. Following Williams with the zeal of an iconoclast, Rolf Dieterich Claus produced a study of BWV 565 that emphasized the dubious nature of the sources and the musical oddities of the work itself, hoping to pry the piece from the grasp of

---

65 Andrew Talle, "J. S. Bach's Keyboard Partitas and Their Early Audience," Ph.D. diss. (Harvard University, 2003).

66 David Yearsley, "The Anna Magdalena Bach Book of 1725 and the Art of Dying," ECM 2 (2005): 231–249; see also David Yearsley, *Bach and the Meanings of Counterpoint* (Cambridge: Cambridge University Press, 2002).

67 Pieter Dirksen, "Het Auterschap van Praeludium en Fuga in f-klein (BWV 534)," *Het Orgel* 96 (2000): 5–14. Dirksen suggests an attribution of the piece to Wilhelm Friedemann Bach.

68 Peter Williams, "BWV 565: a Toccata in D Minor for Organ by J. S. Bach?" EM 9 (1981): 330–337.

Keyboard Music   315

the Bach canon, if not the popular imagination.[69] Christoph Wolff rejoined in his magisterial Bach biography from 2000 that the Toccata was "refreshingly imaginative, varied, and ebullient" even if "structurally undisciplined and un-mastered."[70] Wolff attempts to account for the exuberant, if stylistically unusual, parallel octaves in the Toccata with the rather far-fetched claim that they were written for Bach's Arnstadt organ, which had no sixteen-foot stops in the manual: thus "the octave doubling reflects an ingenious solution for making up for that deficiency and for creating the effect of an *organo pleno*."[71] In a subsequent article, Wolff added a coda to this enthusiastic reading of the piece, claiming that since the scribe of the principle source, Johannes Ringk, made no mistakes in his other attributions to Bach, the attribution of BWV 565 to Bach should not be questioned.[72] It seems, then, that the scholarly question of authorship and style remains open. But the wider implications of this debate are worth considering. If the piece is a transcription of a violin work, as Williams suggests—or a lute piece as others have ventured[73]—then the famous Toccata and Fugue becomes a fascinating document in the reception of "Bach's music" as well as creative modes of performance at the organ and away from it.

Understood as the dissemination of manuscripts and the web of personal relationships that sponsored their exchange and ensured the ultimate survival of much of Bach's output, reception has long been a concern of Bach scholarship.[74] Andrew Talle again deserves mention for illuminating the ways the partitas (Bach's first printed collection of keyboard works) engaged with consumers, their social backgrounds, and musical abilities.[75] Important findings have been made in the case of Germany,[76] and significant work has been done on the Bach Revival in England, most significantly in *The English Bach Awakening* edited by Michael Kassler, which makes a vital contribution, especially with the chapters on the Well-Tempered Clavier by Yo Tomita.[77] That organists long played these preludes and fugues on the organ from Bach's time onward[78] shows the distance

---

69 Rolf Dietrich Claus, *Zur Echtheit von Toccata und Fuge d-moll BWV 565* (Cologne: Dohr, 1995).

70 Wolff BLM, 169.

71 Ibid., 72.

72 Christoph Wolff, "The Authenticity Problem of Bach's D-Minor Toccata," *Perspectives on Organ Playing and Musical Interpretation: Essays in Honor of Heinrich Fleischer,* eds. Ames Anderson et al. (New Ulm: Martin Luther College, 2003): 87–99.

73 Eric Lewin Altschuler, "Were Bach's Toccata and Fugue in BWV 565 and the Ciaccona from BWV 1004 lute pieces?" MT 146 (2005): 77–86.

74 See, for example, Russell Stinson, *The Bach Manuscripts of Johann Peter Kellner and His Circle; A Case Study in Reception History* (Durham: Duke University Press, 1989).

75 Talle, "J. S. Bach's Keyboard Partitas and Their Early Audience."

76 See Michael Heineman, et al, ed. *Bach und die Nachwelt*, 4 vols. (Laaber: Laaber, 1997–2005).

77 Michael Kassler, ed., *The English Bach Awakening: Knowledge of J. S. Bach and his Music in England, 1750–1830* (Aldershot: Ashgate, 2004).

78 Andrew McCrea, "A Note on Thomas Adams and His Showroom Demonstrations," *Journal of the British Institute of Organ Studies* 25 (2001): 78–95; Andrew McCrea's "Professorial Annotations: William Crotch's Study of the '48'," *Journal of the British Institute of Organ Studies* 28 (2004): 47–65.

traveled between the eighteenth century and the appearance of Marshall's article. In general reception studies help to weaken the rigidity that has encroached in the division of Bach's music between organ and keyboard over the last century. Vast reaches of nineteenth-century performance practice and research of the vital Bachian keyboard tradition, especially at the organ, remain untouched by music historians. The ideological and the political dimensions of Bach's keyboard music in the nineteenth century will emerge from this work, as will the changing status of the various keyboard instruments and the sound of Bach's music as heard on them. Further research into the reception of Bach's music will prove a crucial way of understanding the changing contexts and meanings of his music, and this work will tell us much about where our own attitudes evolved from and what they reacted against. Future research will help elucidate not only the distance between our attitudes and those of earlier musicians, but it will also amplify the resonance of Bach's music in our own time.

13 Instrumental Chamber and Ensemble Music

David Ledbetter

As with virtually all aspects of Bach's life and works, the literature dealing with the instrumental music is so extensive and rich that I can do no more here than single out some general themes and points of contention, provide brief notes on individual work groups, and suggest further avenues of investigation. The expansion of Bach research in the later twentieth century dates from the initiation of the *Neue Bach Ausgabe* in 1950. A useful selection of foundation articles for the first twenty years of this period was published by Walter Blankenburg in 1970.[1] Blankenburg has also provided an excellent survey of literature and associated debates, covering the period from around 1960–1982.[2] A full and detailed survey of literature up to the Bach year 2000 is included as part of the compendium on the ensemble music by Siegbert Rampe and Dominik Sackmann.[3]

Aspects of Performance

It would not be too much to say that the most remarkable development with regard to Bach's instrumental music since 1960 has been in performance. The sound-world we take for granted now has changed utterly since then, even for those who play "modern" instruments. The central publications in English before 1960 were those of Arnold Dolmetsch (1915) and Thurston Dart (1954).[4] In these, much attention is given to details of ornamentation, and to rhythmic features such as *notes inégales*, over-dotting, and tempo. The culmination of this phase was Robert Donington's monumental *The Interpretation of Early Music* (1963), with several subsequent ancillary publications and a substantially revised edition

---

1 Walter Blankenburg, ed., *Wege zur Forschung Band CLXX. Johann Sebastian Bach* (Darmstadt: Wissenschaftliche Buchgesellschaft, 1970).

2 Walter Blankenburg, "Die Bachforschung seit etwa 1965. Ergebnisse, Probleme, Aufgaben, Teil II," AcM 54 (1982): 162–207, continued in "Teil III," 55 (1983): 30–33.

3 Siegbert Rampe and Dominik Sackmann *Bachs Orchestermusik: Entstehung, Klangwelt, Interpretation: ein Handbuch* (Kassel: Bärenreiter, 2000).

4 Arnold Dolmetsch, *The Interpretation of the Music of the Seventeenth and Eighteenth Centuries* (London: Novello, 1915; 2nd ed. 1946); Thurston Dart, *The Interpretation of Music* (London: Hutchinson, 1954; 2nd ed., 1955). Since Dolmetsch's book consists mainly of translations of original sources it has a classic quality; Dart was a prime mover in combining performance and musicology.

318   *David Ledbetter*

in 1974.[5] Donington's work represented a summary rather than a new beginning and its shortcomings were quickly apparent: throwing together evidences from vastly different styles and dates (a feature shared by his article "Ornamentation" in NG[1], 1980), and a concentration on what are essentially surface details.[6] Meanwhile a long-running and acerbic debate surrounding *notes inégales* and over-dotting ran through the 1960s and 1970s between proponents Sol Babitz, Michael Collins, and David Fuller, and opponent Frederick Neumann.[7] This debate was well summarized in 1993 by Stephen Hefling, who proposed a more nuanced approach.[8] In citing evidences it is essential to differentiate between ordinary dance music and sophisticated, virtuoso solo music, and music in the "mixed style." Unequal rhythm, for example, is an expressive resource of infinite subtlety, as described in an instructive manuscript by Quantz.[9]

In addition to conventions of rhythmic notation, Neumann objected to what he regarded as a specious orthodoxy with regard to the performance of appoggiaturas and trills, as represented in the writings of Dolmetsch, Dart and Donington. In all this, Neumann's ultimate focus was the music of Bach. As a violinist who had studied with Otakar Ševčík, Carl Flesch, Max Rostal and Adolf Busch, Neumann passionately believed that this orthodoxy, which was not that of his upbringing, had to be rebutted. His passion resulted in a work of quite exceptional erudition (1978).[10] The information Neumann presented is invaluable but must be read in the light of his *parti pris*. His citing of evidence is selective and anybody using his work should first read David Fuller's review (1980).[11] A critical reading of this debate, because it affects Bach's instrumental music, would be very revealing of attitudes in two crucial decades of the historical-performance movement, quite apart from the value of the great amount of information from performance sources that emerged in its course.

---

5   Robert Donington, *The Interpretation of Early Music* (London: Faber, 1963; 2nd ed., 1974; 3rd ed., 1989; new ed., 1990).

6   These shortcomings are very apparent if one compares his article with Georg von Dadelsen's more historically based "Verzierungen" in MGG 13: cols. 1526–1556 (1966).

7   The main articles in this debate are listed in the bibliography of David Fuller's article "*Notes inégales*" in NG[Online].

8   Stephen E. Hefling, *Rhythmic Alteration in Seventeenth- and Eighteenth-Century Music: Notes inégales and Overdotting* (New York: Schirmer, 1993).

9   See Claire A. Fontijn, "Quantz's *unegal*: Implications for the Performance of 18th-Century Music," EM 23 (1995): 55–62; the Quantz MS, *Dk-Kk* C I 45 (Gieddes Samling I, 16), is edited by Winfried Michel and Hermien Teske in *Solfeggi Pour La Flute Traversiere avec l'enseignement Par Mons[r.] Quantz* (Winterthur: Amadeus, 1978). The first part of Quantz's career (1719–1741) was spent at the Dresden court, at the time when Bach had most dealings with it, and Dresden was Bach's ideal of musical standards; Dok 1: 63 (No. 22): NBR 150 (No. 151).

10 Frederick Neumann, *Ornamentation in Baroque and Post-Baroque Music: With Special Emphasis on J. S. Bach* (Princeton: Princeton University Press, 1978; 3rd ed., 1983).

11 David Fuller, JAMS 33 (1980): 394–402. Neumann's most important articles are reprinted in Frederick Neumann, *Essays in Performance Practice* (Ann Arbor: UMI, 1982), and *New Essays on Performance Practice* (Ann Arbor: UMI, 1989). A recent application of Neumann's principles is in Jerome Carrington, *Trills in the Bach Cello Suites: A Handbook for Performers* (Norman: University of Oklahoma Press, 2009).

Instrumental Chamber and Ensemble Music 319

French Overtures

One particularly long-running debate has concerned the performance of overtures in French style, in regard to dotted rhythms and also tempo. New thinking was startlingly demonstrated by William Malloch in a recording of Bach's Overture-suites (BWV 1066–1069), issued in 1991.[12] Malloch argued that the first and second sections of the overture should share the same basic tempo that, he claimed, solved the over-dotting problem.[13] Although this was refreshing in view of the ponderous tempi of old-fashioned performances, much of Malloch's evidence concerned the overtures of Lully and his immediate French followers, in a relatively straightforward dance style. These were not sufficiently differentiated from the later mixed-style overtures of Telemann, Handel and Bach, particularly Bach's multilayered contrapuntal textures.[14] In addition, Malloch's tempi were all on the fast side (based on various eighteenth-century evidences for dance tempi), giving a driven effect and lacking the nuance that is one of the principal benefits of using period instruments. The debate continued in two articles of 1997, by Matthew Dirst and Ido Abravaya.[15] Dirst considers Bach's changes in rhythmic notation between the Allemande of the C minor cello Suite (BWV 1011/2; before 1726) and Bach's lute version of the same piece (BWV 995/2; ca. 1727–1731); and also between Anna Magdalena Bach's copy of the French Overture for harpsichord (BWV 831a/1, in C minor, ca. 1725–1731) and the version in B minor (BWV 831/1) that Bach prepared for publication in *Clavier-Übung II* (1735). He posits that Bach's concept of the French overture changed after 1730, that the older notation was more schematic, but that the newer, seemingly more dotted style reflected Bach's interest in the 1730s in the leading musical fashion in his environment, that of the Dresden court, for which there is much evidence. According to Dirst this change of notation was therefore "political."

Performance Analysis

Whatever the theory, the proof is in the performance. Abravaya considers performances of various Bach overtures, notably Reinhard Goebel's of the overtures BWV 1066/1, 1068/1, and 1069/1, which dispense with over-dotting.[16] The evolution

---

12   William Malloch, The Boston Early Music Soloists, *Bach: Suites for Dancing* (CD Koch International Classics, 1991), 3–7073–2H1. I have used the term overture-suite, common in writing about Telemann who pioneered the genre in Germany, since the word "Ouvertüre" in the sources is awkward in English.

13   William Malloch, "Bach and the French Overture," MQ 75 (1991): 174.

14   See David Ledbetter, *Unaccompanied Bach: Performing the Solo Works* (New Haven: Yale University Press, 2009), 85–87.

15   Matthew Dirst, "Bach's French Overtures and the Politics of Overdotting," EM 25 (1997): 35–44, and Ido Abravaya, "A French Overture Revisited: Another Look at the Two Versions of BWV 831," EM 25 (1997): 47–61. Abravaya's *Bach's Rhythm and Tempo* (Kassel: Bärenreiter, 2006) gives a dispassionate account of modern controversies, and sensibly sides with Kirnberger's concept of *Bewegung* and *mouvement* as deciding factors.

16   Musica Antiqua Köln, Archiv CD 289415671–2 (recorded 1982, 1985).

320   David Ledbetter

of performance approaches to Bach's music, as represented in recordings, is considered by Martin Elste (2000), and with a particularly scientific approach based on computer analysis by Dorottya Fabian (2003).[17] Fabian has recently found, in a series of controlled experiments, that "listeners... are deceived by tempo and articulation in their perception of rhythm."[18] In what has sometimes been a rather theoretical debate, this practical finding, together with the variety of approaches now available in recordings, is welcome confirmation that the perception of rhythm is anything but straightforward. Technical analysis of this sort is becoming ever more sophisticated and anybody wishing to engage in it should contact field leaders such as the Centre for the History and Analysis of Recorded Music (CHARM).[19]

A nontechnical, but illuminating, account of the evolution of performance style from the 1960s until now, from a performer who has been a main participant, is by the oboist Bruce Haynes (2007).[20] Haynes's description of a trajectory from what he terms "strait" (i.e., "Urtext") style to "eloquent" (i.e., free and richly nuanced expressively) and back is supported by sound clips from Telefunken Bach recordings that give vivid confirmation of his argument.[21] This is essential reading for anybody considering the recent history of performance practice of Bach's music.

Instruments

More than musicologists, even than performers, the new sound world for Bach's music is the responsibility of organologists and instrument makers, the two skills often combined in one person. The Brandenburg Concertos alone provide a number of conundrums, since a connoisseurish peculiarity of instrumentation is part of their point. The meaning of "Fiauti d'echo" in BWV 1049 has long been a matter for contention, partly because of the terminology and partly because of the note f♯''', not easily available on F treble recorders. Arnold Dolmetsch proposed recorders in G, but the second recorder goes down to f', so one suggestion has been to have one recorder in G and one in F.[22] Thurston Dart, in an elegantly

---

17 Martin Elste, *Meilensteine der Bach-Interpretation 1750–2000* (Stuttgart: Metzler, 2000), including historic recordings of BWV 1004, 1017, 1043, 1047; Dorottya Fabian, *Bach Performance Practice, 1945–1975: A Comprehensive Review of Sound Recordings and Literature* (Aldershot: Ashgate, 2003), who considers the Brandenburg Concertos, and also the Overture-suites; also Dorottya Fabian and Eitan Ornoy, "Identity in Violin Playing on Records: Interpretation Profiles in Recordings of Solo Bach by Early Twentieth-Century Violinists," *Performance Practice Review*, 14 (2009): 1–40, which considers the *Sei Solo* for violin.

18 Dorottya Fabian and Emery Schubert, "A New Perspective on the Performance of Dotted Rhythms," EM 38 (2010): 585–588, the piece considered being BWV 988/16.

19 http://www.charm.rhul.ac.uk/index.html.

20 Bruce Haynes, *The End of Early Music: A Period Performer's History of Music for the Twenty-First Century* (Oxford: Oxford University Press, 2007); for a critical assessment see David Schulenberg's review in JAMS 63 (2010): 169–178.

21 http://www.oup.com/us/companion.websites/9780195189872/?view=usa.

22 Tushaar Power, "On the Pitch Dispositions of Bach's Fiauti d'echo and Other Treble Recorders," *The Galpin Society Journal*, 47 (1994): 155–160. Power's finding that recorder parts in Bach cantatas that have the f♯''' do not go below g' is suggestive (ibid., 156).

Instrumental Chamber and Ensemble Music 321

argued essay (1960), proposed French bird-flageolets at 4' pitch, which he identifies with the "echo flute" promoted by James Paisible in London in the 1710s.[23] Dart ingeniously found musical and dynastic links between London and Berlin in that decade, but his theory did not find favor. More suggestive has been the idea, first proposed in 1989, of a double instrument (two linked recorders, one quieter than the other) of which an example survives in the Museum für Musikinstrumente of Leipzig University.[24] This theory was not accepted by Ulrich Prinz in 1994, but in the most recent summary of information about Bach's instrumentarium (2005), he accepted it on account of the advocacy by Siegbert Rampe and Michael Zapf.[25] This in turn has been rejected by Josef Wagner (2009) who finds the *Doppelflöte* neither necessary nor playable in this piece and that recorders in F are meant. Whether the term "Fiauti d'Echo" applies solely to the function of the recorders in the slow movement, or means a special instrument, requires further investigation.[26]

Keyboard instruments are not the concern of this chapter, but the harpsichord in BWV 1050 deserves a brief comment. In March 1719, Bach made a trip to Berlin to collect a harpsichord for the Cöthen court, apparently by the maker Michael Mietke.[27] Since Sheridan Germann (1985) identified two harpsichords in the Charlottenburg Palace, Berlin, as instruments from the Mietke workshop, these two instruments have become a magnet for harpsichord makers to copy.[28] How the acquisition of this instrument may have affected the composition history of the Fifth Brandenburg Concerto has long been a subject for speculation.[29] Prince Leopold's summer visits to the spa at Carlsbad (Karlovy Vary in Bohemia) have also been adduced as possible platforms for Bach to exhibit his prowess as Germany's foremost keyboard virtuoso. Recent research (2006) has shed further light on these visits. The only mention of taking a harpsichord is for the visit in May–June 1718, which cannot have been the Mietke, and nothing is known of the instrument other than that it took three men to move it so it must have been fairly substantial. There is no information about music for the Prince's visit in 1720, although Bach must have gone, because the 1720 autograph of the *Sei*

---

23 Thurston Dart, "Bach's 'Fiauti d'echo'," ML 41 (1960): 331–341.

24 See Josef Wagner, "Die 'Fiauti d'Echo' in Johann Sebastian Bachs viertem Brandenburgischen Konzert," *Tibia*, 34 (2009): 576–585.

25 Ulrich Prinz, "Zum Instrumentarium in den Brandenburgischen Konzerten," Pavol Polák, ed., *Mitteleuropäische Kontexte der Barockmusik. Bericht über die Internationale Musikwissenschaftliche Konferenz Bratislava 23.–25. März 1994* (Bratislava: Musikunion, 1997), 227–233; Ulrich Prinz, *Johann Sebastian Bachs Instrumentarium* (Kassel: Bärenreiter, 2005), 203–205; see also Rampe and Sackmann, *Bachs Orchestermusik*, 279–280.

26 Wagner, "Die 'Fiauti d'Echo'," 582.

27 For datings of Bach's activities, see Chapter 20.

28 Sheridan Germann, "The Mietkes, the Margrave and Bach," Peter Williams, ed., *Bach Handel Scarlatti Tercentenary Essays* (Cambridge: Cambridge University Press, 1985), 119–148.

29 See in particular Alfred Dürr, "Zur Entstehungsgeschichte des 5. Brandenburgischen Konzerts," BJ 61 (1975): 63–69; and Pieter Dirksen, "The Background to Bach's Fifth Brandenburg Concerto," Pieter Dirksen, ed., *The Harpsichord and its Repertoire* (Utrecht: Foundation for Historical Performance Practice, 1992), 157–185.

322   David Ledbetter

Solo for violin is uniquely on paper from a mill 20 km from Carlsbad, and this is the visit from which, according to Bach's obituary, he returned to find his first wife Maria Barbara already dead and buried.[30] Little is known of the Mietke, though it is surely the instrument that appears in a 1784 court inventory as "the large harpsichord with two manuals by Michael Mietke in Berlin, 1719."[31] The Mietke workshop produced at least two instruments with 16' stop, and this may also be the case here.[32]

The most radical development in recent Bach organology has been the revivification of the violoncello da spalla (cello played on the shoulder) by Dmitry Badiarov, with associated recording of the cello Suites by the violinist Sigiswald Kuijken.[33] Speculation about the nature of the violoncello piccolo and viola pomposa, an instrument said to have been invented by Bach, continued throughout the twentieth century.[34] With a shoulder-played cello the Suites can be played by a violinist, thus answering Dominik Sackmann's (2008) wish that both the violin Solos and the cello Suites could be played by the same person, to solve problems of technical feel and illuminate the relationship between the two sets.[35] Badiarov has produced a wealth of evidence in support of the instrument, and this is further extended in Kuijken's booklet notes for his recording, in which he comes to the bold conclusion that, up to around 1740, when Bach wrote violoncello he meant *da spalla*. Against that it has to be said that the situation regarding bass stringed instruments in Bach's environment was complex. Iconographical evidence for Germany points to the violoncello played *da gamba*, with viol-style underhand bow hold. The bass viol had a virtuoso repertory in the German area until well into the eighteenth century and that tradition has an undoubted bearing on Bach's Suites both stylistically and in terms of instrumental technique.[36] The cello Suites themselves are for at least two different instruments. The revival of the violoncello *da spalla* is a most refreshing development. No doubt further

---

30 Maria Hübner, "Neues zu Johann Sebastian Bachs Reisen nach Karlsbad," BJ 92 (2006): 93–107.

31 Dok 2: 73–74 (No. 95); NBR 87 (No. 77).

32 See John Koster, "The Quest for Bach's *Clavier*: an Historical Interpretation," *Early Keyboard Journal* 14 (1996): 71; also John Koster, "The Harpsichord Culture in Bach's Environs," BP 4 (1999): 57–77.

33 Dmitry Badiarov, "The Violoncello, Viola da spalla and Viola pomposa in Theory and Practice," *The Galpin Society Journal* 60 (2007): 121–145; also Dmitry Badiarov, "Errata, and More on the Violoncello da spalla of the Italians," *The Galpin Society Journal* 61 (2008): 324–5. Sigiswald Kuijken, *Johann Sebastian Bach Cello Suites BWV 1007–1012*, (CD Accent, 2007, 2009), ACC 24196.

34 For a summary of arguments, see Ledbetter, *Unaccompanied Bach*, 42–46.

35 Dominik Sackmann, *Triumph des Geistes über die Materie. Mutmassungen über Johann Sebastian Bachs "Sei Solo a Violino senza Basso accompagnato" (BWV 1001–1006) mit einem Seitenblick auf die "6 Suites a Violoncello Solo" (BWV 1007–1012)* (Stuttgart: Carus, 2008), 52.

36 For a general survey, see Ledbetter, *Unaccompanied Bach*, 36–43, 46; also Fred Flassig, *Die solistische Gambenmusik in Deutschland im 18. Jahrhundert* (Göttingen: Cuvillier, 1998), 240.

Instrumental Chamber and Ensemble Music   323

research will ultimately give us a fuller picture of the variety of instruments in Bach's environment.[37]

Half of Bach's cantata oboe parts are for oboe d'amore.[38] Because it is in A (so sharp keys such as B minor and F sharp minor are fingered as D minor and A minor on the normal oboe), and extends a minor third lower than the oboe, it has come into the frame for the reconstruction of putative "original" versions of concertos surviving only in late sources, such as the A major harpsichord Concerto (BWV 1055 ca. 1739–1742).[39] This concerto is a good example of how arguments about chronology and genesis can flow back and forth. Hans-Joachim Schulze (1981) associated the putative original oboe d'amore concerto with Bach's visit to the court at Schleiz in August 1721, where the instrument had recently been introduced, and this was hailed as biographical research joining with stylistic study to give precision to chronology.[40] There are, however, technical difficulties with the reconstruction for this instrument and more recently Kai Köpp (2000) has made a convincing case for the viola d'amore, also in A, where these difficulties melt away.[41] The reconstruction of "lost originals" is a contentious issue which will be discussed next.

Pitch and Intonation

Pitch has traditionally been discussed in relative rather than absolute terms. Basing his conclusions on the pitch of wind instruments, Bruce Haynes concluded that pitch at Cöthen was roughly one and a half or two equal-tempered semitones below a' = 440 Hz (i.e., ca. 403 or ca. 392).[42] The latter was the usual pitch of French woodwind instruments in the early eighteenth century, and the Brandenburg Concertos have been recorded at that pitch by Siegbert Rampe; 403, a difficult pitch level nowadays for those with acute pitch sense, was used for the *Sei Solo* for violin by Elizabeth Wallfisch.[43]

Intonation and temperament are as critical for instrumentalists as for keyboard players, particularly the tuning of open strings. Eighteenth-century views on

---

37 For stringed bass instruments generally, see Laurence Dreyfus, *Bach's Continuo Group* (Cambridge: Harvard University Press, 1987); see also Prinz, *Johann Sebastian Bachs Instrumentarium*.

38 See Bruce Haynes, "Questions of Tonality in Bach's Cantatas: the Woodwind Perspective," *Journal of the American Musical Instrument Society* 12 (1986): 53–54.

39 Bruce Haynes, "Johann Sebastian Bachs Oboenkonzerte," BJ 78 (1992): 23–43.

40 Hans-Joachim Schulze, "Johann Sebastian Bachs Konzerte – Fragen der Überlieferung und Chronologie," *Beiträge zum Konzertschaffen Johann Sebastian Bachs* (Leipzig: Breitkopf & Härtel, 1981), 14–15; see also Rampe and Sackmann, *Bachs Orchestermusik*, 135.

41 Kai Köpp, "Die Viola d'amore ohne Resonanzsaiten und ihre Verwendung in Bachs Werken," BJ 86 (2000): 163–165.

42 Bruce Haynes, *A History of Performing Pitch: The History of 'A'*, (Lanham: Scarecrow, 2002), 236; also Rampe and Sackmann, *Bachs Orchestermusik*, 315–316.

43 Siegbert Rampe, La Stravaganza Hamburg, *Bach: Brandenburgische Konzerte I*, (CD Intercord, 1994) INT 860.882; Elizabeth Wallfisch, *Bach: Sonatas and Partitas for Solo Violin* (CD Hyperion, 1997), CDD 22009.

324   David Ledbetter

whether or not to tune pure or tempered fifths, and intonation generally have been collected by Patrizio Barbieri and Bruce Haynes (1991).[44]

Forces

The title of NBA Series VII (*Orchesterwerke/Orchestral Works*) is really not acceptable nowadays because it relates to a modern concept of the orchestra that has little to do with Bach's performing circumstances. What is meant are more properly called Ensemble Works. Bach himself used the term *Orchestre* in 1733, when offering his services to the Elector of Saxony "in *Componir*ung der Kirchen *Musique* sowohl als zum *Orchestre*."[45] Robert L. Marshall has explored the implications of the word *Orchestre* in Bach's background, where the most usual meaning was the place where musicians play in an opera theatre.[46] It is unlikely that this is quite what Bach meant; more probably, it was his version of the common designation "for church or chamber" (as in Biber's "tam aris quam aulis"[47]). Joshua Rifkin has pointed out that Bach probably includes voices, and that he was thinking of the cantatas (more properly called serenatas) that he wrote for birthdays and name-days of the Saxon ruling family.[48]

There are a number of traditions of ensemble music in Bach's background. In the French opera orchestra of Lully, the multiple manning of parts was an integral part of the effect, with viola inner parts mere *parties de remplissage*. German consort music of the seventeenth century, with lively concertato viola parts, was essentially for one instrument to a part. Italian concertos were very flexible in the size of the ensemble, depending on the occasion, from large groups with multiple manning of ripieno parts to a mere trio-sonata group.[49] Any of these could be adapted to local circumstances. Neal Zaslaw's question, whether or not stylistic reference has a bearing on instrumentation (for example, if in the French dances of the Overture-suites (BWV 1066–1069) a 16' bass is inappropriate because it was not fully integrated into the French opera orchestra until after 1720), is hardly

---

44 Patrizio Barbieri, "Violin Intonation: A Historical Survey," EM 19 (1991): 69–88; Bruce Haynes, "Beyond Temperament: Non-Keyboard Intonation in the 17th and 18th Centuries," EM 19 (1991): 357–381; for Quantz's temperament, see Mary Oleskiewicz, "The Flute at Dresden: Ramifications for Eighteenth-Century Woodwind Performance in Germany," Peter Holman and Jonathan Wainwright, eds., *From Renaissance to Baroque. Change in Instruments and Instrumental Music in the Seventeenth Century* (Aldershot: Ashgate, 2005), 164.

45 Dok 1: 74 (No. 27).

46 Robert L. Marshall, "Bach's *Orchestre*," EM 13 (1985): 176–179, reprinted in Robert L. Marshall, *The Music of Johann Sebastian Bach* (New York: Schirmer, 1989), 59–63.

47 *Sonatae tam aris quam aulis servientes* (Salzburg, 1676).

48 Joshua Rifkin, "More (and Less) on Bach's Orchestra," *Performance Practice Review*, 4/1 (1991): 5–13.

49 See Georg Muffat's *Vorred* to *Außerlesener...Instrumental-Music Erste Versamblung* (Passau, 1701), in David K. Wilson, *Georg Muffat on Performance Practice: the Texts from Florilegium primum, Florilegium secundum, and Auserlesene Instrumentalmusik: a New Translation with Commentary* (Bloomington: Indiana University Press, 2001).

Instrumental Chamber and Ensemble Music   325

relevant.[50] Bach wrote in the German "mixed style" of the early eighteenth century, and stylistic reference is not bound to instrumentation; a solo cello or a lute could recreate a French overture (BWV 1011/1, 995/1), or a solo violin an Italian concerto (BWV 1003/3, 1005/2).

The issue of single manning of parts has been almost as hotly debated with regard to Bach's instrumental ensemble music as it has been for his vocal music. There is nothing new about the concept; Heinrich Besseler and Hans Grüß proposed in 1956 that all the Brandenburg Concertos could have been played by the instrumental group known to have been available to Bach at Cöthen with one to a part, and Thurston Dart recommended it in 1960 for BWV 1049.[51] The textures of the string writing are themselves suggestive. There are places in the Overture-suites where the two violins and viola coalesce into a unison, giving a tutti effect, before going their separate ways, a contrast of texture lost with multiple manning. Two sorts of evidence have been adduced to illuminate Bach's intentions: surviving sets of parts, and the forces known to have been available to him at various stages.[52] For the first, there is the obvious caveat that parts may have gone missing or otherwise been disposed of; for the second, it is by no means certain that the musicians on, for example, a court payroll were all that was available. The issue became live in the 1980s when Joshua Rifkin, in line with his landmark recording of the B minor Mass with single voices (1981), performed the Overture-suites with single manning of parts. This in turn inspired William Malloch to record them with exactly the number of instruments as there are surviving parts.[53] In the C major BWV 1066, for example, the only bass parts are the bassoon and harpsichord, without the expected violoncello and violone. Besseler and Grüß (KB VII/1, 1967) assumed that if duplicate parts for violins and continuo are not present they must have been lost. Rifkin (1997, 2007) has shown that this is a fallacy.[54] In BWV 1066, it is most unlikely that there ever were more parts because the wrapper, prepared by one of the scribes who copied the set, does not list any more.[55] Circumstances differed in different places, however, and Bach had duplicate parts copied for Weimar and Cöthen works when he revived them in Leipzig. As Rifkin points out, this in itself implies that

---

50 Neal Zaslaw, "When Is an Orchestra not an Orchestra?" EM 16 (1988): 485; also Mary Cyr, "*Basses* and *basse continue* in the Orchestra of the Paris Opéra 1700–1764," EM 10 (1982): 156–157.

51 KB VII/2: 7–8: for details of Besseler's view, and the views of those who have taken a similar position, see John Spitzer and Neal Zaslaw, *The Birth of the Orchestra: History of an Institution, 1650–1815* (New York: Oxford University Press, 2004), 147; Dart, "Bach's 'Fiauti d'echo'," 331.

52 For a summary of forces available to Bach at Weimar, Cöthen and Leipzig, see Siegbert Rampe and Günther Hoppe in Rampe and Sackmann, *Bachs Orchestermusik*, 31–54.

53 Malloch, *Bach: Suites for Dancing*.

54 Joshua Rifkin, "Benutzung – Entstehung – Überlieferung: Bemerkungen zur Ouvertüre BWV 1068," BJ 83 (1997): 172; Joshua Rifkin, "The 'B-Minor Flute Suite' Deconstructed: New Light on Bach's Ouverture BWV 1067," BP 6 (2007): 2.

55 Rifkin, "More (and Less)," 9.

326   David Ledbetter

there were only single parts originally.[56] Rifkin was writing in answer to one of the main proponents of more than one-to-a-part, Hans-Joachim Schulze (1989). Schulze's argument is based on variety of practice and he presented information not only about the places where Bach was employed, but also any place with which he had a connection.[57] When Bach visited Dresden in 1717, he would have found around thirty-three instrumentalists in the court *Capelle*, far more than he had at his disposal at Weimar or Cöthen.[58] Often quoted is Quantz's prescription for orchestral forces, which are not concerned with absolute numbers but relative numbers according to the overall size of the group.[59] Group size depended on the type of piece and the circumstances of the performance, as Georg Muffat specified for Italian-style concertos in 1701.

A further element in the argument is whether or not players shared parts. Kai Köpp (2005) has shown that, in the luxurious circumstances of the Dresden court opera in 1731–1732, musicians did not share parts since there was the same number of seats as music stands. Another feature of the Dresden court was the practice of putting the instrumentalist's name on the part, from which we can see that, for example, in a 1712 performance of a Telemann concerto for two violins, the ripieno had four first violins, two seconds, one viola, and one violone, plus a musician who swapped between viola and violone. On the other hand, Telemann and J. G. Walther tell us that part-sharing was common in Hamburg churches and at the Weimar court.[60] The most extreme position, that the number of printed or manuscript parts was the number of musicians required for a performance, has been taken by Richard Maunder (2001, 2004).[61] He has adduced a great deal of information, but in forming an assessment of his interpretation it is advisable to read Michael Talbot's review of the 2004 book.[62] Talbot's main point is that if, for example, Vivaldi issued a concerto in six part-books, that was the minimum number of musicians needed to perform the work, not necessarily an exclusive prescription.

---

56 Rifkin, "More (and Less)," 8; the first movement the First Brandenburg Concerto also acquired duplicate violin parts when reused as the opening Sinfonia of Cantata 52 (1726).

57 Hans-Joachim Schulze, "Johann Sebastian Bach's Orchestra: Some Unanswered Questions," EM 17 (1989): 3–15.

58 Ortrun Landmann, "The Dresden Hofkapelle during the Lifetime of Johann Sebastian Bach," EM 17 (1989): 20; for a survey of forces in courts in Bach's environment, see Samantha Owens et al., eds., *Music at German Courts, 1715–1760: Changing Artistic Priorities* (Woodbridge: Boydell, 2011).

59 Johann Joachim Quantz, *Versuch einer Anweisung die Flöte traversiere zu spielen* (Berlin: Voß, 1752; facsimile, Wiesbaden: Breitkopf & Härtel, 1988), 185 (XVII/i.16); ET *On Playing the Flute*, 2nd ed., trans. Edward R Reilly (Boston: Northwestern University Press, 2001), 214.

60 Kai Köpp, *Johann Georg Pisendel (1687–1755) und die Anfänge der neuzeitlichen Orchesterleitung* (Tutzing: Schneider, 2005), 309–312.

61 Richard Maunder, "Bach's Concertos: Orchestral or Chamber Music?" *Early Music Performer* 8/3 (2001): 1–6; Richard Maunder, *The Scoring of Baroque Concertos* (Woodbridge: Boydell, 2004).

62 Michael Talbot, review of Maunder, *The Scoring of Baroque Concertos*, ML 86 (2005): 287–290.

Instrumental Chamber and Ensemble Music 327

It can be difficult to see quite what the argument is about. The concept of an exclusive intention is hardly relevant to Bach, who was constantly producing new music and reviving old. The score was a blueprint from which the requisite number of parts could be copied for any particular performance. Variety of practice must be taken into account, as testified by Georg Muffat and Quantz. As far as modern concert life is concerned, one-to-a-part performance has long been common. The combination of period instruments and single manning of parts has restored a more humane, nuanced and acutely expressive sound world for Bach, surely the underlying quest of the debate.

Analytical Approaches

Analytical writing about Bach's music is endless and there are many approaches. I shall concentrate on two aspects where the analysis serves a purpose beyond itself: analysis of style, which has a bearing on performance; and analysis of genre and form, which can illuminate the genesis and compositional history of works, and their place in the general chronology of Bach's career.

Styles

The style that is most likely to affect performance is French dance, with its highly characteristic performing conventions. A good listing of French things known to Bach was published long ago by André Pirro (1907), and the best more recent general listing is by Victoria Horn (1986).[63] New possible avenues of influence are constantly surfacing, as in contacts with Pisendel in Dresden, a musician with a similar connoisseur's cast of mind who may have provided Bach with works of François Couperin.[64]

In 1991, Meredith Little and Natalie Jenne published a detailed examination of dance types in Bach's music. Regrettably, they limited the discussion to pieces with dance titles, so although they give much useful information they did not address what is perhaps the most interesting aspect of Bach's use of dance elements, his incorporation of them into genres of sonata, concerto, or fugue. A revised version in 2001 went some way towards rectifying this.[65] Dance meters

---

63 André Pirro, "J.-S. Bach et la musique française', *Musica* 6 (1907): 149–150; Victoria Horn, "French Influences in Bach's Organ Works," George Stauffer and Ernest May, eds., *J. S. Bach as Organist* (London: Batsford, 1986), 256–273; Pirro makes an excellent and original point about psychological imitation, later writers tend to concentrate on technical details. See also Dominik Sackmann, "'Französischer Schaum und deutsches Grundelement' – französisches in Bachs Musik," BJHM 28 (2004): 81–93; and Rampe and Sackmann, *Bachs Orchestermusik*, 250–256, for a summary of French influences in Bach's environment.

64 Kerstin Delang, "Couperin – Pisendel – Bach. Überlegungen zur Echtheit und Datierung des Trios BWV 587 anhand eines Quellenfundes in der Sächsischen Landesbibliothek-Staats- und Universitätsbibliothek Dresden," BJ 93 (2007): 197–207.

65 Meredith Little and Natalie Jenne, *Dance and the Music of J. S. Bach* (Bloomington: Indiana University Press, 1991; 2nd expanded ed., 2001).

328   *David Ledbetter*

and characters are endemic in Bach's style, blended with Italian styles and genres into what Quantz described as the "mixed style," even the "German style." But, as Laurence Dreyfus has pointed out, Bach's compositional method cannot be construed just as yet another realization of the "united tastes."[66] Bach was unique among his contemporaries in his obsessive, radical "research" of musical materials. To an extent this was a product of the "musikalisch denken," which Forkel claims that Bach learnt from Vivaldi, as Christoph Wolff has demonstrated, not in the usual Vivaldian concerto allegro, but in a slow movement (Op. 3 No.3/2, arranged by Bach for harpsichord as BWV 978/2), where two contrasting motifs are elaborated into a rhetorically cogent structure.[67] This is a less obvious working of the "invention" principle than in, for example, a fugue. Bach's treatment of dance elements can be yet more subtle, and radical. The B minor violin Allemanda (BWV 1002/1) takes the *notes inégales* of the French allemande and galant-style triplets as its *inventio* and develops them in an Italianate sonata structure; the C minor cello Allemande (BWV 1011/2) clothes a similar structure with features of a French *entrée*.[68] In the case of the B minor Allemanda, a modern violinist sees large leaps and dissonant intervals, and takes the piece to be highly dramatic and over-dotted; a lutenist sees *style brisé* and written-out *notes inégales* with a quite opposite expression. A broad exploration of context is needed to find out what Bach most probably intended. Knowledge of the French dances is vital, but there is much more to explore in Bach's extraordinary use of dance elements. Our increasing understanding of Bach's contemporaries provides ever more context for this.[69]

Genres

The categorization of genres (*Gattungen*), a form of scientific taxonomy, has been a fundamental part of German musicology since the nineteenth century, enshrined by Guido Adler (1919) as "Historische Grundklassen."[70] The problem is that categories must not be too rigidly applied, and a full view of context and variety of treatments is essential. Besseler and Grüß, for example, in their edition of the Brandenburg Concertos for NBA VII/2 (1956), proposed various criteria for establishing a chronology of composition, one of the main ones being that group concertos ("Gruppenkonzerte") antedate solo concertos.[71] This is based on a

---

66 See Dreyfus, *Bach and the Patterns of Invention*, 131–133, for some penetrating comments on Bach and "mixed style."

67 Wolff Essays, 75–78.

68 See the commentaries in Ledbetter, *Unaccompanied Bach*, 109–113, 218–221; the second chapter is an introduction to some basic concepts of style and structure.

69 See for example Steven Zohn, *Music for a Mixed Taste: Style, Genre, and Meaning in Telemann's Instrumental Works* (New York: Oxford University Press, 2008).

70 Guido Adler, *Methode der Musikgeschichte* (Leipzig: Breitkopf & Härtel, 1919), 7.

71 For a general view of Besseler's chronology, see Heinrich Besseler, "Zur Chronologie der Konzerte Joh. Seb. Bachs," Walter Vetter, ed., *Festschrift Max Schneider zum achzigsten Geburtstag* (Leipzig: Deutscher Verlag für Musik, 1955), 115–128; for a detailed critique, see

Instrumental Chamber and Ensemble Music 329

textbook view of Corelli's concerti grossi giving way to Vivaldi's solo concertos. In Besseler's view, the Sixth Brandenburg Concerto is stylistically the oldest, though he distributed the concertos in three very narrow time bands of around one year each, from 1718 to 1721. Martin Geck (1970) put it back to Weimar around 1713.[72] Michael Marissen (1995) suggested that it may be one of the very latest concertos Bach wrote at Cöthen.[73] The only firm date for the Concertos is the *terminus ante quem* of 24 March 1721, when Bach penned the dedication to the Margrave. There are then what appear to be earlier versions, significantly of the First and Fifth Concertos (BWV 1046a, 1050a), although the copies they survive in date from much later. At the same time, there is always the thought that Bach as concertmaster at Weimar must surely have composed more music than one cantata a month, and that Weimar instrumental works are either lost or survive in later arrangements.[74] Opinions of genesis and chronology are therefore based on style and genre analysis, and there have been many attempts to work out a firm chronology. Such attempts tend to reveal more about the preconceptions of the writer than about Bach's activities. Only gradually has understanding of context broadened enough to provide the basis for a true evaluation of what Bach was doing. The undoubted influence of Vivaldi, for example, was for long based mainly on the concertos that Bach arranged for organ or clavier, mostly from Op. 3. Now a great deal more is known about Vivaldi's originality and variety.[75] In addition, chronological systems tend to base hypothesis upon hypothesis. To take a random example, Dominik Sackmann (2008) proposes a date of between 1715 and 1717 for the Fuga of the A minor violin Solo (BWV 1003/2).[76] This is based on formal similarities to the organ Fugue in A minor (BWV 543/2), whose earliest source (not autograph) dates from the later 1720s. But opinions have differed about the dating of the organ Fugue, and 1715–1717, though based on Bach's practice in datable cantatas of that period, is essentially a guess.[77] The *terminus*

Werner Breig, "Probleme der Analyse in Bachs Instrumentalkonzerten," Reinhold Brinkmann, ed., *Bachforschung und Bachinterpretation heute: Wissenschaftler und Praktiker in Dialog. Bericht... 1978... Marburg* (Kassel: Bärenreiter, 1981), 133–136.

72 Martin Geck, "Gattungstraditionen und Altersschichten in den Brandenburgischen Konzerten," Mf 23 (1970): 150.

73 Michael Marissen, *The Social and Religious Designs of J. S. Bach's Brandenburg Concertos* (Princeton: Princeton University Press, 1995), 55.

74 See Siegbert Rampe, "'Monatlich neüe Stücke' – Zu den musikalischen Voraussetzungen von Bachs Weimarer Konzertmeisteramt," BJ 88 (2002): 61–104.

75 See for example, Simon McVeigh and Hehoash Hirschberg, *The Italian Concerto 1700–1760: Rhetorical Strategies and Style History* (Woodbridge: Boydell, 2004).

76 Sackmann, *Triumph des Geistes*, 31–32.

77 Siegbert Rampe, ed., *Das Bach-Handbuch Band 4/2. Bach's Klavier- und Orgelwerke* (Laaber: Laaber, 2008), 768; the point is about Bach's use of 5th cycles in those years, observed by Jean-Claude Zehnder in an attempt to develop stylistic criteria for dating based on a very detailed study of Weimar organ works, "Zum späten Weimarer Stil Johann Sebastian Bachs," Martin Geck and Werner Breig, eds., *Bachs Orchesterwerke. Bericht über das 1.Dortmunder Bach-Symposion 1996* (Witten: Klangfarben Musikverlag, 1997), 80–124, on this basis Zehnder dates BWV 1046a, 1050a, and the putative original of BWV 1064, around 1716.

330   David Ledbetter

ante quem for the violin Solos is that of the autograph fair copy (1720). Because there is a clear process of increasing formal elaboration through the three fugues of the Solos, one could equally argue that the order of composition was that in the autograph. A frequently expressed opinion is that works of similar formal cut belong together chronologically, but this is by no means necessarily so. Alfred Dürr (1977) observed that it was possible to date Bach's cantatas by stylistic features up to around 1716 when his style firmed up, but much less so after that. It cannot be said that Bach did not move back and forth; stylistic features cannot be erected into a rule.[78] In 1999, Hans-Joachim Schulze voiced a general frustration with endless debates about "Gattungstraditionen und Altersschichten," picking over the same material as before, with no new hard information.[79]

Since the 1980s, a more extensive view of context, and a more nuanced view of influences on Bach, have led to a fuller understanding of Bach's handling of style and genre. In 1957, Ulrich Siegele proposed that, given the concerto style of the first movement of the G minor gamba Sonata (BWV 1029, the earliest surviving source dates from 1753), the entire sonata may well be an arrangement of a concerto for two flutes of about the time of the Brandenburg Concertos.[80] The notion that style, genre and scoring are all necessarily connected does not do justice to Bach's connoisseurship of musical materials, and his predilection for referring to one medium in terms of another as an ultimate development of the German "mixed style." In answer to a perceived problem with BWV 1029, Laurence Dreyfus (1983) adduced the genre of *Sonate auf Concertenart* from a description of current genres published by Johann Adolph Scheibe (1740).[81] This has had a long and fruitful career. Dreyfus's original opinion that BWV 1029 as *Sonate auf Concertenart* "makes no sense before the 1730s," and was therefore a guide to chronology, soon needed revision.[82] Michael Marissen (1985) proposed a lost Trio Sonata *auf Concertenart* in C major as the original of the A major Sonata for flute and obbligato harpsichord (BWV 1032), a solution to the problem of the Sonata's unusual key scheme (three movements with the same

---

78   Alfred Dürr, *Studien über die frühen Kantaten Johann Sebastian Bachs*, 2nd ed. (Wiesbaden: Breitkopf & Härtel, 1977), 176; see also Breig, "Probleme der Analyse," 135.

79   Hans-Joachim Schulze, review of Geck and Breig, eds., *Bachs Orchesterwerke,* BJ 85 (1999): 201–204.

80   Dissertation of 1957, published unaltered as Ulrich Siegele, *Kompositionsweise und Bearbeitungstechnik in der Instrumentalmusik Johann Sebastian Bachs* (Stuttgart: Hänssler, 1975), 97–100 (page numbers are from the 1975 imprint). Reconstructions of BWV 1029 as a concerto have been attempted by John Hsu and others; see Peter Williams, "Bach's G Minor Sonata for Viola da Gamba and Harpsichord. A Seventh Brandenburg Concerto?" EM 12 (1984): 345–354.

81   Paper given to the American Musicological Society; the concept was developed in print in the "Concluding Remarks" in Laurence Dreyfus, ed., *Joh. Seb. Bach. Drei Sonaten für Viola da Gamba (Violoncello) und Cembalo BWV 1027–1029* (Leipzig: Peters, 1985), 63, and more fully in "J. S. Bach and the Status of a Genre: Problems of Style in the G-minor Sonata BWV 1029," JM 5 (1987): 55–78, expanded and revised in Chapter 4 of *Bach and the Patterns of Invention.* For a detailed listing of literature, see David Schulenberg, "The *Sonate auf Concertenart*: A Postmodern Invention?" BP 7 (2008): 56, footnote 1.

82   Dreyfus, "Concluding Remarks," 64.

Instrumental Chamber and Ensemble Music 331

tonic).[83] Perspectives of time and place were greatly extended by Jeanne Swack (1993), who put what is essentially the same idea back beyond Vivaldi's chamber concertos to Telemann's early experiments around 1710.[84] Most intriguing were Dresden Trios *auf Concertenart* by Quantz, seemingly dating from the early 1730s, one of which in E flat major (QV 2:18) seems closely related to the Sonata in the same key for flute and obbligato harpsichord (BWV 1031), long doubted to be a work of Bach's and excluded from NBA VI/3. Swack was undecided as to whether BWV 1031 was by Bach or by Quantz.[85] Hans Eppstein (1981) had definitely excluded Bach on grounds of "un-Bach-like" features such as lack of density of musical thought, of transformation of material, very thin textures, and lack of dissonance.[86] These are subjective judgments based on a narrow view of Bach's style. It is a measure of the current greater acceptance of Bach's diversity and flexibility that Sackmann and Rampe (1997) proposed it as a work of Bach's of around 1745, trying the Berlin galant style, which was ultimately to come to fruition in the *Musical Offering* Trio Sonata (1747), in the relative key C minor.[87] This is of course very arguable, but the presentation of Bach as an exceptionally flexible, many-faceted polyglot composer was a sign of the times.

The hunt for mixed genres was now on. Steven Zohn (2004) extended Swack's (1993) perspectives yet further.[88] In 2007, he explored concepts of *Concert en ouverture* (the B minor flute Suite BWV 1067) and in 2008 the *Concerto en suite* (for example the First Brandenburg Concerto).[89] Meanwhile, Gregory Butler (1999) found the blend of trio sonata and the Vivaldi type of chamber concerto so finely balanced in the Fourth Brandenburg Concerto that he reversed Scheibe's terms in a *Concerto auf Sonatenart*; and Swack (2007) invented the neat "aria *auf Ouvertürenart*" for Telemann's cantatas.[90] Matthias Geuting (2006) attempted a typology for mixed genres in an effort to cover Bach's very fluid practice.[91] Finally, David Schulenberg (2008) questioned Scheibe's mixed categories as in

---

83 Michael Marissen, "A Trio in C Major for Recorder, Violin and Continuo by J. S. Bach?" EM 13 (1985): 384–390; extended in "A Critical Reappraisal of J. S. Bach's A-Major Flute Sonata," JM 6 (1988): 367–386.

84 Jeanne Swack, "On the Origins of the *Sonate auf Concertenart*," JAMS 46 (1993): 369–414.

85 Jeanne Swack, "Quantz and the Sonata in E♭ Major for Flute and Cembalo BWV 1031," EM 23 (1995): 31–53; see also KB VI/5: 23–37.

86 Hans Eppstein, "Zur Problematik von Johann Sebastian Bachs Flötensonaten," BJ 67 (1981): 77–90; see also Robert Marshall's reply in *The Music of Johann Sebastian Bach*, 225.

87 Dominik Sackmann and Siegbert Rampe, "Bach, Berlin, Quantz und die Flötensonate Es-Dur BWV 1031," BJ 83 (1997): 51–85.

88 Steven Zohn, "The *Sonate auf Concertenart* and Conceptions of Genre in the Late Baroque," ECM 1 (2004): 205–247.

89 Steven Zohn, "Bach and the *Concert en Ouverture*," BP 6 (2007): 137–157; *Music for a Mixed Taste*, 47.

90 Gregory G. Butler, "The Question of Genre in J. S. Bach's Fourth Brandenburg Concerto," BP 4 (1999): 9–32; Jeanne Swack, "A Comparison of Bach's and Telemann's Use of the Ouverture as Theological Signifier," BP 6 (2007): 99–135.

91 Matthias Geuting, *Konzert und Sonate bei Johann Sebastian Bach. Formale Disposition und Dialog der Gattungen* (Kassel, 2006).

332   David Ledbetter

turn too bound to the definition of *Gattung*. Rather than taking BWV 1029 as a fusion of sonata and concerto, "we might see it as employing a fluid combination of compositional techniques and musical signs that only later crystallized to represent separate and distinct formal principles."[92]

Did Bach really think of the definition of genre as a "problem," that he was "destabilizing his material," and other common locutions of current analysis? Research can penetrate further the subtlety of Bach's treatments, particularly in relation to his contemporaries whose lesser complexity throws his into relief.

Improvisation

A fruitful direction to look for new approaches is in improvisation practices, which have yielded much new insight into other eighteenth-century repertories.[93] Too often, common traditions may be misinterpreted as significant influence. The ritornello pattern of *Vordersatz – Fortspinnung – Epilog*, as described by Wilhelm Fischer (1915) and that lies behind much Bach analysis, is a common improvisation pattern going back at least to Thomas de Sancta Maria (1565).[94] Its background in improvisation is more evident in the lute works of Silvius Leopold Weiß, another great *Extemporaneus*, than in the more highly wrought works of Bach. Joel Lester's fruitful concept of parallel sections (1999), demonstrated with regard to the Siciliana of the G minor violin Sonata (BWV 1001/3), can also be seen as an improvisation practice, involving repetition and variation, in an obviously improvised piece such as the lute Fuga in E flat major (BWV 998/2).[95] It is a more fruitful analytical concept than trying to torture pieces into tutti/solo ritornello patterns.[96]

---

92   Schulenberg, "The *Sonate auf Concertenart*," 59.

93   See, for example, Robert O. Gjerdingen, ed., "*Partimenti*," *Journal of Music Theory* 51/1 (Spring 2007), and *Music in the Galant Style* (New York: Oxford University Press, 2007); Dirk Moelants and Kathleen Snyers, eds., *Partimento and Continuo Playing in Theory and Practice* (Leuven: Leuven University Press, 2010); Giorgio Sanguinetti, *The Art of Partimento: History, Theory, and Practice* (New York: Oxford University Press, 2012); also John Kenneth Lutterman, "Works in Progress: J. S. Bach's Suites for Solo Cello as Artifacts of Improvisatory Practices," Ph.D. diss. (University of California at Davis, 2006).

94   Wilhelm Fischer, "Zur Entwicklungsgeschichte des Wiener klassischen Stils," *Studien zur Musikwissenschaft* 3 (1915): 24–84; Thomas de Sancta Maria, *Libro llamado arte de tañer fantasia* (Valladolid, 1565), Sancta Maria's model was Josquin (*segunda parte*, 64).

95   Joel Lester, *Bach's Works for Solo Violin: Style, Structure, Performance* (New York: Oxford University Press, 1999); the concept is more fully worked out in "Heightening Levels of Activity in J. S. Bach's Parallel-Section Constructions," JAMS 54 (2001): 49–96; Ledbetter, *Unaccompanied Bach*, 261–262. Dreyfus, *Bach and the Patterns of Invention*, 208, etc. uses the term "rotations," more commonly associated with the composing methods of Bruckner and Sibelius; James Hepokoski, *Sibelius: Symphony No. 5* (Cambridge: Cambridge University Press, 1993), denies the relevance of the term to Bach, yet it may equally have an origin in Bruckner's improvisation practice.

96   Hans Eppstein, for example, wondered why Bach in sonatas used a form dependent on tutti/solo contrast in a medium where it is impossible: "Über die Beziehungen zwischen Konzert und Sonate bei Johann Sebastian Bach," *Bach-Studien* 6 (1981): 89.

Interpretations

Hermeneutic interpretations need to be carefully handled. To take one obvious example, the descending chromatic tetrachord clearly has a traditional association with laments, used as such in BWV 78/1, BWV 992, and elsewhere for that purpose. All three Fugues of the violin Solos use it, but it could hardly be said to have this expressive association there. It is a traditional building block for invertible counterpoint, and in addition has technical advantages for double-stopping on stringed instruments.[97] Exegesis of musical symbolism has a long history with regard to Bach's vocal music, and the instrumental music has by no means escaped the attention of hermeneuts, a particular favorite being the D minor violin Ciaccona (BWV 1004/5). Helga Thoene (2002, etc.), following in the footsteps of Hertha Kluge-Kahn (1985), has discerned chorale quotations in a number of the violin Solos, and deduced biographical and theological intentions.[98] The problem with this line of argument is that common musical outlines can be made to work various ways.[99] Henry Schmidt's (1976) theory that the Overture-suite in C major (BWV 1066) is a variation suite based on a chorale melody of Bach's (BWV 299) was rejected by Irving Godt (1990) for this reason.[100] Godt preferred vaguer outlines as a more likely basis for variation, taking the B minor Overture-suite (BWV 1067) as an example. Less highly evolved than Thoene's reading of the Ciaccona is Heinrich Poos's (1993), placing it in the perspective of Bach's religious convictions, with a wide-ranging frame of reference.[101] Anybody attempting this type of analysis should read John Butt's salutary critique, including "impersonations," of hermeneutic interpretations of the opening chorus of the Saint Matthew Passion.[102]

---

97 See Williams's comments on Raymond Monelle's interpretation of BWV 886/2, Peter Williams, *The Chromatic Fourth During Four Centuries of Music* (Oxford: Clarendon, 1997), 100–103; also Ledbetter, *Unaccompanied Bach*, 151–153.

98 Helga Thoene, *Johann Sebastian Bach, Ciaccona – Tanz oder Tombeau?* (Oschersleben: Ziethen, 2002), also *Morimur*, with chorales sung by The Hilliard Ensemble (CD ECM New Series, 2001), 461 895–2; Hertha Kluge-Kahn, *Johann Sebastian Bach: Die verschlüsselten theologischen Aussagen in seinem Spätwerk* (Wolfenbüttel: Möseler, 1985).

99 Raymond Erickson shows that "God rest ye merry gentlemen" works as well as "Christ lag in Todesbanden" with the beginning of the Ciaccona, "Secret Codes, Dance and Bach's Great 'Ciaccona'," *Early Music America* 8/2 (2002): 34–43.

100 Henry Schmidt, "Bach's C Major Orchestral Suite: A New Look at Possible Origins," ML 57 (1976): 152–63; Irving Godt, "Politics, Patriotism, and a Polonaise: A Possible Revision in Bach's Suite in B Minor," MQ 74 (1990): 610–622.

101 Heinrich Poos, "J. S. Bach's Chaconne für Violine solo aus der Partita d-moll BWV 1004. Ein hermeneutischer Versuch," *Jahrbuch des Staatlichen Instituts für Musikforschung, Preußischer Kulturbesitz 1993*: 151–203.

102 John Butt, *Bach's Dialogue with Modernity: Perspectives on the Passions* (Cambridge: Cambridge University Press, 2010), Chapter 3; also Matthias Wendt, "Bach und die Zahl 13. Marginalien zu einem Randthema," Kollegium des Johann-Sebastian-Bach-Instituts Göttingen, eds., *Acht kleine Präludien und Studien über BACH. Georg von Dadelsen zum 70. Geburtstag am 17. November 1988* (Wiesbaden: Breitkopf & Härtel, 1992), 86–91; and Sven Hiemke, *Johann Sebastian Bach. Orgelbüchlein* (Kassel: Bärenreiter, 2007), Chapter II.4.

334   *David Ledbetter*

Number symbolism has also been a faithful companion since the mid-twentieth century. Here the most fruitful results have been produced by Ruth Tatlow (1991, etc.), who does not regard numbers as having occult meaning but rather as structural scaffolding, particularly in defining cycles.[103] On the basis of numerical correspondences, she has proposed the six Sonatas for violin and obbligato harpsichord (BWV 1014–1019) as the *Libro Secondo* implied by Bach's "*Libro Primo*" on the 1720 title-page of the *Sei Solo* for violin. The *Libro Secondo* is usually thought to be the cello Suites, but the numbers do not support this.[104] It has to be said, though, that the cello Suites do seem to form a cycle, with a rational key scheme, a progression of technical sophistication, and the systematic inclusion of scordatura and a five-stringed instrument. The fundamental discussion of cycles in Bach's instrumental music is by Rudolf Eller (1969), and there have been many since.[105] Whether or not the Brandenburg Concertos constitute a cycle has long been a subject of debate. The most fanciful suggestion is by Vincent Dequevauviller, who proposes a scheme based on Bach's quasi-palindromic spelling of "Marggraf."[106]

Political interpretations of music generally were common enough in the old Soviet bloc. They came to the fore in the West in respect of Bach with the rise of the New Musicology, just around the time when the Berlin Wall fell. Most striking was Susan McClary's (1987) attempt to bring Bach down from his transcendent pedestal into the political arena.[107] The harpsichord in the first movement of the Fifth Brandenburg Concerto, the ensemble's lackey as continuo player, becomes "a genuine deviant" from the service department, hijacking all in its final solo in a manner she likens to the storming of the Bastille. This Beaumarchais-esque scenario is constructed in sublime indifference to historical

---

103 Ruth Tatlow, *Bach and the Riddle of the Number Alphabet* (Cambridge: Cambridge University Press, 1991); Ruth Tatlow, *Bach's Numbers: Compositional Proportion and Significance* (Cambridge: Cambridge University Press, 2016).

104 Ruth Tatlow, booklet notes for Maya Homburger, *J. S. Bach. Sonata in G minor BWV 1001, Partita in B minor BWV 1002* (CD Maya Recordings, 2003), MCD 0301; also Ruth Tatlow, "Collections, Bars and Numbers: Analytical Coincidence or Bach's Design?" UB 2 (2007): 37–58: Tatlow, *Bach's Numbers*, 146–149.

105 Rudolf Eller, "Serie und Zyklus in Bachs Instrumental-Sammlungen," Martin Geck, ed., *Bach-Interpretationen* (Göttingen: Vandenhoeck & Ruprecht, 1969), 126–143.

106 Vincent Dequevauviller, "Le secret des *Concertos Brandebourgeois*," *Musurgia* 4 (1997): 39–46. For a survey of interpretations of the Brandenburg concertos as a cycle, see Peter Schleuning, "Bach und die Natur. Beobachtungen an den Brandenburgischen Konzerten," *Österreichische Musikzeitschrift* 55 (2000): 32–3; Peter Schleuning, "Sind die Brandenburgischen Konzerte ein Zyklus?" *Jahrbuch des Staatlichen Instituts für Musikforschung, Preußischer Kulturbesitz*, (2004): 62–74, including his own theory that the horn calls at the beginning of BWV 1046 constitute a "Herrschergruß" that unites all six concertos motivically; see also Peter Schleuning, *Johann Sebastian Bach. Die Brandenburgischen Konzerte* (Kassel: Bärenreiter, 2003).

107 Susan McClary, "The Blasphemy of Talking Politics During the Bach Year," Richard D. Leppert and Susan McClary, eds., *Music and Society: The Politics of Composition, Performance and Reception* (Cambridge: Cambridge University Press, 1987), 13–62.

Instrumental Chamber and Ensemble Music 335

reality. The luxurious Mietke harpsichords at Charlottenburg never belonged to the service department. The Electress Sophie Charlotte was noted for playing the works of François Couperin, for whom playing the harpsichord was inherently so grand an activity as to be described as "toucher, rather than the "jouer" of common fiddlers.[108] The social inversion theme was continued by Michael Marissen (1995, etc.), who saw the humble violas take the limelight over the aristocratic soloistic viol in the Sixth Brandenburg Concerto, and the horns of the First Concerto gradually losing their social identity to become part of the general group.[109] Whatever one thinks of these interpretations, they do point to new directions in identifying social dimensions in Bach's music, at a time when analysis of this sort was yielding rich results for music of the Classical period.[110] The French operatic *passacaille* expresses a broadly social emotion (BWV 78/1), whereas the Italian operatic lament expresses intense personal anguish (BWV 154/1), genres also traversed in the D minor violin Ciaccona. Another approach is to see how musical materials and even structures grow out of the nature of instruments. The harmonic proportion 2:1 that dominates the first movement of the Second Brandenburg Concerto derives from the harmonic series of the trumpet. The final bar of the first movement of the First Concerto reveals that the auxiliary figure in the oboes and violins is a variation on the horns' "huffing" idiom, and that the main theme of the first section of the movement is in fact a division variation constructed from this and the hunting fanfares. There is still much to be said about instruments and social implications.

Work Groups

Instrumental Solos BWV 1001–1013

Much important work has recently been done on the German background to the violin Solos, notably by Clemens Fanselau (2000) and Thomas Drescher (2004).[111] Because so much writing about these works is concerned with style and influences as indicators of genesis and chronology, there is always scope for

---

108 See David Ledbetter, *Harpsichord and Lute Music in 17th-Century France* (London: Macmillan, 1987), 13–14.

109 Marissen, *The Social and Religious Designs*.

110 For example Wye Jamison Allanbrook, *Rhythmic Gesture in Mozart: Le nozze di Figaro and Don Giovanni* (Chicago: University of Chicago Press, 1983).

111 Clemens Fanselau, *Mehrstimmigkeit in J. S. Bachs Werke für Melodieinstrumente ohne Begleitung* (Sinzig: Studio, 2000); Thomas Drescher, *Spielmännische Tradition und höfische Virtuosität* (Tutzing: Schneider, 2004); Pauline Nobes has usefully published editions with facsimiles of some little-known German violin solos in: *Klagenfurt Manuscript, Dances and Scordatura Suites* (Ipswich: Rhapsody, 1999); *6 Vilsmaÿr Partitas (Salzburg, 1715)* (Ipswich: Rhapsody, 2000); see also "Neglected Sources of the Solo Violin Repertory before ca. 1750: With Special Reference to Unaccompanied Performance, Scordatura and Other Aspects of Violin Technique," Ph.D. diss. (University of Exeter, 2000); for a summary, see Ledbetter, *Unaccompanied Bach*, chapter One, section 2.

336   *David Ledbetter*

further work on context. To take an example, Dominik Sackmann (1999) has proposed an important influence of the graces of the 1710 Amsterdam publication of Corelli's Op. 5 violin Sonatas on movements such as the Adagio of the violin Sonata in G minor (BWV 1001/1).[112] A further influence of Corelli's Op. 5 has been proposed for the cello Suites by David Watkin.[113] Although the Amsterdam graces could well have been influential, they were part of a tradition of such improvisation with manifestations perhaps closer to Bach in violin works of Johann Pachelbel, and Fantasias by Nicola Matteis the younger and Angelo Ragazzi in Pisendel's collection in Dresden, a tradition that needs exploring.[114]

In common with virtually all Bach's instrumental music, the main bone of contention has been chronology. Günther Haußwald (1957), NBA editor of the violin Solos, considered that the works as represented in the 1720 autograph were the result of a long process of refinement and consolidation going back to Bach's Weimar days, and indeed this would make sense in that the violin assumed a new importance for Bach in 1714 with his appointment as concertmaster.[115] Many, starting with Alfred Dörffel in BG (1879), have noted that one source of the later 1720s uses the flat sign (♭) rather than the natural (♮) to cancel the sharp (♯).[116] Since Alfred Dürr showed that Bach abandoned this form of notation in the summer of 1714, this has been taken as evidence that the copyist's *Vorlage* must have originated before that date.[117] But Georg von Dadelsen (1991) has shown that this cannot be regarded as a sure dating criterion since a conservative copyist may put Bach's script back.[118] It is not impossible, though most unlikely, that the Solos

---

112   Dominik Sackmann, *Bach und Corelli: Studien zu Bachs Rezeption von Corellis Violinsonaten op. 5 unter besonderer Berücksichtigung der "Passaggio-Orgelchoräle" und der langsamen Konzertsätze* (Munich: Katzbichler, 1999); for a survey of views on the authenticity of "Corelli's graces," see Cristina Urchueguía, ed., *Arcangelo Corelli. Historisch-kritische Gesamtausgabe der musikalischen Werke Band III. Sonate a Violino e Violone o Cimbalo Opus V* (Laaber: Laaber, 2006), 15–16, 167, who concludes that Roger used a manuscript compiled by Corelli, or under his supervision.

113   David Watkin, "Corelli's Op.5 Sonatas: 'Violino e violone *o* cembalo'?" EM 24 (1996): 645–663.

114   See Ledbetter, *Unaccompanied Bach*, 22, 29–31, and Appendix 3.

115   Günther Haußwald, "Zur Stilistik von J. S. Bachs Sonaten und Partiten für Violine allein," AfMw 14 (1957): 320. Wollny in NBA[rev] 3, *Kammermusik mit Violine* (2014): 244, doubts that Bach led from the violin as concertmaster at Weimar; for a contrary opinion about this and P267, see Clemens Fanselau in Siegbert Rampe and Dominik Sackmann, eds., *Das Bach-Handbuch* 5/2 (Laaber: Laaber, 2013), 224–228.

116   D-B Mus. Ms.Bach P 267; Peter Wollny has proposed Georg Gottfried Wagner, a violinist in Bach's Leipzig church music between 1723 and 1726, as the copyist (KB VI/5: 90).

117   See Sackmann, *Triumph des Geistes*, 29.

118   Georg von Dadelsen, "Bach der Violinist. Anmerkungen zu den Soli für Violine und für Violoncello," Andreas Glöckner, et al., eds., *Johann Sebastian Bach: Schaffenskonzeption, Werkidee, Textbezug. Bericht... Leipzig... 1989* (Leipzig: Nationale Forschungs- und Gedenkstätten Johann Sebastian Bach, 1991), 71–72; see also Hans-Joachim Schulze, "Johann Sebastian Bachs Konzerte," 18–19. Bach used the old convention in the harpsichors part of BWV 1050, as well as in other Cöthen works, and later, for example, the bass figuring he added in BWV 1021 (1732).

Instrumental Chamber and Ensemble Music 337

were composed before the summer of 1714, but this notational feature cannot be taken as hard evidence for that.

A further point of debate is whether the violin Solos or the cello Suites were composed first. Haußwald (1958) considered that the cello Suites came first, though not by much, since they do not break formal boundaries as much as the Solos.[119] A similar point is made by Eppstein (1976): that Bach's trend is towards growing freedom in the treatment of form.[120] Fanselau (2000) neatly remarks that this argument could equally well be reversed.[121] As with virtually all the instrumental works, the chronological debate washes back and forth and it is unlikely that anything can be fixed in the absence of composing scores or other hard evidence.[122]

Otherwise, the main thrust of current new research is on sources that have hitherto been considered late and peripheral, and the amount of light they can shed on subsequent influence and reception history, as outlined by Yo Tomita in Chapter 3.

Duo Sonatas BWV 1014–1019, 1025, 1027–1032

The Six Sonatas for obbligato harpsichord and violin (BWV 1014–1019), in spite of being one of Bach's finest chamber collections, have received less attention than others in this category, probably because they are a rational series and the question of prior origins in other media has not been so pressing.[123] The main object of discussion has been the G major Sonata (BWV 1019), which breaks the pattern of the previous five Sonatas and exists in three versions. NBA VI/1 was one of the earliest NBA volumes (1958, 2/1974), and Rudolf Gerber, editor of these Sonatas, did not have available the detailed information about copyists and sources that later became general. He placed what was in fact the first version second. Hans-Joachim Schulze (1984) showed that the hand of the harpsichord part for BWV 1014–1019/2 was that of Bach's Ohrdruf nephew Johann Heinrich Bach in 1725.[124] Movements 3 to 5 of BWV 1019[1] are Bach autograph. This

---

119 KB VI/1: 62–63.
120 Hans Eppstein, "Chronologieprobleme in Johann Sebastian Bachs Suiten für Soloinstrument," BJ 62 (1976): 47.
121 Fanselau, *Mehrstimmigkeit*, 320.
122 For comment on J. P. Kellner's versions of the Solos and Suites, and on Martin W.B. Jarvis's proposal that the cello Suites were composed by Anna Magdalena Bach, see Chapter 3; for BWV 1013, see Ledbetter, *Unaccompanied Bach*, chapter Six.
123 Analytical essays on individual movements are in Jürgen Asmus, "Zur thematischen Arbeit und Formbildung in Bachschen langsamen Sonatensätzen (Sonaten für Violine und obligates Cembalo, BWV 1014–1019)," *Bach-Studien* 9 (1986): 151–164; and Geuting, *Konzert und Sonate*; for a survey of sonatas with obbligato keyboard in the seventeenth and eighteenth centuries, see Alfred Wierichs, *Die Sonate für obligates Tasteninstrument und Violino bis zum Beginn der Hochklassik in Deutschland* ([n.p.: copy of typescript doctoral dissertation, Wilhelms-Universität Münster, 1980], 1981).
124 Schulze, 110–119, updated from "Ein 'Dresdner Menuett' im zweiten Klavierbüchlein der Anna Magdalena Bach. Nebst Hinweisen zur Überlieferung einiger Kammermusikwerke Bachs," BJ 65 (1979): 45–64.

338   *David Ledbetter*

version contains two movements in common with the E minor clavier Partita (BWV 830/3) and 6 (BWV 1019[1]/3 and 5). Hans Eppstein (1964) argued that the violin versions of these came first, partly because of a variation element he detected between these two movements and BWV 1019[1]/2, and partly because Bach omitted them from the Sonata after the Partita was published in 1730/31.[125] Since only an unfigured bass part survives for BWV 1019[1]/5, Eppstein suggested this movement as a duo for violin and bass viol, balancing the harpsichord solo BWV 1019[1]/3. Eppstein's views have since been disputed by Andrew Talle, who gives cogent reasons for the Sonata having been assembled from disparate, preexisting elements.[126]

Eppstein and others have proposed trio-sonata or ensemble originals for various movements in these sonatas. There are suggestive features, such as that the harpsichord right-hand part in the C minor Sonata (BWV 1018/2) does not go below g in a movement similar in character to the D minor Concerto for two violins (BWV 1043/1), for which a trio-sonata origin has been proposed.[127] Peter Williams (1984) considered that "no harpsichord player can believe his part in the opening movement of the E major Violin Sonata (BWV 1016) was originally conceived for harpsichord."[128] These are subjective judgments. Bach seems in these Sonatas to be exploring possible relationships between violin and harpsichord in his usual systematic way. He may well be alluding to other media here as he demonstrably does elsewhere, particularly in the second WTC, something in which he was not alone, judging by other harpsichord music of the period.

Two more recent editions, by Richard Jones (1993) and Peter Wollny (2004), are based on accurate source assessment.[129] Jones prioritizes the manuscript score by Johann Christoph Altnickol, presumably copied during the last three years of Bach's life or shortly thereafter; in view of the sparsity of performance indications in Altnickol's copy, Wollny also prioritizes copies by Johann Friedrich Agricola (1739–1740 and after 1741, this source was unknown to Rudolph Gerber in NBA VI/1) and the Berlin copyist Schlichting (ca. 1745). Wollny's edition, with some differences and a great deal more detailed source information, is also in NBA[rev] 3 (2014).

The essentially provisional nature of theories about origins is demonstrated by the curious "Trio" for violin and obbligato harpsichord (BWV 1025). In 1992, it was revealed to be an arrangement by Bach of a lute Sonata by Silvius Leopold

---

125 Hans Eppstein, "Zur Problematik von J. S. Bachs Sonate für Violine und Cembalo G-Dur (BWV 1019)," AfMw 21 (1964): 217–242.

126 Andrew James Talle, 'J. S. Bach's Keyboard Partitas and Their Early Audience', Ph.D. diss, (Harvard University, 2003), 75–77. See also Tatlow, *Bach's Numbers*, 146–149.

127 See Rampe and Sackmann, *Bachs Orchestermusik*, 108–110. The RH part of BWV 1019/1 shows signs of having been transposed down an octave in places.

128 Williams, "Bach's G Minor Sonata," 346.

129 Richard D. P. Jones, ed., *J. S. Bach. The Music for Violin and Cembalo/Continuo* (Oxford: Oxford University Press, 1993); Peter Wollny, ed., *J. S. Bach. Six Sonatas for Violin and Obbligato Harpsichord BWV 1014–1019* (Kassel: Bärenreiter, 2004).

Instrumental Chamber and Ensemble Music   339

Weiß in which Bach transferred the lute part to the harpsichord and composed a new violin part to go with it.[130] It is therefore of considerable interest for Bach's technique of composition, along with works such as BWV 1021 in which Bach transformed what seems to be borrowed material by additions of his own. The extant source of Weiß's Sonata lacks the initial Fantasia of BWV 1025, but lute versions of parts of it have since been identified.[131]

Unlike the sonatas for violin and obbligato harpsichord, those for gamba (BWV 1027–1029) and flute (BWV 1030–1032) do not form coherent series. At the same time, these have complex backgrounds and are some of the most discussed of Bach's instrumental chamber works. Theories of a concerto origin for the G minor gamba Sonata (BWV 1029) have been mentioned previously. The G major Sonata (BWV 1027) is the only one of the gamba Sonatas to survive in a Bach autograph (ca. 1742, the earliest sources for the other two Sonatas are copies dated 1753).[132] It also survives as a trio Sonata for two flutes and continuo (BWV 1039), in parts made by two unknown copyists, and the relationship between the two versions has been the main point of debate. Siegele (1957), on grounds that the bass goes below cello C and what he regarded as the unusually low tessitura of the flutes, proposed a lost original in B flat major for two recorders.[133] But there are places in the version for flutes where the melodic line is deflected because of instrumental range ("Stimmknickungen"), so Eppstein (1965) supposed two violins in G major for the putative original, the various anomalies explained by BWV 1027 being an arrangement of BWV 1039, but with reference to the original.[134] An organ arrangement probably made by J. P. Kellner after 1730 seems to have been based on this original, a view endorsed by Russell Stinson (1989) in his study of Kellner's Bach copies.[135]

On the question of "Stimmknickungen," both Siegele and Eppstein proposed many lost originals for works that survive only in late copies, using this as one of the criteria for identifying a piece as an arrangement. Alfred Dürr (1968) voiced some important caveats about this methodology, for example that Bach often transposes material in the course of a movement, in which case adaptations of line need not necessarily imply an arrangement.[136] As we have seen with reference to BWV 1031, Eppstein had difficulty in accepting galant features as part of Bach's stylistic palette, and for this reason he also doubted the authenticity of

---

130 See Christoph Wolff, "Das Trio in A-Dur BWV 1025," BJ 79 (1993): 47–67.

131 Karl-Ernst Schröder, "Zum Trio A-Dur BWV 1025," BJ 81 (1995): 47–60; also KB VI/5: 75.

132 Kobayashi, 50.

133 Siegele, *Kompositionsweise*, 67–69.

134 Hans Eppstein, "J. S. Bachs Triosonate G-dur (BWV 1039) und ihre Beziehungen zur Sonate für Gambe und Cembalo G-dur (BWV 1027)," Mf 18 (1965): 126–137.

135 Russell Stinson, "Three Organ-Trio Transcriptions from the Bach Circle: Keys to a Lost Bach Chamber Work," Don O. Franklin, ed., *Bach Studies* (Cambridge: Cambridge University Press, 1989), 125–159; Russell Stinson, *The Bach Manuscripts of Johann Peter Kellner and his Circle: A Case Study in Reception History* (Durham: Duke University Press, 1989), chapter IV.

136 Alfred Dürr, "Zu Hans Eppsteins 'Studien über J. S. Bachs Sonaten für ein Melodieinstrument und obligates Cembalo',"Mf 21 (1968): 332–340.

340   *David Ledbetter*

the D major gamba Sonata (BWV 1028).[137] Dürr's critique of Eppstein is salutary in stressing the need for firm stylistic criteria, and for keeping open a full range of possibilities, while bearing in mind that unproven things must be treated as problems, not facts to build on.

The B minor Sonata for flute and obbligato harpsichord (BWV 1030) has inspired a particularly complex set of theories. It exists in an autograph score in B minor (ca. 1736/37), and a later copy of just the harpsichord part in G minor that nonetheless clearly reflects an earlier state of the work. The original solo instrument is therefore open to speculation. Theories regarding origins were the subject of a sharply worded exchange between Hans Eppstein and Alfred Dürr. In an effort to explain differences of texture between the first and second movements, Eppstein (1966) first proposed a Cöthen trio sonata in G minor for two flutes and continuo, based on an original concerto for flute.[138] Dürr (1968) objected to the idea of two flutes in the same register at the beginning of the first movement, particularly since the harpsichord right-hand part is a typical *Spielfigur*, and also to the inconvenience of key and tessitura for flute.[139] Eppstein ultimately (1969) came up with a tortuous theory of origins for the first movement: possibly an aria idea—short concerto or sonata movement for melody instrument (flute?)—trio in G minor—harpsichord and flute in G minor (BWV 1030a).[140] More recently, Klaus Hofmann (1998) has proposed an even more ingenious theory of origin. On grounds of the range and tessitura of the G minor harpsichord part he suggests a trio for melody instrument, lute and bass, in line with trios for this combination by Philippo Martino and Johann Kropfgans that Bach may have known.[141] Hofmann considered the unveiling (1992) of BWV 1025 as an arrangement of a lute Sonata by Weiß to be further evidence in support of his theory.[142] He did not escape a "Kritische Nachbemerkung" from Eppstein, repeating answers to Dürr and preferring Eppstein's own concept of a trio for two flutes and continuo.[143]

Such elaborate theories have been encouraged by the situation that, apart from the violin Solos, the Brandenburg Concertos and the Fuga in G minor for violin and continuo (BWV 1026), all the surviving sources for the instrumental

---

137   Hans Eppstein, *Studien über J. S. Bachs Sonaten für ein Melodieinstrument und obligates Cembalo* (Uppsala: Almquist & Wiksell, 1966), 135–136; Hans Eppstein, "Zur Problematik von Johann Sebastian Bachs Flötensonaten," 85, where he links BWV 1028 and BWV 1031.

138   Eppstein, *Studien*, 75–88.

139   Dürr, "Zu Hans Eppstein's 'Studien'," 335.

140   Hans Eppstein, "Erwiderung auf Alfred Dürr's Besprechung der 'Studien über J. S. Bachs Sonaten für ein Melodieinstrument und obligates Cembalo',"Mf 22 (1969): 206–208.

141   Klaus Hofmann, "Auf der Suche nach der verlorenen Urfassung: Diskurs zur Vorgeschichte der Sonate in h-Moll für Querflöte und obligates Cembalo von Johann Sebastian Bach," BJ 84 (1998): 31–59.

142   There is still a question about Bach's involvement in BWV 1025, whether it derives from a trio by Weiß (of which there are many), or a duo for lute and harpsichord; see Tim Crawford, ed., *Silvius Leopold Weiss (1687–1750), Sämtliche Werke für Laute* 8 (Kassel: Bärenreiter, 2007), 286–287.

143   Ibid., 60–62.

Instrumental Chamber and Ensemble Music   341

chamber and ensemble works date from Bach's Leipzig period, mostly from 1730 and later, and roughly one third in copies from after Bach's lifetime. At the same time, a number of works demonstrably derive from earlier ones, and others give good reason to think that they do. A reaction came in 1985 when Christoph Wolff developed the theory that works in Leipzig sources were actually composed in Leipzig, rather than the older idea that most of the instrumental chamber and ensemble music originated in Cöthen.[144] But theories of early origins did not go away, and in 1994 Martin Geck questioned Wolff's logic.[145] Since then, the time scale has been extended backwards well into Bach's Weimar days, notably by Rampe and Sackmann (2000).[146]

The remaining work in this category is the A major Sonata for flute and obbligato harpsichord BWV 1032. Two peculiarities of the autograph manuscript (ca. 1736/37) have given rise to speculation. The first movement of the Sonata is written on spare staves beneath the score of the Concerto in C minor for two harpsichords (BWV 1062, an arrangement of BWV 1043), but approximately forty-six bars towards the end of the movement have been cut away. Hans-Joachim Schulze (1980) suggested that this was done by Bach perhaps to replace an overcorrected passage, or to avoid repeating perceived formal deficiencies at the beginning of the movement. The replacement would have been on a separate piece of paper, now lost.[147] The other peculiarity is that all three movements have the same tonic (the second movement is in A minor), which led Hans Eppstein to suppose an original trio for flute, violin and continuo in which the outer movements were in C major; or a concerto, since Eppstein (as with BWV 1031) applied his subjective judgment of Bach's style and found the first movement lacking the "intensiv dreistimmige Satzstruktur" of a trio sonata.[148] A trio-sonata origin is nonetheless plausible and the key-scheme argument is compelling. Michael Marissen (1985, 1988) proposed a trio for treble recorder, violin and continuo, with the first movement completed by transposing material from earlier in the movement, and an ingenious theory of Bach cutting out a section of the movement to facilitate copying.[149] Jeanne Swack (1995) addressed the problem of the missing bars with two more nuanced suggestions for completion, based on the concept of the *Sonate auf Concertenart*.[150] In view of Schulze's suggested reason

---

144 Christoph Wolff, "Bach's Leipzig Chamber Music," EM 13 (1985): 165–175; reprinted in Wolff Essays, 223–238.

145 Martin Geck, "Köthen oder Leipzig? Zur Datierung der nur in Leipziger Quellen erhaltenen Orchesterwerke Johann Sebastian Bachs," Mf 47 (1994): 17–24.

146 Rampe and Sackmann, *Bachs Orchestermusik*.

147 Hans-Joachim Schulze, ed., *Johann Sebastian Bach. Konzert c-Moll für zwei Cembali und Streichorchester BWV 1062. Sonate A-Dur für Flöte und Cembalo BWV 1032. Faksimile der autographen Partitur* (Kassel: Bärenreiter, 1980), 16–17.

148 Eppstein, *Studien*, 90–102.

149 Michael Marissen, "A Trio in C Major for Recorder, Violin and Continuo by J. S. Bach?" expanded in "A Critical Reappraisal of J. S. Bach's A-Major Flute Sonata."

150 Jeanne Swack, "J. S. Bach's A Major Flute Sonata BWV 1032 revisited," Daniel R. Melamed, ed., *Bach Studies 2* (Cambridge: Cambridge University Press, 1995), 154–174; Gerhard

342   *David Ledbetter*

for the excision as recomposition rather than transposed repetition, these may be nearer the mark. The relationship of this Sonata and BWV 1031 (discussed previously) is intriguing, and the last word has by no means been said.

The Sonata in G minor (BWV 1020) is now thought to be neither by Sebastian nor Emanuel Bach.[151]

Chamber Music with Continuo: BWV 1021, 1023, 1026, 1034–1035

The two Sonatas for violin and continuo each present different problems. Doubts have been expressed about the authorship of the E minor Sonata (BWV 1023), though Wolff (1991) accepted it and dated it "after 1723."[152] It is in the tradition of the late seventeenth-century German violin sonata, though with updated harmony, and most commentators have supposed a Weimar origin: Günter Haußwald (1958) thought 1714–1717; Pieter Dirksen (2003) ca. 1714; Peter Wollny (2005) perhaps for Pisendel's visit to Weimar in 1709, since the only source was made by a Dresden copyist apparently at Pisendel's request.[153] In this case it would join the only chamber work definitely datable to Weimar: the much more assured and virtuoso Fuga in G minor (BWV 1026), which Wollny suggests may also reflect a meeting with Pisendel. The source of BWV 1026 is a copy by J. G. Walther dating from after ca. 1712, and Jean-Claude Zehnder (1995) has suggested a composition date of ca. 1712–1714 on grounds of style.[154] Other chamber works suggested for around this time have included a putative original trio sonata in G minor for oboe, viola/bass viol and continuo for the organ Sonata (BWV 528) (ca. 1730).[155]

The G major Sonata (BWV 1021) is part of a complex of works using the same bass about which opinions have differed. The source is a copy by Anna

---

Kirchner lists 38 editions since 1860 (BG IX), with 22 completions and comments on theories for completing the movement: "Ein Schnitt und seine Folgen. Zum ersten Satz der Sonate BWV 1032," Andreas Eichhorn, ed., *Festschrift Hans-Peter Schmitz zum 75. Geburtstag* (Kassel: Bärenreiter, 1992), 117–134.

151   KB VI/5: 87–89.

152   Wolff Essays, 228.

153   KB VI/1: 128ff; Pieter Dirksen, "Ein verschollenes Weimarer Kammermusikwerk Johann Sebastian Bachs? Zur Vorgeschichte der Sonate e-Moll für Orgel (BWV 528)," BJ 89 (2003): 35; Peter Wollny, ed., *J. S. Bach. Sonatas in G Major, E Minor. Fugue in G Minor for Violin and Basso continuo BWV 1021, 1023, 1026* (Kassel: Bärenreiter, 2005), Preface; Wollny, in NBA[rev] 3, revised his identification of the copyist.

154   KB VI/5: 64; Jean-Claude Zehnder, "Zu Bachs Stilentwicklung in der Mühlhäuser und Weimarer Zeit," Karl Heller and Hans-Joachim Schulze, eds., *Das Frühwerk Johann Sebastian Bachs* (Cologne: Studio, 1995), 338.

155   Dirksen, "Ein verschollenes Weimarer Kammermusikwerk," 35; for other putative early originals of organ Sonatas, see Klaus Hofmann, "Ein verschollenes Kammermusikwerk Johann Sebastian Bachs. Zur Fassungsgeschichte der Orgelsonate Es-Dur (BWV 525) und der Sonate A-Dur für Flöte und Cembalo (BWV 1032)," BJ 85 (1999): 67–79; and the summaries of literature in Peter Williams, *The Organ Music of J. S. Bach*, 2nd ed. (Cambridge: Cambridge University Press, 2003), 2ff., and Siegbert Rampe, "Triosonaten," *Das Bach-Handbuch Band 4/2*, 797–811.

Instrumental Chamber and Ensemble Music 343

Magdalena Bach made in 1732, with additions by Bach including the bass figuring. Siegele (1957) questioned whether Bach composed the bass or added parts to an existing one.[156] Either way, the Sonata seems to have been part of Bach's method of teaching composition by giving a figured bass to students, to which they composed upper parts, a written version of a normal way of teaching improvisation. BWV 1021 looks like a model provided by Bach. Wollny suggests around 1715 for the bass since its brevity (for Bach) matches the type of Telemann's influential *Six Sonates* (Frankfurt, 1715) for violin and continuo, dedicated to Prince Johann-Ernst of Sachsen-Weimar. Klaus Hofmann (2004) suggests 1710 or before.[157] The same bass is used in two other works: a trio Sonata in G major for flute, scordatura violin and continuo (BWV 1038), and a Sonata in F major for scordatura violin and obbligato harpsichord (BWV 1022). BWV 1038 exists in three autograph parts of 1732–1735, but it has long been thought a student work of C. P. E. Bach's.[158] Hofmann concludes that both may originate in a Trio for violin, viola and bass described as "mit Johann Sebastian Bach gemeinschaftlich verfertigt" in the 1790 listing of Emanuel Bach's estate.[159] More recently, Wollny has proposed it as a genuine work of Bach's, using an existing bass to save having to invent a new structure, and with lesser instrument-technical demands than usual in response to a request from an amateur.[160]

Of the two Sonatas for flute and continuo, in E minor (BWV 1034) and E major (BWV 1035), BWV 1034 was the subject of an altercation between Hans Eppstein and Robert L. Marshall that again revealed the weaknesses of attempting too precise a dating on grounds of style. Eppstein (1972) put it in Cöthen; Marshall (1979) preferred to place it around 1724, at a time when Bach was writing a number of virtuoso flute obbligatos in cantatas.[161] Eppstein then (1981) berated Marshall for ignoring the findings of style analysis, to which Marshall rightly (1989) pointed to problematic aspects of Eppstein's criteria, and that the earliest source dates from 1726/27.[162] The Sonata is indeed slightly mysterious; the stylistic mismatch between the somewhat formulaic Andante and the first two movements has been the subject of comment (the Andante is of a common

---

156 Siegele, *Kompositionsweise*, 23, 31.

157 Klaus Hofmann, "Zur Echtheit der Triosonate G-Dur BWV 1038," BJ 90 (2004): 68.

158 Ibid., 43–44; Ulrich Leisinger and Peter Wollny, "'Altes Zeug von mir.' Carl Philipp Emanuel Bachs kompositorisches Schaffen vor 1740," BJ 79 (1993): 192.

159 Hofmann, "Zur Echtheit," 70–79; see also KB VI/5: 51–61; for further discussion see Barthold Kuijken, ed., *Johann Sebastian Bach (?). Trio Sonata for Flute, Violin and Basso Continuo in G major BWV 1038* (Wiesbaden: Breitkopf & Härtel, 2012).

160 *J. S. Bach. Trio Sonata for Flute, Violin and Continuo in G major BWV 1038*, ed. Peter Wollny (Munich: Henle, 2013), Preface; the edition may be consulted on the Henle Verlag website (30/10/2013).

161 Hans Eppstein, "Über J. S. Bachs Flötensonaten mit Generalbaß," BJ 58 (1972): 16–17; Robert Lewis Marshall, "J. S. Bachs Compositions for Solo Flute: A Reconsideration of their Authenticity and Chronology," JAMS 32 (1979), reprinted in *The Music of Johann Sebastian Bach*, 213, 216.

162 Eppstein, "Zur Problematik," 89–90; Marshall, "Postscript," *The Music of Johann Sebastian Bach*, 225.

344   *David Ledbetter*

aria type, with examples by Handel, Quantz, Graupner and others), nonetheless Marshall's dating is now generally accepted.

A nineteenth-century comment that BWV 1035 was written in Potsdam for Michael Gabriel Fredersdorf, private secretary and flute partner of Frederick II, matches the style of the piece so well that most have associated it with Bach's visits to Berlin in 1741 or 1747, though its commission and delivery could have been mediated by C. P. E. Bach at any time after 1738.[163]

Eppstein and Marshall crossed swords again over the dubious C major flute Sonata (BWV 1033). The source is in the hand of the young Emanuel Bach, but attributed "di Joh. Seb. Bach." Eppstein (1972) doubted Sebastian's authorship and few would disagree.[164] Marshall (1979), in an attempt to make sense of the source attribution, proposed an original unaccompanied flute sonata (on the lines of BWV 1013), to which Emanuel was asked to provide a bass as an exercise, something that was evidently common in Sebastian's teaching of composition.[165] Eppstein (1981) with good reason doubted the flute part to be by Sebastian, showed the bass part to be essential to the composition, and thought it most unlikely that the Sonata was originally for flute.[166] More recently it has been thought that the piece is too weak even for Emanuel before 1735, so its origin is unclear.[167]

Of other dubious pieces, the violin Sonata in C minor (BWV 1024) was enthusiastically promoted as a work of Bach's by Rolf van Leyden (1955), but doubted by Alfred Dürr and Ulrich Siegele (1956); the D minor trio Sonata (BWV 1036) has long been known to be a work of C. P. E. Bach; and the C major trio Sonata (BWV 1037) was convincingly shown by Alfred Dürr (1953) to be a work of Johann Gottlieb Goldberg.[168]

Brandenburg Concertos BWV 1046–1051

The title "Brandenburg Concertos" goes back no further than Spitta. It derives from Bach's inaccurate "Marggraf de Brandenbourg" on the title-page of the dedication autograph score (1721), but there was in reality no such person. Christian Ludwig's title was Margrave of Schwedt.[169] It is nonetheless well to consider Bach's actual title for the collection: "Six Concerts Avec plusieurs Instruments." Bach used French as the language of the court, but even so the French "concert"

---

163 Dok. 3: 623 (Anhang I, 3); Marshall, *The Music of Johann Sebastian Bach*, 220–22.
164 Eppstein, "Über J. S. Bachs Flötensonaten," 12.
165 Marshall, *The Music of Johann Sebastian Bach*, 207.
166 Eppstein, "Zur Problematik," 78–83.
167 Leisinger and Wollny, "Altes Zeug," 196; KB VI/5: 15–21.
168 BWV 1024: Rolf van Leyden, "Die Violinsonate BWV 1024," BJ 42 (1955): 73–102; Alfred Dürr, review of Leyden's 1955 edition, Mf 9 (1956): 367–368; Ulrich Siegele, "Noch einmal: Die Violinsonate BWV 1024," BJ 43 (1956): 124–139. BWV 1036: Leisinger and Wollny, "Altes Zeug," 174–181; Christoph Wolff, "Carl Philipp Emanuel Bachs Trio in d-Moll (BWV 1036/Wq 145)," BJ 95 (2009): 177–190. KB VI/5: 89–93.
169 As distinct from the family name Brandenburg-Schwedt, see Rampe and Sackmann, *Bachs Orchestermusik*, 90–91.

Instrumental Chamber and Ensemble Music   345

had nothing of the formal connotations of the Italian "concerto," and meant simply a piece of chamber or ensemble music. Bearing this in mind might have saved some argumentation in the literature. Having said that, Bach's title is essentially a transliteration into French of titles such as the *6 Concerti a più istrumenti*, concertos of variable instrumentation by the cosmopolitan Munich capellmeister Evaristo Felice Dall'Abaco (Amsterdam, ca. 1719). As Michael Talbot (1999) has pointed out, Bach could have distributed his concertos in a set of twelve part-books as Dall'Abaco did.[170] Much attention has been given to purely Italian composers such as Albinoni and Vivaldi in an effort to define Bach's stylistic development. Important as these are, his place in the context of more cosmopolitan composers working in the German area is only now becoming clearer.[171]

As with most of the instrumental works, the main debate has been about style and chronology, the outlines of which have been discussed previously.[172] The most obvious cases for early origins are Concertos 1 and 5. The early version of No. 1 (BWV 1046a) survives in a copy dated 1760, which is no help in dating the piece. Attempts at dating have centered on the known availability of horns, at Weißenfels in conjunction with Cantata 208 either in 1716 or 1713 (or 1712), but there are known to have been horns at Weimar in 1715 and 1716, and at Cöthen, though after March 1721.[173] The connection with Cantata 208 has been doubted with good reason by Michael Marissen (1992) and Jean-Claude Zehnder (1997), and given that horns at that stage were also played by trumpeters, Bach could have had them available at any time.[174] With regard to the Fifth Concerto, Besseler (1955) and many others have found it the latest stylistically, but Pieter Dirksen (1992) found the notion of the concerto's modernity shattered by the earlier version (BWV 1050a), and developed an ingenious theory that it was composed for Bach's competition with Louis Marchand in Dresden in autumn 1717.[175] Dirksen's comments on the relation of this concerto to Vivaldi's violin concertos are penetrating, but the fact that both hand and paper of the autograph parts of BWV

---

170   Michael Talbot, "Purpose and Peculiarities of the Brandenburg Concertos," Martin Geck and Klaus Hofmann, eds., *Bach und die Stile. Bericht über das 2. Dortmunder Bach-Symposion 1998* (Dortmund: Klangfarben, 1999), 256.

171   There is much new work on Telemann and Johann Friedrich Fasch, and the inclusion of Albicastro (Johann Heinrich von Weißenburg) in Rampe's and Sackmann's (2000) survey of stylistic context is welcome.

172   Summaries of views are in Hans-Joachim Schulze, "Johann Sebastian Bachs Konzerte"; Malcolm Boyd, *Bach, The Brandenburg Concertos* (Cambridge: Cambridge University Press, 1993); Rampe and Sackmann, *Bachs Orchestermusik*.

173   Johannes Krey, "Zur Entstehungsgeschichte des ersten Brandenburgischen Konzerts," Eberhardt Klemm, ed., *Festschrift Heinrich Besseler zum sechzigsten Geburtstag* (Leipzig: Deutscher Verlag für Musik, 1961), 337–342; also Prinz, *Johann Sebastian Bachs Instrumentarium*, 121–122.

174   Michael Marissen, "On Linking Bach's F-Major Sinfonia and his Hunt Cantata," BACH 23/2 (1992): 31–46; Zehnder, "Zum späten Weimarer Stil," 100, 112.

175   Besseler, "Zur Chronologie," 126; Dirksen, "The Background to Bach's Fifth Brandenburg Concerto," 157–185.

346 *David Ledbetter*

1050a date from Cöthen does not support his theory.[176] There are two different harpsichords involved in the two versions, and it would make sense for the first to be the instrument brought to Carlsbad in 1718, and the second the Berlin instrument of 1719. In the absence of hard evidence, opinions fluctuate. In the Bach year 2000, Christoph Wolff thought there was no reason why most or all the Concertos could not have originated in Weimar, whereas Rampe and Sackmann moved back to a rather tight chronology in Cöthen, full circle from Besseler.[177]

The exceptionally connoisseurish nature of these Concertos needs always to be borne in mind. Not only does each Concerto have something exquisitely unusual about its instrumentation, but Bach also seems to have exerted himself to the fullest compositionally; whether specifically for the "gout fin et delicat" of the Margrave or for the other fine connoisseurs who employed him is immaterial. This in itself makes the set a cycle rather than just a collection of things Bach happened to have in stock. The first movements of the Second and Third Concertos are particularly finely wrought: as Jeanne Swack (1999) has observed, the first movement of the Second Concerto is such a subtle piece that Boyd (1993) and Dreyfus (1996) came to quite different conclusions about its use of the ritornello/episode pattern.[178] Some numerical things are obvious, such as the 3×3 of the Third Concerto (representing Apollo and the nine Muses according to some); less so the binary nature of the Second Concerto, based on the two voices of the trumpet ("heroic" and "musical" according to Altenburg), and the fact that the octaves of the harmonic series are multiples of 2 (1 2 4 8 16).[179] The structure of the movement is therefore binary, based on a division of the octave in 2, with 2 matching key schemes (F C d B♭ | c g a F). Klaus Hofmann (1997) developed a hypothesis that the Concerto was originally for the four soloists and continuo only.[180] This is possible, but not necessarily so and there is no hard evidence for it; similar hypotheses have been proposed for other Concertos, such as BWV 1043 and 1061.

Other Concertos BWV 1041–1045, 1052–1065

This group of works has the most complex source situation of all those surveyed in this section, with corresponding complexity of argumentation. Earliest sources for individual concertos fall in a range from around 1730 to 1760, yet many are arrangements, some of works plainly earlier than 1730. Versions of movements are dotted around Leipzig cantatas of the 1720s, and one (BWV 1057) is an

---

176 Alfred Dürr, "Zur Entstehungsgeschichte des 5. Brandenburgischen Konzerts," 63.
177 Wolff BLM, 169; Rampe and Sackmann, *Bachs Orchestermusik*, 88–102.
178 Jeanne Swack, "Modular Structure and the Recognition of Ritornello in Bach's Brandenburg Concertos," BP 4 (1999), 42. For a nuanced view of the Third Brandenburg Concerto, see Bettina Varwig, "One More Time: J. S. Bach and Seventeenth-Century Traditions of Rhetoric," ECM 5 (2008): 179–208.
179 Johann Ernst Altenburg, *Versuch einer Anleitung zur heroisch-musikalischen Trompeter- und Pauker-Kunst* (Halle: Hendel, 1795; facsimile, Amsterdam: Antiqua, 1966); Altenburg's father was a trumpeter at Weißenfels in Bach's day.
180 Klaus Hofmann, "Zur Fassungsgeschichte des zweiten Brandenburgischen Konzerts," Martin Geck and Werner Breig, eds., *Bachs Orchesterwerke*, 185–192.

Instrumental Chamber and Ensemble Music   347

arrangement of the Fourth Brandenburg Concerto (at latest 1721). Origins are therefore even hazier than for the chamber music, which at least has a substantial number of sources from the 1720s.

As for other works in this section, most discussion has centered on formal and stylistic analysis, combined with biographical study, with a view to establishing a chronology. With the greatly increased sophistication of source study following the establishment of the NBA in 1950, the foundation literature from the 1950s is by Besseler (1955) and Siegele (1957).[181] Besseler included a number of other works in his temporal grid for the Brandenburgs; Siegele, as for the duo Sonatas, set criteria for identifying arrangements in terms of instrumental ranges, melodic distortion and reorganization. Besseler's chronology was soon attacked, and over the next two decades there were hearty disagreements based on stylistic assessments. A flavor of the debate is conveyed by the discussion printed at the end of Schulze's 1981 article on concerto chronology.[182] This phase is well summed up by Werner Breig (1983), who offered a classic chronological outline as then understood: (1) twenty-two keyboard arrangements of concertos made at Weimar for Prince Johann Ernst; (2) still probably at Weimar, original concerto compositions, extended at Cöthen; (3) early Leipzig conversion of pre-Leipzig concerto movements into cantata movements; (4) 1729–ca. 1740, concertos for the Leipzig Collegium musicum.[183] Breig's contribution here was to point out that similar things do not necessarily belong together chronologically; there are many realities to be taken into account, such as commissions, stipulations of various sorts, new instruments and so on.

In 1985, a new chapter opened with Christoph Wolff's argument that most of the instrumental works surviving in Leipzig sources were in fact composed in Leipzig. Bach's involvement with the Collegium musicum may have begun before 1729, and the old compartmentalization of instrumental works at Cöthen/ sacred vocal music at Leipzig is untenable. Bach's activities were a varied continuum.[184] Wolff has continued to defend this view, in 1997 in answer to Martin Geck's defense of earlier datings (1994), and in 2008, commenting on Rampe and Sackmann (2000).[185] As far as Leipzig sources are concerned, vital information about performances at the Collegium musicum is given by Andreas Glöckner (1981), and for the dating of Bach's autographs of the 1730s and 1740s by Yoshitake Kobayashi (1988).[186] A snapshot of debates about the concertos in the

---

181   Besseler, "Zur Chronologie"; Siegele, "Kompositionsweise."

182   Schulze, "Johann Sebastian Bachs Konzerte."

183   Werner Breig, "Zur Chronologie von Johann Sebastian Bachs Konzertschaffen. Versuch eines neuen Zugangs," AfMw 40 (1983): 77–101.

184   Wolff, "Bach's Leipzig Chamber Music."

185   Christoph Wolff, "Die Orchesterwerke J. S. Bachs: Grundsätzliche Erwägungen zu Repertoire, Überlieferung und Chronologie," in Geck and Breig, eds., *Bachs Orchesterwerke*, 17–30; Christoph Wolff, "Sicilianos and Organ Recitals: Observations on J. S. Bach's Concertos," BP 7 (2008): 97–114; Geck, "Köthen oder Leipzig?"

186   Andreas Glöckner, "Neuerkenntnisse zu Johann Sebastian Bachs Aufführungskalender zwischen 1729 und 1735," BJ 67 (1981): 43–75; summarized in "Bachs Leipziger Collegium musicum und seine Vorgeschichte," Christoph Wolff, ed., *Die Welt der Bach Kantaten Band II*.

348   *David Ledbetter*

1990s is in the report of the first Dortmund Bach-Symposion (1996), and the entire literature up to the Bach year is expertly surveyed in detail by Rampe and Sackmann (2000).[187] Rampe and Sackmann drew together a vast amount of material, particularly with regard to Bach's context and possible influences in the Weimar and Cöthen periods, with a view to offering a new, more nuanced chronology based on all available factors (as Breig and others had pleaded for in the 1980s). This is distilled in a table of seventeen concertos, mostly dated to the year, ranging from 1712 to 1721.[188] The precision of this chronology, and the theory that Bach ceased writing concertos in 1721, have of course been strongly questioned, notably by Geck (2003) and Wolff (2008), but there is no denying the sheer amount of information and grist for argument that went into it.[189]

Of the three surviving original violin Concertos (BWV 1041, 1042, 1043) the A minor (BWV 1041) and the E major (BWV 1042) are a classic case of the problem with these works. The earliest source for the A minor is a set of parts of around 1730, which may or may not be close to its date of composition; for the E major it is a score and parts dated 1760, though it must have existed around 1738 when Bach arranged it for harpsichord as BWV 1054. Nonetheless, Wolff, in his argument for Leipzig origins (1985), found the A minor notably more advanced than the E major, the result of Bach's experience of writing cantata Sinfonias in the 1720s, therefore the later of the two.[190] Rampe and Sackmann (2000) agreed with the ordering, but for entirely different reasons, and put the E major in 1718 and the A minor in 1719/20.[191] They also proposed a trio-sonata "auf Concertenart" origin for the D minor double Concerto (BWV 1043), which they dated 1718/19 (the earliest source dates from 1730/31, entitled *"Concerto à 6"*); whereas Wolff (2008) found the trio-sonata concept unconvincing, and no pre-Leipzig examples of the long-breathed lyrical type of melody of the slow movement, a characteristic of Leipzig cantatas of 1724–1725.[192] Possible objections to all these arguments are obvious and have duly been made; the debate will continue. Geck's (1994) suggestion of a G minor origin for (BWV 1041), on account of a few corrections in the second violin part, has not found favor in view of the bariolage patterns and the fact that the harpsichord arrangement BWV 1058 was copied from an A minor original.[193]

The pastiche Concerto in A minor for flute, violin and harpsichord (BWV 1044) has aroused particularly conflicting opinions. The sources (scores of the first two movements copied by J. F. Agricola, and anonymous parts that belonged to

---

    Johann Sebastian Bachs weltliche Kantaten (Stuttgart: Metzler, 1997), 105–117; Kobayashi, *passim.*

187 Geck and Breig, eds., *Bachs Orchesterwerke*; Rampe and Sackmann, *Bachs Orchestermusik.*

188 Rampe and Sackmann, *Bachs Orchestermusik*, 241–243.

189 Martin Geck, review of Rampe and Sackmann, *Bachs Orchestermusik*, Mf 56 2003): 421–423; Wolff, "Sicilianos."

190 Wolff Essays, 234–237.

191 Rampe and Sackmann, *Bachs Orchestermusik*, 102–110.

192 Wolff, "Sicilianos," 106–107.

193 Geck, "Köthen oder Leipzig?" 19.

Instrumental Chamber and Ensemble Music 349

J. G. Müthel, both dating from around 1750) are little help in dating the Concerto, or in deciding who made the arrangement (both Agricola and Müthel have been credited, apart from Bach himself). The outer movements are based on the Prelude and Fugue in A minor for harpsichord (BWV 894, earliest source after 1714). Schulenberg (2006) has pointed to formal similarities between the Prelude and the first movement of the D minor harpsichord Concerto (BWV 1052), generally thought to have originated in a mid-Weimar violin concerto.[194] Eppstein (1971) proposed that the Prelude was itself an arrangement of a concerto movement, and Rampe and Sackmann (2000) discerned influence of Albinoni's Op.1 and Op.5 (1700, 1707).[195] The second movement is a version of the second movement of the D minor organ Sonata BWV 527. Eppstein thought both versions derived from a common trio-sonata movement on account of the simplification of line in the bass for the organ pedals. The most suggestive thing in this movement is the harpsichord's range (up to f'''), most unusual for Bach and implying a late origin. The rather wearisome moto perpetuo triplets of both Prelude and Fugue, together with the uninspired ripieno parts (lacking the galant touches in the ripieno of BWV 1064), raise the question of the purpose of the arrangement, if it was indeed made by Bach. Wollny (1997) proposed a brilliant showpiece for Bach's 1741 or 1747 visits to Berlin, extended by Wolff in the ensuing discussion to any of Bach's concert appearances in Dresden, Berlin, or Carlsbad.[196]

The harpsichord concertos BWV 1052–1059 have provided one of the richest sources of speculation and disagreement. They exist in autograph scores of ca. 1738, currently bound together (P 234).[197] Breig (1988) showed that BWV 1052–1057 are a set of six concertos, and suggested BWV 1058 as a preliminary stage between the very straightforward arrangement of BWV 1043 as BWV 1062 (autograph score 1736) and the much more sophisticated BWV 1052. BWV 1059 is a fragment of nine bars (related to Cantata 35/1).

Why did Bach compile a set of harpsichord concertos around 1738? The traditional answer was for the Leipzig Collegium musicum, but Bach gave up directing the Collegium between March 1737 and October 1739. In any case both Schulze and Wolff have questioned the traditional motivation for Leipzig instrumental music as the Collegium musicum, just as earlier works were invariably dated to Cöthen. Schulze (1988) suggested that Bach needed works for his appearances in Dresden, the most prestigious musical center in his environment, in this case for his visit in May 1738; Dadelsen (1988) suggested that they were for Bach family use, specifically Gottfried Heinrich Bach, described by C. P. E. Bach

---

194 David Schulenberg, *The Keyboard Music of J. S. Bach*, 2nd ed. (New York: Schirmer, 2006), 145–146, 464.

195 Hans Eppstein, 'Zur Vor- und Entstehungsgeschichte von J.S. Bachs Tripelkonzert a-Moll (BWV 1044)', *Jahrbuch des Staatlichen Instituts für Musikforschung, Preußischer Kulturbesitz*, 3 (1970): 34–44 (Berlin, 1971); Rampe and Sackmann, *Bachs Orchestermusik*, 148–150.

196 Peter Wollny, 'Überlegungen zum *Tripelkonzert* a-Moll BWV 1044', in Geck and Breig (eds), *Bachs Orchesterwerke*, 283–291.

197 *D-B* Mus.ms.Bach P 234.

350   David Ledbetter

as a "großes Genie" who unfortunately did not develop; Wolff (2000) thought the fact that copies were made by C. F. Penzel, one of Bach's last pupils, implies that Bach may have used his concertos as exercises.[198] This set seems to belong with other keyboard compendia Bach was putting together at this time such as the second *Well-tempered Clavier*, the third part of the *Clavier-Übung*, and the so-called Eighteen Chorales for organ.

Three of the Concertos are arrangements of the violin Concertos, as discussed previously. Others have movements in common with cantata Sinfonias of the 1720s, and it seems reasonable to assume that, just as Bach revived pre-Leipzig works such as Weimar cantatas and Brandenburg Concerto movements in these cantatas, so he revived things from a putative stock of pre-Leipzig concertos, otherwise now lost. Wolff (2008) questioned this orthodoxy, proposing that the D minor Concerto (BWV 1052) and the E major Concerto (BWV 1053) may have been written for Bach's recitals in Dresden in September 1724, where he is reported to have played "preludes and various concertos, with intervening soft instrumental music in all keys."[199] In other words they were for organ and strings, as in the cantata Sinfonias (BWV 146/1–2, 188/1, 169/1+5, 49/1). This would solve the problem of BWV 1052, hitherto reckoned an arrangement of an early violin concerto. Partly because the violin writing in various reconstructions was unlike Bach's violin writing generally, Siegele (1957) doubted it to be a work of Bach's but by an Italian-influenced contemporary, a shocking allegation about a work considered since the nineteenth century as an iconic Bach masterpiece.[200] Wolff's proposal neatly solved the problem by linking it to keyboard works that imitate violin idiom.[201] That notwithstanding, most still consider BWV 1052 as having originated as a mid-Weimar violin concerto.[202]

For the other concertos, numerous efforts have been made to reconstruct their supposed original versions. Wilfried Fischer, in NBA VII/7 (1970), attempted to establish objective criteria for divining original details, based on Siegele's (1957) criteria for arrangements and on Bach's own keyboard arrangements of known violin pieces.[203] The results are not ideal. BWV 1052R has not found much favor with violinists, and BWV 1055R is awkward for oboe d'amore (as discussed previously). The fragmentary BWV 1059 has inspired some ingenious argumentation. Siegele and Dürr saw the two Sinfonias of Cantata 35/1+5 as the outer

---

198 Schulze, "Johann Sebastian Bachs Konzerte," 12–13; Georg von Dadelsen, "Bemerkungen zu Bachs Cembalokonzerten," Winfried Hoffmann and Armin Schneiderheinze, eds., *Bericht über die Wissentschaftliche Konferenz zum V. Internationalen Bachfest der DDR in Verbindung mit dem 60. Bachfest der Neuen Bachgesellschaft, Leipzig, 25. bis 27. März 1985* (Leipzig: VEB Deutscher Verlag für Musik, 1988), 237–240; Wolff BLM, 250; Jane R. Stevens, *The Bach Family and the Keyboard Concerto: The Evolution of a Genre* (Warren: Harmonie Park, 2001).

199 Wolff, "Sicilianos," 107.

200 Siegele, *Kompositionsweise*, 101–115.

201 Wolff, "Sicilianos," 110.

202 For a summary of debates, see Dreyfus, *Bach and the Patterns of Invention*, 195–202.

203 KB VII/7 (1971): 12–34.

Instrumental Chamber and Ensemble Music   351

movements of a lost oboe concerto in D minor. Joshua Rifkin (1978) proposed the slow movement of the F minor concerto (BWV 1056, one of Bach's best-known movements) as the second movement of the putative original, transposed from A flat to F major.[204] Bruce Haynes (1992) thought the second movement of the D minor Concerto for three harpsichords (BWV 1063, in F major), omitting the first violin and the second and third harpsichords, would make an excellent slow movement to go with BWV 35/1+5 as a BWV 1059R.[205] In 1999 a new avenue was opened up by Steven Zohn and Ian Payne, who identified the second movement of BWV 1056 (also the Sinfonia of Cantata 156/1) as a reworking of a Telemann concerto movement (TWV51:G2/1).[206] This is just the sort of contextual work that can shed refreshing new light on old problems, and provide badly needed links between the untypical Bach and his contemporaries. One has to ask, though, how much standard treatments of standard materials (in this case the Romanesca bass with standard upper-part outlines) can really count as influence rather than parallel workings (as with the Andante of BWV 1034 discussed previously). More work needs to be done on improvisation gambits to assess this.

Of the remaining harpsichord Concertos, the putative original for violin and oboe of the two-harpsichord Concerto in C minor (BWV 1060) is unlikely to have been in D minor in view of oboe range and violin bariolage.[207] Both the two-harpsichord Concerto (BWV 1061) and the three-harpsichord Concerto (BWV 1064) in C major are thought to have originated without ripieno, BWV 1064 as a chamber concerto for three violins and continuo in D major, of which Breig (1983) considered the Third Brandenburg Concerto to be a "transcendental" reworking.[208] The D minor Concerto for three harpsichords is more of a problem. It is difficult to see what the original instruments may have been, and the Alla Siciliano second movement seems to date from considerably later than the outer ones.[209]

Overture-suites (Ouvertüren) BWV 1066–1069

The question of terminology for these pieces has been discussed under *Aspects of Performance* above. The origin of the type lies in suites of dances drawn from Lully's stage works in which, notionally at any rate, a five-part string band is

---

204 Joshua Rifkin, "Ein langsamer Konzertsatz Johann Sebastian Bachs," BJ 64 (1978): 140–147.

205 Haynes, "Johann Sebastian Bachs Oboenkonzerte," 40.

206 Steven Zohn and Ian Payne, "Bach, Telemann and the Process of Transformative Imitation in BWV 1056/2 (156/1)," JM 17 (1999): 546–584.

207 Haynes, "Johann Sebastian Bachs Oboenkonzerte," 39–40; Rampe and Sackmann, *Bachs Orchestermusik*, 162–163.

208 Karl Heller, "Zur Stellung des Concerto C-Dur für zwei Cembali BWV 1061 in Bachs Konzert-Oeuvre," Hoffmann and Schneiderheinze, eds., *Bericht über die Wissenschaftliche Konferenz... 1985*, 241–252; Rampe and Sackmann, *Bachs Orchestermusik*, 153–159, 202–203; Zehnder, "Zum späten Weimarer Stil," 91, 112; KB VII/6: 42–63; Breig, "Zur Chronologie," 83–95.

209 KB VII/6: 11–31; Rampe and Sackmann, *Bachs Orchestermusik*, 173, 205–207.

352   *David Ledbetter*

doubled by oboes, though exactly how they were performed depended on local availabilities. Many collections of these were published in Amsterdam around 1700, and a version for oboe band developed in the later seventeenth century. The German reception of the type between 1650 and 1706 has been thoroughly explored by Michael Robertson (2009).[210] The end of Robertson's survey neatly coincides with the beginning of the next wave of development, led by Telemann who, from his appointment as Capellmeister at Sorau (Upper Silesia) in 1705 and subsequently Eisenach (1708), produced large numbers of overture-suites (TWV55) featuring the newer fashionable dance types from Campra and other of Lully's French successors, with an admixture of Italian elements in a style so influential as to be known as "Telemannischer Geschmack." An equivalent survey to Robertson's of this stage, including works of Fux, J. F. Fasch, J. B. Bach, Zelenka, Telemann, Heinichen, Handel and others would be useful in pinpointing quite how untypical Bach is in his treatment of the genre.[211]

Typical of Bach is the separation of the string and oboe bands into independent concertante groups, as in the D major Overture-suite (BWV 1069) and to a certain extent in the C major (BWV 1066), as well as in the First Brandenburg Concerto and many cantatas from BWV 71 (1708) on. This may have something to do with the dating of BWV 1066 and 1069 in that they are in the earliest surviving sources (1724/1725), whereas the earliest sources for the D major (BWV 1068) and the B minor (BWV 1067) are 1730/31 and ca. 1738/39, respectively. The latter two come into a different category, related by Zohn (2007) to Scheibe's *Concertouverture* with a single solo instrument, flute in BWV 1067 and "Violino concertato" in BWV 1068, a type cultivated particularly in the 1720s and 1730s.[212]

Otherwise, theories of chronology have been as for Bach's other instrumental works that survive only in Leipzig sources. Besseler and Grüß (KB VII/1, 1967) slotted them into Besseler's pre-Leipzig grid. Besseler had a penchant for adducing four stylistic reasons to support any particular dating, on the principle that each extra reason added security to his hypothesis. In doing so he used some very shaky criteria. He related the fanfare figure in the strings in Gavotte II of BWV 1066 to a similar figure in Cantata 70a/1 (1716) and to the horns in BWV 1046a (which he dated 1716–1717); and BWV 1068 was dated ca. 1722 on account of two Airs in the French Suites for clavier BWV 813/4 and 815/5 in

---

210 Michael Robertson, *The Courtly Consort Suite in German-Speaking Europe, 1650–1706* (Farnham: Ashgate, 2009); Michael Robertson, "Internet Resources for Researching Seventeenth- and Eighteenth-Century German and Austrian Music," *Early Music Performer*, 20 (2007): 16–18.

211 In 1961 Martin Bernstein attributed BWV 1066 to J. F. Fasch on grounds that its quality was weak for Bach; Besseler and Grüß (KB VII/1: 6) rejected this on the basis of an examination of six of Fasch's 87 known overture-suites; see Blankenburg, ed., *Wege der Forschung Band CLXX*, 416–418; a good brief survey of the German background to Bach's Overture-suites is in Rampe and Sackmann, *Bachs Orchestermusik*, 250–256.

212 Zohn, "Bach and the *Concert en ouverture*"; Penzel's score and parts (after 1753) for BWV 1068 seem to represent an earlier version of the work, with Violin I as "Violino concertato" in the Overture and Air (KB VII/1: 11).

Instrumental Chamber and Ensemble Music   353

Anna Magdalena Bach's first *Clavier-Büchlein* (1722).[213] But a standard fanfare pattern can hardly be evidence of anything, and the Airs of the French Suites are allegro movements, quite unlike the Air of BWV 1068/2. Wolff (1985) preferred Leipzig origins, including (2008) linking the Air of BWV 1068/2 to the long, lyrical melody of BWV 1043/2 as typical of 1724–1725 cantatas.[214] Geck (1994) favored pre-Leipzig origins for all but BWV 1067, and Rampe and Sackmann (2000) for all four.[215]

As regards individual works, Besseler and Grüß (1967) posited an early version of BWV 1069 without trumpets and drums. These are almost certainly a later addition to BWV 1068 for a performance around 1730.[216] The suggestion that oboes were also a later addition to BWV 1068 (because they do not have an independent concertante role as in BWV 1066 and 1069) is less convincing, given that oboes *colla parte* with strings was a standard instrumentation of the time. Here again, the objections of Schulze and Wolff to the constant assignment of Leipzig instrumental works to the Collegium musicum are in order. Geck (1994) wondered how trumpets and drums would have fitted into a coffee-house.[217] The concerts operated outdoors in summer, but even so there were many occasions when they could have been used. In 1729 Bach had several contacts with the court at Weißenfels (where he held the title of Capellmeister) when festal music would have been in order, and name-days and birthdays of the Saxon ruling family were publicly celebrated in Leipzig with his music.

Most attention has focused on the B minor flute Suite (BWV 1067). This seemed to be the least problematical as regards origins (its galant style and flute solo accorded well with the ca. 1738/39 date of the earliest source), until Joshua Rifkin (1996) pointed to mistakes in the copyists' parts, implying that it had been transposed from A minor.[218] Bariolage patterns then suggested a violin origin, although Steven Zohn (2007) argued for a flute with C-foot.[219] The Suite duly appeared in a violin "reconstruction" by Werner Breig (2003).[220] Breig's decision to reduce the five-part B minor version to four parts, on the model of BWV 1068 without the trumpets, drums and oboes and with Penzel's Violino concertato,

---

213 KB VII/1: 13.

214 Wolff Essays, 229; "Sicilianos," 102.

215 Geck, "Köthen oder Leipzig?"; Rampe and Sackmann, *Bachs Orchestermusik*, 276.

216 KB VII/1: 15; see also Joshua Rifkin, "Benutzung – Entstehung – Überlieferung: Bemerkungen zur Ouvertüre BWV 1068," 169–176; Joshua Rifkin, "Klangpracht und Stilauffassung. Zu den Trompeten der Ouvertüre BWV 1069," Geck and Hofmann, eds., *Bach und die Stile*, 327–345.

217 Geck, "Leipzig oder Köthen?" 22.

218 Paper given at the 1. Dortmunder Bach-Symposion (1996), expanded and published in "The 'B-Minor Flute Suite' Deconstructed: New Light on Bach's Ouverture BWV 1067," BP 6 (2007): 1–98; see also Siegbert Rampe, *Das Bach-Handbuch* 5/1 (Laaber: Laaber, 2013), 22.

219 Zohn, "Bach and the *Concert en ouverture*," 140–147.

220 Werner Breig, *J. S. Bach. Overtüre (Suite) für Streicher und Basso continuo a-moll nach BWV 1067* (Wiesbaden: Breitkopf & Härtel, 2003).

354 *David Ledbetter*

was strongly criticized in a review by Tassilo Erhardt (2004).[221] Erhardt adduced an Overture-suite in G minor by Johann Bernhard Bach, with performance parts datable to 1730 and strong thematic similarities to BWV 1067, which is for solo violin and four-part strings so five parts in all.[222] Breig's reply to this, and an extended article in the *Bach-Jahrbuch* (2004), together with the articles of Rifkin and Zohn, provide a useful introduction to current debates concerning Bach's Overture-suites generally.[223]

Summary

It has not been possible in this brief survey to report each and every view of these works expressed in the very extensive literature. For further information about recent literature dealing with particular works, see the second volume of Richard Jones, *The Creative Development of Johann Sebastian Bach* (New York: Oxford University Press, 2013); and the two volumes of *Bachs Orchester und Kammermusik* edited by Rampe and Sackmann (2013) that updates their 2000 volume on the *Orchestermusik*.[224]

Directions for future research have been mentioned under the individual headings above. It will be seen that much of the literature since 1950 has been concerned with questions of chronology and this avenue is unlikely to yield much more of benefit until new concrete evidence emerges. There is a danger of circular argument (style – date – style), of hypothesis built on hypothesis, and theories tend to reflect the preconceptions of the writer. A sign of the progress of musicology has been the way in which Bach has come to be viewed in more recent decades as a more complex, flexible and in the end more interesting figure than before, and this is where the future lies. Given the quality of the works considered in this section, and the fact that they have in general received less attention than, say, the vocal and keyboard works, the scope is enormous.

The headings of performance, analysis, hermeneutics, and reception are all interrelated and shed light on each other. Performance can in itself be a form of research. Currently an important area is mixed styles and genres, the study of which is of vital importance for performers, but it is also vital for understanding Bach's expressive and structural intentions as a composer.[225] The treatment of individual dance genres in Bach's environment, and Bach's treatments in relation

---

221 Tassilo Erhardt, "Transposition Good – Excision Bad," *Early Music Review*, 97/2 (2004): 4–5.

222 See Glöckner, "Neuerkenntnisse," 48–49.

223 Werner Breig, "What is a Reconstruction?" *Early Music Review* 99/4 (2004): 6; Werner Breig, "Zur Vorgeschichte von Bachs Ouvertüre h-Moll BWV 1067," BJ 90 (2004): 41–63. For an assessment of the *Ouvertüre* in G minor BWV 1070 see, David Schulenberg, *The Music of Wilhelm Friedemann Bach* (Rochester: University of Rochester Press, 2010), 164–165.

224 *Das Bach-Handbuch Band 5/1–2*, ed. S. Rampe and D. Sackmann (Laaber: Laaber, 2013).

225 For a useful collection of quotations about mixed style from Bach's environment, see Hartmut Krones, "Johann Georg Pisendel und der 'vermischte Geschmack'," Ortrun Landmann and Hans-Günter Ottenberg, eds., *Johann Georg Pisendel – Studien zu Leben und Werk* (Hildesheim: Olms, 2010), 383–400.

Instrumental Chamber and Ensemble Music   355

to that, is important. Yet more so is the nature of dance elements in pieces that mix styles and genres, in order to get a firmer analytical grasp, but also how this may affect performance. Organology can always be refined, as in the current debate about the nature of the violoncello. How Bach builds his material on the nature of the instrument he is writing for, and his ingenuity in exploring possibilities, has hardly been discussed, even in the case of brass instruments whose limitations dictate particular types of material. The expressive nature of musical gesture, including the physical act of playing an instrument, is acquiring a large literature which so far has not considered these works to any extent, even though the unaccompanied solos provide an obvious focus.[226] Analysis of recorded performances by means of technologies such as the "sonic visualizer" will become more sophisticated. They are fruitful so long as the things being compared are comparable, and they require a solid grounding in style and genre, and in performance matters generally. Especially for the time before recorded performances, "instructive" and other editions with the editor's personal performance markings have recently proved a fruitful research terrain.[227] Archives of notable modern performers have become available digitally from the libraries that hold them, and are as yet underused.[228]

Analysis has gained greatly in subtlety and penetration, partly through work on composers in Bach's environment and partly through more far-reaching concepts explored by, for example, Laurence Dreyfus.[229] Common formal strategies are subservient to Bach's exceptionally searching treatment of his materials, and concepts for formal strategies have themselves been refined.[230] Many of the works considered in this chapter have yet to be examined in this light. The range of Bach's care in composition needs to be explored. This is obvious in the keyboard works, but in the instrumental ones one could plot a spectrum from, say, the Third Brandenburg Concerto as an example of a highly finished work, to BWV 1021 and related pieces, composed on a preexistent bass that is possibly not by Bach. Some guesses about chronology have been vitiated by not taking this variety into account. Similarly, an assessment of the works that have come

---

226 For an introduction, see *Music and Gesture*, ed. A. Gritten and E. King (Aldershot: Ashgate, 2006); also Elizabeth Le Guin, *Boccherini's Body: An Essay in Carnal Musicology* (Berkeley: University of California Press, 2006); for organ pedals, see David Yearsley, *Bach's Feet: the Organ Pedals in European Culture* (Cambridge: Cambridge University Press, 2012); for Bach and gesture on the bass viol, see Jonathan Gibson, "Hearing the Viola da Gamba in 'Komm, süsses Kreuz'," Claire Fontijn and Susan Parisi, eds., *Fiori Musicali: liber amicorum Alexander Silbiger* (Sterling Heights: Harmonie Park, 2010), 419–450.

227 See the website for the Collection of Historical Annotated String Editions (CHASE) http://chase.leeds.ac.uk/.

228 See for example Daniel Sarlo, "Investigating Performer Uniqueness: The Case of Jascha Heifetz," Ph.D diss. (Goldsmith's, University of London, 2011; available online).

229 For example, Gregory G. Butler, "J. S. Bach's Reception of Tomaso Albinoni's Mature Concertos," Melamed, ed., *Bach Studies 2*, 20–46; Dreyfus is cited under relevant headings previously.

230 For example Jean-Claude Zehnder, 'Ritornell – Ritornellform – Ritornellkonstruktion – Aphorismen zu einer adäquaten Beschreibung Bachscher Werke," BJ 98 (2012): 95–106.

356   David Ledbetter

in and out of the Bach canon over the years could be revealing; why were they accepted as Bach works, and why were they subsequently rejected?[231] A particularly fruitful recent development has been the growth of interest in traditions of improvisation, and how they may affect Bach's methods of composition. Features have sometimes been thought of as influences that are in fact simply parallel manifestations of a common tradition. Some work has been done on the vocal and keyboard works in this direction, but the instrumental works have not so far received much attention even though such an analytical commonplace as Wilhelm Fischer's *Vordersatz – Fortspinnung – Epilog* pattern (see Analytical Approaches) is in reality an improvisation formula going back at least to the time of Josquin.[232]

The history of analytical traditions as they relate to Bach's music is in itself a rich field. This overlaps with reception history, which is probably the area of research that is moving forward most significantly at the moment.[233] The study of late and peripheral sources of, for example, the violin Solos can be very revealing of opinions and performances.[234] Hearing and listening have been a growing topic in music of the Classical period, but have not so far dealt with Bach's instrumental works to any extent.[235] The use of Bach's music in films, etc., has also been a fruitful topic. The evolution of Bach scholarship itself provides rich materials for research, as do the writings of individual leading figures.

Cultural studies have developed greatly since the 1980s and there is a growing literature viewing Bach from perspectives outside the musicological "silo."[236] They are illuminating so long as they do not dispense with a sound technical

---

231 This is a suggestion of John Butt's in *Bach's Dialogue with Modernity*, 1.

232 It has ancient antecedents in Aristotle, Cicero and Quintilian. For improvisation patterns in Bach's cantatas, see Alexander A. Fisher, "Combinatorial Modeling in the Chorus Movement of Cantata 24, *Ein ungefärbt Gemüte*, Gregory G. Butler, George B. Stauffer, Mary Dalton Greer, eds., *About Bach* (Urbana: University of Illinois Press, 2008), 35–52; Giorgio Sanguinetti has pointed to keyboard works, *The Art of Partimento*, Epilogue; also David Ledbetter, "Fugal Improvisation in the Time of J. S. Bach and Handel," *The Organ Yearbook* (2013): 53–75; for the cello Suites, see John Lutterman, "'Cet art est la perfection du talent': Chordal Thoroughbass Realization and Improvised Solo Performance on the Viol and the Cello in the Eighteenth Century," Rudolf Rasch, ed., *Beyond Notes: Improvisation in Western Music of the Eighteenth and Nineteenth Centuries* (Turnhout: Brepols, 2011), 111–128.

233 See Michael Heinemann and Hans-Joachim Hinrichsen, eds., *Bach und die Nachwelt*, 4 vols. (Laaber: Laaber, 1997–2005).

234 See Chapter 3 above; also Tanja Kovačević and Yo Tomita, "Neue Quellen zu Johann Sebastian Bachs Violinsoli (BWV 1001–1006). Zur Rekonstruktion eines wichtigen Überlieferungszweigs," BJ 95 (2009): 49–74.

235 For a useful summary of nineteenth- and twentieth-century approaches, see Adolf Nowak, "Bachs Werke für Violine allein: Ihre Rezeption durch Aufführung, Theorie und Komposition," Hermann Danuser and Friedhelm Krummacher, eds., *Rezeptionsästhetik und Rezeptionsgeschichte in der Musikwissenschaft* (Laaber: Laaber, 1991), 223–237.

236 For a survey of recent trends, see the Introduction to *The Oxford Handbook of the New Cultural History of Music*, ed. J. F. Fulcher (New York: Oxford University Press, 2011); some examples of social and political concepts applied to the instrumental works are considered under Aspects of Performance and Analytical Approaches.

knowledge of music and are firmly based on historical evidence. John Butt has provided a notable recent example in relation to the Passions in *Bach's Dialogue with Modernity*. The variety of possible approaches is great, depending on the interests and outlook of the writer, and there is no reason why they should not be applied to untexted music if argued at the appropriate level. The aim should always be to illuminate these great works. In the end, as Hans-Georg Gadamer says: "Der Interpret, der seine Gründe beibrachte, verschwindet, und der Text spricht."[237]

---

237 Hans-Georg Gadamer, "Text und Interpretation," Jean Grondin, ed., *Gadamer Lesebuch* (Tübingen: Mohr Siebeck, 1997), 171.

14 Chorales[1]

Robin A. Leaver

The chorales of Bach appear to be well-known; after all they have been used for generations for the teaching of keyboard harmony and counterpoint. Yet for all their familiarity, their background, the contexts within which they originated, their transmission by Bach's sons and pupils, as well as other issues, there is more to be discovered. The primary thesis of this chapter is that our knowledge of Bach's understanding and use of chorales, texts as well as melodies, is fragmentary and incomplete, and that much research still needs to be done in order to enlarge the picture of Bach's knowledge of, involvement in, and use of the Lutheran chorale.

The corpus of Bach chorales may well have been more diverse than the Kirnberger-C. P. E. Bach edition published by Breitkopf between 1784 and 1787 might suggest. Twenty years earlier, in his new year catalog of 1764, Breitkopf offered two different manuscript collections of chorales harmonized by Bach:

> Bach, J. S. Capelmeisters und Musikdirectors in Leipzig, 150 Choräle, mit 4 Stimmen. *a* 6 thl.[150 Chorales in 4 parts] (p. 7)...[2]
>
> Bachs, J. S. Vollständiges Choralbuch mit Noten aufgesetzten General-basse an 240 in Leipzig gewöhnlichen Melodien. 10 thl. [Complete Choral Book with notes set with figured bass comprising 240 melodies in use in Leipzig] (p. 29).[3]

What seems to have gone generally unnoticed is that these two anthologies represent different types of chorale settings: the first was a collection of 150 vocal settings in four parts and the second an anthology of 240 keyboard settings in which the melodies were given with figured bass.[4] Spitta reported that both of

---

1 The chapter is a revision of the article "Suggestions for Future Research into Bach and the Chorale: Aspects of Repertoire, Pedagogy, Theory and Practice," BACH 42/1 (2011): 40–63.
2 Spitta 2: 596, note 23; Spitta ET 3: 115, note 170.
3 Spitta 2: 589, note 1; Spitta ET 3: 108, note 148.
4 Kirnberger's pupil and collaborator J. A. P. Schulz recognized two different approaches to the harmonization of chorale melodies among the pupils of Bach. On the one hand, there was the intensive harmonic explorations of the familiar melodies that formed the basis of learning how

Chorales 359

these manuscripts had been lost, though hints that the 150 four-part chorales may have had some relationship with Marpurg's manuscript of 100 chorales that formed the basis of Birnstiel's collection, published between 1765 and 1769, and ultimately led to the edition of Kirnberger and C. P. E. Bach.[5] The manuscript of 150 four-part chorales, which Spitta thought lost, has been identified as Ms. R.18 in the Musikbibliothek der Stadt Leipzig,[6] but the manuscript *Vollständiges Choralbuch* containing 240 melodies with figured bass has not been located.

Apart from the sixty-nine melodies with figured bass in the Schemelli Gesangbuch of 1736, and perhaps the no longer extant eighty-eight chorales in Bach's hand that were with C. P. E. Bach's copy of the Schemelli *Musikalisches Gesangbuch*,[7] the concentration has been almost entirely focused on vocal settings of chorales, epitomized in the Breitkopf edition of 1784–1787. But before the possibility of figured bass chorales by Bach can be addressed, it is necessary to review the further groundwork that needs to be done with regard to the background of Bach's knowledge and experience of the chorale.

The chapter is in three sections. The first deals with the need to establish the chorale repertory that Bach was first exposed to as a boy, that was later built upon when he was in Lüneburg, Arnstadt, Mühlhausen, and Weimar. The second section focuses on Bach's figured bass chorale accompaniments in Leipzig, especially those of the Schemelli *Gesangbuch*. The third section draws attention

---

to compose. On the other hand, there was the more simple approach necessary for supporting the singing of a congregation. Schulz wrote: "In arranging a simple chorale the greatest harmonists of the Bach school sought rather to display their erudition by multiplying unexpected and dissonant progressions—often rendering the melody quite unrecognizable—than to regard that simplicity, which is necessary to render the chorale intelligible to the common people." Johann Abraham Peter Schulz, *Gedanken über ein Einfluss der Musik auf die Bildung eines Volks, und über deren Einführung in den Schulen der Königlich Dänischen Staaten* (Copenhagen: Prost, 1790), 19; Spitta ET, 3: 129.

5 On the complexities of editions of Bach's four-part chorales, see Gerd Wachowski, "Die vierstimmigen Choräle Johann Sebastian Bachs. Untersuchungen zu den Druckausgaben von 1765 bis 1932 und zur Frage der Authentizität," BJ 69 (1983): 51–79.

6 See Friedrich Smend, "Zu den ältesten Sammlungen der vierstimmigen Choräle J. S. Bachs,"*Bach-Studien: Gesammelte Reden und Aufsätze*, ed., Christoph Wolff (Kassel: Bärenreiter, 1969), 237–269; originally appeared in BJ 52 (1966): 5–40. See also, Hans-Joachim Schulze, "'150 Stück von den Bachischen Erben': Zur Überlieferung der vierstimmigen Choräle Johann Sebastian Bachs," BJ 69 (1983): 81–100.

7 "Naumburgisches gesangbuch mit gedruckten und 88 vollstimmigen geschriebenen Chorälen," CPEB NV, 73; the term "vollstimmigen" implies four-part settings rather than melodies with figured bass. Because the Schemelli *Gesangbuch* was prepared for the Naumburg churches, the reference to "Naumburgisches gesangbuch" in C. P. E. Bach's *Nachlass* is usually taken as a reference to the Schemelli hymnal. But that is not the only identification that can be made. There was a specific *Naumburgisches Gesangbuch*, first published in 1712, with a new edition issued the year before the Schemelli *Gesangbuch*: *Neuvermehrtes und wohleingerichtetes Naumburgisches Gesangbuch* (Naumburg: Boßögel, 1735), preface dated 1 September. 1735. Therefore the reference in the 1790 *Nachlass* could mean that Bach in addition to his work on the Schemelli *Gesangbuch* he had produced eighty-eight settings in connection with an edition of the *Naumburgisches Gesangbuch*.

360   *Robin A. Leaver*

to recent research into chorale collections compiled by Bach's pupils that give multiple alternative basses and figures, and what light these settings might shed on Bach's pedagogy.

Bach's Earliest Chorale Repertory

Born in Eisenach, where his father, Ambrosius (1645–1695), was a leading court, town, and church musician, and his father's cousin, Johann Christoph (1642–1703), was the organist of the Georgenkirche in the town,[8] Johann Sebastian was introduced to the music of worship at a young age. When old enough, he attended the Latin school and sang in the church services. In both church and school, he would have sung from the *Neues vollständiges Eisenachisches Gesangbuch* published in 1673 by Johann Günther Rörer, court printer in the town:

> *Neues vollstandiges Eisenachisches Gesangbuch Worinnnen/ in ziemlich bequeemer und füglicher Ordnung/ vermittels fünffacher Abteilung/ so wol die alte/ als neue/ doch mehrenteils bekante Geistliche Kirchenlieder und Psalmen/ D. Martin Luthers/ und anderer Gottseeligen Männer befindlich. Mit besonderem Fleiß auserlesen und zusammen getragen: samt darzu gehörigen Registern. Unter Fürstl. Sächs. Absonderlichem gnädigsten Schutz und Befreyung. EISENACH/ Gedruckt von Johann Günther Rörern/ Fürstl. S. Buchdrucker daselbst. Im Jahr Chr. 1673.[9]*

The volume was embellished with twelve full-page engravings by Johann David Herlicius (ca. 1640–1693), the local artist who also painted the portrait of Bach's father, Ambrosius.[10]

   The hymnal contains a large repertory of hymns in Latin as well as German but contains no music. There has been a tendency to regard such word-only hymnals as of limited value with regard to revealing answers to musical questions. But in the same way that printed opera libretti can often supply valuable information with regard to what was included or excluded from particular performances of individual operas, so word-only hymnals can be researched to discover the repertory of chorale melodies required for their hymn texts. This is possible because it was customary in these word-only hymnals to include in the heading

---

8 See Martin Petzoldt, "Johann Sebastian Bach in theologischer Interaktion. Persönlichkeiten in seinem beruflichen Umfeld," *Über Leben, Kunst und Kunstwerke: Aspekte musikalischer Biographie: Johann Sebastian Bach im Zentrum.* [Festschrift für Hans-Joachim Schulze zum 65. Geburtstag], ed. Christoph Wolff (Leipzig: Evangelische Verlagsanstalt, 1999), 135.

9 See Conrad Freyse, "Sebastians Gesangbuch," BJ 45 (1958): 123–126; Conrad Freyse, "Johann Sebastian Bachs erstes Gesangbuch," *Jahrbuch für Liturgik und Hymnologie* 6 (1961): 138–142; Hans Dieter Ueltzen, "Johann Sebastian Bachs Kinder-Bilder-Gesangbuch," *Gottesdienst und Kirchenmusik* 5 (1986): 143–144.

10 See Conrad Freyse, "Das Portrait Ambrosius Bachs," BJ 46 (1959): 149–155, and Petzoldt, "Bach in theologischer Interaktion," 144–145.

Chorales 361

of a hymn a reference to the melody to which the text was to be sung. As with other processes of musicological research, it involves a boring, painstaking and detailed collection of data but when completed becomes a vital source of information. This is research that has yet to be undertaken, but when it is done it will provide the detailed repertory of the chorale melodies that the young Bach was exposed to during his earliest years. This basic core repertory will establish a valuable perspective to his later compositions that employ chorale melodies. For example, we will be able to know with reasonable certainty whether Bach knew a specific melody from his earliest years or whether he encountered it in later life. But the fruits of this research will also encourage further research with regard to the other hymnals that Bach encountered later, establishing chorale melody repertories in Lüneburg, Arnstadt, Mühlhausen, and Weimar, especially the Arnstadt Gesangbuch,[11] reissued when Bach was organist of the Neuekirche, and in Weimar when in the middle of his tenure at court a new hymnal was introduced, thus providing two Weimar hymnals that need to be researched for their specific chorale repertories. The same kind of research needs to be undertaken with regard to Leipzig and Dresden hymnals Bach must have known and used. Here the concern is with the *Eisenachisches Gesangbuch,* the earliest hymnal Bach encountered.

The ducal boundaries of Saxe-Eisenach, Saxe-Weimar and Saxe-Gotha were intertwined during the seventeenth century, a complex web that fluctuated with the actual or nonexistent heirs and successors of the various princes. But, however the boundaries were drawn, Gotha remained a cultural center for Thuringia, and Eisenach, while maintaining its distinctiveness, looked to Gotha for many things. The *Neues vollständiges Eisenachisches Gesangbuch* is a case in point, in that it was clearly linked to the educational and religious reforms of Andreas Reyher (1601–1673)[12] that were carried out on behalf of Ernst der Fromme (1601–1675), who became Duke of Saxe-Gotha in 1640.

Duke Ernst faced the task of rebuilding the physical and cultural life of his domain after the ravages of the Thirty Years' War. Reyher, the rector of the Gotha Gymnasium since 1639, influenced by the educational theories of Jan Comenius, worked closely with the general superintendent Salomon Glass (1593–1656) in the educational reforms that had a specific religious content. First came the visitation articles of 1641, which called for instruction in both "Choral und Figuralgesang." The following year, Reyher published his *Spezial- und Sonderbarer Bericht, Wie nechst Göttlicher verleyhung die Knaben und Mägdelein auff den Dorffschaften und in den Städten die unter dem untersten Hauffen der Schul-Jugend begriffene Kinder im Fürstenthumb Gotha kurtz- und nützkich unterrichtet werden können und sollen.* (Gotha: Peter Schmieder, 1642). [A special and particular report showing how, under the guidance of God, school-children,

---

11 Edited by one of the Arnstadt clergy, Johann Christoph Olearius, a pioneer Lutheran hymnologist; see Robin A. Leaver, "The Organist Encounters the Hymnologist: J. S. Bach and J. C. Olearius in Arnstadt," UB 7 (2012): 21–28.

12 Petzoldt, "Bach in theologischer Interaktion," 150–151.

362   *Robin A. Leaver*

the boys and girls of villages and towns, and children of the lower classes in this principality of Gotha, can and shall be efficiently and effectively instructed.] This curriculum included for the first time such practical and scientific disciplines as natural science, botany, geography, etc., but regular instruction in the theory and practice of singing was also strongly promoted. Having created the new curriculum, over the next few years Reyher worked on creating a collection of congregational and choral hymns and motets (Choral und Figuralmusik). This was published between the years 1646 and 1648 as:

> Cantionale Sacrum, Das ist/ Geistliche Lieder/ von Christlichen und Trostreichen Texten/ Mit 3. 4. 5. oder mehr Stimmen unterschiedlicher Autorum, Für die Fürstl. Land- und andere Schulen im Fürstenthum Gotha Auff gnädige Fürstl. Verordnung in dieses bequeme Format zusammen gebracht/ | Und gedruckt zu Gotha im Jahr 1646. Durch Johann Michael Schalln.[13] (Cantionale sacrum, that is, spiritual songs of Christian and comfort-rich texts, in 3, 4, 5, or more parts by various authors...)

The *Cantional* had three sections. These are described thus in the Vorrede:

> Erste in sich begreiffe die Fest-Lieder/ nach Ordnung der fürnembsten Feste durch das gantze Jahr... Der Anderer Theil hält in sich andere Christliche Kirchen- und Schul-Gesänge/ welche nach der Ordnung des Heilgen Catechißmi eingetheilet werden ... In den Dritten Theil werden solche Gesänge gesamblet/ welche man bey Christlichen Leichbestattungen füglichen gebrauchen kan/ und auch guten theils allbereit zu gebrauchen pfleget...[14] (First comprises the festival-songs according to the special feasts throughout the whole year... The second part contains other Christian songs for church and school arranged according to the structure of the holy catechism... In the third part are assembled such songs that may conveniently be used for Christian burials, and are appropriate for such use...)

The *Cantional* was intended primarily for use in the schools that would provide the choirs for the worship of the churches to which the schools were attached. Thus the first section provided music for the Sundays, feasts and fasts of the church year that was required, though not exclusively, for the morning Hauptgottesdienst. The second section, based on the structure of the catechism, provided settings of Kirchenlieder that would often be sung at Vespers, the worship

---

13 See Walter Blankenburg, "Das Gothaer Cantionale Sacrum," *Jahrbuch für Liturgik und Hymnologie* 15 (1970): 145–153; see also Zahn 6: 165–166 (No. 540). The title pages of two further sections indicate that this first edition was printed by Johann Michael Schall but were published by Andreas Reyher: "Typis Reyherianis." The *Cantional* was reissued by Schall in 1651–1657.

14 *Cantionale Sacrum [I.], Das ist/ Geistliche Lieder/ von Christlichen und Trostreichen Texten/ Mit 3. 4. 5. oder mehr Stimmen unterschiedlicher Autorum .... Und zum andernmal gedruckt* (Gotha: Schall, 1651), sig. Aiij^r-Aiv^r.

context for the preaching and teaching of the catechism. The third section of funeral music was particularly important because of the long-standing tradition of the school choirs singing in funeral procession from house to church, and from church to cemetery, as well as in the funeral services, part of the "Kurrenden" tradition. The settings found in all three sections of the *Cantional* were also regularly sung at various points each school day, as directed in the Gotha curriculum.

When the structure of the 1673 *Eisenachisches Gesangbuch* is compared with that of the Gotha *Cantional*, it becomes clear that the former is closely based on the latter. Although the *Eisenachisches Gesangbuch* has five sections compared with the three sections of the Gotha *Cantional*, a closer inspection reveals that much of the material found in sections three and four of the *Eisenachisches Gesangbuch* has been rearranged largely from the second section of the Gotha *Cantional*. The additional matter found in the *Eisenachisches Gesangbuch* is generally the inclusion of more congregational chorales; otherwise, the content of both is very similar.

In common with elsewhere in Thuringia, as well as in other areas in Germany, Eisenach closely followed the educational reforms of Reyher in its schools, not only in following the basic curriculum, but also in modeling its *Gesangbuch* on the Gotha *Cantional*, the cantional that had been created in direct response to the educational reforms that Reyher had introduced. The principal difference between the two anthologies is that although the Gotha *Cantional* includes music, the *Eisenachisches Gesangbuch* does not, though it does include references to the melodies to which the texts are to be sung. The question is: What musical source (or sources) did the Eisenach Cantor, Andreas Christian Dedekind (1658–1706),[15] use with the *Eisenachisches Gesangbuch* in the Latin school that the young Sebastian Bach attended? Given the similarity of content, Latin as well as German, between the Gotha and Eisenach anthologies of Kirchenlieder and other liturgical texts and melodies,[16] the Gotha *Cantional* must have been the primary musical source for both the Latin school and the Georgenkirche in Eisenach during Bach's early school years. The Gotha *Cantional* therefore assumes a particular importance with regard to Bach's earliest experience of Lutheran chorales.

On the one hand, the Gotha *Cantional* provides the form of each melody that Bach first experienced. Therefore there is here a significant research project—comparing the forms of the chorale melodies that Bach employed in his compositions with those of the Gotha *Cantional* to see how far he retained those forms, and if he did differ from them, were the variants of his own making, or did he follow another hymnal? Alfred Dürr has recorded many of the variant forms of chorale melodies used by Bach but did not relate them to the forms found in the Gotha *Cantional*.[17] It is a complex issue but it would seem that there might be greater clarity if research was carried out *a priori* rather than *a posteriori*; that

---

15 Petzoldt, "Bach in theologischer Interaktion," 137.

16 See Blankenburg, "Das Gothaer Cantionae Sacrum," 152 (Tabelle A & B).

17 Alfred Dürr, "Melodienvarianten in Johann Sebastian Bachs Kirchenliedbearbeitung," *Das protestantische Kirchenlied im 16. Und 17. Jahrhundert: Text-, musik und theologiegeschichtliche*

364   *Robin A. Leaver*

is, starting not with the variants but beginning with the forms that Bach first encountered and then dealing with the variants.

On the other hand, the Gotha *Cantional* contains the vocal settings, the harmonic expositions, of these melodies that Bach apparently first encountered. They therefore establish the background to Bach's own chorale harmonizations. The corpus of chorale settings found in the Gotha *Cantional* was not the product of one or two composers but rather a whole range of different composers. Of the 324 settings, 213 are in the homophonic "Cantional" style and forty-five are contrapuntal settings.[18] Many of the settings in the Gotha *Cantional* are by Thuringian composers:

> 56 items, previously unpublished, were the work of Bartholomäus Helder (ca. 1585–1635),[19] pastor of parishes near Gotha, hymn-text poet and composer;
> 34 settings were by Melchior Vulpius taken from his *KirchenGeseng und Geistliche Lieder... Mit vier/etliche mit fünff stimmen... contrapuncts weise also gesetzt...* (Erfurt: Birnstil, 1604);
> 15 settings were from Michael Altenburg, *Christlicher lieblicher und andechtiger newer Kirchen und Hauss Gesänge...*
> (Erfurt: Röhbock, 1620–1622).

From further afield:

> 30 settings came from Johann Hermann Schein, *Cantional, Oder Gesangbuch Augspurgischer Confession... Lieder und Psalmen... mit 4. 5. und 6. Stimmen* ([Leipzig]: Schein, 1627; 2nd ed, Leipzig: Schuster & Ritzsch, 1645);
> 30 came from Melchior Franck, *Psalmodia sacra, das ist: ... geistlichen Gesäng ... mit 4 u. 5 St. in contrapuncto simpliciter componiert...* (Nürnberg: Endter, 1631);
> 9 from Heinrich Schütz, *Psalmen Davids... durch D. Cornelium Beckern... Nach gemeiner Contrapuncts art in 4. Stimmen gestellet...*
> (Freiberg: Hoffman, 1628; 2nd ed., Güstrow: Jäger, 1640).

Taken together the settings of these composers amount to more than 50% of the total of 324 items.

The thirty settings from Johann Hermann Schein's *Cantional* raise an interesting question. It can be demonstrated that in one or two of his Leipzig cantatas for the concluding chorale Bach began with the four-part setting found in Vopelius's *Neu Leipziger Gesangbuch* (Leipzig, 1682), and then continued in his

---

Probleme, ed. Alfred Dürr and Walther Killy [Wolfenbütteler Forschungen 31] (Weisbaden: Harrassowitz, 1986), 149–163.

18   Blankenburg, "Das Gothaer Cantionae Sacrum," 152.

19   See Friedrich Wilhelm Bautz, ed., *Biographisch-bibliographisches Kirchenlexikon*, Bd 2 (Hamm: Bautz, 1990), col. 696.

own way. The tacit assumption is that he did so by opening up a copy of Vopelius, but since Vopelius took over many settings from Schein's *Cantional*, as did the Gotha *Cantional*, Bach may well have been relying on memory rather than directly consulting Vopelius.[20]

At a 2008 conference on Michael Praetorius, held at the Herzog August Bibliothek, Wolfenbüttel, I presented a paper that investigated the possible influence of the settings of Praetorius on the young Bach via the Gotha *Cantional*.[21] The initial discovery was that Praetorius is not represented with as many settings as one might have expected. There are just four named Praetorius items in the Gotha *Cantional*: three in the first section, one in the second, and none in the third.

The first is a setting of the German version of the liturgical Sanctus that first appeared, with this four-part setting, in Praetorius's *Musae Sioniae. Geistlicher deutscher in der Christlichen Kirchen ublicher Lieder und Psalmen mit II. III. IV. V. VI. VII. VIII. Stimmen, fünffter Theil* ([Wolfenbüttel: Fürstlicher Druckerei], 1607). It is the very first item in the Gotha *Cantional* in which the text is given under the bass part in the four-part open score. The text is also found in the *Eisenachisches Gesangbuch* but there is no reference to Praetorius. However, the heading is "Ein ander," a reference back to the previous item, "Preiß/ Lob und Herrlichkeit," which is headed "Ein ander Advents Lied vor der Predigt" (Another Advent hymn before the sermon). Therefore in the *Eisenachisches Gesangbuch* the single stanza is an alternative "Predigtlied" sung as part of the *Exordium* of sermons preached during Advent in any given year, and as such would have been sung many times during the four weeks of Advent. Those singing from the *Eisenachisches Gesangbuch* would not be aware of the Praetorius connection, but the schoolboys singing from the Gotha *Cantional* could not avoid the name at the top of the page.

The second Praetorius setting is found as the first item under the rubric "Auffs das Fest der Offenbahrung (Epiphanius]" in the Gotha *Cantional*: the German version of *Quem pastores*, "Den die Hirten Lobten sehre," which alternates with the German version of *Nunc angelorum*, "Heut sind die lieben Engelein." Both texts and settings are also taken from the fifth volume of Praetorius's *Musae Sioniae*. The two texts also appear in the *Eisenachisches Gesangbuch*, assigned to the same feast and headed: "*Nunc Angelorum gloria*, Verteutscht und verbeßert durch *Mich. Praet*."

---

20 Where Bach took over a setting without alteration, such as BWV 43/11, his source would clearly have been Vopelius; see Emil Platen, "Zur Echtheit einiger Choralsätze Johann Sebastian Bachs," BJ 61 (1975): 50–62; and Wolfgang Wiemer, "Ein Bach-Doppelfund: Verschollene Gerber-Abschrift (BWV 914 und 996) und unbekannte Choralsammlung Christian Friedrich Penzels," BJ 73 (1987): 29–73.

21 See Robin A Leaver, "Michael Praetorius, the Gotha Cantional, and Johann Sebastian Bach," *Michael Praetorius - Vermittler europäischer Musiktraditionen um 1600*, ed. Susanne Rode-Breymann and Arne Spohr [*Ligaturen: Musikwissenschaftliches Jahrbuch der Hochschule für Musik und Theater Hannover*, 5] (Hildesheim: Olms, 2011), 239–253.

366   *Robin A. Leaver*

The third named Praetorius setting in the Gotha *Cantional* is another four-part setting from the fifth volume of *Musae Sioniae*, the sixteenth-century Passion hymn *O Wir armen Sünder*. The text is also included in the *Eisenachisches Gesangbuch*, among "Fasten Lieder," except that it begins with the vocative "Ach" rather than "O," and there is no reference to Praetorius. Thus again the connection with Praetorius would presumably only have been known to those using the Gotha *Cantional* as the source of music for the *Eisenachisches Gesangbuch*.

The fourth named Praetorius setting in the Gotha *Cantional* is the four-part setting of the morning hymn *Ich danck dir schon durch deinen Sohn* that first appeared in a Leipzig Gesangbuch of 1586, but in the seventeenth century was thought to have been written by Michael Praetorius. The text and setting were taken from volume 8 of Praetorius, *Musae Sioniae. Deutscher geistlicher in Kirchen und Häusern gebreuchlicher Lieder und Psalmen ... mit 4. Stimmen, in contrapuncto simplici nota contra notam ... gesetzet* ([Wolfenbüttel: Fürstlicher Druckerei], 1610). In the *Eisenachisches Gesangbuch* it is included with other morning hymns but the Praetorius connection was hardly disguised in that his name appears in uppercase letters. The intention seems to have been to especially draw attention to Praetorius because elsewhere such names usually appear in lower case letters with only the initial letters capitalized.

Although only four settings are specifically identified in the Gotha *Cantional* as being by Praetorius, there were undoubtedly others. No less than fifty-two settings are labeled "Incèrti autoris" (uncertain composer). Further research may well discover that many of these anonymous settings were taken from Praetorius's *Musae Sioniae* because he incorporated the work of other composers unknown to him and identified them simply as "Incèrti." Similarly, Praetorius also included settings by other composers who are named, and therefore the editor of the Gotha *Cantional* most likely took them from the publications of Praetorius rather than from the sources in which they originally appeared. For example, settings by Joachim à Burck are found in *Musae Sioniae* volumes 6, 7 and 8, which are the most likely sources for Burck's twenty-four settings that are found in the Gotha *Cantional*; settings by Bartholomäus Gesius occur in *Musae Sioniae* volumes 5 and 8, which are the probable the sources for the nine Gesius settings in the Gotha *Cantional*. Thus here is another research project—discovering how many chorale settings by different composers in the Gotha *Cantional* can be traced to the earlier volumes edited by Praetorius. Such research is likely to confirm that Bach grew up knowing the principal vocal settings of the Lutheran cantional tradition, and that much of that was due to the work of Michael Praetorius.

Bach's Figured Bass Chorales in Leipzig.

From his earliest years, Bach was exposed to the many-faceted role of the organ in relation to the chorale within the Lutheran liturgy: in Eisenach, with his father's cousin, Johann Christoph Bach (1642–1703), organist of the Georgenkirche; in Ohrdruf, with his brother Johann Christoph (1671–1721), who had studied with Pachelbel; and in Lüneburg with Georg Böhm (1661–1733), organist of the

Chorales 367

Johanniskirche. He also encountered the chorale compositions of earlier members of the Bach family as well as other north German composers, and the young Bach took the opportunity to travel to hear such masters as Reincken in Hamburg and Buxtehude in Lübeck.

Bach, of course, was never professionally an organist after he left Weimar in 1717. Nevertheless he continued to play and compose for the organ, as well as act as organ consultant and recitalist, so much so that when he died in 1750 he was characterized in the first sentence of the heading of the obituary written by C. P. E. Bach and Johann Friedrich Agricola as "The world famous organist."[22] Much of this organ playing was improvised, which would have included organ accompaniments for congregational singing, which explains why there are so few examples of Bach's chorale settings, such as *Allein Gott in der Höh sei Ehr* (BWV 715), *Herr Jesu Christ dich zu uns wend* (BWV 726), and *In dulci jubilo* (BWV 729)—all three transmitted by Bach's pupils and were almost certainly written-out improvisations.[23] That such accompaniments would have been improvised appears confirmed by the advice Bach gave his pupils. In 1746 Johann Gotthilf Ziegler reported that

> As concerns the playing of chorales, I was instructed by my teacher, Capell-meister Bach, who is still living, not to play the hymns [*Lieder*] merely off-hand but according to the sense [*Affekt*] of the words.[24]

Since the *Affekt* of the words changed from stanza to stanza, and sometimes from line to line, implies that Bach's practice was to improvise his chorale accompaniments in close relation to the respective texts. In responding to questions about his father from Johann Nikolaus Forkel, C. P. E. Bach wrote the following in a letter, dated 13 January 1775:

> Since he [Bach senior] himself had composed the most instructive pieces for the clavier, he brought up his pupils on them. In composition he started his pupils right in with what was practical, and omitted all the *dry species* of counterpoint that are given in Fux and others. His pupils had to begin their studies by learning pure four-part thorough bass. From this he went to chorales; first he added the basses to them himself, and they had to invent the alto and tenor. Then he taught them to devise the basses themselves. He particularly insisted on the writing out of the thorough bass in parts... The realization of a thorough bass and the introduction to chorales are without doubt the best method of studying composition, as far as harmony is concerned.[25]

---

22 Dok 3: 80 (No. 666); NBR, 297 (No. 306); see also Dok 7: 93.
23 BWV 715 and BWV 726 in D-B Mus. ms. Bach P 804; BWV 729 in D-B Mus. ms. Bach P 1108 and D-B Mus. ms. Bach P 802.
24 Dok 3: 423 (No. 542); NBR 336 (No. 340).
25 Dok 3: 289 (No. 803); NBR 399 (No. 395).

368   *Robin A. Leaver*

The harmonic language that Bach expected in thorough bass realization was full and adventurous, as is reported by Johann Christian Kittel, reputed to have been his last pupil:

> One of his most capable pupils always had to accompany on the harpsichord [*Flugel*]. It will easily be guessed that no one dared to put forward a meager thorough-bass accompaniment. Nevertheless, one always had to be prepared to have Bach's hands and fingers intervene among the hands and fingers of the player and, without getting in the way of the latter, furnish the accompaniment with masses of harmonies that made an even greater impression than the unsuspected close proximity of the teacher.[26]

What is clear from these reminiscences is that even though Bach insisted on the writing out of these compositional exercises they were grounded in keyboard technique. The impression one has is that Bach had his pupils begin with realizing chorales at the keyboard, filling in the harmonies with the inner parts, and then progressing to composing more developed realizations in which all four parts had distinctive lines more akin to vocal rather than keyboard music. One of the persistent complaints about Bach's four-part chorales, as we know them, is that they are difficult to play on a keyboard; the parts do not fall naturally under the fingers. Significantly, most of the four-part chorales in the Kirnberger/C. P. E. Bach collection can be identified as originating in Bach's vocal works; only around eighty have no such connection and even they may have come from the 100 or so cantatas that have presumably not survived.[27]

There is therefore the suggested scenario that there were two strands of Bach chorales, the written-out chorales that originated in connection with his vocal works, which are preserved in the Kirnberger/C. P. E. Bach printed collection (together with several manuscript collections), and the improvised chorale accompaniments that by their very nature have not been preserved, except in very few examples.

However, that said, while it is impossible to recover such improvised keyboard chorale harmonizations, we can at least begin to come to terms with the likelihood that some may have been preserved, and there is the firmer possibility that we may be able to reconstruct a possible repertory of keyboard chorales that grew out of Bach's expertise in improvisation.

The Schemelli *Musicalisches Gesangbuch* was one of Breitkopf's earliest ventures into music publishing:

> *Musicalisches Gesang-Buch, Darinnen 954 geistreiche, sowohl alte als neue Lieder und Arien, mit wohlgesetzten Melodien, in Discant und Baß, befindlich sind; Vornemlich denen Evangelischen Gemeinen im Stifte Naumburg-Zeitz*

---

26 NBR 323 (No.317).
27 However, a few of the chorales in the Kirnberger/C. P. E. Bach collection are clearly keyboard rather than vocal settings; see Wolff Essays, 388–389.

gewidemt... herausgegeben von Georg Christian Schemelli, Schloß-Cantore daselbst... Leipzig 1736. Verlegts Bernhard Christoph Breitkopf, Buchdr. [Musical Hymn Book, wherein 954 spiritual songs and arias, old as well as new, with well-set melodies, in soprano and bass are to be found. Specially dedicated to the Evangelical [=Lutheran] congregations of the diocese of Naumburg Zeitz... edited by Georg Christian Schemelli, cantor at the castle [Schloß] in that place... Leipzig 1736. Published by Bernhard Christoph Breitkopf, Bookprinter.][28]

Bach was the music editor of the project as is made clear in the preface written by the Zeitz superintendent, Friedrich Schultze, dated 24 April 1736:

> The melodies to be found in this musical song book have been in part quite newly composed and in part improved in the thorough bass by the most noble Mr. Johann Sebastian Bach, Electoral Saxon Capellmeister and *Director Chori Musici* in Leipzig.[29]

Up until this time Bach had no personal need to create a corpus of chorale melodies with figured bass; for him accompanying chorales was an exercise in improvisation. But the commission to work on the Schemelli *Gesangbuch* gave him the opportunity of providing for the less gifted keyboard player good bass lines with appropriate figured harmonies for the chorale melodies. But the published volume contained only sixty-nine melodies, each with figured bass (BWV 439–507), although some of them were assigned to more than one text: thirteen were associated with two texts; six with three texts; two with four texts; and one, *Ermuntre dich, mein schwacher Geist* (BWV 454), was assigned to no less than nine different texts—making a total of 108 texts covered by the published melodies, that is, only a little more than 10 percent of the total of texts in the hymnal.

None of the published melodies is the older traditional chorale tunes, which goes against the statement on the title page that the hymnal contains old as well as new texts and tunes, suggesting that at a fairly late stage in the production of the hymnal, a decision was made to include only newer melodies. The sixty-nine melodies are representative of the more recent freer style of chorale tune, epitomized in Freylinghausen's *Geistreiches Gesangbuch* published in Halle in 1704 and 1714; indeed, some of the melodies for which Bach supplied figured basses first appeared in the Freylinghausen Pietist hymnal. They are by nature more "Arien" rather than "Lieder," the two terms that occur on the title page. This has led some to regard the Schemelli *Musicalisches Gesangbuch* as a Pietist collection and as evidence that Bach was moving away from the traditional chorale

---

28 NBR 170 (No.178).

29 George Christian Schemelli, *Musicalisches Gesangbuch* (Leipzig: Breitkopf, 1736; facsimile, Hildesheim: Olms, 1975), sig. **4ᵛ; NBR 170 (No.179).; see also Robin A. Leaver, "Bach's Choral-Buch? The Significance of a Manuscript in the Sibley Library," BP 10 (2016): 16–38.

370   *Robin A. Leaver*

in the 1730s.[30] But such a judgment does not take into account several factors. First, these newer tunes were intended to complement rather than replace the older chorale tunes, as is clear from the fact that the stanzas of *Kommt, seelen dieser Tag* (BWV 479) were intended to be sung in alternation with the stanzas of Luther's *Komm, Gott Schöpfer, heiliger Geist* (1524), and similarly, the stanzas of *Kommt wieder aus der finstern Gruft* (BWV 480) were to be sung in alternation with the stanzas of *Heut triumphiret Gottes Sohn* (1607).[31] Second, the melodies that were published were new and either could only be found in a few hymnals, or not at all. As the preface makes clear, the decision to restrict the number of tunes was an economic one. Each tune was separately engraved, a costly process, hence Breitkopf's determination to include only those tunes that could not easily be found elsewhere, if at all. It was a decision that was made after Bach had worked on the complete corpus of tunes for the hymnal; the familiar chorale melodies were to be omitted for economic reasons, but if there was sufficient demand and the first print run was exhausted, a second expanded edition including all the edited melodies could then be issued. This is spelled out at the end of Schultze's preface:

> One should not doubt that many more [melodies] would have made the book too expensive. While no extensive edition is made at this time, the hope is that the present example of this musical hymnal will soon be sold out. The publisher has around 200 melodies completely prepared and ready for engraving, so that no single hymn, that does not have a familiar melody, will be found without notes [in the new edition].[32]

Even though only a small proportion of Bach's edited melodies with figured bass were included, there is nevertheless evidence of his careful work with regard to the melodies that were omitted. In many instances, a capital letter occurs to the left of the hymn number. One does not have to proceed too far into the volume

---

30 See, for example, Alfred Dürr, "Bach's Chorale Cantatas," *Cantors at the Crossroads: Essays on Church Music in Honor of Walter E. Buszin*, ed. Johannes Riedel (St. Louis: Concordia, 1967), 119; see also the German version, "Gedanken zu Bachs Choralkantaten," *Johann Sebastian Bach*, ed. Walter Blankenburg (Darmstadt: Wissenschaftliche Buchgesellschaft, 1970), 517.

31 See Robin A. Leaver, "Congregational Hymn and Soloistic Aria in the Music of Johann Sebastian Bach,." *The Hymnology Annual: An International Forum on the Hymn and Worship*, 3 (1993): 109–119.

32 Schemelli, *Musicalisches Gesangbuch*, sig. **4[v]: "Man hätte deren noch mehrer beyfügen können, wenn man nicht bedencken müssen, daß hiedurch manchem das Buch zu theuer werden mögen. Indem man aber vor dießmal keine große Auflage gemachet, und daher zu hoffen ist, daß die vorhandenen Exemplaren dieses musicalischen Gesangbuches bald abgehen dörften; so ist der Verleger gesonnen, bey 200 Meldodien, die zum Stechen bereits fertig liegen, noch hinzu zu thun: Daß alsdenn kein einzig Lied in diesem Gesangbuche, wenn es nicht eine gantz bekannte Melodie hat, ohne Noten wird befindlich seyn."

Chorales 371

to realize that these indicate the preferred keys for the respective melodies.[33] Usually the same key is indicated when the tune is assigned to other texts, but some melodies are linked with different keys for different texts. For example, the melody *Ach Gott, wie manches Herzeleid* is to be in F at No. 155 and G at No. 772; *An Wasserflüssen Babylon* is assigned to the key of G for seven texts but at No. 587 it is to be in D; *Erschienen ist der herrliche Tag* is usually in D but at No. 9 it is indicated to be in G and at No. 353 it is in E. Here it seems likely that Bach was being guided by the meaning of the respective texts, assigning keys that reflected the nature of the substance of the hymn.

In any event, the *Gesangbuch* did not sell enough copies to warrant a new, expanded edition. Therefore Breitkopf, and presumably Bach himself, had manuscript copies of the omitted melodies with figured bass that, according to the preface of the Schemelli *Gesangbuch*, numbered "around 200."[34]

In order to discover the kind of repertory that these "lost" settings might have covered, I worked through the Schemelli *Gesangbuch*, carefully noting the tune assignments at the head of each hymn text. When no tune was assigned, it was taken to mean that the tune associated with the first line of the text was intended. The total number of tunes required to be able to sing all the texts included in the Schemelli *Gesangbuch* appears to be 302. Of that number, sixty-nine were published in 1736, which means that the "lost" manuscript of these additional tunes should number 233—very close to the "around 200" referred to in the preface to the hymnal, and even closer to Breitkopf's manuscript, advertised in the new year of 1764, of a "Complete Choral Book with notes set with figured bass comprising 240 melodies."

Thus with reasonable certainty the complete repertory of melodies that Bach edited for the Schemelli *Gesangbuch* can be compiled, even though the forms of these melodies, their basses, and how they were figured cannot be known, since Bach's manuscript collection of these melodies is no longer extant. But the later activities of some of his significant pupils may well shed some light on how Bach approached the realization of figured bass chorales.

---

33 See further, Robin A. Leaver, "Letter Codes Relating to Pitch and Key for Chorale Melodies and Bach's Contributions to the Schemelli Gesangbuch," BACH 45/1 (2014):15–33. On the need to establish correct keys for congregational singing, see Jacob Adlung, *Anleitung zu der musikalischen Gelahrtheit* (Erfurt: Jungnicol, 1758; facsimile, Kassel: Bärenreiter, 1953), 676–678 (§ 338); and Daniel Gottlob Türk, *Von der wichtigsten Pflichten eines Organisten: Ein Beytrag zur Verbesserung der musikalische Liturgie* (Halle: [Türk], 1787), 9–10; ET, *Daniel Gottlob Türk On the Role of the Organist in Worship* (1787), trans & ed. Margot Anne Greenlimb Woolard (Lanham: Scarecrow, 2000), 3–4.

34 See Markus Jenny, "Zweihundert verschollen Bach-Werke," *Mededelingen van het Insituut voor Liturgiewetenschap van de Rijksuniversiteit Gronigen* 18 (September, 1984): 20–29; see also Robin A. Leaver, "Bach, Hymns and Hymnbooks," *The Hymn: The Journal of the Hymn Society of America* 36/4 (October 1985): 7–13; see also the German version, "Bach, Kirchenlieder und Gesangbücher," *Theologische Bachforschung heute: Dokumentation und Bibliographie der Internationalen Arbeitsgemeinschaft für theologische Bachforschung 1976 –1996*, ed. Renate Steiger (Berlin: Galda + Wilch, 1998), 277–293.

372   *Robin A. Leaver*

Bach's Pupils and Pedagogy

Johann Christian Kittel (1732–1809) was reputedly Bach's last pupil (or at least, Bach's last surviving pupil), studying in Leipzig between 1748 and Bach's death in 1750. Forkel, in his list of Bach's celebrated former pupils, refers to him thus: "Organist in Erfurt. He is a very solid (though not very ready [obgleich nicht sehr fertiger]) organ player. As a composer, he has distinguished himself by several trios for the organ, which are so excellent that his master himself would not have been ashamed of them."[35] Kittel is noted for his important organ tutor *Der angehende praktische Organist* (The Prospective Practical Organist), published in Erfurt between 1801 and 1808, a work that covers all aspects of the organist's art but has a particular stress on preluding on and accompanying chorales.[36] Throughout he states that he is passing on what he himself had learned from his teacher Bach and gives many alternative examples of how to harmonize individual phrases of chorale melodies.

In 2007, a manuscript *Choralbuch* was offered for sale by a German antiquarian book dealer, described as "Uraltes Choralbuch von Johann Christ. Kittel, ca. 1780–1810." It contains 189 chorale melodies with figured basses and is now in the personal collection of Professor Yo Tomita of Queen's University, Belfast. The handwritten title reads: *Choralbuch von Johann Christ. Kittel, Organist an der PredigerKirche in Erfurt*. The title was inscribed by an early owner of the manuscript who added: *Poß: J. G. Anhalt*. Above it in another larger hand the name of a later owner appears: *Poß Ludwig Christian*. The melodies, basses and figures are in yet another hand, but not that of Kittel, and are presumably the work of one of Kittel's pupils.

While chorale collections by Kittel, both manuscript and in print, are known and recorded, the existence of this manuscript was totally unknown before this time. No reference to it is found in either Zahn's *Die Melodien der deutschen evangelischen Kirchenlieder*, or John Philip Anthony's 1978 Yale dissertation on Kittel's organ works.[37]

The antiquariat description of the manuscript dated it between 1780 and 1810, but it is possible to be more specific concerning the period not when the manuscript was copied but when the chorale basses and figures were created. Kittel's first appointment in Erfurt was in 1756 when he became the organist of the Barfüßerkirche, then six years later (1762) he became the organist of the Predigerkirche, a position he held until his death in 1809. There is another

---

35   NBR 458; Dok 7: 56.

36   Johann Christian Kittel, *Der angehende praktische Organist: oder, Anweisung zum zweckmässigen Gebrauch der Orgel bei Gottesverehrungen in Beispielen* (Erfurt: Beyer und Maring, 1801–1808; facsimile, Leipzig: VEB Deutscher Verlag für Musik, 1986). See Charles Stagmeier Brown, "The Art of Chorale-preluding and Chorale Accompaniment as Presented in Kittel's *Der angehende praktische Organist*" (DMA diss., University of Rochester, 1970).

37   John Philip Anthony, "The Organ Works of Johann Christian Kittel," PhD diss. (Yale University, 1978).

Chorales 373

Kittel manuscript *Choralbuch* that is in his own hand and dated 1790,[38] formerly owned by Carl Ferdinand Becker[39]—the editor of the first modern edition of the Schemelli chorales and Breitkopf's third edition of Bach's *371 vierstimmige Choralgesänge*, both published in 1832. A significant characteristic of this 1790 manuscript is that the chorale melodies are given in alphabetical order according to the first lines of the associated texts. This contrasts with the Tomita-Kittel manuscript that, like Bach's projected *Orgelbüchlein*, is structured the same way as a regular *Gesangbuch*, with the first primary section comprising chorales according to the order of the church year.

A hymnal was published in Erfurt in 1778: *Vollständiges Neu aufgelegtes und vermehrtes Evangelisches Gesang-Buch, darinnen 1031. geistreiche Alte und Neue Lieder und Psalmen wie solche sowol in denen Chur- und Fürstl. Sächsis. als auch in denen Thüringischen Landen und andern Orten*, and reprinted in 1785. The chorale settings in the Becker-Kittel 1790 manuscript have inscribed numbers that correspond to those in these Erfurt imprints. However, these Erfurt *Gesangbücher* were reprints of the Langensalza collection that was published in 1765 and again in 1772, and which in turn can be traced back to a series of hymnals issued in Sonderhausen from 1721:[40]

Vollständiges Neu aufgelegtes und vermehrtes Evangelisches Gesang-Buch, Darinnen 851. Geistreiche... Lieder (Sondershausen: Bock, [ca. 1735]).
Other imprints: Sonderhausen, 1736
                    Jena, 1750, 1770, 1775, 1780, 1782, 1789
                    Langensalza, 1750, 1772, 1784, 1788, 1790, 1791
                    Erfurt, 1751, 1778, 1780, 1785, 1795

It therefore seems likely that these Sonderhausen/Langensalza hymnals were in use in the Erfurt churches before the specific Erfurt editions were published from the late 1770s, and that the content of the Tomita-Kittel manuscript, with its 189 chorale settings in topical order, originated at a much earlier period than the Becker-Kittel 1790 comprehensive manuscript of 1049 chorales in alphabetical order. There is also an Erfurt manuscript chorale book, comprising 352 melodies, that must have been created by Kittel sometime around 1760, probably in

---

38 Musikbibliothek der Stadt Leipzig. Ms. II/1/4° 69.

39 Carl Ferdinand Becker, *Die Choralsammlungen der verschiedenen christlichen Kirchen* (Leipzig: Fleischer, 1845), 206: "107 Blätter. Enthält 375 Choräle mit bezifferten Bässen. Handschrift des Bearbeiters."

40 *Vollständiges Neu aufgelegtes und vermehrtes Evangelisches Gesang-Buch, darinnen 1031. geistreiche Alte und Neue Lieder und Psalmen* (Langensalza: [s.n.], 1765 and 1772; and Erfurt: Freytagen, 1778, and Erfurt: Müller, 1785); *Vollständiges Neu aufgelegtes und vermehrtes Evangelisches Gesang-Buch, Darinnen 734. Geistreiche Alte und Neue Lieder und Psalmen* (Sondershausen: Bock, [1721]). Information from the Mainz University database: http://www.blogs.uni-mainz.de/gesangbuchforschung/gesangbuchbibliographie/

374   *Robin A. Leaver*

connection with his move to the Predigerkirche in 1762.[41] Like later Kittel chorale books, these melodies with figured bass are arranged alphabetically, which seems to suggest that the content of the Tomita-Kittel manuscript dates from an earlier period, indeed, Susan McCormick has argued that it should be dated ca. 1750–1760, that is, the decade immediately following Kittel's studies with Bach in Leipzig.[42]

A very interesting feature of the Tomita-Kittel *Choralbuch* is that most of these melodies appear with multiple bass-lines, usually ranging from between four or five alternatives, and each different bass-line has its own set of figures. That in itself is not surprising because there are at least two other Kittel manuscripts that include mostly eight alternative basses and figures for each melody: one of twenty-five melodies (dated 1791) in Eastman's Sibley Library,[43] and another of twenty-four melodies (which are not always the same as those of the Sibley manuscript) in the Beinecke Rare Book and Manuscript Library, Yale University.[44] The Yale manuscript was owned by Kittel's pupil Johann Heinrich Christian Rinck (1770–1846) who edited it for Johann André, who in turn issued the settings in Offenbach as *24 Choräle, mit acht verschiedenen Bässen über eine Melodie*, published early in the nineteenth century.[45] Until the discovery of the Tomita-Kittel manuscript, it was generally thought that the alternative basses and figures were primarily compiled for pedagogical purposes, that Kittel created them as examples for his pupils. This was almost certainly the aim of André and Rink in their published edition of Kittel's twenty-four chorales with alternative basses. But the Tomita-Kittel manuscript provides a much more extensive corpus of alternative basses and harmonizations that, given the fact that it is structured according to the usual sequence found in hymnals, implies that they were also intended for practical use in accompanying congregational singing of chorales Sunday by Sunday—the alternative basses and figures supplying different harmonic expositions that could be matched to the meaning of different stanzas. This is also confirmed in the Beinecke Kittel manuscript of twenty-four melodies. The final cadence of the last alternative figured bass is given in a variant form for two of the chorales that have this attached note: "for the last verse"

---

41   Zahn 6: 546–547 (No. 44).

42   Susan Rebecca McCormick, "Johann Christian Kittel and the Long Overlooked Multiple Bass Chorale Tradition," PhD diss. (Queen's University Belfast, 2015), 299. Confirming evidence for the Tomita-Kittel manuscript predating Kittel's other chorale collections is to be found in the fact that the latter contain a number of melodies distinct to Erfurt, whereas the former includes melodies reflecting usage beyond the Erfurt churches; ibid., 297–298.

43   *25 Chorale, mit achterley General Baessen.* Eastmann Sibley Music Library, accession no.: 150596.

44   *24 Choräle* [mit verschiedenen Bässen]. Ms. Yale. LM 4745.

45   *24 Choräle mit acht verschiedenen Bässen über eine Melodie von | J. Ch. Kittel, letzten Schüler von Joh. Seb. Bach. 2897 Neue, auf das Sorgfaltigste von Wgd. Oppel durchgesehene Ausgabe. Pr. M.5,20. Eigenthum des Verlegers Offenbach a/M, bei Joh. André. Die erste Ausgabe dieser Choräle wurde con Ch. H. Rinck, Gr. Hess. Hof Organisten u. Cantor – einem Schuler Kittel's – zum Druck befördert.*

Chorales 375

("zum letzten Verse"). Thus while these alternative basses and figures had an obvious pedagogical use they also had a practical purpose as examples of how to harmonize chorale melodies for the accompaniment of different stanzas.

Until the Tomita-Kittel manuscript *Choralbuch* came to light, the phenomenon of multiple chorale basses was thought to have been relatively rare. But in a dissertation that began as a basic study of this new source, Susan McCormick has been able to locate approaching thirty sources (sixteen manuscripts and twelve prints) dating from between 1715 and 1860, and nine pedagogical or theoretical writings (mostly manuscripts) that promote alternative basses and harmonizations of chorale melodies.[46] As further research is undertaken, it is likely that more such sources will be located, especially manuscripts that are currently simply listed in catalogs and databases as "Choralbuch mit beziffertem Bass" but without reference to whether each melody has multiple basses and figures.

What is particularly significant from McCormick's research is that a good number of these identified sources of chorales with multiple basses originated either from Bach's pupils or from their pupils. One example is the manuscript *Choralbuch*, formerly owned by Carl Ferdinand Becker, now in the Musikbibliothek der Stadt Leipzig, with settings by Johann Philipp Kirnberger, who appears to have studied with Bach around 1739–1741. It is a manuscript very similar to the Tomita-Kittel *Choralbuch* in that each of its 245 melodies is supplied with up to ten different bass-lines, each with its own set of figures.[47] McCormick compared these Kirnberger multiple bass settings with an earlier manuscript of similar settings, now in Hamburg, and discovered that every bass of these multiple bass settings also occurs in the Kirnberger manuscript.[48] This discovery led to a reassessment of the origin of the earlier manuscript—which has been variously dated between the late seventeenth century and early eighteenth century—to suggest that it originated within the Bach circle in Leipzig in the second quarter of the eighteenth century, and that Kirnberger acquired it while studying with Bach, 1739–1741.[49]

That there appear to have been two of Bach's primary pupils who produced manuscripts of chorales with alternative basses and figures, as well as theoretical

---

46 McCormick, "Kittel and the Long Overlooked Multiple Bach Chorale Tradition," 41–184.

47 Musikbibliothek der Stadt Leipzig. Ms. III/6/82ª; Becker, *Die Choralsammlungen der verschiedenen christlichen Kirchen*, 206: "Dieses Choralbuch... dass einer jeder Melodie drei, vier, fünf bis zehn bezifferte Bässe untergelegt sind, soll von Ph. Kirnberger in Berlin ausgearbeitet sein." Similarly Kirnberger's treatise on composition, *Die Kunst des reinen Satzes in der Musik*, includes no less than 26 alternative basses and figures for the stollen of the chorale melody *Ach Gott und Herr, wie groß und schwer*, but these are composition exercises rather than models for accompanying congregational singing. Johann Philipp Kirnberger, *Die Kunst des reinen Satzes in der Musik: aus sicheren Grundsätzen hergeleitet und mit deutlichen Beyspielen* (Berlin and Königsberg: Decker & Hartung, 1776–1779; reprint, Hildesheim: Olms, 2010), 2: 22–29.

48 Staats- und Universitätsbibliothek Hamburg Carl von Ossietzky, shelfmark 2366; see McCormick, "Kittel and the Long Overlooked Multiple Bach Chorale Tradition," 197–206.

49 McCormick, "Kittel and the Long Overlooked Multiple Bach Chorale Tradition," 206–210.

376 *Robin A. Leaver*

works promoting the practice, may well be indicative of Bach's own pedagogy. Thus by researching these later examples of keyboard chorales, more light may be shed on Bach's own approaches to the pedagogy and practice of harmonizing chorales, especially in the last decade or so of his life. As reviewed earlier in this chapter, Bach's approach to the harmonization of chorale melodies began with keyboard studies, teaching his pupils by first giving them melodies with basses for which they would create the inner parts, and then when they were proficient, he required them to compose their own basses as well as the harmony. The Tomita-Kittel *Choralbuch*, and other Kittel manuscripts, together with the *Choralbuch* of Kirnberger, suggest that Bach was part of an established and continuing tradition of organ chorale harmonizations for congregational singing that runs in parallel with the more familiar four-part vocal chorales.

15 Counterpoint, Canons and the Late Works

Paul Walker

This chapter is a discussion of significant research into the complexity, logic and ingenuity of Bach's counterpoint published since around 1975.

Bach's Compositions of His Last Years

Christoph Wolff's 1968 dissertation was on Bach's relationship to the *stile antico*,[1] and in the years following he pursued systematic study of most of the major works from Bach's last decade, when the composer turned to older music and strict counterpoint for study, performance, and inspiration. In the article, "Toward a Definition of the Last Period of Bach's Work," first published in 1988, Wolff considered the validity of identifying a "late period" in Bach and concluded that the composer's success in "clearing his plate" of significant official duties in the late 1730s, due in part to a certain disenchantment with his superiors, provided him the opportunity to explore certain compositional projects purely of his own interest.[2] The controversy with Scheibe, begun in 1737 and credited by many scholars with inciting Bach to explore ever more conservative and esoteric compositional projects, is seen by Wolff as less important than has been assumed.

Already in the 1970s, study of the sources for the *Art of Fugue* had begun to cast doubt on that piece's proper place in the chronology of Bach's last compositions, as will be seen later, but in 1988 Yoshitake Kobayashi used a close analysis of paper types, handwriting identification, and some manuscripts with reliable dates, to offer a fresh and detailed chronology of Bach's last decade of composition.[3] Kobayashi was able to confirm suspicion that the *Art of Fugue* was indeed primarily composed early in the 1740s and that it was probably the concluding parts of the B-Minor Mass that represented Bach's last major compositional efforts.

---

1 Wolff St. ant.

2 Christoph Wolff, "Toward a Definition of the Last Period of Bach's Work," Wolff Essays, 359–367; originally published in German: "Bachs Spätwerk: Versuch einer Definition," *Johann Sebastian Bachs Spätwerk und dessen Umfeld: Prespektiven und Probleme. Bericht über das wissenschalftliche Sumposion anläßlich des 61. Bachfestes der Neuen Bachgesellschaft, Duisburg, 1986* (Tutzing: Schneider, 1985), 15–22.

3 Kobayashi, esp. 35–65.

378 *Paul Walker*

Although each of the three multimovement works of Bach's final years—the Goldberg Variations, the Musical Offering, and the Art of Fugue—has since 1975 generated a vast amount of scholarly writing, a few authors have chosen to write about all of Bach's last works in a single volume. These efforts include Kluge-Kahn (1985), with primary emphasis on theology as a mirror through which to see the entire corpus,[4] the dissertation by Kamatani (2004),[5] where the emphasis is on science, philosophy, Mizler's society, and the influence of Leibniz, and the more standard summary account offered by Sprondel (1999).[6]

A rare attempt to apply the more unusual kinds of methods and topics characteristic of New Musicology is David Yearsley's *Bach and the Meanings of Counterpoint* (2002),[7] a work focused specifically on Bach's last works. Yearsley's provocative chapters explore such diverse topics as Bach's final chorale prelude and its relationship to Lutheran ideas of dying, the role of canons in musicians' thinking of the time, and ways in which Bach's contemporaries understood and interpreted contrapuntal technique. It remains to be seen whether Yearsley's ideas will engender further work of this sort.

Music Theory and Compositional Process

One of the great ironies of Bach's compositional legacy is the contrast between its centrality for the study of tonal counterpoint today and the almost complete lack of anything from the composer's pen explaining how he thought about counterpoint or approached its challenges. The idea of the last decade of Bach's life as one of contrapuntal writing and study at the very highest, most rarified level is virtually universally accepted, and yet the circumstantial evidence that we are able to put together regarding Bach's attitude towards what one might expect to be the theoretical, even mathematical principles behind it, paints a contradictory picture. According to his son, Carl Philipp Emmanuel, Bach "did not... occupy himself with deep theoretical or speculative matters in music," nor was he a "lover of dry mathematical stuff,"[8] and yet he joined the learned musical society of his pupil Lorenz Christoph Mizler and was clearly proud to have his portrait painted while holding the canon that he wrote for his entrance into the society.

Thomas Christensen goes a long way towards clarifying the reasons behind these apparent contradictions in his cleverly titled article "Bach Among the Theorists" (2000).[9] Indeed, Christensen identifies the very lack of writings by the

---

4 Hertha Kluge-Kahn, *Johann Sebastian Bach: Die verschüsselten theologischen Aussagen in seinem Spätwerk* (Wolfenbüttel: Möseler, 1985).

5 Pamela M. Kamatani, "Science, Metaphysics, and the Late Works of J. S. Bach," Ph.D. diss. (University of California, Berkeley, 2004).

6 Friedrich Sprondel, "Die rätselhafte Spätwerk: Musikalisches Opfer; Kunst der Fuge; Canons," *Bach Handbuch*, ed. Konrad Küster (Bärenreiter: Kassel, 1999), 937–975.

7 David Yearsley, *Bach and the Meanings of Counterpoint* (Cambridge: Cambridge University Press, 2002).

8 NBR 398 (No. 395); Dok 3: 288 (No. 803).

9 Thomas Christensen, "Bach Among the Theorists," BP 3 (1998): 23–46.

Counterpoint, Canons and the Late Works   379

composer about his craft as the necessary blank slate upon which his later disciples and enthusiasts could then project their own explanations of what Bach must have been thinking. Christensen traces today's almost ubiquitous pedagogical use of Bach's four-part chorales to the writings of Bach's student Kirnberger and quarrels in Germany over the relative merits and meaning of the composer's contrapuntally conceived music vs. the harmonic basis lying at the heart of Jean Philippe Rameau's treatise of 1722. The article offers many important insights, not least of which is that much of the blame for Bach's misleading reputation as primarily an intellectual, mathematical composer can be placed at the door of some of his most ardent admirers in the half century following his death. Although Christensen's title is inspired by Jaroslav Pelikan's *Bach Among the Theologians*, he could also have chosen a take-off on the title of Theodor Adorno's much discussed article "Bach Defended Against his Devotees."[10]

In the years since Christensen's article, two extremely important finds have helped us to penetrate further than ever before into Bach's renewed engagement with sophisticated counterpoint during his last decade. Both sources comprise manuscript pages in Bach's hand filled with counterpoint exercises: one comprising two separate such sets of pages from the possessions of Peters Verlag and the other a manuscript fragment in the recently rediscovered collection of the Berlin Sing-Akademie. The focus of all of these manuscripts is on invertible counterpoint at the octave, tenth, and twelfth.

Writing about the two sources from Peters Verlag, Walter Werbeck (2003)[11] notes how Bach's explorations of invertible counterpoint move well beyond those of Christoph Bernhard and J. G. Walther before him in sophistication and complexity. Using Kobayashi's work on the progression of Bach's penmanship, Werbeck dates the two manuscripts to 1739–1742. He finds the shorter, simpler one almost certainly intended for teaching, but the second, longer manuscript, based in part on Calvisius's Latin translation of Zarlino and incorporating many canonic examples, Werbeck considers most likely to represent Bach's own study of contrapuntal possibilities in preparation for his last great learned works.

The manuscript in the Sing-Akademie collection is thoughtfully evaluated by Peter Wollny (2002).[12] Scholars' initial impressions of the source's relative unimportance changed once Wollny determined that the hands of both J. S. and W. F. Bach were present and that the sketches represented a kind of musical dialogue between father and son on possibilities in invertible counterpoint. Handwriting analysis and biographical details suggest a date of 1736–1738, and of special interest is the presence of examples in *stile antico* counterpoint and engagement with the pretonal modes of Renaissance music. As Wollny notes, the

---

10 Jaroslav Pelikan, *Bach Among the Theologians* (Philadelphia: Fortress, 1986); "Bach Defended from his Devotees," Theodor Adorno, *Prisms* (London: Spearman, 1967), 133–146; originally published in German in 1951.

11 Walter Werbeck, "Bach und der Kontrapunkt: Neue Manuskript-Funde," BJ 89 (2003): 67–95.

12 Peter Wollny, "Ein Quellenfund in Kiew: Unbekannte Kontrapunktstudien von Johann Sebastian und Wilhelm Friedemann Bach," LBB 5 (2002): 275–287.

380   *Paul Walker*

practical consequences of these studies can be seen in Bach's handling of modal chorale melodies in *Clavier-Übung III* and of Gregorian chant in the Credo of the *B-Minor Mass*. Wollny also sees in this manuscript the "clearly recognizable contours" of the *Art of Fugue*.

The two finds just discussed appear as part of the recently-published Supplement volume of the *Neue Bach Ausgabe* devoted to Bach's surviving sketches and theoretical writings, edited by Peter Wollny.[13] Based on his work as editor of that volume, Peter Wollny gave a preliminary description of Bach's compositional process as revealed in these sources, painting a picture of Bach's approach to composition that is both deceptively simple and astonishingly revealing.[14] Wollny takes the emphasis on invertible counterpoint revealed in the Peters Verlag and Sing-Akademie manuscripts and shows its central role for Bach's compositional strategy. As the author perceives it, Bach employed a two-stage process, neatly described by the rhetorical terms "invention" and "elaboration." The first involved the jotting down of the initial idea of the piece (e.g., an opening ritornello or the first contrapuntal entries), a process often accompanied by much tinkering. At the second stage of "elaboration," often undertaken long after the first, Bach attempted to extract all that he could from the "invention" that he had created, and for that purpose his most potent tool was invertible counterpoint, the focus of the recently discovered theoretical sketches. Wollny's article only scratches the surface of this exciting new insight into the composer's thought processes and working methods. Follow-up work would be most welcome.

Bach and Fugue

Fugue has been the ultimate goal of the study of counterpoint since before Johann Joseph Fux published his classic *Gradus ad Parnassum* in 1725. Paul Walker's *Theories of Fugue from the Age of Josquin to the Age of Bach* (2000)[15] traces the development of this pedagogical approach, which forms the backdrop for Bach's epoch-making essays in the genre. The book offers insights into what "fugue" meant to Bach's predecessors and contemporaries as well as the ways in which they described its proper handling. Another important contribution to the meaning of "fugue" is Dreyfus's essay "Matters of Kind" in his *Bach and the Patterns of Invention* (1996).[16] Dreyfus dismisses the unhelpful debate about whether fugue is a form or a technique and returns fugue to its original status as

---

13 NBA Supplement: *Beiträge zur Generalbaß- und Satzlehre, Kontrapunktstudien, Skizzen und Entwürfe* (2011).

14 Peter Wollny, "On Johann Sebastian Bach's Creative Process: Observations from His Drafts and Sketches," *The Century of Bach and Mozart: Perspectives on Historiography, Composition, Theory, and Performance*, eds., Sean Gallagher and Thomas Forrest Kelly (Cambridge: Harvard University Press, 2008), 217–238; see also Giorgio Sanguinetti, *The Art of Partimento: History, Theory, and Practice* (New York: Oxford University Press, 2012), 316–341.

15 Paul Walker, *Theories of Fugue from the Age of Josquin to the Age of Bach* (Rochester: University of Rochester Press, 2000).

16 Laurence Dreyfus, *Bach and the Patterns of Invention* (Cambridge: Harvard University Press, 1996), 135–168

Counterpoint, Canons and the Late Works 381

a genre, using an overview of early nineteenth-century writing to explain how the "fugue as form" idea arose at that time.

Johann Mattheson's *Der vollkommene Capellmeister* appeared in 1739, just as Bach was about to delve intensely into the abstract contrapuntal genres of fugue and canon that played such a central role in his final decade. Butler (1983)[17] finds much in Mattheson's text that shows parallels with Bach's late fugal work, especially part II of the *Well-Tempered Clavier* and the *Art of Fugue*, and he offers many musical examples in support of his arguments.

In 1980 one could still read (in the article on "Fugue" NG[1]) that "[i]n his vocal works Bach introduced an apparently new technique, the 'Permutationsfuge'..." Walker's article "Die Entstehung der Permutationsfuge" (1989)[18] overturns this misconception by exploring the technique's roots in the counterpoint studies pursued by Bernhard, Weckmann, Reinken, Buxtehude, and Theile in the 1660s and 1670s and pointing to examples of permutation fugue in these composers' works. The article argues that the theoretical writings of Johann Theile are the channel through which Bach most likely encountered the technique.

C. P. E. Bach described his father's pedagogical method of teaching of fugue as one arising out of the teaching of figured bass. William Renwick identified in Berlin Mus. ms. Bach P 296 a collection of "partimento fugues," that is, fugues represented on a single staff with continuo figures, that fit this description closely. His article (1999)[19] makes the case for these pieces as representative of Bach's method of teaching fugue, despite the lack of solid evidence linking them to the composer himself. (Renwick offers various candidates for possible authorship of the pieces.) In 2000, Renwick published a monograph treating the manuscript in greater detail and including editions of all of the fugues.[20] Sanguinetti (2010)[21] provides a study of partimento fugues in Italy, where the pedagogical approach appears to have originated.

Finally, Joseph Kerman (2005)[22] offers a series of music-critical essays on selected fugues of Bach, written in the tradition of Donald Francis Tovey. Included are fugues from the *Well-tempered Clavier*, the *Art of Fugue*, and Bach's organ repertory.

17　Gregory G. Butler, "*Der vollkommene Capellmeister* as a Stimulus to J. S. Bach's Late Fugal Writing" *New Mattheson Studies*, eds., George J. Buelow and Hans Joachim Marx (Cambridge: Cambridge University Press, 1983), 293–305.

18　Paul Walker, "Die Entstehung der Permutationsfuge," BJ 75 (1989): 21–42; trans. and expanded, "The Origin of the Permutation Fugue," *Studies in the History of Music 3: The Creative Process* (New York: Broude, 1992), pp. 51–91. An example of an earlier study is Carl Dahlhaus, "Zur Geschichte der Permutationsfuge," BJ 46 (1959): 95–110.

19　William Renwick, "'39. Praeludia et Fugen del Signor Johann Sebastian Bach?': The Langloz Manuscript, SBB Mus. Ms. Bach P 296," BP 4 (1999): 137–158.

20　William Renwick, *The Langloz Manuscript: Fugal Improvisation through Figured Bass* (Oxford: Oxford University Press, 2000).

21　Georgio Sanguinetti, "Partimento-fugue: the Neapolitan Angle," *Partimento and Continuo Playing in Theory and Practice*, ed. Dirk Moelants (Leuven: Leuven University Press, 2010), 71–111.

22　Joseph Kerman, *The Art of Fugue: Bach Fugues for Keyboard, 1715–1750* (Berkeley: University of California Press, 2005).

382   *Paul Walker*

Goldberg Variations

Since 1900, Bach's Clavierübung IV (though the words "Vierter Theil" do not appear on the title page), the Goldberg Variations, has been among his most admired keyboard works, perhaps most famously championed by Wanda Landowska (before World War II) and Glenn Gould (after). Because the piece was published during Bach's lifetime in a clean edition, scholars and performers presumed there to be little likelihood of problems with either its musical text or its dating. This sanguine picture began to change in 1975, when a copy of the original print surfaced (in a private collection) that turns out to have been Bach's own copy and that includes, in his hand, fourteen additional canons written on the first eight notes of the opening bass line. The manuscript was acquired in that year by the Bibliothèque nationale in Paris and assigned the number 17669, and in the following year Christoph Wolff published a report on these findings in JAMS under the title "The Handexemplar of the Goldberg Variations" (now included in *Bach: Essays*).[23] Wolff noted that Bach added a few handwritten details to his copy of the piece (including tempo indications, articulation marks, and ornaments) and corrected a few mistakes, but of much greater significance are the fourteen canons appended at the end (BWV 1087). Wolff further argued that the number of canons was deliberate and inspired by the numerical total arrived at by adding up the letters of Bach's last name according to a standard number alphabet (BACH = 2+1+3+8). Basic realization of the canons appeared to pose few problems.

At almost the same time, Werner Breig published an article (1975)[24] in which he took a closer look at various structural principles discernible in the work and offered the hypothesis that Bach may have originally planned for only twenty-four variations. Of his several arguments, perhaps the most persuasive is that such a plan would conclude the cycle of canons at the octave, certainly a more natural stopping point than the ninth. This plan would also put the canons at the fourth and fifth in the middle of the piece, and in general the symmetrical layout of the canons would be perfect. To test this hypothesis, for which he conceded that no concrete evidence exists, Breig considered questions of order in the variations of the *Canonic Variations on "Vom Himmel hoch"* and the *Musical Offering*. Given the two different orderings of the variations in the former and the uncertainties still surrounding the order of movements in the latter, Breig's hypothesis about Bach's original conception of the Goldberg Variations has necessarily remained speculative and somewhat controversial.

In a relatively lengthy monograph dedicated to the Goldberg Variations (1986), Rolf Dammann expressed considerable skepticism towards Breig's hypothesis.[25] As counterarguments Dammann pointed to the obvious symmetry of

---

23   Christoph Wolff, "Bach's Handexemplar of the Goldberg Variations," JAMS 29 (1976): 224–241; Wolff Essays, 162–177, German: "Bachs Handexemplar der Goldberg-Variationen: eine neue Quelle," *Bericht uber die Wissenschaftliche Konferenz zum III. Internationalen Bach-Fest der DDR, Leipzig 18./19. September 1975* (Leipzig: VEB Deutscher Verlag für Musik, 1977), 79–89.

24   Werner Breig, "Bachs Goldberg-Variationen als zyklisches Werk," AfMw 32 (1975): 243–265.

25   Rolf Dammann, *Johann Sebastian Bachs "Goldberg-Variationen"* (Mainz: Schott, 1986), 68–70.

Counterpoint, Canons and the Late Works 383

the print, especially the use of a French Overture to begin the work's second half, and the rather anticlimactic way that the calm, pastoral canon at the octave would have ended it. His book then proceeds as a thorough analysis, movement by movement, of the work in its final, published form.

A decade after Dammann, Vered Cohen offered support for Breig's hypothesis with an article in *Israel Studies in Musicology* (1996)[26] exploring in greater detail the interconnections exhibited in the first eight canons and the symmetrical layout that they create. Among his observations in support of Breig's hypothesis is the awkwardness engendered by Bach's inclusion of canons at both the second and the ninth (i.e., essentially the same interval) in the finished work.

Concrete information bearing on the question of origins has since been provided by Yo Tomita in two articles. In the first (1999),[27] Tomita reveals the existence of an earlier version of Variation V in a manuscript that also includes earlier versions of two preludes from WTC II. The author examines closely the differences between this manuscript version and Variation V in the publication before arguing convincingly for its status as an earlier version rather than a later simplification. Then, in something of a follow-up (2007),[28] Tomita notes the existence of a set of canons over a cantus firmus written by Jan Dismas Zelenka that incorporates precisely the intervals from unison to ninth (although notated by Zelenka in descending order). Seen together, these two articles offer hard evidence that could be seen to support Breig's idea: the existence of an earlier version of one variation reinforcing the possibility of an earlier conception of the whole cycle and Bach's possible knowledge of Zelenka's canonic cycle suggesting an impetus for expanding it. Tomita's own conclusions are cautious, and he encourages further research.

The Goldberg Variations have been particularly fertile ground for analysis based on numbers, including already in the 1970s Wolff's speculation about Bach's use of number alphabet in choosing to add precisely fourteen canons to his personal copy and Breig's subdivisions of the variations into ten groups of three (each group culminating in a canon), three groups of ten (i.e., grouped as variations 1, 4, 7, etc. 2, 5, 8, etc., and the canons), and two groups of fifteen (with a French Overture to signal the beginning of the second group). In a small monograph entitled *Vom Wirken der Zahl in J. S. Bachs Goldbergvariationen* (1985),[29] Bernhard Kistler-Liebendörfer focuses entirely on such uses of number in this piece. He explores at length all of the numbers elucidated by Wolff and Breig:

---

26 Vered Cohen, "Interrelationships Among the Canons of J. S. Bach's Goldberg Variations," *Israel Studies in Musicology* 6 (1996): 115–132.

27 Yo Tomita, "Bach and His Early Drafts: Some Observations on Little Known Early Versions of Well-Tempered Clavier II and the Goldberg Variations from the Manfred Gorke Collection," BACH 30/2 (1999): 49–72.

28 Yo Tomita, "Bach and Dresden: A New Hypothesis on the Origin of the Goldberg Variations (BWV 988)," *Music and Theology: Essays in Honor of Robin A. Leaver*, ed. Daniel Zager (Lanham: Scarecrow, 2007), 169–191.

29 Bernhard Kistler-Liebendörfer, *Vom Wirken der Zahl in J. S. Bachs Goldbergvariationen* (Frankfurt: Fischer, 1985).

384 *Paul Walker*

2, 3, 10, 14, and 15. The book includes information about the Hebrew number alphabet and ways in which the author feels Bach intentionally employed it. A more standard approach to analysis and the use of number, without the mysticism of numerology, appears in Kaußler and Kaußler (1985).[30]

Hertha Kluge-Kahn's study of Bach's late works (1985) takes as its thesis that the "purely instrumental late cycles contain content taken from the Bible and from Bach's deepest personal beliefs toward his God."[31] Thus, although her explication of the Goldberg Variations abounds in numbers of various kinds, she argues that Bach conceived the work as a whole by analogy to the structure and contents of Psalm 119, the longest Psalm in the Bible. Naturally the writings of theologians and religious mystics figure prominently alongside the numerology.

Going further into the question of number is Walter Schenkman's "Notes and Numbers in the *Goldberg* (2007).[32] Schenkman uses the standard number alphabet described previously to single out the numbers 14 (derived from B-A-C-H) and 41 (derived from J-S-B-A-C-H), then identifies instance after instance of fourteen- and forty-one-note melodies. Most of this has, in the end, little to do with the canons or Bach's counterpoint, however. Anyone interested in this subject should consult Ruth Tatlow's thorough overview (1991).[33]

Bach and Canon

Wolff's discovery of the fourteen puzzle canons appended to Bach's own copy of the Goldberg Variations has unleashed a frenzy of activity among scholars that belies both the relatively small number of notes that Bach put on paper and the apparent straightforwardness of their realization. The principal activity has been a search for further solutions not offered by Wolff in his edition for the NBA, and an amazing number of such solutions have been put forward. The list of scholars includes Gárdonyi (1986), Harrow (1990), Hartmann (1990), and Bietti and Bizzi (2008),[34] but by far the prize goes to Reinhard Böß, who has published (1996)[35]

---

30 Ingrid Kaußler and Helmut Kaußler. *Die Goldberg-Variationen von J. S. Bach* (Stuttgart: Freies Geistesleben, 1985).

31 Hertha Kluge-Kahn, *Johann Sebastian Bach. Die verschlüsselten theologischen Aussagen in seinem Spätwerk* (Wolfenbüttel: Möseler, 1985), 7.

32 Walter Schenkman, "Notes and Numbers in the Goldberg Variations," *Ad Parnassum: A Journal of Eighteenth- and Nineteenth-Century Instrumental Music*, 5/9 (2007): 41–70.

33 Ruth Tatlow, *Bach and the Riddle of the Number Alphabet* (Cambridge: Cambridge University Press, 1991); see also the more recent study, Ruth Tatlow, *Bach's Numbers: Compositional Proportion and Significance* (Cambridge: Cambridge University Press, 2016), esp. 190–203. See also Ulrich Siegele, *Johann Sebastian Bach komponiert Zeit: 1. Grundlegung und Goldberg-Variationen* (Hamburg: Tredition, 2014).

34 Zoltán Gárdonyi, "Zu einigen Kanons von J. S. Bach," *Studia musicologica Academiae Scientiarum Hungaricae* 28 (1986): 321–324; Peter Harrow, "New Solutions to Canon 10 of J. S. Bach's Fourteen Canons BWV 1087," *College Music Symposium* 30 (1990): 90–99: Günter Hartmann, "BWV 1087/10: 'Evolutiones' eines Bach-Kanons," *Musiktheorie* 5 (1990): 85–83; Giovanni Bietti and Giancarlo Bizzi, Etcetera: "L''arte del canone" – Uno studio sul pensiero canonico di J. S. Bach," *Nuova rivista musicale italiana* 42 (2008): 421–464.

35 Reinhard Böß, *Verschiedene Canones... (BWV 1087) von J. S. Bach* (Munich: Text und Kritik, 1996).

what he calls an "edition" of the fourteen canons that runs to 2149 [sic] measures and 134 pages. In a review (2001),[36] Werner Breig rejects the designation "edition" for such an effort, and the scholarly community has largely dismissed Böß's work as fanciful. One author, Crean (2009),[37] has found sufficient parallels between these canons and a treatise by Stölzel to suggest the latter as a possible inspiration for Bach's efforts.

One of the fourteen canons has long been known from the famous Haußmann portrait and thus carries its own BWV number 1076. Clement (2007) considers this canon in detail, discusses its relationship to Mizler's society and the Canonic Variations, and draws connections between it and Bach's theology.[38]

Melamed (1995)[39] explores the history of a thirty-six voice canon copied out by C. P. E. Bach and ties it convincingly to J. S. Bach's interest in abstract counterpoint and *stile antico* in his last years. The manuscript ascribes the canon to Thomas Selle, the mid-seventeenth-century Hamburg Cantor, but its real creator was the Roman composer Romano Micheli, and the piece appeared as the frontispiece of Athanasius Kircher's *Musurgia universalis* of 1650. Clearly Bach's interest in canon in his later years extended to works from the historical past as well as to his own explorations of the technique.

Musical Offering

The NBA edition of the Musical Offering, edited by Christoph Wolff, appeared in 1976. In the course of the volume's preparation, Wolff examined all of the surviving copies of the original print and produced three articles delving into three important aspects of the piece and its history. The first (1967)[40] addressed Bach's use of the word "ricercar" in this piece, a word that the composer otherwise is not known to have used. The second and most thorough (1971)[41] considered at length the piece's intended structure, with particular attention to clues provided by the various surviving exemplars. The third (1973)[42] looked more closely at the royal theme itself and its relationship to Frederick the Great, who is said to have created it, and Bach. Each of these three articles has since spawned considerable scholarly engagement and a wealth of speculation and interpretation.

---

36 Mf 54 (2001): 216–217.

37 Elise Crean, "G. H. Stölzel's Practischer Beweiss: A Hitherto Unconsidered Source for J. S. Bach's Fourteen Canons," BACH 40/2 (2009): 1–21.

38 Albert Clement, "Johann Sebastian Bach and the Praise of God: Some Thoughts on the Canon Triplex (BWV 1076)," Zager, ed., *Music and Theology*, 147–168. See also the earlier study, Friedrich Smend, *J. S. Bach bie seinem Namen gerufen* (Kassel: Bärenreiter, 1950).

39 Daniel R. Melamed, "A Thirty-six Voice Canon in the Hand of C. P. E. Bach," Daniel R. Melamed, ed., *Bach Studies 2* (Cambridge: Cambridge University Press, 1995), 107–118.

40 Christoph Wolff, "Der Terminus 'Ricercar' in Bachs Musikalischem Opfer," BJ 53 (1967): 70–81.

41 Christoph Wolff, "New Research on the Musical Offering," MQ 57 (1971): 71–77; Wolff Essays, 239–258.

42 Christoph Wolff, "Überlegungen zum 'Thema Regium'," BJ 59 (1973): 33–38. A combined ET of the 1967 and 1973 articles appeared as: "Apropos the Musical Offering: The Thema Regium and the Term Ricercar," Wolff Essays, 324–331.

386 *Paul Walker*

Wolff's first article noted that the easiest conceivable explanation for the use of "ricercar," namely that Bach at some point hit upon the idea of the well-known acrostic and decided to incorporate it, could not be the case, since the original sources show that the acrostic was something of a last-minute addition, after the word "ricercar" had already been chosen. Wolff then speculated that Bach had been inspired to choose the word by the two contrasting definitions of "ricercar," both found in Walther's *Musicalisches Lexikon*: its original use for free, improvisatory, preludial pieces, primarily for lute, in the early sixteenth century and its later, more common use to designate keyboard fugues of the strictest sort. Because the three-voice Ricercar was, according to all reports, the one that Bach improvised for the king, and because it features adventuresome and wide-ranging harmonic movement, Wolff associated it with the older definition. The six-voice Ricercar, composed after Bach's Berlin visit and notated in open score—the notation of choice for strict, fugal ricercars—Wolff associated with the second definition.

In 1979 Warren Kirkendale[43] took the "ricercar as prelude" argument one step further when he argued that the genre of ricercar had retained its preludial function throughout the Baroque era even as it came primarily to designate fugal pieces of the strictest sort without hint of improvisation. To do so he associated the ricercar with the exordium of classical rhetoric, and in an article published the following year, his wife Ursula took his conclusions as the jumping-off point for her own hypothesis that the entire Musical Offering had been conceived by Bach as the musical embodiment of a classical oration as outlined by the late-Classical author Quintilian.[44] Warren Kirkendale's conclusions were challenged by Paul Walker (1995),[45] who found almost no persuasive evidence associating the strict, imitative ricercar with preludial or exordial functions. Walker also speculated that Bach chose the word "ricercar" primarily for its reputation as the designation of choice for the strictest fugues, that is, as a way of emphasizing (for the king?) their special nature. Two years later (1997),[46] Kirkendale subsequently vigorously defended his original thesis.

Beyond the question of their genre designation, the two ricercars have not drawn the level of scholarly scrutiny that one might have imagined given their central importance for both the original meeting between Bach and the King

---

43 Warren Kirkendale, "Ciceronians versus Aristotelians on the Ricercar as Exordium, from Bembo to Bach," JAMS 32 (1979): 1–44.

44 Ursula Kirkendale, "The Source for Bach's Musical Offering: The *Institutio oratoria* of Quintilian," JAMS 33 (1980): 88–141; abridged German trans. (with some updating) as "Bach und Quintilian: Die *Institutio oratoria* als Modell des Musikalischen Opfers," *Quellen und Studien zur Musikgeschichte von der Antike bis in die Gegenwart* (Frankfurt: Lang, 1987), 1: 85–107.

45 Paul Walker, "Rhetoric, the Ricercar, and Bach's Musical Offering," Melamed, ed., *Bach Studies 2*, 175–191.

46 Warren Kirkendale, "On the Rhetorical Interpretation of the Ricercar and J. S. Bach's Musical Offering," *Studi musicali* 26 (1997): 331–376; also included in Kirkendale, *Music and Meaning: Studies in Music History and the Neighbouring Disciplines* (Florence: Olschki, 2007).

Counterpoint, Canons and the Late Works 387

and the resulting print. Ulrich Siegele (2001)[47] has offered a long and extremely thorough analysis of the Ricercar a 3, and an amateur scholar from Washington Grove, Maryland, named Humphrey Sassoon has argued in a very brief article (2003)[48] that Bach based the structure of the Ricercar a 6 on Handel's Fugue V from his *Six Fugues or Voluntarys* of 1735. Primarily, however, scholarly attention has focused on other aspects of the *Musical Offering*, especially (1) the question of Bach's original conception for the piece and its "meaning," (2) Frederick the Great's role in the royal theme and Bach's attitude towards the King and the entire project, and (3) the ten canons that Bach incorporated into various parts of the print.

The structure of the *Musical Offering* has been a topic of intense study and scholarly disagreement since Hans David published in 1945 a monograph[49] arguing that Philipp Spitta's conclusions regarding an "installment" publication history for the work could not be correct given the otherwise careful planning evident in Bach's other late works. David's hypothetical reconstruction of the original plan of movements relied primarily on a presumption of symmetry, with the trio sonatas in the middle flanked by the two ricercars with the ten canons interspersed. In the second of his seminal articles, based on his examination of the extant copies, Wolff took issue with David's conclusions. He demonstrated first that not a single copy survived complete, then drew conclusions concerning order that found something of a middle ground between Spitta and David. On the one hand, he concluded that the print was produced in three distinct fascicles in a particular order: the first with the Ricercar a 3 and a few canons, the second with the Trio Sonata and one canon, the third with the Ricercar a 6 and the remaining canons, a finding consistent with Spitta's installment theory. On the other hand, the order of the three fascicles largely matched David's symmetrical plan. Finally, however, Wolff concluded that "there is no hint whatsoever at any intended order for a complete cyclical performance."[50]

Ursula Kirkendale's 1980 article, mentioned previously, agreed with David's contention that Bach always had an overarching conception for his large-scale pieces, and it took serious issue with Wolff's conclusions. Her thesis, controversial from that day to this, was that the inspiration behind Bach's conception was the classical oration as described by Quintilian, and she drew analogies at the most detailed level between the various parts of an oration and the various movements or pieces of the *Musical Offering*. Only in 1991, on the occasion of the republication of his original article, did Wolff respond to her idea in the form

---

47 Ulrich Siegele, "Technik des Komponisten vor der Größe des Herrschers: Das dreistimmige Ricercar aus dem Musikalischen Opfer von J.S. Bach," *Musik als Klangrede: Festschrift zum 70. Geburtstag von Günter Fleischhauer* (Cologne: Böhlau, 2001), 156–193.

48 Humphrey F. Sassoon, "Royal Peculiar: J. S. Bach's Musical Offering and the Source of its Theme," MT 144 (Winter 2003): 38–39.

49 Hans T. David, *J. S. Bach's Musical Offering: History, Interpretation, and Analysis* (New York: Schirmer, 1945; reprint, New York: Dover, 1972).

50 Wolff Essays, 257.

388   *Paul Walker*

of a two-page rebuttal at the end of the article's footnotes.[51] In the meantime, and continuing on to the present day, other scholars have continued to offer their own theories on the overall conception and meaning of the work.

Two scholars, Siegbert Rampe (1993)[52] and Jacques Chailley (1985),[53] have expressed doubt about any sort of intended overall plan for the work at all. Chailley contrasted the circumstances within which the piece came into being, requiring a reactive approach from the composer, with those surrounding the Art of Fugue, for which Bach remained in control from inception to final form. Rampe found no fault with Wolff's conclusions and opined that Bach left the order of movements unspecified.

Subsequent to Wolff's 1971 article, an additional bit of hard evidence surfaced when Wolfgang Wiemer (1977)[54] demonstrated that not one but two Schübler brothers had worked on the engraving of the *Musical Offering*. In 1994 Michael Marissen[55] followed the implications of this information to argue for a different ordering of the whole that follows the original written announcement of the work's availability: first the two fugues, then the sonata, and finally the ten canons.

The most important work on this question since the appearance of Wolff's article has been done by Gregory Butler, who published his results in 2002.[56] Butler undertook a thorough reexamination of all of the original sources and their paper, and, as a result, argued that three, not two, of the Schübler brothers participated in the work's engraving. He also noted that one page of the Ricercar a 6 showed a significant number of corrections. From this information Butler theorizes that this troublesome page required reengraving in the course of the production process, and thus that Bach had no opportunity to correct it until later. In Butler's view, this delay made necessary the completion of the work in installments, as Spitta had originally speculated, and it also gave Bach time to expand his original, more modest conception of the collection—which Butler argues was simply the two ricercars with their appended canons—through the addition of the trio sonata with its canon and the larger group of canons that form a separate unit. These new findings make Wolff's wrapper theory untenable, and Butler provides further evidence that Bach apparently allowed buyers to purchase only the parts of the whole that they wanted. He therefore agrees with Marissen that the two

---

51 Wolff Essays, 421–423.

52 Siegbert Rampe, "Bach, Quantz und das 'Musicalische Opfer,'"*Concerto: Das Magazin für Alte Musik* 10/84 (1993): 15–23.

53 Jacques Chailley, "Peut-on restituer le plan de L'offrande musicale? *Education musical* 40/319 (1985): 45–48.

54 Wolfgang Wiemer, *Die wiederhergestellte Ordnung in Johann Sebastian Bachs Kunst der Fuge: Untersuchungen am Originaldruck* (Wiesbaden: Breitkopf & Haertel, 1977).

55 Michael Marissen, "More Source-Critical Research on Bach's Musical Offering," BACH 25/1 (1994): 11–27.

56 Gregory Butler, "The Galant Style in J. S. Bach's Musical Offering: Widening the Dimensions," BACH 33/ 1 (2002): 57–68.

Counterpoint, Canons and the Late Works 389

ricercars belong together and that Bach did not have a single, symmetrical plan in mind when he conceived the work.

The question of movement order for the purpose of a full performance served as motivation for two publications in the years leading up to the Bach year 1985. In conjunction with a performance mounted in Ansbach in 1979, Wolff advocated beginning with the two ricercars, followed by the ten canons, and concluding with the trio sonata for a satisfying finish. Bernhard Kistler-Liebendörfer's monograph (1985)[57] argued for segregating the two styles—strict/contrapuntal and galant—by grouping the two ricercars, along with their associated canons, together at the beginning, and concluding the performance with the trio sonata and the canon perpetuus.

Although a number of scholars reject not only Ursula Kirkendale's thesis but the very idea that any sort of extra-musical "programme" lay behind the Musical Offering, Michael Marissen (1995)[58] has found common cause with Kirkendale while proposing an entirely different programme based in theology. In Marissen's interpretation, since Frederick was presumed to be an enthusiast neither of fugue and the learned style nor of religion, Bach took the opportunity of this piece to "preach" to the King, through both the use of the title "ricercar," the strictest style of fugue, and the incorporation of many canons, which Bach often associated with the Law and the Ten Commandments. (Here he draws to some extent on work done by Eric Chafe.) In an article focused primarily on the Musical Offering's trio sonata, Mary Oleskiewicz (1999)[59] has taken issue with this interpretation, primarily because of J. J. Quantz's (Frederick's teacher's) considerable cultivation of music in learned style. She is skeptical of Frederick's supposed dislike of the style and feels that, far from preaching to the King, Bach almost certainly gave the King precisely what he wanted.

Questions surrounding the royal theme, the trio sonata, and Quantz lie at the heart of two contributions from the 1990s. Wolff had speculated, in the last of his three seminal articles, that the original form of the royal theme was likely simpler than Bach's final version, and had offered a hypothetical original version with a more straightforward second half. Both Rampe (1993) and Oleskiewicz (1999) have followed up this line of reasoning through their own investigations of Quantz's music and have found there a number of similar themes. Oleskiewicz's particularly thorough search leads her to conclude that, contrary to Wolff's and other scholars' skepticism about Frederick's ability to craft such a theme, Frederick had plenty of exposure to just this sort of chromatic melodic material and could easily have conceived such a sophisticated theme either by himself or in consultation with his teacher. Rampe's research focuses on a single Quantz

---

57 Berhard Kistler-Liebendörfer, *Quaerendo invenietis: Versuch über J.S. Bachs Musikalisches Opfer* (Frankfurt: Fischer, 1985).

58 Michael Marissen, "The Theological Character of J. S. Bach's Musical Offering," Melamed, ed., *Bach Studies 2*, 85–106.

59 Mary Oleskiewicz, "The Trio in Bach's Musical Offering: A Salute to Frederick's Tastes and Quantz's Flutes?" BP 4 (1999): 79–110.

390   *Paul Walker*

sonata discovered in the Dresden Library that shows not only a theme quite close to the royal theme but also another one very similar to the opening of Bach's sonata. From this Rampe draws the conclusion that the royal theme was taken directly from this sonata and that Bach knew the piece and modeled his own on it. Another hypothesis, perhaps inspired by Wolff's theory, appears in an article on Frederick the Great and music, whose author, Elmar Budde, argues that Frederick wrote only the first half of the theme and that Bach supplied the second half.[60]

The ten canons have also attracted their share of scholarly attention. Among the most interesting contributions is Gregory Butler's contention (2002) that some of the canons—among which he includes the Fuga canonica, the Canon perpetua, and the Canon 2 a 2 violini—belong not to the category of strict works along with the two ricercars but to the galant category together with the trio sonata. Easily the most controversial is again Reinhard Böß's two-volume "edition" (1991) of all ten canons in vastly expanded versions incorporating additional contrapuntal manipulations beyond those called for in Bach's original. Böß's work has been sharply criticized by Joachim Brügge (1994),[61] who finds that, although for the most part these solutions technically "work," they show little of Bach's usual handling of harmonic progression. Another controversial thesis is that of Thomas Op de Coul (2006),[62] who claims that the Canon 4 per augmentationem and contrario motu was meant to be played through twice so that the entire augmented voice would sound from beginning to end. Denis Collins has cast doubt on this thesis[63] by searching for precedents for such a handling of augmentation canon and finding only a few examples from Elizabethan England that Bach almost certainly did not know. The Canon 5 per tonos has also attracted attention in articles by Joachim Brügge (1992),[64] and Denis Collins and Andrew Schloss (2001),[65] both focused on the meaning and effect of this particular canon. Rounding out the list is Michael Kopfermann's detailed analysis (1981)[66] of the Canon 1 cancrizans

---

60 Elmar Budde, "Für Kenner und Liebhaber: Friedrich der Große und die Musik," *Neue Musik und Tradition: Festschrift Rudolf Stephan zum 65. Geburtstag* (Laaber: Laaber, 1990), 123–134.

61 Joachim Brügge, "Johann Sebastian Bach, Musikalisches Opfer (BWV 1079): Bemerkungen zum Canon a 2 per tonos," BJ 78 (1992): 91–100.

62 Thomas Op de Coul, "The Augmentation Canon in Bach's Musical Offering," BACH 37/1 (2006): 50–77.

63 Denis Collins, "From Bull to Bach: In Search of Precedents for the 'Complete' Version of the Canon by Augmentation and Contrary Motion in J. S. Bach's Musical Offering," BACH 38/2 (2007): 39–63.

64 Joachim Brügge, "Zum Problem der 'Mehrfachlösungen' in den Kanons des Musikalischen Opfers: Eine kritische Studie zu Reinhard Böss, Die Kunst des Rätselkanons im Musikalischen Opfer," *Neues musikwissenschaftliches Jahrbuch* 3 (1994):81–101.

65 Denis Collins and Andrew Schloss, "An Unusual Effect in the Canon per Tonos from J. S. Bach's Musical Offering," *Music Perception: an Interdisciplinary Journal* 19 (2001): 141–153.

66 Michael Kopfermann, "Über den Zählsinn. Analytische Erörterung zum Begriff der Architektonik der Form, am Beispiel des Krebskanons aus Johann Sebastian Bachs Musikalischem Opfer," *Musik-Konzepte* 17–18 (1981) [*Johann Sebastian Bach: Das spekulative Spätwerk*]: 20–82.

Counterpoint, Canons and the Late Works 391

and the most unusual Petri-Net graph of the Canon perpetuus offered by Degli Antoni and Haus (1985).[67]

Finally, the *Musical Offering* has figured prominently in two works of more popular writing: Douglas Hofstadter's *Gödel, Escher, Bach* (1979) and James Gaines's *Evening in the Palace of Reason* (2005).[68] Hofstadter engages especially with the Canon 5 per tonos; Gaines's entire book explores the occasion of Bach's meeting with the King.

Canonic Variations on Vom Himmel hoch

Like the *Art of Fugue*, Bach's *Canonic Variations on Vom Himmel hoch* exist in two versions, one printed, the other in manuscript, although in this case the manuscript postdates the print. The two versions differ sufficiently to warrant two catalog numbers (BWV 769 and 769a), and most speculation about the piece has focused on the question of which version represents Bach's final, most mature thinking. In his book *The Organ Music of J. S. Bach* (1980; 2nd ed. 2003),[69] Peter Williams offers several possible explanations for the differing versions, including that the print may be more "to the performer's [taste]," the manuscript more "to the composer's."[70] Zacher (1981)[71] characterizes the print as Bach's "official publication," the manuscript as his "last and clearest opinion (*Meinung*) about the piece." Clement (1989)[72] uses the phenomena of *Figurenlehre* and number symbolism to argue that the printed version represents Bach's true intentions for the piece. At the end of his detailed analysis of the piece and its sources, Butler (2000)[73] proposes that the whole idea of a "Fassung letzter Hand" for this piece, i.e., that one and only one of the two versions can represent Bach's ultimate intention, be abandoned as "counterproductive for understanding the piece." The result is two versions of equal validity, much like the two versions of the *Art of Fugue*.

---

67 Giovanni Degli and Goffredo Haus, "Netz-Repräsentation von Musikstücken," *Musikpsychologie: Ein Handbuch in Schlüsselbegriffen* (Munich: Urban und Schwarzenberg, 1985), 141–148.

68 Douglas Hofstadter, *Gödel, Escher, Bach: an Eternal Golden Braid* (New York: Basic, 1979); James R. Gaines, *Evening in the Palace of Reason: Bach Meets Frederick the Great in the Age of Enlightenment* (London: Fourth Estate, 2005).

69 Peter Williams, *The Organ Music of J. S. Bach*, 2nd ed. (Cambridge: Cambridge University Press, 2003), 512–524.

70 Williams, *The Organ Music of J. S. Bach*, 516.

71 Gerd Zacher, "Canonische Veränderungen, BWV 769 und 769a," *Johann Sebastian Bach: Das spekulative Spätwerk* [*Musik-Konzepte* 17/18] (Munich: Text und Kritik, 1981), 3–19.

72 Albert Clement, "O Jesu, du edle Gabe: Studien zum Verhältnis von Text und Musik in den Choralpartiten und den Kanonischen Veränderungen von Johann Sebastian Bach," Ph.D. diss. (University of Utrecht, 1989).

73 Gregory Butler, "J. S. Bachs Kanonische Veränderungen über Vom Himmel hoch (BWV 769): Ein Schlußstrich unter die Debatte um die Frage der 'Fassung letzter Hand,'" BJ 86 (2000): 9–34; see also Chapter 4 of the present volume.

392   *Paul Walker*

Aside from questions surrounding the existence of two versions, little about the *Canonic Variations* incites controversy. It is clear that Bach wrote it originally for Mizler's society, to which fact John Butt (1995)[74] adds speculation that the composer may have been influenced by some of the chorale preludes in J. G. Kauffmann's *Harmonische Seelenlust*. Detailed analyses are offered by Williams, Zacher (1981 with particular attention to the text of the chorale itself), Kluge-Kahn (1985, a number-based analysis), and chapter 3 of David Yearsley's *Bach and the Meanings of Counterpoint*.

Art of Fugue

The years 1975–1983 witnessed a fundamental transformation of our understanding of Bach's *Art of Fugue*. Before this time the scholarly community had taken for granted that it was the last piece that Bach composed and that he died before finishing it. Summing up this view was Hans Gunter Hoke, editor of a facsimile edition of both the autograph manuscript P 200 of the Berlin Library and the print, who wrote (1975)[75] that the piece was almost certainly conceived with Mizler's musical society in mind and thus after Bach's induction in 1747. In the same year as Hoke's article, however, a seminar class at Columbia University led by Christoph Wolff published a group report that cast doubt on several aspects of the received wisdom concerning the piece's dating.[76] Most surprising was the observation that the collection of primarily autograph manuscript materials, including Bach's fair copy of much of the piece plus three appendices with additional materials, showed enough variety in the composer's handwriting to suggest that the bulk of the work had been completed in the early part of the 1740s, when Bach's hand was still steady and firm.

The musicological world soon came to accept that *The Art of Fugue* was not Bach's last creation but rather the first in the composer's final decade of exploration into counterpoint at the highest and most sophisticated level, as Wolff summarized in his article of 1983.[77] And yet, when near the end of his life Bach decided to publish the piece, he incorporated certain substantial revisions, including several additional movements and some rewriting of existing ones. A portion of this work is evident in the three manuscript appendices, which are working copies rather than fair copies and show the unsteadiness of handwriting associated with Bach's final years. Bach's original version of the work is now

---

74   John Butt, "J. S. Bach and G. F. Kauffmann: Reflections on Bach's Later Style," Melamed, ed., *Bach Studies 2*, ed. 47–61.

75   Hans Gunter Hoke, "Neue Studien zur Kunst der Fuge, BWV 1080," *Beiträge zur Musikwissenschaft* 17/2–3 (1975): 95–115.

76   Stauffer, George, et al., "Seminar Report: Bach's Art of Fugue, an Examination of the Sources," *Current Musicology* 19 (1975): 47–77. The report also includes Wolff's article, "The Last Fugue: Unfinished?" ibid., 71–77, reprinted in Wolff Essays, 259–264.

77   Christoph Wolff, "Zur Chronologie und Kompositionsgeschichte von Bachs Kunst der Fuge," *Beiträge zur Musikwissenschaft* 25 (1983): 130–142; ET "The Compositional History of the Art of Fugue," Wolff Essays, 265–281.

Counterpoint, Canons and the Late Works　393

perceived to be of sufficient interest and quality to warrant its own edition, which Wolff provided in 1986[78] alongside an edition of the later print. Meanwhile, it remains clear that Bach indeed did not live to see the print through to publication. Already in 1977 Wolfgang Wiemer argued convincingly that most of the final print nonetheless reflected Bach's intentions for it,[79] and Wolff concurred in his 1983 article that fugues 1–13 were certainly in the order Bach had planned. The order and placement of the four canons and of the final, unfinished fugue, on the other hand, remain uncertain. Based on a close examination of the print, Gregory Butler argued in 1983[80] that Bach had intended for the fugue to be placed before the canons, an ordering that puts all fugues together ending with the unfinished, then all of the canons together ending with that in augmentation. Few scholars believe that the chorale added to the print "in compensation for the incompleteness of the final fugue," was actually intended to go with the rest.

Opinions about the proper understanding and purpose of the unfinished fugue, on the other hand, vary widely. Such widespread disagreement comes in part from the discrepancy between C. P. E. Bach's characterization of the final, unfinished fugue as a quadruple fugue on four subjects and the movement's ultimate title in the print ("Fugue with Three Subjects"), as well as from the principal theme's complete absence from the movement. In his contribution to the Seminar Report of 1975, Wolff nonetheless expressed confidence that this fugue was the one intended by Bach as the final quadruple fugue and that the final section was to have brought in the work's principal theme against the other three, a possibility that Wolff demonstrated with a musical example combining all four themes. Wolff went on to make the more controversial argument, based on evidence found in the manuscript, that Bach had almost certainly already worked out the fugue's completion on a separate sheet of paper, but that after his death those responsible for the work's publication remained unaware of this fragment and were thus unable to incorporate it.

Several alternative explanations have been put forward for the unfinished fugue. Writing a few years after Wolff, Ulrich Siegele (1988)[81] maintained that it was not intended as the final movement, but rather that Bach planned the *Art of Fugue* as a twenty-four movement work, capped not by one fugue with four themes but by four fugues with four themes each. In a series of articles that same year, the Belgian scholar Walter Corten offered the hypothesis, based largely on

---

78　Johann Sebstian Bach, *Die Kunst der Fuge, BWV 1080*, 2 vols. (I: earlier edition; II: later edition), ed. with Foreword, Christoph Wolff (Frankfurt: Peters, 1986).

79　Wolfgang Wiemer, *Die wiederhergestellte Ordnung in Johann Sebastian Bachs Kunst der Fuge. Untersuchungen am Original-Druck* (Wiesbaden: Breitkopf & Härtel, 1977).

80　Gregory G. Butler, "Ordering Problems in J. S. Bach's Art of Fugue Resolved," MQ 69 (1983): 44–61.

81　Ulrich Siegele, "Wie unvollständig ist Bachs Kunst der Fuge?" *Johann Sebastian Bach: Weltbild, Menschenbild, Notenbild, Klangbild* (Leipzig: VEB Deutscher Verlag für Musik, 1988), 219–225.

394   Paul Walker

number analysis, that Bach purposely chose not to complete the fugue.[82] Another Belgian scholar, Charles Dewulf (1996),[83] followed this theory several years later with the argument that Bach did in fact intend the chorale as the close of the collection, just as it appears in the final print, and that the ending of the unfinished fugue as it stands serves as a bridge leading directly into it. Equally provocative, perhaps, is the argument recently offered by Gregory Butler (2008)[84] that the unfinished fugue was not intended for the *Art of Fugue* at all and was never planned to incorporate the piece's principal theme, but was instead to have been Bach's annual contribution to Mizler's musical society.

Attempts to complete the unfinished fugue, generally accompanied by arguments about its intended original length, have constituted something of a cottage industry over the years. Since 1975, scholars who have taken up this challenge have included Adel Heinrich (1986),[85] Zoltán Göncz (1996),[86] Yngve Jan Trede (1996),[87] Thomas Walz (2000),[88] and Herbert Anton Kellner (2002).[89]

Despite the uncertainties surrounding placement of the concluding canons and the meaning of the unfinished fugue, the general consensus among scholars that the first thirteen fugues as they appear in the print represent Bach's final intentions has made the writing of monograph-length works on the *Art of Fugue* much more feasible than comparable efforts on the *Musical Offering*. A number of these monographs offer lengthy, detailed analyses of the whole, including Adel

---

82 Walter Corten, "'Un renversement peut en cacher un autre,' ou Un aspect inédit du contrepoint 18 de L'art de la fugue," *Revue de musicologie* 73 (1987): 203–226; Walter Corten, "L'Art de la fugue de J.S. Bach: Un plan a déchiffrer?" *Analyse musicale* 13 (1988): 75–79; Walter Corten, "Du microcosme au macrocosme: Le lien numérique et initiatique chez Bach," *Musique ed claviers* (Rouen: CIREM, 1988), 9–17; Walter Corten, "La dernière fugue: Pièce inachevée ou ouverture sur l'infini? Contribution a l'etude du contrepoint BWV 1080, 19 de l'Art de la fugue de J. S. Bach," *Analyse musicale* 11 (1988): 61–65; Walter Corten, "Clefs numériques dans L'art de la fugue de J. S. Bach?" *Revue belge de musicologie/Belgisch tijdschrift voor muziekwetenschap* 42 (1988): 199–221.

83 Charles Dewulf, "L'art de la fugue: Testament de Johann Sebastian Bach," *Revue de la Société Liégeoise de Musicologie* 4 (1996) 41–60.

84 Gregory G. Butler, "Scribes, Engravers, and Notational Styles: The Final Disposition of Bach's Art of Fugue," Gregory G. Butler, George B. Stauffer, and Mary Dalton Greer, eds., *About Bach* (Urbana: University of Illinois Press, 2008), 111–123.

85 Adel Heinrich, " Bach's Die Kunst der Fuge: A Living Compendium of Fugal Procedures," Ph.D. diss. (University of Wisconsin, 1976).

86 Zoltán Göncz, "Reconstruction of the Final Contrapunctus of The Art of Fugue," *International Journal of Musicology* 5 (1996): 25–93; see also Zoltán Göncz, *Bach's Testament: On the Philosophical and Theological Background of the Art of Fugue*, trans. Peter Laki and Erzsébet Mészáros (Lanham: Scarecrow, 2013).

87 Yngve Jan Trede, "Beobachtungen zu Zeitstruktur und Formanlage der mehrthematischen Sätze in Johann Sebastian Bachs Kunst der Fuge," *Dansk årbog for musikforskning* 24 (1996): 11–29.

88 Thomas Walz, "Die Kunst der Fuge: Bachs Gradus ad Parnassum – Sechs Thesen und eine Rekonstruktion," *Musiktheorie* 15 (2000): 349–364.

89 Herbert Anton Kellner, *Die Kunst der Fuga: How Incomplete is the Fuga a 3 sogetti? (BWV 1080/19, Contrapunctus 14)* (Darmstadt: [the author], 2002).

Counterpoint, Canons and the Late Works 395

Heinrich (1983 publication of his 1976 dissertation),[90] Walter Kolneder (1977)[91], Robert Kreft (1977),[92] Erich Bergel (1980),[93] and Pierre Vidal (1984).[94]

A number of scholars have offered their own personal responses to the piece, often attempting as well to draw out extra-musical meaning and in the process probably revealing more about themselves than about Bach or his music. Bergel (1980),[95] for instance, sees in the piece a dialectic between the divine (represented musically by the diatonic) and the human (represented by the chromatic). For Peter Schmiedel (1986)[96] the whole follows a kind of narrative representing the unfolding of a human life, a *Persönlichkeitsentfaltung*. Thomas Schmögner (1994)[97] focuses on symbolism and finds relationships to certain Psalm texts. The most provocative is undoubtedly the monograph of Hans-Eberhard Dentler (2004),[98] whose thesis, inspired by Ursula Kirkendale's interpretation of the *Musical Offering*, argues for Pythagorean theory and the ancient phenomenon of the riddle as the extra-musical inspiration and basis for the *Art of Fugue*. More focused on more purely musical meanings are the monographs of Hans Heinrich Eggebrecht (1975),[99] Peter Schleuning (1993),[100] and Pieter Dirksen (1994).[101]

Certain of the individual movements have also engendered scholarly articles offering detailed analyses. The most interest has been shown in *Contrapuncti I–IV*, including articles by Rivera (1978),[102] Wiemer (1981),[103] Traub (1990),[104]

---

90 See note 84.

91 Walter Kolneder, *Die Kunst der Fuge. Mythen des 20. Jahrhunderts* (Wilhelmshaven: Heinrichshofen, 1977).

92 Robert Kreft, *Johann Sebastian Bach. Die Kunst der Fuge und ihre B-A-C-H – Elemente. Werkanalyse* (Tutzing: Schneider, 1977).

93 Erich Bergel, *Johann Sebastian Bach, die Kunst der Fuge. Ihre geistige Grundlage im Zeichen der thematischen Bipolarität* (Bonn: Brockhaus, 1980).

94 Pierre Vidal, *L'origine thématique de L'Art de la Fugue et ses incidences* (Paris: La Flûte de Pan, 1984).

95 Erich Bergel, *Johann Sebastian Bach, die Kunst der Fuge. Ihre geistige Grundlage im Zeichen der thematischen Bipolarität* (Bonn: Brockhaus, 1980).

96 Peter Schmiedel, "Dynamische Formentwicklung als Keim zukünftiger Persönlichkeitsentfaltung: Zur Kunst der Fuge Johann Sebastian Bachs," *Bach Studien* 9 (1986): 25–28.

97 Thomas Schmögner, "Assoziative Symbolik in Johann Sebastian Bachs Kunst der Fuge," *"Musik muß man machen:" Eine Festgabe für Josef Mertin zum neunzigsten Geburtstag am 21. März 1994* (Vienna: Pasqualatihaus, 1994), 149–171.

98 Hans-Eberhard Dentler, *Johann Sebastian Bachs Kunst der Fuge: Ein pythagoreisches Werk und seine Verwirklichung* (Mainz: Schott, 2004).

99 Hans-Heinrich Eggebrecht, *Bachs Kunst der Fuge: Erscheinung und Deutung* (Munich: Piper, 1984).

100 Peter Schleuning, *Johann Sebastian Bachs Kunst der Fuge: Ideologie, Entstehung, Analyse* (Munich: DTV, 1993).

101 Pieter Dirksen, *Studien zur Kunst der Fuge von Johann Sebastian Bach: Untersuchungen zur Entstehungsgeschichte, Struktur und Aufführungspraxis* (Wilhelmshaven: Noetzel, 1994).

102 Benito Rivera, "Bach's Use of Hitherto Unrecognized Types of Countersubjects in The Art of Fugue," *JAMS* 31 (1978): 344–362.

103 Wolfgang Wiemer, "Eine unbekannte Frühfassung des 'Contrapunctus 2' im Autograph der Kunst der Fuge – mit einigen Anmerkungen zur Grossform des Werks," *Mf* 34 (1981): 413–422.

104 Andrea Traub, "Zur Kunst der Fuge," *Festschrift: Rudolf Bockholdt zum 60. Geburtstag* (Pfaffenhofen: Ludwig, 1990), 183–192.

396   *Paul Walker*

Gerd Zacher (1992 and 1993),[105] and Nimczik and Orgass (1999). Zacher has also written about *Contrapuncti VI* and *VII* (both 1993),[106] Traub (1990) has focused on *Contrapunctus XIII*, and Walter Corten (1987)[107] on *Contrapuncti XVIII, 1 & 2*. The last of these introduces an element of controversy: the author claims that both mirror fugues were conceived by Bach as reversible, despite the absence of any evidence for this.

Several scholars have engaged with Bach's curious choice of the words *contrapunctus* and *canon* in a work said to be about the art of *fugue*. Writing in 1976,[108] Kathryn Bailey proposed that Bach chose the word *contrapunctus* because the individual movements were not meant as entire fugues at all, but as sections of a fugue, some representing opening expositions, some later sections (for which she used the word *development*), an idea not picked up by later writers. Wolff (1983) cited Mattheson's definition of *contrapunctus* as "the adroit combination of several melodies sounding simultaneously"[109] in arguing that Bach chose the word because of the significant engagement with multiple themes; in other words, in contrast to the *Well-Tempered Clavier*, in which Bach explored the genre of fugue, here Bach was exploring the possibilities of "harmony" (i.e., invertible counterpoint). Butler drew a similar conclusion in his article on *Der vollkommene Capellmeister* from the same year.[110] Dirksen asserted that Bach used the two words *contrapunctus* and *canon* as stand-ins for the older terms *fuga soluta* (tied fugue, i.e., non-canonic) and *fuga ligata* (canonic).

In the late 1970s and early 1980s, a few scholars (Kolneder 1977, Hoke 1977, and Breig 1982)[111] addressed the question of performance. The general consensus quickly became that Bach envisioned performance of the work on harpsichord, with his later arrangement of two of the earlier fugues for two harpsichords as a principal point of the argument. This conclusion has remained largely

---

105   Gerd Zacher, "Der geheime Text des Contrapunkts IV von Bach: Anregungen der Sprache für die Ausprägung von Musik," *Beiträge zur Gregorianik: Forschung und Praxis* 13–14 (1992): 219–237; Gerd Zacher, "Der verdrehte Baß in Contrapunctus I aus der Kunst der Fuge," *Musik-Konzepte* 79–80 (1993): 7–11.

106   Gerd Zacher, "Die Metrik in Contrapunctus VII: Per augmentationem et diminutionem," and "Über den Rhythmus 'in Stylo Francese;: Contrapunctus VI aus der Kunst der Fuge,"*Musik-Konzepte* 79–80 (1993): 115–125 and 126–142, respectively.

107   See note 82.

108   Kathryn Bailey, "The Art of Fugue: A New Explanation," *Studies in Music from the University of Western Ontario* 1 (1976): 31–42.

109   Wolff *Essays*, 277.

110   See note 17.

111   Walter Kolneder, *Die Kunst der Fuge: Mythen des 20. Jahrhunderts* (Wilhelmshaven: Heinrichshofen, 1977); Hans Gunter Hoke, "Wissenschaftliche contra idealistische Hypothesen zur Kunst der Fuge," *Bericht über die Wissenschaftliche Konferenz zum III. Internationalen Bach-Fest der DDR, Leipzig 18./19. September 1975* (Leipzig: VEB Deutscher Verlag für Musik, 1977), 245–252; Werner Breig, "Bachs Kunst der Fuge: Zur instrumentalen Bestimmung und zum Zyklus-Charakter," BJ 68 (1982): 103–124.

Counterpoint, Canons and the Late Works   397

unchallenged in the intervening years. To it Edward Aldwell (1989)[112] has added some thoughts concerning the proper tempo for performance, and two scholars, Kolneder (1977)[113] and Markham (2001),[114] have surveyed the work's reception history, with special focus on the nineteenth century.

Finally, regarding the chorale with which the print closes: In addition to the original version of this piece in the *Orgelbüchlein* and its reworking in the *Art of Fugue*, a third version, incomplete, is found at the end of the so-called Leipzig autograph album of chorale preludes (Berlin Mus. ms. autogr. P 271). It is this last version, not the published version, that shows Bach's most sophisticated thinking about this piece, and therefore the chorale published with the *Art of Fugue* cannot be Bach's final composition dictated on his death bed. These arguments are laid out in Wolff (1974).[115]

---

112 Edward Aldwell, "Tempo in The Art of Fugue: An Approach Through Figured Bass," *Journal of the Conductors Guild* 10/3–4 (1989): 88–92.

113 Kolneder, *Die Kunst der Fuge*.

114 Michael Markham, "'The Usefulness of Such Artworks": Expression, Analysis, and Nationalism in The Art of Fugue," *Repercussions* 9 (2001): 33–75.

115 Christoph Wolff, "Bachs Sterbechoral. Kritische Fragen zu einem Mythos," *Essays in Renaissance and Baroque Music in Honor of Arthur Mendel*, ed. Robert Marshal. (Kassel: Bärenreiter, 1974), 283–297; ET "The Deathbed Chorale: Exposing a Myth,"Wolff Essays, 282–294.

16 Compositional Technique

Ulrich Siegele

The present volume pursues a pioneering concept. It challenges an entire scientific branch to stop, to reflect on the achievements of sixty years of research, and to contrive future tasks. If I, having reached four score years, participate in such a project (as compared with someone thirty or sixty years younger), both reflection and contrivance take on a different character. I refrain from providing an historical depiction, especially since the field of research has become too complex even for someone who has personally experienced and partly shaped this time. What I can achieve is a personal report, a source that is subject to all the problems inherent in oral history. Moreover, I can point to desiderata that I will indeed only be able to redeem to a certain extent. Therefore, I would above all request lenience towards my individual perspective, and I hope that subjective experience and contrivance will include enough objective merit in order to introduce the specific area of Bach's compositional technique and its investigation.

Furthermore, it will be useful for the understanding of the following remarks to keep in mind two scientific-cultural differences, especially for readers in the United States. First, musical analysis in Germany has never been possessed of an autonomous status as it has in the English-speaking countries. Neither Schenkerian analysis nor Set Theory has ever played a role worth mentioning. This has led to less dependence on established norms and consequently to more freedom and variety. Analysis does not constitute a discipline on its own; while it is hardly ever linked to music theory, it is usually regarded as belonging to historical musicology. Second, any positivism and formalism—which obviously did exist in Germany— were questioned through the extensive activities of Theodor W. Adorno. Since his return from his years in exile, he fundamentally changed musicology in Germany without being a musicologist in the strict sense of the word, despite the reservations musicologists felt towards him. He did so not only through his philosophical, sociological, and aesthetic viewpoints, but especially through his proposition that social prerequisites do affect the inner structure of every composition.

This postulation was decisive for my work from its early beginnings and gave me a specific task. I understood the necessity to provide a methodological foundation with comprehensible steps for Adorno's "physiognomic view," which at a glance bridged the span between social and compositional conditions. Therefore, I have, among other projects, investigated Bach's compositions on the one hand, and the political and social context of his life on the other. At times, I have also parquelleled both areas in order to elucidate the structural correlation between the condition of his life and the condition of his music. Thus musicology in Germany has, without much ado, already anticipated and incorporated many crucial positions of New Musicology since the early 1950s. During an unforgettable evening at the Millennium Music Conference in the year 2000 at Toronto, it became obvious to me how eager New Musicology was to present Adorno as its patron once his writings became available in English in the 1990s. A target of blame is hereby created, which allows the (would-be) New Musicology in the United States to establish itself and to break out of a scientific tradition, which has been considered troublesome. In the following remarks, I try to take into account the different branches of discourse on both sides of the Atlantic. To which extent I succeed in this will be left to the judgment of respective readers. However, my remarks on the development of Bach research and the description of my own concept of composition-technical (kompositionstechnisch) investigations should be read against this background.

The State of Composition-Technical Investigations

1950 was a key year for Bach research. The bicentenary of Bach's death provided the occasion to issue the New Bach Edition (Neue Bach-Ausgabe, NBA). This project engrossed the forces of Bach research for more than half a century. Furthermore, it established a hierarchy of areas for Bach research. It is only understandable and reasonable that, after the destruction of war, the desire arose to preserve, to document, and to supply access to all that had been saved. Nevertheless, it should not be overlooked that a new edition of Bach's works became part of not just the cultural but also the economic reconstruction of West Germany. It did so by meeting the demands of the publishing industry to use its capacities in a long-ranging and accountable manner. Therefore, Karl Vötterle, the owner of the Bärenreiter publishing house, declared the "Moment of the Complete Edition" ("Die Stunde der Gesamtausgabe").[1] On the other hand, dealing with the prerequisites and the production of an edition guaranteed an escape from any political compromise. The focus on the project of an edition was a retreat into a clearly defined terrain. It made a reflection on the time of National Socialism redundant, even though every edition includes cultural-political positioning.[2] In order to avoid a misunderstanding: I sincerely and absolutely appreciate and acknowledge the achievements stimulated by the New Bach Edition, and admire everyone who played a decisive role in this field of research; I myself would not have been capable of such renunciation. What has been achieved in the areas of the comprehension and evaluation of the sources has become an essential part of Bach scholarship that embraces studies of watermarks, handwriting and scribes, and the like, as well as the differentiation of source layers and the resulting chronology.

---

1 Karl Vötterle, "Die Stunde der Gesamtausgabe," *Musica* 10 (1956): 33–36.
2 Ulrich Siegele, "Ein Editionskonzept und seine Folgen," AfMw 52 (1995): 337–346.

400　*Ulrich Siegele*

Thus Bach research has, somewhat proudly, incorporated methods of philological text criticism, which nevertheless were developed in relation to sources of a completely different structure. In consequence, a limited efficiency of these methods could be anticipated, especially when only one source (possibly written by a copyist and even corrupt) or a huge number of sources were handed down. In the second case (which mostly concerned keyboard music), the use of the manuscripts as teaching material has created a confusion of readings. This thwarts an unequivocal verification of the dependence of sources. Consequently, an unambiguous stemma of the tradition and an unambiguous text of first or last hand cannot be obtained. In fact, it is more appropriate to comprehend the progress of tradition as an encompassing net and the quality of the resulting information as a broad field.[3] Alfred Dürr's decade-long experience and his pragmatic procedure were indispensable for achieving the edition of both volumes of WTC. But even he failed with the French Suites, and reluctantly had to add a virtual version, produced by blending different sources, to the older version transmitted by Altnickol.[4] In both cases of either one or many sources, the establishment of an edition is dependent on inner criticism, namely on criteria of compositional technique (which Alfred Dürr had already made use of for the French Suites). If just two sources exist for one composition, whose interrelation cannot be determined with methods of source criticism, only a composition-technical evaluation of the divergent readings can decide if one of them depends on the other, or whether both depend on a preceding third and lost source. This, however, requires a distinct notion of compositional technique.

The dominant enterprise of the NBA had prioritized questions of source criticism, text criticism, and edition technique; it had elevated auxiliary procedures into main issues. The criticism of authenticity is important for an edition. However, it only concerns the border areas, not the center of a composer's work. Starting with the investigations of Georg von Dadelsen and Alfred Dürr (and later of Yoshitake Kobayashi), the results of chronology are spectacular.[5] Nevertheless, at first, there were no (and later only hesitant) attempts to perceive the new chronology as implying compositional development. The demands of the NBA eclipsed other areas. Even Alfred Dürr, whose life achievement shaped the NBA, has acknowledged this with a tinge of regret in regard to compositional technique.[6] But questions of biography were also being neglected. Every single discovery of documents closely related to Bach has to be welcomed. But it must be recognized that there is little hope of discovering comprehensive hitherto unknown holdings of sources that could lead to a new view on Bach—for instance, the minutes of the Leipzig consistory, which would be pertinent, were pulped a long time ago. As for

---

3　For an instructive example from around 1600, see Ulrich Siegele, ed., *Johann Ulrich Steigleder, Ricercar Tabulatura (1624)*, 2 vols. (Kassel: Bärenreiter, 2008), 2: 30–55 together with v–xii (German) and xvii–xxiv (English).

4　NBA V/6.1 and 6.2 (1989 and 1995/1996); NBA V/8 (1980/1982).

5　Dürr 1957/1976, Dadelsen 1958, Kobayashi 1988.

6　Alfred Dürr, *Johann Sebastian Bach – Das Wohltemperierte Klavier* (Kassel: Bärenreiter, 1998), 25.

Compositional Technique   401

me, I see only the strategy of investigating, as thoroughly as possible, the institutional and cultural, social and political contexts in which Bach lived and worked, and to determine his status within these very contexts. By means of the indirect method, facts that lack direct sources can be ascertained, even if a scholarship that is addicted to positive sources denies this possibility. Thanks to the purposive activities of Walter Blankenburg and Renate Steiger, theological Bach research was stepping forward on its path that had been hardly affected by the NBA.[7]

The discussion I had with Walter Gerstenberg regarding the topic of my PhD thesis in early 1954 is symptomatic of the direction of post-war Bach research. I had suggested the arrangements in Bach's instrumental music based on the consideration that the limited differences between the various versions render perceptible compositional categories. In response, Gerstenberg proposed investigations into the handwriting of Bach and the copyists of his works, which Georg von Dadelsen eventually executed in his inaugural dissertation with widespread success. In view of this proposal, I answered: "I have been studying musicology, not graphology." Thereupon Gerstenberg responded: "The advantage of your topic is that you found it; the advantage of my topic is that I found it." Immediately, I concluded: "Then we will pick mine." This discussion shows the degree to which even a scholar with an intimate relation to Bach's music felt obliged to conform to the general trend. And even then I felt a strong pressure to draw conclusions not just on dependence and evolution of the pieces in question, but also, based on these observations, to explore chronology and authenticity for

---

7   Concerning my contributions to the contextualization of biography, see the following: "Bachs Endzweck einer regulierten und Entwurf einer wohlbestallten Kirchenmusik," *Festschrift Georg von Dadelsen* (Stuttgart: Hänssler 1978), 313–351; reprinted in *The Garland Library of the History of Western Music 6: Baroque Music II: Eighteenth Century* (New York: Garland, 1985), 195–233; "Bachs Stellung in der Leizpiger Kulturpolitik seiner Zeit," BJ 69 (1983): 7–50, BJ 70 (1984): 7–43, and 72 (1986): 33–67, abridged ET (Carol K. Baron), "Bach's Situation in the Cultural Politics of Contemporary Leipzig," Carol K. Baron, ed., *Bach's Changing World. Voices in the Community* (Rochester: University of Rochester Press, 2006), 127–173; "Johann Sebastian Bach – Zur Entstehung und Kritik einer Identifikationsfigur," Hermann Danuser, ed., *Gattungen der Musik und ihre Klassiker* (1988) (Laaber: Laaber, 1998), 59–85; "'Ich habe fleißig sein müssen…' Zur Vermittlung von Bachs sozialem und musikalischem Charakter," MuK 61 (1991): 73–78, also in *Beiträge zur Bach-Forschung* 9/10 (Leipzig 1991), 13–19, ET (Gerhard Herz), "'I had to be industrious…' Thoughts about the Relationship between Bach's Social and Musical Character," BACH 22/2 (1991): 5–12; "Bach and the Domestic Politics of Electoral Saxony," John Butt, ed., *The Cambridge Companion to Bach* (Cambridge: Cambridge University Press, 1997), 17–34; "Bachs politisches Profil oder Wo bleibt die Musik?" Konrad Küster, ed., *Bach-Handbuch* (Kassel: Bärenreiter, 1999), 5–30; "Bach und Händel: Zwei Lebensläufe," *Händel-Jahrbuch* 47 (2001): 315–334; "Wandlungen der Politik – Wandlungen Bachs," LBB 5 (2002): 465–477.

Concerning the development of Bach research, see Hans-Joachim Schulze, "Zum Themenbereich der neueren Bach-Forschung," Johann Trummer and Rudolf Flotzinger, eds., *Johann Sebastian Bach und Johann Joseph Fux. Bericht über das Symposion 1983 in Graz* (Kassel: Bärenreiter 1985), 25–37; Hans-Joachim Hinrichsen, "Universalität und Zersplitterung. Wege der Bachforschung 1945–2005," Michael Heinemann and Hans-Joachim Hinrichsen, eds., *Johann Sebastian Bach und die Gegenwart. Beiträge zur Bach-Rezeption 1945–2005* (Cologne: Dohr, 2007), 117–164; and the introduction to this volume.

402   *Ulrich Siegele*

supporting composition-technical investigations.[8] I was not able to free myself before 1960 with my essay on the Gigue of the Sixth English Suite: a mirror piece of horizontal and vertical inversions that pushes the limits of possibilities. This essay was ordered, kindly but firmly, by Hans Heinrich Eggebrecht for the *Archiv für Musikwissenschaft*; I still consider it to be one of my best.[9] But here I faced a headwind from a different direction. Despite his appreciation, my former teacher Hermann Keller expressed his regret that the construction of such a magnificent piece was being exposed to this extent. Investigations into composition-technique do not progress easily. They hang around at the margin of Bach research, whereas they should be at its center. Laurels of general appreciation cannot be expected, since compositional craft, which is the main concern, demands the expert knowledge of the qualified specialist.

Two questions are usually being asked in connection with these investigations. The first one is if Bach (or any other composer) worked consciously or subconsciously. For me this question is irrelevant. The problem does not lie in the level of awareness, but in the competence of action. We do not think about grammar when using a language we know. However, grammatical structures exist, and it is possible for a speaker or writer to become aware of them in special circumstances. This is true for composition as well as for any other craft. Someone with little experience will have to think about this frequently. Someone with much experience is able to act quickly and correctly without much specific thought. In any case, structures are being created that can be assessed and accounted for by analytical consideration. Those structures are the center of interest, not a psychology of creative activity. The subject is Bach's works as objectifications of his extraordinary compositional competence.

The other objection, that an analysis investigates aspects not mentioned by the composer (and, in a larger realm, by contemporary music theory), also has no importance for me. I always ask myself which aspects of his highly developed compositional technique Bach (or any other first-rate composer) was able to formulate by himself. The medium through which a composer communicates his music-theoretical concerns and documents his music-theoretical ideas is the composition. It is up to us to read compositions as music-theoretical texts. This means to extract the regulatory system with which a composer composed from the composition itself, and to verbalize this regulatory system. In doing this, we do not have to accept any limits set by the ability or inability of contemporary formulation. (Apart from that, the social and economic context has to be taken into account as well: how many people were interested in works that display a

---

8   Ulrich Siegele, "Kompositionsweise und Bearbeitungstechnik in der Instrumentalmusik Johann Sebastian Bachs," PhD. diss. (Tübingen University, 1957; published as *Tübinger Beiträge zur Musikwissenschaft 3*, Stuttgart: Hänssler, 1975)

9   Ulrich Siegele, "Die musiktheoretische Lehre einer Bachschen Gigue," AfM 17 (1960): 152–167. Fifty years later, certainly I would avoid speaking of a "zwölfstufige gleichschwebend temperierte Skala" (a scale of twelve equally tempered degrees), but would replace "gleichschwebend temperiert" (equally tempered) with "wohltemperiert" (well-tempered), meaning an unequally tempered scale, which allows to use all the keys and also enharmonic changes.

highly developed compositional technique in order to remunerate the trouble of composing and the costs of publishing?) I imagine that teaching composition consisted not so much of promoting rules, but rather of deleting mistakes. The instruction was based on the student writing an exercise and the teacher correcting and communicating how it had to be done. If the student was intelligent, he understood, and from then on applied the acquired knowledge himself. If he did not understand, that was the end of it. This would partly explain why so little of what constituted Bach's compositional status can be found in the music of his sons and students. Of course, we have to take note of contemporary music theory. But what exists in handwritten or printed form can only serve as an introduction to highly developed compositional practice for beginners.

In the spring of 1976, I met the English composer Alexander Goehr. He exerted another decisive influence on the development of my methodological principles. I showed him my formal and structural analysis of the six-part Ricercar of the Musical Offering. He remarked that it would be impossible to just compose something like that without having a plan. At that very moment, it became clear to me that we must not approach a piece of music with our preconceived questions, because this way we only receive answers determined by these questions that are designed to solve our own problems. We rather must try to put ourselves in the position of the composer; we must try to reach clarity with regard to the compositional problems he was facing, and then try to define how he solved those problems. This includes an awareness of all possible solutions available to the composer and why he chose one specific possibility over the others. A historical grammar of music does not provide directives; it does not determine the composition, and does not limit itself only to one possibility. Rather, it provides a wide spectrum of possibilities at any given moment and location, out of which a selection is being made in each and every specific case. It must be the goal to understand the accomplished composition as the result of a decision-making process, as the final consequence of a series of musical arguments, following each other step by step. Ideally, the specific place of every note could be accounted for. To stress the point: what is at stake is the problems presented to the composer and his strategies in resolving them.

This concept of investigating Bach's (and any other composer's) compositional technique distances itself from an analytical tradition that understands the result of compositional activity as an organism that adheres to the opinion of being capable of proving its coherence and unity. On the contrary, the concept faces discrepancies and breaks, which claim recognition as attributes of the compositional work, because it is these very discrepancies and breaks that point to the location of compositional problems and their resolution (or nonresolution). The concept does not postulate universal ideas, general notions, or archetypes subliminally roaming around, and it does not strive after acquiring any of these items. An all-embracing universal spirit and transcendental will of music are as alien to this concept as the masterpiece itself, created by a genius. The regulatory system, which the concept undertakes to construct, is not a normative and prescribing grammar. Instead, it is a historical grammar, which reveals information about the regulatory system of a specific composer. And because a composer is able to change his regulatory system over time, and often does, it also reveals

404   *Ulrich Siegele*

information about the specific regulatory system that forms the basis for a specific piece or a group of pieces. The differentiation of genre and chronology eventually combine into the peculiarity of a composer's work.

The concept under discussion does not worship crude nominalism, and it does not renounce universals from the outset. Rather, it determines the interrelation between the general and the specific in the manner of a limited repertoire of basic musical ideas—untreated work blocks, so to speak—standing at the beginning of the compositional activity. These blocks, however, are unspecific because of their general nature, and therefore they are being treated every time in differentiated steps of specific procedures in order to be individualized. Nevertheless, the concept is not content with a positive description of available basic ideas and procedures. Rather, the concept evaluates their function and interdependence within the regulatory system as well as the individual composition. This essentially historical approach positions the concept among the subdisciplines of musicology: neither does it aim to save the individuality of a specific composition in front of the generalizations of music theory (which were originally didactically motivated); nor does it consider itself to be the supplier of raw material for music theory, which refines the material through systematic integration. Rather, the concept is decisively siding with historical musicology, and it is confident enough to claim a central position within this sub-discipline. What could be more relevant to a musicology that intends to do justice to its own subject matter than a history of the changing system of categories valid in compositional activities?

However, this concept is not a plea for a detached formalism, for a one-sided fixation on the musical composition in its state of being, for an autonomous condition of compositional technique and its history. The prerequisites for the compositional facts insist on their authority. This is true for musical prerequisites (for example, the tradition of genres and their blending, the resources of performance, their possibilities and connotations, the words of the text and the conventions of their musical realization) as well as extra-musical prerequisites (for example, the institutions, social and cultural contexts, economic conditions, as well as aesthetic, philosophical, and theological concepts). However, I resolutely believe that the impact of those factors can only be reliably determined through clarity about the compositional facts. Otherwise, there is the danger of arbitrary parallels. There is no interpretation without a positive base, unless it enjoys the creation of fictitious castles in the air. In dealing with the facts of musical composition, musicology has a deficit. It will take a long time until neglected tasks will be addressed and for even the most pressing tasks to be achieved.

Incidentally, my analyses of historical music have profited from my extensive investigations into contemporary Western music of the fifties, sixties, and early seventies of the previous century.[10] There, I learned to analyze out of the

---

10   Ulrich Siegele, "Entwurf einer Musikgeschichte der sechziger Jahre," Rudolf Stephan, ed., *Die Musik der sechziger Jahre. Zwölf Versuche* (Mainz: Schott 1972), 9–25; Ulrich Siegele, *Zwei Kommentare zum 'Marteau sans maître' von Pierre Boulez* (Stuttgart: Hänssler, 1979); Ulrich Siegele, "Planungsverfahren in György Ligetis 'Aventures & Nouvelles Aventures,'" *Musik & Ästhetik* 6/2 (2002): 40–51.

Compositional Technique 405

composition itself, without the prerequisites of common music theory, without harmony, counterpoint, and form. I have applied this access, which is liberated from the music-theoretical burden, to the analysis of historical music. This allowed me to discover things that until then had remained hidden. At the same time, it always gives me pleasure when composers of the present time not only approach with interest the compositional procedures of their past colleagues, but also deem them useful for their own work.

The Scope of Composition-Technical Investigations

What has been achieved in the field of compositional technique, and how has it been done? Because this essay is designed for erecting signposts in this field of research, the literature references do not aim at a complete bibliography. Instead, they are limited to representative rather than exhaustive examples that illustrate respective possibilities. In some cases, of course, other titles of one or many authors could also have been mentioned. However, I do have to record and regret the declining consideration of German publications in English-speaking literature that has been observable since the mid-1990s. Isolating national discourses certainly prejudices any field of research.

The intention of composition-technical investigations is not to neglect the documentary sources that must be encountered, if not at the beginning then at least at an appropriate juncture of the ongoing work. Where various arrangements or versions exist, a comparison can offer clues with regard to compositional technique—drafts, sketches, and corrections (in English terminology combined in the catchword "compositional process"). Gregory Butler specializes in the examination of original prints of Bach's works by methods that are normally applied to manuscripts.[11] This technique has not only enabled him to shed light on the history of publication, but also to reveal the history of the published work. Names such as Alfred Dürr, Hans Eppstein, Wilfried Fischer, Joshua Rifkin, Klaus Hofmann, and myself may be mentioned for investigations into the wide area of arrangements and versions.[12] For the area of parodies (which should be

---

11 Gregory G. Butler, *Bach's Clavier-Übung III: The Making of a Print. With a Companion Study of the Canonic Variations on 'Vom Himmel hoch' BWV 769* (Durham: Duke University Press, 1990); see also Chapter 4 of this volume.

12 Alfred Dürr, "Gedanken zu J. S. Bachs Umarbeitungen eigener Werke," BJ 43 (1956): 93–104; Hans Eppstein, *Studien über J. S. Bachs Sonaten für ein Melodieinstrument und obligates Cembalo* (Stockholm: Almquist and Wiksells, 1966); Hans Eppstein, "Grundzüge in J. S. Bachs Sonatenschaffen," BJ 55 (1969): 5–30; Hans Eppstein, "Chronologieprobleme in Johann Sebastian Bachs Suiten für Soloinstrument," BJ 62 (1976): 35–57; Fischer NBA VII/7 (1970/1971); Joshua Rifkin, "Besetzung – Entstehung – Überlieferung: Bemerkungen zur Ouvertüre BWV 1068," BJ 83 (1997): 169–176; Joshua Rifkin, "Verlorene Quellen, verlorene Werke. Miszellen zu Bachs Instrumentalkomposition," Martin Geck, ed., *Bachs Orchesterwerke. Bericht über das 1. Dortmunder Bach-Symposion 1996* (Witten: Klangfarben Musikverlag, 1997), 59–75; Joshua Rifkin, "Klangpracht und Stilauffassung. Zu den Trompeten der Ouvertüre BWV 1069," Martin Geck, ed., *Bach und die Stile. Bericht über das 2. Dortmunder Bach-Symposion 1998* (Dortmund: Klangfarben Musikverlag, 1999), 327–345; Joshua Rifkin, "The 'B-Minor

406 *Ulrich Siegele*

included here as well), the names of Werner Neumann, Ludwig Finscher, Georg von Dadelsen, Klaus Häfner, and Stephen A. Crist may be added.[13] This preoccupation with arrangements created the side branch of reconstruction. Either because of peculiarities in the sources, or of the compositional structure, earlier but lost versions, often for differing performance forces, were not just postulated and outlined, but also realized and performed (designated by "R" following the respective BWV number). Such reconstructions, and especially their specific decisions, are sometimes more and sometimes less (and sometimes not at all) justified.

Based on the autographs of the vocal works, Robert L. Marshall's examination of drafts, sketches, and corrections resulted in fruitful findings with regard to the understanding of Bach's compositional process (findings that were made available in two splendidly published volumes).[14] With the help of this methodology and after extensive research, Werner Breig was able to draw an extraordinarily differentiated picture regarding the compositional evolution of the concertos for single harpsichord and orchestra.[15] By the way, the critical reports of the NBA offer rich material, which has only partially been exploited. However, a restriction of composition-technical investigations to the compositional process, namely to data transmitted in the sources, entails a contraction of the perspective, similar to the restrictions of contemporary music theory.

On the one hand, it is essential for composition-technical investigations to consider the results of source criticism and chronology.[16] On the other hand, three

---

Flute Suite' Deconstructed. New Light on Bach's Ouverture BWV 1067," BP 6 (2007), 1–98; Klaus Hofmann, "Zur Fassungsgeschichte des zweiten Brandenburgischen Konzerts," Geck, ed., *Bachs Orchesterwerke*, 185–192; Siegele, *Kompositionsweise und Bearbeitungstechnik in der Instrumentalmusik... Bachs.*

13 Werner Neumann, "Über Ausmaß und Wesen des Bachschen Parodieverfahrens," BJ 51 (1965): 63–85; Ludwig Finscher, "Zum Parodieproblem bei Bach," Martin Geck, ed., *Bach-Interpretationen* (Göttingen: Vandenhoeck & Ruprecht, 1969), 94–105; Georg von Dadelsen, "Anmerkungen zu Bachs Parodieverfahren," Wolfgang Rehm, ed., *Bachiana et alia musicologica. Festschrift Alfred Dürr zum 65. Geburtstag* (Kassel: Bärenreiter, 1983), 52–57; Georg von Dadelsen, "Die 'Fassung letzter Hand' in der Musik," Georg von Dadelsen, *Über Bach und anderes. Aufsätze und Vorträge 1957–1982*, eds. Arnold Feil and Thomas Kohlhase (Laaber: Laaber, 1983), 55–67; Klaus Häfner, *Aspekte des Parodieverfahrens bei Johann Sebastian Bach. Beiträge zur Wiederentdeckung verschollener Vokalwerke* (Laaber: Laaber, 1987); Stephen A. Crist, "The Question of Parody in Bach's Cantata *Preise dein Glücke, gesegnetes Sachsen*, BWV 215," BP 1 (1995): 135–161; Ulrich Siegele. "Das Parodieverfahren des Weihnachtsoratoriums von J. S. Bach als dispositionelles Problem," *Studien zur Musikgeschichte. Eine Festschrift für Ludwig Finscher* (Kassel: Bärenreiter, 1995), 259–266.

14 Robert L. Marshall, *The Compositional Process of J. S. Bach. A Study of the Autograph Scores of the Vocal Works*, 2 vols. (Princeton: Princeton University Press, 1972).

15 NBA VII/4 (1999/2001).

16 Reinmar Emans, "'Äußere' Chronologie – 'Innere' Chronologie – 'Relative' Chronologie. Überlegungen zu methodologischen Voraussetzungen," Geck, ed., *Bachs Orchesterwerke*, 9–16; Hans-Joachim Schulze, "Probleme der Werkchronologie bei Johann Sebastian Bach," Martin Staehelin, ed., *"Die Zeit, die Tag und Jahre macht," Zur Chronologie des Schaffens von Johann Sebastian Bach. Bericht über das Internationale wissenschaftliche Colloquium*

objections must be taken into account. Source criticism and chronology serve to preorder the material on which composition-technical investigations are based. They are prerequisites for composition-technical investigations, not their goal. It is not the task of composition-technical investigations to corroborate or to complete the results of source criticism and chronology. (If accidentally encountered, however, such corroborations and completions should not be ignored either.) The application and the development of compositional procedures do not necessarily follow a timeline. They can be influenced by leaps and breaks, experiments and regresses, genre traditions and instrumental possibilities, occasions and capacities of the musicians: all in contradiction to the dependence of sources and chronology. It is important to accept this contradiction, to turn it into productivity, and to understand it as an invitation to elucidate its reasons. Besides, only a portion of compositional traits enables statements of chronological proof, as mentioned on various occasions: it is said that details are more pertinent than formal design.[17] Therefore, a focus of composition-technical investigations on chronology prefers certain compositional characteristics. But on the other hand, it can miss important aspects and be in danger of preventing an integrated comprehension. After all, source criticism always only allows dating the source, which does not have to coincide with the date of the first formation of the transmitted composition in each case. Therefore, the preconditions of source criticism and chronology can provide an aid, but they cannot set limits. It is decisive to acknowledge the self-reliance of composition-technical investigations. Their subject matter is the compositional facts. These facts are within the musical text. This text in its turn can and must be read as evidence for the composer's work, for the chosen and rejected possibilities.

Whoever attempts composition-technical investigations takes a preliminary decision which is guided by his cognitive interest and so far sets a frame for possible results. As usual, this preliminary decision relates to the choice of material on which the investigation is based. Projects that view the whole of Bach's work articulate the ultimate claim. This has been done by Richard D. P. Jones and announced by Christoph Wolff.[18] Elke Krüger, Jean-Claude Zehnder, and Heinrich Deppert have dealt with a specific creative period, in this case the early production; however, both approaches stress the perspective of chronology.[19] It is common to look at a specific group of works. Werner Breig's typological order of

---

aus Anlaß des 80. Geburtstages von Alfred Dürr, Göttingen 1998 (Göttingen: Vandenhoeck & Ruprecht, 2001), 11–20.

17 Reinmar Emans, "Die solistischen Choralbearbeitungen Bachs. Erneute Überlegungen zu Ansätzen einer stilkritischen Theorie," LBB 5 (2002): 139–154; Jean-Claude Zehnder, *Die frühen Werke Johann Sebastian Bachs. Stil – Chronologie – Satztechnik. Teilband A: Werkbetrachtungen, Teilband B: Stilmerkmale und weitere chronologische Indizien* (Basel: Schwabe, 2009), A: 6.

18 Richard D. P. Jones, *The Creative Development of Johann Sebastian Bach*, 2 vols. (Oxford: Oxford University Press, 2007–2013).

19 Elke Krüger, *Stilistische Untersuchungen zu ausgewählten frühen Klavierfugen Johann Sebastian Bachs* (Hamburg: Wagner, 1970); Zehnder, *Die frühen Werke Johann Sebastian Bachs*; Heinrich Deppert, *Studien zum Frühwerk Johann Sebastian Bachs. Untersuchungen*

408   Ulrich Siegele

the free organ works, especially with regard to fugues can be mentioned as an example. It is complemented by a corresponding order of the preludes by George B. Stauffer. Christian Martin Schmidt yielded original contributions. Meanwhile, Russell Stinson has devoted himself to the chorale settings for organ.[20] Daniel R. Melamed explores at the motets.[21] The WTC received detailed attention by Ludwig Czaczkes (whose observations regarding aspects of formal design deserve preference over his hypotheses on motivic relationships), Siglind Bruhn, Alfred Dürr, David Ledbetter, Joseph Groocock, and myself.[22] In this connection, Carl Dahlhaus, Werner Breig, and Siegfried Oechsle pursue selected issues.[23] An essay by Peter Schleuning[24] is attractive from a methodological point of view, especially as he speaks less about what Bach did than about what Bach was able to do but chose not to do so. This fascinating perspective frequently occupied Ferruccio Busoni in his edition of the WTC with commentary.

---

zur Chronologie auf der Grundlage der Kompositionstechnik in den Werken der Möllerschen Handschrift und der sogenannten Neumeister-Choräle (Tutzing: Schneider 2009).

20 Werner Breig, "Freie Orgelwerke," Küster, ed., *Bach-Handbuch*, 613–712; George B. Stauffer, *The Organ Preludes of Johann Sebastian Bach* (Ann Arbor: UMI, 1980); Christian Martin Schmidt, "Zur Entwicklung der Form im emphatischen Sinne. Bachs Orgelpräludium h-moll BWV 544," *Musiktheorie* 1 (1986): 195–204; Christian Martin Schmidt, "Analyse und Geschichtsauffassung. Bachs Präludium und Fuge für Orgel BWV 552," Joseph Kuckertz, et al., eds., *Neue Musik und Tradition. Festschrift Rudolf Stephan* (Laaber: Laaber, 1990), 99–111; Russell Stinson, *Bach: The Orgelbüchlein* (New York: Schirmer, 1996; reissued, Oxford: Oxford University Press, 1999); Russell Stinson, *J. S. Bach's Great Eighteen Organ Chorales* (Oxford: Oxford University Press, 2001); Russell Stinson, "Neues über Bachs Leipziger Orgelchoräle," LBB (2002): 109–129.

21 Daniel R. Melamed, *J. S. Bach and the German Motet* (Cambridge: Cambridge University Press, 1995).

22 Ludwig Czaczkes, *Analyse des Wohltemperierten Klaviers. Form und Aufbau der Fuge bei Bach*, 2 vols. (Wien: Kaltschmid – later Österreichischer Bundesverlag, 1956–1963, 2nd ed., 1982); Siglind Bruhn, *J. S. Bach's Well-Tempered Clavier. In-Depth Analysis and Interpretation*, 4 vols. (Hong Kong: Mainer, 1993); Alfred Dürr, *Johann Sebastian Bach – Das Wohltemperierte Klavier* (Kassel: Bärenreiter, 1998); David Ledbetter, *Bach's Well-tempered Clavier. The 48 Preludes and Fugues* (New Haven: Yale University Press, 2002); Joseph Groocock, *Fugal Composition: A Guide to the Study of Bach's '48,'* ed. Yo Tomita (Westport: Greenwood, 2003); Ulrich Siegele, "Zu Bachs Fugenkomposition," Reinhard Szeskus, ed., *Johann Sebastian Bachs Traditionsraum* (Leipzig: Breitkopf & Härtel, 1986), 19–24; Ulrich Siegele, "Kategorien formaler Konstruktion in den Fugen des Wohltemperierten Klaviers," Siegbert Rampe, ed., *Bach, Das Wohltemperierte Klavier I. Tradition, Entstehung, Funktion, Analyse. Ulrich Siegele zum 70. Geburtstag* (Munich: Katzbichler, 2002), 321–471.

23 Carl Dahlhaus, "Bemerkungen zu einigen Fugen des Wohltemperierten Klaviers," BJ 41 (1954): 40–45; Carl Dahlhaus, "Bachs konzertante Fugen," BJ 42 (1955): 45–72; Werner Breig, "Beobachtungen an einigen späten Klavierfugen Bachs," LBB 5 (2002): 207–218; Siegfried Oechsle, "Zum Formbegriff einiger Fugen des Wohltemperierten Klaviers," Martin Geck, ed., Bachs *Musik für Tasteninstrumente. Bericht über das 4. Dortmunder Bach-Symposion 2002* (Dortmund: Klangfarben, 2003), 199–212.

24 Peter Schleuning, "'Sinnreiche Verbrämungen' und 'versteckte Zierrathen.'' Beobachtungen und Gedanken zu zwei Präludien und zwei Fugen des Wohltemperierten Klaviers mit zwei kunsthistorischen Anmerkungen von Werner Busch," Peter Schleuning, *Über Bach... Gesammelte Aufsätze* (Dortmund: Klangfarben Musikverlag, 2006), 91–111.

Questions of compositional technique take up much space in two publications edited by Siegbert Rampe, the one on Bach's keyboard music, the other, edited together with Dominik Sackmann, on Bach's orchestral music.[25] The two authors have specifically compared the evolution of the ritornello forms in the cantatas and concertos, including pieces by other composers as well. Based on this comparison, they inferred from the cantatas, whose dates are established for the most part, to the first versions of the concertos with orchestra, whose dates are disputable on the whole, providing the single concertos with more accurate dates in the time frame between 1712 (Weimar) and 1720/21 (Cöthen). Siegbert Rampe has extended this method to the keyboard music, so far as it makes use of ritornello forms. Chamber music can be included, too. Hio-Ihm Lee classified the forms of the ritornellos in general; Jeanne Swack and Gregory Butler, Hans Eppstein and Matthias Geuting inquired into the topic of genres and their blending; Clemens Fanselau discussed the problem of polyphony in the works for melodic instruments without accompaniment on different lines.[26]

Werner Neumann's PhD thesis on Bach's choral fugues, written in 1934–1935 and published for the first time in 1938,[27] represents an early (if not the first) structural investigation into Bach's compositional technique. It determines the feature of the vocal fugue as permutation fugue, opposite to instrumental fugues destined for keyboard instruments. The vocal fugue is based on a thematic texture of several subjects, which is formed as both *dux* and *comes*. Entries of this thematic texture follow each other on ascending or descending fifths, without intervening episodes. After all voices have entered, the subjects are being exchanged, that is to say permutated. However, in the meantime it has turned out that the principle of voice-permutation within a fugue is neither limited to vocal music nor to Bach, especially when episodes are permitted between the entries of the thematic texture. Alfred Dürr explicitly conforms to Werner Neumann's methodical principles in the formal analyses of his studies on Bach's early cantatas; on this line Emil Platen explored the choral settings of chorale melodies.[28]

---

25 Siegbert Rampe, ed., *Bachs Klavier- und Orgelwerke. Das Handbuch 4/1–2* (Laaber: Laaber, 2007–2008); Siegbert Rampe and Dominik Sackmann, *Bachs Orchestermusik. Entstehung – Klangwelt – Interpretation. Ein Handbuch* (Kassel: Bärenreiter, 2000).

26 Hio-Ihm Lee, *Die Form der Ritornelle bei Johann Sebastian Bach* (Pfaffenweiler: Centaurus, 1993); Jeanne Swack, "Modular Structure and the Recognition of Ritornello in Bach's Brandenburg Concertos," BP 4 (1999): 33–53; Gregory G. Butler, "The Question of Genre in J. S. Bach's Fourth Brandenburg Concerto," BP 4 (1999): 9–32; Gregory G. Butler, "The Prelude to the Third English Suite BWV 808: an Allegro Concerto Movement in Ritornello Form," Anne Leahy and Yo Tomita, eds., *Bach Studies from Dublin* (Dublin: Four Courts, 2004), 93–101; Hans Eppstein, "Konzert und Sonate," Geck, ed., *Bachs Orchesterwerke*, 145–149; Matthias Geuting, *Konzert und Sonate bei Johann Sebastian Bach. Formale Disposition und Dialog der Gattungen* (Kassel: Bärenreiter, 2006); Clemens Fanselau, *Mehrstimmigkeit in J. S. Bachs Werken für Melodieinstrumente ohne Begleitung* (Sinzig: Schewe, 2000).

27 Werner Neumann, *J. S. Bachs Chorfuge. Ein Beitrag zur Kompositionstechnik Bachs* (Leipzig: Kistner & Siegel, 1938, 2nd and 3rd eds., Leipzig: Breitkopf & Härtel, 1950 and 1953).

28 Dürr St, and Dürr St 2.

410   *Ulrich Siegele*

To all appearances, the new chronology of the vocal works has encouraged the precipitate proclamation of a new Bach image on the one hand, but initially blocked a comprehensive investigation into the cantatas on the other. Then, the shock of the new chronology concentrated on the B minor Mass. The discussion of this paradigm became personalized, and indeed took on a tragic trait. The new chronology turned up approximately at the same time that Friedrich Smend's edition was published,[29] and ruined the life work of this impressive Lutheran scholar. Only thirty years later, with the distance of one generation, a series of composition-technical investigations began that benefited from the new chronology. On this basis, Werner Breig in 1988 outlined a history of Bach's four-part chorale settings.[30] He differentiated the corpus, until then regarded as homogeneous, into several evolutionary stages assigned to the pre-Weimar, Weimar and Leipzig periods, with the Leipzig period further subdivided within Bach's first year, and finally at the end of the regular cantata production.

Reinmar Emans, starting in the early nineties, looked into the development of soloistic movements, in particular examining continuo arias, ariosi, secco and accompagnato recitatives, as well as arias based on chorales, whereas Martin Geck discussed the *Vox Christi* movements in the cantatas;[31] furthermore, Geck's special approach is documented in a volume of collected essays.[32] Actually, Martin Geck's Dortmund Bach symposiums gave way to a multifarious and intensive discussion of composition-technical issues, as substantiated in the reports (published in the series *Dortmunder Bach-Forschungen*). Paul Brainard and Stephen A. Crist turned to a special approach regarding the arias; for once, they did not emphasize the rhetorical and affective, but the formal aspect of the text, one author investigating the translation of the metrics of the text into the metrics of music, the other exploring the influence of the line structure of a given poem on the musical form.[33] In 1995, Friedhelm Krummacher pursued the unfolding of compositional problems in Bach's cycle of chorale cantatas, posed on the one hand by connecting the words and the melody of the chorale with the heterogeneous forms of the recitative and the aria, on the other hand (with particular respect to the opening choruses) by inserting the chorale with its motet texture into the concertante texture dominated by instrumental ritornellos; later, he examined choruses from the viewpoint of thematic combination and concentration of text-related

---

29   NBA II/1 and KB (1954/1956).

30   Werner Breig, "Grundzüge einer Geschichte von Bachs vierstimmigem Choralsatz," AfM 45 (1988): 165–185, 300–319.

31   Emans, *Die solistischen Choralbearbeitungen Bachs*; Martin Geck, "Die vox-Christi-Sätze in Bachs Kantaten," Geck, ed., *Bach und die Stile*, 79–101.

32   Martin Geck, *"Denn alles findet bei Bach statt." Erforschtes und Erfahrenes* (Stuttgart: Metzler, 2000).

33   Paul Brainard, "The Regulative and Generative Roles of Verse in Bach's 'thematic' invention," Don O. Franklin, ed., *Bach Studies* [1] (Cambridge: Cambridge University Press, 1989), 54–74; Stephen A. Crist, "Aria Forms in the Cantatas from Bach's First Leipzig Jahrgang," Franklin, ed., *Bach Studies* [1], 36–53.

Compositional Technique 411

vocal and autonomous instrumental parts.[34] In 1999, Konrad Küster displayed the narrative of the compositional evolution of the church cantatas on the basis of their chronological order.[35] Instrumental cantata sinfonias had been examined earlier in connection with concertos but now all forms of composition-technical studies of the cantatas were undertaken.

From a methodical perspective, such investigations range from isolation to contextualization. It is possible to take a single piece, to isolate it, and to judge it according to its own merits. That has been done many times. The next step is to view pieces that are related to each other, for example the pair "Prelude and Fugue," or the movements of a suite, a sonata, or a concerto. Such combinations of two or more movements can be considered as new units themselves, especially when several of these new units are put together in successive combinations. In this case it is decisive whether the result of putting together is, on the one hand, a mere collection, compiled without any discernible structures itself, or, on the other hand, a well-ordered arrangement, furnished with more or less obvious structural features. The second possibility results in a noticeable methodical advantage, since structures exist on two levels: on the subordinate level of the new units, and on the higher level of their combination. If these two levels are correlated, they are able to explain and to control each other, and therefore provide an increasing reliability of understanding.

Common research issues concerning the structure of arrangements are the order of keys and the sequence of movement types, for example the order of dance types in suites.[36] In this regard, Bach's late monothematic works, such as the Goldberg Variations, the Canonic Variations, the Musical Offering, and the Art of Fugue, are popular objects, even if the results are variable. On the other hand, my attempt to award the status of an arrangement, structured on several levels, to the two volumes of the WTC has been met with reservation. Nevertheless, cantatas, passions, oratorios, and masses are also open to an examination from the viewpoint of a structured arrangement. Much has been done in this respect,

---

34 Friedhelm Krummacher, *Bachs Zyklus der Choralkantaten. Aufgaben und Lösungen* (Göttingen: Vandenhoeck & Ruprecht, 1995); Friedhelm Krummacher, *Bachs Weg in der Arbeit am Werk. Eine Skizze* (Göttingen: Vandenhoek & Ruprecht, 2001).

35 Konrad Küster, "Geistliche Kantaten," Küster, ed., *Bach-Handbuch*, 95–391.

36 As to ordering principles of arrangements in general, see: Rudolf Eller, "Serie und Zyklus in Bachs Instrumentalsammlungen," Geck, ed., *Bach-Interpretationen*, 126–143; Walter Gerstenberg, "Tonart und Zyklus in Bachs Musik. Anmerkungen zu Suite, Konzert und Kantate," Geck, ed., *Bach-Interpretationen*, 119–125; Christoph Wolff, "Ordnungsprinzipien in den Originaldrucken Bachscher Werke," Geck, ed., *Bach-Interpretationen*, 144–167; Rudolf Stephan, "J. S. Bach und das Problem des musikalischen Zyklus," BJ 59 (1973): 39–52; Klaus Hofmann, "Überlegungen zum Aufbau Bachscher Suiten- und Sonatensammlungen," *Beiträge zur Bach-Forschung* 9/10 (1991): 85–94; Hans Eppstein, "Fragen der Ordnungsprinzipien in Bachs Köthener und Leipziger Instrumentalsammlungen," LBB 5 (2002): 131–135. As to ordering principles in the field of dance types see: Doris Finke-Hecklinger, *Tanzcharaktere in Johann Sebastian Bachs Vokalmusik* (Trossingen: Hohner, 1970); Meredith Little and Natalie Jenne, *Dance and the Music of J. S. Bach*, revised and expanded edition (Bloomington: Indiana University Press, 2001).

412   *Ulrich Siegele*

but much more is possible. As mentioned previously, an equally developed con-textualization according to creative periods complements the contextualization in consideration of work groups and even the whole work. More often, however, the contextualization refers to pieces of the same kind, in singling out a group of similar and therefore comparable pieces. Finally, pieces of different kinds can be related to each other, and even pieces by other composers can be included. The decision between the isolation of a single piece and the various possibilities of contextualization will be regulated by the intention of the investigation, whose progress however may demand revision.

Another approach to the material placed at our disposal by Bach's compo-sitional output is to make use of composition-technical notions, as it has been illustrated by permutation fugue or ritornello form. Christoph Wolff has been engaged in the *stile antico* during Bach's late period, followed in this field by Siegfried Oechsle. Heinrich Deppert has written on cadence and clausula, har-mony and key. Don O. Franklin examined the notation of Bach's music in or-der to extract evidence about its temporal structure. I myself investigated the key structure governing the sequence of movements in cantatas.[37] The compass "vocal-instrumental" has played an outstanding role in the thinking of Werner Neumann right from the outset, who was later followed by Friedhelm Krum-macher. Paul Brainard added a thoughtful contribution and Marianne Danck-wardt a specific study.[38] Laurence Dreyfus extended the term "inventio" from the invention of thematic material to the preparatory exploration of the implied

---

37   Wolff St. ant.; Siegfried Oechsle, "Johann Sebastian Bachs Rezeption des stile antico. Zwischen Traditionalismus und Geschichtsbewußtsein," Geck, ed., *Bach und die Stile*, 103–122; Siegfried Oechsle, "Doppelte Historisierung des Komponierens. Die motettischen Chorfugen in Bachs I. Jahrgang," Martin Geck, ed., *Bachs 1. Leipziger Kantatenjahrgang. Bericht über das 3. Dort-munder Bach-Symposion 2000* (Dortmund: Klangfarben, 2002), 239–251; Siegfried Oechsle, "Johann Sebastian Bachs Auseinandersetzung mit dem Stylus antiquus und die musikalisch-liturgischen Traditionen in Leipzig," LBB 5 (2002): 413–425; Heinrich Deppert, *Kadenz und Klausel in der Musik von J. S. Bach. Studien zu Harmonie und Tonart* (Tutzing: Schneider, 1993); Don O. Franklin, "Das Verhältnis zwischen Taktart und Kompositionstechnik im Wohltemperierten Klavier I," Rampe, ed., *Bach, Das Wohltemperierte Klavier I*, 147–160; Don O. Franklin, "The Role of Time Signatures in Bach's Composition of Jahrgang I," Geck, ed., *Bachs 1. Leipziger Kantatenjahrgang*, 329–347, plus discussion, 347–356; Don O. Franklin, "Aspekte von Proportion und Dimension in Johann Sebastian Bachs Missa von 1733," LBB 5 (2002) 235–272; Don O. Franklin, "Viewing the Goldberg Variations as a Musico-Mathematical Matrix," Geck, ed., *Bachs Musik für Tasteninstrumente*, 231–250; Don O. Franklin, "Compos-ing in Time: Bach's Temporal Design for the Goldberg Variations," Leahy and Tomita, eds., *Bach Studies from Dublin*, 103–128; Ulrich Siegele, "Planungsverfahren in Kantaten J. S. Bachs," Geck, ed., *Bachs 1. Leipziger Kantatenjahrgang*, 95–113, plus discussion, 113–120.

38   Neumann, "Über Ausmaß und Wesen"; Werner Neumann, "Das Problem 'vokal – instrumental' in seiner Bedeutung für ein neues Bach-Verständnis," Reinhold Brinkmann, ed., *Bachforschung und Bachinterpretation heute. Wissenschaftler und Praktiker im Dialog. Bericht über das Bachfest-Symposium 1978 der Philipps-Universität Marburg* (Leipzig: Neue Bachgesellschaft, 1981), 72–85; Paul Brainard, "The Aria and Its Ritornello: The Question of 'Dominance' in Bach," Rehm, ed., *Bachiana et alia musicologica*, 39–51; Marianne Danckwardt, *Instrumen-tale und vokale Kompositionsweisen bei Johann Sebastian Bach* (Tutzing: Schneider, 1985).

Compositional Technique 413

possibilities concerning its use, and examined how the compositional repertoire gained that way may be arranged and integrated for producing integral pieces, especially a concert movement in ritornello form or a fugue.[39] Finally, Michael Marissen and Peter Schleuning undertook—both reflecting upon the Brandenburg concertos, but each in his own way—to open structural accomplishments to semantic interpretation.[40]

The occupation with questions of texture, especially counterpoint, by Bach and his circle provides its own area of research. The material has been considerably augmented by the fourteen canons that Bach added as a supplement at the end of his personal copy of the Goldberg Variations, as well as by new findings presented by Peter Wollny, Walter Werbeck, and Christoph Wolff.[41] These findings point to the last fifteen years of Bach's life. They have been published (2011), together with notes on figured bass and the craft of setting as well as sketches and drafts, as a supplement to the NBA, edited by Peter Wollny. This will offer new perspectives on the setup of the curriculum Bach developed for his teaching activities—a continuing consideration that could include the approach by Klaus-Jürgen Sachs.[42]

I am skeptical to attempts that exploit analyses for proving a preconceived goal going beyond the intent of the analysis. It is not to be doubted that compositional procedures can be interpreted aesthetically, philosophically, politically and theologically. However, it should be thoroughly examined whether such interpretations are justified, and whether they influenced the analyses beforehand. Therefore, I increasingly prefer to focus on the compositional technique, its procedures, and its results. In this regard, much still has to be done. However, I always find it stimulating to ponder on the statements of people who are composers or have studied composition. An historical view of Bach's compositional technique cannot be expected, but the actual interest is based on competence for craft. In earlier times, in addition to Ferruccio Busoni, August Halm should be mentioned, later on René Leibowitz, Erwin Ratz, Philipp Herschkowitz, and Jurij Cholopov, who follow the tradition of Arnold Schönberg and Anton Webern in sharing their teleological approach; Sigismund Toduţă pursues a different trajectory.[43]

---

39 Laurence Dreyfus, *Bach and the Patterns of Invention* (Cambridge: Harvard University Press, 1996).

40 Michael Marissen, *The Social and Religious Designs of J. S. Bach's Brandenburg Concertos* (Princeton: Princeton University Press, 1995); Peter Schleuning, *Johann Sebastian Bach. Die Brandenburgischen Konzerte* (Kassel: Bärenreiter, 2003).

41 Peter Wollny, "Ein Quellenfund in Kiew. Unbekannte Kontrapunktstudien von Johann Sebastian und Wilhelm Friedemann Bach," LBB 5 (2002): 275–287; Walter Werbeck, "Bach und der Kontrapunkt. Neue Manuskript-Funde," BJ 89 (2003): 67–95; Christoph Wolff, "Johann Sebastian Bachs Regeln für den fünfstimmigen Satz," BJ 90 (2004): 87–99.

42 Klaus-Jürgen Sachs, "Die 'Anleitung…, auff allerhand Arth einen Choral durchzuführen,' als Paradigma der Lehre und der Satzkunst Johann Sebastian Bachs," AfM 37 (1980): 135–154.

43 René Leibowitz, "La dialectique structurelle de l'œuvre de J.-S. Bach, *La revue internationale de musique* 8 (1950): 55–67; Erwin Ratz, "Einführung in die musikalische Formenlehre. Über Formprinzipien in den Inventionen J. S. Bachs und ihre Bedeutung für die

414   *Ulrich Siegele*

Approaches to Composition-Technical Investigations

The outline of a methodology for investigating compositional technique is to be understood as an aid. It offers the coordinates that provide orientation to such investigations, and it communicates an idea of the richness of this research area, as well as of the great variety of approaches that lead to results. It is specifically not the aim to recommend one single method. On the contrary, it is important to sharpen the awareness that methods cannot be arbitrarily applied: they must be developed and controlled in relationship to a specific object. Therefore, I would like to plea for a decisive historization of the realm of methodology as well as for pluralism of methods. Methods are not universally valid dogmatic truths, which seek confirmation. They are tools for gaining insight into reality, and their validity will be proved by how much reality they disclose in each and every case—in the present context how much insight into the craft of a specific composer they bring to light. The more they achieve in this regard, the higher is the credit they may claim.

Only a general scheme can be offered for research on a musical text, since, depending on the formulation of the question and the intention of the investigation, a considerable range of strategies is at our disposal. In each special case, it is essential to secure the genre and the function in reality (or, as biblical studies put it, "Sitz im Leben," the setting in life), namely the location and the occasion at which the present piece of music is directed, as well as its specific liturgical or secular utilization. These prerequisites provide the general frame in which the compositional technique unfolds. In regard to vocal music, it is important to gain a clear understanding of the verbal text, namely of its origin, whether it is prose or poetry, of its syntactic structure, and, where pertinent, of the poetic genre, the number of syllables, the meter, and the rhyme scheme, the content and affect in general and in particular. If the words are in a foreign language, a careful translation is necessary, which for this purpose has to maintain closeness to the original language. A consultation with the score serves to obtain clarity regarding the performing forces, the key, and the musical meter. If a chorale melody, whether Gregorian chant or hymn, is involved, it is necessary to determine its origin, its

---

Kompositionstechnik Beethovens," (Vienna: Österreichischer Bundesverlag, 1951, 2nd and 3rd eds. Vienna: Universal-Edition, 1968 and 1973); Filip Gerškovi, "Ob odnoj invencii Ioganna Sebast'jana Bacha. K voprosu o proischoždenii klassi eskoj venskoj sonatnoj formy," *U ènye zapiski Tartuskogo Gosudarstvennogo Universiteta 467: Trudy po znakovym sistemam* 11 (Tartu, 1979): 44–70; ET "Philipp Herschkowitz: On an Invention of Johann Sebastian Bach [BWV 795]. To the Problem of the Genesis of Viennese Classical Sonata Form,"; Jurij Cholopov, "Koncertnaja forma u J. S. Bacha" *O Muzyke* (1974): 119–149; Juri Cholopow, "Prinzipien der musikalischen Formbildung bei J. S. Bach. Die Struktur der Bachschen Instrumentalfuge im Kontext der Entwicklung von Harmonik und Thematismus," *Beiträge zur Musikwissenschschaft* 25 (1983): 97–104; Sigismund Toduţă (with Hans Peter Türk and Vasile Herman), *Formele muzicale ale barocului în operele lui J. S. Bach*, 3 vols. (Bucharest: Editura muzical a uniunii compozitorilor, 1969–1978); Sigismund Toduta and Hans Peter Türk, "Bachs Inventionen und Sinfonien – Ästhetisch-stilistische Beiträge," *Bericht über die Wissenschaftliche Konferenz zum III. Internationalen Bach-Fest der DDR, Leipzig 1975*, eds. Werner Felix et al. (Leipzig: VEB Deutscher Verlag für Musik 1977), 189–204.

Compositional Technique   415

variants, and its mode or key (which does not always have to be in accordance with the key of the accompanying polyphonic texture).

The inspection of the musical text itself can be divided into two areas, namely the stratification in the vertical dimension of pitches and the succession in the horizontal dimension of time, or, in other words, the achievement of texture and the production of form. The goal of a composition-technical investigation, however, is not the separation of single features, but the interplay of all features, the interconnection of pitch and time, texture and form. Therefore, the division into these aspects does not intend to isolate objects, but rather to organize procedural steps. In any case, it has turned out to be practical to gain clarity regarding the considered categories and their interrelationships. This clarity, however, appears only step by step in the course of investigation; but when gained, it can be of use for checking and revising the results retroactively. Naturally, these categories must be developed anew for every object of investigation. Nevertheless, I consider it to be convenient to provide an example by describing the categories of formal construction which obtruded in the course of scrutinizing the fugues of both volumes of the WTC.[44]

These categories, divided into structural factors of the horizontal and vertical dimension, are related to each other pair by pair. Two times two categories designate basic facts of Bach's fugue writing. The determinations of these two pairs constitute not only every single fugue, they also constitute the ensemble of the two times twenty-four pieces: these determinations constitute the work plans of each of the two volumes of the WTC. The first pair names general determinations: particularly meter and key, which are neither limited to fugues and the WTC nor to Bach, although they unfold their effectiveness in the WTC as well. The second pair names specific determinations: particularly the number of entries and the number of voices, which are distinctive of fugues (and, in their peculiar use, possibly distinctive of Bach's fugues).

Two times two more categories unfold these basic facts. The first pair on the one hand concretizes the number of entries by assigning definite scale degrees, that way stating fundamental possibilities of scale degree order. On the other hand, it concretizes the number of voices by assigning definite registers, and thus stating fundamental possibilities of voice order (or part succession). Consequently, this pair connects the two structural factors of the horizontal and vertical dimension, the entries disposed in time being represented by the voices disposed in register. The second pair aims at the thematic structure. On the one hand, it refers to the relationship of thematic and nonthematic time. Thematic time means the presence of the subject as an entity and unity. Nonthematic time means the absence of the subject as an entity and unity. Certainly, this does not exclude the processing of thematic material within nonthematic time. On the other hand, the second pair refers to the range of the voices and the texture. Besides the aspect of time, the aspect of register also participates in the relationship of thematic and nonthematic areas, namely areas of range occupied by the subject, and

---

44 Ulrich Siegele, "Kategorien formaler Konstruktion in den Fugen des Wohltemperierten Klaviers," Rampe, ed., *Bach, Das Wohltemperierte Klavier I*, 331–333.

416   *Ulrich Siegele*

areas of range disregarded by the subject. Incidentally, the last item draws attention to the display of register in general, especially during the course of a piece.

The enclosed chart represents the categories of formal construction, namely the two pairs of the basic facts and the two pairs of their unfolding, which may be applied to the observation of the fugues of the WTC (see Table 16.1).

From an overall point of view, Bach seems to have fewer problems with the achievement of texture than with the production of form. He had mastered counterpoint early. However, he was occupied with form repeatedly and over a long period, understood as organization of the duration of the segments of a piece on the one hand, and the functional differentiation of these segments (for example in thematic and nonthematic time) on the other. This factual difference is reflected in the state of research. Aspects of texture are more easily comprehended and better ascertained than aspects of form, which seem to me more interesting, productive, and significant, besides being more challenging. Nevertheless, much has to be investigated and clarified in the area of texture as well. At least some topics should be mentioned, although it is impossible to deal with them in detail in the present context.

Bach regarded the condition of his compositional accomplishments as "intricate."[45] Remarks by contemporaries—supporters as well as critics—agree with Bach's self-characterization. The consequent application of Monteverdi's attainment of dividing texture into harmonic background and melodic foreground results in the intricacy of the obbligato parts. In fact, individual parts do not have to be contrapuntally coordinated each with each at any moment. From time to time, an individual part in itself can relate to the harmonic background, independently from the other parts.[46] That is the reason for the abundance of dissonances in Bach's texture, which settles so infrequently in a full consonance. This is also the reason why this texture is so difficult to understand, because it frequently

Table 16.1   Categories of formal construction in the Fugues of the Well-Tempered Clavier

	Structural Factors of the Horizontal Dimension	*Structural Factors of the Vertical Dimension*
General Determinations of the Work-Plan	Meter	Key
Specific Determinations of the Work-Plan	Number of Entries	Number of Voices
Representation of the Entries in Time through the Voices in Register	Degrees of Entries and Order of Degrees	Register of Entries and Order of Voices
Thematic Structure	Time, Thematic and Nonthematic	Range of Voices, Thematic and Nonthematic

45   Dok 1: 88 (No. 34); NBR 176 (No. 183).

46   Ulrich Siegele, "Cruda Amarilli, oder: Wie ist Monteverdis 'seconda pratica' satztechnisch zu verstehen?" *Claudio Monteverdi: vom Madrigal zur Melodie* (Munich: Edition Text + Kritik, 1994), 31–102.

demands the distinction of harmonic and nonharmonic tones: its comprehension depends on the recognition of the different significance of tones. Certainly, this condition makes the texture interesting, and secures its history of influence as well as the attention, which attracts us to this day. The possibility of this specific kind of texture did generally exist at Bach's time. But it is only he who turned it into a principle. By looking at the C major Fugue of the first volume of the WTC (BWV 846/2), one would find many, and also surprising, examples for one voice parting intervallically with the others and relating independently to the harmonic background. Especially within four-note groups, whose succession guarantees coherence, the significance of each single sixteenth note (semiquaver) can vary between consonance and dissonance, dependent on the context. At times, the correct continuation of a dissonant note results in a completely different environment than expected, because the contrapuntal progression had developed in another direction. There are many tough nuts to crack if the focus for once is not the thematic structure but the contrapuntal texture.

The Sinfonia (or three-part Invention) in F minor (BWV 795) is designed on a thematic texture of three subjects, with the descending chromatic fourth forming the first subject and the foundation. The harmonic model, connected with the descending chromatic fourth in this case, puts the relationship between consonance and dissonance into a peculiar twilight. Within the thematic texture, intervallic consonances can be chordal dissonances, and conversely intervallic dissonances chordal consonances. The three subjects must be interchangeable in consideration of the compositional device of invertible counterpoint, used in the Sinfonia. But the harmonic model prevents such interchanges since it includes triads. If one of the three obbligato voices takes up the fifth of the triad and turns to the bass, a six-four chord will emerge. Bach does not choose the cheap way of avoiding the fifth of a triad in the obbligato voices at all. He rather takes compositional countermeasures that place the six-four chords on an even (and therefore weak) eighth note (quaver). In addition, he lets one note of the offensive fourth enter as the resolution of a suspension at the end of a figure, whereas the other note enters as an upbeat in the beginning of a figure. Thus, for perception, both voices separate, dissociating the interval of the fourth. If the harmonies of a figured bass would be added to this texture of obbligato voices, the incorrect six-four chord would obtrude. Consequently, Bach composed a piece, to which it is not only redundant to add a figured bass, but simply impossible. This fact presents the occasion to consider the significance of figured bass in Bach's musical thinking. Did he seek to unequivocally complete his texture of obbligato voices, so a harmonic filling would be redundant? In this case, he would have retained the executed figured bass only when demanded by a convention or the direction of an ensemble, but would have dismissed otherwise.[47]

---

47 Ulrich Siegele, "Erfahrungen bei der Analyse Bachscher Musik," *Bachforschung und Bachinterpretation heute. Wissenschaftler und Praktiker im Dialog. Bericht über das Bachfest-Symposium 1978 der Philipps- Universität Marburg*, ed. Reinhold Brinkmann (Leipzig: Neue Bachgesellschaft, 1981), 137–145.

418   *Ulrich Siegele*

Bach's four-part chorale settings accomplished a double function from early on. Besides their utilization in liturgical vocal works, they also served the purpose of teaching, as Bach himself had used in his own teaching. Mastering four-part texture was the first demand, which was achieved in two stages. The elaboration of three upper voices to a given bass line was taught through figured bass realization. The elaboration of three lower voices to a given melody was taught through chorale melody harmonization. This second stage was divided into two steps. In the first place, Bach added a bass line to the melody, which resulted in the exercise of inserting two middle voices into a given texture of two outer voices. Then he provided the melody only; consequently, the responsibility of the student was extended to the addition of the bass line as well. This basic course, which pursued the positive goal of gaining command over the normative four-part texture, bypassed at first a training in the capacity of disposing musical form, since the formal design was given with both a figured bass line and a chorale melody. The contrapuntal lessons were followed by instruction in formal disposition, which was based on keyboard fugues. Therefore, it can be concluded that Bach considered keyboard fugues to be especially suitable from a didactic point of view. He supposedly started with two-part fugues because of their straightforward formal design, which was in any case simpler than in fugues with more parts. Maybe a reconstruction of Bach's compositional technique should follow his own paradigm and demonstrate the principles of counterpoint with regard to four-part chorales and the principles of form with regard to keyboard fugues.[48]

Soprano and bass form the primary framework in Bach's four-part chorale settings. In the first instance, the relationship between the added bass line and the given melody is intervallically determined. It is based—of course, outside of cadential areas—on the rules of invertible counterpoint. At least with respect to chorale settings, this relationship is not an absolute norm, but a commonly valid regulative which from case to case must give way to other aspects. Since both the voices do not actually exchange in chorale settings, here the use of invertible counterpoint is merely figurative. But nevertheless, the bass, within the bounds of the regulative, is written mostly in a way that it possesses the quality of a melody and therefore would be acceptable as an upper voice.[49] It should be examined whether a development can be detected in Bach's work regarding the intervallic relationship of the bass line to the melody, insofar as this relationship makes use of the rules of invertible counterpoint. The result should be compared with the

---

48 Dok 3: 289 (No. 803, figure 9).

49 Jutta Schmoll-Barthel, "Bachs Choralsatz – aus kontrapunktischer Perspektive betrachtet," *Festschrift Ulrich Siegele zum 60. Geburtstag*, ed. Rudolf Faber (Kassel: Bärenreiter, 1991), 87–104. On Bach's chorale settings, see also Robert L. Marshall, "How J. S. Bach Composed Four-part Chorales," MQ 56 (1970): 198–220; Walter Heimann, *Der Generalbaß-Satz und seine Rolle in Bachs Choral-Satz* (Munich: Katzbichler, 1973); Rudolf Bockholdt, "Zum vierstimmigen Choralsatz J. S. Bachs," *International Musicological Society, Report of the Eleventh Congress Copenhagen 1972* (Copenhagen: Hansen, 1974), 1: 277–287; Elmar Seidel, *Johann Sebastian Bachs Choralbearbeitungen in ihren Beziehungen zum Kantionalsatz* (Mainz: Schott, 1998); Thomas Daniel, *Der Choralsatz bei Bach und seinen Zeitgenossen. Eine historische Satzlehre* (Cologne: Dohr, 2000).

Compositional Technique 419

development of chorale setting, presented by Werner Breig. Furthermore, the general aspect might be traced, whether (and when) it is a principle of Bach's contrapuntal writing to base the texture on the two outer voices outlined in invertible counterpoint, whereas the middle voices (alto and tenor to begin with) are inserted into the primary framework of the outer voices. Finally, the specific technicality of this contrapuntal procedure is worthwhile to be investigated as well.

The two-part Inventions present an example for the dominating validity of invertible counterpoint as a regulative for Bach's texture outside of cadential areas. I understand these Inventions as an ideal transcription of a duet for two equal voices to a keyboard instrument with one manual.[50] Such a transcription demands—with respect to the technical possibilities of playing—the separation of two voices using one and the same register into two different registers. This is effectuated by transposing one of the two voices to the lower octave (besides occasional further octave transpositions in order to use the entire range of the instrument). The device of invertible counterpoint, governing the texture of the two-part Inventions, allows without much effort, to aesthetically experience the ideal model of two equal parts by rescinding the supposed octave transpositions; at times, small adjustments are necessary at the cadences. Correspondingly, the three-part Sinfonias can be understood as trios for two equal voices and bass. The transposition one octave down of one of the two upper voices in comparison with the ideal model proves, apart from the demands of the technical possibilities of playing, how important it was for Bach to equally cover the registers of the entire range of the keyboard instrument. Incidentally, the inner genealogy leads to an interpretation of the catch-phrase "cantabile Art im Spielen" (playing in a singing manner), which is recommended by Bach's title-page. Each voice is to be performed on the keyboard instrument as if performed by a melodic instrument. This sheds light on not just the increasing requirements in composition technique, but also in playing technique. The two-part Inventions demand independence of the two hands. The three-part Sinfonias in turn demand independence of the individual fingers of each hand (since one hand will have to take over two voices at once when all three voices are active).

The existence of multiple settings of the same chorale melody leads to another research approach. A comparison brings to view that in a group of such settings the framework texture between melody and bass completely or closely coincides, maybe not within the entire chorale, but within individual lines. At times, two such models are available for a single line. These models may be differently combined from one chorale setting to another. Moreover, select lines can be set specifically, in the light of the wording or of the connection with a preceding movement or also for other reasons. Seemingly, Bach, like any organist, had a chorale book in mind, which of course included variants. Predominantly, the memory referred to the framework texture of the outer voices, the middle voices being inserted and possibly varying from case to case. Concerning chorale setting, Bach used an identical procedure in his own activities as well as in his teaching.

---

50 Siegele, "Bachs vermischter Geschmack," 9.

420   *Ulrich Siegele*

Proportioning as a Compositional Tool

The perspective of compositional technique circumscribes the problem of musical form in a specific way: how is form being produced, and how is the production process being controlled? The answer I offer reads: by means of proportioning. At this very moment, I emphasize that, in the present context, proportioning is to be understood exclusively as a compositional tool to produce form, in particular to produce the durational segmentation and the functional differentiation in the course of a musical piece. The theological and philosophical, political and social implications of the procedure can rest for the time being. Proportioning as a tool does not intend to superimpose a sublime meaning, transcending the compositional fact; proportioning is satisfied with producing the compositional fact of form. A piece of music is not the means to represent proportioning. Rather, proportioning is a means to produce a piece of music. Despite all misinterpretations, I emphasize for a certainty: proportioning is not the end, but the means. The end of the means of proportioning is the accomplished composition. If proportioning were an end, namely the materialization of an idea (as it would be according to the Pythagorean-Platonic tradition), then each divergence of the materialization would mean an adulteration and the collapse of the system. As a tool, on the other hand, its validity is limited to a definite task. Once this task has been fulfilled, other tools are introduced for other tasks. They, in turn, have the right to change the proportioning in fulfilling their particular tasks. Proportioning can be compared with a geometric delineation in architecture. Its lines cannot be built simply because walls demand a certain thickness. Even though the measurements of the delineation have to be matched to the constructive necessities, they persist in constituting the foundation for the dimensions of the realized building.

The condition of form is the decisive question from a music-theoretical point of view. Is form only and at all times to be understood as a product of a thematic process, or do other procedures exist which produce form? Serial music in particular opened the perspective on alternatives to the thematic process. An understanding of form as a product of a thematic process implies a one-sided fixation on the thematic material: it defines form as a function of this material. But, according to the present approach, the thematic process does not at all remain detached. Rather, proportioning offers a formal frame for the material elaboration of the thematic process. Both interrelate and are able to flexibly react to each other. Proportioning does not determine the material elaboration, but it opens up a space where the elaboration can unfold on its own account. Certainly, proportioning obligates the elaboration to desist from arbitrariness, and to fill the available space with a coherent context, which is musically meaningful. Proportioning enables coherent context, but it does not guarantee it. Those interested may look at the interrelation of formal proportioning and material elaboration in the Aristotelian-scholastic tradition under the keyword *universalia in re*. In any case, the knowledge of proportioning enables valid statements concerning the formal condition of a piece, which cannot be achieved in any other way.

As an example for illustrating how proportioning functions, I choose the three-part fugue in A major of the second volume of the WTC (BWV 888/2). Its basic

Compositional Technique 421

pattern includes $4 \times 2 = 8$ entries, that is eight times the duration of the subject which lasts three half-measures, or eight thematic units. The same number of nonthematic units has been added. Consequently, the basic pattern balances thematic and nonthematic time. This balance, however, is unspecific due to its high degree of generality. Therefore, it demands individualization. This individualization is achieved by processing the basic pattern, at first by dividing the eight thematic units and the corresponding nonthematic units into two halves, then by augmenting the thematic units of the first half by two, the nonthematic units of the second half by one, and thus the whole piece by three units (see Table 16.2).

As a result of this process, the first half relates to the second half as the thematic time to the nonthematic time. Duration and thematic structure, segmentation and functional differentiation correspond. The durational and functional areas coincide: they exhibit conformity in proportion. Since this conforming proportioning concerns two layers, which are superimposed within the piece, it cannot be an unintentional effect of the compositional act. On the contrary, it requires a plan, or, to put it with poignancy, it results intentionally. This corroborates the conviction that proportioning is a compositional tool.

Each half of the scheme can be subdivided, thereby clarifying its inner structure (see Table 16.3). The three-part fugue in A major of the second volume of the WTC is not the only fugue that is based on this proportional pattern. The same pattern is valid for the four-part fugue in F minor of its first volume, except for the unit of the subject lasting three measures instead of three half-measures (BWV 857/2). A comparison of these two fugues proves the remarkable difference in material elaboration permitted of the same proportional pattern. Procedural steps referring to the lower level of measures or half-measures continue the procedural steps referring to the higher level of the duration of the subject, namely the thematic units—the lower level implying less structural but more pragmatic weight. Concerning the fugue in A major, a nonthematic half-measure of the

Table 16.2 Fugue in A major, *WTC* II (BWV 888/2): Basic Proportional Pattern and its Individualization

	1ˢᵗ Half	*2ⁿᵈ Half*	*Sums*
Thematic	4+2	4	8+2
Nonthematic	4	4+1	8+1
Sums	8+2	8+1	16+3

Table 16.3 Fugue in A major, *WTC* II (BWV 888/2): Inner Structure of the Halves

	1ˢᵗ Half		*2ⁿᵈ Half*		*Sums*
	1ˢᵗ Subdivision	*2ⁿᵈ Subdivision*	*1ˢᵗ Subdivision*	*2ⁿᵈ Subdivision*	
Thematic	4	0+2	2	2	8+2
Nonthematic	4–2	0+2	2+1	2	8+1
Sums	8–2	0+4	4+1	4	16+3

422 *Ulrich Siegele*

first subdivision of the first half is given to its second subdivision. The last half-measure with the final of the concluding cadence completes the eighth (quaver) rest of the beginning, and therefore will not be counted. Incidentally, the proportioning and the procedure of processing it is by no means a question of arithmetic. On the contrary, numbers are a shorthand notation of musical facts, and they are trusted to be understood this way. Within the formal frame, the material elaboration of this fugue performs a twofold development, which can be understood as an intensification, on the one hand in the area of the thematic entries by the varying contrapuntal furnishing, on the other hand in the area of nonthematic time by processing the last half-measure of the subject, using changing devices.

A second example is the basic proportional pattern of the six-part Ricercar of the Musical Offering (BWV 1079). The values in the chart that follows refer to measures containing four half notes (minims). The last measure of the piece, measure 103, will not be considered from the aspect of proportioning, since the final of the subject always exceeds its proportional length of four measures. Therefore, the concluding note of the last thematic entry, which terminates the piece, necessitates its special measure for pragmatic reasons; but in fact, it is a structural surplus (see Table 16.4).

Apart from the sums of the thematic and nonthematic areas, these numbers belong to an excerpt of the later so-called Fibonacci series, multiplied by three. I am aware that with this statement I incur the judgment of Ruth Tatlow.[51] However, I have only respected the segmental and functional differentiation Bach has applied to the piece, and have counted and summed up the measures. The compositional goal, which Bach was pursuing with this series of numbers, is obvious. The subject, lasting four measures of four half notes (minims), enters, according to the number of voices, six times in each of the two parts. The resulting periodicity of the thematic entries is balanced by the aperiodicity of the nonthematic segments. As otherwise, it would be possible to achieve this aperiodicity of the nonthematic segments based on the equal distribution of thematic and nonthematic time, but only in a secondary way. The so-called Fibonacci series, however, exhibits the necessary requirements in a primary way. It combines the (even continual) proportioning with aperiodicity, and it does this with integer numbers, corresponding to whole measures as an indispensable prerequisite for the possibility of managing a proportion compositionally. In the light of this obvious goal, questions as to how Bach knew of the so-called Fibonacci series, what he called it, and whether or not

Table 16.4 Six-part Ricercar of the Musical Offering (BWV 1079/2): Basic Proportional Patterns

	1st Part	*2nd Part*	*Sums*
Thematic	24	24	48
Nonthematic	15	39	54
Sums	39	63	102

51 Ruth Tatlow, "The Use and Abuse of Fibonacci Numbers and the Golden Section in Musicology Today," *Understanding Bach* 1 (2006): 69–85.

Compositional Technique   423

he connected any connotations or philosophical interpretations to it, are rendered irrelevant. Bach was not a historian of mathematics, but a composer, and what mattered to him was the compositional benefit of this number series. It also enabled the formation of two parts with a corresponding number of thematic entries, the nonthematic time falling behind the thematic time in the first part and surpassing it in the second part. The proportioning of the six-part Ricercar in line with the so-called Fibonacci series, which I observed and mentioned for the first time some thirty years ago, did not happen by chance, but was designed on purpose.[52]

Concerning the fugues of the WTC, it surprises me how rarely people are disturbed by the fact that the subject of so many fugues (half of them in each volume) does not undergo any contrapuntal procedures. Since Marpurg, contrapuntal devices had been accepted as a common characteristic of a good fugue. Are the fugues belonging to the other half therefore bad fugues? Joseph Groocock, thanks to his systematic approach, makes a point of this widely unrecognized and even unknown problem. He perceives the first two fugues of the first volume as representatives of two types, the first type being a stretto fugue without episodes, the second type being an episodic fugue without strettos. Most of the fugues of the two volumes tend towards the one or the other type. However, the two principles of stretto and episode do not oppose each other, as they blend in some fugues. David Ledbetter, a student of Groocock's, refers to Marpurg's distinction of *fuga obligata* and *fuga libera* when describing both types (Marpurg, however, having directed his distinction towards Bach and Handel). Ledbetter also connects the *fuga libera* with the ritornello form of the concerto originating in Vivaldi.[53]

My suggestion for a solution follows a similar path. Bach cultivated two different types of fugue. One was the traditional kind. This kind of fugue employs a contrapuntal definition of its formal segments. Its characteristics include augmentation

---

52 Concerning the six-part Ricercar, see: Ulrich Siegele, "Erfahrungen bei der Analyse Bachscher Musik," 137–145; Ulrich Siegele, "Bachs Ort in Orthodoxie und Aufklärung," MuK 51 (1981): 3–14; Ulrich Siegele, *Bachs theologischer Formbegriff und das Duett F-Dur. Ein Vortrag* (Stuttgart: Hänssler, 1978), ET (abridged) by Alfred Clayton, "Bach's Theological Concept of Form and the F Major Duet, *Music Analysis* 11/ 2–3 (1992): 245–278; Ulrich Siegele, "Schöpfungs- und Gesellschaftsordnung in Bachs Musik," *Im Gespräch: der Mensch. Ein interdisziplinärer Dialog: Joseph Möller zum 65. Geburtstag*, ed. Heribert Gauly et al. (Düsseldorf: Patmos, 1981), 276–285. For discussions concerning proportioning in Monteverdi, see Siegele, "Cruda Amarilli," 31–102; for proportioning in Schütz, see Ulrich Siegele, "Musik als Zeugnis der Auslegungsgeschichte: Heinrich Schützens Motette 'Die mit Tränen säen' aus der *Geistlichen Chormusik*," *Schütz-Jahrbuch* 4–5 (1982/83): 50–56: for proportioning in Beethoven, see Ulrich Siegele, *Beethoven: Formale Strategien der späten Quartette* (Munich: Edition Text + Kritik, 1990), and Ulrich Siegele, "Klaviersonate C-Dur 'Waldsteinsonate' Op. 53 (zusammen mit dem Andante favori F-Dur WoO 57)," *Beethoven. Interpretationen seiner Werke* I, ed. Albrecht Riethmüller, et al. (Laaber: Laaber, 1994), 370–379.

53 Groocock, *Fugal Composition*, 2; Ledbetter, *Bach's Well-tempered Clavier*, 101–103; Dahlhaus, "Bachs konzertante Fugen," 45–72. Concerning the following paragraphs, see Siegele, "Kategorien formaler Konstruktion," 462–471, and Ulrich Siegele, "Von zwei Kulturen der Fuge: Ritornellform und kontrapunktische Definition im Wohltemperierten Klavier von J. S. Bach," *Musik & Ästhetik* 10/40 (October 2006): 63–69.

424   *Ulrich Siegele*

or diminution of the subject, stretto, contrapuntal addition of a certain number of other voices in certain note values and certain registers, also with certain figures, and so forth. The other kind resulted from Bach's occupation with ritornello form, but earlier than Vivaldi's. This occupation made Bach aware of the imperfection of the treatment of keys and episodes in fugues, especially for keyboard instruments. Therefore, he took advantage of the organizational procedures he found in the ritornello form by expanding the scale degree order of the thematic entries beyond *dux* and *comes*, and by aiming at a balanced relationship of thematic and nonthematic time. He regarded thematic entries as ritornellos, nonthematic segments as episodes, and he usually assigned harmonic stations to the thematic entries, and modulations to the nonthematic segments. By doing so, proportioning became part of the fugue, since, as far as I can see, proportioning originated in arias and especially in concertos, where it could be employed in a freer and therefore more elaborate way. By modeling fugue in accordance with ritornello form, Bach gave fugue a form, which (except for the polyphony of the texture) was independent from contrapuntal procedures, as far as they concern the subject. This is Bach's specific contribution to the theory and practice of fugue. It probably included the didactic benefit of teaching the basics of ritornello form by means of keyboard fugue.

However, Bach did not substitute the contrapuntally defined fugue by the ritornello fugue. He let both kinds coexist and manifested their equal value by assigning each kind one half of the fugues in both volumes of the WTC. But the contrapuntally defined fugue took over characteristics of the ritornello fugue, namely the balanced relationship of episodes and the harmonic disposition, although these never became fully integrated. On the other hand, the ritornello fugue adopted contrapuntal procedures, which did not affect the subject but the episodes. The two cultures of the contrapuntally defined fugue and the ritornello fugue approached each other, but never merged completely. Finally, Bach returned to the contrapuntal definition in the Art of Fugue—now, however, not concerning the segments of a single fugue, but concerning the sequence of self-contained fugues. He had probably sensed that in the long run it would not be the ritornello form but rather contrapuntal workmanship that would continue.

The fugue in C major of the first volume of the WTC (BWV 846/2), however, shows no influence of the ritornello form, except maybe for the cadence on the sixth scale degree in the middle of the piece. At any rate, it is conceived without episodes, and in this sense it is unique. At the beginning of the work, Bach presents the tradition of the contrapuntally defined fugue without any compromise, in order to oppose it programmatically with his new paradigm of a ritornello fugue through the next fugue in C minor (BWV 847/2). Without any regard to its uniqueness, the fugue in C major is used as a representative model of a Bach fugue over and over again. At times, far-reaching conclusions are being drawn, which however can claim only limited validity because of the unique status of the specimen. The opinion has been voiced that the succession of the contrapuntal devices is not coherent, but sauntering around in a circle. Even if this should be true in the case of the present fugue, the opinion can be confronted with other fugues, which in this regard follow a straight, arrow-like line.

Compositional Technique   425

In a study on the fugue in C minor of the first volume of the WTC, I have undertaken to represent the structural layers of the piece as genetic stages, and have actually elaborated these stages for opening up the structural layering to the aesthetic perception in this special case.[54] Later, the least conspicuous, if not problematic, form of the three-part Ricercar of the Musical Offering (BWV 1079/1), which is a ritornello fugue just like the six-part Ricercar, induced me to investigate how the real situation, which gave rise to a musical piece, can influence its compositional outcome. I envisage the three-part Ricercar as a conversation between Bach and Frederick II, king in Prussia, about their musical and social interrelationship. Bach, in this artistic dialogue, claims equality of aesthetic and political action, similar to Beethoven with his Eroica Symphony.[55]

In denoting the harmonic disposition of the thematic entries, I prefer numbers peculiar to the scale degree. It is often possible to interpret the order of degrees functionally, especially when the *dux* on the first and the *comes* on the fifth scale degrees are supplemented by the two relative keys with identical scales, but changing mode. However, there are always degree successions which can only be understood by the notion of modality. Therefore, I advocate the neutral designation by scale degrees, which leaves a functional interpretation to discretion, but does not exact it automatically. Incidentally, it is my opinion that with regard to harmonic progressions in Bach's music, at least in his fugues, the dominant of the dominant of a key should be named differently. It rather concerns one of the many appearances of the fourth scale degree (in functional interpretation the subdominant), in this case by raising the fundamental note and substituting the interval of the fifth by the interval of the sixth. Furthermore, the third scale degree, if not accompanied by the sixth scale degree in major or the seventh scale degree in minor, should not be understood as relative of the dominant or the tonic respectively, but, as current in English (but also in Schönberg's) terminology, as mediant, namely as the triad based on the middle note of the tonic triad, and the third in the order of precedence, following the tonic and the dominant.

Sequence building, particularly the sequence of falling fifths, demands a special interest, this being true not only regarding fugues, but also in general. On the one hand, the sequence of falling fifths, especially when forming a complete circle, serves the representation of a key, in which case time passes, without harmonic progression, the corresponding initial and final degrees, however, changing from a weak to a strong or from a strong to a weak position. On the other hand, the sequence of falling fifths serves as a means of modulation if one (or rarely several) changes of the basic scale take place in its course.

54 Ulrich Siegele, "Zur Analyse der Fuge c-Moll aus dem ersten Teil des Wohltemperierten Klaviers," *Cöthener Bach-Hefte* 4 (1986): 101–136; ET by Don O. Franklin, "The Four Conceptual Stages of the Fugue in C Minor, WTC I," *Bach Studies* [1], ed. Don O. Franklin, (Cambridge: Cambridge University Press, 1989), 197–224.
55 Ulrich Siegele, "Technik des Komponisten vor der Größe des Herrschers. Das dreistimmige Ricercar aus dem 'Musikalischen Opfer' von J. S. Bach, *Musik als Klangrede: Festschrift Günter Fleischhauer*, ed. Wolfgang Ruf (Cologne: Böhlau, 2001), 156–193.

426   *Ulrich Siegele*

Apart from some insignificant exceptions, measure numbers belong to the many and diverse ordering factors of structured arrangements comprising combinations of two or more movements, especially in instrumental music, but also in the B minor Mass. The concern, however, is not primarily the measure numbers of single, individual pieces, but the sums, which develop from groups of pieces, as well as averages which can be drawn from these sums. The meaning of these numbers becomes clear when they are distributed into their structural components, namely in basic numbers as well as in large or structural and small or pragmatic modifications. Starting with the foundation of the basic numbers, modifications allow a sensible reaction to composition-technical as well as external requirements. Therefore, measure numbers are not an abstract, irrevocable precondition. They are rather a flexible technical aid and an instrument of control. They provide information about two compositional parameters: the sum total according to which a structured arrangement is contrived, and the imagined standard values on which the combinations of movements as well as single pieces, possibly of different kind, are based.

A specific aspect of this procedure is that measure numbers establish a connection to the general measurement of time, with the common index of 162 measures of any meter corresponding to 7½ minutes (formerly a common subdivision value of time). This correspondence relates neither to the actual duration of performance, nor to the composed duration. It should rather be seen as the dispositional duration which serves as an orientation for the outline. A frequently chosen basic value is 1944 measures, which aim at 90 minutes. Normative notions regarding the extent of structured arrangements, combinations or pairs of movements, and single movements as well shaped the frame in which Bach's compositional activities unfolded. These investigations also enable a new view on the genesis and the intended final state of the Art of Fugue. Incidentally, such use of measure numbers can be shown for other composers as well.[56] While my interest in the significance of measure

---

56 Ulrich Siegele, "Taktzahlen als Ordnungsfaktor in Suiten- und Sonatensammlungen von J. S. Bach. Mit einem Anhang zu den Kanonischen Veränderungen über *Vom Himmel hoch*, AfMw 63 (2006): 215–240; Ulrich Siegele, "Taktzahlen als Schlüssel zur Ordnung der Klavierübung III von J. S. Bach. Ein Vorschlag für die Aufführung," MuK 76 (2006): 344–351; Ulrich Siegele, "Some Observations on the Formal Design of Bach's B-minor Mass, *Exploring Bach's B-Minor Mass*, eds. Yo Tomita, Robin A. Leaver, and Jan Smaczny (Cambridge: Cambridge University Press, 2013),107–124; Ulrich Siegele, "Taktzahlen der Präludien und Fugen in Sammlungen mit Tastenmusik von J. S. Bach, *Bach und die deutsche Tradition des Komponierens: Wirklichkeit und Ideologie, Festschrift Martin Geck zum 70. Geburtstag*, eds. Reinmar Emans and Wolfram Steinbeck (Dortmund: Klangfarben, 2009), 77–107; Ulrich Siegele, "Zum Aufbau von Telemanns Passionsoratorium *Seliges Erwägen*," *Georg Philipp Telemanns Passionsoratorium 'Seliges Erwägen' zwischen lutherischer Orthodoxie und Aufklärung: Theologie und Musikwissenschaft im Gespräch*, ed. Martina Falletta et al. (Frankfurt: Haag & Herchen, 2005), 125–155; Ulrich Siegele, "Johann Ulrich Steigleders 'Ricercar Tabulatura' (1624) als Kunstbuch. Eine Einführung in Formprinzipien imitatorischer Tastenmusik," *Schütz-Jahrbuch* 28 (2006): 157–206 (NB on p. 205, line 1, the two figures should be changed into 210 and 105); Ulrich Siegele, Johann Ulrich Steigleders Vaterunser-Variationen (1626/27). Eine Kunst der organistischen Choralbearbeitung im Spannungsfeld zwischen ober- und niederdeutscher Tradition (Stuttgart: Cornetto, 2012); Ulrich Siegele, "Wie unvollständig ist Bachs 'Kunst der Fuge'?" *Bericht über die Wissenschaftliche Konferenz zum V. Internationalen Bachfest der DDR in Verbindung mit dem 60. Bachfest der Neuen Bachgesellschaft Leipzig*

Compositional Technique 427

numbers is directed at the outline of a structured arrangement and its components, Ruth Tatlow in her "Theory of Proportional Parallelism" is concerned with the final result of the compositional process. Numerical correspondences within the succession of movements, within collections and even among different collections tend towards round numbers and simple proportions of measures.[57]

Time Structure

In conclusion, I would like to discuss an area of compositional technique which on the one hand leads into the inner condition of Bach's music (maybe more than any other area), but on the other hand is highly controversial: the structure of time. Methodically, the investigation originates in characteristics such as meter, layering of note values in upper, middle and fundamental voices, rhythm of changing harmonies and meter of textual declamation in relationship to the framework of musical meter. A classification of Bach's compositional output in consideration of these characteristics creates a synoptic view of movement types. Apart from their chronological layering, these characteristics are marked more distinctly in ensemble music; in soloistic music, however, they are more individualized. Therefore, the success of an investigation depends mainly on the correct diagnosis of the movement types, for whose differentiation analytical tools are yet to be developed, for the most part. Already a preliminary inspection reveals the compositional connection of such types, for example the connection of the recitative with the chorale, where two declamatory units of the recitative (namely two eighth notes [quavers]) usually equal one declamatory unit of the chorale (namely one quarter note [crotchet]). Or the connection of the chorale with the Siciliana and the Pastorale, if the declamatory unit of a quarter note (crotchet) in the chorale is divided into three eighth notes (quavers) instead of two and thus notated as a dotted quarter note (crotchet). The task consists in combining such particular connections to a comprehensive network, where each movement type occupies a definite place and each piece of the compositional output participates in a specific movement type.

At this point, it seems reasonable to assign a certain tempo to each movement type. In this sense, the concern is the composed tempo. Tempo is not unconditionally submitted to the competence of performance. Rather, it is an indispensable quality of composition and therefore a criterion for performance, just as much as the other notated parameters. Tempo as an integral constituent of composition is a representative signature for the sum of all the structural time characteristics, essential to a defined movement type. Inasmuch, my approach is related to Rudolf Kolisch's

---

1985, ed. Winfried Hoffmann and Armin Schneiderheinze (Leipzig: VEB Deutscher Verlag für Musik, 1988), 219–225.

57 Ruth Tatlow, "Bach's Parallel Proportions and the Qualities of the Authentic Bachian Collection," *Bach oder nicht Bach? Bericht über das 5. Dortmunder Bach-Symposion 2004*, eds. Reinmar Emans and Martin Geck (Dortmund: Klangfarben, 2009), 135–156; Ruth Tatlow, "Parallel Proportions, Numerical Structures and *Harmonie* in Bach's Autograph Score," Tomita, Leaver, Smaczny, eds., *Exploring Bach's B-minor Mass*,142–162; Ruth Tatlow, *Bach's Numbers: Compositional Proportion and Significance* (Cambridge: Cambridge University Press, 2016).

428   *Ulrich Siegele*

investigations into tempo and character in Beethoven's music around seventy years ago; Erwin Bodky's proposals regarding tempi in Bach's keyboard music are a result of similar considerations.[58] The interrelationship between tempo and movement types, rooted in the characteristics of time structure, results in the fact that tempo is ordered in types, namely in specific degrees, as well. These tempo degrees are related to each other proportionally, justified by the network of movement types.

The decided concern in types is due to a change in the comprehension of time. The younger concept of time determines the duration of the unit, the beat. It adds beat units to measures, and measures to theoretically infinite musical pieces. Its symbol is the pendulum clock, its instrument the metronome. The older concept determines the overall duration of time, limited by the musical piece itself, the special occasion, or in general (and conforms to the original sense of the word, which is documented in the antonym of "time and eternity"). It divides this finite time into the number of contained measures. Its symbol is the hourglass. The younger kind is able to change the tempo continuously, at least in imagination (although the scale of the metronome divides the minute step by step). The older kind changes the tempo in proportional degrees. It is tied to the cycle of the liturgical year, to reiteration and model. The younger kind relates to the secularized progress, unexpected newness, the individual and the original genius.[59]

This interpretation has been touched by thoughts Karol Berger expressed in a publication with the title *Bach's Cycle, Mozart's Arrow.*[60] It seems, however, that the change in the comprehension of time, though prepared long ago, was only completed at the end of the early modern period, taking place in the span between the French Revolution in 1789 and the Viennese Congress in 1814–1815. This span also included the end of the old German Empire. As late as 1802, Heinrich Christoph Koch (based on Jean-Jacques Rousseau, and differing from Johann Joachim Quantz's four-degree scale) was able to order tempi gradually in five principal types, sufficient for the correct motion of each musical piece without many noticeable deviations.[61] And even the metronome markings which Beethoven added in 1817 to his Eroica Symphony—the work written during the decline of the old Empire

---

58   Rudolf Kolisch, "Tempo and Character in Beethoven's Music," MQ 29 (1943):169–187 and 291–312; Rudolf Kolisch, *Tempo und Charakter in Beethovens Musik* (Munich: Edition Text + Kritik, 1992); Rudolf Kolisch, "Tempo and Character in Beethoven's Music," MQ 77 (1993): 90–131 and 268–342; Erwin Bodky, *The Interpretation of Bach's Keyboard Works* (Cambridge: Harvard University Press, 1960).

59   Ulrich Siegele, "Vortrag," MGG 14: cols. 16–31. For a another approach to questions of tempo and proportion, see the articles of Don O. Franklin, for example: Aspekte von Proportion und Dimension in Johann Sebastian Bachs Missa von 1733," LBB (2000): 235–272; "Composing in Time: Bach's Temporal Design for the Goldberg Variations," *Bach Studies from Dublin*, eds. Anne Leahy and Yo Tomita (Dublin: Four Courts, 2004), 103–128.

60   Karol Berger, *Bach's Cycle, Mozart's Arrow: An Essay on the Origins of Musical Modernity* (Berkeley: University of California Press, 2007).

61   Heinrich Christoph Koch, *Musikalisches Lexikon* (Offenbach: André, 1802), q.v. "Zeitmaaß," 1755 et seq., and "Adagio," 62–66; Ulrich Siegele, "La Cadence est une qualité de la bonne Musique," *Studies in Renaissance and Baroque Music in Honor of Arthur Mendel* (Kassel: Bärenreiter, 1974), 124–135.

and, by its compositional stature, programmatically enunciated the revolutionary claim of the symphonic genre appertaining to the high style—are still proportionally organized. The dotted half notes (minims) of the first movement equal 60, the eighth notes (quavers) of the second movement 80, the dotted half notes (minims) of the third movement 116, and the half notes (minims) of the fourth movement 76, turning later to eighth notes (quavers) equaling 108, and finally to quarter notes (crotchets) equaling 116. It should be allowed, in accordance with Koch, to view 116 as a minimal deviation from 120, and 76 as a minimal deviation from 80. Only 108 could be assessed as a noticeable retardation of 120. Looking at the numbers this way, the metronome markings of 60, 80, and 120 relate to each other as 3 : 4 : 6. (Incidentally, the first movement of the symphony belongs to the same movement type and to the same tempo degree as the first movement of Bach's fourth Brandenburg Concerto (BWV 1049/1), except that Beethoven notates note values one degree larger than Bach.) Only in 1826, in the middle of the Restoration Period, Beethoven writes: "We are hardly able to have ordinary tempi (*"tempi ordinarij"*— note the plural) any longer, since one has to follow the ideas of the freer genius."[62] Together with the movement types, the tempo types have disappeared.

This change is the reason why it is so difficult for us, who stand on the other side of the line, to understand the time structure of Bach's music, to make sense of it, and to accept it. The widespread lack of comprehension of such investigations into the time structure of Bach's music and its composed tempo is a result of this difficulty. The reluctance is understandable, since the issue achieves—to use fashionable terms—a deconstruction in the original sense of the notion, namely a reversal of a binary hierarchic relationship, in this case of the relationship of performance and composition. A deep fear seems to be involved as well, the fear that a definition of some few tempo degrees will lead to impoverishment. However, this fear misunderstands the fact that a different mechanism of tempo determination is inherent in a different structure of time. The fixed degrees of tempo enable the composer to differentiate the perception of the same tempo degree to a considerable extent by means of different densities of texture, namely the changing number and kind of its events. The composer himself has authority to determine the perception of a specific tempo degree. He does not have to leave the choice of tempo to the performer, but can establish the nuances in the composition himself. The fixed degrees of tempo are the prerequisite for the compositional stylization of the movement types—so to speak, the foil to which stylization has to be related. Only on this basis can the stylization be recognized and become evident in performance. The remark that Bach usually performed his own pieces at a rather lively tempo makes sense in this context.[63] He probably adhered accurately to the fixed degrees of tempo, but the high activity and the high density of his music evoked the impression of a tempo that was faster than normal.

---

62 Ludwig van Beethoven, *Briefwechsel Gesamtausgabe 6: 1825–1827*, ed. Sieghard Brandenburg (Munich: Henle, 1996), 330 (No. 2244); Emily Anderson, ed. *The Letters of Beethoven* 3 (London: Macmillan, 1961), 1325 (No. 1545).

63 Dok 7: 30 (Forkel); NBR 436; also Dok 3: 87 (No. 666); NBR 305–306 (No. 306).

430   *Ulrich Siegele*

Incidentally, since the topic of this essay is compositional technique, a discussion of how this tempo of composition is to be transferred to practical performance is not necessary, especially since the tradition of reception is legitimate on its own, and each performance is responsible for determining its place between the unattainable limits of historicity and actuality. But I am skeptical of the common practice to slow down the tempo if the density increases, and to speed it up if the density decreases, and in that way to deviate from the tempo degree attached to a movement type. Thus, the characteristic differences are leveled off: they disappear, they blur, and they become unrecognizable. However, historical tempi can lead to new and unexpected realizations of musical pieces, as can the use of period instruments, the number of singers and players, tunings, as well as playing and singing techniques.

Four different domains contribute their traditions of genre with the inherent traditions of tempo to Bach's work: the domain of liturgical and chorale music, the domain of motet and figural music, the domain of the concerto, and the domain of dances. Presumably, each of those four domains (especially the domain of dances) possessed a specific tradition of movement and tempo types, which were not easily compatible. In Bach's work, however, these different traditions were combined into a consistent system. This demanded a process of adaptation on all sides, except perhaps for the domain of liturgical and chorale music. At the same time, it created the indispensable prerequisite for the blending of genres which is so characteristic for Bach's work.

As far as I can see, this tempo system is based on a scale of six degrees, the terms of which relate to each other in the alternating ratios of the intervals of the fifth and the fourth, namely, 2 : 3 : 4 : 6 : 8 : 12. For the absolute fixation of this proportional scale, I refer to Michael Praetorius regarding the term 3 and to Lorenz Christoph Mizler regarding the term 4, raising their respective values of 80 and 105 measures in 7½ minutes (or half a quarter hour) to 81 and 108 measures in order to exactly depict the ratio of 3 : 4.[64] The origin of the scale is the term 4, whose 108 measures in 7½ minutes result in a metronome marking of 57.6 beats per minute. I designate this principal value of the scale, from which the proportional markings of the other terms result, with p (and no one should be offended that here, where tempo degrees of single pieces are concerned, I use another absolute fixation than earlier in this essay, where comprehensive values for structured arrangements are concerned). Experience tells us even today that tempo degrees could be achieved exactly with some practice, so much the more as no systematic possibility to find a tempo existed outside of these defined degrees. By the way, tempo degrees always refer to the basic tempo; they do not limit the variety of the performance.

Three of the terms are labeled as basic values of a domain, the term 3 for the liturgical and chorale music, the term 4 for the motet and figural music, and the

---

64 Michael Praetorius, *Syntagma musicum tomus tertius* (Wolfenbüttel: Holwein 1619; facsimile,Kassel: Bäreneiter, 1954) 87–88, ET *Syntagma Musicum III*, trans. and ed. Jeffery Kite-Powell (Oxford: Oxford University Press, 2004), 100; Lorenz Christoph Mizler, *Musikalische Bibliothek* (Leipzig: Mizler, 1739–1754; reprint, Hilversum: Knuf, 1966), 4/1: 108 et seq. (the figure "400" on page 109, line 4, is a paleographically understandable misprint instead of the correct figure "490").

Compositional Technique 431

term 6 for the concerto, each presupposing common 4/4 meter. Understandably, such a general basic value cannot be assigned to the domain of dances. The liturgical and chorale domain is self-contained and includes, besides chorale and recitative, also the turbae of the oratorical works; at least as long as they are marked with 4/4 meter, these turbae have to be understood (and performed) as recitatives expanded to polyphony. The motet and figural domain takes advantage of the possibilities of proportional relationships by equalizing measures of different meter (or its subdivisions) on the one hand, and note values on the other. The concerto chooses among the available degrees of tempo, whereas each dance type remains attached to a characteristic tempo type. Incidentally, examples exist that, in a successive combination of movements, the proportionality of tempo degrees results in a proportionality of duration—at times even in the orientation towards round values of the general time measurement. These interrelationships demand special consideration. The examples regarding these interrelationships are found in concertos, and likewise in cantatas: besides the oratorical works, the cantatas exhibit the most elaborate dispositions in Bach's compositional output, displayed on manifold layers. Here and elsewhere, structured time joins as an equally entitled ordering factor the forms of text and music (particularly the chorale as the specific formal element of Lutheran church music), keys and scoring (comprising the vocal and instrumental forces).[65] The chart that follows provides a general view of the system of time structure, contained in and derived from Bach's music. It should be added that the subdivision of a quarter note (crotchet) of the term 6 into eight thirty-seconds (demisemiquavers), and the subdivision of an eighth note (quaver) of the term 12 into four thirty-seconds (demisemiquavers), as it is common in soloistic zones of Bach's music, result in 11.52 beats per second, thus reaching the limit of acoustic and physiological possibilities (see Table 16.5).

A few examples mainly taken from dance movements for keyboard instruments—the English Suites (E), the French Suites (F) along with the two Suites in A minor and E-flat major, the Partitas (P), and the French Overture—illustrate how the system of time structure operates. I disregard external statements by theorists and rely exclusively on the internal statements of Bach's

---

65 Ulrich Siegele, "Proportionierung als kompositorisches Arbeitsinstrument in Konzerten J. S. Bachs," *Bachs Orchesterwerke. Bericht über das 1. Dortmunder Bach-Symposion 1996*, ed. Martin Geck (Witten: Klangfarben, 1997), 159–171; and Siegele, "Planungsverfahren in Kantaten J. S. Bachs." See also the earlier studies: Ulrich Siegele, "Bemerkungen zu Bachs Motetten," BJ 49 (1962): 33–57; Ulrich Siegele, "Zur Verbindung von Präludium und Fuge bei J. S. Bach," *Bericht über den internationalen musikwissenschaftlichen Kongreß Kassel 1962* (Kassel: Bärenreiter, 1963), 164–167; Ulrich Siegele, "Von Bachschen Modellen und Zeitarten," *Festschrift Walter Gerstenberg zum 60. Geburtstag: im Namen seiner Schüler*, eds. Georg von Dadelsen and Andreas Holschneider (Wolfenbüttel: Möseler, 1964), 162–165; Ulrich Siegele, "Bachs Motette 'Jesu, meine Freude.' Protokoll einer Aufführung," MuK 39 (1969): 170–183. Since I wrote the present essay in summer 2012, two more extensive studies of tempo and duration in Bach's music have been published: Ulrich Siegele, *Johann Sebastian Bach komponiert Zeit. Tempo und Dauer in seiner Musik*, vol. 1: *Grundlegung und Goldberg-Variationen*, and vol 2: *Johannes- und Matthäus-Passion* (Hamburg: Tradition, 2014 and 2016).

432   *Ulrich Siegele*

Table 16.5 The System of Time Structure in Bach's Music

Term of the Scale	Ratio of the Degree	Metronome Marking	Basic Value of a Domain
12	Threefold (= 3p)	172.8	
8	Twofold (= 2p)	115.2	
6	Three Halves (= 3/2p)	86.4	Concerto
4	The Principal Value (= p)	57.6	Motet and Figural
3	Three Quarters (= 3/4p)	43.2	Liturgical and Chorale
2	The Half (= 1/2p)	28.8	

music, true to the composition-technical approach. In addition to tempo degree, the individual dance types are defined by meter. In German, the fixed combination of tempo degree and meter can be named "Zeitart" (time species), analogous to "Tonart" (key species). Time species is a primary concept in shaping the horizontal dimension, as key species is a primary concept in shaping the vertical dimension.

Many dance types exhibit proper tempo degrees in proper meters: the Allemande the degree p in quadruple meter; the Sarabande the same degree p, yet in triple meter; the Gavotte and the Bourrée the degree 3/2p in duple meter; the Menuet (also the Burlesca and the Polonaise) the degree 2p in triple meter; the Passepied (also the Rondeaux of Partita II) the degree 3p in triple meter; Air or Aria, Capriccio, Scherzo, and Echo the degree 3/2p, in either quadruple or duple meter. Each of the named dance types is related to one specific tempo degree only. It is not contradictory that the "Tempo di Gavotta" movement of Partita VI has been decreased to the degree p. The sixfold subdivision values of the half notes result in the same speed as the fourfold subdivision values of the half notes in the Gavottes belonging to the degree 3/2p.

Courante and Gigue, however, are differentiated, the Courante into two types, namely the French and the Italian. The French type, the Courante proper, exhibits the degree p related to the half notes, even if the usual time signature of 3/2 turns to 6/4 (F III). Embracing this Courante type, the first three core movements of a suite—Allemande, Courante, and Sarabande—invariably keep to the principal tempo degree p. They only differ concerning the meter (and its internal configuration). This calls attention to an issue worthwhile its special investigation: how are movement and tempo types ordered in the course of an individual suite performing its dramaturgy?

The Italian type is still missing in the English Suites. It appears for the first time in the French Suites with the questionable designation Courante, and later in the Partitas with the proper designation Corrente. This type always exhibits triple meter. However, the inner subdivision and the tempo degree vary reciprocally; their interaction aims at the maintenance of the same constant speed concerning the smallest subordinate note values in continuous motion (as has been shown in the previously mentioned movement with the designation "Tempo di Gavotta"). For comparing the speed of the smallest subordinate note values in continuous motion regarding different pieces, the speed may be related to the scale of tempo degrees through multiplying the particular tempo degree by the number of notes subordinate to the beat in the specific case. It then turns out that the range of speed of the smallest note values stretches from 3/2 for the eighth notes (quavers) of the chorale and the recitative (namely 3/4 × 2) to 12 for the thirty-second notes (demisemiquavers) in a basic concerto movement (namely 3/2 × 8), the range of speed consequently exhibiting the ratio 1 : 8.

The characteristics of the Italian Corrente rest on the constant speed of the smallest note values. For achieving the constant speed 6 p varying possibilities are at hand: 3/4 meter with continuous eighth note (quaver) motion (F II) or 3/8 meter with continuous sixteenth note (semiquaver) motion (P V), both with the degree 3p; 3/4 meter with continuous triplet subdivision and the degree 2p (F IV and P I); 3/4 meter with continuous sixteenth note (semiquaver) motion and the degree 3/2p (F V and F VI). The Correntes of two Partitas, the one in 3/4, the other in 3/8 meter (P III and P VI), decrease the degree from 3p to 2p in view of the fourfold subdivision of the beat resulting in continuous sixteenth and thirty-second note motion respectively; on the other hand, they increase the speed of the smallest subordinate note values in continuous motion by one third in comparison with the other Correntes, namely from 6 to 8. Incidentally, just these two Partitas had already been enclosed in the Keyboard Book for Anna Magdalena Bach from 1725.

The Gigues prefer the tempo degree 2p, which always refers to the comprehensive value of the triplet subdivision, in particular to the dotted quarter note (crotchet) in 6/8 meter (E II and F IV) as well as in 12/8 meter (E III, E IV, and P III), to the dotted eighth note (quaver) in 12/16 meter (E VI and F V) as well as in 9/16 meter (P IV), and to the quarter note (crotchet) in 4/4 meter (P I), always leading to the speed 6p of the subdivision values. Two Gigues intensify the triplet subdivision in the ratio 2 : 1 to a dotted rhythm in the ratio 3 : 1, in particular to dotted eighth note plus sixteenth note (semiquaver) in 4/4 meter (F I) or to dotted quarter note (crotchet) plus eighth note (quaver) in 4/2 meter (P VI), in this way changing the threefold subdivision of triplets into the fourfold subdivision of sixteenth notes (semiquavers) or eighth notes (quavers) respectively. In both cases, the comprehensive value, quarter note (crotchet) or half note (minim) respectively, is being decreased from degree 2p to degree 3/2p. This retardation of the comprehensive value results in the constant speed 6p of the subdivision values, due to the change into the fourfold subdivision. By the way, the Gigue of the Partita VI was, previous to the publication, written down one note value smaller in both the Keyboard Books for Anna Magdalena Bach, concordant with the Gigue of the French Suite I.

Especially within Bach's keyboard works, several examples are handed down for the notation of a piece in two adjoining degrees of note values, one of them smaller and the other larger. For my part, a philosophical superstructure should not be insisted upon to explain this fact, at least when discussing tempo. Rather, two pragmatic reasons should be taken into account, a graphic and an economic

434   *Ulrich Siegele*

one. In notating an intricate polyphonic structure, in particular for more than four parts, on the two systems of the keyboard notation, the beams are a substantial obstacle which can be considerably diminished when choosing a notation one note value degree larger, especially changing consecutive eighth notes (quavers) into quarter notes (crotchets). This may be a reason why the five-part fugues in C-sharp minor (BWV 849/2) and B-flat minor (BWV 867/2) of the first volume of the WTC are written in 2/2 meter. And in preparing a copper-plate publication, saving beams meant reducing costs.

Four Gigues are notated in 6/8 meter (E I and P V) or in 3/8 meter (E V and F III). Their comprehensive value of a dotted quarter note (crotchet), however, is not subdivided into three eighth notes (quavers) but into six sixteenth notes (demiquavers). The tempo degree of the comprehensive value of the dotted quarter note (crotchet) is further decreased to p, which results in the degree 3p for the eighth note (quaver) beat including two of the six subdivision units. Again, the speed of the subdivision values remains constant. This constant speed 6p of the subdivision values does not only group the seventeen Gigues together, but also connects them with the main group of the Correntes, exhibiting the same speed of subdivision values. The decisive criterion for both dances is the constant speed of subdivision values, whose varying configurations cause changing tempo degrees of the comprehensive values.

The main group of seventeen Gigues is confronted with two other Gigues which increase the speed of the smallest subdivision values by half, namely from 6 to 9 p. Indeed, the main groups of Correntes and Gigues share a corresponding speed of the subdivision values. Concerning the increase of the speed, however, the Gigues surpass the Correntes by a sixth of the original value (the Correntes increasing not by half, but by one third from 6 to 8 p only). These two Gigues (F VI and A minor) are notated in 6/8 meter; with regard to the comprehensive value of a dotted quarter note (crotchet), they should be associated with the degree 2p. However, they introduce sixteenth notes (semiquaver) into the triplet division of the dotted quarter note (crotchet) to a larger extent. Therefore, their degree is being decreased to 3/2 p, what actually leads to the increased speed 9 p of the subdivision values.

This concerns the two Gigues as well, which belong to the type of the Canarie. They are notated in 3/8 meter (F II) or in 6/8 meter (French Overture), but intensify the triplet subdivision of the three equal eighth notes by dotting the first note and correspondingly shortening the second note to a sixteenth note, in that way assuming a subdivision into six sixteenth notes. Finally, the Loure (F V) can rhythmically be regarded as a slow complement to the vivacious Canarie. The quarters of the 6/4 meter are related to the degree 3/2p, its dotted halves (minims) to the degree 1/2p. Therefore the ratio of the Loure to the Canarie is 1 : 2.

The response that this is not Bach's systematization of time structure defining his music, but mine, can be anticipated. Although I should be flattered by such an objection, I ungrudgingly acknowledge Bach's authorship of this extraordinary music-theoretical achievement. It is an achievement that needs to be acknowledged as an indispensable feature of his outstanding compositional competence.

Translated by Reiko Füting

Part V
Dissemination

17 Sons, Family and Pupils[1]

Stephen Roe

The tumultuous history of the last decades of the twentieth century helped re-shape Bach studies. The restoration of displaced manuscript and printed sources to their former homes in Germany and the opening up of archives in the former DDR long closed to scholars have added considerably to knowledge of J. S. Bach and his family. The work of the sons, pupils and followers of Johann Sebastian is seen in a new light. This impetus, which shows no sign of flagging, has trans-formed our view of the Bach family and its *Rezeptionsgeschichte*. Even before the Berlin Wall crumbled, scholars and researchers on both sides of the Atlantic had begun to examine the lives and careers of the Bach sons more scrupulously and with greater ease: biographies, collections of letters, thematic catalogs and complete editions cascaded from the presses. These were complemented by re-cordings and performances: works such as the operas of Johann Christian Bach, which had only received a handful of performances even in the 1760s and 1770s, were edited and performed with success on professional stages of Europe and elsewhere. They have now received many more performances in the twenty-first century than in the eighteenth.

In 1999 the reemergence and return to Berlin from Kiev of the Bach sources of the Sing-Akademie, including the so-called Alt-Bachisches Archiv, threw all the cards in the air again. With three hundred "new" manuscripts of Emanuel Bach and fifty of Wilhelm Friedemann, the worklists of these two composers had to be revised and rewritten.[2] The new C. P. E. Bach edition (superseding an aborted attempt begun by Oxford University Press) reflects these new discoveries. Originally planned to be completed for the tricentenary of the composer's birth in 2014, it publishes for the first time the twenty-one Hamburg passion settings of C. P. E. Bach, their texts almost completely unknown hitherto.[3] They reveal

---

1 I am enormously grateful for the help of Christoph Wolff and Peter Wollny and the kindness of their colleagues at the Bach-Archiv, Leipzig.

2 See LBB 8 (2006); and Elias N. Kulukundis, "C. P. E. Bach in the Library of the Singakademie zu Berlin," *C. P. E. Bach Studies*, ed. Stephen L. Clark (Oxford: Oxford University Press, 1988), 159–176, which includes a reconstructed listing of the Singakademie's Emanuel Bach holdings, published before the recovery of the collection.

3 *Carl Philipp Emanuel Bach: the Complete Works*, managing editor Paul Corneilson (Cambridge, MA, 2005–), 8 series, in 56 volumes with six supplements of facsimiles.

438   *Stephen Roe*

Emanuel to be an extraordinarily "pragmatic" man even by late eighteenth-century standards, brushing up the oratorios of Homilius and Telemann and performing them under his own name. Unlike his father, the composition of passions was no summation of his greatest work, but simply a commission, raising questions about Emanuel's spirituality, which may have been more elastic than his father's religious devotion.

The reputations of nearly all the Bach composer sons have been affected by the new source material, which had not been available for study for at least sixty years, and had been little known then. It was not just the Alt-Bachisches Archiv. There were other discoveries: all the missing autographs of J. C. Bach's Milanese church music returned from Yerevan, Armenia, to their home in Hamburg, a similarly transformative moment for students of his works.[4] These fascinating scores solved a number of outstanding problems and raised a few more.

Another important event at the beginning of the present century was the concentration of research in the Bach-Archiv, Leipzig, which inevitably led to the closing of the Bach-Institut in Göttingen in 2006, which had been a powerful centre in the post-war years. The transferring of scholars, musical sources and resources and research materials from Göttingen, including contemporary copies and printed editions, as well as facsimiles of all the manuscripts relating to Johann Sebastian and the Bach family housed in Berlin, established and reaffirmed Leipzig as the premiere research centre for Bach studies.

The Bach-Archiv is a private foundation supported by the city of Leipzig and the state of Saxony, as well as receiving generous subventions from private foundations and individuals. It has a substantial number of autographs of J. S. Bach, but in 2011 received as a deposit the extraordinarily rich collection of printed music, autograph manuscripts, letters, documents and memorabilia relating to the Bach sons, the wider Bach family and their contemporaries formed by Elias N. Kulukundis, of Greenwich, Connecticut. The hundreds of items collected from the mid-1950s make the Bach-Archiv the greatest depository of Bach family material outside the Staatsbibliothek, Berlin. A collection of essays in honour of Dr Kulukundis is in preparation which will shed light on many aspects of this diverse and rich assemblage.[5]

Even before the arrival of the Kulukundis collection in Leipzig, Bach research had taken on a new lease of life in the 1990s with the establishment of several projects, such as the Expedition Bach,[6] aimed at a detailed examination of the libraries of churches and other formerly closed municipal and ecclesiastical institutions around Leipzig, in Saxony, Thuringia and their hinterlands to find new

---

4   See Stephen Roe, "Wiederaugefundene Autographe von Johann Christian Bachs Mailander Kirchenmusik in der Staats-und Universitätsbibliothek Hamburg (ND VI 540 Bd 1–4)," BJ 88 (2002): 139–164.

5   The volume edited by Peter Wollny and Stephen Roe is forthcoming.

6   See the exhibition catalogue prepared by Michael Maul, *Expedition Bach: Katalog zur Sonderausstellung im Bach-Museum Leipzig vom 21. September 2006 bis 17. Januar 2007* (Leipzig: Bach Archiv, 2006).

Sons, Family and Pupils 439

sources and records of Bach, his sons and pupils. This has proved extremely successful: each *Bach-Jahrbuch*, the house journal of the Archiv, brims with new information and documentation covering Bach's entire career, his friends and pupils. A glance at the indexes over the past twenty-five years reveals discovery upon discovery, new sources and perhaps even as important, new pupils and the identification of their handwriting among the copyists of Johann Sebastian Bach.

Another far-reaching project in Leipzig is the Bach Repertorium, producing thematic catalogs of all the composers of the Bach clan, aimed at "collecting and making accessible both music sources and relevant archival and literary documents on the work of the Bach family over five generations." Several volumes have appeared so far, beginning with the Bach sons whose output is relatively manageable: Wilhelm Friedemann[7] and Johann Christoph Friedrich.[8] Catalogs for the more tricky sons, from the point of view of their vast outputs, C. P. E. and J. C. Bach, are either in the planning stage, or slowly appearing.[9] Both composers have stop-gap catalogs by Helm[10] and Warburton[11] though neither of them is dependable and both are poorly organized. Volumes dealing with all the Bach sons are planned, as well as the one composer grandson, Wilhelm Friedrich Ernst, and younger and older more distant members of the family. This is an immense project, one which for the first time will bring together research on all the important members of the Bach family and their sources.

The tenuous threads of ownership of these sources have gradually been gathered into public institutions. A feature of the twentieth century has been the amassing of the sources in the comparative safety of libraries, mostly in Germany. A concomitant problem for the custodians of the Bach sources, new and old, was how to undo the neglect of decades and in many cases to deal with the bungled restorations of the 1920s and 1930s, where efforts to silk or otherwise preserve the precious Bach autographs had gone spectacularly awry. Treasures such as Anna Magdalena's *Notenbuch* (1725 and later)[12] had been seriously damaged by such restorations and were not in good shape.

All the manuscripts returned to Germany from the Soviet Union had been marked by the authorities with ownership stamps and sometimes with call numbers in colored crayons, but had otherwise been treated with benign neglect and were not in worse condition than when they were originally transported. In many of the J. S. Bach sources the high tannin content in the ink caused the eating away of the paper and the inevitable loss of notes, particularly where the dense

---

7 BR-WFB.

8 BR-JCFB.

9 BR-CPEB. The Bach-Archiv published an online *C. P. E. Bach Works Catalogue* (Christine Blanken, Solvej Donadel, Wolfram Enßlin, August 2013): http://www.cpebach.de/en/about-bach/works-catalogue

10 E. Eugene Helm, *Thematic Catalogue of the Works of Carl Philipp Emanuel Bach* (New Haven: Yale University Press, 1989).

11 Ernest Warburton, *Johann Christian Bach Thematic Catalogue = The Collected Works*, 48/1 (New York: Garland, 1999).

12 D-B Mus. ms. Bach P 225.

440 *Stephen Roe*

writing involved much deletion or correction. The only solution was to restrict the handling of these fragile documents. At the end of the twentieth century, an ambitious program of irreversible restoration was begun on many of these sources in Eastern Germany, involving the splitting of individual leaves and insertion of acid-free membranes. This process caused the manuscripts to become stiff, like card, and the notes seemingly to sink into the paper. Sometimes this led to the manuscripts resembling photographic facsimiles, many of which seemed to be able to stand up by themselves. This program was at first conceived in the DDR, in Leipzig and in the former Deutsche Staatsbibliothek, Berlin; but to mark the Millennium and the 250th anniversary of Bach's death, the process was extended to all the J. S. Bach sources in the Staatsbibliothek Preussischer Kulturbesitz, Berlin, and to many of the other Bach family sources, where there were no particularly pressing conservation problems. There was a small, vociferous outcry at the time, and the program was halted in Leipzig, but continued in Berlin. Only time will tell whether such bold treatment was justified or whether we have lost more than we gained.

Another similarly radical process was applied in the Berlin Staatsbibliothek: each Bach family autograph was split into its component bifolia, acid-free paper inserted between the leaves and each unit inserted into folders, the now enormous manuscripts housed in large boxes. The autograph of the five early concertos of J. C. Bach composed in Berlin, once in a relatively slim volume bound in the nineteenth century, is now delivered in a large acid-free box many times bigger than in its pre-2004 incarnation.[13] The manuscripts are now beautifully preserved and should survive the most insensitive treatment, but would they not have fared equally well without being split up, and with less handling, more careful supervision and more acid-free materials to form a barrier between the pages? What has been lost in the process? Can one ever talk about Anna Magdalena's *Notenbuch* again, when it is no longer a book, the early binding now protecting a dummy of blank pages, the music leaves separated and disbound? It seems that at the end of the twentieth century, the conservationists got the upper hand and were given rein to do what they liked, including carrying out experimental and irreversible work on primary sources. The pendulum has swung back a little now, but we are left to deal with the aftermath. For J. S. Bach, the manuscript is the primary means of transmission of his music and was a teaching aid for his sons and his pupils. As far as the manuscript sources in the major repositories in Germany, we can no longer see the autographs as Bach, his pupils and his sons saw them. That is a loss.

Anna Magdalena Bach

All the Bach sons were Sebastian's pupils to a greater or lesser extent. The elder received the complete attention of their father, probably also supplemented with assistance from Maria Barbara or Anna Magdalena. The musical studies of the younger sons, Johann Christoph Friedrich and Johann Christian, were probably

---

13 D-B Mus. ms. Bach P 390.

Sons, Family and Pupils 441

overseen by their father, but the day-to-day activities supervised by others such as Johann Elias Bach or Johann Christoph Altnikol. All the sons were influenced by the works and attitudes of Johann Sebastian; all possessed important sources of their father's music; and all reacted to his influence and reputation.

The transmission of Bach's music is mostly due to Anna Magdalena, Wilhelm Friedemann and Carl Philipp Emanuel Bach, with the assistance of a number of Johann Sebastian's pupils. Johann Christoph Friedrich and Johann Christian may well have played a minor role. No systematic work has yet been done on determining exactly which son received which manuscript. There is still a good deal of research to be done on the early (and later) provenances of the Bach sources. Much of the writing on provenance in the NBA *Kritische Berichte* is out of date, most being accomplished in the pre-computer age. The absence of indexes in many of the volumes makes cross-referencing somewhat haphazard. The identification of handwriting is similarly inaccurate and superseded.

Surviving documents relating to J. S. Bach's inheritance provide no details of the division of his compositions or music library. His theological tomes are listed, valued and distributed amongst his children male and female.[14] Bach's widow evidently retained a substantial part of the music, eventually acquired by St. Thomas's, comprising the parts of the cantatas stored in the church archives for future use. Many of these are now on deposit in the Bach-Archiv, some on regular exhibit in the Bach Museum. It is not known when these manuscripts were deposited in the church library, before or after Anna Magdalena's death. She had a hand in the division of the other remaining Bach sources: at least one manuscript contains the name "Christel," the familiar name of Johann Christian Bach, in her handwriting.[15] Other sources are similarly marked by her. There was a division of the manuscripts after 1750. The majority devolved to the two elder sons, W. F. and C. P. E. Bach, who as adults, considerably older, professional composers, may have been in a stronger position to acquire them than their younger siblings. Both made use of these sources in their own musical activities and enterprises, in some cases mercilessly plundering them.

Anna Magdalena Bach remains a shadowy figure. Regarded by many as neglected by her sons and stepsons in her widowhood, she lingered in frugal retirement until her own demise in Leipzig in 1760. She played a significant role in her husband's life and career, not least as a zealous and effective copyist, particularly when time was short and the workload great. She was not a regular copyist in Bach's Leipzig years. A list of the works she transcribed, as well as the most comprehensive account of her life and times, was published in 2004.[16] New speculation about her early life by Hans-Joachim Schulze has recently appeared.[17]

---

14 Dok 2: 490–514 (Nos. 627 and 628).

15 The B minor Prelude and Fugue for organ (BWV 544); Robert O. Lehman Deposit, Pierpont Morgan Library, New York, NY.

16 Maria Hübner, ed., *Anna Magdalena Bach Ein Leben in Dokumenten und Bildern*, with a biographical essay by Hans-Joachim Schulze (Leipzig: Evangelische Verlagsanstalt, 2004); see also, Yo Tomita, "Anna Magdalena as Bach's Copyist," UB 2 (2007): 59–76.

17 Hans-Joachim Schulze, "Anna Magdalena Wilcke: Gesangsschülerin der *Paulina*," BJ 99 (2013): 279–295.

442   *Stephen Roe*

Among the most important manuscripts in her hand is the primary source of the Six Cello Suites (BWV 1007–1012). In 2002 Professor Martin W. B. Jarvis, an Australian conductor and composer, began to suggest that Anna Magdalena was somehow involved in the composition of the cello suites. By 2008 what began as a possibility was being promoted as an actuality and Anna Magdalena was thrust into the limelight. No longer was she considered the forgotten manager of the Bach household but rather the *éminence grise*, responsible not only for copying the Cello Suites but was the composer herself. This bombshell, relayed by news services at a quiet moment, ricocheted around the world. A *jeu d'esprit* became a *cause célèbre,* gaining far greater weight in the process than it deserved.

Jarvis interprets the later inscription on the title-page: "Ecrit par Madame Bachen Son Epouse," as a statement of authorship. Anna Magdalena's title-page firmly attributes the suites to her husband, but Jarvis thinks otherwise. His theories were rehearsed at a conference in Melbourne and elaborated in an incessant stream of articles.[18] His thesis does not rely on the manuscript alone: he contends that the musical style is "immature" and the suites sound like exercises for the cello, which in a sense they are. The absence of compositions firmly attributed to Anna Magdalena argues against any such reattribution. The willfulness of Jarvis's contention recalls the wilder elaborations of number theorists for J. S. Bach and the tedious nineteenth- and twentieth-century enthusiasts who will the authorship of Shakespeare's plays to others on similarly specious grounds. Jarvis's case relies on a misreading, misunderstanding or distortion of the evidence, and has not found favor anywhere. It has at least turned the spotlight on Anna Magdalena as a transmitter of her husband's work.

She was among the longest surviving close observers of Johann Sebastian's musical activity, remaining in the Thomaskirchhof apartment long after her stepsons Wilhelm Friedemann and Carl Philipp Emanuel had left the family home. Anna Magdalena was well-regarded by her husband as a singer and musician, referring to her in a letter as "gar einen sauberen Soprano"[19] Without Anna Magdalena's transcriptions, the cello suites and a number of other works might not have survived. She assisted her husband on a number of occasions, including in the parts of the St. Matthew Passion[20] and the later versions of the St. John Passion.[21] She worked so closely with him that her handwriting took on many of the characteristics of Sebastian's script as can be seen in her transcript of

---

18 Examples of Jarvis's many publications on the topic include: "'1720 Autograph' of the Violin Sonatas & Partitas What it Purports to Be?" *Stringendo* 30/2 (2008), 27–30; "The Application of Forensic Document Examination Techniques to the Writings of J. S. Bach and A. M. Bach," UB 3 (2008): 87–92; *Written by Mrs Bach: The Amazing Discovery That Shocked the Music World* (Sydney: ABC Books, 2011). In 2014 a documentary film was made, with a similar title, promoting Jarvis's theory; see the critique of Ruth Tatlow, "A Missed Opportunity: Reflections on *Written by Mrs. Bach*," UB 10 (2015): 141–157.

19 Letter to Georg Erdmann in Danzig, 28 October 1730; Dok 1: 67–68 (No. 23); NBR 151–152 (No. 152).

20 D-B Mus. ms. Bach St.110.

21 D-B Bach Mus. ms. Bach St 111.

the Sonata for Solo Violin BWV 1001.[22] There is much work still to be done on Anna Magdalena and her contribution as a copyist. Her work as a composer is not worth exploration.

Among the main achievements of the past 60 years has been the disentangling of the various scripts found in Bach's manuscripts, ascertaining Bach's role, what he wrote first, what was added later, and what belonged to his family and pupils. An examination of the development of Bach's hand and the paper of the scores and parts themselves has helped problems of chronology and dating, as well as raising new questions about his worklist. Through the pioneering work of Dürr, Dadelsen, Schulze and Kobayashi, amongst others, we now can discriminate between the hand of Anna Magdalena and her husband; also Christian Gottlob Meissner, a pupil of the Thomasschule, whose handwriting took on characteristics of his master, and many other hands of family members and disciples. Bach's other pupils and sons did not imitate their teacher's hand to the same extent as Meissner, but there is always cause to be wary. The instrumental and vocal parts for the St. John Passion contain twenty or more hands, including the young and old scripts of the author. Friedemann's and Emanuel's handwriting was fairly distinct from their father's script. Yet both men added to the manuscripts of their father that they owned, causing confusions of a different sort.

Wilhelm Friedemann Bach

J. S. Bach and his eldest son Wilhelm Friedemann (1710–1784) enjoyed a close relationship, closer than any of the other children. Friedemann never completely emerged from his father's shadow. In early adulthood he allowed Sebastian to further his career. Letters of application for a position at the Sophienkirche, Dresden, in June 1733, were written by his father and merely signed by his son. The reappearance of the Sing-Akademie sources sheds light on the relationship in many fascinating ways. A new group of manuscripts from around 1738, when Friedemann was in Dresden, shows both father and son collaborating on projects and exercises, composing canons and other experiments in counterpoint. The relationship seems not so much as a master and pupil, but as equals, an indication certainly of the high regard of father for son and also a mutual dependence when the pursuit of the extremes of counterpoint was musically unfashionable.[23] David Schulenberg has described these manuscript exercises as follows: "Sebastian

---

22 Bach's original is at D-B Mus. ms. Bach P 967; Anna Magdalena's transcript is at D-B Mus. ms. Bach P 268; both are illustrated next to each other in *Johann Sebastian Bach Life, Times, Influence*, eds. Barbara Schwendowius and Wolfgang Dömling (Kassel: Bärenreiter, 1977), 124.

23 See Peter Wollny, "Eine Quellenfund in Kiew: unbekannte Kontrapunktstudien von Johann Sebastian Bach und Wilhelm Friedemann Bach," LBB 5:(2002): 275–287; these sketches are published in a supplementary volume to the *NBA: Beiträge zur Generalbass-und Satzlehre, Kontrapunktstudien, Skizzen und Entwürfe*, ed. P. Wollny (Kassel: Bäreneiter, 2011), 67–86. These exercises may have had a competitive element, see Robert L. Marshall, "Bach at Mid-Life: The Christmas Oratorio and the Search for New Paths," BACH 43/1 (2012): 1–28.

444   *Stephen Roe*

does not seem to have set these up as exercises (*Übungen*) to be completed by Friedemann. Rather, what we have is something akin to a written version of the 'double fugues' that Mattheson and Handel worked out *da mente non da penna* (improvisatorily, without writing them down), as they traveled together from Hamburg to Lübeck to visit Buxtehude in 1703."[24]

Much earlier, father and son worked together on the manuscript of the *Clavierbüchlein für Wilhelm Friedemann Bach*, containing early versions of the inventions, preludes from the Well-tempered Clavier, dances and a variety of other short pieces, even though W. F. Bach was only nine years old.[25] The manuscript, begun as an instructional manual prepared by J. S. Bach, became a joint effort, with copying duties about equal. Occasionally, the transcription of individual pieces is shared, indicating a very close collaboration, adumbrating their later work together on the contrapuntal studies. The collection was begun in Cöthen in 1720, when W. F. Bach was nearly ten years old. Even earlier, in a manuscript now lost, Bach wrote lovingly of his elder son, not yet ten years of age: "Du bist [m]ein gutes Jüngelchen"[26] ("You are a [my] good little boy").

Friedemann later assisted his father as a copyist for cantatas in Leipzig. He transcribed the cornetto parts of *Ich freue mich in dir* (BWV 133), performed in 1724. Friedemann learnt about such compositions from the inside, a skill put to good use in the twenty-two sacred works he wrote for Halle in the 1740s. Around the same time, Friedemann began a collection of virtuoso organ pieces by his father for his own use as a keyboard soloist, drawing comparison with Sebastian's similar youthful enterprise at his elder brother's home in Ohrdruf at the beginning of the century. Forkel indicates that the Six Trio Sonatas for organ (BWV 525–30) were written for W. F. Bach: a manuscript survives of the set in Friedemann's hand, though completed by Anna Magdalena, dating from around 1735.[27]

Thanks to Peter Wollny, more is known about Friedemann's early career and his place in the transmission of his father's music. W. F. Bach, already a sensitive and complete musician, had a grandstand view of his father's musical development. In addition to the *Clavierbüchlein*, the first book of the Well-tempered Clavier was assembled for his and his brothers' use in the 1720s. Wollny writes that apart from hearing the Brandenburg Concertos in Cöthen, "he had been among the first listeners to the three Leipzig cantata cycles (and probably had vivid recollections of his father's continuous stress, having to compose a new piece every week and then to make copies, rehearse and perform it). He had

---

24   David Schulenberg, *The Music of Wilhelm Friedemann Bach* (Rochester: University of Rochester Press, 2010), 37.

25   See Peter Wollny, *Wilhelm Friedemann Bach "Der hochbegabte, wunderliche Liebling des Vaters,"* catalogue of the Wilhelm Friedemann Bach exhibition at the Bach Museum (Leipzig: Bach-Archiv, 2010). The *Clavierbüchlein* manuscript is in Yale University Library; facsimile, ed. Ralph Kirkpatrick (New Haven: Yale University Press, 1959).

26   See Christoph Wolff, "Decandants of Wilhelm Friedemann Bach in the United States," BP 5: *Bach in America*, ed. Stephen A. Crist (2003): 123–130, esp. p. 130.

27   Dok 7: 80. The manuscript survives at D-B Mus. ms. Bach P 272.

Sons, Family and Pupils   445

listened to the first and second versions of the St. John Passion and helped prepare the dedicatory copy of the Kyrie-Gloria Mass which his father presented to the Dresden court in 1733. There was probably no other musician of his generation who in his childhood and youth already commanded such a wealth of musical experience…"[28] J. S. Bach also assisted in disseminating his son's music, copying out the Concerto for two Harpsichords (FK10/ BR-WFB A 12) composed about 1742. It is thought that both men may have performed the work in Leipzig, perhaps at a private or public concert.

W. F. Bach's early and prominent role in the advancement and distribution of his father's music can be seen in his espousal of cantatas by J. S. Bach in the 1740s and 1750s in Halle. The reemergence of the Sing-Akademie manuscripts has been crucial in elucidating Friedemann's role. New autograph scores of W. F. Bach and evidence from printed libretti in the Halle archives build up a picture of his early endeavors on his father's behalf. Wollny notes Friedemann combining his own music with works by his father, "performing one in the morning and one in the afternoon. This was the case for example on 3 October 1756… W. F. Bach presented his valedictory cantata *Der Höchste erhöret das Flehen der Armen* (FK 86/BR-WFB F 21) and in the afternoon J. S. Bach's Michaelmas cantata *Man singet mit Freuden vom Sieg* (BWV 149)."[29] Whether Wilhelm Friedemann transcribed his father's cantata from an autograph score he owned is not known, but it is highly likely.[30] The original score and parts are lost and the work only comes down via contemporary transcripts. Friedemann was by no means as careful as Carl Philipp Emanuel in preserving the sources entrusted to him. He was forced to sell much of his inheritance over the years. Most of the manuscripts owned by C. P. E. Bach ended up in institutional libraries relatively soon after his death. Those owned by Friedemann were generally scattered: most of the autographs of Bach in the salerooms of the nineteenth and twentieth centuries derive from him.

Recently, curious features of certain manuscripts in Friedemann's possession have come to light. He annotated his father's manuscripts elucidating or disguising the authorship. On the autograph of the Prelude and Fugue in G major (BWV 541), W. F. Bach adds correctly "per manum Autoris."[31] Elsewhere he obfuscates the authorship: he attributes works by his father to himself and vice versa. Wollny draws attention to the autograph of Friedemann's chorus *Dienet dem Herrn mit Freuden* (FK 84/BR-WFB F 25), from around 1755, on which W. F. Bach scratched out his own initials, replacing them with his father's, reattributing the

---

28 Wollny, *"Der hochbegabte, wunderliche Liebling des Vaters,"* 9.
29 Wollny, *"Der hochbegabte, wunderliche Liebling des Vaters,"* 21; for a fuller discussion of W. F. Bach's cantatas and those by his father in Halle, see P. Wollny: "Wilhelm Friedemann Bach's Halle Performances of Cantatas by his Father," *Bach Studies 2*, ed. Daniel R. Melamed (Cambridge, 1995), 202–228.
30 NBA KB I/30: 106ff.
31 D-B N. Mus. ms. 378. The title and inscription are reproduced in *Die Handschrift Johann Sebastian Bachs. Ausstellung in Berlin zum 300. Geburtstag von J. S. Bach 22 März bis 13 Juli 1985* [Staatsbibliothek preussischer Kulturbesitz, 1985] (Wiesbaden: Reichart, 1985), 115.

446   *Stephen Roe*

entire work to J. S. Bach.[32] This manuscript is in the Sing-Akademie collection.[33] Carl Friedrich Zelter, founder of the institution, queried Friedemann's attribution, adding his doubts to the manuscript. The autograph of W. F. Bach's Kyrie (FK 100/BR-WFB E 1), a work also from his Halle period, contains a similar alteration and false attribution to J. S. Bach.[34]

Sebastian's organ transcription of D minor violin concerto of Vivaldi (BWV 596) shows the reverse. The autograph, once owned by Friedemann, dates from around 1714. It contains not only his addition to the title of "di W. F. Bach," but also "manu mei Patris descript," asserting that the composer was Friedemann, the transcriber Sebastian.[35] This led to some early misattributions to W. F. Bach. The next owner of the manuscript, J. N. Forkel, believed it to be a work of Friedemann and it was published by Forkel's pupil F. C. Griepenkerl with the false attribution.

Borrowing is a common practice in the eighteenth century. Failure to acknowledge it is unexceptionable: J. S. Bach does not mention Vivaldi in the manuscript of the organ work. Deliberate misattribution is rarer and requires explanation. The poverty experienced by Friedemann in his final years in Berlin brought about the need to acquire new pieces, and assuming his father's works as his own was a convenient expedient. Attributing his own works to his father requires more explanation. Perhaps Friedemann felt Sebastian Bach's religious compositions to be more admired than his own, attracting a more enthusiastic and sympathetic audience and market. Friedemann's flexible attitude towards authorship is unique among the sons of J. S. Bach. Emanuel used his father's music without revealing his sources, but never annotated the many autographs of his father to disguise the composer. Friedemann seems to have suffered from psychological problems: his attitude reveals a complex dependence on his father and on his music. It also shows the need for posthumous approbation, which the success of his own music passed off as his father's might convey.

He acquired a large number of his father's autographs after 1750. Forkel claims he received a greater proportion than the others. Living in Halle, he was close enough to ensure a generous share. Following the researches of Dürr and Dadelsen, it is believed that he owned the whole second series of church cantatas and possibly later series as well, if they existed. By comparison with Emanuel, most of the autographs owned by Friedemann were disposed of in his lifetime. C. P. E. Bach retained practically all his and they were dispersed after his death in an auction by his widow. Many were bought by Georg Pölchau who kept them together and they were acquired en bloc by the Königliche Bibliothek, Berlin in the 1840s. The earlier dissemination by W. F. Bach, all through private sales rather than auction, resulted in a wider distribution of sources, many now being lost.

---

32 Wollny, *"Der hochbegabte, wunderliche Liebling des Vaters,"* 21.
33 D-Bsa 271.
34 Now part of the Kulukundis Deposit at the Bach-Archiv, Leipzig.
35 D-B Mus. ms. Bach P 330. Title reproduced in *Die Handschrift Johann Sebastian Bachs*, 65.

Wollny has described the importance of the friendship between Friedemann and Sara Levy, née Itzig. She was his keyboard pupil in Berlin, an important collector of Sebastian Bach's manuscripts and supporter of his music.[36] She was also a friend of J. F. Reichardt, who wrote in his autobiography of the art-loving connoisseurs of the Itzig household and the "veritable Bach cult" to be found there. Her circle included Abraham, father of Felix Mendelssohn, who also became a collector of Bach manuscripts, including several autographs. The view of the Bach revival as a sudden explosion in the early nineteenth century has now been modified. J. S. Bach was always admired in circles of *Kenner und Liebhaber* around the two elder sons, both supporting performances of their father's music through rich patrons. The Bach revival was a broadening out of these tributaries rather than a sudden shock of discovery.

The reappearance of the Sing-Akademie material has refined the focus on W. F. Bach, Sara Levy and the dissemination of the sources of J. S. Bach. Part of Levy's collection was gradually presented to the Sing-Akademie from 1813 onwards, including autographs of W. F. Bach, such as the concerto for two keyboards in E flat (FK 46/BR-WFB C11),[37] probably performed at private concerts in Berlin by Sara and her sister Zippora. There are also autographs and other sources of Emanuel Bach and important early manuscripts of J. C. F. and J. C. Bach. Peter Wollny has recently reconstructed a catalog of the manuscripts and printed scores owned by Levy and other brothers Daniel, Benjamin, Isaak, Moses and sisters Zippora, Fanny, Rebecca and Rachel.[38] Not all the collection reached the Sing-Akademie: after Sara's death in 1854, there were sales. A number of items were lost or were acquired by other libraries, including the autograph of Emanuel's Double Concerto for Fortepiano and Harpsichord (Wq 47),[39] probably composed for Sara and her sister. She does not seem to have owned any autographs of J. S. Bach, but many important early copies, including fragments of both books of the Well-tempered Clavier[40] and manuscripts (now lost) of the Triple Concerto (BWV 1044) and the Fifth Brandenburg Concerto (BWV 1050).[41] As a keyboard pupil of W. F. Bach, Sara Levy was the direct recipient of the distillation of the keyboard practice of Sebastian. She was considered by contemporaries to be a keyboard virtuoso, but nothing is known of her playing style and technique.

---

36 See Peter Wollny, *"Ein förmliche Sebastian und Philipp Emanuel Bach-Kultus": Sara Levy und ihr musikalisches Wirken* (Wiesbaden: Breitkopf & Härtel, 2010).

37 D-Bsa 2365.

38 Wollny, *Sara Levy und ihr musikalisches Wirken*, 63–107.

39 Now at D-Bsa 4; the first page of music is reproduced in *Er ist Original! Carl Philipp Emanuel Bach: sein musikalisches Werk in Autographen und Erstdrucken aus der Musikabteilung der Staatsbibliothek Preussischer Kulturbesitz Berlin. Ausstellung zum 200. Todestag des Komponisten, 14. Dezember 1988 bis 11. Februar 1989* (Wiesbaden: Reichart, 1988), 95.

40 See Wollny, *Sara Levy und ihr musikalisches Wirken*, 70–71; BWV 846, 851 and 852 at B-Bc 25,448; BWV 850/2 at D-B, N. Mus. Ms. 10488; and BWV 892/2 at Newberry Library, Chicago, Case MS 6A 72.

41 Both listed in Wollny, *Sara Levy und ihr musikalisches Wirken*, 71.

448   *Stephen Roe*

The new catalog of W. F. Bach's works in *Bach-Repertorium* series (BR-WFB) supersedes Falck's study of the last century (FK). The publication of a Complete Edition is moving slowly, not with the lightning appearance of the *C. P. E. Bach Collected Works*, but in beautiful, clear and carefully produced scores.[42]

Carl Philipp Emanuel Bach

C. P. E. Bach was the major force in publishing his father's works and publicizing his life and output. Friedemann had only limited relationships with publishers. Very little of his output was printed, despite living close to the centre of music publishing, Leipzig. Perhaps Friedemann was too impoverished to contemplate the expense of publishing any of his own or his father's scores. They were too valuable to him as a resource to cede them to others. Perhaps he was also afraid to put the final double-bar to a piece, which a printed edition would inevitably impose. Fastidiousness in composers such as Brahms and Dukas often resulted in a limited number of publications. Friedemann was perhaps similarly inclined.

Sebastian's selectively worded obituary, prepared by Emanuel and the Bach pupil J. F. Agricola, was published in Lorenz Mizler' s *Neu-eröffnete Musikalische Bibliothek* (1754). This account is the paradigm for one of the more illuminating Bach biographies of recent years by Peter Williams, where passages from the obituary are stripped out and subjected to analysis and expansion, using knowledge of Bach in the late twentieth century.[43] Emanuel's account emphasizes Bach the autodidact, the self-trained musician. Sebastian appears to have had no real teacher, apart from immediate family members. Writing to J. N. Forkel on 13 January 1775 about the planned biography, Emanuel provided the following information: "...besides Froberger, Kerl and Pachhelbel, he loved and studied the works of Frescobaldi, the Baden Capellmeister Fischer, Strungk, some good old Frenchmen, Buxtehude, Reincken, Bruhnsen and [crossed out: his teacher Böhm], the Lüneburg organist Böhm...".[44]

C. P. E. Bach's account is contradicted by the recent discovery of the earliest surviving manuscripts by Sebastian, comprising transcriptions of works by Pachelbel, Buxtehude and Reincken, as well as a chorale prelude by Bach himself.[45] The Reincken manuscript dates from the time J. S. Bach spent in Lüneburg (1700–1702), and is written on Dutch paper, the very same used by Böhm specifically between 1698 and 1700. The clinching evidence is found at the end of the manuscript with Bach's inscription: "Il fine â Dom[ino]. Georg Böhme descriptum

---

42 Four volumes of a proposed 11-volume series had appeared by the beginning of 2014, published by Carus-Verlag, Stuttgart.

43 Peter Williams, *J. S. Bach, A Life in Music* (Cambridge: Cambridge University Press, 2007).

44 This version of the text, slightly different from that provided by Williams, is in *The Letters of C.P.E. Bach*, translated and edited by Stephen L. Clark, (Oxford: Clarendon, 1997), 72–75 (No.76).

45 Peter Wollny and Michael Maul, "The Weimar Organ Tablature: Bach's Earliest Autographs," UB 3 (2008): 67–74.

Sons, Family and Pupils   449

a[nn]o. 1700 Lunaburgi." Bach lived in Böhm's house and studied with him in Lüneberg. Emanuel's attempt at obfuscation has now been confounded.

The efforts Emanuel made to add Sebastian's name to the pantheon of the great and to promote the cause of the entire family (Emanuel succeeded his father as the family genealogist) is clear in recent publications of Emanuel's letters, especially those to Johann Nikolaus Forkel.[46] W. F. Bach took a similar interest in his father's life, assisting the biographer. Forkel himself acquired some of the Bach autographs Friedemann had owned.

Few compositions of J. S. Bach were printed in the second half of the eighteenth century; most appeared under the auspices of Emanuel. The most beautiful score produced by C. P. E. Bach is the first edition of the *Art of Fugue* (1751). It is entirely engraved, an uncommon practice for the time, the music embellished with flowers and fruits in the manner of a Renaissance manuscript. It was not a commercial success and the plates were sold for scrap in 1756. The appearance at auction of a completely unbound set of the first edition, second issue (with a preface by Marpurg), in 1999,[47] with loose and unpressed leaves, suggests that this edition was published on demand, as the first printings of the Partitas in the 1720s and 1730s, and bound up as necessary. The sets of four-part chorales published by Emanuel in 1765 and 1769 were more successful commercially and helped establish these extraordinary compositions as mainstays of composition instruction, based as they were on the familiar melodies of the Lutheran liturgy. Despite the studies of Schulze and Wachowski, there is still much work to be done on the later publications of J. S. Bach.[48]

No comprehensive listing exists of the scores owned by W. F. Bach. The situation is clearer with the sources belonging to Emanuel listed in his *Nachlass*.[49] These include both passions, orchestral music including the A minor violin concerto, the Christmas and Easter oratorios and a sizeable amount of organ music. As with Friedemann, C. P. E. Bach was an early copyist of his father's music before and after 1750. Emanuel went to great lengths to transcribe manuscripts and scores and to gather together and collate them,[50] preserving the family heritage, including the Alt-Bachisches Archiv. He is the only son whose antiquarian, genealogical and historical interests matched those of Sebastian himself.

---

46   *Carl Philipp Emanuel Bach: Briefe und Dokumente: Kritische Gesamtausgabe*, ed. Ernst Suchalla (Göttingen: Vandenhoeck & Ruprecht, 1994); see also footnote 44.

47   *Fine Printed and Manuscript Music*, Sotheby's London, 21 May 1999, lot 18.

48   Hans-Joachim Schulze, "'150 Stück von den Bachischen Erben': zur Überlieferung der vierstimmigen Choräle Johann Sebastian Bachs," BJ 68 (1983): 81–100; and Gerd Wachowski, "Die vierstimmigen-Choräle Johann Sebastian Bachs: Untersuchungen zu den Druckausgaben von 1765 bis 1932 und zur Frage der Authentizität," BJ 68 (1983): 51–79.

49   CPEB NV.

50   For example there are a number of manuscripts in D-B which are gathered together and annotated by Emanuel. These manuscripts do not always contain only his father's music, but also works by other members of the Bach family, such as Johann Christoph Bach, as for example Mus. ms. Bach St 4/2, where Johann Christian Bach has transcribed one motet of his ancestor.

450   *Stephen Roe*

Emanuel and his elder brother assisted the wider dissemination of Bach's music by circulating manuscript copies to their pupils and friends, extending these scores over a large part of Germany. Late eighteenth-century subscription lists in his publications show that Emanuel's contacts throughout Germany and further afield were extensive. The network was probably used to channel his father's music to *Kenner* and *Liebhaber* around Europe. Yo Tomita's study of early copies of the Well-tempered Clavier in the United Kingdom reveals an extensive relay of sources, several emanating from Emanuel and Friedemann.[51] Emanuel presented a number of manuscripts to Charles Burney in Hamburg in 1772, including a copy of part 1 of the Well-tempered Clavier, now lost since the auction sale after Burney's death in 1814.[52] A manuscript fragment of the second book which came to England via Sara Levy survives in the British Library.[53] This manuscript is believed to have been presented to her complete; it was later divided among her musical friends in Germany. More important is the autograph of the second volume of the Well-Tempered Clavier.[54] Tomita suggests this derived from Friedemann and was acquired by Clementi on his marriage in 1804 to Caroline Lehmann, daughter of a prominent church musician in Berlin and friend of W. F. Bach.[55]

There was a ready market for keyboard music in manuscript in the eighteenth century. It is more surprising that an early copy of the Symbolum Nicenum [Credo] of the B minor mass migrated probably in the 1780s to the Royal Library, London.[56] According to Tomita, it was transcribed from a copy owned by Charles Burney, now in Berlin.[57] This Berlin source probably corresponds to the score listed in the sale catalog of Burney's library in 1814.[58] This manuscript must derive originally from J. S. Bach's autograph, possibly seen by Burney when he met C. P. E. Bach in 1772. The Berlin version is not transcribed by Burney, though it is annotated by him, and is of British provenance. There must have been an intervening source. Both London and Berlin transcripts are on paper used in Britain in the late eighteenth century (though not the same type). The London score is slightly later, dating from ca. 1790, the paper similar to the endpapers of some manuscripts of J. C. Bach bound around then. Tomita rules out that the Royal manuscript source belonged to Queen Charlotte, many of whose scores are inscribed by her librarian "This Volume belongs to the Queen 1788." This does not entirely rule out her ownership: not all her books and manuscripts

---

51   Yo Tomita, "The Dawn of the English Bach Awakening Manifested in Sources of the '48,'" *The English Bach Awakening: Knowledge of J. S. Bach and his Music in England 1750–1830*, ed. Michael Kassler (Aldershot: Ashgate, 2004), 35–168.

52   Tomita, "The Dawn of the English Bach Awakening," 42 (Table 1.2, No. 1).

53   Tomita, "The Dawn of the English Bach Awakening," 42 (Table 1.1, No. 2), and also 82–85. The manuscript comprises the Prelude and Fugue No. 15 (BWV 880), at GB-Lbl Add ms. 38,068.

54   GB-Lbl Add Ms 35,021.

55   Tomita, "The Dawn of the English Bach Awakening," 73.

56   GB-Lbl R.M. 21.e.27. See also the discussion in Yo Tomita, "Bach's *Credo* in England: an Early History," *Irish Musical Studies 8: Bach Studies from Dublin,* ed. Anne Leahy and Yo Tomita (Dublin: Four Courts Press, 2004), 205–228.

57   Tomita, "Bach's *Credo* in England," 218, and footnote 42; DB Mus. ms. Bach P 1212.

58   See Tomita "Bach's *Credo* in England," 211 (source D1).

Sons, Family and Pupils 451

bear this inscription.[59] Tomita also notes many annotations in pencil, correcting errors and providing performance instructions, surmising that "it was used for the preparation of public performance."[60] This manuscript can have only been a study score. It is too big and unwieldy for a conductor or continuo player: with only two bars per page in some sections, including fast movements, it would be impossible to use for a practical purpose. Besides, the annotations seem to be much later than the manuscript, perhaps from the 1820s, when the Bach revival was in fuller swing.

The B minor Mass is among the many autographs owned by Emanuel Bach now in the Staatsbibliothek, Berlin.[61] Much work has been done recently on its composition history.[62] It is now believed that certain sections, notably the Crucifixus, were among the last music written by Bach. There is no evidence that the mass was performed in its entirety in Bach's lifetime. Sections were used for performance by C. P. E. Bach during his Hamburg years and were annotated by him. It is extremely difficult to determine which markings are by the father or son. Modern techniques, ink analysis and crystal spectography have been employed to determine the inks of Emanuel and his father: the new critical edition of the Mass strips away Emanuel's accretions, the equivalent of sand-blasting the stones of a medieval cathedral. The monument is revealed in all its glowingly original glory.[63]

The extent of Emanuel's use of his father's manuscripts is revealed in the discoveries in the Sing-Akademie and through the Bach-Expedition. Some 300 new sources of Emanuel's music returned to Berlin, including manuscripts of nineteen of the twenty-one recorded passions. All are in fact pasticcios, using (unacknowledged) music from other such pieces by G. H. Stölzel, G. A. Homilius, Benda, Telemann and J. S. Bach himself. Emanuel supplies chorales simply harmonized and some recitatives; the borrowed music is left virtually unaltered. Sebastian's two surviving passions contained the best of him; Emanuel simply cobbled his own together. Perhaps he felt unable to compete with his father's output and, as with Friedemann and his misattributions, the inheritance was as much a burden as a boon. Perhaps Emanuel was also less moved by the passion narrative. He lived in a more skeptical age and was au fait with contemporary philosophy and thought. Diderot was a correspondent and Voltaire lived in Potsdam during Emanuel's time at the court of Frederick the Great. In Berlin, he inhabited a world of intellectual rigor and discussion. Much more is known about this through recent publications of his letters and papers.[64]

---

59 To be discussed in my forthcoming *Descriptive Catalogue of the Autograph Manuscripts of Johann Christian Bach*.

60 Tomita, "Bach's *Credo* in England," 220.

61 D-B Mus. ms. Bach P 180.

62 See for example *Exploring Bach's B-minor Mass*, ed. Yo Tomita, Robin A. Leaver and Jan Smaczny (Cambridge: Cambridge University Press, 2013).

63 *Frühfassungen der H-moll Messe*, ed. Uwe Wolf, NBA[rev] II/1A (2005), with KB.

64 See Clark, *Letters of C.P.E. Bach*, 50–51 where two letters from Diderot to C. P. E. Bach are printed.

452   *Stephen Roe*

Neither of the two thematic catalogs of C. P. E. Bach is satisfactory. Wotquenne (Wq) makes no claim to be a complete record of Emanuel's output and Helm's work (H) appeared before the rediscovery of the Sing-Akademie material. Bibliographers ruefully joke that it is only clear how a catalog should be organized once it is published; but very few enjoy the luxury of a second edition. All thematic catalogs are fragile constructs, rendered obsolete by the abrupt appearance of a new cache of sources or a single major autograph. Helm's catalog suffers from these tribulations and more. The catalog has not been accepted by Emanuel's bibliographers. It is scarcely used in the new *Collected Edition*.[65] A thematic catalog of the vocal works of C. P. E. Bach appeared in 2014 in the *Bach Repertorium* series (BR-CPEB 2).

Emanuel published the first edition of the *Versuch* in 1753.[66] This important keyboard treatise incorporates the ideas and practice of Johann Sebastian Bach. One immediate beneficiary was Johann Christian Bach who studied with his half-brother Emanuel in Berlin from the end of 1750 until 1755. His keyboard studies, begun in Leipzig, were refined under his brother's tuition. He performed publicly in Berlin and composed six keyboard concertos, all strongly influenced by Emanuel Bach.[67] These early concertos are probably the most technically demanding the composer ever wrote. All Emanuel's keyboard pupils absorbed the techniques outlined in the *Versuch*, techniques honed from the practice of Johann Sebastian, now increasingly regarded as the most important teacher in Germany in the eighteenth century.

Johann Gottfried Bernhard

Bach's third surviving musician son Johann Gottfried Bernhard (1715–39) predeceased his father, dying in semi-disgrace in Jena. None of his compositions have survived and the extent of the paternal influence can only be speculated. The Bach sons, Johann Gottfried Bernhard included, began their apprenticeship as copyists and helpmates for their father around their thirteenth or fourteenth year. Gottfried Heinrich Bach (1724–1763) was the exception: no authenticated example of his musical hand survives. Though a talented keyboard player, he suffered from some mental incapacity and was unable to live alone after his stepmother's death.

---

65 See note 3 above.

66 Carl Philipp Emanuel Bach, *Versuch über die wahre Art das Clavier zu spielen... Erster Theil* (Berlin: Winter, 1753), *Zweiter Theil* (Berlin: Winter, 1762); facsimile, ed W. Horn (Kassel: Bärenreiter, 1994).

67 See, for example, Stephen Roe, *The Keyboard Music of J. C. Bach: Source Problems and Stylistic Development in the Solo and Ensemble Works* (New York: Garland, 1989), 115–124; Jane R. Stevens, "Concerto No.6 in F minor: by Johann Christian Bach?" *RMA Research Chronicle* 21 (1988): 53–55; Jane R. Stevens, *The Bach Family and the Keyboard Concerto: the Evolution of a Genre* (Warren: Harmonie, 2001).

Johann Christoph Friedrich Bach

Johann Christoph Friedrich Bach (1732–1795) was an important copyist for his father. His lively and exuberant handwriting has been identified in some late manuscripts such as the instrumental parts for the St. John Passion in 1749. The hypothesis that J. C. F. Bach was the scribe of the "Aria di Giovannino," written in a childish and inexpert hand in Anna Magdalena's notebook, is definitively disproved by Wollny, who identifies the hand of Bernhard Dietrich Ludewig (1707–40), a pupil and secretary of Sebastian, who served as tutor for some of the younger Bach children at the end of the 1730s.[68] In 1750, J. C. F. Bach was appointed to the court of Schaumburg-Lippe, Bückeburg, near Hanover. He was absent from Leipzig when his father died and may not have been around for the division of the music. He inherited a few manuscripts from his father, notably the autograph of the Second Partita for Violin (BWV 1001–1004), which eventually came to the Berlin Staatsbibliothek, via Friedrich Wilhelm Rust (1739–1796), a pupil of C. P. E. Bach. Wollny provides the definitive account of J. C. F. Bach's inheritance[69] and Ulrich Leisinger has produced the most up-to-date and authoritative edition of letters and documents relating to Christoph Friedrich. More is now known about this composer than at any other time.[70] The new thematic catalog, also prepared by Leisinger,[71] replaces Wohlfarth's study.[72]

J. C. F. Bach visited Johann Christian in London in 1778, leaving his son Wilhelm Friedrich Ernst there for some months. Christoph Friedrich made his living as a keyboard virtuoso and was noted for his skill and virtuosity on the instrument. His musical style was dictated by the Italianate taste of his patron and his music remains a halfway house between the rigor of C. P. E. Bach and the pleasing *galanteries* of Johann Christian. There has recently come to light a fragmentary manuscript of the Chromatic Fantasia and Fugue in D minor (BWV 903) in J. C. F. Bach's hand, dating from the 1740s, one of the few sources of this early work from the composer's lifetime.[73] The work can be added to the roster of compositions by Johann Sebastian used by the younger Bach children. A similar manuscript in the hand of Bach's pupil, Johann Friedrich Agricola, dates from around 1740.[74]

---

68 Peter Wollny, "Tennstädt, Leipzig, Naumburg, Halle: Neuerkenntnisse zur Bach-Ueberlieferung in Mitteldeutschland," BJ 88 (2002): 29–60.

69 Peter Wollny, "Johann Christoph Friedrich Bach und die Teilung des väterlichen Erbes," BJ 87 (2001): 55–68.

70 LBB 9 (2011).

71 See note 8.

72 Hannsdieter Wohlfarth, *Johann Christoph Friedrich Bach: ein Komponist im Vorfeld der Klassik* (Bern: Francke, 1971).

73 Now in the Bach Archiv, Leipzig; see Peter Wollny, "Fundstücke zur Lebensgeschichte Johann Sebastian Bachs 1744–1750," BJ 97 (2011): 35–50.

74 D-B Mus.ms. Bach P.651.

454   *Stephen Roe*

J. C. F. Bach outlived all his brothers and was survived by his wife, Lucia Elisabeth (1728–1803), daughter Christina Louisa (1762–1852), who owned the manuscript of the sonatas and partitas for solo violin (BWV 1001–1006),[75] and his son. Wilhelm Friedrich Ernst (1759–1845), on returning to Germany from London, lived in Berlin for the remainder of his life and assisted in the rediscovery of his grandfather's music as his last surviving musical heir. He is described as owning manuscripts of J. S. Bach and as being an accomplished organist. Nothing is known of the manuscripts of his forbears which he owned, but he has been identified as a copyist of his father's music. W. F. E. Bach did not achieve greatness as a composer: his music is insipid and lacking in quality, a feeble codetta to the Bach dynasty.[76]

Johann Christian Bach

Johann Christian is the most intriguing of the Bach sons: alone in traveling extensively, a truly cosmopolitan artist, equally at home in Germany, Italy, France and England, fluent in their languages and musical styles. More is now known of his early life and influences. His first and only major biographer, C. S. Terry,[77] was unable to find details of Christian's attendance at the Thomasschule. There can be no doubt that he studied there: as an *externus*, a boy who did not board, he would not be listed among the pupils. J. C. Bach was born in an apartment in the school.[78] It is inconceivable that he did not receive instruction in the building in which he lived with his family.

Christian was musically gifted. Terry speculates that Sebastian probably only supervised his tuition, leaving most to others such as Johann Christoph Altnickol (1720–1759),[79] married to Christian's elder half-sister Elisabeth Juliana Friderica in 1749, having been appointed to a post in Naumburg the year before. There were several other Bach pupils living close by who may equally have served as tutor.

Sebastian's music was the staple diet of his earliest instruction. Manuscript copies survive of five of the English suites annotated by him.[80] These are in the hands of Johann Nathaniel Bammler, a pupil and student of Johann Sebastian who often deputized for him at the Thomaskirche in his final years.[81] He is also a likely candidate as a teacher of Johann Christian. A printed copy of the third

---

75 Wollny, "Johann Christoph Friedrich Bach," 55. The autograph survives at D-B Mus.ms. Bach P 967.

76 See also Lowell Mason, *Musical Letters from Abroad* (Boston: Mason, 1853; reprint, ed. Elwyn A. Weinandt, New York: Da Capo, 1967), esp. 98.

77 Charles Sanford Terry, *John Christian Bach* (London: Oxford University Press, 1929; 2nd ed. rev. H.C. Robbins Landon, 1967).

78 Information kindly supplied by Michael Maul; see also his *"Dero berühmbter Chor" – Die Leipziger Thomasschule und ihre Kantoren (1212–1804)* (Leipzig: Lehmstedt, 2012).

79 Terry, *John Christian Bach*, 3.

80 D-B N.Mus Ms 365.

81 The handwriting is identified by Peter Wollny, "Neue Bach-Funde," BJ 83 (1997): 7–50.

Sons, Family and Pupils 455

keyboard Partita also survives similarly marked by Johann Christian.[82] This first edition is a particularly interesting source: it is very badly printed, the music not centered on the page; too sloppily produced to be released for sale, it was retained by the family for private use. Both the English Suites and the Partita contain doodles, the young Johann Christian experimenting with his pen and rastrum.

Christian assisted his father in his final months, not only as a musical amanuensis, but also in various secretarial duties, especially as Sebastian's eyesight diminished. Christian's hand is also found in the altered parts for the final version of the St. John Passion performed on Good Friday 1749, and probably in the following year as well. Christian's contributions to the parts are generally on added leaves and relate to three numbers, "Ach mein Sinn," the F minor aria "Zerfliesse, mein Herze," and the final choral, "Ach Herr." On Sebastian's death in July 1750, Christian received three keyboard instruments (or perhaps more likely a pedal harpsichord with two manuals) from his father, which evidently displeased his elder brothers. Christian owned at least one autograph by J. S. Bach: the manuscript of the B minor Prelude and Fugue for organ (BWV 544).[83] Recent research on other manuscripts believed to be owned by him, including the Toccata and Fugue in F (BWV 540)[84] and the Prelude and Fugue in G minor (BWV 535), shows they were not in his possession. They belonged to another J. C. Bach, Johann Christoph Bach, the Bindersleben Bach.[85] Other sources said to be owned by the London Bach include a fragment of the Fantasia and Fugue in C minor (BWV 562).[86] This too probably belonged to the other J. C. Bach. Only the autograph of the B minor Prelude and Fugue can be firmly ascribed to Christian Bach's ownership. Christian played the organ in Milan and in London, but whether he ever played an instrument with a pedal-board is not known.

No evidence suggests that Christian retained much affection for his father's music or did anything to propagate it. Once he left Germany, his musical style changed towards the Italianate manner, transforming his aesthetic towards the high Classical style which was soon to influence the young Mozart. There are some surviving fugues by him, notably in the Italian church works written for Milan and in one keyboard sonata (Op. 5 No. 6). All these stem from the teaching of Padre Martini, his mentor in counterpoint and much else in Bologna. The old-fashioned keyboard sonata is modeled on Martini's early keyboard pieces.[87] In a letter to Martini, Bach indicates that more keyboard fugues existed and are

---

82 A-Wn Sammlung Hoboken J. S. Bach 51; see also *Katalog der Sammlung Anthony van Hoboken in der Musiksammlung der Oesterreichischen Nationalbibliothek, i. Johann Sebastian Bach und Seine Söhne*, ed. T. Leibnitz (Tutzing: Schneider, 1982), No.82.

83 MS now in the Pierpont Morgan Library, New York, Lehman Deposit; see also NBA KB IV/5–6, 35–37.

84 A manuscript apparently in the private collection of G. M. D. Esser, Brunswick.

85 Unpublished information from Peter Wollny. For information on the Bindersleben Bach, see Helga Brück, "Die Erfurter Bach-Familien von 1635 bis 1805," BJ, 82 (1996): 101–132.

86 See NBA KB IV/5–6, 27. The manuscript is at D-B Mus.ms. Bach P 490.

87 For further discussion, see Roe, *The Keyboard Music of Johann Christian Bach*, 154–173.

456   *Stephen Roe*

now lost.[88] J. C. Bach's models were Italian rather than German. He was too young in Leipzig to be much influenced by his father's contrapuntal writing and he seems to have learnt strict counterpoint only through Martini. He composed a Kyrie and Gloria in Italy in 1758; neither movement reveals any connection with the B minor Mass, completed eight years before, save only in the massive length. Fleeting influences of J. S. Bach can be seen in the gigue-like finales of Christian's keyboard sonatas and notably in the first movement of the accompanied sonata in B flat (Op. 10, No. 1) which quotes the opening of J. S. Bach's keyboard partita in the same key (BWV 825). Christian probably played the partita in Leipzig in the 1740s.

In England, where Christian settled in 1762, knowledge and appreciation of J. S. Bach grew slowly, through the visits to Germany of English musicians such as Burney and the influx to London of Germans who had come into contact with Sebastian Bach's music. Karl Friedrich Horn (1762–1830) brought some of J. S. Bach's works to the English court. From 1789 he was the queen's music master, successor to Christian Bach who had died in 1782 (there was no replacement for him in the interim). Some of Horn's music in manuscript can be found in a newly discovered (and little-known) part of the British Royal Music Library which had migrated to Hanover and is now at the Beinecke Library, Yale University. Horn was a good organist, noted for his performances of Sebastian Bach's trio sonatas and published an edition of the Well-Tempered Clavier in London between 1810 and 1813.

J. C. Bach was close to the queen and knew Charles Burney. He was in limited contact with his brothers Emanuel, Friedemann and Johann Christoph Friedrich Bach.[89] There is no evidence that any of the manuscript sources in the Royal Library derived from Johann Christian. Frederick Nicolay, the queen's librarian, was of German origin, a copyist of Christian Bach's music,[90] and a custodian of some J. S. Bach sources now in the British Library. Christian Bach probably regarded his father's music as outdated and shared Carl Friedrich Abel's view that Sebastian's music might have been more effective if it were less complicated. He supplied Padre Martini with not-entirely accurate biographical details of his father and the Bach family,[91] which seems to be the extent of his involvement in his father's genealogical interests. Alone amongst the Bach sons, Christian was unencumbered by the weight of family heritage.

---

88 See the letter of Bach to Martini, 14 July 1759, Terry, *John Christian Bach*, 34 (misdated to 7 July).

89 See the letters of introduction to his brothers published in Betty Matthews, "The Davies Sisters, J. C. Bach and the Glass Harmonica," ML 56 (1975): 150–169.

90 For example, the manuscript of J. C. Bach's *Orione*, of which he made an important early transcript now at GB-Ob D.I.84, formerly Tenbury MS 348.

91 See annotations by Martini on a draft of a letter to Pompeo Sales, giving biographical materials on the Bach family. The letter is dated 31 May 1761. Martini notes that J. C. Bach was then present with Martini in Bologna. I-Bc H.84.105a. See Anne Schnoebelen, ed., *Padre Martini's Collection of Letters in the Civico Museo Bibliografico Musicale in Bologna* (New York: Pendragon, 1979), No. 4864.

Johann Christian's music is now more popular and held in greater esteem than at any time since the eighteenth century. As a forerunner of Mozart, he is regarded as an important link between the Baroque and Classical eras. Ernest Warburton, an indefatigable researcher, was almost the sole worker on the monumental editions that appeared in the final decades of the twentieth century.[92] Warburton's editions are not the fruit of careful assessment of sources, but use any complete text available. The scores are facsimile copies of eighteenth-century editions or manuscripts and/or elegant transcriptions made by Warburton himself.[93] None of the editions were peer-assessed or reviewed by other scholars. Warburton's work stimulated performances of this often great music on disc, radio and in live performance; but the texts leave a lot to be desired. Two volumes of Thematic Catalogue form volume 48 of the edition. Poorly produced and organized, the catalog has no guiding bibliographical principles and not much in the way of cross-referencing: it is often necessary to look in three or more different places to get a full picture of a single work. It is a compendium of information rather than an organized catalog.

There is now a great need for a scholarly catalog of Johann Christian Bach's music. The present author is preparing a detailed catalog of the composer's autographs which will illuminate his working methods and date and redate many works, as well as containing accurate transcriptions of the letters in their original languages and in English translation. Warburton's edition of the letters in the *Collected Works* is inaccurate and incomplete. He did not examine the originals, but (tacitly) relied on the transcriptions of others, such as Riccardo Allorto, who silently modernizes the Italian of Bach's letters to Martini, omits words and parts of sentences, and fails to convey their wonderful character and exuberance.[94] I hope to complete a new biography of the composer, in which Johann Christian will appear, not only as one of the most important composers of his generation, but also as a figure admired by the major thinkers and artists of his age in Germany, Italy, France and England.[95]

The Bach Daughters

Johann Sebastian's daughters were musical, though none was able to pursue a professional career. Catherina Dorothea (1708–1774), his eldest child, lived most of her life within the family, never marrying, and was described by her father

---

92 *The Collected Works of Johann Christian Bach, 1735–1782*, ed. Ernest Warburton, 48 volumes (New York: Garland, 1984–1989).

93 Though the facsimiles are often not exact: the autograph of the opera *Carattaco*, (Vol. XX) all the blank leaves are silently omitted in the reproduction, giving an inaccurate picture of the structure of the manuscript.

94 Riccardo Allorto, ed., *Gli anni milanesi di Giovanni Cristian Bach e le sue composizioni sacre* (Milan: Ricordi, 1992).

95 *A Descriptive Catalogue of the Autograph Manuscripts, Letters, Documents, ephemera and memorabilia of J. C. Bach (1735–1782)*, forthcoming.

458 *Stephen Roe*

as "musically... not bad at all," probably high praise. Catherina may have acted as an extra mother to the many children of the second marriage. The last child, Regina Susanna (1742–1809), evidently inherited much of her mother's estate, including unpublished sources of Johann Sebastian and of her brothers. She lived in straitened circumstances in Leipzig, unmarried and childless and was later assisted financially by the publishers Breitkopf and Härtel and J. F. Rochlitz. She was approached by the Swiss music publisher Georg Nägeli to buy her manuscripts and publish them in a special Bach edition. Nägeli did print a number of works of Johann Sebastian and played an important role in the Bach revival in the early nineteenth century, producing an edition of the Well-tempered Clavier and other works.

The Bach Pupils

The sons and perhaps the daughters of J. S. Bach can be counted as his primary pupils: he had no more talented disciples than his composer sons. Other Bach relatives entered his orbit, eager to take advantage of his teaching and the wider opportunities of the Thomasschule or the University of Leipzig. These included Johann Ernst Bach (1722–1777), who studied in the early 1730s, and Johann Elias (1705–1755), the Schweinfurt Bach. He was a theology student at the university, served as an assistant to Sebastian, writing discreet but gently revealing letters surviving in draft, about life in the environs of the Thomaskirche between 1738 and 1743, a selection of which have recently been published.[96] They are written to a wide range of correspondents, including his close family and other friends. Though they build a picture of life in the Bach household, they have relatively little musical content. They serve as an incomparable witness to the life of the Bachs and life in Leipzig in general. Johann Elias is regarded as another possible early teacher of Johann Christoph Friedrich and Johann Christian Bach.[97]

An earlier family member from Schweinfurt, Johann Lorenz (1695–1773) was a pupil of Bach in Weimar from 1715–1717. Bach's nephews from Ohrdruf, Johann Bernhard (1700–1743) and Johann Heinrich Bach (1707–1783) were both pupils and copyists for their uncle. Bernhard helped out in Cöthen, while Heinrich worked with Johann Sebastian in the mid- to late 1720s in Leipzig. Formerly known as Hauptkopist C, his handwriting was identified by Hans-Joachim Schulze.[98] He was not the most successful of Bach's pupil copyists: his work is often corrected or rewritten by Sebastian, or the underlay altered, possibly to the accompaniment of several cuffs around the ear. Another Ohrdruf Bach, Johann Andreas (1713–1779) was not a pupil, even though he owned a major source of

---

96 LBB 3 (2005). This second, expanded edition, takes advantage of new finds. The original edition dates from 2000. The letters published are the retained drafts and copies.

97 Terry, *John Christian Bach*, 2.

98 Hans-Joachim Schulze, "Ein 'Dresdner Menuett' im zweiten Klavierbüchlein der Anna Magdalena Bach. Nebst Hinweisen zur Überlieferung einiger Kammermusikwerke Bachs," BJ 65 (1979): 45–64, esp. 58–62.

his Johann Sebastian's music, the so-called "Johann Andreas Bach Buch," a manuscript collection inherited from his father Johann Christoph. Christoph's two other sons Thomas Friedrich (1695–1768) and Johann Christoph (1702–1756) did not study in Leipzig.

What constituted being a pupil of Johann Sebastian Bach? Attending one-to-one sessions, being in a general class, observing from a distance a great teacher, or even just being in the same room with him? We should think of the teacher/pupil relationship as being direct one-to-one contact with Sebastian, even sharing in musical composition, as with Wilhelm Friedemann; or being a major participant, but at a distance, as with Johann Christian. Clearly there were degrees of contact and various levels of his being a teacher. His tuition covered keyboard studies, organ and composition, encompassing harmony, counterpoint and figured bass-realization. His activities as a teacher began as early as Mühlhausen and ended at his death in Leipzig, with at least one student attending his deathbed. He had hundreds of pupils, not least at the Thomasschule, where many of them would go on to become professional musicians.

Bach can now be regarded as the most important teacher in Germany in the first half of the eighteenth century. His methods cascaded through his family and formal pupils and disseminated through C. P. E. Bach's *Versuch*, his elder sons' pupils such as F. W. Rust and the Levys and through the teaching of J. C. F. and J. C. Bach. Christian was able to carry forward the principles of his father's tuition far and wide in Europe, where he had students in Italy, England and Paris, his most famous being the young Mozart in London in 1764–1765.

The first study of J. S. Bach's pupils records about eighty names,[99] among which are famed musicians such as Krebs, Nichelmann and Gerber. His first pupil was apparently Johann Martin Schubert (b. 1690) in Mühlhausen and the last Johann Georg Voigt (1728–1765) in Leipzig. Löffler omits Johann Friedrich Schweinitz, the Göttingen organist, Bach's pupil in the mid-1730s. His career is captured by Hans-Joachim Schulze in a recent article.[100] A useful survey of the pupils is provided by Stephen Daw. It is difficult to dispute his main thesis that "the substantial body of evidence concerning his [Bach's] teaching and teaching methods is far from complete or authoritative."[101] There is clearly a book to be written on the subject of Bach and his pupils, encompassing the new material recently emerged from the studies made in the Bach-Archiv.

Of the several hundred pupils who passed through the Thomasschule during Bach's time in Leipzig, it has been estimated that at least three hundred went on to have careers as musicians and became teachers themselves. The churches and courts around Saxony and beyond were seeded with direct and indirect pupils

---

99 Hans Löffler, "Die Schüler Johann Sebastian Bachs," BJ 40 (1953): 5–28.

100 Hans-Joachim Schulze, "Johann Friedrich Schweinitz: 'A Disciple of the Famous Herr Bach in Leipzig,' *About Bach*, ed. Greg G.Butler, George B. Stauffer and Mary D.Greer (Urbana: University of Illinois Press, 2008), 81–88.

101 Stephen Daw, "Bach as a Teacher and Model," *The Cambridge Companion to Bach*, ed. John Butt (Cambridge: Cambridge University Press, 1997), 195–202.

460   *Stephen Roe*

of Sebastian Bach.[102] These musicians published little; they were hidden away in their churches or courts and next to nothing is known about them. They were Bach's immediate legacy, and to an extent the guardians of his works. Not only were they composers, but many were copyists for Bach himself and transcribed his music for performance in their churches. It is through this angle that so much work has been done, much of it by Peter Wollny, but also by colleagues and associates of the Bach-Archiv and elsewhere. In several elegantly penned, modestly titled but explosive articles in the *Bach Jahrbuch,* Wollny has revealed the names of pupils and copyists who were known hitherto by pseudonyms, such as Anon A, B, C, etc., and as a result shed light on a world which was formerly obscure or otherwise completely unknown. Wollny's work on the pupils and copyists, including Altnikol, pseudo-Altnikol, and Bammler, has provided new perspectives, new information and new answers to Bach's relationship with the musicians surrounding him, and specifically on the dissemination of his music through manuscript copies prepared by his pupils.[103] Much of Wollny's work has been stimulated by discussion with and reaction to the work of Hans-Joachim Schulze, the former head of the Bach-Archiv, whose pioneering work and research over fifty years has germinated much fine work by Andreas Glöckner, Wollny and Michael Maul.

There are relatively few anonymous copyists now and only a handful to be identified. This expansion of range of pupils has led to new perspectives on Bach as a teacher. The last years have seen more emphasis on the little-known pupils than on the famous, such as the Krebs, Kirnberger, Kittel and Heinrich Nikolaus Gerber, from whom we know most about the experience to be a Bach pupil, through the testimony of his son, the musical lexicographer Ernst Ludwig Gerber (1746–1819). The rediscovery of Gerber's transcripts of four of the English Suites (BWV 806, 808, 810 and 811) is of some significance, especially when no autograph exists. They reappeared in a Sotheby catalog in London and were acquired by an English collector.[104] Another exception is Johann Friedrich Agricola (1720–1774), the composer, theorist and obituarist of his teacher. Some new pieces of information have come to light in the newly published correspondence of Christian Gottfried Krause, a fellow member of the First Berlin School of song composition.[105]

Much work of the past years has centred on the copying work of Bach's pupils, how the different copies varied from each other, what represented the most

---

102 See for example Walter Hüttel, "Schüler und Enkelschüler Johann Sebastian Bachs im ehemaligen schönburgischen Territorium," BJ 74 (1988): 111–121.

103 See, for example, "Neue Bach-Funde,"BJ 83 (1997): 7–50; "Alte Bach-Funde," 84 (1998): 137–148; "Überlegungen zur Bach-Überlieferung in Naumburg," BJ 86 (2000): 87–100; "Neuerkenntnisse zur Bach-Ueberlieferung in Mitteldeutschland," BJ 88 (2002): 29–60.

104 See Stephen Roe, *The Kohn Collection of Music: Autograph Manuscripts, Letters, Printed Music, Books and Iconography* (London, December 2001). The Sotheby's sale was *Fine Printed and Manuscript Music*, London, 5 December 1997, lot 4.

105 *The Correspondence of Christian Gottfried Krause: A Music Lover in the Age of Sensibility*, ed. Darrel M. Berg (Farnham: Ashgate, 2009).

Sons, Family and Pupils 461

accurate version. The major strides in determining these copyists were taken by Georg von Dadelsen[106] and others in the 1950s, pioneers in the new era of Bach studies. This research too has had an important bearing on matters of authenticity. The Eight short Preludes and Fugues (BWV 553–560) for organ have plausibly been attributed to Johann Ludwig Krebs on the basis of watermark studies and also on musical style by Alfred Dürr.[107] Peter Williams, in the revision of his great study of Bach's organ works, while considering Krebs as a possibility, suggests that they might be more convincingly attributed to a south German composer such as J. K. F. Fischer, who had little or no connection with Sebastian Bach.[108] Another Bach work teetering on the brink of the J. L. Krebs catalog is the Fugue in C minor (BWV537/2). John O'Donnell claims that the last forty measures were not only transcribed but composed by the younger Krebs,[109] though as usual, these claims are far from uncontested.[110] Williams also attributes the chorale prelude *Das Jesulein soll dich mein Trost* (BWV 702) to Bach's favorite pupil.[111] The tricentenary of Krebs's birth in 2013 caused some excitement in his native Thuringia with a series of concerts, performances and recordings of his music. But there has so far been little in the way of re-assessment of his position and output.

A pupil who has been somewhat side-lined, even ignored, is Carl Friedrich Abel (1723–1787), friend and collaborator of Johann Christian Bach, who later founded the Bach-Abel concerts with him in 1765. His position as a pupil of J. S. Bach, probably in the late 1730s or early 1740s, is established by Burney.[112] Abel has been identified as the author of a somewhat critical assessment of his teacher relayed by Burney in his article "Fuga" in Abraham Rees's *Cyclopaedia*.[113] A member of a major German music dynasty often intertwined with the Bachs, Abel's father, Christian Ferdinand, was a gamba player in Cöthen and is a candidate to be the first performer of the Cello Suites. Sebastian Bach was the godfather of Abel's daughter, Sophie-Charlotte, and both men accompanied the prince of Anhalt-Cöthen on the fateful trip to Karlsbad. On his return from this visit, Bach discovered that his first wife had been taken ill and died.

---

106 TBSt 1, and TBSt 4/5.

107 *Acht kleine Praeludien und Fugen: BWV 553–560 für Orgel / früher Johann Sebastian Bach zugeschrieben*, ed. Alfred Dürr (Kassel: Bäreneiter, 1987), 34.

108 Peter Williams, *The Organ Music of J. S. Bach*, 2nd ed. (Cambridge: Cambridge University Press, 2003), 142.

109 John O'Donnell, "Mattheson, Bach, Krebs and the Fantasia and Fugue in C minor," *Organ Yearbook* 20 (1989): 88–94.

110 See Russell Stinson, "Studies and Discoveries," *J. S. Bach at his Royal Instrument: Essays on His Organ Works* (Oxford: Oxford University Press, 2012), 5.

111 See Stinson, *Bach at his Royal Instrument*, 5; Williams, *The Organ Music of J. S. Bach*, 442.

112 Charles Burney, *A General History of Music, from the Earliest Ages to the Present Period* (London: "Printed for the Author," 1776–1789) 4: 678: "Charles Frederick Abel, a disciple of J. S. Bach."

113 See Tomita, "The Dawn of the English Bach Awakening," 59–60.

462 Stephen Roe

Given the close connections of the Bach and Abel clans, it seems entirely plausible that Carl Friedrich should take lessons with Johann Sebastian in Leipzig. Some have questioned whether Abel was a pupil, but the testimony of Burney, personally acquainted with the gambist and author of his obituary, is paramount. What Abel studied is unknown. The possibility that he played the gamba solo in the St. John Passion in Leipzig cannot be excluded. Later in life he was critical of Johann Sebastian's harmonic complexity and his old-fashioned style of music-making. Burney himself was not much of a fan of Sebastian's music for much of his life, only recanting in old age.[114]

The most recent discovery concerns Gottfried Benjamin Fleckeisen, who in 1751 applied for a job in the small town of Döbeln, not far from Leipzig. His letter of application was discovered by Michael Maul in the town archives. Fleckeisen states he was a former member of the Thomanerchor and pupil of Bach and makes the claim that he "had to lead and conduct" musical performances in the St. Thomas and Nikolai churches in Leipzig for "two entire years" and "completed that service with honour." This news was trailed in John Eliot Gardiner's recent book, and Maul's detailed account later appeared in the *Bach Jahrbuch*.[115] The years in contention are probably from 1744–1746. Bach may have abrogated many of his responsibilities in his last years. As today, the job was exacting, politically delicate and exhausting, and it is no surprise that Bach needed some breaks. There are wider resonances. If Bach did not conduct much in his final years, what was performed? Did the annual cantata sequences 4 and 5, mentioned by C. P. E. Bach in the obituary, actually exist or were the later cycles simply of revised and rehashed material? Are Emanuel's claims for lost cantatas merely exaggerated or mistaken? Does this exonerate Wilhelm Friedemann from apparently losing the autograph manuscripts of the later cantata sequences, estimated at about one hundred works, a third of the known cantatas?

Bach did direct in his last years: the surviving parts for the St. John Passion from 1749/1750 and other parts annotated by him in his later hand prove that to be the case. The composition of church music did dry up and he turned his attention to concert works, orchestral music and the concentration on fugal and contrapuntal artifices.

Who can blame him if he chose to hang up his surplice in his last years? The twenty-first-century press reported this as "Bach burnt out," but applying modern concepts to eighteenth-century artists is of little use, especially on the slender evidence of a former pupil. The testimony of the music composed in Bach's last years, the Goldberg Variations, much of the Credo of the B minor Mass, The Musical Offering and the Art of Fugue, more eloquently denotes Bach's mental shape than any musician from Döbeln.

---

114 Tomita, "The Dawn of the English Bach Awakening," 59.

115 John Eliot Gardiner, *Music in the Castle of Heaven: a Portrait of Johann Sebastian Bach* (New York: Knopf, 2013), 540–541. Michael Maul, "...zwey ganzer Jahr die Music an Statt des Capelmeisters aufführen, und dirigiren müssen"—Überlegungen zu Bachs Amtsverständnis in der 1740er Jahren," BJ 101 (2015): 75–97.

Sons, Family and Pupils 463

There are groups of pupils who did not proceed to musical careers, but relayed the Bach flame in other ways. Johann Tobias, brother of Johann Ludwig Krebs, became an educator and author of works on the New Testament and Josephus; and Carl August Thieme, another educator and philologist—who has evaded the lists of Bach pupils. This is an immensely fluid area of research with many opportunities to dig into primary and secondary sources. Recent research shows that Bach's place as a teacher in his lifetime and through his sons and pupils, was of supreme importance in Saxony, Thuringia and Germany as a whole, fanning out to the whole of Europe and then the world. We are all Bach's pupils now.

18 Early Posthumous Printed Editions

Matthew Dirst

During the 100 years between Bach's death in 1750 and the founding of the Bach Gesellschaft in 1850, most of his keyboard and organ music and a number of the chamber and church works appeared in print from a variety of publishers across Europe. With a few exceptions, these editions followed the pattern set by Bach himself with his four-volume *Clavier-Übung* series—that is, with works demonstrating the utter mastery of didactic or domestic genres like the dance suite and variations—and in a series of highly learned publications from his last decade. Bach's posthumous editors and publishers followed suit with the Well-Tempered Clavier, the organ trio sonatas, the "French" and "English" Suites, the sonatas for violin and obbligato harpsichord, and new editions of most of the *Clavier-Übung* volumes, among other works. The sustained focus on Bach's keyboard and organ works reflects both the marketplace for musical editions during the late eighteenth and early nineteenth centuries, when German church works had little potential outside their immediate locale, and the longstanding preference among Bach devotees for works that could be studied and savored on one's own and shared with like-minded enthusiasts.

The First Posthumous Editions

The second half of the eighteenth century was hardly a propitious time for publishing the music of J. S. Bach. Tastes had changed dramatically, making much of the elder Bach's output seem anachronistic even to his most fervent admirers. By mid-century the sheer complexity of his work stood in stark contrast to the simpler, more tuneful style embraced by the younger generation: the genres in which Bach trafficked, moreover, held little appeal for musical consumers who preferred simple sonatas, rondos, or songs. Thus despite his fame as the greatest organist Germany had ever produced, there were few publishers willing to risk precious resources on volumes whose potential audience was rather limited. Hand copies of the keyboard and organ works continued to circulate among family members, former students, and the musically well-connected, and publishers continued to offer manuscripts and published editions of Bach's music from his own day, but there were few new editions. Just two collections of Sebastian's music appeared in print during this fifty-year period: *The Art of Fugue* and the four-part chorales.

Early Posthumous Printed Editions   465

By virtue of their exceptional status and remarkable contents, these volumes are among the most thoroughly documented first editions in the Bach canon. As a result, source-critical questions about these editions have mostly been answered; the story of their reception and influence, on the other hand, is still being written.

Bach may have labored for the better part of a decade on *The Art of Fugue*, but its printing was not yet complete at his death, for reasons we may never understand. An extant autograph of most of the collection suggests that Bach began work on it sometime around 1740, not during his last years as many once thought, while the engraved print shows how thoroughly he reworked the volume's contents over perhaps as much as a decade.[1] Divergences between the *Handexemplar* and the 1751/52 edition are discussed in a series of essays by Christoph Wolff and Gregory Butler that settles the intended order of the various contrapuncti and canons and summarizes what is known about the engraving process for the volume.[2] Bach himself supervised its copperplate engraving, the most expensive and the most artful method for publishing music in the eighteenth century, but its completion fell to Emanuel Bach and Johann Friedrich Agricola, who assumed responsibility for it at Sebastian's death in 1750. Announcing its imminent publication in May of 1751, C. P. E. Bach commended *The Art of Fugue* to connoisseurs, who "have a concept of what is possible in art and who desire original thought and its special, unusual elaboration."[3] Novelty, not extreme learnedness, was the selling point: "such a work, in which the entire study of fugue is so thoroughly elaborated upon a single theme, has so far nowhere appeared."[4] Nor has anything quite like *The Art of Fugue* appeared since. Its singularity was no guarantee of a commercial market in the middle of the eighteenth century, however, when fugues were regarded by many as more artifice than art; indeed, the title alone may have irritated those who regarded learned counterpoint as hopelessly outdated. And yet its posthumous editors in Berlin offered it the next year for subscription, seemingly confident that this last great example of the elder Bach's genius would find a grateful audience among at least connoisseurs of the art.

For once money was not the problem. Most of the engraving expenses had already been paid by Sebastian himself; all that remained was to cover the cost of the paper on which the edition was printed. Selling the work proved more of a challenge. Bach had neither provided a title nor made any kind of provision for distributing *The Art of Fugue*, likely intending to present a number of copies to

---

1 For specifics, see Klaus Hofmann, NBA VIII/2, KB, 16–76.

2 Christoph Wolff, "Zur Chronologie und Kompositionsgeschechte von Bachs *Kunst der Fuge*," *Beiträge zur Musikwissenschaft* 25 (1983): 130–142, revised ET, "The Compositional History of the Art of Fugue," Wolff Essays, 265–281; and Gregory Butler, "Ordering Problems in J. S. Bach's *Art of Fugue* Resolved," MQ 69 (1983): 44–61, "Scribes, Engravers, and Notational Styles: The Final Disposition of Bach's Art of Fugue," *About Bach*, ed. Gregory Butler et al. (Urbana: University of Illinois Press, 2008), 111–123, and Chapter 4 of this volume.

3 NBR, 257 (No. 281); Dok 5: 182 (No. C 638a).

4 Ibid., see also the announcement in the *Leipziger Zeitungen*, 1 June 1751; NBR, 258 (No. 282); Thomas Wilhelmi, "Carl Philipp Emanuel Bachs 'Avertissement' über der Kunst der Fuge," BJ 78 (1992): 101–105.

466   *Matthew Dirst*

colleagues and patrons, as was the custom.[5] Based on print run figures and recent estimates for Bach's previous keyboard publications,[6] one may assume that at least 100 copies of the work were planned, though far fewer were actually drawn. Bach's widow presented a few exemplars to the Leipzig town council, who "in consideration of her poverty" compensated her generously for them.[7] The rest were available via subscription, the most common method of music sales during this time. The project was helped along by no less a figure than the eminent Hamburg authority Johann Mattheson, who confidently predicted that the work "will one day throw all French and Italian fugue makers into astonishment—to the extent that they can really penetrate and understand it, not to speak of playing it."[8] Alas, few chose to "risk [their] louis d'or on this rarity," Mattheson's enthusiasm for it notwithstanding, probably for the very reason he suggests: the market for such sophisticated music was small indeed. To the dismay of its editors, the first edition of *The Art of Fugue* attracted only a handful of subscribers. A detailed preface to the 1752 print by music theorist Friedrich Wilhelm Marpurg seems to have had little effect on sales. In 1756 C. P. E. Bach offered to sell the engraved plates, perhaps because of the penalty that such a pile of copper could have brought upon its owner at the outbreak of the Seven Years' War.[9]

What to make of such a lackluster showing for Bach's greatest contrapuntal achievement? Perhaps the most important thing to note about this edition is the sense of obligation clear not only from the publication itself but from the way his disciples characterized this most unusual work. Obligation explains, at least in part, the participation in this enterprise of Emanuel Bach and his Berlin colleagues, several of whom had studied in Leipzig with J. S. Bach. *The Art of Fugue* needed to be published, both out of respect for its creator and for its inestimable value as a grand summation of the high style. Like no other work, it showed what could be achieved by a superior composer working within a system based in species counterpoint but writing fully developed fugues and canons of every

5 Bach reports in a 1748 letter to Johann Elias Bach that he gave away most of the prints of the *Musical Offering* as gifts to friends; Dok 1: 117–118 (No 49); NBR 234 (No. 257).

6 Of the works J. S. Bach himself had printed, there are print run records only of the *Musical Offering*, but these documents are inconclusive. A 1747 receipt from Bernhard Christoph Breitkopf for 200 copies of the title page and preface of this work (Dok 2: 436 [No. 556]) stands at odds with Bach's own 1748 comment (Dok 1: 117–119 [No. 49]) that he had only 100 copies of the work produced. Estimating the size of print runs for the *Clavier-Übung* series, Peggy Daub doubts that Bach ever sold more than 200 copies of any of his published works; see Peggy Daub, "The Publication Process and Audience for C. P. E. Bach's *Sonaten für Kenner und Liebhaber*," BP 2 (1996): 76. Similarly Andrew Talle is of the opinion that the number of exemplars of each of Bach's publications amounted to "several hundred"; Andre Talle, "A Print of *Clavierübung* I from J. S. Bach's Personal Library," Butler, ed., *About Bach*, 157.

7 Dok 3: 17 (No. 650).

8 Dok 3: 13–13 (No. 647); NBR 377 (No. 375).

9 When C. P. E. Bach disposed of the plates he took pains to note their great weight, not the fact that they represented any kind of financial drain. During wartime, any such precious metal became a highly controlled commodity, and could bring their owner no small amount of trouble if discovered in his possession; see Dok 3: 113–114 (No. 683).

Early Posthumous Printed Editions   467

conceivable kind, all derived from permutations of a single theme. Marpurg, who was relatively unknown at this time, had additional reasons for supporting the edition. Noting in his preface to the 1752 print that "in [it] are contained the most hidden beauties possible in the art of music,"[10] Marpurg effectively paved the way for the first volume of his *Abhandlung von der Fuge*, which appeared in print the very next year. How exactly Marpurg's acquaintance with *The Art of Fugue* affected his thoughts on the subject, as expressed in this treatise or elsewhere, remains an open question.

The first editors of *The Art of Fugue* were careful to characterize this collection in terms that would appeal to connoisseurs while not putting off mere enthusiasts. In advance press notices and edition prefaces, C. P. E. Bach, Marpurg, and Agricola proudly point to its comprehensive range of fugal devices and canonic species while stressing those aspects of this "perfect work" that might have pleased partisans of the more tuneful operatic style of Hasse and Graun. Their repeated insistence that *The Art of Fugue* is in fact "throughout practical," its ideas "spontaneous and natural," that each part of every fugue is "singable throughout,"[11] displays considerable chutzpah but also perhaps a certain anxiety about its commercial potential. The meager number of advance orders shows just how ineffective such descriptions were as public relations. As witnesses to changing tastes, on the other hand, these buzzwords show how Bach's compositional style could be reevaluated over the course of the eighteenth century as the exemplification of the most fashionable aesthetic ideals.[12] At the very least, the first editors of *The Art of Fugue* managed to establish its extraordinary worth as a compendium of counterpoint and fugue while bringing it to the attention of experts, some of whom republished excerpts from the work in their treatises.[13] That the 1751 and 1752 prints were highly valued by those who owned them seems clear from the large number of surviving exemplars: although C. P. E. Bach reports that only thirty or so prints were drawn, the NBA KB lists twenty-three extant copies of this edition and dozens of surviving hand copies made from it during the late eighteenth and early nineteenth centuries.[14] Interest in the work prompted new editions after the turn of the century by Vogt (Paris, 1801), Nägeli (Zurich, 1802), and an ill-fated edition by Breitkopf & Härtel (Leipzig, 1838) that had to be reissued the next year under a different editor to address complaints about Carl

---

10 Dok 3: 14 (No. 648); NBR, 375 (No. 374).

11 Dok 5: 182–183 (No. 638a); Dok 3: 114–116 (No. 648); NBR, 256–258 and 275–377 (Nos. 281 and 374).

12 On this topic, see my own *Engaging Bach: The Keyboard Legacy from Marpurg to Mendelssohn* (Cambridge: Cambridge University Press, 2012), 3–33.

13 Excerpts from *The Art of Fugue* appeared in Friedrich Wilhelm Marpurg, *Abhandlung von der Fuge* (Berlin: Haude & Spener, 1753–1754; reprint, Hildesheim: Olms, 1970); John Casper Heck, *The Musical Library and Universal Magazine of Harmony* (London: Welcker, ca. 1780); and Augustus Frederic Christopher Kollmann, *Essay on Practical Musical Composition* (London: Kollmann, 1799; reprint, New York: Da Capo, 1973); see NBA VIII/2, KB, 75.

14 NBA VIII/2, KB, 16–20, 62–75.

468   *Matthew Dirst*

Czerny's heavy editorial hand.[15] Given the number of surviving sources from this time, it is somewhat surprising to note that investigation into the work's reception has favored only the best-known cases of compositional influence—as one of many works of Bach known to Beethoven for instance[16]—over broader questions about its role in the musical thought and practice of a crucial era in Western music. Does the rise of the "school fugue" in early nineteenth-century pedagogy, for example, owe anything in particular to reception of *The Art of Fugue*?

We know more about the academic fugue's debt to the Well-Tempered Clavier, hand copies of which likewise proliferated as this seminal collection of preludes and fugues passed from teacher to pupil and among connoisseurs from London to Moscow during the second half of the eighteenth century. Like *The Art of Fugue*, the WTC acquired a reputation before it became part of the repertory, but in this case, detailed explanations of individual fugues preceded published editions.[17] Publication of the work occurred only after 1800, despite announcements from as many as ten years earlier that two editions were imminent.[18] Why did it take so long to produce an edition? For didactic works like the WTC, hand copying made a certain amount of sense, since the act of copying encourages careful study of the notes. Publication came only at the turn of the century, thanks to the sustained advocacy of influential German and English devotees.[19]

The connections Bach himself had established with various music publishers and engravers also helped to keep his music in circulation during the second half of the eighteenth century. The Breitkopf firm of Leipzig, whose founder Bernhard Christoph Breitkopf had published text sheets for various Bach cantatas and a small handful of his chorale harmonizations,[20] offered virtually all Bach's original prints and manuscript copies of various works for sale in catalogs published

---

15 On the latter edition, see especially Karen Lehmann, *Die Anfänge einer Bach-Gesamtausgabe: Edition der Klavierwerke durch Hoffmeister und Kühnel (Bureau de Musique) und C. F. Peters in Leipzig 1801–1865* (Hildesheim: Olms, 2004), 157–161.

16 Martin Zenck, *Die Bach-Rezeption des späten Beethoven: zum Verhältnis von Musikhistoriographie und Rezeptionsgeschichtsschreibung der "Klassik"* (Wiesbaden: Steiner, 1986).

17 For example, Kirnberger's analysis of the B-minor Fugue from Book 1 (Dok 3: 258–262 [No. 781]), and Reichardt's impressionistic thoughts on the the the F-Minor Fugue from Book 2 (Dok 3: 357–361 [No. 864]).

18 In a foreword to C. P. E. Bach's *Preludio e Sei Sonate pel* [sic] *Organo*, Op. V (1790), Berlin music dealer J. C. F. Rellstab announced his intention to publish the WTC, describing Bach's preludes and fugues as "the first and most lasting musical works of art the German nation can display" (Dok 3: 487; see Hans T. David and Arthur Mendel, *The Bach Reader... Revised, with a Supplement* (London: Dent, 1966), 454). Kollmann, a German organist living in London, announced his phantom edition in his *Essay on Practical Music Composition*, 97–98 (Dok 3: 582 [No. 1021]). On Kollmann's failure to publish the work, see Stephen L. Clark, ed. and trans., *The Letters of C. P. E. Bach* (Oxford: Clarendon, 1997), 228–232, 234–235 (Nos. 274 and 277).

19 See Dirst, *Engaging Bach*, chapters 4 and 5.

20 The former are listed in Ernest May, "Connections between Breitkopf and J. S. Bach," BP 2 (1996): 11 (Table 1). The latter appeared in Georg Christian Schemelli's *Musicalisches Gesangbuch* (1736), for which Bach served as music editor.

Early Posthumous Printed Editions 469

in the 1760s and 1770s. A more energetic music publisher and seller than his father, Johann Gottlob Immanuel Breitkopf was also an assiduous collector: by the 1770s his library included nearly all the editions Bach himself supervised (the *Clavier-Übung* series, for example) plus a number of autograph scores and parts, which his firm copied out and sold on demand.[21]

Though Breitkopf printed a number of volumes of C. P. E. Bach's keyboard works in the 1770s and 1780s,[22] he resisted issuing any new editions of J. S. Bach's music until Johann Philipp Kirnberger and Emanuel Bach prevailed on him to publish Sebastian's four-part chorales in four volumes between 1784 and 1787. The Breitkopf edition of the chorales was a significant improvement over an earlier edition from the Berlin publisher Friedrich Wilhelm Bernstiel (in two volumes, 1765–1769), and it served as the basis for subsequent editions of the works. These were the first volumes devoted solely to Bach's harmonized chorales, as culled from his concerted church works and teaching material. Whether Bach ever intended to collect and prepare such workaday music for publication will probably never be known, and this seems not to have mattered much to his heirs, who decided that his large corpus of chorales—which by contemporary standards were unusually complex—deserved to be published. Because both the Birnstiel and Breitkopf editions have been discussed at length numerous times in the literature, most recently by the present author,[23] only the principal areas of inquiry into their nature and significance need be mentioned here.

Detailed source studies by Frieder Rempp and Friedrich Smend track the expansion of the Bernstiel volumes, which comprise some 200 chorales, to Breitkopf's four books totaling 371 individual settings.[24] Both editions relied on manuscript collections of the chorales from members of Bach's inner circle, including those copied by C. P. E. Bach and Johann Ludwig Dietel, a pupil at the Leipzig Thomasschule during Bach's tenure there. While the origins of many of the chorales have been established, others remain a mystery and may stem from either one-time or occasional use either in church or domestically. Rempp usefully summarizes current thinking about the sources of the melodies and the origins of each harmonization in his Critical Report to the relevant volume of the NBA,[25] and Robin A. Leaver gives a detailed report about the current state of

---

21 BP 2 is the most complete source of information on the provenance, copying, and sale of the Bach sources acquired by Breitkopf, especially: May, "Connections," 12–26; Andreas Glöckner, "Church Cantatas in the Breitkopf Catalogs," BP 2 (1996): 27–33; Hans-Joachim Schulze, "J. S. Bach's Vocal Works in the Breitkopf Nonthematic Catalogs of 1761 to 1836," ibid., 35–49; and Yoshitake Kobayashi, "On the Identification of Breitkopf's Manuscripts," ibid., 107–121.

22 Daub, "The Publication Process," 65–83.

23 Dirst, *Engaging Bach*, 34–54.

24 Frieder Rempp, NBA III/2.1, KB, and Friedrich Smend, "Zu den ältesten Sammlungen der vierstimmigen Chorale J. S. Bachs," BJ 52 (1966): 5–40. On the relationship of the Bernstiel and Breitkopf volumes to later editions of the chorales, see Gerd Wachowski, "Die vierstimmigen Choräle Johann Sebastian Bachs. Untersuchungen zu den Druckausgaben von 1765 bis 1932 und zur Frage der Authentizität," BJ 69 (1983): 51–79.

25 NBA III/2.1, KB, 39–101; and NBA III/2.2, KB, 134–331.

470   *Matthew Dirst*

knowledge (or lack thereof) in three crucial areas: Bach's acquaintance with the chorale genre from a young age, his teaching of chorale harmonization, and the continued cultivation of the harmonized chorale by his followers.[26]

The first champions of these little miracles of harmony and voice leading emphasized the broad potential utility of the Bach chorales and their surprising inherent worth: Bach had transformed the most plain-spoken of musical genres by infusing the simple harmonized chorale with the same kind of polyphonic rigor found in his organ works.[27] At once apologetic and enthusiastic, Agricola notes (in a 1766 review of Part I of the Birnstiel edition) that "while [Bach's] melodies may not be as charming and touching as others, they are all controlled by the richest harmonies in such a natural and unconstrained manner; one would break into quite a sweat trying to write something of their equal."[28] In his preface to Birnstiel's first volume, C. P. E. Bach encourages subscribers to sing, play, and use the chorales as models for composition (something Marpurg and Kirnberger stressed as well), despite the fact that few were still learning musical composition from chorales in the 1760s.[29] At any rate, contemporary music theorists took note and occasionally reproduced a Bach chorale or two in their treatises and tutors as concise examples of his extraordinary *Harmonie*.[30] These miniature "masterpieces," as Emanuel Bach described them, elevated the humble chorale while providing a "practical textbook" for composers and serious students of the art.[31] Notwithstanding the enthusiasm of Marpurg, Kirnberger and their circle, it took some time before "the Bach chorale" became normative for either keyboard practice or harmonic pedagogy.[32] The eventual acceptance of the chorales as practical music—something we take for granted, having grown up with them in our hymnals and theory texts—happened only gradually, as musicians and theorists argued their virtues in the first half of the nineteenth century especially.[33] Much of this story has yet to be told, though various aspects of performance and reception are addressed in the literature.[34]

---

26 Robin A. Leaver, "Suggestions for Future Research into Bach and the Chorale: Aspects of Repertoire, Pedagogy, Theory, and Practice," BACH 42/2 (2011): 40–63; a revised version appears as Chapter 14 of this volume.

27 A point made by Christoph Wolff, Wolff Essays, 388.

28 Dok 3: 187–188 (No. 733), ET Thomas Christensen, "Bach among the Theorists," BP 3 (1998), 34.

29 NBR, 379–380.

30 For a concise yet comprehensive summary, see Christensen, "Bach among the Theorists," 23–46.

31 Dok 3: 179–181 and 202 (Nos. 723 and 753); NBR, 379–380 (Nos. 378 and 379).

32 Wolff overestimates, I think, the influence of the Berlin group when he asserts that the Bach chorale "became a norm for harmonic elaboration no later than Marpurg's [*Handbuch bey dem Generalbasse und der Composition*, Part III] of 1758"; Wolff Essays, 389.

33 NBA III/2.2, KB, 76–81, lists publications by Abbé Georg Vogler/Carl Maria von Weber (1811), Carl Ferdinand Becker (1830), Johann Anton André (1832), and Adolf Bernhard Marx (1841), and others that reproduce various Bach chorales as models of tonal harmony.

34 See, for example, Glenn Stanley, "Bach's 'Erbe': The Chorale in the German Oratorio of the Early Nineteenth Century," *19th-Century Music* 11/2 (1987): 121–149; David Schildkret,

Early Nineteenth-Century Editions

Bach's posthumous reputation as the "patriarch" of German keyboard music[35] finally found practical realization just after the turn of the century, when editions of his keyboard and organ works began to appear in earnest. The most eagerly anticipated of these were multiple editions of the WTC by Simrock (Bonn and Paris, ca. 1801),[36] Nägeli (Zurich, 1801), Imbault (Paris, 1801, fugues only), and by Franz Anton Hoffmeister and Ambrosius Kühnel as part of their ambitious *Œuvres complettes de Jean Sebastien Bach* (Vienna and Leipzig, 1801–04), the first attempt at a "complete works" edition though its actual aim was to publish just the keyboard and organ works. During the four-year run of the *Œuvres complettes*, Hoffmeister and Kühnel's *Bureau de musique* published some sixteen separate fascicles comprising the following single works and entire collections by Bach:

> Toccata in D minor (BWV 913a)
> Inventions and Sinfonias (BWV 772–801)
> Well-Tempered Clavier (BWV 846–869 and 870–893)
> Chromatic Fantasie and Fugue (BWV 903)
> Six "little" Preludes (BWV 933–938)
> Fantasie in C minor (BWV 906/1)
> "French" Suites (BWV 812–817)
> *Clavier-Übung* Parts 1, 3 (omitting the four Duets BWV 802–805), and 4 (Partitas BWV 825–830, "Organ Mass" BWV 669–689, and "Goldberg" Variations BWV 988).

For unknown reasons this series ceased production well short of its goal. Other publishers took up where Hoffmeister & Kühnel left off, producing first editions of the Bach motets (Leipzig, 1803), the unaccompanied violin works (Bonn, 1803), the sonatas for violin and obbligato keyboard (Zürich, 1803), and the organ trio sonatas (London, 1809–10). The next two decades saw numerous other works of Bach into print for the first time: the *Magnificat* BWV 243a (Bonn, 1811), six of the large preludes and fugues for organ BWV 543–548 (Vienna, 1813), the A-Major Mass BWV 234 (Bonn, 1818), *Ein feste Burg ist unser Gott* BWV 80 (Leipzig, 1821), the cello suites (Leipzig, 1826), and the G-Major Mass BWV 236 (Bonn, 1828), among others. A number of the keyboard works were available in multiple editions by mid-century, with the WTC leading the pack: my own recent

---

"Toward a Correct Performance in Bach's Chorales," BACH 9 (1988): 21–27; and Stephen Crist, "The Role and Meaning of the Bach Chorale in the Music of Dave Brubeck," BP 5 (2003): 179–215.

35 From an anonymous 1766 "Essay on Musical Taste"; Dok 3: 184 (No. 727).

36 This publisher's description of the WTC, as a "German masterwork, whose eternal worth had long been unanimously confirmed by all nations," confirms that an edition was overdue; Nicolaus Simrock, *Allgemeine Musikalische Zeitung*, Jg. 3, *Intelligenz-Blatt* V (4 Feb. 1801), 17–18; Dok 3: 617–618 (No. 1045).

472　*Matthew Dirst*

count lists more than thirty editions of this seminal work (not including reprints) before 1845.[37]

What do we know about this sudden outpouring of editions? The field of Bach studies excels at source histories, including those that trace the origins of early nineteenth-century editions. The most detailed of these, by Yo Tomita, address dissemination and publication of the WTC in two particularly important geographic centers: Vienna and England.[38] Dated but still useful are studies by Alfred Dürr and Magali Philippsborn that likewise focus on sources and early editions of the WTC.[39] Essays by Michael Kassler on the first English editions of the WTC and on the first-ever edition of the organ trio sonatas provide varied models for further work on other Bach editions from this time, whether single publications or parts of a series.[40] Good candidates for such investigations are not in short supply; perhaps most promising in this regard are the big organ preludes and fugues, esteemed by generations of organists and which Mendelssohn did much to champion,[41] and the "Goldberg" Variations, bits and pieces of which caught the attention of writers on music and certain composers during this time.[42]

37　See the lists of early nineteenth-century Bach editions in Dirst, *Engaging Bach*, 92 and 113 (Tables 4.1 and 4.2); and in Zenck, *Die Bach-Rezeption*, 4–19.

38　Yo Tomita's many contributions to this area of Bach studies include: "Bach Reception in Pre-Classical Vienna: Baron van Swieten's Circle Edits the 'Well-Tempered Clavier' II," ML 81 (2000): 364–391; "Most Ingenious, Most Learned, and yet Practicable Work: The English Reception of Bach's The WTC in the First Half of the Nineteenth Century seen through the Editions Published in London," *The Piano in Nineteenth-Century British Culture: Instruments, Performers and Repertoire*, eds. Therese Ellworth and Susan Wollenberg, (Aldershot: Ashgate, 2007), 33–67; "The Dawn of the English Bach Awakening Manifested in Sources of the '48'," *The English Bach Awakening: Knowledge of J. S. Bach and his Music in England 1750–1830*, ed. Michael Kassler (Aldershot: Ashgate, 2004), 35–167; "Pursuit of Perfection: Stages of Revision of the Wesley/Horn '48'," *The English Bach Awakening*, ed. Kassler, 341–377; "Veiled Aspects of Bach Reception in the Long Nineteenth Century Exposed through a Macro-examination of Printed Music: with Particular Focus on The Well-Tempered Clavier," *Understanding Bach* 7 (2012): 29–53.

39　Alfred Dürr, "On the Earliest Manuscripts and Prints of Bach's WTC in England," *A Bach Tribute: Essays in Honor of William H. Scheide*, ed. Paul Brainard and Ray Robinson (Kassel: Bärenreiter; 1994), 121–134; and Magali Philippsborn, *Die Frühdrucke der Werke Johann Sebastian Bachs in der ersten Hälfte des 19. Jahrhunderts: Eine kritisch vergleichende Untersuchung anhand des Wohltemperierten Klaviers I* (Thesis, Frankfurt-am-Main, 1975).

40　Michael Kassler, "The Bachists of 1810: Subscribers to the Wesley/Horn Edition of the '48'," and "The Horn/Wesley Edition of Bach's 'Trio' Sonatas," *The English Bach Awakening*, 315–340 and 417–429, respectively; and "Broderip, Wilkinson and the First English Edition on the '48'," MT 147 (Summer 2006): 67–76.

41　On Mendelssohn's reception of Bach's organ music, see Russell Stinson, *The Reception of Bach's Organ Works from Mendelssohn to Brahms* (Oxford: Oxford University Press, 2006), 7–75.

42　Three movements appear in John Hawkins, *A General History of the Science and Practice of Music* (London, 1776), for example, and the entire set inspired a similar compositional effort from Forkel. On the latter musical curiosity, see Donald Francis Tovey, "Bach: Goldberg

Early Posthumous Printed Editions   473

Documentary studies like Karen Lehmann's book on the Hoffmeister & Kühnel and C. F. Peters editions provide a similar wealth of detail for further research into the particular readings, reception, and significance of these first efforts to publish a comprehensive portion of Bach's output. In this book and in an earlier essay,[43] Lehmann marshals a large body of documentary evidence to relate how Breitkopf & Härtel, Nicolaus Simrock, Hans-Georg Nägeli, Hoffmeister & Kühnel and eventually the C. F. Peters firm advanced the Bach cause bit by bit, with editions of varying quality and ambition. Lehmann's primary objective is to show how the goal of a truly complete Bach edition emerged gradually, as first one and then another German publisher worked systematically through the keyboard and organ works. It was only with the founding of the Bach Gesellschaft in 1850 that the fledgling Bach industry finally found the academic and financial wherewithal to publish all his extant music. Anyone working on the Hoffmeister & Kühnel edition will also benefit from a volume edited by George Stauffer of correspondence between Johann Nikolaus Forkel, who served as advisor and *de facto* editor of the *Œuvres complettes*, and the Leipzig publishers.[44] Of course, Forkel did more than just edit a few volumes of Bach's music. Author of the first biography of the composer, he was one of several prominent turn-of-the-century figures who effectively argued Bach's music into print and into bourgeois musical practice. The most important of these advocates—in addition to Forkel, both Friedrich Rochlitz (founding editor of the *Allgemeine musikalische Zeitung*), and Samuel Wesley (the English "Bach disciple") were central to this movement— have received the lion's share of scholarly attention,[45] but even lesser known publishers like Nägeli and Simrock are of interest to specialists in Bach editions and reception.[46] And that is a good thing, since a detailed accounting of the surviving exemplars of just the WTC editions from the first decade or two of the century might alter our sketchy picture of this work's reach during a crucial time in its historical trajectory. Even more work remains to be done on the earliest editions

---

Variations," *Essays in Musical Analysis: Chamber Music*, ed. Hubert J. Foss (London: Oxford University Press, 1944), 48–49 and 73–75.

43 Lehmann, *Die Anfänge einer Bach-Gesamtausgabe*, and "Die Idee einer Gesamtausgabe: Projekte und Probleme," *Bach und die Nachwelt Band*, ed. Michael Heinemann and Hans-Joachim Hinrichsen (Laaber: Laaber, 1997–1999), 1: 255–303.

44 George B. Stauffer, ed., *The Forkel – Hoffmeister & Kühnel Correspondence: A Document of the Early 19th-Century Bach Revival* (New York: Peters, 1990).

45 In addition to Part II of my own *Engaging Bach*, which describes how early nineteenth-century Bach editions were part of a larger program of cultural awareness and education in early nineteenth-century Germany and England, the most recent publications that address these editions and/or the campaigns that accompanied them include most of the essays in Michael Kassler, ed., *The English Bach Awakening*; Hans-Joachim Hinrichsen, "Johann Nikolaus Forkel und die Anfäge der Bachforschung," Heinemann and Hinrichsen, eds., *Bach und die Nachwelt*, 1: 193–253; and Celia Appelgate, *Bach in Berlin: Nation and Culture in Mendelssohn's Revival of the St. Matthew Passion* (Ithaca: Cornell University Press, 2005).

46 Both Simrock and Nägeli's Bach editions are referred to with some frequency in Lehmann, *Die Anfänge einer Bach-Gesamtausgabe*, for example.

474 *Matthew Dirst*

of Bach's church music: the six motets or the Magnificat, for example, whose publication preceded by decades the 1829 revival of the St. Matthew Passion.[47]

Outside these German and English orbits in the early nineteenth century, a noticeably slower growth of interest in Bach means that less has been written about, say, the first French or Italian Bach editions. And yet, the French fascination with Bach's organ works especially—which led to a newly serious compositional aesthetic among organist-composers Jacques-Nicolas Lemmens, Alexandre Boëly, and eventually César Franck and the whole French "symphonic" school—grew substantially during the 1820s and 1830s with Belgian critic François-Joseph Fétis' support of the new German editions and French reprints of the same.[48] This was long before Albert Schweitzer and Charles-Marie-Widor created their all-too-durable edition of the Bach organ works for G. Schirmer Inc, leaving much fertile ground for further work on the first French editions and their audience. Ferrucio Busoni's work as a Bach editor has also begun to attract scholarly attention, especially as regards the production and use of "interpretive" editions of old music in the nineteenth century.[49] Given the sheer number of volumes of Bach's music published during the nineteenth century and the variety of editorial philosophies behind them, there should be no shortage of productive topics for further research in this area especially.

---

47 On Beethoven's reception of various Bach's mass settings, see Zenck, *Die Bach-Rezeption*, 232–263.

48 On which see especially Josef Burg, "Notizen zu den französischen Ausgaben der Orgelwerke von J. S. Bach und ihrer Geschichte," *Ars Organi* 34/4 (1986): 211–217, and 35/1 (1987): 22–27.

49 See, for example, Chiara Bertoglio, *Instructive Editions and Piano Performance Practice: A Case Study* (Saarbrücken: Lambert, 2012).

19 Recent Research Developments

Manuel Bärwald

Over the course of 200 years of Bach research not only did the view of Bach and his music change, and change repeatedly, the nature of our knowledge became more complex and sophisticated. It has now become a very specialized discipline of historical musicological research. One reason for this is that, compared to lives of other composers, the information we have access to is limited. The paucity of biographical and other documents has compelled us to borrow methodologies and techniques from other disciplines. Such primary research includes the identification of the development of Bach's handwriting, as well as the handwriting of his copyists, and the examination of the watermarks of the paper he used for his compositions. These were the methodologies employed by Alfred Dürr and Georg von Dadelsen in the 1950s to establish the "New Chronology" of Bach's vocal compositions.[1] On the other hand, many Bach scholars since Johann Nikolaus Forkel have attempted to unearth new documentary sources. For example, Forkel by corresponding with Bach's son Carl Philipp Emanuel, and Philipp Spitta by his pioneering research in archival resources. Here in a way is exemplified the two-sided nature of Bach research: the exploration of new archival resources, and the utilization of modern technologies as they become available.

New Bach Edition (NBA)—Revised

Until the Second World War, Bach scholarship was largely conducted by individual scholars and authors, but since the early 1950s, with the founding of the Bach-Archiv Leipzig and the Johann-Sebastian-Bach-Institut Göttingen, it has become a much more institutionalized discipline. These two institutions—one each in the DDR and BRD—were primarily concerned with the editing of the Neue Bach Ausgabe (NBA), which began publication in 1954.[2] The complete edition of the Bach-Gesellschaft, published between 1850 and 1900 in forty-six volumes, contained much incorrect and sketchy information concerning the authenticity and dating of many works, problems that the NBA sought to resolve

---

1 Dürr Chr, and TBSt 1.
2 NBA, Kassel und Leipzig, 1954–2007.

476   *Manuel Bärwald*

and correct by creating an accurate historical-critical edition based on up-to-date research. Thus Bach's complete works were published in more than 100 volumes during the second half of the twentieth century. In the process the understanding of Bach's music and his biography in many details became—yet again—radically altered as new musical sources came to light, new works were discovered, and new analytical methods were applied to research. Because of these new developments in methodology and the discovery of new sources some of the NBA volumes had been rendered out-of-date when its publication came to an end in 2007, hence the need for some revised volumes. For example, while Arthur Mendel identified four different versions of the St. John Passion, described in his NBA edition of 1974, under the terms of the NBA "to present the St. John Passion in a 'final form',"[3] he was obliged to conflate these versions into one, idealized non-historical form. Thus the St. John Passion is being re-edited for the new revised NBA edition (NBA[rev]) that will present two reconstructable authentic performance versions—those from 1725 and 1749. The first revised volume to be published, on the B-minor Mass, benefits from recent developments in technology, especially X-ray fluorescence analysis of the ingredients of the ink used in the autograph source.[4] Altogether the Bach-Archiv expects to revise 15 volumes,[5] including a new edition of the *Bilddokumente zur Lebensgeschichte J. S. Bachs*,[6] and revision of the libretti of the vocal works.[7]

The organ works were among the earliest sections of the NBA to have been completed (NBA IV/1–11), and there have been significant discoveries of source material since these volumes were published, but there is no plan for the organ works to be included in NBA[rev]. However, two new editions, taking full account of recent discoveries and alternative editorial procedures, are currently being prepared by different publishers, whose first volumes both appeared in 2010: *Bach: Complete Organ Works,* edited in 10 volumes by Werner Breig, Pieter Dirksen, and Reinmar Emans published by Breitkopf & Härtel, Wiesbaden, each volume including a detailed critical commentary and a CD-ROM of printable alternative versions; and *Johann Sebastian Bach: The Complete Organ Works. Leupold Critical Urtext Edition*, edited in 15 volumes by Christoph Wolff, George B. Stauffer and Quentin Faulkner, published by Wayne Leupold Editions, Colfax, North Carolina, each volume being supplied with critical commentaries, facsimiles and alternative versions, and three supplemented volumes documenting sources, chorales and performance issues.

---

3 Johann Sebastian Bach, *Johannespassion. Passio secundum Joannem. Fassung IV* (1749), ed. Peter Wollny (Stuttgart: Carus, 2001), ix.

4 NBA[rev] 1, ed. Uwe Wolf (2010); see also Uwe Wolf, "Many Problems, Various Solutions: Editing Bach's B-minor Mass," Yo Tomita, Robin A. Leaver and Jan Smaczny, eds., *Exploring Bach's B-minor Mass* (Cambridge: Cambridge University Press, 2013), 165–185.

5 Two further volumes have been published to date: Weimar cantatas (NBA[rev] 2), ed. Andreas Glöckner (2012), and violin chamber music (NBA[rev] 3), ed. Peter Wollny (2014).

6 Werner Neumann, *Bilddokumente zur Lebensgeschichte Johann Sebastian Bachs* = Dok 4, pictorial documents of the life of Johann Sebastian Bach.

7 Werner Neumann, *Sämtliche von Johann Sebastian Bach vertonte Texte* (Leipzig: VEB Deutscher Verlag für Musik, 1974).

Recent Research Developments   477

Bach Digital

Initially Bach Digital was conceived as a catalog of Bach sources that would be an addendum to the NBA. During the 1990s the decision was made to create such a catalog as an electronic database published on CD-ROM; later, these plans were modified to become instead an internet project including a digital library of selected autographs.[8] This database was based at the Johann-Sebastian-Bach-Institut, Göttingen, and became known as the Göttinger Bach-Katalog.[9] It went online in 2001 and comprises information about every Bach work and all the known sources.

In 2004 a common purpose and collaboration was forged between the Staatsbibliothek zu Berlin – Preußischer Kulturbesitz (SBB–PK), the Sächsische Landesbibliothek- Staats- und Universitätsbibliothek Dresden (SLUB), the Bach-Archiv Leipzig, and the Universitätsrechenzentrum Leipzig with the concept of Bach Digital, that is, a digital library based on the Göttinger Bach-Katalog. At the same time the Bach-Archiv had the opportunity to restore and digitize their original Bach sources: forty-four parts of Bach's Chorale Cantata Cycle, additional autographs from Bach and his family, and other valuable music manuscripts from the seventeenth and eighteenth centuries.[10] The SLUB owns four autograph Bach manuscripts: Kyrie and Gloria of the Mass in B Minor (BWV 232[1]), the Fantasia and Fugue in C minor (BWV 906), as well as two autograph transcriptions of works by Georg Philipp Telemann (TWV 8:6 and TWV 52:G2).[11] The largest number of Bach autographs is located today in the Staatsbibliothek, Berlin (SBB–PK), which holds about 80 percent of Bach's original manuscripts—including the Christmas Oratorio (BWV 248), the St. John and St. Matthew Passions (BWV 245 and 244 respectively), the Mass in B Minor (BWV 232), and the Brandenburg Concertos (BWV 1046–1051).[12] Together the three mentioned institutions own more than 90 percent of all the Bach sources.

The systematic digitization of Bach's autographs and original manuscripts began in 2008 and was sponsored by the Deutsche Forschungsgemeinschaft, which already had supported the Göttinger Bach-Katalog. After a two-year period of preparation Bach Digital went online in 2010, and the digitization and uploading of the images continued with the number of digitized sources constantly being increased. Information held in the Göttinger Bach-Katalog was updated, enhanced and transferred into a more user-friendly database.

A second project—planned to last three years—was begun in 2013. After Bach's autograph and original manuscripts, the project partners are now digitizing

---

8   For an overview of the history of Bach Digital, see www.bachdigital.de
9   www.bach.gwdg.de
10 "Bach Digital," *Concerto. Das Magazin für Alte Musik* 192 (April 2004): 11.
11 Christine Blanken, Christiane Hausmann, Jens Kupferschmidt, et al., "Bach Digital. Digitalisierung der Werkautographen und der originalen Aufführungsmaterialien Johann Sebastian Bachs, Leipzig 2013" (online publication).
12 Martina Rebmann, "Bach-Forschung am Bildschirm. Bach digital in der Staatsbibliothek zu Berlin," *Bibliotheks Magazin. Mitteilungen aus den Staatsbibliotheken in Berlin und München* (2010/3): 8–11.

478   *Manuel Bärwald*

and investigating early manuscript copies of Bach's works. This is particularly important because more than half of Bach's works were not transmitted in autograph sources. In these instances copies made by his sons, students and friends are the most valuable replacements for the lost original materials. This is particularly important since, in contrast to a good number of the autographs, there are currently no facsimile imprints of these sources.[13] By combining images of original manuscripts and early manuscript copies Bach Digital will eventually become a database that provides not only information on every Bach work but also digital images of their main sources.

Bach Bibliography

The roots of Bach bibliography go back to the early twentieth century when Max Schneider presented two catalogs of published literature about Johann Sebastian Bach which contained about 800 records of predominantly German publications.[14] First, in 1953, the editors of the *Bach-Jahrbuch* started publishing a cumulative Bach bibliography using a systematic classification.[15] Its final issue was presented in the *Bach-Jahrbuch 2011*. For the continuation of Bach bibliography the Bach-Archiv Leipzig now collaborates with Yo Tomita (Queen's University Belfast, Northern Ireland), who started building a database in 1985, which went online as an open-access internet source in 1997.[16] Tomita's *Bach Bibliography* presented for the first time the possibility for access, in real time, to an almost complete overview of the recent state of Bach literature. In April 2014 the database contained about 57,000 entries, comprising published books, scholarly articles (including reviews and correspondence), published facsimiles, printed editions of music (focusing on pre-1950), as well as unpublished dissertations from universities and unpublished papers read at significant conferences or meetings.[17] The collaboration between Tomita and the Bach-Archiv means that the bibliography can be continued and expanded with the broad staff and institutional base of the Bach-Archiv, continuing the recording of significant worldwide literature about J. S. Bach and the whole Bach family, irrespective

---

13 Martina Rebmann, "Fortsetzungsantrag für das Digitalisierungsprojekt 'Bach Digital' bei der Deutschen Forschungsgemeinschaft (DFG) erfolgreich," *Forum Musikbibliothek* 34/3 (2013): 41–43.

14 Max Schneider, "Verzeichnis der bisher erschienen Literatur über Johann Sebastian Bach," BJ 2 (1905): 76–110; Max Schneider, "Neues Material der bisher erschienenen Literatur über Johann Sebastian Bach," BJ 7 (1910): 133–159.

15 Wolfgang Schmieder, "Das Bachschrifttum 1945–1952," BJ 40 (1953): 119–168; continued by Schmieder (BJ 1958), Eberhard Franke (BJ 1967), Rosemarie Nestle (BJ 1973, 1976, 1980, 1984, 1989 and 1994), Karin Germerdonk (BJ 2000) and Marion Söhnel (BJ 2005 and 2011). The bibliographies published in BJ between 1905 and 1984 were reissued, with a supplement and index, as *Bach Bibliographie*, ed. Christoph Wolff (Kassel: Merseburger, 1985).

16 Yo Tomita, "About the Project" (www.music.qub.ac.uk/tomita/bachbib/bb-intro.html; accessed on April 7, 2014).

17 Yo Tomita, "Scope of Data," ibid.

Recent Research Developments   479

of the language, country of origin, or the date of publication. The new *Bach Bibliography*—combining the information from Tomita's database with the records from the library catalog of the Bach-Archiv—contains now (as of Fall 2015) 60,000 records.

Archival Studies and the Development of New Sources

The institutionalization of Bach scholarship since the 1950s brought with it a broadened research for hitherto unknown archival sources and a systematic elaboration of existing material. Between 1963 and 1979 Werner Neumann and Hans-Joachim Schulze from the Bach-Archiv published the four-volume *Bach-Dokumente* as a supplement to the NBA:

> The series was designed to incorporate all archival and iconographical material on Bach.... Volume 1 of the *Bach-Dokumente* (1963) comprises the written material originating with Bach himself—that is, all autograph letters, reports, testimonials, receipts, and the like. Volume 2 (1969) contains all documents dating from 1685 to 1750 that are related to Bach's life and work but that did not originate with the composer himself. Volume 3 (1972) includes all documents from the time of Bach's death in 1750 until 1800. Volume 4 (1979) is an iconographical documentation.[18]

Earlier projects—such as the edition of Bach's letters edited by Erich H. Müller von Asow[19] or *The Bach Reader* by Hans T. David and Arthur Mendel[20]—provided only a selection of documents which were given without systematic commentary. By contrast the volumes of the *Bach-Dokumente*, the series of supplements to NBA, provide a comprehensive anthology of transcribed documents, some of which are culled from later sources as the original documents are no longer extant.[21] But even these volumes have their limitations. For example, Volume 2 includes only documents that mention Johann Sebastian Bach by name, but ignores corresponding material that relates to his musical environment; Volume 3 ceases at the quite randomly defined year 1800. New research developments will no doubt solve these problems in different ways. Initially Volume 5 of the *Bach-Dokumente*, which was published in 2007, edited by Hans-Joachim Schulze, submits amendments and revisions to Volumes 1–3; many of them are results of Expedition Bach (see later in this chapter). Three additional volumes (*Bach-Dokumente 6–8*) cover the chronological gap between 1800 (the end of documentation in *Bach-Dokumente 3*) and 1850 (the founding of the Bach-Gesellschaft and beginning of the first critical edition of Bach's complete works).

---

18 Christoph Wolff, Preface, NBR, viii.
19 Johann Sebastian Bach, *Gesammelte Briefe*, ed. Erich H. Müller von Asow (Regensburg: Bosse, 1938).
20 The first edition of NBR was published in 1945.
21 Dok 1: 8.

480 *Manuel Bärwald*

Volume 6 (documents on the residual effect of Johann Sebastian Bach between 1801 and 1850) is thus the logical continuation of Volume 3. But while the older documentation is organized strictly chronologically and intended to present a complete edition, Volume 6 is based on a five-part thematic systematic order of the documents (biography, aesthetics and analysis, editions, performances, and performance practice) and comprises a selection of the most significant texts. Volume 7 is a critical edition of Johann Nikolaus Forkel's Bach biography *Ueber Johann Sebastian Bachs Leben, Kunst und Kunstwerke* (Leipzig 1802). Finally the forthcoming Volume 8, edited by Peter Wollny, will present documents relating to the transmission of Bach sources between 1800 and 1850.

None of the *Bach-Dokumente* volumes include general documents relating to the Leipzig Thomaskantorate. As an outcome of the celebration of the 800th anniversary of the Thomanerchor in 2012,[22] the Bach-Archiv sponsored two volumes of documentary sources, dating from the Reformation to the end of the tenure of August Eberhard Müller as Thomaskantor in 1810, presented along the lines of the *Bach-Dokumente*: letters and historical biographies of the cantors, music inventories, lists of choir members, and rules of the school.[23]

Expedition Bach[24]

Discovering new documents about Bach and his environment will not be ended with the completion of the *Bach-Dokumente* volumes. Volume 5 already includes several results of the so-called Expedition Bach—a research project planned by the Bach-Archiv in 2001, a systematic search for hitherto unknown Bach documents in historic archives and libraries of central Germany.

Up until this time the majority of documents that had been discovered—Bach's organ reports, testimonials for his students, receipts for some of his guest performances, etc.—were somewhat accidental findings. It was only in the Bach cities of Eisenach, Ohrdruf, Lüneburg, Arnstadt, Mühlhausen, Weimar, Cöthen, and Leipzig that scholars undertook intense and systematic searches for Bachiana. Expedition Bach was planned to leave nothing to chance and in 2002 a systematic and comprehensive search for Bach sources within the public, municipal, and ecclesiastical archives in 400 central German cities was begun. To date the high points of Expedition Bach discoveries have been the previously unknown

---

22 See *800 Jahre Thomana. Glauben – Singen – Lernen. Festschrift zum Jubiläum von Thomaskirche, Thomanerchor und Thomasschule*, eds. Stefan Altner and Martin Petzoldt (Halle: Stekovics, 2012).

23 Michael Maul, *Dokumente zur Geschichte des Thomaskantorats I. Von der Reformation bis zum Amtsantritt Johann Sebastian Bachs* (forthcoming); and Andreas Glöckner, *Dokumente zur Geschichte des Thomaskantorats II. Von Johann Sebastian Bach bis zum Ende der Amtszeit von August Eberhard Müller* (forthcoming).

24 Michael Maul, *Expedition Bach. Katalog zur Sonderausstellung im Bach-Museum Leipzig vom 21. September 2006 bis 17. Januar 2007* (Leipzig: Bach Archiv, 2006).

Recent Research Developments 481

Bach strophic aria *Alles mit Gott und nichts ohn' ihn*[25] by Michael Maul, and the *Weimar Organ Tablature*[26] by Michael Maul and Peter Wollny. Both sources were discovered within the holdings of the Weimar Anna-Amalia-Bibliothek—an archive that had previously been researched by generations of musicologists. This demonstrates the necessity of systematic searches even in well-explored places. However, the cumulative results at numerous smaller archives and libraries have already proved to be quite extensive. One of Maul's first discoveries was the identification of the Thomaner Carl Friedrich Barth first as a general prefect of the Thomanerchor and then the interim cantor after Gottlob Harrer's death in 1755. At that time Barth copied several of Bach's chorale cantatas and initiated the first renaissance of Bach's music after 1750.[27] Already in 1997 Peter Wollny was able to identify the last of Bach's unknown main copyists by name: Johann Nathanael Bammler, Thomaner and also a prefect from the mid-1740s. Bach included Bammler in the production of the parts to several cantatas, the score of the St. John Passion, and his copy of Handel's Brockes Passion.[28]

Bach's Thomaner

These successes of Expedition Bach encouraged the Bach-Archiv to start another research project in the 800th anniversary year of the St. Thomas Boys Choir in 2012: biographies of Bach's Thomaner were now being systematically researched. It was believed that the screening of the lives of Bach's students would also reveal more information about Bach himself—an expectation that has already been fulfilled. The project was initiated by Michael Maul's rediscovery of the matriculation register of the Thomasschule in the Leipzig city archive. The document had been lost since the Second World War; it records the names, matriculation dates, and short Latin biographies of all the Thomaner between 1729 and 1800. Since these entries are autograph documents we now have specimens of the handwriting of every Bach student between 1729 and 1750. When Peter Wollny discovered an autograph Bach copy of Francesco Gasparini's *Missa canonica* within the music manuscript collection of the Weißenfels St. Nicholas Church, he was able to show by consulting the handwritten entries of the matriculation register that Bach copied the piece with the assistance of his student Johann Gottlieb August Fritzsche, who became a Thomaner in 1740, and was one of Bach's most ambitious students.

---

25 See Michael Maul, "Alles mit Gott und nichts ohn' ihn" – Eine neu aufgefundene Aria von Johann Sebastian Bach," BJ 91 (2005): 7–34; NBA Supplement, *Beiträge zur Generalbass- und Satzlehre, Kontrapunktstudien, Skizzen und Entwürfe*, ed. by Peter Wollny (2011): 231–243.

26 *Weimarer Orgeltabulatur. Die frühesten Notenhandschriften Johann Sebastian Bachs sowie Abschriften seines Schülers Johann Martin Schubart. Mit Werken von Dietrich Buxtehude, Johann Adam Reinken und Johann Pachelbel*, ed. Michael Maul and Peter Wollny (Kassel: Bärenreiter, 2007).

27 Michael Maul and Peter Wollny, "Quellenkundliches zu Bach-Aufführungen in Köthen, Ronneburg und Leipzig zwischen 1720 und 1760," BJ 89 (2003): 97–141.

28 Peter Wollny, "Neue Bach-Funde," BJ 83 (1997): 7–50, esp. 47.

482   *Manuel Bärwald*

On leaving the school in 1745, he took a leading role in Leipzig concert life and composed many *Singspiele* for the coffee houses.[29] These matriculation entries establish our view of the typical biography of a Bach-Thomaner: after they left the Thomasschule they usually attended Leipzig University and later became cantor or organist in a central German city.[30] One notable example is Gottfried Benjamin Fleckeisen, who in 1751 applied for the post of cantor in the Saxon town of Döbeln. In his application letter, which Michael Maul was able to find in the Döbeln archive, Fleckeisen claimed he conducted and performed concerted music at Leipzig's two main churches, St. Thomas and St. Nicholas, substituting for Capellmeister Bach for two whole years.[31] These remarks cast a completely new light on Bach's activities during the 1740s when Fleckeisen was a prefect, and when Bach had composed no more church cantatas and was concentrating on music unrelated to his post as Cantor, such as the Art of Fugue (BWV 1080), the Well-Tempered Clavier (BWV 846–893) or the Musical Offering (BWV 1079).

Central German Sources in the Territory of the Former Soviet Union

Within the past two decades—after the dissolution of the Soviet Union in 1991— several discoveries of former central German sources came to light in archives and libraries especially in Kiev and St. Petersburg.

The most significant recovery of musical sources connected with the Bach family was the rediscovery of the historical music collection of the Berlin Sing-Akademie, which was made by Christoph Wolff "in collaboration with the Russian Research Center of Harvard University and, in particular, the Harvard Ukrainian Research Institute."[32] Inherited from the estate of Carl Philipp Emanuel Bach during the first half of the nineteenth century the Sing-Akademie held the most important Bach collection in the world. After the Sing-Akademie sold its autograph J. S. Bach manuscripts to the Berlin Royal Library in 1854 music scholars only occasionally took notice of its collection—in the early twentieth century especially Martin Falck and Heinrich Miesner, who devoted their research to the Bach sons Wilhelm Friedemann and Carl Philipp Emanuel. Since the Second World War, the fate of the Sing-Akademie's music collection was completely unknown. It was long after the Second World War when the scholarly interest in the Bach sons significantly increased, especially in the 1990s when

---

29 Peter Wollny, "Eine unbekannte Bach-Handschrift und andere Quellen zur Leipziger Musikgeschichte in Weißenfels," BJ 99 (2013): 129–170, esp. 130–133.

30 Manuel Bärwald, "Johann Sebastian Bachs Thomaner. Einblicke in ein Forschungsprojekt," *Bach-Magazin* 23/1 (2014): 24–25; see also Bernd Koska, "Cantors, Schoolmasters, and Directors: New Research on Bach's Students," UB 10 (2015): 161–170.

31 Michael Maul reported on this discovery in BJ 101 (2015): 75–97.

32 Christoph Wolff, "Recovered in Kiev: Bach et al. A Preliminary Report on the Music Collection of the Berlin Sing-Akademie," *Notes. Quarterly Journal of the Music Library Association* 58 (2001): 259–271, esp. 259.

Recent Research Developments 483

plans were made for a collected edition of the works of Carl Philipp Emanuel Bach. The loss of the Sing-Akademie's music archive that held many of C. P. E. Bach's works in unique copies was particularly acute. But with the rediscovery and the repatriation of the Sing-Akademie manuscripts to Berlin in 2001, many new scholarly opportunities could now be pursued. The planned publication of C. P. E. Bach's collected works was extended to a complete edition as a project of the Packard Humanities Institute, in cooperation with the Bach-Archiv Leipzig, the Sächsische Akademie der Wissenschaften zu Leipzig, and Harvard University.[33] A collected edition of Wilhelm Friedemann Bach's works, edited by Peter Wollny and published by the Bach-Archiv, was begun in 2009.[34] Wolfram Enßlin prepared a catalog of the entire Bach sources of the Sing-Akademie, which was published in 2006.[35] One of the first special studies of the Sing-Akademie's collection was presented by Peter Wollny.[36]

Another group of central German sources in Eastern Europe libraries concerns the many discoveries Tatiana Schabalina was able to make in the collection of St. Petersburg's National Library beginning in 2008.[37] The main corpus of her findings thus far consists of more than a dozen libretti textbooks for music performances in the Leipzig main churches, which establishes with accuracy Bach's Leipzig cantata performances and their dates, notably: the Ratswahl cantata *Wünschet Jerusalem Glück* (BWV Anh. 4), composed for 27 August 1725; the passion oratorio *Ein Lämmlein geht und trägt die Schuld* by Gottfried Heinrich Stölzel, performed in St. Thomas's Church on Good Friday 1734; and the St. Mark Passion (BWV 247), revised reperformance on Good Friday 1744. A complete documentation of the findings of Schabalina's research will be published in the near future.[38] Like the historical music collection of the Sing-Akademie found in Kiev, the repository of the St. Petersburg sources is similarly the result of looted arts, but in the eighteenth rather than in the twentieth century. The libretto booklets from Leipzig are ranked among the oldest holdings of the St. Petersburg

---

33 Carl Philipp Emanuel Bach, *The Complete Works* (Los Altos: The Packard Humanities Institute, 2005–).

34 Wilhelm Friedemann Bach, *Gesammelte Werke*, ed. by Peter Wollny (Stuttgart: Carus, 2009–).

35 LBB 8 (2006).

36 Peter Wollny, *"Ein förmlicher Sebastian und Philipp Emanuel Bach-Kultur": Sara Levy und ihr musikalisches Wirken; mit einer Dokumentensammlung zur musikalischen Familiengeschichte der Vorfahren von Felix Mendelssohn Bartholdy* (Wiesbaden: Breitkopf & Härtel, 2010).

37 Tatiana Schabalina, "'Texte zur Music' in Sankt Petersburg. Neue Quellen zur Leipziger Musikgeschichte sowie zur Kompositions- und Aufführungstätigkeit Johann Sebastian Bachs," BJ 94 (2008): 33–98; Tatiana Schabalina, "'Texte zur Music' in Sankt Petersburg: Weitere Funde," BJ 95 (2009): 11–48; Tatiana Schabalina, "Die 'Leges' des 'Neu aufgerichteten Collegium musicum' (1729). Ein unbekanntes Dokument zur Leipziger Musikgeschichte," BJ 98 (2012): 107–119; Tatiana Shabalina, "Discoveries in St Petersburg: New Perspectives on Bach and Poland," UB 9 (2014): 25–48.

38 Tatiana Schabalina, *"Texte zur Music" in Sankt Petersburg. Gedruckte Quellen zu Werken von J. S. Bach und anderen deutschen Komponisten des 17. und 18. Jahrhunderts* = LBB 12, forthcoming.

484 *Manuel Bärwald*

Imperial Public Library, where many of them were obtained by the brothers Andrzej Stanisław and Józef Andrzej Załuski, who founded Poland's first public library in Warsaw. They created a significant collection of published sources from all over Europe to create the library, which was brought in its entirety from Warsaw to St. Petersburg by the Russian army in 1795.

When Andreas Glöckner published a reconstructed inventory of the old music library of the Leipzig Thomasschule he assumed that this collection may well have shared a similar fate to that of the Sing-Akademie collection and hoped that it would be discovered somewhere in the former USSR. The forty-four original parts of Bach's choral cantatas that are today safely housed in the Bach-Archiv, Leipzig, were originally part of this collection but were separated from it during the Second World War, when the main parts of the manuscripts were evacuated from the Thomasschule to the Saxon castle of Belgershain. The Bach sources remained with the Thomaskantor, Günther Ramin, and fortunately survived the war. For the rest of the manuscripts, it is unclear whether they were destroyed during the war or whether they were taken to the Soviet Union by the Red Army.[39] This issue may possibly be resolved by further research in the future.

As Bach scholarship is ongoing and continuous, no final conclusions can be drawn. In the highly specialized and sophisticated world of Bach research, the expansion of our knowledge is incrementally slow as our findings are subjected to the scrutiny of other Bach scholars, the evaluation of new technological procedures, the development of new methodologies, as well as the improvement of old ones. My remarks in this final chapter of this Research Companion serve only to cast light on random points of the scholarly quest. The conclusion of any project and the solution of any problem rather than bringing a sense of closure instead underscores the incompleteness of our knowledge and raises a multitude of new questions—and for Bach research there is no end in sight.

39 LBB 11 (2011): 9–13.

Part VI

Chronology

20 Life and Works 1685–1750

Robin A. Leaver

Other chronologies of Bach's life can be found elsewhere. On the one hand, there are the briefer accounts in NBR, xli–lii, and Wolff, *Bach, The Learned Musician*, 525–534, and, on the other hand, there are the more detailed chronologies of Dok 5, 1–45, and *Kalendarium zur Lebensgeschichte Johann Sebastian Bachs*, ed. Andreas Glöckner (Leipzig: Evangelische Verlagsanstalt, 2008, effectively the third edition of the work first issued in 1970). This latter has formed the basis of what is presented here, but with some abbreviation and revision. Not included in this chronology are many payments for services rendered, and the regular installments of income from various sources. Also missing are most of Bach's testimonials for pupils, and others, though a few are recorded. Similarly, not every occasion when Bach stood as godparent will be found here. Some of the information in the *Kalendarium* has been revised to take account of the sources that have been discovered since that work was committed to the press, information that has subsequently appeared in issues of BJ.

In references to Dok and NBR, numbers without preceding punctuation or following a colon refer to item numbers; those following a comma refer to page numbers.

Eisenach 1685–1695

1685

21 Mar	Johann Sebastian Bach is born, the eighth child of the town and court musician Johann Ambrosius Bach and his wife Elisabeth (née Lämmerhirt). Dok 2: 232; NBR 304
23 Mar	Baptism in St. George's Church, Eisenach. Dok 2: 1; NBR 2

1693

Pupil in the Quinta (fifth class) of the Latin School. Listed as forty-seventh in the class of eighty-one; absent ninety-six hours.
Dok 2: 2; NBR 6

1694

Pupil in the Quinta (fifth class) of the Latin School. Listed as fourteenth in the class of seventy-four; absent fifty-nine hours.

Dok 2: 2; NBR 6

3 May — Burial of his mother, Elisabeth Bach (aged 50).

BJ 24 (1927): 149; NBR 3

23 Oct — Marriage of his eldest brother, Johann Christoph (1671–1721), to Dorothea von Hof, in Ohrdruf. Performances by members of the Bach family, including Johann Ambrosius Bach, and Johann Christoph's teacher, Johann Pachelbel.

BJ 71 (1985): 55–81

27 Nov — Marriage of his father Johann Ambrosius Bach to Barbara Margaretha Bartholomaei (née Keul).

BJ 24 (1927): 149: NBR 4

1695

Pupil in the Quarta (fourth class) of the Latin School. Listed as 23rd in the class of 45; absent 103 hours.   Dok 2: 2; NBR 6

20 Feb — Death of his father Johann Ambrosius Bach (aged 50); buried 24 Feb.   Dok 2: 3; BJ 24 (1927): 149; NBR 5

Spring? — Johann Sebastian and his brother Johann Jacob move to Ohrdruf to live with their eldest brother, Johann Christoph Bach.

Ohrdru3f 1685–1700

1696

Pupil in the Tertia (third class) of the Lyceum. Listed as fourth in the class.   Dok 2: 4; NBR 8

1697

Pupil in the Tertia (third class) of the Lyceum. Listed as first in the class of twenty-one.   Dok 2: 4; NBR 8

1698

Pupil in the Secunda (second class) of the Lyceum. Listed as second in the class.   Dok 2: 4; NBR 8

1699–1703 489

1699

Pupil in the Secunda (second class) of the Lyceum. Listed as fourth in the class; transferred to the Prima (first class).

Dok 2: 4; NBR 8

1700

Feb-Mar

Protestant Germany changed from the "old style" Julian calendar to the "new style" Gregorian calendar. Thursday 18 Feb (Thursday after Sexegesima Sunday) was followed immediately by 1 March (Monday before Reminiscere Sunday); the intervening days (including Estomihi and Invocavit Sundays) were thus "lost."

15 Mar

With his school friend Georg Erdmann, leaves Ohrdruf for Lüneburg; arrives in time to celebrate Holy Week and Easter. (4–11 April)

Dok 2: 4; NBR 8

Lüneburg 1700–1703

Ms. of the chorale prelude *An Wasserflüssen Babylon*, by Johann Adam Reinken, in tablature in Bach's hand, copied in the house of Georg Böhm and dated: "a[nn]o. 1700 Lunaburgi."

Dok 5, 272 [Anhang. Notizen, Besitzmerke No. 17]

1 May

Receives fees for singing in the Mettenchor (Mattins choir) of St. Michael's Church for the month of April (beginning on 3 April).

Dok 2: 5

29 May

Receives fees for singing in the Mettenchor (Mattins choir) for the month of May.

Dok 2: 4; NBR 11

1702

Sept/Oct?

Attempted to become the successor to Gottfried Christoph Gräffenhayn (?–1702) as organist of St. James Church, Sangerhausen.

Dok 1: 38

It is not known where Bach was living at this time: Was he still in Lüneburg or had he returned to Ohrdruf?

Weimar 1703

20 Dec 1702

↓

"Laquey [lackey] Baach" employed by Duke Johann Ernst von Saxe-Weimar (1664–1707), probably through the influence of Johann Effler (1635–1711), the Weimar court organist.

490   *1703–1707*

31 May 1703   Dok 2: 6; NBR 13; see also BJ (2004): 157–168, and Dok 5, 289

1703

ca. 3 July   Examination and inauguration of the new Wender organ in the New Church, Arnstadt.   Dok 2: 7; NBR 15

Arnstadt 1703–1707

9 Aug   Bach appointed organist of the New Church, Arnstadt.
                    Dok 2: 8–10; NBR 16

1705

Aug   Deliberations of the Arnstadt Consistory concerning the brawl between Bach and Johann Heinrich Geyersbach.
                    Dok 2: 14; NBR 19

Oct/Nov   Visit to Lübeck "to comprehend one thing and another about his art"; in his absence, his cousin Johann Ernst Bach undertook his duties in Arnstadt.   Dok 2: 16; NBR 20

2/3 Dec   In Lübeck for the Abendmusiken when Buxtehude's *Castrum doloris* (BuxWV 134) and *Templem honoris* (BuxWV 135) were performed.   Dok 2: 16; NBR 20

1706

Jan/Feb   Return to Arnstadt after three or four months' absence; on 2 Feb Bach received Communion in Arnstadt.   Dok 2: 15

21 Feb   Rebuked by the Arnstadt Consistory for his extended absence from Arnstadt and for confusing organ playing on his return.   Dok 2: 16; NBR 20

4 Apr   (Easter Day). Performance of the earliest version of *Christ lag in Todesbanden* (BWV 4)?

11 Nov   Rebuked by the Arnstadt Consistory for unwillingness to make music with students, and for taking a young lady into the organ loft.   Dok 2: 17; NBR 21

28 Nov   (Advent 1) Participates in the examination of the new organ at Langewiesen.   Dok 2: 18

1707

4 Apr   (Easter Day) Tests the renewed organ in the St. Blasius Church, Mühlhausen. Probably performs *Christ lag in Todesbanden* (BWV 4).   Dok 2: 19

24 May	Bach is suggested as the successor of Johann Georg Ahle as organist of the St. Blasius Church, Mühlhausen.
	Dok 2: 19; NBR 22a
14/15 June	Bach is appointed organist of the St. Blasius Church, Mühlhausen.
	Dok 2: 20; NBR 22b-c
15 June	Announcement of Bach's appointment in Mühlhausen.
	Dok 2: 21; NBR 23
22/23 June	Johann Ernst Bach became a candidate for Sebastian's position in Arnstadt, and is subsequently chosen.
	Dok 2: 22–23; see also Dok 2: 34–35
29 June	Bach requests the Arnstadt Consistory for his dismissal and returns the organ key. Dok 2: 25; NBR 24
July	Removal to Mühlhausen.

Mühlhausen 1707–1708

	The Quodlibet fragment, *Was seind das vor große Schlösser* (BWV 524) dates from Bach's Mühlhausen period. Date and place of performance are unknown, but was probably "composed" for a wedding of a member of the Bach family.
Aug	Takes up his duties as organist of the St. Blasius Church, Mühlhausen.
2 Oct	(Trinity 15) First reading of the banns of marriage in the New Church, Arnstadt, for Johann Sebastian Bach and Maria Barbara, youngest daughter of Johann Michael Bach, organist in Gehren.
	Dok 2: 28; NBR 26
17 Oct	Marries Maria Barbara in Dornheim. Dok 2: 28–29; NBR 26

1708

4 Feb	Performance of the *Gott is mein König* (BWV 71), for the inauguration of the new town council, Bach's first publication.
	Dok 2: 30–31; NBR 27, 28a; see also Dok 1, 268 and NBA I/32.1 KB, 61
21 Feb	Suggested specification, and explanation of improvements, for the St. Blasius Church organ.
	Dok 1: 83; Dok 2: 32; NBR 29–31
20 June	Bach is chosen as the successor to Johann Effler as organist and chamber musician at the court of dukes Wilhelm Ernst and Ernst August of Saxe-Weimar. Dok 5: 35a
By 25 June	First performance of *Aus der Tiefe rufe ich, Herr, zu dir* (BWV 131). Dok 3, 638
25 June	Bach requests dismissal from the position of organist of the St. Blasius Church. Dok 1: 1; NBR 32

492   *1708–1711*

| 26 June | Dismissal granted. | Dok 2: 36; NBR 33 |
| 4 July | Johann Friedrich Bach chosen as Sebastian's successor in Mühlhausen. | Dok 2: 37; NBR 34 |

Weimar 1708–1717

| 14 July | Bach takes up his duties at the Weimar court. | Dok 2: 38 |
| 29 Dec | Baptism of the firstborn daughter, Catherina Dorothea Bach. | Dok 2: 42 |

1709

1709→1712	Bach makes a handwritten copy of de Grigny, *Premier Livre d'Orgue* (Paris, 1699): Universitätsbibliothek Frankfurt am Main. Mus. Hs. 1538.	Dok 2: 409; Dok 3: 147a
4 Feb	Performance of Bach's second town council cantata (BWV Anh. I.192) in St. Mary's Church, Mühlhausen; score, parts and print no longer extant.	Dok 2: 43; NBR 28b & d; see also NBA I/32.1, KB, 85
10 Feb	Second performance of Bach's second town council cantata (BWV Anh. I.192) in St. Blasius Church, Mühlhausen.	See NBA I/32.1, KB, 85
March	Johann Georg Pisendel visits Bach in Weimar.	Dok 3: 735

1710

4 Feb	First performance of Bach's third town council cantata in St. Mary's Church, Mühlhausen; composition lost.	See NBA I/32.1, KB, 87
10 Feb	Second performance of Bach's third town council cantata (BWV Anh. I.192) in St. Blasius Church, Mühlhausen.	See NBA I/32.1, KB, 87
26 Oct	(Trinity 19) Participates in the examination of the new organ at Taubach, near Weimar.	Dok 2: 50–50a
22 Nov	Birth of son, Wilhelm Friedemann Bach.	Dok 2: 51: NBR 41
24 Nov	Baptism of son, Wilhelm Friedemann.	Dok 2: 51; NBR 41

1711

??	Bach is guest performer at the court of Gotha.	Dok 5: B 52b
16 Feb	Bach writes testimonial for organ builder Heinrich Nicolaus Trebs, the builder of the organ in Taubach that he examined on 26 Oct 1710.	Dok 1: 84; NBR 42
3 Jun	Bach's salary is increased.	Dok 5: B 52a; NBR 38

_1712–1713_ 493

1712

Bach makes a handwritten copy of Du Mage, _Livre d'Orgue_ (Paris, 1708); no longer extant. Dok 2: 409; NBR 344

30 Apr Philipp David Krauter begins studying with Bach.
Dok 5: B53b

27 Sept Bach stands godfather to Johann Gottfried Walther, jun., son of Bach's cousin, Johann Gottfried Walther, organist of the town church in Weimar. Dok 2: 54

Oct Johann Gotthilf Ziegler concludes his studies with Bach.
See Dok 2: 324

1713

The cantata _Mein Herz schwimmt im Blut_ (BWV 199) probably composed sometime in 1713.

19 Feb (Sexagesima). Probable first performance of _Gleichwe der Regen und Schnee vom Himmel_ fällt (BWV 18).

21–22 Feb Bach is guest performer at the court of Weissenfels, which may not have been his first visit. He seems to have established a significant connection with the Weissenfels court around this time, though the documentary evidence is incomplete.
Dok 2: 55; Dok 5, 290; NBR 44

23 Feb Birth and emergency baptism of the twins Maria Sophia and Johann Christoph Bach; Johann Christoph died the same day.
Dok 2: 56

27 Feb First performance of the Hunting Cantata, _Was mir behagt, ist nur die muntre Jagd_ (BWV 208), celebrating the birthday of Duke Christian of Saxe-Weissenfels, in the duke's hunting lodge. NBA I/35, KB, 40

15 Mar Burial of Maria Sophia, three weeks old. Dok 2: 57

2 Aug Bach enters a four-part perpetual canon (BWV 1073) in an autograph album. Dok 1: 147; NBR 45

Sept/Oct Johann Lorenz Bach begins studying with Bach.
Dok 2: 82; NBR 66

Before 3 Sept First performance of the motet _Ich lasse dich nicht, du segnest mich denn_ (BWV Anh. III.159)

3 Sept Philipp David Kräuter concludes his studies with Bach.
Dok 2: 58; Dok 5: B 58a

30 Oct _Alles mit Gott und nichts ohn' ihn_ (BWV 1127) composed for the fifty-third birthday of Duke Wilhelm Ernst of Saxe-Weimar. Dok 5: B 59a

6 Nov Participant in the consecration of the restored St James Church, Weimar. Dok 2: 60

1–15 Dec Bach in Halle. Dok 1: 4; Dok 2: 62; NBR 46–47

494   *1713–1714*

3 or 10 Dec	Performance of a trial cantata in the Church of Our Lady, Halle; music unknown. Dok 2: 62; NBR 46a
13 Dec	Bach is chosen as the successor of the late Friedrich Wilhelm Zachow as organist of the Church of Our Lady, Halle.
	Dok 2: 63; NBR 48

1714

	Bach makes a handwritten copy of Frescobaldi, *Fiori musicali* (Venice, 1635), dated "J. S. Bach 1714"; no longer extant.
	Dok 1, 269
14 Jan	Bach requests changes in the proposed Halle contract; letter to August Becker. Dok 1: 2; NBR 49
Before 19 Mar	Bach declines the position in a no-longer-extant letter.
	Dok 1:3; Dok 2: 65
2 Mar	Bach is promoted to Concertmaster, with an increased salary, with the added duties of composing one cantata a month for performance in the court chapel. Dok 2: 66; NBR 51
8 Mar	Birth of son Carl Philipp Emanuel Bach. Dok 2: 67
10 Mar	Baptism of son Carl Philipp Emanuel (Georg Philipp Telemann was godfather). Dok 2: 67; NBR 55
19 Mar	Bach refutes the accusation that he acted dishonestly over his dealings with the church officials in Halle concerning the position of organist; letter to August Becker. Dok 1: 4; NBR 50
23 Mar	New rules introduced for rehearsals in connection with Bach's increased responsibilities. Dok 2: 66
25 Mar	(Palm Sunday) First performance of *Himmelskönig, sei willkommen* (BWV 182).
22 Apr	(Jubilate) First performance of *Weinen, Klagen, Sorgen, Sagen* (BWV 12).
1 May	Following Bach's rejection of the Halle organist position, the Halle church council undertake to find another; eventually (30 July 1714) Gottfried Kirchhoff is chosen. Dok 2: 70
20 May	(Pentecost) First performance of *Erschallet, ihr Lieder, erklinget, ihr Saiten* (BWV 172).
17 June	(Trinity 3) Performance of *Ich hatte viel Bekümmernis* (BWV 21), designated for "in ogni tempi," which may have been composed earlier.
12 Aug	(Trinity 11) Reperformance of *Mein Herz schwimmt im Blut* (BWV 199) [see under 1713].
2 Dec	(Advent 1) First performance of *Nun komm der Heiden Heiland* (BWV 61).
25 Dec	(Christmas Day) Possible first performance of *Christen, ätzet diesen Tag* (BWV 63).
30 Dec	(Sunday after Christmas) First performance of *Tritt auf die Glaubensbahn* (BWV 152).

1715–1716 495

1715

24 Feb	(Sexagesima) Possible first performance of *Gleichwie der Regen und Schnee vom Himmel fällt* (BWV 18).
20 Mar	Bach's salary is increased. Dok 2: 73; NBR 73
24 Mar	(Oculi) First performance of *Alles, was von Gott geboren* (BWV 80a).
21 Apr	(Easter Day) First performance of *Der Himmel lacht! die Erde jubilieret* (BWV 31).
11 May	Birth of son, Johann Gottfried Bernhard Bach. Dok 2: 74; NBR 56
12 May	Baptism of son, Johann Gottfried Bernhard. Dok 2: 74; NBR 56
16 June	(Trinity Sunday) First performance of *O heilige Geist- und Wasserbad* (BWV 165).
14 July	(Trinity 4). First performance of *Barmherziges Herze der ewigen Liebe* (BWV 185).
1 Aug	Death of Prince Johann Ernst of Saxe-Weimar. BJ 71 (1985): 159
11 Aug ↓ 2 Feb 1716	Period of mourning for Prince Johann Ernst of Saxe-Weimar during which time no celebrations were permitted and little music allowed. The ban was partially lifted on 10 Nov (Trinity 21), from which date concerted church music could resume. BJ 71 (1985): 159–161
24 Nov	(Trinity 23) First performance of *Nur jedem das Seine!* (BWV 163).
22 Dec	(Advent 4) First performance of *Bereitet die Wege, bereitet die Bahn* (BWV 132).

1716

Jan ??	Bach makes a manuscript copy of the cantata *Languet anima mea* by Francesco Bartolomeo Conti. BJ 64 (1978): 55–57
19 Jan	(Epiphany 2) First performance of *Mein Gott, wie lang, ach lange* (BWV 155).
2 Feb	Remaining mourning restrictions lifted. BJ 71 (1985): 161
4 Feb	Memorial sermon with suitable funeral music for Prince Johann Ernst of Saxe-Weimar, *Was ist, das wir Leben nennen* (BWV deest); music lost.
31 Mar ↓ 28 Apr	Bach is invited by the church council to examine the new organ in the Church of Our Lady, Halle, built by Christoph Contius. Dok 2: 76, 78
22 Apr	Bach accepts the invitation to inspect the new Halle organ; letter to August Becker. Dok 1: 5; NBR 58
29 Apr–1 May	Examination and inauguration of the new Contius organ in the Church of Our Lady, Halle, with Johann Kuhnau, Cantor in

496   *1716–1717*

	Leipzig, and Christoph Friedrich Rolle, organist in Quedlinburg. Dok 2: 76
1 May	Report on the new Halle organ submitted by Kuhnau, Rolle, and Bach. Dok 1: 85; NBR 59
	Inauguration of the new organ. Dok 1: 85, 108; Dok 2: 76, 78, 594; NBR 59–61
31 July	Bach and Johann Anton Weise, organ builder in Arnstadt, write a testimonial for Johann Georg Schröter, builder of the new organ in the Augustinian Church, Erfurt, which they had tested and evaluated. Dok 1: 86; Dok 2: 79; NBR 62
27 Sept	(Trinity 16) First performance of *Komm, du süße Todesstunde* (BWV 161).
25 Oct	(Trinity 20) First performance of *Ach! Ich sehe, ietz, da ich zur Hochzeit gehe* (BWV 162).
1 Dec	Death of the Weimar Court Capellmeister, Johann Samuel Drese.
6 Dec	(Advent 2) Probable first performance of *Wachet! betet! betet! wachet!* (BWV 70a).
13 Dec	(Advent 3) Probable first performance *Ärgre dich, o Seele, nicht* (BWV 186a).
20 Dec	(Advent 4) Incomplete manuscript of *Herz und Mund und Tat und Leben* (BWV 147a), suggesting that it was not performed in the Weimar court chapel at this time.

1717

	Earliest printed reference to Bach: Mattheson's request for an autobiography from Bach in *Das Beschützte Orchestre* (Hamburg, 1717), 222. Dok 2: 83
26 Mar	(Good Friday) Bach directs Passion music in the chapel of the Gotha court; composition unknown. Dok 5: B 81a; NBR 63–65
Aug/Sept?	Visit to Dresden; correspondence with the French organist, Louis Marchand (no longer extant), and the abortive attempt to arrange a competition between the two virtuosi at the Dresden court. Dok 1: 6; Dok 2: 441; NBR 67; Dok 3: 666; NBR 306
5 Aug	Bach pledged to become the successor of Augustin Reinhard Stricker as court Capellmeister to Leopold of Anhalt-Cöthen. Dok 2: 128
7 Aug	Bach's expenses paid retrospectively by the Cöthen court later in the year (29 Dec), since at the time Bach's new position had yet to be ratified. Dok 2: 86
30 Oct	Fifty-seventh birthday of Wilhelm Ernst of Saxe-Weimar, and eve of the celebration of the bicentenary of the Reformation, 1517–1717.

31 Oct–1 Nov	Jubilee festival of the 200th anniversary of the Lutheran Reformation, held over three days, throughout Germany but especially in Saxony, where it began. Wilhelm Ernst issued detailed instructions on how the three days should be celebrated at court as well as in the churches of Saxe-Weimar.
6 Nov	Bach arrested and detained for forcing the issue of his dismissal. Dok 2: 84; NBR 68
2 Dec	Bach released from detention with an unfavorable discharge from the Duke Wilhelm Ernst's service. Dok 2: 84; NBR 68

Cöthen 1717–1723

16 Dec	Bach examines the new organ, built by Johann Scheibe of Leipzig, in the university church of St. Paul. Dok 1: 109; Dok 2: 85, 87–89; NBR 73
17 Dec	Bach's written report on the organ. Dok 1: 87; NBR 72

1718

19 Apr	Maria Barbara Bach in Halle, as godparent at the baptism of Christiana Renata Ziegler, daughter of Bach's pupil Johann Gotthilf Ziegler. Dok 2: 90
9 May	Leaves for a visit to Carlsbad with Prince Leopold. BJ 92 (2006): 97
29 June?	Return from Carlsbad. BJ 92 (2006): 98
15 Nov	Birth of son, Leopold August Bach. Dok 2: 94; NBR 78
17 Nov	Baptism of son, Leopold Augustus. Dok 2: 94; NBR 78
10 Dec	Birthday of Prince Leopold of Anhalt-Cöthen. Performance of *Der Himmel dacht auf Anhalts Ruhm und Glück* (BWV 66a); music only partially known. Also performance of *Lobet den Herrn, all seine Heerscharen* (BWV Anh. I, 5); music lost.

1719

	Johann Mattheson again requests Bach to supply biographical details. *Exemplarische Organisten-Probe* ... (Hamburg, 1719), 120. Dok 2: 98
1 Jan	(New Year) Performance of *Die Zeit, die Tag und Jahre macht* (BWV 134a).
1 Mar	Bach visits Berlin to purchase a large two-manual harpsichord for the Cöthen court. Dok 2: 95; NBR 94
May–July	Abortive attempt to meet Georg Friedrich Handel in Halle. Dok 3: 927
28 Sept	Burial of Leopold Augustus, just 10 months old. Dok 2: 96

498   *1720–1721*

10 Dec	Birthday of Prince Leopold of Anhalt-Cöthen. Celebratory poem by Menantes, and music from Bach and chamber musicians. Dok 2: 97

1720

	Fair copy of the sonatas and partitas for unaccompanied violin (BWV 1001–1006) dated "1720."
1 Jan	(New Year) Performance of *Dich loben die lieblichen Strahlen der Sonne* (BWV Anh. I, 6); music lost.
10 Jan	Godparent at baptism of Sophia Charlotta Abel, daughter of the Cöthen gamba player, Christian Ferdinand Abel. Dok 2: 99
22 Jan	Date on title page of the *Clavierbüchlein für Wilhelm Friedemann Bach* (aged 9). Dok 1: 149; NBR 79
25 May	Leaves for a visit to Carlsbad with Prince Leopold. BJ 92 (2006): 105
7 June	Burial of Bach's wife, Maria Barbara. Dok 2: 100; NBR 80
7 June?	Return from Carlsbad. Dok 3: 666; BJ 92 (2006): 107
12 Sept	Death of Heinrich Friese, organist of St. James Church, Hamburg. Dok 2: 102; NBR 81
By 21 Sept	Bach applies for the organist's position in Hamburg. Dok 2: 102; NBR 81
ca. 23 Nov	Bach visits Hamburg and performs in the presence of Johann Adam Reinken. Dok 2: 102; NBR 81 Almost certainly performs *Ich hatte viel Bekümmernis* (BWV 21). Dok 2: 200, 253; NBR 82, 319
23 Nov	Bach returns to Cöthen. Dok 2: 102; NBR 81
10 Dec	Birthday of Prince Leopold of Anhalt-Cöthen. Performance of *Heut ist gewiß ein guter Tag* (BWV Anh. I, 7); music lost.
By 19 Dec	Letter from Bach to the council of the St. Jacobi Church, Hamburg; no longer extant. Dok 1: 7; Dok 2: 102; NBR 81
19 Dec	Johann Joachim Heitmann chosen as organist of the St. James Church, Hamburg. Dok 1: 7; Dok 2: 102; NBR 81

1721

22 Feb	Death of his older brother, Johann Christoph Bach, who had effectively been Sebastian's guardian after the death of their parents 1694–1695. BJ 42 (1955): 103
24 Mar	Dedication of the "Brandenburg" Concerti (BWV 1046–1051) to the Margrave Christian Ludwig of Brandenburg. Dok 1: 150; NBR 84
7–13 Aug	Bach visits the court of Count Heinrich XI in Schleiz, Thuringia. Dok 2: 107; NBR 85

_1722–1723_ 499

25 Sept	Anna Magdalena Wilcke, "fürstl. Sängerin allhier," and Johann Sebastian Bach are godparents at the baptism of Johann Christian Hahn, son of a footman of the Prince. Dok 2: 108
3 Dec	Marriage of Johann Sebastian Bach and Anna Magdalena Wilcke, "in Hause." Dok 2: 110; NBR 86
10 Dec	Birthday of Prince Leopold of Anhalt-Cöthen.
11 Dec	Marriage of Prince Leopold of Anhalt-Cöthen and Friederica Henrietta von Anhalt-Bernburg. Dok 1: 23

1722

	Title page of the first _Clavier-Büchlein_ for Anna Magdalena Bach, "Anno 1722." Dok 1, 268; NBR 88
	Title page of Well-Tempered Clavier I, "Anno 1722." Dok 1: 152
15 Mar	Bach petitions the Erfurt town council, on behalf of himself and his brother, Johann Jacob Bach (then in Stockholm) concerning a matter of inheritance. Dok 1: 8; NBR 89
16 Apr	Death of his brother, Johann Jacob, in Stockholm, the brother who went with Sebastian to live with their older brother, Johann Christoph, on the death of their parents, 1694–1695. Dok 2: 118
5 Jun	Death of Johann Kuhnau, Cantor in Leipzig.
9 Aug	Birthday of Prince Johann August of Anhalt-Zerbst, for which Bach composed _O vergnügte Stunden_ (BWV deest); music lost. It is uncertain whether Bach visited Zerbst at this time. Dok 2: 114; Dok 5: B 113a
10 Dec	Birthday of Prince Leopold of Anhalt-Cöthen. Performance of _Durchlauchster Leopold_ (BWV 173a). Dok 2: 115
By 21 Dec	Bach applies for the vacant Cantorate in Leipzig. Dok 2: 119

1723

	Title page of the Inventions, "Auffrichtige Anleitung … Anno Christi 1723." Dok 1: 153; NBR 92
	Title page of the _Orgelbüchlein_. Dok 1: 148
Mid-year?	Birth of daughter Christiana Sophia Henrietta (see 29/30 Jun 1726).
1 Jan	(New Year) Performance of a celebratory cantata of which only the title page of the libretto is known (BWV Anh. I, 8). Dok 2, 115, 120
15 Jan	Bach's candidacy confirmed. Dok 2: 121; NBR 94b
2 Feb	(Estomihi) For his audition, Bach performs two cantatas in the St. Thomas Church, Leipzig: _Jesu nahm zu sich die Zwölfe_ (BWV 22) and _Du wahrer Gott und Davids Sohn_ (BWV 23). Dok 2: 122–125; NBR 95

500   *1723*

9 Apr	Councillor Plaz: "Since the best could not be obtained [i.e., Georg Philipp Telemann from Hamburg; Christoph Graupner from Darmstadt], mediocre ones would have to be accepted [i.e., Bach from Cöthen; or Georg Friedrich Kauffmann from Merseberg; or Georg Balthasar Schott from Leipzig]."
	Dok 2: 127; NBR 94c
By 13 Apr	Bach invited to become Kuhnau's successor; he thus petitioned Prince Leopold for dismissal.
13 Apr	Prince Leopold of Anhalt-Cöthen grants Bach's petition.
	Dok 2:128; NBR 96
19 Apr	Bach's preliminary acceptance, addressed to the Leipzig town council. Dok 1: 91; NBR 97
22 Apr	Formal election by the combined three councils in Leipzig.
	Dok 2: 129–130; NBR 98
23 Apr	Public announcement of Bach as the successor of Kuhnau.
	Dok 2: 130
5 May	Bach's final acceptance of the terms of his appointment; addressed to the town council. Dok 1: 92; NBR 100
	Bach's appointment entered into the records of the St. Thomas School. Dok 2: 133; NBR 99
By 8 May	Theological examination, conducted in Latin, by professors Johann Schmid and Salomon Deyling. Dok 2: 134; NBR 101
13 May	As required of all school teachers and church officials, Bach affirms his Lutheran theology, first by signing that he accepts the *Formula of Concord* (1577) and the Saxon *Visitation Articles* (1592), both of which are found in the *Book of Concord*, the anthology of Lutheran confessions.
	Dok 3: 92a; Dok 2: 136
16 May	(Pentecost) Beginning of the new school year at the St. Thomas School; the original date for Bach to have begun his Cantorate.
	Dok 1: 91; NBR 97
	Performance of a cantata (by Bach?) in the University Church of St. Paul. Dok 5: B 137a

Leipzig 1723–1750

22 May	The Bach family moves to Leipzig. Dok 2: 138; NBR 102
30 May	(Trinity 1) Bach begins his duties in the Leipzig churches with a cantata in the St. Nicholas Church: *Die Elenden sollen essen* (BWV 75). Dok 2: 139–142; NBR 103, 105
1 Jun	Official installation as Cantor in the St. Thomas School.
	Dok 2: 144–148, 152; NBR 104
6 Jun	(Trinity 2) *Die Himmel erzählen der Ehre Gottes* (BWV 76), the first cantata to be heard in the St. Thomas Church by the newly appointed Cantor.

13 Jun	(Trinity 3) Reperformance of *Ich hatte viel Bekümmernis* (BWV 21).
14 June	Wilhelm Friedeman and Carl Philipp Emanuel enrolled in the St. Thomas School. Dok 2: 149; NBR 111
20 Jun	(Trinity 4) First performance of *Ein ungefärb Gemüthe* (BWV 24); reperformance of *Barmherziges Herze* (BWV 185).
24 Jun	(St. John the Baptist) First performance of *Ihr Menschen, rühmet Gottes Liebe* (BWV167); and possible first performance of the Sanctus in C major (BWV 237).
2 Jul	(Visitation) Performance of *Herz und Mund und Tat und Leben* (BWV 147), composed in Weimar but may not have been performed there (BWV 147a). First performance of Magnificat in E-flat (BWV 243a). BJ 89 (2003): 37–45
11 Jul	(Trinity 7) First performance of the reworked *Ärgre dich, o Seele, nicht* (BWV 186), originally composed in Weimar (BWV 186a).
13 Jul	Cantata performed at the marriage of Johann Gottfried Hübner and Beata Regina Hennig; composition unknown. NBA I/33, KB, 12
18 Jul	(Trinity 8) First performance of *Erforsche mich, Gott, und erfahre mein Herz* (BWV 136).
25 Jul	(Trinity 9) First performance of *Herr, gehe nicht ins Gericht mit deinem Knecht* (BWV 105).
1 Aug	(Trinity 10) First performance of *Schauet doch und sehet, ob irgendein Schmerz sei* (BWV 46)
8 Aug	(Trinity 11) First performance of *Siehe zu, dass deine Gottesfurcht nicht Heuchelei sei* (BWV 179) and reperformance of *Mein Herze schwimmt im Blute* (BWV 199).
9 Aug	University celebration of the birthday of Friedrich II of Saxon-Gotha-Altenburg; Latin ode; composition unknown. Dok 2: 156; Dok 5: B 156a
15 Aug	(Trinity 12) First performance of *Lobe den Herren, meine Seele* (BWV 69a).
22 Aug	(Trinity 13) First performance of *Du sollst Gott, deinen Herren, lieben* (BWV 77).
29 Aug	(Trinity 14) First performance of *Es ist nichts Gesundes an meinem Liebe* (BWV 25).
30 Aug	Inauguration of the Leipzig town council, first performance of *Preise, Jerusalem, den Herrn* (BWV 119) in the St. Nicholas Church. Dok 5: B 157a
5 Sept	(Trinity 15) First performance of *Warum betrübst du dich, mein Herz* (BWV 138).
12 Sept	(Trinity 16) First performance of *Christus, der ist mein Leben* (BWV 95).

502 *1723–1724*

	Cantata performed at the marriage of Johann Christoph Krause and Maria Barabara Blechschmidt; composition unknown.
	NBA I/33, KB, 12
19 Sept	(Trinity 17) Possible first performance of *Bringet dem Herrn Ehre seines Namens* (BWV 148) (see also 23 Sept 1725).
3 Oct	(Trinity 19) First performance of *Ich elender Mensch, wer wird mich erlösen* (BWV 48).
10 Oct	(Trinity 20) Reperformance of *Ach! ich sehe, jetz, da ich zur Hochzeit gehe* (BWV 162).
17 Oct	(Trinity 21) First performance of *Ich glaube, lieber Herr, hilf meinem Unglauben* (BWV 109).
24 Oct	(Trinity 22) First performance of *Was soll ich aus dir machen, Ephraim?* (BWV 89).
2 Nov	Examination and inauguration of the new Hildebrandt organ in the church at Störmthal, near Leipzig; and first performance of *Höchsterwünschtes Freudenfest* (BWV 194).
	Dok 2: 163–164; Dok 5: B 164
7 Nov	(Trinity 24) First performance of *O Ewigkeit, du Donnerwort* (BWV 60).
13 Nov	New regulations for the St. Thomas School issued. Dok 2: 165
14 Nov	(Trinity 25) First performance of *Es reißet euch ein schrecklich Ende* (BWV 90).
21 Nov	(Trinity 26) First performance of the reworked *Wachet! betet! betet! wachet!* (BWV 70), originally composed in Weimar (BWV 70a).
28 Nov	(Advent 1) Reperformance of *Nun komm der Heiden Heiland* (BWV 61). Liturgical order for the Divine Service on the first Sunday in Advent entered on the cover of the autograph score of Cantata 61, probably at a later date. Dok 1: 178; NBR 113
5–12 Dec	(Advent 2–4) *Tempus clausum*, no concerted music during the penitential season.
25 Dec	(Christmas Day) Reperformance of *Christen ätzet diesen Tag* (BWV 63); first performance of the Sanctus in D major (BWV 238); Magnificat (BWV 243a), with the Christmas interpolations.
26 Dec	(St. Stephen's Day) First performance of *Dazu ist erschienen der Sohn Gottes* (BWV 40).
27 Dec	(St. John's Day = Sunday after Christmas) First performance of *Sehet, welch eine Liebe hat uns der Vater erzeiget* (BWV 64).

1724

1 Jan	(New Year) First performance of *Singet dem Herrn ein neues Lied* (BWV 190); some of the music is missing.

1724 503

2 Jan	(Sunday after New Year) First performance of *Schau, lieber Gott, wie meine Feind* (BWV 153)
6 Jan	(Epiphany) First performance of *Sie werden alle aus Saba kommen* (BWV 65).
9 Jan	(Epiphany 1) First performance of *Mein liebster Jesu ist verloren* (BWV 154).
16 Jan	(Epiphany 2) Reperformance of *Mein Gott, wie lang, ach lange* (BWV 155); in the St. Thomas Church.
23 Jan	(Epiphany 3) First performance of *Herr, wie du willt, so schick's mit mir* (BWV 73); in the St. Nicholas Church.
30 Jan	(Epiphany 4) First performance of *Jesu schläft, was soll ich hoffen?* (BWV 81); in the St. Thomas Church.
2 Feb	(Purification) First performances of *Erfreute Zeit im neuen Bunde* (BWV 83); in the St. Nicholas Church (morning) and St. Thomas Church (afternoon).
6 Feb	(Septuagesima) First performance of *Nimm, was dein ist, und gehe hin* (BWV 144); in the St. Thomas Church.
8 Feb	Cantata performed at the marriage of Johann Gottlieb Hoffmann and Johanna Gertraude Bösch; composition unknown.

NBA I/33, KB, 12

13 Feb	(Sexagesima) First performance of *Leichtgesinnte Flattergeister* (BWV 181); in the St. Nicholas Church; and reperformance of *Gleichwie der Regen und Schnee vom Himmel fällt* (BWV 18)?
20 Feb	(Estomihi) Reperformance of *Jesu nahm zu sich die Zwölfe* (BWV 22); in the St. Thomas Church; and reperformance of *Du wahrer Gott und Davids Sohn* (BWV 23)?
26 Feb	Birth of son, Gottfried Heinrich Bach. Dok 2: 176
27 Feb	Baptism of son, Gottfried Heinrich. Dok 2: 176; Dok 5 A 92a
27 Feb–2 Apr	(Lent) *Tempus clausum*, no concerted music during the penitential season.
25 Mar	(Annunciation) First performances of *Siehe, eine Jungfrau ist schwanger* (BWV Anh. I, 199); in the St. Thomas Church (morning) and St. Nicholas Church (afternoon); music lost.

BJ 59 (1973): 16–17

	Reperformance of *Himmelskönig sei willkommen* (BWV 182).
7 Apr	(Good Friday) First performance of the St. John Passion (BWV 245) in the St. Nicholas Church.

Dok 1: 179; Dok 2: 179–180; NBR 114–116

9 Apr	(Easter Day) Reperformance of *Der Himmel lacht! die Erde jubiliert* (BWV 31); in the St. Nicholas Church (morning) and St. Thomas Church (afternoon); reperformance of *Christ lag in Todesbanden* (BWV 4).

504   *1724*

10 Apr	(2 Easter) First performance of the reworking of *Erfreut euch, ihre Herzen* (BWV 66); in the St. Thomas Church (morning) and St. Nicholas Church (afternoon).
11 Apr	(3 Easter) First performance of the reworking of *Ein Herz, das seinen Jesum lebend weiß* (BWV 134); in the St. Nicholas Church.
16 Apr	(Quasimodogeniti) First performance of *Halt im Gedächtnis Jesum Christ* (BWV 67); in the St. Thomas Church.
23 Apr	(Misericordias Domini) First performance of *Du Hirte Israel, höre* (BWV 104); in the St. Nicholas Church.
30 Apr	(Jubilate) Reperformance of *Weinen, Klagen, Sorgen, Zagen* (BWV 12).
7 May	(Cantate) First performance of *Wo gehest du hin?* (BWV 166).
14 May	(Rogate) First performance of *Wahrlich, Wahrlich, ich sage euch* (BWV 86).
18 May	(Ascension) First performance of *Wer da gläubet und getauft wird* (BWV 37).
21 May	(Exaudi) First performance of *Sie werden euch in dem Bann tun* (BWV 44).
28 May	(Pentecost) Reperformances of *Erchallet ihr Lieder* (BWV 172) and *Wer mich liebet, der wird mein Wort halten* (BWV 59); (re?-) performance of the Missa in a minor by Johann Christoph Pez (BWV Anh. III, 24). BJ 44 (1957): 71
29 May	(2 Pentecost) Possible first performance of the re-working of *Erhöhtes Fleisch und Blut* (BWV 173) (see also 2 Jun 1727).
30 May	(3 Pentecost) First performance of *Erwünschtes Freudenlicht* (BWV 184).
4 Jun	(Trinity) Reperformance of *O heilges Geist- und Wasserbad* (BWV 165); and possible reperformance *of Höchsterwünschtes Freudenfest* (BWV 194).
11 Jun	(Trinity 1) First performance of *O Ewigkeit, du Donnerwort* [II] (BWV 20).
18 Jun	(Trinity 2) First performance of *Ach Gott, vom Himmel sieh darein* (BWV 2).
24 Jun	(St. John the Baptist) First performance of *Christ unser Herr zum Jordan kam* (BWV 7).
25 Jun	(Trinity 3) First performance of *Ach Herr, mich armen Sünder* (BWV 135).
2 Jul	(Visitation = Trinity 4) First performance of *Meine Seel erhebt den Herren* (BWV 10).
9 Jul	(Trinity 5) First performance of *Wer nurden lieben Gott läßt walten* (BWV 93).
18 Jul	Johann Sebastian and Anna Magdelena perform in Cöthen.
	Dok 2: 184; NBR 117a

1724 505

23 Jul	(Trinity 7) First performance of *Was willst du dich betrüben* (BWV 107).
30 Jul	(Trinity 8) First performance of *Wo Gott der Herr nicht bei uns hält* (BWV 178).
6 Aug	(Trinity 9) First performance of *Was frag ich nach der Welt* (BWV 94).
13 Aug	(Trinity 10) First performance of *Nimm von uns, Herr, du treuer Gott* (BWV 101).
20 Aug	(Trinity 11) First performance of *Herr Jesu Christ, du höchstes Gut* (BWV 113).
28 Aug	Inauguration of the Leipzig town council in the St. Nicholas Church. Libretto and music lost.　　　　　Dok 5: B 184a
3 Sept	(Trinity 13) First performance of *Allein zu dir, Herr Jesu Christ* (BWV 33); in the St. Thomas Church.
10 Sept	(Trinity 14) First performance of *Jesu, der du meine Seele* (BWV 78); in the St. Nicholas Church.
17 Sept	(Trinity 15) First performance of *Was Gott tut, das ist wohlgetan* [I] (BWV 99); in the St. Thomas Church.
24 Sept	(Trinity 16) First performance of the early version of *Liebster Gott, wenn werd ich sterben?* (BWV 8); in the St. Nicholas Church.
29 Sept	(St. Michael) First performance of the early version of *Herr Gott, dich loben alle wir* (BWV 130); in the St. Thomas Church (morning) and St. Nicholas Church (afternoon).
1 Oct	(Trinity 17) First performance of *Ach, lieben Christen, seid getrost* (BWV 114).
8 Oct	(Trinity 18) First performance of *Herr Christ, der einge Gottessohn* (BWV 96).
15 Oct	(Trinity 19) First performance of *Wo soll ich fliehen hin* (BWV 5).
22 Oct	(Trinity 20) First performance of *Schmücke dich, o liebe Seele* (BWV 180).
29 Oct	(Trinity 21) First performance of *Aus tiefer Not schrei ich zu dir* (BWV 38).
31 Oct	(Reformation). (Re-?) Performance of Georg Philipp Telemann's *Der Herr ist König* in the University Church of St. Paul.　　　　　BJ 84 (1998): 90
5 Nov	(Trinity 22) First performance of *Mache dich, mein Geist, bereit* (BWV 115).
12 Nov	(Trinity 23) First performance of *Wohl dem, der sich auf seinem Gott* (BWV 139).
19 Nov	(Trinity 24) First performance of *Ach wie flüchtig, ach wie nichtig* (BWV 26).
26 Nov	(Trinity 25) First performance of *Du Friedefürst, Herr Jesu Christ* (BWV 116).

506   *1724–1725*

3 Dec	(Advent 1) First performance of *Nun komm der Heiden Heiland* [II] (BWV 62).
10–24 Dec	(Advent 2–4) *Tempus clausum*, no concerted music during the penitential season.
25 Dec	(Christmas Day) First performances of the early version of *Gelobet seist du, Jesu Christ* (BWV 91a) and Sanctus in D major (BWB 232III).
26 Dec	(St. Stephen's Day) First performance of *Christum wir sollen loben schon* (BWV 121).
27 Dec	(St. John's Day) First performance of *Ich freue mich in dir* (BWV 133).
31 Dec	(Sunday after Christmas) First performance of *Das neugeborne Kindelein* (BWV 122).

1725

	Second *Clavier-Büchlein* for Anna Magdalena Bach begun this year.
	Johann Joseph Fux's *Gradus ad Parnussum* is published in Vienna; Bach obtains a copy but the date he did so is unknown. Dok 1, 270
1 Jan	(New Year) First performance of *Jesu, nun sei gepreiset* (BWV 41).
6 Jan	(Epiphany) First performance of *Liebster Immanuel, Herzog der Frommen* (BWV 123).
7 Jan	(Epiphany 1) First performance of *Meinen Jesum laß ich nicht* (BWV 124).
14 Jan	(Epiphany 2) First performance of *Ach Gott, wie manches Herzeleid* [I] (BWV 3).
21 Jan	(Epiphany 3) First performance of *Was mein Gott will, das g'scheh allzeit* (BWV 111).
28 Jan	(Septuagesima) First performance of *Ich hab in Gottes Herz und Sinn* (BWV 92).
2 Feb	(Purification) First performance of *Mit Fried und Freud ich fahr dahin* (BWV 125).
4 Feb	(Sexagesima) First performance of *Erhalt uns, Herr, bei deinem Wort* (BWV 126).
11 Feb	(Estomihi) First performance of *Herr Jesu Christ, wahr Mensch und Gott* (BWV 127).
12 Feb	Cantata performed at the marriage of Christoph Friedrich Lösner and Johanna Gertraude Bösch (BWV Anh. I, 14); music lost. Dok 2: 186
13 Feb	Cantata performed at the marriage of Christian Heinrich Hennig and Amelia Rosina Küttner; composition unknown. NBA I/33, KB, 12

18 Feb–25 Mar	(Lent) *Tempus clausum*, no concerted music during the penitential season.
23 Feb	Birthday cantata for Duke Christian of Saxe-Weissenfels, *Entfliehet, verschwindet, entweichet, ihr Sorgen* (BWV 249a); performance in Weissenfels.
25 Mar	(Palm Sunday = Annunciation) First performance of *Wie schön leuchtet der Morgenstern* (BWV 1).
30 Mar	(Good Friday) Performance of the St. John Passion (BWV 245, second version) in the St. Thomas Church.
Apr→Jul	First performance of a birthday cantata; probably for a Leipzig University professor: *Schwingt freudig euch empor* (BWV 36c).
1 Apr	(Easter Day) First performance of the reworking of BWV 249a: *Kommt, eilet und laufet, ihr flüchtigen Füße* (BWV 249); re-performance of *Christ lag in Todesbanden* (BWV 4).
2 Apr	(2 Easter) First performance of *Bleib bei uns, denn es will Abend werden* (BWV 6).
8 Apr	(Quasimodogeniti) First performance of *Am Abend aber desselbigen Sabbats* (BWV 42); incomplete sketch of an alternative 1st movement (BWV 42a).
14 Apr	Baptism of son, Christian Gottlieb Bach. Dok 2: 188; Dok 5: A 92b
15 Apr	(Misericordia) First performance of *Ich bin ein guter Hirt* (BWV 85).
22 Apr	(Jubilate) First performance of *Ihr werdet weinen und heulen* (BWV 103).
ca.22 Apr	Johann Francisci, Cantor in Neusohl (Upper Hungary), visits Bach in Leipzig. Dok 2: 469; NBR 469
29 Apr	(Cantate) First performance of *Es ist euch gut, daß ich hingehe* (BWV 108).
6 May	(Rogate) First performance of *Bisher habt ihr nichts gebeten in meinem Namen* (BWV 87).
10 May	(Ascension) First performance of *Auf Christi Himmelfahrt allein* (BWV 128).
13 May	(Exaudi) First performance of *Sie werden euch in dem Bann tun* [II] (BWV 183); incomplete sketch of an aria or arioso (BWV 183a).
20 May	(Pentecost) First performance of *Wer mich liebet, der wird mein Wort halten* [II] (BWV 74).
21 May	(2 Pentecost) First performance of *Also hat Gott die Welt geliebt* (BWV 68).
22 May	(3 Pentecost) First performance of *Er rufet seinen Schafen mit Namen* (BWV 175).
ca.25 May–6 Jun	Visit to Gera. Dok 5: B 189a and 189c

508   *1725*

26 May	Examination of the organ in St. John's Church, Gera; organ recital in St. Saviour's Church, Gera. Dok 2: 183, 183a; Dok 5: B 189b
27 May	(Trinity) First performance of *Es ist ein trostzig und verzagt Ding* (BWV 176).
10 Jun	(Trinity 2) Possible re-performance of the second part of *Die Himmel erzählen die Ehre Gottes* (BWV 76).
17 Jun	(Trinity 3) Performance of *Ich ruf zu dir, Herr Jesu Christ* in the St. Nicholas Church; composer unknown. BJ 59 (1973): 21
24 Jun	(Trinity 4 = St. John the Baptist) Performance of *Gelobet sei der Herr, der Gott Israel*, by Georg Philipp Telemann (?); in the St. Thomas Church (morning) and St. Nicholas Church (afternoon). BJ 59 (1973): 21
1 Jul	(Trinity 5) Performance of *Der Segen des Herrn machet reich ohne Mühe*, by Georg Philipp Telemann (?); in the St. Nicholas Church. BJ 59 (1973): 21
2 Jul	(Visitation) Performance of *Meine Seele erhebt den Herrn*, composed by either Reinhard Keiser or Johann Mattheson; in the St. Thomas Church (morning) and St. Nicholas Church (afternoon). BJ 59 (1973): 21; BJ 92 (2006): 109–125
8 Jul	(Trinity 6) Performance of *Wer sich rächet, an dem wird sich der Herr wieder rächen*, by Georg Philipp Telemann (?); in the St. Nicholas Church. BJ 59 (1973): 21
15 Jul	Cantata performed at the marriage of Christian Rother and Johanna Magdalena Hartmann; composition unknown. NBA I/33, KB, 12
29 Jul	(Trinity 9) First performance on *Tue Rechnung! Donnerwort* (BWV 168).
3 Aug	Cantata performed on the name day of August Friedrich Müller, professor of philosophy and law: *Zerreißet, zersprenget, zertrümmert die Gruft* (BWV 205).
13 Aug	Cantata performed at the marriage of Anton Francke and Johanna Christiana Baßler; composition unknown. NBA I/33, KB, 13
19 Aug	(Trinity 12) First performance of *Lobe den Herren, den mächtigen König zu Ehren* (BWV 137).
26 Aug	(Trinity 13) First performance of *Ihr, die ihr euch von Christo nennet* (BWV 164).
27 Aug	Inauguration of the Leipzig town council in the St. Nicholas Church; first performance of *Wünschet Jerusalem Glück* (BWV Anh. I, 4); music lost. Dok 2: 264; BJ 94 (2008): 61–64
9 Sept	Cantata performed at the marriage of Johann Christoph Frenzius and Johanna Sophia Lohrengel; composition unknown. NBA I/33, KB, 13
14 Sept	First letter to the King-Elector, Friedrich Augustus I, concerning musical responsibilities for the "New Service" in St. Paul's University Church. Dok 1: 10; NBR 119a

1725–1726 509

17 Sept	Response to Bach's letter on behalf of the King-Elector.
	Dok 2: 192
19–20 Sept	Recital on the Silbermann organ in St. Sophia's Church, Dresden. Dok 2: 193; NBR 118
23 Sept	(Trinity 17) Possible first performance of *Bringet dem Herrn Ehre seines Namens* (BWV 148) (see also 19 Sept 1723).
31 Oct	(Reformation) First performance of *Gott der Herr ist Sonn und Schild* (BWV 79).
2 Nov	Entered a canon in an autograph book of which only the date, dedication, and motto are known. Dok 1: 154
3 Nov	Second letter to the King-Elector, Friedrich Augustus I, concerning musical responsibilities for the "New Service" in St. Paul's University Church. Dok 1: 11; NBR 119b
27 Nov	Cantata performed at the marriage of Peter Hohmann, the younger, and Christiana Sibylla Mencke, *Auf! süß-entzückende Gewalt* (BWV Anh I, 196); music lost.
30 Nov	Birthday of Princess Charlotte Friederica Amelia of Anhalt-Cöthen; possible first performance of *Steigt freudig in die Luft* (BWV 36a) (see also 30 Nov 1726).
4 Dec	Cantata performed at the marriage of Benedictus Hieronymus Dicell and Johanna Catharina Böttger; composition unknown. NBA I/33, KB, 13
10–24 Dec	(Advent 2–4) *Tempus clausum*, no concerted music during the penitential season.
By 10 Dec	Bach and Anna Magdalena visit Cöthen to celebrate the birthday of Prince Leopold of Anhalt-Cöthen. Dok 2: 199; NBR 117b
25 Dec	(Christmas Day) First performance of *Unser Mund sie voll Lachens* (BWV 110).
26 Dec	(St. Stephen's Day) First performance of *Selig ist der Mann* (BWV 57).
27 Dec	(St. John's Day) First performance of *Süßer Trost, mein Jesu kömmt* (BWV 151).
30 Dec	(Sunday after Christmas) First performance of *Gottlob! Nun Geht das Jahr zu Ende* (BWV 28).
31 Dec	Third letter to the King-Elector, Friedrich Augustus I, concerning musical responsibilities for the "New Service" in St. Paul's University Church. Dok 1: 12; NBR 119c

1726

1 Jan	(New Year) First performance of *Herr Gott, dich loben wir* (BWV 16).
13 Jan	(Epiphany 1) First performance of *Liebster Jesu, mein Verlangen* (BWV 32).
20 Jan	(Epiphany 2) First performance of *Meine Seufzer, meine Tränen* (BWV 13).

510 *1726*

21 Jan	The King's decision concerning musical responsibilities for the "New Service" in St. Paul's University Church. Dok 2: 202; NBR 120
27 Jan	(Epiphany 3) First performance of *Alles nur nach Gottes Willen* (BWV 72).
2 Feb–3 Mar	During the period embracing Epiphany 3 to Estomihi Bach performed six cantatas by his cousin Johann Ludwig Bach. BJ 46 (1959): 52–94; BJ 48 (1961): 5–24; BJ 49 (1962): 5–32
10 Mar–14 Apr	(Lent) *Tempus clausum*, no concerted music during the penitential season.
4 Apr	Baptism of daughter, Elisabeth Juliana Friderica. Dok 2: 204; Dok 5: A 92c
19 Apr	(Good Friday) Performance of the St. Mark Passion, attributed to "Reinhard Keiser," in the St. Nicholas Church.
21 Apr–19 May	During the period embracing Easter Day to Cantate, Bach performed six cantatas by his cousin Johann Ludwig Bach. BJ 46 (1959): 52–94; BJ 48 (1961): 5–24; BJ 49 (1962): 5–32
24 Apr	Cantata performed at the marriage of Christian Gottfried Petermann and Eleanora Sophia Scipio; composition unknown. NBA I/33, KB, 13
7 May	Cantata performed at the marriage of Johann Georg Schmidlein and Maria Dorothea Stöpß; composition unknown. NBA I/33, KB, 13
12 May	(Jubilate) Possible first performance of *Wir müssen durch viel Trübsal in das Reich Gottes eingehen* (BWV 146) (see also 18 Apr 1728).
30 May	(Ascension) First performance of *Gott fähret auf mit Jauchzen* (BWV 43).
16 Jun	(Trinity) Reperformance of *Höchsterwünschtes Freudenfest* (BWV 194); and possible first performance of *Gelobet sei der Herr, mein Gott* (BWV 129) (see also 31 Oct 1726).
23 Jun	(Trinity 1) First performance of *Brich dem Hungrigen Brot* (BWV 39).
24 Jun–2 Jul	During the period embracing John the Baptist Day to the Visitation Bach performed two cantatas by his cousin Johann Ludwig Bach. BJ 46 (1959): 52–94; BJ 48 (1961): 5–24; BJ 49 (1962): 5–32
29 Jun	Death of daughter Christiana Sophia Henrietta, 3 years old. Dok 2: 207
1 Jul	Burial of Christiana Sophia Henrietta. Dok 2: 207
2 Jul	(Visitation) Cantata by Johann Ludwig Bach performed. BJ 46 (1959): 52–94; BJ 48 (1961): 5–24; BJ 49 (1962): 5–32
21 Jul	(Trinity 5) First performance of *Siehe, ich will viel Fischer aussenden* (BWV 88).
28 Jul	Letter to school friend Georg Erdmann in Danzig. Dok 5: A 13; NBR 121

28 Jul	(Trinity 6) First performance of *Vergnügte Ruh, beliebte Seelenlust* (BWV 170) and performance of a cantata by Johann Ludwig Bach.
	BJ 46 (1959): 52–94; BJ 48 (1961): 5–24; BJ 49 (1962): 5–32
4 Aug	(Trinity 7) First performance of *Es wartet alles auf dich* (BWV 187).
11 Aug	(Trinity 8) First performance of *Es ist dir gesagt, Mensch, was gut ist* (BWV 45).
25 Aug	Cantata for the birthday of Count Joachim Friedrich von Fleming: *Verjaget, zerstreuet, zerrüttet, ihr Sterne* (BWV 249b); music only partially known.
25 Aug	(Trinity 10) First performance of *Herr, deine Augen sehen nach dem Glauben* (BWV 102).
26 Aug	Inauguration of the Leipzig town council in the St. Nicholas Church; music lost.
8 Sept	(Trinity 12) First performance of *Geist und Seele wird verwirret* (BWV 35).
After 12 Sept	Publication of Partita I of *Clavierübung* I (BWV 825), dedicated to the Prince of Anhalt-Cöthen, Emanuel Ludwig, born on 12 Sept; with dedicatory poem. Dok 1: 155; NBR 127–128
14 Sept	In a letter Bach acknowledges the request of the town council of Plauen for him to find a suitable candidate for the position of Cantor then vacant. Dok 1: 14; NBR 123
15 Sept	(Trinity 13) Cantata by Johann Ludwig Bach performed.
	BJ 46 (1959): 52–94; BJ 48 (1961): 5–24; BJ 49 (1962): 5–32
22 Sept	(Trinity 14) First performance of *Wer Dank opfert, der preiset mich* (BWV 17).
26 Sept	Letter to the town council of Plauen concerning the vacant position of Cantor. Dok 1: 15
29 Sept	(St. Michael's Day = Trinity 15) First performance of *Es erhub sich ein Streit* (BWV 19).
6 Oct	(Trinity 16) First performance of *Wer weiß, wie nahe mir mein Ende* (BWV 27).
13 Oct	(Trinity 17) First performance of *Wer sich selbst erhöhet, der soll erniedriget werden* (BWV 47).
20 Oct	(Trinity 18) First performance of *Gott soll allein mein Herze haben* (BWV 169).
21 Oct	In a letter Bach commends Christoph Gottlob Wecker for consideration for the position of Cantor in Plauen. (Wecker was not chosen.) Dok 1: 16
27 Oct	(Trinity 19) First performance of *Ich will den Kreutzstab gerne tragen* (BWV 56).
31 Oct	(Reformation) Possible first performance of *Gelobet sei der Herr, mein Gott* (BWV 129) (see also 16 Jun 1726).
1 Nov	Advertisement for Partita I of *Clavierübung* I (BWV 825) in the Leipzig paper *Nouvellen*. Dok 2: 214

512   *1726–1727*

By 2 Nov	Beginning of repairs or alterations to Bach's dwelling in the St. Thomas School. Dok 2: 215
3 Nov	(Trinity 20) First performance of *Ich geh und suche mit Verlangen* (BWV 49).
5 Nov	Cantata performed at the marriage of Christian Schindler and Johanna Magdalena Stuhlmacher; composition unknown. NBA I/33, KB, 13
10 Nov	(Trinity 21) First performance of *Was Gott tut, das ist wohlgetan* [II] (BWV 98).
15 Nov	Letter to the Plauen town council recommending Georg Gottfried Wagner as a suitable candidate for the position of Cantor. (Wagner was chosen.) Dok 1: 17; NBR 126
17 Nov	(Trinity 22) First performance of *Ich armer Mensch, ich Sündenknecht* (BWV 55).
24 Nov	(Trinity 23) First performance of *Falsche Welt, dir trau ich nicht* (BWV 52).
From 25 Nov	Visit of the Eisenach court musician, Johann Christian Hertel, to Bach in Leipzig. Dok 3: 688
30 Nov	Possible first performance of the birthday cantata, *Steigt freudig in die Luft* (BWV 36a), for Princess Friederica Amalia of Anhalt-Cöthen (see also 30 Nov 1725).
8–22 Dec	(Advent 2–4) *Tempus clausum*, no concerted music during the penitential season.
ca.11 Dec	Cantata composed in honour of Docent Gottlieb Kortte on his appointment as Professor of Roman Law at Leipzig University: *Vereinigte Zweitracht der wechselnden Saiten* (BWV 207).

1727

5 Jan	(Sunday after New Year) First performance of *Ach, Gott, wie manches Herzeleid* (BWV 58).
2 Feb	(Epiphany 4 = Purification) First performance of *Ich habe genung* (BWV 82), and possible reperformance of *Erfreute Zeit im neuen Bunde* (BWV 83).
4 Feb	Cantata performed at the marriage of Christoph Gottlieb Grabß and Johanna Christiana Hillmer; composition unknown. NBA I/33, KB, 13
6 Feb	Memorial service for Johann Christoph von Ponickau in Pomßen, near Leipzig. Probably first performance of *Ich lasse dich nicht, du segnest mich denn* (BWV 157), directed by Christoph Gottlob Wecker.
9 Feb	(Septuagesima) First performance of *Ich bin vergnügt mit meinem Glücke* (BWV 84).

26 Feb	Letter to the town council of Chemnitz recommending Christoph Gottlob Wecker for the vacant position of Cantor.

Dok 1: 18; NBR 129; see also Dok 1: 120; NBR 130,
and Dok 1: 60; NBR 131

2 Mar–6 Apr	(Lent) *Tempus clausum*, no concerted music during the penitential season.
11 Apr	(Good Friday) First performance of the early version of the St. Matthew Passion (BWV 244b); in the St. Thomas Church.

Dok 2: 180; NBR 114

Before 12 Apr	Completion of repairs or alterations in Bach's dwelling in the St. Thomas School. Dok 2: 215
13 Apr	(Easter Day) Reperformance of the Sanctus in D major (BWV 232^{III}).
12 May	Birthday cantata for the King-Elector, Friedrich Augustus I: *Entfernet euch, ihr heitern Sterne* (BWV Anh. I, 9); music lost.

Dok 2: 219–220; NBR 132

1 Jun	(Pentecost). Probable first performance of *O ewiges Feuer! o Ursprung der Liebe* (BWV 34); in the St. Nicholas Church (morning) and St. Thomas Church (afternoon).

BJ 96 (2010): 61–77

2 Jun	(2 Pentecost) Reperformance, or the first performance of *Erhöhtes Fleisch und Blut* (BWV 173) (see also 29 May 1724); in the St. Thomas Church (morning) and St. Nicholas Church (afternoon). BJ 94 (2008): 61–77
3 Jun	(3 Pentecost) Reperformance of *Erwünschtes Freudenlicht* (BWV 184); in the St. Nicholas Church. BJ 94 (2008): 61–77
8 Jun	(Trinity) Reperformance or first performance of *Gelobet sey der Herr* (BWV 129); in the St. Thomas Church (morning) and St. Nicholas Church (afternoon) (see also 31 Oct 1726).

BJ 94 (2008): 61–77

30 Jun	Cantata performed at the marriage of Christian Lange and Christiana Gottvertreu Schultze; composition unknown.

NBA I/33, KB, 13

3 Aug	Cantata performed on the name day of the King-Elector, Friedrich Augustus I: *Ihr Häuser des Himmels, ihr scheinenden Lichter* (BWV 193a); music incomplete. Dok 2: 221
Before 18 Aug	Four-voice canon (BWV 1074) entered into an autograph book (no longer extant), dedicated to "Monsieur Hudemann."

Dok 1: 158; NBR 133

25 Aug	Inauguration of the Leipzig town council in the St. Nicholas Church; first performance of *Ihr Tore zu Zion* (BWV 193); music survives incomplete.
31 Aug	(Trinity 20) Probable reperformance of *Lobe den Herrn, meine Seele* (BWV 69a).

514   *1727–1728*

5 Sept	Death of Electress of Saxony, Christiane Eberhardine.
7 Sept	Beginning of the period of mourning for the deceased Electress.
19 Sept	The availability of Partitas II and III of *Clavierübung* I (BWV 826–827) advertised in the Leipzig paper *Nouvellen*.
	Dok 2: 224
ca.3–13 Oct	Dispute concerning Bach's involvement in the memorial service for the deceased Electress in St. Paul's University Church.
	Dok 2: 225–228; NBR 135
15 Oct	Bach finishes the composition of the *Trauerode* (BWV 198).
	Dok 2: 226
17 Oct	The university memorial service for Queen-Electress Christiane Eberhardine in St. Paul's University Church at which *Laß Fürstin, laß noch einen Strahl* (BWV 198) was performed.
	Dok 2: 229–235; NBR 136
30 Oct	Baptism of son, Ernestus Andreas Bach.
	Dok 2: 236; Dok 5: A 92d
1 Nov	Death of Ernestus Andreas, two or three days old. Dok 2: 237
2 Nov	Burial of Ernestus Andreas. Dok 2: 237
7–21 Dec	(Advent 2–4) *Tempus clausum*, no concerted music during the penitential season.
27 Dec	Burial of Bach's sister, Maria Salome Wiegand, in Erfurt.
	BJ 82 (1996): 126

1728

Jan?	Publication of Partita IV of *Clavierübung* I (BWV 828).
	Dok 1: 162
5 Jan	Honorarium for visit to Cöthen, which probably included the performance of a cantata on New Year's Day.
	Dok 2: 241; NBR 117c
6 Jan	End of the period of mourning for the deceased Electress.
5 Feb	Cantata performed at the marriage of Johann Heinrich Wolff and Susana Regina Hempel: *Vergnügte Pleißen-Stadt* (BWV 216).
	BJ 90 (2004): 199–208
15 Feb–21 Mar	(Lent) *Tempus clausum*, no concerted music during the penitential season.
26 Mar	(Good Friday) Passion performance in the St. Nicholas Church; composition unknown. Dok 2: 180; NBR 114
18 Apr	(Jubilate) Possible first performance of *Wir müssen durch viel Trübsal in das Riech Gottes eingehen* (BWV 146) (see also 12 May 1726).
24 Jun	(St. John the Baptist's Day). Christian Friedrich Henrici [Picander] dedicates his annual cycle of cantata texts to Bach: *Cantaten Auf die Sonn- und Fest-Tage durch das gantze Jahr*.
	Dok 2: 243

30 Aug	Inauguration of the Leipzig town council in the St. Nicholas Church; music lost.
7–20 Sept	Dispute concerning the choice of hymns at Vespers. Dok 1: 19; Dok 2: 246; NBR 137–138
21 Sept	Death of son, Christian Gottlieb Bach, aged 3½. Dok 2: 247
22 Sept	Burial of Christian Gottlieb. Dok 2: 247
10 Oct	Baptism of daughter, Regina Johanna Bach. Dok 2: 248; Dok 5: A 92e
17 Oct	(Trinty 21) Possible first performance of *Ich habe meine Zuversicht* (BWV 188) (see also 6 Nov 1729).
19 Oct	Cantata performed at the marriage of Gottlob Vodel and Rosina Elisabeth Berthold; composition unknown. NBA I/33, KB, 14
8 Nov	Cantata performed at the marriage of Friedrich Schultze (Naumburg deacon) and Joanna Elisabeth Weiß; composition unknown. NBA I/33, KB, 14
19 Nov	Death of Prince Leopold of Anhalt-Cöthen.
5–19 Dec	(Advent 2–4) *Tempus clausum*, no concerted music during the penitential season.
25 Dec	(Christmas Day) Probable first performance of *Ehre sei Gott in der Höhe* (BWV 197a); music incomplete.

1729

	Purchase of Bodenschatz's collection of motets, *Florilegium Portense* (1621) for the St. Thomas School. Dok 2: 271 Purchase of four string instruments for the St. Thomas Church. Dok 2: 272
1 Jan	(New Year) Probable first performance of *Gott, wie dein Name, so ist dein Ruhm* (BWV 171).
12 Jan	Cantata in homage to the Duke of Saxe-Weissenfels, *O! Angenehme Melodie* (BWV 210a), performed during the Duke's visit to Leipzig. Dok 5: B 253a
18 Jan	Cantata performed at the marriage of Johann Friedrich Höckner and Jacobina Agnetha Bartholomaei; composition unknown. Dok 5: 253b
23 Jan	(Epiphany 3) Possible first performance of *Ich steh mit einem Fuß im Grabe* (BWV 156).
14 Feb	Cantata performed at the marriage of Johann Jacob Straube and Catharina Regina Weiß; composition unknown. NBA I/33, KB, 14
ca.15–ca.23 Feb	Visit to the Court of Weissenfels to celebrate the birthday of the Duke of Saxe-Weissenfels; Bach away from Leipzig for three weeks. It is probable that during this period that he was named honorary Capellmeister to the court of Saxe-Weissenfels. BDK 1: 20; NBR 130; Dok 2: 254

516   *1729*

27 Feb	(Estomihi) Possible first performance of *Sehet, wir gehn hinauf gen Jerusalem* (BWV 159).
5 Mar	Matriculation of Wilhelm Friedemann Bach at the University of Leipzig. Dok 2: 149
6 Mar–10 Apr	(Lent) *Tempus clausum*, no concerted music during the penitential season.
From 20 Mar	Bach takes over the direction of the Collegium Musicum from Georg Balthasar Schott, who was moving to Gotha as Cantor; continues until the early 1740s. Dok 1: 20; NBR 130
23 Mar	Music in memory of Prince Leopold of Anhalt-Cöthen performed at the Cöthen court; libretto and music unknown. Dok 2: 259
24 Mar	Memorial service for Prince Leopold of Anhalt-Cöthen; *Klagt, Kinder, klagt es aller Welt* (BWV 244a) (score lost); Bach, Anna Magdalena, and son (presumably Wilhelm Friedemann) at the Cöthen court. Dok 2: 258–259; Dok 5: B 259a
15 Apr	(Good Friday) Reperformance of the early version of the St. Matthew Passion (BWV 244b); in the St. Thomas Church. Dok 2: 180; NBR 114
18 Apr	Report in the Leipzig *Post-Zeitungen* that copies of Johann David Heinichen's *General-Bass* and Johann Gottfried Walther's *Musicalisches Lexicon* can be purchased from Bach in Leipzig. Dok 260; NBR 140
18 Apr	Wedding cantata for an unidentified couple, *Herr Gott, Beherrscher aller Dinge* (BWV 120a); music incomplete.
19 Apr	(3 Easter) Possible first performance of *Ich lebe, meine Herze, zu deinen Ergötzen* (BWV 145).
3–10 May	Bach recommends Carl Gotthelf Gerlach for the vacant position of organist of the New Church, Leipzig. Dok 2: 261
ca.18 May–Jun 3	Bach reports on the musical abilities of boys in the St. Thomas School. Dok 1: 63–66; NBR 142–145; Dok 1: 180
18 May	Letter from the chairman of the school board, Dr. Christian Ludwig Stieglitz, concerning the state of the school choirs. Dok 2: 262; NBR 141
5 Jun	(Pentecost) Completion of the performing parts of *Ich liebe den Höchsten von ganzem Gemüte* (BWV 174). NBA I/14, KB, 92
6 Jun	(2 Pentecost) First performance of *Ich liebe den Höchsten von ganzem Gemüte* (BWV 174).
12 Jun	Funeral music for Nicolaus Ernst Bodinus, with the Collegium Musicum: *Was spielt ihr denn, ihr straffen Saiten* (BWV deest); composition unknown, composer uncertain. Dok 5: B 262b
5 Jul	Cantata performed at the marriage of Johann Georg Artopae and Joanna Judith Hertel; composition unknown. NBA I/33, KB, 14

1729–1730 517

26 Jul	Cantata performed at the marriage of Christoph Georg Winckler and Caroline Wilhelmina Jöcher; *Vergnüende Flammen, verdoppelt die Macht* (BWV Anh. I, 212). Dok 5: B 262c
29 Aug	Inauguration of the Leipzig town council in the St. Nicholas Church; possible first performance of *Gott, man lobet dich an der Stille* (BWV 120). Dok 2: 264
29 Sept	(St. Michael's Day) First performance of *Man singet mit Freuden vom Sieg* (BWV 149).
Autumn	First performance of *Geschwinde, ihr wirbelnden Winde* (BWV 201) (Pheobus and Pan) by Bach's Collegium Musicum.
20–21 Oct	Funeral of Johann Heinrich Ernesti, rector of the St. Thomas School; first performance of the motet *Der Geist Hilft unser Schwachheit auf* (BWV 226), in St. Paul's University Church.
6 Nov	(Trinity 21) Possible first performance of *Ich habe meine Zuversicht* (BWV 188) (see also 17 Oct 1728).
4–18 Dec	(Advent 2–4) *Tempus clausum*, no concerted music during the penitential season.
Before 24 Dec	Member of the commission to find an organist for the St. Nicholas Church in Leipzig. Dok 2: 446

1730

1 Jan	Baptism of daughter, Christiana Benedicta Louise Bach. Dok 2: 273
4 Jan	Death of Christiana Benedicta Louise Dok 2: 273a
5 Jan	Burial of Christiana Benedicta Louise Dok 2: 273a
16 Feb	Letter of the Consistory to Superintendent Deyling censuring the omission of the chanting of the Latin Nicene creed in Advent (1729) and the introduction of new hymns. NBR 149
26 Feb–2 Apr	(Lent) *Tempus clausum*, no concerted music during the penitential season.
7 Apr	(Good Friday) Possible performance of the St. Luke Passion (BWV Anh. II, 246), composer unknown, in the St. Nicholas Church; composition unknown. Dok 2: 180; NBR 114; see BJ 92 (2006): 161–169
1 May	Announcement of the publication of Partita V of *Clavierübung* I (BWV 829) in the *Leipziger Post-Zeitungen*. Dok 2: 276
25 Jun	(Trinity 3 = Bicentennial of the Augsburg Confession I) First performance of *Singet dem Herrn ein neues Lied* (BWV 190a) in the St. Nicholas Church; music partly known. Dok 2: 279
26 Jun	(Bicentennial of the Augsburg Confession II) First performance of *Gott, man lobet dich an der Stille* (BWV 120b) in the St. Thomas Church; music partly known. Dok 2: 279

518   *1730–1731*

27 Jun	(Bicentennial of the Augsburg Confession III) First performance of *Wünschet Jerusalem Glück* (BWV Anh. I, 4a) in the St. Nicholas Church; music lost. Dok 2: 279
2 Aug	The town council charges Bach with indolence. Dok 2: 280; NBR 150a
23 Aug	Bach's "Short But Most Necessary Draft for a Well-Appointed Church Music" addressed to the Leipzig town council. Dok 1: 22; NBR 151
25 Aug	Further report to the town council of problems with the Cantor. Dok 2: 281; NBR 150b
28 Aug	Inauguration of the Leipzig town council in the St. Nicholas Church; first performance of *Gott, gib dein Gerichte dem Könige* (BWV Anh. I, 3); music lost.
17 Sept	(Trinity 15) Probable reperformance of *Jauchzet Gott in allen Landen!* (BWV 51)
1 Oct	Letter to his school friend, Georg Erdmann, in Danzig. Dok 1: 23; NBR 152
31 Oct	(Reformation) Reperformance of *Gott der Herr ist Sonn und Schild* (BWV 79).
21 Nov	Cantata performed at the marriage of Johann Georg Michael Teutzschner and Christiana Elisabeth Reich; composition unknown. NBA I/33, KB, 14
10–24 Dec	(Advent 2–4) *Tempus clausum*, no concerted music during the penitential season.

1731

	Johann Mattheson again requests biographical details from Bach. Dok 2: 303
	Publication of the complete *Clavierübung I* (BWV 825–830). Dok 1: 165; NBR 155
1 Jan	(New Year) Reperformance of *Herr Gott, dich loben wir* (BWV 16).
2 Feb	(Purification) Reperformance of *Ich habe genung* (BWV 82).
11 Feb–18 Mar	(Lent) *Tempus clausum*, no concerted music during the penitential season.
18 Mar	Baptism of daughter, Christiana Dorothea Bach. Dok 2: 286; Dok 5: A 92g
23 Mar	(Good Friday) Performance of the St. Mark Passion (BWV 247) in the St. Thomas Church; music lost. Dok 2: 180; NBR 114
25 Mar	(Easter Day) Reperformance of *Der Himmel lacht! die Erde jubiliert* (BWV 31); in the St. Nicholas Church (morning) and St. Thomas Church (afternoon).

26 Mar	(2 Easter) Reperformance of *Erfreut euch, ihre Herzen* (BWV 66); in the St. Thomas Church (morning) and St. Nicholas Church (afternoon).
27 Mar	(3 Easter) Reperformance of *Ein Herz, das seinen Jesum lebend weiß* (BWV 134); in the St. Nicholas Church.
1 Apr	(Quasimodogeniti) Reperformance of First performance of *Am Abend aber desselbigen Sabbats* (BWV 42).
4 Apr	Testimonial for his pupil Johann Adolph Scheibe.
	Dok 1: 68; NBR 153
8 Apr	(Misericordias Domini) First performance of *Der Herr is mein getreuer Hirt* (BWV 112).
9 Apr	Birthday of the rector of the St. Thomas School, Johann Matthias Gesner; probable reperformance of *Schwingt freudig euch empor* (BWV 36c).
15 Apr	(Jubilate) Reperformance of *Ihr werdet weinen und heulen* (BWV 103).
16 Apr	Alterations to the St. Thomas School begun; Bach and his family are relocated for the duration. Dok 2: 290–291
3 May	(Ascension) Reperformance of *Wer da gläubet und getauft wird* (BWV 37).
13 May	(Pentecost) Reperformance of *Erschallet, ihr Lieder, erklinget, ihr Saiten!* (BWV 172) in the St. Nicholas Church (morning) and St. Thomas Church (afternoon); possible reperformance of *Wer mich liebet, der wird mein Wort halten* [I] (BWV 59).
14 May	(2 Pentecost) Reperformance of *Erhöhtes Fleisch und Blut* (BWV 173) in the St. Thomas Church (morning) and St. Nicholas Church (afternoon).
15 May	(3 Pentecost) Reperformance of *Erwünschtes Freudenlicht* (BWV 184) in the St. Nicholas Church.
20 May	(Trinity) Reperformance of *Höchsterwünschtes Freudenfest* (BWV 194) in the St. Thomas Church (morning) and St. Nicholas Church (afternoon).
24 Jun	Cantata performed at the marriage of Carl Gottlob Hoffmann (substitute deacon of the St. Nicholas Church) and Joanna Elisabeth Jerre; composition unknown. NBA I/33, KB, 14
25 Aug	Cantata for the birthday of Count Joachim Friedrich von Fleming: *So kämpfet nur, ihr muntern Töne* (BWV Anh. I, 10); music lost.
27 Aug	Inauguration of the Leipzig town council in the St. Nicholas Church; first performance of *Wir danken dir, Gott, wir danken dir* (BWV 29).
13 Sept	First performance of Johann Adam Hasse's opera *Cleofide* in Dresden; Bach was probably among the audience.

520   *1731–1732*

14 Sept	Recital on the Silbermann organ in the St. Sophia Church, Dresden, and performance at the Dresden court. Dok 2: 294–294a; NBR 307
1 Oct	Matriculation of Carl Philipp Emanuel Bach at the University of Leipzig. Dok 2: 149
6 Oct	Participates in the funeral of Georg Heinrich Bose. Dok 2: 295
12 Nov	Examination of the not-yet-completed organ in the church of Stöntzsch, near Leipzig. Dok 2: 298
18 Nov	(Trinity 26) Reperformance of *Wachet! betet! betet! wachet!* (BWV 70).
25 Nov	(Trinity 27) First performance of *Wachet auf, ruft uns die Stimme* (BWV 140).
2 Dec	(Advent) First performance of *Schwingt freudig euch empor* (BWV 36) containing music composed earlier.
9–23 Dec	(Advent 2–4) *Tempus clausum*, no concerted music during the penitential season.
25 Dec	(Christmas Day) Possible reperformance of *Gelobet seist du, Jesu Christ* (BWV 91) (see also 25 Dec 1732).

1732

4 Jan	Second examination of the completed organ in the church of Stöntzsch, near Leipzig. Dok 2: 298
After 16 Feb	Publication of Johann Gottfried Walther's *Musikalisches Lexicon*, which includes a short biography of Bach. Dok 2: 323; NBR 304
2 Mar–6 Apr	(Lent) *Tempus clausum*, no concerted music during the penitential season.
11 Apr	(Good Friday) Performance of the third version of the St. John Passion (BWV 245) in the St. Nicholas Church. Dok 2: 180; NBR 114
By 24 Apr	The Cantor and family return to their apartment in the renewed St. Thomas School. Dok 2: 308
25 May	Cantata performed at the marriage of Christian Nicolaus Schneider and Sophia Charitas Petermann; composition unknown. NBA I/33, KB, 14
30 May	In a letter, Louise Adelgunde Victorie Kulmus (later Frau Gottsched) comments on the difficulty of Bach's keyboard works. Dok 2: 309
5 Jun	Dedication of the renewed and expanded St. Thomas School; first performance of *Froher Tag, verlangte Stunden* (BWV Anh. I, 18), music lost. Dok 2: 311
21 Jun	Birth of son, Johann Christoph Friedrich Bach. Dok 1: 184; NBR 303

23 Jun	Baptism of Johann Christoph Friedrich.
	Dok 2: 312; Dok 5: A 92h
6 July	(Trinity 4) First performance of *Ich ruf zu dir, Herr Jesu Christ* (BWV 177).
3 Aug	Cantata performed on the name day of the King-Elector, Friedrich Augustus I: *Es lebe der König, der Vater im Lande* (BWV Anh. I, 11); music lost. Dok 2: 313
5 Aug	Cantata performed at the marriage of Jacob Friedrich Schröter and Christiana Sophia Lünig; composition unknown.
	NBA I/33, KB, 14
25 Aug	Inauguration of the Leipzig town council in the St. Nicholas Church; composition unknown.
Dok 2: 264	
31 Aug	Death and burial of daughter Christiana Dorothea, aged 1½.
	Dok 2: 314
21 Sept	Travels to Kassel with Anna Magdalena.
	Dok 2: 315, 318; NBR 158
22–28 Sept	Examination of the rebuilt organ in St. Martin's Church, Kassel.
	Dok 2: 316; NBR 157
28 Sept	Dedication of the organ in St. Martin's Church, Kassel, in the presence of the 12-year-old Prince Friedrich von Hessen-Kassel.
	Dok 2: 316, 522; NBR 157, 338
7–21 Dec	(Advent 2–4) *Tempus clausum*, no concerted music during the penitential season.
25 Dec	(Christmas Day) Probable reperformance of *Gelobet seist du, Jesu Christ* (BWV 91) (see also 25 Dec 1731).

1733

	Personal monogram entered into the main title pages of Abraham Calov's three-volume Bible commentary, based on the writings of Martin Luther.
	Dok 1: 183; Dok 3, 647–648; Dok 5, 288–289
	The Leipzig town council issues a revision of the regulations for the St. Thomas School.
4 Jan	(Sunday after New Year) Possible reperformance of *Ach Gott, wie manches Herzeleid* [II] (BWV 58) (see also 3 Jan 1734).
6 Jan	Concert of Bach's Collegium Musicum in Gottfried Zimmermann's coffee house in the Katharinenstraße; program unknown.
	Dok 5: B 327a
1 Feb	Death in Warsaw of Friedrich Augustus I, King of Poland, Elector of Saxony.
15 Feb	(Estomihi) Beginning of the period of mourning for the deceased King-Elector.

522   *1733*

22 Feb–29 Mar	(Lent) *Tempus clausum*, no concerted music during the penitential season.
3 Apr	(Good Friday) Because no concerted music was permitted during the period of mourning, no passion was performed. Dok 2: 180; NBR 114
21 Apr	Service of fealty to the new ruler, Friedrich Augustus II, in the St. Nicholas Church.
25 Apr	Death of daughter Regina Johanna, aged 4½. Dok 2: 328
26 Apr	Burial of Regina Johanna. Dok 2: 328
7 Jun	Bach writes to the Dresden town council and church consistory commending his son, Wilhelm Friedemann, for the vacant position of organist of St. Sophia's Church, Dresden. Dok 1: 25–26
17 Jun	Restrictions of mourning temporarily lifted, allowing the first performance of Bach's Collegium Musicum in Zimmermann's coffee garden; program unknown. Dok 2: 331; NBR 160
23 Jun	Wilhelm Friedemann chosen as the successor to Christian Petzold for the vacant position of organist of St. Sophia's Church, Dresden. Dok 1: 25
2 Jul	(Visitation) Mourning restrictions completely removed. Possible first performance of the later version of the Magnificat (D major) (BWV 243). Dok 2: 331; NBR 160
Before 27 Jul	Bach travels to Dresden. Dok 1: 27; NBR 162
27 Jul	Bach sent to Friedrich Augustus II the performing parts of the Missa, Kyrie and Gloria (BWV 232I), with a covering letter requesting a court title. Dok 1: 166; NBR 161; Dok 1: 27; NBR 162
3 Aug	Cantata performed on the name day of the Saxon Elector, Friedrich Augustus II, *Frohes Volk, vergnügte Sachsen* (BWV Anh. I, 11); performed by Bach's Collegium Musicum in Zimmermann's coffee garden; music lost. Dok 2: 333–334
9 Aug	Carl Philipp Emanuel writes a letter of application for the position of organist of St. Wenceslas Church, Naumburg; with corrections by his father. Dok 1, 271
25 Aug	Cantor, organist, and rector write to the town council regarding wedding fees. Dok 1: 28; NBR 163
31 Aug	Inauguration of the Leipzig town council in the St. Nicholas Church; composition unknown. Dok 2: 264
5 Sept	Birthday of the electoral Prince, Friedrich Christian; *Laßt uns sorgen, laßt uns wachen* (BWV 213) performed by Bach's Collegium Musicum in Zimmermann's coffee garden. Dok 2: 336–337
Before 23 Sept	Cantor, organist, and rector write again to the town council regarding wedding fees. Dok 1: 29; NBR 164

1733–1734 523

5 Nov	Baptism of son, Johann August Abraham Bach.
	Dok 2: 340; Dok 5: a 92i
6 Nov	Death of Johann August Abraham. Dok 2: 341
7 Nov	Burial of Johann August Abraham. Dok 2: 341
11 Nov	Town Council responds to the matter raised by cantor, organist, and rector. Dok 2: 342
6–20 Dec	(Advent 2–4) *Tempus clausum*, no concerted music during the penitential season.
7 Dec	Completion of the original score of *Tönet, ihr Pauken! Erschallet, Trompeten!* (BWV 214).
8 Dec	Birthday of Electress, Maria Josepha; *Tönet, ihr Pauken! Erschallet, Trompeten!* (BWV 214) performed by Bach's Collegium Musicum, probably in Zimmermann's coffee house.
	Dok 2: 343–344

1734

3 Jan	(Sunday after New Year) Possible reperformance of *Ach Gott, wie manches Herzeleid* [II] (BWV 58) (see also 4 Jan 1733).
10 Jan	Two-part canon (BWV 1075) entered into an autograph album for a godchild, perhaps Johann Gottfried Walther, jun. (born 1712).
	Dok 1: 167; NBR 166; BJ 53 (1967): 87–88
17 Jan	Elector Friedrich Augustus II crowned King of Poland at Krakow. The event celebrated in Leipzig by Bach's Collegium Musicum in Zimmermann's coffee house: first performance of *Blast Lärmen, ihr Feinde! verstärket die Macht* (BWV 205a); music lost. Dok 2: 346–348; BJ 93 (2007): 205–212
By 13 Mar	Visit to Bach in Leipzig by violinist Franz Benda. Dok 3: 731
14 Mar–18 Apr	(Lent) *Tempus clausum*, no concerted music during the penitential season.
23 Apr	(Good Friday) Performance of the Passion-Oratorio, *Der Gläubigen Seele Geistliche Betrachtungen Ihres leidenden Jesu*, in the St. Thomas Church; composer Gottfried Heinrich Stölzel. Dok 2: 180; NBR 114; BJ 94 (2008): 77–84
Jun/Jul	First performance of the Coffee Cantata, *Schweigt stille, plaudert nicht* (BWV 211) by Bach's Collegium Musicum.
22 Jun	Cantata performed at the marriage of Johann Caspar Zeisig and Catharina Elisabeth Olearius; composition unknown.[1]
	NBA I/33, KB, 14

---

1 A manuscript full score of a wedding cantata in Bach's hand comprising "20 folio pages" and dated "1734," was sold by London auction houses in 1847 (Puttock, 30 Mar, Lot 48) and 1872 (Sotheby, 12 Jul, Lot 97); current location unknown.

524   *1734*

28 Jun	Lorenz Christiph Mizler dedicates his *Dissertatio quod musica ars sit pars eruditionis philosophicae* ... to Johann Mattheson, Johann Sebastian Bach, Georg Heinrich Bümler, and Johann Samuel Ehrmann. Dok 2: 349; NBR 168–169
25 July	(Trinity 5) Probable first performance of *In allen meinen Taten* (BWV 97).
3 Aug	Cantata performed on the name day of the Saxon Elector, Friedrich Augustus II, performed by Bach's Collegium Musicum in Zimmermann's coffee garden; composition unknown. Dok 2: 350; NBR 170
30 Aug	Inauguration of the Leipzig town council in the St. Nicholas Church; composition unknown. Dok 2: 264
9 Sept	Matriculation of Carl Philipp Emanuel Bach at the University of Frankfurt/Oder. Dok 1: 1674
4 Oct	Cantata honoring the rector of the St. Thomas School, Johann Matthias Gesner, who was leaving to become professor of poetry and eloquence at the University of Göttingen: *Wo sind meine Wunderwerke* (BWV Anh. I, 210); music lost. Dok 5: B 350a
5 Oct	Cantata marking the first anniversary of the election of Friedrich Augustus as King of Poland, *Preise dein Glücke, gesegnetes Sachsen* (BWV 215), performed by Bach's Collegium Musicum outside the "Apelischen Hause," Leipzig, in the presence of the King and Queen. Dok 2: 351–353: NBR 171–172
6 Oct	Death of the town trumpeter, Gottfried Reiche, who had performed the virtuoso trumpet part of the cantata presented to the King-Elector the night before. Dok 2: 352
24 Oct	(Trinity 18) Possible reperformance of *Herr Christ, der einige Gottessohn* (BWV 96).
2 Nov	Bach's conduct in the affairs of the St. Thomas School criticized. Dok 2: 355
21 Nov	Introduction of the new rector of the St. Thomas School, Johann August Ernesti, with the performance of *Thomana saß annoch betrübt* (BWV Anh. I, 19); music lost. Dok 2: 357–358
28 Nov	(Advent) Performance of Georg Philipp Telemann's *Machet die Tore Weit* (TWV 1: 1074).
5–19 Dec	(Advent 2–4) *Tempus clausum*, no concerted music during the penitential season.
25 Dec	(Christmas Day) First performances of *Jauchzet, frohlocket, auf, preiset die Tage* (BWV 248^I) in the St. Nicholas Church (morning) and St. Thomas Church (afternoon). Dok 2: 360
26 Dec	(St. Stephen's Day) First performances of *Und es waren Hirten in derselben Gegend* (BWV 248^{II}) in the St. Thomas Church (morning) and St. Nicholas Church (afternoon). Dok 2: 360
27 Dec	(St. John's Day) First performance of *Herrscher des Himmels, erhöre das Lallen* (BWV 248^{III}) in the St. Nicholas Church. Dok 2: 360

1735

| | Bach compiles the manuscript genealogy "Origin of the Musical Bach Family." Dok 1: 184; NBR 303 |

1 Jan (New Year) First performances of *Fallt mit Danken, fallt mit Loben* (BWV 248^{IV}) in the St. Thomas Church (morning) and St. Nicholas Church (afternoon). Dok 2: 360

2 Jan (Sunday after New Year) First performance of *Ehre sei dir Gott gesungen* (BWV 248^{V}) in the St. Nicholas Church. Dok 2: 360

6 Jan (Epiphany) First performances of *Herr, wenn die stolzen Feinde schnauben* (BWV 248^{VI}) in the St. Thomas Church (morning) and St. Nicholas Church (afternoon). Dok 2: 360

30 Jan (Epiphany 4) First performance of *Wär Gott nicht mit uns diese Zeit* (BWV 14).

2 Feb (Purification) Possible reperformance of *Ich habe genung* (BWV 82).

27 Feb–3 Apr (Lent) *Tempus clausum*, no concerted music during the penitential season.

8 Apr (Good Friday) Passion performance in the St. Nicholas Church; composition unknown. Dok 2: 180; NBR 114

11 Apr (2 Easter) Possible reperformance of *Erfreut euch, ihr Herzen* (BWV 66).

12 Apr (3 Easter) Possible reperformance of *Ein Herz, das seinen Jesum lebend weiß* (BWV 134).

ca.1 May Publication of *Clavierübung II* (BWV 971 and 831) for the Easter Fair in Leipzig. Dok 1: 168; Dok 2: 323; NBR 174

2 May Bach writes to councilor Tobias Rothschier in Mühlhausen recommending his son Johann Gottfried Bernhard Bach for the vacant position of organist in the town. Dok 1: 30; NBR 175

5 May Report in the *Leipziger-Zeitungen* that published keyboard works by Conrad Friedrich Hurlebusch can be purchased from Bach in Leipzig. Dok 363; see also Dok 2: 373

19 May (Ascension) First performance of *Lobet Gott in seinen Reichen*, Ascension Oratorio (BWV 11).

21 May Bach writes to burgermaster Christian Petri in Mühlhausen recommending his son Johann Gottfried Bernhard Bach for the vacant position of organist in the town.
Dok 1: 31; Dok 2: 364; NBR 176

By 9 Jun Audition by Gottfried Bernhard Bach on the organ of St. Mary's Church, Mühlhausen; Johann Sebastian in Mühlhausen for two weeks. Dok 2: 363, 365

By 16 Jun Bach's examination of the organ in St. Mary's Church, Mühlhausen. Dok 2: 365

22 Jun Testing the renovated organ of the Church of St. Peter and St. Paul, Weissensee. Dok 5: B 365a

17 Jul (Trinity 6) Possible reperformance of *Es ist das Heil uns kommen her* (BWV 9).

526   *1735–1736*

3 Aug	Cantata performed on the name day of the King-Elector, Friedrich Augustus II, performed by Bach's Collegium Musicum in Zimmermann's coffee garden; probably *Auf, schmetternde Töne der muntern Trompeten* (BWV 207a). Dok 2: 367–368
13 Aug	*Clavierübung II* (BWV 971 and 831) advertised in the Leipzig newspaper *Nouvellen.* Dok 2: 370; see also Dok 2: 366
29 Aug	Inauguration of the Leipzig town council in the St. Nicholas Church; composition unknown. Dok 2: 264
4 Sept	(Trinity 13) Performance of *O! Wie selig sind die Blicke*, in the St. Nicholas Church; composed by Gottfried Heinrich Stölzel, Capellmeister at the court of Gotha. BJ 94 (2008): 99–122; see also BJ 95 (2009): 95–115
5 Sept	Birth of son, Johann Christian Bach. Dok 1: 261
7 Sept	Baptism of Johann Christian. Dok 2: 371; Dok 5: A 92k
11 Sept	(Trinity 14) Performance of *Schnöder Aussatz meiner Sünden*, in the St. Thomas Church; composed by Gottfried Heinrich Stölzel. BJ 94 (2008): 99–122
18 Sept	(Trinity 15) Performance of *Sorgen, Sorgen, sind die Steine*, in the St. Nicholas Church; composed by Gottfried Heinrich Stölzel. BJ 94 (2008): 99–122
25 Sept	(Trinity 16) Performance of *Mein Jesu, deine Wunder-Hand*, in the St. Thomas Church; composed by Gottfried Heinrich Stölzel. BJ 94 (2008): 99–122
29 Sept	(St. Michael's Day) Performances of *Michael, wer ist wie Gott*, in the St. Nicholas Church (morning) and St. Thomas Church (afternoon); composed by Gottfried Heinrich Stölzel. BJ 94 (2008): 137–158
2 Oct	(Trinity 17) Performance of *Du Artzt in Israel*, in the St. Thomas Church; composed by Gottfried Heinrich Stölzel. BJ 94 (2008): 137–158
9 Oct	(Trinity 18) Performance of *Leite mich in Liebes-Seilen*, in the St. Nicholas Church; composed by Gottfried Heinrich Stölzel. BJ 94 (2008): 137–158
16 Oct	(Trinity 19) Performance of *Jesu, hier ist deine Stadt*, in the St. Thomas Church; composed by Gottfried Heinrich Stölzel. BJ 94 (2008): 137–158
4–18 Dec	(Advent 2–4) *Tempus clausum*, no concerted music during the penitential season.

1736

3 Jan	Performance of wedding music in Ohrdruf that included movements from Bach's cantatas BWV 195 and 34a; probably not performed under Bach's direction. Dok 5: B 376a

1736 527

19 Feb–25 Mar	(Lent) *Tempus clausum*, no concerted music during the penitential season.
30 Mar	(Good Friday) Reperformance of the St. Matthew Passion (BWV 244) in the St. Thomas Church; "with both organs." Dok 2: 180; NBR 114
ca. Apr	Publication of the Schemelli Gesangbuch in time for the Easter Fair in Leipzig. Dok 2: 378; NBR 178
24 Apr	Bach's role as musical editor of the Schemelli Gesangbuch acknowledged in the preface. Dok 2: 379; NBR 179
ca.15 Jun	Rector Johann August Ernesti appoints Johann Gottlob Krause as first prefect, displacing Bach's choice. Dok 2: 282
10 Jul	Beginning of the conflict over appointment of prefects. Dok 2: 282; see Dok 3: 820; NBR 180
19 Jul–2 Aug	Bach away from Leipzig for two weeks; place and purpose unknown. Dok 2: 282; NBR 184; see also Dok 2: 162
12 Aug	Bach's first complaint to the town council in the dispute with Ernesti. Dok 1: 32; NBR 181
13 Aug	Bach's second complaint to the town council in the dispute with Ernesti. Dok 1: 33; NBR 182
15 Aug	Bach's third complaint to the town council in the dispute with Ernesti. Dok 1: 34; NBR 183
17 Aug	Ernesti's response to the town council. Dok 2: 382; NBR 184
19 Aug	(Trinity 12) Bach's fourth complaint to the town council in the dispute with Ernesti. Dok 1: 35; NBR 185
27 Aug	Inauguration of the Leipzig town council in the St. Nicholas Church; composition unknown. Dok 2: 264
Sept	Announcement in Lorenz Christoph Mizler's *Neue eröffnete musikalische Bibliothek* of weekly concerts by Bach's Collegium Musicum in Zimmermann's coffee house. Dok 2: 387; NBR 187
3 Sept	Cantata performed at the marriage of Johann August Zeisig and Helena Reinhardt; composition unknown. NBA I/33, KB, 15
13 Sept	Ernesti's rebuttal of Bach's third complaint. Dok 2: 383; NBR 186
By 27 Sept	Bach petitions for the title "Hofcompositeur" (court composer) to the King-Elector, Friedrich Augustus II; original document no longer extant. Dok 1: 36
7 Oct	Cantata performed on the birthday of the Saxon Elector, Friedrich Augustus II, performed by Bach's Collegium Musicum in Zimmermann's coffee house; *Schleicht, spielende Wellen, und murmelt gelinde!* (BWV 206). Dok 2: 386
30 Oct	Bach's first letter to the Sangerhausen town council in connection with the organ position at the St. James Church, then vacant. Dok 1: 37; NBR 188

528   *1736–1737*

18 Nov	Bach's second letter to the Sangerhausen town council recommending his son (Johann Gottfried Bernhard) for the vacant position of organist of St. James Church. Dok 1: 38; NBR 189
19 Nov	Bach is appointed "Hofcompositeur" (court composer) to the King-Elector, Friedrich Augustus II. Dok 2: 388; NBR 190
1 Dec	Bach gives a recital on the recently built Silbermann organ of Our Lady's Church, Dresden. Dok 2: 389; NBR 191
2 Dec	(Advent) Possible reperformance of *Nun komm, der Heiden Heiland* [II] (BWV 62); the order of the Hauptgottesdienst listed on the cover of the ms. score. Dok 1: 181
9–23 Dec	(Advent 2–4) *Tempus clausum*, no concerted music during the penitential season.

1737

	Purchase of Bodenschatz's *Florilegium* of either motets or Latin hymns for the St. Thomas Church. Dok 2: 407
14 Jan	Johann Gottfried Bernhard Bach appointed the organist of St. James Church, Sangerhausen. Dok 2: 396
6 Feb	Decree of the town council regarding the dispute with Ernesti over the appointment of prefects. Dok 1, 99–100; Dok 2: 392
12 Feb	Bach's first appeal to the consistory regarding the dispute with Ernesti over the appointment of prefects. Dok 1: 39; NBR 193
13 Feb	Response of the consistory Dok 2: 394
10 Mar–14 Apr	(Lent) *Tempus clausum*, no concerted music during the penitential season.
10 Apr	In the St. Nicholas Church, the "Praecentor" began a hymn too low for the congregation to join in; Bach instructed to deal with the issue. Dok 2: 399
19 Apr	(Good Friday) Passion performance in the St. Nicholas Church; composition unknown. Dok 2: 180; NBR 114
14 May	Johann Adolph Scheibe is critical of Bach's compositional style in *Der Critische Musicus. Sechstes Stück.* Dok 2: 400; NBR 343
8 Jul	Cantata performed at the marriage of Johann Gottlob Winckler and Johanna Eschert; composition unknown. NBA I/33, KB, 15
21 Aug	Bach's second appeal to the consistory regarding the dispute with Ernesti over the appointment of prefects. Dok 1: 40; NBR 194
26 Aug	Inauguration of the Leipzig town council in the St. Nicholas Church; composition unknown. Dok 2: 264
28 Aug	First performance of cantata composed in honor of Johann Christian, Count von Hennicke *Angenehmes Wiederau, freue dich in deinen Auen!* (BWV 30a). Dok 2: 402
By 18 Oct	Johann Elias Bach becomes house teacher to the family and personal secretary to Bach. Dok 1: 49

1737–1738 529

18 Oct	Bach's appeal to the King-Elector regarding the dispute with Ernesti over the appointment of prefects. Dok 1: 41; NBR 195
30 Oct	Baptism of daughter Johanna Carolina Bach. Dok 2: 405; Dok 5: A 921
8–22 Dec	(Advent 2–4) *Tempus clausum*, no concerted music during the penitential season.
16 Dec	Examination of the new organ built by Conrad Christian Schäfer in the Church of St. Peter and St. Paul, Weissensee, Thuringia. Dok 5: B 425a, 427a, 428a
17 Dec	The King-Elector's decree regarding Bach's complaint regarding the dispute with Ernesti over the appointment of prefects. Dok 2: 406; NBR 196

1738

By 8 Jan	Johann Abraham Birnbaum, lecturer in rhetoric at Leipzig University, publishes a defense of Bach against the criticism of Johann Adolph Scheibe. Dok 2: 409; NBR 344
5 Feb	The consistory responds in connection with the dispute with Ernesti over the appointment of prefects. Dok 2: 412
23 Feb–30 Mar	(Lent) *Tempus clausum*, no concerted music during the penitential season.
18 Feb	Johann Adolph Scheibe replies to Johann Abraham Birnbaum's defense of Bach. Dok 2: 417; NBR 345
4 Apr	(Good Friday) Passion performance in the St. Thomas Church; composition unknown. Dok 2: 180; NBR 114
28 Apr	"Abendmusik" in honor of the King-Elector, Friedrich Augustus II and his family, *Willkommen! Ihr herrschenden Götter der Erden* (BWV Anh. I, 13), performed by Bach's Collegium Musicum outside the "Apelischen Hause," Leipzig; music lost. Dok 2: 424, 424a, 436
ca.29 Apr	Johann Elias Bach writes to his mother in Schweinfurt for presents for Johann Sebastian and Anna Magdalena. Dok 2: 423; NBR 202
May	Bach subscribes to Georg Philipp Telemann's "Paris Quartets." Dok 2: 425
22 May	Bach returns from a visit to Dresden. Dok 1: 42
24 May	Letter to Johann Friedrich Klemm, Burgermaster in Sangerhausen, concerning the debts of his son Johann Gottfried Bernhard. Dok 1: 42; NBR 203
26 May	Letter to Burgermaster Klemm's wife in Sangerhausen concerning the debts of son. Dok 1: 43; NBR 204
By 30 Jul	Receives copies of the recently engraved chorale variations on *Allein Gott in der Höh sei Ehr* from the composer, his cousin Johann Gottfried Walther. Dok 2: 427

530   *1738–1739*

25 Aug	Inauguration of the Leipzig town council in the St. Nicholas Church; composition unknown. Dok 2: 264, 428
7–21 Dec	(Advent 2–4) *Tempus clausum*, no concerted music during the penitential season.

1739

10 Jan	Bach is reported to be planning to publish "some clavier pieces"; presumably *Clavierübung III*. Dok 2: 434; NBR 205
28 Jan	Matriculation of Johann Gottfried Bernhard Bach at the University of Jena. Dok 1: 42; NBR 203
15 Feb–22 Mar	(Lent) *Tempus clausum*, no concerted music during the penitential season.
Mar	Publication of Johann Abraham Birnbaum's response to Johann Adolph Scheibe's criticisms of Bach. Dok 2: 441
17 Mar	Bach protests the decision of the town council against the performance of a particular Passion. Dok 2: 439
27 Mar	(Good Friday) Whether there was a Passion performance is uncertain. Dok 2: 439; NBR 208
2 Apr	Johann Adolph Scheibe publishes a satire against Johann Abraham Birnbaum and Bach. Dok 2: 442; NBR 347
7 Apr	Performance of *Schweigt stille, plaudert nicht* (BWV 211), the Coffee Cantata, by the Collegium Musicum in Frankfurt/Oder, probably directed by Carl Philipp Emanuel Bach. Dok 5: B 442a
17 May	(Pentecost). Bicentenary of the introduction of the Reformation into Leipzig when Luther preached in the St. Thomas Church at Pentecost 1539.
27 May	Death of Bach's son, Johann Gottfried Bernhard Bach, in Jena, aged 24. Dok 2: 323
Before 11 Aug	Wilhelm Friedemann spends four weeks in Leipzig; house music with the Dresden lutanists, Sylvius Leopold Weiss and Johann Kropffgans. Dok 2: 448; NBR 209
12 Aug	Bicentenary of the adoption of Reformation theology and practice by Leipzig University.
31 Aug	Inauguration of the Leipzig town council in the St. Nicholas Church; reperformance of *Wir danken dir, Gott, wir danken dir* (BWV 29). Dok 2: 452
Early Sept	Visit to Altenburg and organ recital in the St. George's Church in the castle. Dok 2: 453
30 Sept	The publication of *Clavierübung III* announced in the *Leipziger Zeitungen*. Dok 2: 462
2 Oct	Bach again takes over the direction of the Collegium Musicum from Carl Gotthelf Gerlach, who had been the leader for a period. Dok 2: 455, 457; NBR 210

1739–1741 531

5 Oct	Johann Elias Bach writes to his sister in Schweinfurt for her to send some wine to Johann Sebastian.
	Dok 2: 458; NBR 211
7 Oct	Cantata performed on the birthday of the King-Elector, Friedrich Augustus II, performed by Bach's Collegium Musicum in Zimmermann's coffee house; composition unknown.
	Dok 2: 459
7–14 Nov	Johann Sebastian and Anna Magdalena visit the court of Weissenfels; chamber music performed in the house of Johann Leberecht Schneider. Dok 2: 456; Dok 1: 169; NBR 206
6–20 Dec	(Advent 2–4) *Tempus clausum*, no concerted music during the penitential season.

1740

18 Jan	Bach reports on candidates for an assistant music teacher's position at the St. Thomas School. Dok 1: 76; NBR 215
6 Mar–10 Apr	(Lent) *Tempus clausum*, no concerted music during the penitential season. Bach was in Halle during Lent, during which time he visited Johann Georg Hille, Cantor in Glaucha.
	Dok 2: 477; NBR 217
Jun	Bach (or Johann Elias Bach) requests a songbird for Anna Magdalena. Dok 2: 477; NBR 217
3 Aug	Cantata performed on the name day of the King-Elector, Friedrich Augustus II, performed by Bach's Collegium Musicum in Zimmermann's coffee garden; reperformance of *Schleicht, spielende Wellen, und murmelt gelinde!* (BWV 206). Dok 2: 479
29 Aug	Inauguration of the Leipzig town council in the St. Nicholas Church; first performance of *Herrscher des Himmels, König der Ehren* (BWV Anh. I, 193); music lost. Dok 2: 452
Oct	Review of *Clavierübung III* by Lorenz Christoph Mizler.
	Dok 2: 482; NBR 333
4–18 Dec	(Advent 2–4) *Tempus clausum*, no concerted music during the penitential season.

1741

19 Feb–26 Mar	(Lent) *Tempus clausum*, no concerted music during the penitential season.
By 29 Apr	Cantata performed in honor of the King-Elector, Friedrich Augustus II, and his family; composition unknown. Dok 2: 487
Jul	Letter to Johann Leberecht Schneider at the court of Weissenfels. Dok 1: 44; NBR 221
Early Aug	Bach in Berlin; Anna Magdalena ill in Leipzig.
	Dok 2: 489–490; NBR 222–223

532   *1741–1742*

28 Aug	Inauguration of the Leipzig town council in the St. Nicholas Church; reperformance of *Wünschet Jerusalem Glück* (BWV Anh. I, 4); music lost. Dok 2: 452
Sept	Anna Magdalena writes to Johann Leberecht Schneider at the court of Weissenfels regretting that due to illness she cannot make a visit to the court. Dok 2: 493; NBR 224
11 Sept	Cantata performed at the marriage of Gottlob Heinrich Pipping and Johanna Eleonora Schütze; composition unknown. NBA I/33, KB, 15
19 Sept	Performance of *O holder Tag, erwünschte Zeit* (BWV 210) at the marriage of Georg Ernst Stahl and Johanna Elisabeth Schrader in Berlin; probably directed by Carl Philipp Emanuel Bach with Johann Friedrich Agricola. Dok 5: C 775a; BJ 87 (2001): 7–22
5 Nov	Cantata performed at the marriage of Johann Gottlob Haußmann and Eleonora Dorothea Eschert; composition unknown. NBA I/33, KB, 15
17 Nov	Johann Sebastian Bach and Johann Elias Bach return from a visit to Dresden. Dok 2: 498
10–24 Dec	(Advent 2–4) *Tempus clausum*, no concerted music during the penitential season.

1742

	Lorenz Christoph Mizler publishes his German translation of Fux's *Gradus ad Parnassum* in Leipzig. Since Bach owned a copy of the Latin edition, and there is evidence that he used the German version in his teaching, he may have influenced Mizler to undertake the translation. BJ 90 (2004): 87–99
11 Feb–18 Mar	(Lent) *Tempus clausum*, no concerted music during the penitential season.
22 Feb	Baptism of daughter Regina Susanna. Dok 2: 505; Dok 5: A 92m
23 Mar	(Good Friday) Reperformance of the St. Matthew Passion (BWV 244) in the St. Thomas Church. BJ 88 (2002): 29–33
27 May–3 Jun	Two weeks mourning (including Trinity 1 and Trinity 2) for Wilhelmina Amalie, widow of Kaiser Joseph I, mother of Maria Josepha, wife of King-Elector, Friedrich Augustus II; no concerted music in the churches. Dok 5: B 508a
3 Aug	Cantata performed on the name day of the King-Elector, Friedrich Augustus II, performed by Bach's Collegium Musicum in Zimmermann's coffee garden; reperformance of *Was mir behagt, ist nur die muntre Jagd!* (BWV 208a). Dok 2: 480
27 Aug	Inauguration of the Leipzig town council in the St. Nicholas Church; composition unknown. Dok 2: 264

30 Aug	Cantata in honor of Carl Heinrich von Dieskau, *Mer hahn en neue Oberkeet* (BWV 212) performed at his estate in Kleinschocher, near Leipzig.
Sept	Bach purchases the multivolume Altenburg edition of Luther's collected writings (1661–1664) at a book auction.
	Dok 1: 123; NBR 228; BJ 61 (1975): 126–128
31 Oct	Johann Elias Bach brings to an end his role as house teacher to the family and personal secretary to Bach, and leaves Leipzig.
	Dok 2: 511; NBR 226
27 Nov	Cantata performed at the marriage of Daniel Siegfried Klaubarth and Johanna Sophia Teutzscher; composition unknown.
	NBA I/33, KB, 15
9–23 Dec	(Advent 2–4) *Tempus clausum*, no concerted music during the penitential season.
25 Dec	(Christmas Day) Performance of *Gloria in excelsis Deo* (BWV 191) in the University's St. Paul's Church.
	BJ 99 (2013): 329–328 and 329–334

1743

3 Mar–7 Apr	(Lent) *Tempus clausum*, no concerted music during the penitential season.
26 Aug	Inauguration of the Leipzig town council in the St. Nicholas Church; composition unknown. Dok 2: 264
ca.27 Aug	Evaluation of the organ of St. Wenceslas Church, Naumburg.
	Dok 1: 88
11 Nov	Letter to Burgermaster Joachim Valentin Ludolph Niedt in Salzwedel, near Magdeburg, on behalf of his pupil Johann Friedrich Doles with regard to the Cantorate vacancy.
	Dok 5: A 45c; BJ 93 (2007): 9–43
8–22 Dec	(Advent 2–4) *Tempus clausum*, no concerted music during the penitential season.
By 13 Dec	Examination of the organ in St. John's Church, Leipzig.
	Dok 2: 519

1744

	Bach obtains, either by purchase or gift, a folio Luther Bible, with engravings by Merian (Frankfurt: Merian, 1704).
	BJ 97 (2011): 37–39, 47–48
	Early in the year marriage of Carl Philipp Emanuel Bach to Johanna Maria Dannemann in Berlin.
16 Feb–22 Mar	(Lent) *Tempus clausum*, no concerted music during the penitential season.

534   *1744–1746*

27 Mar	(Good Friday) Performance of the second version of the St. Mark Passion (BWV 247) in the St. Thomas Church; music lost. BJ 95 (2009): 30–48
29 Mar–13 May	Five-week absence from Leipzig; purpose and location unknown. Dok 5: A 45d
16 May	Letter to Burgermaster Joachim Valentin Ludolph Niedt in Salzwedel, near Magdeburg, on behalf of his pupil Gottlob Friedrich Türsch. Dok 5: A 45d
17 May	Lists compiled of the four choirs of the St. Thomas School alumni. BJ 92 (2006): 34
31 Aug	Inauguration of the Leipzig town council in the St. Nicholas Church; composition unknown. Dok 2: 264
6–20 Dec	(Advent 2–4) *Tempus clausum*, no concerted music during the penitential season. Between 1744 and 1746, Bach's duties of directing the music in the two principal churches were undertaken by the Thomaner, Gottfried Benjamin Fleckeisen. BJ 101 (2015): 75–97

1745

7 Mar–11 Apr	(Lent) *Tempus clausum*, no concerted music during the penitential season.
13 Jun	Cantata performed at the marriage of Christian Gottlieb Ludwig and Sophia Regina Reichel; composition unknown. NBA I/33, KB, 15
30 Aug	Inauguration of the Leipzig town council in the St. Nicholas Church; composition unknown. Dok 2: 264
29 Sept	(St. Michael's Day) From this time, Johann Christoph Altnickol was regularly used by Bach as an instrumentalist and vocal bass. Dok 1: 81; Dok 2: 553; NBR 240
30 Nov	Prussian troops, under Leopold of Anhalt-Dessau, occupy Leipzig during the Second Silesian War.
5–19 Dec	(Advent 2–4) *Tempus clausum*, no concerted music during the penitential season.
10 Dec	Baptism in Berlin of Johann August Bach, oldest son of Carl Philipp Emanuel Bach. Dok 2: 540
25 Dec	(Christmas Day) Peace concluded between Austria and Prussia in Dresden, bringing the Second Silesian War to an end.

1746

	The Saxon court painter, Elias Gottlob Haussmann, paints Bach's portrait. BJ 11 (1914): 6
1 Jan	Departure of Prussian troops from Leipzig

27 Feb–3 Apr	(Lent) *Tempus clausum*, no concerted music during the penitential season.
16 Apr	Wilhelm Friedemann Bach appointed the organist of Our Lady's Church, Halle. BJ 7 (1910): 117–119
7 Aug	Bach examines and inaugurates the new Johann Scheibe organ in Zschortau. Dok 1: 89; Dok 2: 545; NBR 235
29 Aug	Inauguration of the Leipzig town council in the St. Nicholas Church; composition unknown. Dok 2: 264
24–29 Sept	Bach in Naumburg. Dok 2: 550a
26 Sept	Bach and Gottfried Silbermann report on the rebuilt organ by Zacharias Hildebrandt in the St. Wenceslas Church, Naumburg. Dok 1: 89–90; Dok 2: 546–548; NBR 235–236
13 Jun	Cantata performed at the marriage of Johann Jacob Bose and Christiana Maria Heydenreich; composition unknown. NBA I/33, KB, 15
4–18 Dec	(Advent 2–4) *Tempus clausum*, no concerted music during the penitential season.

1747

19 Feb–26 Mar	(Lent) *Tempus clausum*, no concerted music during the penitential season.
9 Apr	Cantata performed at the marriage of Carl Ludewig Jacobi and Christiana Helena Lievers; composition unknown. NBA I/33, KB, 15
7–8 May	Bach visits the court of Frederick the Great, King of Prussia, in Potsdam. Dok 2: 554; NBR 239
8 May	Organ recital in the Church of the Holy Spirit, Potsdam. Dok 2: 554; NBR 239
After 8 May	Bach probably visits the new opera house in Berlin. Dok 2: 554; NBR 239; Dok 3: 803
15 May	A report of Bach's visit to Potsdam appears in the *Leipziger Zeitungen*. Dok 5, 297
21 May	(Pentecost) Possible performance of *O ewiges Feuer, o Ursprung der Liebe* (BWV 34) by Wilhelm Friedemann Bach in Halle.
25 May	Testimonial for his pupil (later son-in-law) Johann Christoph Altnickol. Dok 1: 81; NBR 240
Jun	Repairs begun on the organ of the St. Thomas Church, undertaken by Johann Scheibe. Dok 2: 561
ca.28 Jun	Lorenz Christoph Mizler visits Bach in Leipzig. Dok 2: 557 Bach becomes a member of Mizler's "Societät der Musikalischen Wissenschaften," founded in 1738. Dok 2: 574; Dok 3: 665; NBR 241 Presentation of the *Canonic Variations on Vom Himmel hoch* (BWV 769) to Mizler's "Society." Dok 1: 176; NBR 243

536   *1747–1748*

7 Jul	Dedication of the *Musical Offering* (BWV 1079) to Frederick the Great, King of Prussia. Dok 1: 173; Dok 2: 556; NBR 244–245
29 Aug	Inauguration of the Leipzig town council in the St. Nicholas Church; composition unknown. Dok 2: 264
4 Sept	Birth of granddaughter, Anna Carolina Philippina Bach, in Berlin. Dok 2: 558
17 Sept	(Trinity 16) Possible reperformance of *Liebster Gott, wann werd ich sterben*? (BWV 8).
30 Sept	Announcement of the publication of the *Musical Offering* (BWV 1079) in the Leipzig journal *Nouvellen*. Dok 3: 558a
1 Oct	(Trinity 18) Possible reperformance of *Herr Christ, der einige Gottessohn* (BWV 96).
15 Oct	Bach enters his five-voice canon (BWV 1077), "Christus Coronabit Crucigeros," into the autograph album of Johann Gottfried Fulde, a theological student. Dok 1: 174; NBR 251
10–24 Dec	(Advent 2–4) *Tempus clausum*, no concerted music during the penitential season.

1748

1 Jan	A second testimonial for his pupil (later son-in-law) Johann Christoph Altnickol. Dok 1: 82; NBR 252
12 Jan	Testimonial for organ builder Heinrich Andreas Contius of Halle. Dok 5 A 90a; NBR 255
18 Feb	Cantata performed at the marriage of Abraham Köhler and Johanna Christiana Schultze; composition unknown. NBA I/33, KB, 15
3 Mar–7 Apr	(Lent) *Tempus clausum*, no concerted music during the penitential season.
24/30 Jul	Bach writes to the Naumburg town council recommending his pupil Johann Christoph Altnickol for the vacant position of organist. Dok 1: 47–48; NBR 253–254
26 Aug	Inauguration of the Leipzig town council in the St. Nicholas Church; first performance of *Lobe den Herrn, meine Seele* (BWV 69).
Aug	Bach begins the fair copy score of the B minor Mass (BWV 232$^{\text{I-IV}}$).
26 Sept	Baptism of his grandson, Johann Sebastian Bach, the younger, in Berlin. Dok 1: 49
6 Oct	Bach writes to Johann Elias Bach concerning a copy of the "Prussian Fugue" from the *Musical Offering*. Dok 1: 49; NBR 257
2 Nov	Bach writes to Johann Elias Bach thanking him for a cask of wine. Dok 1: 50; NBR 258

1748–1749 537

8–22 Dec	(Advent 2–4) *Tempus clausum*, no concerted music during the penitential season.
26 Dec	Publication of the banns of marriage for Johann Christoph Altnickol and Elisabeth Juliana Friderica Bach in Naumburg.

Dok 2: 578

1749

1 Jan	(New Year) Reperformance of *Herr Gott, dich loben wir* (BWV 16).
5 Jan	Publication of the banns of marriage for Johann Christoph Altnickol and Elisabeth Juliana Friderica Bach in Leipzig.

Dok 2: 579a

20 Jan	Marriage of Johann Christoph Altnickol and Elisabeth Juliana Friderica Bach in the St. Thomas Church, Leipzig.

Dok 2: 579a

17 Feb	Cantata performed at the marriage of Johann Friedrick Schubert and Rosina Elisabeth Salina; composition unknown.

NBA I/33, KB, 16

23 Feb–30 Mar	(Lent) *Tempus clausum*, no concerted music during the penitential season.
1 Mar	Autograph album entry of seven-voice canon BWV 1078, probably dedicated to Benjamin Gottlieb Faber.

Dok 1: 177; Dok 5: 587; NBR 259

2 Apr	Bach receives a commission from Count Johann Adam von Questenberg. Dok 5: B 581a; NBR 261
Apr?	Correspondence with the organ builder Heinrich Andreas Contius. Dok 2: 582, 589
4 Apr	(Good Friday) Performance of the fourth version of the St. John Passion (BWV 245), in the St. Nicholas Church.
6 Apr	(Easter Day) Reperformance of the Easter Oratorio, *Kommet, eilat und laufet, ihr flüchtigen Füße* (BWV 249).
12 Apr	Testimonial for his pupil Johann Nathanael Bammler.

Dok 5: A 82a; NBR 263

6 May	Bach acts as agent for the purchase of a "Piano et Forte."

Dok 3: 142a

12 May	Possible reperformance of *Geschwinde, ihr wirbelnden Winde* (BWV 201) (Pheobus and Pan).
Mid-May	Sudden critical illness.
2 Jun	Count Heinrich von Brühl recommends his Dresden Capellmeister, Gottlob Harrer, as Bach's successor in Leipzig.

Dok 2: 583; NBR 265

8 Jun	The Leipzig town council arranges for Gottlob Harrer to audition in the concert room of the "Three Swans"; Harrer's cantata, *Der Reiche starb, und ward begraben*, was performed.

Dok 2: 584; Dok 5: 584a; NBR 266

538   *1749–1750*

20 Jul	(Trinity 7) Possible reperformance of *Es wartet alles auf dich* (BWV 187).
25 Aug	Inauguration of the Leipzig town council in the St. Nicholas Church; reperformance of *Wir danken dir, Gott, wir danken dir* (BWV 29). Dok 2: 585
Oct?	Completion of the manuscript score of the B minor Mass (BWV 232).
4 Oct	Birth of grandson Johann Sebastian Altnickol in Naumburg. Dok 2: 587
6 Oct	Baptism of grandson Johann Sebastian Altnickol in Naumburg; Bach not present. Dok 2: 587
27 Oct	Letter of thanks to Count Wilhelm von Schaumburg-Lippe in Bückeburg, with commendation of his son Johann Christoph Friedrich Bach. Dok 1: 54; NBR 267
Before 19 Nov	Burgermeiser Jacob Born criticizes the singers of the second choir of the St. Thomas School. Dok 5: B 587a
30 Nov	(Advent) Performance of Wilhelm Friedemann Bach's cantata *Lasset uns ablegen die Werke der Finsternis* (Fk 80), perhaps an attempt for him to become his father's successor.
7–21 Dec	(Advent 2–4) *Tempus clausum*, no concerted music during the penitential season.
10 Dec	Letter to Cantor Georg Friedrich Einicke in Frankenhausen. Dok 1: 53; Dok 2: 592; NBR 268
11 Dec	Second testimonial for his pupil Johann Nathanael Bammler. Dok 5: A 82b; NBR 264
21 Dec	Burial in Naumburg of grandson Johann Sebastian Altnickol, barely three months old. Dok 2: 587

1750

1 Jan	Johann Christoph Friedrich Bach is appointed court musician to the Count Wilhelm von Schaumburg-Lippe in Bückeburg. Dok 1: 54; NBR 267
2 Feb	(Purification; or 25 Mar, Visitation) Performance of C. P. E. Bach's *Magnificat* (Wq 215/ H 773) in Leipzig, almost certainly as a bid to succeed his father.
15 Feb–22 Mar	(Lent) *Tempus clausum*, no concerted music during the penitential season.
23 Mar	(Good Friday) The fourth version of the St. John Passion (BWV 245) may have been performed in the St. Thomas Church, and most likely directed by a prefect (Johann Nathanael Bammler?).
28–30 Mar	First eye surgery by the London oculist John Taylor. Dok 2: 598; NBR 269a
5–8 Apr	Second eye surgery by the London oculist John Taylor. Dok 2: 599; NBR 269b

9 Apr	Letter (presumably dictated) to Cantor Georg Friedrich Einicke in Frankenhausen. Dok 2: 592; NBR 268
14 Apr	In a letter, Padre Giovanni Battista Martini in Bologna lists manuscripts and prints of Bach's music he has in his possession. Dok 2: 600; NBR 385
4 May	Johann Gottfried Müthel, court organist in Schwerin, begins studying with Bach and dwells in Bach's apartment for the duration. Dok 2: 603; Dok 3 777
26 May	Letter (presumably dictated) to Cantor Georg Friedrich Einicke in Frankenhausen. Dok 1: 55; Dok 2:592; NBR 268
22 Jul	Following a stroke, receives the Sacrament of the Altar for the last time; received in his home ("Priv. Commun."). Dok 2: 605
28 Jul	Johann Sebastian Bach dies, "a little after" 8:15 pm. Dok 2: 606–607
29 Jul	A hearse is provided for the funeral. Dok 2: 608
30 or 31 Jul	Burial in the churchyard of St. John's Church; the whole St. Thomas School attended. Dok 609; NBR 271
31 Jul	Announcement of Bach's death read from the pulpit of the St. Thomas church. Dok 2: 611; NBR 272
6 Aug	Obituary notice in the *Berlinische Nachrichten*: "The loss of this uncommonly able man is greatly mourned by all true connoisseurs of music." Dok 2: 612; NBR 273

Index

Abel, Carl Friedrich 456, 461–2
Abel, Christian Ferdinand 198, 461, 498
Abravaya, Ido 319
Adami, Johann Christian 183
Adler, Guido 328
Adlung, Jakob 1, 223, 303; *Anleitung zu der musikalischen Gelahrtheit* 298–9; *Musica mechanica organoedi* 303
Adorno, Theodor 398; "Bach Defended Against his Devotees" 298, 379
Agricola, Johann Friedrich 76, 94, 338, 460, 470, 532; *Art of Fugue,* assistance in completion of 465, 467; as copyist 348, 453; obituary of J. S. Bach by 36, 56, 237, 299, 367, 448
Ahle, Johann Georg 162, 491
Albinoni, Tomaso 248; Opus 1 239, 251, 349; Opus 2 250; Opus 5 349; Opus 7 262; Opus 9 262
Albrici, Vincenzo 224
Aldwell, Edward 397
Allendorf, Johann Konrad Ludwig: *Cöthenisch Lieder* 174
Allorto, Riccardo 457
Alt-Bachisches Archiv 105, 213–36, 281, 437, 449; categories of compositions in 221; contents of 214–15, 217–20; history of 213–16; influence of 226–9; music of 220–6; reception of 229–36
Altenburg: St. George's Church 530
Altenburg, Michael: *Christlicher lieblicher und andechtiger newer Kirchen und Hauss Gesänge* 364
Altner, Stefan 136
Altnickol, Johann Christoph 4, 38–9, 242, 441, 454, 534; as copyist 71, 76, 80, 338; marriage of 177, 537; testimonial for 32, 535, 536
Altnickol, Johann Sebastian 72, 538

Ammon, Christoph F. 188
André, Johann 374
Andreae, Valentin 122
"Andreas Bach Book" 76, 248, 309–10, 459
Anhalt-Bernburg, Friederica Henrietta von 173, 201, 499
Anhalt-Cöthen, Prince Emanuel Ludwig of 201, 511
Anhalt-Cöthen, Prince Leopold of 171–2, 194, 198, 321, 497, 498, 499, 500, 509, 516; death of 515; employment by 170–1, 197, 270, 496; marriage of 173, 201, 499
Anhalt-Cöthen, Princess Charlotte Friederica Amelia of 509, 512
Anhalt-Dessau, Leopold of, 534
Anhalt-Zerbst, Prince Johann August of 208, 499
Ansermet, Ernest 9
Anthony, John Philip 372
Antoni, Degli 391
"Apelischen Hause," Leipzig 524, 529
Aries, Philippe: *Centuries of Childhood* 103–4
Arndt, Johann 122; *Wahres Christenthum* 180
Arnold, Johann Heinrich 130–1
Arnstadt 270, 490–1; Barfüsserkirch 153; clergy in 152–9; Neuen Kirche 40, 152–3, 195, 219, 302, 490, 491; students, contact with 116, 133–4, 140
Art of Fugue, The (BWV 1080) 72, 189, 295, 380, 381, 392–7, 424, 426, 482; C. P. E. Bach comment on 64, 393; composition date of 377, 392; *Contrapuncti I–IV* 395–6; *Contrapuncti VI* 396; *Contrapuncti VII* 396; *Contrapuncti VIII* 67;

542 *Index*

Contrapuncti XIII 396; *Contrapuncti
XVIII* 396; performance of 396–7;
printed editions of 91–2, 93, 449, 464,
465–8; unfinished nature of 393–4
Avenarius, Johann 288
Axmacher, Elke 267, 287; *"Aus Liebe will
mein Heyland Sterben"* 17, 289
Ayrton, William 267

Baal, Johann: Mass in A major 251
Babitz, Sol 318
Bach, Anna Carolina Philippina 40, 536
Bach, Anna Magdalena Wilcke 30, 32, 40,
100, 109, 111, 180, 184, 440–3, 531; as
copyist 54, 57, 73, 75, 109, 113, 241,
342–3, 441–3; correspondence by 532;
as godmother 499; handwriting of 67,
68, 73; marriage of 103, 172, 199, 203,
499; as performer 112–13, 442, 504;
role of 112; travels of 504, 509, 516,
521, 531
Bach, Barbara Margaretha Bartholomaei
103, 112, 488
Bach, Carl Philipp Emanuel 29, 32,
35, 37, 64, 105, 106, 142, 294, 309,
344, 349–50, 442, 448–52, 470, 482,
530, 536; Alt-Bachisches Archiv and
217, 230, 231–2, 449; *Art of Fugue*
publication by 465, 466, 467; Berlin
employment of 207; birth and baptism
of 40, 494; *Briefe und Dokumente* 30;
care for Johann Christian Bach 72,
101; as chronicler of J. S. Bach 1, 44,
216, 247, 367, 378, 381, 393, 441, 446,
449–50, 465, 469; as copyist 61, 75,
241, 385, 449; education of 501, 520,
524; employment of 522; ink used by
66; Kittel, altercation with 36; marriage
of 533; obituary of J. S. Bach by 36, 56,
202, 233, 237, 299, 367, 448, 462; *see
also* Bach, Carl Philipp Emanuel – works
Bach, Carl Philipp Emanuel – works
86–7, 343, 368, 437–8, 439, 447,
451–2, 469, 483; Concerto in a minor
for harpsichord and orchestra 259;
D minor trio Sonata (BWV 1036) 344;
Double Concerto for Fortepiano and
Harpsichord 447; *Magnificat* 538;
Nachlass 81–2, 449; *Versuch* 452, 459
Bach, Catherina Dorothea 457–8, 492
Bach, Christiana Benedicta Louise
178, 517
Bach, Christiana Dorothea 177, 518, 521

Bach, Christiana Sophia Henrietta 499, 510
Bach, Christian Gottlieb 177, 507, 515
Bach, Christina Louisa 454
Bach, Dorothea von Hof 488
Bach, Elisabeth Juliana Friderica 71, 72,
454; baptism of 177, 510; marriage of
177, 537
Bach, Ernestus Andreas 178, 514
Bach, Friedelena 112
Bach, Georg Christoph 213; *Siehe, wie fein
und lieblich* 214, 221, 224
Bach, Gottfried Heinrich 349–50, 452;
baptism 177, 503; birth 503
Bach, Heinrich 153, 213, 218, 219, 223, 231
Bach, Johann 213; *Sei nun wieder
zufrieden* 214, 218; *Unser Leben ist ein
Schatten* 214, 224, 228, 229; *Weint nicht
um meinen Tod* 214, 218
Bach, Johanna Carolina 178, 529
Bach, Johann Ambrosius 101, 105–6, 111,
114, 213, 218, 221, 360, 488; death of
100, 488; marriage of 488
Bach, Johann Andreas 458–9
Bach, Johann August 534
Bach, Johann August Abraham 177, 523
Bach, Johann Bernhard 259, 458;
Overture-suite in G minor 354
Bach, Johann Christian 72, 441, 453,
454–7, 458, 461; birth and baptism of
177, 526; compositions by 437, 438,
447, 455–6, 457; as copyist 38, 75, 455;
education of 101, 440, 452, 454–5
Bach, Johann Christoph (brother) 153, 247,
366, 459; care of J. S. Bach 101, 129,
131, 149, 488; as copyist 75–6; death of
498; marriage of 488; Pachelbel, pupil
of 248
Bach, Johann Christoph (first cousin once
removed) 213, 218, 219, 222–3, 224,
226, 232, 233, 235, 360, 366; *Ach,
daß ich Wassers gnug hätte* 214, 217,
219, 221, 224, 225–6, 227, 232; *An
Wasserflüssen Babylon* 225, 226; *Der
Gerechte* 214, 218, 219, 226, 230, 231,
232; *Es erhub sich ein Streit* 214, 217,
219, 221, 222, 227, 230, 232; *Es ist nun
aus mit meinem Leben* 214, 224, 230;
Ich lasse dich nicht (BWV Anh. III.159)
215, 217, 220, 233, 493; *Lieber Herr
Gott* 214, 217, 218, 230, 231–2, 233;
Meine Freundin, du bist schön 214,
221–2, 224, 228, 229, 230; *Mit Weinen
hebt sichs an* 214

Index 543

Bach, Johann Christoph (son) 439, 493
Bach, Johann Christoph (uncle) 106, 221, 222
Bach, Johann Christoph Friedrich 181, 441, 447, 453–4; birth and baptism 178, 520; as copyist 75, 453; education of 440, 458; employment of 538
Bach, Johann Elias 531, 536; correspondence of 30, 57, 105, 458, 529, 531, 532; role in J. S. Bach household 441, 458, 528, 533
Bach, Johann Ernst 219, 458, 490, 491
Bach, Johann Friedrich 492
Bach, Johann Gottfried Bernhard 29–30, 452, 525, 528, 529; birth and baptism of 495; death of 452, 530; education of 530
Bach, Johann Heinrich 75, 337, 458
Bach, Johann Jacob 101, 102, 488, 499
Bach, Johann Lorenz 53n18, 458, 493
Bach, Johann Ludwig 194, 223; *Allein Gott in der Höh sei Ehr* 256; cantatas 253, 254, 272, 510, 511
Bach, Johann Michael 213, 218, 219, 222, 223, 226, 231, 233, 235; *Ach, wie sehnlich wart ich der Zeit* 214, 224, 229; *Auf, laßt uns den Herren loben* 215, 224, 229, 232; *Das Blut Jesu Christi* 215, 218, 221, 233; *Der Herr ist König* 222; *Die Furcht des Herrn* 215, 219, 222; father-in-law of J. S. Bach 213, 491; *Herr, wenn ich nur dich habe* 215, 218, 221, 224; *Ich weiß, daß mein Erlöser lebt* 215; *Nun hab ich überwunden* 215, 233; *Revange* 222
Bach, Johann Nicolaus 231
Bach, Johann Sebastian (grandson) 536
Bach, Johann Sebastian – works: **BWV 1** *(Wie schön leuchtet der Morgenstern)* 507; **BWV 2** *(Ach Gott, vom Himmel sieh darein)* 504; **BWV 3** *(Ach Gott, wie manches Herzeleid* [I]*)* 506; **BWV 4** *(Christ lag in Todesbanden)* 490, 503, 507; **BWV 5** *(Wo soll ich fliehen hin)* 505; **BWV 6** *(Bleib bei uns, denn es will Abend werden)* 507; **BWV 7** *(Christ unser Herr zum Jordan kam)* 504; **BWV 8** *(Liebster Gott, wenn werd ich sterben?)* 80, 505, 536; **BWV 9** *(Es ist das Heil uns kommen her)* 525; **BWV 10** *(Meine Seel erhebt den Herren)* 290, 504; **BWV 11** (Ascension Oratorio) 282, 290, 525; **BWV 12** *(Weinen, Klagen, Sorgen, Zagen)* 494, 504; **BWV 13**

(Meine Seufzer, meine Tränen) 509; **BWV 14** *(Wär Gott nicht mit uns diese Zeit)* 525; **BWV 16** *(Herr Gott, dich loben wir)* 509, 518, 537; **BWV 17** *(Wer Dank opfert, der preiset mich)* 511; **BWV 18** *(Gleichwie der Regen und Schnee vom Himmel fällt)* 493, 495, 503; **BWV 19** *(Es erhub sich ein Streit)* 511; **BWV 20** *(O Ewigkeit, du Donnerwort* [II]*)* 504; **BWV 21** *(Ich hatte viel Bekümmernis)* 202, 208, 494, 498, 501; **BWV 22** *(Jesu nahm zu sich die Zwölfe)* 499, 503; **BWV 23** *(Du wahrer Gott und Davids Sohn)* 499, 503; **BWV 24** *(Ein ungefärb Gemüthe)* 501; **BWV 25** *(Es ist nichts Gesundes an meinem Liebe)* 501; **BWV 26** *(Ach wie flüchtig, ach wie nichtig)* 505; **BWV 27** *(Wer weiß, wie nahe mir mein Ende)* 511; **BWV 28** *(Gottlob! Nun Geht das Jahr zu Ende)* 509; **BWV 29** *(Wir danken dir, Gott, wir danken dir)* 519, 530, 538; **BWV 30a** *(Angenehmes Wiederau, freue dich in deinen Auen!)* 528; **BWV 31** *(Der Himmel lacht! die Erde jubilieret)* 495, 503, 518; **BWV 32** *(Liebster Jesu, mein Verlangen)* 509; **BWV 33** *(Allein zu dir, Herr Jesu Christ)* 505; **BWV 34** *(O ewiges Feuer, o Ursprung der Liebe)* 279–80, 513, 535; **BWV 34a** *(O ewiges Feuer, o Ursprung der Liebe)* 145n11, 279–80, 526; **BWV 35** *(Geist und Seele wird verwirret)* 350, 351, 511; **BWV 36** *(Schwingt freudig euch empor)* 520; **BWV 36a** *(Steigt freudig in die Luft)* 201, 509, 512; **BWV 36c** *(Schwingt freudig euch empor)* 507, 519; **BWV 37** *(Wer da gläubet und getauft wird)* 504, 519; **BWV 38** *(Aus tiefer Not schrei ich zu dir)* 505; **BWV 39** *(Brich dem Hungrigen Brot)* 510; **BWV 40** *(Dazu ist erschienen der Sohn Gottes)* 502; **BWV 41** *(Jesu, nun sei gepreiset)* 506; **BWV 42** *(Am Abend aber desselbigen Sabbats)* 507, 519; **BWV 42a** 507; **BWV 43** *(Gott fähret auf mit Jauchzen)* 272, 510; **BWV 44** *(Sie werden euch in dem Bann tun)* 504; **BWV 45** *(Es ist dir gesagt, Mensch, was gut ist)* 511; **BWV 46** *(Schauet doch und sehet, ob irgendein Schmerz sei)* 501; **BWV 47** *(Wer sich selbst erhöhet, der soll

544 *Index*

erniedriget werden) 43, 511; **BWV 48**
*(Ich elender Mensch, wer wird mich
erlösen)* 287, 502; **BWV 49** *(Ich geh
und suche mit Verlangen)* 350, 512;
BWV 51 *(Jauchzet Gott in allen
Landen!)* 518; **BWV 52** *(Falsche Welt,
dir trau ich nicht)* 512; **BWV 55** *(Ich
armer Mensch, ich Sündenknecht)* 203,
512; **BWV 56** *(Ich will den Kreutzstab
gerne tragen)* 511; **BWV 57** *(Selig ist
der Mann)* 509; **BWV 58** *(Ach Gott, wie
manches Herzeleid)* 512, 521, 523;
BWV 59 (*Wer mich liebet, der wird
mein Wort halten* [I]) 504, 519; **BWV
60** *(O Ewigkeit, du Donnerwort)* 502;
BWV 61 *(Nun komm der Heiden
Heiland)* 53, 494, 502; **BWV 62** (*Nun
komm, der Heiden Heiland* [II]) 506,
528; **BWV 63** *(Christen, ätzet diesen
Tag)* 494, 502; **BWV 64** *(Sehet, welch
eine Liebe hat uns der Vater erzeiget)*
502; **BWV 65** (*Sie werden alle aus Saba
kommen)* 503; **BWV 66** *(Erfreut euch,
ihre Herzen)* 200, 504, 519, 525; **BWV
66a** *(Der Himmel dacht auf Anhalts
Ruhm und Glück)* 200, 497; **BWV 67**
(Halt im Gedächtnis Jesum Christ) 504;
BWV 68 *(Also hat Gott die Welt geliebt)*
507; **BWV 69** *(Lobe den Herrn, meine
Seele)* 536; **BWV 69a** *(Lobe den Herrn,
meine Seele)* 501, 513; **BWV 70**
(Wachet! betet! betet! wachet!) 502,
520; **BWV 70a** *(Wachet! betet! betet!
wachet!)* 169, 352, 496, 502; **BWV 71**
(Gott is mein König) 163, 352, 491;
BWV 72 *(Alles nur nach Gottes Willen)*
510; **BWV 73** *(Herr, wie du willt, so
schick's mit mir)* 503; **BWV 74** (*Wer
mich liebet, der wird mein Wort halten*
[II]) 507; **BWV 75** *(Die Elenden sollen
essen)* 271, 500; **BWV 76** *(Die Himmel
erzählen die Ehre Gottes)* 500, 508;
BWV 77 *(Du sollst Gott, deinen Herren,
lieben)* 501; **BWV 78** *(Jesu, der du
meine Seele)* 333, 335, 505; **BWV 79**
(Gott der Herr ist Sonn und Schild) 4,
509, 518; **BWV 80** *(Ein feste Burg ist
unser Gott)* 471; **BWV 80a** *(Alles, was
von Gott geboren)* 495; **BWV 81** *(Jesu
schläft, was soll ich hoffen?)* 503; **BWV
82** *(Ich habe genung)* 512, 518, 525;
BWV 83 *(Erfreute Zeit im neuen Bunde)*
503, 512; **BWV 84** *(Ich bin vergnügt mit*

meinem Glücke) 512; **BWV 85** *(Ich bin
ein guter Hirt)* 507; **BWV 86** *(Wahrlich,
Wahrlich, ich sage euch)* 504; **BWV 87**
*(Bisher habt ihr nichts gebeten in
meinem Namen)* 507; **BWV 88** *(Siehe,
ich will viel Fischer aussenden)* 510;
BWV 89 *(Was soll ich aus dir machen,
Ephraim?)* 502; **BWV 90** *(Es reißet
euch ein schrecklich Ende)* 502; **BWV
91** *(Gelobet seist du, Jesu Christ)* 520,
521; **BWV 91a** *(Gelobet seist du, Jesu
Christ)* 506; **BWV 92** *(Ich hab in Gottes
Herz und Sinn)* 506; **BWV 93** *(Wer nur
den lieben Gott läßt walten)* 504; **BWV
94** *(Was frag ich nach der Welt)* 505;
BWV 95 *(Christus, der ist mein Leben)*
501; **BWV 96** *(Herr Christ, der einig
Gottessohn)* 505, 524, 536; **BWV 97** *(In
allen meinen Taten)* 524; **BWV 98** (*Was
Gott tut, das ist wohlgetan* [II]) 512;
BWV 99 (*Was Gott tut, das ist
wohlgetan* [I]) 505; **BWV 101** *(Nimm
von uns, Herr, du treuer Gott)* 505;
BWV 102 *(Herr, deine Augen sehen
nach dem Glauben)* 511; **BWV 103** *(Ihr
werdet weinen und heulen)* 507, 519;
BWV 104 *(Du Hirte Israel,höre)* 504;
BWV 105 *(Herr, gehe nicht ins Gericht
mit deinem Knecht)* 61, 501; **BWV 107**
(Was willst du dich betrüben) 505; **BWV
108** *(Es ist euch gut, daß ich hingehe)
glaube, lieber Herr, hilf meinem
Unglauben)* 502, 507; **BWV 110** *(Unser
Mund sie voll Lachens)* 272, 509; **BWV
111** *(Was mein Gott will, das g'scheh
allzeit)* 506; **BWV 112** *(Der Herr is
mein getreuer Hirt)* 519; **BWV 113**
(Herr Jesu Christ, du höchstes Gut) 505;
BWV 114 *(Ach, lieben Christen, seid
getrost)* 505; **BWV 115** *(Mache dich,
mein Geist, bereit)* 505; **BWV 116** *(Du
Friedefürst, Herr Jesu Christ)* 505;
BWV 119 *(Preise, Jerusalem, den
Herrn)* 501; **BWV 120** *(Gott, man lobet
dich an der Stille)* 517; **BWV 120a**
(Herr Gott, Beherrscher aller Dinge)
145n11, 516; **BWV 120b** *(Gott, man
lobet dich an der Stille)* 517; **BWV 121**
(Christum wir sollen loben schon) 506;
BWV 122 *(Das neugeborne Kindelein)*
506; **BWV 123** *(Liebster Immanuel,
Herzog der Frommen)* 506; **BWV 124**
(Meinen Jesum laß ich nicht) 506;

BWV 125 *(Mit Fried und Freud ich fahr dahin)* 506; BWV 126 *(Erhalt uns, Herr, bei deinem Wort)* 506; BWV 127 *(Herr Jesu Christ, wahr Mensch und Gott)* 147, 506; BWV 128 *(Auf Christi Himmelfahrt allein)* 507; BWV 129 *(Gelobet sei der Herr, mein Gott)* 510, 511, 513; BWV 130 *(Herr Gott, dich loben alle wir)* 505; BWV 131 *(Aus der Tiefe rufe ich, Herr, zu dir)* 162, 491; BWV 132 *(Bereitet die Wege, bereitet die Bahn)* 495; BWV 133 *(Ich freue mich in dir)* 444, 506; BWV 134 *(Ein Herz, das seinen Jesum lebend weiß)* 504, 519, 525; BWV 134a *(Die Zeit, die Tag und Jahre macht)* 200, 497; BWV 135 *(Ach Herr, mich armen Sünder)* 504; BWV 136 *(Erforsche mich, Gott, und erfahre mein Herz)* 501; BWV 137 *(Lobe den Herren, den mächtigen König zu Ehren)* 508; BWV 138 *(Warum betrübst du dich, mein Herz)* 501; BWV 139 *(Wohl dem, der sich auf seinem Gott)* 505; BWV 140 *(Wachet auf, ruft uns die Stimme)* 520; BWV 144 *(Nimm, was dein ist, und gehe hin)* 503; BWV 145 *(Ich lebe, meine Herze, zu deinen Ergötzen)* 516; BWV 146 *(Wir müssen durch viel Trübsal in das Reich Gottes eingehen)* 350, 510, 514; BWV 147 *(Herz und Mund und Tat und Leben)* 501; BWV 147a *(Herz und Mund und Tat und Leben)* 169, 496, 501; BWV 148 *(Bringet dem Herrn Ehre seines Namens)* 502, 509; BWV 149 *(Man singet mit Freuden vom Sieg)* 445, 517; BWV 151 *(Süßer Trost, mein Jesu kömmt)* 509; BWV 152 *(Tritt auf die Glaubensbahn)* 494; BWV 153 *(Schau, lieber Gott, wie meine Feind)* 503; BWV 154 *(Mein liebster Jesu ist verloren)* 335, 503; BWV 155 *(Mein Gott, wie lang, ach lange)* 495, 503; BWV 156 *(Ich steh mit einem Fuß im Grabe)* 515; BWV 157 *(Ich lasse dich nicht, du segnest mich denn)* 512; BWV 159 *(Sehet, wir gehn hinauf gen Jerusalem)* 516; BWV 161 *(Komm, du süße Todesstunde)* 496; BWV 162 *(Ach! ich sehe, ietz, da ich zur Hochzeit gehe)* 496, 502; BWV 163 *(Nur jedem das Seine!)* 495; BWV 164 *(Ihr, die ihr euch von Christo nennet)* 508; BWV 165

(O heilges Geist- und Wasserbad) 495, 504; BWV 166 *(Wo gehest du hin?)* 504; BWV 167 *(Ihr Menschen, rühmet Gottes Liebe)* 501; BWV 168 *(Tue Rechnung! Donnerwort)* 508; BWV 169 *(Gott soll allein mein Herze haben)* 350, 511; BWV 170 *(Vergnügte Ruh, beliebte Seelenlust)* 511; BWV 171 *(Gott, wie dein Name, so ist dein Ruhm)* 515; BWV 172 *(Erschallet, ihr Lieder, erklinget, ihr Saiten!)* 494, 504, 519; BWV 173 *(Erhöhtes Fleisch und Blut)* 504, 513, 519; BWV 173a *(Durchlauchster Leopold)* 200, 499; BWV 174 *(Ich liebe den Höchsten von ganzem Gemüte)* 516; BWV 175 *(Er rufet seinen Schafen mit Namen)* 507; BWV 176 *(Es ist ein trostzig und verzagt Ding)* 508; BWV 177 *(Ich ruf zu dir, Herr Jesu Christ)* 521; BWV 178 *(Wo Gott der Herr nicht bei uns hält)* 505; BWV 179 *(Siehe zu, dass deine Gottesfurcht nicht Heuchelei sei)* 501; BWV 180 *(Schmücke dich, o liebe Seele)* 505; BWV 181 *(Leichtgesinnte Flattergeister)* 503; BWV 182 *(Himmelskönig, sei willkommen)* 270, 494, 503; BWV 183 *(Sie werden euch in dem Bann tun* [II]*)* 507; BWV 183a 507; BWV 184 *(Erwünschtes Freudenlicht)* 200, 504, 513, 519; BWV 185 *(Barmherziges Herze der ewigen Liebe)* 495, 501; BWV 186 *(Ärgre dich, o Seele, nicht)* 169, 501; BWV 186a *(Ärgre dich, o Seele, nicht)* 496, 501; BWV 187 *(Es wartet alles auf dich)* 511, 538; BWV 188 *(Ich habe meine Zuversicht)* 350, 515, 517; BWV 190 *(Singet dem Herrn ein neues Lied)* 502; BWV 190a *(Singet dem Herrn ein neues Lied)* 517; BWV 191 *(Gloria in excelsis Deo)* 55, 176, 190, 533; BWV 193 *(Ihr Tore zu Zion)* 513; BWV 193a *(Ihr Häuser des Himmels, ihr scheinenden Lichter)* 513; BWV 194 *(Höchsterwünschtes Freudenfest)* 33, 200, 502, 504, 510, 519; BWV 195 145n11, 526; BWV 196 *(Der Herr denket an uns)* 145n11, 158; BWV 197a *(Ehre sei Gott in der Höhe)* 515; BWV 198 *(Laß Fürstin, laß noch einen Strahl)* 514; BWV 198 *(Trauerode)* 42, 45, 176, 514; BWV 199 *(Mein Herze schwimmt

546   *Index*

im Blut) 493, 494, 501; **BWV 200**
(Bekennen will ich seinen Namen) 245;
BWV 201 *(Geschwinde, ihr wirbelnden
Winde)* (Pheobus and Pan) 517, 537;
BWV 205 *(Zerreißet, zersprenget,
zertrümmert die Gruft)* 291, 508; **BWV
205a** *(Blast Lärmen, ihr Feinde!
verstärket die Macht)* 275, 291, 523;
BWV 206 *(Schleicht, spielende Wellen,
und murmelt gelinde!)* 527, 531; **BWV
207** *(Vereinigte Zweitracht der
wechselnden Saiten)* 512; **BWV 207a**
*(Auf, schmetternde Töne der muntern
Trompeten)* 526; **BWV 208** *(Was mir
behagt, ist nur die muntre Jagd)* 196,
203, 493; **BWV 208a** *(Was mir behagt,
ist nur die muntre Jagd!)* 532; **BWV 210**
(O holder Tag, erwünschte Zeit) 532;
BWV 210a *(O! Angenehme Melodie)*
515; **BWV 211** *(Schweigt stille, plaudert
nicht)* 275, 523, 530; **BWV 212** *(Mer
hahn en neue Oberkeet)* 533; **BWV 213**
(Laßt uns sorgen, laßt uns wachen) 275,
276, 522; **BWV 214** *(Tönet, ihr Pauken!
Erschallet, Trompeten!)* 275, 276, 523;
BWV 215 *(Preise dein Glücke,
gesegnetes Sachsen)* 275, 524; **BWV
216** *(Vergnügte Pleißen-Stadt)* 291, 514;
BWV 216a 291; **BWV 226** *(Der Geist
Hilft unser Schwachheit auf)* 517; **BWV
232**[III] (Sanctus in D major) 506, 513;
BWV 233a *(Christe, du Lamm Gottes)*
147; **BWV 237** (Sanctus in C major)
501; **BWV 238** (Sanctus in D major)
502; **BWV 239** (Sanctus in D minor)
257; **BWV 240** (Sanctus in G major)
257; **BWV 242** (Christe eleison in G
minor) 257; **BWV 243** (Magnificat in D
major) 275, 290, 522; **BWV 243a**
(Magnificat in E-flat major) 275, 290,
471, 501, 502; **BWV 244a** *(Klagt,
Kinder, klagt es aller Welt)* 9, 516; **BWV
246/40a** *(Aus der Tiefen)* 254; **BWV 248**
(Christmas Oratorio) 275, 276, 290,
477; **BWV 248**[I] *(Jauchzet, frohlocket,
auf, preiset die Tage)* 524; **BWV 248**[II]
*(Und es waren Hirten in derselben
Gegend)* 524; **BWV 248**[III] *(Herrscher
des Himmels, erhöre das Lallen)* 524;
BWV 248[IV] *(Fallt mit Danken, fallt mit
Loben)* 525; **BWV 248**[V] *(Ehre sei dir
Gott gesungen)* 525; **BWV 248**[VI] *(Herr,
wenn die stolzen Feinde schnauben)*

525; **BWV 249** (Easter Oratorio) 290,
507, 537; **BWV 249a** *(Entfliehet,
verschwindet, entweichet, ihr Sorgen)*
507; **BWV 249b** *(Verjaget, zerstreuet,
zerrüttet, ihr Sterne)* 511; **BWV 299**
333; **BWV 454** *(Ermuntre dich, mein
schwacher Geist)* 369; **BWV 479**
(Kommt, seelen dieser Tag) 370; **BWV
480** *(Kommt wieder aus der finstern
Gruft)* 370; **BWV 524** *(Was seind das
vor große Schlösser)* 145, 146, 491;
BWV 532 251; **BWV 535** (Prelude and
Fugue in G minor) 455; **BWV 536**
(Prelude and Fugue in A major) 250;
BWV 537/2 (Fugue in C minor) 461;
BWV 540 (Toccata and Fugue in F
major) 302, 455; **BWV 541** (Prelude
and Fugue in G major) 445; **BWV 543**
(Prelude and Fugue in A minor) 329,
471; **BWV 543–548** (Preludes and
Fugues) 471; **BWV 544** (Prelude and
Fugue in B minor) 441n15, 455, 471;
BWV 552 (Prelude and Fugue in E-flat
major) 307, 309; **BWV 553–560** (8
short Preludes and Fugues) 461; **BWV
562** (Fantasia and Fugue in C minor)
455; **BWV 565** (Toccata and Fugue in D
minor) 74, 296, 297, 314–16; **BWV
592–596** (Concertos transcribed for
organ) 53–4, 239, 241, 250, 446; **BWV
596** (D-minor Concerto for organ) 53–4,
239, 446; **BWV 645–650** *(Schübler
Chorales)* 52, 94, 308; **BWV 702** *(Das
Jesulein soll dich mein Trost)* 461;
BWV 715 *(Allein Gott in der Höh sei
Ehr)* 367; **BWV 726** *(Herr Jesu Christ
dich zu uns wend)* 367; **BWV 729** *(In
dulci jubilo)* 367; **BWV 806–811**
(English Suites) 81, 402, 460; **BWV 830**
(Clavierübung I, Partita 6) 338; **BWV
894** (Prelude and Fugue in A minor)
349; **BWV 903** (Chromatic Fantasia and
Fugue in D minor) 453, 471; **BWV 906**
(Fantasia and Fugue in C minor) 471,
477; **BWV 910–916** (Toccatas) 300,
471; **BWV 933–938** (Six Little
Preludes) 81, 471; **BWV 946** 239, 251;
BWV 950 239, 251; **BWV 951** 239,
251; **BWV 954** 239, 251; **BWV 965/2**
239, 251; **BWV 966/2** 239; **BWV 978/2**
(Concerto in F major) 328; **BWV 985**
(Concerto in G minor) 251; **BWV 992**
(Capriccio sopra il lontananza del suo

fratello dilettissimo) 228, 333; **BWV 995** (C minor lute Suite) 319, 325; **BWV 998/2** (Fuga in E flat major) 332; **BWV 1021** (G major Sonata) 53, 57, 336n118, 339, 342–3, 355; **BWV 1022** (Sonata for Violin and Basso Continuo in F major) 343; **BWV 1023** (E minor Sonata) 342; **BWV 1024** (Violin Sonata in C minor) 344; **BWV 1025** (Suite in A major for Violin and Harpsichord) 246, 338–9, 340; **BWV 1026** (Fuga in G minor for violin and continuo) 340, 342; **BWV 1030** (Sonata in B minor for Flute) 340; **BWV 1030a** (Sonata in G minor for Flute and Harpsichord) 340; **BWV 1031** (Sonata in E-flat major for Flute) 331, 341, 342; **BWV 1032** (Sonata for Flute in A major) 330–1, 341; **BWV 1033** (Sonata for Flute in C major) 344; **BWV 1034** (Sonata for Flute and Continuo in E minor) 343–4; **BWV 1035** (Sonata for Flute and Continuo in E major) 343, 344; **BWV 1038** (Trio Sonata in G major) 343; **BWV 1039** (Trio Sonata in G major for two flutes and continuo) 339; **BWV 1041** (Violin Concerto in A minor) 348; **BWV 1042** (E major Concerto) 348; **BWV 1043** (D minor Concerto for two violins) 338, 341, 346, 348, 349, 353; **BWV 1044** (Triple Concerto) 348, 447; **BWV 1052** (D minor harpsichord Concerto) 56, 305, 349, 350; **BWV 1052–1059** (Harpsichord Concertos) 349; **BWV 1053** (E major Concerto) 305, 350; **BWV 1054** 348; **BWV 1055** (Harpsichord Concerto in A major) 323, 350; **BWV 1056** (Concerto in F minor) 351; **BWV 1057** 346–7; **BWV 1058** 348, 349; **BWV 1059** (Concerto in D minor) 349, 350, 351; **BWV 1060** (Concerto for two harpsichords in C minor) 351; **BWV 1061** (Concerto for two harpsichords) 346, 351; **BWV 1062** (Concerto in C minor for two harpsichords) 341, 349; **BWV 1063** (Concerto in D minor for three harpsichords) 351; **BWV 1064** (Concerto for three harpsichords) 351; **BWV 1065** (Concerto for four harpsichords) 259; **BWV 1073** (four-part perpetual canon) 493; **BWV 1074** 513; **BWV 1075** 523; **BWV 1076**

(Canon in G major) 385; **BWV 1077** ("Christus Coronabit Crucigeros") 536; **BWV 1078** (Canon in F major) 537; **BWV 1081** (Credo intonation) 257; **BWV 1087** (Fourteen Canons) 86, 382, 413; **BWV 1112** *(Christus, der ist mein Leben)* 228; **BWV 1121** (Fantasia in C Minor) 295; **BWV 1127** *(Alles mit Gott und nichts ohn' ihn)* 87, 165, 196, 481, 493; **BWV 1128** *(Wo Gott der Herr nicht bei uns hält)* 295, 310–11; **BWV Anh. I, 3** *(Gott, gib dein Gerichte dem Könige)* 518; **BWV Anh. I, 4** *(Wünschet Jerusalem Glück)* 483, 508, 532; **BWV Anh. I, 4a** *(Wünschet Jerusalem Glück)* 518; **BWV Anh. I, 5** *(Lobet den Herrn, all seine Heerscharen)* 200, 497; **BWV Anh. I, 6** *(Dich loben die lieblichen Strahlen der Sonne)* 200, 498; **BWV Anh. I, 7** *(Heut ist gewiß ein guter Tag)* 200, 498; **BWV Anh. I, 8** 200, 499; **BWV Anh. I, 9** *(Entfernet euch, ihr heitern Sterne)* 513; **BWV Anh. I, 10** *(So kämpfet nur, ihr muntern Töne)* 519; **BWV Anh. I, 11** *(Es lebe der König, der Vater im Lande)* 521; **BWV Anh. I, 11** *(Frohes Volk, vergnügte Sachsen)* 522; **BWV Anh. I, 13** *(Willkommen! Ihr herrschenden Götter der Erden)* 529; **BWV Anh. I, 14** 506; **BWV Anh. I, 18** *(Froher Tag, verlangte Stunden)* 520; **BWV Anh. I, 19** *(Thomana saß annoch betrüt)* 524; **BWV Anh. I, 23** *(Concerto a cinque)* 250; **BWV Anh. I, 192** (town council cantata) 492; **BWV Anh. I, 193** *(Herrscher des Himmels, König der Ehren)* 531; **BWV Anh. I, 196** *(Auf! süß-entzückende Gewalt)* 509; **BWV Anh. I, 199** *(Siehe, eine Jungfrau ist schwanger)* 503; **BWV Anh. I, 210** *(Wo sind meine Wunderwerke)* 524; **BWV Anh. I, 212** *(Vergnüende Flammen, verdoppelt die Macht)* 517; **BWV Anh. II, 25** (Mass in C major) 257; **BWV Anh. II, 29** (Kyrie-Gloria Mass in C minor) 252; **BWV Anh. II, 30** (Magnificat in C major) 257; **BWV Anh. II, 167** (Mass in G major) 257; **BWV deest** *(O vergnügte Stunden)* 208, 499; **BWV deest** *(Was ist, das wir Leben nennen)* 495; **BWV deest** *(Was spielt ihr denn, ihr straffen Saiten)* 516; *Ursprung der musicalisch-Bachischen Familie* 40,

548   Index

44, 104, 105, 213, 525; *see also Art of Fugue, The* (BWV 1080); B minor Mass (BWV 232); *Brandenburg Concerti* (BWV 1046–1051); Canonic Variations on Vom Himmel hoch (BWV 769); Cello Suites (BWV 1007–1012); Clavier-Büchlein for Anna Magdalena Bach; *Clavierbüchlein für Wilhelm Friedemann Bach*; *Clavierübung* I; Clavierübung II; Clavierübung III; Concertos for organ or harpsichord (BWV 572–587); *Entwurff eine wohlbestallten Kirchen Music*; French Suites (BWV 812–817); *Fuga à tre*; *Goldberg Variations* (BWV 988); *Gottes Zeit ist die allerbeste Zeit*; "Great Eighteen" Chorales (BWV 651–668); Inventionen und Sinfonien (BWV 772–801); Latin Masses (BWV 233–236); Musical Offering (BWV 1079); "Neumeister" Chorales (BWV 1090–1120); *Orgelbüchlein* (BWV 599–644); Overture-suites (BWV 1066–1069); St. John Passion (BWV 245); St. Mark Passion (BWV 247); St. Matthew Passion (BWV 244); Six Sonatas for Violin and Harpsichord (BWV 1014–1019); Sonatas and Partitas for Solo Violin (BWV 1001–1006); Sonatas for Viola da Gamba and Harpsichord (BWV 1027–1029); *Tilge, Höchster, meine Sünden*; Trio Sonatas for organ (BWV 525–530); *Well-Tempered Clavier*
Bach, Leopold August 497
Bach, Lucia Elisabeth 454
Bach, Maria Barbara 112, 197, 440, 497; as copyist 249; death and burial of 100, 199, 322, 498; early life of 100, 101, 111; marriage of 102, 157–8, 159, 491
Bach, Maria Elisabeth 100, 112, 487, 488
Bach, Maria Sophia 165, 493
Bach, Regina Johanna 177, 515
Bach, Regina Susanna 178, 458, 522, 532
Bach, Veit 104, 231
Bach, Wilhelm Friedemann 36, 72, 184, 199, 207, 442, 443–8, 462, 482, 530, 535; birth and baptism of 492; as copyist 75, 444, 445; education of 501, 516; Our Lady's Church employment 535; St. Sophia's Church employment 443, 522; transmission of J. S. Bach's works by 1, 142, 441, 445–7, 449; *see also* Bach, Wilhelm Friedemann – works

Bach, Wilhelm Friedemann – works 437, 439, 444, 445–6, 483; Concerto for Two Harpsichords 260, 445; Concerto for two keyboards in E flat 447; *Der Höchste erhöret das Flehen der Armen* 445; *Dienet dem Herrn mit Freuden* 445; Kyrie 446; *Lasset uns ablegen die Werke der Finsternis* 538
Bach-Archiv, Leipzig 10, 438; *Bach Bibliography* 478–9; collections of 50, 185, 477, 484; Expedition Bach 87, 438–9, 451, 480–1; publications by 10, 25, 475–6, 480, 483
Bach Bibliography 478–9
Bach Digital 50, 477–8
Bachfests 4, 9, 10
Bachgesellschaft 3
Bach-Gesellschaft Ausgabe 26, 473, 475
Bach-Institut, Göttingen 438
Bach Network UK 87
Backhaus, Wilhelm 9
Badiarov, Dmitry 322
Bailey, Kathryn 396
Bammler, Johann Nathanael 189, 538; as copyist 53, 75, 255, 454, 481; J. S. Bach testimonial for 537, 538
Barbieri, Patrizio 324
Baron, Carol 292
Barth, Carl Friedrich 481
Bassani, Giovanni Battista 256; *Acroama missale* 256–7
Becker, August 494, 495
Becker, Carl Ferdinand 373, 375
Beethoven, Ludwig van 428–9
Beißwenger, Kirsten 75
Benda, Franz 451, 523
Bergel, Erich 395
Berger, Karol: *Bach's Cycle, Mozart's Arrow* 428
Berger, Paulus 172
Berlin 207, 497, 535; *see also* Frederick II ("The Great") of Prussia
Bernstiel, Friedrich Wilhelm 469, 470
Bertling, Rebekka 281
Besseler, Heinrich 71, 325, 328, 329, 352, 353; "Das Erbe deutscher Musik" 235; "Zur Chronologie der Konzerte Joh. Seb. Bachs" 328n71, 345, 347
Bibles 16, 66, 149, 181–3, 521, 533
Bietti, Giovanni 384
Biffi, Antonio: *Amante moribondo* 240, 253
Binder, Caspar 288

Birnbaum, Johann Abraham 249; dispute with Scheibe 28, 529, 530
Birnbaum, Johann Gottlieb 28
Birnstiel 359, 470
Bitter, Carl Heinrich 1, 158
Bizzi, Giancarlo 384
Blanken, Christine 87, 247
Blankenburg, Walter 9, 401; "Die Bachforschung seit etwa 1965" 17; "Handreichung zum Bach-Jahr 1950 für Pfarrer, Organisten und Chorleiter ..." 15–16; "Tendenzen der Bachforschung seit den 1960er Jahren" 17; *Wege zur Forschung Band CLXX* 317; "Zehn Jahre Bachforschung" 17; "Zwölf Jahre Bachforschung" 17
Blume, Friedrich 10, 21–2, 298; *J. S. Bach im Wandel der Geschichte* 16–17; "Present State of Bach Research, The" 18–19; *Syntagma Musicologicum II* 19–20; *Two Centuries of Bach* 8; "Umrisse eines neuen Bachbildes" 13–14
B minor Mass (BWV 232) 8–9, 43, 190, 275, 276–7, 410, 477; *Confiteor* 263; *Credo* 263–4, 380, 450; *Crucifixus* 267, 451; editions of 12, 268, 451, 476; manuscripts of 52, 62, 66, 536, 538; *Missa* 57, 61, 206, 256, 275, 276, 477, 522; performances of 325, 451; revisions to 55–6, 231, 451; *Sanctus* 57
Bodenschatz: *Florilegium Portense* 515, 528
Bodinus, Nicholaus Ernst 516
Bodky, Erwin 428
Boëly, Alexandre 474
Böhm, Georg 228, 248, 310, 448–9, 489; influence on J. S. Bach 227, 261, 366
Boineburg-Lengsfeld, Christoph Ernst Abraham Albrecht Freiherr von 77
Boje, Johann Jacob 152
Bokemeyer, Heinrich 29, 260
Bonporti, Francesco: *La Pace* 258
Born, Jacob 538
Böß, Reinhard 384–5, 390
Bose, Christiana Sybilla 184
Bose, Georg Heinrich 520
Böttiger, Johann Jeremias 130
Boyd, Malcolm 346
Boyvin, Jacques: *Premier Livre d'Orgue* 250; *Second Livre d'Orgue* 250
Brainard, Paul 410, 412

Brandenburg Concerti (BWV 1046–1051) 58, 196, 207, 334, 340, 344–6; dedication of 498; editions of 328–9; Fifth (BWV 1050) 63, 70–1, 321, 329, 334, 336n118, 345–6, 447; First (BWV 1046) 329, 331, 335, 345, 352; Fourth (BWV 1049) 320–1, 325, 331, 347, 429; instrumentation for 320–1, 325; manuscripts of 57, 63, 447, 477; pitch of 323; Second (BWV 1047) 335, 346; Sixth (BWV 1051) 329, 335; Third (BWV 1048) 346, 351, 355; versions of 70, 329, 345–6, 352
Braun, August 132
Braun, Friedrich Nicolaus 247
Braunschweigisch-Lüneburgische Schulordnung 137
Breig, Werner 349, 351, 385, 406, 407–8, 419, 476; *"Bachs Goldberg-Variationen als zyklisches Werk"* 382; "Bach und Marchand in Dresden" 36n61; "Freie Orgelwerke" 408n20; "Grundzüge einer Geschichte von Bachs vierstimmigem Choralsatz" 410; *J. S. Bach* 353; "Zur Chronologie von Johann Sebastian Bachs Konzertschaffen" 347
Breitkopf, Bernhard Christoph 468–9
Breitkopf, Johann Gottlob Immanuel 469
Breitkopf & Härtel 87, 358, 370, 371, 458, 467, 468–9, 473, 476
Briegel, Wolfgang Carl 154
Britten, Benjamin 9
Brockes, Barthold Heinrich 289
Brügge, Joachim 390
Brühl, Count Heinrich von 537
Bruhn, Siglind 408
Bruning, Jens 126, 141
Brunner, Otto 110
Brunswick-Calenberg, Duke Ernest August of 193
Brunswick-Lüneburg, Duke Georg Wilhelm of 202
Bückeburg, 538
Budde, Elmar 390
Buddeus, Johann Franz 138
Bümler, Georg Heinrich 39, 524
Bunge, Rudolph 32
Buno, Johann 123, 129
Bünting, Heinrich 183
Burck, Joachim à 366
Burney, Charles 37, 450, 456, 462; "Fuga" 461; *Tagebuch seiner musikalischen Reisen* 40

550   *Index*

Büsche, Magister Johannes 132
Busoni, Ferrucio 408, 413, 474
Butler, Gregory 388–9, 390; *Bach's Clavier-Übung III* 92, 307, 405; *Der vollkommene Capellmeister* 381, 396; "Engravers of Bach's *Clavier-Übung II,* The" 92; "Engraving of Bach's *Six Partitas*" 92; "Galant Style in J. S. Bach's Musical Offering, The" 388; "J. S. Bach and the Schemelli *Gesangbuch* Revisited" 92; "J. S. Bachs Kanonische Veränderungen über Vom Himmel hoch (BWV 769)" 93, 307, 391; "J. S. Bach's Reception of Tomaso Albinoni's Mature Concertos" 262; "Leipziger Stecher in Bachs Frühdrucken" 92; "Ordering Problems in J. S. Bach's *Art of Fugue* Resolved" 92, 465; "Printing of J. S. Bach's *Musical Offering,* The" 93; "Question of Genre in J. S. Bach's Fourth Brandenburg Concerto, The" 331, 409; "Scribes, Engravers, and Notational Styles" 93, 394, 465
Butler, Lynn Edwards 303
Butt, John 125, 267; *Bach: Mass in B Minor* 284; *Bach's Dialogue with Modernity* 124, 286, 333, 357; "J. S. Bach and G. F. Kauffmann" 309, 392; *Music Education and the Art of Performance in the German Baroque* 118
Buttstett, Johann Heinrich 222, 223
Buxtehude, Dieterich 157, 227, 248, 251, 261, 310, 367, 448; *Castrum doloris* 490; *Nun freut euch, lieben Christen g'mein* 240, 248, 310; Prelude and Fugue in G minor 248; *Templem honoris* 490; Toccata in G major 250

Caldara, Antonio 256; Magnificat in C major 257
Calov, Abraham 287, 288; *Die Deutsche Bibel* 16, 66, 182, 183, 189, 521
Calvisius, Sethus 134
Canonic Variations on Vom Himmel hoch (BWV 769) 147, 189, 295, 309, 382, 391–2, 535; engraving of 90–1; versions of 90, 93, 307, 391
Capricornus, Samuel 154
Carissimi, Giacomo 224
Carlsbad 321–2, 497, 498
Carlstadt, Andreas 179

Carpzov, Johann Gottlob 178–9; "Gewissens-Unterricht" 178
Casals, Pablo 9
Cello Suites (BWV 1007–1012) 79, 335–7, 442; Cello Suite in C minor (BWV 1011) 319, 325, 328; printed edition of 471
Cembalo d'amore 298
Centre for the History and Analysis of Recorded Music (CHARM) 320
Chafe, Eric 267, 287, 389; *Analyzing Bach's Cantatas* 289; "Bach's *Ascension Oratorio*" 282; *J. S. Bach's Johannine Theology* 173; *Tonal Allegory in the Vocal Music of J. S. Bach* 281–2
Chailley, Jacques 388
chamber music *see* instrumental chamber and ensemble music
Chemnitz 513
Chemnitz, Martin: *Examen Concilii Tridentini* 184
Cholopov, Jurij 413
chorales 358–76; earliest influences 360–6; figured bass 366–71
Chorlieder 221
Christenius, Johannes: *Kirchen Quotlibet* 147
Christensen, Thomas: "Bach Among the Theorists" 378–9
chronologies 12–13, 269–77, 406–8, 410, 487–539
church 142–90; Beichvaters 176–7; clergy, impact on J. S. Bach 148–79; family association with 142–8; music, role in 143–4
Claus, Rolf Dieterich 314
clavichord 297, 298, 301; pedal 304
Clavier-Büchlein for Anna Magdalena Bach 200, 314, 353, 433, 439, 506; binding of 62; influences on 258; title page of 173, 499
Clavierbüchlein für Wilhelm Friedemann Bach 62, 81, 199–200, 258, 444, 498
Clavierübung I 92, 299; Partita I (BWV 825) 201, 456, 511; Partita II (BWV 826) 514; Partita III (BWV 827) 514; Partita IV (BWV 828) 514; Partita V (BWV 829) 517; printed editions of 92, 94, 309, 471, 518
Clavierübung II 526; *French Overture* (BWV 831) 299, 312, 319; Italian Concerto (BWV 971) 77, 299; printed editions of 92, 309, 525

Index 551

Clavierübung III 307, 380, 530, 531;
   Chorale Preludes (BWV 669–689)
   471; Duet in F-major (BWV 803) 127;
   Duettos (BWV 802–805) 127, 295–6,
   307, 471; Prelude and Fugue in E-flat
   major (BWV 552) 307, 309; printed
   editions of 92, 94, 95, 309, 471, 531
Clement, Albert 385, 391
Clementi, Muzio 450
Coberger, Johann Sigismund 149
Cohen, Vered 383
Collegium Musicum 258, 273, 516, 530;
   performances by 206, 275, 517, 521, 522,
   523, 524, 526, 527, 529, 530, 531, 532
Collins, Denis 390
Collins, Michael 318
Comenius, Jan Amos 122, 123, 128, 136,
   361; *Janua linguarum reserata* 123,
   125; *Orbis sensualium pictus* 123, 125,
   141; *Vestibulum* 123, 129
compositional technique investigations
   54, 55, 398–434; approaches to
   414–19; proportioning 420–7; scope
   of 405–13; state of 399–405; time
   structure 427–34
Concertos for organ or harpsichord (BWV
   572–587) 239, 241, 250; Aria in F major
   (BWV 587) 53, 241, 250; Fugue (BWV
   579) 239, 251
Conti, Francesco Bartolomeo: cantata 253;
   Languet anima mea 253, 495
Contius, Christoph 495
Contius, Heinrich Andreas 536, 537
copyists 74–7, 113, 114; Agricola, Johann
   Friedrich 348, 453; Altnickol, Johann
   Christoph 71, 76, 80, 338; Bach, Anna
   Magdalena Wilcke 54, 57, 73, 75, 109,
   113, 241, 342–3, 441–3; Bach, Carl
   Philipp Emanuel 61, 75, 241, 385,
   449; Bach, Johann Christian 38, 75,
   455; Bach, Johann Christoph 75–6;
   Bach, Johann Christoph Friedrich 75,
   453; Bach, Maria Barbara 249; Bach,
   Wilhelm Friedemann 75, 444, 445;
   Bammler, Johann Nathanael 53, 75, 255,
   454, 481; of St. John Passion 442, 443,
   455, 481; of St. Matthew Passion 442
Corelli, Arcangelo 329; Opus 3 239, 251;
   Opus 5 263, 336
Corten, Walter 393–4, 396
Cöthen 116, 198–202, 497–500;
   Agnuskirche 172, 199; Charlotte
   Friederica Amelia, Princess of

Anhalt-Cöthen 509, 512; clergy in 172–4;
   Emanuel Ludwig, Prince of Anhalt-
   Cöthen 201, 511; Jacobskirche 202;
   pitch of organ in 323; responsibilities at
   199–200, 270–1; visit to 504, 509, 514,
   516; *see also* Anhalt-Cöthen, Prince
   Leopold of
counterpoint 380, 385, 413
Couperin, François 327, 335; *L'impériale*
   53, 241–2, 250; *Second Livre des Pièces
   de Clavecin* 241
courts, influence on J. S. Bach 191–209;
   see also Cöthen; Weimar
Cox, Howard 66, 287
Crean, Elise 385
Crist, Stephen 267, 281, 287, 406, 410;
   "Historical Theology and Hymnology
   as Tools for Interpreting Bach's Church
   Cantatas" 287–8
Crowell, Greg 305
cultural representation 192
Cusick, Suzanne 21
Czaczkes, Ludwig 408
Czerny, Carl 467–8

Dadelsen, Georg von 13, 70, 269,
   278, 401, 443, 446; "Anmerkungen
   zu Bachs Parodieverfahren" 406;
   "Bach der Violinist" 336; *Beiträge
   zur Chronologie* 12, 13, 47, 69,
   267, 400, 461; "Bemerkungen zu
   Bachs Cembalokonzerten" 349–50;
   *Bemerkungen zur Handschrift Johann
   Sebastian Bachs* 47, 69, 461, 475
Dahlhaus, Carl 408
Dähnert, Ulrich 303, 304
Dall'Abaco, Evaristo Felice 345
Dammann, Rolf 382–3
Danckwardt, Marianne 412
d'Anglebert, Jean Henri: *Pièces de
   Clavecin* 250
Dannemann, Johanna Maria 533
Danz, Johann Andreas 131
Dart, Thurston 317, 318, 320–1, 325
databases, online 50
David, Hans Theodor 25, 387, 479
Daw, Stephen 459
Decker, Georg Jacob 33
Dedekind, Andreas Christian 363
Degrada, Francesco 258
de Grigny, Nicolas: *Premier Livre d'Orgue*
   249, 492
Dehné, Jean Christoph 92

552 *Index*

Delang, Kersten 242
Dentler, Hans-Eberhard 395
Deppert, Heinrich 407, 412
Dequevauviller, Vincent 334
Deutsch, Otto Erich 25
Deutsche Forschungsgemeinschaft 477
Dewulf, Charles 394
Deyling, Salomon 175–6, 180, 189, 500, 517
Dieskau, Carl Heinrich von 533
Dietel, Johann Ludwig 75, 469
Dieupart, François: *Six Suittes de Clavessin* 250
Dirksen, Pieter 342, 345, 395, 396, 476
Dirst, Matthew 319
documents: accuracy of 39–46; collections 25–6; completeness of 28–35; credibility of 35–9; use of 26–8
Doles, Johann Friedrich 34, 232, 533
Dolmetsch, Arnold 317, 318, 320
Donington, Robert 318; *Interpretation of Early Music, The* 317–18
Doppelflöte 321
Dörffel, Alfred 336
Dornheim 491
Dortmund Bach-Symposion 348, 410
Drescher, Thomas 335
Dresden 204–6, 496; Frauenkirche 206, 528; Sophienkirche 206, 305, 509, 520, 522; visit to 519–20, 522, 529
Drese, Adam: *Nun ist alles überwunden* 215, 219, 220
Drese, Johann Samuel 167, 169, 195, 197, 270, 496
Drese, Johann Wilhelm 167, 169, 270
Dreyfus, Laurence 330, 346, 355; *Bach and the Patterns of Invention* 311–13, 328, 380–1, 412–13; *Bach's Continuo Group* 278
Drobisch, Johann Friedrich 42
Dülmen, Richard van: *Kultur und Alltag* 110
Du Mage, Pierre: *Livre d'Orgue* 250, 493
Dumpf, Johann Carl Wilhelm 42
Durante, Francesco 256; Kyrie-gloria Mass in C minor 257
Dürr, Alfred 10, 13, 17, 73, 269, 336, 344, 350, 443, 446; *Acht kleine Praeludien und Fugen* 461; *Cantatas of J. S. Bach with their Librettos in German-English Parallel Text, The* 15; "Gedanken zu J. S. Bachs Umarbeitungen eigener Werke" 405; *Johann Sebastian Bach – Das Wohltemperierte Klavier* 400, 408;

"Melodienvarianten in Johann Sebastian Bachs Kirchenliedbearbeitung" 363; "On the Earliest Manuscripts and Prints of Bach's WTC in England" 472; *Studien über die frühen Kantaten J. S. Bachs* 70n81, 330, 409; "Tastenumfang und Chronologie in Bachs Klavierwerken" 302; "Zu Hans Eppstein's 'Studien'" 339–40; "Zum Wandel des Bach-Bildes" 15; *Zur Chronologie der Leipziger Vokalwerke J. S. Bachs* 12, 47, 68, 70, 74–5, 267, 278

Ebata, Nobuaki 88
Eccard, Johann 233
Eckelt, Valentin 248
Edelmann, Johann Christian 193
Edler, Arnfried 108
education 111, 116–41; by J. S. Bach 134–40; of J. S. Bach 101–2, 116, 128–34, 487–9; Lutheran Reformation impact on 119–22; 17th century reforms of 122–7; types of schools 120
Effler, Johann 40, 489, 491
Eggebrecht, Hans Heinrich 395, 402
Ehrmann, Johann Samuel 524
Eichenauer, Richard 235
Eichler, Christian Gottlob 178
Eilmar, Georg Christian 159, 161–3
Einicke, Georg Friedrich 538, 539
Eisenach 142, 352, 361, 363, 487–8; clergy in 148–9; education in 128–9; Georgenkirche 129, 360, 487
Eisenachisches Gesangbuch 363
Eisenhardt, Benjamin 162
Elfeld, Eberhard Joachim 132
Eller, Rudolph 262, 334
Ellis, Mark 226
Elste, Martin 320
Emans, Reinmar 21, 410, 476
Emery, Walter 68, 90
Emmerling, Johannes Andreas 152
ensemble music *see* instrumental chamber and ensemble music
Enßlin, Wolfram 217, 483
Entwurff eine wohlbestallten Kirchen Music 37, 285
Eppstein, Hans 339–40; "Chronologieprobleme in Johann Sebastian Bachs Suiten für Soloinstrument" 337, 405; "J. S. Bachs Triosonate G-dur (BWV 1039) und ihre Beziehungen zur Sonate für Game und

Index   553

Cembalo G-dur (BWV 1027)" 339;
"Konzert und Sonate" 409; *Studien
über J. S. Bachs Sonaten* 340, 341, 405;
"Über J. S. Bachs Flötensonaten mit
Generalbaß" 343, 344; "Zur Problematik
von Johann Sebastian Bachs
Flötensonaten" 331, 338, 343, 344; 'Zur
Vor- und Entstehungsgeschichte von
J. S. Bachs Tripelkonzert a-Moll (BWV
1044)' 349
Erdmann, Georg 14, 29, 37, 42, 102, 104,
112, 116, 173, 201, 489, 510, 518
Erfurt 496, 499; *Vollständiges
Neu aufgelegtes und vermehrtes
Evangelisches Gesand-Buch* 373
Erhardt, Tassilo 354
Erickson, Raymond 292
Ernesti, Johann August 43, 136, 140, 189,
524; *Initia doctrinae solidioris* 139, 187;
Institutio interpretis novi testamenti
187–8; "Präfektenstreit" 27, 43, 139–40,
185–7, 527, 528, 529
Ernesti, Johann Heinrich 137, 517
Ernst, Wilhelm Friedrich 439, 453, 454
Eschert, Johanna 528
Expedition Bach 87, 438–9, 451, 480–1

Faber, Benjamin Gottlieb 537
Fabian, Dorottya 320
Falck, Martin 448, 482
family, Bach: gatherings of 142–3, 145–6;
musicality of 104–5, 111–12; religion
of 142; *Ursprung der musicalisch-
Bachischen Familie* 40, 44, 104, 105,
213, 525; *see also* Alt-Bachisches Archiv
Fanselau, Clemens 335, 337, 409
Farlau, Johann Christoph 71, 77
Fasch, Johann Friedrich 170, 294
Faselius, Anton Günther 164
Faulkner, Quentin 303, 476
Fétis, François-Joseph 474
Finke-Heckllinger, Doris 281
Finscher, Ludwig 406
Fischer, Johann Caspar Ferdinand 248,
310, 461
Fischer, Kurt von 9–10
Fischer, Wilfried 350, 405
Fischer, Wilhelm 332, 356
Fleckeisen, Gottfried 185, 188
Fleckeisen, Gottfried Benjamin 38, 185,
462, 482, 534
Fleming, Count Joachim Friedrich von
511, 519

Fletin, Jonas de 218
Florilegium portense 232
flute, echo 321
Forkel, Johann Nikolaus 1, 3, 35, 145,
231, 233, 328, 372, 444, 446, 473, 475;
Bachs Leben, Kunst und Kunstwerke 26,
104–5, 142–3, 146, 207, 297, 299–300,
480; correspondence of 237, 247, 309,
367, 448, 449, 473
fortepiano 303
Fowler, Alistair 312
Francisci, Johann 507
Franck, César 474
Franck, Melchior: *Psalmodia sacra* 364
Franck, Salomo 168, 180, 292
Francke, August Hermann 123, 126, 138,
160, 173, 183, 288
Frankfurt/Oder, 530
Franklin, Don 267, 287, 412; "Role of the
'Actus Structure' in the Libretto of J. S.
Bach' Matthew Passion, The" 288
Frederick II ("The Great") of Prussia 35,
207, 385, 389–90, 535, 536
Fredersdorf, Michael Gabriel 344
French Suites (BWV 812–817) 81, 200, 352,
471; No. 2 in C minor (BWV 813) 352;
No. 4 in E flat major (BWV 815) 352
Frescobaldi, Girolamo: *Fiori musicali*
249, 494
Freylinghausen, Johann Anastasius 161;
Geistreiches Gesangbuch 369
Friedrich Augustus I, King-Elector 508,
509, 513, 521, 521
Friedrich Augustus II, King-Elector 524,
526, 527, 528, 529, 531, 532; coronation
of 523; Kyrie and Gloria of B-minor
Mass sent to 61, 206, 275, 276, 522
Friedrich Christian, Prince 275, 522
Friedrich Wilhelm I of Prussia 198
Friese, Heinrich 498
Fritzsche, Johann Gottlieb August 481–2
Froberger, Johann Jacob 247
Frohne, Johann Adolph 159, 161, 163
Fuga à tre 94
fugue 380–1, 423–6
Fulde, Johann Gottfried 536
Fuller, David 318
Fux, Johann Joseph: *Gradus ad Parnussum*
380, 506, 532

Gadamer, Hans-Georg 357
Gaines, James: *Evening in the Palace of
Reason* 391

554   *Index*

Gardiner, John Eliot 462
Gárdonyi, Zoltán 384
Gasparini, Francesco: *Missa Canonica* 481
Gaudlitz, Gottlieb 178
Geck, Martin: *Bach: Leben und
    Werk* 21; *"Denn alles findet bei
    Bach statt"* 410; *Die Vokalmusik
    Dietrich Buxtehudes und der frühe
    Pietismus* 221; "Gattungstraditionen
    und Altersschichten in den
    Brandenburgischen Konzerten" 329;
    Johann Sebastian Bach 21; "Köthen
    oder Leipzig?" 341, 347, 348, 353
Geier, Martin 183, 288; *Zeit und
    Ewigkeit* 180
Geiringer, Karl 226–7
genealogy, interest in 104
genres 328–32
Gera: Johanniskirche 208, 508; St. Savior's
    Church 508
Gerber, Ernst Ludwig 223, 460;
    *Historisch-biographisches Lexicon der
    Tonkünstler* 26, 200
Gerber, Heinrich Nikolaus 1, 26, 76, 194,
    459, 460
Gerber, Rudolf 337, 338
Gerhard, Johann 165; *Schola Pietatis* 180
Gerlach, Carl Gotthelf 88, 258, 516, 530
Germann, Sheridan 321
German schools 120
Gerstenberg, Walter 401
Gesius, Bartholomäus 366
Gesner, Johann Matthias 34, 136, 137,
    140, 169, 187, 519, 524; *"Institutiones
    Rei Scholasticae"* 137–8; *Programma de
    interrogandi in studiis litterarum ratione
    atque utilitate* 138–9
Geuting, Matthias: *Konzert und Sonate bei
    Johann Sebastian Bach* 331, 409
Geyer, Helen 209
Geyersbach, Johann Heinrich 490
Glassius, Salomon 361; *Philologia sacra*
    188
Glöckner, Andreas 254, 267, 286, 460,
    484; "Ein weiterer Kantatenjahrgang
    Gottfried Heinrich Stözels in Bachs
    Aufführungsrepertoire?" 245;
    *Kalendarium zur Lebensgeschichte
    Johann Sebastian Bachs* 28, 487;
    "Neuerkenntnisse zu Johann Sebastian
    Bachs Aufführungskalender zwischen
    1729 und 1735" 347; "Neues zum
    Thema Bach und die Oper seiner
    Zeit" 246

Godt, Irving 333
Goebel, Reinhard 319
Goehr, Alexander 403
Goldberg, Johann Gottlieb: C major trio
    sonata (BWV 1037) 344
Goldberg Variations (BWV 988) 77, 94,
    189, 299, 382–4; fourteen additional
    canons, discovery of 86, 94, 308, 382,
    384, 413; number alphabet in 383–4;
    performances of 297; publication of 471,
    472; Variation 5 383; Variation 28 80;
    Variation 29 80; Variation 30 146
Göncz, Zoltán 394
Gotha 170, 202–3, 361, 492, 496
Gottes Zeit ist die allerbeste Zeit (Cantata
    106) 229
Göttinger Bach-Katalog 50, 477
Gottsched, Johann Christoph 27, 45–6, 292
Götze, Georg Heinrich 157; *Lübeckisches
    Gesang-Buch* 157
Gould, Glenn 297, 382
Graun, Carl Heinrich 29
Graupner, Christoph 31, 194, 294, 500
"Great Eighteen" Chorales (BWV 651–668)
    71, 231, 306; "Vor deinen Thron tret
    ich" (BWV 668) 71
Greer, Mary 158–9, 230
Greulich, Karl 4, 5
Greyerz, Kaspar von 144
Griepenkerl, F. C. 446
Grimstead, Patricia Kennedy 216, 280
Groocock, Joseph 408, 423
Grüß, Hans 325, 328, 352, 353

Häfner, Klaus 406
Hahn, Johann Christian 499
Halle 493, 531, 535; Church of Our Lady
    494, 495
Halle Paedagogium 126
Halle Pietism 123, 126, 159–63, 173
Halm, August 413
Hamburg 498; St. Jacobi Church 498;
    St. James Church 498
Hammerschmidt, Andreas 154; *Ach Gott
    vom Himmel sieh darein* 147; *Gott hat
    das Evangelium* 147; *Kirchen- und
    Tafel-Music* 147
Hammerstein, Notger 118
*Handbuch der deutschen
    Bildungsgeschichte* 118
Handel, Georg Friedrich 309, 497; *Armida
    abbandonata* 259; Brockes Passion 246,
    255, 481; *Six Fugues or Voluntarys* 387
Handexempläre 89, 94–5

Index 555

handwriting: of J. S. Bach 67–73; neat 56; rough 56
Harnoncourt, Nikoloaus 283
harpsichord 297, 299, 301, 321–2
Harrer, Gottlob 38, 71, 481, 537; *Der Reiche starb, und ward begraben* 537
Harrington, Joel 102; *Unwanted Child, The* 101
Harrow, Peter 384
Hartmann, Günter 384
Hartwig, Carl 41
Harvard University 483; Russian Research Center 482; Ukranian Research Institute 482
Haselböck, Lucia: *Bach-Textlexikon* 291
Hasse, Johann Adam: *Cleofide* 519
Hässler, Johann Wilhelm 305; *Deus noster refugium* 4
Haupt, Carl Ephraim 43
Hauptkopist 75n112
Hauptschreiber 75n112
Haus, Goffredo 391
Hauser, Franz 250
Haussmann, Elias Gottlob 534
Haußwald, Günther 336, 337, 342
Haynes, Bruce 320, 323, 324, 351
Hebenstreit, Pantaleon 298
Hecker, Johann Wilhelm 165
Hefling, Stephen 318
Heidorn, Peter 248
Heindorff, Ernst Dietrich 218, 219, 221
Heinichen, Johann David: *General-Bass* 516
Heinrich, Adel 394–5
Heinrich, Johann Georg 43, 44
Heinrich XI, Count of Reuß 208, 498
Heitmann, Johann Joachim 498
Helbig, Johann Georg 43
Helder, Bartholomäus 364
Hennicke, Count Johann Christian von 528
Henrici, Christian Friedrich 279, 292; *Cantaten Auf die Sonn- und Fest-Tage durch das gantze Jahr* 272–3, 514
Herda, Elias 102, 131, 151, 152
Herlicius, Johann David 360
hermeneutics 6–7, 311–14
Herschkowitz, Philipp 413
Hertel, Johann Christian 512
Herz, Gerhard 16
Hessen-Kassel, Prince Friedrich von 521
Heunisch, Caspar 183; *Haupt-Schlüssel über die hohe Offenbahrung S. Johannis* 150
Heussner, Horst 91

Hildebrandt, Zacharias 41, 303, 535; organs 502
Hill, Robert 309–10
Hille, Johann Georg 531
Hobohm, Wolf 253
Hoffmann-Erbrecht, Lothar 91
Hoffmeister, Franz Anton 471
Hoffmeister & Kühnel 471, 473
Hofmann, Klaus 17, 70, 340, 343, 346, 405
Hofstadter, Douglas: *Gödel, Escher, Bach* 391
Hoke, Hans Gunter 93, 392
Hollaz, David: *Examen theologicum acromaticum* 177
Holy Roman Empire of the German Nation 191
Homilius, Gottfried August 41, 232, 438, 451
Hoppe, Günther 201
Horn, Karl Friedrich 1, 456
Horn, Victoria 327
households 99–115; composition of 101, 106–7, 110; female roles in 109, 111, 112–13; male roles in 113–14; musical 106–7, 108, 110–12, 114–15; training in 111; *see also* family, Bach
Hübner, Maria 109
Hülsemann, Martin Georg 133, 151–2
Hunnius, Nicholas: *Apostasia Ecclesiae Romanae* 184
Hurlebusch, Conrad Friedrich 308–9, 525
Hutter, Leonhard 126; *Compendium* 127, 129, 133

Imhof, Arthur 100, 103
improvisation 332
instrumental chamber and ensemble music 317–57; analytical approaches to study of 327–35; forces in 324–7; genres of 328–32; improvisation in 332; instrumentation in 320–3; interpretations of 333–5; intonation in 323–4; performance aspects of 317–27; pitch in 323–4; styles of 327–8
Integrated Automated Fingerprint Identification System (IAFIS) 60
Internationale Arbeitsgemeinschaft für theologische Bachforschung 16–18
Internationale Bach-Gesellschaft 9
International Musicological Society 13
intonation 323–4
Inventionen und Sinfonien (BWV 772–801) 200, 295, 499; bound version 62; Invention in B minor (BWV 786) 80;

556 Index

Invention in C major (BWV 772) 295, 311; Invention in C minor (BWV 773) 77n131; Invention in G minor (BWV 797) 77n131; printed edition of 471; Sinfonia in F minor (BWV 795) 417
Itzig, Zippora 447

Jacob, Benjamin 1
Jahrgäng 271–3
Jarvis, Martin W. B. 73, 442
Jenne, Natalie 281, 327
Joachim, Joseph 5
Johann-Sebastian-Bach-Institut,Göttingen 10, 12, 475, 477
Jones, Richard 94, 95, 227, 228, 281, 338, 407; *Creative Development of Johann Sebastian Bach, The* 354
Juncker, Johann Christian 129

Kaemmel, Otto: *Geschichte des Leipziger Schulwesens* 117, 135, 136
Kaiser, Rainer 128
Kamatani, Pamela M. 378
Kaprowski, Richard 91, 92, 93
Kassel: St. Martin's Church 521
Kassler, Michael 472; *English Bach Awakening, The* 315
Kauffmann, Georg Friedrich 309, 500; *Harmonische Seelenlust* 309, 392
Kaußler, Helmut 384
Kaußler, Ingrid 384
Kayn, Georg Rudolph von 208
Kayser, Bernhard Christian 76, 258
Keiser, Reinhard 508; St. Mark Passion 246–7, 253, 274, 510
Keller, Hermann 402
Kellner, Herbert Anton 394
Kellner, Johann Peter 74, 339
Kerl, Johann Caspar 247; *Missa superba* 257
Kerman, Joseph 297, 313, 381
Kevorkian, Tanya 18, 144–5; *Baroque Piety* 293–4
keyboard music 295–316; hermeneutical criticism of 311–14; influences on 308–11; instruments, hierarchies of 296–306; organological matters in 302–6; source studies of 306–8
Kiesewetter, Johann Christoph 130, 151, 168
Kinsky, Georg 89, 90
Kircher, Athanasius: *Musurgia universalis* 385
Kirchhoff, Gottfried 494

Kirkendale, Ursula 386, 387, 389, 395
Kirkendale, Warren 386
Kirnberger, Johann Philipp 1, 87, 359, 368, 460, 470; correspondence of 33; promotion of J. S. Bach music by 469; pupil of J. S. Bach 375, 379
Kistler-Liebendörfer, Berhard 389; *Vom Wirken der Zahl in J. S. Bachs Goldbergvariationen* 383–4
Kittel, Johann Christian 1, 372–5, 460; altercation with C. P. E. Bach 36; *Choralbuch* 372–5; as copyist 76; *Der angehende praktische Organist* 372; pupil of J. S. Bach 305, 368, 372
Klein, Hans-Günter 262
Kleinschocher 533
Klemm, Johann Friedrich 529
Klessen, Johann 165; *Die Weimarische Kleine Bibel* 165
Klotz, Hans 90, 91
Kluge, Johann Christian 41
Kluge-Kahn, Hertha 333, 378, 384, 392
Knauer, Johann Oswald 292
Knüpfer, Sebastian 134; *Enforsche mich, Gott* 220, 232, 258
Kobayashi, Yoshitake 17, 69, 72, 269, 278, 379, 400, 443; *Bach to no Taiwa* 65, 67; *Die Kopisten Johann Sebastian Bachs* 75; "Quellenkundliche Überlegungen zur Chronologie der Weimarer Vokalwerke Bachs" 267; "Zur Chronologie der Spätwerke Johann Sebastian Bachs" 70, 267, 347, 377
Koch, Heinrich Christoph 428, 429
Koch, Johann Wilhelm 57
Köhler, Johann Friedrich 36
Kolisch, Rudolph 427–8
Kollmann, A. F. C. 1
Kolneder, Walter 395, 397
Koopman, Ton: "Bach's Choir" 284
Kopfermann, Michael 390–1
Köpp, Kai 323, 326
Kortte, Gottlieb 512
Kramer, Lawrence 21
Krauß, Gottfried Theodor 43
Krause, Christian Gottfried 460
Krause, Johann Gottlob 43, 527
Kräuter, Philipp David 31, 197, 220, 493
Krebs, Johann Ludwig 75, 88, 302n22, 459, 460, 461, 463
Krebs, Johann Tobias 76, 196, 463
Kreft, Robert 395
Kretzschmar, Hermann 3, 5, 6–7

Index 557

Krickeberg, Dieter: *Struktur, Funktion und Bedeutung* 108
Kromayer, Johann Abraham 150, 152
Kromayer, Melchior 150
Kropfgans, Johann 340, 530
Krüger, Elke 407
Krüger, Johann Christian 43–4
Krügner, Johann Gottfried 92, 309
Krull, Christoph 198
Krummacher, Friedhelm 410, 412
Kuhnau, Johann 134, 177, 230, 248, 495, 496, 499, 500; Biblical Sonatas 228
Kuhnau, Johann Andreas 75
Kühnel, Ambrosius 471
Kuijken, Sigiswald 322
Kulmus, Louise Adelgunde Victorie 520
Kulukundis, Elias N. 438
Küster, Konrad 21, 131, 132, 219, 411

Lage, Georg Wilhelm von der 164–5
Lairitz, Johann Georg 164, 167
Landowska, Wanda 382
Langewiesen 490
Latin Masses (BWV 233–236) 8, 190, 256; F major Mass (BWV 233) 32; G major Mass (BWV 236) 471; A major Mass (BWV 234) 471
Latin schools 120–1, 128–9
Lautenwerk 298
Leaver, Robin A. 267, 290; "Bach's 'Clavierübung III'" 313; *J. S. Bach and Scripture* 287; *Theologische Bibliothek* 287
Le Bègue, Nicolas Antoine 248
Lebrecht, Emanuel 171
Ledbetter, David 408, 423
Lee, Hio-Ihm 409
Lehmann, Caroline 450
Lehmann, Karen 473
Lehms, Georg Christian 292
Lehmus, Georg Michael 150
Leibowitz, René 413
Leipzig 107, 173, 499, 500–39; clergy in 174–9; compositions during 269, 271; New Church 134, 179, 516; St. John's Church 134, 533, 539; *see also* St. Nicholas Church, Leipzig; St. Paul's University Church; St. Thomas Church, Leipzig; St. Thomas School, Leipzig
Leipziger Post-Zeitungen 516, 517
Leipziger-Zeitungen 525, 530, 535
Leisinger, Ulrich 453
Lemmens, Jacques-Nicolas 474

Leo, Leonardo 233
Leonhardt, Gustav 283
Lester, Joel 332
Levy, Sara Itzig 447, 450
Leyden, Rolf van 344
library of J. S. Bach 179–85, 238–40
Linicke, Christian Bernhard 198
Little, Meredith 281, 327
Locatelli, Pietro Antonio: Concerto grosso in f minor 259
Löffler, Hans 459
Lohmann, Heinz 300, 301
Lotti, Antonio 256; *Crucifixus* 233; *Missa à 4, 5, et 6 voci* 257
Lübeck 156–7
Ludewig, Bernhard Dietrich 33, 453
Ludwig, Albrecht Christian 170
Ludwig, Margrave Christian 58, 63, 207, 344, 498
Lully, Jean-Baptiste 248, 319; *Armide* 220
Lundgren, Peter 125; *Schulhumanismus* 117, 128
Lüneburg 116, 202, 448, 489; clergy at 151–2; Michaeliskirch 151–2, 489; Michaelisschule 102, 124, 130, 131–3, 202
Luther, Martin 2–3, 180–1, 288; "An die Ratsherren aller Städte deutschen Landes, daß sie christliche schulen aufrichten und erhalten sollen" 119; cult of 2–4, 8; *Ein feste Burg* 4; *Erhalt uns, Herr, bei deinem Wort* 168; *Hauspostille* 181, 183; *Herr Gott dich loben wir* 167; *Heut triumphiret Gottes Sohn* 370; *Kirchenpostille* 181; *Komm, Gott Schöpfer, heiliger Geist* 370; *O Gott vom Himmel sieh darein* 155; Sermons *(Postillen)* 180; Small Catechism 124, 126, 143, 165; *Tischreden* 143, 181
Lutheran Church *see* church
Lütkemann, Joachim: *Corpus Doctrinae Catecheticae Augustum* 152

McClary, Susan 21, 334
McCormick, Susan 374, 375
Malloch, William 319, 325
manualiter 301, 307
manuscripts 47–88; approaches to study of 48–9; autograph 52, 54; Bach's classification of 56–8; Bach's handwriting 67–73; binding of 60–3; classifying 51–8; collation of pages in 60–3; compositional stage of 54–6; copy

558   *Index*

52–3; copyists of 74–7; critical editions of 82–4; locating 49–51; musical evidence in 77–8; neatness of 56; notational evidence on 67–77; original 54; paper used for 58–60; as physical artifact 58–67; primary sources 51–2; reception history of 85–6; secondary sources 51–2; sources for 49–58; stave ruling on 63–5; study of 48–58; for teaching 81–2

Marais, Marin 248

Marcello, Alessandro 239, 250

Marcello, Benedetto 239, 250

Marchand, Louis 36, 204, 345, 496

Maria Josepha, Electress 206, 275, 523

Marissen, Michael 21, 267, 287; *Bach's Oratorios* 290; *Lutheranism, Anti-Judaism, and Bach's St. John Passion* 289; "More Source-Critical Research on Bach's Musical Offering" 93, 388; "On Linking Bach's F-Major Sinfonia and his Hunt Cantata" 345; *Social and Religious Designs of J. S. Bach's Brandenburg Concertos, The* 18, 329, 335, 413; "Theological Character of J. S. Bach's Musical Offering, The" 389; "Trio in C Major for Recorder, Violin and Continuo by J. S. Bach, A?" 330–1, 341

Markham, Michael 397

Marpurg, Friedrich Wilhelm 1, 359, 423, 466, 470; *Abhandlung von der Fuge* 467; *Legende einiger Musikheilgen* 204–6

marriage 102, 157–8, 159, 491; remarriage 103, 172

Marshall, Robert 267, 302; "Bach's Chorus" 284; "Bach's Orchestre" 324; *Compositional Process of J. S. Bach, The* 278, 406; "J. S. Bachs Compositions for Solo Flute" 343; *Music of Johann Sebastian Bach, The* 344; "Organ or 'Klavier'?" 300–1, 304

Martini, Padre Giovanni Battista 44, 455, 456, 539

Martino, Philippo 340

Martius, Herrn 38

Martius, Johann Christoph Gottfried 38

Marx, A. B. 88

Matteis, Nicola 336

Mattheson, Johann 104, 181, 233, 396, 466, 496, 508, 518, 524; *Das neu-eröffnete Orchestre* 298; *Der vollkommene Capellmeister* 298, 381;

Exemplarishe Organisten-Probe 497; *Grundlage einer Ehren-Pforte* 40, 231; *Muscialische Patriot* 161; *Vollkommener Capellmeister* 108

Maul, Michael 34–5, 38, 240, 460, 462, 482; "Alles mit Gott und nichts ohn' ihn" 280, 481; "Quellenkundliches zu Bach-Aufführungen in Köthen, Ronneburg und Leipzig zwischen 1720 und 1760" 481; *Weimar Orgeltabulatur* 87, 248, 249, 310, 481

Maunder, Richard 326

Mayer, Johann Friedrich 182

Meine Seele soll Gott loben (BWV 223) 162–3

Meißner, Christian Gottlob 68, 75, 443

Melamed, Daniel 267; "Constructing Johann Christoph Bach (1642–1703)" 219; *Hearing Bach's Passions* 247, 286; *J. S. Bach and the German Motet* 218, 220, 227, 230, 408; "Thirty-six Voice Canon in the Hand of C. P. E. Bach, A" 385

Melanchton, Philipp 119, 143; *Unterricht der visitatoren* 120

Mendel, Arthur 13, 25, 476, 479

Mendelssohn, Abraham 447

Mendelssohn, Felix 26, 52, 267, 294

Michel, Johann Heinrich 232

Micheli, Romano 385

Miesner, Heinrich 482

Mietke, Michael 199, 207, 321, 322

Millennium Music Conference 399

Mintz, Donald 13

Mitterauer, Michael 104

Mizler, Lorenz Christoph 1, 39, 87, 299, 531, 532; *Die Musicalische Bibliothek* 299; *Dissertatio quod musica ars sit pars eruditionis philosophicae* 524; *Musikalische Bibliothek* 430; *Neue-eröffnete Musikalische Bibliothek* 448, 527; "Societät der Musikalischen Wissenschaften" 378, 535

"Möller Manuscript" 76, 248, 309–10

Monteverdi, Claudio 281, 416

Moser, Hans Joachim 235–6

motets 221, 232–3

Muffat, Georg 326, 327

Mühlhausen 157, 249, 270, 491–2; Blasiuskirche 159, 302, 490–1, 492; clergy in 159–63; Marienkirche 159, 162, 492, 525; responsibilities in 116, 133–4

Müller, August Eberhard 480
Müller, August Friedrich 508
Müller, Heinrich 183, 288; *Evangelische
Schluß-Kette* 180
Müller von Asow, Erich H. 479
Mund, Frank: *Lebenskrisen als Raum der
Freiheit* 139
musical hermeneutics 6–7, 311–14
Musical Offering (BWV 1079) 89, 189,
295, 382, 385–91, 482, 536; Canon 1
cancrizans 390; Canon 2 a 2 violini 390;
Canon 4 390; Canon 5 per tonos 390,
391; canons 387, 390–1; dedication
of 536; engraving of 93, 388; printed
editions of 91, 92–3, 385; Ricercar a 3
386, 387, 425; Ricercar a 6 386, 387,
403, 422; "ricercar" in 385, 386–7; royal
theme 389–90; structure of 387–9; Trio
Sonata 331, 387
Musikbibliothek der Stadt Leipzig 359
Müthel, Johann Gottfried 349, 539

Nagel, Maximilian 41, 43
Nägeli, Hans Georg 277, 458, 467,
471, 473
Naue, Johann Friedrich 220, 233
Naumburg 535, 536, 538; St. Wenceslas
Church 41, 522, 533, 535
Nepo, Cornelius: *Biographien führender
Gestalten* 129
Neue Bach Ausgrabe (NBA) 10, 268, 317,
399, 475–6; *Kritische Berichte* 49, 50,
441; Series VII 324, 328; Supplement
380; Volume I 12; Volume II 12;
Volume IV/1–11 476
Neue Bachgesellschaft 3–5, 6, 7;
Direktorium 5, 6n25
Neugebauer, Wolfgang 118, 125
Neumann, Frederick 318
Neumann, Werner 406, 409, 412, 479
Neumeister, Erdmann 160, 168, 227, 292;
Tisch des Herrn 185; *Wasserbad im
Worte* 185
"Neumeister" Chorales (BWV 1090–1120)
227, 228, 295; *Christus, der du bist der
helle Tag* (BWV 1120) 228; *Herr Gott,
nun schleuß den Himmel auf* (BWV 1092)
228; *Ich hab mein Sach Gott heimgestellt*
(BWV 1113) 228, 229; *O Jesu, wie ist
dein Gestalt* (BWV 1094) 228
Nichelmann, Christoph 43, 459
Nicolai, Friedrich: *Allgemeine Deutsche
Bibliothek* 29

Nicolay, Frederick 456
Niedt, Joachim Valentin Ludolph 533, 534
Niitsuma, Masahiro 65, 73
Nikolaikirche *see* St. Nicholas Church,
Leipzig
Nitsche, Gotthelf Engelbert 43
notation: chronology of 73–4; conventions
73–4; *see also* handwriting
notes inégales 318
number symbolism 334, 383–4

Obituary 36, 56, 202, 233, 237–8, 268,
271, 299, 302, 367, 448, 462
oboe d'amore 323
Ochs, Siegfried 5
O'Donnell, John 461
Oechsle, Siegfried 263–4, 408, 412
Ohrdruf 102, 488–9, 526; clergy in
149–51; Lyceum 101, 116, 129–31, 151;
Michaeliskirche 149–50
Olearius, Gottfried 153
Olearius, Johann 288; *Biblische Erklärung*
181–2, 288
Olearius, Johann Christoph 153,
154–7, 179–80, 288; *Arnstadtisches
Gesangbuch* 155; *Evangelischer Lieder-
Schatz* 156, 157
Olearius, Johann Gottfried 153–4, 163
Oleskiewicz, Mary 389
Oley, Johann Christoph 77
Op de Coul, Thomas 390
organ 298–306; compasses of 302;
positive 305
Orgelbüchlein (BWV 599–644) 62, 156,
306, 397; *Da Jesus an dem Kreuze
stund* (BWV 621) 80; *Es ist das heil
uns kommen her* (BWV 638) 80; *Ich
ruf zu dir, Herr Jesu Christ* (BWV
639) 80; period of composition of 45,
196, 200; quavers in 80; title page of
45, 499
orphaned children, care of 101–2
Oswald, Andreas 148
over-dotting 318, 319
Overture-suites (BWV 1066–1069) 324,
351–4; manning of parts for 325;
performance of 319; Suite in B minor
(BWV 1067) 331, 333, 352, 353, 354;
Suite in C major (BWV 1066) 325, 333,
352, 353; Suite in D major (BWV 1068)
352, 353; Suite in D major (BWV 1069)
352, 353
Owens, Samantha 209

560   Index

Pachelbel, Johann 4, 131, 227, 241, 247, 248, 251, 261, 336, 366, 448, 488; *An Wasserflüssen Babylon* 242, 249; *Fuga* 242, 249; *Kyrie Gott Vater in Ewigkeit* 242, 249
Packard Humanities Institute 483
Paczkowski, Szymon 291; "Bach and Poland in the 18th Century" 87
Paisible, James 321
Palestrina, Giovanni Pierluigi da 252, 256, 281; Missa *Ecce sacerdos manos* 242; *Missarum liber primus cum quatuor, quinque, ac sex vocibus, iber primus* 242
Papyraceae Historiam Illustrantia 59
Parrott, Andrew 284, 285, 286
Pasquini, Bernardo 250
Paulinerkirche *see* St. Paul's University Church
Paulsen, Friedrich 122; *Geschichte des gelehrten Unterrichts* 117
Payne, Ian 351
pedaliter 307
Pelikan, Jaroslav: *Bach Among the Theologians* 379
Penzel, C. F. 350; *Violino concertato* 353
Penzel, Christian Friedrich 76
Peranda, Marco Giuseppe 224, 252; Missa in a (Kyrie and gloria) 243
performance of works: manuscript evaluation implication for 78–81
Pergolesi, Giovanni Battista: *Stabat Mater* 258
Peters, Mark 290
Petri, Christian 525
Petzold, Christian 522
Petzoldt, Martin 127, 148, 152, 267; *Bach-Commentar* 287; "Ut probus & doctus reddar" 117, 125, 132
Pez, Johann Christoph 256; Missa (BWV Anh. III, 24) 504; *Missa San Lamberti* 252
Pfau, Marc-Roderich 244, 254
Pfeiffer, August 183, 184, 288; *Anti-Calvinismus* 173; *Antimelancholicus* 173, 180; *Christen Schule* 173; *Evangelische Aug-Apfel* 185
Philippsborn, Magali 472
piano 297, 303
Picander *see* Henrici, Christian Friedrich
Pietism 123, 126, 138, 159–63, 173, 293–4
Pirro, André 327
Pisendel, Johann Georg 103, 241, 250, 492
pitch 323–4
PIXE 66

Platen, Emil 409
Plauen 31, 511, 512
Pölchau, Georg 216, 446
Pomßen 512
Ponickau, Johann Christoph von 512
Poos, Heinrich 333
Potsdam: Church of the Holy Spirit 535
Praetorius, Michael 146–7, 365; *Musae Sioniae* 365, 366; *Syntagma musicum tomus tertius* 430
Preuß, Hans 7
primary sources 51–2
printed editions 89–95, 405; posthumous 464–74
Prinz, Ulrich 321
proportioning 420–7
pupils of Bach 458–63
Puschner, Johann Georg 92

Quantz, Johann Joachim 318, 327, 328, 389; Dresden Trios *auf Concertenart* 331; *Versuch einer Anweisung die Flöte traversiere zu spielen* 186
Questenberg, Count Johann Adam von 32, 194, 537
Quintilian 387
quodlibets 145–8

Rabener, Justus Gotthard 177
Ragazzi, Angelo 336
Ram, Johann Paul 177
Rambach, Johann Jacob 183–4; *Betrachtungen über das gantze Leiden Christi* 184
Rameau, Jean Philippe 379; *Nouvelles Suites de Pieces de Clavecin* 243
Ramin, Günther 484
Rampe, Siegbert 323, 347, 389–90; "Bach, Berlin, Quantz und die Flötensonate Es-Dur BWV 1031" 331; "Bach, Quantz und das 'Musicalische Opfer'" 388; *Bachs Klavier- und Orgelwerke* 296–7, 409; *Bachs Orchestermusik* 317, 321, 341, 346, 348, 349, 353, 409; *Das Bach-Handbuch Band 5/1–2* 354
rastrum 63–5
Rath, Gisela Agnes von 171–2, 173
Rathey, Markus 267–8, 287, 290; "Drama and Discourse" 288–9
Ratke, Wolfgang 123
Ratz, Erwin 413
realia 124, 125, 132, 137, 139, 141
reception history 85–6
recorders 320–1

Index   561

Rees, Abraham: *Cyclopaedia* 461
Reichardt, J. F. 447
Reiche, Gottfried 106, 524
Reineccius, Georg Theodor 116, 166, 167, 169
Reinhardt, Helena 527
Reinken, Johann Adam 248, 261, 367, 448, 498; *An Wasserflüssen Babylon* 240, 242, 243–4, 248, 310, 489; *Hortus musicus* 239, 251
Rempp, Frieder 469
Renwick, William 381
Reul, Barbara 209
Reutz, Caspar 229–30
Reyher, Andreas 123, 124–5, 128, 136, 361; *Cantional* 362–4, 365–6; *Dialogi seu Colloquia puerilia* 129; "Kleine Dialoge" 125; *Methodus oder Bericht wie [die] Schuljugend [...] unterrichtet werden soll* 124; *Spezial- und Sonderbarer Bericht* 361–2; *Systema logicum* 133
Richter, Bernhard Friedrich 34, 106
Riemer, Johann Salomon 38
Rietschel, Georg 5, 6, 7; *Lehrbuch der liturgik* 5–6
Rifkin, Joshua 268, 285, 286, 354; "Bach's Chorus" 78, 283, 284; "Besetzung – Entstehung – Überlieferung" 325, 405; "Ein langsamer Konzertsatz Johann Sebastian Bachs" 351; "More (and Less) on Bach's Orchestra" 324, 325–6; "The 'B-Minor Flute Suite' Deconstructed" 353, 405
Rinck, Johann Heinrich 374
Ringk, Johannes 74, 315
Rivera, Benito 395
Robertson, Michael 352
Rochlitz, J. Friedrich 458, 473
Rollberg, Fritz 106
Rolle, Christoph Friedrich 496
Roper, Lyndal 102, 112, 113; *Holy Household, The* 110
Rörer, Johann Günther: *Eisenachisches Gesangbuch* 360–1, 363, 365, 366
Rose, Stephen 107, 114
Rothschier, Tobias 525
Rovetta, Giovanni 233
Rufus, Curtius 129
Rust, Friedrich Wilhelm 158, 238, 453, 459

Sachs, Klaus-Jürgen 413
Sackmann, Dominik 262, 347; "Bach, Berlin, Quantz und die Flötensonate

Es-Dur BWV 1031" 331; "Bachs langsame Konzertsätze unter dem Einfluß von Arcangelo Corelli" 263; *Bachs Orchestermusik* 317, 341, 346, 348, 349, 353, 409; *Bach und Corelli* 336; *Das Bach-Handbuch Band 5/1–2* 354; *Triumph des Geistes über die Materie* 322, 329
St. John Passion (BWV 245) 203, 268, 290, 445, 453, 462; copyists of 442, 443, 455, 481; manuscripts of 53, 477; "Mein teurer Heiland" 289; Version I 274, 503; Version II 274, 507; Version III 274, 520; Version IV 274, 537, 538; versions of 274, 476
St. Luke Passion (BWV Anh. II, 246) 254, 274, 517
St. Mark Passion (BWV 247) 268, 290; performance of 254, 483, 518, 534; revisions to 255
St. Matthew Passion (BWV 244) 9, 268, 288, 290, 294, 333; copyists of 442; early version of (BWV 244b) 76–7, 84, 513, 516; manuscript of 63, 477; Mendelssohn performance of 26, 267; notation in 73, 74; performances of 513, 516, 527, 532, 534; versions of 274
St. Nicholas Church, Leipzig 134, 482, 517; clergy of 174, 178, 184; organ of 41; performances in 500, 501, 503, 504, 505, 508, 510, 511, 513, 514, 515, 517, 518, 519, 520, 521, 522, 524, 525, 526, 527, 528, 530, 531, 532, 533, 534, 535, 536, 537, 538
St. Paul's University Church 508, 509, 510, 514; organ of 41, 497, 500; performances in 176, 505, 517, 533
St. Thomas Church, Leipzig 134, 482, 528, 530; clergy of 175, 176–7, 178; instruments of 515, 535; performances in 483, 499, 503, 504, 505, 507, 508, 513, 516, 517, 518, 519, 523, 524, 525, 526, 527, 529, 532, 534, 538, 539
St. Thomas School, Leipzig 106, 117, 127, 134–40, 174, 481, 500, 501, 515, 516, 524, 531, 534; alterations to 519, 520; apartment in 512, 513, 520; Boys Choir 134, 481–2, 534; pedagogy at 135–9; regulations of 502, 521; responsibilities at 135, 139–40
Salmen, Walter: *Social Status of the Professional Musician* 108; *Zu Tisch mit Johann Sebastian Bach* 107
Sancta Maria, Thomas de 332

562 *Index*

Sangerhausen: St. James Church 489, 527–8
Sanguinetti, Georgio 381
Sassoon, Humphrey 387
Saxe-Weimar, Duke Ernst August I of 194, 491
Saxe-Weimar, Duke Ernst Ludwig of 194
Saxe-Weimar, Duke Johann Ernst of 165, 194, 220, 251, 270, 347, 489, 495
Saxe-Weimar, Duke Wilhelm Ernst of 165, 194, 196, 491, 493, 496, 497
Saxe-Weissenfels, Duke Christian of 193, 203, 493, 507, 515
Saxon-Gotha-Altenburg, Friedrich II of 501
Saxony, Elector August the Strong of 176, 204
Saxony, Electress Christiane Eberhardine of 31, 45, 176, 514
Saxony-Gotha, Duke Ernst the Pious of 124, 125, 361
Schabalina, Tatjana 245, 278–80; "Neue Erkenntnisse zur Entstehungsgeschichte der Kantaten BWV 34 and 34a" 279–80; "Recent Discoveries in St Petersburg" 279; "'Texte zur Music' in Sankt Petersburg" 279, 483; "'Texte zur Music' in Sankt Petersburg: Weitere Funde" 279, 483
Schäfer, Conrad Christian 529
Schaumburg-Lippe, Count Wilhelm von 538
Scheibe, Johann 331, 377, 497, 535; *Concertouverture* 352
Scheibe, Johann Adolph 330, 519; *Der Critische Musicus* 528; dispute with Birnbaum 28, 529, 530
Scheibler, Christoph: *Aurifodina Theologica* 185
Scheide, William H. 268
Scheidt, Samuel 154
Schein, Johann Hermann 134, 364; *Cantional* 364, 365
Schelle, Johann 134, 230
Schemelli *Musicalisches Gesangbuch* 90, 92, 155–6, 359, 368–71, 527
Schenker, Heinrich 6, 312
Schenkman, Walter: "Notes and Numbers in the *Goldberg*" 384
Schering, Arnold 11–12, 106, 283, 285
Schicht, Johann Gottfried 220
Schindel, Ulrich 138; *Johann Matthias Gesners aufgeklärte Pädagogik* 137
Schleiz 208, 498

Schleuning, Peter 395, 408, 413
Schlichting 338
Schloss, Andrew 390
Schmeider, Wolfgang 304; *Bach-Werke-Verzeichnis* 295, 296
Schmid, Balthasar 90–1, 92
Schmid, Ernst Fritz 33
Schmid, Johann 175, 500
Schmidt, Christian Martin 408
Schmidt, Henry 333
Schmidt, Johann Christoph: *Auf Gott hoffe ich* 253
Schmiedel, Peter 395
Schmögner, Thomas 395
Schmolck, Benjamin 244; *Das Saiten-Spiel des Hertzens* 253–4
Schneider, Christian Nicolaus 235, 520
Schneider, Johann Leberecht 531
Schneider, Max 216, 217–18, 478; *Das Erbe deutscher Musik* 217
Schönberg, Arnold 413
schools *see* education
Schorn-Schütte, Luise 112
Schott, Georg Balthasar 500, 516
Schramm, Sebastian 149
Schröder, Karl-Ernst: "Zum Trio A-dur BWV 1025" 246
Schrön, Valentin 149
Schröter, Christoph Gottlieb 28
Schröter, Johann Georg 496
Schubart (Schubert), Johann Martin 249, 459
Schubert, Johann Friedrick 537
Schübler, Johann Georg 93, 388
Schübler, Johann Heinrich 93
Schübler, Johann Jacob 93
Schulenberg, David 331–2; *Keyboard Music of J. S. Bach, The* 296, 349; *Music of Wilhelm Friedemann Bach, The* 443–4
Schultze, Friedrich 369, 370, 515
Schulze, Hans-Joachim 10, 17, 109, 117, 268, 330, 353, 443, 460, 479; "150 Stück von den Bachischen Erben" 449; "Anna Magdalena Wilcke" 441; "Bach und Buxtehude" 248; "Die Bachen stammen aus Ungarn her" 231; *Die Thomasschule in Leipzig* 139; "Ein 'Dresdner Menuett'" 458; "Johann Friedrich Schweinitz" 459; *Johann Sebastian Bach. Konzert c-Moll für zwei Cembali und Streichorchester BWV 1062* 341; "Johann Sebastian Bachs Konzerte" 323, 347; "Johann Sebastian

Bach's Orchestra" 326; "Studenten als Helfer bei der Leipziger Kirchenmusik 286; *Studien zur Bach-Überlieferung im 18* 337; "The B minor Mass—Perpetual Touchstone for Bach Research" 277; "Zumahln da meine itzige Frau" 113
Schütz, Heinrich: *Psalmen Davids* 364
Schütze, Johanna Eleonora 536
Schweinitz, Johann Friedrich 459
Schweitzer, Albert 9, 226, 474
Seckendorf, Veit Ludwig von 124
Seiber, Urban Gottfried 177
Selle, Thomas 385
Sicul, Christoph Ernst 278
Sieder, Reinhard 104
Siegele, Ulrich 401–2, 412; *Bachs theologischer Formbegriff und das Duett F-dur* 127; "Johann Sebastian Bach – Deutschlands großter Kirchenkomponist" 7; *Kompositionsweise* 330, 339, 343, 347, 350; "Noch einmal" 344; "Technik des Komponisten vor der Größe des Herrschers" 387; "Wie unvollständig ist Bachs Kunst der Fuge?" 393; "Zu Bachs Fugenkomposition" 408
Silbermann, Gottfried 35, 41, 298, 303, 535; organs by 305, 509, 520, 528
Silbermann, Johann Andreas 41
Simrock, Nicolaus 471, 473
Sing-Akademie zu Berlin 294, 451; collection of 216, 217, 443, 445, 446, 447; rediscovery of collection 86, 269, 280, 379, 437, 482–3
Six Sonatas for Violin and Harpsichord (BWV 1014–1019) 334, 337–8; Sonata in C minor (BWV 1018) 338; Sonata in E major (BWV 1016) 338; Sonata in G major (BWV 1019) 337, 338
Smend, Friedrich 5, 12, 13, 52, 410; *Bach in Köthen* 11; "Bachs h-moll-Messe" 8–9; "Bach's Kanonwsie über 'Vom Hommel hoch da komm ich her'" 90; "What's Left?" 15; "Zu den altesten Sammlungen der vierstimmigen Chorale J. S. Bachs" 469
Smend, Julius 3–4, 5, 6, 7
Söderblom, Nathan 7
Sonata in G minor (BWV 1020) 342
Sonatas and Partitas for Solo Violin (BWV 1001–1006) 85, 200, 321–2, 323, 335–7; manuscripts of 453, 454, 498; notation in 79; Sonata in A minor (BWV 1003) 325, 329; Sonata in B minor (BWV 1002)

328; Sonata in C major (BWV 1005) 325; Sonata in D minor (BWV 1004) 83n159, 333; Sonata in G minor (BWV 1001) 332, 336, 443
Sonatas for Viola da Gamba and Harpsichord (BWV 1027–1029) 339–40; Sonata in D major (BWV 1028) 340; Sonata in G major (BWV 1027) 339; Sonata in G minor (BWV 1029) 330, 332, 339
Sonate auf Concertenart 331–2
Sophie Charlotte, Electress 335
Speerstra, Joel 304
Spener, Philipp Jacob 160; *Gerechter Eifer wider das Antichristische Pabstthum* 184
Speratas, Sigismund Scholze: *Singende Muse and der Pleisse* 90, 95
Spitta, Friedrich 5, 7
Spitta, Philipp 1, 3, 8, 15, 19, 33, 34, 40, 47, 58, 67, 69, 81, 89, 91, 93, 150, 158, 159, 162, 216, 226, 234, 249, 260–1, 269, 344, 359, 387
Spohr, Louis 85
Sponheuer, Bernd 234
Spork, Count Franz Anton von 57–8
Sprondel, Friedrich 378
Stauber, Johann Lorenz 158
Stauffer, George 268, 303–4, 408, 476; "Boyvin, Grigny, D'Angelbert, and Bach's Assimilation of French Classical Organ Music" 309; "Ein neuer Blick auf Bachs 'Handexemplar'" 95; *Forkel – Hoffmeister & Kühnel Correspondence, The* 473; "Free Organ Preludes of Johann Sebastian Bach, The" 251
Steffani, Agostino 248; *Il zelo di Leonato* 259
Steglich, Rudolf 9
Steiger, Renate 268, 287, 401
Stenger, Nicolaus 183; *Grund-Feste der Augspurgischer Confession* 185
Stieglitz, Christian Ludwig 186–7, 516
Stiehl, Herbert 34
stile antico 20, 263, 377, 379, 385, 412
Stiller, Günther 287
Stinson, Russell 306, 309, 339, 408
Stockigt, Janice 209
Stoecker, Adolf 2
Stölzel, Gottfried Heinrich 170, 193, 294, 385, 451; *Der Gläubigen Seele Geistliche Betrachtungen Ihres leidenden Jesu* 245, 274, 279, 523; *Diomedes oder die triumphierende*

564 *Index*

Unschuld 245–6; *Du Artzt in Israel* 526; *Ein Lämmlein geht und trägt die Schuld* 245, 255, 483; *Jesu, hier ist deine Stadt* 526; *Leite mich in Liebes-Seilen* 526; *Mein Jesu, deine Wunder-Hand* 526; *Michael, wer ist wie Gott* 526; *Namen-Buch* Jahrgang 244–5, 254; *O! Wie selig sind die Blicke* 526; *Schnöder Aussatz meiner Sünden* 526; *Sorgen, Sorgen, sind die Steine* 526
Stöntzsch 520
Störmthal 502
Straube, Karl 5
Streck, Harald 291
Stricker, Augustin Reinhard 170–1, 197, 198, 496
Swack, Jeanne 331, 341, 346, 409
Swieten, Baron Gottfried van 1, 35

Talbot, Michael 326, 345
Talle, Andrew 95, 338; *Social Background for Bach's Partitas* 313–14
Tangentenflügel 298
Tatlow, Ruth 334, 384, 422; "Theory of Proportional Parallelism" 427
Taubach 492
Tauler, Johannes 179
Taylor, John 538
Telemann, Georg Philipp 31, 40, 95, 103, 104, 170, 193, 274, 294, 326, 352, 438, 451, 494, 500; Concerto for two violins in G major 477; correspondence of 29; *Der Herr ist König* 253, 477, 505; *Der Segen des Herrn machet reich ohne Mühe* 508; *Gelobet sei der Herr, der Gott Israel* 508; influence on J. S. Bach's works 239, 250, 251, 351; *Machet die Tore Weit* 253, 524; "Paris Quartets" 529; Quartet for flute, violin, violoncello, and continuo 260; *Six Sonates* 343; *Wer sich rächet, an dem wird sich der Herr wieder rächen* 508
Teller, Romanus 176–7
tempo 427–34
Terry, Charles Sanford 45, 454
Thiele, Johann 381
Thieme, Carl August 38, 463
Thirty Years' War 191
Thoene, Helga 333
Thomasius, Jakob 136
Thomaskirch *see* St. Thomas Church, Leipzig
Tilge, Höchster, meine Sünden 258
time structure 427–34

Toduta, Sigismund 413
Tomita, Yo 315, 337, 372, 450–1; "Anna Magdalena as Bach's Copyist" 109, 113; "Bach and Dresden" 383; "Bach and His Early Drafts" 383; *Bach Bibliography* 478–9; "Bach Reception in Pre-Classical Vienna" 472; "Dawn of the English Bach Awakening Manifested in Sources of the '48, The" 472; *J. S. Bach's "Das Wohltemperierte Clavier II"* 306
Torelli, Guiseppe: *Concerti grossi* 263; influence on J. S. Bach's works 239, 250, 308
Tovey, Donald Francis 381
transmission 85
Traub, Andrea 395, 396
Trebs, Heinrich Nicolaus 492
Trede, Yngve Jan 394
Treuner, Johann Philipp 164
Trio Sonatas for organ (BWV 525–530) 295, 444; D minor organ Sonata (BWV 527) 349; Trio Sonata for Organ in E minor (BWV 528) 342
Türsch, Gottlob Friedrich 534

Uthe, Justus Christian 152–3

Van Elferen, Isabella 287
Vetter, Walthar: *Der Kapellmeister Bach* 11
Vidal, Pierre 395
viola d'amore 323
viola pomposa 322
violoncello da spalla 322–3
violoncello piccolo 322
Vivaldi, Antonio 227; D minor violin concerto 446; influence on Bach's works 239, 262, 308, 328, 329, 345, 423; *L'Estro Armonico*, Op. 3 54, 250
vocal music 278–94; chronology of 269–77; completeness of oeuvre 268; concertos 221; contextual analysis of 292–4; musical analysis of 280–2; number of singers per voice 268; performance practice 283–6; source study of 278–80; textual analysis of 290–2; theological perspectives on 286–90
Vogler, Johann Caspar 76, 82, 250
Voigt, Johann Georg 459
Volumier 204
Vopelius: *Neu Leipziger Gesangbuch* 364–5
Vötterle, Karl 399
Vulpius, Melchior: *KirchenGeseng und Geistliche Lieder* 364

Wachowski, Gerd 449
Wagner, Georg Gottfried 31, 39, 512
Wagner, Josef 321
Wagner, Richard: *Tristan und Isolde* 281
Walker, Paul 386; "Die Entstehung der
 Permutationsfuge" 381; *Theories of
 Fugue from the Age of Josquin to the
 Age of Bach* 380
Wallfisch, Elizabeth 323
Walter, Meinrad 287; *Musik-Sprach des
 Glaubens* 289
Walther, Johann Gottfried 29, 39, 196,
 304, 326, 493; *Allein Gott in der
 Höh sei Ehr* 529; as copyist 76, 342;
 Harmonische Denck-und Danckmahl
 260; *Musicalisches Lexicon* 39, 40, 167,
 386, 516, 520; music collection of 242,
 252; Weimer employment of 164
Walther, Johann Gottfried, Jun. 493, 523
Walz, Thomas 394
Warburton, Ernest: *Collected Works of
 Johann Christian Bach, The* 457
watermarks 58–60
Watkin, David 336
Webern, Anton 413
Wecker, Christoph Gottlob 32, 511, 512, 513
Weimar 116, 194–8, 249, 270, 489–90,
 492–7; clergy in 163–70; *Herzogin Anna
 Amalia Bibliothek* 196; imprisonment
 at 197–8, 200; Jakobskirche 164,
 493; *LandRichter-stube* 197–8, 200;
 responsibilities at 195, 270; Saxe-
 Weimar, Duke Ernst August I of
 194, 491; Saxe-Weimar, Duke Ernst
 Ludwig of 194; Schlosskirche 197, 302;
 Stadtkirche of SS. Peter and Paul 164; *see
 also* Saxe-Weimar, Duke Johann Ernst of;
 Saxe-Weimar, Duke Wilhelm Ernst of
Weimarische Grosse Bibel 165
Weiß, Joanna Elisabeth 176n194, 515
Weiß, Silvius Leopold 332, 338–9, 340,
 530; Lute suite in A major 246, 260
Weiß, Wisso: *Katalog der Wasserzeichen
 in Bachs Originalhandschriften* 59, 60
Weise, Christian 116
Weise, Johann Anton 496
Weiss, Christian, Sr. 176, 180
Weissenfels 203–4; court chapel organ
 in 302; performance at 196, 203,
 493, 507; Saxe-Weissenfels, Duke
 Christian of 193, 203, 493, 507, 515;
 visit to 515, 531
Weissensee: Church of St. Peter and
 St. Paul 525, 529

Weldig, Adam Immanuel 197, 203
Well-Tempered Clavier 57, 295, 301, 423,
 472, 482; period for composition of
 36–7, 45; printed editions of 456, 468;
 see also Well-Tempered Clavier I;
 Well-Tempered Clavier II
Well-Tempered Clavier I 200, 444;
 binding of 62; Fugue in B-flat minor
 (BWV 867/2) 434; Fugue in C major
 (BWV 846/2) 417, 424; Fugue in C
 minor (BWV 847/2) 424–5; Fugue in
 C-sharp major (BWV 848/2) 80; Fugue
 in C-sharp minor (BWV 849/2) 434;
 Fugue in F minor (BWV 857/2) 421;
 manuscripts of 450; Prelude in B-flat
 major (BWV 866/1) 80; Prelude in F
 minor (BWV 857/1) 80; Prelude in
 F-sharp minor (BWV 859/1) 80; Prelude
 in G major (BWV 860/1) 80; Prelude
 in G minor (BWV 861/1) 80; printed
 editions of 471, 473; title page of 499
Well-Tempered Clavier II 77, 306–7,
 381; binding of 62; Fugue in A
 major (BWV 888/2) 420–2; "London
 autograph" 54, 73; manuscripts of 450;
 Prelude in A minor (BWV 889/1) 80;
 Prelude in C major (BWV 870a/1) 82;
 Prelude in D-minor (BWV 875/1) 53,
 56; Prelude in F minor (BWV 881/1)
 58, 80; Prelude in F-sharp minor (BWV
 883/1) 56; printed editions of 471, 473
Welter, Friedrich 132
Wentzel, Eugen 194
Werbeck, Walter 379, 413
Werner, Arno: *Vier Jahrhunderte im
 Dienste der Kirchenmusik* 108
Werner, Friedrich: *Der richtige und
 untrügliche Himmels-Weg eines
 Christen* 184
Wesley, Samuel 1, 473
Whittaker, W. G.: *Cantatas of Johann
 Sebastian Bach, The* 15
Widor, Charles-Marie 474
Wiegand, Maria Salome 514
Wiemer, Wolfgang 92, 388, 393, 395
Wiermann, Barbara 242, 252
Wild, Friedrich Gottlieb 44
Wilderer, Johann Hugo von: Mass in G
 minor 256
Wilhelm, Margrave Georg 245
Wilhelmina Amalie 532
Williams, Peter 303, 392; "Bach's G Minor
 Sonata" 338; "BWV 565: a Toccata in D
 Minor for Organ by J. S. Bach?" 314; *J. S.*

566 *Index*

Bach, A Life in Music 21, 220, 230, 231, 448; *Life of Bach, The* 21; *Organ Music of J. S. Bach, The* 228, 296, 391, 461
Winckler, Andreas 180
Winckler, Johann Gottlob 528
"Winkelschulen" 120
Witt, Christian Friedrich 169
Wolf, Johann Christoph 150
Wolf, Uwe 66, 286
Wolff, Christoph 20, 21, 102, 217, 238–9, 268, 281, 349, 383, 384, 389, 407, 476; *Bach: Essays on His Life and Music* 328, 342, 353, 387, 396; "Bach's Leipzig Chamber Music" 341, 347; "Bach's Personal Copy of the Schübler Chorales" 308; *"Bachs Sterbechoral"* 397; "Das Trio A-Dur BWV 1025" 246; *Der Stile antico in der Musick Johann Sebastian Bachs* 412; "Der Terminus 'Ricercar'" 385, 386; Expedition Bach 87; "Handexemplar of the Goldberg Variations, The" 382; "Images of Bach in the Perspective of Basic Research and Interpretive Scholarship" 15; "Johann Adam Reinken und Johann Sebastian Bach" 261; *Johann Sebastian Bach: The Learned Musician* 99, 128, 131, 132, 135, 140, 202, 231, 263, 273, 315, 346; "Johann Sebastian Bachs Regeln für den fünfstimmigen Satz" 413; *Klavierübung I-IV* facsimile edition 93; "Last Fugue, The: Unfinished" 64, 67, 392; *Musical Offering* facsimile edition 92–3; "New Research on Bach's Musical Offering" 91, 385; "Recovered in Kiev" 482; rediscovery of Sing-Akademie collection 86, 216, 280; "Sicilianos and Organ Concerts" 305, 348, 350, 353; "Textkritische Bemerkungen zum Originaldruck der Bachschen Partiten" 94–5; "Toward a Definition of the Last Period of Bach's Work" 377; "Überlegungen zum 'Thema Regium'" 385; "Zur Chronologie und Kompositionsgeschichte von Bachs Kunst der Fuge" 392, 465
Wolle, Christoph 177
Wollny, Peter 209, 217, 218–19, 240, 268, 342, 343, 460, 480, 481, 483; "Alt-Bach Funde" 218, 219, 220; "Bekennen will ich seinen Namen" 244; *"Der hochbegabte, wunderliche Liebling des Vaters"* 444–5; "Ein förmliche Sebastian

und Philipp Emanuel Bach-Kultus" 447; "Ein Quellenfund in Kiew" 379, 413; "Geistliche Musik" 230; "Italian and German Influences in the Thuringian Motet" 234; *J. S. Bach. Six Sonatas for Violin and Obbligato Harpsichord BWV 1014–1019* 338; "Johann Christoph Friedrich Bach un die Teilung des väterlichen Erbes" 453; *Marco Gioseppe Peranda, Missa in a* 243, 252; "Neue Bach-Funde" 240; "Tennstädt, Leipzig, Naumburg, Halle" 71n89, 76–7, 453; "Überlegungen zum *Tripelkonzert* a-Moll BWV 1044" 349; *Weimar Orgeltabulatur* 87, 248, 249, 310, 481; "Zur Rezeption französischer" 241, 243; "Zwei Bach-Funde in Mügeln" 246, 273
Wörthmüller, Willi 91
Wunder, Heide 112; *He is the Sun, She is the Moon* 110
Würben, Graf von 31
Wustmann, Gustav 89

Yearsley, David: *Bach and the Meanings of Counterpoint* 378, 392

Zacher, Gerd 391, 392, 396
Zachow, Friedrich Wilhelm 154, 494
Zaluski, Andrzej Stanislaw 484
Zaluski, Józef Andrzej 484
Zapf, Michael 321
Zaslaw, Neal 324
Zehnder, Jean-Claude 224, 227, 228, 261, 262–3, 342, 345, 407
Zeidler, Georg Friedrich 172
Zeisig, Johann August 527
Zelenka, Jan Dismas 383
Zelter, Carl Friedrich 85, 233, 294, 446
Zerbst 208
Zerbst, Johann Christoph: *Biblia, Das ist* 149; *Neues vollständiges Eisenachisches gesangbuch worinnen* 148–9
Ziegler, Christiana Renata 497
Ziegler, Christiane Mariane von 272, 292
Ziegler, Johann Gotthilf 92, 367, 493, 497
Zimmermann, Gottfried 521
Zimmermann's coffee house/garden (Leipzig), performances at 521, 522, 523, 524, 526, 527, 531, 532
Zohn, Steven 95, 331, 351, 352, 353, 354
Zschortau 535
Zwingli, Ulrich 179